Optimal and Self-Optimizing Control

Optimal and Self-Optimizing Control

Edited by Rufus Oldenburger

THE M.I.T. PRESS
Massachusetts Institute of Technology
Cambridge, Massachusetts, and London, England

Permission to reproduce previously published material has been obtained.

Library of Congress Catalog Card Number: 66-21356
Printed in the United States of America

Foreword

Between 1950 and the present over three hundred articles and books on optimal and self-optimizing control have been published. Most of these were authored by experts in the United States and the Soviet Union. The field received substantial impetus with the introduction of the maximum principle by L. S. Pontryagin in 1957. Since then the volume of papers on the subject has grown at a rapidly increasing rate. Optimal and self-optimizing control has become the major area of automatic control research in the world today. The field is so vast that no single book or paper now available to the student can possibly give him an adequate picture of the principal results. This volume is intended to fill the need for a single source of information on major aspects of the subject. To this end thirty-nine papers have been selected from the literature and reprinted here. A few papers with more historical than scientific interest are included to show the logical development of the field and thus give the reader a better understanding of the purpose and importance of various developments. The collection contains papers on both theory and application. Since very few articles on applications have been published, the volume is necessarily heavily weighted in the direction of the mathematical theory of optimal and self-optimizing control.

This book was compiled to serve as a basic or supplementary text for undergraduate and graduate courses on nonlinear, optimal and adaptive control. The papers range from introductory to advanced mathematical treatises, so that they will fit the needs of introductory as well as advanced courses in the area. They are grouped into five parts or categories. Some publications belong in more than one category; in such case one category was selected as representative. Part I is devoted to optimal control with unbounded inputs. Work was initiated on this problem long before optimal control of systems with bounded inputs was studied, in fact Pontryagin was naturally led from an investigation of systems with unbounded inputs to systems with bounded inputs and the maximum principle. Part II is concerned with papers on the optimal control of systems with bounded inputs where the point of view is that of the automatic control expert who wishes to keep the error in a controlled variable at a minimum. He is interested in the entire response to a system disturbance, although he may achieve optimal response by minimizing a single property of this response. Part III concerns systems with bounded inputs for which a functional is minimized. Examples of such a functional are time, fuel, and terminal error. The papers of Part III were largely inspired by the maximum principle. Part IV is devoted to papers in which statistical methods are employed. Part V is a collection of papers on self-optimizing control and belong in the area of adaptive control where the controller must seek the maximum or minimum of a function.

The editor hopes that this volume will hasten the general industrial application of optimal and self-optimizing control, a field in which theory has far outstripped practice.

Purdue University
Lafayette, Indiana

RUFUS OLDENBURGER, *Editor*
April 1, 1966

Contents

Foreword v

Chapter 1. R. Oldenburger, A survey of the literature on optimal and self-optimizing control. 1

PART I

Optimal control of systems with unbounded inputs

Chapter 2. D. Graham and R. C. Lathrop, The synthesis of "optimum" transient response: criteria and standard forms, Transactions of the American Institute of Electrical Engineers, Vol. 72, 1953, pp. 273–288. 51

Chapter 3. A. M. Letov, Analytical controller design, I, Avtomatika i Telemekhanika, Vol. 21, No. 4, April, 1960, pp. 436–441. 65

PART II

Optimal transients for systems with bounded inputs

Chapter 4. D. McDonald, Nonlinear techniques for improving servo performance, Proceedings of the National Electronics Conference, Chicago, Illinois, Vol. 6, 1950, pp. 400–421. 71

Chapter 5. I. Bogner and L. F. Kazda, An investigation of the switching criteria for higher order contactor servomechanisms, Transactions of the American Institute of Electrical Engineers, Part II, Applications and Industry, Vol. 73, July, 1954, pp. 118–127. 93

Chapter 6. R. E. Kalman, Analysis and design principles of second and higher order saturating servomechanisms, Transactions of the American Institute of Electrical Engineers, Part II, Applications and Industry, Vol. 74, November, 1955, pp. 294–310. 102

Chapter 7. R. Oldenburger, Optimum nonlinear control, Transactions of the American Society of Mechanical Engineers, Vol. 79, 1957, pp. 527–546. 119

Chapter 8. P. Chandaket and C. T. Leondes, The synthesis of optimum type II nonlinear control systems, Proceedings of the National Electronics Conference, Chicago, Illinois, Vol. 16, 1960, pp. 79–95. 139

Chapter 9. R. Oldenburger and N. P. Smith, Optimum nonlinear control for arbitrary disturbances, American Institute of Electrical Engineers, Paper CP63–122, 1963, pp. 1–22. 156

PART III

Minimization of a functional for systems with bounded inputs

Chapter 10. A. A. Fel'dbaum, Optimal processes in automatic control systems, Avtomatika i Telemekhanika, Vol. 14, No. 6, 1953, pp. 712–728. 179

Chapter 11. R. Bellman, I. Glicksberg, and O. Gross, On the "bang-bang" control problem, Quarterly of Applied Mathematics, Vol. 14, No. 1, April, 1956, pp. 11–18. 202

Chapter 12. L. I. Rozonoér, L. S. Pontryagin's maximum principle in the theory of optimum systems, I, Avtomatika i Telemekhanika, Vol. 20, No. 10, October, 1959, pp. 1320–1334. 210

Chapter 13. L. I. Rozonoér, L. S. Pontryagin's maximum principle in the theory of optimum systems, II, Avtomatika i Telemekhanika, Vol. 20, No. 11, November, 1959, pp. 1441–1458. 225

Chapter 14. L. I. Rozonoér, L. S. Pontryagin's maximum principle in the theory of optimum systems, III, Avtomatika i Telemekhanika, Vol. 20, No. 12, December, 1959, pp. 1561–1578. 242

Chapter 15. J. P. LaSalle, The "bang-bang" principle, Proceedings of the First International Congress of the International Federation of Automatic Control, Moscow, 1960, published by Butterworths, London, England, Vol. 1, pp. 493–497. 258

Chapter 16. V. G. Boltyanskii, R. V. Gamkrelidze, E. F. Mishchenko, and L. S. Pontryagin, The maximum principle in the theory of optimal processes of control, Proceedings of the First International Federation of Automatic Control, Moscow, 1960, published by Butterworths, London, England, Vol. 1, pp. 454–459. 262

Chapter 17. A. M. Letov, Analytical controller design, II, Avtomatika i Telemekhanika, Vol. 21, No. 5, May, 1960, pp. 561–568. 267

Chapter 18. A. M. Letov, Analytical controller design, III, Avtomatika i Telemekhanika, Vol. 21, No. 6, June, 1960, pp. 661–665. 272

Chapter 19. A. M. Letov, The analytical design of control systems, Avtomatika i Telemekhanika, Vol. 22, No. 4, April, 1961, pp. 425–435. 276

Chapter 20. A. G. Butkovskii, Optimum processes in systems with distributed parameters, Avtomatika i Telemekhanika, Vol. 22, No. 1, January, 1961, pp. 17–26. 286

Chapter 21. L. D. Berkovitz, Variational methods in problems of control and programming, Journal of Mathematical Analysis and Applications, Vol. 3 (1961), pp. 145–169. 295

Chapter 22. L. D. Berkovitz, On control problems with bounded state variables, Journal of Mathematical Analysis and Applications, Vol. 4 (1962), pp. 488–498. 320

Chapter 23. A. G. Butkovskii, The method of moments in the theory of optimal control of systems with distributed parameters, Avtomatika i Telemekhanika, Vol. 24, No. 9, September, 1963, pp. 1217–1225. 331

Chapter 24. I. Flügge-Lotz and H. Marbach, The optimal control of some attitude control systems with different performance criteria, Transactions of the American Society of Mechanical Engineers, Vol. 85, Series D, No. 2, June, 1963, pp. 165–176. 339

Chapter 25. M. Athanassiades, Optimal control for linear time-invariant plants with time, fuel, and energy constraints, Institute of Electrical and Electronics Engineers, Transactions on Applications and Industry, Vol. 81, No. 64, January, 1963, pp. 321–325. 351

Chapter 26. W. M. Wonham and C. D. Johnson, Optimal bang-bang control with quadratic performance index, Transactions of the American Society of Mechanical Engineers, Vol. 86, Series D, No. 1, March, 1964, pp. 107–115. 356

Chapter 27. H. O. Ladd, Jr., and B. Friedland, Minimum fuel control of a second-order linear process with a constraint on time-to-run, Transactions of the American Society of Mechanical Engineers, Vol. 86, Series D, March 1, 1964, pp. 160–168. 365

Chapter 28. Y. Sakawa, Solution of an optimal control problem in a distributed-parameter system, Institute of Electrical and Electronics Engineers, Transactions on Automatic Control, Vol. AC–9, No. 4, October, 1964, pp. 420–426. 374

PART IV

Statistical methods in optimal control

Chapter 29. R. C. Booton, Jr., An optimization theory for time-varying linear systems with nonstationary statistical inputs, Proceedings of the Institute of Radio Engineers, Vol. 40, No. 8, August, 1952, pp. 977–981. 383

Chapter 30. L. A. Zadeh and J. R. Ragazzini, Optimum filters for the detection of signals in noise, Proceedings of the Institute of Radio Engineers, Vol. 40, No. 10, October, 1952, pp. 1223–1231. 388

Chapter 31. N. N. Krasovskii, Optimal control under conditions of lagging feedback, Avtomatika i Telemekhanika, Vol. 24, No. 8, August, 1963, pp. 1021–1036. 397

PART V

Self-optimizing control

Chapter 32. C. S. Draper and Y. T. Li, Principles of optimalizing control systems and an application to the internal combustion engine, American Society of Mechanical Engineers, September, 1951, 160 pp. Pages 1–16 are reproduced here. 415

Chapter 33. H. S. Tsien and S. Serdengecti, Analysis of peak-holding optimalizing control, Journal of the Aeronautical Sciences, Vol. 22, No. 8, August, 1955, 561–570. 430

Chapter 34. R. E. Kalman, Design of a self-optimizing control system, American Society of Mechanical Engineers Transactions, Vol. 80, No. 2, February, 1958, pp. 468–478. 440

Chapter 35. A. A. Fel'dbaum, Statistical theory of gradient systems of automatic optimization for objects with quadratic characteristics, Avtomatika i Telemekhanika, Vol. 21, No. 2, February, 1960, pp. 167–179. 450

Chapter 36. A. A. Fel'dbaum, Dual control theory, I, Avtomatika i Telemekhanika, Vol. 21, No. 9, September, 1960, pp. 1240–1249. 458

Chapter 37. A. A. Fel'dbaum, Dual control theory, II, Avtomatika i Telemekhanika, Vol. 21, No. 11, November, 1960, pp. 1453–1464. 465

Chapter 38. A. A. Fel'dbaum, The theory of dual control, III, Avtomatika i Telemekhanika, Vol. 22, No. 1, January, 1961, pp. 3–16. 472

Chapter 39. A. A. Fel'dbaum, The theory of dual control, IV, Avtomatika i Telemekhanika, Vol. 22, No. 2, February, 1961, pp. 129–143. 484

Index 497

Optimal and Self-Optimizing Control

A Survey of the Literature on Optimal and Self-Optimizing Control*

R. Oldenburger

Prior to the last decade, emphasis in the automatic control field was largely on qualitative rather than quantitative aspects. Thus the designer was concerned primarily with whether or not a control system would work at all, would be stable, would return a disturbed system to equilibrium within a reasonable time, would keep system errors within reasonable values, would not have transients with excessive over- and underswings and would not give response that is too oscillatory. He did not try to attain optimum performance. He usually treated linear systems; for nonlinear ones he used approximate linear models. The mathematical tools for studying nonlinear systems were meager, and since optimum performance can usually be obtained only by the use of nonlinear controllers he avoided the question of optimality.

Where such questions were treated they were restricted to linear systems. Thus Norbert Wiener (1)† solved the problem of the opti-

* Except for some minor changes, this chapter is identical with an article by R. Oldenburger which appeared in the book *Applied Mechanics Surveys* published by Applied Mechanics Reviews with the support of the Office of Naval Research, 1966.

† Numbers in parentheses refer to items in bibliography, pp. 27–48.

mum filtering of noise from signal plus noise, keeping the root-mean-square value of the error to a minimum.

In 1944 R. Oldenburger found the optimum control transients for aircraft engine-propeller systems. In such a system it is desired to hold the speed of the engine constant regardless of disturbances. The pitch angle of the propeller is varied by a governor so as to keep engine speed at the reference value. Thus, if the engine speeds up the propeller pitch is increased and the propeller bites more air, increasing the load on the engine and tending to return the speed to its reference values. The propeller pitch is varied by a hydraulic servomotor containing a piston in a cylinder. A valve controls oil flow to the piston. If this valve is fully open in one direction, the piston will travel at full speed in one direction except for lags and other factors which play a secondary role. Similarly full piston speed in the opposite direction is attained if the valve is fully open the other way. Here the time rate of change of the controlling variable, namely piston velocity, is subject to a saturation condition, in that it cannot exceed a certain maximum numerical value. In addition, maximum speed is for practical purposes the same in each direction, and the piston speed may at any time be made to take on any value between zero and maximum in either direction. The problem of optimum transients is thus, given an initial nonequilibrium state of the system, to determine the optimum return to the desired equilibrium state with the controlling variable arbitrary except that it is subject to the saturation condition. In treating this problem the author asked the following questions:

1. Does an optimum transient exist that is better than all others?
2. Is this optimum unique?
3. Is the optimum obtained by operating at all times at saturation or zero?
4. Does the transient satisfy all reasonable engineering criteria for optimum at the same time?
5. Do control functions depending only on the error in the controlled variable and mathematically derived quantities exist that will automatically yield the optimum transient?
6. Will a single function do?

For the kinds of systems and disturbances that arise in normal practice the author proved that the answer to the first five questions is yes. For the last question the answer is also yes in the case of second-

and third-order systems. For higher-order systems, multiple functions and higher time derivatives, such as the third, arise. In practice noise prevents taking the third or higher derivatives; for this reason the higher-order optimal theory is largely of academic rather than of practical interest. Fortunately, in first-approximation studies higher-order systems may generally, although not always, be treated as second or third. The results will then be almost optimal, i.e., suboptimal Neglected factors will of course always arise, compromising performance, so that the optimal theory for second- and third-order systems is adequate. It is supposed that a load fluctuation, a change in the setting of the controlled variable, or some other external disturbance causes the system to leave equilibrium. The transient is understood to occur after the disturbance has died out. Since the control functions are nonlinear the control is termed "optimum nonlinear." Because of proprietary considerations involved in securing patents and developing hardware to exploit the discovery, the results of this study were not published until 1957 (2).

A control may be constructed that simultaneously minimizes the first overswing (respectively, underswing); yields no second swing that causes the solution to be aperiodic; and minimizes the duration of the transient, the average absolute value of the error, the area between the error curve and the time axis, etc. In his work Oldenburger developed the theory of optimum nonlinear control as far as appeared practical for industry. Although the main results obtained were stated in the 1957 paper, most of the proofs have not yet been published, but are being prepared for publication (3). This theory concerns both step changes in the setting of the controlled variable as well as step load disturbances. It shows that higher-order systems may be treated as third order in an auxiliary variable, which is brought to its equilibrium value in an optimum manner. The given system is then allowed to coast to equilibrium. A limit cycle near equilibrium will always arise with bang-bang control, because of secondary factors. To avoid this a linear band is introduced so that the control is linear near equilibrium and yields stable response. A practical compromise control function is employed that automatically becomes linear near equilibrium. This function is only a linear combination of the error in the controlled variable, its derivative and absquare (signed square). Extensive industrial-application efforts indicate that it is not feasible to complicate this function further. Discontinuities and unintentional nonlinearities in the system controlled are treated. The area in which the optimal nonlinear will give better practical results than linear theory is definitely limited and is spelled out in the paper. Sinusoidal and other disturbances are studied. Systems with pure delays are also treated.

Oldenburger's work on optimum control was preceded by studies of on-off or bang-bang control, as obtained with a relay. In 1942, H. G. Doll developed a programmed controller for a third-order system resulting in a patent application (4) in 1943. He was concerned with operating a ship's rudder at maximum speed to achieve better steering. In this effort he treated the second-order system as a special case of third order. He did not attempt to find optimum control where operation between limits is allowed. This was permitted by R. Oldenburger.

The first paper published on the optimal control of systems subject to saturation appeared in 1950 (5). In it D. McDonald treated a second-order servomechanism with an electric motor. He assumed that this system has no lags or leads. By means of a three-position switch this motor can be made to run at full speed in either direction or stand still. This is an on-off bang-bang type servomechanism where the controlling variable, namely torque, is either at saturation or zero. His problem differed from that of the author in that the controlling variable could not take values between zero and maximum or minimum. Also the controlling variable rather than its time rate of change was bounded. Nevertheless the control function was the same as for the simplest second-order systems of Oldenburger since the time rate of change of the controlling variable may be considered to be the controlling variable; thus, McDonald's second-order system corresponds to a system actually termed first order in Oldenburger's paper. The control or "switching" function is a linear combination of the error in the controlled variable and the absquare of the time derivative of this error. McDonald was concerned with minimizing the duration of the transient, and therefore his work belongs to the area of time optimal control. In the paper he used a heuristic phase plane argument. McDonald applied the theory to hardware. The publication of McDonald's results started an avalanche of papers on optimal control that by now has numbered in the hundreds.

McDonald's paper was followed in 1951 by one by A. M. Hopkin (6) on an empirical phase-plane analysis of a servomotor subject to saturation. A computer study of the subject was published by R. C. Lathrop (7) in the same year. At the Cranfield Conference in England in 1951 A. M. Uttley and P. H. Hammond (8) presented the same solution of time optimal switching for an on-off servomechanism, employing the absquare, as obtained by McDonald and Oldenburger. However, they required that there be no overshoot. In 1953, T. M. Stout (9) showed how incorrect switching affects the response time and the integrated absolute or squared error. His study was inspired in part by the fact that in applications switching will usually be late. He found that imperfections in the switching device are less serious if the switching is done early.

In 1953, L. F. Kazda (10) and T. M. Stout (11) showed how friction affects time optimal bang-bang servomechanisms. In 1954, J. R. Burnett and P. E. Kendall (12) presented a paper on linear approximations to the nonlinear approach of McDonald. Together with I. Bogner (13), Kazda found in 1954 that results indicate that as the order of the servomechanism goes up by one, so does the number of switching functions and switching. In 1954, L. M. Silva (14) treated higher-order bang-bang servomechanisms by lumping all but the dominant lag into an auxiliary variable yielding a second-order system in this variable for which optimal minimal time transients were obtained. After this variable reaches equilibrium, the system-controlled variable is allowed to coast to equilibrium. This approach was developed and published independently by R. Oldenburger (2). S. S. L. Chang (15) in 1955 treated second- and higher-order bang-bang servomechanisms and gave switching functions for minimal time response. A. A. Fel'dbaum (16) in the Soviet Union used phase space to synthesize optimal systems the same year. In 1956 A. M. Hopkin and M. Iwama (17) studied the optimal attitude control of an airplane by phase space methods. The same year, R. W. Bass (18) published a report on optimization and the equivalent linearization of nonlinear circuit analysis.

In 1957, H. G. Doll and T. M. Stout (19) presented a paper on third-order systems, which constitutes an extension of the early work of Doll. Here second-order systems are studied where the controlling variable is either at saturation or else the time rate of change of this variable is plus or minus a given constant. This constant arises because it is assumed that a fixed time is required for the controlling variable to go from one saturation limit to the other. The usual assumption of symmetrical saturation limits, that the minimum value of the controlling variable is the negative of the maximum, is made here. The problem studied is largely second rather than third order in that the system controlled is second order when the controlling variable is at saturation. A switching surface is obtained by associating with each point of the error-versus-error-rate-phase plane the value of the second derivative of the error required for optimum response. This surface in phase space passes through the origin, which represents the equilibrium state. When the system state is on the switching surface, bang-bang control will bring the system to equilibrium, thereby minimizing the duration of the transient from this state. If the system state is not on the switching surface the rate of change of the controlling variable is made to operate at one saturation value or the other to bring the system to the switching surface. A two-variable function generator with a photoelectric tube was employed to represent the switching function.

In 1958, C. L. Smith and C. T. Leondes (20) published a compromise between linear and bang-bang, that is "predictor," servomechanisms. They use variable damping that is a function of the absolute value of the error in the controlled variable. As this value increases, the coefficient of a damping term in the second-order differential equation of the system is diminished, giving rapid system response when the error is far from zero, and slow action for numerically small errors. In 1958, F. W. Nesline, Jr., (21) extended the bang-bang theory to multiposition devices. The same year S. F. Schmidt and E. V. Harper (22) surveyed the optimum nonlinear control of systems subject to input saturation for plants to the fourth order and to suboptimal approximations. In 1960, C. T. Leondes and P. Chandaket (23) treated higher-order bang-bang systems using the technique of Silva (14) and Oldenburger (2) whereby two intervals of operation at saturation are followed by a period of coasting to equilibrium. The authors term this a Type II system as constrasted to Type I where minimal time is attained. They compare the durations of the transients for Types I and II and show that they are not far apart for typical cases. They also extend the earlier results of Silva and Oldenburger restricted to dominant real roots to systems with predominant complex roots. In 1960 T. Mitsumaki (24) published a paper on suboptimal nonlinear control.

In 1961, R. Oldenburger, J. C. Nicklas, and E. H. Gamble (25) published a technical note on the optimum nonlinear control of second-order systems based on a thesis of Nicklas (26), extending the earlier work of R. Oldenburger on second-order systems with nonlinear damping. Here the damping is taken proportional to the absquare of the controlled variable. With the aid of Bessel functions the optimum response is obtained for step inputs. This response is bang-bang. In contrast to the optimum control of linear systems there are three distinct types of optimum transients instead of one, classified according to the first and second derivatives of the controlled variable. In the case of second-order linear systems there is at most one change in sign of the second derivative, whereas there may be two changes in sign for the second-order nonlinear case. In his thesis, Nicklas showed that in the case of third-order nonlinear systems not only are switching functions involved, but a decision-making process must be incorporated by which the controller determines which of several types of transients will bring the system to equilibrium in an optimum manner. Practical approximations to the complicated switching functions are given as well as electronic means for accomplishing the control operations. In 1962 J. C. Nicklas and H. C. Vivian (27) modified optimal nonlinear control theory for attitude control of spacecraft. The same year C. N. Shen (28) studied ramp inputs to high-order nonlinear control systems using the describing function, and L. B. Scheiber and O. I. Elgerd (29) applied Boolean algebra to the switching of second order on-off systems. U. I. Utkin (30) obtained switching curves for simple second-order relay systems. V. N. Novoseltsev (31) derived switching functions for the minimal time optimal control of second-order pulse-relay systems. In 1962, R. Oldenburger (32) reported, at a Wright Field conference on optimal control, on the applicability of optimum nonlinear control theory and presented patented means employed successfully in industry. In 1963, he published similar papers (33, 34) and, together with N. P. Smith (35), announced unexpected laboratory findings. They first solved the optimum nonlinear control problem for linear systems subject to step or ramp load disturbances, or step, ramp or parabolic changes of the reference value of the controlled variable. An analogue computer setup was employed to generate the optimum switching function, called the ramp control function. When the system under study was subjected to a random disturbance, response was obtained that was remarkably better than could be obtained for the same system and same disturbance, but with other known switching functions, such as a linear function, or the function optimal for step changes. To explain this discovery the authors distinguished between two types of disturbances or portions of disturbances, "controllable" and "uncontrollable." An uncontrollable disturbance is one that a perfect controller cannot keep up with. A system error will result. Otherwise the disturbance is controllable. In good design a controller can keep up with the disturbance a large part of the time, and uncontrollable portions are followed by sufficiently long controllable portions so that during the controllable intervals an ideal controller can return the system to equilibrium. The ramp control function appears to work so well because a practical disturbance curve may be approximated by straight line segments of sufficient length. The control function optimal for ramps yields suboptimal response for such a disturbance if the disturbance is sufficiently controllable. D. E. Bass in unpublished work reported at the Wright Field optimal control conference that he independently discovered the optimal switching function for ramps to give remarkably good results for arbitrary disturbances. Mr. O. Rubin of the South African National Research Institute also did work in the area.

In a 1963 Ph.D. thesis, K. Okamura (36) treated the optimum nonlinear control of systems with two inputs and one output where the rates of change of the inputs are subject to saturation. He showed that switching functions as well as a logic are involved in an optimum controller.

Except for the work of R. Oldenburger and his associates, almost all of the contributions mentioned are restricted to systems operating only at saturation, that is bang-bang, where the authors were concerned with selecting switching instants to give time optimal control.

With one or two exceptions the papers listed belong essentially to a school arising from industrial need. There has been a parallel development by a second school of optimal control whose approach has been largely mathematical.

This school has its inception in a 1952 mathematics Ph.D. thesis by D. W. Bushaw (37) who made a topological study of transients for the case of torque saturation controlled by switching functions, in particular, linear. As is the case of the work of the industrial school, Bushaw studied one-degree-of-freedom problems only, thus restricting himself to one controlled variable. The one-degree-of-freedom case is of primary concern to industry. He confined his study to bang-bang systems only and, for the special systems studied, proved the existence of time optimal control of bang-bang systems. In 1953, A. A. Fel'dbaum (38) made the classical formulation of the time optimal control problem for systems subject to saturation. The same year J. P. LaSalle (39) proved that the best bang-bang system is the optimum of all systems subject to the same saturation limitations, where now the system is allowed to operate below saturation if necessary. In 1960, he published (40) a proof of the time optimality for systems with one or more controlling variables subject to saturation limits. He employed the matrix approach and variational methods and reported his results at the 1960 Moscow Congress of the International Federation of Automatic Control. In 1955, R. E. Kalman (41) treated second- and higher-order saturating servomechanisms. He represented nth order differential equation systems with constant coefficients as a set of first-order equations and employed the matrix approach. He gave simple means for approximating in a plane the cardinal features of trajectories in an n-dimensional phase space, and applied the approach to several examples. In 1956, R. Bellman, I. Glicksberg and O. Gross (42) gave a general treatment of the optimal problem. They were concerned with reaching the origin, that is equilibrium, in minimum time from any given initial state while the system experiences no external disturbances during the transition. In 1957, R. V. Gamkrelidze (43) considered the same problem proving the existence and uniqueness of optimal steering. In a series of papers beginning with 1957 N. N. Krasovskii (44, 45, 46) treated the more general problem of hitting a moving particle. In the papers of Bellman *et al.*, Gamkrelidze, Krasovskii, and LaSalle one matrix is associated with the controlled variables and a second with the controlling variables or steering functions. In treating the optimal problems these authors divide the study into cases depending on the nature of the characteristic roots associated with the first matrix and the nonsingularity or singularity of the second. Much of the work is concerned with optimal steering employing switching functions that can be expressed in terms of the state variables and are independent of time.

A great advance on the problem of optimal control was made by the Soviet mathematician L. S. Pontryagin (47) and presented in a 1957 paper. His approach was explained in a series of articles by L. I. Rozonoér (48) which appeared in 1959 and in a paper and a book by

Pontryagin and associates (49) translated into English in 1962. Pontryagin introduced the maximum principle. He is concerned with a system of ordinary first-order differential equations in the controlling and controlled variables where the latter are subject to saturation limitations. He minimizes an integral functional (a time integral from the initial time to the final time of a function of the controlling and controlled variables). The minimization is done for the process of transferring the system, represented by the differential equations, from an initial to a final state. He introduces auxiliary variables and constructs an adjoint system and a Hamiltonian. The optimal solution reduces to the determination of the maximum of the Hamiltonian. Many extensions of Pontryagin's results have been obtained. In 1960, A. M. Letov (50) showed how the optimal control problem can be transformed to one without saturation limitations. He treated (51) linear systems with servomotor speed limitations when the integral of a quadratic form is minimized, and in 1961 (52) he applied dynamic programming to the case of a bounded controlling variable. The same year E. B. Lee (53) treated the synthesis of linear time optimal controllers. In 1960, S. Tszyan (54) applied the maximum principle to a rotary amplifier and d-c motor. That year A. G. Butkovskii and A. Ya. Lerner (55) employed the maximum principle to minimize a functional for a system with distributed parameters. The maximum principle was also applied by A. G. Butkovskii (56, 57) in 1961 in a general study to this same problem and to a thermal conductivity problem (58). That year A. E. Bor-Ramenskii and S. Chien (59), A. N. Filatov (60), F. Albrecht (61), V. K. Isaev (62), and C. Jen-Wei (63) applied the maximum principle, respectively, to a time optimal servo drive with two bounded controlling variables, to minimal time systems not requiring switching, to the general problem of minimal time control of linear systems, to the optimal programming of rocket thrust, and to the synthesis of linear optimal systems with the integral of a quadratic form minimized. With a Lyapunov function, L. D. Berkovitz (64) in 1961 and 1962 applied the theory of the Bolza problem to obtain the maximum principle and developed a Hamilton-Jacobi theory which he also related to this principle. In 1961, V. N. Novoseltsev (65) found optimum switching curves for second-order pulsed relay systems in the presence of random disturbances. That same year S. S. L. Chang (66) published a survey of optimal control techniques for systems with and without saturation limitations, and C. A. Desoer and J. Wing (67) minimized the number of sampling points in a minimal time problem. In 1961, E. F. Mishchenko and L. S. Pontryagin (68) treated a statistical optimal control problem, H. L. Groginsky (69) discussed time optimal controllers, and F. B. Smith, Jr. (70) studied time optimal control of higher-order systems. In 1961, W. Kipiniak (71) applied the calculus of variations to control problems involving continuous disturbances.

In 1962, Y. Takahashi (72) and his associates applied the maximum principle to second-order systems subject to input saturation, minimizing different functionals, such as time, the integrated absolute error, and the integrated effort. They compared the optimal solutions and show that it does not usually make much difference as to which functional is minimized. More or less similar solution trajectories were obtained.

During the same year, G. Leitman, R. Bellman, R. Kalaba, and others (73) treated optimization techniques applicable to aerospace systems. The requirements of space vehicles have created a great current interest in the Pontryagin maximum principle. In applying this principle the major concern is with guidance problems rather than with control. Thus one may wish to bring a vehicle from one point in space to another using a minimum weight of fuel in the process. In many such problems, minimizing one variable is enough, in contrast to control problems where it is not sufficient to focus on minimizing one quantity only. Here there are actually infinitely many optimum criteria. Unless one can satisfy all of them, one must search for a compromise to give best over-all response. In the work under discussion, Bellman and Kalaba applied dynamic programming to some general optimizing problems. Leitman examined optimum rocket trajectories with mass flow rate, propulsion power or thrust acceleration limited but operating at constant power. Reference was already made to a symposium on optimum system synthesis held at Wright Field in 1962 (74). One objective of this meeting was to explore the applicability of optimum control. Solutions of the problems of minimizing the time integrals of the magnitudes of error and thrust vectors, of minimizing transient duration for the pitch attitude control of flexible launch vehicles, and of optimizing related quantities were presented by A. V. Balakrishnan, J. S. Meditch, J. A. Lovingood, and others. The approach was primarily that of guidance rather than control with emphasis on mathematical considerations, such as the calculus of variations and the maximum principle, rather than on hardware. At this meeting R. Oldenburger showed that even in simple two-input–two-output problems minimal time may not yield unique optimum transients.

In 1962, B. Friedland (75) applied the standard calculus of variations to the problems considered by Bellman and Pontryagin, and treated minimal time control for amplitude energy constraints. That year L. Markus and E. B. Lee (76) studied the existence of optimal controls minimizing a given cost functional. Y. C. Ho (77) presented an approximation technique to optimal control for systems subject to saturation limitations. J. H. Eaton and L. A. Zadeh (78) treated optimal pursuit. W. L. Nelson (79) covered minimal time optimal on-off sampling systems. E. Polak (80) studied minimal time control of second-order pulse-width-modulated sampled data systems. E. R. Rang (81) gave a rule for computing initial relay positions for time optimal control. N. Kallay (82) minimized the energy needed for the optimal start-up sequence of satellite power plants. L. S. Kirillova (83) applied the maximum principle to optimizing the final state of a linear system and gave an airplane landing example. D. L. Kelendzheridze (84) used dynamic programming and the maximum principle for minimal time tracking where one object knows all of the alternatives to the other. Yu. I. Paraev (85) discussed conditions under which singular control yields optimality for a system linear in the controlling variables. G. M. Ostrovskii (86) gave an approximate method of solution for the case where extrema may lie on boundaries. He eliminated the constraints so that the problem could be solved by the calculus of variations. G. A. Nadzhafova (87) minimized transient time for a servomechanism with driving torque and speed of rotation bounded. N. N. Krasovskii and A. M. Letov (88) used dynamic programming to minimize a functional associated with a linear system. V. S. Balakirev (89) applied the maximum principle to second-order systems and extended the results to systems with pure delays. V. K. Isaev and V. V. Sonin (90) applied the maximum principle to rocket dynamics where the power and jet velocity are limited. B. Friedland (91) treated the minimal time, terminal error and minimum fuel problems for a space vehicle. R. L. Stratonovich (92) obtained switching lines for optimal tracking in the presence of noise. C. Jen-Wei (93) used dynamic programming to minimize the integral of a quadratic form for a linear system with a pure delay. V. N. Novoseltsev

(94) solved a minimal time problem for expected values and random disturbances. He published a similar study (95) in 1963. K. Stahl (96) treated special cases where a functional is minimized for linear and nonlinear systems. O. A. Solheim (97, 98) applied the calculus of variations to optimizing a performance index in controlling batch processes.

In 1963 M. Athans and associates (99) minimized time and fuel for certain nonlinear systems. W. H. Foy, Jr., (100) used Pontryagin's maximum principle to minimize fuel for a single-axis rigid body flight vehicle attitude controller. F. J. Elbert and C. W. Merriam III (101) synthesized linear time varying feedback control for an aircraft landing system using parametric expansions. S. S. L. Chang (102) treated third-order control systems with both the controlled variable and its rate of change bounded. E. Polak (103) used state space to treat pulse-width-modulated regulator systems. T. R. Benedict and G. W. Bordner (104) applied the calculus of variations to a radar problem. C. A. Desoer and others (105) treated two input linear time invariant minimal time discrete systems, minimizing the sampling period. M. Athanassiades (106) used the maximum principle and showed the difference for bang-bang control of time and fuel. Here the control signal is linearly related to the state of the plant for the minimum energy case. M. Athans (107) minimized the time integral of the effort for a bang-bang control system using the maximum principle. H. C. Hsieh (108) sought the direction of the gradient at a point in applying the steepest descent method in Hilbert space to a quadratic functional. I. Flügge-Lotz and H. A. Titus (109) obtained the minimal time response of third-order bang-bang systems, employing matrices. G. M. Kranc and P. E. Sarachik (110) applied functional analysis to the optimum control problem treated by Fel'dbaum and others. M. Aoki (111) discussed a successive approximation technique to constructing minimizing sequences of functionals in extremal problems for variables in Banach spaces. T. L. Gunckel II, and G. F. Franklin (112) used a quadratic measure of the error to optimize linear sampled-data control problems. E. Polak (113) studied the equivalence of time optimal discrete systems. J. J. Florentin (114) studied optimal control with a quadratic performance index for systems with Poisson inputs. Nonsymmetric steering functions were treated by R. Oldenburger and G. Thompson (115) for time optimal control.

In 1963, L. S. Kirillova (116) optimized the final state of a linear system with a bounded control function and proved (117) the existence of the minimum of a sum of a function of the final state and functional of the whole trajectory for linear systems with input saturation. V. F. Demyanov and V. V. Khomenyuk (118) minimized a functional of one coordinate for a linear system. B. G. Pittel (119, 120) applied the maximum principle to linear systems with minimal time and other optimality criteria. Minimal time problems were solved by A. Ya. Dubovitskii and A. A. Milyutin (121) for linear systems, by V. S. Balakirev (122) with the aid of digital computer control, by I. Flügge-Lotz and H. Marbach (123) for single-axis attitude control systems with the aid of the maximum principle, also treating the minimum fuel case, by B. Friedland (124) who also solved the problems of minimum terminal error and energy consumption for both discrete and continuous cases, by P. A. Meschler (125) for the state vector rendezvous of two controlled tracking systems and by H. K. Knudsen (126) using parametrization in terms of initial conditions of the adjoint differential equation. Knudsen published (127) similar results in 1964. M. E. Salukvadze (128) solved the problem of optimum control of variable linear systems with constant disturbances. D. Gieseking (129) minimized the integral of a quadratic form for stable linear missile autopilot systems. A. G. Butkovskii (130) extended the maximum principle to distributed systems with the aid of Banach spaces. M. Gavrilovic, R. Petrovic, and D. Siljak (131) employed the maximum principle to determine the sensitivity of optimal trajectories to perturbations in the controlled process. E. Polak (132) studied optimal linear systems with one mode a saturating sampled-data relay and the other mode continuous or discrete. H. H. Rosenbrock (133) showed how on-off and proportional-plus-integral control are extreme forms of the optimal control of linear systems in the presence of Gaussian white noise, where the integral of a quadratic form is minimized. A. G. Butkovskii (134) obtained an extended maximum principle for discrete control systems. Y. C. Ho (135) surveyed the optimal control field, and established conditions (136) under which time optimal-operation is bang-bang at all times in either the controlled or state variables. F. Haberstock (137) studied second-order sampling systems where the system error is to be corrected in minimum time. In 1964, the maximum principle was employed by F. A. Shatkhan (138) to solve the minimal time and maximum degree of conversion problems for chemical reactions, by T. K. Sirazetdinov

(139) to solve the optimal problems for systems with distributed parameters, by A. I. Egorov (140) for the same purpose, by Y. Takahashi and H. Thal-Larsen (141) to optimize the start-up time of a dual heat-exchanger, by W. M. Wonham and C. D. Johnson (142) to obtain bang-bang and linear modes for the optimal control of linear systems where an integral of quadratic form is minimized, by Y. Takahashi and H. Sutabutra (143) to optimize a computer model of a system where repeated computations is employed, and by D. R. Howard and Z. V. Rekasius (144) to determine the maximum value of the error in worst-error-analysis problems. Minimum fuel problems were treated by H. O. Ladd, Jr., and B. Friedland (145) and by M. Athans (146) for second-order systems with a constraint on total transient time, and by J. S. Meditch (147) for single axis control. F. M. Kirillova and R. Gabasov (148) solved the problem of minimizing the terminal error for linear systems. G. N. Milshtein (149) used successive approximations to minimize the integral of a quadratic form. P. K. C. Wang and F. Tung (150) treated continuous and discrete optimal distributed parameter systems with and without constraints. R. A. Rohrer and M. Sobral, Jr. (151) obtained necessary and sufficient conditions for optimal partially or totally singular systems where an integral of a quadratic form is minimized. B. Paiewonsky and associates (152) published a survey of optimal synthesis techniques in 1964. V. A. Petrov and G. V. Skvortsov (153) applied the maximum principle to a simple second-order system where a functional in the energy consumption is to be minimized. Yu. B. Popov (154) used dynamic programming and an optimal Lyapunov function to minimize an integral of a quadratic form for the design of an optimal controller to stabilize the angular position of vertical take-off and landing vehicles. V. N. Novoseltsev (155) treated optimal switching surfaces with a delay by first ignoring the delay and then correcting for it. A. B. Savvin (156) solved the degenerate problem of minimizing the time to bring a system from one state to another with two bounded controlling variables. R. L. Häussler and Z. V. Rekasius (157) used a Lyapunov function to treat globally asymptotically stable systems where an integral of a positive definite or semipositive-definite form is minimized. A. Leonhard (158) showed that time optimal second-order relay systems are sensitive to random disturbances. J. T. Tou (159) studied time optimal control of discrete systems with bounded controlling variables. H. Weischedel (160) applied the maximum

principle to linear time-varying systems with a quadratic error criterion. C. D. Johnson and J. E. Gibson (161) applied the maximum principle to obtain time-invariant nonlinear control for a quadratic performance index. M. Athans and M. D. Canon (162) employed this principle for second-order systems with absquare damping. Z. V. Rekasius and T. C. Hsia (163) obtained necessary and sufficient conditions for the existence of optimal control laws for a quadratic performance index. J. J. O'Donnell (164) studied limit cycles due to inaccurate switching. W. L. Nelson (165) used multiple performance bounds instead of a single index. J. S. Meditch (166) applied the maximum principle to minimum fuel thrust programming of a lunar vehicle.

All of the publications mentioned up to now concern the optimal control of systems with constraints on the controlling variables. Many of them were logical consequences of earlier work in which the controlling variables were unconstrained. These will be discussed later.

In 1951, C. S. Draper and Y. T. Li (167) published a monograph on an optimalizing control for internal combustion engines where the control searches for the maximum value of a function and attempts to hold the system at the peak value. This work inspired a wave of papers on self-optimizing systems. J. R. Shull (168) and W. K. Genthe (169) in 1952 and 1957 gave results on the peak-holding type of aircraft cruising control. H. S. Tsien and S. Serdengecti (170) in 1955 analyzed the limitations of peak-holding controls.

Self-optimalizing control systems were treated extensively by A. A. Fel'dbaum (171*a*). In 1958, R. E. Kalman gave a method for automatic system identification and optimization by sampling techniques (171*b*). At the 1960 Congress of the International Federation of Automatic Control, R. I. Stakhovskiy, L. N. Fitsner, and A. B. Shubin (172) presented automatic electronic optimizers for finding the minimum of a function of several variables by the gradient method. At the same Congress, A. Y. Lerner (173) discussed the use of the method of steepest descent remote from the extremum and from gradients in the immediate vicinity of the extremum. In 1960, A. A. Fel'dbaum (174) employed gradient methods to the search for the extremum, in this case minimum, of a function in the presence of noise. The same year he (175, 176) published his dual-control theory, followed by additional papers (177, 178, 179, 180) in 1961, 1962, and 1964. This is adaptive control where in the first place the controller must investigate and learn the characteristics of the controlled system or ways of controlling it, and in the second place it must direct the system to the desired state, deviation from this state being measured by a loss function. In 1960, I. S. Morosanov (181) treated the self-oscillations of extremum systems. A. A. Pervozanskii (182) employed trial periodic pulses to search for a drifting extremum in the presence of high-frequency disturbances. L. N. Fitsner (183) treated scanning in minimum time or for the minimum value of a dynamic error integral. He continued this study (184, 185, 186) in 1961 and 1962. In 1961, A. P. Yurkevich (187) treated extremal searches for systems with memory, and N. V. Grishko (188) gave a method of searching for the extremum of a parabolic function where the mean error measured as the deviation of the function from its critical value is minimized. He assumed the presence of random disturbances. T. I. Tovstykha (189) discussed the gradient search for an extremum in the case of a discrete optimization system with independent inputs. I. I. Perelman (190) compared extrapolation and gradient methods of tracking an extremum employing the steady mean error. V. Ya. Katkovnik and A. A. Pervozanskii (191) studied the effect of noise in tracking an extremum for relay self-oscillating systems.

V. N. Zhigulev (192) in 1962 employed Fel'dbaum's dual control theory approach in minimizing the statistical dispersion of the system output at a given time. Ts. Ts. Paulauskas (193) applied the gradient method to a discrete optimizer and (194, 195) employed quickest descent for large deviations from the extremum and the gradient method for small ones (194, 195). I. N. Bocharov and A. A. Fel'dbaum (196) used steepest descent, gradient and other methods for searching for the smallest of several minima, giving experimental results. A. V. Netushil (197) studied the effect of statistical characteristics on self-oscillations in sampled-data extremum systems. M. Yu. Gadzhiev (198) solved a game problem for linear systems. One player selects his controlling variable to minimize a cost functional and the other attempts to maximize this functional. L. G. Pliskin (199) minimized the expenditure of raw material for an arbitrary number of interconnected chemical reactors. I. Sh. Pinsker and B. M. Tseitlin (200) studied ravines where the method of steepest descent is ineffective. V. P. Putsillo, V. P. Strakhov and L. I. Feigin (201) used the gradient method and dynamic programming to optimize a blooming mill. K. Brammer (202) treated step by step search for the minimum mean square of the deviation of the controlled variable with the aid of a model. P. Eykhoff and O. J. M. Smith (203) in 1962 used sinusoidal test signals to find the top of a parabola. The same year J. S. Frait and D. P. Eckman (204) discussed perturbations to search automatically for an optimum of a function. In 1963, H. J. Kushner (205) applied gradient and relaxation processes to the self-optimization of a multiparameter noise disturbed system. That year E. G. Golshtein and D. B. Yudin (206, 207) solved an extremum problem by pulse-width amplitude modulation. L. A. Rastrigin (208) treated the convergence of a random search method, preferred to the gradient method. Yu. I. Bobrov, R. V. Kornilov, and V. P. Putsillo (209) used the second derivative for an extremal control relay system. N. N. Krasovskii (210) treated quasi-stationary continuous extremal systems with bounded plant coordinates. I. I. Perelman (211) compared gradient and extrapolation search methods for extremal problems. D. C. Karnopp (212) employed random search of the absolute maximum or minimum of a reward function. Yu. S. Popkov (213) classified existent kinds of extremal regulators. H. Chestnut, R. R. Duersch, and W. M. Gaines (214) studied the effectiveness of different models of poorly defined processes for the extremum problem and considered strategies with and without noise. G. M. Rakovchuk (215) presented a sequential multistep parameter regulator for sampled-data servosystems, with adjustment dependent on the value of the dynamic error for an assigned noise intensity. J. J. G. Guignabodet (216) minimized a function of the actual discrete state sequence and desired state sequence. He employed dynamic programming. T. L. Gunckel II and G. F. Franklin (217) studied sampled-data control systems with a quadratic function of the error as a performance index. P. H. Hammond and M. J. Duckenfield (218) used continuous parameter perturbation to minimize an even function of the controlled variables.

In 1964, V. F. Demyanov (219) gave a convergent successive approximation method for minimizing a quadratic form. V. P. Zhivoglyadov (220) applied dual control to optimize a plant with a pure delay. M. H. Hamza (221) alternately reversed polarity to locate an extremum and measured resultant discontinuities in an appropriate derivative of the system output. G. A. Medvedev (222) synthesized dual control systems by finding an optimum estimate of system parameters. H. J. Kushner (223) gave a search method for locating a maximum point defined by a Gaussian stochastic process. F. J. Mullin and J. de Barbeyrac (224) solved the problem of bringing a sampled-data system from a given to a final state with a minimum number of sampling periods. M. Aoki (225) treated discrete time systems with unknown constants or stochastic parameters. F. H. Kishi (226) employed a coordinate-wise gradient method in computing at each sampling instant optimum control with bounded controlling variables where a Euclidean norm is minimized. M. D. Mesarovic (227) treated partially unknown systems and disturbances and the automatic minimization of a functional of the controlled and controlling variables. B. Widrow (228) discussed minimizing a mean-square error in pattern recognition. K. S. Narendra and L. E. McBride (229) used the method of steepest descent in minimizing a mean-square error. N. E. Nahi (230) used the calculus of variations to optimize each step in bringing a linear system to a final state under an energy constraint. H. J. Kushner (231) determined the optimum timing of observations, where the total number is given, and where a quadratic total cost function is minimized. A. H. Sephahban (232) employed a digital differential analyzer for the time-optimal attitude control of a space vehicle. R. F. Drenick and L. Shaw (233) used the mean-square error as the performance criterion for optimizing linear systems for which the coefficients and reference signals are random processes. J. M. Nightingale (234) studied the stability of an adaptive loop where the mean square error is minimized and disturbances are random. H. H-y Chien and R. Aris (235) treated the adaptive sampled-data control of a batch reactor with greatest conversion in a given time or a given conversion in least time.

A major effort on the optimization of completely linear systems was inspired by N. Wiener's work on prediction and filtering (1). This effort demonstrated the usefulness of statistical correlation techniques. Wiener solved the problem of optimum filtering and prediction where the input to the system is a signal plus noise and it is desired to extract the present or future signal. The transfer function of the fixed components, and the random characteristics of the signal and noise are assumed known. Wiener determines the optimum transfer function of the system in the sense of minimizing the mean-square error. This error is the difference between the actual and desired system output. In a servomechanism problem it is desired to have the output follow the input or reference setting. Wiener's theory is for stationary random inputs to time-invariant systems. R. C. Booton, Jr., (236) in 1952 generalized this theory to linear time-varying systems subject to statistically nonstationary random processes. In 1952, L. A. Zadeh and J. R. Ragazzini (237) used three distance concepts to separate signal and noise. In 1956, R. C. Booton, Jr., (238) treated final-value systems where it is desired to minimize the terminal or final error. Such a problem arises in the yaw control of an aircraft landing system. The input is a signal plus noise. Correlation functions are employed to solve the problem. In 1960, P. S. Matveev (239) determined the optimal impulsive response function in the presence of noise, where the mean-square error in following an input is minimized. In 1961, E. L. Peterson (240) used statistical methods for the multiple-input multiple-output case, minimizing mean-square errors of the outputs. The inputs contain noise. He employed approximations to correlation functions. The same year S. A. Doganovskii (241) treated the automatic search for a minimum of a function of mathematical expectancies for steady random disturbances. N. N. Krasovskii and E. A. Lidskii (242, 243, 244) studied the minimization of an integral of the expectation of a positive definite function by employing a positive definite Lyapunov function. Their solution is approximate. R. L. Stratonovich (245) solved the optimum filter problem for a telegraph signal plus white noise. R. I. Stakhovskii (246) minimized the mathematical expectation of a performance function for coupled control systems subject to stationary random noise. S. N. Diligenskii (247) showed that discrete filters with memory were better approximations to optimal filters than continuous with infinite memory. He used a mean-square performance index. In 1962, P. E. Fleischer (248) considered small sensitivity to plant variations and insensitivity to instrument noise. He minimized the mean-square error. A. N. Sklyarevich (249) employed an algebraic method to determine the transfer function minimizing the root-mean-square error. N. N. Korobov (250) optimized the weighting function of a linear sampled-data system where the signal is a power series in time and noise is stationary random. H. Schlitt (251) used a Wiener criterion to optimize a filter for satellite receiving stations.

In 1963, V. I. Schmalgauzen (252) by dynamic programming obtained an approximate solution to the optimum tracking of a random diffusion signal, the signal being observed in white noise. That year G. E. Kolosov and R. L. Stratonovich (253) treated a tracking problem with a pulse signal. I. I. Perelman (254) studied the problem of ensuring the maximum probability of attaining a given control without prior knowledge of certain system parameters and statistical knowledge of random disturbances. He continued this investigation (255, 256) in 1964 in approximating the optimal search for an extremum. In 1963, I. B. Chelpanov (257) synthesized optimal filters for signals with changing statistical properties. M. R. Elistratov (258) used minimum dispersion of random system error and minimum total reproduction error as performance indices for discrete systems with input noise. I. B. Chelpanov (259) determined best filters in the mean-square-error sense when the interval of observation is random or continuously changing. A. N. Sklyarevich (260) used an algebraic method to optimize a transfer function by minimizing the second-order moment of the signal reproduction error. A. G. Zaitsev (261) determined an optimal filter in the sense of minimizing an integral of the sum of the weighted error squared and random error dispersion. He also treated (262) the design of controllers with a similar performance index. V. I. Ivanenko (263) minimized the mean-square error of a servosystem. In 1964, O. M. Kozlov (264) studied the conditions under which optimality with respect to one criterion entails optimality relative to all criteria in a class. He treated random processes where the criteria are functions of the absolute value of the difference between actual and desired values of system variables. That year V. Ya. Katkovnik and R. P. Poluéktov (265) showed that an optimum filter can be attained with time-invariant elements for the transmission of continuous signals through sampled-data circuits. V. P. Zhivoglyadov (266) applied statistical solution theory to optimal control systems whose parameters can be measured in definite time intervals. The theory is applicable to Markov plants and delay systems. Yu. S. Popkov (267) made a statistical study of the error effect on periodic states with independent search. A. B. Kurzhanskii (268) used the moment method for minimizing a standard deviation.

Early work on optimal control was concerned with completely linear problems in which some performance index was to be optimized for the response to step or other deterministic inputs. In 1943, A. C. Hall (269) minimized the time integral of the square of the area. P. T. Nims (270) in 1951 studied the minimization of the time integral of the error and that of the product of the error by time. F. C. Fickerson and T. M. Stout (271) in 1952 minimized the time integral of the absolute error. D. Graham and R. C. Lathrop (272) in 1953 discussed minimizing the time integral of the product of the absolute value of the error by time or time squared, and the integral of the product of the error squared by time or by time squared. They preferred the first integral. In 1956, J. M. L. Janssen (273) used the deviation ratio as a measure of the quality of the control. This is the quotient of the deviation with control divided by the deviation without control for step disturbance. The same year R. C. Oldenbourg and H. Sartorius (274) studied the integral of the quadratic measure of the area and gave a practical optimum criterion. These were efforts to select the best response to a linear system on the basis of one criterion. This approach has not been completely satisfactory since an engineer must look at many criteria in each problem.

Numerous papers have been published on systems not subject to saturation limitations on the controlling variables. In 1960, A. M. Letov (275) minimized the integral of a positive definite quadratic form with one controlling variable where there is no bound on this variable. In 1962, he employed (276) dynamic programming to minimize an integral of the product of a function of time by a quadratic form in the controlled and controlling variables. In 1960, S. V. Emelyanov and A. I. Fedotova (277) used the phase plane approach for a minimal time problem for second-order systems where only certain coefficients are bounded. The same year I. A. Litovchenko (278) treated a tracking problem with a proportional search law. In 1961, V. D. Matytsin (279) minimized the flight time of aircraft with the aid of the calculus of variations, and Ya. Kurtsveil (280) used the matrix approach to minimize an integral of a quadratic form for a linear system. M. E. Salukvadze (281) minimized such a functional for a linear system in the presence of known decaying forcing functions. He followed this (282, 283) by similar studies in 1962. In 1961, I. A. Litovchenko (284) applied the calculus of variations to the optimal control of a linear system with an isoperimetric constraint. The same year W. Kipiniak (285) made a general calculus-of-variations study of minimizing a function for discrete systems and a functional for continuous systems. In 1962, V. F. Krotov (286) used the calculus of variations to minimize the sum of a function of initial and final states and a functional. R. Gabasov (287) treated minimal time problems for coupled digital systems with bounds on one output.

In 1963, N. N. Krasovskii (288) minimized the mathematical expectation of a functional, using dynamic programming and Lyapunov functions for systems with pure delay in a feedback path. That year A. G. Butkovskii (289) applied the method of moments to the optimal control of systems with distributed parameters. E. M. Vaisbord (290) gave an approximate method for synthesizing optimal systems based on Lyapunov's second method and a method of successive approximations in a strategy space. V. M. Popov and A. Khalanaj (291) treated linear systems with a pure delay where an integral of a quadratic form is minimized. V. D. Matytsin (292) minimized the integral-square estimate of maximum error for autopilot control. V. F. Krotov (293) formulated an optimality principle for a case where there is no minimal in the class of permissible functions. R. Gabasov and F. M. Kirillova (294) minimized time for transients in one system and bounded phase coordinates for another coupled to the first. G. Rabow (295) minimized time for a partially unknown system. L. E. Weaver and W. E. Cooper (296) minimized the mean-square value of the random variations in the flux of a nuclear power reactor. S. S. L. Chang (297) used the calculus of variations to minimize a return function. A. I. Propoi (298) minimized the transient response area for sampled-data control systems. R. Gabasov and F. M. Kirillova (299) used the maximum error as a performance index and optimized discrete systems with pure delays by first treating continuous systems. M. Aoki (300) treated the final-value optimal control problem. J. Mekswan and G. J. Murphy (301) time-optimized discrete systems with zero memory nonlinearities. W. J. Culver (302) studied the use of optimal control models.

In 1964, N. E. Kirin (303) time-optimized linear systems by approximations, and R. P. Parsheva (304) used dynamic programming and Lyapunov functions to minimize an integral of the product of an exponential function by a positive definite quadratic form. Yu. I. Paraev used the maximum principle (305) and dynamic programming (306) to bring a linear system to a partially defined terminal point where an integral of a quadratic form is minimized. M. E. Salukvadze (307) treated the invariance of optimal regulators. Here an integral of a quadratic form is minimized for a linear system. The author proves that the solution cannot be invariant under constantly acting disturbances. V. F. Krotov (308) optimized distributed parameter systems. Yu. B. Popov (309) used a Lyapunov function to minimize an integral of a quadratic form. A. Ya. Yasiliev (310) treated optimal problems involving the control rate. Yu. M. Volin and G. M. Ostrovsky (311) minimized a functional associated with chemical processes described by partial differential equations. V. F. Krotov (312) gave an approximate synthesis of optimal control where a functional is minimized. V. F. Demyanov (313) gave a converging successive approximation minimization procedure for linear systems. L. N. Volgin (314) studied the programming of digital computers for optimal control of linear systems. R. E. Kalman (315) treated the problem of determining all performance indices for which a given control law is optimal. To solve the problem he restricted himself to certain classes of linear systems, a linear control law, and a certain type of functional. P. K. C. Wang (316) used dynamic programming for the optimal control of distributed parameter systems with pure delays. F. B. Bailey (317) applied a parametric expansion method to the control of a space vehicle with an error performance criterion. F. Tung (318) minimized the expected value of the square of the control effort to attain given terminal accuracy of a space vehicle. F. B. Tuteur and J. S. Tyler, Jr., (319) used dynamic programming and a random quadratic cost function to track a randomly moving target. J. S. Tyler, Jr., (320) employed models for optimal control. Y. Sakawa (321) studied a heat-conduction problem described by a partial differential equation. He minimized the deviation in temperature distribution from an assigned distribution, at a given time.

The major approaches to optimal control thus are minimizing some performance index depending on the system error and time for completely linear systems, minimizing the root-mean-square error for statistical inputs, minimizing time for bang-bang systems, minimizing a functional for systems subject to saturation limitations, selecting optimum response for such systems on the basis of the entire response, and searching for the maximum or minimum of a function in self-optimizing control.

Due largely to the demand of the space effort, major emphasis in the optimum control field is currently on the mathematical solution of problems by the Pontryagin and related methods. Since the weight of the fuel used to guide a vehicle from one position to another can often be expressed, at least approximately, as a time integral, it is to be expected that space scientists will be seriously concerned for a long time to come with the problem of minimizing such integrals. The elegant mathematical techniques available for treating such problems are encouraging work in this area. However, this picture may change as the limitations of the approach become clear to the space scientist. It is likely that after the major guidance problems are solved he will turn his attention to questions of control. Many fundamental problems that arise are singular in the Pontryagin sense and for them the maximum principle fails. Further, the solutions obtained by minimizing a functional usually involved mathematical operations that cannot be performed physically and are therefore more of academic than practical interest. Experience in industry shows that nonlinear switching and control functions for optimum control can be replaced often, if not always, at the cost of little or no sacrifice in performance, by linear functions, or piecewise linear with few linear segments. Because such functions are relatively easy to produce in hardware it is to be expected that in future serious attention will be given to the minimization of time integrals with linear or piecewise linear control functions. At present it appears that for every person trying to apply optimal control theory, where a single performance index is to be minimized or maximized, there are several working on the general mathematical theory. The field has been dominated so much by mathematicians that guidance and control engineers refer to numerical calculations of examples as "applications." Actual applications, with the theory reduced to successful hardware, in competition with hardware designed by other methods, are needed to justify the intense theoretical effort which has far outstripped practice. It is to be expected that the ratio of theoreticians to engineers applying the mathematics will change in favor of the latter.

Control problems play an important role in space vehicles as well as elsewhere, in that flow, temperature, pressure, and other variables must be kept at desired values regardless of disturbances. It is to be expected that techniques used in applying the maximum principle successfully to guidance will be employed for these control problems since many properties of the response of the controlled variable to the disturbance, such as the area between the error curve and the time axis, can be treated by the maximum principle.

Since in a control problem the designer must satisfy many criteria for optimality at the same time, or select a compromise, more attention will be devoted to optimizing on the basis of the entire response of the controlled variable rather than of a single property of the response that can be treated by the maximum principle. One promising approach is to assume a disturbance to be known in advance and to determine the response of the controlled variable that is optimum in an engineering sense. This response serves as a guide and limit on performance. Sometimes engineers will disagree as to what the optimum is, but in many cases it is unique and well defined. The problem is now, from information available to the controller through measurements of system variables, to perform mathematical operations on these measurements from which the controlling variable is determined so as to give response as near optimum as possible. In this approach entire curves, that is, the actual response and the optimum, are compared. This may be done by using the concept of distance between curves introduced by the mathematician Frechet. If two curves are close together, the Frechet distance between them is small. Sometimes the optimum response for a given disturbance can be found where the controller has information about the past and present only. Actual response should then be compared with this optimum.

The disturbance to which a system is subjected is usually not known in advance, but, in practice some properties, such as the maximum possible value and maximum possible rate of change of the disturbance, are known. The control expert thus must design for a given class of disturbances defined by these properties and select a controller that will give responses near the optimum regardless of what disturbance of the class is the one that will actually occur. Often he is more concerned with designing the system that is to be optimum for certain portions of the disturbance, such as large step changes, and will select a controller to give as near to optimum response for these portions as possible. Both deterministic and statistically defined disturbances may be treated.

In the event that several variables are to be controlled simultaneously the maximum principle promises to be especially useful in selecting optimum sets of responses for these variables. Here the problem of geometrically comparing sets of curves becomes difficult, although still desirable. The maximum principle may be employed to reduce the problem to the study of a smaller class of response curves. In applying the maximum principle to control problems the integrands in the integrals to be minimized depend only on the errors in the controlled variables and derived quantities, in contrast to guidance studies where they may also involve the controlling variables, i.e., steering functions, and time. It seems likely that the impetus given to the optimum control field by space experts will carry over to industry in general, with resulting benefits.

Relatively little attention has been given to self-optimizing control where the controller automatically searches for a maximum or minimum. This area shows considerable promise for the process field. It is to be expected that progress will soon be made on the major problems of stability and rapidity of search. Increased use of digital computers will facilitate the industrial application of self-optimizing control.

The contributions of mathematicians to the automatic-control field have been profound. The introduction of the calculus of variations has changed the optimum control picture completely. It is to be expected that the introduction of other mathematical techniques will provide the solution of optimal problems that are now still too difficult to treat. Widespread application will be made of the maximum principle, which so far has barely been exploited. The maximum principle is ushering in a new era of automatic control.

The author wishes to express his appreciation to the Information Systems Branch of the Office of Naval Research of the United States Navy for support of Contract Nonr-1100(20) in connection with the survey of this chapter.

The papers in the volume are reprinted with the permission of the respective societies, journals, and publishing houses involved, namely, the American Society of Mechanical Engineers, the Institute of Electrical and Electronics Engineers, the American Institute of Aeronautics and Astronautics, the National Electronics Conference, Butterworths, Quarterly of Applied Mathematics, and the Academic Press. The translations of the Russian papers are reproduced with the permission of the Instrument Society of America.

References

1. The extrapolation, interpolation and smoothing of stationary time series with engineering applications, N. Wiener, 163 pp., The Technology Press and John Wiley & Sons, New York, 1948. Also published in paperback as *Time Series,* The Technology Press, Cambridge, Mass., 1964.

2. Optimum nonlinear control, R. Oldenburger, ASME Trans., Vol. 79, No. 3, 527–546, April, 1957, AMR* 10 (1957), Rev. 3541.
3. Monograph on "Optimal control," R. Oldenburger, to be published by Holt, Rinehart & Winston, New York.
4. Automatic control system for vehicles, H. G. Doll, U. S. Patent No. 2,643,362 (1943).
5. Nonlinear techniques for improving servo performance, D. McDonald, National Electronics Conference, Vol. 6, pp. 400–421, 1950.
6. A phase-plane approach to the compensation of saturating servomechanisms, A. M. Hopkin, AIEE Trans. (Communications and Electronics), Vol. 70, Part I, pp. 631–639, 1951.
7. A topological and analog computer study of certain servomechanisms employing nonlinear electronic components, R. C. Lathrop, Ph.D. thesis, University of Wisconsin, 1951.
8. The stabilization of on-off controlled servomechanisms, A. M. Uttley and P. H. Hammond, "Automatic and manual control," 1951 Cranfield Conference, pp. 285–307, 1952, AMR 5 (1952), Rev. 2772.
9. Switching errors in an optimum relay servomechanism, T. M. Stout, National Electronics Conference, Vol. 9, pp. 188–198, 1953.
10. Errors in relay servomechanisms, L. F. Kazda, AIEE Trans. (Applications and Industry), Vol. 72, Part II, pp. 323–328, Nov., 1953.
11. Effects of friction in an optimum relay servomechanism, T. M. Stout, AIEE Trans. (Applications and Industry), Vol. 72, Part II, pp. 329–336, Nov., 1953.
12. Linear compensation of saturating servomechanisms, J. R. Burnett and P. E. Kendall, AIEE Trans. (Applications and Industry), Vol. 73, Part II, No. 11, pp. 6–10, March, 1954.
13. An investigation of the switching criteria for higher order servomechanisms, I. Bogner and L. F. Kazda, AIEE Trans. (Applications and Industry), Vol. 73, Part II, No. 13, pp. 118–127, July, 1954.
14. Predictor servomechanisms, L. M. Silva, IRE Trans., Vol. CT–1, No. 1, pp. 56–70, March, 1954.
15. Optimum switching criteria for higher order contactor servo with interrupted circuits, S. S. L. Chang, AIEE Trans. (Applications and Industry), Vol. 74, Part II, No. 21, pp. 273–276, Nov. 1955.
16. Synthesis of optimum systems with aid of the phase space, A. A. Fel'dbaum, Avtomatika i Telemekhanika, Vol. 16, No. 2, pp. 129–149, 1955, AMR 10 (1957), Rev. 629.
17. A study of a predictor-type air-frame controller designed by phase-space analysis, A. M. Hopkin and M. Iwama, AIEE Trans. (Applications and Industry), Vol. 75, Part II, No. 23, pp. 1–9, March, 1956.

* The symbol AMR refers to a review in Applied Mechanics Reviews published by the American Society of Mechanical Engineers. Thus Reference No. 2 was reviewed in Vol. 10 of Applied Mechanics Reviews, 1957, and the review is No. 3541.

18. Equivalent linearization of nonlinear circuit analysis and the stabilization and optimization of control systems, R. W. Bass, "Proceedings of the Symposium on Nonlinear Circuit Analysis," Polytechnic Institute of Brooklyn, Vol. 6, 1956, pp. 163–198.
19. Design and analog computer analysis of an optimum third order nonlinear servomechanism, H. G. Doll and T. M. Stout, ASME Trans. Vol. 79, No. 3, pp. 513–525, April, 1957.
20. On a compromise approach to servomechanism dynamic response optimization, C. L. Smith and C. T. Leondes, National Electronics Conference, Vol. 14, pp. 100–122, 1958.
21. Optimum response of discontinuous feedback control system, F. W. Nesline, Jr., AIEE Trans. (Applications and Industry), Vol. 77, Part II, pp. 651-658, Jan., 1958.
22. The design of feedback control systems containing a saturation type nonlinearity, S. F. Schmidt and E. V. Harper, NASA TN D–324; AMR 15 (1962), Rev. 3791.
23. The synthesis of optimum type II nonlinear control systems, C. T. Leondes and P. Chandaket, National Electronics Conference, Vol. 16, pp. 79–95, 1960.
24. Modified optimum nonlinear control, T. Mitsumaki, AIEE Trans. (Applications and Industry), Vol. 79, Part II, No. 47, pp. 10–14, 1960.
25. Optimum nonlinear control of a second order nonlinear system, R. Oldenburger, J. C. Nicklas, and E. H. Gamble, NASA TN D–825, 89 pp., 1961, AMR 14 (1961), Rev. 5854.
26. Predictor control of a second- and third-order nonlinear system, J. C. Nicklas, Ph.D. thesis, Purdue University, June, 1960.
27. Derived-rate increment stabilization: Its application to the attitude control problem, J. C. Nicklas and H. C. Vivian, ASME Trans. 84 D (J. Basic Eng.), Vol. 1, pp. 54–60, Mar. 1962; AMR 16 (1963), Rev. 40.
28. Synthesis of high order nonlinear control systems with ramp input, C. N. Shen, IRE Trans. on Automatic Control, Vol. AC–7, No. 2, pp. 22–37, Mar. 1962.
29. A study of optimum switching of on-off type control systems through logic, L. B. Scheiber and O. I. Elgerd, Proceedings of the National Electronics Conference, Vol. 17, pp. 203–209, 1962.
30. The construction of a class of optimal automatic control systems without using "pure" undistorted derivatives in the control law, U. I. Utkin, Avtomatika i Telemekhanika, Vol. 23, No. 12, pp. 1631-1642, Dec. 1962.
31. Optimal Processes in second-order pulse-relay systems. V. N. Novoseltsev, Avtomatika i Telemekhanika, Vol. 21, No. 5, pp. 569–574, May, 1960.
32. Applications and applicability of optimum nonlinear control, R. Olden-

burger, Proceedings of the Optimum System Synthesis Conference, Sept., 1962, ASD–TDR 63–119, pp. 323–342, Feb., 1963.
33. Theorie und Anwendung optimaler nichtlinearer Regelungen, R. Oldenburger, Regelungstechnik, Vol. 11, No. 4, pp. 158–165, Jan., 1963.
34. Nonlinear theory and application, R. Oldenburger, ISA Trans. 2, 3, 257–265, July, 1963.
35. Optimum nonlinear control for arbitrary disturbances, R. Oldenburger and N. P. Smith, IEEE Conference Paper No. 63–122, 22 pp., 1963.
36. Optimum nonlinear control of a system with two inputs and one output, K. Okamura, Ph.D. thesis, Purdue University, June, 1963.
37. Differential equations with a discontinuous forcing term, D. W. Bushaw, Report No. 469, Experimental Towing Tank, Stevens Institute of Technology, Hoboken, New Jersey, Jan., 1953.
38. Optimum processes in automatic regulation systems, A. A. Fel'dbaum, Avtomatika i Telemekhanika, Vol. 14, No. 6, pp. 712–728, 1953.
39. Study of the basic principle underlying the "bang-bang" servo, J. P. LaSalle, Goodyear Aircraft Corporation Report CER–5518, July, 1953.
40. The bang-bang principle, J. P. LaSalle, Proceedings of the 1960 Moscow Congress of the International Federation of Automatic Control, Butterworths, London, Vol. 1, pp. 493–497, 1960.
41. Analysis and design principles of second and higher order saturating servomechanisms, R. E. Kalman, AIEE Trans. (Applications and Industry), Vol. 74, Part II, No. 21, pp. 294–310, Nov. 1955.
42. On the bang-bang control problem, R. Bellman, I. Glicksberg, and O. Gross, Quart. Appl. Mathematics, Vol. 14, No. 1, pp. 11–18, April, 1956, AMR 10 (1957), Rev. 23.
43. Concerning optimal process theory, R. V. Gamkrelidze, Akad. Nauk SSSR Doklady, Vol. 116, No. 5, 1957.
44. Concerning the theory of optimal control, N. N. Krasovskii, Avtomatika i Telemekhanika, Vol. 18, No. 11, pp. 960–970, Nov. 1957.
45. On one optimal control problem, N. N. Krasovskii, Prikl. Mat. Mekh., Vol. 21, No. 5, pp. 670–677, Oct. 1957.
46. On a problem of optimal control of nonlinear systems, N. N. Krasovskii, Prikl. Mat. Mekh., Vol. 23, No. 2, pp. 209–229, Apr. 1959; AMR 15 (1962), Rev. 5694.
47. Some mathematical problems arising in connection with the theory of optimal automatic control systems. Basic problems of automatic regulation and control, L. S. Pontryagin, Proceedings of the Session of the AN SSSR on the Scientific Problems of the Automation of Production, Izvestiya, AN SSSR, 1957.
48. L. S. Pontryagin's maximum principle in the theory of optimum systems, L. I. Rozonoér, Avtomatika i Telemekhanika, Parts I-III, Vol. 20, Nos. 10–12, October–December, 1959, pp. 1320–1334, pp. 1441–1458, and pp. 1561–1578; AMR 14 (1961), Rev. 3426.

49. The maximum principle in the theory of optimal processes of control, V. G. Boltyanskii, R. V. Gamkrelidze, E. F. Mishchenko, and L. S. Pontryagin, Proceedings of the First International Federation of Automatic Control, Moscow 1960, published by Butterworths, England, Vol. 1, pp. 454–459. The mathematical theory of optimal processes (book), L. S. Pontryagin, V. G. Boltyanskii, R. V. Gamkrelidze, and E. F. Mishchenko, John Wiley & Sons, New York, 1962, 360 pp.; AMR 16 (1963), Rev. 3161.
50. Analytical controller design, A. M. Letov, Avtomatika i Telemekhanika, Vol. 21, No. 5, pp. 436–441, May, 1960.
51. Analytical controller design, III, A. M. Letov, Avtomatika i Telemekhanika, Vol. 21, No. 6, pp. 661–665, June, 1960.
52. Analytical design of control systems, IV, A. M. Letov, Avtomatika i Telemekhanika, Vol. 22, No. 4, pp. 425–435, April, 1961.
53. Mathematical aspects of the synthesis of linear minimum response-time controllers, E. B. Lee, IRE Trans. on Automatic Control, Vol. AC–5, No. 4, pp. 283–290, September, 1960.
54. Optimal control of a nonlinear system, Sun Tszyan, Avtomatika i Telemekhanika, Vol. 21, No. 1, pp. 3–14, Jan., 1960.
55. The optimal control of systems with distributed parameters, A. G. Butkovskii and A. Ya. Lerner, Avtomatika i Telemekhanika, Vol. 21, No. 6, pp. 682–691, June, 1960.
56. Optimum Processes in systems with distributed parameters, A. G. Butkovskii, Avtomatika i Telemekhanika, Vol. 22, No. 1, pp. 17–26, January, 1961.
57. The maximum principle of optimum systems with distributed parameters, A. G. Butkovskii, Avtomatika i Telemekhanika, Vol. 22, No. 9, pp. 1288–1301, September, 1961.
58. Some approximate methods for solving problems of optimal control of distributed parameter systems, A. G. Butkovskii, Avtomatika i Telemekhanika, Vol. 22, No. 12, pp. 1565–1575, Dec., 1961.
59. Optimum servo drive with two control parameters, A. E. Bor-Ramenskii and Sung Chien, Avtomatika i Telemekhanika, Vol. 22, No. 2, pp. 157–170, Feb., 1961.
60. The problem of speed of response without switching for an arbitrary number of control functions, A. N. Filatov, Avtomatika i Telemekhanika, Vol. 22, No. 7, pp. 831–833, July, 1961.
61. On a certain problem in the theory of processes with an optimal speed of response in linear systems, F. Albrecht, Avtomatika i Telemekhanika, Vol. 22, No. 7, pp. 838–844, July, 1961.
62. L. S. Pontryagin's maximum principle and optimal programming of rocket thrust, V. K. Isaev, Avtomatika i Telemekhanika, Vol. 22, No. 8, pp. 986–1000, Aug., 1961.
63. A problem in the synthesis of optimal systems using maximum principle, Chang Jen-Wei, Avtomatika i Telemekhanika, Vol. 22, No. 9,

pp. 1302–1308, Sept., 1961. Synthesis of relay systems from the minimum integral quadratic deviation, Chang Jen-Wei, Avtomatika i Telemekhanika, Vol. 22, No. 12, pp. 1601–1607, Dec., 1961.

64. Variational methods in problems of control and programming, L. D. Berkovitz, Journal of Mathematical Analysis and Applications, Vol. 3 (1961), pp. 145–169. On control problems with bounded state variables, L. D. Berkovitz, Journal of Mathematical Analysis and Applications, Vol. 4 (1962), pp. 488–498.
65. Optimum control characteristics of a pulsed relay system in the presence of random disturbances, V. N. Novoseltsev, Avtomatika i Telemekhanika, Vol. 22, No. 7, pp. 865–875, July, 1961.
66. Synthesis of optimum control system, S. S. L. Chang, McGraw-Hill Book Co., New York, 381 pp., 1961.
67. A minimal time discrete system, C. A. Desoer and J. Wing, IRE Trans. on Automatic Control AC–6, No. 2, pp. 111–124, May, 1961.
68. On a statistical optimal control problem, E. F. Mishchenko and L. S. Pontryagin, Izv. Akad. Nauk SSSR, Seriia Mat. Vol. 25, No. 4, pp. 477–498, July–Aug., 1961.
69. On a property of optimal controllers with boundedness constraints, H. L. Groginsky, IRE Trans. on Automatic Control, AC–6, No. 2, pp. 98–110, May, 1961.
70. Time optimal control of higher-order systems, F. B. Smith, Jr., IRE Trans. on Automatic Control, AC–6, No. 1, pp. 16–21, Feb., 1961.
71. Dynamic optimization and control, W. Kipiniak, John Wiley & Sons, New York, 1961, 233 pp.; AMR 15 (1962), Rev. 5696.
72. Some applications of the maximum principle to second order systems, subject to input saturation, minimizing error, and effort (J. Basic Eng.), G. Boyadjieff, D. Eggleston, M. Jacques, H. Sutabutra and Y. Takahashi, ASME Trans., 86 D (J. Basic Eng.), No. 1, pp. 11–22, March, 1964.
73. Optimization Techniques with application to aero-space systems, G. Leitmann (Editor), Academic Press, New York, 1962, 453 pp.; AMR 16 (1963), Rev. 3162.
74. "Feedback Design and Optimal Control Theory," J. G. Truxal and P. Dorato, pp. 1–9; "Function Space Methods in Control Systems Optimization," A. V. Balakrishnan and H. C. Hsieh, pp. 10–40; "The Problem of Optimal Mode Switching," R. A. Nesbit, pp. 41–54; "Optimal Thrust Programming for Minimal Fuel Midcourse Guidance," J. S. Meditch, pp. 55–68; "The Synthesis of Optimal Controllers," B. H. Paiewonsky, pp. 69–97; "An Application of Time-Optimal Control Theory to Launch Vehicle Regulation," F. B. Smith, Jr., and J. A. Lovingood, pp. 99–118; "The Equivalent Minimization Problem and the Newton-Raphson Optimization Method," D. K. Scharmack, pp. 119–158; "Application of Optimal Linear Control Theory to the Design of Aerospace Vehicle Control Systems," P. A. Reynolds and E. G.

Rynaski, pp. 159–188; "Sortie Boost and Glide Trajectors Determined for Specific Mission Requirements by the Steepest Ascent Technique," K. Mikami, C. T. Battle, and R. S. Goodell, pp. 189–240; "Optimal Programming of Multivariable Control Systems in the Presence of Noise," A. E. Bryson, Jr., pp. 343–352; "Smoothing for Linear and Nonlinear Dynamic Systems," A. E. Bryson, Jr., and M. Frazier, pp. 353–364; "On Optimal Control for Systems with Numerator Dynamics," C. A. Harvey, E. B. Lee, and L. Markus, pp. 383–395; "The Doliac Macro-Micro Control Logic, Its Synthesis, Evaluation, Potential and Problems," D. O. Dommasch, pp. 241–268; "The Approximate Realization of Optimum Control Systems," S. S. L. Chang and F. J. Alexandro, pp. 269–322; "Applications and Applicability of Optimum Nonlinear Control," R. Oldenburger, pp. 323–342; "First Order Implications of the Calculus of Variations in Guidance and Control," R. E. Kalman, pp. 365–372; "A Synthesis Method for Optimal Controls," L. W. Neustadt, pp. 373–382; all from the Proceedings of the Optimum System Synthesis Conference, September, 1962, Technical Documentary Report No. ASD-STR-63-119, Feb., 1963.

75. The structure of optimum control systems, B. Friedland, ASME Trans. 84 D (J. Basic Eng.), Vol. 1, pp. 1–11, Mar., 1962; AMR 16 (1963), Rev. 1981.
76. On the existence of optimal controls, L. Markus and E. B. Lee, ASME Trans. 84 D (J. Basic Eng.), Vol. 1, pp. 13–20, Mar., 1962.
77. A successive approximation technique for optimal control systems, subject to input saturation, Y. C. Ho, ASME Trans. 84 D (J. Basic Eng.), Vol. 1, pp. 33–40, Mar. 1962.
78. Optimal pursuit strategies in discrete-state probabilistic systems, J. H. Eaton and L. A. Zadeh, ASME Trans. 84 D (J. Basic Eng.), Vol. 1, pp. 23–29, Mar., 1962.
79. Optimal control methods for on-off sampling systems, W. L. Nelson, ASME Trans. 84 D (J. Basic Eng.), Vol. 1, pp. 91–200, Mar., 1962; AMR 16 (1963), Rev. 5657.
80. Minimum time control of second order pulse-width-modulated sampled-data systems, E. Polak, ASME Trans. 84 D (J. Basic Eng.), Vol. 1, pp. 101–109, Mar., 1962; AMR 16 (1963), Rev. 5010.
81. A switching criterion for certain time-optimal regulating systems. E. R. Rang, ASME Trans. 84 D (J. Basic Eng.), Vol. 1, pp. 30–32, Mar., 1962; AMR 16 (1963), Rev. 3163.
82. An example of the application of dynamic programming to the design of optimum control programs, N. Kallay, IRE Trans. on Automatic Control AC-7, No. 2, pp. 10–21, April, 1962.
83. The problem of optimizing the final state of a controlled system, L. S. Kirillova, Avtomatika i Telemekhanika, Vol. 23, No. 12, pp. 1584–1594, Dec., 1962.

84. On a problem of optimal tracking, D. L. Kelendzheridze, Avtomatika i Telemekhanika, Vol. 23, No. 8, pp. 1008–1013, Aug., 1962.
85. On singular control in optimal processes that are linear with respect to the control inputs, Yu. I. Paraev, Avtomatika i Telemekhanika, Vol. 23, No. 9, pp. 1202–1209, Sept., 1962.
86. On a method of solving variational problems, G. M. Ostrovskii, Avtomatika i Telemekhanika, Vol. 23, No. 10, pp. 1284–1289, Oct., 1962.
87. The optimal transfer number for a reducer in high speed servomechanisms, G. A. Nadzhafova, Avtomatika i Telemekhanika, Vol. 23, No. 3, pp. 342–347, March, 1962.
88. The theory of analytic design of controllers, N. N. Krasovskii and A. M. Letov, Avtomatika i Telemekhanika, Vol. 23, No. 6, pp. 713–720, June, 1962.
89. The principle of the maximum in the theory of second-order optimal systems, V. S. Balakirev, Avtomatika i Telemekhanika, Vol. 23, No. 8, pp. 1014–1022, Aug., 1962.
90. A nonlinear problem in optimum control, V. K. Isaev and V. V. Sonin, Avtomatika i Telemekhanika, Vol. 23, No. 9, pp. 1117–1129, Sept., 1962.
91. Optimum space control and guidance, B. Friedland, Melpar Technical Note 62/3, June, 1962.
92. On the theory of optimal control, An asymptotic method for solving the diffusive alternative equation, R. L. Stratonovich, Avtomatika i Telemekhanika, Vol. 23, No. 11, pp. 1439–1447, Nov., 1962.
93. The problem of synthesizing an optimal controller in systems with time delay, Chang Jen-Wei, Avtomatika i Telemekhanika, Vol. 23, No. 2, pp. 133–137, Feb., 1962.
94. Time-optimal control systems in the presence of random noise, V. N. Novoseltsev, Avtomatika i Telemekhanika, Vol. 23, No. 12, pp. 1620–1630, Dec., 1962.
95. Finding of control algorithms in time-optimal systems with random noise disturbances, V. N. Novoseltsev, Avtomatika i Telemekhanika, Vol. 24, No. 4, pp. 510–520, April, 1963.
96. Non-linear optimization of control loops, K. Stahl, Regelungstechnik, Vol. 10, No. 1, pp. 7–12, Jan., 1962.
97. On optimizing control of batch-processes, Part I, O. A. Solheim, Regelungstechnik, Vol. 10, No. 6, pp. 241–245, June, 1962.
98. On optimizing control of batch-processes, Part II, O. A. Solheim, Regelungstechnik, Vol. 10, No. 7, pp. 299–302, July, 1962.
99. Time-, fuel- and energy-optimal control of nonlinear norm-invariant systems, M. Athans, P. L. Falb, and R. T. La Cross, IEEE Trans. on Automatic Control AC–8, No. 3, pp. 196–201, July, 1963.
100. Fuel minimization in flight vehicle attitude control, W. H. Foy, Jr., IEEE Trans. on Automatic Control AC–8, No. 2, pp. 84–88, Apr. 1963; AMR 16 (1963), Rev. 6279.

101. Synthesis of feedback controls using optimization theory — An example, F. J. Elbert and C. W. Merriam III, IEEE Trans. on Automatic Control AC–8, No. 2, pp. 89–103, Apr., 1963.
102. Minimal time control with multiple saturation limits, S. S. L. Chang, IEEE Trans. on Automatic Control AC–8, No. 1, pp. 35–42, Jan., 1963.
103. Minimal time control of a discrete system with a nonlinear plant, E. Polak, IEEE Trans. on Automatic Control AC–8, No. 1, pp. 49–55, Jan., 1963; AMR 16 (1963) Rev. 5008.
104. Synthesis of an optimal set of radar track-while-scan smoothing functions, T. R. Benedict and G. W. Bordner, IRE Trans. on Automatic Control AC–7, No. 4, pp. 27–32, July, 1962.
105. The multiple-input minimal time regulator problem (general theory), J. Wing and C. A. Desoer, IEEE Trans. on Automatic Control AC–8, No. 2, pp. 125–136, April, 1963.
106. Optimal control for linear time-invariant plants with time, fuel, and energy constraints, M. Athanassiades, IEEE Trans. (Applications and Industry), Vol. 82, Part II, No. 64, pp. 321–324, Jan., 1963.
107. Minimum-fuel feedback control systems, M. Athans, IEEE Trans. (Applications and Industry), Vol. 82, Part II, No. 65, pp. 8–16, March, 1963.
108. Synthesis of optimum multivariable control systems by the method of steepest descent, H. C. Hsieh, IEEE Trans. (Applications and Industry), Vol. 82, Part II, No. 66, pp. 125–130, May, 1963.
109. The optimum response of full third-order systems with contactor control, I. Flügge-Lotz and H. A. Titus, ASME Trans. 84 D (J. Basic Eng.), No. 4, pp. 554-558, Dec., 1962; AMR 16 (1963), Rev. 6274.
110. An application of functional analysis to the optimal control problem, G. M. Kranc and P. E. Sarachik, ASME Trans. 85 D (J. Basic Eng.), No. 2, pp. 143–150, June, 1963; AMR 17 (1964), Rev. 1282.
111. On a successive approximation technique in solving some control system optimization problems, M. Aoki, ASME Trans. 85 D (J. Basic Eng.), No. 2, pp. 177–180, June, 1963; AMR 17 (1964), Rev. 0664.
112. A general solution for linear, sampled-data control, T. L. Gunckel II and G. F. Franklin, ASME Trans. 85 D (J. Basic Eng.), No. 2, pp. 197–203, June, 1963; AMR 17 (1964), Rev. 037.
113. On the equivalence of discrete systems in time-optimal control, E. Polak, ASME Trans. 85 D (J. Basic Eng.), No. 2, pp. 204–210, June, 1963.
114. Optimal control of systems with generalized Poisson inputs, J. J. Florentin, ASME Trans. 85 D (J. Basic Eng.), Vol. 2, pp. 217–221, June, 1963; AMR 17 (1964), Rev. 041.
115. Introduction to time optimal control of stationary linear systems, R. Oldenburger and G. Thompson, Automatica, Vol. 1, No. 2/3, pp. 177–205, Aug., 1963; AMR 17 (1964), Rev. 1276.

116. Optimizing the final state of a control system, L. S. Kirillova, Avtomatika i Telemekhanika, Vol. 24, No. 8, pp. 1050–1055, Aug., 1963.
117. An existence theorem in terminal control problems, L. S. Kirillova, Avtomatika i Telemekhanika, Vol. 24, No. 9, pp. 1178–1182, Sept., 1963.
118. The solution of a linear problem in optimal control, V. F. Demyanov and V. V. Khomenyuk, Avtomatika i Telemekhanika, Vol. 24, No. 9, pp. 1174–1177, Sept., 1963.
119. Some problems of optimum control, I, B. G. Pittel, Avtomatika i Telemekhanika, Vol. 24, No. 9, pp. 1183–1186, Sept., 1963.
120. Some problems of optimum control, II, B. G. Pittel, Avtomatika i Telemekhanika, Vol. 24, No. 11, pp. 1441–1453, Nov., 1963.
121. Certain optimality problems for linear systems. A. Ya. Dubovitskii and A. A. Milyutin, Avtomatika i Telemekhanika, Vol. 24, No. 12, pp. 1616–1625, Dec., 1963.
122. On a way of optimum system realization with the help of a digital computer, V. S. Balakirev, Avtomatika i Telemekhanika, Vol. 24, No. 4, pp. 521–530, April, 1963.
123. The optimal control of some attitude control systems for different performance criteria, I. Flügge-Lotz and H. Marbach, ASME Trans., Vol. 85, Series D, No. 2, pp. 165–176, June, 1963.
124. The design of optimum controllers for linear processes with energy limitations, B. Friedland, ASME Trans., Vol. 85, Series D, No. 2, pp. 181–196, June, 1963.
125. Time optimal rendezvous strategies, P. A. Meschler, IEEE Trans. on Automatic Control AC–8, No. 4, pp. 279–283, Oct., 1963.
126. An iterative procedure for computing time-optimal controls, Harold K. Knudsen, Institute of Electrical and Electronic Engineers, Wescon Technical Papers, Paper No. 12.4, 1963.
127. An iterative procedure for computing time-optimal controls, Harold K. Knudsen, IEEE Transactions on Automatic Control AC–9, No. 1, pp. 23–30, Jan., 1964.
128. Concerning analytical design of optimal controller, M. E. Salukvadze, Avtomatika i Telemekhanika, Vol. 24, No. 4, pp. 437–446, April, 1963.
129. An optimum bistable controller for increased missile autopilot performance, Darrell Gieseking, IEEE Transactions on Automatic Control AC–8, No. 4, pp. 306–311, Oct., 1963.
130. Broadened principle of maximum for optimum control problems, A. G. Butkovskii, Avtomatika i Telemekhanika, Vol. 24, No. 2, pp. 314–327, Feb., 1963.
131. Adjoint method in the sensitivity analysis of optimal systems, M. Gavrilovic, R. Petrovic, and D. Siljak, Journal of the Franklin Institute, Vol. 276, No. 1, pp. 26–38, July, 1963.
132. An application of discrete optimal control theory, E. Polak, Journal of the Franklin Institute, Vol. 276, No. 2, pp. 118–127, Aug., 1963.

133. The formulation of optimal control, with an application to large systems, H. H. Rosenbrock, Automatica, Vol. 1, No. 4, pp. 263–288, Dec., 1963.
134. The necessary and sufficient conditions for optimality of discrete control systems, A. G. Butkovskii, Avtomatika i Telemekhanika, Vol. 24, No. 8, pp. 1056–1064, Aug., 1963.
135. A short introduction to optimal control theory, Y. C. Ho, Regelungstechnik, Vol. 11, No. 1, pp. 6–8, Jan., 1963.
136. Optimal control problems with input and output constraints, Y. C. Ho, Regelungstechnik, Vol. 11, No. 4, pp. 151–157, April, 1963.
137. Synthesis of an optimized relay-type controller for sampling systems, F. Haberstock, Regelungstechnik, Vol. 11, No. 5, pp. 210–215, May, 1963.
138. Application of the maximum principle to the optimization of parallel chemical reactions, F. A. Shatkhan, Avtomatika i Telemekhanika, Vol. 25, No. 3, pp. 368–373, March, 1964.
139. On the theory of optimal processes with distributed parameters, T. K. Sirazetdinov, Avtomatika i Telemekhanika, Vol. 25, No. 4, pp. 463–472, April, 1964.
140. Optimal control of processes in certain systems with distributed parameters, A. I. Egorov, Avtomatika i Telemekhanika, Vol. 25, No. 5, pp. 613–623, May, 1964.
141. Time optimal start-up of a dual heat-exchanger, Y. Takahashi and H. Thal-Larsen, ASME Preprint Paper No. 64–WA/AUT–17, pp. 1–7, 1964.
142. Optimal bang-bang control with quadratic performance index, W. M. Wonham and C. D. Johnson, ASME Trans., Vol. 86, Series D, No. 1, pp. 107–115, March, 1964.
143. Control based upon repeated computation, Yasundo Takahashi and Haris Sutabutra, ASME Preprint No. 64–WA/AUT–9, pp. 1–14.
144. Error analysis with the maximum principle, D. R. Howard and Z. V. Rekasius, IEEE Trans. on Automatic Control AC–9, No. 3, pp. 223–229, July, 1964.
145. Minimum fuel control for a second-order linear process with a constraint on time-to-run, H. O. Ladd, Jr., and Bernard Friedland, ASME Trans., Vol. 86, Series D, No. 1, pp. 160–168, March, 1964.
146. Fuel-optimal control of a double integral plant with response time constraints, Michael Athans, IEEE Trans. (Applications and Industry), Vol. 83, No. 73, pp. 240–246, July, 1964.
147. On minimal-fuel satellite attitude controls, J. S. Meditch, IEEE Trans., Vol. 83, No. 71, pp. 120–128, March, 1964.
148. On a method of solving certain optimal control problems, R. Gabasov and F. M. Kirillova, Avtomatika i Telemekhanika, Vol. 25, No. 3, pp. 312–320, March, 1964.
149. Successive approximations for solution of one optimal problem. G. N.

Milshtein, Avtomatika i Telemekhanika, Vol. 25, No. 3, pp. 321–329, March, 1964.

150. Optimum control of distributed-parameter systems, P. K. C. Wang and F. Tung, ASME Trans. Vol. 86, Series D, No. 1, pp. 67–79, March, 1964.

151. Optimal singular solutions for linear multi-input systems, R. A. Rohrer and M. Sobral, Jr., ASME Preprint No. 64–WA/AUT–15, pp. 1–16.

152. A study of synthesis techniques for optimal controllers, Bernard Paiewonsky *et al.*, U. S. Air Force Technical Documentary Report No. ASD–TDR–63–239, June, 1964.

153. On a controller analytical design problem, V. A. Petrov and G. V. Skvortsov, Avtomatika i Telemekhanika, Vol. 25, No. 10, pp. 1399–1403, Oct., 1964.

154. Analytical design of an optimal controller for stabilizing angular position of vertical take-off, Yu. B. Popov, Avtomatika i Telemekhanika, Vol. 25, No. 4, pp. 452–462, April, 1964.

155. On optimal control in the presence of a delay, V. N. Novoseltsev, Avtomatika i Telemekhanika, Vol. 25, No. 11, pp. 1545–1548, Nov., 1964.

156. Simultaneous operation of two optimum-speed automatic devices, A. B. Savvin, Avtomatika i Telemekhanika, Vol. 25, No. 1, pp. 12–15, Jan., 1964.

157. On the sub-optimal design of nonlinear control systems, R. L. Häussler and Z. V. Rekasius, Regelungstechnik, Vol. 12, No. 7, pp. 290–296, July, 1964.

158. "Optimum" two-position control, A. Leonhard, Regelungstechnik, Vol. 12, No. 10, pp. 437–441, Oct., 1964.

159. Time optimal control for discrete systems subject to saturation, J. T. Tou, Regelungstechnik, Vol. 12, No. 11, pp. 481–486, Nov., 1964.

160. Optimizing linear control systems with transient parameters applying Pontryagin's maximum principle, H. Weischedel, Regelungstechnik, Vol. 12, No. 11, pp. 487–490, November, 1964.

161. Optimal control with quadratic performance index and fixed terminal time, C. D. Johnson and J. E. Gibson, IEEE Trans. on Automatic Control AC–9, No. 4, pp. 355–360, Oct., 1964.

162. On the fuel optimal singular control of nonlinear second-order systems, M. Athans and M. D. Canon, IEEE Trans. on Automatic Control, Vol. AC–9, No. 4, pp. 360–369, Oct., 1964.

163. On an inverse problem of optimal control, Z. V. Rekasius and T. C. Hsia, IEEE Trans. on Automatic Control AC–9, No. 4, pp. 370–374, Oct., 1964.

164. Bounds on limit cycles in two-dimensional bang-bang control systems with an almost time-optimal switching curve, John J. O'Donnell, IEEE Trans. on Automatic Control AC–9, No. 4, pp. 448–457, Oct., 1964.

165. On the use of optimization theory for practical control system design, Winston L. Nelson, IEEE Trans. on Automatic Control AC–9, No. 4, pp. 469–476, October, 1964.
166. On the problem of optimal thrust programming of a soft lunar landing, James S. Meditch, IEEE Trans. on Automatic Control AC–9, No. 4, pp. 477–484, October, 1964.
167. Principle of optimalizing control systems with an application to the internal combustion engine, C. S. Draper and Y. T. Li, ASME Monograph, 1951, 160 pp.
168. An automatic cruise control computer for long range aircraft, J. R. Shull, IRE Trans. on Electronic Computers, Vol. EC–1, pp. 47–57, December, 1952.
169. Optimalizing control—design of fully automatic cruise control system for turbojet aircraft, W. K. Genthe, 1957 IRE WESCON Convention Record, Vol. 1, Part 4, pp. 47–57, 1957.
170. Analysis of peak-holding optimalizing control, H. S. Tsien and S. Serdengecti, J. Aerospace Sci., Vol. 22, No. 8, pp. 561–570, August, 1955.
171*a*. Rechengeräte in automatischen Systemen, A. A. Fel'dbaum, R. Oldenbourg Verlag, Munich, 1962, 469 pp. Automatic optimizer, A. A. Fel'dbaum, Avtomatika i Telemekhanika, Vol. 19, No. 8, August, 1958, pp. 731–743. An automatic optimizer for the search for the smallest of several minima (a global optimizer), I. N. Bocharov and A. A. Fel'dbaum, Avtomatika i Telemekhanika, Vol. 23, No. 8, March, 1962, pp. 289–302.
171*b*. Design of a self-optimizing system, R. E. Kalman, ASME Trans. Vol. 80, No. 2, Feb., 1958, pp. 468–478.
172. Automatic optimizers and their use for solving variational problems and for automatic signals, R. I. Stakhovskiy, L. N. Fitsner, and A. B. Shubin, Proceedings of the 1960 Moscow Congress of the International Federation of Automatic Control, Butterworths, London, Vol. 3, pp. 141–148, 1960.
173. The use of Self-Adjusting Automatic Control Systems, A. Y. Lerner, Proceedings of the 1960 Moscow Congress of the International Federation of Automatic Control, Butterworths, London, Vol. 4, pp. 226–230, 1960.
174. Statistical theory of gradient systems of automatic optimization for objects with quadratic characteristics, A. A. Fel'dbaum, Avtomatika i Telemekhanika, Vol. 21, No. 1, pp. 167–179, Feb., 1960.
175. Dual control theory, I, A. A. Fel'dbaum, Avtomatika i Telemekhanika, Vol. 21, No. 9, pp. 1240–1249, Sept., 1960.
176. Dual control theory, II, A. A. Fel'dbaum, Avtomatika i Telemekhanika, Vol. 21, No. 11, pp. 1453–1464, Nov., 1960.
177. The theory of dual control, III, A. A. Fel'dbaum, Avtomatika i Telemekhanika, Vol. 22, No. 1, pp. 3–16, Jan., 1961.

178. The theory of dual control, IV, A. A. Fel'dbaum, Avtomatika i Telemekhanika, Vol. 22, No. 2, pp. 129–143, Feb., 1961.
179. On the optimal control of Markov objects, A. A. Fel'dbaum, Avtomatika i Telemekhanika, Vol. 23, No. 8, pp. 993–1007, Aug., 1962.
180. One class of self-organizing systems with dual control, A. A. Fel'dbaum, Avtomatika i Telemekhanika, Vol. 25, No. 4, pp. 433–444, April, 1964.
181. Investigation of the periodic behavior of relay systems with extremum regulation, I. S. Morosanov, Avtomatika i Telemekhanika, Vol. 21, No. 7, pp. 951–957, July, 1960.
182. Continuous extremum control systems in the presence of random noise, A. A. Pervozanskii, Avtomatika i Telemekhanika, Vol. 21, No. 7, pp. 958–964, July, 1960.
183. Two types of optimum extremal systems, L. N. Fitsner, Avtomatika i Telemekhanika, Vol. 21, No. 8, pp. 1115–1122, Aug., 1960.
184. Automatic optimization of space distribution, II, L. N. Fitsner, Avtomatika i Telemekhanika, Vol. 22, No. 7, pp. 857–864, July, 1961.
185. Automatic optimization of space distribution, III, L. N. Fitsner, Avtomatika i Telemekhanika, Vol. 22, No. 8, pp. 1001–1012, Aug., 1961.
186. The automatic optimalization of space distribution, IV, L. N. Fitsner, Avtomatika i Telemekhanika, Vol. 23, No. 2, pp. 148–157, Feb., 1962.
187. Transitional processes in a system of extremal control with a dynamic sensitive unit, A. P. Yurkevich, Avtomatika i Telemekhanika, Vol. 22, No. 2, pp. 176–184, Feb., 1961.
188. The determination of optimal characteristics for an extremal system with random disturbances. N. V. Grishko, Avtomatika i Telemekhanika, Vol. 22, No. 8, pp. 1013–1026, Aug., 1961.
189. On the question of choice of parameters in the control part of a gradient-type automatic optimization system, T. I. Tovstykha, Avtomatika i Telemekhanika, Vol. 22, No. 8, pp. 1027–1037, Aug., 1961.
190. The statistical investigation of extrapolation extremal-control systems for an object with a parabolic characteristic, I. I. Perelman, Avtomatika i Telemekhanika, Vol. 22, No. 11, pp. 1453–1465, Nov., 1961.
191. Dynamics of relay self-oscillating extremum control systems, V. Ya. Katkovnik and A. A. Pervozanskii, Avtomatika i Telemekhanika, Vol. 22, No. 12, pp. 1576–1584, Dec., 1961.
192. Synthesis of a certain class of optimal system, V. N. Zhigulev, Avtomatika i Telemekhanika, Vol. 23, No. 11, pp. 1431–1438, Nov., 1962.
193. The investigation of a gradient system of automatic optimization with random interference at the input and output of the object, Ts. Ts. Paulauskas, Avtomatika i Telemekhanika, Vol. 23, No. 1, pp. 34–44, Jan., 1962.
194. Automatic sampled-data optimizer, I, Ts. Ts. Paulauskas, Avtomatika i Telemekhanika, Vol. 23, No. 5, pp. 610–619, May, 1962.

195. A digital automatic optimizer, II, Ts. Ts. Paulauskas, Avtomatika i Telemekhanika, Vol. 23, No. 11, pp. 1497–1506, Nov., 1962.
196. An automatic optimizer for the search for the smallest of several minima (A global optimizer), I. N. Bocharov and A. A. Fel'dbaum, Avtomatika i Telemekhanika, Vol. 23, No. 3, pp. 289–301, March, 1962.
197. Self-oscillations in sampled-data extremum systems, A. V. Netushil, Avtomatika i Telemekhanika, Vol. 23, No. 3, pp. 302–311, March, 1962.
198. Application of the theory of games to some problems of automatic control I, M. Yu. Gadzhiev, Avtomatika i Telemekhanika, Vol. 23, No. 8, pp. 1023–1036, Aug., 1962.
199. Conditional optimization of a chemical factory on the basis of matching the reactor modes, L. G. Pliskin, Avtomatika i Telemekhanika, Vol. 23, No. 10, pp. 1362–1374, Oct., 1962.
200. A nonlinear optimization problem, I. Sh. Pinsker and B. M. Tseitlin, Avtomatika i Telemekhanika, Vol. 23, No. 12, pp. 1611–1619, Dec., 1962.
201. The use of a method of linear programming for solving the transport problem of optimal feed of metal to a blooming mill, V. P. Putsillo, V. P. Strakhov, and L. I. Feigin, Avtomatika i Telemekhanika, Vol. 23, No. 8, pp. 1067–1077, Aug., 1962.
202. Self-optimization of a cascade control loop with a deviation model, K. Brammer, Regelungstechnik, Vol. 11, No. 7, pp. 306–311, July, 1963.
203. Optimalizing control with process-dynamics identification, P. Eykhoff and O. J. M. Smith, IRE Trans. on Automatic Control, Vol. AC–7, No. 2, pp. 140–155, March, 1962.
204. Optimizing control of single input extremum systems, J. S. Frait and D. P. Eckman, ASME Trans., 84 D (J. Basic Eng.), Vol. 1, pp. 85–90, Mar., 1962; AMR 16 (1963), Rev. 3160.
205. A simple iterative procedure for the identification of the unknown parameters of a linear time-varying discrete system, H. J. Kushner, ASME Trans., 85 D (J. Basic Eng.) Vol. 2, pp. 227–235, June, 1963.
206. Methods for calculating and synthesizing sampled-data automatic systems I, E. G. Golshtein and D. B. Yudin, Avtomatika i Telemekhanika, Vol. 24, No. 7, pp. 921–928, July, 1963.
207. Methods for calculating and synthesizing sampled-data automatic systems II, E. G. Golshtein and D. B. Yudin, Avtomatika i Telemekhanika, Vol. 24, No. 12, pp. 1643–1659, Dec., 1963.
208. The convergence of the random search method in the extremal control of a many-parameter system, L. A. Rastrigin, Avtomatika i Telemekhanika, Vol. 24, No. 11, pp. 1467–1473, Nov., 1963.
209. Determination of optimizer control law with object relaxation taken into account, Yu. I. Bobrov, R. V. Kornilov, and V. P. Putsillo, Avtomatika i Telemekhanika, Vol. 24, No. 2, pp. 183–192, Feb., 1964.
210. Quasi-stationary processes of extremal continuous control in the case

of bounded coordinates, N. N. Krasovskii, Avtomatika i Telemekhanika, Vol. 24, No. 12, 1633–1642, Dec., 1963.

211. Comparative investigation of simplest gradient and extrapolation extremal systems with real static characteristics, I. I. Perelman, Avtomatika i Telemekhanika, Vol. 24, No. 4, pp. 493–509, April, 1963.

212. Random search techniques for optimization problems, D. C. Karnopp, Automatica, Vol. 1, No. 2/3, pp. 111–121, Aug., 1963.

213. Motion equations for sampled-data extremal systems with constant repetition period, Yu. S. Popkov, Avtomatika i Telemekhanika, Vol. 24, No. 4, 472–481, April, 1963.

214. Automatic optimizing of a poorly defined process, I, H. Chestnut, R. R. Duersch and W. M. Gaines, IEEE Transactions (Applications and Industry), No. 65, pp. 32–41, March, 1963.

215. Sequential multistep parameter regulator for self-adjusting systems, G. M. Rakovchuk, Vol. 24, No. 11, pp. 1501–1513, Nov., 1963.

216. Dynamic programming: cumulative errors in the evaluation of an optimal policy, J. J. G. Guignabodet, ASME Transactions, Vol. 85, Series D, No. 2, pp. 151–156, June, 1963.

217. A general solution for linear sampled-data control, T. L. Gunckel II and G. F. Franklin, ASME Transactions, Vol. 85, Series D, No. 2, pp. 197–203, June, 1963.

218. Automatic optimization by continuous perturbation of parameters, P. H. Hammond & M. J. Duckenfield, Automatica, Vol. 1, No. 2/3, pp. 147–175, Aug., 1963.

219. Determination of the optimum program of a linear system, V. F. Demyanov, Avtomatika i Telemekhanika, Vol. 25, No. 1, pp. 3–11, Jan., 1964.

220. Optimal dual control of plants with pure delay, V. P. Zhivoglyadov, Avtomatika i Telemekhanika, Vol. 25, No. 1, pp. 54–66, Jan., 1964.

221. Synthesis of extremum-seeking regulators, M. H. Hamza, Avtomatika i Telemekhanika, Vol. 25, No. 8, pp. 1156–1161, Aug., 1964.

222. Synthesis of asymptotic optimum dual control systems, G. A. Medvedev, Avtomatika i Telemekhanika, Vol. 25, No. 8, pp. 1170–1181, Aug., 1964.

223. A new method of locating the maximum point of an arbitrary multipeak curve in the presence of noise, H. J. Kushner, ASME Trans., Vol. 86, Series D, No. 1, pp. 97–106, March, 1964.

224. Linear digital control, F. J. Mullin and J. de Barbeyrac, ASME Transactions, Vol. 86, Series D, No. 1, pp. 61–66, March, 1964.

225. Optimal control of some class of imperfectly known control systems, Masanao Aoki, ASME Preprint No. 64–WA/AUT–7, pp. 1–12, 1964.

226. A suboptimal on-line discrete controller with bounded control variables, F. H. Kishi, IEEE Transactions (Applications and Industry), Vol. 83, No. 73, pp. 216–222, July, 1964.

227. Self-organizing control systems, M. D. Mesarovic, IEEE Trans. on Applications and Industry, Vol. 83, No. 74, pp. 265–269, Sept., 1964.
228. Pattern recognition and adaptive control, Bernard Widrow, IEEE Trans. (Applications and Industry), Vol. 83, No. 74, pp. 269–277, September, 1964.
229. Multiparameter self-optimizing systems using correlation techniques, K. S. Narendra and L. E. McBride, IEEE Transactions on Automatic Control, Vol. AC–9, No. 1, pp. 31–39, January, 1964.
230. Optimum control of linear systems with a "modified" energy constraint, N. E. Nahi, IEEE Transactions on Automatic Control AC–9, No. 2, pp. 137–143, April, 1964.
231. On the optimum timing of observations for linear control systems with unknown initial state, H. J. Kushner, IEEE Transactions on Automatic Control AC–9, No. 2, pp. 144–150, April, 1964.
232. Digital implementation of time-optimal attitude control, A. H. Sephahban, IEEE Transactions on Automatic Control AC–9, No. 2, pp. 164–174, April, 1964.
233. Optimal control of linear plants with random parameters, R. F. Drenick and L. Shaw, IEEE Transactions on Automatic Control AC–9, No. 3, pp. 236–244, July, 1964.
234. Practical optimizing systems, J. M. Nightingale, Control Engineering, Vol. 11, No. 12, pp. 76–81, Dec., 1964.
235. The adaptive control of a batch reactor II, Optimal path control, H. H-y Chien and R. Aris, Automatica, Vol. 2, No. 1, pp. 59–71, June, 1964.
236. An optimization theory for time-varying linear systems with non-stationary statistical inputs, R. C. Booton, Jr., IRE Proc., 40, 8, 977–981, Aug., 1952.
237. Optimum filters for the detection of signals in noise, L. A. Zadeh and J. R. Ragazzini, Proceedings of the Institute of Radio Engineers, Vol. 40, No. 10, Oct., 1952, pp. 1223–1231.
238. Optimum design of final-value control systems, R. C. Booton, Jr., Proceedings of the Symposium on Nonlinear Circuit Analysis, Polytechnic Institute of Brooklyn, Vol. 6, pp. 233–241, April, 1956.
239. Determination of the optimal impulsive response function in the presence of internal noise, P. S. Matveev, Avtomatika i Telemekhanika, Vol. 21, No. 3, pp. 286–292, March, 1960.
240. Statistical analysis and optimization of systems, E. L. Peterson, John Wiley & Sons, New York, 1961; AMR 15, Rev. 4468, 190 pp., 1962.
241. Optimization of automatic systems by statistical criteria, S. A. Doganovskii, Avtomatika i Telemekhanika, Vol. 22, No. 7, pp. 845–856, July, 1961.
242. Analytical design of controllers in systems with random attributes I, Statement of the problem, method of solving, N. N. Krasovskii and

E. A. Lidskii, Avtomatika i Telemekhanika, Vol. 22, No. 9, pp. 1145–1151, Sept., 1961.
243. Analytic design of controllers in systems with random attributes, II, N. N. Krasovskii and E. A. Lidskii, Avtomatika i Telemekhanika, Vol. 22, No. 9, pp. 1273–1278, Sept., 1961.
244. Analytical control design in systems with random properties, III, N. N. Krasovskii and E. A. Lidskii, Avtomatika i Telemekhanika, Vol. 22, No. 11, pp. 1425–1431, Nov., 1961.
245. Optimum filter discrimination of telegraph signals, R. L. Stratonovich, Avtomatika i Telemekhanika, Vol. 22, No. 9, pp. 1163–1174, Sept., 1961.
246. On the statistical autonomy of dynamic processes in optimalization objects containing control systems. R. I. Stakhovskii, Avtomatika i Telemekhanika, Vol. 22, No. 9, pp. 1179–1186, Sept., 1961.
247. Methods for realizing optimal filters with a finite memory, S. N. Diligenskii, Avtomatika i Telemekhanika, Vol. 22, No. 11, pp. 1441–1452, Nov., 1961.
248. Optimum design of passive-adaptive, linear feedback systems with varying plants, P. E. Fleischer, IRE Trans. on Automatic Control, Vol. AC–7, No. 2, pp. 117–128, Mar., 1962.
249. Algebraic method of determining the optimum transfer function, A. N. Sklyarevich, Avtomatika i Telemekhanika, Vol. 23, No. 9, pp. 1154–1164, Sept., 1962.
250. The synthesis of optimal characteristics for sampled-data servosystems, N. N. Korobov, Avtomatika i Telemekhanika, Vol. 23, No. 9, pp. 1215–1223, Sept., 1962.
251. Optimum design of following controllers using Wiener's criterion, H. Schlitt, Regelungstechnik, Vol. 10, No. 5, pp. 193–200, May, 1962.
252. Synthesis of an optimum servosystem, V. I. Schmalgauzen, Avtomatika i Telemekhanika, Vol. 24, No. 8, pp. 1057–1064, Aug., 1963.
253. A problem in the synthesis of an optimal control solved by the method of dynamic programming, G. E. Kolosov and R. L. Stratonovich, Avtomatika i Telemekhanika, Vol. 24, No. 9, pp. 1165–1173, Sept., 1963.
254. Optimal controls based on maximum probability, I, I. I. Perelman, Avtomatika i Telemekhanika, Vol. 24, No. 10, pp. 1317–1329, Oct., 1963.
255. Optimal controls based on maximum probability, II, I. I. Perelman, Avtomatika i Telemekhanika, Vol. 25, No. 9, pp. 1273–1284, Sept., 1964.
256. Optimization of control on the basis of the criterion of likelihood maximum, III, I. I. Perelman, Avtomatika i Telemekhanika, Vol. 25, No. 11, pp. 1549–1556, Nov., 1964.
257. Synthesis of optimal filters for signals changing their statistical properties in successive time intervals, I. B. Chelpanov, Avtomatika i Telemekhanika, Vol. 24, No. 10, pp. 1330–1337, Oct., 1963.

258. The problem of synthesizing discrete systems with the method of polynomial equations, M. R. Elistratov, Avtomatika i Telemekhanika, Vol. 24, No. 11, pp. 1474–1486, Nov., 1963.
259. Design of optimum stationary filter with finite memory for random time interval, I. B. Chelpanov, Avtomatika i Telemekhanika, Vol. 24, No. 1, pp. 47–52, January, 1963.
260. Optimum transfer function with recurrent methematical expectation actions, A. N. Sklyarevich, Avtomatika i Telemekhanika, Vol. 24, No. 1, pp. 53–64, Jan., 1963.
261. Analytical design of system reproducing signal in the presence of noise, A. G. Zaitsev, Avtomatika i Telemekhanika, Vol. 24, No. 2, pp. 143–150, Feb., 1963.
262. Analytical design of optimal controllers with random outer disturbances, A. G. Zaitsev, Avtomatika i Telemekhanika, Vol. 24, No. 4, pp. 447–454, April, 1963.
263. Synthesis of optimum compensation according to servosystem input signal, V. I. Ivanenko, Avtomatika i Telemekhanika, Vol. 24, No. 6, pp. 764–768, June, 1963.
264. The problem of conditions for identity of systems that are optimal with respect to different criteria, O. M. Kozlov, Avtomatika i Telemekhanika, Vol. 24, No. 11, pp. 1454–1460, Nov., 1963.
265. Optimum transmission of continuous signals through a sampled-data circuit, V. Ya. Katkovnik and R. P. Poluéktov, Avtomatika i Telemekhanika, Vol. 25, No. 2, pp. 201–206, Feb., 1964.
266. Application of statistical solution theory to problems of indirect control, V. P. Zhivoglyadov, Avtomatika i Telemekhanika, Vol. 25, No. 10, pp. 1451-1461, Oct., 1964.
267. Intensive errors effect on periodic states in sampled-data extremal systems, with independent search, Yu. S. Popkov, Avtomatika i Telemekhanika, Vol. 25, No. 10, pp. 1462–1471, Oct., 1964.
268. Optimal control design using a method of moments and minimizing the standard deviation, A. B. Kurzhanskii, Avtomatika i Telemekhanika, Vol. 25, No. 5, pp. 624–630, May, 1964.
269. The analysis and synthesis of linear servomechanisms, A. C. Hall, The Technology Press, Massachusetts Institute of Technology, Cambridge, 1943, 193 pp.
270. Some design criteria for automatic controls, P. T. Nims, AIEE Trans., Vol. 70, Part I, pp. 606–611, 1951.
271. Analogue methods for optimum servomechanism design, F. C. Fickerson and T. M. Stout, AIEE Trans. (Applications and Industry), Vol. 71, Part II, No. 3, pp. 244–250, Nov., 1952.
272. The synthesis of "optimum" transient response: Criteria and standard forms, D. Graham and R. C. Lathrop, AIEE Trans. (Applications and Industry), Vol. 72, Part II, pp. 273–288, 1953.
273. Control-system behavior expressed as a deviation ratio, J. M. L. Jans-

sen, "Frequency Response," edited by R. Oldenburger, The Macmillan Company, New York, pp. 131–140, 1956; AMR 10 (1957), Rev. 19.
274. A uniform approach to the optimum adjustment of control loops, R. C. Oldenbourg and H. Sartorius, "Frequency Response," edited by R. Oldenburger, The Macmillan Company, New York, pp. 211–225, 1956.
275. Analytical controller design, I, A. M. Letov, Avtomatika i Telemekhanika, Vol. 21, No. 4, pp. 416–441, April, 1960.
276. The analytic design of controls V, A. M. Letov, Avtomatika i Telemekhanika, Vol. 23, No. 11, pp. 1405–1413, Nov., 1962.
277. Constructing optimal second-order automatic control systems using limiting values of control loop element gains, S. V. Emelyanov and A. I. Fedotova, Avtomatika i Telemekhanika, Vol. 21, No. 1, pp. 56–63, Jan., 1960.
278. On a problem of optimal control, I. A. Litovchenko, Avtomatika i Telemekhanika, Vol. 21, No. 8, pp. 1123–1133, Aug., 1960.
279. Determination of aircraft control equation for the optimum path under variable flight conditions. V. D. Matytsin, Avtomatika i Telemekhanika, Vol. 22, No. 1, pp. 47–56, Jan., 1961.
280. The analytical design of control systems, Ya. Kurtsveil, Avtomatika i Telemekhanika, Vol. 22, No. 6, pp. 688–695, June, 1961.
281. Analytic design of regulators (constant disturbances), M. E. Salukvadze, Avtomatika i Telemekhanika, Vol. 22, No. 9, pp. 1279–1287, Sept., 1961.
282. The analytical design of an optimal control in the case of constantly acting disturbances, M. E. Salukvadze, Avtomatika i Telemekhanika, Vol. 23, No. 6, pp. 721–731, June, 1962.
283. Concerning the synthesis of an optimal controller in linear delay systems subjected to constantly acting perturbations, M. E. Salukvadze, Avtomatika i Telemekhanika, Vol. 23, No. 12, pp. 1595–1601, Dec., 1962.
284. Isoperimetric problem in analytic design, I. A. Litovchenko, Avtomatika i Telemekhanika, Vol. 22, No. 12, pp. 1553–1559, Dec., 1961.
285. Dynamic optimization and control, Walerian Kipiniak, The M.I.T. Press and John Wiley & Sons, 233 pp., 1961.
286. Methods for solving variational problems on the basis of the sufficient conditions for an absolute minimum, I, V. F. Krotov, Avtomatika i Telemekhanika, Vol. 23, No. 12, pp. 1571–1583, Dec., 1962.
287. On optimal processes in coupled digital systems, R. Gabasov, Avtomatika i Telemekhanika, Vol. 23, No. 7, pp. 872–880, July, 1962.
288. Optimal control under conditions of lagging feedback, N. N. Krasovskii, Avtomatika i Telemekhanika, Vol. 24, No. 8, pp. 1021–1036, Aug., 1963.
289. The method of moments in the theory of optimal control of systems with distributed parameters, A. G. Butkovskii, Avtomatika i Telemekhanika, Vol. 24, No. 9, pp. 1217–1225, Sept., 1963.

290. An approximate method for the synthesis of optimal controls, E. M. Vaisbord, Avtomatika i Telemekhanika, Vol. 24, No. 12, pp. 1626–1632, Dec., 1963.
291. On a problem in time-delay optimal systems theory, V. M. Popov and A. Khalanaj, Avtomatika i Telemekhanika, Vol. 24, No. 2, pp. 133–135, Feb., 1963.
292. Analytical method of determination of static and astatic autopilot optimal parameters, V. D. Matytsin, Avtomatika i Telemekhanika, Vol. 24, No. 4, pp. 455–464, April, 1963.
293. Methods of solving variational problems II, Sliding regimes, V. F. Krotov, Avtomatika i Telemekhanika, Vol. 24, No. 5, pp. 581–598, May, 1963.
294. Concerning optimum processes in coordinated control systems, R. Gabasov and F. M. Kirillova, Avtomatika i Telemekhanika, Vol. 24, No. 6, pp. 757–763, June, 1963.
295. Performance limits for feedback control systems, G. Rabow, IEEE Trans. (Applications and Industry), No. 69, pp. 351–356, Nov., 1963.
296. Minimization of reactor noise through external control, L. E. Weaver and W. E. Cooper, IEEE Transactions on Automatic Control, Vol. AC–8, No. 4, pp. 366–370, October, 1963.
297. Optimal control in bounded phase space, S. S. L. Chang, Automatica, Vol. 1, No. 1, pp. 55–67, Jan.–March, 1963.
298. Use of linear programming methods for synthesizing sampled-data automatic systems, A. I. Propoi, Avtomatika i Telemekhanika, Vol. 24, No. 7, pp. 912–920, July, 1963.
299. Optimum control of linked discrete systems, R. Gabasov and F. M. Kirillova, Avtomatika i Telemekhanika, Vol. 24, No. 7, pp. 900–905, July, 1963.
300. Synthesis of optimal controllers for a class of maximization problems, Masanao Aoki, Automatica, Vol. 1, No. 1, pp. 69–80, Jan.–March, 1963.
301. Optimum design of nonlinear sampled-data control systems, J. Mekswan and G. J. Murphy, Regelungstechnik, Vol. 11, No. 7, pp. 195–299, July, 1963.
302. A modeling theory for a class of optimal control systems, Walter J. Culver, Report SRC–38–A–68–15, Systems Research Center, Case Institute of Technology, Sept., 1963.
303. On solving the general problem of linear speed of response, N. E. Kirin, Avtomatika i Telemekhanika, Vol. 25, No. 1, pp. 16–22, Jan., 1964.
304. The problem of using dynamic-programming methods for construction of optimal regulators, R. P. Parsheva, Avtomatika i Telemekhanika, Vol. 25, No. 1, pp. 30–40, Jan., 1964.
305. A problem in analytical design of controllers, Yu. I. Paraev, Avtomatika i Telemekhanika, Vol. 25, No. 2, pp. 167–176, Feb., 1964.

306. Solution of a problem in analytical controller design, Yu. I. Paraev, Avtomatika i Telemekhanika, Vol. 25, No. 4, pp. 445–451, April, 1964.
307. The problem of invariancy of optimal regulators, M. E. Salukvadze, Avtomatika i Telemekhanika, Vol. 25, No. 5, pp. 650–652, May, 1962.
308. Methods for variational problem solution based on absolute minimum sufficient conditions, III, V. F. Krotov, Avtomatika i Telemekhanika, Vol. 25, No. 7, pp. 1037–1046, July, 1964.
309. Some aspects of control quality in problems of optimum controllers analytical design, Yu. B. Popov, Avtomatika i Telemekhanika, Vol. 25, No. 9, pp. 1263–1272, Sept., 1964.
310. On necessary and sufficient conditions of optimality for controlled systems, A. Ya. Yasiliev, Avtomatika i Telemekhanika, Vol. 25, No. 10, pp. 1404–1413, Oct., 1964.
311. On an optimum problem, Yu. M. Volin and G. M. Ostrovsky, Avtomatika i Telemekhanika, Vol. 25, No. 10, pp. 1414–1420, Oct., 1964.
312. Approximate synthesis of optimal control, V. F. Krotov, Avtomatika i Telemekhanika, Vol. 25, No. 11, pp. 1521–1527, Nov., 1964.
313. Minimization of convex flat functionals in linear systems at convex flat constraint of phase coordinates, V. F. Demyanov, Avtomatika i Telemekhanika, Vol. 25, No. 11, pp. 1528–1537, Nov., 1964.
314. Programming of optimal processes for control of linear objects, L. N. Volgin, Avtomatika i Telemekhanika, Vol. 25, No. 11, pp. 1538–1544, Nov., 1964.
315. When is a linear control system optimal?, R. E. Kalman, ASME Transactions, Vol. 86, Series D, No. 1, pp. 51–60, March, 1964.
316. Optimum control of distributed parameter systems with time delays, P. K. C. Wang, IEEE Transactions on Automatic Control AC–9, No. 1, pp. 13–22, Jan., 1964.
317. The application of the parametric expansion method of control optimization to the guidance and control problem of a rigid booster, F. B. Bailey, IEEE Trans. on Automatic Control, Vol. AC–9, No. 1, pp. 74–81, Jan., 1964.
318. Linear control theory applied to interplanetary guidance, F. Tung, IEEE Trans. on Automatic Control, Vol. AC–9, No. 1, pp. 82–89, Jan., 1964.
319. Optimal-control theory applied to a probabilistic intercept problem, J. S. Tyler, Jr., and F. B. Tuteur, IEEE Trans. on Automatic Control AC–9, No. 4, pp. 498–507, Oct., 1964.
320. The characteristics of model-following systems as synthesized by optimal control, J. S. Tyler, Jr., IEEE Transactions on Automatic Control AC–9, No. 4, pp. 485–498, Oct., 1964.
321. Solution of an optimal control problem in a distributed-parameter system, Y. Sakawa, IEEE Trans. on Automatic Control AC–9, No. 4, pp. 420–425, Oct., 1964.

PART I

Optimal Control of Systems with Unbounded Inputs

The Synthesis of "Optimum" Transient Response: Criteria and Standard Forms

DUNSTAN GRAHAM
MEMBER AIEE

R. C. LATHROP
ASSOCIATE MEMBER AIEE

Synopsis: Methods for synthesizing servomechanisms are reviewed, and it is pointed out that stability criteria, frequency, and root-locus methods reduce to conditions on the transfer-function constants. These may be made mathematically specific following Whiteley's suggestion of "standard forms." Eight mathematical criteria for optimum transient responses are critically examined, and the clear superiority of the minimum integral of time-multiplied absolute-value of error is demonstrated. The application of this criterion results in the selection of standard forms, which are presented in tables.

TRANSIENT BEHAVIOR is an attribute of many measurement, control, and communication devices. Engineering design of such physical systems often involves the choice of design variables which will insure optimum transient behavior. Mathematical techniques applicable to this engineering design problem have been rapidly developed and extended during the past ten years. The lack of a practical mathematical definition of optimum transient behavior, however, has forced empiricism into the design procedures, and the procedures themselves, for the most part, are esoteric and laborious. Development of a unitary figure of merit for transient behavior and the tabulation of optimum system characteristics would be valuable to the designer.

Mathematical methods applied to the problem of optimizing the transient behavior of physical systems depend uniformly on the concept of the response of a transfer system.[1–3] A transfer system which is characterized by an input and a related output is illustrated in Fig. 1. The block may be conceived of as an operator which metamorphoses a given input $r(t)$ to produce a unique output $c(t)$. The most fundamental relationship which gives the dependence of the output (response or effect) on the input (cause) is usually the differential equation which describes the physical system. A simple positioning servomechanism, its linear second-order equation, and its transfer function are illustrated in Fig. 2. The transfer functions of the linear systems considered in this paper are always reduced to the normalized form

$$\frac{C(s)}{R(s)}=\frac{p_m s^m+\ldots+p_2 s^2+p_1 s+p_0}{s^n+q_{n-1}s^{n-1}+\ldots+q_2 s^2+q_1 s+1} \qquad (1)$$

Procedures for deriving the normalized transfer function from the system differential equation are outlined in Appendix I.

Three distinct problems occur in the application of differential equations and operational mathematics to physical systems. These problems have been named the analysis, instrument, and synthesis problems.

1. The analysis problem is: Given the input and the mathematical description of the system, find the output.
2. The instrument problem is: Given the output and the mathematical description, find the input.
3. The synthesis problem is: Given the input and the desired output, determine the mathematical description.

It is clear that the synthesis problem is intimately related to engineering design. Typical inputs are often known and the "desired" output may be subject to specification. The mathematical description of the required system is a preliminary to its physical realization. Realization of the physical system is excluded from consideration in this paper, however, and attention will be confined to what Bubb[4] has termed the "mathematical attorney" of the system. Attention will be further confined to the class of linear transfer systems called "duplicators," that is, those systems in which the shape of the output approximately duplicates the shape of the input.

The synthesis of duplicators has suffered, generally, from an inadequate definition of desired output. The desired output of a duplicator usually is perfect reproduction of the shape of the input, but this is physically impractical. The desired output is, therefore, often formulated rather loosely on a frequency-response basis in terms of gain margin and phase margin, or on a transient basis in terms of intuitive concepts of rise time and overshoot.

Nomenclature

$r(t)$ = input to a transfer system
$c(t)$ = output, or response, of a transfer system
$e(t)=r(t)-c(t)$ = transfer system error
$E(s)=R(s)-C(s)$ = Laplace transform of error
$w(t)$ = transfer-system weighting function
$W(s)=C(s)/R(s)$ = transfer function of a linear system
$j=\sqrt{-1}$
ω = angular frequency
ω_0 = natural angular frequency
λ = Laplace complex variable
$s=\lambda/\omega_0$ = normalized Laplace variable
t = time
P_i, Q_i = transfer-function coefficients
p_i, q_i = normalized transfer-function coefficients
$a_i, b, c, d, \ldots$ = normalized transfer-function coefficients
ζ = damping ratio
$\alpha+j\beta$ = a root of a transfer-system characteristic equation
C_i = error coefficient

Synthesis Methods

The first and most obvious condition on the output is stability. The output of a duplicator is unequivocally desired to be stable. Fortunately, stability can be precisely defined, and conditions for stability can be rather easily calculated. There are certain conditions on the coefficients of the characteristic equation which must be satisfied in order to insure that the system is stable.

The functional relations between the coefficients defined by the Routh-Hurwitz criterion must hold. These test functions are tabulated for the various orders of normalized characteristic equations through the eighth order in Table I. Theoretically, $n-1$ test functions have to be applied to each characteristic equation. It has been shown, however, by Frazer and Duncan,[5] that the conditions tabulated are practically all that are necessary since they will first indicate the change in the character of the roots on going from a stable to an oscillatorily divergent system. The change on going from a stable system to an aperiodically

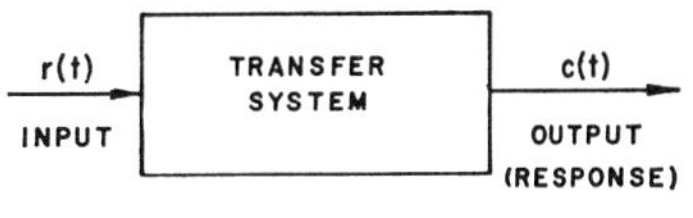

Fig. 1. A transfer system

$$C(t)=\int_{-\infty}^{+\infty} r(\tau)w(t-\tau)d\tau$$
$$C(s)=R(s)W(s)$$

Paper 53-249, recommended by the AIEE Feedback Control Systems Committee and approved by the AIEE Committee on Technical Operations for presentation at the AIEE Summer General Meeting, Atlantic City, N. J., June 15–19, 1953. Manuscript submitted March 19, 1953; made available for printing May 5, 1953.

DUNSTAN GRAHAM and R. C. LATHROP are with the Wright Air Development Center, Wright-Patterson Air Force Base, Ohio.

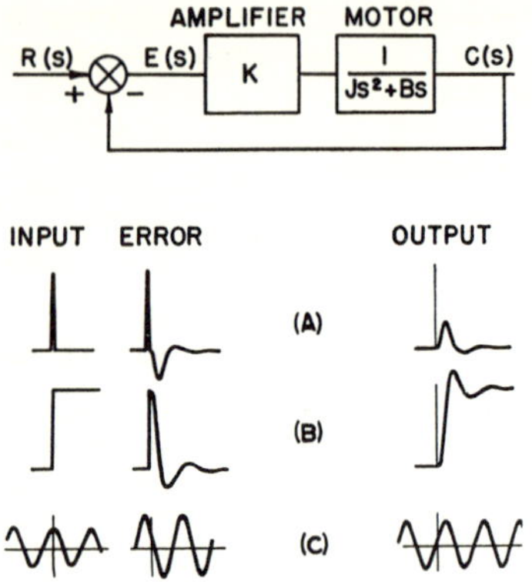

Fig. 2. A linear positioning servomechanism defined by the differential equation $J\frac{d^2c}{dt^2}+B\frac{dc}{dt}+Kc=Kr$ and the transfer function $\frac{C(s)}{R(s)}=\frac{K}{Js^2+Bs+K}$

Typical responses illustrated are:

A. The impulse response, or weighting function

B. The step-function response

C. The sinusoidal response

Table I. The Routh-Hurwitz Stability Criterion

Characteristic Equation	Criterion
$s^2+bs+1=0$	$b>0$
$s^3+bs^2+cs+1=0$	$bc-1>0$
$s^4+bs^3+cs^2+ds+1=0$	$bcd-d^2-b^2>0$
$s^5+bs^4+cs^3+ds^2+es+1=0$	$bcd+b-d^2-b^2e>0$
$s^6+bs^5+cs^4+ds^3+es^2+fs+1=0$	$(bcd+bf-d^2-b^2e)e+b^2c-bd-bc^2f-f^2+bfe+cdf>0$
$s^7+bs^6+cs^5+ds^4+es^3+fs^2+gs+1=0$	$(bcd+bf-d^2-b^2e)e+b^2cg-bdg-bc^2f-f^2-bc+d+bfe+cdf>0$
$s^8+bs^7+cs^6+ds^5+es^4+fs^3+gs^2+hs+1=0$	$(bcde+b^2cg+bef-bdg-b^2e^2-bc^2f-d^2e-f^2--bch+dh+bfe+cdf)f+b^2cfg+bc^2dh-b^2ceh-bcd^2g-b^3g-b^2cd+b^3e+b^2edg+b^2gh+bd^2-b^2f-bdfg-cd^2h+cdf^2+d^3g+b^2gh-bfdg-bh^2+dfh>0$

divergent one is first indicated by a change in the sign of the last coefficient. Familiar theorems of the theory of equations point out additional relations between the roots and the coefficients of the characteristic equation.

A method much in vogue among aerodynamicists for the approximate synthesis of airplane dynamics involves plotting the Routh-Hurwitz test function, equated to zero, as a function of two design variables, with all others held fixed. This gives a graphical representation, called a stability diagram, of the boundary between stable and unstable combinations of the two selected variables. An extension of this method due to W. Brown[6] enables one, at the cost of considerable labor, to superimpose lines of constant oscillatory period and lines of constant logarithmic decrement (damping) on such a plot. The degree of stability provided by a selected combination may be determined in this fashion. A stability diagram for third-order systems is shown in Fig. 3, which may be used for the solution of the cubic equation, since the real and imaginary parts of the complex pair of roots are available directly, and the third root is the negative inverse of $\alpha^2+\beta^2$.

In the case of closed loop systems, such as servomechanisms and feedback amplifiers, the Nyquist criterion is often applied to determine stability.[7] The shape of the complex frequency-response function

$$\frac{C(j\omega)}{R(j\omega)}=\left[\frac{P_m\lambda^m+P_{m-1}\lambda^{m-1}+\ldots+P_1\lambda+P_0}{Q_n\lambda^n+Q_{n-1}\lambda^{n-1}+\ldots+Q_1\lambda+Q_0}\right]_{\lambda=j\omega} \quad (2)$$

is, of course, dependent on the various coefficients of the numerator and denominator polynomials. It appears that, as in the case of the Routh-Hurwitz criterion, the stability and degree of stability of the system, judged by the Nyquist criterion, depend on certain relations between the coefficients of the transfer function.

The synthesis of servomechanisms is often carried out using the logarithmic plots of the frequency-response function developed by Bode[8] and Nichols.[2] Appropriate rules governing maximum amplitude ratio, gain margin, phase margin, and the length of asymptotes between break points, if applied with care, may result in a system with adequate transient performance. The outcome of the analysis, however, is not necessarily the optimum system, and the result indicates only approximately the changes in the system which would bring about improved transient performance. All this is in decided contrast to the situation usually facing an amplifier or filter designer, to whom the frequency response is all important and is susceptible to precise specification.

The root-locus method developed by Evans[9,10] is also widely used in the synthesis of closed-loop systems. Both the frequency and transient responses of the system may be inferred from such a plot. There are, however, no generally known

Table II. Methods of Servomechanism Synthesis

Method	Author	Assumed Input	Criterion	Remarks
Stability Diagram	Routh and Hurwitz Brown	None necessary	Stability	Determines stability only. Brown shows how the degree of stability may be determined.
Frequency Response	Nyquist Bode Nichols	Constant amplitude sinusoids of all frequencies	Stability, maximum gain, stability margins	Most widely used method. Depends on rules of thumb for shaping the frequency response. Essentially a cut and try method.
Root Locus	Evans Moore	None necessary	Stability and degree of stability. Transient and frequency response may be inferred and suitable criteria applied.	Criteria are not explicit. A graphical method easy to apply. Only one gain may be adjusted at a time.
Rms-Error	Wiener Phillips Bubb	Input and noise must be stationary time series. Power spectral density must be known	Minimum root mean square error.	A powerful method, but difficult to apply. Leads explicitly to required transfer characteristic.
Transient Response	Draper, *et al.* Brown and Hall Oldenbourg and Sartorius Bretoi Others	Step function or other simple type	Speed of response, overshoot, minimum $\int e^2$, error coefficients	Charts available for first, second and third order systems. Higher ordered systems must be cut and tried. Analog computers a great help.
Standard Forms	Whiteley	Step function	Maximally flat frequency response, or a given peak overshoot.	The standard form essentially is the desired transfer characteristic. Very easy to apply. The criteria may be questioned.

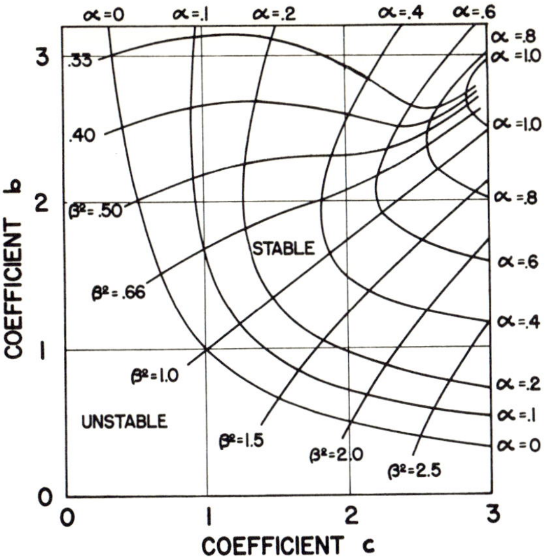

Fig. 3. Stability diagram for third-order systems defined by the transfer function $\frac{C(s)}{R(s)}=\frac{1}{s^3+bs^2+cs+1}=\frac{1}{\left(s+\frac{1}{\alpha^2+\beta^2}\right)[(s+\alpha)^2+\beta^2]}$ **showing contours of constant logarithmic decrement** α **and undamped frequency, squared** β^2

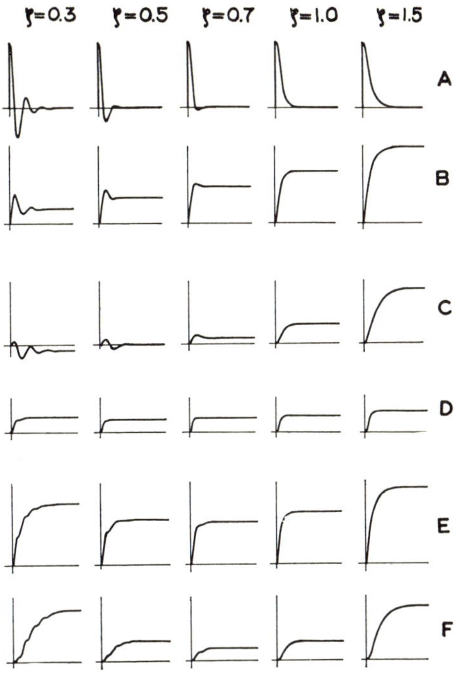

Fig. 4. Step-function responses of second-order systems and figures of merit

(A). $e(t)$ (D). $\int_0^t e^2dt$

(B). $\int_0^t e(t)dt$ (E). $\int_0^t |e|dt$

(C). $\int_0^t tedt$ (F). $\int_0^t t|e|dt$

specifications for the optimum location of the poles and zeros beyond the bare specification of stability or degree of stability (damping ratio, time to damp). If it were possible to specify the optimum location of the poles and zeros, that would amount to the specification of the form and the coefficients of the system transfer function.

In the design of filters (or servomechanisms) operating on noisy inputs, the elegant mathematical methods of Wiener[11] may be applied. The result is an explicit mathematical statement of the desired weighting function for the system. Phillips[2] has simplified the application of this method to the synthesis of duplicator servomechanisms by assuming a form for the system transfer function, and leaving only one parameter open to adjustment so as to obtain the minimum rms error.

For a few cases, the direct synthesis of transient response is possible. Charts showing the transient responses as functions of nondimensional system parameters are given by Draper and Schliestett,[12] G. Brown,[13] Bretoi,[14] and others for first and some second- and third-order systems. In very special cases, as in the synthesis of pulse-amplifier interstage circuits, Wallman[15] and others[16,17] have presented such charts for transient responses of higher-ordered systems. Note that the method of specifying the exact form of the transient response in terms of the system parameters is equivalent to the specification of a desired system transfer function.

Whiteley[18] has taken the indicated step and has tabulated the coefficients of the polynomial denominators of system transfer functions for desirable systems of various orders, and with three different kinds of numerators. He has named these explicit numerical functions for the polynomial denominators standard forms. The criteria which Whiteley[18] used to judge the "goodness" of desired outputs were, in one case, a maximally flat frequency response, and in others, the magnitude of the peak overshoot.

Some other criteria of goodness for transient responses which have been applied by the authors of transient-response charts and by users of such charts and of differential analyzers are:

1. Delay time.
2. Solution time.
3. Time to first zero.
4. Peak ratio.
5. Overshoot.

While suitable values for all these or other applicable quantities may be known in general, this knowledge usually does not give much insight into the most favorable adjustments to make to the system. In many cases where several figures of merit are applied, it is possible to "trade" part of one for a better value of another. The direct synthesis of transient responses, whether from charts, from Whiteley's[18] standard forms, or by means of a differential analyzer, is subject to the objection that the desired output has not been defined precisely enough.

Table II summarizes the various methods of synthesizing servomechanisms (and other dynamic systems) which have been discussed above, cites the criteria which are applied, and summarizes the limitations of each method.[19]

Criteria for Transfer System Response

The choice of specific design variables in the synthesis of duplicators depends completely on the criteria which are applied in judging how well the output follows the input. Speed and stability of response are desirable. These qualities may be indicated numerically by defining solution time, time to first zero, overshoot, and so forth. A more fruitful approach to the problem, however, would be to develop a unitary figure of merit or criterion

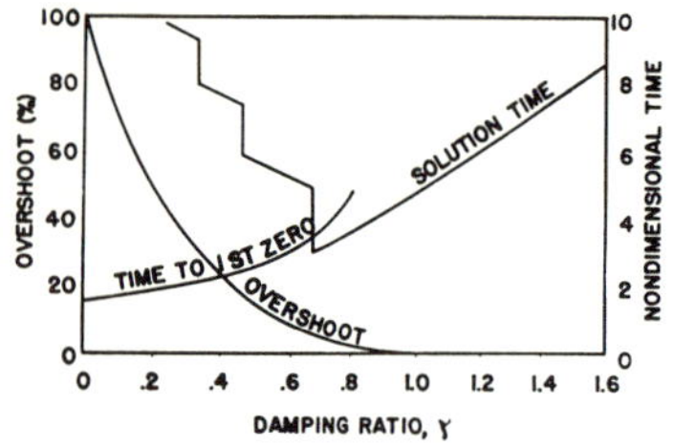

Fig. 5. Measures of the transient performance of second-order systems

of goodness for the transient response which would take most of its characteristics into account. Ideally, such a criterion should have three basic attributes:

1. Reliability.
2. Ready applicability.
3. Selectivity.

This paper is concerned with the transient performance of servomechanisms or similar transfer systems. Only those systems which have a steady-state displacement error of zero when subjected to an input step function are considered. An example of such a system would be a simple linear second-order system which has the normalized transfer function

$$\frac{C(s)}{R(s)}=\frac{1}{s^2+2\zeta s+1} \qquad (3)$$

Fig. 4(A) shows the error responses of this system for various values of ζ, when the input is a unit step function. These responses differ from a perfect response in various ways. Certain characteristics of the responses provide a measure of the degree to which the responses approximate the ideal response. Three commonly used characteristics are:

1. The time for the error to reach its first zero.
2. The amount of the first overshoot, expressed as a percentage of the initial error.
3. The solution time (time for the error to reach and remain within only 5 per cent of its initial value).

These three quantities are plotted in Fig. 5 as functions of the damping ratio ζ. It is clear that the per-cent overshoot and the time to first zero are conflicting characteristics, in that their minimum values occur at different damping ratios. If these two characteristics of the simple second-order responses were used as criteria, the design problem would consist of selecting that value of ζ which affords the best compromise between small overshoot and fast rise time. On the other hand, the solution time can be used alone as a criterion of performance, since it combines, in a sense, the properties of the other two characteristics. Applied to a linear second-order system, it appears to have some of the characteristics of an ideal criterion. It is reliable, in that it selects a damping ratio of about 0.7, a value which is commonly considered to be optimum. It is fairly easy to apply, given the time responses of a system. It is also selective, in that the difference between the optimum value and other values is easy to distinguish. It gives an exaggerated picture, however, of the difference between the goodness of a system with a damping ratio slightly less than the optimum, and one with a damping ratio slightly greater than optimum.

Several other criteria have been used for evaluating the transient performance of zero-displacement-error transfer systems which are subjected to input step functions. Oldenbourg and Sartorius[3] and Nims[20] have suggested a criterion based on the minimization of the integral

$$I_1=\int_0^\infty e\,dt \qquad (4)$$

This criterion, called the control area, appears to be satisfactory for system responses which do not overshoot. For systems which have a characteristically underdamped response, however, the control area gives an erroneous indication of merit, since overshoots decrease rather than increase the value of the integral.

Curve A of Fig. 6 shows the value of the criterion I_1 as a function of the parameter ζ for a system with the transfer function of equation 3 subjected to a unit step function of input. It can be seen that the minimum value of I_1 occurs at the damping ratio $\zeta=0$, a value which is certainly not optimum. The failure of this criterion to select a reasonable linear second-order system is sufficient grounds for its rejection from further consideration.

A modification of this criterion to provide for weighting of the error with time was proposed by Nims.[20] This modified criterion is defined by the integral.

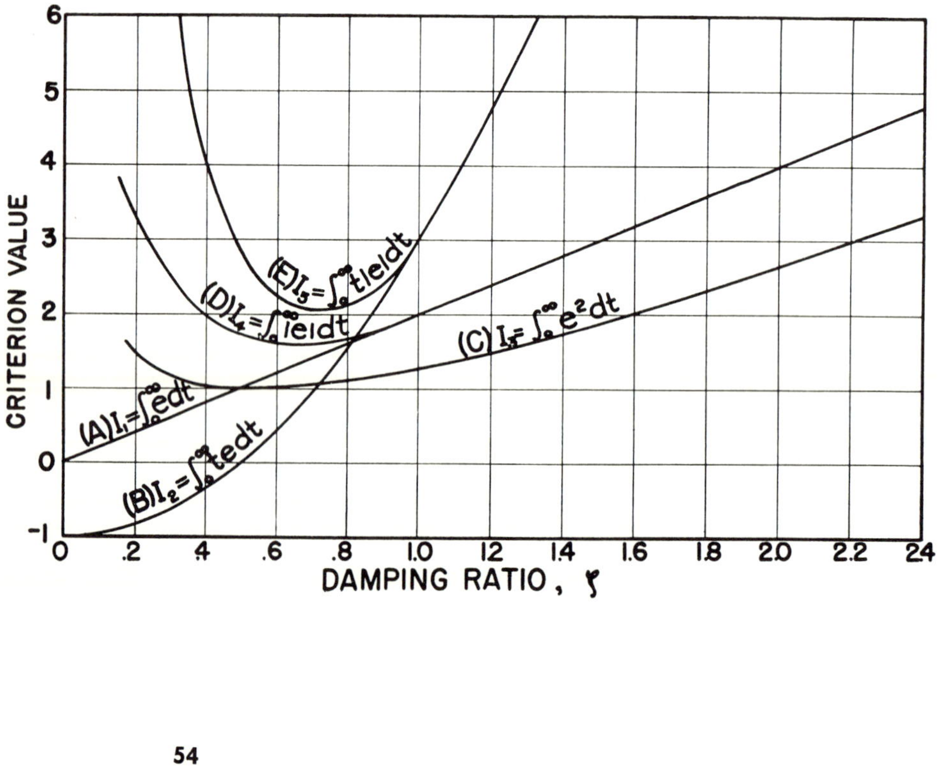

Fig. 6. Criteria for the step-function responses of second-order systems $\frac{C(s)}{R(s)}=\frac{1}{s^2+2\zeta s+1}$

Curve A: Integral of error, the control area

Curve B: Integral of time-multiplied error, the weighted control area

Curve C: Integral of squared error

Curve D: Integral of absolute value of error

Curve E: Integral of time-multiplied absolute value of error

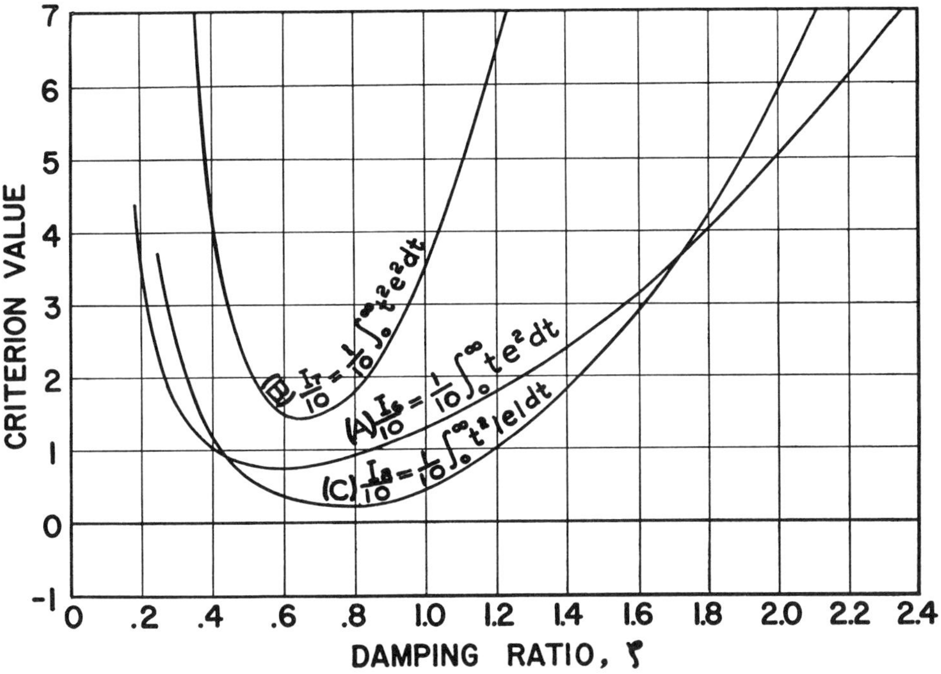

Fig. 7. Three additional criteria for the step-function responses of second-order systems

Curve A: integral of time-multiplied squared error
Curve B: integral of time-squared error-squared
Curve C: integral of time-squared absolute value of error

$$I_2=\int_0^\infty tedt \tag{5}$$

The weighted control area I_2 provides an increasingly heavy penalty for a sustained error. As before, that system is considered optimum which produces a minimum value of I_2. Curve *B* of Fig. 6 is a plot of the value of this criterion applied to the second-order system. It can be noted that the minimum value of the weighted control area occurs at the damping ratio $\zeta=0$. Therefore, this criterion fails in the same way as the control area.

Hall[21] has suggested the integral

$$I_3=\int_0^\infty e^2dt \tag{6}$$

as a figure of merit. In this case either positive errors or negative errors due to overshoots will produce positive contributions to the value of the integral. If this criterion is applied to the step-function responses of the simple linear second-order transfer system, curve *C* of Fig. 6 is the result. The minimum criterion value occurs at $\zeta=0.5$, which is not an obviously undesirable damping ratio. Furthermore, the criterion can be handled analytically or mechanized with relative ease on a differential analyzer. It also exhibits limited selectivity.

Another figure of merit which has been investigated is given by the integral

$$I_4=\int_0^\infty |e|dt \tag{7}$$

Curve *D* of Fig. 6 shows the results of testing this criterion in connection with the transient response of the simple linear second-order transfer system. The minimum value of the criterion occurs at about $\zeta=0.7$. It is moderately selective, and although it is not analytic, it is easily mechanized on an analogue computer.

If time weighting is introduced, this criterion is modified to

$$I_5=\int_0^\infty t|e|dt \tag{8}$$

This function is known as the integral of time-multiplied absolute-value of error (ITAE) criterion. If, as before, it is tested on the simple second-order system, curve *E* of Fig. 6 is the result. The minimum occurs at $\zeta=0.7$. The ITAE criterion is selective and easy to mechanize on an analog computer. Applications to other systems to test its reliability will be discussed later.

Still other figures of merit can be formed with more complex combinations of error and time weighting. Three such criteria are

$$I_6=\int_0^\infty te^2dt,\ I_7=\int_0^\infty t^2e^2dt,\ I_8=\int_0^\infty t^2|e|dt \tag{9}$$

The values of these criteria as functions of ζ for the step-function responses of the simple second-order system are presented in Fig. 7. Although these criteria show promise with respect to reliability and selectivity, they are excluded from further consideration because they are difficult to handle, either analytically or on the analogue computer.

Of the several criteria mentioned here, only those defined by equations 6, 7, and 8 are considered worthy of further investigation. In order to test the general applicability of these three criteria, they are applied to a second-order linear zero-velocity-error system, which has the normalized transfer function

$$\frac{C(s)}{R(s)}=\frac{2\zeta s+1}{s^2+2\zeta s+1} \tag{10}$$

This transfer function describes a second-

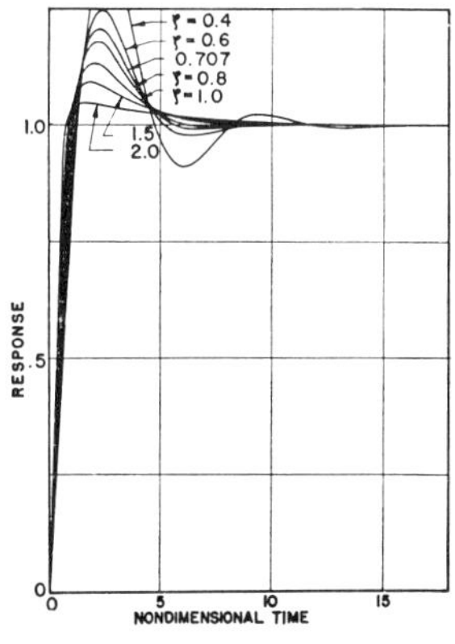

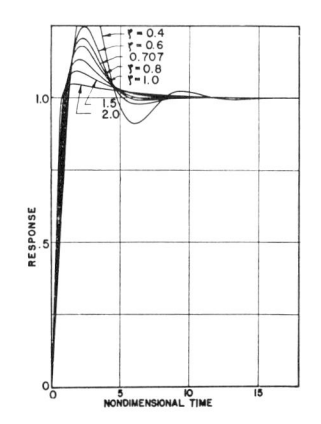

Fig. 8. Step-function responses of zero-velocity-error second-order systems

order servomechanism in which all of the damping is mathematically pure error rate damping. The responses of such a system to a unit step function of input displacement are shown in Fig. 8 for various values of the damping ratio. It is interesting to note that, as the damping ratio is increased above one, the response continues to improve. The values of the three criteria are plotted as functions of the damping ratio ζ in Fig. 9. All three criteria indicate improvement in performance as the damping ratio is increased. The ITAE criterion shows the greatest over-all selectivity.

As a further test of the general applicability of the criteria defined by equations 6, 7, and 8, they have been applied to linear third-order systems characterized by the transfer function

$$\frac{C(s)}{R(s)}=\frac{1}{s^3+bs^2+cs+1} \tag{11}$$

The responses of such a system to a unit step function of input displacement are shown in Fig. 10 for various combinations of the parameters b and c. The results of the integral of error-squared and integral of absolute-value-of-error criteria as applied to this system are presented in Fig. 11. It is clear that these two criteria fail to achieve selectivity. Additional tests indicate that these criteria become even less selective for higher-order systems, and it is doubtful that they are suitable for evaluating the transient performance of general transfer systems.

The ITAE criterion, on the other hand, retains good selectivity for the third-order system, as is evidenced by Fig. 12. A sharp minimum of the criterion occurs for the third-order system which has the parameters $b=1.75$ and $c=2.15$. It is gratifying to note that the step-function response of a system with these parameters appears qualitatively to have excellent characteristics of fast rise time and small overshoot.

A number of proposals for nonlinear modifications of the basic second-order linear servomechanism to improve the transient performance have appeared in the literature.[22,23] The step function responses of three such nonlinear systems, together with the corresponding values of the ITAE criterion, are shown in Fig. 13. A decreasing value of the criterion is seen to correspond to a general improvement in the transient-response characteristics.

In the case of higher-ordered linear transfer systems with unit-numerator transfer functions (also called zero-displacement-error systems) the ITAE criterion may be represented as a surface in a multidimensional space which has the dimensions of the transfer-function coefficients. The surface (line), its shape, and minimum point have already been illustrated for the second- and third-order cases in Figs. 6 and 12. The multidimensional surface itself cannot be graphically represented for systems of order higher than the third. Instead, Figs. 14 and 15 show sections through the surface for the fourth- and fifth-order systems. These sections are obtained by adjusting all but one of the coefficients of the system transfer function to their optimum values. This one coefficient is then varied throughout a range on either side of its optimum value, and the corresponding variation in the value of the ITAE criterion is plotted. In Figs. 14 and 15, the curves denoted by the letters b, c, etc., are the sections through the multidimensional surface obtained by varying the indicated coefficients in this manner. Several step-function responses which result from the nonoptimum adjustment of a transfer-function constant are illustrated, adjacent to the corresponding nonminimum value of the criterion function. It may be seen from these figures that the adjustment of the coefficients of the lowest powers of the complex variable in the transfer-function denominator is the most critical, both with respect to the character of the step-function response and with respect to the value of the criterion. The same situation obtained throughout the investigation, although the still-higher-ordered cases are not illustrated in this way. It appears that the application of the ITAE criterion to step-function responses results in the selection of optimum transfer-function constants. Systematic tabulations of numerical values for the transfer function constants become standard forms.

Filter Responses and Standard Forms

A low-pass filter is a duplicator, and other duplicators, including servomechanisms, may be designed by analogy to filters.[2] In general, transfer systems with good low-pass filter characteristics have correspondingly good transient responses. One of the simplest possible low-pass filters is an n-stage resistance-capacitance-coupled pulse amplifier, in which the stages are identical.[15] The characteristic function of such a system is the binomial expansion of an appropriate order. The response of a physical system with such a characteristic equation is composed of equally and critically damped modes. This response has been suggested by Imlay[24] as an optimum in connection with the response of an aircraft under the control of an automatic pilot, and by Oldenbourg and Sartorius[8] in connection with regulators and servomechanisms.

The precise definition of desired output afforded by the requirement that all modes of the response be equally and

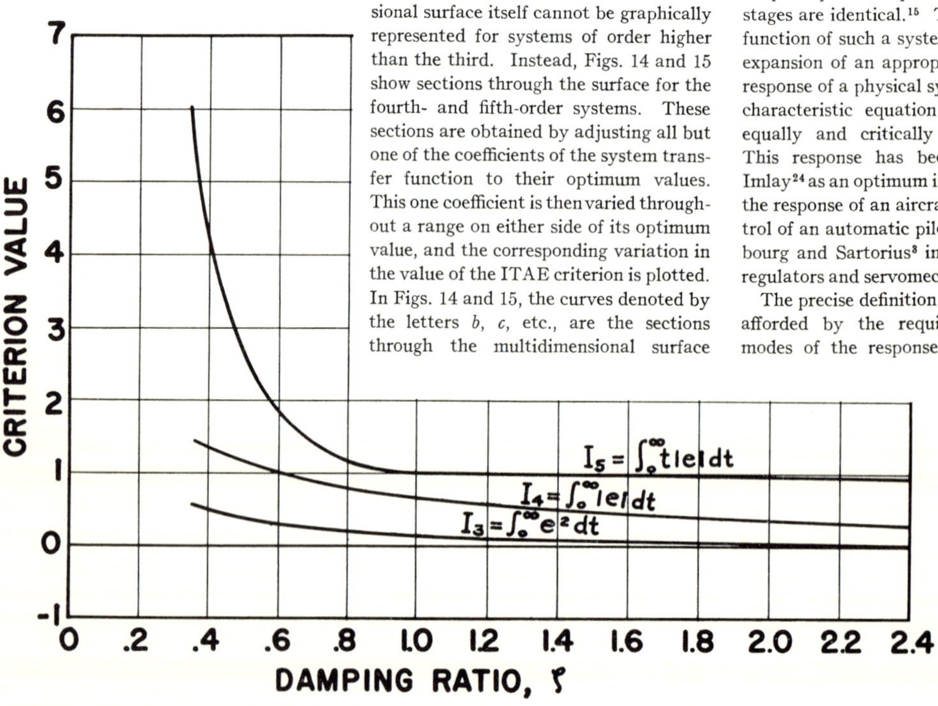

Fig. 9. Criteria applied to the step-function responses of zero-velocity - error second - order systems

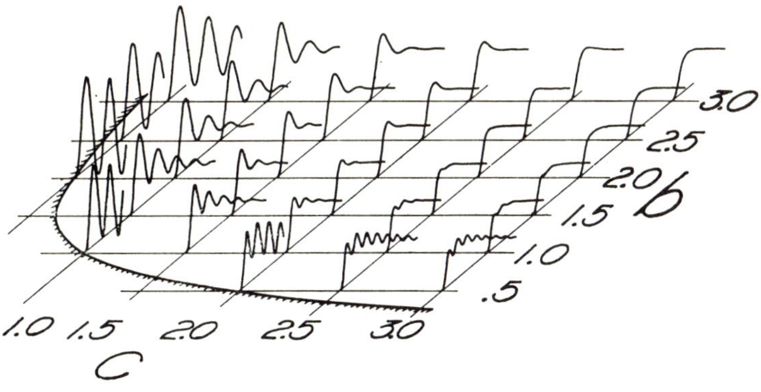

Fig. 10. Step-function responses of third-order systems with the transfer function

$$\frac{C(s)}{R(s)} = \frac{1}{s^3+bs^2+cs+1}$$

critically damped leads readily and explicitly to the required system transfer function. The coefficients of these characteristic functions are the binomial coefficients. The polynomial characteristic functions with binomial coefficients are tabulated in Table III. They might be considered to be a set of standard forms for the synthesis of duplicators with unit-numerator transfer functions. In fact, lacking more suitable forms, Whiteley[18] has suggested the binomial coefficients for certain higher-order system transfer-function constants. The step-function responses of the binomial filters are shown in Fig. 16, and the corresponding frequency-response functions in Fig. 17. It has been noted that, in the language of operational mathematics, these methods of describing the response are equivalent. Therefore, the adjustment of a linear transfer system's parameters, resulting in a transfer function with a unit numerator and a characteristic equation with binomial coefficients, guarantees the responses indicated. The transient responses of the binomial filters are not optimum for many applications, in the sense that they are relatively slow. The frequency-response characteristics show a corresponding attenuation of even the relatively low frequencies.

Another rather simple configuration for the interstage couplings of a pulse amplifier has been suggested by Butterworth.[25] These interstage circuits are designed so that the poles of the normalized system transfer function are evenly distributed on the unit circle in the left half of the complex plane. Such a location of the poles is illustrated for systems of orders one through eight in Fig. 18. The corresponding step-function and frequency responses are shown in Figs. 19 and 20. The standard forms for the Butterworth filters are shown through the eighth order in Table IV. It would be possible to extend this table by analysis, since the definition of the distribution of the poles implies the definition of the characteristic function.

The standard forms for the Butterworth[25] filters are similar to those for the binomial filters, in that the coefficients are symmetrical. This phenomenon is indeed typical of all characteristic functions whose poles lie on the unit circle in the complex plane. (The binomial characteristic equations are special cases, whose roots all lie at the minus one point.)

The step function responses of the Butterworth[25] filters are, by comparison with the responses of the binomial filters, faster, and not surprisingly, more oscillatory. Nevertheless, for many purposes, they represent a close approach to intuitive concepts of optimum duplicator responses. They served, in each case, as the starting point for the iterative experimental determination of the optimum unit-numerator transfer functions by the application of the minimum ITAE criterion.

When the minimum ITAE criterion is applied to the determination of the optimum unit-numerator transfer functions of various orders, the standard forms of Table V are obtained. The corresponding pole locations, step-function responses, and frequency responses are shown in Figs. 21, 22, and 23. With regard to these various mathematical equivalents, it can be seen that the application of this arbitrary criterion has not resulted in the selection of a family of systems with similar and progressive characteristics as the order of the system is increased. This is, in a way, a disappointing result, for it had been hoped that it would be possible to extrapolate the experimental results to the selection of standard forms for systems of still higher orders than it was possible to investigate. In general, the standard forms defined here have coefficients which are slightly higher for the

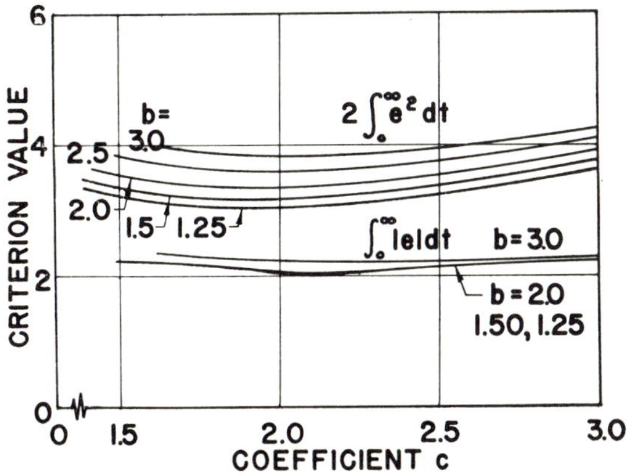

Fig. 11. Integral of squared error and integral of absolute value of error criteria applied to the step-function responses of third-order systems

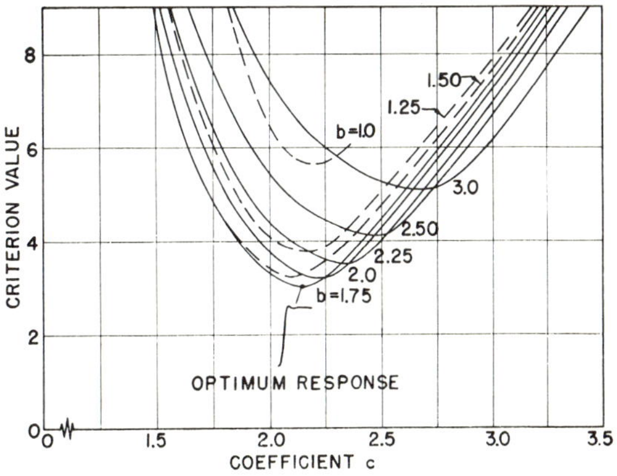

Fig. 12. The integral of time-multiplied absolute value of error criterion applied to the step-function responses of third-order systems

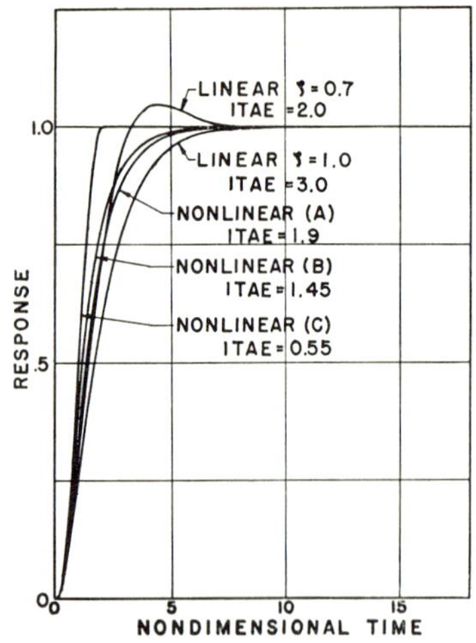

Fig. 13 (left). Step-function responses of linear and nonlinear second-order servomechanisms

Servo A:

$$\frac{d^2e}{dt^2}+\frac{2}{1+4\left(e+\frac{de}{dt}\right)}\frac{de}{dt}+e=0$$

Servo B:

$$\frac{d^2e}{dt^2}+k\frac{de}{dt}+e=0 \qquad k=0;\ e+\frac{de}{dt}\neq 0 \qquad k=2;\ e+\frac{de}{dt}=0$$

Servo C:

$$\frac{d^2e}{dt^2}+k=0 \qquad k=1;\ 2e+\frac{de}{de}\left|\frac{de}{dt}\right|>0 \qquad k=-1;\ 2e+\frac{de}{dt}\left|\frac{de}{dt}\right|<0$$

low orders of the complex variable, and slightly lower for the higher orders of the complex variable than the corresponding Butterworth[25] standard forms. No inferences on this basis, however, seem warranted.

The criterion has selected responses which are much faster than those of the binomial filters, but which are less oscillatory than those of the Butterworth[25] filters. The goodness of the selected responses might be classed as a fortunate phenomenon of engineering science. Presumably, the value of the congruent standard forms is correspondingly high.

Zero-Velocity and Zero-Acceleration-Error Systems

The class of linear duplicators with unit-numerator transfer functions, while basic, represents only a small fraction of the possible linear systems. The numerators of possible system transfer functions are almost infinitely variable. By confining attention, however, to duplicators with no steady-state displacement error, the normalized transfer-function numerator polynomials are limited to those which include a constant term of unit magnitude. This would still leave open for consideration a large number of polynomial numerators, of an order equal to or less than the corresponding denominator, if an arbitrary choice of polynomial coefficients were allowed. In servomechanism design practice, however, there are two limiting cases, the zero-velocity-error and zero-acceleration-error systems.

The steady-state error of a servomechanism may be shown[2] to be

$$\underset{t\to\infty}{e(t)}=C_0r+C_1\frac{dr}{dt}+\frac{C_2}{2}\frac{d^2r}{dt^2}+\ldots \qquad (12)$$

In terms of the generalized transfer-function constants shown in the transfer function

$$\frac{C(\lambda)}{R(\lambda)}=\frac{P_m\lambda^m+P_{m-1}\lambda^{m-1}+\ldots+P_2\lambda^2+P_1\lambda+P_0}{Q_n\lambda^n+Q_{n-1}\lambda^{n-1}+\ldots+Q_2\lambda^2+Q_1\lambda+Q_0} \qquad (13)$$

Displacement error coefficient $C_0=0$, when $P_0=Q_0$

Velocity error coefficient $C_1=0$, when $P_1=Q_1$

Acceleration error coefficient $C_2=0$, when $P_2=Q_2$

Therefore, in considering the zero-velocity and zero-acceleration-error systems as limiting cases from among all the possible systems with polynomial-numerator transfer functions, only two different numerators for each order of the denominator will be selected. The optimum transfer functions (standard forms) for systems with normalized transfer functions

$$\frac{C(s)}{R(s)}=\frac{1}{s^n+q_{n-1}s^{n-1}+\ldots+q_2s^2+q_1s+1} \qquad (14)$$

have already been found by applying the ITAE criterion. The possibilities of finding standard forms for zero-velocity-error systems characterized by the transfer function

$$\frac{C(s)}{R(s)}=\frac{q_1s+1}{s^n+q_{n-1}s^{n-1}+\ldots+q_2s^2+q_1s+1} \qquad (15)$$

and zero-acceleration-error systems with the transfer function

$$\frac{C(s)}{R(s)}=\frac{q_2s^2+q_1s+1}{s^n+q_{n-1}s^{n-1}+\ldots+q_2s^2+q_1s+1} \qquad (16)$$

will now be examined in turn.

It may be noted that $C_1=\int_0^\infty e\,dt$ and

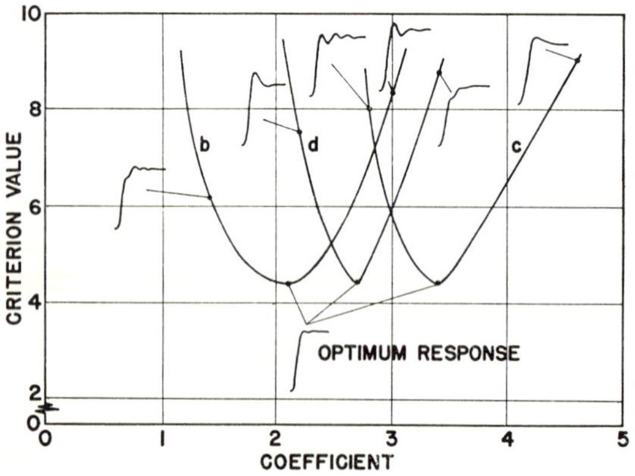

Fig. 14. Sections through the minimum point of the ITAE surface, fourth-order unit-numerator system

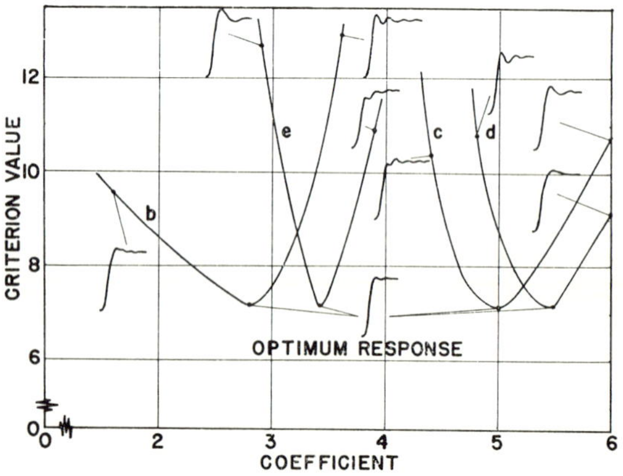

Fig. 15. Sections through the minimum point of the ITAE surface, fifth-order unit-numerator system

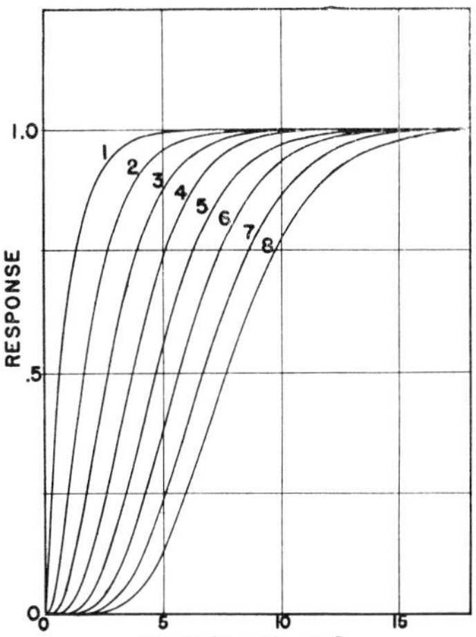

Fig. 16. Step-function responses of the binomial filters, defined by the transfer functions

$$\frac{C(s)}{R(s)}=\frac{1}{(s+1)^n}\quad (n=1, 2, \ldots 8)$$

Table III. The Binomial Standard Forms

$$s+\omega_0$$
$$s^2+2\omega_0 s+\omega_0^2$$
$$s^3+3\omega_0 s^2+3\omega_0^2 s+\omega_0^3$$
$$s^4+4\omega_0 s^3+6\omega_0^2 s^2+4\omega_0^3 s+\omega_0^4$$
$$s^5+5\omega_0 s^4+10\omega_0^2 s^3+10\omega_0^3 s^2+5\omega_0^4 s+\omega_0^5$$
$$s^6+6\omega_0 s^5+15\omega_0^2 s^4+20\omega_0^3 s^3+15\omega_0^4 s^2+6\omega_0^5 s+\omega_0^6$$
$$s^7+7\omega_0 s^6+21\omega_0^2 s^5+35\omega_0^3 s^4+35\omega_0^4 s^3+21\omega_0^5 s^2+7\omega_0^6 s+\omega_0^7$$
$$s^8+8\omega_0 s^7+28\omega_0^2 s^6+56\omega_0^3 s^5+70\omega_0^4 s^4+56\omega_0^5 s^3+28\omega_0^6 s^2+8\omega_0^7 s+\omega_0^8$$

Table IV. The Butterworth Standard Forms

$$s+\omega_0$$
$$s^2+1.4\omega_0 s+\omega_0^2$$
$$s^3+2.0\omega_0 s^2+2.0\omega_0^2 s+\omega_0^3$$
$$s^4+2.6\omega_0 s^3+3.4\omega_0^2 s^2+2.6\omega_0^3 s+\omega_0^4$$
$$s^5+3.24\omega_0 s^4+5.24\omega_0^2 s^3+5.24\omega_0^3 s^2+3.24\omega_0^4 s+\omega_0^5$$
$$s^6+3.86\omega_0 s^5+7.46\omega_0^2 s^4+9.13\omega_0^3 s^3+7.46\omega_0^4 s^2+3.86\omega_0^5 s+\omega_0^6$$
$$s^7+4.5\omega_0 s^6+10.1\omega_0^2 s^5+14.6\omega_0^3 s^4+14.6\omega_0^4 s^3+10.1\omega_0^5 s^2+4.5\omega_0^6 s+\omega_0^7$$
$$s^8+5.12\omega_0 s^7+13.14\omega_0^2 s^6+21.84\omega_0^3 s^5+25.69\omega_0^4 s^4+21.84\omega_0^5 s^3+13.14\omega_0^6 s^2+5.12\omega_0^7 s+\omega_0^8$$

Table V. The Minimum ITAE Standard Forms, Zero-Displacement-Error Systems

$$s+\omega_0$$
$$s^2+1.4\omega_0 s+\omega_0^2$$
$$s^3+1.75\omega_0 s^2+2.15\omega_0^2 s+\omega_0^3$$
$$s^4+2.1\omega_0 s^3+3.4\omega_0^2 s^2+2.7\omega_0^3 s+\omega_0^4$$
$$s^5+2.8\omega_0 s^4+5.0\omega_0^2 s^3+5.5\omega_0^3 s^2+3.4\omega_0^4 s+\omega_0^5$$
$$s^6+3.25\omega_0 s^5+6.60\omega_0^2 s^4+8.60\omega_0^3 s^3+7.45\omega_0^4 s^2+3.95\omega_0^5 s+\omega_0^6$$
$$s^7+4.475\omega_0 s^6+10.42\omega_0^2 s^5+15.08\omega_0^3 s^4+15.54\omega_0^4 s^3+10.64\omega_0^5 s^2+4.58\omega_0^6 s+\omega_0^7$$
$$s^8+5.20\omega_0 s^7+12.80\omega_0^2 s^6+21.60\omega_0^3 s^5+25.75\omega_0^4 s^4+22.20\omega_0^5 s^3+13.30\omega_0^6 s^2+5.15\omega_0^7 s+\omega_0^8$$

$C_2=2\int_0^\infty tedt$ for the error response to a unit step input, and that low (or zero) values of these integrals have already been rejected as suitable criteria for optimum response. On an experimental basis, at least, no suitable combination of system parameters could be found which would give displacement step-function responses in accord with intuitive concepts of a good response for many of the zero-velocity and zero-acceleration-error systems. This is by no means to say, however, that the ITAE criterion may not be applied to select the best possible response.

Figs. 8 and 9 have already been presented to show the possible responses of second-order zero-velocity-error systems and the corresponding values of the ITAE criterion. An arbitrary selection of the damping parameter $\zeta=1.6$, as optimum, may be made on the basis that further increases in the damping parameter result in a negligible improvement in the response.

Very much the same situation obtains with regard to the third-order zero-velocity-error system with the transfer function

$$\frac{C(s)}{R(s)}=\frac{cs+1}{s^3+bs^2+cs+1}\qquad(17)$$

For any given value of b, the step-function response will improve indefinitely as the parameter c is increased. The value $b=1.75$ is optimum, according to the ITAE criterion, and the value $c=3.25$ may be selected as marking the onset of diminishing returns.

The standard forms corresponding to the minimum value of the ITAE criterion for the zero-velocity-error systems, through the sixth order, are shown in Table VI. The corresponding responses to step functions of input displacement are illustrated in Fig. 24. Large peak overshoots and rapid accelerations are a concomitant of zero-velocity error. The alternatives suggested by Whiteley,[18] who used peak overshoot as a criterion, tend to have a persistent error which the ITAE criterion will not tolerate. A compromise which may have some merit in this case is afforded by the zero-velocity-error systems which have transfer-function denominators identical to those of the binomial filters, Table III. The step function responses of these systems are presented in Fig. 25. Note that while the responses exhibit less overshoot and less rapid ac-

Fig. 17. Frequency-response functions of the binomial filters

$$\frac{C(j\omega)}{R(j\omega)}=\frac{1}{(j\omega+1)^n}\quad (n=1, 2, \ldots 8)$$

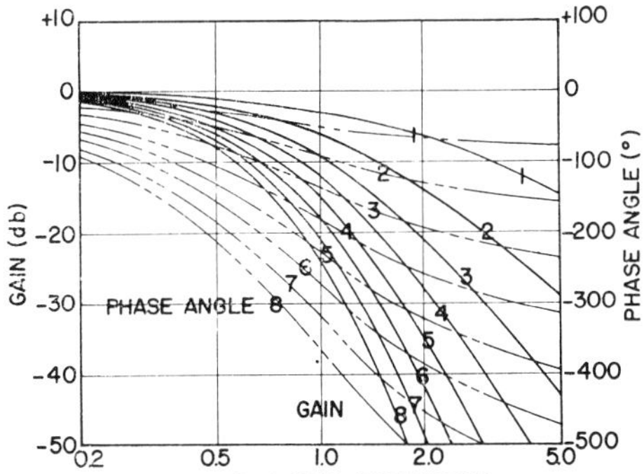

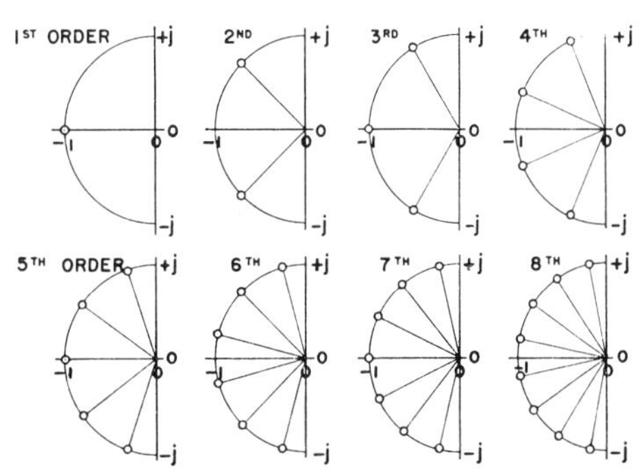

Fig. 18 (right). Pole locations of the Butterworth filters, first to eighth orders

celerations than the optimum responses of Fig. 24, they are, at the same time, appreciably slower.

The case of the third-order zero-acceleration-error transfer system is similar to the third-order zero-velocity-error system, in that the ITAE criterion diminishes in value indefinitely as the value of the b parameter is increased. The value $c=4.9$ is optimum, and the value $b=3.0$ marks the point where little improvement in response results from further increases in this parameter.

Other optimum standard forms for the zero-acceleration-error systems through the sixth order are shown in Table VII, and the corresponding step-function responses appear in Fig. 26. As in the case of the zero-velocity-error systems, the step-function responses, while best according to the ITAE criterion, may still leave something to be desired with respect to peak overshoot. The systems defined by Whiteley's[18] standard forms suffer from the same defect as before; that is, they tend to have a persistent error. Binomial zero-acceleration-error systems, therefore, may again prove to be a suitable compromise. The step-function responses of the binomial zero-acceleration-error systems are shown in Fig. 27.

It is worth reiterating that while these responses are relatively slow, they may,

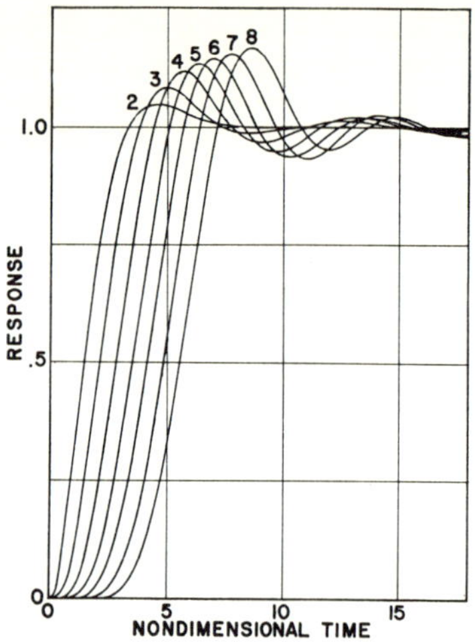

Fig. 19. Step-function responses of the Butterworth filters, second to eighth orders

theoretically at least, be reproduced to an arbitrary time scale. The ITAE criterion lays heavy emphasis on a rapid response in nondimensional time, and the overshoots, undershoots, and rapid accelerations are an inevitable feature, if rapid responses of zero-acceleration-error systems are required. Another criterion, such as $\int_0^\infty |e|\, dt$, would penalize the first overshoot more heavily, but it is dubious that this criterion would select a zero-acceleration-error system response clearly superior to the one selected by the ITAE criterion $\int_0^\infty t|e|dt$.

None of the higher-ordered zero-velocity or zero-acceleration-error systems have good responses, as adjudged by intuition. It may be that the procedure of optimizing the response to a step function of input displacement for zero-velocity and zero-acceleration-error systems is misleading. Optimizing the responses to velocity and acceleration inputs, however, would lead to not greatly different standard forms, and the responses to step functions of input displacement would still be relatively poor. Design compromises are indicated. Systems with good responses to step functions of input displacement, and small but finite velocity and acceleration errors, probably represent an over-all optimum. Standard forms for such systems remain to be discovered.

Suggested Application of the Criterion and of Standard Forms to Design

If a standard form is available for the type of transfer function involved in a particular design problem, its use repre-

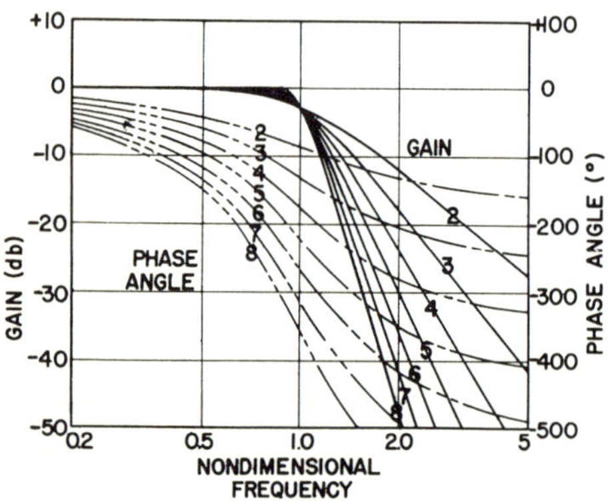

Fig. 20 (left) Frequency - response functions (amplitude and phase) of the Butterworth filters, second to eighth orders

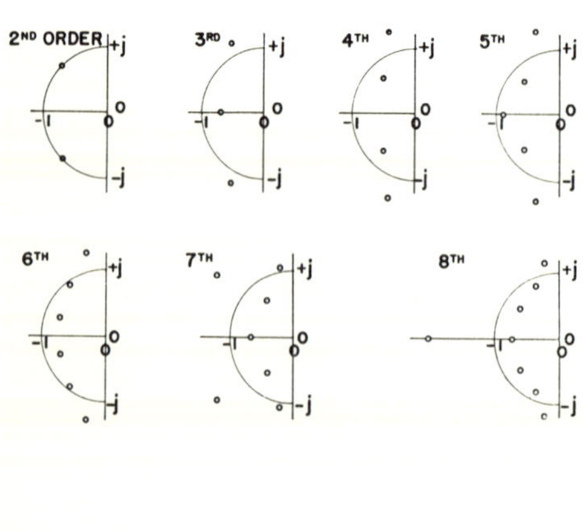

Fig. 21 (left). Pole locations of the optimum unit - numerator transfer systems, second to eighth orders

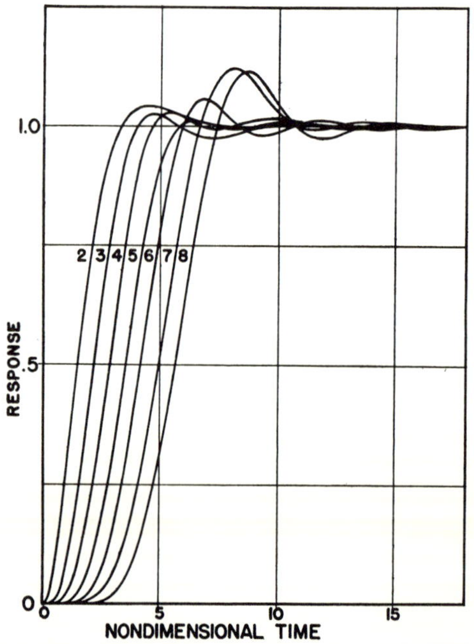

Fig. 22. Step-function responses of the optimum unit-numerator transfer systems, second to eighth orders. These responses have a minimum integral of time-multiplied absolute value of error

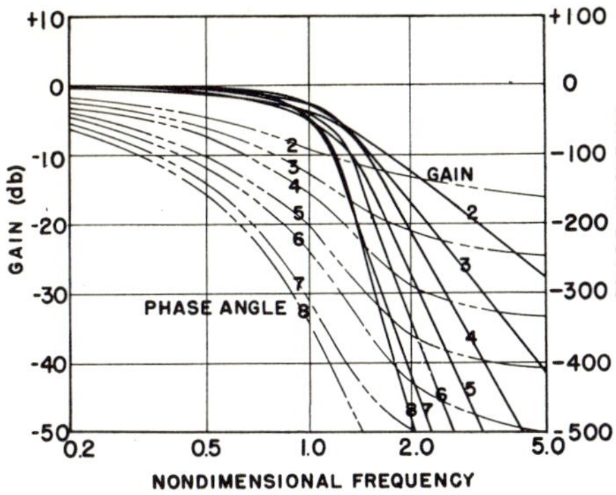

Fig. 23 (left). Frequency-response functions of the optimum unit-numerator transfer systems, second to eighth orders

sents a simple, powerful, and accurate synthesis procedure. The elementary steps involved would be:

1. Write the differential equations of the system.

2. Develop the system transfer function, leaving in literal form the constants which may be adjusted by design.

3. Normalize the transfer function (equivalent to a time-scale change in the time domain).

4. Solve algebraically for the values of the design variables which will make the transfer-function denominator conform numerically to the appropriate standard form.

5. If it is a matter of choice, the real time scale of the response may be adjusted by the selection of suitable design variables.

6. The system will have the desired response.

Mathematical operations involved comprise the simplest algebra and the direct Laplace transformation (usually accomplished by inspection). The use of standard forms does not involve solving for the roots of equations, plots or graphical constructions, integration, or inverse Laplace transformations. It is a true synthesis method, in that it leads directly and unequivocally to a description of the required system in terms of its design parameters.

The standard forms for the zero-displacement-error systems appear to have immediate application to the design of the many servomechanisms, regulators, and instruments which have transfer functions with unit numerators. They further give rise to a new class of multistage pulse amplifiers with a novel and unique adjustment for optimum response. In those cases where standard forms are unavailable for the exact type of transfer function involved, the use of the most nearly approximate standard form will lead to a very rapid estimate of suitable system adjustments. This estimate may then be refined by other methods. Of course, it may be hoped that standard forms will eventually be developed for all cases of practical interest to the designer of linear systems.

If analogue computation is employed in the study of linear or nonlinear systems for which no standard forms are available, the ITAE criterion may still be used as a unitary figure of merit for the rapid evaluation of a large number of configurations. In the case of systems with multiple outputs, such as an aircraft under automatic control, the criterion, suitably weighted, could be applied to the several outputs simultaneously and the sum of the weighted ITAE criterion values would be an over-all figure of merit for the system.

Finally, since the application of the criterion requires an origin in time, it may appear that the standard forms developed from it are not suitable for the optimum synthesis of servomechanisms operating

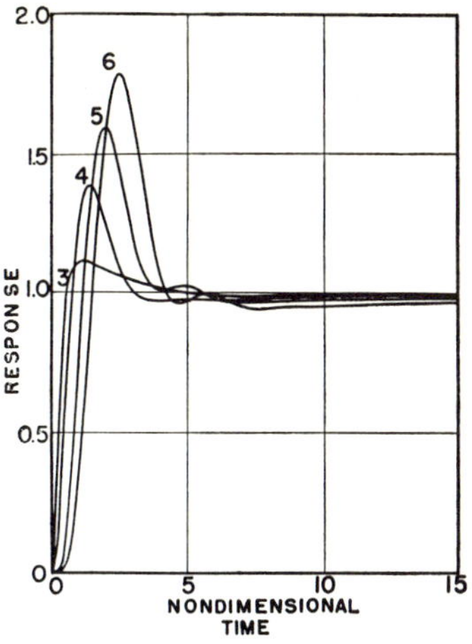

Fig. 26. Step-function responses of the optimum zero-acceleration-error systems, third to sixth orders

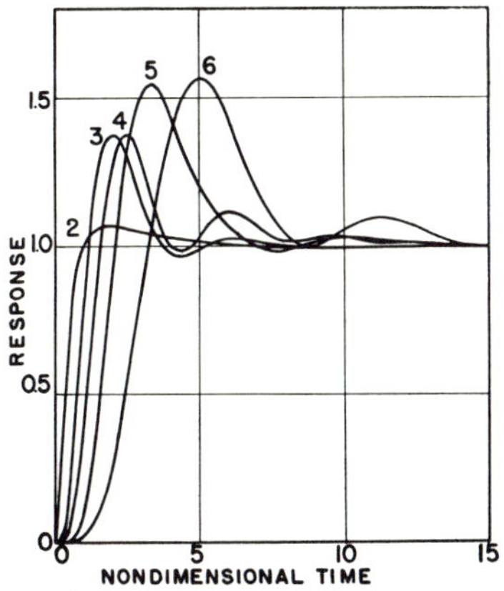

Fig. 24. Step-function responses of the optimum zero-velocity-error systems, second to sixth orders

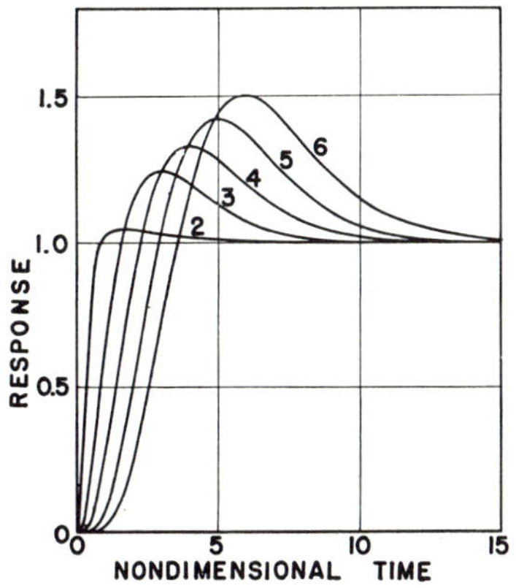

Fig. 25. Step-function responses of the binomial zero-velocity-error systems, second to sixth orders

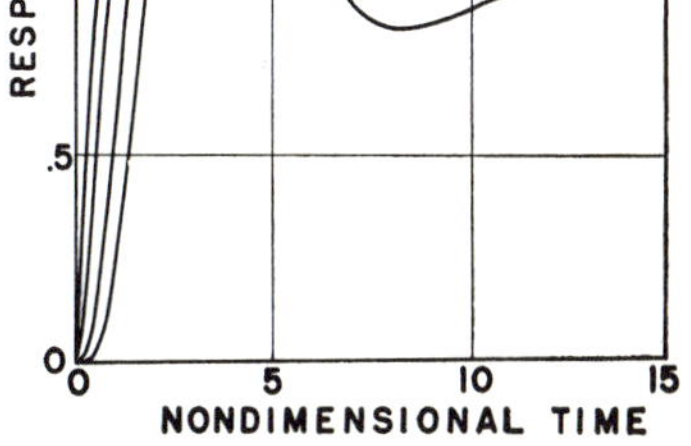

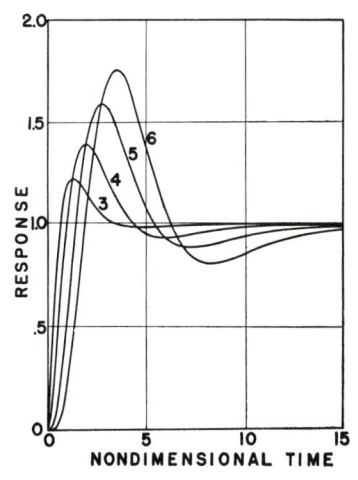

Fig. 27. Step-function responses of the binomial zero-acceleration-error systems, third to sixth orders

Table VI. The Minimum ITAE Standard Forms, Zero-Velocity-Error Systems

$s^2+3.2\omega_0 s+\omega_0^2$
$s^3+1.75\omega_0 s^2+3.25\omega_0^2 s+\omega_0^3$
$s^4+2.41\omega_0 s^3+4.93\omega_0^2 s^2+5.14\omega_0^3 s+\omega_0^4$
$s^5+2.19\omega_0 s^4+6.50\omega_0^2 s^3+6.30\omega_0^3 s^2+5.24\omega_0^4 s+\omega_0^5$
$s^6+6.12\omega_0 s^5+13.42\omega_0^2 s^4+17.16\omega_0^3 s^3+14.14\omega_0^4 s^2+6.76\omega_0^5 s+\omega_0^6$

Table VII. The Minimum ITAE Standard Forms, Zero-Acceleration-Error Systems

$s^3+2.97\omega_0 s^2+4.94\omega_0^2 s+\omega_0^3$
$s^4+3.71\omega_0 s^3+7.88\omega_0^2 s^2+5.93\omega_0^3 s+\omega_0^4$
$s^5+3.81\omega_0 s^4+9.94\omega_0^2 s^3+13.44\omega_0^3 s^2+7.36\omega_0^4 s+\omega_0^5$
$s^6+3.93\omega_0 s^5+11.68\omega_0^2 s^4+18.56\omega_0^3 s^3+19.3\omega_0^4 s^2+8.06\omega_0^5 s+\omega_0^6$

on continuous signals in the presence of statistical noise. The fundamental concept of linear filter theory, however, is discrimination against the noise on a frequency basis. Phillips,[2] as has been pointed out, suggests the selection of a form for the servomechanism system transfer function, and subsequent adjustment of a design parameter to minimize the rms error in the presence of given spectra of signal and noise. There is no reason why the form which is selected should not be one of the standard forms defined by application of the ITAE criterion. The design parameter which is reserved for the optimizing process is the time scale of the standard-form response. This is the equivalent of saying that the natural frequency of the system is placed between the signal and noise frequencies in a way which gives the least rms error in following the signal and rejecting the noise.

Conclusion

Standard forms can provide a quick and easy method for the synthesis of optimum dynamic response in a variety of applications. Where, as in very-high-ordered linear, nonlinear, or multiple-output systems, the available standard forms themselves are not applicable, the ITAE criterion still has exceptional merit of its own, and permits the rapid and unequivocal experimental selection of optimum system adjustments. There does not, however, appear to be any theoretical limit to the number of standard forms which may be developed for both general and special applications to linear systems. Eventually a table of standard forms similar to a complete table of Laplace transforms should be available for all cases of interest; at that time the synthesis of linear systems to have optimum transient response will become a simple, straightforward matter of algebra instead of the involved and often baffling problem which it has been in the past.

Appendix I. Derivation of the Normalized Transfer Function

In general, linear transfer systems of the class known as duplicators may be described by an explicit differential equation of the form

$$\left(Q_n\frac{d^n}{dt^n}+Q_{n-1}\frac{d^{n-1}}{dt^{n-1}}+\dots+Q_2\frac{d^2}{dt^2}+Q_1\frac{d}{dt}+Q_0\right)c(t)=\left(P_m\frac{d^m}{dt^m}+P_{m-1}\frac{d^{m-1}}{dt^{m-1}}+\dots+P_2\frac{d^2}{dt^2}+P_1\frac{d}{dt}+P_0\right)r(t) \quad (18)$$

in which P_i and Q_i are constants and $m\leqq n$. The corresponding transfer function is

$$\frac{C(\lambda)}{R(\lambda)}=\frac{P_m\lambda^m+\dots+P_2\lambda^2+P_1\lambda+P_0}{Q_n\lambda^n+\dots+Q_2\lambda^2+Q_1\lambda+Q_0} \quad (19)$$

Equation 19 may be put in a more convenient form for some purposes by a normalization process, which is accomplished as follows:

1. Define a constant ω_0 such that

$$\omega_0^n=\frac{Q_0}{Q_n} \quad (20)$$

2. Define new coefficients for the denominator terms in equation 19 by

$$q_i=\frac{Q_i}{\omega_0^{n-i}Q_n} \qquad i=1, 2, \dots n \quad (21)$$

and new coefficients for the numerator terms by

$$p_i=\frac{P_i}{\omega_0^{n-i}Q_n} \qquad i=0, 1, 2, \dots m \quad (22)$$

3. Divide the numerator and denominator of equation 19 by Q_n and apply the definitions of equations 20, 21, and 22. The transfer function then becomes

$$\frac{C(\lambda)}{R(\lambda)}=\frac{p_m\omega_0^{n-m}\lambda^m+\dots+p_2\omega_0^{n-2}\lambda^2+p_1\omega_0^{n-1}\lambda+p_0\omega_0^n}{\lambda^n+q_{n-1}\omega_0\lambda^{n-1}+\dots+q_2\omega_0^{n-2}\lambda^2+q_1\omega_0^{n-1}\lambda+\omega_0^n} \quad (23)$$

4. Introduce a new complex variable s such that

$$s=\frac{\lambda}{\omega_0} \quad (24)$$

Then the transfer function reduces finally to the normalized form

$$\frac{C(s)}{R(s)}=\frac{p_m s^m+\dots+p_2 s^2+p_1 s+p_0}{s^n+q_{n-1}s^{n-1}+\dots+q_2 s^2+q_1 s+1} \quad (25)$$

Equation 24 is equivalent to the substitution of a new independent variable τ in the original differential equation, where $\tau=\omega_0 t$. It is important to note that the transfer function of the system has been reduced to a form in which the coefficients of the first and last terms of the denominator are unity.

Appendix II. Analogue Computer Techniques

The development of the standard forms outlined in this paper depended on the availability of the transient responses associated with a very large number of combinations of transfer function coefficients. The computational labor necessary to obtain these responses by conventional operational methods would have been prohibi-

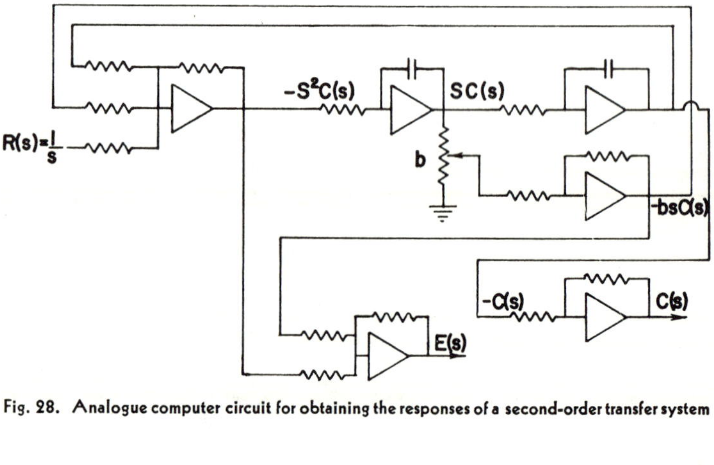

Fig. 28. Analogue computer circuit for obtaining the responses of a second-order transfer system

tive, especially for the higher-order systems. An electronic analogue computer afforded the only practical means for obtaining the transient responses and the corresponding criterion values.

Fig. 28 shows the basic computer circuit diagram for obtaining the response of a second-order zero-displacement-error system which has the normalized transfer function

$$\frac{C(s)}{R(s)}=\frac{1}{s^2+bs+1} \qquad (26)$$

If $r(t)$ is a unit step function applied at $t=0$, then $R(s)=1/s$, and the transform of the output response is

$$C(s)=\frac{1}{s(s^2+bs+1)} \qquad (27)$$

The transform of the error response is given by

$$E(s)=R(s)-C(s)=\frac{1}{s}-\frac{1}{s(s^2+bs+1)}$$
$$=\frac{s^2+bs}{s(s^2+bs+1)}=(s^2+bs)C(s) \qquad (28)$$

It is possible, with the aid of a computer technique developed by Beck,[26] to simultaneously extract the error response from the basic computer circuit, which is used to generate the output response without using differentiators. The method involves summing selected responses which are available within the computer loop, as illustrated in Fig. 28.

The Laplace transforms of the output response and error response of a second-order zero-velocity-error system are given by

$$C(s)=\frac{bs+1}{s(s^2+bs+1)} \qquad (29)$$

and

$$E(s)=\frac{s^2}{s(s^2+bs+1)} \qquad (30)$$

for an input step function. Beck's[26] method may be applied to extract these responses from the basic computer circuit of Fig. 28, although the required connections are not shown. In a similar manner, the output and error responses of zero-displacement, zero-velocity, and zero-acceleration-error systems of higher orders may be developed without using differentiators. Only one basic computer circuit is required for each order.

The criteria discussed in this paper were mechanized on the analogue computer using the circuits of Fig. 29. Criterion values were produced simultaneously with the associated responses. The absolute-value device utilized a high-speed relay, in a circuit similar to the one described by Bennett and Fulton.[27]

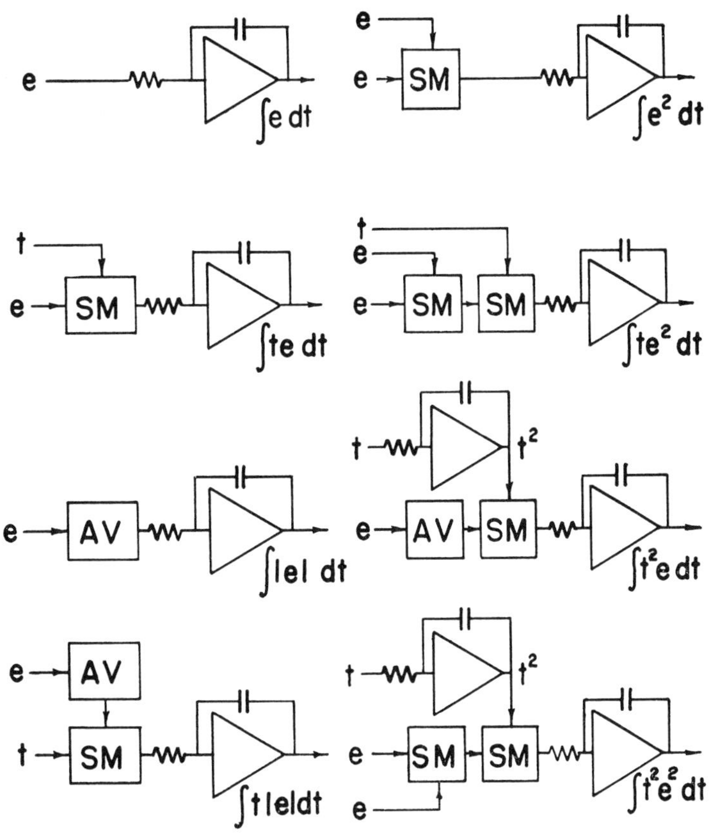

Fig. 29. Circuits for mechanizing performance criteria on an electronic analogue computer

SM = servo multiplier AV = absolute value unit

References

1. Response of Physical Systems (book), **J. D. Trimmer.** John Wiley and Sons, Inc., New York, N. Y., 1950.

2. Theory of Servomechanisms (book), **H. M. James, N. B. Nichols, R. S. Phillips.** McGraw-Hill Book Company, Inc., New York, N. Y., 1947.

3. The Dynamics of Automatic Controls (book), **R. C. Oldenbourg, H. Sartorius.** The American Society of Mechanical Engineers, New York, N. Y., 1948.

4. A New Linear Operational Calculus, **F. W. Bubb.** United States Air Force *TR No. 6581*, Wright Air Development Center, Wright-Patterson Air Force Base, Ohio, May 1951.

5. On the Criteria for the Stability of Small Motions, **R. A. Frazer, W. J. Duncan.** *Proceedings*, Royal Society of London, England, vol. A-124, 1929, pp. 642–54.

6. A Simple Method of Constructing Stability Diagrams, **W. S. Brown.** *R and M No. 1905*, British Aeronautical Research Committee, London, England, 1942.

7. Regeneration Theory, **H. Nyquist.** *Bell System Technical Journal*, New York, N. Y., vol. 11, 1932, pp. 125–47.

8. Network Analysis and Feedback Amplifier Design (book), **H. W. Bode.** D. Van Nostrand Co., Inc., New York, N. Y., 1945.

9. Control System Synthesis by Root Locus Method, **W. R. Evans.** *AIEE Transactions*, vol. 69, pt. I, 1950, pp. 66–69.

10. Aerodynamic Stability and Automatic Control, **W. Bollay.** *Journal*, Institute of the Aeronautical Sciences, New York, N. Y., vol. 18, 1951, pp. 569–617.

11. The Extrapolation, Interpolation, and Smoothing of Stationary Time Series (book), **N. Wiener.** John Wiley and Sons, Inc., New York, N. Y., 1949.

12. General Principles of Instrument Analysis, **C. S. Draper, G. V. Schliestett.** *Instruments*, Pittsburgh, Pa., vol. 12, 1939, pp. 137–42.

13. Dynamic Behaviour and Design of Servomechanisms, **G. S. Brown, A. C. Hall.** *Transactions*, American Society of Mechanical Engineers, New York, N. Y., vol. 68, 1946, pp. 503–22.

14. Automatic Flight Control—Analysis and Synthesis of the Lateral Control Problem, **R. N. Bretoi.** *Transactions*, American Society of Mechanical Engineers, New York, N. Y., vol. 74, 1951, pp. 415–30.

15. Vacuum Tube Amplifiers (book), **G. E. Valley, Jr., H. Wallman.** McGraw-Hill Book Company, Inc., New York, N. Y., 1948.

16. Networks Designed to Approximate a Specified Transient Response, **J. A. Blickensderfer, H. P. Blanchard.** *Technical Report No. 1*, Electronics Research Laboratory, Stanford University, Palo Alto, Calif., March 1950.

17. The Synthesis of Lumped-Element Circuits for Optimum Transient Response, **G. W. C. Mathers.** *Technical Report No. 38*, Electronics Research Laboratory, Stanford University, Palo Alto, Calif., Nov. 1951.

18. The Theory of Servo Systems, With Particular Reference to Stabilization, **A. L. Whiteley.** *Journal*, Institution of Electrical Engineers, London, England, vol. 93, 1946, pp. 353–72.

19. A Survey of Stability Analysis Techniques for Automatically Controlled Aircraft, **A. L. Jones, B. R. Briggs.** National Advisory Committee for Aeronautics *TN 2275*, Ames Aeronautical Laboratory, Moffett Field, Calif., Jan., 1951.

20. Some Design Criteria for Automatic Controls, **Paul T. Nims.** *AIEE Transactions*, New York, N. Y., vol. 70, 1951, pt. I, pp. 606–11.

21. The Analysis and Synthesis of Linear Servomechanisms (book), **A. C. Hall.** The Tech-

nology Press, Massachusetts Institute of Technology, Cambridge, Mass., 1943.

22. Non-Linear Techniques for Improving Servo Performance, **D. MacDonald.** *Proceedings*, National Electronics Conference, Inc., Chicago, Ill., vol. 6, 1951, pp. 400–21.

23. A Topological and Analog Computer Study of Certain Servomechanisms Employing Non-Linear Electronic Components, **R. C. Lathrop.** *Thesis*, University of Wisconsin, Madison, Wis., 1951.

24. A Theoretical Study of Lateral Stability with an Automatic Pilot, **F. H. Imlay.** National Advisory Committee for Aeronautics *TR 693*, Washington, D. C., 1940.

25. On the Theory of Filter Amplifiers, **S. Butterworth.** *Wireless Engineer*, London, England, vol. 7, 1930, pp. 536–41.

26. Symposium I on REAC Techniques. Reeves Instrument Corporation, New York, N. Y., "A Method for Solving Problems on the REAC by the Use of Transfer Functions Without Passive Networks," **C. Beck.** March 15–16, 1951, pp. 131–36.

27. The Use of High-Speed Relays in Electric Analogue Computers, **R. R. Bennett, A. S. Fulton.** *AIEE Transactions*, vol. 70, pt. II, 1951, pp. 1553–55.

ANALYTICAL CONTROLLER DESIGN. I

A. M. Letov

(Moscow)

Translated from Avtomatika i Telemekhanika, Vol. 21, No. 4, pp. 436-441, April, 1960
Original article submitted December 23, 1959

A solution is presented for the problem of analytical controller design in accordance with a given optimizing functional. The solution is given for the open region of definition of the system's differential equations. The cases of closed regions are worked out in Parts II and III of the present work, which are to be published in succeeding numbers of this journal.

1. Two Classes of Problems in Optimal System Theory

The construction of optimal systems leads to the solution of the allied mathematical problems, which are divided into two classes. The first of these is comprised of those problems which are related to the determination and calculation of the undisturbed modes of motion. Here, one has to do with those programs of automatic control for which the given undisturbed motion possesses the requisite extremal properties. We shall call such systems optimal with respect to control mode.

Systems for which the concept of optimality connotes the arrival at a given state in minimal time we shall find it convenient to call brachistochrone.

In the other class of problems fall those controllers which guarantee the existence of given properties of the disturbed motions (transient processes).

We shall call such systems optimal with respect to transient response. The set consisting of the object of control, the optimal programming element, and the optimal controller comprises an optimal automatic control system. In both cases the optimization problem can be treated as a two-point boundary problem, for the solution of which one may apply all the methods of the variational calculus and, in particular, the latest methods, developed in [1-7]. However, certain differences do exist between these two classes of problems. Thus, in the first case, the problem's solution is obtained in the form of a known function of time, which then becomes the basis for the design of the programming elements. In the second case, the analytical form of the control law appears as some function of the original coordinates of the control system, i.e., the problem consists of the construction of the controller's differential equation. Of course, the process of analytic controller construction is nothing else than the synthesis process. In particular, the synthesis process is here given the same meaning as in [1-5]. However, we choose not to use this term since many other authors use it with differing interpretations. On the other hand, the equivalent terminology "analytic construction" must suggest itself more strongly to engineers, since this terminology implies merely the search, by means of the tools of mathematical analysis, for the form of the controller's differential equation which will answer to the accepted criterion of optimality. In the present paper we consider the problem of the analytical construction (design) of optimal systems which are defined in open regions. In the succeeding papers we shall deal with the same problem as formulated for closed regions.

2. Initial Posing of the Analytical Design Problem

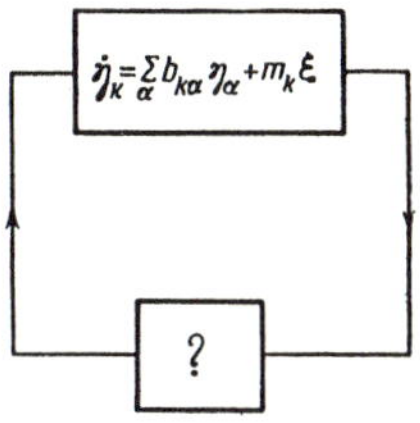

We consider a closed controlled system (cf. Fig. 1) in which the object's disturbed motion is given by the set of equations

$$g_k = \dot{\eta}_k - \Big(\sum_\alpha b_{k\alpha}\eta_\alpha + m_k\xi\Big) = 0 \qquad (2.1)$$

$$(k = 1, \ldots, n)$$

in the generalized coordinates η_k, while the equation of the controller for the coordinate ξ remains unknown. For definiteness, we shall assume that all the $b_{k\alpha}$ and m_k are given constants on which no restraints have as yet been imposed.

Let N be the open region in which (2.1) are given; any conditions in N of the form

$$\eta_1(0) = \eta_{10}, \ldots, \eta_n(0) = \eta_{n0}, \quad \xi(0) = \xi_0, \qquad (2.2)$$
$$\eta_1(\infty) = \ldots = \eta_n(\infty) = \xi(\infty) = 0$$

we shall call natural boundary conditions of the problem. They mean simply this, that whatever the transient response which arises in N, it must terminate, for $t = \infty$, with the system being found at the origin of coordinates.

As the criterion for system optimality, we choose the integral

$$I(\xi) = \int_0^\infty V\,dt \qquad (2.3)$$

of the positive definite quadratic form

$$V = \sum_k a_k \eta_k^2 + c\xi^2. \tag{2.4}$$

We shall seek such continuous functions $\xi, \eta_1 \dots \eta_n$ (class C_1) with continuous first derivatives which give the integral in (2.3) a minimum value. The existence and uniqueness of the solution of this problem were proven in [7]. We now give ourselves the task of determining the form of this solution as well as the possibilities of using it for the purpose of an analytic design. The integral $I(\xi)$ is a functional defined on class C_1 of functions, and its value characterizes the integral of the squared error, weighted by the constants a_k and c, which the system will have in the course of the transient response lasting until $t^* = \infty$. The problem consists in writing in analytic form

$$F(\dot{\xi}, \xi, \eta_1, \dots, \eta_n) = 0 \tag{2.5}$$

the control law which, in conjunction with (2.1), will form a stable system and will guarantee the existence of a minimum for the integral in (2.3).

---

3. Solution of the Problem

We are dealing with the Lagrange variational problem, the procedures for the solution of which are very well known. Specifically, we first set up the function

$$H = V + \sum_k \lambda_k g_k, \tag{3.1}$$

where the λ_k are arbitrary multipliers.

Then,

$$\frac{\partial H}{\partial \dot{\eta}_k} = \lambda_k, \quad \frac{\partial H}{\partial \eta_k} = 2a_k\eta_k - \sum_\alpha \lambda_\alpha b_{\alpha k}; \quad \frac{\partial H}{\partial \dot{\xi}} = 0, \tag{3.2}$$

$$\frac{\partial H}{\partial \xi} = 2c\xi - \sum_\alpha m_\alpha \lambda_\alpha. \tag{3.2}$$

The equations of the variational problem have the form

$$\dot{\lambda}_k = -\sum_j b_{jk}\lambda_j + 2a_k\eta_k, \quad 0 = 2c\xi - \sum_j m_j\lambda_j. \tag{3.3}$$

To these, (2.1) should be adjoined.

The further steps in the procedure for analytic design (excluding singular cases) are as follows:

1. The equations of the variational problem must be solved jointly for the functions η_k and λ_k.

Let

$$\Delta(\mu) = \begin{vmatrix} b_{11} - \mu, \dots, & b_{1n}, & \dfrac{m_1^2}{2c}, \dots, & \dfrac{m_1 m_2}{2c} \\ \dots & \dots & \dots & \dots \\ b_{n1}, \dots, & b_{nn} - \mu, & \dfrac{m_n m_1}{2c}, \dots, & \dfrac{m_n^2}{2c} \\ 2a_1, \dots, & 0, & -b_{11} - \mu, \dots, & -b_{n1} \\ \dots & \dots & \dots & \dots \\ 0, \dots, & 2a_n, & -b_{1n}, \dots, & -b_{nn} - \mu \end{vmatrix} \tag{3.4}$$

be the system's characteristic determinant. It is easily proven that, if $\mu_1, \dots, \mu_n$ are simple roots of the equation $\Delta(\mu) = 0$, then the numbers $-\mu_1, \dots, -\mu_n$ are also simple roots. We assume that $\mu_1, \dots, \mu_n$ are simple roots, $\mathrm{Re}\,\mu_k \neq 0$, and the roots are numbered in accordance with the inequalities

$$\mathrm{Re}\,\mu_k < 0 \quad (k = 1, \dots, n). \tag{3.5}$$

This latter step is always possible by virtue of the aforementioned property of determinant (3.4). The general solution of the equations of the problem will consist of a linear combination of exponential functions of the form $c_k e^{\mu_k t}$ and $c_{n+k} e^{-\mu_k t}$ $(k = 1, \dots, n)$, and will contain 2n arbitrary constants

$$c_1, \dots, c_n, c_{n+1}, \dots, c_{2n}.$$

2. By virtue of (2.2)* at infinity we set

$$c_{n+k} = 0 \ (k = 1, \dots, n)$$

where the constants c_k can be chosen from the initial conditions. However, this operation is not necessary.

3. In the remaining 2n formulas which define the functions $\eta_1, \dots, \eta_n, \lambda_1, \dots, \lambda_n$, we eliminate the n functions of time $c_k e^{\mu_k t}$, as a result of which we find that

$$\lambda_j = \sum_\alpha \Delta_{j\alpha} \eta_\alpha \quad (j = 1, \dots, n), \tag{3.6}$$

where the $\Delta_{j\alpha}$ are completely defined constants.

4. We substitute the values found for the λ_j in the last equation of (3.3), thus finding the controller's equation

$$\xi = p_1\eta_1 + p_2\eta_2 + \dots + p_n\eta_n. \tag{3.7}$$

It remains to verify that (3.7), in conjunction with the initial equations (2.1), forms a stable† automatic control system. This verification is easily carried out. Indeed, the optimal system found has a general solution which is a linear combination of the exponential functions $c_k e^{\mu_k t}$ $(k = 1, \dots, n)$. Consequently, the numbers μ_k $(k = 1, \dots, n)$ are the roots of the characteristic equation of system (2.1), (3.7). We obtained ideal controller (3.7) with rigid feedback and with an infinitely fast servomotor [8]. Thus, we arrive at the conclusion that functionals like (2.3) lead to controllers which can not be realized.

4. Possible Generalizations of Functional (2.3)

We now consider an indefinite quadratic form such as

$$T = \sum_k \sum_j c_{kj}\dot{\eta}_k\dot{\eta}_j + \dot{\xi}^2 \qquad (4.1)$$

and repeat the formulation of the Lagrange problem for the functional

$$I(\xi) = \int_0^\infty (T + V)\,dt.$$

The value of the functional $I(\xi)$ characterizes the integral of the squared position and velocity errors which the system will have in the course of the transient response lasting until $t^* = \infty$.

We remark that the solution of the problem may be simplified by eliminating the derivatives $\dot{\eta}_k$ in accordance with the original equations. It is reasonable, therefore, to consider first the simpler functional of the form

$$I(\xi) = \int_0^\infty (V + \dot{\xi}^2)\,dt. \qquad (4.2)$$

The computation will differ from the foregoing only in that now the expression $\partial H/\partial\dot{\xi} = 2\dot{\xi}$ and does not equal zero. Therefore, instead of the last equation of (3.3), we get

$$2\ddot{\xi} = 2c\xi - \sum_j m_j\lambda_j. \qquad (4.3)$$

This equation, in conjunction with (2.1) and the first n equations of (3.3), solves the given problem. The solution procedure reduces to the implementation of the following operations:

1. The equations of the problem must be solved for the functions η_k, λ_k and ξ.

Let

$$\overline{\Delta}(\mu) = \begin{vmatrix} b_{11}-\mu, \ldots, & b_{1n}, & 0, \ldots, & 0, & m_1 \\ \cdots & \cdots & \cdots & \cdots & \cdots \\ b_{n1}, \ldots, & b_{nn}-\mu, & 0, \ldots, & 0, & m_n \\ 2a_1, \ldots, & 0, & -b_{11}-\mu, \ldots, & -b_{n1}, & 0 \\ \cdots & \cdots & \cdots & \cdots & \cdots \\ 0, \ldots, & 2a_n, & -b_{1n}, \ldots, & -b_{nn}-\mu, & 0 \\ 0, \ldots, & 0, & -m_1, \ldots, & -m_n, & 2c-\mu^2 \end{vmatrix} \qquad (4.4)$$

be the system's characteristic determinant. As in the case of (3.4), it possesses the property that $\overline{\Delta}(\mu) = \overline{\Delta}(-\mu)$. Therefore, the equation $\Delta(\mu) = 0$ will have the roots $\mu_1, \ldots, \mu_{n+1}$ (which we assume to be simple), with the property enunciated by (3.5), plus the roots $-\mu_1, \ldots, -\mu_{n+1}$. The system's general solution will consist of a linear combination of exponential functions of the form $c_k e^{\mu_k t}$ and $c_{n+1+k}e^{-\mu_k t}$ ($k = 1, \ldots, n+1$) and will contain $2n+2$ arbitrary constants.

2. By virtue of (2.2) at infinity we set $c_{n+1+k} = 0$ ($k = 1, \ldots, n+1$). The remaining constants can be determined from the initial conditions.

3. We now take the solution found for the function ξ. In the $n+2$ formulas found for the functions $\eta_1, \ldots, \eta_n$, ξ and $\dot{\xi}$, we eliminate the functions of time $c_1e^{\mu_1 t}, \ldots, c_{n+1}e^{\mu_{n+1}t}$, as a result of which we find the controller's equation

$$\dot{\xi} = \sum_\alpha p_\alpha \eta_\alpha - r\xi. \qquad (4.5)$$

Here, the p_α and r are completely defined constants, determined in the course of implementing the enumerated operations. In conjunction with (2.1), (4.5) forms a stable optimal system. The stability, as in the previous case, is a consequence of the fact that the numbers $\mu_1, \ldots, \mu_{n+1}$ are roots of the optimal system's characteristic equation.

In contradistinction to the solution of Section 3, we obtained a linear controller with a limited variable servomotor speed. Such controllers can be realized if the region N is sufficiently small. The analytic design procedure in the case when the motion of the system is in a closed region N, when the optimal solution can be found on the region's boundary, will be considered in the subsequent papers.

5. Examples

For a first-order system, the equations of the variational problem will be

$$\dot{\eta} = b\eta + m\xi, \quad \dot{\lambda} = -b\lambda + 2a\eta, \quad 2\ddot{\xi} = 2c\xi - m\lambda. \qquad (5.1)$$

To these there correspond the characteristic equation

$$\mu^4 - (b^2 + c)\mu^2 + am^2 + cb^2 = 0 \qquad (5.2)$$

and the solution

$$\eta = c_1e^{\mu_1 t} + c_2e^{\mu_2 t},$$
$$\xi = \frac{\mu_1 - b}{m}c_1e^{\mu_1 t} + \frac{\mu_2 - b}{m}c_2e^{\mu_2 t}, \qquad (5.3)$$
$$\dot{\xi} = \frac{\mu_1(\mu_1 - b)}{m}c_1e^{\mu_1 t} + \frac{\mu_2(\mu_2 - b)}{m}c_2e^{\mu_2 t}.$$

The controller's equation has the form

$$\begin{vmatrix} 1 & 1 & \eta \\ \frac{\mu_1 - b}{m} & \frac{\mu_2 - b}{m} & \xi \\ \frac{\mu_1(\mu_1 - b)}{m} & \frac{\mu_2(\mu_2 - b)}{m} & \dot{\xi} \end{vmatrix} = 0$$

or, in expanded form,

$$\dot{\xi} = -\frac{(\mu_1 - b)(\mu_2 - b)}{m}\eta + (\mu_1 + \mu_2 - b)\xi. \quad (5.4)$$

For a second example, we consider the second-order system

$$\dot{\eta}_1 = b_{11}\eta_1 + b_{12}\eta_2 + m_1\xi, \quad \dot{\eta}_2 = b_{21}\eta_1 + b_{22}\eta_2 + m_2\xi. \quad (5.5)$$

To obtain the equations of the variational problem, we must append

$$\begin{aligned} \dot{\lambda}_1 &= -b_{11}\lambda_1 - b_{21}\lambda_2 + 2a_1\eta_1, \\ \dot{\lambda}_2 &= -b_{12}\lambda_1 - b_{22}\lambda_2 + 2a_2\eta_2, \\ 2\ddot{\xi} &= 2c\xi - m_1\lambda_1 - m_2\lambda_2. \end{aligned} \quad (5.6)$$

The characteristic equation has the form

$$\bar{\Delta}(\mu) = \begin{vmatrix} b_{11}-\mu, & b_{12} & 0, & 0, & m_1 \\ b_{21}, & b_{22}-\mu, & 0, & 0, & m_2 \\ 2a_1 & 0, & -b_{11}-\mu, & -b_{21}, & 0 \\ 0, & 2a_2, & -b_{12}, & -b_{22}-\mu, & 0 \\ 0, & 0, & -m_1, & -m_2 & 2c-2\mu^2 \end{vmatrix} = 0.$$

Let μ_1, μ_2, and μ_3 be the three roots for which $\mathrm{Re}\,\mu_s < 0$. We then have

$$\begin{aligned} \eta_1 &= \sum_{s=1}^{3} \Delta_1(\mu_s) e^{\mu_s t} c_s, \quad \eta_2 = \sum_{s=1}^{3} \Delta_2(\mu_s) e^{\mu_s t} c_s, \\ \xi &= \sum_{s=1}^{3} \Delta_5(\mu_s) e^{\mu_s t} c_s, \quad \dot{\xi} = \sum_{s=1}^{3} \mu_s \Delta_5(\mu_s) e^{\mu_s t} c_s. \end{aligned} \quad (5.8)$$

Here, Δ_1, Δ_2, and Δ_5 are the minors of the first, second, and fifth elements of the first row of the determinant in (5.7). It is obvious that the equation sought for the optimal controller will have the form

$$\begin{vmatrix} \Delta_1(\mu_1) & \Delta_1(\mu_2) & \Delta_1(\mu_3) & \eta_1 \\ \Delta_2(\mu_1) & \Delta_2(\mu_2) & \Delta_2(\mu_3) & \eta_2 \\ \Delta_5(\mu_1) & \Delta_5(\mu_2) & \Delta_5(\mu_3) & \xi \\ \mu_1\Delta_5(\mu_1) & \mu_2\Delta_5(\mu_2) & \mu_3\Delta_5(\mu_3) & \dot{\xi} \end{vmatrix} = 0. \quad (5.9)$$

The author sincerely thanks E. A. Barbashin and N. N. Krasovskii for their active participation in the discussions of the present problem, and for their helpful suggestions.

LITERATURE CITED

1. L. S. Pontryagin, "Some mathematical problems arising in connection with the theory of optimal automatic control systems. Basic problems of automatic regulation and control," Proceedings of the Session of the AN SSSR on the Scientific Problems of the Automation of Production [in Russian] (Izd. AN SSSR, 1957).
2. N. N. Krasovskii, "Concerning optimal control theory, Avtomatika i Telemekhanika 18, No. 11 (1957).‡
3. R. V. Gamkrelidze, "Concerning optimal process theory," Doklady Akad. Nauk SSSR 116, No. 1 (1957).
4. N. N. Krasovskii, "On one optimal control problem," Prikl. Matem. i Mekh. 21, No. 5 (1957).
5. N. N. Krasovskii, "On one problem in the optimal control of nonlinear systems," Prikl. Matem. i Mekh. 23, No. 2 (1959).
6. R. Bellman, Dynamical Programming (Princeton University Press, 1957).
7. R. Bellman, J. Glicksberg, and O. Gross, "Some aspects of the mathematical theory of control processes," Report 313, RAND Corporation (1958).
8. A. M. Letov, Stability of Nonlinear Controlled Systems [in Russian] (Gostekhizdat, 1955).

*For the given case, the boundary condition for the function ξ is superfluous.

†The author wishes to thank M. A. Aizerman for the advice which permitted him to avoid an erroneous judgment on this property, which was contained in the first version of the paper.

‡See English translation.

PART II

Optimal Transients for Systems with Bounded Inputs

NONLINEAR TECHNIQUES FOR IMPROVING SERVO PERFORMANCE

DONALD McDONALD

Cook Research Laboratories, Chicago, Illinois

Abstract.—Speed of response and accuracy of servomechanisms have greatly improved in the last ten years resulting from the development of highly refined techniques of linear analyses for closed loop systems and from the improvement of servo motors and controllers. Fundamental limitations in these factors will be discussed. If nonlinear elements are used in servomechanisms, system performance can be improved without improvements in the characteristics of existing controllers and servo motors. This practice has been neglected because of the extreme difficulty encountered in handling and solving nonlinear differential equations. Phase plane and space analysis applied to nonlinear servo problems give an analytical interpretation of the effect of nonlinear elements and assist in the design of nonlinear servos.

I. INTRODUCTION

The speed of response and accuracy of servomechanisms have been greatly increased in the last ten years. Such an increase has resulted from the development of highly refined techniques of linear analyses for closed loop systems and from the improvement of servo motors and controllers.

It is becoming more difficult to improve any further the transient performance of servomechanisms designed upon the basis of linear system analysis without (1) reducing the time delays or energy storages of existing controllers and servo motors, and (2) improving the acceleration characteristics of existing servo motors. Significant improvements in controllers and servo motors are now being made less frequently and with less ease than they were made during the first half of the past decade.

If nonlinear elements are used in servomechanisms, system performance can sometimes be improved without increased improvements in the characteristics of existing controllers and servo motors. Unfortunately, the use of nonlinear elements in a closed loop system has been neglected because of the extreme difficulty encountered in handling and solving nonlinear differential equations. Phase plane analysis and, more generally, phase space analysis, when applied to servo problems of a nonlinear nature, give a analytical interpretation of the effect of nonlinear elements and assist in the design of nonlinear servos.

II. PHASE PLANE ANALYSIS

The phase space representation of a single-degree-of-freedom system becomes a phase plane. Curves in this phase plane are plots of the velocity versus the position of the system. In the phase plane, time has been eliminated from both of the usual velocity and the position equations, and a single equation of velocity as a function of position is used. As an example, the phase plane representation of a simple single-degree-of-freedom servo with error rate damping, having the characteristic equation of motion of

$$\ddot{E} + 2cw_n\dot{E} + w_n^2E = 0 \tag{1}$$

may be used to explain the properties of the phase plane.[1] Figure 1 shows the phase plane representation of this system for a damping ratio c of 1.

The ordinate of Fig. 1 is the error rate divided by w_n, the undamped natural frequency of the system, and the abscissa is the error. In this graph the error rate divided by w_n represents the non-dimensionalized velocity of the system. If the system were subjected to a step function of input position equal to 5, the error would immediately jump to 5. The response of the system to such a step function of the input position is shown in Fig. 1 by the curve A, starting at $E = 5$ and proceeding in the fourth quadrant to $E = 0$ and $\dot{E} = 0$. This curve shows that the system with an initial positive error and zero error rate approaches zero error, first by increasing the magnitude of the error rate, and then by slowly decreasing the magnitude of this error rate to zero, as is to be expected of a critically-damped system. In addition the representation shows that the error rate is negative, which is the polarity required to reduce a positive error to zero.

If the system were subjected to an input velocity step function of approximately $1.5w_n$ rad/sec, the response of the system would be represented by curve B in the phase plane, starting at $E = 0$ and $\dot{E}/w_n = 1.5$, and proceeding to a maximum error of three where the error rate is zero. From this point the response is proportionately the same as the response to a step function of 5, and is represented by curve B from $E = 3$ to the origin lying totally in the fourth quadrant.

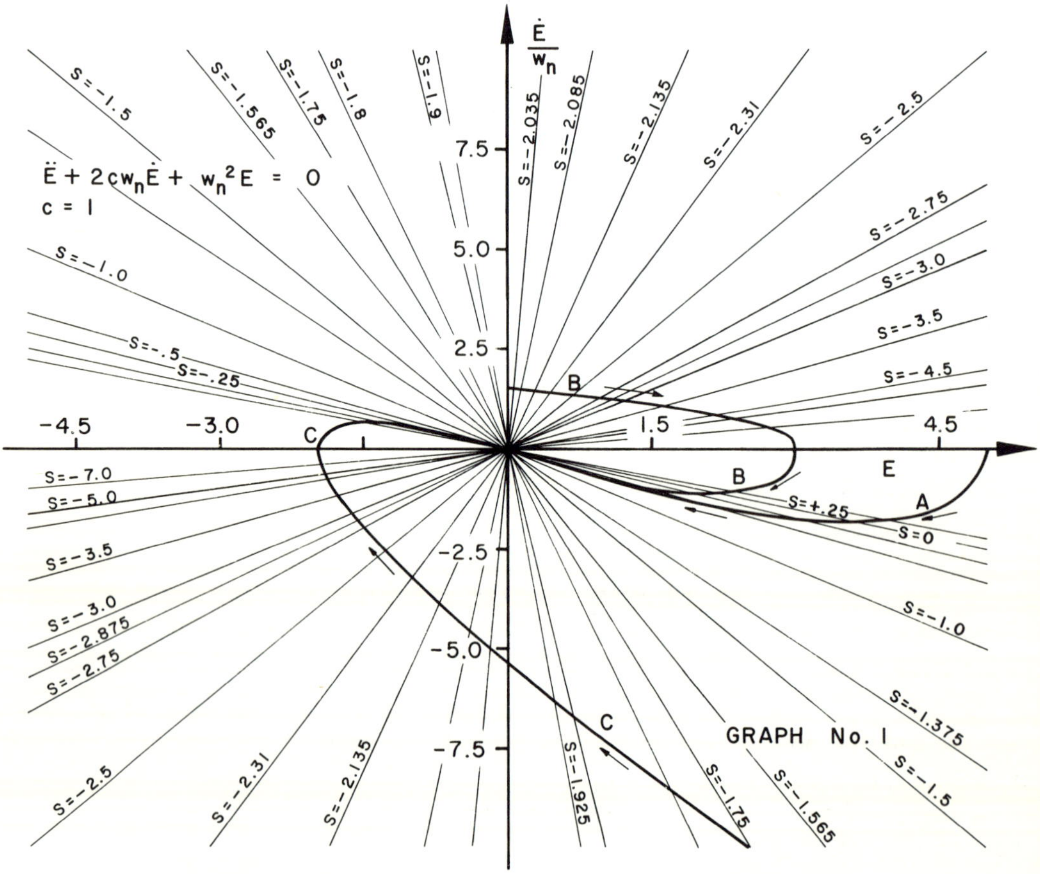

Fig. 1—Nondimensionalized plot of error rate versus error of an elementary error-rate-damped servo.

Lastly, if the system were subjected simultaneously to a step function of input position of 2.5 rad and a step function of input velocity of $-10w_n$ rad/sec, the response of the system would be represented in the phase plane by the curve C, starting at $E = 2.5$ and $\dot{E}/w_n = -10$ and proceeding into the third quadrant, reaching a maximum negative error of approximately -2 rad where the error rate is zero. From this point the system reaches zero error and zero error rate by following a path similar to those followed by the system in responding to step functions of 5 and 3 rad; with the exception that this part of the curve now lies in the second quadrant, inasmuch as a positive error rate is required to reduce a negative error to zero.

As shown in Appendix 1, the direction of motion of the point representing the velocity and position of the system is indicated by the arrows on the curve.

The phase plane representation of a single-degree-of-freedom system is a particularly useful device because, as is shown in Appendix 2, the phase portrait (plots of velocity versus position) may be created even when nonlinearities in the equation of motion make it impossible to obtain solutions for the velocity and position as functions of time. Furthermore, as time can be obtained from the phase portrait, plots of position and velocity as a function of time may be obtained from the portrait.

III. NONLINEAR SERVOS DERIVED FROM LINEAR SERVOS

Figure 2 shows the approximate response of four different types of single-degree-

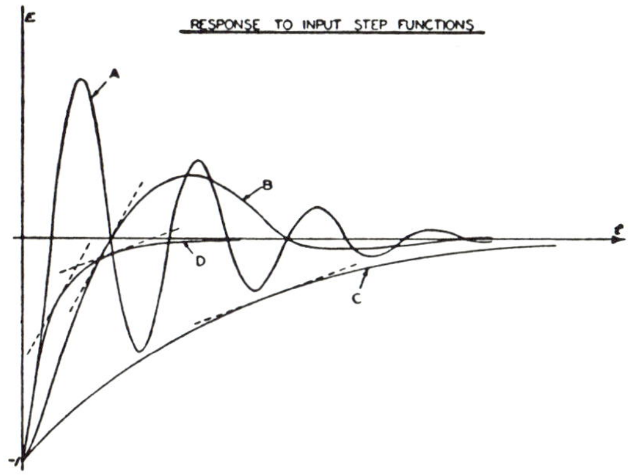

Fig. 2—Transient responses to step functions of input position.

of-freedom servos when subjected to input step functions. Curves A, B, and C are the response of servos similar to the one used for Fig. 1, but having damping ratios of approximately 1/3, ¾, and 2, respectively. A desirable characteristic for such responses to an input step function is for the error to be reduced to a minimum value as quickly as possible and thereafter to be maintained below this value. Curve A causes the error to go to zero in the shortest time interval. However, the error does not remain at zero, but builds up to a large value before again returning to zero. This process is carried out several times before the error remains less than some minimum value. Curve C, which is the other extreme, takes the longest time to bring the error to a value smaller than the minimum error, but once having reached this value, the error continues to decrease. Curve B is a compromise between these two cases. Curve D represents the response of a modified version of this servo wherein the response initially follows curve A, then as the error is reduced, takes on a slope approximately that of curve B for that magnitude of error, and later, as the error approaches the minimum value, the slope of the response becomes similar to that of C near the minimum error. As is evident from curve D, this response is the most satisfactory from the standpoint that the error reaches and remains less than a minimum value in the shortest interval. It is possible that another system with response, composed of portions of curves A, B, and C, and having one overshoot, might produce even more desirable results. However, for the purpose of demonstrating the use of the phase plane analysis and of nonlinear elements in simple servos, the system having the response of D will be considered. Such a system is not necessarily an optimum one, but lends itself easily to a demonstration of the effect of nonlinear elements.

$$\ddot{E} + \frac{2cw_n\dot{E}}{1 + a\,|E|} + w_n{}^2E = 0 \tag{2}$$

Equation 2 is the characteristic equation of motion of a single-degree-of-freedom servo with error rate damping proportional to the error rate and inversely proportional to the magnitude of the error. The system represented by this equation will have the characteristic that the damping ratio is small for large values of error and progressively increases as the error is reduced. This variation of the damping ratio with error yields a response similar to that of curve D of Fig. 2. Equation 3

$$Y = \frac{-x}{s' + \dfrac{2c}{1 + |X|}} \tag{3}$$

$$\text{where } Y = \frac{a\dot{E}}{w_n},\ X = aE, \text{ and } s' = \frac{s}{w_n}$$

is the equation of the isocline for this servo, and Fig. 3 is its phase plane portrait which was constructed using the isoclines of (3).

Figure 3 shows only the first and fourth quadrants of the phase plane. Inasmuch as the isoclines for the third quadrant are the same as the isoclines for the first quadrant reflected first about the abscissa and then about the ordinate, and the isoclines for the second quadrant are similarly related to the isoclines of the fourth quadrant, the phase portrait in the second and third quadrants may be easily predicted by consideration of the first and fourth quadrant alone. The ordinate of Fig. 3 is proportional to the nondimensionalized error rate, and the abscissa is proportional to the error. Curve A represents the response of the system to an input step function of $5/a$, and Curve B represents the response to a step function of velocity input of approximately $8w_n/a$. As may be noted, the general configuration of these two curves is the same as that of Fig. 1. (Curves A and B should pass through the origin before touching the abscissa. The fact that this does not occur is the result of poor geometrical construction of the curve near the origin.) It is interesting to note that if a is set equal to 1, the response of the system between $aE = E = 3$ and 2.5 of curve B is almost identical to that portion of the curve B of Fig. 4 between $E = 3$ and 2.5. This is to be expected because (1) the phase portrait from 3 to 2.5 in the fourth quadrant of curve B of both graphs is independent of previous motion of the system, and (2) the damping ratio of 2 in Fig. 3 is reduced by a factor of approximately 4 in this region by the term $1 + a|E|$, resulting in an effective c of 1/2, which is the value of the damping ratio for Fig. 4.

If a were set equal to 5/3, curve A of Fig. 3 would then represent the response of the system to an input step function of 3 rad, and the resulting nondimensionalized error rate $\dot{E}/w_n$ for this curve should now be multiplied by $1/a$ or $3/5$.

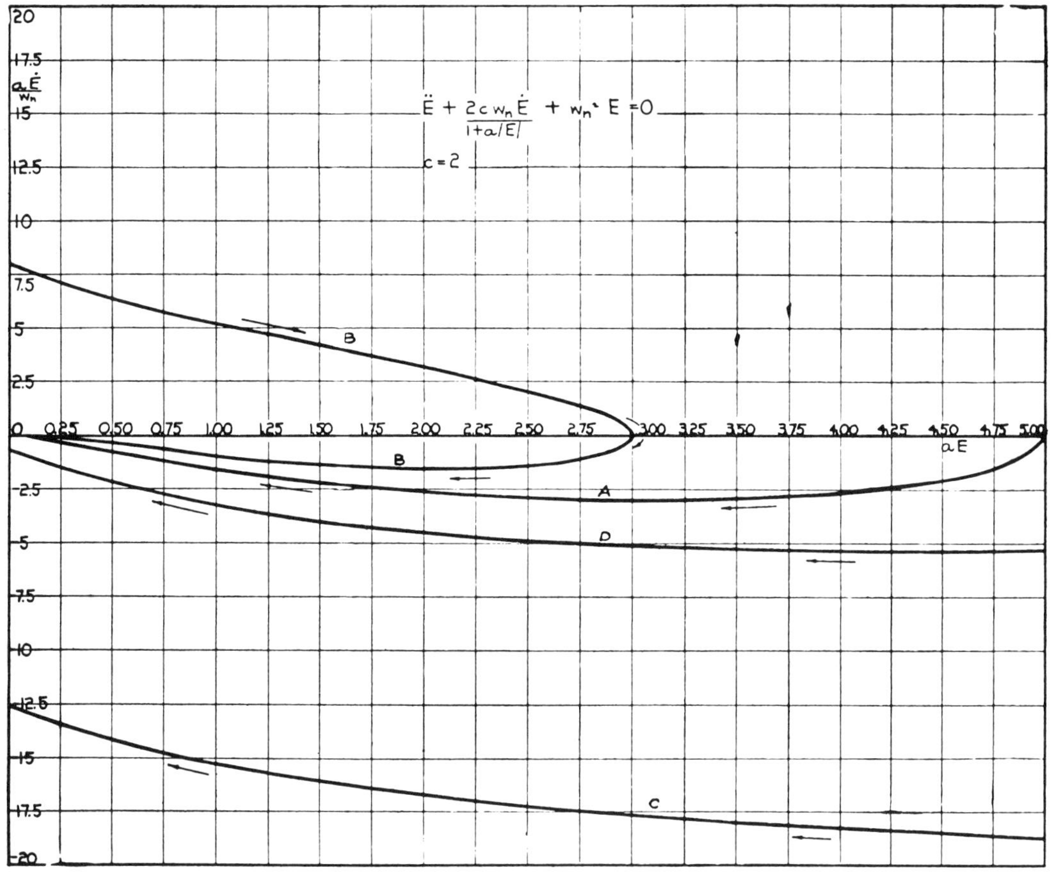

Fig. 3—Nondimensionalized plot of error rate versus error for an elementary servo with nonlinear damping.

Comparisons of that portion of curves A and B in the fourth quadrant for both Figs. 3 and 4 show that the response of the system of Fig. 3 to an input step function starts out with a low damping ratio of the order of $c = 1/2$. Furthermore, as the error approaches zero, comparison of Fig. 3 with Figs. 5 and 4 shows that the response progressively approaches the response of a system with a higher damping ratio.

It is worth noting that curve D of Fig. 3 is a portion of the response of this nonlinear system to a step function of input of approximately $aE = 10$ and that for such a large step function the system tends to overshoot—that is, the error rate is not zero when the error goes to zero, as is indicated by the fact that curve D does not pass through the origin the first time, $aE = 0$, but reaches the origin further on, as did curve C of Fig. 1.

In addition to having response characteristics similar to those of curve D of Fig. 2, the response of this type of nonlinear servo to noise is reduced when the error is small, when the ratio of noise to error can become appreciable. This reduction in the effect of noise is also produced by overdamped systems. but at the cost of reduction of response to input transients which the output should follow. The possible application of nonlinear terms to reducing the effect of noise on servos without reducing their normal transient performance should not be overlooked.

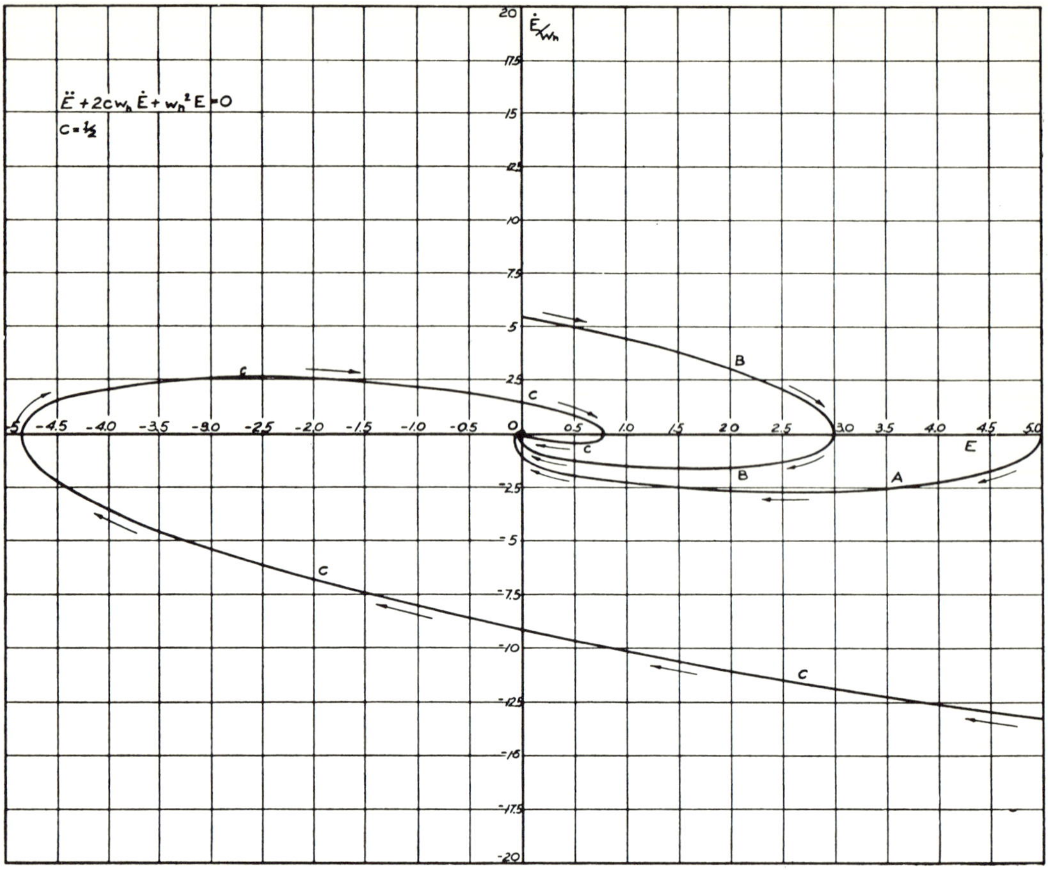

Fig. 4—Nondimensionalized plot of error rate versus error of an elementary error-rate-damped servo.

It is interesting to note that w_n does not affect the shape of the phase portraits, but only changes the time scale.

Comparisons of curves B in the first quadrant of both Figs. 3 and 5 show that the maximum value of error resulting from a step function of input velocity is greater for the nonlinear system of Fig. 3 than for the linear system of Fig. 5. However, the response of the two systems from that point on is better for the nonlinear system. These results are as to be expected because in the first quadrant the error rate damping assists the output in catching up with the input, thus making faster the response of the linear system which has higher damping. On the other hand, in the fourth quadrant the error rate damping impedes the overspeeding of the output which is required to overtake the input, and consequently the nonlinear system has better response in this quadrant. It would therefore be desirable to modify further the nonlinear system so that the damping term is (1) linear when the error rate and error have the same sign (first quadrant) and (2) nonlinear when the error rate and error have opposite signs (fourth quadrant). By similar reasoning it may be shown that the damping term should be linear in the third quadrant and nonlinear in the fourth quadrant. Thus, in general, a linear damping term for this type of servo is best when the error and error rate have the same signs, and a nonlinear damping term is more satisfactory when the error and error rate have opposite signs. A network for achieving this operation is shown in Appendix III.

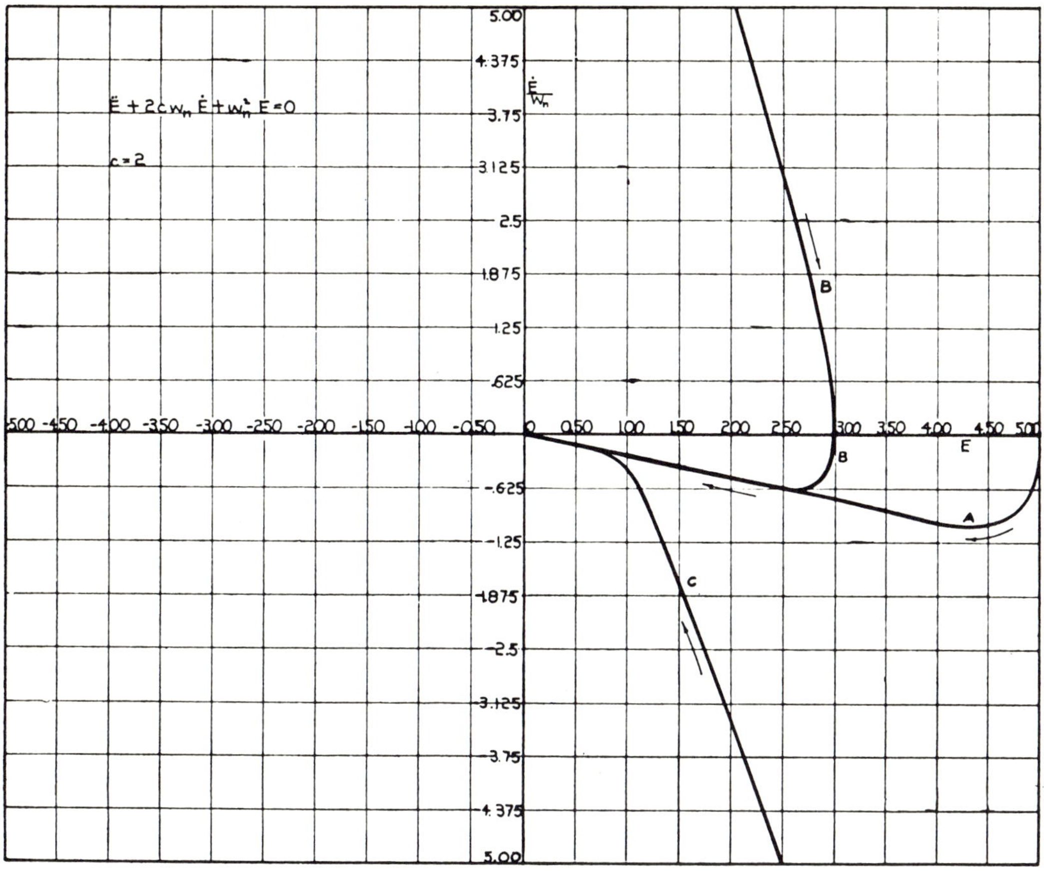

Fig. 5—Nondimensionalized plot of error rate versus error of an elementary error-rate-damped servo.

The response of the servo of Fig. 3 overshoots for step functions of input position of the order of $aE = 10$ or greater. While this is not necessarily undesirable, the servo may be modified so as to extend the upper limit for step functions of aE, for which overshooting does not take place, by the use of the nonlinear damping term shown in (4).

$$\ddot{E} + \frac{2cw_n\dot{E}}{1 + a|E + b\dot{E}|} + w_n^2 E = 0 \tag{4}$$

Equation (4) is the characteristic equation of motion of a single-degree-of-freedom servo with error rate damping proportional to error rate and inversely proportional to the magnitude of the sum of error and error rate. The isoclines for such a system are given by

$$Y = \frac{-X}{s' + \dfrac{2c}{1 + |X + b'Y|}} \tag{5}$$

$$\text{where } Y = \frac{a\dot{E}}{w_n},\ X = aE,\ s' = \frac{s}{w_n},\ \text{and } b' = bw_n$$

Figure 6 which was constructed from these isoclines is a partial phase portrait of this system. Again the nondimensionalized error rate and the error are used as the ordinate and abscissa respectively. This phase portrait is a partial one because only that portion of the phase portrait lying in the fourth quadrant between the abscissa and the line-marked boundary is given. The portrait has not been given in the first quadrant because it can be shown that a linear damping term is again more desirable for the first quadrant. The boundary in the fourth quadrant is the line

$$E + bE = 0. \tag{6}$$

All curves between the abscissa and this boundary are those for which $E + bE$ has the sign of E and is greater than zero. Curves below this boundary would be those for which $E + b\dot{E}$ would bear the sign of $\dot{E}$ and would be less than zero. Therefore, curves below this boundary would tend to have very low effective damping when the error is small and the error rate is high. Such a condition would surely lead to multiple overshoots and reduction in speed of response. Consequently, it is more desirable that a linear damping term be used for values of E and $\dot{E}$ which fall below the boundary line.

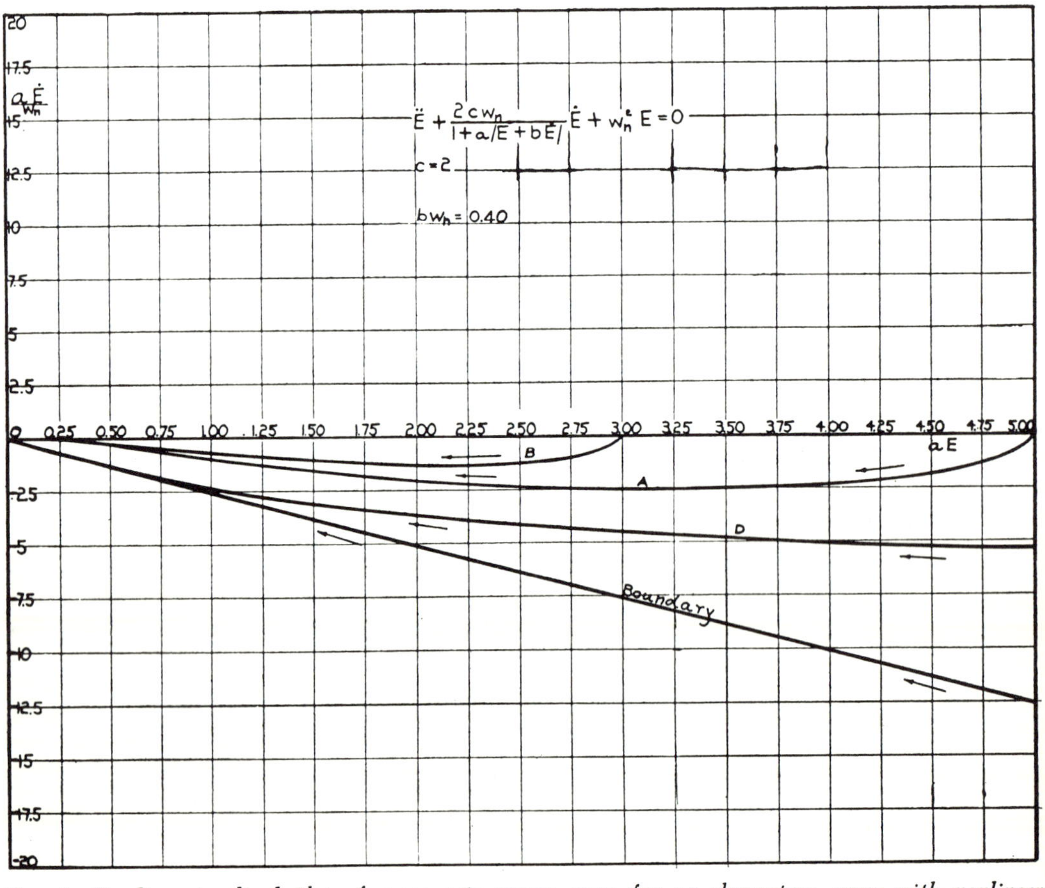

Fig. 6—Nondimensionalized plot of error rate versus error for an elementary servo with nonlinear damping.

Curve D of Fig. 6 is a portion of the response of this type of nonlinear servo to a step function of input which is larger than that producing curve D in Fig. 3. It will be noted that even with this larger step function of input, the system of Fig. 6 does not overshoot as does the one of Fig. 3.

The quantity bw_n has been chosen equal to 0.4 for the system shown in Fig. 6. Therefore, in the region of aE from 4 to 2.5 of curve A, where $a\dot{E}/w_n$ is equal to approximately —2.5, the sum of $E + b\dot{E}$ is smaller than E by $1/a$. Consequently, in this region the damping coefficient is proportionately increased for this system over the one of Fig. 3.

Another type of nonlinear, single-degree-of-freedom servo is one with a nonlinear restoring term rather than a nonlinear damping term. Equation 7

$$\ddot{E} + 2cw_n\dot{E} + \frac{w_n{}^2E}{1 + a\dot{E}} = 0 \qquad (7)$$

is the characteristic equation of motion of such a single-degree-of-freedom servo where the restoring term is directly proportional to the error and inversely proportional to the magnitude of the error rate. Equation 8

$$X = (2c + s')(Y^2 - Y) \qquad (8)$$

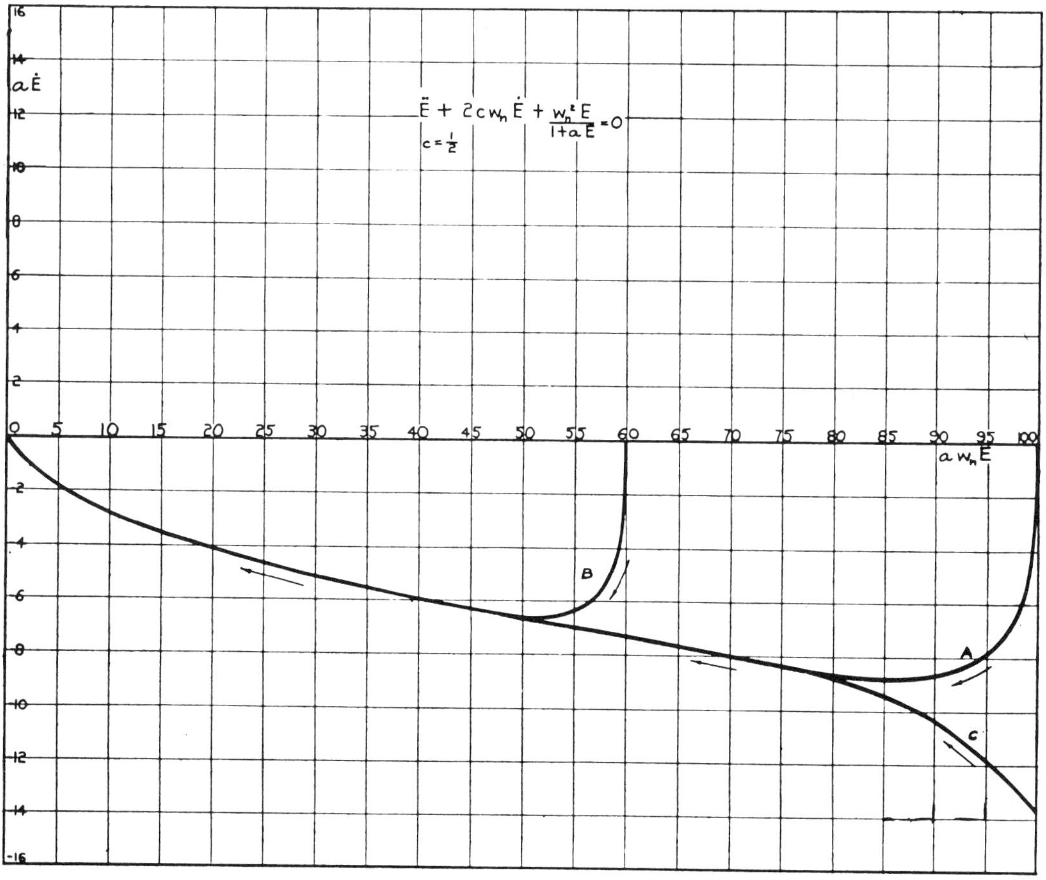

Fig. 7—Nondimensionalized plot of error rate versus error for an elementary servo with a nonlinear restoring torque.

where $X = aw_nE$, $Y = a\dot{E}$, $s' = s/w_n$ represents the isoclines for this servo in the fourth quadrant only, and Fig. 7 is its partial phase portrait. The phase portrait has not been plotted for the first quadrant, because it may be shown that a linear restoring term produces better response in this quadrant. Similar reasoning may be used for the second and third quadrants, with the isoclines of the second quadrants being mirror images of the isoclines of the fourth quadrant reflected first about the abscissa and then about the ordinate.

In this servo the response to step functions of input position starts out with a high effective natural frequency, and as the velocity increases, the effective natural frequency is reduced until the phase curve approaches the origin. This response is different from curve D of Fig. 2 in that the variation of the nonlinear term is a function of error rate rather than of error.

The servo systems of Figs. 3, 6, and 7 are stable systems because all the curves of the phase portrait end at the origin and it can be shown that the origin constitutes a stable focus.

Other types of nonlinear terms for single-degree-of-freedom servos exist. Some which appear to have promise are damping terms proportional to the square root of the error rate and restoring terms proportional to the square root of the error. It seems highly probable that undesirable performance would be obtained if the square of the error rate and the square of the error were used in these terms instead. The several Figs. 1, 3-7 show the phase portraits of three linear, single-degree-of-freedom servos and three nonlinear, single-degree-of-freedom servos. There are many other variations in addition to these plotted or suggested where both the damping and restoring terms are nonlinear.

IV. OFF-ON-OR-CONTACTOR SERVOS

The off-on or contactor servo is the most commonly used nonlinear servo. Its operation may be represented well by a single-degree-of-freedom, characteristic equation of motion. This type of servo is not usually considered to be capable of optimum response because of its nonlinear operation. However, if the off-on servo is controlled by a procedure which is different from the conventional procedure, its nonlinear operation will result in the maximum speed of response obtainable with any servo motor having a limited torque output. This fact will be demonstrated in the following paragraphs along with a discussion of the performance of the off-on servo with conventional controllers.

The most elementary contactor servo has the characteristic equation of motion

$$(9)\qquad J\ddot{E} = -T \qquad E > 0$$

$$J\ddot{E} = T \qquad E < 0$$

In this system the restoring torque is of constant magnitude and opposite in polarity to the error. Equation 10

$$(10)\qquad \dot{E} = -\frac{T}{sJ} \qquad E > 0$$

$$\dot{E} = \frac{T}{sJ} \qquad E < 0$$

represents the isoclines for this elementary contactor servo. Figure 8 is the phase portrait for such a system. This graph was derived directly from (9) without using the isoclines. When this elementary contactor servo is subjected to a step function of input position, 14 rad for example, its phase portrait starts on the abscissa at +14 and proceeds in the fourth quadrant along curve A until its intersects the ordinate at approximately 3.7. Here the restoring torque reverses, resulting in (1) a reversal of the error rate and of the slope of the phase portrait, and (2) the system decelerating again to zero error rate at an equal negative distance from the origin. The phase portrait continues from there on the same curve through quadants 2 and 1 and back to +14 of the abscissa, where this sequence is again repeated. Curves B and C are phase portraits of the response for smaller values of a step input. It may be noted that all of the phase portraits are made up of segments of parabolas and are closed paths having a common "center" at the origin. A system having a phase portrait with a "center" at the origin represents a stable oscillatory motion.

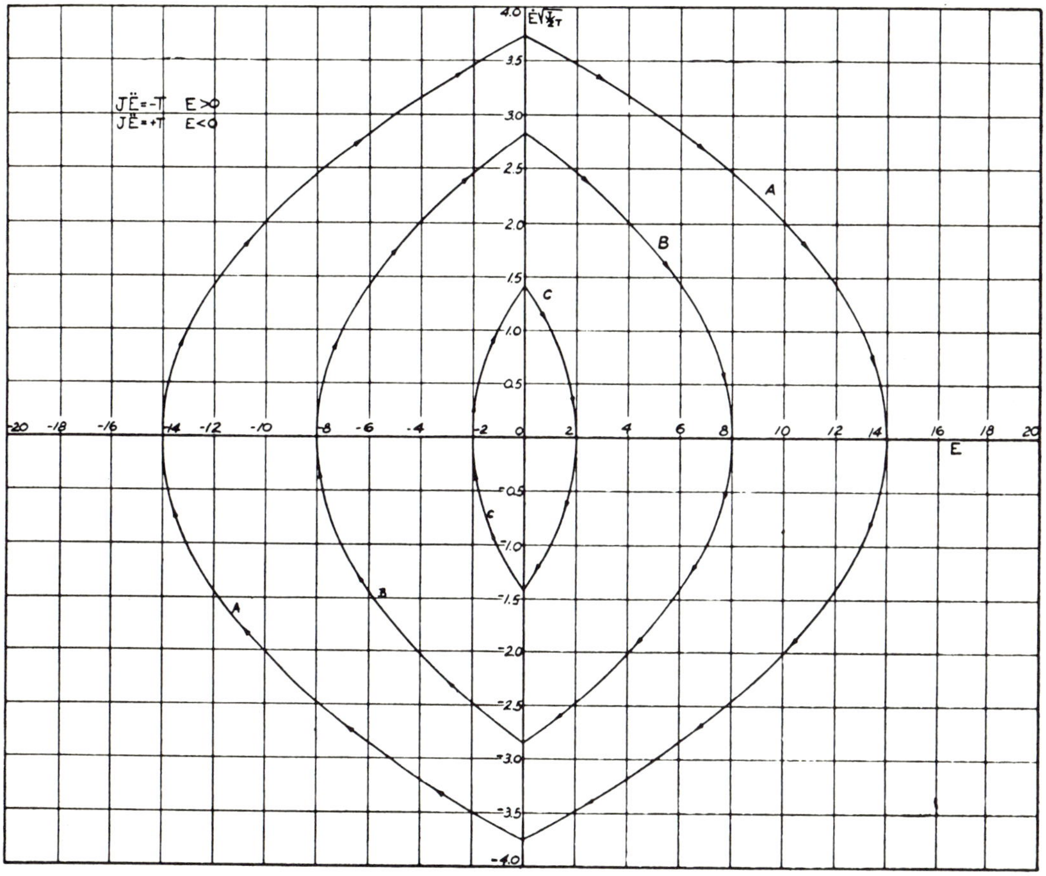

Fig. 8—Nondimensionalized plot of error rate versus error for an elementary off-on servo.

Inasmuch as any one of the phase curves is continuous, the same curves could be interpreted as the response to step functions of input velocities. For example, when the system is subjected to a step function of input velocity of $3.7\sqrt{2T/J}$, the phase portrait would begin on the ordinate at 3.7 and proceed along curve A in quadrant 1 toward the abscissa. From there on the system would continue to oscillate, always remaining on curve A.

The performance of contactor servos may be improved if the point of torque reversal is not where the error changes sign, but where a certain value of error rate exceeds a certain value of error. Equation 11

$$(11) \qquad J\ddot{E} = -T \qquad KE + L\dot{E} > 0$$
$$J\ddot{E} = T \qquad KE + L\dot{E} < 0$$

is the characteristic equation of motion for such a system. This type of control of the motor is normally achieved by the insertion of a simple lead network into the proportional amplifier controlling the relay or switch which energizes the servo motor. Figure 9 is a phase portrait of this system, and the graph was again derived from (11).

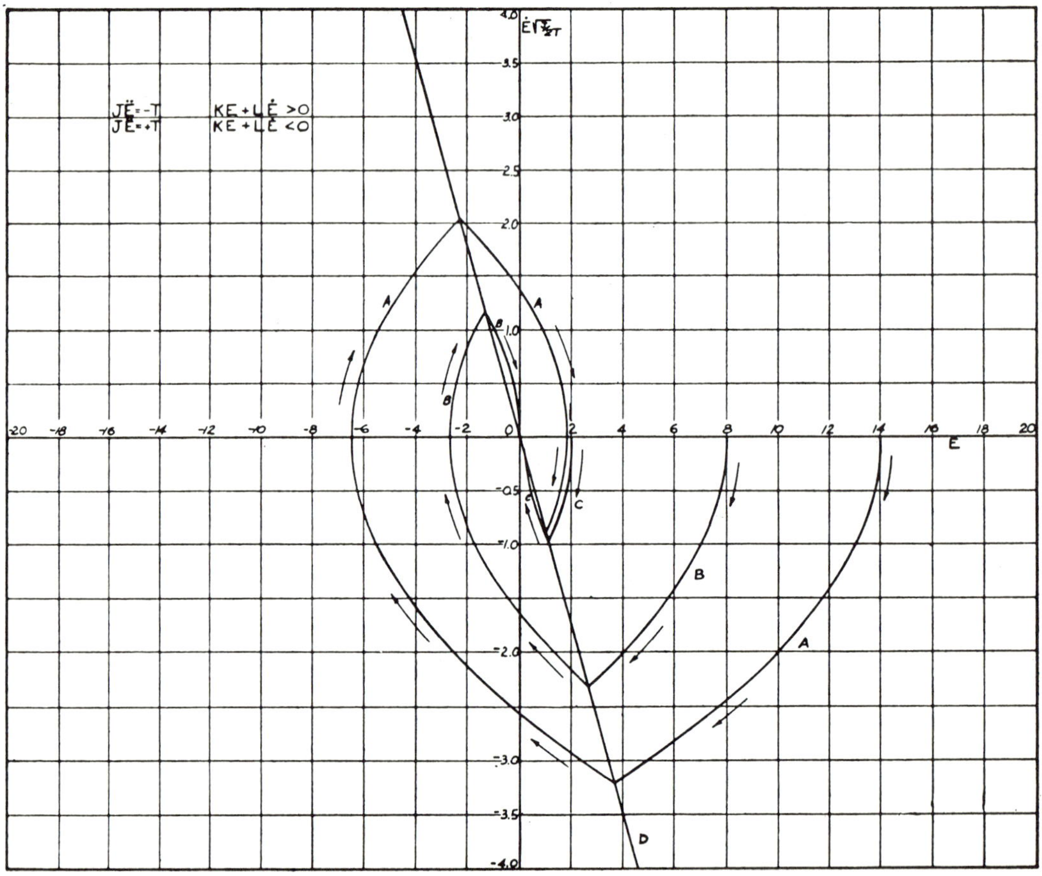

Fig. 9—Nondimensionalized plot of error rate versus error for an elementary off-on servo with a linear lead network.

If this contactor servo with an error lead network in its controller amplifier were subjected to a step function of input position, 14 radians for example, the response of the system would be represented by curve A. Curve A starts at the abscissa, where $E = 14$, and proceeds with increasing velocity until the phase curve meets the straight line D. The equation for D is

$$(12) \qquad KE + L\dot{E} = 0$$

and represents the boundary between the regions of positive and negative torque. For that portion of the phase plane lying above and to the right of line D the restoring torque is always negative, and it is positive for that portion of the phase plane to the left and below D.

The phase curve, on intersecting D, changes slope and passes through the third and second quadrants. The curve again intersects line D in the second quadrant, where the restoring torque is reversed in polarity and the error rate and error are further reduced.

Curves B and C are responses of the same system to smaller step functions of input position. Curve B appears to reach the origin with less overshoots than does A. Curve C has not been completed, but the response, although overshooting, would tend to reach the vicinity of zero more rapidly. It should be pointed out that although all of the phase curves tend to approach the origin in the form of a spiral, the origin is not a focus of this phase portrait. Close inspection of the phase portrait around the origin on an expanded scale would show that this portion of the portrait is made up of paths which circle the origin but do not pass through it except for a special case. Consequently, this system is stably oscillatory, but has a much smaller amplitude of oscillation when disturbed than has the elementary system of Fig. 8.

The performance of the off-on servo is noticeably improved by the introduction of a lead network into the amplifier controlling the off-on servo. Another type of network yielding a characteristic equation of motion

$$(13)\quad \left.\begin{aligned} J\ddot{E} &= -T \qquad \dot{E}^2 + \frac{2T}{J}E > 0 \\ J\ddot{E} &= T \qquad \dot{E}^2 + \frac{2T}{J}E < 0 \end{aligned}\right\} \text{where } E \text{ and } \dot{E} \text{ have the same sign and the sign of } \dot{E}^2 \text{ is that of } \dot{E}$$

$$\left.\begin{aligned} J\ddot{E} &= -T \qquad E > 0 \\ J\ddot{E} &= T \qquad E < 0 \end{aligned}\right\} \text{where } E \text{ and } \dot{E} \text{ have opposite signs}$$

for the contactor servo, produces the optimum response possible from a contactor type servo. In fact, the speed of response demonstrated by this type of system is the maximum obtainable with any type of servo motor having a limited torque, whether operated in a linear or nonlinear system.

Figure 10 is the phase portrait of this optimum off-on servo. As will be noted from (13), the torque has one polarity when $\dot{E}^2 + (2T/J)E$ is greater than zero and reverses when it becomes less than zero. Curves D and D′ of Fig. 10 represent this boundary condition and have the equations

$$(14)\qquad -\dot{E}^2 + \frac{2T}{J}E = 0$$

$$(15)\qquad \dot{E}^2 + \frac{2T}{J}E = 0$$

When this off-on servo is subjected to an input step function, 14 rad for example, the phase curve starts on the abscissa at 14 and proceeds along curve A in the fourth quadrant until this curve crosses curve D, at which point the torque reverses. Upon the torque reversing, the phase curve then follows D into the origin. Contrary to the operation of the system in Fig. 9 using a lead network, the line of torque reversal is also the path along which the representative point moves to the origin.

Curves B and C, starting from the positive abscissa, represent the response of the servo to smaller step functions of input angle. For both of these curves the phase portrait follows along B and C until they intersect D, and then again D becomes the remainder of the phase portrait carrying the system to zero error and zero error rate. The dotted lines in the fourth quadrant, which are the continuations of curves A, B, and C, do not represent a portion of the phase portrait, but have been included only to assist in interpreting the overall operation of the system.

When this servo is subjected to step function of input velocities, $3.7\sqrt{2T/J}$ for example, the response starts at 3.7 on the ordinate. The phase curve then follows curve A through quadrant 1 to the abscissa at 14. From this point on the phase curve is the same as that previously described for a step function of input position of 14. It will be noted from both the characteristic equation of motion, (13), and Fig. 10 that curve D does not exist in the first quadrant. Curve D is shown dotted in the first quadrant, and the torque does not reverse when curve A intersects D in this quadrant. If torque reversal did take place at this intersection, the representative point on the phase curve would not reach the origin, but would follow D out and away from the origin.

By similar reasoning the response of the servo to negative step functions of input velocity and of input position may be represented by the curves in quadrants 3 and 2, with the same restriction imposed upon curve D.

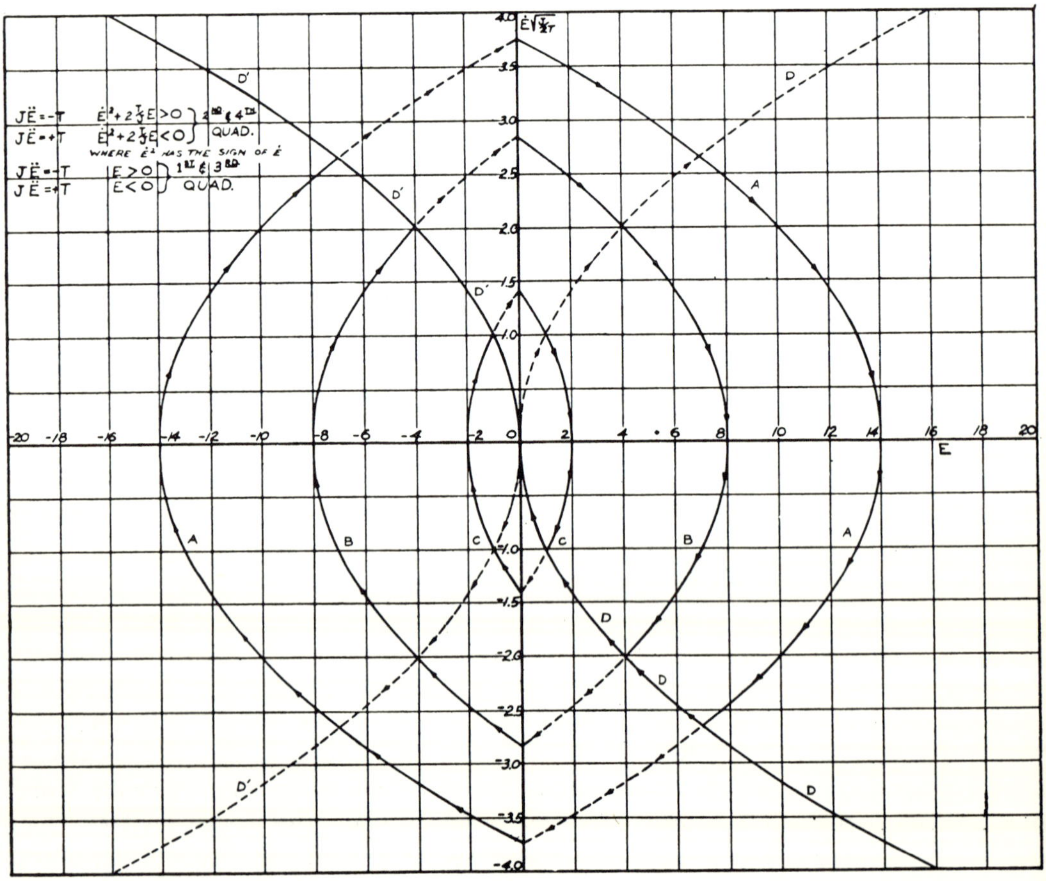

Fig. 10—Nondimensionalized plot of error rate versus error for an elementary off-on servo with a square law lead network.

The response of this type of off-on servo, as represented by the phase portrait of Fig. 10, is the most rapid possible for a servo motor with limited torque. This type of operation results in the motor being used first to accelerate the output at top acceleration for half of the distance the output must travel, and then to decelerate it at top deceleration for the remainder of the distance. Such a sequence necessarily takes the shortest possible time.

V. SERVOS WITH OUTPUT DAMPING

Servo systems with output damping have not been considered so far, because, with the exception of several special cases, the output damping existing in practical systems is too small to produce a first order effect in the dynamic response. These special cases are (1) hydraulic servos and some electric motor servos operating with comparatively small load moments of inertia, and (2) servos obtaining their stabilization from tachometer feedback. In the first of these special cases the output damping cannot be varied. For the systems using tachometer feedback, which is the equivalent of output damping, the damping can be varied by changing the magnitude of the voltage feedback from the tachometer.

The response of servos employing tachometer feedback to step functions of input position is the same as that of servos employing error rate, whether linear or nonlinear in operation. For step functions of input velocity the response of nonlinear servos using tachometer feedback is different from that of error rate damped servos, and a discussion of this response is beyond the scope of this article.

There is however a case of output damping which is inherently nonlinear, that of Coulomb friction, which has received very little consideration in the literature. If Coulomb friction damping or Coulomb damping is properly added to the servo system of Fig. 10, the response of this servo can be improved further. To the best of the author's knowledge, this servo using Coulomb damping is a new type of servo.

Figure 11 is a combined phase portrait of the servo of Fig. 10 with and without Coulomb damping. This Coulomb damping is added only in the fourth and second quadrants when the servo begins to decelerate. If the curves E and E′ of Fig. 11 are disregarded, Coulomb damping not added, the response point of this servo to step functions of input position and velocity starts on curves A, B, C, or other similar curves and follows around on these curves until it intersects D or D′ where it follows D or D′ into the origin.

If a representative point denoting the response, for example a point on A, could travel beyond the intersection of A and D until it intersects curve E and then follow curve E to the origin, the response would be faster than for the system as originally described for Fig. 10. This increased response is the result of a higher negative error rate or over speeding existing without overshooting of the output. Such operation could be achieved if a Coulomb damper were coupled to the output and the motor torque reversed at the intersection of curves A and E. For the case plotted in Fig. 11, the magnitude of the Coulomb damping added is twice the magnitude of the motor torque T. As will be noted from the characteristic equations of motion on Fig. 11, the braking torque is $3T$ and occurs when

$$\dot{E}^2 + 6\,\frac{T}{J}\,E = 0 \tag{16}$$

which is the formulae for curve E. The operation of the system in quadrant two is similar to that in quadrant four. As before, curves E and E′ do not exist in the first and third quadrants.

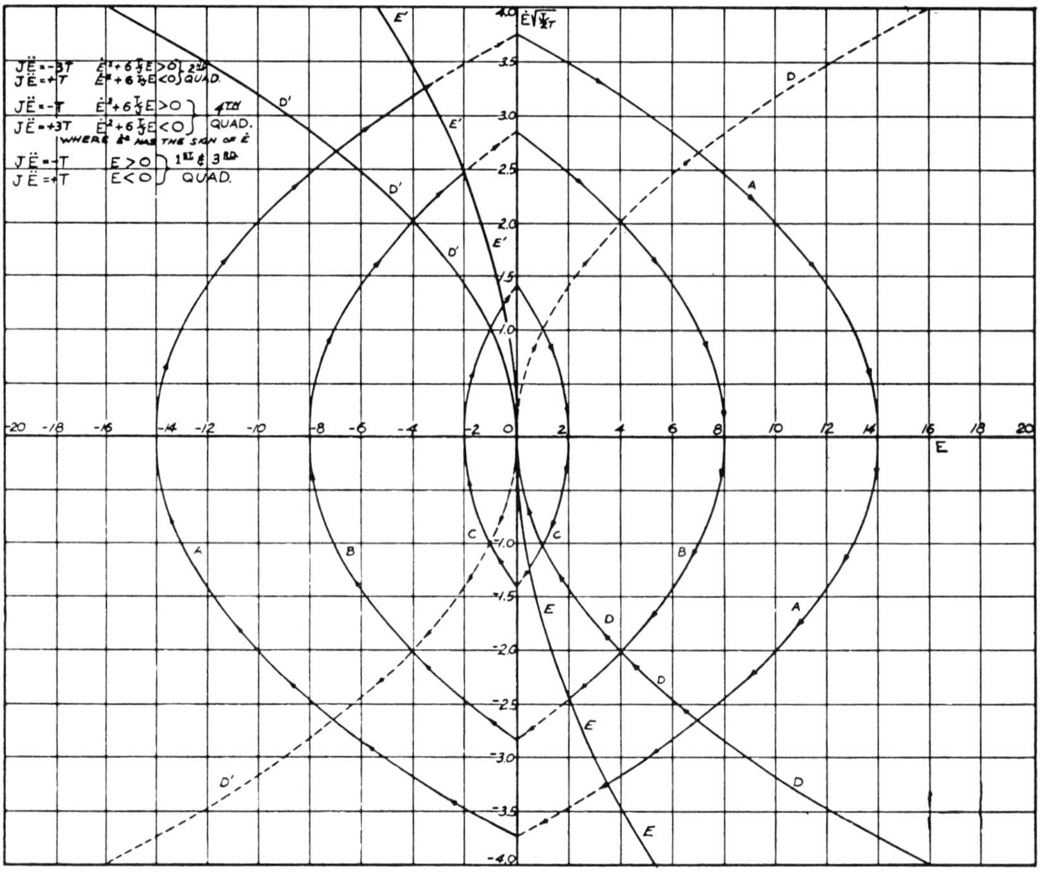

Fig. 11—Nondimensionalized plot of error rate versus error for an elementary off-on servo with a square law lead network and a Coulomb brake.

The Coulomb damper when employed this way is put into operation only at the intersection of curves A, B, C, and other similar curves with curves E or E′. Thus this damper operates only during the interval that the servo motor is braking or decelerating. For the case of step functions of input position, the damper plus the motor must dissipate during deceleration the total energy the servo motor has added to the system up to the deceleration point. This energy which must be dissipated by the damper during deceleration is less than that it must dissipate for step functions of input velocity.

Simple disk or drum brakes or capstan brakes can serve as Coulomb dampers and can be engaged to the output through clash or positive engagement clutches.

The performance of the servos of Fig. 10 and Fig. 11 will be improved further if a third equation

$$(17) \qquad J\ddot{E} = 0 \qquad \text{when } \dot{E} = 0$$

is added to their characteristic equations of motion.

VI. SEVERAL CONSIDERATIONS

The characteristics of the nonlinear servos derived from linear servos and the characteristics of the servo of Fig. 11 if combined, should yield a truly optimum servo. Although the servo of Fig. 11 has the maximum obtainable speed of response, its operation in the vicinity of zero error and zero error rate will be erratic even with the addition of (17). Consequently, a servo with the characteristic equation of motion of (4) for small errors and the characteristic equation of motion of Fig. 11 for any larger errors would eliminate a large portion of the erratic motion of the off-on servo near zero error and zero error rate.

VII. CLOSURE

1. Appendix 1 contains the derivation of the generalized characteristic equation of motion for such a servo system.

2. In Appendix 2 the procedure for constructing the phase plane of a single-degree-of-freedom system is presented and the isocline and its use in plotting the phase portrait are described in detail. The procedure carried out here is paraphrased from Reference 1.

3. Appendix 3 comprises account of some circuits for producing nonlinear terms.

ACKNOWLEDGMENT

I should like to express my appreciation to the Drafting Department of Cook Research Laboratories for the assistance given me in the preparation of the figures; and to Mr. K. C. Mathews of Cook Research Laboratories for the time he spent discussing with me the material for this article.

APPENDIX 1

The equation of motion of the system of Fig. 12 is

$$\frac{T}{E} = k + lp \tag{18}$$

where J = combined moment of inertia of servo motor and load
T = torque developed by servo motor
k = steady state gain of controller
l = error rate damping coefficient
$p = \dfrac{d}{dt}$
$E = A_i - A_o =$ error

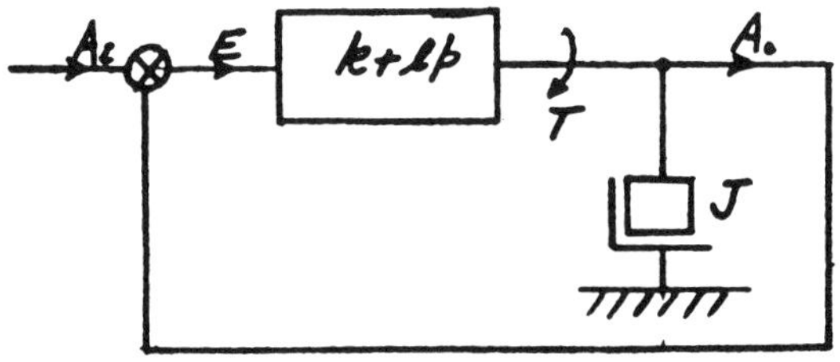

Fig. 12—Block diagram of an elementary error-rate-damped servo.

The characteristic equation of motion for the system is

$$Jp^2E + lpE + kE = 0 \tag{19}$$

Dividing (19) by J and substituting

(20) $$c = \frac{l}{2\sqrt{Jk}} = \text{damping ratio}$$

$$w_n = \sqrt{\frac{k}{J}} = \text{undamped natural frequency}$$

yields

(21) $$p^2E + 2cw_npE + w_n{}^2E = \ddot{E} + 2cw_n\dot{E} + w_n{}^2E = 0$$

APPENDIX 2

The general procedure for plotting velocity versus position curves or portraits of a single-degree-of-freedom servo is best described by considering the case of the linear servo for which the characteristic equation of motion was derived in Appendix 1.

There are three methods for plotting the phase portrait of a system as follows:

a. When time solutions for $\dot{E}$ and E can be obtained by integrating (21), $\dot{E}$ as a function of E may be obtained by eliminating time from the individual time solutions for $\dot{E}$ and E. Then the resulting relationship of $\dot{E}$ as a function of E may be directly plotted.

b. Instead of the differential equation (21) being solved, a new differential equation in terms of $d\dot{E}$ and dE may be formed, which when solved, yields $\dot{E}$ as a function of E directly. This new differential equation is obtained from the time differential equation as follows:

Let us substitute

(22) $$\begin{aligned} v &= \dot{E} \\ x &= E \\ g &= 2cw_n \\ h &= w_n{}^2 \end{aligned}$$

into (21) and obtain

(23) $$\dot{v} + gv + hx = 0$$

Now

(24) $$\frac{\dot{v}}{v} = \frac{dv/dt}{dx/dt} = \frac{dv}{dx}\,.$$

Solving (23) for $\dot{v}$ and substituting it into (24) yields

(25) $$vdv + (gv + hx)dx = 0,$$

which may be integrated by a well-known procedure for homogeneous equations and the resulting equation plotted.

c. There are times when the form of (25) is such that the solution of (25) is extremely difficult or impossible. This condition is the case when the original characteristic equation of motion is nonlinear. However, there is a graphical method of obtaining the solution to (25) from (24) which yields directly a plot of v versus x or $\dot{E}$ versus E.

Equation (24) may be written as

$$\frac{\dot{v}}{v} = \frac{dv}{dx} = s \tag{26}$$

where s = slope of paths in phase plane.

Substituting $\dot{v}$ from (23) into (26) yields

$$-\frac{gv + hx}{v} = s \tag{27}$$

which is the equation of the family of isoclines of the system in the phase plane. An isocline is a locus of points where the paths have a given slope.

Equation (27) is the equation of a family of straight lines passing through the origin of the phase plane. These lines have been plotted on Fig. 2 and have the following equations

$$Y = -\frac{E}{S + 2c} \tag{28}$$

where $Y = \dot{E}/w_n$ and $S = s/w_n$

The use of the isocline in plotting the phase portrait can best be explained by reference to Fig. 13, which is a plot of several isoclines on a phase plane. These isoclines have been chosen arbitrarily and are not related to (28).

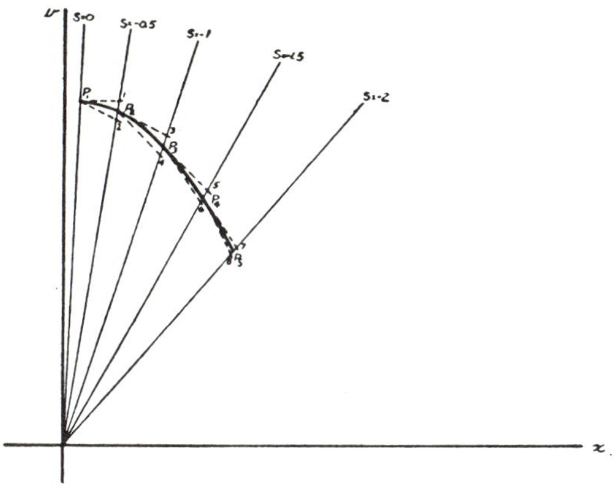

Fig. 13—Phase portrait construction.

The construction of a path can be started by arbitrarily beginning with point P_1 on $s = 0^a$. Two straight lines having slopes of 0 and —½ respectively should be drawn through P_1 intersecting $s = -½$ at 1 and 2. Part of the path can then be drawn as a straight line between P_1 and P_2, which is the midpoint between points 1 and 2. This process may be repeated by drawing two more straight lines with slopes of —½ and —1 respectively through P_2 intersecting $s = -1$ at 3 and 4. The next section of the path can then be drawn between P_2 and P_3, which is the midpoint of points 3 and 4.

This procedure may be continued until the path under consideration is completed and a resulting plot of v versus x obtained. The accuracy of this procedure can be increased by increasing the number of isoclines used.

It is important to note that time, t, can be obtained from the phase portrait. Even though the original characteristic equation of motion cannot be solved for $\dot{E}$ and E

as functions of time, the phase portrait, when created graphically as described under heading (c) above, can be used to obtain time relations as follows:

$$t = \int \frac{dx}{v} = \int \frac{dx}{dx/dt} = \int dt \tag{29}$$

If the resulting phase portrait is replotted with the ordinate as $1/v$, then the area under the reciprocal path represents the time. Plots of both v and x versus t can then be obtained.

APPENDIX 3

All of the nonlinear terms and sequences described in the text require four types of operations to be performed. These operations are (1) obtaining the magnitudes of E, $\dot{E}$, or $E + b\dot{E}$; (2) dividing $\dot{E}$ or E by $1 + a|E|$, $1 + a|\dot{E}|$, or $1 + a|E + b\dot{E}|$; (3) switching the nonlinear terms in or out of the circuit according to the quadrant location; and (4) developing $\dot{E}^2 + KE$. The following sections describe how each of these basic operations may be performed:

A. *Magnitudes*

Figure 14 (a) shows a circuit for developing a voltage proportional to the magnitude

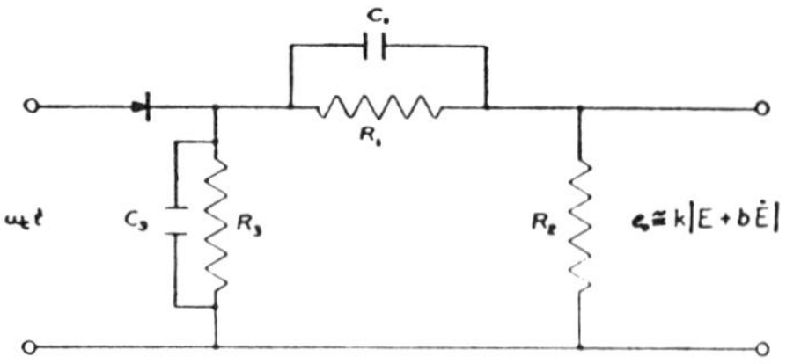

Fig. 14(a)—Circuit for generating the magnitude of the error plus error rate.

of the error plus the error rate. In this circuit, the error in the form of a suppressed-carrier-modulated-voltage is applied to the input terminals and detected by the rectifier. This rectifier permits only the magnitude of E to appear across R_3 and C_3. The conventional lead network composed of R_1, C_1, and R_2 then produces a proportional and approximate derivative term of E. The magnitude of either E or $\dot{E}$ may be obtained alone if the form of the lead network is modified.

B. *Division*

In general, division of the quantities required in the nonlinear terms may be considered simply to be the problem of obtaining the quotient $X/(1 + Y)$. Figures 14 (b) and 14 (c) show two networks which perform this operation. As an example, let $X = E$ and $Y = a|E + b\dot{E}|$. Further, for simplicity, set $e_1 = Y$ and $e_2 = X$. Upon reference to Fig. 14 (b), it will be noted that e_1 is applied to the network controlling the second grid, while e_2 is applied to the network controlling the first grid of a variable-μ tube. (A 6SK7 tube is a good example of a variable-μ tube.) The network of Fig. 14 (a) will supply e_1, and e_2, a suppressed-carrier-modulated-voltage, will be supplied directly from the error input. The voltage e_5, as plotted in Fig. 14 (b), has the general shape of the function $1/(1 + e_1)$. By proper choice of the value of R and of the type of nonlinear resistor, this approximation can be made excellent for a limited range of e_1. In addition, if e_6 is correctly adjusted, the μ of the tube can be made linearly proporitonal to e_5 and e_0 made linearly proportional to μe_2. Consequently, as shown in Fig. 14 (b), e_0 is approximately proportional to the quotient $X/(1+Y)$. The circuit of Fig. 14 (c) does not use a nonlinear resistor to obtain the reciprocal of $1+Y$, but uses the familiar feedback amplifier with a variable-μ tube in the feedback path. The operation of this figure is self-explanatory.

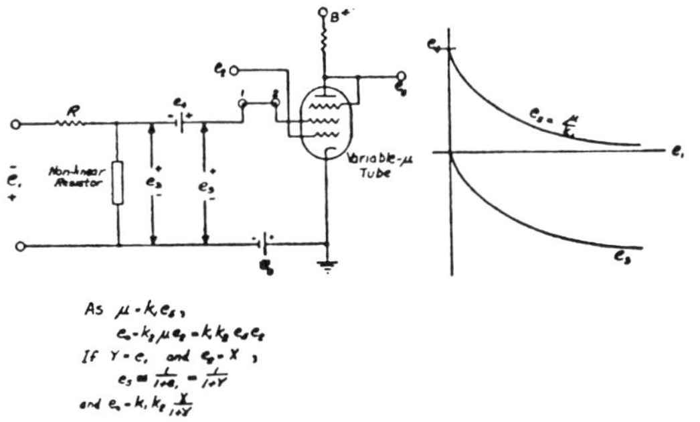

Fig. 14(b)—Circuit for taking the quotient of two variables.

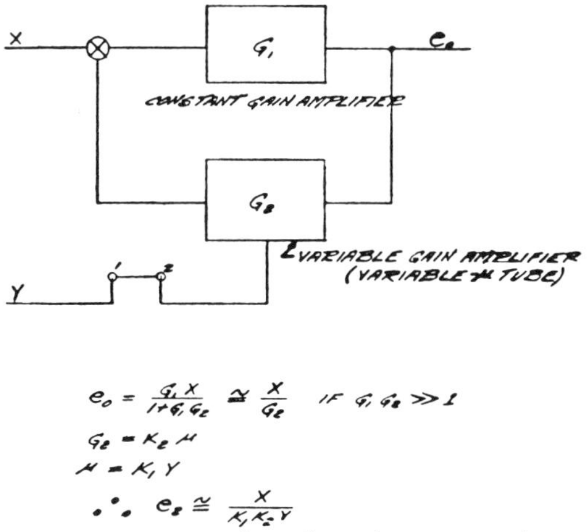

Fig. 14(c)—Circuit for taking the quotient of two variables.

C. *Quadrant Switching*

As noted previously, the nonlinear terms of the characteristic equation of motion of the servos are replaced by linear terms when the signs of E and $\dot{E}$ are the same. Figure 14 (d) is a circuit for changing the operation of circuits of Figs. 14 (b) and 14 (c) from linear to nonlinear operation. The operation of the circuit of Fig. 14 (d) is as follows: The error signal E is applied to the network at the left-hand terminal. The rectifier in series with the coil of Relay No. 1 permits only positive values of E to be applied to the coil. Consequently, this relay remains in the normally open position for negative values of E. The network of R_1 and C apply an approximate $\dot{E}$ to the rectifier and coil of Relay 2 in series. This rectifier permits only negative values of $\dot{E}$ to be applied to the coil of the relay. Consequently, the relay remains in the normally open position for all positive values of $\dot{E}$.

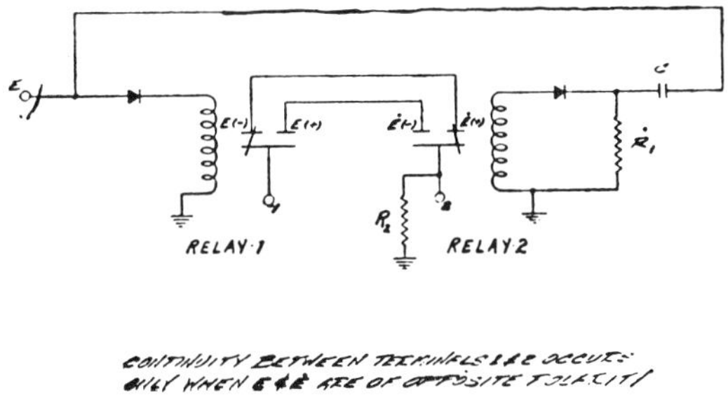

Fig. 14(d)—Quadrant switching system.

Continuity between terminals 1 and 2 exists only when E and $\dot{E}$ are of opposite polarity. If the connections between terminals 1 and 2 of Figs. 14 (b) and 14 (c) are removed, and terminals 1 and 2 of the circuit of Fig. 14 (d) connected to the corresponding terminals of either of the circuits of b and c, the operation of the circuits of Fig. 14 (b) and Fig. 14 (c) will become nonlinear only when E and $\dot{E}$ have opposite signs. This change will take place because the No. 2 grid of the variable-μ tube in both of the circuits will receive a signal which is a function of E or $\dot{E}$ only when E and $\dot{E}$ have opposite signs.

D. *Circuit for Obtaining $\dot{E}^2 + kE$*

The circuit of Fig. 14 (e) is a circuit for producing the square of the error rate

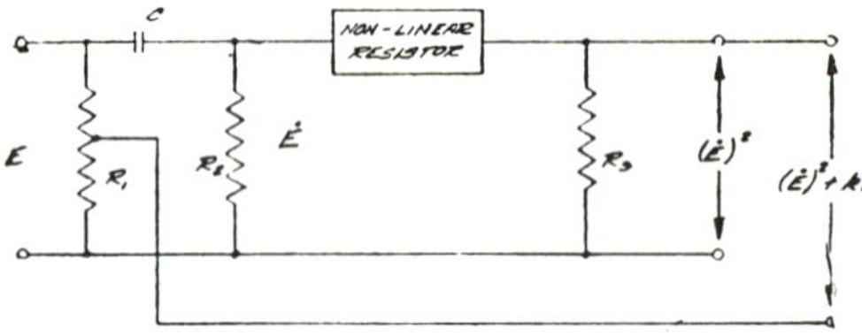

Fig. 14(e)—Square-law lead network.

plus the error. In this circuit R_2 and C develop an output approximately proportiona to $\dot{E}$. By proper choice of the nonlinear resistor and R_3, $\dot{E}$ is squared in magnitude, but retains the polarity of $\dot{E}$. Finally, a portion of E is obtained from R_1 and added to the output across R_3 to obtain the desired sum.

REFERENCE

[1]A. A. Andronow and C. E. Chaikin, "Theory of Oscillations," Princeton University Press, Princeton, N. J., pp. 248-250; 1949.

An Investigation of the Switching Criteria for Higher Order Contactor Servomechanisms

IRVING BOGNER
ASSOCIATE MEMBER AIEE

LOUIS F. KAZDA
MEMBER AIEE

Synopsis: The use of a linear anticipatory switching network in an on-off servomechanism, while improving system stability, does not result in optimum response. Mathematical analysis of second order systems indicates that the network should be a nonlinear function of error and error rate. This paper describes a method for deriving the switching criterion for a "piecewise" linear on-off servo of order greater than two, when the input variable is limited to a step function of position and velocity. The switching criterion results in system error and in derivatives of error reducing to zero in a minimum time. System behavior is described in the principal co-ordinate phase space. Starting at a point in the phase space corresponding to the initial conditions, the representative point moves in a series of discontinuous trajectories determined by the sign of the controlled variable, eventually reaching the origin. The sequence of sign reversals represents the desired switching criterion.

Results indicate that: 1. a unique switching criterion is possible when the number of sign reversals is one less than the order of the system; and 2. although any arbitrary number of reversals greater than the above minimum may be used, in the examples considered minimum switching resulted in minimum response time. All the recorded data and photographs were obtained from an analogue computer study.

Paper 54-44, recommended by the AIEE Feedback Control Systems Committee and approved by the AIEE Committee on Technical Operations for presentation at the AIEE Winter General Meeting, New York, N. Y., January 18–22, 1954. Manuscript submitted October 20, 1953; made available for printing November 17, 1953.

IRVING BOGNER is with the Cook Research Laboratories, Skokie, Ill.; LOUIS F. KAZDA is with the University of Michigan, Ann Arbor, Mich.

The authors wish to acknowledge the assistance received from the engineering faculty at the University of Michigan and the staff at Cook Research Laboratories.

This work in part was sponsored by the United States Air Force under Contract No. *AF 33(038)-21673*, and contains part of the results of a thesis submitted by Irving Bogner in partial fulfillment of the requirements for the degree of Doctor of Philosophy at the University of Michigan

FEEDBACK control theory may be divided into two major categories, depending upon the type of control that exists. The continuous control type of servo is defined by Brown and Campbell[1] as being "linearly and continuously error sensitive." Such systems, described by a linear differential equation with real constant coefficients, are discussed extensively in the literature. The assumption of linearity permits one to employ methods of analysis not applicable to nonlinear systems. Since the linear servo is in many respects similar to a feedback amplifier, the frequency response methods of Nyquist[2] and Bode[3] represent powerful tools in linear design.

The characterization of a physical system as linear has resulted in the development of fast and accurate servos, which are satisfactory in many applications. Frequently, however, control systems possess nonlinearities, inherent or inserted, which are not linear in the sense that they can be described by a linear differential equation.

The past decade has brought forth important contributions to the study of nonlinear servomechanisms, particularly in the field of contactor or on-off servos. In the earlier analyses by MacColl[4] and Weiss,[5] phase plane[6,7] techniques are used to determine the responses of second-order on-off servos possessing such nonlinearities as finite torque reversal time and coulomb damping. Kochenburger[8] and Johnson[9] modified existing linear frequency response techniques to analyze nonlinear systems.

Emphasis in much of the literature pertaining to contactor servos has been on methods of improving system stability. Exceptions are the methods suggested by Neiswander and MacNeal,[10] and before them by Hopkin[11] and McDonald,[12] in which phase plane analysis is used to optimize performance. In McDonald's method a torque-reversing criterion is developed in which the sign of the torque applied to the load is determined by a nonlinear function of error and error rate.

It is the purpose of this paper, in extending the suggestions put forth by McDonald, to present a method for obtaining unique switching criteria for contactor servomechanisms of order greater than two. The analysis presupposes a discontinuous forcing function, fixed in magnitude and reversible in sign, supplied to a dynamic system which is describable over every interval, of its operation by a linear differential equation. This type of control, while nonlinear in the general sense of the term, is more accurately described as being sectionally or piecewise linear. The discussion which follows makes use of phase plane and phase space analysis in describing the system behavior, the particular phase space of interest being one in which servo error is plotted against its higher derivatives.

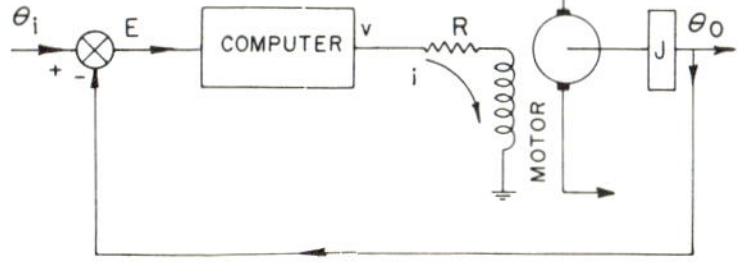

Fig. 1 (right). Second-order contactor servomechanism. The voltage v reverses in sign, as a nonlinear function of E and (dE)/(dt) in a manner which reduces E_0 or $[(dE)/(dt)]_0$ to zero in a minimum time. The motor field time constant is neglected

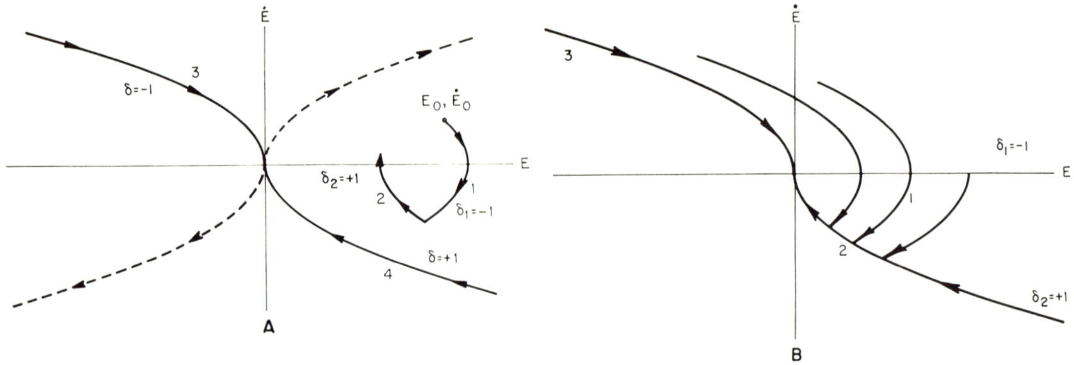

Fig. 2. Phase portraits for the second-order contactor servo of Fig. 1. Curves 1 and 3 in Fig. 2(A) represent trajectories for a positive value of v; curves 2 and 4 for a negative value. Curves 2 and 3 in Fig. 2(B) are the sign reversal curves for optimum system response to step inputs of position and velocity.

Subsequent analysis makes use of what is referred to in the literature as the principal co-ordinate[13] phase space.

Definition of Symbols

a = number of controlled variable sign reversals in excess of the minimum required
b_n = real coefficients in the differential equation describing system dynamics
C = constant of integration
E = servomechanism position error
E_0 = servomechanism position error at time equal to zero
ϵ = dimensionless position error
$F(\ )$ = function of ( )
$h_n(\ )$ = equation of a trajectory projection
i = motor field current
I_a = motor armature current, assumed constant
J = moment of inertia of motor and load
K_ϕ = ratio of flux to field current
K_2 = ratio of torque to flux
L = inductance of motor field
P = number of sign reversals of controlled variable
R = resistance of motor field
S_n = switching curves defined by equations 45 and 46
t = time
T = motor torque
T_M = motor saturation torque
u_n = phase space co-ordinates corresponding to $\dfrac{d^{n-1}E}{dt^{n-1}}$
v_n = principal co-ordinate of a system
v_{12} = variable v_1 at point 2 in the phase space
v = voltage output of the servomechanism computer, the controlled variable
V = magnitude of v
δ = sign determining factor for the controlled variable
Δ = increment of a variable
θ_i = servomechanism input variable
Θ_i = dimensionless input variable
θ_0 = servomechanism output variable
Θ_0 = dimensionless output variable
$\sum_n$ = summation on n
τ = dimensionless time
τ_ϕ = motor field time constant
ϕ = field flux

Optimum Switching for Second-Order Systems

For the idealized system shown in Fig. 1, the load differential equation of motion is

$$\pm T = J\frac{d^2\theta_0}{dt^2} \tag{1}$$

Under the assumption that the inputs are limited to step functions of position and velocity, equation 1 when expressed in terms of the error becomes

$$\mp T = J\frac{d^2E}{dt^2} \tag{2}$$

The solution of equation 2 results in the general phase trajectory equation

$$\left(\frac{dE}{dt}\right)^2 \pm \frac{2T}{J}E = C \tag{3}$$

The $\pm$ sign, which determines the direction of motor torque, may be replaced by δ, i.e.

$$\delta = \begin{cases} +1 \text{ for } T<0 \\ -1 \text{ for } T>0 \end{cases} \tag{4}$$

Equation 2 may then be written as

$$\delta = \frac{J}{T}\frac{d^2E}{dt^2} \tag{5}$$

from which one obtains

$$\left(\frac{dE}{dt}\right)^2 - \delta\frac{2T}{J}E = C \tag{6}$$

Equation 6 can be represented by parabolas 1, 2, 4, shown in Fig. 2(A). At $t=0$, the representative point is at a point in the phase plane corresponding to initial conditions E_0, $\left(\frac{dE}{dt}\right)_0$. Assuming the first delta δ_1, is equal to minus one, the representative point moves along the trajectory 1. If at some time later the delta is changed to plus one, the representative point will follow trajectory 2. The problem is to establish a program for the sign reversal of δ such that the representative point reaches the origin in minimum time.

There is a mathematical theorem[14] which states that for each value of δ there is only one phase trajectory which passes

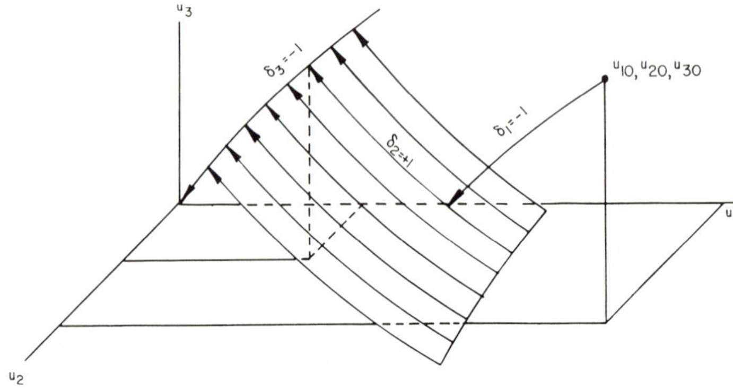

Fig. 3. Phase portrait for a general third-order contactor servo

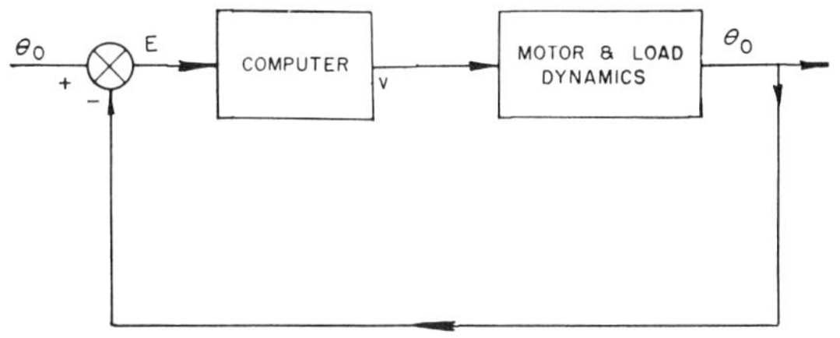

Fig. 4. Block diagram of a general higher order system

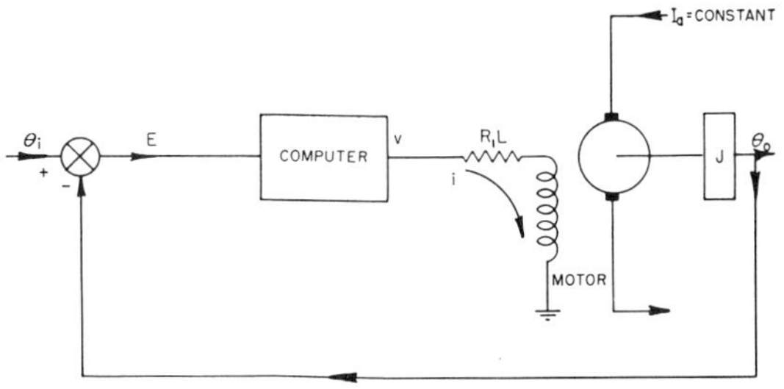

Fig. 6. Third-order contactor servo. The order of the system is increased by accounting for the lag in the motor field

through a given point in the phase plane. Since there exist two possible deltas in the present problem; i.e., $\delta=+1$ and $\delta=-1$, there will be two trajectories which pass through any point, and in particular the origin. These are shown as curves 3 and 4 in Fig. 2(A) and will be referred to as zero trajectories. Every representative point starting at $E_0, \left(\frac{dE}{dt}\right)_0$ to reach the origin, must eventually reach either curve 3 or 4 through some switching sequence. To simplify the analysis, it will be assumed that the initial conditions E_0 and $\left(\frac{dE}{dt}\right)_0$ are in a particular section of the phase plane so that, when proper switching occurs, the representative point reaches the origin along the $\delta=+1$ zero trajectory.

Fig. 2(B) shows the final $\delta_2=+1$ trajectory as 2, a plane curve, extending from the origin. It may be noted that from every point along 2, there radiates a $\delta_1=-1$ trajectory such as 1. The family of these trajectories form a surface whose initial conditions fill the entire upper-half phase plane bounded by curves 2 and 3. For this half of the phase plane the switching criterion would be to let $\delta_1=-1$ until the representative point reaches curve 2, at which time $\delta_2=+1$. The corresponding criterion exists for the other half phase plane where $\delta_1=+1$ and $\delta_2=-1$.

This point of view can be extended to a purely hypothetical third-order system whose differential equation is of the form

$$\delta=F_1\left(E, \frac{dE}{dt}, \frac{d^2E}{dt^2}, \frac{d^3E}{dt^3}\right) \tag{7}$$

and whose general phase trajectory is defined by

$$F_2(\delta, u_1, u_2, u_3)=0 \tag{8}$$

$$F_3(\delta, u_1, u_2, u_3)=0 \tag{9}$$

Equations 8 and 9 form a space curve in the 3-dimensional phase space with coordinates u_1, u_2, and u_3, where

$$u_1=E \tag{10}$$

$$u_2=\frac{dE}{dt} \tag{11}$$

$$u_3=\frac{d^2E}{dt^2} \tag{12}$$

$$\delta=+1 \text{ or } -1 \tag{13}$$

As in the preceding example, there are two trajectories which pass through the origin, one for $\delta=+1$ and one for $\delta=-1$. The discussion is therefore temporarily restricted to initial conditions, u_{10}, u_{20}, u_{30}, in a given half of the phase space such that when proper switching occurs, the representative point reaches the origin along the $\delta=-1$ zero trajectory.

Fig. 3 shows the zero trajectory ($\delta_3=-1$) extending from the origin in the form of a space curve. From every point along the δ_3 curve there radiates a $\delta_2=+1$ curve. The family of δ_2 trajectories forms a surface which terminates in the zero trajectory. The final step is to consider this surface as the termination of a family of trajectories whose initial conditions fill the entire 3-dimensional half-phase space mentioned earlier. The switching criterion for this region is to choose $\delta_1=-1$ until the representative point reaches the switching surface formed by the δ_2 space curves. At the surface, the δ changes sign so that the representative point, traveling in the surface, reaches the zero trajectory and then moves into the origin. As in the previous example, there exists an analogous switching criterion in the other half phase space, where $\delta_1=+1$, $\delta_2=-1$, and $\delta_3=+1$.

The preceding paragraphs represent an effort to create a point of view which can be extended to a phase space of dimensions greater than three. The idea, essentially one of working backwards from the origin of the space, may be summarized for a 3-dimensional space as follows: From the origin there extends the zero trajectory, e.g., $\delta_3=-1$. This path is the termination of a surface composed of a family of trajectories having a driving term δ, of opposite sign to that of the zero trajectory; finally this surface is the termination of a family of trajectories whose initial condition fill in the half-phase space.

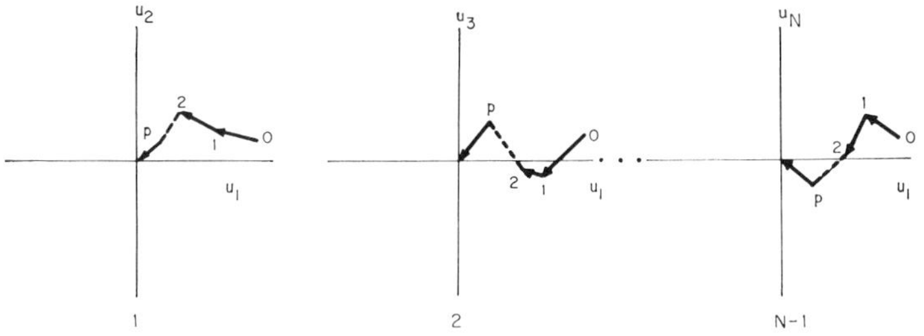

Fig. 5. Phase space projections for an Nth-order system. The representative point, starting at zero, and following P sign reversals of the controlled variable v, reaches the origin of the phase space

Mathematical Derivation

It is the purpose of the following section to lend mathematical credence to the material in the previous section. Fig. 4 represents an *N*th order system in block form. The motor and load behavior can be defined by the following differential equation

$$-\delta=\sum_{n=0}^{N} b_n \frac{d^n\theta_0}{dt^n} \tag{14}$$

where all system constants are lumped into the b_n coefficients. In terms of the error E, equation 14 becomes

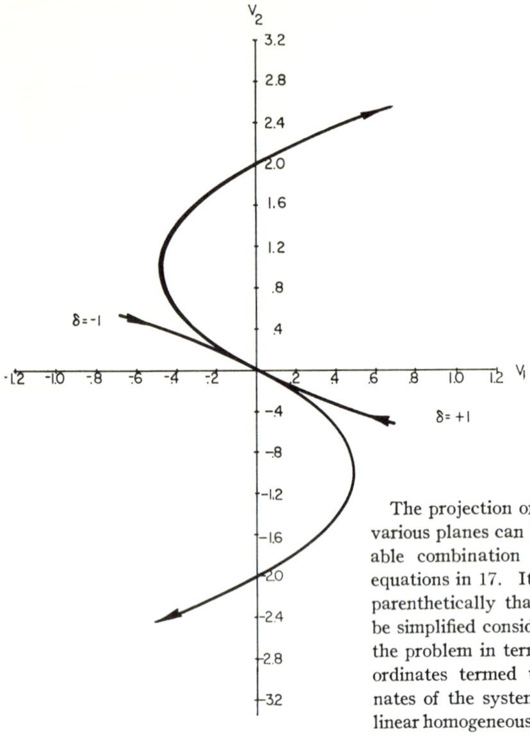

Fig. 7 (left). The v_1-v_2 projection of the zero trajectories for the third-order contactor servo

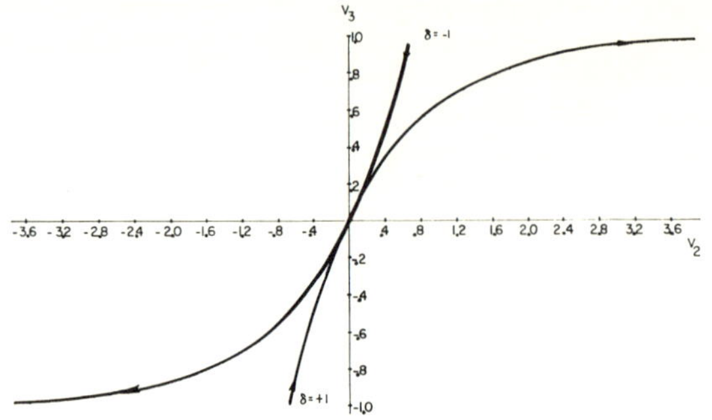

Fig. 8. The v_2-v_3 projection of the zero trajectories for the third-contactor servo

$$\sum_{n=0}^{N} b_n \frac{d^n E}{dt^n} = \delta + \sum_{n=0}^{N} b_n \frac{d^n \theta_i}{dt^n} \qquad (15)$$

an Nth order differential equation in E whose phase space has as co-ordinates

$$u_1 = E$$
$$u_2 = \frac{dE}{dt} \qquad (16)$$
$$\cdots$$
$$u_n = \frac{d^{N-1}E}{dt^{N-1}}$$

Equations 15 and 16 are used to establish a system of differential equations, which, when solved, yield the trajectory of the representative point

$$\frac{du_1}{dt} = u_2$$
$$\frac{du_2}{dt} = u_3$$
$$\cdots \qquad (17)$$
$$\frac{du_{N-1}}{dt} = u_N$$
$$\frac{du_N}{dt} = \sum_{n=0}^{N-1} -\frac{b_n}{b_N} u_{n+1} + \frac{\delta}{b_N} + \sum_{n=0}^{N} \frac{b_n}{b_N} \frac{d^n \theta_i}{dt^n}$$

The projection of the trajectory in the various planes can be obtained by a suitable combination and solution of the equations in 17. It should be noted here parenthetically that such a solution can be simplified considerably by considering the problem in terms of a new set of co-ordinates termed the principal co-ordinates of the system, obtained through a linear homogeneous transformation. Since the transformation is not pertinent to this discussion, it will be assumed that the appropriate equations have been solved for the N-1 projections of the general trajectory in all the planes common to the u_1 axis, as shown in Fig. 5.

$$h_1(u_1, u_2, \delta) = 0$$
$$h_2(u_1, u_3, \delta) = 0 \qquad (18)$$
$$\cdots\cdots$$
$$h_{N-1}(u_1, u_N, \delta) = 0$$

The object is to determine the loci of points at which δ changes sign, such that the final trajectory passes through the origin. If points 1, 2 . . . P, represent the switching points, let $\delta = \delta_1$; e.g., $\delta_1 = -1$, between 0 and 1, $\delta_2 = -\delta_1$ between 1 and 2, etc. The problem then resolves itself into the solution of equation 18 (with the proper δ's inserted) for the unknown co-ordinates of the P points.

The following is noted from Fig. 5:

N = order of the system
$N-1$ = number of independent phase planes
P = number of switchings
$P+1$ = number of equations per plane

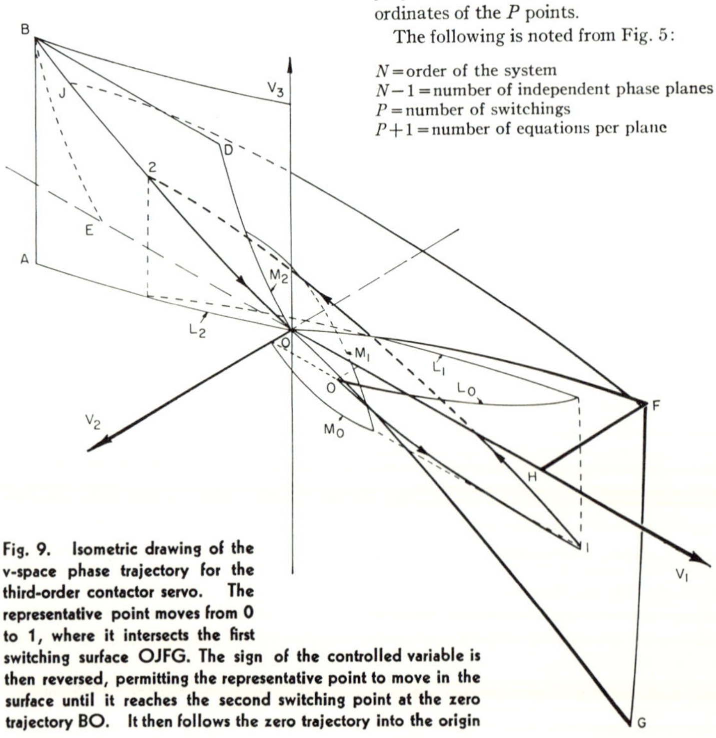

Fig. 9. Isometric drawing of the v-space phase trajectory for the third-order contactor servo. The representative point moves from 0 to 1, where it intersects the first switching surface OJFG. The sign of the controlled variable is then reversed, permitting the representative point to move in the surface until it reaches the second switching point at the zero trajectory BO. It then follows the zero trajectory into the origin

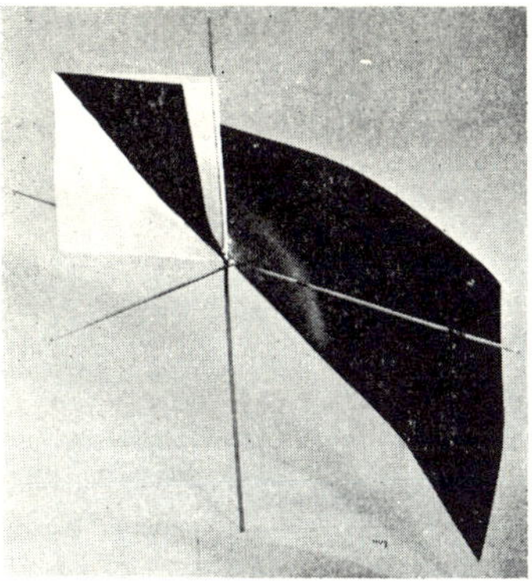

Fig. 10. Model of the switching surface in Fig. 9

$(P+1)(N-1)$ = total number of equations
NP = number of unknowns

Let a be defined by

$$NP-(P+1)(N-1)=a \tag{19}$$

$$(\text{variables})-(\text{equations})=a \tag{20}$$

or

$$P=N-1+a \tag{21}$$

The following can be stated for possible values of a:

When $a<0$, assuming the equations are independent, there is no solution.

When $a>0$, assuming there is a solution, it has a arbitrary constants and therefore is not unique.

When $a=0$ there is a solution provided the equations are independent.

It can therefore be concluded that a unique solution is possible when

$$P=N-1 \tag{22}$$

Thus in general a second-order system requires one switching, a third-order system requires two switchings, etc. The loci of P points must of necessity be the zero trajectory; the family of P-1 points form the final switching surface, etc. It also follows that if the initial conditions place the representative point on the mth switching surface, the number of switchings required to reach the origin reduces to $P-m$.

It is to be noted that for the case of $a>0$, a solution is possible provided a switching points are arbitrarily decided upon. In specific examples considered, it was found that increasing the number of switching points resulted in an increase in response time.

The method of analysis requires that the sign of the first δ be decided upon. This may be done by noting that it is desirable to begin reducingthe error or error rate immediately following a step input. On this basis, for either positive position or velocity input $\delta_1=-1$.

In summarizing, it has been shown that the behavior of an Nth order contactor servo may be represented as a trajectory in an N-dimensional phase space. A unique switching criterion can be derived when the number of switching points P is one less than N, the order of the system. For given initial conditions, the problem of establishing the switching criterion then resolves itself into a solution of NP equations in as many unknowns.

Application of Phase Space Analysis

The method proposed in the previous section is applied to the third-order on-off servomechanism shown in Fig. 6. The increase in order as shown by equation 23 is based upon the inclusion of the motor field time lag in the analysis.

$$\frac{d^3\epsilon}{d\tau^3}+\frac{d^2\epsilon}{d\tau^2}=\delta \tag{23}$$

By making the substitutions

$$u_1=\epsilon \tag{24}$$

$$u_2=\frac{d\epsilon}{d\tau} \tag{25}$$

$$u_3=\frac{d^2\epsilon}{d\tau^2} \tag{26}$$

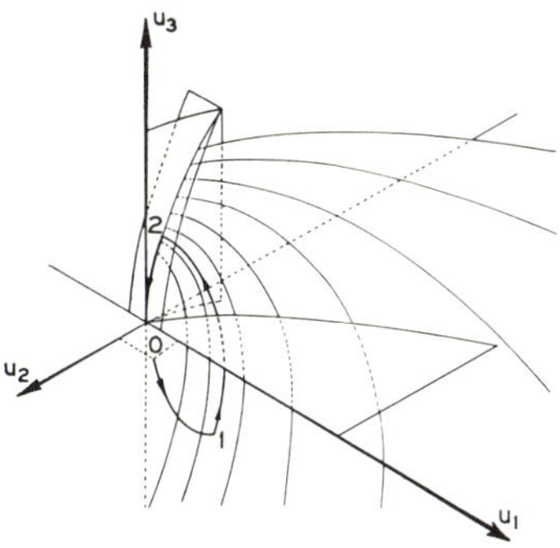

Fig. 11 (left). Isometric drawing of the u-space phase trajectory derived from a co-ordinate transformation of Fig. 9

Fig. 12. Model of the switching surface in Fig. 11

the following set of equations may be written

$$\frac{du_1}{d\tau}=u_2 \tag{27}$$

$$\frac{du_2}{d\tau}=u_3 \tag{28}$$

$$\frac{du_3}{d\tau}=-u_3+\delta \tag{29}$$

These equations represent the differential equations which must be solved to yield the general trajectory. To simplify the mathematics the principal co-ordinates defined by

$$v_1=u_1-u_3 \tag{30}$$

$$v_2=u_2+u_3 \tag{31}$$

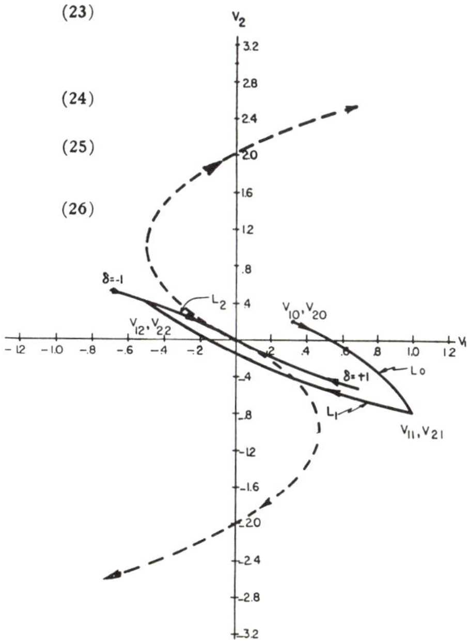

Fig. 13 (right). The v_1-v_2 projection of a trajectory resulting from a combined step input of position and velocity

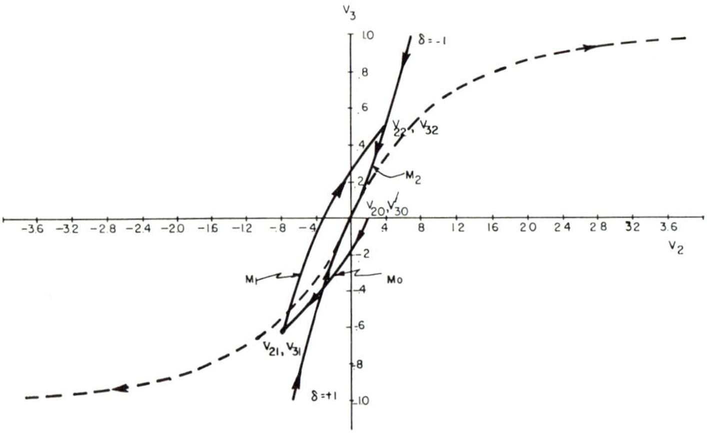

Fig. 14. The v_2-v_3 projection of a trajectory resulting from a combined step input of position and velocity

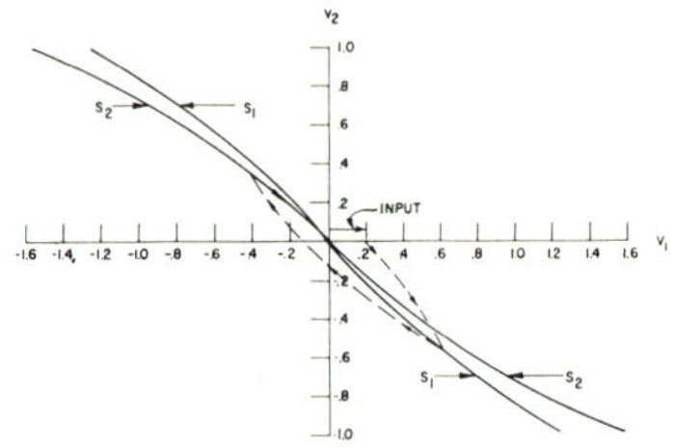

Fig. 15. The v_1-v_2 projection of the switching curves for a step input of position. The representative point projection travels along the dashed line

$$v_3 = u_3 \tag{32}$$

are used in the remainder of the analysis.

By properly combining equations 27 through 32, the following set of equations is obtained

$$\frac{dv_1}{d\tau} = v_2 - \delta \tag{33}$$

$$\frac{dv_2}{d\tau} = \delta \tag{34}$$

$$\frac{dv_3}{d\tau} = -v_3 + \delta \tag{35}$$

The simultaneous solution of equations 33, 34, and 35 yields

$$2v_1 - \delta(v_2 - \delta)^2 = C_1 \tag{36}$$

and

$$v_2 + \delta \ln(1 - \delta v_3) = C_2 \tag{37}$$

which are the projections of the phase trajectory in the v space. The initial conditions v_{10}, v_{20}, v_{30} serve to determine C_1 and C_2. It should be noted that a change in initial conditions results only in the translation of the trajectory projections in the $v_1 - v_2$ and $v_2 - v_3$ planes.

The trajectories passing through the origin, given by equations 38 and 39

$$(2v_1 + \delta) - \delta(v_2 - \delta)^2 = 0 \tag{38}$$

$$v_2 + \delta \ln(1 - \delta v_3) = 0 \tag{39}$$

are plotted in Figs. 7 and 8.

The arrows, which indicate increasing time, were determined by solving equation 34.

$$v_2 - v_{20} = \delta\tau \tag{40}$$

If Δ is defined as an increment, then

$$\Delta v_2 = \delta(\Delta\tau) \tag{41}$$

Equation 41 enables one to find the total time expended in moving between two points along any combination of trajectories.

Fig. 9 represents an isometric view of a phase trajectory having an initial step input combination of position and velocity v_{10}, v_{20}, designated as the point 0. The representative point moves along the path until the first point of switching is reached. This point, point 1 on the drawing, occurs when the trajectory intersects the surface *OJFG*. The representative point then follows a curve in the surface *OJFG* until it reaches the second switching point 2, which is the intersection of the trajectory 1-2 and the zero trajectory *BO*. It then follows *BO* into the origin. The curves L_0, L_1, L_2, are projections of the trajectory in the plane of axes v_1, v_2, and curves M_0, M_1, M_2 are projections of the trajectory in the v_2, v_3 plane.

The final switching curve *BO* is represented as the intersection of two surfaces *OABC* and *OEBD*. Curve *OA* corresponds to the curve $\delta = -1$ in Fig. 7, and *OABC* is the surface through *OA* with vertical elements parallel to the v_3 axis. Curve *OD* corresponds to $\delta = -1$ in Fig. 8, and *OEBD* is the surface through *OD* with horizontal elements parallel to the v_1 axis. Curve *OF* is the intersection of the $v_1 - v_2$ plane and the switching surface *OJFG*.

Applying the theory presented earlier, it may be seen that *BO* is the zero trajectory. The switching surface which terminates in *BO* was obtained by graphically constructing in the $v_1 - v_2$ and $v_2 - v_3$ planes a family of trajectories which terminate on the zero trajectory projections. The results were transferred to the isometric drawing. Fig. 11 shows the same trajectory and switching surface in the u-phase space. Both drawings are accompanied by photographs of models which were built to represent the switching surface.

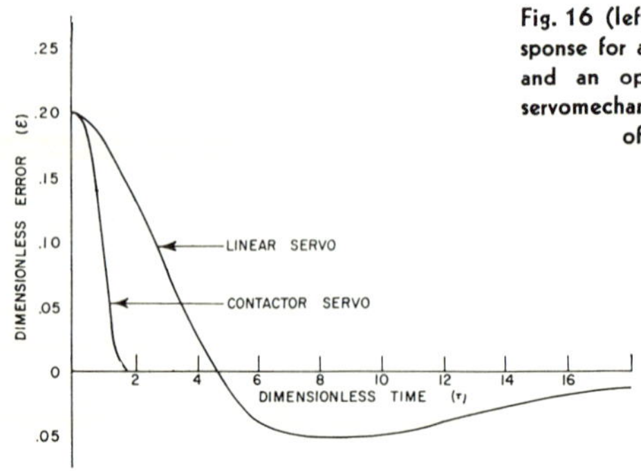

Fig. 16 (left). Computed response for a third-order linear and an optimized contactor servomechanism for a step input of position

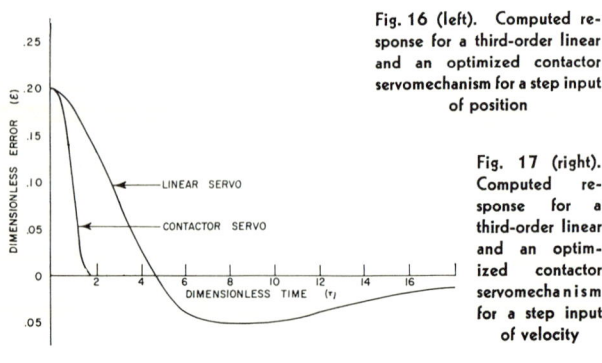

Fig. 17 (right). Computed response for a third-order linear and an optimized contactor servomechanism for a step input of velocity

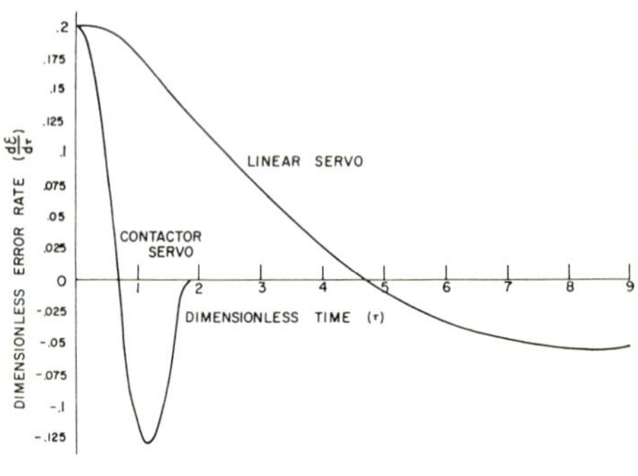

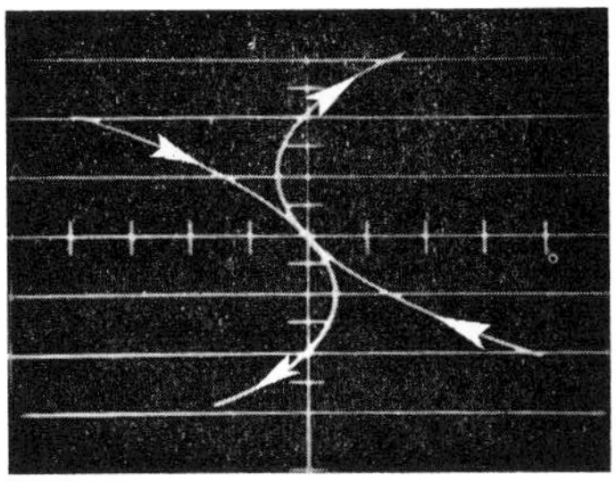

Fig. 18. The v_1-v_2 projection of the zero trajectories

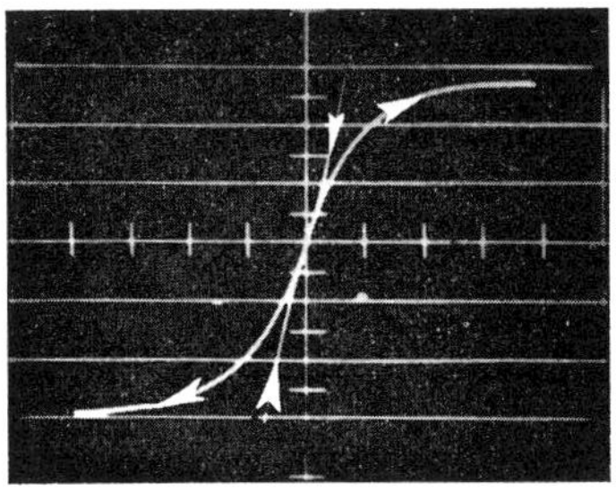

Fig. 19. The v_2-v_3 projection of the zero trajectories

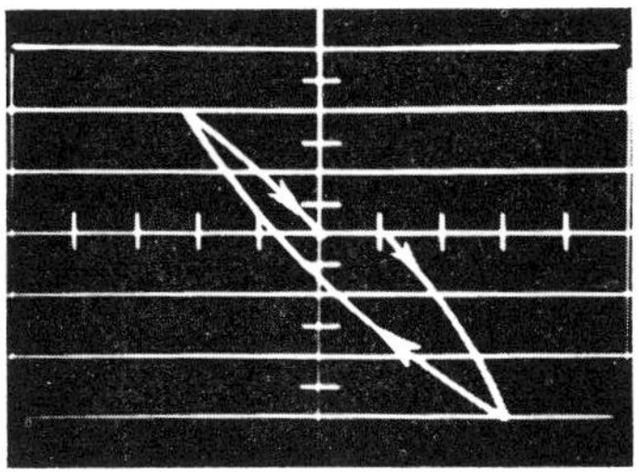

Fig. 20. The v_1-v_2 projection of a trajectory resulting from a step input of position

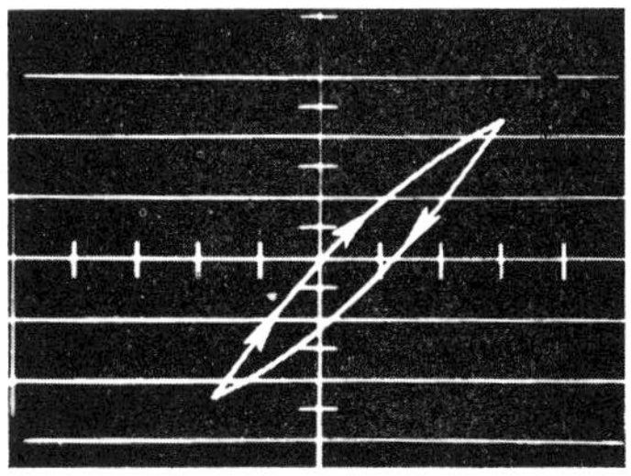

Fig. 21. The v_1-v_3 projection of a trajectory resulting from a step input of position

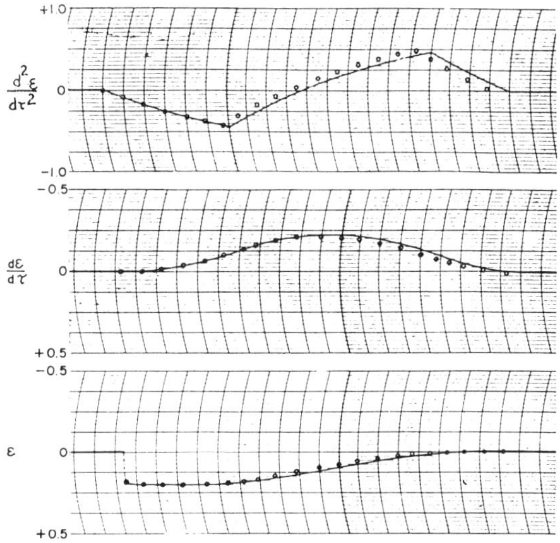

Fig. 22 (right). Recorded response of the optimized third-order servo to a step input of position

. . . . Calculated
——— Recorded

It has been pointed out that the reasoning can be extended to systems of orders larger than three. It is obvious, however, that the analyses for higher order systems must be carried out in terms of the projections in the various planes that make up the N-dimensional space. The remainder of the analysis will therefore be devoted to obtaining the switching criteria in terms of one particular plane, in this case the v_1-v_2 plane. Where necessary, the plane-switching criterion will be correlated with the surface and space-curve-switching criterion.

Figs. 13 and 14, which display the trajectory projections, were derived on the following basis: As a third-order system, two switchings are required. The final path (also the final switching curve) is the zero trajectory, and because the input is positive the initial path must be along a path corresponding to $\delta_1=-1$. The problem remaining, to determine the locus of v_{11}, v_{21}, is solved as follows. Equations 36 and 37 are used to write six equations corresponding to the L and M projections. The simultaneous solution of these equations yields

$$2v_{11}-\delta_1\left\{1+2\ln^2\left[1+\sqrt{1-e^{-\delta_1 v_{21}}(2-e^{-\delta_1(v_{21}-v_{20})})}\right]\right\}+\delta_1(v_{21}+\delta_1)^2=0 \quad \textbf{(42)}$$

If $v_{20}=0$, equation 42 becomes

$$2v_{11}-\delta_1-\delta_1 2\ln^2(2-e^{-\delta_1 v_{21}})+\delta_1(v_{21}-\delta_1)^2=0 \quad \textbf{(43)}$$

Equations 42 and 43 are the first switching curves for a particular class of step inputs, namely for which $v_{10}=u_{10}$; $v_{20}=u_{20}$; and $v_{30}=0$. The concept of a first switching curve and the earlier one of a first switching surface may seem to clash; they are, however, part of the same pattern which may be explained as follows: Consider only the class step input of position. The locus of first switching points forms a space curve in the switching surface whose projection in the v_1-v_2 plane is given by equation 43. Similarly for a class of step inputs of position plus velocity, where the velocity is specified, the locus of first switching points forms a space curve in the switching surface, which when projected in the v_1-v_2 plane becomes the curve given by equation 42. Note that there is a different projection for each value of v_{20}.

The second sign reversal curve may be obtained from equation 38, the zero trajectory projection in the v_1-v_2 plane.

$$2v_1+\delta_3-\delta_3(v_2-\delta_3)^2=0 \quad \textbf{(44)}$$

These sign reversal curves, plotted in Fig. 15 for $v_{20}=0$, were obtained as follows

$$S_1(v_1, v_2)=\begin{cases}\text{equation 43 } \delta_1=-1 \; v_{21}<0\\ \text{equation 43 } \delta_1=+1 \; v_{21}>0\end{cases} \quad \textbf{(45)}$$

$$S_2(v_1, v_2)=\begin{cases}\text{equation 44 } \delta_3=-1 \; v_2>0\\ \text{equation 44 } \delta_3=+1 \; v_2<0\end{cases} \quad \textbf{(46)}$$

The switching sequence is then

$$1\begin{cases}\delta_1=-1 & S_1>0\\ \delta_1=+1 & S_1<0\end{cases} \quad \textbf{(47)}$$

$$2\begin{cases}\delta_2=-1 & S_2>0\\ \delta_2=+1 & S_2<0\end{cases} \quad \textbf{(48)}$$

The servo computer, comparing the v_1-v_2 trajectory projection to S_1 applies the proper sign to δ_1. When the representative point crosses S_1, the sign of δ is reversed. The computer then compares the representative point to S_2 so that the sign of δ may again be reversed when S_2 is reached.

A comparison of the response of this system to that of an equivalent linear system, shown in Figs. 16 and 17, clearly indicates the improvement to be expected

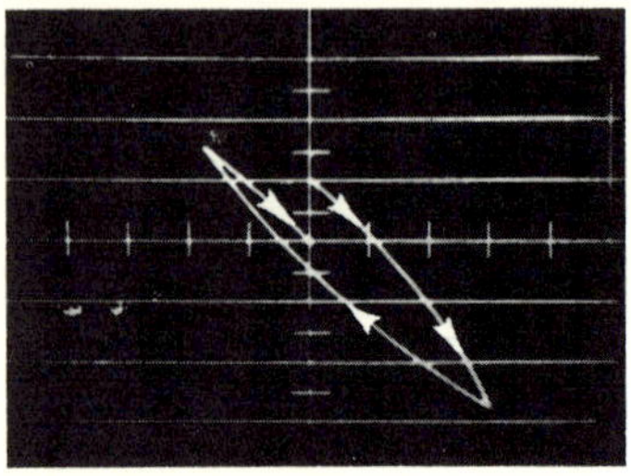

Fig. 23. The v_1-v_2 projection of a trajectory resulting from a step input of velocity

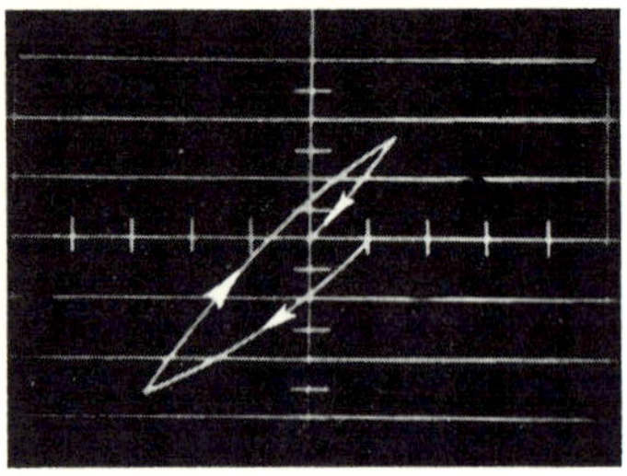

Fig. 24. The v_2-v_3 projection of a trajectory resulting from a step input of velocity

Fig. 25 (right). Recorded response of the optimized third-order servo to a step input of velocity

. . . . Calculated
——— Recorded

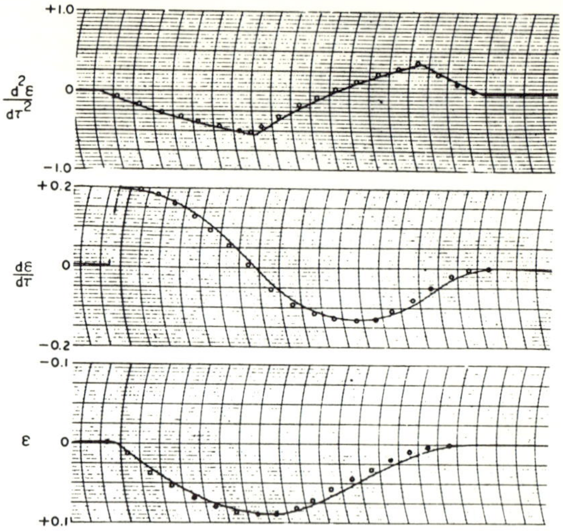

from the use of an optimum-switching on-off servo.

Computer Study

Figs. 18 through 25 represent results obtained from an analogue computer study of a third-order on-off servo in which the foregoing switching criterion was employed. In all cases data taken from the photographs were found to agree with calculated behavior to within experimental accuracy.

An examination of Fig. 22 leads, in this particular example, to what at first appears to be a new interpretation of the concept of a unique switching criterion. The curve of error acceleration may be viewed as one of torque build-up. It can therefore be seen that the derived switching criterion is essentially a program of torque modulation such that the torque and its two time integrals reduce to zero simultaneously. The condition for the case of velocity input, as demonstrated by Fig. 25 is quite similar. The torque in this case must be manipulated to permit the error rate to overshoot, since the error, the time integral of error rate, begins and must eventually terminate at zero.

A re-examination of the switching criterion for the second-order on-off servo leads to similar results, the major differences being that for the second-order system torque build-up is assumed instantaneous while for the third-order system it is exponential.

Summary Conclusions

The purpose of this paper is to describe a method for obtaining the switching criterion for an Nth order on-off servo which reduces system error and derivatives of error to zero in a minimum time.

System behavior is described in the principal co-ordinate phase space. A switching criterion is then established from the simultaneous solution of a number of equations representing trajectory projections; the first trajectory passing through a point defined by the initial conditions, and the final one passing through the origin.

The mathematical analysis employed imposes two restrictions on the results: 1. inputs are limited to step-functions; 2. the system must be describable over every interval of its operation by a linear differential equation.

Most of the data presented were obtained from an analogue computer study. In view of the results, it is felt that the method merits further development to the point where it forms a basis for the design of on-off control systems.

Appendix I. Derivation of Third-Order System Differential Equations

The following equations describe each section of the third-order on-off servo shown in Fig. 6.

$$v = -\delta V \tag{49}$$

$$v = Ri + L\frac{di}{dt} \tag{50}$$

$$\phi = K_\phi i \tag{51}$$

$$T = K_2 \phi \tag{52}$$

$$T = J\frac{d^2\theta_0}{dt^2} \tag{53}$$

V is the magnitude of the computer output voltage; δ is a function of the error, error rate, and error acceleration, having a value of $+1$ or -1, as determined by the computer.

The combination of equations 49 through 52 results in

$$-\delta V\frac{K_2K_\phi}{R} = T + \tau_\phi\frac{dT}{dt} \tag{54}$$

and the combinatio n of equations 53 and yields

$$-\delta V\frac{K_2K_\phi}{RJ} = \tau_\phi\frac{d^3\theta_0}{dt^3} + \frac{d^2\theta_0}{dt^2} \tag{55}$$

It will be assumed that V is large enough to drive the motor to torque saturation T_M. From equation 54, therefore

$$T_M = V\frac{K_2K_\phi}{R} \tag{56}$$

New dimensionless variables may be defined as follows

$$\tau = \frac{t}{\tau_\phi} \tag{57}$$

$$\Theta_i = \frac{J}{\tau_\phi^2 T_M}\,\theta_i \tag{58}$$

$$\Theta_0 = \frac{J}{\tau_\phi^2 T_M}\,\theta_0 \tag{59}$$

$$\epsilon = \frac{J}{\tau_\phi^2 T_M}\,\mathrm{E} \tag{60}$$

Equation 55 may then be written

$$-\delta = \frac{d^3\Theta_0}{d\tau^3} + \frac{d^2\Theta_0}{d\tau^2} \tag{61}$$

The dependent variables are related by

$$\frac{d^n\Theta_0}{d\tau^n}=\frac{d^n\Theta_i}{d\tau^n}-\frac{d^n\epsilon}{d\tau^n} \quad n=0, 1, 2\ldots \tag{62}$$

Under the assumption that

$$\frac{d^n\Theta_i}{d\tau^n}=0 \quad n\geqq 2 \tag{63}$$

the substitution of equations 62 and 63 into equation 64 yields

$$\frac{d^3\epsilon}{d\tau^3}+\frac{d^2\epsilon}{d\tau^2}=\delta \tag{64}$$

References

1. PRINCIPLES OF SERVOMECHANISMS (book), **G. S. Brown, D. P. Campbell.** John Wiley and Sons, Inc., New York, N. Y., 1948.

2. REGENERATION THEORY, **H. Nyquist.** *Bell System Technical Journal*, New York, N. Y., Jan. 1932, pp. 126–47.

3. NETWORK ANALYSIS AND FEEDBACK AMPLIFIER DESIGN (book), **H. W. Bode.** D. Van Nostrand and Company, Inc., New York, N. Y., 1945.

4. FUNDAMENTAL THEORY OF SERVOMECHANISMS (book), **L. A. MacColl.** D. Van Nostrand and Company, Inc., New York, N. Y., 1945.

5. ANALYSIS OF RELAY SERVOMECHANISMS, **H. K. Weiss.** *Journal of the Aeronautical Sciences*, Easton, Pa., vol. 13, no. 7, July 1946, pp. 364–76.

6. NONLINEAR MECHANICS (book), **N. Minorsky.** J. W. Edwards Bros., Ann Arbor, Mich., 1947.

7. THEORY OF OSCILLATIONS (book), **A. A. Andronow, C. E. Chaiken.** Princeton University Press, Princeton, N. J., 1949.

8. A FREQUENCY RESPONSE METHOD FOR ANALYZING AND SYNTHESIZING CONTACTOR SERVOMECHANISMS, **R. J. Kochenburger.** *AIEE Transactions*, vol. 69, pt. I, 1950, pp. 270–84.

9. SINUSOIDAL ANALYSIS OF FEEDBACK-CONTROL SYSTEMS CONTAINING NONLINEAR ELEMENTS, **E. Calvin Johnson.** *AIEE Transactions*, vol. 71, pt. II, July 1952, pp. 169–81.

10. OPTIMIZATION OF NONLINEAR CONTROL SYSTEMS BY MEANS OF NONLINEAR FEEDBACKS, **R. S. Neiswander, R. H. MacNeal.** *AIEE Transactions*, vol. 72, pt. II, Sept. 1953, pp. 262–72.

11. A PHASE-PLANE APPROACH TO THE COMPENSATION OF SATURATING SERVOMECHANISMS, **Arthur M. Hopkin.** *AIEE Transactions*, vol. 70, pt. I, 1951, pp. 631–39.

12. NONLINEAR TECHNIQUES FOR IMPROVING SERVO PERFORMANCE, **D. McDonald,** *Proceedings*, National Electronics Conference, Inc., Chicago, Ill., vol. 6, pp. 400–21.

13. THE MATHEMATICS OF PHYSICS AND CHEMISTRY (book), **H. Marganau, G. M. Murphy.** D. Van Nostrand and Company, Inc., New York, N. Y., 1948.

14. THEORY OF FUNCTIONS OF A REAL VARIABLE (book), **L. M. Graves.** McGraw-Hill Book Company, Inc., New York, N. Y., 1946, chap. 9.

Analysis and Design Principles of Second and Higher Order Saturating Servomechanisms

R. E. KALMAN
STUDENT MEMBER AIEE

Synopsis: This paper presents an extension and generalization of the phase-plane method to automatic control systems governed by high-order nonlinear differential equations. A unified procedure of analysis is outlined. It is based on linear transformations in the phase space, correlated with the partial-fraction expansion of transfer functions to separate natural frequencies, and makes use of the root-locus method for the qualitative study of closed-loop stability. The analysis leads to replacing a high-order system with a second-order system which closely approximates the former. Excellent insight is obtained into difficult problems. The method is applied to a study of control systems subject to saturation. Appendix II summarizes the current state of knowledge concerning second-order optimum saturating systems.

SINCE about 1950, there has been an awakening of serious interest in the problems of analysis and design of nonlinear automatic control systems, i.e., systems where the principle of superposition is not applicable. Already, considerable clarification of such problems has been possible by the use of the powerful phase-plane (topological) method.[1–16]

It is generally believed at present that the phase-plane method is suitable only for the analysis of second-order systems. As will be seen, however, the advantages of the method may be retained even in the analysis of high-order systems, provided that simple means can be found for approximating in a plane the cardinal features of trajectories in n-dimensional phase space. The purpose of this paper is to outline such an approximation technique, and to illustrate it by numerous applications to the problem of saturation. This paper covers the second stage of a long-range study of nonlinear control systems.

Essentials of the Saturation Problem

The engineer is vitally and urgently interested in developing a good theory of nonlinear dynamic systems because he wants to understand fully the effects on system performance of the various inevitable physical limitations and imperfection of practical equipment. The most obvious limitation may be termed "saturation." It is everywhere present. For example, the voltages in a transformer are limited by magnetic saturation; the amplitudes of signals handled by electronic amplifiers are always finite; the flow-rate through a hydraulic or pneumatic valve, under constant pressure conditions, reaches limits when the valve is fully opened or closed; no one may work for more than 24 or less than zero hours a day, etc. Thus saturation may be defined as an upper or lower limit or both on a physical quantity. In control systems, saturation in the output element will always limit the speed of response.

What is the physically realizable maximum speed of response of a system for a given level of saturation and how can optimum performance be attained or approximated? These questions are being answered by the recently developed optimum relay servomechanism theory discussed in Appendix II. The realization of optimally fast transient response, if at all possible, requires nonlinear compensation. Such compensation may present grave engineering difficulties, and it is important to know how closely the optimum can be approached by use of standard linear compensation methods. In this paper, the capabilities of some such methods (gain adjustment, tachometer feedback, cascaded lead or lag networks, etc.) will be explored in particular cases. This will be done so as to obtain as much insight as possible about various aspects of transient behavior without explicitly solving the nonlinear differential equations.

Paper 55-551, recommended by the AIEE Feedback Control Systems Committee and approved by the AIEE Committee on Technical Operations for presentation at the AIEE Summer General Meeting, Swampscott, Mass., June 27–July 1, 1955. Manuscript submitted October 21, 1954; made available for printing May 19, 1955.

R. E. KALMAN is with the E. I. du Pont de Nemours and Company, Wilmington, Del.

A part of the work reported here, carried out while the author was with the Servomechanisms Laboratory, Massachusetts Institute of Technology, was sponsored by the U. S. Navy under Contract NOrd 11799. A part of the section, "Nearly Optimally Compensated Third-Order Saturating Servomechanism" is based on a thesis by John L. Preston;[14] Figs. 8(A) and (B) are reproduced by his permission. The author is indebted to Mr. Preston and Dr. James M. Mozley for helpful discussions.

Principles of Analysis

The ensuing discussion rests on the following fundamental considerations:

1. To represent all solutions of an autonomous (time-invariant) ordinary nonlinear differential equation of the nth order, it is necessary to use an n-dimensional space, called the phase space. Each point in the phase space corresponds to a particular set of initial conditions and therefore determines a unique solution (trajectory) of the differential equation.

2. The trajectories of a nonlinear differential equation may be approximated with arbitrary accuracy by breaking up the phase space into a sufficiently large number of regions, such that within each region the trajectories obey a linear differential equation with constant coefficients. This is equivalent to approximating nonlinear characteristic curves by straight-line segments.[13] In particular, it will be convenient to describe saturation, from the start, by the idealized curve of Fig. 3.

3. To be able to deal with linear systems in n-dimensional phase space, as required by the scheme of the foregoing point 2, a further approximation is essential. It consists of replacing an nth-order linear system by a second-order one which accounts for the dominant (slowly-decaying) transient terms; the same idea is frequently used in linear servomechanism theory. If this approximation were carried out at the beginning of the analysis, all the interesting properties of high-order nonlinear systems which are not possessed by second-order systems would be lost. But if the approximation is postponed until the end of the analysis, the error committed will be very small and, as will be shown, the distinguishing features of high-order systems can be preserved.

It is necessary to develop a fairly elaborate mathematical apparatus for this second type of approximation. The central idea is the linear normal co-ordinate transformation, discussed in the following.

It should be emphasized that the results of this paper concerning the practical design of saturating control systems will be primarily qualitative, revealing phenomena but not usually supplying numerical answers. Such is the proper task of the phase-space method.[13] Even though all the phase-space analysis will be carried out in precise, quantitative terms, for the point-by-point calculation of transients various specialized graphical or numerical techniques may prove more suitable.[13]

Nomenclature

Symbols in Text

$\mathcal{C}$ = actual (physical) phase space
$\mathcal{U}$ = saturation-region normal co-ordinate phase space
$\mathcal{V}$ = linear-region normal co-ordinate phase space
$\mathcal{W}$ = arbitrary phase space
A, B_u, B_v, B_w = system matrices
$\mathbf{c}$; c_1, c_2, c_3 = output variables, i.e., a vector in $\mathcal{C}$ and its components
e; $\dot{e}$, $\ddot{e}$ = error and its time derivatives
f or $f(x)$ = saturation function
K_1, K_2, K_3 = gain parameters
P_u, P_v, P_w, P_u^{-1}, P_v^{-1}, P_w^{-1} = linear transformations or their matrix representations
$\mathbf{r}$, r_1, r_2, r_3 = inputs, i.e., the forcing-function vector in $\mathcal{C}$ and its components
s = Laplace-transform variable
s_i = eigenvalue (natural frequency)
T, T_c, T_r = time constants
$\mathbf{u}$; u_1, u_2, u_3 = a vector in $\mathcal{U}$ and its components
$\mathbf{v}$; v_1, v_2, v_3 = a vector in $\mathcal{V}$ and its components
$\mathbf{w}$; w_1, w_2, w_3 = a vector in $\mathcal{W}$ and its components
σ, ω = real and imaginary parts of s
ζ = damping ratio

Symbols in Figures

L = linear region in phase plane
$+$, $-$ = saturation regions in phase plane, corresponding to $f=\pm 1$
N^+, N^- = stable, unstable node
F^+, F^- = stable, unstable focus

Properties and Representation of Linear Systems

The following will be the principal tools of analysis:

1. Theory of second-order nonlinear differential equations in the phase plane.[13,17–19] In particular, the terminology of reference 13 will be followed throughout and its contents assumed familiar. For convenience, a review of the phase-plane trajectories of standard second-order linear differential equations is given in Appendix I.

2. The root-locus method for studying the variation of the eigenvalues (roots of the characteristic equation) as a function of loop gain or other parameters.[20,21]

3. Vector representation of linear differential equations in the phase space.[22,23] A comprehensive discussion of this technique, interpreted with the aid of the signal-flow graphs, is the subject of the present section. Basic concepts of vector algebra, vector spaces, and linear transformations are treated from the modern point of view by Halmos[24] and Birkhoff and MacLane.[25]

Standard Form Related to Signal-Flow Graph

Every ordinary, nth-order, linear differential equation system with constant coefficients can be written in the standard form

$$\frac{dc_i}{dt}\equiv\dot{c}_i=\sum_{j=1}^{n} a_{ij}c_j+r_i \quad (i=1, 2, \ldots n)$$

or

$$\frac{d\mathbf{c}}{dt}\equiv\frac{d\mathbf{c}}{dt}=A\mathbf{c}+\mathbf{r} \tag{1}$$

where $\mathbf{c}=\|c_1, c_2, \ldots c_n\|$ denotes the components of a vector, drawn from the origin, locating a point in relation to an orthogonal Cartesian co-ordinate system in the n-dimensional phase space $\mathcal{C}$;

$$A=\|a_{ij}\|=\begin{Vmatrix} a_{11} & a_{12} & \ldots & a_{1n} \\ a_{21} & a_{22} & \ldots & a_{2n} \\ \ldots & \ldots & & \ldots \\ a_{n1} & a_{n2} & \ldots & a_{nn} \end{Vmatrix}$$

is an $n\times n$ matrix with real constant elements; the vector $\mathbf{r}=\|r_1, r_2, \ldots r_n\|$ denotes the forcing terms.

For the servo engineer, it is natural to visualize equations 1 by means of a signal-flow graph[26,27] (generalized block diagram), as shown in Fig. 1(A), where $1/s$ symbolizes integration. The signal-flow graph may be regarded as an abstract picture of the interconnections in an analogue computer[28] set up to simulate solutions of equations 1. Each little circle (node) represents one of the variables in equations 1. The r_i's are the independent variables and correspond to function generators in the analogue computer. The $\dot{c}_i$'s and c_i's are dependent variables and correspond to the output of adders and integrators respectively in the analogue computer. Branches directed toward a circle mean that the variable above the circle is a linear combination of those variables where the branches originate, each of the latter variables being weighted by the constant (or the operator $1/s$) which appears along the branch. Thus in Fig. 1(A)

$$\dot{c}_3=0.c_1+a_{32}c_2+a_{33}c_3+1.r_3$$

Note that it would be superfluous and even confusing to have branches connecting the $\dot{c}_i$'s among themselves.

Eigenvalues and Eigenvectors

It is well known that particular solutions of equations 1 have the form $c_i=$ constant $\epsilon^{s\mu t}$. What are the permissible values of s? Substituting in the differential equation shows

$$s\mathbf{c}=A\mathbf{c} \tag{2}$$

The n homogeneous linear algebraic equations 2 have a nonzero solution if and only if their determinant vanishes

$$|A-sI|=0 \tag{3}$$

where I is the unit matrix.

Expanding the determinant leads to an nth-degree algebraic equation in s. The n (not necessarily distinct) roots s_i of this equation are called the eigenvalues of the matrix A. Equation 3 is called the eigenvalue equation (or characteristic equation, or secular equation). Alternately, the s_i will be called the natural frequencies of the dynamic system represented

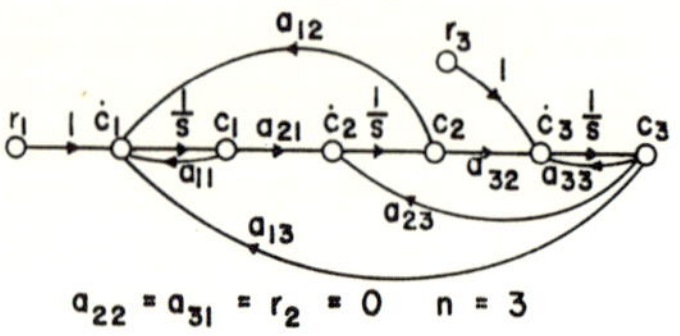

(A)

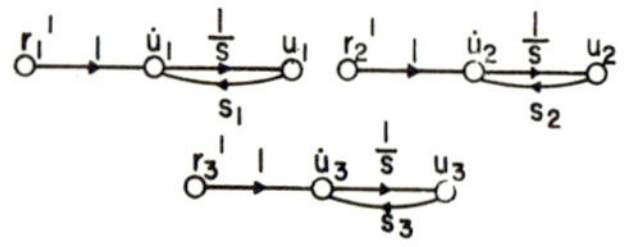

(B)

Fig. 1. Signal-flow graph representation of linear systems

A—A particular third-order system
B—Third-order system with real, distinct eigenvalues shown in normal co-ordinate phase space

by A^{29}; this is a plausible generalization of the fact that if the s_i are pure imaginary, the terms e^{s_it} give rise to sinusoids with angular frequency $|s_i|$. In the past, the concept of the eigenvalue has frequently been referred to also by the names characteristic value or root, latent root, proper value, etc.

Substituting the eigenvalues s_i given by equation 3 into equations 2, it is seen that any set of $n-1$ components of $\mathbf{c}$ may be expressed in terms of the remaining nth component of $\mathbf{c}$. If s_i is real, the resulting expressions are simply the equations of a line through the origin in the phase space. This line is called the eigenvector of the matrix A. The names characteristic or proper vectors, principal axes or directions, eigenmodes, or principal modes have also been used in the past. Note that the eigenvector is a trajectory since equations 2 satisfy the original differential equations 1.

Linear Transformations

What happens to the eigenvalues under a linear transformation (change of variables, change of co-ordinate system)? A linear transformation may be written as

$$\mathbf{c} = P_w\mathbf{w}$$

or

$$\mathbf{w} = P_w^{-1}\mathbf{c} \qquad (4)$$

where P_w is an $n \times n$ matrix with real elements and P_w^{-1} its inverse, $P_wP_w^{-1} = I$. A simple calculation shows

$$P_w^{-1}\frac{d\mathbf{c}}{dt} = \frac{d(P_w^{-1}\mathbf{c})}{dt} = \frac{d\mathbf{w}}{dt} = P_w^{-1}A\mathbf{c} = P_w^{-1}AP_wP_w^{-1}\mathbf{c} = P_w^{-1}AP_w\mathbf{w} = B_w\mathbf{w} \qquad (5)$$

that the matrix A transforms as $B_w = P_w^{-1}AP_w$. Then

$$|B_w - sI| = |P_w^{-1}AP_w - sI| = |P_w^{-1}(A-sI)P_w| = |P_w^{-1}|\cdot|A-sI|\,|P_w| = |A-sI| = 0 \qquad (6)$$

Thus the eigenvalues of A are the same as the eigenvalues of B_w, and A and B_w are therefore called similar matrixes. Two dynamic systems whose matrixes are A and B_w differ only superficially; they represent the same equations of motion, referred to different co-ordinate systems. It may also be said that A and B_w describe the motion of the system in two different phase spaces $\mathcal{C}$ and $\mathcal{W}$, in each of which a point is described by its orthogonal Cartesian co-ordinates. Of course, if a point in $\mathcal{C}$ is given, the corresponding point in $\mathcal{W}$ may be calculated by means of equations 4, and vice versa. The latter point of view will be used throughout the paper.

A particularly simple phase space is one whose matrix B_u contains only diagonal elements; it is the normal co-ordinate phase space $\mathcal{U}$. The corresponding linear transformation P_u is called the normal co-ordinate or diagonalizing transformation. The signal-flow graph corresponding to $\mathcal{U}$ has n disjoint parts, as shown in Fig. 1(B). The diagonal elements of B_u are the eigenvalues, and the differential equations in $\mathcal{U}$ have the simple form (off-diagonal elements of B_u being zero)

$$u_i(t) = u_i(t_0)\epsilon^{s_it}, \quad t \geq t_0 \ (i = 1, 2, \ldots n) \qquad (7)$$

The initial conditions and the forcing function transform according to

$$\mathbf{u}(t_0) = P_u^{-1}\mathbf{c}(t_0)$$

and

$$\mathbf{r}'(t) = P_u^{-1}\mathbf{r}(t) \qquad (8)$$

In other words, a separate differential equation may be written along each of the co-ordinate axes in $\mathcal{U}$, with initial conditions and forcing function determined by equations 8. This means that in any m-dimensional subspace of $\mathcal{U}$, formed by picking out $m \leq n$ co-ordinate axes, the trajectories are governed by an m-dimensional linear differential equation. Thus it is possible to isolate convenient sets of eigenvalues and define thereby smaller phase spaces which are contained in $\mathcal{U}$.

In particular, assume that the transient behavior of the linear system may be approximated after some time $t_1 > t_0$ by two dominant eigenvalues. Then all the trajectories in $\mathcal{U}$ may be approximated by the trajectories in that plane of $\mathcal{U}$ which

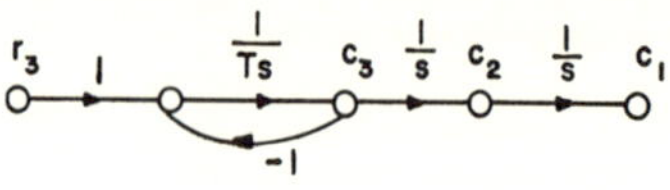

(A)

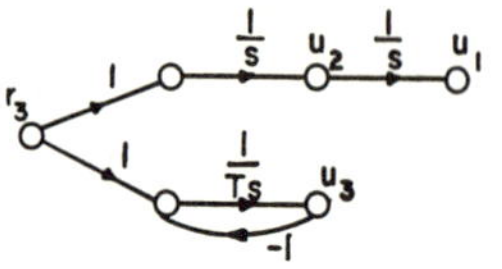

(B)

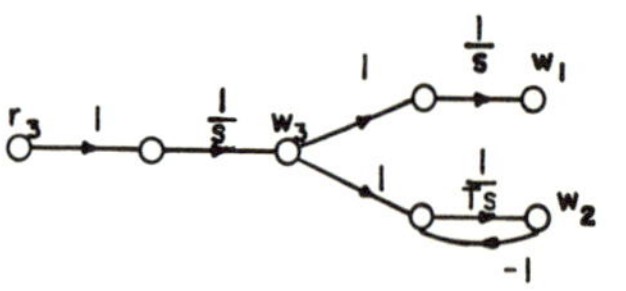

(C)

Fig. 2. Example of computation of transformation matrix

A—Original system
B—System in normal co-ordinate phase space
C—System in another phase space

contains the two eigenvalues. The trajectories in this plane, being governed by a second-order linear differential equation, are easily calculated. Finally, by projecting on some convenient plane in $\mathcal{C}$, by means of P_u, an approximate but physically meaningful 2-dimensional picture of the transient behavior is obtained. This procedure represents one of the contributions of the present paper.

Note that if the eigenvalues are all real, then the eigenvectors in $\mathcal{C}$ are simply the co-ordinate axes of $\mathcal{U}$ transferred into $\mathcal{C}$. If the dominant eigenvalues are real, then the trajectories in a suitable plane of $\mathcal{C}$ are determined uniquely by the eigenvalues and the projections of the corresponding eigenvectors on the plane; computation of P_u, etc., is unnecessary.

Only very little use has been made so far of normal-co-ordinate transformations in studying nonlinear systems in the phase space.[12,30,31] This is partly because of the difficulty of obtaining the transformations by standard computational methods. A new point of view is necessary. This is developed next.

Diagonalization Process Related to Transfer Functions

Complete diagonalization of the matrix A may not be possible or desirable. The process fails if A has multiple eigenvalues. Also, if any eigenvalues of A are complex,

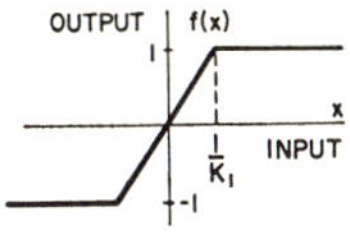

Fig. 3. Definition of saturation

then the diagonalizing transformation P_u may contain complex elements. For reasons of simplicity, it is best to work exclusively with real numbers. Complex numbers may be avoided if 2×2 submatrixes (with complex eigenvalues but real elements) are permitted to remain along the diagonal. The same device also allows consideration of double eigenvalues; eigenvalues of multiplicity three or higher are excluded in this paper.

The foregoing requirements are readily met and the computational steps for obtaining the matrix P_u are very much simplified by the following considerations. Notice that the diagonalizing transformation decomposes a complicated system into its natural frequencies (cf. equation 7). This is analogous to expanding a transfer function into partial fractions. The expansion can always be carried out if the natural frequencies are known; to compute P_u by any method, the natural frequencies must always be known also. As before, the process is considerably clarified if it is related to signal-flow graphs.

The following example illustrates the steps required in determining the components of P_u. Consider the transfer function $G(s)=1/s^2(Ts+1)$. The transfer function is represented by the signal-flow graph of Fig. 2(A), which defines the variables in $\mathcal{C}$. Since $G(s)$ has a double eigenvalue at $s=0$, complete diagonalization is not possible and only the eigenvalue $s=-1/T$ may be separated. This leads to Fig. 2(B).

A check on whether or not Fig. 2(B) was set up correctly is the verification of the known theorem

$$\text{trace } A \equiv \sum_i a_{ii} = \text{trace } B_u = \sum_i b_{ii} = \sum \text{eigenvalues}$$

Expanding the transfer functions relating c_1, c_2, and c_3 to r_3 leads to

$$\frac{C_1(s)}{R_3(s)}=\frac{1}{s^2(Ts+1)}=\frac{1}{s^2}-\frac{T}{s}+\frac{T^2}{Ts+1}$$

$$\frac{C_2(s)}{R_3(s)}=\frac{1}{s(Ts+1)}=\frac{1}{s}-\frac{T}{Ts+1} \qquad (9)$$

$$\frac{C_3(s)}{R_3(s)}=\frac{1}{Ts+1}=\frac{1}{Ts+1}$$

The coefficients in equations 9 make up the transformation matrix

$$\mathbf{c}=P_u\mathbf{u}=\begin{Vmatrix}1 & -T & T^2\\ 0 & 1 & -T\\ 0 & 0 & 1\end{Vmatrix}\mathbf{u} \qquad (10)$$

The foregoing result may be checked by computing the identity $AP_u=P_uB_u$, where A and B_u are the system matrixes in Figs. 2(A) and (B)

$$A=\begin{Vmatrix}0 & 1 & 0\\ 0 & 0 & 1\\ 0 & 0 & -1/T\end{Vmatrix}$$

$$B_u=\begin{Vmatrix}0 & 1 & 0\\ 0 & 0 & 0\\ 0 & 0 & -1/T\end{Vmatrix}$$

It is useful to have also the inverse P_u^{-1}, which is readily obtained by rearranging equations, since P_u is triangular

$$\mathbf{u}=P_u^{-1}\mathbf{c}=\begin{Vmatrix}1 & T & 0\\ 0 & 1 & T\\ 0 & 0 & 1\end{Vmatrix}\mathbf{c} \qquad (11)$$

In general, an analytic form of P_u^{-1} can always be obtained directly by reversing the process of the partial fraction expansions shown in equations 9, which leads to equating of coefficients of powers of s. If P_u is given numerically and is of moderate order (up to about the fifth or sixth), a recent method advanced by Andree[32] is recommended for the computation of P_u^{-1} as particularly quick and simple.

A short calculation reassures that

$$P_u^{-1}AP_u=B_u$$

In setting up the signal-flow graphs in the phase spaces $\mathcal{C}$ and $\mathcal{U}$, care must be taken to select the variables c_i and u_i so that all transfer functions approach 0 as $s\rightarrow\infty$. Otherwise, the partial-fraction expansions will contain impulsive terms which would complicate the algebra.

This procedure for calculating the transformation matrix is obviously applicable not only to the signal-flow graph of Fig. 2(B) but to any other graph which contains the same natural frequencies, e.g., Fig. 2(C). The corresponding transformation matrix is

$$P_w=\begin{Vmatrix}1 & -T & 0\\ 0 & 1 & 0\\ 0 & -1/T & 1/T\end{Vmatrix}$$

The following is a semirigorous justification of the transformation process described. First observe that a step input is equivalent, as far as the computation of trajectories is concerned, to a transient generated by some initial condition $\mathbf{c}_0(t_0)$, provided no degeneracy is involved, i.e., a step input excites all of the natural frequencies of the system. Since the transformation $\mathbf{c}=P_u\mathbf{u}$ decomposes one particular forced solution $\mathbf{c}_0(t)$ (not identically zero) in terms of its natural frequencies, it will decompose all others because of linearity. The proof of the last assertion follows easily by noting that solutions of equations 1 form a vector space.[22]

Idealizing Assumptions

Definition of Saturation

Saturation is represented by an idealized curve; see Fig. 3. The saturation levels are normalized at ±1; the gain in the linear region is K_1. The letter f in the signal-flow graphs symbolizes the functional dependence depicted by Fig. 3.

Phase-Space Regions

In view of the foregoing definition, and in accordance with the author's generalized method of phase-plane analysis,[13] it is logical to subdivide the phase space into two distinct types of regions:

1. Saturation Regions. The trajectories are governed by the differential equations of the output element, excited by ±1. The poles and zeros of the transfer function of the output element are assumed to be known. The regions are labeled by ± signs according to the saturation polarity; their boundaries are shown by dash-dotted lines.

2. Linear Region. The trajectories are governed by the linear closed-loop differential equations; it is in each case necessary to determine approximately the closed-loop eigenvalues. The linear region is labeled L; its boundaries are shown by dash-dotted lines.

Permissible Inputs

The simplest and presently only workable method of introducing forcing functions in phase-plane analysis is by considering them as initial conditions.[13] In general, combinations of step and ramp inputs $r+\dot{r}t$ $(t\geq 0)$ are considered, although frequently the ramp component is set identically zero to simplify the discussion.

To identify step or ramp inputs with initial conditions, the following procedure is used: Investigate the dependence of critical points in $\mathcal{C}$ on r and $\dot{r}$, and then translate the co-ordinate system so as to leave the critical point always at the origin, if possible. For instance, if for a step input $c_1=r$ in the steady state, the variable c_1 is changed to $r-c_1=e$; the steady-state equilibrium point is then always at $e=0$. This process is possible only if the error in $\mathcal{C}$ remains finite, which is not the case, e.g., when a nonzero position-error servomechanism is subjected to a ramp input $\dot{r}t$. The method pre-

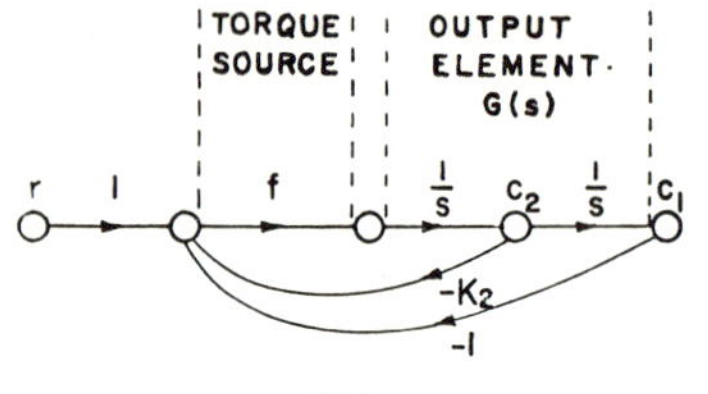

(A)

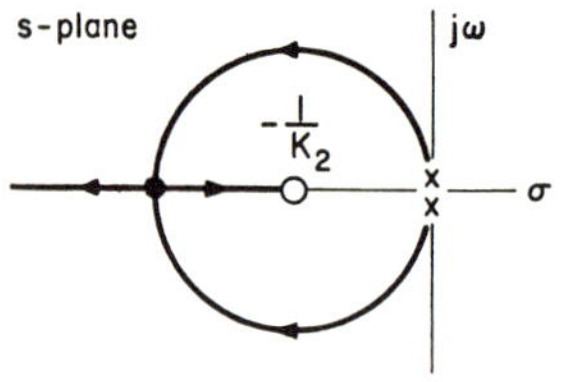

(B)

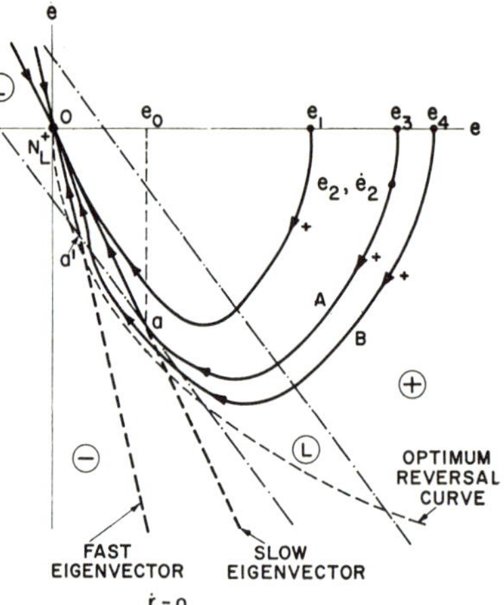

(C)

Fig. 4. Example 1

A—Signal-flow graph
B—Root locus
C—Phase-plane trajectories

sented for the analysis of high-order systems shows excellent promise also for the treatment of arbitrary (but nonrandom) inputs.

Analysis of Second-Order Saturating Systems

Example 1. Position Control Servo Consisting of a Saturating Torque Source Driving Pure Inertia

Consider an idealized system with the following parts: a torque source (motor, etc.) whose dynamics are negligible but which is subject to saturation with a transfer function f, and a purely inertial linear output element with a transfer function $G(s)=1/s^2$. To assure stability, it is necessary to introduce some form of compensation, for instance, a lead network or velocity (tachometer) feedback. Any physical lead network possesses not only a zero but also a pole which makes the system third-order; discussion of the effect of the pole is postponed until Example 4. If velocity feedback is chosen, the signal-flow graph for the system is as shown in Fig. 4(A).

In the saturation region, the feedback is not effective; the system is simply a double integration excited by ± 1. The trajectories are parabolas. The optimum reversal curve for both steps and ramps is $2e=-\dot{e}|\dot{e}|$; see Appendix II.

In the linear region, the system is governed by the following differential equation, written down by inspection from the graph

$$\frac{dc}{dt}=\begin{Vmatrix}0 & 1\\ -K_1 & -K_1K_2\end{Vmatrix}c+\begin{Vmatrix}0\\ K_1r\end{Vmatrix}=Ac+\text{constant}$$

The eigenvectors of A are the straight lines

$$s_ic_1=-\frac{K_1}{K_1K_2+s_i}c_1=c_2 \quad (i=1,\ 2) \tag{12}$$

The locus of the eigenvalues s_i, i.e., the locus of the closed-loop poles, is shown in Fig. 4(B). Increasing the gain K_1 results first in two complex and then in two real roots; one of the real roots goes to the zero and the other to $-\infty$ as $K_1\rightarrow\infty$.

The boundaries of the linear region are the straight lines

$$-K_2c_2+(r-c_1)=\pm 1/K_1$$

To eliminate dependence on the input, set $r-c_1=e$ and $\dot{r}-c_2=\dot{e}$; then

$$e+K_2\dot{e}=\pm 1/K_1+\dot{r}K_2 \tag{13}$$

With this change of variables, the critical point in the linear region will remain at the origin for all step and ramp inputs.

With the knowledge of the optimum reversal curve, the eigenvectors, the root locus, and the eigenvalues and boundaries of the linear region, a complete solution of the problem is possible. Restrict the input to steps ($\dot{r}_2\equiv 0$), and consider first the case of real eigenvalues. Noting that the slope of the slow eigenvector, defined in Appendix I, is always larger than the slope of the linear region, i.e.,

$$-s_1>1/K_2 \quad (s_1>s_2)$$

it is clear that, for sufficiently large K_2, the situation in the $(e,\ \dot{e})$ phase plane must be as depicted in Fig. 4(C). A transient trajectory will remain in the linear region and go to zero without overshoot if it moves sufficiently close to the slow eigenvector after entering the linear region. The largest such trajectory is denoted by A in Fig. 4(C). Trajectory A may have resulted from a step error e_3 or a combination of step and ramp errors e_2 and $\dot{e}_2$. If the error is larger (e_4), the resulting trajectory B may still reach the origin without overshoot if it re-enters the linear region in the segment between the two eigenvectors (a and a' in the figure), in which case it will become asymptotic to the slow eigenvector from the other side.

If the magnitude of the error is further increased, the response will deteriorate as the trajectories enter and leave the linear region more and more times. This is because the effective reversal of saturation takes place later and later than required by the optimum reversal curve. The question arises as to how such poor performance can be minimized by proper selection of K_2.

Fig. 4(C) shows that the largest error for which the trajectory still remains in the linear region is roughly proportional to e_0, the intersection of the slow eigenvector with the boundary of the linear region. From the geometry and equations 12 and 13

$$-e_0=1/K_1(1+K_2s_1)=1/K.\times\left[1-K_2\left(\frac{K_1K_2}{2}-\sqrt{\frac{K_1^2K_2^2}{4}-K_1}\right)\right]$$

$$=1/K_1\left[1-\frac{K_1K_2^2}{2}\left(\frac{2}{K_1K_2^2}+\frac{2}{K_1^2K_2^4}+\frac{4}{K_1^3K_2^6}+\dots\right)\right]$$

Hence if $4/K_2^2\leq K_1<\infty$

$$e_0\approx K_2^2 \tag{14}$$

Equation 14 reveals the dilemma of the situation: to have a good step response to large errors, e_0 should be made as large as possible; on the other hand, since $-s_1\approx 1/K_2$, this would result in very slow response of the system after it leaves saturation, or for small inputs. The designer must compromise between the requirements of nonoscillatory response to large and sufficiently fast response to small errors. For a previous treatment of the same problem, see Kendall and Marquardt.[11]

When ramp inputs $\dot{r}_2\neq 0$ are also admitted in addition to steps, the location of the linear region in the $(e,\ \dot{e})$ phase plane will shift. This represents a further departure from the optimum reversal curve requirements. The shift can be eliminated only by measuring the derivative of the input, i.e., using a lead network which operates on the error signal. The ensuing analysis is similar to the foregoing.

The discussion becomes somewhat less straightforward if the eigenvalues in the

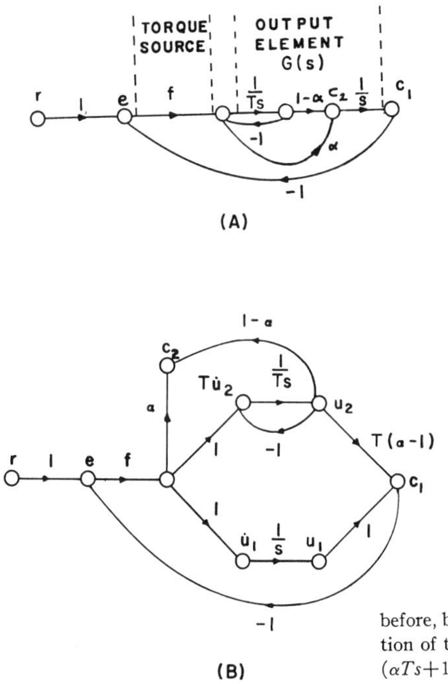

Fig. 5. Example 2

A—Signal-flow graph in $\mathcal{C}$
B—Signal-flow graph in $\mathcal{U}$

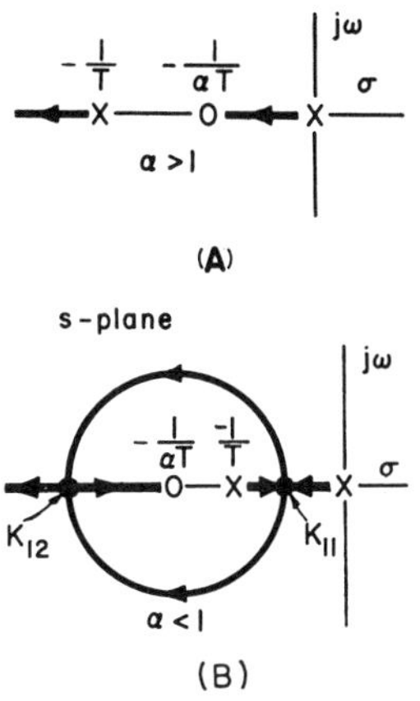

Fig. 6. Example 2; root loci

A—$\alpha>1$
B—$\alpha<1$

linear region are complex. Then the simplest representation of the trajectories is a logarithmic spiral, see Appendix I, which has to be transformed from the normal co-ordinate system to the actual phase plane (e, $\dot{e}$). In the present example, however, the root locus shows that the time of response will decrease with the gain until about critical damping is reached. Hence it is not desirable in this case to keep K_1 so small that complex eigenvalues result.

The most important aspects of nonlinear system design are now apparent. It is meaningless to attempt to formulate hard and fast criteria for the adjustment of the parameters K_1 and K_2, such as the M_p criterion, phase margin, etc., used in linear systems, because the whole design must be predicated on some compromise between the desired responses to particular classes of signals. At the present state of the theory, only step or ramp-type signals can be treated and this restricts the analysis to consideration of signal magnitudes only. Moreover, linear compensation may be inadequate altogether and a better approximation to the optimum reversal line may be necessary.

Example 2. Servo with Zero in Open-Loop Transfer Function

Consider the same type of system as before, but assume that the transfer function of the output element is now $G(s)=(\alpha Ts+1)/s(Ts+1)$; see Fig. 5(A). It will be convenient to carry out the entire analysis in terms of the normal co-ordinates of the saturation region. The appropriate transformation is obtained by expanding into partial fractions the transfer functions

$$G(s)=\frac{C_1(s)}{\pm 1/s}=\frac{1}{s}+\frac{T(\alpha-1)}{Ts+1}$$

and

$$sG(s)=\frac{C_2(s)}{\pm 1/s}=\alpha+\frac{1-\alpha}{Ts+1}$$

Fig. 5(B) is the revised signal-flow graph showing the old variables c_1 and c_2 in terms of the new variables u_1 and u_2.

The dependence of the critical points in the linear region of the (u_1, u_2) phase plane on the inputs may be deduced from steady-state considerations as follows. For steps, $r-c_1=e=0$ implies $r-u_1=0$, $u_2=0$. For combinations of steps and ramps, $r-c_2=\dot{e}=0$ together with $e=\dot{r}/K_1$ implies $r-u_1=\dot{r}[T(\alpha-1)+1/K_1]$ and $\dot{r}-u_2=0$. Hence it is logical to work in the $(r-u_1, \dot{r}-u_2)$ phase plane which is similar to the usual (e,$\dot{e}$) phase plane. For simplicity, the following discussion is limited to step inputs, $\dot{r}\equiv 0$, since then the critical point is always at the origin.

The trajectories in the saturation region are given by $u_2=\pm[1\mp$ constant $\exp(\mp u_1/T)]$ and have the same qualitative shape as in case 2, Appendix II.

The boundaries of the linear region are the straight lines

$$(r-u_1)-T(\alpha-1)(-u_2)=\pm 1/K_1 \qquad (15)$$

Two distinct types of root loci are possible, depending on whether $\alpha>1$ or $\alpha<1$, and are shown in Figs. 6(A) and (B). As in the previous example, only real roots will be of interest, and thus the critical point at the origin will always be a stable node N_L^+. Assuming first $\alpha>1$, consider the effect of gain adjustments on the transient behavior in the linear region. The equation of the eigenvectors is

$$(1+s_i/K_1)(r-u_1)=-T(\alpha-1)(-u_2) \qquad (i=1, 2) \quad (16)$$

As the eigenvalues vary in accordance with the root locus, the eigenvectors rotate around the origin. The slow eigenvector starts on the $(r-u_1)$ axis, swings into the second and fourth quadrants, and approaches the line $(r-u_1)=-T(\alpha-1)(-u_2)$ as $K_1\rightarrow\infty$. The fast eigenvector starts on the $(-u_2)$ axis, swings into the first and third quadrants, and approaches the line $(r-u_1)=T(-u_2)$. See Fig. 7(A). It is also necessary to know whether the intersection A of the slow eigenvector with the line $-u_2=\pm 1$ falls inside or outside the linear region. Using equations 15 and 16, the condition $a<b$ becomes

$$T(\alpha-1)+1/K_1<-1/s_1, \ (s_2<s_1) \qquad (17)$$

Since from the eigenvalue equation $1/K_1+\alpha T=T_1+T_2$, where $s_1=-1/T_1$, and $s_2=-1/T_2$ are the closed-loop poles in Fig. 6(A), inequality 17 becomes

$$T-T_2>0$$

In view of the root locus, the inequality is satisfied for all K_1. It is now possible to sketch a typical trajectory by inspection, as had been done in Fig. 7(A), without the danger of having omitted any important details.

If $\alpha<1$, the only essential difference from the previous case is because of the new root locus, Fig. 6(B). By carrying out simple calculations, analogous to the foregoing, the phase-plane sketches shown in Figs. 7(B) and (C) are arrived at. As $K_1\rightarrow\infty$, the eigenvectors first swing toward one another in the second and fourth quadrants as in Fig. 7(B) and coincide when $K_1=K_{11}$. If K_1 is further increased, the eigenvalues become complex conjugate, which case is not analyzed. When $K=K_{12}$, the eigenvectors again coincide, this time in the first and third quadrants and separate with K_1 increasing still further, as shown in Fig. 7(C).

Note that in all the computations which determine the qualitative features of Fig. 7 and, in particular, the location of the point A and the position of the eigenvectors, it is only necessary to use the eigenvalue equation and the qualitative form of the root locus No explicit com-

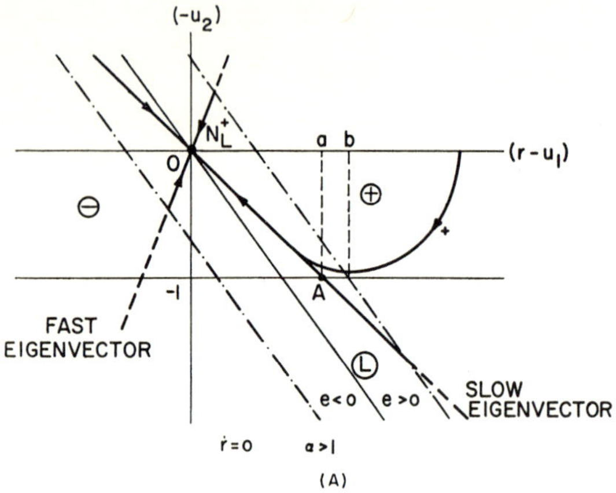

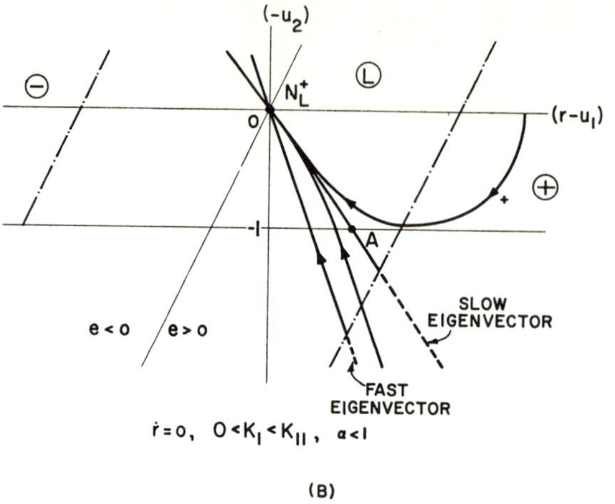

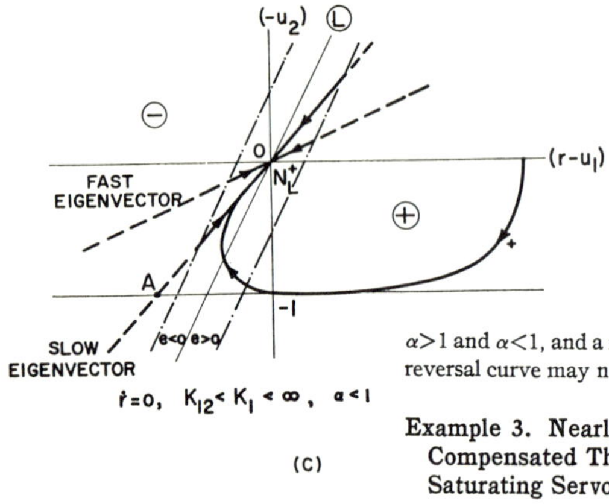

Fig. 7. Example 2, phase-plane trajectories

A—$\alpha>1$
B—$\alpha<1$; $0<K_1<K_{11}$
C—$\alpha<1$; $K_{12}<K_1<\infty$

putation of either the eigenvalues or the corresponding value of K_1 is necessary.

The end results of the analysis shown in Fig. 7 contain few surprises. The optimum relay servomechanism theory is not applicable in this case because of the presence of the zero in the transfer function; see Appendix II. The large-signal response in Fig. 7(A) is acceptable and quite insensitive to wide variations in K_1 or α. The response in Fig. 7(B) is very poor; it may be improved by increasing K_1 which leads to Fig. 7(C). The transient in this figure will always overshoot, but the effect is easily minimized by choosing a large value of K_1.

As a final point, notice the intrinsic difference between putting the term $\alpha Ts+1$ before or after the saturation. In the first case, the servo has error-rate feedback and the linear region may be adjusted so that it will contain the entire optimum reversal curve between the limits $\dot{c}=\pm 1$. As shown by Kendall and Marquardt[11] this is equivalent to setting $\alpha \approx 1-ln\ 2=0.307$. In the second case, discussed in the foregoing, the response may be entirely acceptable for both $\alpha>1$ and $\alpha<1$, and a meaningful optimum reversal curve may not even exist.

Example 3. Nearly Optimally Compensated Third-Order Saturating Servomechanism

Analogue Computer Study

The following is a summary of an analogue computer study of the optimum control of a saturating third-order servomechanism, carried out by J. L. Preston.[14] The problem is characterized by a transfer function $G(s)=1/s^2(Ts+1)$. Such a problem may arise when it is impossible to reverse instantaneously the torque in the system of Example 1 because of the unavoidable energy storage in the torque source.

As pointed out in Appendix II, the optimum nonlinear compensation scheme calls for three reversals of the signal to the output element: the first occurs when the trajectory intersects a reversal surface, the second when the trajectory moving in the reversal surface intersects a reversal line, and the third on reaching the origin of the $(e, \dot{e}, \ddot{e})$ phase space. The equations of the reversal surface and line may be derived by utilizing a normal coordinate transformation[12] or by computing the solutions of the output-element differential equation backwards in time, using the substitution $t'=-t$.

The reversal surface was approximated on a real-time analogue computer by means of a function generator and a servo multiplier. A typical step response of the optimally compensated system and the corresponding signal to the output element (control effort) are shown by the solid curves of Fig. 8(A). A striking feature of these curves, supported by detailed investigation of the author, is that at the second reversal the output is very near its steady-state value. In other words, the second reversal is of negligibly small significance as far as in-the-large behavior of the transient is concerned. Moreover, in any practical system it is necessary to provide a small linear region near zero error since otherwise small inaccuracies in the reversal surface and/or noise would seriously impair the steady-state performance. The second reversal will then be brought about while the system behaves linearly.

In view of these considerations, a simplified compensation was arrived at. It consists of: 1. a small linear zone, of width $2/K_1=2T$; and 2. a reversal curve in the $(e, \dot{e})$ phase plane, which is simply the intersection of the reversal surface with $\ddot{e}=-1$ in the fourth quadrant and $\ddot{e}=+1$ in the second quadrant.

Step 2 is based on the assumption that $\ddot{e}$ has reached its steady-state value at the time of the first reversal; this is certainly an excellent approximation for large signals and is of no interest for small signals since then the trajectory stays in the linear region. The dash-dotted curves in Fig. 8(A) show the response obtainable with this nearly optimum compensation. The response follows the optimum transient curve until entering the linear region, when a slight oscillation (somewhat exaggerated in the figure) develops. The last part of the transient is approximately the same for all magnitudes of the input.

The reversal curve in the $(e, \dot{e})$ phase plane is shown by the solid curve in Fig. 8(B). It is seen that the signal to the third-order output element must be reversed much earlier than in the case of the second-order transfer function $1/s^2$ (dash-dotted line), since the actual reversal o f the acceleration $-\ddot{e}=c_3$ takes place wit h a lag $1/(Ts+1)$. The signal-flow grapih of the nearly optimum system is shown n Fig. 8(C) where the equation $g(e)+K_2\dot{e}=0$ represents the reversal curve.

Finally, the dash-d curves in Fig. 8(A) show the response of a saturating linear system, with the parameters adjusted experimentally so as to minimize the performance-criterion expression[33]

$$\int_0^\infty t|e|\,dt$$

in response to a step during entirely linear operation. The following optimum values were found: loop gain $K_1=0.186/T^2$ and velocity-feedback gain $K_2=3.76T$. Notice that while the nearly optimum control effort, dash-dotted curve, is quite different from the optimum control effort, solid curve, the output responses are very nearly the same. By contrast, although the dash-dotted control effort closely resembles the dashed one, the corresponding output responses are very different as the linear saturating system has large overshoot and effectively twice as long speed of response, because the acceleration is reversed too late.

Simplified Analysis and Design Procedure

The preceding discussion shows that very nearly optimum response may be achieved by using an appropriate reversal curve for the first reversal, and satisfying the need for a second reversal near the origin by leading the trajectory into a small linear region. This suggests the following simplified derivation of the reversal curve which at the same time lends excellent insight into the principal quantitative questions involved. It is simply the implementation of the approximation stated under point 3 in the section entitled "Principles of Analysis."

First, calculate the normal co-ordinate transformation for the transfer function $G(s)=1/s^2(Ts+1)$. This was discussed in the foregoing in connection with Figs. 2(A) and (B). The transformation matrix P_u is given by equation 10.

In $\mathfrak{U}$, the plane (u_1, u_2) containing the transfer function $1/s^2$ is optimally compensated in the usual fashion, while along the u_3 axis the transient is assumed to have reached its steady-state value at the time of the first reversal. The assumption

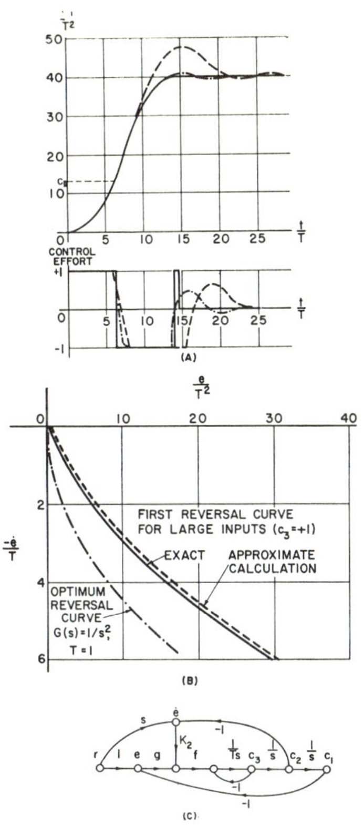

Fig. 8. Example 3

A—Transient responses
B—Reversal curves
C—Signal-flow graph of nearly optimally compensated system

concerning u_3 was also implicit in deriving the first reversal curve from the reversal surface in the analogue computer study. Optimum compensation in the (u_1, u_2) plane is not identical with optimum compensation in the $(e, \dot{e}, \ddot{e})$ phase space; the error involved in the procedure, however, is only the neglection of the second reversal and, as mentioned in the foregoing, this is totally unimportant.

The optimum reversal curve in the (u_1, u_2) plane consists of two half-parabolas

$$2u_1=-u_2|u_2| \tag{18}$$

Substituting the transformation equation 11 into equation 18 and $u_3=\pm 1$ leads to two equations in c_1, c_2, and c_3 from which c_3 may be eliminated. Finally, a shift in the origin yields the analytic expression of the reversal curve in the $(e, \dot{e})$ phase plane

$$2e=-(|\dot{e}|^2+4T|\dot{e}|+T^2)|\dot{e}|/\dot{e} \tag{19}$$

Geometrically, the foregoing calculation is equivalent to projecting the reversal curve from $\mathfrak{U}$ onto the (c_1, c_2) plane of $\mathfrak{C}$. Equation 19 is shown by the dashed curve in Fig. 8(B); agreement with the solid reversal curve, which is the intersection of the exact reversal surface with $c_3=+1$, is very close.

Application of the normal co-ordinate transformation eliminates the necessity of computing the reversal surface. The first reversal curve is determined very quickly from the well-known second-order cases. It is not even necessary to express the reversal curve in the $(e, \dot{e})$ plane analytically; by means of P_u^{-1}, it may be transferred from the (u_1, u_2) plane point by point.

Other relevant information is equally readily calculated:

1. Time of response: This must be roughly the time of response of the optimum second-order system in the (u_1, u_2) plane, plus the time required to reduce u_3 from ± 1 to zero on reversing the relay polarity, about T seconds. Hence the approximate time of response to step r is

$$2\sqrt{|r|}+T \tag{20}$$

2. Error at first reversal: In the (u_1, u_2) phase plane the reversal occurs when $(r-u_1)=r/2$, $u_2=-\sqrt{|r|}$. Hence

$$|e_{11}|=|r-c_{11}|=|r|/2+T\sqrt{|r|}+T^2$$

These results also agree closely with Fig. 8(A).

Examples of Third-Order Saturating Control Systems

General

Example 3 showed that the crucial difference between the analysis of second- and high-order systems lies in determining how the trajectories enter and leave the two different saturation regions. When there is also a linear region, the following further considerations arise:

1. The transformation from $\mathfrak{C}$ to the saturation-region normal co-ordinate phase space $\mathfrak{U}$ is not the same as from $\mathfrak{C}$ to the linear-region normal co-ordinate phase space $\mathfrak{V}$. Hence, while all the approximations concerning the neglect of fast transient terms must be carried out in the normal co-ordinate phase spaces, to have a complete picture of the solutions the results of the approximations are to be projected onto some one phase plane in any of the spaces $\mathfrak{U}$, $\mathfrak{V}$, and $\mathfrak{C}$. It will be usually convenient to refer everything to the (u_1, u_2) or $(e, \dot{e})$ phase planes. Thus, the analysis leads to an approximately equivalent second-order nonlinear system, defined in any convenient phase plane.

2. The linear region in the equivalent phase plane will have two different types of boundaries:

a. Points where trajectories leave one of the saturation regions and enter the linear region, derived under the assumption

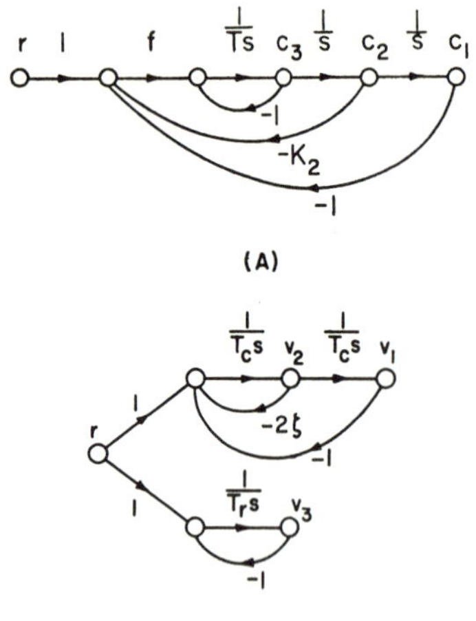

Fig. 9. Example 4

A—Signal-flow graph in $\mathcal{C}$
B—Signal-flow graph in $\mathcal{U}$

that the fast transients in $\mathcal{U}$ have reached their steady states.

b. Points where trajectories leave the linear region and enter one of the saturation regions, derived under the assumption that the fast transients in $\mathcal{V}$ have reached their steady states.

A geometric picture is helpful here. During saturation, all trajectories in $\mathcal{C}$ tend asymptotically to a certain plane which corresponds to, say, the (u_1, u_2) plane in $\mathcal{U}$. The intersection of this plane with that boundary plane of the linear region in $\mathcal{C}$ where the trajectories enter is a line. The projection of this line on the equivalent phase plane is the boundary of type a. During linear operation, the trajectories in $\mathcal{C}$ tend to a different plane which corresponds to, say, the (v_1, v_2) plane in $\mathcal{V}$. The intersection of this plane with that boundary plane of the linear region in $\mathcal{C}$ where the trajectories leave, projected on the equivalent phase plane, is the boundary of type b.

The following examples have been chosen to illustrate these considerations and also to reveal some of the peculiar differences which distinguish higher order systems from their second-order counterparts.

Example 4. Velocity Feedback in Third-Order Servo

This is the problem of the preceding section, but here the interest centers on the effect of linear velocity feedback. The signal-flow graph is shown in Fig. 9(A). The appropriate transformations from $\mathcal{C}$ to $\mathcal{U}$ and vice versa have already been derived in equations 10 and 11. The boundaries of the linear region referred to $\mathcal{U}$ are

$$r-c_1-K_2c_2=r-u_1+Tu_2-T^2u_3-K_2(u_2-Tu_3)=\pm 1/K_1 \quad (21)$$

Assuming that u_3 is very near its steady-state value, i.e., substituting $u_3 \cong \pm 1$ in equation 21, gives the approximate boundary lines (type a) where the trajectories enter the linear region

$$(r-u_1)+(K_2-T)(\dot{r}-u_2)=\mp T(K_2-T)\pm 1/K_1+(K_2-T)\dot{r} \quad (22)$$

To find the boundaries where the trajectories leave the linear region (type b), it is necessary to have the transformation between $\mathcal{C}$ and $\mathcal{V}$. For convenience, the co-ordinates in $\mathcal{V}$ are selected as shown in Fig. 9(B). The quantities T_r, T_c, and ζ are to be determined from the root locus for any particular value of K_1; if all the eigenvalues are real, $-1/T_r$ will denote the most negative eigenvalue. The transformation matrixes are

$$\mathbf{c}=P_v\mathbf{v}=\frac{1}{T_r^2+T_c^2-2\zeta T_rT_c}\times \begin{Vmatrix} T_c^2 & -2\zeta T_rT_c & -T_rT_c & T_r^2 \\ & T_r & T_c & -T_r \\ & -1 & T_r/T_c-2\zeta & 1 \end{Vmatrix}\mathbf{v} \quad (23)$$

and

$$\mathbf{v}=P_v^{-1}\mathbf{c}=\begin{Vmatrix} 1 & T_r & 0 \\ 0 & T_c & T_rT_c \\ 1 & 2\zeta T_c & T_c^2 \end{Vmatrix}\mathbf{c} \quad (24)$$

From equation 23, the boundaries of the linear region referred to $\mathcal{V}$ are

$$r-c_1-K_2c_2=\pm 1/K_1=r-\frac{[T_c^2+T_r(K_2-2\zeta T_c)]v_1+T_c(K_2-T_r)v_2+T_r(T_r-K_2)v_3}{T_r^2+T_c^2-2\zeta T_rT_c} \quad (25)$$

Using the linear transformation $\mathbf{v}=P_v^{-1}P_u\mathbf{u}$ and the assumption that $v_3 \cong 0$ when the trajectories leave the linear region, equation 25 may be referred to $\mathcal{U}$ and u_3 eliminated. Thus the equation of the boundaries of type b in the (u_1, u_2) phase plane is

$$(TK_2-2\zeta TT_c+T_c^2)(r-u_1)+T_c^2(K_2-T)(\dot{r}-u_2)\pm(T^2-2\zeta TT_c+T_c^2)/K_1=T_c^2(K_2-T)\dot{r}$$

Using the eigenvalue equation, T_c and ζ may be eliminated by introducing T_r

$$(T_r^2K_1+1)(r-u_1)+(K_2-T)(\dot{r}-u_2)\pm[1/K_1+(T+T_r-K_2)T_r]=(K_2-T)\dot{r} \quad (26)$$

During saturation, the situation in the $(r-u_1, \dot{r}-u_2)$ phase plane is similar to that in the $(e, \dot{e})$ phase plane of example 1, but now K_2 is replaced by (K_2-T) in equation 13. If $1/K_1 \approx 0$, i.e., the linear region is very small, the system becomes a relay servo. The condition for this relay servo to be stable for all inputs is a negatively sloping reversal line in the $(r-u_1, \dot{r}-u_2)$ plane

$$K_2>T \quad (27)$$

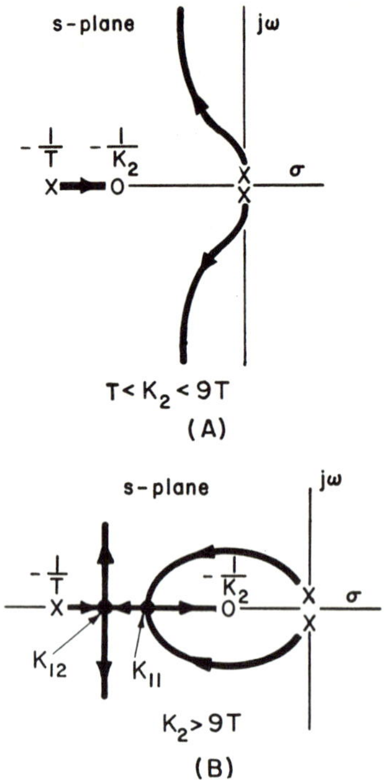

Fig. 10. Example 4, root loci

A—$T<K_2<9T$
B—$K_2>9T$

Now examine the linear region. If $K_2/T>1$, two qualitatively different root loci are possible depending on the magnitude of K_2/T, as shown in Figs. 10(A) and (B). In both cases, the eigenvalues remain in the left-half plane for all values of $K_1>0$. Hence inequality 27 which guarantees the stability in the saturation region also implies stability in the linear region. Conversely, if $K_2/T<1$, i.e., the pole and zero in Fig. 10(A) are interchanged, which is equivalent (approximately) to reflecting about the $j\omega$ axis the root loci starting at the double pole at the origin, there will be two complex eigenvalues in the right-half plane for any $K_1>0$. Thus violation of inequality 27 implies instability in both the saturation and linear regions.

Since equation 26 was derived by the assumption $v_3 \cong 0$, it is valid only if the real eigenvalue $-1/T_r$ represents a transient which can be neglected in comparison with the other two poles. This is

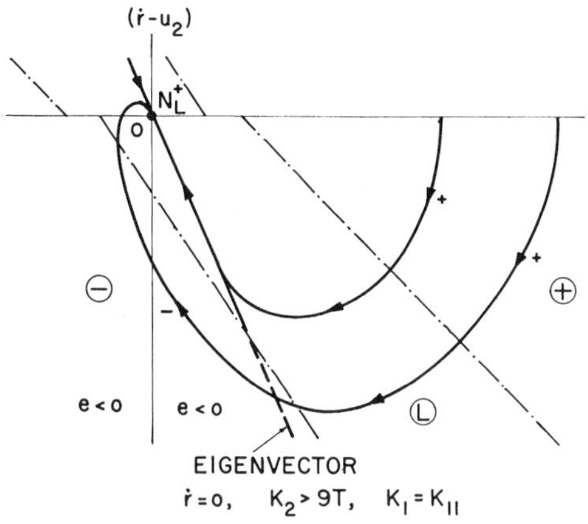

Fig. 11 (left). Example 4; phase-plane trajectories

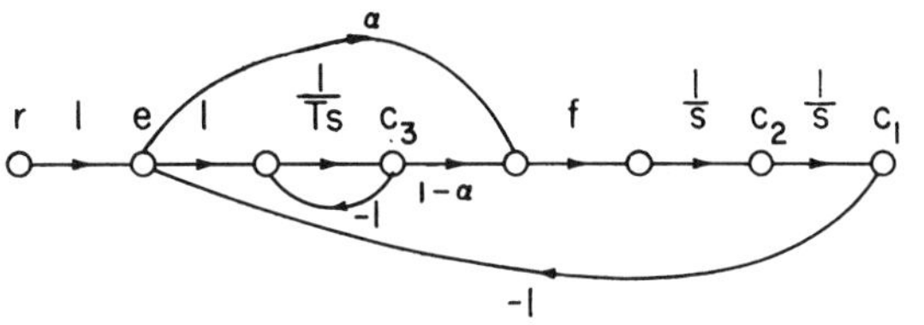

Fig. 12 (above). Example 5; signal-flow graph in $\mathcal{C}$

true in Fig. 10(A) for $K_1>0$ and in Fig. 10(B) for $0<K_1<K_{12}$.

If, however, $K_1>K_{12}$ in Fig. 10(B), the obvious assumption would be $v_1=v_2\cong 0$. If the assumption is correct, it means that the trajectories will have synchronized to the slow eigenvector before leaving the linear region. But if the trajectory has already synchronized to the eigenvector, it will move along the eigenvector closer and closer to the origin, and therefore cannot leave the linear region. It should be remembered that the boundary of the linear region here is a plane; if it were a more complicated surface, the conclusion would not necessarily hold. In reality, if the trajectories start sufficiently far from the origin, however, they will not synchronize to the eigenvector before leaving the linear region, so that the assumption $v_1=v_2\cong 0$ is untenable and a more detailed analysis is necessary. The latter case is too complicated to be considered in this paper.

Fig. 11 shows the boundaries of the linear region in the $(r-u_1,\ \dot{r}-u_2)$ phase plane. As in example 3, the usual optimization theory for the transfer function $1/s^2$ applies in this plane.

To appraise the situation in the linear region, it is necessary to project the dominant eigenvector from $\mathcal{C}$ into the $(r-u_1,\ \dot{r}-u_2)$ plane. In $\mathcal{C}$ the eigenvectors are defined by the equations

$$s_i c_1=c_2$$

$$s_i c_2=c_3$$

Hence, making use of P_u

$$s_i(u_1-Tu_2+T^2u_3)=u_2-Tu_3$$

$$s_i(u_2-Tu_3)=u_3 \tag{28}$$

Eliminating u_3 from equation 28 gives the projection of the eigenvector on the $(r-u_1,\ \dot{r}-u_2)$ plane

$$s_i(r-u_1)=\dot{r}-u_2 \tag{29}$$

The fact that this equation is the same in both the $(r-u_1,\ \dot{r}-u_2)$ and $(e,\ \dot{e})$ phase planes is merely an accident.

It remains to investigate the quantitative effects of changes in K_1 and K_2/T. If the root locus of Fig. 10(B) applies, the complex roots which arise when $0<K_1<K_{11}$ are of no interest, for the same reason as in example 1. If $K_{11}\le K_1<K_{12}$, the simplified analysis is admissible. Letting $K_1=K_{11}$ for convenience ($\zeta=1$) and bearing in mind that $0<T<K_2/9$, manipulation of the eigenvalue equation shows

$$K_2/3<T_c<K_2/2 \text{ and } 1<1+T_r^2K_1<4/3 \tag{30}$$

Comparing equations 22, 26, 29, and 30 shows that the relative slopes of the boundaries of the linear region and of the dominant eigenvector must be as sketched in Fig. 11. Even large variations of K_2/T cannot affect the situation. The resulting transient response is not very good. Some improvement might be had by increasing K_1 beyond K_{12}, but too large a value of K_1 would result in the trajectories cutting across the linear region because of more and more poorly damped complex poles, and transients caused by large errors may overshoot several times. Thus it appears that too much velocity feedback is not beneficial.

If the root locus of Fig. 10(A) applies, the analysis may be carried analogously, although the spiral trajectories in the linear region corresponding to the complex eigenvalues are not as readily handled quantitatively. In this case again, if K_1 is increased indefinitely, more and more trajectories will be leaving the linear region; see Figs. 15(D), (E), and (F).

With a moderate value of K_1, fairly satisfactory large-signal performance can be expected. The precise optimum relation between K_1 and K_2/T is probably best obtained by an analogue computer study guided by the foregoing considerations.

Example 5. Lead-Network Compensation

Now consider the lead-network compensation of the servomechanism of example 1. The development of the analysis is similar to but not identical with the preceding example. The lead network is inserted before the saturation; it is necessary to eliminate the zero by expanding the transfer function $(\alpha Ts+1)/(Ts+1)$ into partial fractions, as shown in Fig. 12.

If the co-ordinates in $\mathcal{U}$ are again defined by Fig. 2(B), the transformation from $\mathcal{C}$ to $\mathcal{U}$ is

$$\mathbf{c}=P_u\mathbf{u}=\begin{Vmatrix} 1 & 0 & 0 \\ 0 & 1 & 0 \\ -1 & T & -T^2 \end{Vmatrix}\mathbf{u} \tag{31}$$

The saturation-region trajectories in the $(r-u_1,\ \dot{r}-u_2)$ phase plane are parabolas as in examples 1 and 3.

The root loci are the same as in the previous example, with αT replacing K_2. The co-ordinates in $\mathcal{V}$ being again defined by Fig. 9(B), the transformation from $\mathcal{C}$ to $\mathcal{V}$ is given by

$$\mathbf{v}=P_v^{-1}\mathbf{c}=$$
$$\begin{Vmatrix} 1 & T_r-\alpha T & -\alpha T(T_r-\alpha T)K_1 \\ 0 & T_c & T_c(T_r-\alpha T)K_1 \\ 1 & 2\zeta T_c-\alpha T & [T_c^2+\alpha T(\alpha T-2\zeta T_c)]K_1 \end{Vmatrix}\mathbf{c}$$

It is readily verified from equation 31 and Fig. 12 that the eigenvector equation in $\mathcal{U}$ is again the same as in $\mathcal{C}$

$$s_i(r-u_1)=\dot{r}-u_2 \tag{32}$$

When entered from saturation, the boundaries of the linear region are

$$(r-u_1)+(\alpha-1)T(\dot{r}-u_2)$$
$$=\pm[1/K_1+T^2(1-\alpha)]+(\alpha-1)\dot{r} \tag{33}$$

More interesting are the boundaries of the linear region for trajectories leaving it

$$[\alpha-1+\alpha(T/T_r+\alpha TT_rK_1)](r-u_1)-$$
$$(\alpha-1)(\dot{r}-u_2)=\mp(1/K_1+\alpha T_r^2)T/T_r+$$
$$(1-\alpha)\dot{r} \tag{34}$$

It is now easy to run down the various cases of interest as far as the variation of both K_1 and α is concerned:

$\alpha>9$. If $0<K_1<K_{11}$, the transient response in the linear region is too slow. Increasing the gain to $K_{11}\le K_1\le K_{12}$ makes the dominant eigenvalues real; by equations 32

through 34 they always remain inside the linear region and therefore the transient never overshoots regardless of the magnitude of the input. If $K_1 > K_{12}$, not only does the linear region contract but the spirals corresponding to the complex eigenvalues may leave it. Hence $K_1 = K_{12}$ is a practical limit on the gain. Note also that a large α tends to slow down the response in the linear region.

$1 < \alpha < 9$. No matter how small $K_1 > 0$ is chosen, the spiral trajectories corresponding to the dominant complex eigenvalues will not lie entirely within the linear region. This imposes a limitation on large signal performance since beyond a certain input magnitude the trajectories will overshoot. On the other hand, reduction of α permits somewhat faster response in the linear region.

$\alpha < 1$. This corresponds to a lag network; the system is totally unstable.

Example 6. Roll-Control of Missile

As a concluding example, consider a missile roll-control problem where the influence of saturation is not immediately clear from physical reasoning The aerodynamic relationship between the control surface deflection c_3 and the actual roll angle c_1 is given approximately by the transfer function $1/s(Ts+1)$; in turn, c_3 is governed by a high-gain hydraulic servomechanism whose input is proportional to the roll-angle error e. To conserve hydraulic fluid, the servomechanism must be velocity-limited; this effect is the nonlinearity to be analyzed. The signal-flow graph is shown in Fig. 13(A).

The transformation from $\mathfrak{C}$ to $\mathfrak{U}$ is similar to that used in examples 3 and 4; it is

$$\mathbf{c} = P_u \mathbf{u} = \begin{Vmatrix} 1 & -T & T^2 \\ 0 & 1 & -T \\ 0 & 1 & 0 \end{Vmatrix} \mathbf{u}$$

provided the co-ordinates in $\mathfrak{U}$ are again selected in accordance with Fig. 2(B).

Since this is a regulating system, it is proper to use the (u_1, u_2) phase plane where initial conditions correspond to disturbances which the system is designed to counteract. The boundaries of the linear region for trajectories entering from saturation are

$$K_3 u_1 + (1 - K_3 T) u_2 = \mp (1/K_1 + K_3 T^2)$$

Assume now that $K_1 >> 1/T$, as is generally the case in practice. The linear zone is then very narrow and, for large inputs, the system behaves as a relay servo in the (u_1, u_2) phase plane with an open-loop transfer function $1/s^2$ and a reversal line of slope $T - 1/K_3$. If the slope is positive, i.e.

$$K_3 > 1/T$$

the relay servo may be made completely unstable by a large, sudden disturbance. However, unlike in examples 4 and 5, the foregoing inequality does not imply instability in the linear region. Since $1/K_1 \cong 0$, the eigenvalue equation is approximately

$$s^2 + s/T + K_3/T = 0 \qquad (35)$$

Setting $K_3 = 1/T$ leads to a damping ratio $\zeta = 0.5$ for the eigenvalues of equation 35. Even for any $K_3 > 1/T$, the transients in the linear region will be stable, provided that K_1 is sufficiently large. Thus small trajectories will converge to the origin while large trajectories diverge to infinity, revealing the presence of an unstable limit cycle. The limit cycle will be composed of half-parabolas and may be calculated exactly in the (u_1, u_2) phase plane by the graphical construction shown in Fig. 13(B). The reversal curve bends toward the origin as indicated, since $|u_3| < 1$ if the reversal takes place near the origin.

The unstable limit cycle defines a stability boundary in $\mathfrak{U}$ as follows: Move the origin of the (u_1, u_2) plane along the u_3 axis, maintaining the orthogonality of the axes. The limit cycle will generate the surface of a cylinder. All trajectories starting within the cylinder will converge to the origin, and all others will diverge to infinity. For very large values of u_3, the cylinder will become distorted since the approximation $u_3 \cong \pm 1$ used in deriving the reversal point will no longer be good.

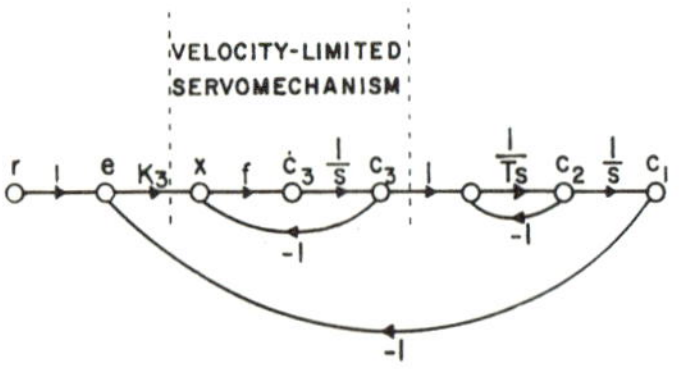

(A)

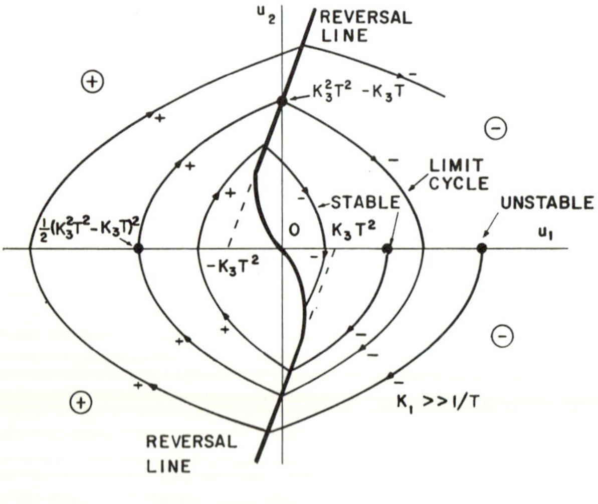

(B)

Fig. 13. Example 6

A—Signal-flow graph in $\mathfrak{C}$
B—Determination of limit cycle

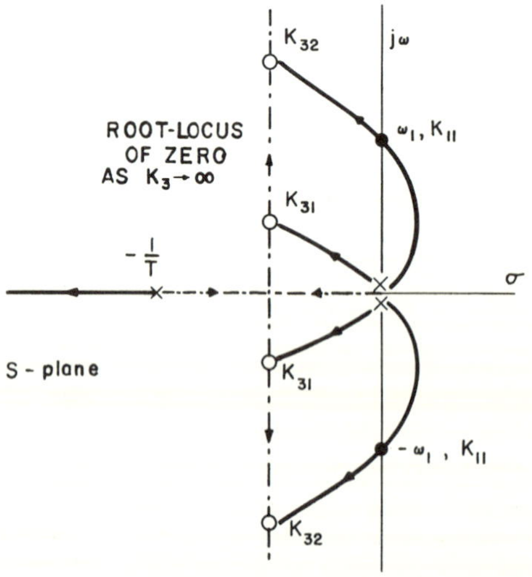

Fig. 14 (above). Example 6; root locus as a function of K_1, with K_3 as parameter

Comparison With Describing-Function Method

It is interesting to consider the question of establishing the existence and of calculating the approximate period and amplitude of the unstable limit cycle by the describing-function method. Johnson[34] has calculated the amplitude and phase of the fundamental harmonic component of c_3 as a function of the amplitude and frequency of a sinusoidal forcing signal e, thereby obtaining a describing function for the velocity-limited servomechanism in Fig. 13(A). He, too, concludes that an unstable limit cycle exists for sufficiently large K_3. An equivalent but conceptually simpler way of proceeding is this.[35] Write the eigenvalue equation for the linear region of the system as

$$K_1\frac{s(Ts+1)+K_3}{s^2(Ts+1)}+1=0 \tag{36}$$

Equation 36 represents a root locus as a function of K_1. The zeros of the root locus in turn depend on K_3, as shown by the dash-dotted line in Fig. 14. For nonlinear operation, K_1 is to be interpreted as some equivalent gain. Thus K_1 will be very large for linear operation (x small) and approach zero for highly nonlinear operation (x large). Now if K_3 is fairly small (K_{31}), the root locus will not cross over into the right-half plane, and the system will be stable for all values of K_1. If K_3 is sufficiently large (K_{32}), however, the root locus will cross and instability will result whenever K_1 is small. Hence, there will be an unstable limit cycle, with its approximate amplitude and frequency being given by the intersection of the root locus with the $j\omega$ axis, as in Fig. 14.

Notice that the foregoing arguments depend crucially on what is meant by equivalent gain. If the a priori assumption is made that a stable or unstable limit cycle exists, then K_1 may be defined as the ratio of the first-harmonic components in $\dot{c}_3=f(x)$ and x, justified by noting that the higher harmonics are attenuated by the transfer function between $\dot{c}_3$ and x. If the limit cycle actually exists and is approximately sinusoidal, the root locus must necessarily intersect the $j\omega$ axis. But intersection of the axis is not sufficient to infer the existence of a limit cycle. Thus the success of the describing-function method may depend on whether a limit cycle actually exists—the very fact that the method is expected to prove. In fact, Nichols[36] has pointed out that the describing-function method applied to a backlash problem indicates the presence of an unstable limit cycle whereas exact analysis shows that none exists. Despite much recent effort,[37] this fundamental weakness of the describing-function method has not been overcome.

By contrast, the phase-space analysis outlined in the foregoing is not dependent on any a priori assumption. The only approximation, concerning u_3, is made in the time domain and is very easily checked in any particular case.

Conclusions

All of the examples of this section were governed by the same saturation-region differential equations, and yet the effect of saturation was quite different in each case. These differences were caused by the manner in which saturation was included in the systems; they were revealed by a detailed consideration of how the trajectories entered and left the linear region.

Summary

This paper presents, apparently for the first time in the engineering literature, a simple approach to high-order nonlinear systems based on linear transformations in the phase space and closely linked to the very useful transfer-function concept in the theory of linear transients. In the present form of the theory, detailed quantitative calculations may be quite laborious. But only a simple analysis of the type discussed is needed to discover characteristic features of the nonlinear system; for this task, the phase-space method is admirably suited.

The author is convinced that the combination of the phase-space representation of nonlinear differential equations, linear transformations linked to the familiar partial-fraction expansion of transfer functions, and the root-locus method of stability study together provide a powerful and modern mathematical apparatus for the study of nonlinear control problems. Much further progress may be expected from the exploitation of these ideas.

Appendix I. Trajectories of Second-Order Linear Systems

For quantitative work in phase-plane analysis, it is very useful to have a set of standard curves of the response of second-order linear systems. A series of such scale plots are reproduced here for ready reference; see Fig. 15. All curves were obtained by means of a real-time analogue computer; accuracy is about ±2 per cent.

The curves represent solutions of the equation often used in servo work

$$\frac{d^2x}{dt^2}+2\zeta\frac{dx}{dt}+x=0 \tag{37}$$

where ζ is a real parameter, the viscous damping coefficient. The qualitative features of Fig. 15 are best discussed in terms of the eigenvalues s_i of equation 37. In view of the diagonalization theorem, this will also take care of the general case where A is a 2×2 matrix.

Case 1. Stable Node: $1\le\zeta<\infty$; or s_1, s_2 are real, negative. The solutions in normal co-ordinates are $u_i(t)=u_i(0)\epsilon^{s_it}$ ($i=1, 2$). From these, the equation of the trajectories is readily obtained by eliminating the time

$$u_2=\text{constant } u_1^{s_2/s_1} \quad s_2<s_1<0 \tag{38}$$

Equation 38 represents a family of parabolas symmetrical around the u_2 axis. Transformation to the $(x, \dot{x})$ phase plane distorts the trajectories, but does not affect the nature of the critical point. Thus in Figs. 15(A) and (C) the trajectories start out as straight lines parallel to the eigenvector corresponding to s_2 (the u_2 axis), and they approach asymptotically the eigenvector corresponding to s_1 (the u_1 axis). This means that the initial rise time of a 2-lag system in response to a step depends primarily on the smaller s_i whereas the final settling time is governed by the larger s_i, as is well known. Bearing these simple physical notions in mind, it is very natural to approximate the trajectories in Fig. 15(A) by two straight lines, as shown in Fig. 15(B), one running parallel to the u_2 axis (the "fast" eigenvector) and the other being the u_1 axis itself (the "slow" eigenvector). Because of the much smaller separation between the eigenvalues, the approximation is less accurate if applied to Fig. 15(C).

Case 2. Stable Focus: $0<\zeta<1$ or s_1, s_2 are complex conjugate, $\sigma<0$. Here it is best to regard one of the solutions in normal co-ordinates

$$u_1(t)=u_1(0)\epsilon^{s_1t}=u_1(0)\epsilon^{(a+jb)t} \tag{39}$$

as a first-order differential equation defined over a 1-dimensional complex space, i.e., the ordinary complex plane. The other solution is merely the complex conjugate of equation 39. The complex quantity $u_1(t)$ is to be regarded as a rotating vector with bt being the angle of rotation in radians and ϵ^{at} the attenuation of the magnitude of the vector. The curve described by the tip of the vector, a logarithmic spiral, is the trajectory in the $(Re[u_1], Im[u_1])$ plane. When translated into the $(x, \dot{x})$ phase plane, the logarithmic spirals appear as in Figs. 15(D), (E), and (F).

It is unfortunately not possible to make use here of the asymptotic behavior of the trajectories as in the case of the node; however, explicit computation of the trajectory is not too difficult in view of the convenient form of equation 39.

Case 3. Center: $\zeta=0$, or s_1, s_2 are pure imaginary. In equation 39, a is set to zero and therefore the rotating vectors describe a circle. The trajectories consist of concentric circles. The system is said to be conservative.

The qualitative difference between parabolic, spiral, and circular trajectories is indeed striking; this is the motivation for

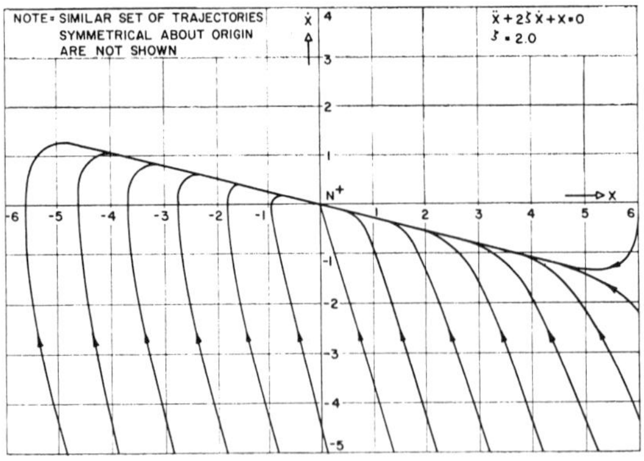

(A)

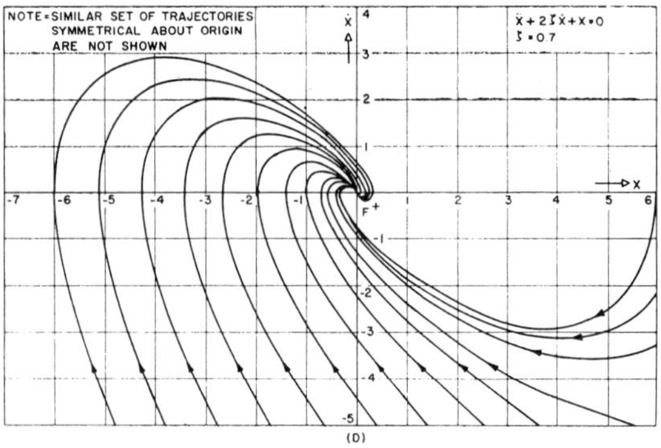

(D)

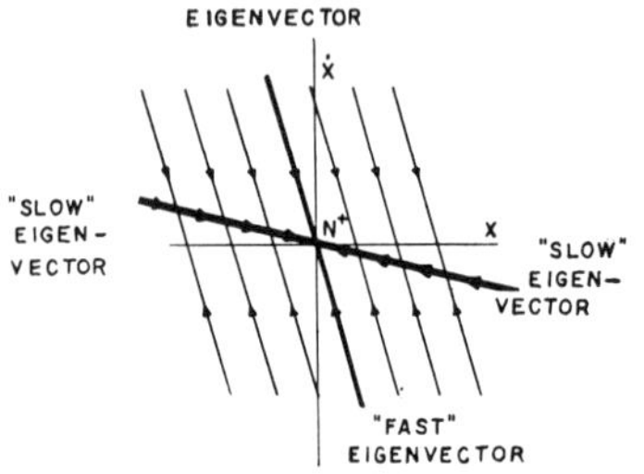

(B)

Fig. 15. Trajectories of the second-order linear differential equation

$$\frac{d^2x}{dt^2}+2\zeta\frac{dx}{dt}+x=0$$

A—$\zeta=2.0$

B—Approximate representation with the help of eigenvectors

C—$\zeta=1.2$

D—$\zeta=0.7$

E—$\zeta=0.4$

F—$\zeta=0.2$

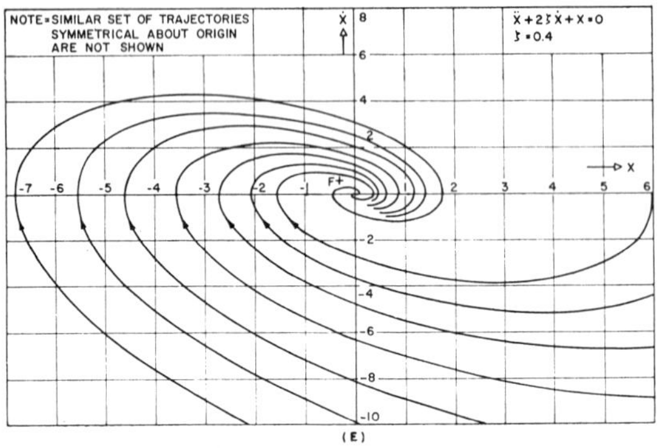

(E)

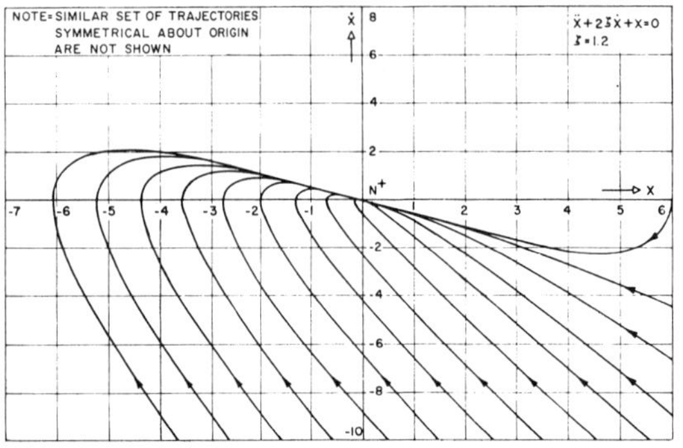

(C)

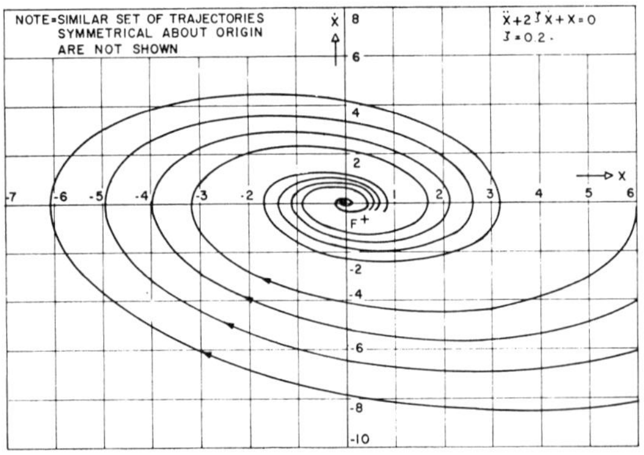

(F)

the insistence in phase-plane theory on sharply differentiating node, focus, and center type of critical points and trajectories.

The case of the saddle point, i.e., s_1, s_2 real, $s_1<0<s_2$, is not treated; it has not been important up to the present in servomechanism theory. Since the eigenvalues are real, the trajectories are easily visualized using the eigenvector concept, as in the case of a node. The degenerate cases when one or both eigenvalues vanish have been treated at some length in connection with optimum relay servos.[3-6,9]

All the trajectories in Fig. 15 represent stable systems, i.e., the trajectories tend to be the critical point as $t \to +\infty$; hence the superscript + over the abbreviation of the critical point.[13] Unstable trajectories may be obtained by reflection about the $\dot{x}$ axis, which corresponds to changing the sign of ζ.

Appendix II. Optimum Relay Servomechanism Theory

Second-Order Systems

The problem of how a relay-controlled or saturating servomechanism is to be designed for optimum speed of response may be completely solved by use of the phase-space approach. The correct solution may be discovered by the following intuitive argument:

To have optimally fast response, it is necessary to exploit fully the power (or torque, etc.) capabilities of the system; hence, the signal into the output element must be maintained at either forward or reverse saturation, corresponding to the two nonzero positions of a polarized relay. This suggests that the signal (forcing function) applied to the output element should be idealized as having only three distinct values: +1, −1, and 0. There will be two different families of trajectories in the phase plane corresponding to the two signs. The problem is to bring the system to rest at zero error as quickly as possible. In the $(e, \dot{e})$ phase plane this is achieved by leading the trajectory into the origin.

Clearly, the transient can reach the origin only by following a trajectory which goes through the origin. There exists one and only one such trajectory in each family since the origin is not a critical point. These trajectories are called reversal curves. They subdivide the phase plane into two regions. In each region the signal polarity is so specified that the resulting trajectories will always intersect the reversal curve, at which instant the signal polarity is reversed. The transient then proceeds along the reversal curve. At the instant of reaching the origin, the signal to the output element is set to zero and the system remains at rest.

This scheme was first proposed and demonstrated with simple examples by McDonald[3] and Hopkin[5] and many other contributions have been recorded since then.[6,15,38–43] In a doctorate thesis, Bushaw[42] has rigorously proved that the intuition which led to the formulation of the theory is indeed correct.

In view of the significance of the optimum relay servomechanism concept in the analysis of saturating systems, the various important special cases of second-order transfer functions are now briefly reviewed. A detailed discussion is given by Tsien.[44]

Case 1. $G(s)=1/s^2$, e.g., ideal torque source driving pure inertia.[3,39] The trajectories are families of parabolas, with vertexes on and symmetrical with the e axis. Representative transient trajectories are sketched in Fig. 16(A). Regions in the phase plane are labeled with $+$ and $-$ signs according to the signal polarity required. The equation of the reversal curve is

$$2e=-\dot{e}|\dot{e}| \tag{40}$$

Case 2. $G(s)=1/s(s+1)$, e.g., armature-controlled d-c motor.[5,39] For small velocities, the trajectories are similar to case 1. Ultimately they become asymptotic to the dashed lines $\dot{c}=\pm 1$; see Fig. 16(B). Note that the trajectories may approach the dotted lines also from the outside. The equation of the reversal curve is

$$\frac{e}{T}=\dot{c}\left(1-\frac{ln\,(1+|\dot{c}|)}{|\dot{c}|}\right) \tag{41}$$

Case 3. $G(s)=1/(s^2+2\zeta s+1)$, $\zeta\geq 1$, e.g., 2-capacity temperature regulation problem.[42] The trajectories tend to the stable nodes $(N_-{}^+)$ and $(N_+{}^+)$, depending on whether they originate above or below the reversal curve; see Fig. 16(C). Only the arc A_+OA_- on the reversal curve is of practical interest, since all large-signal trajectories having converged to the slow eigenvector of $(N_+{}^+)$ will intersect the reversal line at A_+. Similary for A_-.

Case 4. $G(s)=1/(s^2+2\zeta s+1)$, $\zeta\leq -1$, unstable open loop. The trajectories belong to the unstable nodes $(N_+{}^-)$ and $(N_-{}^-)$ respectively. Connecting $(N_+{}^-)$ with trajectory Γ_- to $(N_-{}^-)$ and $(N_-{}^-)$ with Γ_+ to $(N_+{}^-)$, Fig. 16(D), it is easily seen that all trajectories originating outside the closed curve $\Gamma_+\Gamma_-$ will diverge to infinity. If the reversal curve is again made up of trajectories going through the origin and terminating at the nodes, stable operation is assured everywhere inside the curve $\Gamma_+\Gamma_-$. For any other choice of the reversal curve, say, a straight line through the

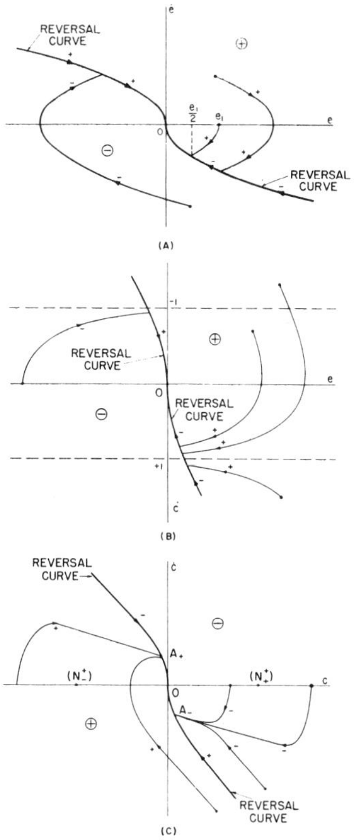

origin realizable by linear velocity feedback, the stable region will be necessarily smaller. The boundary $\Gamma_+\Gamma_-$ is analogous to an unstable limit cycle.

In the foregoing cases, optimum control is achieved by a total of two polarity reversals, including in the count the fact that the signal must be set to zero on reaching the origin. The case of a second-order transfer function with complex roots is in a sense exceptional since only a part of the optimum reversal curve is a trajectory; more and more reversals are necessary as the magnitude of the initial error is increased.

Case 5. $G(s)=1/(s^2+2\zeta s+1)$, $0<\zeta<1$, e.g., aircraft regulation problem.[42] The trajectories are spirals, belonging to the stable foci $(F_+{}^+)$ and $(F_-{}^+)$. The two trajectories leading into the origin intersect one another an infinite number of times; moreover, they do not subdivide the phase plane into two distinct parts. The problem requires serious mathematical investigation.

According to Bushaw's solution,[42] the reversal curve consists of arcs of trajectories constructed as follows: Take a trajectory belonging to $(F_+{}^+)$ and follow it backwards in time from the origin until it intersects the c axis at c_p where $p=1$. Now magnify the arc so obtained by the factor exp $p(\pi\zeta/\sqrt{1-\zeta^2})$ and displace it; c_p units to the right, continuing the process with $p=1, 2, 3, \ldots$. In other words, that trajectory of $(F_-{}^+)$ which goes through the origin is cut at each intersection with the c axis, and the arcs so obtained are placed side by side. The reversal curve for $c<0$

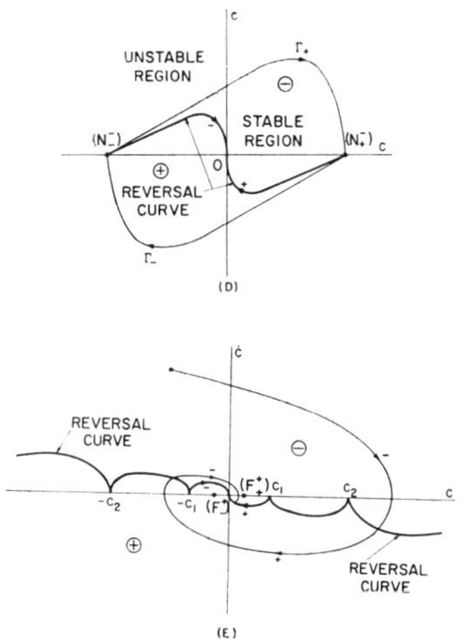

Fig. 16. Reversal curves for optimally compensated second-order systems classified according to output element transfer function

A—$1/s^2$
B—$1/s(Ts+1)$
C—$1/(s^2+2\zeta s+1)$, $\zeta>1$
D—$1/(s^2+2\zeta s+1)$, $\zeta<-1$
E—$1/(s^2+2\zeta s+1)$, $0<\zeta<1$

is determined similarly; see Fig. 16(E). If the initial point lies on the c axis between $c_{p-1}<|c|<c_p$, the number of reversals will be $p+1\geq 2$.

It is difficult to approach optimum performance in this case by linear compensation. A thorough treatment of the many phenomena encountered in relay servos with velocity feedback and this transfer function is given by Flügge-Lotz.[10]

Remark on Inputs

Because of considerations of steady-state error, if the locations of the optimum reversal curves are to be independent of the input, only the following types of inputs are admissible to servomechanisms (follow-up systems) incorporating the transfer functions discussed in the foregoing:

Case 1. Steps and/or ramps.
Case 2. Steps only.
Cases 3 through 5. Neither steps nor ramps.

The axes in Fig. 16 have been labeled accordingly.

Since arbitrary inputs may be approximated by means of steps and ramps, the response of systems of the type 1 and 2 may be regarded as generally acceptable though not always optimum, provided that in the steady state the inputs behave as listed in the foregoing. In cases 3 through 5, only inputs which are identically zero in the steady state are allowed; hence these cases are of interest mainly in connection with regulating systems.

On the other hand, system 1 is capable of following both step and ramp inputs with zero steady-state errors and nonovershooting transients. This contrasts with the well-known fact that a linear servo which has zero steady-state error to a ramp input necessarily overshoots in response to a step.

Remark on Zeros

A further unexpected difficulty appears when the transfer function is allowed to have a zero. The reversal curve, composed of the trajectories leading into the origin of the normal co-ordinate phase plane, depends only on the poles and not on the zero. On the other hand, the transformation which takes the reversal curve back to the $(e, \dot{e})$ phase plane is a function of the zero. By proper selection of the zero, the reversal curve may be rotated by an arbitrary angle in $(e, \dot{e})$; in particular, it may be made to intersect the line $e=0$ so that the transient will overshoot once. Under such circumstances, the response cannot be regarded as optimum and it may be mandatory to introduce a linear zone. The foregoing statements are easily checked by considering an optimum relay servo with the transfer function $(Ts+1)/s^2$, which will have an overshooting step response if $T>0$. These remarks should emphasize the fact that, while an optimum response may always be defined, the existence of meaningful optimum system depends on both the nature of the transfer function and of the inputs.

Systems of Arbitrary Order

If the concept of second-order optimum relay servomechanisms is thoroughly understood, there is no basic difficulty in extending it to arbitrarily high-order systems. Because of the unpleasant complications which have arisen in connection with case 5, only open-loop transfer functions with real poles have been considered so far.[12,14,43]

The argument proceeds backwards: In n-dimensional phase space, the $\pm$ trajectories through the origin constitute the reversal curve. Each point on this reversal curve may be reached (is intersected) by a trajectory of the opposite polarity; the latter trajectories generate a 2-dimensional reversal surface. This process may be continued until the trajectories intersecting the last $(n-1)$-dimensional reversal surface fill the entire n-dimensional phase space. Hence n reversals are necessary in the n-dimensional case. Take a third-order system such as in examples 3 and 4. The first reversal occurs when the trajectory intersects the 2-dimensional surface; after that, the trajectory remains in that surface until intersecting the trajectory through the origin, when the polarity is again reversed. By definition, the third reversal occurs when the signal becomes zero on reaching the origin.

The equations describing the reversal surface may be readily obtained by means ol the normal co-ordinate transformation. The problem has been worked out for the transfer function $1/s^2(Ts+1)$ by Bogner.[12] A more general treatment is due to Rose.[43]

The incorporation of a reversal surface in a practical system is cumbersome because of the necessity of simulating the 1, 2, ... $(n-1)$-dimensional reversal surfaces. Moreover, it would be necessary to measure accurately the first $(n-1)$ derivatives of the error. Herein lies the importance of the approximation scheme discussed in the foregoing. Still, in a difficult control problem, crude simulation of a reversal surface by a diode network may well be the only adequate method of compensation.

Notice also that the optimum compensation assumes precise knowledge of an unchangeable transfer function. The optimum system is a calibrated system. Much further work is necessary before practical equipment can be built which will reliably approach optimum performance even when subjected to noise, slight changes in parameters, etc.

References

1. Fundamental Theory of Servomechanisms (book), **L. A. MacColl.** D. Van Nostrand Company, Inc., New York, N. Y., 1945, Appendix.

2. Analysis of Relay Servomechanisms, **H. K. Weiss.** *Journal of the Aeronautical Sciences*, Easton, Pa., vol. 13, 1946, pp. 364–76.

3. Nonlinear Techniques for Improving Servo Performance, **D. C. McDonald.** *Proceedings*, National Electronics Conference, Chicago, Ill., vol. 6, 1950, pp. 400–21.

4. Multiple-Mode Operation of Servomechanisms, **D. C. McDonald.** *Review of Scientific Instruments*, New York, N. Y., vol. 23, 1952, pp. 22–30.

5. A Phase-Plane Approach to the Design of Saturating Servomechanisms, **A. M. Hopkin.** *AIEE Transactions*, vol. 70, pt. I, 1951, pp. 631–39.

6. Automatic and Manual Control (book). Academic Press, New York, N. Y., 1952, "The Stablization of On-Off Controlled Servomechanisms," **A. M. Uttley, P. H. Hammond**, pp. 285–308.

7. Analysis of a Friction Damper for Clutch-Type Servomechanisms, **H. K. Weiss.** *Journal of the Aeronautical Sciences*, Easton, Pa., vol. 18, 1951, pp. 676–82.

8. Graphical Solution of Some Automatic-Control Problems Involving Saturation Effects with Application to Yaw Dampers for Aircraft, **W. H. Phillips.** *NACA Technical Note No. 3034*, National Advisory Committee for Aeronautics, Washington, D. C., 1953.

9. The Application of Nonlinear Techniques to Servomechanisms, **K. C. Mathews, R. C. Boe.** *Proceedings*, National Electronics Conference, Chicago, Ill., vol. 8, 1952, pp. 10–21.

10. Discontinuous Automatic Control (book), **I. Flügge-Lotz.** Princeton University Press, Princeton, N. J., 1953.

11. Design Considerations of a Saturating Servomechanism, **P. E. Kendall, J. F. Marquardt.** *Proceedings*, National Electronics Conference, Chicago, Ill., vol. 9, 1953, pp. 178–87.

12. An Investigation of Switching Criteria for Higher Order Contactor Servomechanisms, **I. Bogner, L. F. Kazda.** *AIEE Transactions*, vol. 73, pt. II, July 1954, pp. 118–27.

13. Phase-Plane Analysis of Automatic Control Systems with Nonlinear Gain Elements, **R. E. Kalman.** *Ibid.*, Jan. 1954, pp. 383–90.

14. Nonlinear Control of a Saturating Third-Order Servomechanism, **J. L. Preston.** *M. S. Thesis*, Massachusetts Institute of Technology, Cambridge, Mass., May 1954.

15. The Effects of the Addition of Some Nonlinear Elements on the Transient Performance of a Simple R. P. C. System Possessing Torque Limitation, **J. C. West, J. L. Douce, R. Naylor.** *Proceedings*, Institution of Electrical Engineers, London, England, vol. 101, pt. II, 1954, pp. 156–65.

16. The Step-Function Response of an R. P. C. Servo Mechanism Possessing Torque Limitation, **J. C. West, I. R. Dalton.** *Ibid.*, pp. 166–73.

17. Theory of Oscillations (book), **A. A. Andronow, C. E. Chaikin.** Princeton University Press, Princeton, N. J., 1949.

18. Introduction to Nonlinear Mechanics (book), **N. Minorsky.** J. W. Edwards, Ann Arbor, Mich., 1947.

19. Geometrical Methods in the Analysis of Ordinary Differential Equations: Introduction to Nonlinear Mechanics, **J. Kestin, S. K. Zaremba.** *Applied Scientific Research*, The Hague, Holland, vol. 3B, 1953, pp. 149–89.

20. Synthesis of Feedback Control Systems by Phase-Angle Loci, **Y. Chu.** *AIEE Transactions*, vol. 71, pt. II, 1952, pp. 330–39.

21. The Study of Transients in Linear Feedback Systems by Conformal Mapping and the Root-Locus Method, **V. C. M. Yeh.** *Transactions*, American Society of Mechanical Engineers New York, N. Y., vol. 76, 1954, pp. 349–61.

22. Lectures on Differential Equations (book), **S. Lefschetz.** Princeton University Press, Princeton, N. J., 1946.

23. Stability Theory of Differential Equations (book), **R. Bellman.** McGraw-Hill Book Company, Inc., New York, N. Y., 1953.

24. Finite Dimensional Vector Spaces (book), **P. R. Halmos.** Princeton University Press, Princeton, N. J., 1942.

25. A Survey of Modern Algebra (book), **G. Birkhoff, S. MacLane.** The Macmillan Company, New York, N. Y., 1946.

26. Feedback Theory. Some Propertirs of Signal Flow Graphs. **S. J. Mason.** *Proceedings*, Institute of Radio Engineers, New York, N. Y., vol. 41, 1953, pp. 1144–56.

27. Automatic Feedback Control System Synthesis (book), **J. A. Truxal.** McGraw-Hill Book Company, Inc., New York, N. Y., 1955.

28. Electronic Analog Computers (book), **G. A. Korn, T. M. Korn.** *Ibid.*, 1952.

29. Introductory Circuit Theory (book), **E. A. Guillemin.** John Wiley and Sons, Inc., New York, N. Y., 1953.

30. Transient Vibration of Linear Multi-Degree-of-Freedom Systems by the Phase-Plane Method, **R. S. Ayre.** *Journal*, Franklin Institute, Philadelphia, Pa., vol. 253, 1952, pp. 153–66.

31. Metrization of Phase Space and Nonlinear Servo Systems, **Chi Lung Kang, G. H. Fett.** *Journal of Applied Physics*, New York, N. Y., vol. 25, 1955, pp. 38–41.

32. Calculation of the Inverse of a Matrix, **R. V. Andree.** *American Mathematical Monthly*, Buffalo, N. Y., vol. 58, 1951, p. 87.

33. The Synthesis of "Optimum" Transient Response: Criteria and Standard Forms, **D. Graham, R. C. Lathrop.** *AIEE Transactions*, vol. 72, pt. II, Nov. 1953, pp. 273–88.

34. Proceedings of the Symposium on Nonlinear Circuit Analysis (book). Polytechnic Institute of Brooklyn, Brooklyn, N. Y., 1953, "Sinusoidal Techniques Applied to Nonlinear Feedback Systems," **E. C. Johnson**, pp. 258–73.

35. *Discussion* of H. Chestnut's paper, **R. E. Kalman.** *Transactions*, American Society of Mechanical Engineers, New York, N. Y., vol. 76, 1954, p. 1362.

36. Backlash in a Velocity Lag Servomechanism, **N. B. Nichols.** *AIEE Transactions*, vol. 72, pt. II, Jan. 1953, pp. 462–67.

37. Recent Advances in Nonlinear Servo Theory, **J. M. Loeb.** *Transactions*, American Society of Mechanical Engineers, New York, N. Y., vol. 76, 1954, pp. 1281–89.

38. On the Comparison of Linear and Nonlinear Servomechanism Response, **T. M. Stout.** *Transactions*, IRE Professional Group for Circuit Theory, Institute of Radio Engineers, New York, N. Y., vol. CT-1, Mar. 1954, pp. 49–55.

39. Effects of Friction in an Optimum Relay Servomechanism, **T. M. Stout.** *AIEE Transactions*, vol. 72, pt. II, Nov. 1953, pp. 329–36.

40. Switching Errors in an Optimum Relay Servomechanism, **T. M. Stout.** *Proceedings*, National Electronics Conference, Chicago, Ill., vol. 9, 1953, pp. 188–98.

41. Predictor Servomechanisms, **L. M. Silva.** *Transactions*, IRE Professional Group for Circuit Theory, Institute of Radio Engineers, New York, N. Y., vol. CT-1, Mar. 1954, pp. 56–70.

42. Differential Equations with a Discontinuous Forcing Term, **D. W. Bushaw.** *Ph.D. Thesis*, Princeton University, Princeton, N. J., 1952.

43. Theoretical Aspects of Limit Control, **N. J. Rose.** *Report No. 459*, Stevens Institute of Technology, Hoboken, N. J., Nov. 1953.

44. Engineering Cybernetics (book), **H. S. Tsien.** McGraw-Hill Book Company, Inc., New York, N. Y., 1954.

Discussion

J. M. Loeb (Schlumberger Instrument Company, Ridgefield, Conn.): The author should be commended for having given a rigorous approach to an approximation method used by some other authors. Since higher order nonlinear systems are dealt with, a constant need for a kind of "phase plane approach" has been experienced.

The existence of computers has changed the aim of theoretical calculations. For all particular problems, i.e., derivation of the solution of a set of nonlinear differential equations being given the necessary limit conditions, no special mathematical concept is necessary. A good analogue or digital computer does the job. As a matter of fact, the phase plane approach, introduced by Cauchy to drive his "unicity theorem," is rarely used for practical computation. However, the control engineer has equally to perform synthesis of equipments and a general visualization becomes necessary.

Mr. Kalman has showed very well how matrix algebra leads to the discovery of independant variables particularly suitable for a phase plane approximation, i.e., that are related by differential equations containing largest time constants. The conception of "projection" of the phase space upon this particular plane is the key to a good understanding of a whole class of interesting systems.

It remains, however, very difficult to cross the gap that separates linear problems from nonlinear ones. All the problems treated in the paper belong to the so-called "piecewise linear" field.

Many systems are devised to supply in due time the best "switching" that changes the configuration of the system. In more complicated diagrams, is it not to be foreseen that the decomposition, or the author's "near-diagonalization," would lead to a different couple of principal variables? If it is so, one would have to operate the inverse transformation each time the representing point crosses the boundary between different configurations of the system.

K. Klotter (Stanford University, Stanford, Calif.): I share the author's opinion (as expressed in the summary) that the "combination of the phase-space representation of nonlinear differential equations, linear transformations linked to the familiar partial-fraction expansion of transfer functions, and the root locus method of stability study together provide a powerful . . . . apparatus for the study of nonlinear control problems," and think that the author did a commendable job in presenting that technique of investigation.

However, in order to keep the limitations of the procedure in the reader's mind, I would like to underline, and also to implement, a few statements in the paper which are apt to become lost in the technical details:

1. The nonlinear systems investigated are replaced by piecewise linear ones. Although it is true that such an approximation may be achieved "with arbitrary accuracy," it is equally true that increased accuracy entails highly increased labor.

2. The driving terms are replaced by constants; they, in turn, by a transformation of co-ordinates, can be eliminated completely. In this way homogeneous linear equations result.

3. The system of nth order finally is replaced by one of second order. Hence, intrinsically, no "extension of the phase plane method to high-order nonlinear differential equations" is involved. The method is as good as the replacement is. Furthermore, all examples given are restricted to third order.

The author, in presenting his case, makes extensive use of the parlance within some circles of communication engineers, including the use of signal flow graphs in lieu of differential equations. In using, and even coining, new expressions for familiar algebraic and analytical concepts, the author at one point, however, transcends the permissible limits: In the paragraph following equation 1 the quantities $\dot{c}_i$ and c_i are referred to as "dependent variables" and the quantities r_i as "independent variables." Such a usage is at variance with well-established mathematical terminology. The c_i are the dependent variables; however, the r_i are the "driving terms" (or "forcing terms" or "perturbation terms," etc.) but certainly not the independent variables. Independent variable is the time t exclusively and throughout.

Y. H. Ku (Moore School of Electrical Engineering, University of Pennsylvania, Philadelphia, Pa.): This paper is a serious attempt to generalize phase-plane methods of dealing with nonlinear systems and appears to pinpoint a promising area of future research. To represent the solutions of nonlinear differential equations of the nth order, it is necessary to use an n-dimensional phase space, in which an n-dimensional space trajectory representing the solution is located.[1,2] The author is to be congratulated for giving a simplified method of approximating the actual trajectory by breaking up the phase space into a number of regions, such that within each region the portions of the approximated trajectory represent the solutions of linear differential equations. However, it may be pointed out that in the general phase-space method, it is not absolutely necessary that such linear approximations are made. It is a straightforward procedure to find the actual trajectory if it needs be found.[3,4] Thus the phase space of n-dimensions offers a seat to the actual trajectory as well as to the approximated portions of the actual trajectory. In fact, while the junctions of the approximated portions have multivalued slopes, the actual trajectory has continuity of slopes at all points. It would be of interest to compare the actual trajectory (with nonlinearities as originally specified or experimentally determined) with the portions of the approximated trajectory. The simplified method would be especially useful in synthesis and design of nonlinear servomechanisms.

References

1. A Method for Solving Third and Higher Order Nonlinear Differential Equations, Y. H. Ku. *Journal*, Franklin Institute, Philadelphia, Pa., vol. 256, no. 3, Sept. 1953, pp. 229–44.

2. Analysis of Nonlinear Systems with More Than One Degree of Freedom by Means of Space Trajectories, Y. H. Ku. *Ibid.*, vol. 259, no. 2, Feb. 1955, pp. 115–31.

3. Analysis of Nonlinear Coupled Circuits, Y. H. Ku. *AIEE Transactions*, vol. 73, pt. I, 1954 (Jan. 1955 section), pp. 626–31.

4. Part II. *Ibid.*, vol. 74, pt. I, Sept. 1955, pp. 439–43.

Herbert K. Weiss (Northrop Aircraft, Inc., Hawthorne, Calif.): This paper represents a definite contribution to the understanding of nonlinear systems. The brief section on co-ordinate transformations and the several examples are particularly helpful.

Since most interesting nonlinearities can be adequately represented by the saturation function shown in Fig. 3 of the paper, the methods developed appear to be of considerable generality. It is not clear, however, that examination of the latter phases of the transient motion only, as accomplished by use of the two dominant eigenvalues, will yield a sufficiently complete picture for all servo analyses. This is a question of the value function by which one defines the performance objectives to be sought in the servo design. One might imagine, for example, a servo subjected to continued and rapid disturbances, or one attempting to follow a signal in the presence of rapidly fluctuating noise. In these cases the long period response to a single step or ramp input might be of minor importance compared with the initial response gradient to signal change.

It is hoped that Mr. Kalman will find time to extend the methods of his present paper to the examination of all stages of servo response.

R. E. Kalman: I wish to thank the discussers for their serious interest in the paper. Indeed, most of the comments deal not with the specific results of the paper, but with the broader questions of motivation and general framework of analysis. These questions are of the greatest importance, especially in a new field such as nonlinear control system analysis, where a well-chosen initial approach is often the key to success. I would like to summarize in some detail the mathematical and intuitive background from which the paper arose. In so doing, I will express some perhaps intensely personal points of view, which can only be justified, strictly speaking, by their apparent success as far as the present paper is concerned.

In linear control system analysis, the task is clear: (*a*) Decide whether the system is stable, i.e., whether all the real parts of the roots of the eigenvalue equation are negative; (*b*) examine in more detail the response to some prototype input, such as a step, calculating initial rise time, settling time, etc.; (*c*) determine the response of the system to broad classes of signals to which the system will actually be called upon to respond and which are defined perhaps only in statistical terms. These questions are readily agreed upon and interest centers mainly on expedient mathematical methods to answer them.

With nonlinear systems, the situation becomes vastly more complicated. Paralleling the approach to the linear case, the difficulties may be outlined as follows:

1. To start, a way must be found of classifying nonlinear systems from the sta-

bility point of view. A linear time-invariant system is either stable or unstable, regardless of the input signals. In nonlinear systems, stability depends directly on the inputs (or initial conditions) and many phenomena occur: several different types of critical points, limit cycles (steady-state oscillations), regions of completely stable and completely unstable operation, regions in which the character of transient response depends strongly on the amplitude of the input signal, systems which appear docile when subjected to a certain class of signals (steps and ramps) but behave very queerly in response to another class of signals (sinusoids), etc. The list is probably incomplete and much more remains to be discovered.

Clearly then, nonlinear systems should be distinguished according to their peculiarities. If they have no peculiarities, they are not, basically, much different from linear systems and should be studied in much the same way as the latter. The situation is similar, though much more complicated, to that in function theory: Functions are classified according to their singularities; if a function has no singularities, it is very "uninteresting."[1]

To discover these peculiarities, it is essential to be able to visualize the qualitative features of the behavior of a nonlinear system over its entire operating range. The appropriate mathematical tool for this task is the phase-plane method. Dr. Loeb emphasizes, as was insisted on also in an earlier paper,[2] that the phase-plane method is primarily an analytical tool. This basic point has been much obscured in the past since the phase-plane idea is often used for constructing graphical methods of solution. If the phase plane is used for such purposes, it competes merely with the already highly developed techniques of machine computation without offering any significant advantages over the latter except for those who have no access to computers. Only rarely does a graphical method also give insight into a problem. These exceptions are, as far as I know, the Liénard[3] construction and a recent generalization of it by G. Cahen.[4] In these methods, the ideas underlying the graphical constructions also aid significantly in the analysis.

Concentrating on qualitative aspects of nonlinear systems is not only useful but absolutely essential. A well-known mathematical theorem[5] states that the characteristics of a nonlinear system are invariant under any bicontinuous sense-preserving transformation (O-homeomorphism). Intuitively, this means the following: If the trajectories of a system are drawn on a rubber sheet, any deformation (stretching) of the rubber will (nonlinearly) distort the trajectories, thereby leading to a superfically new system, which, however, differs in no essential way from the original one. Thus, for any given nonlinear system there are an infinite number of others which have basically the same properties but are described by different equations, contain different nonlinearities, etc. The theorem certainly agrees with common sense for it would hardly be expected that the dynamic behavior of a control system containing a saturating amplifier will be altered substantially by replacing the saturating amplifier with another one having a somewhat different saturation curve. For this reason, it is very naive to try to obtain quantitative analytic solutions for most nonlinear problems. The matter of a quantitative solution should and must be left up to a computer or to measurement on a model, and mathematical investigations should be directed toward obtaining general qualitative insight. As a result of these considerations, even crude approximations of nonlinear differential equations will be satisfactory, provided that the approximation retains all the qualitative characteristics of the original system. This idea may be called "approximation in the large."

Discussers have commented on the approximation by straight-line segments. This method stems from the arguments just mentioned, and has been considered in a broader setting in an earlier paper.[2]

Professor Klotter's comment that "increased accuracy entails highly increased labor" is of little significance. The purpose of the straight-line (in-the-large) approximation is to capture in as simple a manner as possible significant aspects of system behavior. Determining the minimum number of segments needed to do this will require further serious mathematical investigation; however, in simple cases, such as the saturation-type nonlinearity (Fig. 3 of the paper), it seems intuitively clear that three segments are adequate. This is not a question of accuracy in the ordinary sense since that problem, as pointed out, should be taken care of by means of a computer.

Professor Ku's remark about the continuity of the trajectories in 3-dimensional phase space should be kept in mind when applying the approximation by dominant terms since otherwise some apparent contradictions may be thought to occur. But in analytical work the precise shape of the trajectories matters little and consideration of the dominant terms in the manner and under the assumptions stated in the paper is quite adequate. For this reason, no check on the accuracy was made, with the exception of the indirect check on the derivation of the quasi-optimum reversal curve in example 3 in the paper, nor is such a check thought to be of particular significance. The conditions under which a dominant-term approximation may be logically used was discussed in some detail in connection with example 4. Again, the guiding principle of the approximation is to retain all essential qualitative features of the original system.

Dr. Loeb's observation that in different regions of the phase space different pairs of principal variables may arise and therefore different normal-co-ordinate transformations are needed, pinpoints a major difficulty, or rather inconvenience, of the analytical procedure as presented. In such a case, e.g., examples 4 and 5 of the paper, it is necessary to resort to much more computation and the interpretation of the approximations may become somewhat delicate. Further improvements can probably be expected as more experience is gained in applying the method to real problems.

Professor Klotter's opinion that "intrinsically, no extension of the phase-plane method to high-order nonlinear differential equations is involved" should not be accepted. The logical criterion by which such a question can be judged is whether the method is capable of explaining problems and phenomena which cannot be predicted or solved on the basis of second-order considerations. Examples 3 and 6 certainly represent inherently higher order systems whose behavior is correctly revealed by the method. The fact that the examples in the paper were all of the third order was intended merely to save algebraic labor.

3. Dr. Weiss brings out many basic and unfortunately unsolved problems. The idea of examining the "latter phases of transient motion," and particularly example 3, was motivated by trying to assess and improve the stability properties of systems subjected to very large signals. By analogy, this means considering the sluing mode of operation of a gun-director (moving from one target to the next), whereas Dr. Weiss's question refers to the tracking mode of operation. These are many practical cases when both modes of operation are equally important.

If the signals in the tracking mode are small, approximately linear operation may be assumed, since any continuous nonlinearity may be considered linear over a small range. This argument merely dodges the problem, although it sometimes closely approximates the practical situation. If the nonlinearity is discontinuous (such as an on-off device), or if the signal, perhaps aided by superposed random noise, makes excursions into the saturation region, the situation becomes very difficult to analyze. Principally, the trouble is that in dealing with a piecewise-linear (in-the-large) approximation of a nonlinear system, it is essential to know when the transient crosses the boundaries of the linear regions. This poses a major problem even when the input is analytically defined (say, a sinusoid). When the input is random the crossing can only be defined in a probabilistic sense, which greatly increases the difficulties. In fact, I am unaware of the existence of a single paper dealing with a probabilistic model of the phase plane.

Much of further success in the nonlinear field depends on vigorous interchange of knowledge about solved or analyzed problems. I would be grateful for any account of instances where the method was applied or where it led to difficulties.

REFERENCES

1. THE MATHEMATICS OF CIRCUIT ANALYSIS (book), **E. A. Guillemin.** John Wiley and Sons, Inc., New York, N. Y., 1949. p. 266.

2. Reference 13 of the paper.

3. ÉTUDE DES OSCILLATIONS ENTRETENUES, (STUDY OF SELF-EXCITED OSCILLATIONS), **A. Liénard.** *Revue Générale d'Électricité*, Paris, France, vol. 23, 1928, pp. 901–12, 946–54.

4. SYSTÉMES ÉLECTROMÉCANIQUES NON LINÉAIRES (NONLINEAR ELECTROMECHANICAL SYSTEMS), **A. Cahen.** *Ibid.*, vol. 62 1953, pp. 277–93.

5. GLOBAL STRUCTURE OF ORDINARY DIFFERENTIAL EQUATIONS IN THE PLANE. **L. Markus.** *Transactions*, American Mathematical Society, New York, N. Y., vol. 76, 1954, pp. 127–48.

Optimum Nonlinear Control

By RUFUS OLDENBURGER,[1] ROCKFORD, ILL.

This paper is concerned with the response of a controlled system after an initiating disturbance has died out. Such a transient is obtained, for example, when the load on a prime mover is suddenly rejected or the speed setting of an engine governor is instantly switched to a new value. It is assumed that the rate of change of the controlling variable with respect to time is bounded, and that the maximum rate of change can be obtained arbitrarily. Thus the speed of a hydraulic governor servo is limited. The best return to equilibrium (minimum over or underswing, minimum duration of the transient, and so on) can be obtained under rather general conditions by having the servo or its equivalent travel only at maximum or zero speed. Control functions exist which give the optimum transients. These functions are nonlinear. The results of theoretical studies to enable the control designer to obtain optimum or nearly optimum transients are given here along with practical compromises. All results have been verified in the laboratory with physical devices (governors) of various kinds and automatically controlled systems.

Introduction

A CONTROL system must be stable. It is natural that much concern in the past has been with the problem of stability. When a controller gives unstable performance the customer will simply not buy it. The use of derivative played an enormous role in the solution of the problem of stability. This problem is normally a linear one. Recently attention has been focusing on the problem of the quality of the control. Substantial improvement can be obtained in many areas by the use of nonlinear control.

To designate the class of controlled systems treated in this paper, the author will sometimes restrict himself to speed-governed prime movers. The results hold equally well for the control of temperature and other variables.

Consider a physical system with a single controlled variable. We consider the response of this system to a given disturbance, where after the disturbance dies out the system attains an equilibrium state S. We let m denote the deviation in the value of the controlled variable from its value in the state S. Similarly, let c be the deviation in the value of the controlling variable from the value it has for the state S. For the state S we then have $m = c = 0$. Let $P(D)$ and $Q(D)$ be polynomials in the derivative D with respect to time where the constant terms are different from zero. Let $e^{-\tau_d D}$ denote the dead-time operator, and let $g(c)$ be a monotonic nondecreasing function of c [this means that as c increases, the function $g(c)$ does not decrease]. By definition, given a function $c(t)$ of time t

$$e^{-\tau_d D}\, c(t) = c(t - \tau_d)$$

[1] Director of Research, Woodward Governor Company. Mem. ASME.

Contributed by the Instruments and Regulators Division of The American Society of Mechanical Engineers and presented at the ASME-AIEE Conference on Nonlinear Control Systems, Princeton, N. J., March 26–28, 1956.

Note: Statements and opinions advanced in papers are to be understood as individual expressions of their authors and not those of the Society. Manuscript received at ASME Headquarters, January 12, 1956. Paper No. 56—IRD-13.

Let $f(m)$ be a monotonic nondecreasing function of m, and let the prime on m' denote the derivative dm/dt of m with respect to t. For systems in a single controlled variable the nonlinear theory developed by the author is devoted to those with the differential equation

$$m' + f(m) = \frac{P(D)e^{-\tau_d D}}{Q(D)}\, g(c) - L \qquad \text{[I]}$$

where L is a given (forcing) function of time. The polynomial $P(D)$ corresponds to leads and the polynomial $Q(D)$ to lags. Equation [I] may be considered to be a torque equation where m', $f(m)$, $[P(D)e^{-\tau_d D}/Q(D)]g(c)$, and L correspond to the inertial, damping, driving, and load torques, respectively, m being the revolutions per minute (rpm) of the prime mover and c the servo (throttle or equivalent) position. The coefficients in $Q(D)$ are assumed to be positive, since otherwise Equation [I] represents an unstable system. All of the applications encountered by the author in the speed-governor field are covered, at least to a first approximation, by Equation [I]. In most of the theory relating to Equation [I] the polynomial $P(D)$ is assumed to be a nonzero constant.

We suppose that the controlled system is at a given instant in a nonequilibrium state, and that the system thereafter reaches equilibrium while L is constant. It is assumed that c' is bounded. In the hydraulic speed-governor field this means the servo speed is bounded, which is always the case. It is also assumed that c' can arbitrarily be made to attain its maximum or minimum value, which is true for practical purposes in the case of hydraulic servos. Under rather general conditions the best transients in every sense (minimum over or underswing, minimum duration, etc.), i.e., *optimum control*, can be obtained by having c' take on only its maximum and minimum values and zero. In the case of speed governors this means that the servo should be permitted to travel at full speed or zero only.

Optimum control for systems with Equation [I] is not attained by having the servo travel at full or zero speed in the case where $P(D)$ is different from a constant. However, if the linear term in $P(D)$ is missing, satisfactory, or nearly optimum transients, may often be attained by having the servo travel at full or zero speed. When water hammer is accurately taken into account in the control of hydroturbines the polynomial $P(D)$ contains a linear term. Optimum transients are also not attained for a class of initial conditions unlikely to occur in practice, where lags are involved and m is approaching its equilibrium value at a numerically large rate m'.

Control functions depending on m and on the results of mathematical operations performed on m can be employed to yield optimum transients. These control functions are nonlinear, and are used to determine the values assigned to c' during a transient. Whether or not nonlinear control will be employed in specific cases depends on performance, engineering, and economic considerations.

In July, 1944, the author wished to determine how far the Woodward governors in use on the Hamilton Standard airplane propellers deviated from ideal ones. He immediately found that the best transients could be obtained by making the servo travel at full speed at all times. That is, for a sudden throttle burst or other instantaneous disturbance the servo should travel at full speed in one direction, then change at the correct instant to full speed in the other direction, and so on. The author obtained the ideal transients and established that the performance of the governors then in use was not too far from ideal, and that they were operating very satisfactorily.

Later the author developed the general theory of control where during transients the servo travels at full speed a maximum amount of time, the direction of motion being controlled by functions chosen to give optimum performance. The theory was checked in the laboratory in all of its details by the construction of controllers operating according to the desired functions.

We shall introduce the term *absquare* of a number x to mean the quantity $|x|x$. Here $|x|$ designates the absolute value of x. We denote the absquare of x by $\{x\}$. Thus the absquare of x is the signed square of x; i.e., $\{x\} = x^2$ when x is positive, and $-x^2$ when x is negative. For the simplest case of a controlled system, with no lags, the control function for optimum performance involves the absquare of the derivative m' of the deviation m of the controlled quantity. When the controlled quantity is prime-mover rpm, the quantity m' is prime-mover acceleration. A portion of a transient during which c' is constant, is termed a *phase*. For every system covered by Equation [I] with $P(D)$ equal to a constant, no dead time ($\tau_d = 0$), and $f(m)$ neglected [neglecting $f(m)$ is justified as theory shows], the absquare also occurs in the control function whose vanishing determines that c' should change sign at the start of the last phase before m reaches equilibrium (see Appendix 2). The same is true when the dead time is included and large load rejections are treated (Appendix 1). Because of these and other considerations it appears to the author that the absquare of the derivative m' may be the next element to be often, if not generally, added to control functions.

In so far as we know the first automatic control was the Watt governor. This control was proportional, then integral and derivative were added to controllers, and it now appears that the absquare may be employed. Finding that $f(m)$ could be neglected was quite important, since neglecting $f(m)$ made an enormous simplification in the theory.

In 1950 Donald McDonald (1)[2] published the control function which yields optimum transients in the simplest case of a system with no lags or leads. In this paper he used a heuristic phase-plane argument. In 1952 he published another paper (2) on the subject. This was a phase-plane study of torque saturation. In 1951 there appeared a paper by A. M. Hopkin (3) on the results of an empirical phase-plane analysis of a servo with limiting or saturation. A computer study of the subject was made by Richard C. Lathrop as part of his PhD thesis (4) the same year. At the Cranfield Conference in England in 1951, A. M. Uttley and P. H. Hammond (5) treated the switching of an on-off servo, employing the absquare. In a PhD thesis in 1953 Donald Wayne Bushaw (6) made a topological study of transients for the case of torque saturation controlled by switching functions, in particular, linear ones. Lawrence M. Silva studied switching functions to enable the servo to travel at full speed, and used an energy approach to find these functions (7 to 9). Irving Bogner and Louis F. Kazda (10) investigated the switching criteria for higher-order servomechanisms using the phase-plane approach, and showed that in general the number of switchings for optimum transients increases by one as the order of the controlled system goes up by one. Further work on higher-order servomechanisms was done by S. S. L. Chang (12) and R. E. Kalman (13). Servomechanisms with friction were treated by Louis F. Kazda (14) and T. M. Stout (15).

All of these contributions touch on the nonlinear theory developed by the author which for proprietary reasons has been kept confidential. The mathematics of this theory is far beyond the limits of this paper. However, for the benefit of the reader, the complete fundamental theory is given for the case of the simplest controlled system. It is proved that a best transient exists for any set of initial conditions, and that a control function Σ exists, such that m is brought to equilibrium along the best transient by having c' take on its minimum value when Σ is negative, its maximum when Σ is positive, and zero when Σ is zero. It is hoped that this treatment will give the reader confidence in the approach, and indicate the questions that must be answered to establish the theory for more complicated systems. Without a rigorous theory one cannot be sure that one has the right control functions and that a competitor will not do better. For more complicated systems the mathematical results are given without proof. The author feels that from these considerations the reader can obtain a fairly complete picture of why and where the nonlinear approach improves the quality of the control, and where the use of nonlinear terms is justified. Linear approximations are often satisfactory. The reader also should learn what compromises of the theory should be made in practice to preserve performance but reduce costs.

Controls in present use involve nonlinearities. Thus in many controllers c' takes on its maximum or minimum value when one is outside of a "control band" based on the value of m. Instead of these "unintentional" nonlinearities the correct ones for desired optimum performance should be built into the control.

It appears to the author that the development of new controls will proceed as follows: The correct control functions for optimum performance will be established by mathematical theory. The inherent complexity of this theory indicates that this will require the services of expert research mathematicians. After the correct control functions or reasonable compromises have been established the development engineer will incorporate them into practical devices.

Simple Control Problem

We shall first develop the theory for the simplest case and then proceed to more complicated problems. The simplest system is one where

$$m' = K_1 c \quad [1]$$

for the controlled quantity m, controlling variable c, and constant K_1. As noted, m' is the derivative given by

$$m' = \frac{dm}{dt} \quad [2]$$

In practice the rate of change c' of the controlling quantity is limited; i.e.

$$|c'| \leqq K_2 \quad [3]$$

for a constant K_2 and absolute value $|c'|$ of c'.

As an example we may have

m = engine rpm
c = throttle position

for a prime mover, where these quantities are deviations from equilibrium values. We use the term "throttle" in a general sense to denote rack position on a diesel engine, gate co-ordinate for a hydraulic turbine, fuel-valve position for a gas turbine, steam-valve position for a steam turbine, or throttle position for a gasoline engine. Equation [1] now says that the engine acceleration m' is proportional to throttle position (deviation from equilibrium). When the engine speed is subject to automatic control

[2] Numbers in parentheses refer to the Bibliography at the end of the paper.

the servo is connected to the throttle. It is therefore convenient to take

$$c = \text{servo position}$$

whence Equation [1] says that the engine acceleration is proportional to servo position.

Relation [3] says that the servo speed c' is bounded by K_2.

For example, in the case of the General Motors diesel GM71, driving a direct-connected alternator, with 1-in. servo movement from no-load to full-load, Equation [1] is (approximately)

$$m' = 600c \qquad [4]$$

Thus if the servo is at the no-load position $c = 0$ and if the servo is moved suddenly to the full-load position $c = 1$, the engine accelerates at 600 rpm/sec. A typical Relation [3] for this case is

$$|c'| \leqq 10 \qquad [5]$$

which means that the servo speed is limited to 10 ips; i.e., the servo will go from no-load to full-load in 1/10 sec when traveling at maximum speed.

The condition that the servo speed is bounded is always true in practice. The power a servo can consume is limited and hence the servo speed is bounded. Sometimes the servo speed is limited by other considerations, such as to prevent excessive water hammer in hydro-power installations. In the case of aircraft-propeller governors, if the propeller changes pitch at too fast a rate, the passengers and pilot experience excessive discomfort. In the case of hydraulic speed governors the servo normally can be operated at full speed at will during a transient. This is also true, at least approximately, for other types of controls.

The problem of optimum transients is: Given any initial condition

$$t = 0,\ m = m_0,\ m' = m_0' \qquad [6]$$

how must the servo c be moved so that equilibrium

$$m \equiv 0$$

will be reached in a minimum time with minimum overswing or underswing, and minimum area between the m-curve and the $m = 0$ axis? We shall show that for each set of initial conditions there is a unique transient with m-curve Γ such that *acceptable criteria of automatic control theory for optimum transients are satisfied simultaneously.*

Optimum Transients for Simple Systems

We shall prove later that for an optimum transient in the case of the System [1] and [3] the servo must travel at all times at full speed until equilibrium is attained. Hence for such a transient

$$c' = \pm K_2 \qquad [7]$$

It will be no restriction on the generality of the method to assume that

$$m_0 \geqq 0$$

whence at the start of the transient one is above or on the t-axis. Let us assume that the m-curve is concave up before equilibrium so that we come into equilibrium from above the t-axis as shown in Fig. 1. The curve Γ leading to equilibrium is thus concave up before equilibrium. Then

$$c' = K_2 \qquad [8]$$

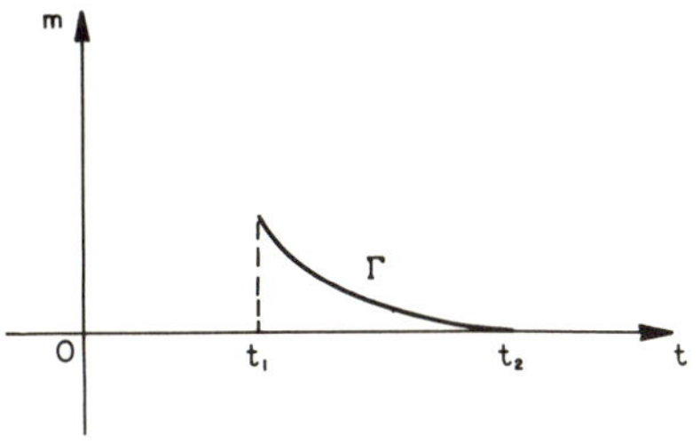

Fig. 1 Arc of Ideal Curve

and by Equation [1] the transient satisfies the equation

$$m'' = K_1K_2 \qquad [9]$$

The second derivative m'', i.e.

$$\frac{d^2m}{dt^2}$$

is the rate of change of acceleration m' with respect to time t.

To solve Equation [9] it will be convenient to make some transformations in the variables t, c, and m. Otherwise the formulas will be excessively complicated. We can write Relations [1] and [3] as

$$\left(\frac{m}{K_1K_2}\right)' = \left(\frac{c}{K_2}\right), \qquad \left|\left(\frac{c}{K_2}\right)'\right| \leqq 1 \qquad [10]$$

Introducing new variables M and C so that

$$M = \frac{m}{K_1K_2}, \quad C = \frac{c}{K_2} \qquad [11]$$

the Relations [10] become

$$M' = C, \qquad |C'| \leqq 1 \qquad [12]$$

which are easier to manipulate. We shall suppose that the curve Γ is concave down before the instant $t = t_1$ and that equilibrium is reached at the instant $t = t_2$. We introduce a new time scale T where

$$T = t - t_1$$

so that at the start of the arc of Fig. 1 we have $T = 0$. We note this does not change Relations [12] since

$$\frac{dM}{dt} = \frac{dM}{dT}, \quad \frac{dC}{dt} = \frac{dC}{dT} \qquad [13]$$

We shall therefore understand that the primes in Relations [12] denote derivatives with respect to T. Equation [9] now becomes

$$M'' = 1 \qquad [14]$$

Let M_1 and M_1' denote the values of M and M' at $T = 0$. By the theory of differential equations (11) the solution of Equation [14] is

$$M' = M_1' + T \qquad [15]$$

$$M = M_1 + M_1'T + \frac{T^2}{2} \qquad [16]$$

When M' reaches zero we want M to reach zero simultaneously;

i.e., the minimum point of the arc in Fig. 1 should be on the t-axis. The three possibilities of solutions that emanate from

$$T = 0, \qquad M = M_1 \ldots\ldots\ldots\ldots\ldots [17]$$

at the point P_1 are shown in Fig. 2.

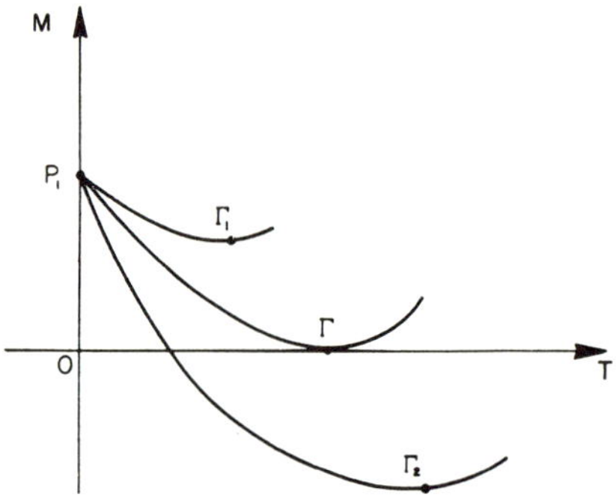

FIG. 2 ARCS FOR DIFFERENT INITIAL SLOPES

If we leave the point P_1 with too steep a slope, we obtain the curve Γ_2 (corresponding to the Equations [15] and [16]) which overshoots the T-axis giving an overswing accordingly. If the slope at P_1 is too little the corresponding curve Γ_1 undershoots the T-axis as shown. The slope M_1' must be chosen so that $M = 0$ at the same instant that $M' = 0$. By Equation [15] we have $M' = 0$ when

$$T = -M_1' \ldots\ldots\ldots\ldots\ldots [18]$$

Substituting T from Equation [18] in Equation [16] and imposing the condition that $M = 0$ when T satisfies Equation [18] we have

$$M_1 - \frac{(M_1')^2}{2} = 0 \ldots\ldots\ldots\ldots\ldots [19]$$

It follows that if M_1 and M_1' are not both zero and are related at any instant by the Equation [19] and if thereafter we keep

$$C' = 1 \ldots\ldots\ldots\ldots\ldots [20]$$

we shall reach $M = 0$ at the same instant that $M' = 0$. If after this instant we keep

$$C' \equiv 0 \ldots\ldots\ldots\ldots\ldots [21]$$

that is, we hold the servo still, the variable M will satisfy the relation

$$M'' \equiv 0 \ldots\ldots\ldots\ldots\ldots [22]$$

whence $M \equiv 0$

so that we remain at equilibrium until the system is disturbed.

If we come into equilibrium from below the T-axis and the servo is traveling in one direction at full speed from $T = 0$ to equilibrium, where equilibrium is reached for some positive value of T, we have

$$C' = -1 \ldots\ldots\ldots\ldots\ldots [23]$$

for this arc, see Fig. 3.

Replacing M_1 by $-M$ we obtain

$$M + \frac{(M')^2}{2} = 0 \ldots\ldots\ldots\ldots\ldots [24]$$

from the Condition [19].

Thus if $M' > 0$ we have Equation [24], and if $M' < 0$, Equation [19] with the subscripts on M_1 and M_1' omitted. These equations can therefore be combined into

$$M + \frac{1}{2}\{M'\} = 0 \ldots\ldots\ldots\ldots\ldots [25]$$

i.e.

$$M + \frac{1}{2}|M'|M' = 0$$

If at any instant M and M' satisfy Equation [25] the Relation [20] or [23] will lead to equilibrium, where Equation [20] is used if $M > 0$, and Equation [23] if $M < 0$.

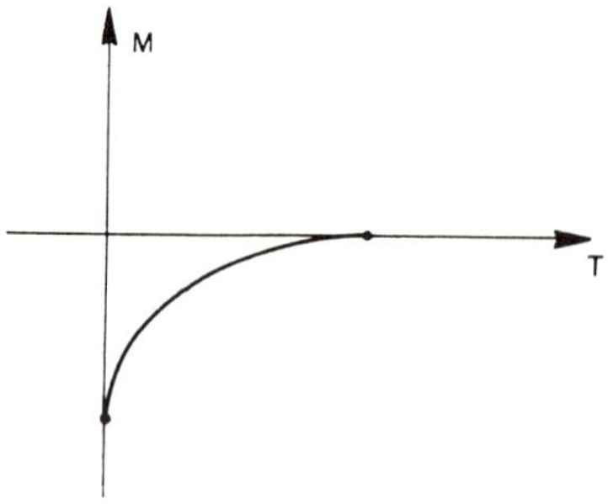

FIG. 3 CURVE CONCAVE DOWN

We introduce the notation Σ where

$$\Sigma = M + \frac{1}{2}\{M'\} \ldots\ldots\ldots\ldots\ldots [26]$$

The *derivative of the absquare* $\{x\}$ is $2|x|x'$. Differentiating Σ with respect to T we obtain

$$\Sigma' = M' \pm M'M'' = (1 \pm M'')M' \ldots\ldots [27]$$

where the $\pm$ sign is $+$ when $M' > 0$ and $-$ when $M' < 0$. For the arcs of Figs. 1 and 3 the sign of M'' is opposite the sign of M'. Thus for these arcs the $\pm$ sign in Equation [27] is opposite the sign of M''. But

$$M'' = \pm 1 \ldots\ldots\ldots\ldots\ldots [28]$$

Hence for the arcs of Figs. 1 and 3 we have

$$\Sigma' = 0 \ldots\ldots\ldots\ldots\ldots [29]$$

whence Σ is a constant. Since $\Sigma = 0$ when equilibrium is reached it follows that

$$\Sigma \equiv 0 \ldots\ldots\ldots\ldots\ldots [30]$$

for these arcs, whence Relation [25] holds everywhere along these arcs.

Suppose that we have a transient curve Γ as in Fig. 1, and that prior to $T = 0$ we have Equation [23] valid. The curve is then concave down before $T = 0$. Keeping Equation [23] valid we trace the curve Γ back to a point Q where $M = 0$ as shown in Fig. 4. There will always be such a point Q as the following argument shows. Since

$$M'' = -1 \ldots\ldots\ldots\ldots\ldots [31]$$

to the left of the M-axis, the slope of the curve Γ extended to the left increases by 1 for each unit of time T as we travel to the left.

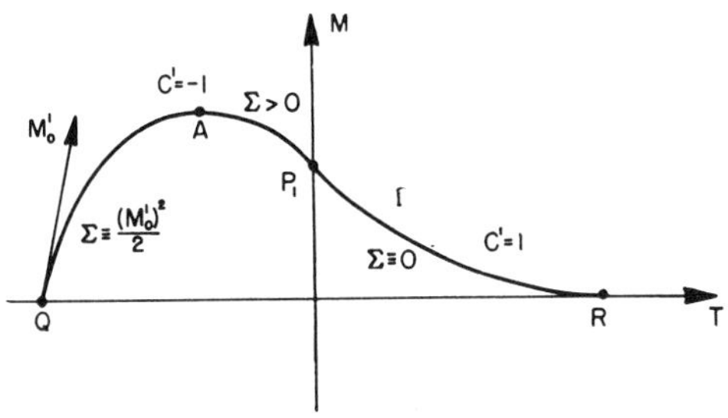

FIG. 4 IDEAL TRANSIENT ABOVE T-AXIS

The slope M' will thus never reach infinity, and eventually the extended curve Γ will cross the M-axis with a positive slope M_0'.

The high point on Γ extended is denoted by A. From Q to A we have $M' > 0$ whence

$$\Sigma' = (1 + M'')M' = 0 \ldots\ldots\ldots\ldots [32]$$

so that Σ is a constant. Since at Q we have

$$M = 0, \qquad M' = M_0' > 0 \ldots\ldots\ldots\ldots [33]$$

it follows that

$$\Sigma \equiv \frac{1}{2}(M_0')^2 > 0 \ldots\ldots\ldots\ldots [34]$$

from Q to A. From A to P_1 we have $M' < 0$ and $M'' = -1$ whence

$$\Sigma' = (1 - M'')M' = 2M' < 0 \ldots\ldots\ldots\ldots [35]$$

Thus Σ is decreasing from the value it has along the arc QA to the value zero, which it has along the arc P_1R.

The curve shown in Fig. 4 leads from the point Q to the equilibrium point R with one switching of the direction of motion of the servo. Suppose now that the system is disturbed so that at a given instant M and M' satisfy Relations [33] where M_0' is an arbitrary positive number. The curve of Fig. 4 (normally the switch point P_1 will not be on the M-axis) will automatically lead to equilibrium if we take

$$\left.\begin{array}{ll} C' = -1, & \Sigma > 0 \\ C' = +1, & \Sigma \equiv 0 \end{array}\right\} \ldots\ldots\ldots\ldots [36]$$

Suppose now that at a given instant T_a we have

$$M = M_a > 0, \qquad M' = M_a', \qquad \Sigma = \Sigma_a > 0 \ldots\ldots [37]$$

With $M'' = -1$ we can trace a curve to the left of $T = T_a$ of the form shown in Fig. 4, until we reach $M = 0$. Thus the element $(M, M') = (M_a, M_a')$ can be associated with a curve that starts at $M = 0$ as shown in Fig. 5. The slope M_a' at the point P_a can be either $+$, 0, or $-$ as long as Relations [37] are satisfied. It follows that we can go from P_a to an equilibrium point R by following a curve as shown in Fig. 4; i.e., by choosing the sign of C' according to Relations [36]. If at P_a the slope M_a' is such that $\Sigma = 0$, instead of > 0, we reach equilibrium along the curve for which $C' = 1$. We have thus taken care of all initial conditions where

$$M_a \geqq 0, \qquad \Sigma_a \geqq 0 \ldots\ldots\ldots\ldots [38]$$

If

$$M_a \leqq 0, \qquad \Sigma_a \leqq 0 \ldots\ldots\ldots\ldots [39]$$

we can take a curve, as shown in Fig. 6, through the point P_a that will lead to the equilibrium point R and when traced to the left originates at a point Q where

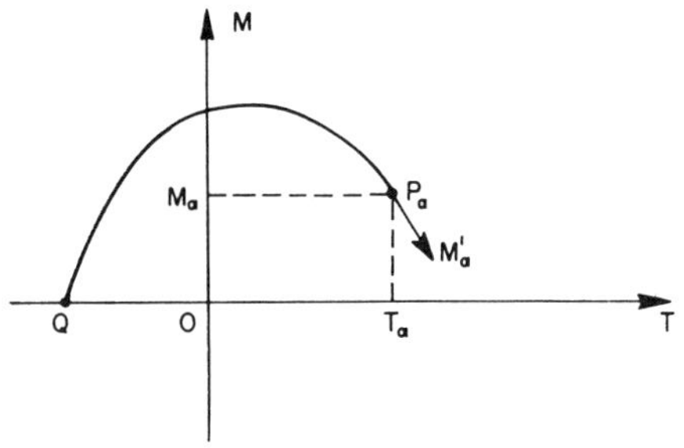

FIG. 5 CURVE TRACED FROM POINT P_a TO Q

$$M = 0, \qquad M' = M_0' < 0 \ldots\ldots\ldots\ldots [40]$$

Suppose now that at the point P_a of Fig. 7 we have

$$M_a > 0, \qquad \Sigma_a < 0 \ldots\ldots\ldots\ldots [41]$$

It follows that

$$M_a' < 0 \ldots\ldots\ldots\ldots [42]$$

From P_a we trace a curve Γ'' to the right for which $C' = 1$. In the Derivative [27] for Σ' we have the minus sign and $M'' = 1$, whence Equation [29] holds. Since M' increases by one unit for each unit increase in T, eventually we will reach a point S where $M' = 0$. But then $M < 0$ since along Γ''

$$\Sigma \equiv \Sigma_a < 0 \ldots\ldots\ldots\ldots [43]$$

It follows that $M = 0$ for some point Q between P_a and S. The

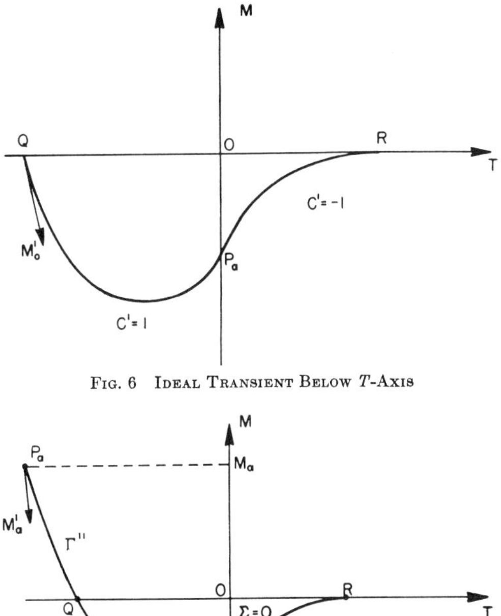

FIG. 6 IDEAL TRANSIENT BELOW T-AXIS

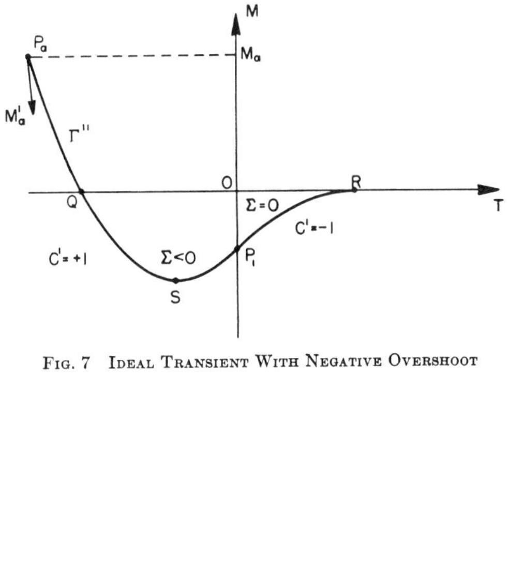

FIG. 7 IDEAL TRANSIENT WITH NEGATIVE OVERSHOOT

curve Γ'' is of the type Γ_2 of Fig. 2. We can now reach equilibrium as in Fig. 6. The entire transient is then as shown in Fig. 7, provided that the T-co-ordinate of the point P_a is chosen properly. For the curve of Fig. 7 $C' = 1$ from P_a to P_1 and $C' = -1$ from P_1 to R. For the arc P_aP_1 we have

$$C' = 1, \quad \Sigma < 0 \qquad [44]$$

and for P_1R

$$C' = -1, \quad \Sigma = 0 \qquad [45]$$

Similarly, if

$$M_a < 0, \quad \Sigma_a > 0 \qquad [46]$$

we have a curve as shown in Fig. 8, provided that the T-co-ordinate of the point P_a is chosen so that the switch point P_1 is on the M-axis.

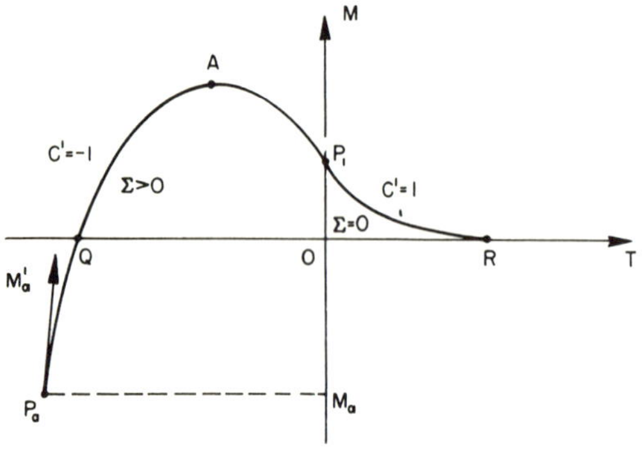

FIG. 8 IDEAL TRANSIENT WITH POSITIVE OVERSHOOT

We have now treated all initial conditions and shown that for all cases

$$C' = 1 \text{ when } \Sigma < 0 \qquad [47]$$

$$C' = -1 \text{ when } \Sigma > 0 \qquad [48]$$

whereas

$$C' = 1 \quad \text{when } \Sigma = 0 \text{ and } M > 0$$
$$C' = -1 \text{ when } \Sigma = 0 \text{ and } M < 0$$

and

$$C' = 0 \text{ when } \Sigma = M = 0$$

The ideal transients of Figs. 4 and 6 to 8 are determined entirely by the sign of Σ except when $\Sigma = 0$.

LOAD REJECTIONS AND SPEED-SETTING CHANGES

Transients of Figs. 4 and 6 starting at the point Q on the T-axis arise when instant load rejections and increases are made on engines. To take care of load we introduce a load term $-l$ into Equation [1] to obtain

$$m' = K_1c - l \qquad [49]$$

which can be written as

$$\left(\frac{m}{K_1K_2}\right)' = \left(\frac{c}{K_2}\right) - \left(\frac{l}{K_1K_2}\right) \qquad [50]$$

from which

$$M' = C - L \qquad [51]$$

when we make the substitution

$$l = K_1K_2L \qquad [52]$$

and the Transformations [11]. In equilibrium $M' = 0$ whence

$$C = L \qquad [53]$$

so that the servo takes a unique position corresponding to the load L. Dropping the load L is equivalent to replacing Equation [51] by

$$M' = C \qquad [54]$$

given in Relations [12]. Suppose that we are in equilibrium before load rejection so that

$$C = L$$

Dropping the load L instantly we have

$$M' = L \qquad [55]$$

from Relation [54] at the start of the transient. Hence at the initial point Q of the transient we have

$$M_0' = L \qquad [56]$$

Thus the curve of Fig. 4 is the response to an instant load rejection. Transients starting at a point off the T-axis may arise when one instant load rejection is followed by another before the response to the first rejection has died out.

Transients starting at a point off from the T-axis with $M' = 0$ arise when there is an instant speed-setting change. Such a transient is shown in Fig. 9 where the transient starts at $T = 0$, $M = -M_0$.

We shall prove in the next section that the curves of Figs. 4, and 6 to 9 are optimum curves.

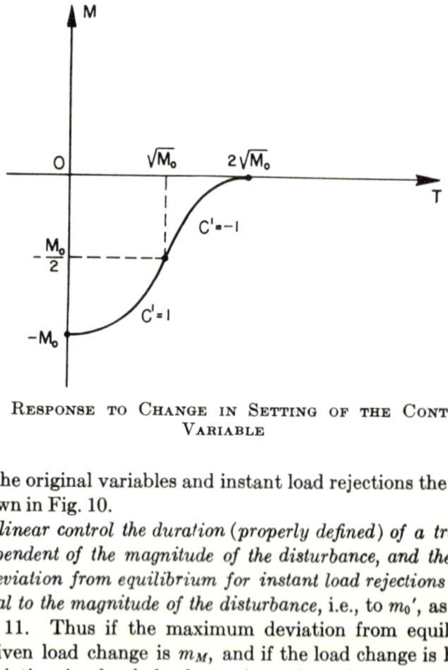

FIG. 9 RESPONSE TO CHANGE IN SETTING OF THE CONTROLLED VARIABLE

For the original variables and instant load rejections the results are shown in Fig. 10.

In a linear control the duration (properly defined) of a transient is independent of the magnitude of the disturbance, and the maximum deviation from equilibrium for instant load rejections is proportional to the magnitude of the disturbance, i.e., to m_0', as shown in Fig. 11. Thus if the maximum deviation from equilibrium for a given load change is m_M, and if the load change is halved, the deviation is also halved to $^1/_2 m_M$, but the maximum still occurs at the same instant t_M.

For the nonlinear control of Fig. 10 if we halve the magnitude of the load rejection, *the deviation m_M from equilibrium goes to* $^1/_4 m_M$, i.e., *as the square of the magnitude of the disturbance*, and

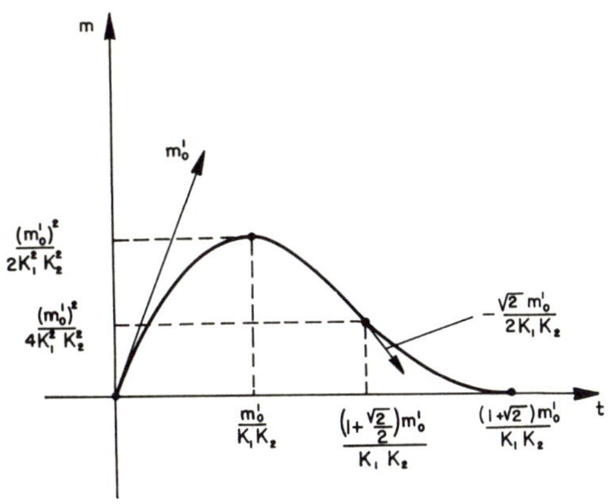

FIG. 10 IDEAL TRANSIENT

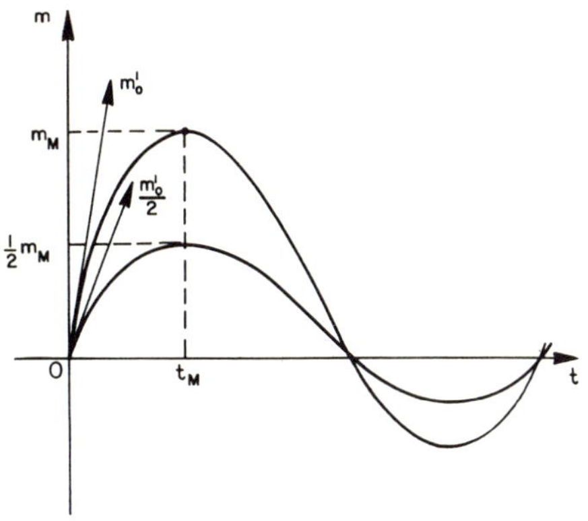

FIG. 11 TRANSIENTS FOR LINEAR CONTROL

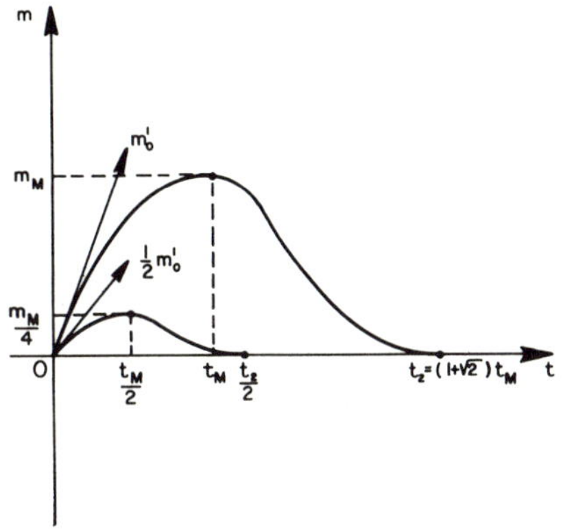

FIG. 12 TRANSIENTS FOR NONLINEAR CONTROL

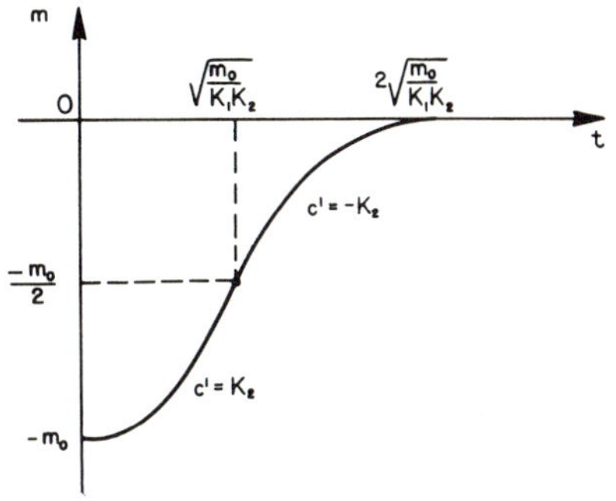

FIG. 13 OPTIMUM TRANSIENT FOR INSTANT CHANGE IN SETTING OF CONTROLLED VARIABLE

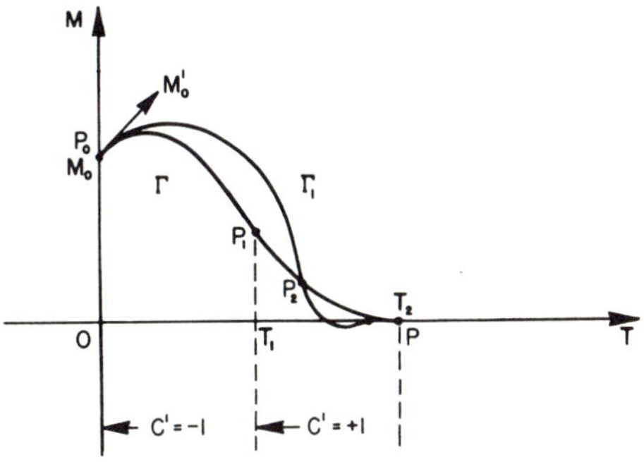

FIG. 14 TRAJECTORIES Γ AND Γ_1 THROUGH GIVEN ELEMENT (M_0, M_0')

the duration of the transient goes down by half, i.e., *in proportion to the magnitude of the disturbance*, as shown in Fig. 12.

For an instantaneous increase in the setting of the controlled variable the optimum curve is shown in Fig. 13.

WHY THE NONLINEAR TRANSIENTS ARE OPTIMUM

To prove that the "nonlinear" transients obtained in this paper are optimum, let us consider any state of the system, i.e., at any time which we may take to be $T = 0$, we have

$$M = M_0, \qquad M' = M_0' \qquad [57]$$

given. This means that the vector in Fig. 14 is given. In this figure we have drawn the "optimum" nonlinear transient Γ as derived in this paper. There is a unique such curve Γ leading to equilibrium at the point P. In Fig. 14 the curve is concave down first ($C' = -1$) up to the point P_1 with $T = T_1$, and then concave up ($C' = +1$). Consider a trajectory Γ_1 that leaves the point $(0, M_0)$ with the slope M_0' but reaches equilibrium before the point P. The curve Γ_1 must then cross or leave the curve Γ at some point P_2 before the time $T = T_2$ associated with P. This point P_2 is to the right of the point P_1 where the concavity of Γ changes. This must be so because the slope cannot change faster along a trajectory than along Γ between the initial point P_0 and the point P_1. If we start at the point P_2 and increase the slope at the maximum rate we cannot reach $M' = 0$ before $T = T_2$. The curve Γ_1 will be below Γ at $T = T_2$ as shown in Fig. 15.

Suppose that the curve Γ undershoots as shown in Fig. 16. Any trajectory leaving P_0 will be below or pass through the point P_1 at the instant $T = T_1$, where the concavity changes, since the slope along Γ is increasing at the maximum rate up to P_1. For a curve Γ_1 starting at the point P_0 with the slope M_0' to reach equilibrium before the instant $T = T_2$ the curve Γ_1 must cross or leave Γ between P_1 and the point P where $T = T_2$. This cannot be so in view of the argument relative to the case of Fig. 14.

The best transient in every case is thus one where equilibrium is reached in one phase with $C' = 1$ or $C' = -1$, or in two phases

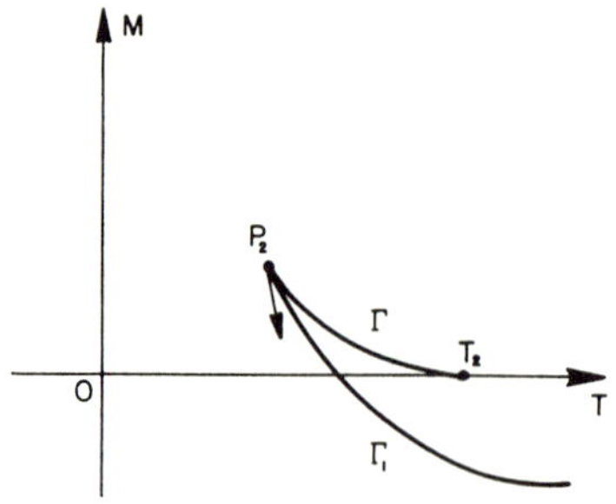

FIG. 15 ARC Γ_1 WITH UNDERSHOOT

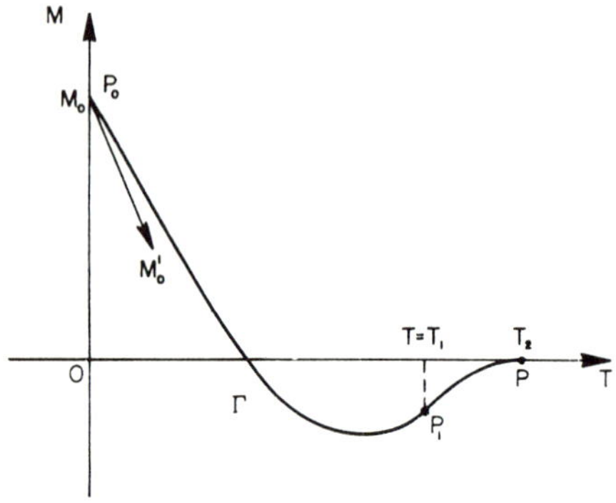

FIG. 16 CURVE Γ WITH UNDERSHOOT

with a phase $C' = 1$ followed by a phase for which $C' = -1$, or a phase with $C' = -1$ followed by a phase with $C' = +1$. Here, as in the introduction, phase refers to a portion of the transient for which C' is a constant (see Figs. 4, 6 to 10, and 13).

CONTROL FUNCTIONS

The problem is now to construct a control which senses M only, and quantities such as M' which depend on M and yields the optimum transients. To do this we consider Σ where

$$\Sigma = M + {}^1/_2 \{M'\} \qquad [58]$$

for the absquare $\{M'\}$ of M'.

Along the arc P_aA of Fig. 8 (from the initial point to the maximum) we have

$$\Sigma' \equiv 0 \qquad [59]$$

whence

$$\Sigma \equiv M_a + {}^1/_2 \{M_a'\} \qquad [60]$$

Along the arc AP_1 from the maximum point A to the point of inflection P_1 we have

$$\Sigma' = 2M' \qquad [61]$$

and from the point P_1 to the equilibrium point R we have

$$\Sigma' \equiv 0 \qquad [62]$$

whence

$$\Sigma \equiv 0 \qquad [63]$$

since at R we have

$$M = M' = 0 \qquad [64]$$

We now use the control

$$C' = -K\Sigma \qquad [65]$$

where K is "infinitely" large, i.e.

$$\left.\begin{aligned} C' &= -1 \text{ for } \Sigma > 0 \\ C' &= 0 \text{ for } \Sigma = 0 \\ C' &= +1 \text{ for } \Sigma < 0 \end{aligned}\right\} \qquad [66]$$

There is an apparent contradiction between the Schedule [66] and $C' = +1$ along the arc P_1R of Fig. 8. However, in practice this is not the case. Consider the inflection point P_1 where we set

$$C' = 0 \qquad [67]$$

in view of Schedule [66]. When Equation [67] holds we have

$$M'' = 0$$

whence M' is a constant. Since M is decreasing Σ will "immediately" become negative. Then by Schedule [66] we have $C' = +1$ and we follow the arc P_1R to equilibrium.

In any physical situation we would have at least

$$\Sigma = -\epsilon \qquad [68]$$

for a small positive number ϵ before we would switch from $C' = -1$ to $C' = +1$. Since Σ is a constant along an arc for which $C' = +1$ and $M' < 0$, when we reach $M' = 0$ we have

$$\Sigma = M = -\epsilon \qquad [69]$$

Thus the transient will undershoot as shown in Fig. 17 where we have taken the initial point at $T = 0$. The amount of undershoot will thus depend on the deadband in the device that controls the servo speed.

Unless a linear zone or equivalent is provided to stabilize the system an on-off servo will hunt forever after a sizable disturbance as can be readily verified by mathematical theory. In practical devices built by the author and his associates for the simple system under discussion, the schedule given by the Formulas [66] is used except that when M is small in absolute value the M-term in Σ is replaced for a constant a by aM and when $|M'|$ is small enough the absquare term is replaced by bM' for a constant b so that the function C' given by

$$C' = -K(aM + bM') \qquad [70]$$

yields good characteristic roots when combined with

$$M'' = C' \qquad [71]$$

For extremely good electronic components, and a system with no lag for practical purposes, one can use a value of K as high as 200, and still have stable transients for disturbances where $M = 0$, $M' = 1$. However, 200 is near the upper limit. See Fig. 18 for the case of optimum transients and instant load rejections obtained in the laboratory. Fig. 18 and Figs. 21 to 27 are photographs of Sanborn oscillograph traces. The RPM-curve of Fig. 18(a) shows the rpm response to instant 25 per cent load rejections and load increases, whereas the RPM-curve of Fig. 18(b) shows the corresponding results for the 50 per cent load case. Note that the RPM-overswing for 25 per cent load rejection is one fourth as much as for 50 per cent load rejection. Note also that there are no RPM-underswings for the load rejections, and that the transients for the 25 per cent load case are over in one half of the time required for the 50 per cent case. The servo

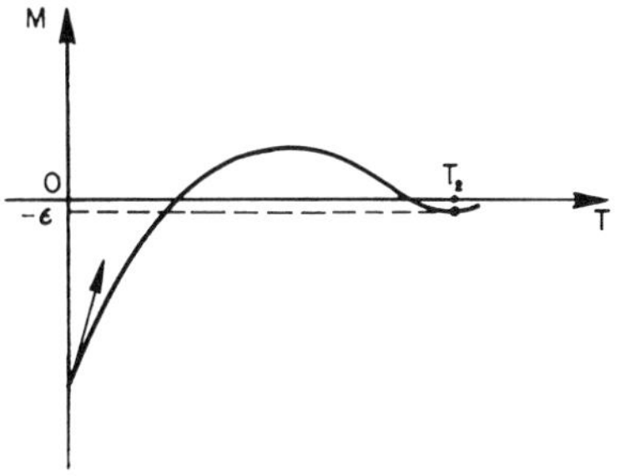

FIG. 17 PRACTICAL TRANSIENT

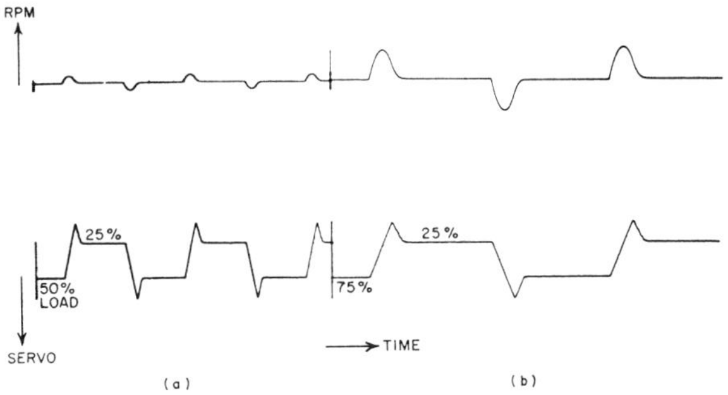

FIG. 18 PHOTOGRAPH OF OPTIMUM NONLINEAR TRANSIENTS IN AN ELECTRONIC CASE

trace of Fig. 18(*a*) is to a different vertical scale from this trace for Fig. 18(*b*). For Fig. 18(*a*) the servo goes from the 50 per cent load level to the 25 per cent load level, then back to the 50 per cent level, etc. The levels for Fig. 18(*b*) are for 75 and 25 per cent load.

The optimum physically realizable characteristic roots can be determined from theory and the limitations of the equipment. The change from M to aM in Σ can normally be made at M between 0.001 and 0.1, and similarly the change from $^1/_2\{M'\}$ to bM' can be made when M' is somewhere in the range from $M' = 0.01$ to $M' = 0.1$. The place where a change in a coefficient is made depends on the magnitude of the disturbances. For the case of Fig. 18 the lags in the system and control were very small so that without a linear control band with the Function [70] the hunt in M was 0.0025 per cent peak to peak. The range of load rejections was 0.625 to 50 per cent, i.e., a range of 80:1 so that the range in overspeeds was 6400:1, namely, from 0.0078 to 50 per cent.

Consider, for the moment, the case where ϵ is infinitely small (to be rigorous one should use a limit process here). Suppose that the system at any instant is in the state $M = M_0$, $M' = M_0'$, say, at $T = 0$. If $\Sigma > 0$, then by the Schedule [66] we have $C' = -1$. Along the trajectory thus obtained Σ will be constant if $M' \geqq 0$. Eventually, $M' < 0$, whence Σ will decrease to $\Sigma = 0$. By the schedule we then have $C' = 0$, and Σ becomes negative immediately, whence by the Schedule [66] we soon have $C' = +1$ and we are brought to equilibrium. At the instant when equilibrium is reached we set $C' = 0$, whence $\Sigma = 0$ thereafter, at least until the next disturbance; similarly, if $\Sigma < 0$ at $T = 0$.

If $\Sigma = 0$ at $T = 0$ and we are not at equilibrium, then

$$M_0' \neq 0 \qquad [72]$$

and with $C' = 0$ immediately Σ becomes + or —, and Schedule [66] will lead to equilibrium along an optimum transient.

Since all transients are optimum when the Schedule [66] is used, we obtain "optimum" transients for instant load rejections as well as for instant changes in the setting of the controlled variable by using this schedule.

EFFECT OF DAMPING IN SYSTEM

The same type of mathematical treatment as used in the simplest case holds for other cases. Because this theory is extremely complicated and beyond the limits of this paper the proofs will be omitted although the results will be summarized.[3]

Consider now the system with the equation

$$M' + \alpha M = C \qquad [73]$$

with $\alpha \geqq 0$ in place of the equation in Formulas [12]. The term αM in this equation is a damping term. We introduce the controlling function Σ where

$$\Sigma = M + \frac{M'}{\alpha} \pm \frac{\ln(1 + \alpha|M'|)}{\alpha^2} \qquad [74]$$

Here the $\pm$ sign is

$$\left.\begin{array}{l} \text{plus when } M' < 0 \\ \text{minus when } M' > 0 \\ \text{either when } M' = 0 \end{array}\right\} \qquad [75]$$

Expanding the ln-term of Equation [74] in powers of $\alpha|M'|$ we obtain

$$\Sigma = \Sigma_1 + \alpha\left(\frac{-\{M'\}|M'|}{3} + \frac{\alpha\{M'\}|M'|^2}{4} - \frac{\alpha^2\{M'\}|M'|^3}{5} \ldots\right) \ldots \qquad [76]$$

where

$$\Sigma_1 = M + {}^1/_2\{M'\} \qquad [77]$$

is the control function for the case with the damping term neglected. If $|M'|$ is small the function Σ can thus be replaced by Σ_1. In any case it is advisable to use the function Σ_1 of Formula [77] in place of the Σ of Formula [74] as if the damping term were missing. *Theory shows that the presence of the damping improves the transients and that the difference in neglecting and not neglecting the damping term is often not too great.* Similarly, if the damping term is $f(M')$ for a monotonic nondecreasing function of M' where

$$f(0) = 0$$

it is advisable to neglect the damping, since theory shows its presence to be beneficial.

Mathematical considerations show that the optimum transient for a load rejection is that given in Fig. 19. Along the arc AP_1 we have

$$\Sigma' = \frac{M'(2 - \alpha M')}{1 - \alpha M'} \qquad [78]$$

whence Σ is decreasing. At the point P_1 (not in general an inflection point) Σ becomes zero. Schedule [66] still applies, however, with the Σ of Formula [74].

[3] The proofs are on hand but have not been written up for publication.

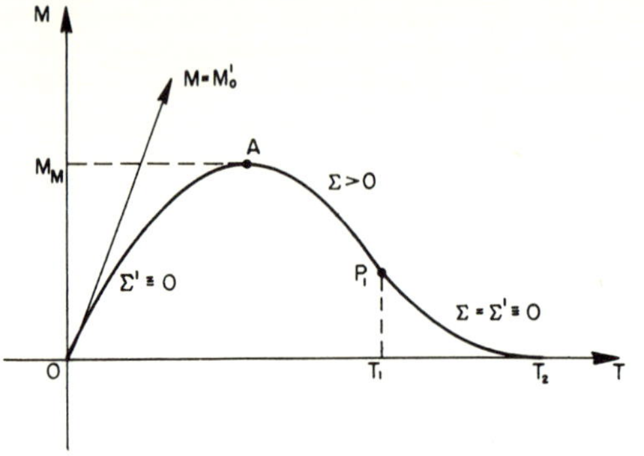

FIG. 19 OPTIMUM TRANSIENT FOR SYSTEM WITH DAMPING

The *maximum* value M_M of M is given by

$$M_M = \frac{M_0'}{\alpha} - \frac{\ln(1 + \alpha M_0')}{\alpha^2} \qquad [79]$$

From theory we can show that the transient is optimum in every sense and unique. The theory holds for transients that start at a point where $M_0 \neq 0$ as well as those where $M_0 = 0$.

SINGLE-LAG SYSTEMS

We now treat a physical system with a lag between servo and torque (in the prime-mover case). This lag is assumed in this section to be one associated with a pure time constant. The equation of the controlled system is now

$$\tau M'' + M' = C \qquad [80]$$

instead of the first equation in Formulas [12]. Here τ is the time constant.

In the simplest prime-mover case the ideal transients are composed of one or two phases. This is no longer true for systems with lags. We introduce the function Σ given by

$$\Sigma = \psi + \frac{\{\psi'\}}{2}$$

$$-(\operatorname{sgn}\psi')\tau^2 \ln^2\left\{1 + \sqrt{1 - (1 + [\operatorname{sgn}\psi']M'')e^{-|\psi'|/\tau}}\right\} \qquad [81]$$

where

$$\psi = M + \tau M' \qquad [82]$$

and

$$\left.\begin{aligned} \operatorname{sgn}\psi' &= +1 \text{ if } \psi' > 0 \\ &= 0 \text{ if } \psi' = 0 \\ &= -1 \text{ if } \psi' < 0 \end{aligned}\right\} \qquad [83]$$

The controlling function Σ for ideal transients involves two functions Σ_1 and Σ_2 where

$$\Sigma_2 = \psi + \frac{\{\psi'\}}{2} \qquad [84]$$

and Σ_1 is the entire expression Σ given in Formula [81]. When Σ_1 becomes imaginary, we take the control function Σ equal to Σ_2. For an instant load rejection the two control functions are needed to bring one to equilibrium along the optimum curve. Here optimum is used in the same sense as before. The ideal transient for instant load rejection is shown in Fig. 20 for the one lag case.

Along the first phase OQ_1 of Fig. 20 we are controlling on the basis of Schedule [66] where

$$\Sigma = \Sigma_1 \qquad [85]$$

Along this arc $\Sigma_1 > 0$ and $C' = -1$. At the point Q_1 the function Σ_1 becomes zero. At a point E after Q, we have $\psi' = 0$. Along the arc Q_1E

$$\Sigma_1 \equiv 0 \qquad [86]$$

and $C' = +1$. Schedule [66] gives $C' = 0$ for this arc. However, after the point Q_1 the function Σ_1 will then become negative

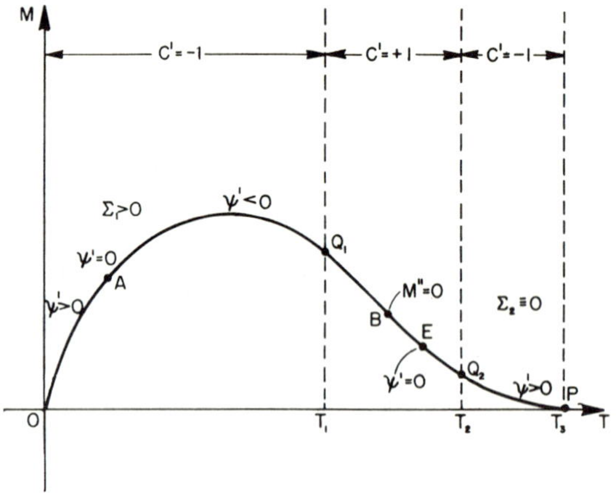

FIG. 20 IDEAL TRANSIENT FOR ONE-LAG CASE

immediately whence by Schedule [66] we have $C' = +1$. At the point E the function Σ_1 becomes imaginary. From the point E to Q_2 the function Σ_2 is negative and increasing. At the point Q_2 the function Σ_2 becomes zero. From E on we control on the basis of the function Σ_2. Schedule [66] with $\Sigma = \Sigma_2$ gives $C' = 0$ for the arc Q_2P. However, again with $C' = 0$ the function Σ will become positive immediately, whence by Schedule [66] we have $C' = -1$. We will now be brought to equilibrium (at least for practical purposes).

At the start we have $\psi' > 0$. This derivative decreases to zero at a point A. From the point A to the point E between Q_1 and Q_2 the quantity $\psi' < 0$. Between the points Q_1 and E there is the inflection point B, for which $M'' = 0$ occurs.

From the point E to the equilibrium point P the quantity ψ' is positive, increasing from the point E to the point Q_2 and decreasing from there to zero at the point P.

Equilibrium can be reached after any disturbance on the basis of Schedule [66] where control is based on the sign of Σ_1 or Σ_2 and during a transient the control function alternates (in the proper manner) between Σ_1 and Σ_2. Equilibrium can be reached on the basis of Schedule [66] in four or less phases. For "most" disturbances three phases suffice. *There are initial conditions for which the optimum transient is not one where the servo travels at full speed.* These would, however, be considered exceptional. Such cases arise when the M-curve is plunging toward the T-axis with a steep slope and reaching equilibrium with maximum servo speed would require the phases $C' = +1, -1, +1, -1$ in this order, or the phases $C' = -1, +1, -1, +1$ putting a hump in the M-curve that could otherwise be avoided.[4]

[4] The complete mathematical theory underlying the foregoing statements for the single-lag case of Formula [80] is quite complicated. It is in the files of the author, but has not been written up for publication.

Higher Lag Cases and Practical Compromises

It can be proved by mathematical considerations that for disturbances of a magnitude normally encountered the log term in Formula [81] is small compared to the rest of Σ, and can therefore be dropped. The controlling function is thus

$$\Sigma = \Sigma_2 \ldots\ldots [87]$$

For a controlled system given by

$$\tau m'' + m' = K_1 c \ldots\ldots [88]$$

and servo speed limitation

$$|c'| \leq K_2 \ldots\ldots [3]$$

the formula for nonlinear control on the basis of Σ_2 becomes

$$c' = -K\left[(m + \tau m') + \frac{\{m' + \tau m''\}}{2K_1K_2}\right] \ldots\ldots [89]$$

where K is as large as possible.

For a two-lag case we have the equation

$$\tau_1\tau_2 M''' + (\tau_1 + \tau_2)M'' + M' = C \ldots\ldots [90]$$

with time constants τ_1 and τ_2. Equation [90] can be written as

$$M' = \frac{C}{(\tau_1 D + 1)(\tau_2 D + 1)} \ldots\ldots [91]$$

where D stands for the derivative with respect to time T. The three controlling functions for this case are quite complicated and will be omitted, except for the analog of Σ_2 in Formula [84]. We let ψ be given by

$$\psi = M + (\tau_1 + \tau_2)M' + \tau_1\tau_2 M'' \ldots\ldots [92]$$

For the last phase of a transient corresponding to a load rejection the quantity $\Sigma_2 \equiv 0$, where Σ_2 is as given in Equation [84], but with ψ as in Formula [92].

More generally, if the equation of the controlled system is given by

$$O(D)M' = C \ldots\ldots [93]$$

for an operator

$$O(D) = (\tau_1 D + 1)(\tau_2 D + 1) \ldots (\tau_n D + 1) \ldots\ldots [94]$$

in the derivative D, for each transient the function Σ_2 vanishes for the last phase, where Σ_2 is given as in Equation [84] and

$$\psi = O(D)M \ldots\ldots [95]$$

Control on the basis of Σ_2 often gives a good approximation to the optimum transients. We can write Equation [93] as

$$\psi' = C \ldots\ldots [96]$$

Control on the basis of Σ_2 and this ψ' *is control on the basis of an auxiliary variable;* namely ψ, instead of M. We make ψ come to equilibrium in an optimum manner. The ψ-system [96] is a no-lag system. When equilibrium is reached with $\psi \equiv 0$, the variable M comes to its equilibrium $M \equiv 0$ according to the differential equation

$$O(D)M = 0 \ldots\ldots [97]$$

For the one-lag case of Equation [80] the variable M comes to equilibrium exponentially according to the law

$$M = M_3 e^{-T/\tau}$$

where M_3 is the value of M at the instant ψ reaches equilibrium.

If in Formula [92] the time constant τ_2 is small compared to τ_1 the Formula [92] can be replaced by the single-lag Formula [82] with $\tau = \tau_1$, or better, with $\tau = \tau_1 + \tau_2$. This is not the case if $\tau_1 = \tau_2$ (see Fig. 22).

If a dead time τ_d is introduced into Equation [93] so that this becomes

$$O(D)e^{-\tau_d D}M' = C \ldots\ldots [98]$$

the dead time may be treated as a time constant unless it is large or dominates the other lags in the system (see Appendix 1 for some results on systems with dead time).

The foregoing theory applies if $O(D)$ has quadratic factors that do not factor further (in the field of real numbers), corresponding to second-order lags. Actually, $O(D)$ in Formula [95] may be any polynomial with positive coefficients.

If a damping term $f(M)$ is included on the left of Equation [93] this term can be dropped as in a previous section on systems with damping, since it improves the transients obtained on the basis of design without it. It is assumed, as in the introduction, that $f(M)$ is a monotonic nondecreasing function of M. Discussion of coulomb damping will be omitted here for the sake of brevity.

If now we have the equation

$$O_1(D)M = O_2(D)C \ldots\ldots [99]$$

for the controlled system, where $O_1(D)$ and $O_2(D)$ are polynomials in D with the linear term missing in $O_2(D)$, all of the terms on the right of Equation [99] may often be dropped except the C-term and an equation of Type [93] used instead, at least when applying the nonlinear approach of this paper to obtain good, though not necessarily, optimum transients.

We remark that in the special case

$$M' = C' + C$$

it is impossible for M' and C to approach zero (equilibrium values) simultaneously while $C' = \pm 1$. It follows that the optimum transients in this case are not obtained by having the M-curve approach the T-axis with maximum $|C'|$.

Because of space considerations the treatment of the case where a term in the integral of M occurs on the left in Equation [99] will be omitted.

Where large lags are involved theory and experiments show that nonlinear control can be used to reduce servo jiggle that arises with linear control and give faster return to equilibrium.

Linear Band

With the control Formula [65] for Σ involving the absquare the system may be unstable. As M, M', etc., become numerically small in Σ their coefficients may be increased or decreased so that when $|M|$ and its derivatives are small, and one is thus near equilibrium, the control formula becomes

$$C' = -K\Sigma_L \ldots\ldots [100]$$

for a sum such as

$$\Sigma_L = aM + bM' + eM'' \ldots\ldots [101]$$

where a, b, and e are constants chosen so as to give good stability.

Practical Compromise

A promising approach for nonlinear control as discussed here is that where a system is treated as a one-lag system and the second derivative is dropped from Formula [89] in the interest of simplification. The control formula is now

$$c' = -K\left[m + \tau m' + \frac{\{m'\}}{2K_1K_2}\right] \ldots\ldots [102]$$

where we use actual variables, rather than per unit quantities, the equation of the controlled system is given by Formula [88], and the servo limitation is given by the Relation [3]. To compensate for dropping the m''-term it is necessary to increase the coefficient of the absquare term so that Formula [102] is replaced by

$$c' = -K[m + (\tau + \beta|m'|)m'] \qquad [103]$$

for a constant β. The coefficient of m' is now a variable, which tends to give a more highly damped response for large values of $|m'|$ than small ones. In practice the value of β is adjusted so that $\beta|m'|_{max}$ dominates τ for the maximum absolute value $|m'|$ of the derivative m' to be encountered in practice. Theory and experiments show that it is desirable to have $\beta|m'|_{max}$ equal to about 10τ or 25τ. The maximum value $|m'|_{max}$ depends on the magnitude of the disturbances encountered by the controlled system. An experimental transient for a case where Formula [103] is used is shown in Fig. 21. The top and bottom curves

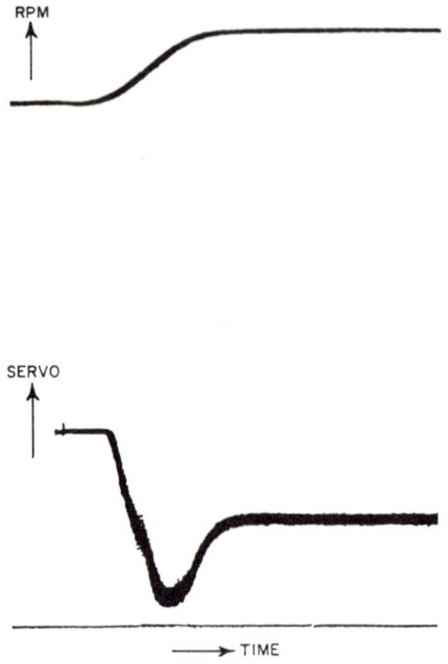

FIG. 21 EXPERIMENTAL NONLINEAR TRANSIENT FOR A CHANGE IN THE SETTING OF THE CONTROLLED VARIABLE

are for engine speed and servo position with respect to time. This figure shows the response to a change in the setting of the controlled variable.

If in Formula [103] we replace $|m'|$ by the "average" value it has for the larger disturbances we obtain a linear control that is at least a rough approximation to the nonlinear.

In practice it is convenient to choose K and τ so that the characteristic roots are optimum when the absquare term is dropped from Formula [103] and then to adjust β so that it is as large as possible without causing hunting of the controlled system after the worst disturbance is made to which the system is to be subjected. The use of absquaring as in Formula [103] allows one to have very poor characteristic roots when the derivative $|m'|$ is large, corresponding to fast movements of the servo, and ideal roots when near equilibrium, yielding optimum stability for small disturbances.

To allow for excessive disturbances it is desirable to bound the value of $|m'|$ or the term $|m'|m'$ in Formula [103].

DISCONTINUITIES

In the theory developed so far no allowance has been made for the fact that the servo stroke is limited. If the maximum servo speed is such that the servo goes through its stroke in a small fraction of the time required for the larger transients, so that application of the nonlinear theory gives essentially two-position control, the nonlinear theory developed here breaks down. Fortunately, this is not the case in many, if not most, applications. If the servo is not at the ends of its stroke during a major part of the transient, the nonlinear performance will normally not deviate too much from theory. If the servo speed is not the same for the two directions of travel of the servo, but is not too different for the two directions (theory and experiment indicate that a 2:1 variation is acceptable), the transients for nonlinear performance on the basis of this paper are still near optimum. The author's theory for the two-speed case will be omitted for the sake of brevity.

Tests of variations of all of the constants show that the nonlinear control treated here is not critical. Variations of 2:1 to 4:1 in the coefficients of Σ and the second power used in the absquare can be tolerated.

AREA OF USEFULNESS

If the lags in a system to be controlled are small, the range of disturbances is large, and the discontinuities are not severe, substantial improvement (by an order of magnitude) over existing control can be obtained for a range of disturbances with the nonlinear control described here. Experiments indicate that definite improvement can also often, if not generally, be obtained when the first two conditions are not satisfied.

A fundamental limitation, from the theoretical point of view, on the use of nonlinear control is that of noise. By "noise" we mean the unwanted part of the signal input to the controller. This signal contains the measurement of the controlled quantity, which is wanted, as well as another portion, which is not wanted. In the absquare $\{m'\}$ of m' the noise is worse than it is in m', and, in fact, may be almost as bad as in m''. On account of noise the gain constant K in Formula [65] is limited, if it is not limited for other reasons. It follows that for the nonlinear control to be effective the quantities m' (or ψ') must be large enough for the bigger disturbances to dominate the noise. *If a system is subject only to very small disturbances* such as those which cause M' to be 0.01 per cent maximum, *the noise may prevent the use of nonlinear control* involving the absquare.

If the noise is too great the servo jiggle will be excessive.

If a system has very large lags relative to the servo-stroke time, such as a ten-second time constant for a three-second servo, a term in M'' can be added to the ψ-term in Formula [84], and the coefficients in ψ can be changed to compensate for dropping the ψ'-term in Formula [84], so that the use of a linear Σ with second derivative is a satisfactory approximation to the performance that can be obtained by the nonlinear Σ of Formula [84], and the employment of a nonlinear Σ with the second derivative term in the absquare is not economically justifiable. However, Formula [103] still applies if the second derivative is not used.

For n sufficiently large, such as $n = 10$ or 100, a dead time τ_d may, for practical purposes, be replaced by n first-order lags in cascade with identical time constants equal to τ_d/n. The corresponding nonlinear theory requires the use of derivatives up to a high order, such as the 11th or more, which noise makes impossible. This difficulty is avoided in the precise dead-time theory of Appendix 1.

With a linear control function the initial overswing (or underswing) for a given instantaneous disturbance can be made the same as would be obtained for the optimum nonlinear control with the same servo, and bounded servo speed. However, nonlinear control with the absquare can be employed to improve the response to maximum disturbances by eliminating or reducing undesired oscillations (after the first swing), and to reduce overswings and underswings in the responses to lesser disturbances. For small disturbances a practical control is normally purely linear. Thus in the case of prime movers the overswing for an instantaneous 100 per cent load rejection may be adjusted to be the same for linear and nonlinear control, whereas for instant load rejections of less than 100 per cent the overswings are reduced. However, the linear control that gives the same overswing as for a satisfactory nonlinear control may be too oscillatory, so that even for 100 per cent load rejections the nonlinear control is to be preferred. *Essentially, by nonlinear control more efficient use is made of the servo.*

Co-operation of the prime-mover manufacturer in reducing lags in the system to be controlled can often result in substantial improvement in the control by permitting the use of a nonlinear governor nearer to that indicated by the theory for the no-lag case. Thus in one application the time constant of a servo (supplied by the governor user) due to trapped air was $1/3$ sec, when it should have been about $1/100$ sec. The result was a different order of magnitude in the speed deviation for the maximum disturbance to be encountered.

Response to Sinusoidal and Other Disturbances

Consider the equation

$$M' = C - \sin \omega T$$

Optimum performance is obtained by letting

$$C = \sin \omega T$$

This condition can be achieved by linear control only for discrete values of ω, and in no case by the nonlinear control of this paper. Frequency-response runs on systems based on optimum nonlinear control and on the best linear control show about the same results except that at large amplitudes of the forcing sine wave the nonlinear control yields a lower resonant frequency where the system response has a peak.

For linear throttle bursts (constant velocity) of 250 to 1000 rpm in $1/2$ to 3 sec on a simulated 3000-rpm airplane engine, connected to a simulated propeller the overspeeds for nonlinear control based on Formula [103] were about half of the overspeeds obtainable by linear control. In this example the servo lag was taken to be 0.02 sec (time constant).

Space does not permit the inclusion of the author's theory for throttle bursts and other kinds of disturbances.

Physical Nonlinear Equipment

Methods of producing the mathematical operations needed to yield the nonlinear control functions of this paper are well known. Thus the use of d-c circuits for differentiating electrically and dashpots for doing this mechanically is classical.

The use of absquaring physical components is also classical. Nonlinear resistors exist for which the current is proportional to the absquare of the voltage. The pressure drop across a sharp-edged orifice is proportional to the absquare of the flow. Thus the absquare is easy to produce by physical devices in common use. However, the improvement of the transients in a problem must be weighed against the cost of including nonlinear terms in the control function.

Experimental Results

All of the points of the theory in this paper have been checked experimentally in the laboratory of the author's company by electronic and other means on simulated and actual engines.

Some experimental results are shown in Figs. 22 and 23. Fig. 22(a) is for a one-lag ($1/5$-sec time constant) system where Formula [89] is used for control. This figure shows the response to instant load rejections and increases. The curves in Fig. 22(b) are the same as for Fig. 22(a) except that the lag with $1/5$-sec time constant has been split into two identical lags with $1/10$-sec time constant. Fig 22(c) is the same thing with the $1/5$-sec lag split into three $1/15$-sec lags. The asymmetry of the rpm swings in Fig. 22(c) is due to minor errors in the equipment and is to be disregarded. The vertical scales for Figs. 22(b) and 22(c) differ a little from those for Fig. 22(a). For Figs. 22(b) and 22(c) the time constants are lumped into one in the control Formula [89]. To eliminate the oscillations near equilibrium in Fig. 22(c) one must employ a sizable linear band about equilibrium or a control formula with higher derivatives, or some other technique such as a deadband. In Fig. 23 is shown the rpm response of an engine to a load increase and a load rejection for the case where the engine and filter in the system have four lags, with time constants 0.4 sec, 0.1 sec, 0.1 sec, and 0.05 sec, respectively, and a control formula of Type [89] with second derivative is used. Here the 0.4-sec lag dominates the others.

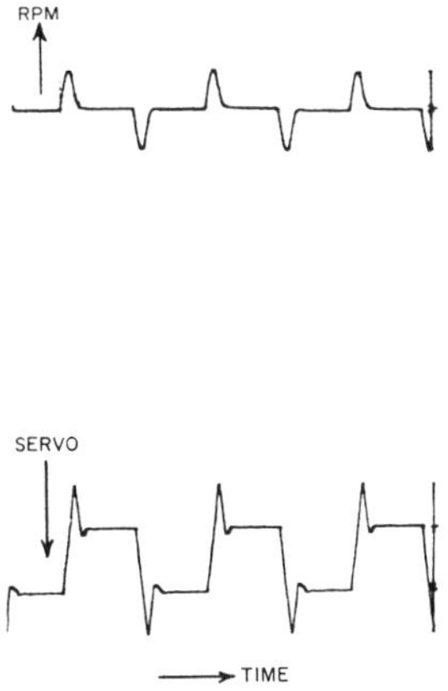

Fig. 22(a) Experimental Response for a Single-Lag System With a Nonlinear Control

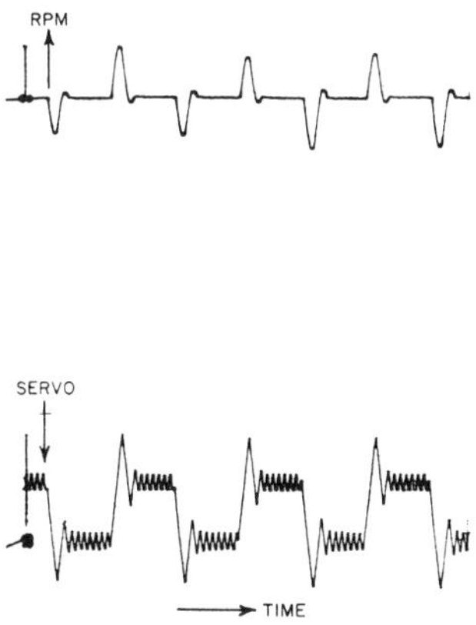

Fig. 22(b) Response of Engine With Two Equal Lags

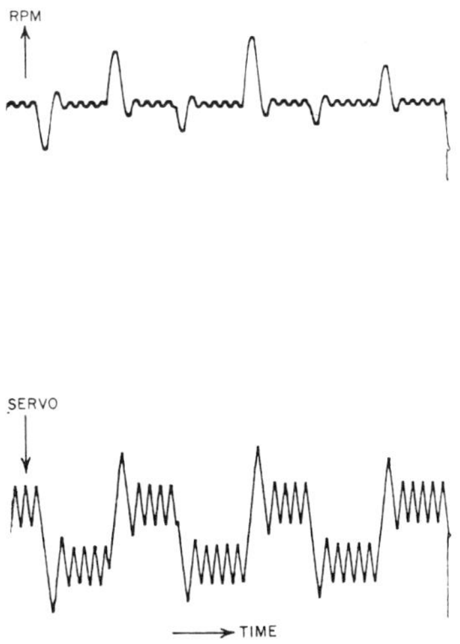

Fig. 22(c) Response of Engine With Three Equal Lags

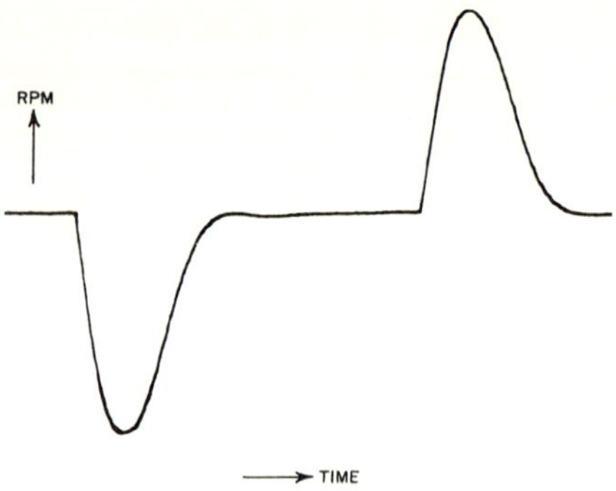

FIG. 23 RESPONSE OF SYSTEM WHERE ONE LAG DOMINATES THREE OTHERS

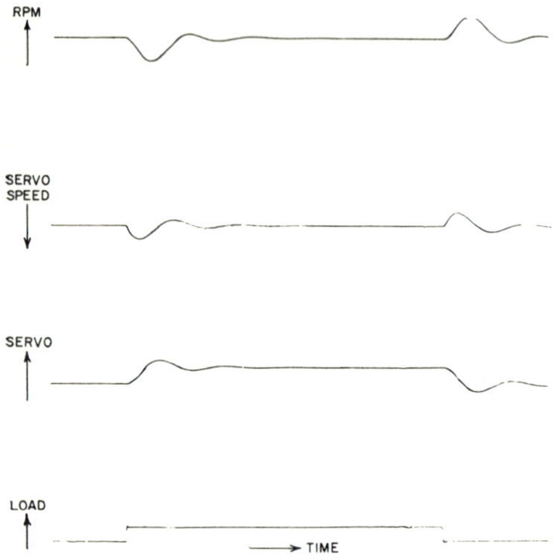

FIG. 24(a) LINEAR RESPONSE TO LOAD REJECTION

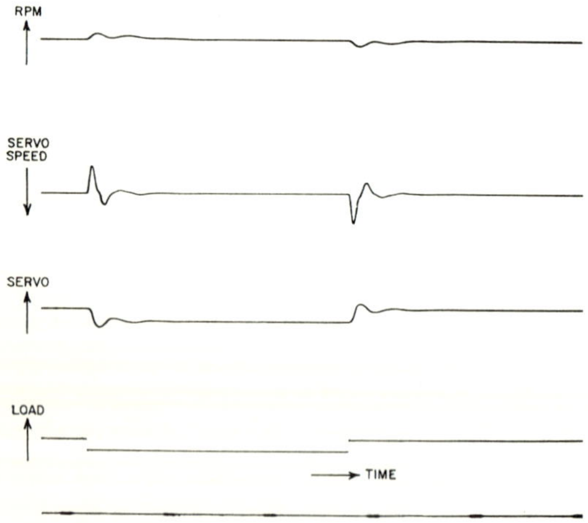

FIG. 24(b) NONLINEAR RESPONSE TO SAME DISTURBANCE

In Figs. 24–27 are shown the experimental results of using an absquare term (Formula [103]) for prime-mover systems where the disturbances are so small that *the servo speed never reaches a maximum value*. Fig. 24(a) gives the response of such a system to load disturbances where the governor is a linear one adjusted to give the best results that can be obtained with a linear control function where servo speed c' is a linear combination of speed deviation m and acceleration m'. In this figure load is taken on and then rejected. In Fig. 24(b) is shown the response of the same system to the same disturbances when a practical amount of absquaring of the acceleration m' is introduced; i.e., Formula [103] is employed. Note the improvement in speed deviation by an order of magnitude. Note also that the part of the transient after the first swing is affected very little because the absquare plays a small role when one is near equilibrium. In Fig. 24(b) the case of load rejection is shown first, whereas in Fig. 24(a) it is shown last.

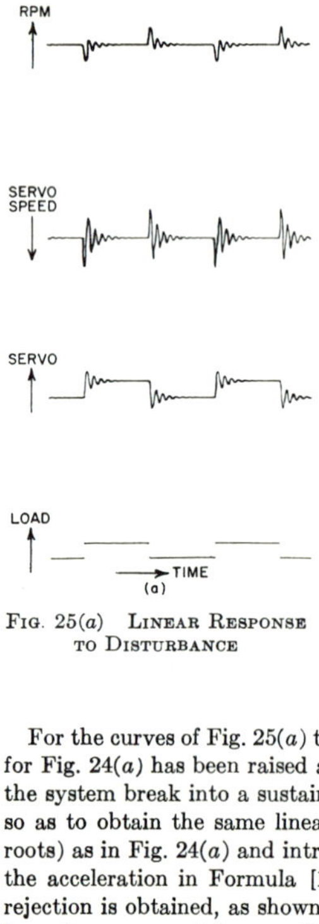

FIG. 25(a) LINEAR RESPONSE TO DISTURBANCE

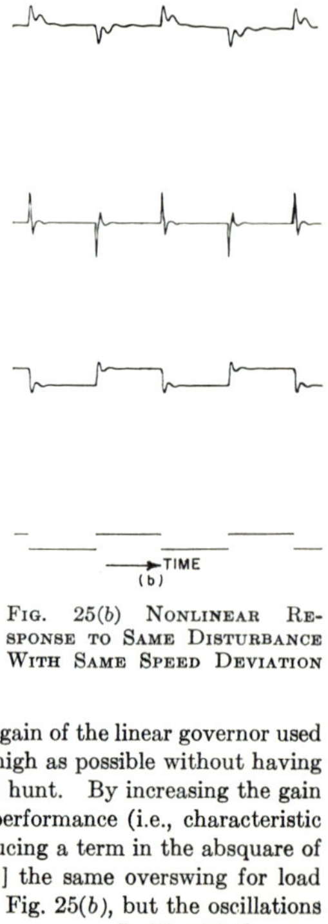

FIG. 25(b) NONLINEAR RESPONSE TO SAME DISTURBANCE WITH SAME SPEED DEVIATION

For the curves of Fig. 25(a) the gain of the linear governor used for Fig. 24(a) has been raised as high as possible without having the system break into a sustained hunt. By increasing the gain so as to obtain the same linear performance (i.e., characteristic roots) as in Fig. 24(a) and introducing a term in the absquare of the acceleration in Formula [103] the same overswing for load rejection is obtained, as shown in Fig. 25(b), but the oscillations have been removed for practical purposes. In Fig. 26 the constants in a linear governor [the governor of Fig. 24(a)] for the same prime-mover system have been adjusted to give the same rpm overswing for load rejection as in Fig. 25(a) and rpm transients as near those of Fig. 25(b) as possible. Note how slowly the rpm curve of Fig. 26 drags in to equilibrium. Note also the oscillations, evident from the servo speed trace.

The response of an engine to quarter-load rejections under linear and nonlinear hydraulic governor control is shown in Fig. 27. The linear governor represented by Equation [70] was adjusted to the border of instability so that a slight numerical increase in the coefficients of the control formula resulted in hunting. This was done to make the overswing a minimum. The nonlinear governor, based on Formula [103], was adjusted so that a good transient was obtained for Fig. 27 without encounter-

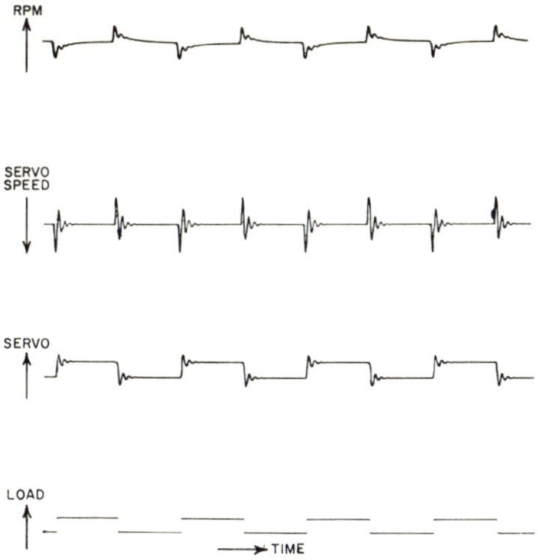

Fig. 26 Linear Response Initially Similar to Nonlinear Response

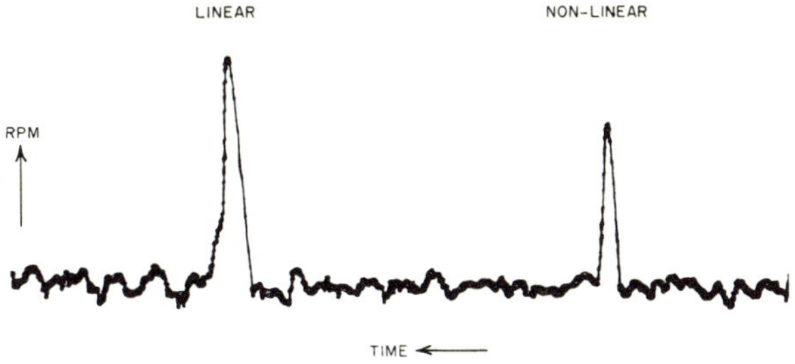

Fig. 27 Partial-Load Rejections on Engine

ing instability. Note that the area under the spike for the nonlinear case is about half of what it is for the linear. For this test the linear and nonlinear governors were actually the same governor except for the physical components generating the absquare in the nonlinear case and the derivative term m' in the linear.

Thus even though *the servo speed does not attain its maximum value* for the disturbances under consideration, the introduction *of the absquare can be used to substantially improve the response* to the "larger" of the disturbances to be encountered.

Summary

In unpublished work the author has treated such topics as the effect of deadband, changing gain in reaching a linear control band about equilibrium, the use of linear and nonlinear approximations to nonlinear control functions, the effect of a second sudden disturbance before the first has died out, the employment of different types of linear control zones near equilibrium, the use of an arbitrary $g(c)$, the determination of control functions for higher-order systems, and other topics which need to be covered in a complete treatment of the subject, but which will be omitted here.

Instant load rejections and the corresponding transients are of considerable concern to the user of speed governors. Let $O(D)$ be a polynomial in D with positive coefficients. To obtain optimum transients in the case

$$O(D)m' = K_1c - l \quad [104]$$

where

$$|c'| \leqq K_2 \quad [3]$$

it is necessary to use control functions which include

$$\Sigma = \psi + \frac{\{\psi'\}}{2K_1K_2} \quad [105]$$

where $\{\psi'\}$ is the absquare $|\psi'|\psi'$ of ψ' and

$$\psi = O(D)m \quad [106]$$

Since Σ in Formula [105] involves the third or higher derivatives of m if $O(D)$ is of the second order or higher, due to noise precise optimum transients cannot be realized physically for higher-lag systems.

Good transients can often be obtained by using

$$c' = -K\Sigma \quad [107]$$

as the only nonlinear control formula, where K is as large as possible, and a linear band, dead zone, or something else is employed to achieve stability where necessary. If the equation is

$$m' + f(m) = \frac{1}{O(D)} K_1c - l \quad [108]$$

with a damping term $f(m)$ that does not decrease as m increases, this term may be dropped and good results obtained by applying the theory for Equation [104]. Let ψ denote $m + \tau m'$. In the case where $O(D)$ is the expression $(\tau D + 1)$ only one control function

$$\Sigma = \psi + \frac{\{\psi'\}}{2K_1K_2}$$
$$-(\operatorname{sgn}\psi')\tau^2K_1K_2 \ln^2\left\{1 + \sqrt{1 - \left(1 + [\operatorname{sgn}\psi']\frac{m''}{K_1K_2}\right)e^{\frac{-|\psi'|}{\tau K_1K_2}}}\right\} \quad [109]$$

is needed to give optimum transients where $\{\psi'\}$ is the absquare of ψ'. When the log term in Formula [109] is imaginary it is dropped.

Formula [105] may often be replaced by

$$\Sigma = m + (\tau + \beta|m'|m') \quad [110]$$

especially where the servo will not attain its maximum speed. Formula [110] may frequently in turn be replaced by a linear expression by using an average value of $|m'|$.

When higher derivative terms in c are introduced on the right of Equation [104] the function Σ of Formula [105] can still be used. If a term in c' is introduced on the right in Equation [104] the nonlinear theory of this paper breaks down. If dead time τ_d is introduced into Equation [104]

$$\Sigma = \psi \pm \tau_d^2K_1K_2 + \frac{\{\psi' \mp 2\tau_dK_1K_2\}}{2K_1K_2} \quad [111]$$

may be used to treat large disturbances.

Acknowledgment

The author is indebted to Mr. William I. Caldwell of the Taylor Instrument Companies, Mr. G. Forrest Drake of the Woodward Governor Company, and others for valuable suggestions which were used to improve the exposition of this paper.

Bibliography

1 "Nonlinear Techniques for Improving Servo Performance,

by Donald McDonald, *National Electronics Conference*, vol. 6, 1950, pp. 400–421.
2 "Multiple Mode Operation of Servomechanisms," by Donald McDonald, *Review of Scientific Instruments*, vol. 23, no. 1, January, 1952, pp. 22–30.
3 "A Phase-Plane Approach to the Compensation of Saturating Servomechanisms," by A. M. Hopkin, Trans. AIEE, vol. 70, part I, 1951, pp. 631–639.
4 "A Topological and Analog Computer Study of Certain Servomechanisms Employing Nonlinear Electronic Components," by R. C. Lathrop, PhD thesis, University of Wisconsin, 1951.
5 "The Stabilization of On-Off Controlled Servomechanisms," by A. M. Uttley and P. H. Hammond, *Automatic and Manual Control*, 1952 publication of the 1951 Cranfield Conference, pp. 285–307.
6 "Differential Equations With a Discontinuous Forcing Term," by D. W. Bushaw, Report No. 469, January, 1953, Experimental Towing Tank, Stevens Institute of Technology, Hoboken, N. J., PhD thesis, Dept. of Math., Princeton University, Princeton, N. J.
7 "Predictor Servomechanisms," by L. M. Silva, Trans. IRE, vol. CT-1, no. 1, March, 1954, pp. 56–70.
8 "Nonlinear Optimization of Relay Servomechanisms," by L. M. Silva, University of California Institute of Engineering Research, series no. 60, issue no. 106, April 15, 1954.
9 "Predictor Control Optimalizes Control-System Performance," by L. M. Silva, Trans. ASME, vol. 77, 1955, pp. 1317–1323.
10 "An Investigation of the Switching Criteria for Higher Order Servomechanisms," by Irving Bogner and L. F. Kazda, Trans. AIEE, vol. 73, part II, Applications and Industry, 1954, pp. 118–127, Paper 54-44.
11 "Differential Equations," by R. P. Agnew, McGraw-Hill Book Company, Inc., New York, N. Y., 1942.
12 "Optimum Switching Criteria for Higher Order Contactor Servo With Interrupted Circuits," by S. S. L. Chang, AIEE 55-549.
13 "Analysis and Design Principles of Second and Higher-Order Saturating Servomechanisms," by R. E. Kalman, AIEE 55-551.
14 "Errors in Relay Servomechanisms," by L. F. Kazda, Trans. AIEE, vol. 72, part II, Applications and Industry, 1953, pp. 323–328.
15 "Effects of Friction in an Optimum Relay Servomechanism," by T. M. Stout, Trans. AIEE, vol. 72, part II, Applications and Industry, 1953, pp. 329–336.

Appendix 1

We shall consider a system with dead time given by the equation

$$M' = e^{-\tau_d D}C - L \qquad [112]$$

with

$$|C'| \leqq 1 \qquad [113]$$

Suppose that

$$L \geqq (\sqrt{2} - 1)\tau_d \qquad [114]$$

If the load L is suddenly dropped at $T = 0$ an optimum transient is obtained where one goes through three phases corresponding to $C' = -1, +1, 0$. Before the disturbance

$$C = L, C' = 0$$

The change from $C' = -1$ to $C' = +1$ must occur when the control function Σ given by

$$\Sigma = M + \tau_d^2 - \frac{(M' - 2\tau_d)^2}{2} \qquad [115]$$

is zero. From $T = 0$ to $T = \tau_d$ we have $M' = L$ and $M = LT$. If L is sufficiently large, as when $L \geqq 2\tau_d$, we have $\Sigma > 0$ and $\Sigma' < 0$ before the instant when C' changes from -1 to $+1$. When

$$M = \frac{\tau_d^2}{2}; M' = -\tau_d \qquad [116]$$

we must switch to $C \equiv 0$. The C-curve reaches equilibrium τ_d units before this happens for M.

Corresponding results are obtained if load is suddenly taken on. For large enough L relative to τ_d we can replace the last term in Formula [115] by the absquare term $\{M' - 2\tau_d\}/2$.

Modifications of the theory apply if L is small relative to τ_d.

Appendix 2

We consider a system with Equation [93] subject to the Condition [113]. Here $O(D)$ is any polynomial with positive coefficients. Introducing ψ as in Formula [95] we derive Equation [96]. Consider the last phase of an optimum transient that leads M to equilibrium. Suppose that $C' = +1$ for this phase, whence $C \equiv 0$ thereafter. We cannot have $\psi = 0$ at the start of the phase since $\psi'' = +1$ until the end of the transient when ψ becomes zero. Thus the shift from $C' = -1$ to $C' = +1$ in entering the last phase (before $M = 0$) occurs when Σ given by

$$\Sigma = \psi + \frac{\{\psi'\}}{2} \qquad [117]$$

becomes zero. Thus *the absquare occurs in the last switching function.*

The foregoing treatment holds equally well when $C' = -1$ before equilibrium.

If Equation [93] is replaced by

$$O(D)M' = e^{-\tau_d D}C \qquad [118]$$

we let

$$U = e^{-\tau_d D}C$$

whence Equation [118] goes into

$$O(D)M' = U \qquad [119]$$

where Relation [113] implies that

$$|U'| \leqq 1 \qquad [120]$$

We can write ψ for $O(D)M$ and obtain

$$\psi' = U \qquad [121]$$

The argument at the beginning of this Appendix applies except that C' must switch values τ_d units of time before it would if the dead time were absent (see Appendix 1). For sufficiently large load rejections or acceptances the final phase before equilibrium (i.e., the last phase for which $\psi'' \neq 0$) is initiated when the control function

$$\Sigma = \psi \pm \tau_d^2 + \frac{\{\psi' \mp 2\tau_d\}}{2} \qquad [122]$$

becomes zero. The absquare thus occurs in the treatment of a system with the Equation [118]. The top signs in Formula [122] apply to load rejections and the bottom to load acceptances.

Discussion

M. J. NOWAK.[5] The author develops the absquare control function, with particular application to the optimum governor speed control of an engine. In general the equation for this type of servo application is

$$O(D)M' = C \qquad [123a]$$

$$|C'| \leqslant 1 \qquad [123b]$$

This general equation represents a large class of servo applica-

[5] Fellow, Engineering Mechanics Division, Stanford University, Stanford, Calif.

tions, for which a particular interpretation is the case where M is an engine-speed deviation and C is the position of a controlling governor; the characteristic of the governor is that its maximum speed is limited (e.g., this may represent the rate of opening of a fuel valve).

For this control situation the intuitive idea of having the servo travel at maximum speed to obtain optimum transient response is used and justified by the author to develop the absquare control function Σ for the case where engine time lags are negligible so that $O(D) = 1$

$$\Sigma = M + {}^1/_2\,|M'|M' \quad [124]$$

In general a control function is a function of the process error and its time derivatives, whose sign determines the direction in which the servo is moving (at maximum speed). These required properties of the motion are sensed and combined into the control function; then the times at which the control function is zero determine the switching points for the servo.

It turns out that absquare control has use not only in the simple case analyzed by the author but also in the general Equation [123]. This more general case will be developed briefly for arbitrary engine time delay and arbitrary initial conditions of engine speed. The result is that even in this general situation the control function has the form

$$\Sigma = M + {}^1/_2 \left|\frac{M'}{C'}\right| M' + 2TM' - 2C'T\hat{T} \quad [125]$$

Thus the exact switching function contains corrections to the absquare function of first and second order in the equivalent time constant of the engine.

For such step switchings involved in this type of discontinuous control the Heaviside transformation theorem is useful; for a differential equation which relates an output y to a step input x

$$y + a_1y^{(1)} + a_2y^{(2)} + \ldots + a_ny^{(n)} = x \quad [126a]$$

$$O(D)y = x \qquad O(D) = (1 + T_1D)\ldots(1 + T_nD) \quad [126b]$$

the usual Heaviside transformation is

$$y(t) = y_s + x\sum_{k=1}^{n}\frac{-T_k}{O'\left(\frac{-1}{T_k}\right)}e^{-t/T_k}$$

$$y_s = [y(t)]_{t=\infty} = \left[\frac{x}{O(D)}\right]_{D=0} \quad [127]$$

The limitation in using this formula is that it applies only to the situation where there is no motion prior to applying the step input, whereas in discontinuous switching control the servo may be reversed several times under arbitrary conditions. However, these arbitrary initial conditions can be taken into account by using operational methods. Thus the original equation can be integrated once by using the operator $\bar{D} = 1/D$ and applying the initial conditions

$$\bar{D}x = \bar{D}y + a_1y + a_2y^{(1)} + \ldots + a_ny^{(n-1)} - (a_1y_0 + a_2y_0^{(1)} + \ldots + a_ny_0^{(n-1)}) \quad [128a]$$

This process can be repeated for n-integrations to obtain

$$\left.\begin{aligned}\bar{D}^nx = {}& \bar{D}^ny + a_1\bar{D}^{n-1}y + a_2\bar{D}^{n-2}y + \ldots + a_ny\\ &- (a_n + a_{n-1}\bar{D} + \ldots + a_1\bar{D}^{n-1})y_0\\ &- (a_n\bar{D} + a_{n-1}\bar{D}^2 + \ldots + a_2\bar{D}^{n-1})y_0^{(1)}\\ &- \ldots\\ &- a_n\bar{D}^{n-1}y_0^{(n-1)}\end{aligned}\right\} \quad [128b]$$

By now applying the operator D^n the result can be put in the following form

$$Oy = x + O_0y_0 + O_1y_0^{(1)} + \ldots + O_{n-1}y_0^{(n-1)} \quad [129]$$

$$\left.\begin{aligned}O(D) &= 1 + a_1D + a_2D^2 + \ldots + a_nD^n\\ O_0(D) &= (a_1 + a_2D + \ldots + a_nD^{n-1})D\\ O_1(D) &= (a_2 + \ldots + a_nD^{n-2})D\\ O_{n-1}(D) &= a_nD\\ O_k(D) &= \sum_{i=k+1}^{n} a_iD^{i-k} = \frac{1}{D^k}\left[O(D) - \sum_{i=0}^{k} a_iD^i\right]\end{aligned}\right\} \quad [130]$$

The output is now produced not only by the applied step but also by steps due to the initial conditions. The usual Transformation [127] can be applied to each step to obtain the complete output; thus the general Heaviside transformation for arbitrary initial conditions is

$$y = y_s - \sum_{k=1}^{n}\frac{T_ke^{-t/T_k}}{O'\left(\frac{-1}{T_k}\right)}\left[x + \sum_{i=0}^{n-1}O_i\left(\frac{-1}{T_k}\right)y_0^{(i)}\right] \quad [131]$$

To facilitate application of the formula the following relations are useful

$$\left.\begin{aligned}O\left(\frac{-1}{T_1}\right) &= 0\\ O'\left(\frac{-1}{T_1}\right) &= \frac{1}{T_1^{n-2}}(T_1 - T_2)(T_1 - T_3)\ldots(T_1 - T_n)\\ O_0\left(\frac{-1}{T_1}\right) &= O\left(\frac{-1}{T_1}\right) - 1 = -1\\ O_1\left(\frac{-1}{T_1}\right) &= -(T_2 + T_3 + \ldots + T_n)\\ O_{k+1}\left(\frac{-1}{T_1}\right) &= -T_1O_k\left(\frac{-1}{T_1}\right) - a_{k+1}\end{aligned}\right\} \quad [132]$$

For the servo application [123] the formula can be applied to the equation

$$O(D)M'' = C'$$

where C' is a step equal to ± 1

$$\left.\begin{aligned}M'' &= C' - \sum_{k=1}^{n}\frac{T_ke^{-t/T_k}}{O'\left(\frac{-1}{T_k}\right)}\left[C' + \sum_{i=0}^{n-1}O_i\left(\frac{-1}{T_k}\right)M_0''^{(i)}\right]\\ M'' &= C' - \tilde{M}''\end{aligned}\right\} \quad [133]$$

The transient term on the right may be denoted by $\tilde{M}''$ and the equation integrated twice with initial conditions applied

$$(M + \tilde{M}) = (M_0 + \tilde{M}_0) + (M_0' + \tilde{M}_0')t + \frac{1}{2}(M_0'' + \tilde{M}_0'')t^2 \quad [134a]$$

$$(M' + \tilde{M}') = (M_0' + \tilde{M}_0') + (M_0'' + \tilde{M}_0'')t \quad [134b]$$

This form of the equation illustrates the author's comment that absquare control for the general case can be applied to the fictitious speed $\hat{M} = M + \tilde{M}$ instead of the actual engine speed. Moreover, this formula can be used to develop a switching criterion for the actual engine speed in this general case.

The general method to determine the switching criterion which leads the system to equilibrium with zero error is to find the time t_1 (in terms of the initial conditions M_0 and M_0') such that the servo forcing can be removed (stepped to zero) and the engine will coast to a final speed with no speed error. For a system with no engine time lags this condition on t_1 is that the speed error and acceleration are zero at t_1; for an engine with time delays the condition is that $M + \tilde{M}$ and $M' + \tilde{M}'$ must be zero at t_1. This important condition can be obtained readily from the general Heaviside transformation applied to the final switching to $C' = 0$.

It turns out that the simplified cases in which the engine time lags are neglected, or a single time lag is included, are insufficient to reveal the essential form of the switching criterion.

In the general case an exact solution can be carried through in terms of two equivalent time constants T, $\hat{T}$ of the order of the engine time constant, which are obtained from the general Heaviside transformation

$$\tilde{M}_0' = -2C'T \qquad \tilde{M}_0 = 2C'T(T - \hat{T}) \ldots\ldots [135]$$

To indicate the development of these equivalent time constants consider first the cases of one and two engine time delays with switching points far enough apart that the engine can settle into its final state of forced motion at $M'' = C'$. In these cases the following substitutions apply

$$\left[C' + \sum_{i=0}^{n-1} O_i \left(\frac{-1}{T_k}\right) M_0''^{(i)}\right] = 2C' \ldots\ldots [136]$$

One delay

$$\tilde{M}' = -2C'T_1 e^{-t/T_1} \qquad \tilde{M}_0' = -2C'T_1$$

$$\tilde{M} = 2C'T_1^2 e^{-t/T_1} \qquad \tilde{M}_0 = 2C'T_1^2$$

$$T = T_1 \qquad \hat{T} = 0 \qquad T\hat{T} = 0$$

Two delays

$$\tilde{M}' = \frac{-2C'}{T_1 - T_2}\left[T_1^2 e^{-t/T_1} - T_2^2 e^{-t/T_2}\right]$$

$$\tilde{M}_0' = -2C'(T_1 + T_2)$$

$$\tilde{M} = \frac{2C'}{T_1 - T_2}\left[T_1^3 e^{-t/T_1} - T_2^3 e^{-t/T_2}\right]$$

$$\tilde{M}_0 = 2C'(T_1^2 + T_1T_2 + T_2^2)$$

$$T = T_1 + T_2 \qquad \frac{1}{\hat{T}} = \frac{1}{T_1} + \frac{1}{T_2} \qquad T\hat{T} = T_1T_2$$

In this method of equivalent time constants C' is the maximum servo speed (± 1) if the switching points are far enough apart; if the switching points are close together C' may have some modified value obtained from Equation [136], depending on the previous switching. In any case Equation [134*b*] can be solved for t_1

$$t_1 = -\frac{1}{C'}(M_0' - 2C'T) \ldots\ldots\ldots\ldots [137]$$

This value of t_1 can be substituted into Equation [134*a*] and the exact equation for the switching criterion is obtained

$$\Sigma = M + {}^1/_2 \left|\frac{M'}{C'}\right| M' + 2TM' - 2C'T\hat{T} \ldots . [125]$$

The equivalent parameters T, $\hat{T}$, C', which can be estimated from the general Heaviside transformation, actually depend on the time delays of the engine, the time between switching points, and the initial conditions of the previous switching; generally it may be too expensive and also unimportant to sense this complicated dependence exactly, and experimental coefficients can be used in the switching criterion. Furthermore, since the constant correction to the switching function is a second-order effect this general analysis supports the author's practical switching criterion

$$\Sigma = M + (T + \beta|M'|)M' \ldots\ldots\ldots\ldots [138]$$

It appears that if a more accurate switching criterion is warranted for large engine time delays a constant bias also should be included in the control function.

T. M. Stout.[6] Many of the previous papers on optimum nonlinear control systems, including those by the writer, have described theoretical or analog computer studies or, in some cases, tests performed on experimental instrument servomechanisms. The author must be among the first to try these concepts in real systems, and his paper is therefore a genuine contribution.

Familiarity may breed a mistaken notion of the complexities of a subject. The writer, nevertheless, considers the statements "The mathematics of this theory is far beyond the limits of this paper" and "this theory is extremely complicated" to be unwarranted. The only permissible values of the manipulated variable that need to be considered are $+1$ and -1. In second-order systems, the corresponding response curves can be plotted in a phase plane. It is easy to visualize what combination of these curves is needed to reach equilibrium from any set of initial conditions and to determine the necessary control or switching function. The resulting transients can be shown to be optimum by making slight alterations in the switching procedure and showing that these increase the response time. For third-order systems, corresponding arguments can be carried out in a three-dimensional phase-space. This essentially graphical but perfectly rigorous approach is extended with difficulty to fourth or high-order systems, because of our inability to draw the multi-dimensional figures required, but the line of reasoning is still applicable. The strictly analytical approach appears unduly cumbersome, even for the simplest systems, so that the phase-plane or phase-space attack seems to be advantageous in all cases.

The paper contains a number of statements and asides which might serve as material for several subsequent papers. The author's remark, "There are initial conditions for which the optimum transient (in the single-lag case) is not one where the servo travels at full speed," deserves elaboration, as does the special case

$$M' = C' + C$$

The discussion of discontinuities, two-speed systems, dead time, dead band, approximations to the ideal control functions, and the effects of multiple, sinusoidal, and other disturbances likewise could be expanded. A question of some importance, not mentioned here, is the effect of intermittent operation on the power rating and life of the actuating device or servo. These matters require investigation before practical applications of optimum nonlinear control systems can be made.

"Compromises to preserve performance but reduce cost" appear essential, and the author correctly stresses the joint importance of performance, engineering, and economic considera-

[6] The Ramo-Wooldridge Corporation, Los Angeles, Calif.

tions. One cannot help wondering whether his optimism concerning the potentialities of optimum nonlinear control is influenced by an apparent, but possibly misleading, simplicity of the governor problems. In the cases discussed, low-order differential equations seem to be adequate to describe the systems, and disturbances of interest seem to be well approximated by step functions. Application of these control concepts to more complicated systems, described by higher-order equations and subjected to less specialized inputs and disturbances, seems less promising. The author would doubtless agree that the theory of optimum nonlinear control should serve only as a guide in the employment of deliberate nonlinearities and should not be applied blindly for its own sake.

T. J. Higgins.[7] This paper deals with what are referred to—at least in electrical engineering—as relay-type (or off-on) servomechanisms. The author cites a number of the principal papers that have been published on the analysis and design of such systems. A substantially equal number of yet other papers on these systems is to be found in the discusser's exhaustive bibliography on nonlinear control systems.[8]

To these many writings on relay-type systems the paper under discussion comprises a most valuable addition. First, the discusser—who has read all of the mentioned published literature on relay servomechanisms—found it to be very clearly written, which is not the case for all the earlier published papers. The theory is developed in considerable detail, so that all points of the theoretical developments are easily understood and grasped. Also, the author has adopted the very excellent procedure of concentrating attention on several of the simpler cases and has examined all possible initial modes of operation of each. Such procedure enables the reader to gain a clear insight into the physical actions through pertinent interpretation of the corresponding mathematical analysis. It also renders very clear (to the qualified reader!) the general procedure to be followed in analyzing more complicated systems such as some of those mentioned, but not taken up by the author, and reveals some of the essential physical phenomena that must be dealt with in designing nonlinear control systems, without obscurement by heavy mathematical manipulation.

Finally, and on the practicing side, the advance of experimental data in confirmation of the analytical work evidences the correctness of the author's work and provides substantial evidence of the great values of analytic procedures for determining optimum performance of complicated nonlinear systems.

In conclusion, the writer would extend to the author his sincere appreciation of the pleasure afforded him by the reading of this well-wrought and lucidly written paper on a difficult and currently interesting phase of control theory.

Author's Closure

The author is in general agreement with the points raised by Mr. Nowak. The theme of Mr. Nowak's discussion is that the absquare used by the author to treat systems without lags also applies to systems with lags. This was actually brought out in the paper in connection with Equation [93]. In fact, Mr. Nowak's equation

$$M'' + \tilde{M}'' = C' \qquad [139]$$

obtained from Relations [133] is identical with the equation

$$O(D)M'' = C'$$

obtained from Equation [93] by differentiation, and the switching function involving the absquare has already been derived in the paper. This function is given by Σ in Formula [26] when M is replaced by ψ where

$$\psi = M + \tilde{M}$$

and is identical with the function Σ in Formula [125]. The author notes that $(M_0'' + \tilde{M}_0'')$ in Equation [134*a*] is C', and hence is equal to ± 1. His treatment of Equation [96], like that of Mr. Nowak, involves control on the basis of a fictitious speed ψ, i.e., $M + \tilde{M}$ (denoted by $\hat{M}$ in the discussion), and after ψ attains the equilibrium condition $\psi \equiv 0$, the engine will coast to the equilibrium value $M = 0$. The theory given in the discussion is thus the same as that of the author except for the point of view.

The author disagrees with the derivation of Equation [129], which is not mathematically rigorous. Starting with Equation [126*a*] by integration and differentiation Mr. Nowak derives Equation [129], which is the same as Equation [126*a*] except that terms have suddenly appeared on the right. From a given equation one cannot derive a new equation that contains more than at the start. Heaviside's work itself was lacking in rigor. This invalidated some of his findings, but did not detract from the over-all value of his work. The same thing can be said about the discussion under consideration.

Dr. Stout possesses a keen and thorough knowledge of the field in which the paper is written, and his remarks are well taken. He states that only the values ± 1 of the servo speed C' need be considered in the argument. This is true if one restricts the theory to on-off servomechanisms. Workers in the field generally have taken this position. If one restricts oneself to the on-off case it is a simple matter to establish whether or not a given transient is optimum in the sense of the paper. In the theory developed by the author it is assumed only that C' is between -1 and $+1$. Since a class of transients, optimum in the sense of this paper, requires that the servo speed C' be in absolute value between 0 and 1, at least during part of the transient, it is not sufficient to consider operation at saturation only.

Although in industry one is primarily concerned with the production of economical engineering designs, regardless of how these designs are obtained, it is nevertheless valuable to have the analytical treatment at hand. The analytical, that is rigorous, mathematical treatment of a theory is absolutely necessary for an understanding of the applications of this theory. This is a point of view that the author knows Dr. Stout shares with him.

The treatment of the case

$$M' = \tau C' + C \qquad [140]$$

for a constant τ is not complicated and will be given here. It is assumed that $|C'|$ is bounded by 1, as in Relations [12]. Suppose that at $T = 0$ we have the initial conditions

$$M = M_0, \quad M' = M_0', \quad C' = 0, \quad C = M_0'$$

The best transient is obtained by letting

$$C' = -(\text{sgn } M)$$

when $M \neq 0$, and

$$C' = -\frac{C}{\tau}$$

when $M = 0$. Note that if $M_0 > 0$ and $C' = -1$ for $T > 0$ we have

$$C = M_0' - T$$

[7] Department of Electrical Engineering, University of Wisconsin, Madison, Wis.

[8] A copy can be obtained by request to the Director, Engineering Experiment Station, Mechanical Engineering Building, University of Wisconsin, Madison, Wis.

$$M' = M_0' - \tau - T$$

$$M = M_0 + (M_0' - \tau)\,T - \frac{1}{2}\,T^2$$

Now $M = 0$ when

$$T = (M_0' - \tau) + \sqrt{[(M_0' - \tau)^2 + 2M_0]}$$

At this value of T

$$C = \tau - \sqrt{[(M_0' - \tau)^2 + 2M_0]}$$

For the next phase we keep $M \equiv 0$ by letting

$$\tau C' + C = 0 \qquad [141]$$

whence

$$C = \{\tau - \sqrt{[(M_0' - \tau)^2 + 2M_0]}\}e^{-T/\tau}$$

where we have taken $T = 0$ at the start of this phase. The initial C' is then

$$\left\{\frac{\sqrt{[(M_0' - \tau)^2 + 2M_0]}}{\tau} - 1\right\}$$

The quantity C' can attain this value only if

$$|\tau - \sqrt{[(M_0' - \tau)^2 + 2M_0]}| \leqq \tau$$

This condition is not satisfied if

$$\sqrt{[(M_0' - \tau)^2 + 2M_0]} > 2\tau \qquad [142]$$

If $M_0 < 0$ the Inequality [142] is replaced by

$$\sqrt{[(M_0' + \tau)^2 - 2M_0]} > 2\tau \qquad [143]$$

Thus C can coast to equilibrium according to Equation [141] only if $|M_0|$ and $|M_0'|$ are sufficiently small.

Thus *even though the ideal transients are not obtained by letting the servo travel at only full or zero speed, there exist control functions* depending on M and C only that yield the ideal transients. In fact, these transients are obtained by letting

$$C' = -K\Sigma$$

where K is very large (infinite in the ideal case) and

$$\Sigma = M$$

for $M \neq 0$ while

$$\Sigma = \frac{C}{K\tau}$$

for $M = 0$, provided that $\tau \neq 0$.

That the author's enthusiasm for the nonlinear approach of the paper is colored by his work on governors is no doubt correct. Customers normally test prime-mover governors by making sudden load rejections or acceptances. Such sudden changes often occur in practice as when a generating unit is separated from the line and concern about the resulting transients is justified. However, the general principles of the paper were verified on a Philbrick analog computer simulating controlled systems of a rather general nature. These studies showed that the use of the absquare is beneficial for a wide range of applications where the disturbances are not necessarily of the step variety.

Dr. Stout is correct in stating that the theory serves as a guide. The improvement that can be obtained in practice by the application of the theory of the present paper was most disappointing to the author, who completed the theory as far as he felt it had to be carried for engineering applications, before initiating the experimental work to verify it. Improvement in maximum overswings of 2:1 for major disturbances without changing the quality of the transients is often about the best that can be attained where the application of the theory is indicated. In comparing linear and nonlinear controls one must be careful to employ the best control with a linear control function involving as many derivatives as is practical (up to the second) and arbitrary coefficients and subject to arbitrary discontinuities.

Professor Higgins is correct in his statement that the paper concerns on-off servomechanisms. The paper actually treats servomechanisms in general where the rate of change of the controlling variable is bounded, and this rate can be made to assume arbitrarily any value between its minimum and maximum. The paper is primarily concerned with transients that can be made optimum by operating a servomechanism as if it were of the on-off variety. Interest in the field of the paper is indicated by the other papers on the subject that are listed in Professor Higgins' superb bibliography on nonlinear control systems.

THE SYNTHESIS OF OPTIMUM TYPE II NONLINEAR CONTROL SYSTEMS*

Prapat Chandaket, Lt. Cmdr.,

Royal Thai Navy

Bangkok, Thailand

and

C. T. Leondes

University of California

Los Angeles, California

ABSTRACT

Techniques have been established for the synthesis of "bang-bang" or relay servos which result in an optimum nonlinear control system for the case where the system under control is of second order. The nonlinear controller in this case utilizes a one variable function generator in its realization. If, however, the controlled system is of third, fourth, fifth, etc. order a two, three, four, etc. variable function generator, respectively, is required in the mechanization of its controller. This imposes a very real practical limitation on the realization of these higher order optimum non linear control systems, and as a result several compromise approaches have been presented in the literature.

In this paper the concept of developing a controller based on the more important roots of the controlled system is examined. Particular emphasis is placed on designing controllers based on the two most important roots of a controlled system, these roots being treated here as those closest to the origin. A control system designed so as to be optimum with this restriction is referred to as an optimum type II* control system. This concept was first introduced by Silva, Ref. 1. In this paper the scope and utility of this method are considerably extended, and a number of significant results are obtained. For example, type I systems require higher rates of changing system velocity, and this would be a limiting factor in using the type I concept in a practical control system. In particular, if a given controlled system is designed for type I or type II operation, and the system acceleration limit is satisfied, the type I system would have a shorter lifetime than a type II system.

I. INTRODUCTION

The concept of Type II predictor control systems was first introduced by Silva, Ref. 1, in 1954 with the intention of achieving near optimum response for systems of order higher than two. The fundamental concept is that the error and its derivatives shall be reduced to zero in three steps for third or higher order systems. These three steps consist of a single period of acceleration toward zero, a single period of deceleration, and finally a force free trajectory which satisfies the requirement that the error and its derivatives shall simultaneously go to zero. It should be pointed out that the concept as stated above is possible only for stationary class systems. For quasi-stationary class systems, a modified dual mode concept must be used, and as a result it is necessary to replace the force-free period by an equilibrium force, Ref. 2.

*The optimum type I nonlinear control system is defined as that system which will reduce the system error and its derivatives to zero in minimum time for the design inputs.

We shall refer to Fig. 1 in the following development. The principal concept in the method is to convert the error differential equation (for systems of order three or higher) to another second order differential equation by introducing a new variable (y). Therefore, a transforming device is needed as shown in the figure to transform e(t) into the new variable y(t). The nonlinear controller is designed to provide the control effort of proper direction to the system to achieve optimum time response in y, namely, y and $\dot{y}$ are to be reduced to zero simultaneously in minimal time. However, at this instant ($y = \dot{y} = 0$) only the y-energies have been reduced to zero, while the error energies which belong to the time constant terms in the transformed box are not yet reduced to zero. For the stationary class system, at $y = \dot{y} = 0$, the nonlinear controller must switch the system to the force free condition and this, as a result, permits all the remaining error energies which belong to the time constant terms in the transformed box to return to zero exponentially and simultaneously.

The main objective of this paper is to present the concept of the Type II optimum nonlinear control system in adequate detail. It will be found that the concept cannot be applied to all types of system functions for good response. The extension of this concept to other system types where the basic concept fails will also be discussed. Therefore, the general area in which Type II designs are effective will be discussed in detail. In addition, the modified dual mode concept will be applied to the design of Type II predictor control system in order to provide a response nearly as good as the optimum system response for both stationary and quasi-stationary class systems. The system response for Type I and Type II will be analyzed theoretically in a typical third order system using a combination input of position and velocity. This analysis is aimed at familiarizing the designer with the technique and it will also permit us to draw some important conclusions. An analog study for a fourth order system will be presented elsewhere, Ref. 3.

II. MATHEMATICAL DEVELOPMENT

To explain the principle of Type II predictor control systems, the system characteristics will be assumed to consist of one integral term and n+1 time constant terms*. After the design principle is presented, it will be clear that this concept is only valid for some system types. Referring to Fig. 1, let the system behavior be described by

$$\delta KF = s(s+\beta)(s+\alpha_1)(s+\alpha_2)\cdots(s+\alpha_n)C_{(t)} \tag{1}$$

where β, $\alpha_1, \alpha_2, \ldots, \alpha_n$ are system characteristic roots

F = maximum control effort

K = gain of the system

Assume a quasi-stationary class input

$$r(t) = a_0 + a_1 t \tag{2}$$

where a_0 and a_1 are constant.

The error equation is described in abbreviated notation by

$$s(s+\beta)\prod_{k=1}^{n}(s+\alpha_k)\, e_{(t)} = \beta\prod_{k=1}^{n}\alpha_k a_1 - \delta KF \tag{3}$$

Due to the system velocity limit, the maximum velocity input should be limited by

$$|a_1| < \frac{KF}{\prod_{k=1}^{n}\alpha_k} \tag{4}$$

Let

$$M = \beta\prod_{k=1}^{n}\alpha_k a_1 - \delta KF \tag{5}$$

and introduce a new variable

$$y_{(t)} = \prod_{k=1}^{n}(s+\alpha_k)\, e_{(t)} \tag{6}$$

*It will be seen later that this assumption does not put any limit on the general conclusion intended to cover all types of systems. In addition, these types of systems are common in practical control systems.

Substitution of equations (5) and (6) into (3) yields

$$s(s+\beta)\, y_{(t)} = M \tag{7}$$

which is an equation on which the design of the nonlinear controller is based. It should be noted that the (n+2)-order error equation (3) is reduced to a second order differential equation in a new variable y(t). The time required to complete the optimum path in the y-y plane can be obtained in straightforward manner, Ref. 2.

If a stationary class input is used*, then $a_1 = 0$ and at the instant $y = \dot{y} = 0$, M should be made zero so that y and $\dot{y}$ will remain zero at all time until the input changes. Then the correcting process in the y-$\dot{y}$ plane will start over. Therefore, for stationary class inputs, the force free period must be switched on when $y = \dot{y} = 0$.

However, for quasi-stationary class inputs* where $a_1 \neq 0$, a new equilibrium force must be applied to the system in order to keep $y = \dot{y} = 0$ at all time. The equilibrium force is obtained from

$$f_e = \frac{\beta\prod_{k=1}^{n}\alpha_k a_1}{K} \tag{8}$$

When using the modified dual mode concept, one switches to the equilibrium mode when $y = \dot{y} = 0$. At this time, according to equation (6)

$$y_{(t)} = \prod_{k=1}^{n}(s+\alpha_k)\, e_{(t)} = 0 \tag{9}$$

Equation (9) gives the behavior of the error under the equilibrium mode control force from equation (8) (or under the force free control in the stationary class) starting from the time at which $y = \dot{y} = 0$.

Let us now consider the error characteristics after y and $\dot{y}$ are brought to zero. From this, one can obtain a justified conclusion as to whether a Type II predictor should be chosen for the system design, and if a Type II system is selected, how close to the optimum response (by Type I) it will come. With the above assumptions concerning the system characteristics and the circuit arrangement, let us determine the error characteristics by classifying the assumed constants in the following manner:

1) $\alpha_k > \beta$ and no repeated roots. (10)

From equation (9), one obtains its independent solution

$$e(t) = \sum_{k=1}^{n} A_k e^{-\alpha_k t} \tag{11}$$

Where the A_k's are functions of $e_0, \dot{e}_0, \ldots, e_0^{(n-1)}$

$$\alpha_1, \alpha_2, \ldots, \alpha_n > \beta$$

2) $\alpha_1 = \alpha_2 = \alpha_3 = \ldots = \alpha_p$ = p repeated roots

$\alpha_{p+1}, \alpha_{p+2}, \ldots, \alpha_n$ (n-p) distinct roots (12)

*See Appendix A.

From equation (9), we obtain

$$e_{(t)} = e^{-\alpha t} \sum_{k=1}^{p} A_k t^{k-1} + \sum_{m=p+1}^{n} A_m e^{-\alpha_m t} \quad (13)$$

where A_k and A_m are functions of $e_0, \dot{e}_0, \ldots e_0^{(n-1)}$

3) $\alpha_1 = \alpha_2 = \ldots = \alpha_p = 0$

$$\alpha_{p-1}, \alpha_{p-2}, \ldots, \alpha_n = (n-p) \text{ distinct roots} \quad (14)$$

We obtain from equation (9)

$$e_{(t)} = \sum_{k=1}^{p} A_k t^{k-1} + \sum_{m=p+1}^{n} A_m e^{-\alpha_m t} \quad (15)$$

Where A_k and A_m are functions of $e_0, \dot{e}_0, \ldots, e_0^{(n-1)}$.

Note: $e_0, \dot{e}_0, \ldots e_0^{(n-1)}$ is the initial error and its derivatives at the time y and $\dot{y}$ are brought to zero, and t from the above solutions should be measured from this time on.

Let us now consider these three cases:

Case (1) After y and $\dot{y}$ are brought to zero the remaining error energies will return to zero according to equation (11). The time required for the error and its derivatives to reach zero is theoretically infinite. However, one can specify the desired level of acceptable error. In that case the time required would depend entirely on the values of α_k's, the initial error and its derivatives. There is no simple way of finding the values of $e_0, \dot{e}_0, \ldots e_0^{(n-1)}$; theoretically however, we can find these values by an analytical technique to be discussed later if the initial conditions of the input and system output are known when the y-correcting process is to be performed. But, with a good guess, if all α_k's are greater than β as assumed, then the error of the system will be corrected in the most efficient way by the y-correcting process. This is because the error energies in the longest time constant terms (∞ and $1/\beta$), which are the predominant characteristic roots of the error equation, are corrected in an optimum manner. Therefore to design the Type II predictor in the most efficient way, it is suggested that the two most predominant roots of the system will be left in the new second order equation so that their energies will be reduced to zero in minimal time.

Attention will now be given to the effects of the α_k's. The solution equation (11) implies that the bigger the values of α_k's, the smaller is the time required for the error and its derivatives to become negligible, and, as a result, the response time of the Type II system will be close to that of the Type I optimum response. This fact will be borne out by the comparisons of the Type I and Type II response to be presented later.

Case (2) Most of the discussion in Case (1) can be applied to this case. Therefore, let us consider the first part of the solution equation (13), that is,

$$e^{-\alpha t} \sum_{k=1}^{p} A_k t^{k-1}$$

These terms result from the repeated roots $\alpha_1 = \alpha_2 = \ldots = \alpha_p$. It should be noted that, even though these terms contain a polynomial function of time, they still have the converging characteristics due to the exponential damping factor. Therefore, Type II predictor design is also suggested if α is sufficiently big.

Case (3) $\alpha_1 = \alpha_2 = \ldots = \alpha_p = 0$. From the solution equation (15), it can be seen that the remaining error and its derivatives will never be reduced to zero. Therefore, systems of this class are not permitted in Type II design. However, if p = 1 (only one zero in the transformed box) we can switch s and $(s + \beta)$ and obtain the second order equation in the new variable as

$$y = -\delta KF \quad (16)$$

where

$$y_{(t)} = (s + \beta) \prod_{k=2}^{n} (s + \alpha_k) e_{(t)} \quad (17)$$

Use of the Type II system is now quite permissible if the rest of the system characteristic roots (β, $\alpha_2, \alpha_3, \ldots, \alpha_n$) are sufficiently far from the origin, and a good system response can be expected. Note that a_1 does not appear on the right side of equation (16) since the system contains two poles at the origin and this is classified as a stationary class system. In this case, after y and $\dot{y}$ reach zero, the system should be switched to force free condition. The discussion presented previously concerns systems whose characteristic roots are all real, and for which the correcting process is performed by only one switching. Only two integral terms are permissible for Type II control systems. Otherwise the remaining error will never return to zero after $y = \dot{y} = 0$ (Case 3). For example, in the design of the Type II system with three integral terms, one infinite time constant term must be put in the transform box, and this will lead to a steady state error.

In conclusion, it should be stated that, the Type II concept is suggested where there are only two predominant roots present, and these two should appear in the transformed second order differential equation of the new variable. The optimum nonlinear controller is then designed to sense the proper control effort to the system in order to correct these predominant error energies in minimal time.

SYSTEMS CONTAINING SOME COMPLEX CHARACTERISTIC ROOTS

From the previous discussion, it can be seen that all terms that are put in the transformed box, after $y = \dot{y} = 0$, will become the control factors in reducing the remaining error. If some complex zeros are put in the transformed box, after the optimum trajectory is completed in the $y - \dot{y}$ plane, the remaining error will return to zero in a damped sinusoidal fashion with possible over-shoot characteristics in the system response. If the damping factor (ζ) is small, it will give a long-tail effect. However, if the damping factor is sufficiently large, the Type II concept will still be acceptable.

In case the system contains no integral terms and the system predominant roots are a pair of complex roots, with the others being sufficiently far to the left of complex plane, then the Type II concept will be very valuable. The approach to this problem is suggested by the following two alternatives.

1) By the usual method. With this technique, all other characteristic roots, except the predominant characteristic roots, are put in the lead transformed box. With this arrangement, the new second order differential equation in y will contain the predominant complex roots. The optimum nonlinear controller is then designed to reduce the predominant error energies to zero in as short a time as possible. However, the optimum switching criterion for the second-order system of complex roots must be used. The optimum switching criterion for this case is derived elsewhere, Ref. 4. The compromise switching boundary is also suggested for the system with low damping factor.

2) By cancellation technique. This technique might prove useful in case a compensation network may be inserted between the nonlinear controller and the system member. A simple approach to the problem is to apply the cancellation method using a simple bridged-T RC network, Ref. 5. The characteristics of the bridged-T will give a pair of complex zeros which can be placed anywhere in the left-half of the s-plane and two poles on the negative real axis. For example, (see Fig. 2), the system function may be represented by

$$G_1(s) = \frac{K}{(s^2 + 2\zeta\omega_n s + \omega_n^2)(s + \alpha_1)(s + \alpha_2)} \quad (18)$$

where α_2 is sufficiently large so that the Type II concept is acceptable. The bridged-T function is represented by

$$G_2(s) = \frac{s^2 + 2\zeta\omega_n s + \omega_n^2}{(s + \gamma_1)(s + \gamma_2)} \quad (19)$$

then the overall system function for Type II to be designed is

$$G_{II}(s) = \frac{K}{(s + \alpha_1)(s + \alpha_2)(s + \gamma_1)(s + \gamma_2)} \quad (20)$$

In this case, the lead transformed box represents $(s + \gamma_2)(s + \alpha_2)$, and the error energies belonging to the γ_1- and α_1-terms are corrected in an optimum manner.

It is interesting to note that the near optimum response for the system containing one integral term, one pair of predominant complex poles and/or other poles sufficiently far to the left in the s-plane might also be obtained by using the bridged-T compensation method. For example (see Fig. 3), the system function is assumed as

$$G'_{II}(s) = \frac{K}{s(s^2 + 2\zeta\omega_n s + \omega_n^2)(s + \alpha_1)(s + \alpha_2)} \quad (21)$$

assume the same bridged-T as in equation (19). The overall system function for applying Type II concept is

$$G'_{II}(s) = \frac{K}{s(s + \gamma_1)(s + \gamma_2)(s + \alpha_1)(s + \alpha_2)} \quad (22)$$

An optimum nonlinear controller is designed to correct the error due to the integral - and γ_1-term. After the y-$\dot{y}$ trajectory is completed, then the remaining error should return to zero exponentially according to the γ_2, α_1 and α_2 terms. Note that the optimum switching criterion for third-order systems containing one pair of complex roots has not been derived, and the suggested procedure might prove very effective at the present time.

EXTENDED-TYPE II CONCEPT

The Type II concept is based on the principle that only one switching is required for a near optimum approach regardless of the system order. The invalidity of this concept for some system types has been discussed in the previous sections. It should be pointed out that the concept can be extended to yield near optimum response in the prohibited types discussed previously, if the required higher order switching criterion for the new variable y is available. For example, the system containing three integral terms and other short-time constant terms, can be transformed into a third-order differential equation in y with three characteristic roots at the origin, the other time-constant terms being inserted in the lead transformed box. In this case, the optimum switching criterion for the third order system K/s^3 is needed to design the nonlinear controller for y-correcting process. This criterion is available at the present time, Ref. 6 and 7. Another example, is the systems containing one integral, two long time constant terms, and additional short time constant terms that can be placed in transform box. The optimum switching criterion required for this case is derived elsewhere, Ref. 2, for the quasi-stationary case and the others, Ref. 8 and 9, for the stationary case.

III. COMPARISON OF TIME RESPONSE IN THIRD-ORDER TYPE I AND TYPE II PREDICTOR CONTROL SYSTEMS

In order to show the method of analyzing the response time for both Type I and Type II systems and to use these results in obtaining conclusions, a numerical example of a third-order system with one integral term and two time constant terms is given. The command input is assumed to be of quasi-stationary class consisting of a step and ramp function. The problem was solved by use of the IBM 709 computer at the Western Data Processing Center, UCLA.

3a Numerical Example

Let the system transfer function be

$$G(s) = \frac{2}{s(s + 1)(s + \alpha)} \quad (23)$$

where

$$\alpha > 1 \quad (24)$$

Let the input be

$$r(t) = 1 + 0.5\, t \quad (25)$$

The system is assumed in the equilibrium state

for $t \leqslant 0$, i.e., $c_0 = \dot{c}_0 = \ddot{c}_0 = 0$, and the maximum control effort is assumed to be

$$F = 1 \qquad (26)$$

To find the effect of α upon the Type II system, the time response will be determined for α = 1.5, 2, 2.5, 3 and 3.5. It is seen that the saturated system velocity equal $2/\alpha$, and the input velocity = 0.5. The highest possible value of α for this assumed input is 4. Now, the method used to obtain the time response for both types will be discussed.

3b Type I Predictor Control System

To illustrate the method assume $\alpha = 2$. The basic diagram of the Type I predictor control system is shown in Fig. 4. Using the notations described in section 3b of Ref. 2, we have

$$\begin{aligned} F &= 1 & a_o &= 1 \\ \alpha &= 2 & a_1 &= 0.5 \\ \beta &= 1 & \gamma &= \frac{\alpha}{\beta} = 2 \\ K &= 2 \end{aligned} \qquad (27)$$

$$\dot{c}_{max} = 1 \qquad (28)$$

$$\mathcal{F} = \frac{\dot{r}}{c_{max}} = 0.5 \qquad (29)$$

Since the system is in the equilibrium condition for $t \leqslant 0$, and the input is applied in the positive direction δ can be taken as +1. A theoretical check can be obtained by consulting section 3b of Ref. 2. The normalized error is $\mathcal{E}(\tau) = \beta^3/KF\, e(\tau)$ according to equation (41) of Ref. 2. From equation (50) of Ref. 2, one obtains the initial condition of the error and its derivatives in normalized form:

$$\begin{aligned} U_{10} &= 0.5 \\ U_{20} &= 0.25 \\ U_{30} &= 0 \end{aligned} \qquad (30)$$

Substitution of equation (30) into equation (69) of Ref. 2 yields the initial condition in W-phase space as

$$\begin{aligned} W_{10} &= 1.75 \\ W_{20} &= 0.5 \\ W_{30} &= -0.5 \end{aligned} \qquad (31)$$

With $\delta = +1$

$$\begin{aligned} N &= \mathcal{F} - \delta = -0.5 \\ P &= \mathcal{F} + \delta = 1.5 \end{aligned} \qquad (32)$$

From equations (115) and 116) of Ref. 2 we obtain

$$K_1 = (N - W_{10})\, e^{\frac{\gamma W_{10}}{N}} = -.00091 \qquad (33)$$

$$K_2 = (N + W_{30})\, e^{\frac{W_{10}}{N}} = -.0315 \qquad (34)$$

Substitution of equation (33) into equation (121) of Ref. 2 yields:

$$(2 - 0.5\, e^{4W_{12}})e^{1.33W_{12}} = (2 - .00091e^{4W_{11}})e^{1.33W_{11}} \qquad (35)$$

Substitution of equation (24) into equation (122) of Ref. 2 yields:

$$(2 - 0.5e^{2W_{12}})e^{.665W_{12}} = (2 - .0315e^{2W_{11}})e^{.665W_{11}} \qquad (36)$$

To obtain the optimum time response, W_{11} and W_{12} must be solved for from equations (35) and (36). This can be done by a graphical method. However, in order to obtain the result as accurately as possible, the computer has been used to solve the problem from the beginning and we obtain for this case

$$\begin{aligned} W_{11} &= -0.520805 \\ W_{12} &= 0.232564 \end{aligned} \qquad (37)$$

Referring to equations (124), (123), and (125) of Ref. 2 one obtains the time required from

the starting point to the first switching	=	4.5416 sec.
the first switching to the second switching	=	0.502 sec.
and from the second switching to the origin	=	0.465 sec.
the total optimum time required	=	5.5086 sec.

The behavior of the error and its derivatives can then be obtained from equation (B-10) in Appendix B. The phase plane behavior of e-ė are plotted in Fig. 8. The time response for the error and its derivatives are shown in Figs. 9, 10 and 11. The results for various values of γ are shown in Table 1. The notation in the Table corresponds to that of Fig. 12. The response time of the error and its time derivatives are plotted in Figs. 9, 10 and 11 for α = 1.5, 2.0, 2.5, and 3.0.

3c Type II Predictor Control System

To demonstrate Type II analytical technique, $\alpha = 2$ will be used. The basic diagram of a Type II predictor control system with $\alpha = 2$ is shown in Fig. 5.

For convenience, the system constants are rewritten as

$$\begin{aligned} F &= 1 & a_o &= 1 \\ \alpha &= 2 & a_1 &= 0.5 \\ \beta &= 1 \\ K &= 2 \end{aligned} \qquad (38)$$

$$r(t) = a_o + a_1 t = 1 + 0.5t \qquad (39)$$

Assuming the system to be in the equilibrium state for $t \leq 0$, one obtains the error initial condition as

$$e_{(o)} = 1$$
$$\dot{e}_{(o)} = 0.5 \quad (40)$$
$$\ddot{e}_{(o)} = 0$$

The error equation is represented by

$$s(s+1)(s+2)\,e(t) = 1 - 2\delta \quad (41)$$

with

$$N = 1 - 2\delta \quad (42)$$

and

$$y(t) = (s+2)\,e(t) \quad (43)$$

The new equation in y for which an optimum nonlinear controller is required, is now

$$\dot{y}(t) + y(t) = N \quad (44)$$

The time required to complete the optimum path in y-$\dot{y}$ plane was derived in Ref. 2. The optimum path in the y-$\dot{y}$ plane is sketched in Fig. 6.

Substituting equation (40) into (43), one obtains

$$y_{oo} = 2.5$$
$$\dot{y}_{oo} = 1 \quad (45)$$

It is seen that the initial point is in the first quadrant, therefore a positive initial force is required. τ_{AB} and τ_{BO} are obtained by solving equations (26) and (27) of Ref. 2 with e_{oo}, $\dot{e}_{oo}$, τ_1, τ_2 replaced by y_{oo}, $\dot{y}_{oo}$, τ_{AB}, τ_{BO} respectively.

The results obtained on the IBM 709 computer are

$$\tau_{AB} = 4.34350 \text{ sec.}$$
$$\tau_{BO} = 0.28117 \text{ sec.} \quad (46)$$
$$\tau_{total\ (y\text{-}\dot{y}\ plane)} = 4.62467 \text{ sec.}$$

and the error and its time derivatives at $y = \dot{y} = 0$ are

$$e(4.62467) = 0.18017$$
$$\dot{e}(4.62467) = -0.36033 \quad (47)$$
$$\ddot{e}(4.62467) = 0.72066$$

After the y-$\dot{y}$ trajectory is completed, the remaining error will return to zero according to the equation

$$e(t) = 0.18017\, e^{-2t} \quad (48)$$

where t, in this case, starts at the instant $y = \dot{y} = 0$. An analytical check of the derived time can be obtained by checking the results of the error and its derivative at the time $y = \dot{y} = 0$. At this point, one would obtain from equation (43) the following relations

$$\dot{e} + 2e = 0$$
$$\ddot{e} + 2\dot{e} = 0 \quad (49)$$

This agrees with the results obtained in equation (47) which has been derived independently. After $y = \dot{y} = 0$ the error and its derivatives will return to zero by equation (49) as shown in Fig. 7. The plot of the error behaviors in the e-$\dot{e}$ and the e-$\ddot{e}$ plane are plotted in Fig. 8 for this case.

The time required for the Type I correcting process is 5.5086 seconds, whereas in the Type II system, the remaining error and its derivatives at this time are reduced to

$$e = 0.02978$$
$$\dot{e} = -0.05956 \quad (50)$$
$$\ddot{e} = 0.11912$$

The time response for the error and its derivatives are obtained from equation (B-10) in Appendix B and plotted in Figs. 9, 10 and 11. It should be noted that the slope of the remaining error in e-$\dot{e}$ and e-$\ddot{e}$ will approach the vertical if α is increased, and this implies that the Type II response will approach the optimum response of the Type I system. The results obtained from the computer are summarized in Table 2.

3d Comparison of Type I and Type II Response

In order to study the behavior of Type I and Type II systems for various values of one system time constant term (α) which is furthermost to the left on the negative real axis, the computer was used to solve for the required time and the error response. The results show that as α was increased the remaining error and its derivatives of Type II system decreased at the time the optimum path was completed. These characteristics are summarized in Table 3. This behavior can be seen also in Fig. 8. When α is increased the slope in the e-$\dot{e}$ plane which represents the error behavior in the equilibrium mode becomes increasingly steep and Type II response will approach Type I response.

The time response for the error, error velocity and error acceleration are plotted in Figs. 9, 10 and 11 for both Type I and Type II systems at α = 1.5, 2.0, 2.5 and 3.0. It should be noted that when α is increased the error correcting process becomes slower. This is normal (for this particular problem) since the system velocity saturation is $2/\alpha$ and the maximum error correction speed is reduced to $2/\alpha - a_1$. Fig. 10 shows that for $\alpha = 2.5$ and 3.0, the system velocity is partly at its maximum limit.

In Fig. 11, the behavior of the error acceleration is shown. Since the input acceleration is zero these curves represent the system acceleration in the negative direction. The system is in an acceleration period (δ^+ - force) from the initial point to the first switching time, deceleration period (δ^- - force) from the first switching to the second, and a final acceleration (δ^+ - force) from the second switching to zero. This behavior takes place for both system types. However, the real acceleration or the rate of increase of the velocity occurs when $\ddot{e} < 0$ and the deceleration or the rate of decrease of the velocity when $\ddot{e} > 0$. From Fig. 11, it can be seen that the Type I system requires a very rapid change of system velocity in the second and third period. It can also be seen that the Type II system does require a rapid change of system velocity in the second period but not as high as Type I, and in the third period, the system is under equilibrium mode control where all the remaining error energies return to zero exponentially. Judging from this fact, one can conclude that the Type I system must be subjected to higher rates of changing velocity than the Type II system. It should be pointed out that the rate of changing system velocity is a very significant property from a practical point of view. The system must be designed on a stronger basis in order to be able to stand higher accelerations or decelerations. This also implies that the quality of the system must be higher (such as better material, more rigid construction) or in other words, the cost and weight must be increased. From another point of view one can state that with the same system being designed for Type I and Type II, the Type I system would have a shorter operational life.

As there is presently no general solution for systems of higher order than the third, we have carried out an analog study of a fourth order Type II system (Ref. 3, Chapter IV). It is the authors' belief that the optimum Type I system of fourth or higher order would again require rapid rate of acceleration between switchings; thus the problem of mechanization and proper construction of a Type I system of higher order should be subject to the same difficulties as in the lower order systems.

IV. CONCLUSIONS

In this paper, the concepts of the Type II system are discussed in detail. This leads to the conditions under which the Type II system can be chosen to give a satisfactory time response when compared to Type I. The concept of the Type II system is also extended to the case where the system function contains predominant complex roots. It has been pointed out that the Type II concept can also be extended to the system containing three predominant roots and where a compensating network cannot be inserted between the nonlinear controller and the system member, if the nonlinear controller can be designed to give optimum correcting process to the transformed third order equation in the new variable. An illustration using simple bridged-T RC network to compensate for the systems containing predominant complex characteristic roots is also shown.

In order to compare the behavior of the response time for the Type I optimum system and the Type II near-optimum system, a numerical example was set up by using a system containing one integral term and two time constant terms. The IBM 709 computer was used to solve for the switching time relations and the time responses of the error, error velocity and error acceleration of both types at various values of the non-predominant time-constant term (α). The results are plotted in Fig. 8, for the e-$\dot{e}$ and e-$\ddot{e}$ trajectory for $\alpha = 2$ and in Figs. 9, 10, and 11 for the response of e(t), $\dot{e}(t)$ and $\ddot{e}(t)$ for α = 1.5, 2, 2.5 and 3. This leads to the conclusion that, as α is increased, the Type II time response does approach Type I response.

A significant conclusion is that the Type I system required higher rates of changing system velocity for all values of α and this would be a limiting factor in using the Type I concept in a practical control system. If the same systems are designed for Type I and Type II operation, and the system acceleration limit is satisfied, the Type I system would have a shorter life when compared to the Type II system.

APPENDIX A

CLASSIFICATION OF OPTIMUM NONLINEAR CONTROL SYSTEM

Nonlinear predictor control systems are classified in Feldbaum's sense, Ref. 8, into three types, namely, stationary, quasi-stationary and non-stationary. The type of input assumed is a polynomial function of time such as

$$r(t) = a_0 + a_1 t + a_2 t^2 + \dots + a_{m-1} t^{m-1} + a_m t^m \tag{A-1}$$

$$G(s) = \frac{K}{s^q(b_0 + b_1 s + b_2 s^2 + \dots + b_n s^n)} \tag{A-2}$$

Let F be the max. controlled effort which takes either equal positive or negative values. The diagram of this control system is shown in Fig. A-1. With the above assumption, the system differential equation becomes

$$b_0 \frac{d^q c(t)}{dt^q} + b_1 \frac{d^{q+1} c(t)}{dt^{q+1}} + \dots + b_n \frac{d^{q+n} c(t)}{dt^{n+q}} = KF \tag{A-3}$$

Since c(t) = r(t) - e(t) we have:

$$b_0 \frac{d^q e(t)}{dt^q} + b_1 \frac{d^{q+1} e(t)}{dt^{q+1}} + \dots + b_n \frac{d^{q+n} e(t)}{dt^{q+n}}$$
$$= b_0 \frac{d^q r(t)}{dt^q} + b_1 \frac{d^{q+1} r(t)}{dt^{q+1}} + \dots + b_n \frac{d^{q+n} r(t)}{dt^{q+1}} - KF \tag{A-4}$$

By substituting (A-1) into (A-4), one obtains the error differential equation from which the optimum switching criterion is derived.

The definition of the class of systems can briefly be stated as follows:

$m < q$ stationary

$m = q$ quasi-stationary

$m > q$ non-stationary

This definition implies that, for a stationary class

$$F = f(e, \frac{de}{dt}, \frac{d^2 e}{dt^2}, \dots, \frac{d^{q+n-1} e}{dt^{q+n-1}}),$$

quasi-stationary class

$$F = f(e, \frac{de}{dt}, \frac{d^2e}{dt^2}, \ldots , \frac{d^{q+n-1}e}{dt^{q+n-1}}, a_m) ,$$

non-stationary class

$$F = f(e, \frac{de}{dt}, \frac{d^2e}{dt^2}, \ldots \frac{d^{q+n-1}e}{dt^{q+n-1}}, a_m, a_{m-1}, \ldots , t)$$

The above statements are confirmed by substituting (A-1) into (A-4), which yields: For $m < q$ (stationary), all time derivatives of input on the right hand side are zero; for $m = q$ (quasi-) only the qth derivative term remains and equals $b_0 a_m \cdot m!$; for $m > q$ (non-stationary), by assuming $m = q + p$, where p can be either of 1, 2,..., then

$$\sum_{k=o}^{p} b_k \frac{d^{q+k}r(t)}{dt^{q+k}}$$

still remain and these terms are functions of $t, t^2, \ldots, t^p, a_m, a_{m-1}, \ldots a_{m-p}$. Therefore, it can be concluded that for the stationary class, the optimum switching criteria are controlled only by the error and its higher time derivatives, whereas in the quasi-stationary class the last coefficient term is added, and in the non-stationary class several coefficients and time are involved.

APPENDIX B

THIRD-ORDER PREDICTOR CONTROL SYSTEM

The error response to the third-order predictor control system containing one integral and two time-constant terms will be needed in the illustrative examples in this paper. For convenience, the error response will be derived here. The basic diagram of the system is shown in Fig. B-1.

Let r(t) be a quasi-stationary class input represented by

$$r(t) = a_o + a_1 t \qquad \text{(B-1)}$$

where a_o and a_1 are constants. The system equation can be written as

$$s(s + \alpha)(s + \beta)\, c(t) = \delta KF \qquad \text{(B-2)}$$

From (B-1) and (B-2) one obtains the error differential equation

$$s(s + \alpha)(s + \beta)\, e(t) = a_1 - \delta KF \qquad \text{(B-3)}$$

Let

$$M = \alpha\beta a_1 - \delta KF \qquad \text{(B-4)}$$

The particular solution for the error is then given by

$$e(t) = A_o t + A_1 + A_2 e^{-\alpha t} + A_3 e^{-\beta t} \qquad \text{(B-5)}$$

where

$$A_o = \frac{M}{\alpha\beta}$$

$$A_1 = -\frac{M(\alpha + \beta)}{\alpha^2\beta^2} \qquad \text{(B-6)}$$

$$A_2 = -\frac{M}{\alpha^2(\alpha - \beta)}$$

$$A_3 = \frac{M}{\beta^2(\alpha - \beta)}$$

The complementary solution can be obtained from

$$s(s + \alpha)(s + \beta) = 0 \qquad \text{(B-7)}$$

Let the initial condition of the error and its derivatives be e_o, $\dot{e}_o$, and $\ddot{e}_o$. The complementary solution is then obtained from solving (B-7) as

$$e(t) = B_1 + B_2 e^{-\alpha t} + B_3 e^{-\beta t} \qquad \text{(B-8)}$$

where

$$B_1 = e_o + \dot{e}_o \frac{(\alpha + \beta)}{\alpha\beta} + \frac{\ddot{e}_o}{\alpha\beta}$$

$$B_2 = \frac{\dot{e}_o \beta + \ddot{e}_o}{\alpha(\alpha - \beta)} \qquad \text{(B-9)}$$

$$B_3 = -\frac{\dot{e}_o \alpha - \ddot{e}_o}{\beta(\alpha - \beta)}$$

Combining (B-5), (B-6), (B-8) and (B-9), one obtains the complete solution for the error as

$$e(t) = A_o t + (A_1 + B_1) + (A_2 + B_2)e^{-\alpha t} + (A_3 + B_3)e^{-\beta t} \qquad \text{(B-10)}$$

where all constant terms are obtained from (B-6) and (B-9). It should be noted that this solution can be used in the general case where the control effort and the initial conditions are known.

ACKNOWLEDGMENTS

The research supported in this paper was made in part by the United States Air Force under Contract No. AF 49(638)-438 monitored by the Air Force Office Of Scientific Research of the Air Research and Development Command.

Dr. Ed Deland of the RAND Corporation was most helpful in making available the analog computing facility of his organization for the study reported herein.

REFERENCES

1. Silva, L. M., "Nonlinear Optimization of Relay Servomechanisms," Electronics Research Laboratory Report, Series No. 60, Issue No. 106, University of California, Berkeley, California, 1954.
2. Chandaket, P. and Leondes, C. T., "The Synthesis Of Optimum Quasi Stationary Nonlinear Control Systems," to be published.
3. Chandaket, P. and Leondes, C. T., "Experimental Studies Of Optimum Type I and Type II Nonlinear Control Systems Of The Stationary and Quasi Stationary Type," to be published.
4. Chandaket, P. and Leondes, C. T., "Optimum Nonlinear Bang Bang Control Systems With Complex Roots," to be published.
5. Chandaket, P. and Rosenstein, A. B., "Bridged-T Complex Conjugate Compensation," Trans. AIEE, Part II, No. 43, pp. 148-162, July 1959.

6. Feldbaum, A. A., "Synthesis Of Optimum Systems With the Aid Of The Phase Space," Avtomatika i Telemekhanika, Vol. XVI, No. 2, 1955.

7. Doll, H. G., Stout, T. M., "Design and Analog Computer Analysis of An Optimum Third Order Nonlinear Servomechanism," Trans. ASME, Vol. 79, pp. 513-526, April 1957.

8. Bogner, I. and Kazda, L. P., "An Investigation of the Switching Criteria for Higher Order Contactor Servomechanisms," Transactions AIEE, Vol. 73, Part II, pp. 118-127, 1954.

9. Kang, C. L. and Fett, G. R., "Metrization of Phase Space and Nonlinear Servo Systems," Jour. Appl. Phys., Vol. 24, pp. 96-97, January 1953.

TABLE I*. OPTIMUM TIME OF TYPE I-THIRD-ORDER SYSTEM

γ	W_{11}	W_{12}	$\tau_{0\to 1}$	$\tau_{1\to 2}$	$\tau_{2\to \text{origin}}$	Total time required
1.5	-0.640316	0.300782	3.22	0.685	0.482	4.387
2.0	-0.520805	0.232564	4.5416	0.502	0.465	5.5086
2.5	-0.397070	0.169903	6.73	0.349	0.453	7.532
3.0	-0.269040	0.112069	11.076	0.218	0.448	11.742
3.5	-0.137293	0.056431	24.1	0.1035	0.446	24.647

*W_{11} and W_{12} and the response time for the error and its derivatives (plotted in Figs. 9, 10 and 11) were obtained on the IBM 709 at the Western Data Processing Center, UCLA.

TABLE II. IBM 709 COMPUTER RESULTS FOR TYPE II SYSTEM

α	τ_{AB} (sec.)	τ_{BO} (sec.)	τ_{total} (sec.) in the y-$\dot{y}$ plane	Remaining error and its derivatives at $y = \dot{y} = 0$		
				e	$\dot{e}$	$\ddot{e}$
1.5	2.96698	0.34863	3.31561	0.34910	-0.52365	0.78548
2.0	4.34350	0.28117	4.62467	0.18017	-0.36033	0.72066
2.5	6.56338	0.20693	6.77031	0.09233	-0.23082	0.57705
3.0	10.93466	0.13352	11.06818	0.04557	-0.13671	0.41012
3.5	23.96808	0.06454	24.03262	0.01824	-0.06386	0.22350

TABLE III. TYPE I OPTIMUM TIME AND TYPE II REMAINING ERROR

α	Type I optimal time	Type II remaining error at optimal time		
		e	$\dot{e}$	$\ddot{e}$
1.5	4.387	0.06705	-.10057	0.15087
2.0	5.5086	0.02978	-.05956	0.11912
2.5	7.532	0.01604	-.04011	0.10028
3.0	11.742	0.00753	-.02260	0.06779
3.5	24.647	0.00223	-.00782	0.02737

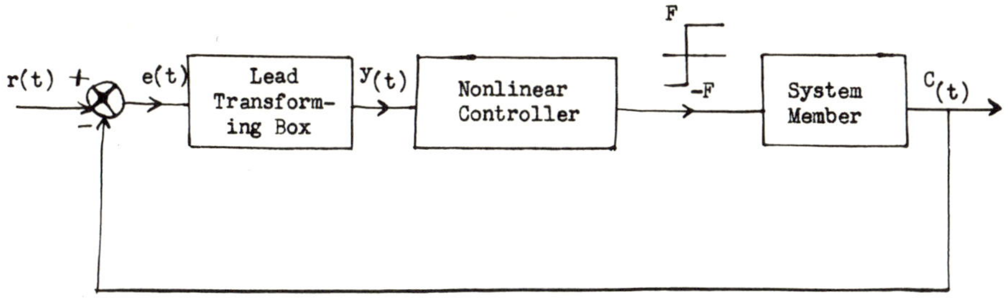

FIG. 1. Basic Diagram for Type II Predictor Control Systems

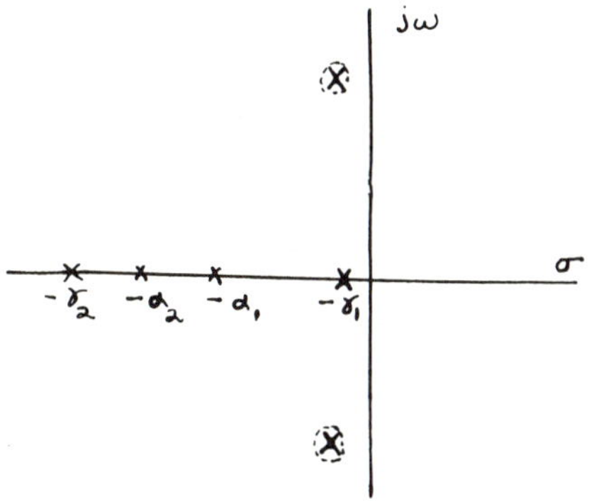

FIG. 2. Bridged-T Compensation for System

$$\frac{K}{(s^2 + 2\zeta\omega_n s + \omega_n^2)(s + \alpha_1)(s + \alpha_2)}$$

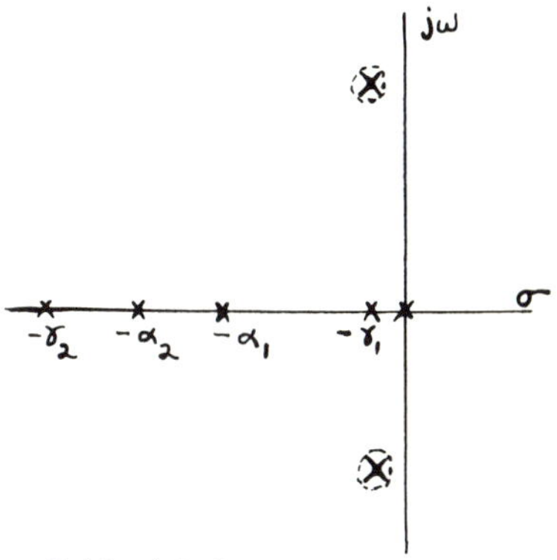

FIG. 3. Bridged-T Compensation for System

$$\frac{K}{s(s^2 + 2\zeta\omega_n s + \omega_n^2)(s + \alpha_1)(s + \alpha_2)}$$

x System Poles
o Bridged-T Zeros
x Bridged-T Poles

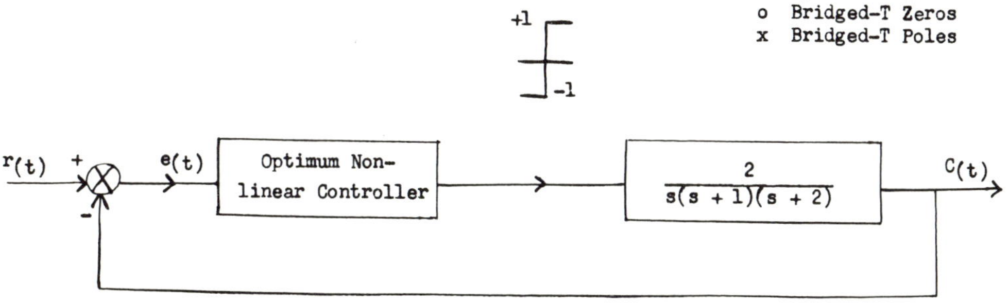

FIG. 4. Type I Third-order Control System with $\alpha = 2$.

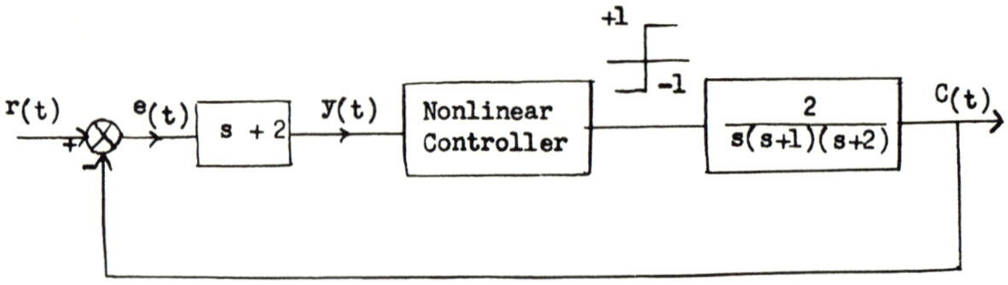

FIG. 5. Type II Third-order System with $\alpha = 2$.

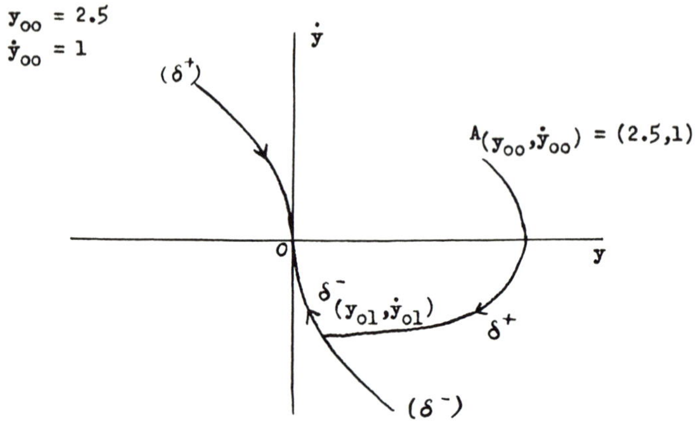

FIG. 6. Sketch of Optimum Path in the y-$\dot{y}$ plane.

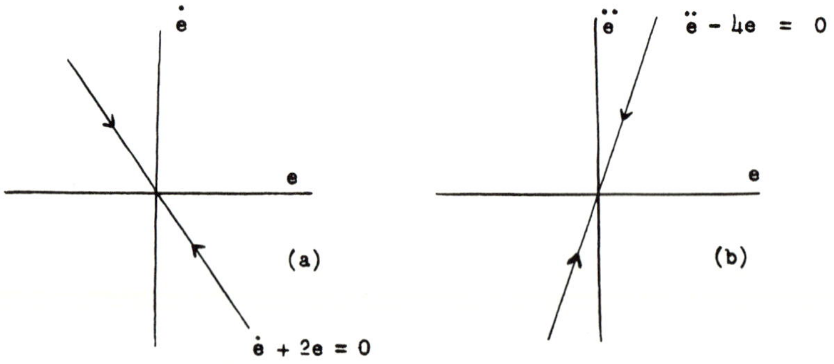

FIG. 7. Slope Characteristics of the Remaining Error as it Approaches Zero in (a) e-$\dot{e}$ plane (b) e-$\ddot{e}$ plane.

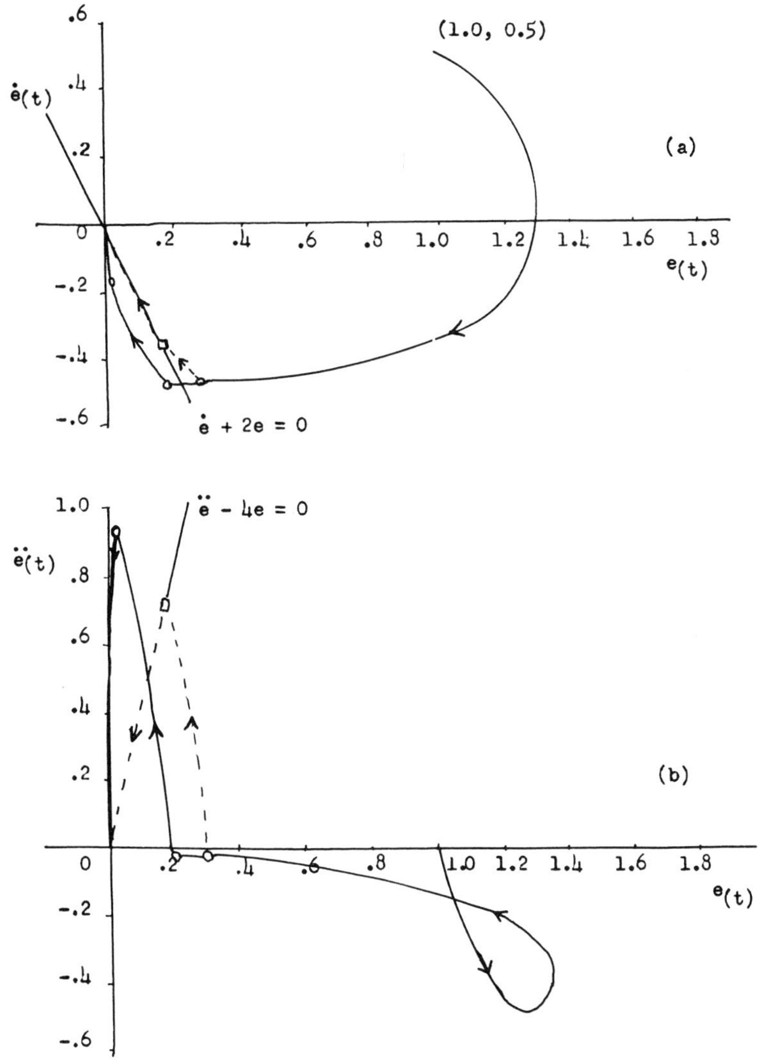

FIG. 8. Phase Plane Characteristics of Error in Type I and Type II Predictor Systems for $\alpha = 2$.

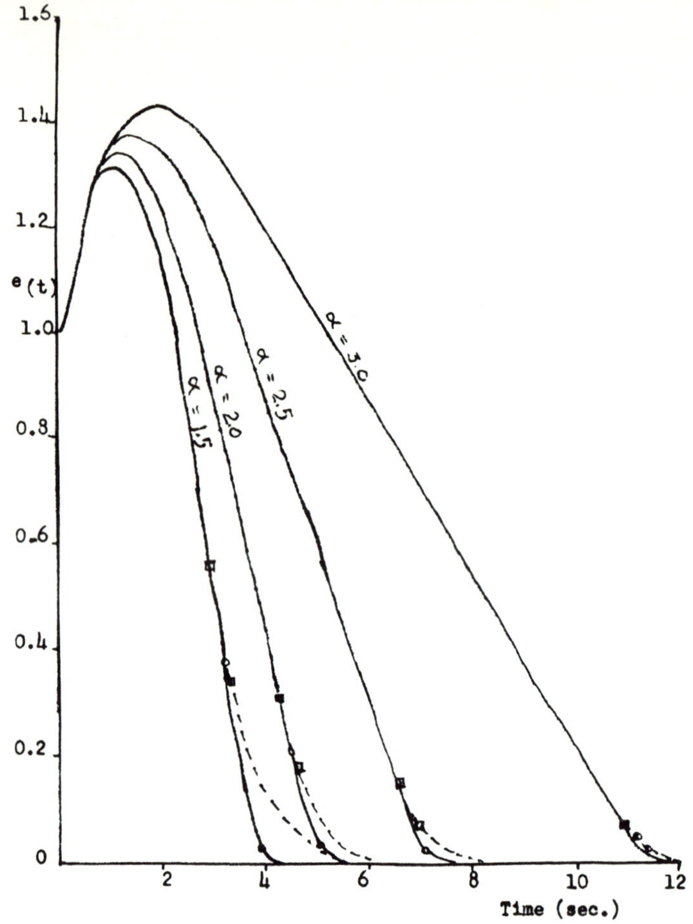

FIG. 9. Error Responses for Type I and Type II Third Order Predictor Control Systems.
o Type I Switching Point
□ Type II Switching Point

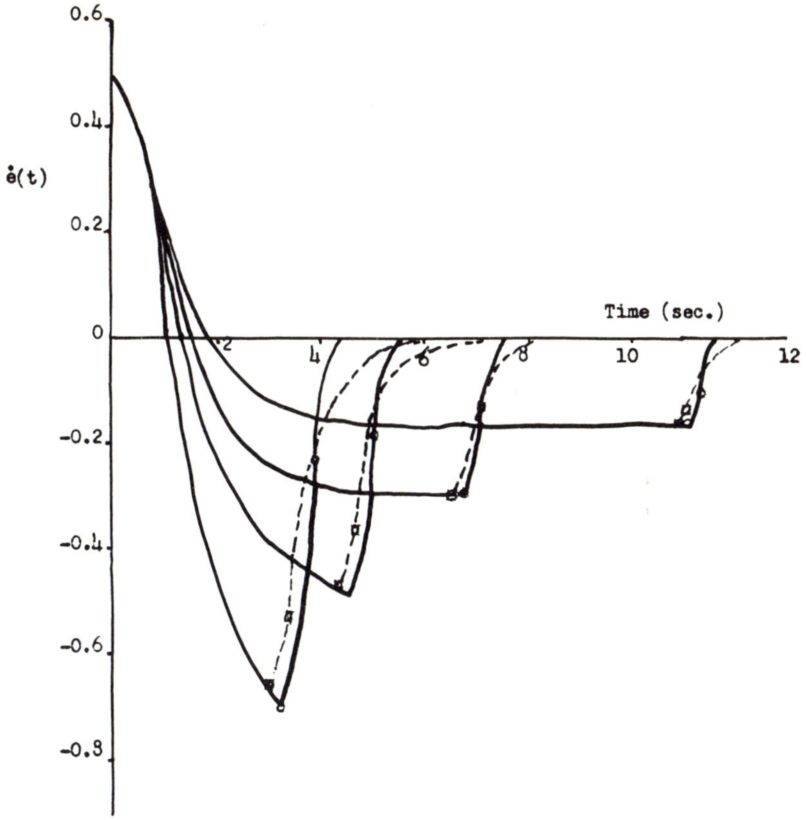

FIG. 10. Error Velocity Responses for Type I and Type II Third Order Predictor Control System.

o Type I Switching Point

□ Type II Switching Point

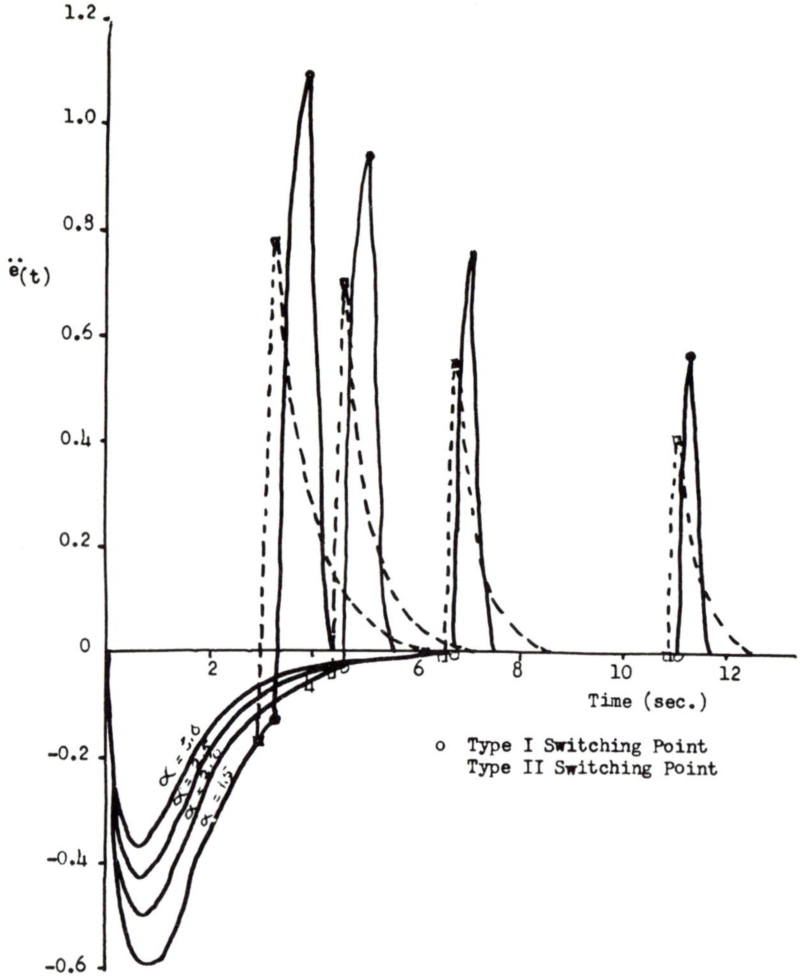

FIG. 11. Error Acceleration Responses for Type I and Type II Third Order Predictor Control Systems.

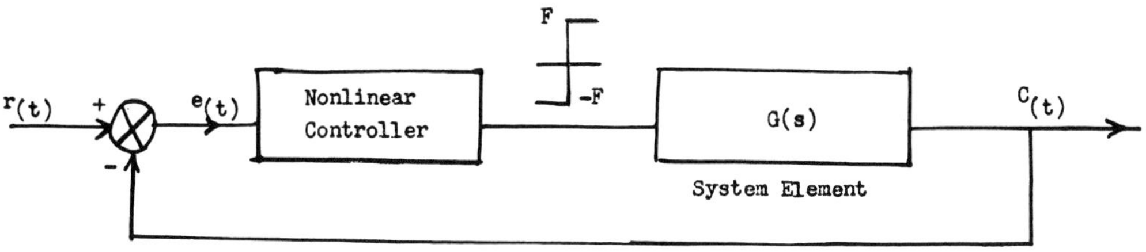

FIG. A-1. Nonlinear Predictor
Control System.

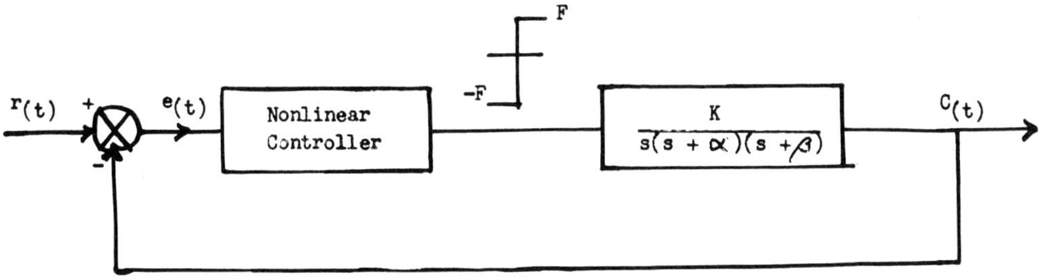

FIG. B-1. Third-Order Nonlinear
Predictor Control System.

OPTIMUM NONLINEAR CONTROL FOR ARBITRARY DISTURBANCES

R. Oldenburger N. P. Smith

SUMMARY

This paper concerns the control of a system variable where the controlling input to the system is bounded, as is normally the case in practice. A control is optimum if the same response is obtained as the best attainable when the system disturbance is known in advance. Disturbances are distinguished between controllable and uncontrollable. The problem of the optimum control for a ramp disturbance is solved. Laboratory tests show that such control applied to arbitrary disturbances yields substantial improvement over known techniques. Approximation of arbitrary disturbances by piecewise linear ones and the solution of the problem of optimum control for random disturbances likely to occur in practice assist here in explaining the improvement obtained in the laboratory. The control described is adaptive in that it adjusts to the rate of change of the disturbance.

INTRODUCTION

A controlled system has an input ℓ where ℓ is a disturbance to which the system is subjected. For convenience this will be called a load disturbance. The system is taken with one output only, this being the controlled variable c. In addition to the disturbance input there is another, namely the manipulated, or controlling, variable m. The quantity m is to be varied by the controller so as to keep c constant or varying with time according to a reference value r, i.e. it is desired to have c = r at all times. Let e denote the error r - c. In the normal equilibrium state r = 0. If the control is perfect c = 0 at the same time.

Let m' denote the rate of change dm/dt of m with respect to time t. In control problems it is desired to keep the error e as near zero as possible regardless of variations in ℓ and r. When in practice $e \equiv 0$ one must have $m' \equiv 0$, whereas when $e \not\equiv 0$ one has $m' \not\equiv 0$. For this reason, in the physical world, wherever precise control is desired the rate m' is made a function of the error e, rather than m. If the error e stays at a non-zero value k one wants m to keep changing. If m did not change for $e \equiv k$ one would have no control. In order to keep e as near zero as possible, it is necessary to have m' depend on quantities such as e' and e" derived from e by mathematical operations.

In first approximation studies many controlled systems may be represented by the equation

$$c' = K_1 m - K_2 \ell \tag{1}$$

where K_1 and K_2 are constants. In physical problems m' is bounded so that

$$|m'| \leq K_3 \tag{2}$$

for a constant K_3 and the absolute value $|m'|$ of m'. In many problems, as where m' is the speed of a hydraulic servomotor piston, one can for practical purposes make m' take on any value between $-K_3$ and K_3 at any time. It is also true that m is bounded, but for large classes of disturbances encountered in practice the variable m does not reach its limits. This is certainly the case for normal control problems and small disturbances, where the control is continuous in the sense that m can take on any value between its maximum and minimum. The limitation (2) is thus the basic saturation condition in control problems, and not the condition

$$|m| \leq K_3$$

assumed in most bang-bang control work.

By the substitutions

$$C = \frac{c}{K_1K_3}, \quad M = \frac{m}{K_3}, \quad L = \frac{K_2\ell}{K_1K_3} \tag{3}$$

relations (1) and (2) become

$$C' = M - L \tag{4}$$

$$|M'| \leq 1 \tag{5}$$

Consider the ramp disturbance

$$L = L_0 + at \qquad\qquad 0 \leq t \leq t_r \tag{6}$$

for constants L_0 and a where the duration t_r of the ramp may be finite or infinite. For $t < 0$ the load L is arbitrary. See Figure 1. There may be a step in L at $t = 0$. Note that $a = 0$ for a step change not superimposed on a ramp. The initial value (at $t = 0$) of M is denoted by M_0. Thus at $t = 0$ the system is in the initial state (C_0, C_0') where

$$C_0' = M_0 - L_0 \tag{7}$$

This state arises from the previous history of the system as, for example, from a step change in L at $t = 0$.

In practical problems the disturbance L on the system is a continuous function $L(t)$ of time t with a continuous derivative $L'(t)$. The Cartesian plot of $L(t)$ versus t being a continuous curve with a tangent line at each point, this plot may be approximated by a broken line made up of straight line segments, each of which is a ramp. For practical purposes the study of the optimum control of a system subject to an arbitrary disturbance reduces to that of a sequence of ramps.

By equation (4)

$$C'' = M' - L' \tag{8}$$

When

$$|L'| < 1 \tag{9}$$

the disturbance is said to be controllable. Such a disturbance is also said to be slowly varying. Perfect, and thus optimum, control is then obtained by letting

$$M' = L' \tag{10}$$

on the assumption that

$$C = C' = 0 \tag{11}$$

at the start of the disturbance. This is true since relations (8) and (10) yield

$$C'' \equiv 0 \tag{12}$$

If now the system starts from the state (11) but

$$|L'| > 1 \tag{13}$$

it follows that $C'' \neq 0$ and a system error C with $C \neq 0$ arises. A perfect control cannot prevent the error, and the disturbance is not controllable. If, finally,

$$|L'| = 1 \tag{14}$$

and relation (10) is satisfied, the system initially in the equilibrium (11) will remain in equilibrium. The control will again be perfect. However, in practice system errors will develop in that after measuring L' directly or indirectly there will be a lag which cannot be compensated for exactly, whence relation (10) will not be satisfied at all times. It follows that a system error C, with $C \neq 0$, will develop. If now relation (10) holds this error will persist. While relation (14) applies one cannot make the difference $(M' - L')$ positive or negative as desired to bring the system back to the equilibrium (11). Thus in practice the cases (13) and (14) are both uncontrollable, whereas the case (9) is controllable. For case (9) there is always an excess of M' over L' available so that $M' - L'$ can be made positive or negative as required.

For controllable disturbances

$$M = L \tag{15}$$

yields perfect control. However, in practice errors in C will develop. If $C \neq 0$, relation (4) gives $C' = 0$ whence the error will persist. If L can be measured one may attempt to schedule the control open loop so that

$$M_1 = L \tag{16}$$

where

$$M = M_1 + M_2 \tag{17}$$

with M_2 as the manipulated variable for the closed loop. The disturbance may now appear smaller than before, i.e. equation (4) is replaced by

$$C' = M_2 - L_1 \tag{18}$$

where

$$L_1 = L - M_1 \tag{19}$$

Suppose that the disturbance L(t) is known not only for the past and present but also for all future time. Suppose that M is determined so that optimum control is obtained. What optimum control is depends on the view-point of the designer. There are disturbances for which control in the case of low order systems can be attained that is optimum simultaneously in every reasonable engineering sense. This is true for a step change. See Figure 2. For optimum nonlinear control the maximum error C_M is a minimum, the duration t_M of the transient is also a minimum, the area between the C-curve and the t-axis is minimized, and all other reasonable optimum criteria are satisfied simultaneously [1][1]. It will be proved here that the same is true for a ramp disturbance as shown in Figure 1, where t_r is large enough for the system to reach equilibrium during the time t_2. More generally, it will be shown in this paper that control optimum in every reasonable sense (such as the C-response in Figure 2 for a step change) can be obtained for a disturbance where the system starts from the equilibrium (11), the disturbance is initially controllable (this phase may be missing), then uncontrollable, followed by a controllable portion of sufficient duration. The optimum control is found on the assumption that the disturbance is known in advance for a sufficient length of time for the system to be returned to equilibrium.

In practice uncontrollable portions are often followed by controllable long enough to return the system to equilibrium.

If a controller knows only the past and present, it is said to give optimum control when the controlled variable C(t) is the same function of time as it would be if the controller gave best response, knowing the future also.

A perfect controller can follow controllable disturbances so as to keep the error zero. Thus if a controller can be built to keep the system error near zero for slowly varying disturbances it will be near optimum for such disturbances.

Suppose that a system is subject to a disturbance L that varies rapidly, i.e. $|L'|$ dominates 1, much of the time. A perfect controller would then not be able to follow the disturbance and the controlled variable C would experience more or less continuous violent fluctuations. This situation cannot happen in successful practice because the control is then ineffective. In the physical world the disturbance L to which a system is subject will normally be controllable a large part of the time. Violent increases in L followed by violent decreases, for example, would be rare. Normally, it is to be expected that a rapid increase or decrease in L will be followed by a slowly varying portion. In practice, a designer should therefore construct a controller that will give nearly optimum response (zero error) for slowly varying disturbances and nearly optimum response for a rapidly varying disturbance followed by a sufficiently long slowly varying portion. In practice an uncontrollable portion is often followed by a controllable section that can be approximated by a broken line made up of two segments. The control of this paper will give nearly optimum response for slowly varying disturbances starting from equilibrium and for rapidly varying disturbances followed by sufficiently long two-segment broken lines unless the second line segment is almost uncontrollable. It is therefore to be expected that the control of this paper will give nearly optimum response in practice much of the time, and definitely better response than can be obtained by known techniques. Extensive analog computer runs bear this out. In fact surprising improvement was obtained in the laboratory when the control, optimum for ramp disturbances, was applied to random disturbances. This

---

[1] The numbers in brackets refer to the bibliography at the end of the paper.

precipitated the current study of the reasons for this improvement.

Consider an arbitrary disturbance $L(t)$ containing uncontrollable portions. There is no single control function that will give optimum response for all such disturbances $\{L(t)\}$. In a given application one does not normally know $L(t)$ in advance. Given two such disturbance functions $L_1(t)$ and $L_2(t)$ it is necessary to switch from one control function to another when $L_1(t)$ is replaced by $L_2(t)$. This is impractical. Since the future is not known there is no solution to the mathematical problem of optimum control for arbitrary disturbances. The best one can do is approximate the optimum as far as possible.

The theory of this paper has been extended to more complicated systems. Where the disturbance can be measured (such as the load on an electric generator), the optimum control given here is attained by the use of control functions involving no derivatives higher than the first, and no higher than the second if the disturbance cannot be measured. Such derivatives can be obtained in practice.

If the reference setting r of the controlled variable is changed this disturbance is equivalent to a load change. The results of this paper thus also apply to such changes in setting. The key to the success of the current approach lies in distinguishing between controllable and uncontrollable disturbances. The control obtained here is adaptive in that it adjusts to the rate of change of the disturbance.

HISTORY

In 1944 one of the authors derived the optimum response of second order systems subject to a saturation limitation on the manipulated variable while trying to optimize governors on aircraft propellers [1]. The object was not to minimize time. An engineer usually must compromise a design to meet several requirements, and looks at many system parameters, in fact he examines the entire response. The parameter normally of most concern is the maximum error in the controlled variable after the initiation of the disturbance. It is fortunate that in the case of low order systems the duration of the system response to step or ramp disturbances is minimized at the same time as the maximum error. Other desirable properties, such as minimum area between the response curve and the time axis, are satisfied simultaneously.

In the hydraulic speed governor field the condition (2) is always satisfied where m is the coordinate of the servomotor piston. Optimum response for step or ramp disturbances is obtained by having the speed of the piston at maximum or zero at all times.

A paper on optimum nonlinear control by Donald MacDonald appeared in 1950 [2]. This was followed by papers of Hopkin [3], Bogner and Kazda [4], Bushaw [5], LaSalle [6], and many others. Hopkin and Wang studied relay systems for random inputs [9]. Rosonoer published a series of papers on the Pontryagin Russian school concerned with minimizing transient duration or other functionals, but this class does not include the maximum error [10].

OPTIMUM CONTROL FOR RAMPS

Derivation of Control Function

The system under study is shown in Figure 3. The control function Σ is computed from measurements of C and R. It is no restriction on the generality of the method to assume that for a controllable ramp disturbance L of formula (6) the controlled variable C reaches equilibrium from above the t-axis at a time $t = t_2$ as is the case for the C-curve of Figure 2, whence this curve is concave up for $t_1 < t < t_2$ and some value t_1 of t. Assume that $M' = 1$ for this section of the C-curve. Let

$$T = t - t_1 \tag{20}$$

for a time coordinate T. The primes in relations (4) and (5) denote derivatives with respect to T (as well as t). The solution of equation (4) with $M' = 1$ and $(C, C') = (C_1, C_1')$ at $T = 0$ is

$$C' = T(1 - a) + C_1' \tag{21}$$

$$C = \frac{T^2}{2}(1 - a) + C_1' t + C_1 \tag{22}$$

When C' reaches zero, C is to reach zero simultaneously, i.e. the minimum point of the arc Γ in Figure 4 starting at the point P_1 for $T = 0$ is on the T-axis. If the initial slope C_1' is numerically too small the corresponding arc Γ_1 for $M' = +1$ will not reach T-axis, whereas if C_1 is numerically too large the corresponding arc Γ_2 will shoot under the T-axis. Elimination of T from the equations (21) and (22) with $C = C' = 0$ yields

$$(1 - a)\, C_1 - \frac{(C_1')^2}{2} = 0 \tag{23}$$

Here $C_1' < 0$ and $C_1 > 0$. It follows that if at any instant (C_1, C_1') satisfies equation (23) the control with $M' = 1$ will automatically bring the system to $(C, C') = (0, 0)$. The system will remain in equilibrium if

$$M' \equiv 0 \tag{24}$$

thereafter.

Similarly, if the C-curve approaches equilibrium with $M' = -1$ from below the T-axis, where

$$(C, C') = (C_1, C_1') \qquad T = 0$$

the relation

$$(1 + a)\, C_1 + \frac{(C_1')^2}{2} = 0 \tag{25}$$

is satisfied. Here $C_1' > 0$ and $C_1 < 0$.

Let $\{C'\}$ denote the <u>absquare</u> of C', where

$$\{C'\} = |C'|\, C' \tag{26}$$

In view of the signs of C_1' relations (23) and (25) may be combined into the single equation

$$\Sigma = 0 \tag{27}$$

where Σ is the control function

$$\Sigma = C - L' |C| + \frac{\{C'\}}{2} \tag{28}$$

Here the subscripts on C_1 and C_1' have been dropped. Let sgn C' be defined by

$$\operatorname{sgn} C' = \begin{cases} 1 & \\ 0 & \text{if} \quad C' = 0 \\ -1 & \end{cases} \qquad \begin{matrix} C' > 0 \\ \\ C' < 0 \end{matrix}$$

The Σ of relation (28) may be replaced by a function Σ_1 where

$$\Sigma_1 = C + \frac{\{C'\}}{2(1 + L' \operatorname{sgn} C')} \tag{29}$$

Relation (27) is plotted in Figure 5 for various values of a. If at any instant C and C' are such that this relation is satisfied the appropriate equation M' = 1 or -1 will lead the system to equilibrium.

Equation (27) can be used to mechanize a controller that will direct the derivative M' to take on the value -1 when the state (C, C') is above the plot of equation (27), and +1 when below.

We shall prove that optimum response in every reasonable engineering sense is obtained with the schedule

$$\begin{aligned} M' &= -\operatorname{sgn} \Sigma && \text{for} \quad \Sigma \neq 0 \\ M' &= 1 && \text{for} \quad \Sigma = 0,\ C > 0 \\ M' &= -1 && \text{for} \quad \Sigma = 0,\ C < 0 \\ M' &= 0 && \text{for} \quad \Sigma = C = 0 \end{aligned} \tag{30}$$

<u>Control Schedule</u>

By relation (28) with L' = a

$$\frac{\partial \Sigma}{\partial C'} = |C'| \tag{31}$$

Thus

$$\frac{\partial \Sigma}{\partial C'} > 0 \qquad \text{for} \quad C' \neq 0 \tag{32}$$

By relation (32) the function Σ increases with C' except when C' = 0. When C' = 0 we have

$$\Sigma = C - a\,|C| \tag{33}$$

Since relation (9) holds, on the assumption that the ramp is controllable,

$$\operatorname{sgn} \Sigma = \operatorname{sgn} C \tag{34}$$

It follows from relations (32) and (34) that $\Sigma > 0$ when (C, C') is above the $\Sigma = 0$ curve and $\Sigma < 0$ below. The control relation

$$M' = -\operatorname{sgn} \Sigma \tag{35}$$

yields the following schedule:

$$\begin{aligned} M' &= 1 &\quad \text{when} \quad \Sigma &< 0 \\ M' &= -1 &\quad \text{when} \quad \Sigma &> 0 \\ M' &= 0 &\quad \text{when} \quad \Sigma &= 0 \end{aligned} \tag{36}$$

The schedule (36) is not identical to the desired schedule (30), but we shall show that in any practical cases schedule (36) yields the same optimum response as schedule (30). Thus for practical purposes schedules (30) and (36) are equivalent.

Proof That Schedule (30) Brings The System To The $\Sigma = 0$ Curve

We shall show that the control function Σ with the schedule (30) will bring the system from any initial state to equilibrium in an optimum manner. We shall prove first that the trajectory will reach the $\Sigma = 0$ control curve from any initial point in the $\Sigma > 0$ region of the phase plane. The proof for the points in the $\Sigma < 0$ region is identical and will be omitted. See Figure 6.

Let the subscript o denote variables in the initial state. Let

$$C_0' > 0, \quad \Sigma_0 > 0 \tag{37}$$

whence by schedule (30)

$$M' = -1 \tag{38}$$

By equation (8)

$$C'' = -1 - a \tag{39}$$

$$C' = C_0' - t - at \tag{40}$$

$$C = C_0 + C_0' t - \frac{t^2}{2} - \frac{at^2}{2} \tag{41}$$

By equations (40) and (41)

$$\lim_{t \to \infty} C' = -\infty \tag{42}$$

$$\lim_{t \to \infty} C = -\infty \tag{43}$$

By relation (28)

$$\lim_{t \to \infty} \Sigma = -\infty \tag{44}$$

Thus at some time Σ changes sign and the trajectory must therefore cross the $\Sigma = 0$ control curve. Let $C \neq 0$. By relation (28) with $L' = a$ the derivative Σ' of Σ is

$$\Sigma = \left[1 - a\,(\text{sgn } C) + (\text{sgn } C') \quad C''\right] \quad C' \tag{45}$$

By relations (37) and (39), while $C' > 0$,

$$\Sigma' = -2aC' \qquad \text{when} \qquad C > 0 \tag{46}$$

$$\Sigma' = 0 \qquad \text{when} \qquad C < 0 \tag{47}$$

Thus when $C < 0$ we have $\Sigma > 0$ and a constant until $C = 0$. When $C > 0$ and $C' > 0$ in view of relation (46) the function Σ will increase or decrease according to the sign of a. In any case C' is decreasing at the maximum possible rate. When $C' = 0$ the variable C attains its maximum value C_M. By relation (40) the time t_M to the maximum point is given by

$$t_M = \frac{C_0'}{1 + a}$$

and by equation (41)

$$C_M = C_0 + \frac{(C_0')^2}{2(1 + a)} \tag{48}$$

If $C_0 < 0$ we have

$$\Sigma_0 = (1 + a)\, C_M \tag{49}$$

Since $\Sigma_0 > 0$ it follows that $C_M > 0$ and the trajectory crosses the C-axis in the phase plane at a point $(C_M, 0)$ where $C_M > 0$. Thus $\Sigma > 0$ to this maximum point.

If $C_0 > 0$ it follows that the trajectory starts in the first quadrant and that $C_M > 0$. Thus in every case where the inequalities (37) hold the trajectory with $M' = -1$ crosses the C-axis in the right half of the phase plane. This trajectory is optimum in that C_M is minimized and all the reasonable criteria for optimum control are satisfied.

Now let

$$C_0' \leq 0, \quad \Sigma_0 > 0 \tag{50}$$

while $M' = -1$, whence the initial state (C_0, C_0') is in the fourth quadrant above the $\Sigma = 0$ control curve. The control function Σ is now given by

$$\Sigma = (1 - a)\, C - \frac{C'^2}{2} \tag{51}$$

Here

$$\Sigma' = 2C' \tag{52}$$

whence Σ is decreasing at a numerically increasing rate. As $t \to \infty$ $\Sigma \to -\infty$ Thus the trajectory eventually reaches the $\Sigma = 0$ curve. Since $C > 0$ when Σ becomes zero, schedule (30) yields $M' = 1$. Then $\Sigma \equiv 0$ until the point $(C, C') = (0, 0)$ is attained. By schedule (30) we have $M' = 0$ thereafter and the system stays in equilibrium.

It follows that the schedule (30) will lead the system to equilibrium from any initial state.

Proof That Schedules (30) And (36) Are Equivalent

We shall show that schedule (36) will bring the system from a point on the $\Sigma = 0$ curve to equilibrium. In practice the trajectory will cross the $\Sigma = 0$ curve before M' changes sign. This may happen, for example, when

$$\Sigma = \pm \mathcal{E} \tag{53}$$

Since Σ is constant until $C = 0$ we have $C' = \pm \sqrt{2\mathcal{E}}$ at $C = 0$. Continuing on the trajectory $M' = \pm 1$ we reach $C' = 0$ when the value of C satisfies

$$C = \frac{\mathcal{E}}{a \pm 1} \tag{54}$$

The trajectory will undershoot or overshoot by the amount C of formula (54). See Figure 7. The amount of overshot will depend on the amount of deadband present. As the deadband $\mathcal{E}$ goes to zero the undershoot or overshoot goes to zero and the trajectory approaches that obtained by using schedule (30) in place of schedule (36).

In practice the system will continue to undershoot or overshoot equilibrium and this will result in a limit cycle about equilibrium.

Continuous Ramp Disturbance

As C and C' are brought to equilibrium $(C, C') = (0, 0)$ the ramp load disturbance may continue and thus cause the system to depart from equilibrium. The system will then be forced back to equilibrium again with schedule (30). This action will take place continually as long as the load disturbance persists and will cause a limit cycle about equilibrium as shown below.

Suppose that the following conditions hold

$$C_0 = 0, \; C_0' = 0, \; \Sigma_0 = 0, \; M_0' = 0 \tag{55}$$

while the ramp (6) continues. By relations (8) and (55)

$$C'' = -a, \quad C' = -at, \quad C = -at^2/2 \tag{56}$$

In view of relations (28) and (56) the variables C and C' both immediately become negative if $a > 0$ or positive if $a < 0$, whence

$$\Sigma \neq 0 \tag{57}$$

and the sign of Σ is opposite that of a. By schedule (30)

$$M' = \operatorname{sgn} a \tag{58}$$

immediately and the system is forced back to equilibrium. The process repeats and in practice results in a limit cycle.

Proof That The Control Is Optimum

The optimum response curve for the ramp will resemble the C-curve shown in Figure 2 obtained for a step change. The proof that the control is optimum in every reasonable sense (time optimum, minimum overswing and underswing, minimum area between the C-curve and t-axis, etc.) will be omitted for the sake of brevity. The argument is the same as used elsewhere by one of the authors [1].

Control Functions In Terms Of Error And Derivatives Of Error

In practice one may not wish or be able to measure the rate of change of the load disturbance. In that case it is necessary to express the control function Σ of formula (28) in terms of C and derivatives of C only. When $|M'| = 1$, by relations (8) and (9)

$$|L'| = \left| 1 - |C''| \right| \tag{59}$$

From equation (8) we have

$$(C'' - C''^3) = (M' - L') - (M' - L')^3 \tag{60}$$

whence when $|M'| = 1$

$$(C'' - C''^3) = L' (L'^2 - 3M'L' + 2) \tag{61}$$

Setting $M' = 1$ in equation (61) yields

$$(C'' - C''^3) = L' (L' - 2) (L' - 1) \tag{62}$$

If $M' = -1$ equation (61) becomes

$$(C'' - C''^3) = L' (L' + 2)(L' + 1) \tag{63}$$

By relations (9), (62) and (63)

$$\operatorname{sgn} L' = \operatorname{sgn} (C'' - C''^3) \tag{64}$$

In view of equations (59) and (64)

$$L' = \left| 1 - |C''| \right| \operatorname{sgn} (C'' - C''^3) \tag{65}$$

Substituting L' from equation (65) into Σ of relation (28) we obtain

$$\Sigma = C - (|C|)\,\Big|1 - |C''|\Big|\ \mathrm{sgn}\,(C'' - C''^3) + \frac{\{C'\}}{2} \tag{66}$$

The control function Σ above is a practical control function that can be obtained entirely from system response. Because of ever present "noise" some filtering of C'' is necessary in order to employ Σ of equation (66).

Relation (59) breaks down when $M' = 0$. However, this happens for an instant only, except when the system is at the equilibrium state $C = C' = 0$ whence equation (66) yields $\Sigma = 0$, which is correct.

Equivalence Of Reference To Load Changes

Let E be the difference between the reference value R of the controlled variable C given by

$$E = C - R \tag{67}$$

The system equation (8) is now replaced by

$$E' = M - L_1 \tag{68}$$

where

$$L_1 = L + R' \tag{69}$$

It follows that a variation in the reference R is equivalent to a variation R' in the load L. The variable C is replaced by the error E. If R is a quadratic function of time, i.e.

$$R = r_0 + bt + ft^2 \tag{70}$$

for constants r_0, b and f, the equivalent load L_1 is a ramp. The quantity R is arbitrary for $t < 0$, and there may be a step in L_1 at $t = 0$. For controllability

$$|M'| > |L' + R''| \tag{71}$$

With

$$L' = a, \quad R'' = 2f \tag{72}$$

the optimum control function Σ of relation (28) becomes

$$\Sigma = E - (L' + R'')\ |E| + \frac{\{E\}}{2} \tag{73}$$

Other Systems

The results above have been extended to more complicated systems, but will be omitted for the sake of brevity.

Practical Control

The schedule (36) is achieved by setting

$$M' = -K\Sigma \tag{74}$$

for $K = +\infty$ with M' subject to the saturation limitation (5). In practice it is convenient to make K as large as possible, such as $K = 100$ (this is near the practical maximum), and for small $|C|$ and $|C'|$ employ a linear Σ in place of the Σ of equation (28) to remove limit cycles and achieve the system stability.

ARBITRARY DISTURBANCES

Uncontrollable Disturbance

Laboratory tests of the use of the control function Σ of relation (28) gave substantial improvement over what could be obtained by known techniques. In an effort to explain this remarkable improvement, optimum control for more general disturbances than ramps and steps was considered. Some of the analysis follows.

Suppose first that the system starts from the equilibrium state $(C, C') = (0, 0)$ at $t = 0$ but that the disturbance L is uncontrollable from $t = 0$ to $t = t_U$ for a value t_U. For optimum control it is then necessary that

$$M' = \operatorname{sgn} L' \tag{75}$$

The rate L' may vary over the interval $(0, t_U)$ but either $L' \geq 1$ over this entire interval, or $L' \leq 1$. In this way the C-curve will bend away from the t-axis a minimum. See the portion from $t = 0$ to $t = t_U$ in Figure 8. Suppose that $L' \geq -1$ whence $C < 0$ as in this figure. Now

$$\Sigma = (1 + L')C + \frac{C'^2}{2} \tag{76}$$

Since $\Sigma < 0$ the schedule (30) yields $M' = 1$. This gives optimum response from $t = 0$ to $t = t_U$. The system equation is

$$C'' = 1 - L' \tag{77}$$

Similarly, if $L' \leq 1$.

Equilibrium Followed By Arbitrary Controllable Disturbance

Suppose that the system is in equilibrium for $t < 0$ and undisturbed and that for $t > 0$ the system is subject to a controllable disturbance L. Suppose that the system leaves equilibrium by having C increase, whence $C > 0$, $C' > 0$. In this case $L' < 0$. The control function Σ of equation (28) satisfies $\Sigma > 0$ whence by the schedule (30) we have $M' = -1$ making $C'' < 0$, whence the C-curve is concave down and returns to the C-axis. Due to physical imperfections there will be an oscillation about equilibrium but this will be negligible unless the imperfections are large.

Uncontrollable Disturbance Followed By Sufficiently Long Controllable Section

Suppose that the system is in equilibrium for $t < 0$ subject to no disturbance or a controllable disturbance. Assume that for $t = 0$ to $t = t_U$ the disturbance is uncontrollable, but that after $t = t_U$ it is controllable for a period of time sufficiently long for the argument to follow. See Figure 8. We shall show that there is a response optimum in every reasonable sense, similar to the optimum response to a step change shown in Figure 2.

It is no restriction to suppose that $L' \geq 1$ for the uncontrollable portion whence C becomes negative as in Figure 9. Until C reaches the minimum value $-C_m$, for $C_m > 0$, the control function Σ of equation (28) is such that $\Sigma < 0$, whence by schedule (30) we have $M' = 1$ and the response is optimum. Let t_m denote the value of t at the minimum point. If

$$C'' = 1 - L' \tag{78}$$

after the minimum point, the inequality $|L'| < 1$ implies that $C'' > 0$. We may assume that there is a number η such that for $t > t_4$ where $t_4 > t_U$

$$|L'| < \eta < 1 \tag{79}$$

It follows that the C-curve will eventually reach the t-axis. Let $t = t_c$ denote the time at the crossing point. For any vertical line ℓ between $t = t_m$ and $t = t_c$ the area A between the C-curve, the t-axis, the line $t = t_m$ and the line ℓ is a minimum. However, at the crossing point $C = 0$, $C' > 0$ whence $\Sigma > 0$. At some point between $t = t_m$ and $t = t_c$ the function Σ changes sign. The schedule (30) then requires that M' switch from +1 to -1. The curve from $t = t_m$ to $t = t_c$ is not optimum in the sense that this results in an overswing after $t = t_c$ with $C = C_M$ at the maximum point. To minimize C_M we must have $C'' = -1 - L'$ valid for $t > t_c$. The value of C_M can be diminished further by letting M' switch from +1 to -1 at a point P_1 and a time $t = t_1$ where $t_1 < t_c$. As P_1 moves to the left the maximum point drops as shown. If P_1 is at the minimum point where $t = t_m$ the C-curve will drop to the right of t_m as shown. It follows that there is a point $t = t_1$ between t_m and t_c where the C-curve to the right of P_1 touches the t-axis. This arc, starting at $t = t_1$, is denoted by Γ in Figures 8 and 9.

The curve in Figure 8 composed of the C-curve from $t = 0$ to $t = t_1$, for which $M' = +1$, and Γ from $t = t_1$ to $t = t_2$, for which $M' = -1$, is optimum. This will be called the Γ-<u>curve</u>. Every other solution Γ_1 passes below the Γ-curve from $t = 0$ to $t = t_1$, or is identical with it up to a value t_3 of t where $t_3 > t_1$, after which it crosses the t-axis, and attains a maximum point above the t-axis at an instant t_M where $t_M > t_2$ as shown in Figure 8. If $\Gamma_1 \equiv \Gamma$ for $0 < t < t_1$, then for $t > t_1$ the curve Γ_1 will lie between the curve $M' = +1$ and Γ. In fact for any t where $t > t_1$

$$-1 - L' \leq C'' \leq 1 - L' \tag{80}$$

The slope C' of the curve with $M' = +1$ increases at the maximum rate whereas for Γ to the right of $t = t_1$ it decreases at the maximum rate. Thus the Γ-curve is optimum in every reasonable engineering sense.

To attain the optimum Γ-curve it is only necessary that the controllable section of L(t) terminate after $t = t_2$ if it terminates at all.

The control schedule (30) will switch M' from +1 to -1 at least once before $t = t_c$. Laboratory runs and broken line approximations to L(t) indicate that the schedule (30) will often give nearly the optimum response of Figure 8. Why this is so can be seen in part from the next section.

Piecewise Linear Disturbance

Suppose that at $t = 0$ the value $-C_m$ of C is at a minimum. If the system started from the equilibrium $(C, C') = (0, 0)$ for some t, $t < 0$, and L was uncontrollable and then controllable to $t = 0$, with the point $(-C_m, 0)$ as the first minimum, this point is attained in an optimum manner by the use of schedule (30). Suppose that the disturbance L after $t = 0$ is made up of a single controllable linear section with $L' = a$. Schedule (30) will yield $M' = +1$ until $t = t_1$ where

$$t_1 = \sqrt{\frac{1 + a}{1 - a}} \sqrt{C_m} \tag{81}$$

Then $M' = -1$ to equilibrium. We remark that

$$C = \frac{(a - 1) C_m}{2} \tag{82}$$

$$C' = \sqrt{1 - a^2} \sqrt{C_m} \tag{83}$$

at the point $t = t_1$. The time t_2 to equilibrium from the point $t = t_1$ is given by

$$t_2 = \sqrt{\frac{1 - a}{1 + a}} \sqrt{C_m} \tag{84}$$

Thus if the linear section with slope a lasts at least as long as $t_1 + t_2$, the schedule (30) will yield a response optimum in every reasonable sense, as in the preceding section.

It may not be possible to approximate $L(t)$ after the minimum point by a sufficiently long single controllable linear section. Suppose therefore that $L(t)$ is made up of two controllable linear sections of total length sufficient to bring the system to equilibrium. Let a_1 and a_2 denote L' for the first and second sections respectively. Normally $a_1 > a_2$ which will be assumed first. Let t_1 and t_2 denote the durations of the first and second sections respectively.

Suppose that Σ with $L' = a_1$ becomes zero at $t = t_s$ during the first section. Let Σ_1 and Σ_2 be the control functions (28) with $L' = a_1$ and $L' = a_2$ respectively. Since when $C < 0$

$$\Sigma_2 = \Sigma_1 + (a_1 - a_2) \ |C| \tag{85}$$

it follows that $\Sigma_2 > \Sigma_1$, whence $\Sigma_2 > 0$ from $t = t_s$ up to the maximum point where $C = C_M$. See Figure 10.

Let C_1 and C_1' denote the values of C and C' at $t = t_1$. Now

$$C_M = \frac{(a_2 - a_1) C_1}{(1 + a_2)} \tag{86}$$

while by $\Sigma_1 = 0$

$$C_1 = \frac{-C_1'^2}{2(1 + a_1)} \tag{87}$$

By equations (82) and (86)

$$C_M < \frac{(a_1 - a_2)(1 - a_1)}{2(1 + a_2)} C_m \tag{88}$$

If a_2 is small compared to 1 and we drop it from $(1 + a_2)$ in inequality (88) we have

$$C_M < \frac{C_m}{8} \tag{89}$$

If a_2 is near -1 the quantity C_M will normally be large, but then the disturbance is practically uncontrollable. If $a_2 \geq -\frac{1}{2}$ inequality (88) yields

$$C_M < 9/16\ C_m \tag{90}$$

regardless of the value of a_1.

The optimum transient with no overshoot is obtained by switching from $M' = +1$ to $M' = -1$ earlier in the first interval. This optimum transient will be little different from that obtained by the schedule (30) unless a_2 is near -1.

If t_1 is so small that $\Sigma_1 < 0$ for the first interval, and a_2 is near enough to a_1, by equation (85) we have $\Sigma_2 < 0$ for a while after $t = t_1$. The schedule (30) will now give optimum response. The same is true if $\Sigma_2 = 0$ at $t = t_1$. If now a_2 is sufficiently less than a_1, we may have $\Sigma_2 > 0$ at $t = t_1$. The schedule (30) will now give an overshoot. The optimum transient with no overswing is obtained by switching from $M' = +1$ to $M' = -1$ in the first interval so that at $t = t_1$ we have $\Sigma_2 = 0$, whence $\Sigma_2 \equiv 0$ until equilibrium $(C, C') = (0, 0)$ is attained. By relations (81) through (83) the maximum value C_M of C obtained with the schedule (30) satisfies inequality (88). Unless a_2 is near -1 the response with schedule (30) will be near the optimum.

If a_2 is not near -1 some designers may prefer the response based on schedule (30) to the optimum, where the optimum has no overswing, since $C = 0$ is attained more rapidly and the net area (difference between areas below and above the t-axis) may be less.

If $a_2 > a_1$ and with schedule (30) we have $\Sigma_1 \neq 0$ during the a_1-section, this schedule gives the optimum transient. This is so since $\Sigma_2 < \Sigma_1$ for $C < 0$. If with schedule (30) the function Σ_1 becomes zero during the a_1-section, at the start of the a_2-section $\Sigma_2 < 0$ whence by schedule (30) there will be no overswing. Thus there will be no overswing in any case for which $a_2 > a_1$. Unless a_1 is very near -1 and a_2 near +1 schedule (30) gives nearly optimum response.

The same type of argument applies if the C-curve initially goes above the t-axis.

Similar analyses hold for disturbances with three or more consecutive linear sections. For the sake of brevity this argument will be omitted. From the above the great improvement obtained experimentally can be better understood.

Optimum control is not obtained by schedule (30) if an uncontrollable disturbance with $L' > 1$ is followed quickly by an uncontrollable portion with $L' < -1$, or vice versa. Such disturbances were studied by Chang and one of the authors [11].

In practice the load L normally varies in a random way about a mean value and occasionally moves from one level to another as shown in Figure 8. This is true, for example, of the load on an engine. The sections marked C in Figure 8 are controllable whereas U denotes an uncontrollable transition portion.

PHYSICAL NONLINEAR EQUIPMENT

Methods for producing the mathematical operations needed to yield the nonlinear control functions of this paper are well known. Thus the use of d-c circuits for differentiating electrically and dashpots for doing this mechanically is classical.

The use of absquaring (signed square $|x| \ x$) physical components is also classical. Nonlinear resistors exist for which the current is proportional to the absquare of the voltage. The pressure drop across a sharp-edged orifice is proportional to the absquare of the flow rate. Thus the absquare is easy to produce by physical devices in common use [12]. The improvement of the transients must be weighed in practice against the cost of including nonlinear terms in the control function.

EXPERIMENTAL RESULTS

The major results of this paper were checked on an analog computer. Figures 11 A - C illustrate the response of the same system to the same ramp disturbance using three different control functions. An initial step change not shown is superimposed. Figure 11 A shows the system response using a linear control function, i.e. $\Sigma = aC + bC'$, where a and b are constants adjusted to give the best system response over the entire range of initial conditions that will typically occur. Figure 11 B shows the response of the same system using the nonlinear control function (28) with $a = 0$, which is optimum for step changes. Note the improvement in the deviation C over the case of Figure 11 A. Figure 11 C shows the response when the control function (28) with schedule (36) is used, the response now being the best obtainable if the ramp were known in advance. Note the large improvement over the transients of Figures 11 A and B. Note also that the part of the transient after the first swing is the portion of the transient which is reduced because the sign of M' in this case is changed at the optimum instant.

In Figure 12 is shown the response to an arbitrary controllable disturbance using schedule (36). For practical purposes this is the same as the best that can be obtained if the disturbance is known in advance. The response to a piecewise linear controllable disturbance is given in Figure 13.

In Figure 14 is shown a typical portion of an experimental run where the same random disturbance is applied to a system with the linear control Σ, where the coefficients a and b in $\Sigma = aC + bC'$ are adjusted to give best overall response (in a practical sense) to large and small disturbances, and applied to the same system with the schedule (36) and Σ of equation (28) taken optimum for ramp changes in the load L. The load trace shown in the figure begins with a large fast change in the level of the load, such as when load is dropped on an electric generator. The random load portion which follows is greatly amplified as are the C-traces. Most of the time much greater improvement was obtained with the nonlinear control than with the best linear, but the portion shown is typical. In Figure 15 there is a typical portion of an experimental run where the linear control function Σ was adjusted to give best response for the "small" disturbance shown and was not tuned to give best overall response for both small and large disturbances. The responses for the best linear and the nonlinear Σ of formula (28) with the same disturbance and system are displayed. Figure 15 indicates that a properly chosen linear control function is a good approximation to the nonlinear. Many other random disturbances were tried and in all cases the control function optimum for ramps gave better performance than the best linear. However, it is necessary to filter high frequency jiggle from L' in computing Σ of formula (28). Otherwise there will be excessive switching and poor performance.

ACKNOWLEDGMENTS

This research was supported by a grant from the National Aeronautics and Space Administration of the United States. Some assistance was also received from the U.S. Office of Naval Research, Information Systems Branch.

BIBLIOGRAPHY

1. Optimum Nonlinear Control, R. Oldenburger, ASME Transactions, Vol. 79, 1957, pp. 527-546.

2. Nonlinear Techniques for Improving Servo Performance, D. MacDonald, National Electronics Conference, Vol. 6, 1950, pp. 400-421.

3. A Phase Plane Approach to The Compensation of Saturating Servomechanisms, A. M. Hopkin, AIEE Transactions, Vol. 70, Part I, 1951, pp. 631-639.

4. An Investigation of the Switching Criteria for Higher Order Servomechanisms, I. Bogner and L. F. Kazda, AIEE Transactions, Vol. 73, Part II, 1954, pp. 118-127.

5. Differential Equations with a Discontinuous Forcing Term, D. W. Bushaw, Report No. 149, Experimental Towing Tank, Stevens Institute of Technology, Hoboken, New Jersey, January, 1953.

6. Optimal Discontinuous Forcing Terms, C. Bushaw, Contributions to The Theory of Nonlinear Oscillations, Vol. IV, 1958, pp. 29-52.

7. The Time Optimal Control Problem, J. P. LaSalle, Contributions to The Theory of Nonlinear Oscillations, Vol. V, 1960, pp. 1-24.

8. Discontinuous Automatic Control (Book), I. Flügge-Lotz, Princeton University Press, Princeton, New Jersey, 1953.

9. A Relay-type Feedback Control System Design for Random Inputs, A. M. Hopkin and P. K. C. Wang, AIEE Transactions, Part II, Applications and Industry, Vol. 78, 1959, pp. 228-233.

10. L. S. Pontryagin's Maximum Principle in the Theory of Optimum Systems, Part I, Part II, Part III, L. I. Rozonoer, Automation and Remote Control, Vol. 20, 1959, pp. 1320-1334, pp. 1405-1421, pp. 1517-1532.

11. Optimum Nonlinear Control for Step and Pulse Disturbances, R. Oldenburger and R. C. C. Chang. This is being prepared for publication.

12. Nonlinear speed and load governor for alternators, U.S. Patent No. 2,908,826, October 13, 1959, R. Oldenburger; Method and apparatus for hydraulic control systems, U.S. Patent No. 2,931,324, April 5, 1960, R. Oldenburger; Method and apparatus for controlling a condition, U.S. Patent No. 2,960,629, November 15, 1960, Canadian Patent No. 610,960, December 20, 1960, R. Oldenburger.

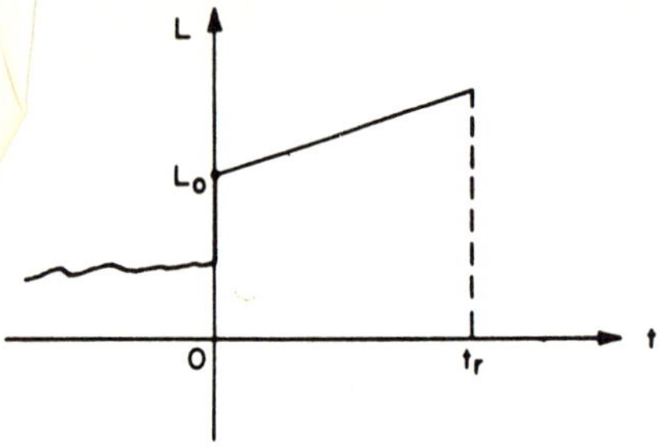

Fig. 1. Ramp disturbance

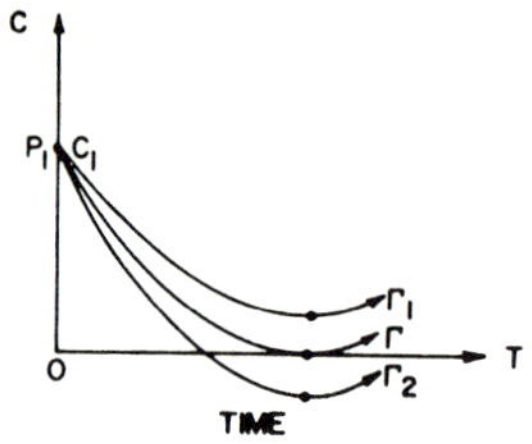

Fig. 4. Arcs for different initial slopes

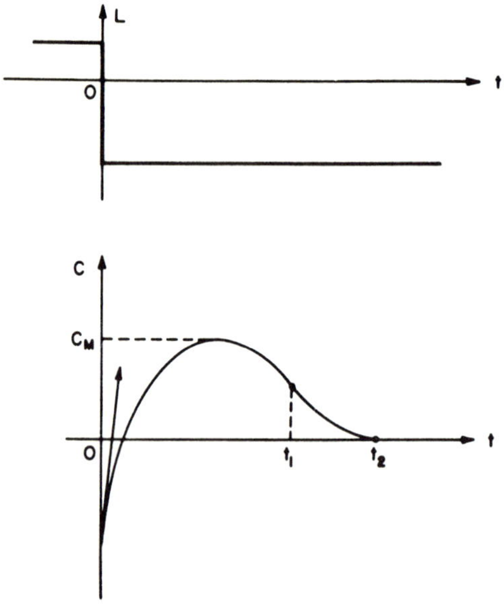

Fig. 2. Response to step change

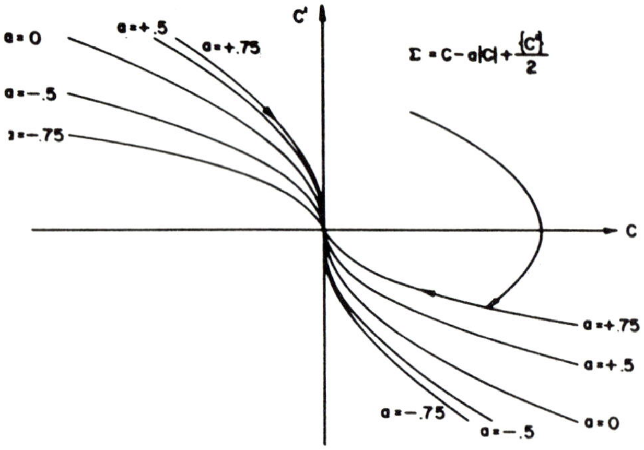

Fig. 5. Control curves for various values of the derivative of the disturbance

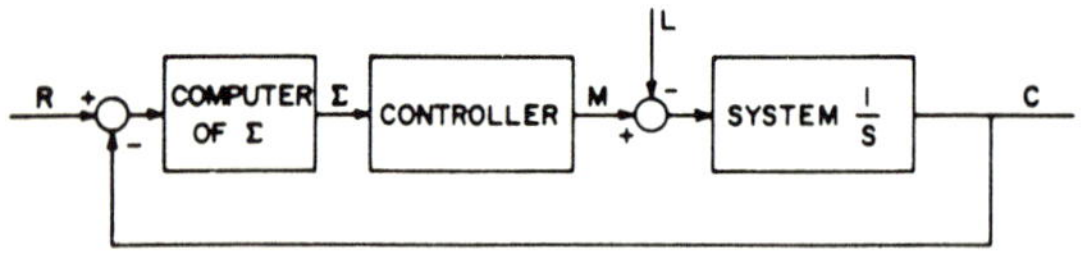

Fig. 3. Closed loop system

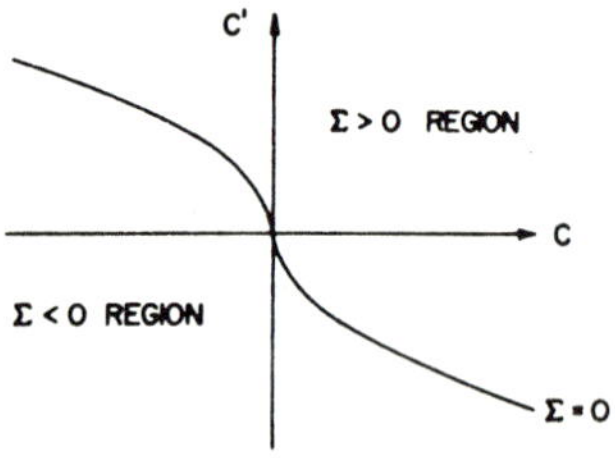

Fig. 6. Sign of control function on phase plane

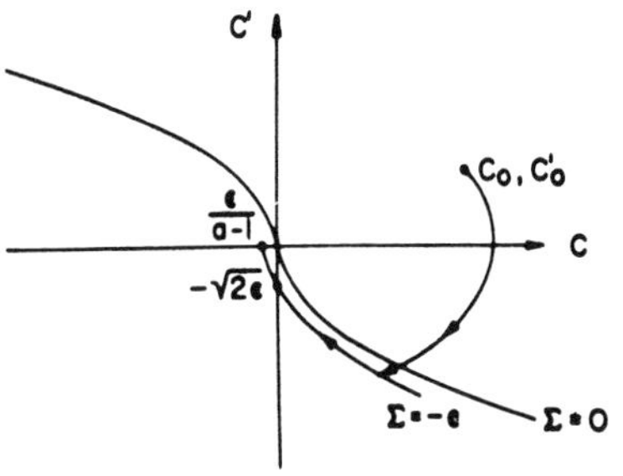

Fig. 7. Trajectory of system with deadband

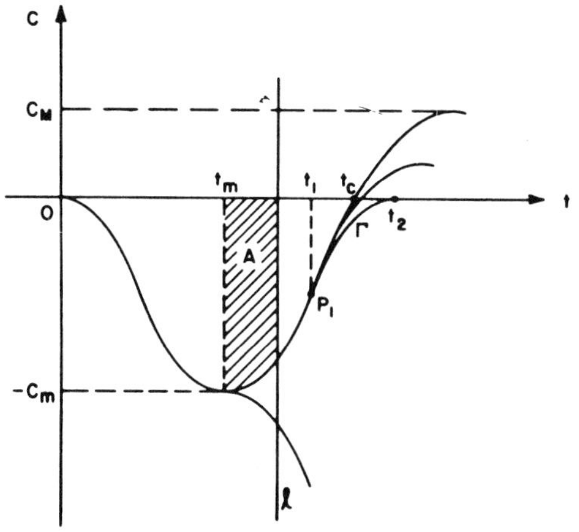

Fig. 9. Curve for $C'' = 1 - L'$ followed by $C'' = -1 - L'$

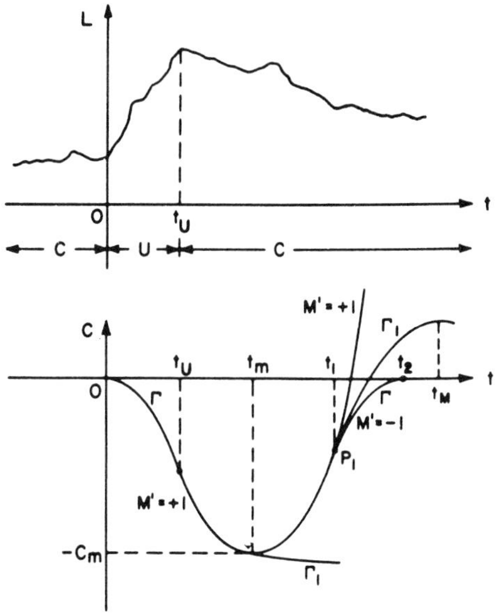

Fig. 8. Response to uncontrollable followed by controllable disturbance

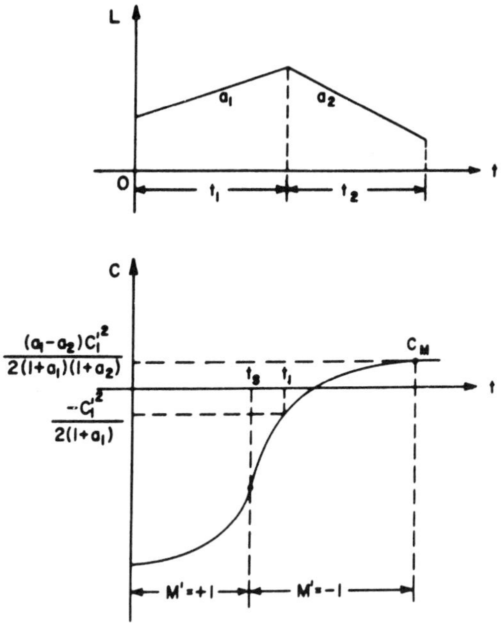

Fig. 10. Piecewise linear disturbance

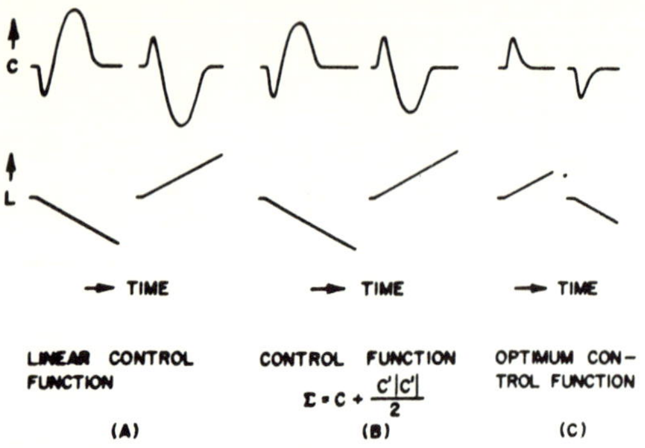

Fig. 11. Response to ramp disturbance

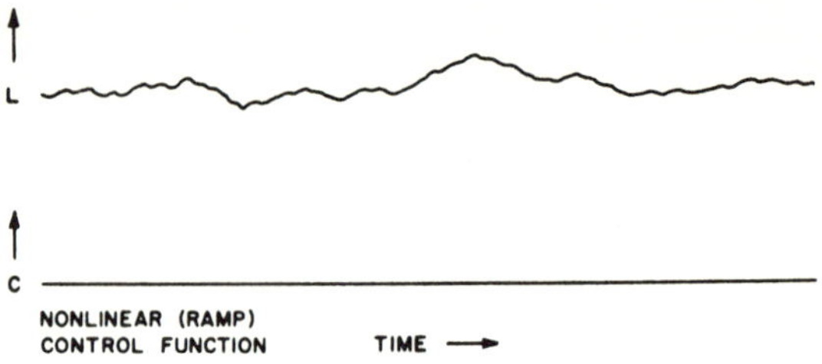

Fig. 12. Response to arbitrary controllable disturbance

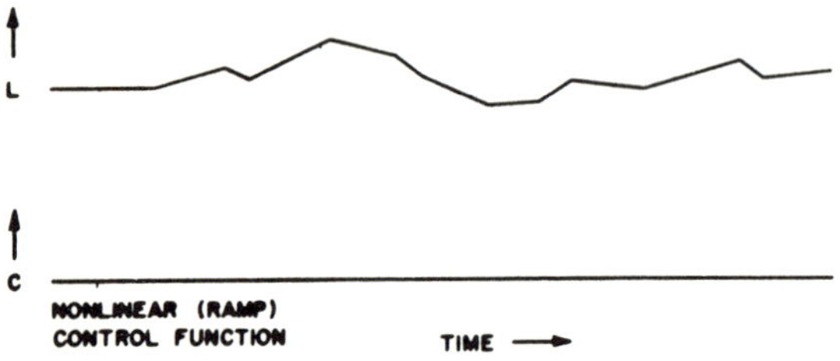

Fig. 13. Response to controllable piecewise linear disturbance

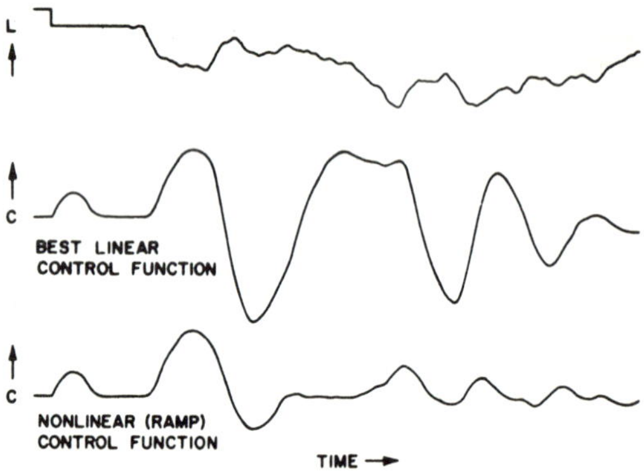

Fig. 14. Response to random disturbance for best linear and optimum nonlinear ramp controls

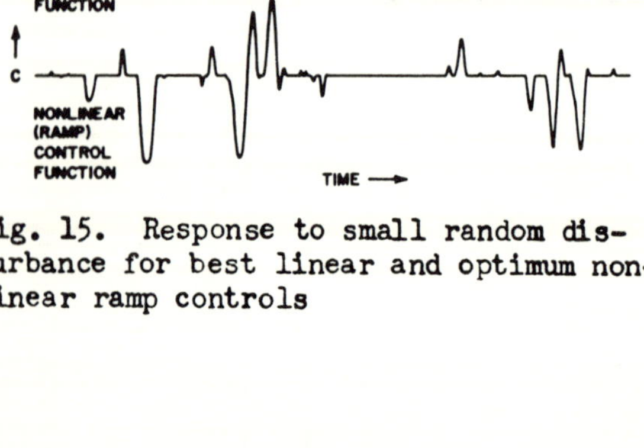

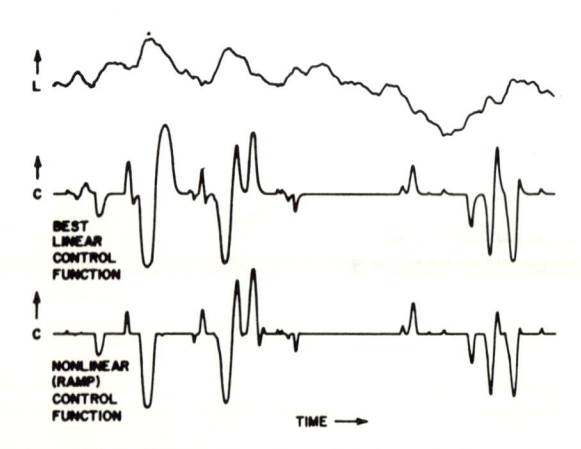

Fig. 15. Response to small random disturbance for best linear and optimum nonlinear ramp controls

PART III

Minimization of a Functional for Systems with Bounded Inputs

OPTIMAL PROCESSES IN AUTOMATIC CONTROL SYSTEMS

BY

A. A. FEL'DBAUM

Translated from Avtomatika i Telemekhanika, Vol. 14, No. 6, pp. 712-728, June, 1953

A generalized concept of the optimal process and the relevant principles of automatic control systems are considered. The form of the optimal process with various types of limitations is determined. An example is given of the application of suggested structural schemes for a practically important class of governing (determined) influences.

1. The Problem of Designing the Best Possible Automatic Control System

The problem of improving the dynamic properties of automatic control systems by means of additional nonlinear couplings has been dealt with in a number of papers. As early as 1935, a quadratic feedback coupling was introduced in the system designed by D. I. Mar'ianovskii and D. V. Svecharnik in order to obtain optimal dynamic characteristics. Automatic potentiometers, relay systems with quadratic feedback coupling, etc., appeared later. The optimal control law for the case of a limited second derivative is given in paper [1], which also gives trajectories in the phase plane. Paper [2] gives experimental data in addition to similar conclusions. The generalization problems for the case of limited higher derivatives were discussed in paper [3], which also showed the realization possibility of processes that are near to the required form in systems containing no relay units. The influence of the parameters of the system and the load on the deviation from the optimal process with limited second derivative is investigated in paper [4]. The same paper gives experimental data for a system with limited second derivative. The processes in this system were found to be smooth and rapid.

Only the special case of continuous influence at zero initial conditions was investigated in the above works. The present paper introduces the general concept of the optimal process for any defining (established) effects $X_0(t)$ and initial conditions, and considers its realization possibilities. The problem is solved with a limitation of any derivative as well as a limitation of the system coordinates (linear combinations of derivatives).

Let us designate by X the magnitude to be controlled, and the established magnitude, i.e., the governing effect, by X_0. The problem of an automatic control system (see, for example [5]) consists in a realization of the equality $X_0 = X$*. Generally speaking, in any real system there exists an error

$$x = X_0 - \dot{X} \tag{1}$$

The value of x equals the sum $x_s + x_d$, where x_s is the established error and x_d is the transient error (which disappears following the transient process in a stable system).

The construction of the best system as shown in the subsequent section reduces to insuring theleast possible duration and occasionally the least possible maximum of the transition process $x_d(t)$ and the least possible values of the established error $x_s(t)$.

*In a tracking system, for example, the magnitude X_0 is the angular position of the governing axis and X is the angular position of the governed axis.

Part of the system (the control target, the actuator and occasionally the last cascade of the control device, i.e., a powerful amplifier) is usually given in practice. The remaining parts of the automatic control system must be designed in such a way that the available power of the system can be utilized to the limit. The lower limit of the transition process duration is given by the limiting values of the variables (the coordinates) that govern the motion of the available power of the system:

$$X_{i1} \leq X_i \leq X_{i2}. \tag{2}$$

In the special case the magnitude X must satisfy the boundary conditions

$$\left| \frac{d^i X}{dt^i} \right| \leq M_i. \tag{3}$$

The acceleration, for example, and occasionally the speed of the servomotor of the tracking system are limited.

Occasionally the limitations are imposed on linear combinations of derivatives.

The values of $x_s(t)$ for a large class of functions $X_0(t)$ may be theoretically decreased to any degree (See [6] , [7] , [8]).

For the subsequent consideration to be concrete it is necessary to limit the functions $X_0(t)$ to a definite class (for example, a class of polynomials, a class of solutions for differential equations of an m-th order with constant coefficients, statistical assignment, etc.). Furthermore, the functions $X_0(t)$ must satisfy the same boundary conditions (for example (3)) as the functions $X(t)$, since otherwise the controlled magnitude $X(t)$ will not be capable of reproducing the function $X_0(t)$.

2. The Generalized Concept of an Optimal Process

Let X be the output magnitude of a system which satisfies the conditions (2) or (3). Let us call such a function $X(t)$ an admissible function. Two types of theoretically feasible optimal processes, in which $X(t)$ are admissible functions, must be distinguished.

1. The ideal optimal process, characterized by the equality $x_s = 0$; here the time t_0, after which the error x_d becomes 0 and thereafter remains 0 at $t > t_0$, is minimal. The time t_0 is known as the control time.

2. The real optimal process characterized by the inequality $|x_s| < \varepsilon_s$, where ε_s is a small magnitude assigned by certain conditions. In this case the control time t_0 must also be minimum, being defined as the time after which the absolute magnitude of the error x_d becomes and henceforth remains smaller than the small magnitude ε_d, i.e., $|x_d| < \varepsilon_d$. At $t > t_0$ the magnitude $x = x_s + x_d$ will then have a smaller modulus than $\varepsilon = \varepsilon_s + \varepsilon_d$.

An additional boundary condition is possible: the largest possible maximum of the magnitude $|x_d|$ must be minimal. This condition, as shown below, in some cases does not contradict the condition for the minimum of t_0. In the general case the minimum of t_0 can be required after the condition for the minimum of the maximum value of $|x_d|$ is satisfied.

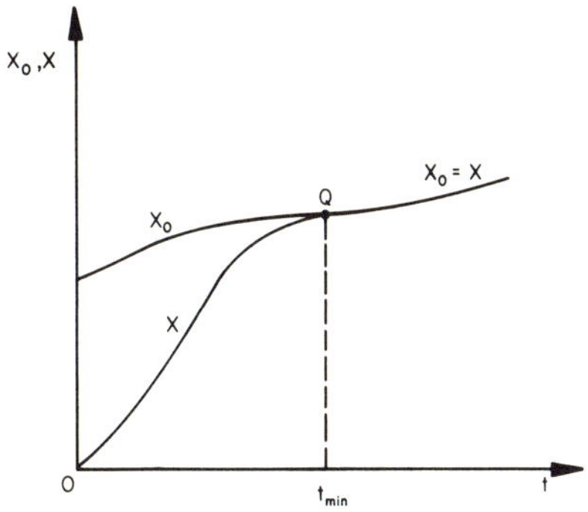

Fig. 1

Let us consider the ideal optimal process (Fig. 1). We assume that both functions $X_0(t)$ and $X(t)$ are admissible, and temporarily consider that the function $X_0(t)$ is known.* Without limiting the generality of thediscussion it can be assumed that $(X)_{t=0} = 0$. If $t_0 = t_{min}$ is the controlled time, then at $t > t_{min}$ both curves coincide. Let X be the initial value of the system characterized by the system of equations of the n-th order, with an input magnitude u. Generally speaking, we then have n + 1 limitations of the type (2). If, for example, n derivatives of the magnitude X are limited, then for the values of the derivatives at the point Q the following equations must be valid:

$$\lim_{\substack{t > t_{min} \\ t \to t_{min}}} \frac{d^i X}{dt^i} = \left(\frac{d^i X_0}{dt^i} \right)_{t=t_{min}} \qquad (i=1, 2, \ldots, n-1) \qquad (4)$$

Otherwise, an infinitely great jump of the higher derivative of X will take place at the point Q. Particularly if the second derivative is limited, then at the point Q not only the curves X and X_0 must coincide, but also the velocities $dX/dt = Y$ and $dX_0/dt = Y_0$.

Considering the magnitude X and n-1 of its derivatives in an n-dimensional phase space (or in the space X, d^iX/dt^i, t) and tracing in the same phase space the trajectory $X_0(t)$, the problem of determining $X(t)$ can be treated as a problem of a contact of points describing the trajectories $X(t)$ and $X_0(t)$ that originate from certain regions of admissible initial values and do not cross the boundaries of the region of admissible maximum deviations characterized by the inequalities (2) and (3). Since the problem to be solved is that of a contact of points after a minimal time t_0 following the beginning of the process, t_0 being a functional of the curve X, we are dealing with a certain variational problem where it is required to find not only the minimal time $(t_0)_{min} = t_{min}$ but also the extremal of $X(t)$.

It is important to stress that the optimal process can be determined knowing only the governing influence of $X_0(t)$ and the boundary conditions (2) or (3) that characterize the class of admissible curves.

It is of interest to find the optimal process not only because the result can be applied in an optimal control system; knowing the process it is possible to evaluate the quality of any type of automatic control system by comparing it with the optimal system.

3. Construction of the Optimal Process

Let us first consider the important class of the optimal processes which correspond to the limitation of the modulus of the second derivative of the controlled magnitude:

$$\left| \frac{d^2 X}{dt^2} \right| \leq M. \qquad (5)$$

---

* As shown below, this function need not be known, but must belong to a known class of functions.

The functions $X_0(t)$ must also satisfy this condition.

As shown below (see Appendix I), it is relatively easy to find the graph of the optimal process X(t) (Fig. 2) by using two parabolas with the equations

$$x = \lambda \pm \frac{M}{2} (t-\mu)^2, \tag{6}$$

where λ and μ can be varied. The acceleration on each of these parabolic trajectories over the molulus is M. Let, for example, these parabolas be cut out of cardboard in the shape of two ovals. Let us set up one of them, P_1P_2 (see Fig. 2), in such a way that the trajectory along the boundary of the oval originates at point 0 and has a given angl of inclination at the origin of coordinates. This angle corresponds to the initial velocity

$$(dX/dt)_{t=0} - (Y)_{t=0}.$$

Then we transpose the second parabola, Q_1Q_2, to the left in such a way that it slides along the curve $X_0(t)$, touching this curve, until it touches the first parabola, P_1P_2. The line OPQ, consisting of sections of the two parabolas, is the required ideal optimal transition process. At $t = t_1$ a transition from the first parabola to the second takes place. At $t > t_{min}$ the curves X(t) and $X_0(t)$ coincide. Fig. 2 shows different examples of the construction of the curves X(t). From these examples it can be seen that two types of processes exist. The first parabola (P_1P_2) for the process of the first type is characterized by the sign (+) in the equation (6), and the second parabola, Q_1,Q_2, by the sign (-) (Fig. 2, A and B). For the processes of the second type, the first parabola is characterize by the sign (-), and the second, by the sign (+) (Fig. 2, C and D). It will be shown in Appendix I that only one of the possible distributions of the parabolas, either of the first or the second type is possible. If by constructing the the process of one type the two parabola touch at the point P that is situated in the left half-plane $(t_1 < 0)$ then this shows that the other type of process applies.

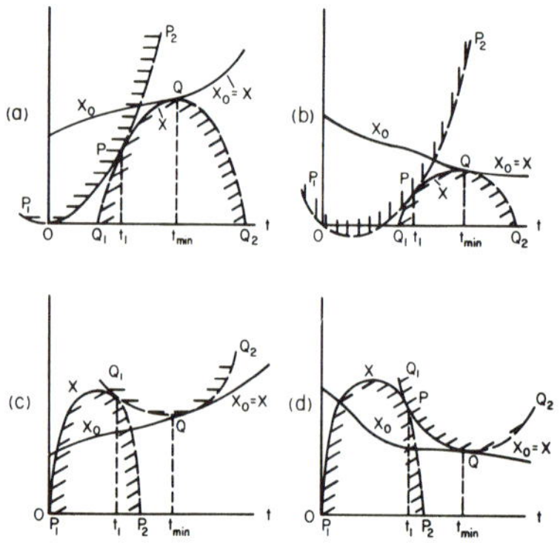

Fig. 2

If only the first derivative is limited, i.e., $|dX/dt| \leq M_0$, then the constructio is made with the aid of the straight line OQ (Fig. 3, A) originating from a point corresponding to $(X)_{t=0} = 0$ and directed to the curve X0. The inclination angle α corresponds to the maximum admissible velocity. It is necessary to choose one of the two straight lines, for which $\tan \alpha = \pm M_0$, where M_0 is the maximum admissible velocity.

If the first and the second derivatives of X are limited, then the figures $P_3P_1P_2P_4$ and $Q_3Q_1Q_2Q_4$ must be used as ovals (see Fig. 3, B). The straight lines P_1P_3

and P_2P_4 are tangents to the parabola $P_5P_1P_2P_6$ and correspond to the maximum admissible velocity M_0. The second figure is formed by the straight lines Q_1Q_3 and Q_2Q_4, which are tangents to the parabola Q_5Q_6, and the section Q_1Q_2 of this parabola. The process OP_2Q_1Q is the optimal process.

If the third derivative of X is limited, then it is convenient to consider the process in the plane Y, t (Fig. 3, C). Let $Y_0 = Y_0(t)$ be represented by the curve $O''R_3SL$. Here it is necessary to apply three parabolas of the type

$$y = \lambda \pm \frac{M_2}{2} (t-\mu)^2, \tag{7}$$

where λ and μ are variable magnitudes and $M_2 > 0$ is the upper limit of the modulus of the third derivative. The first parabola, P_1P_2, passes through the point O', which corresponds to $(Y)_{t=0}$, at an angle that corresponds to the initial value of the second derivative

$$\left(\frac{d^2X}{dt^2}\right)_{t=0} = \left(\frac{dY}{dt}\right)_{t=0}$$

The third parabola, S_1S_2, which is characterized by the same sign in the equation (7) as the first, touches the curve $Y_0(t)$ at the point S. The second parabola, Q_1Q_2, touches the first and the third. An additional condition is that the area

$$\int_0^{t_{min}} Y dt,$$

which is bounded by the curve $O'R_1R_2S$, must amount to

$$(X_0)_{t=0} + \int_0^{t_{min}} Y_0 dt,$$

i.e., it must amount to the sum of the constant magnitude $(X_0)_{t=0}$ and the area bounded by $O''R_3S$. Here also, processes of the first and second type are possible.

Finally, Figure 3D shows a case where the first, second and third derivatives are limited. In view of the above, construction of this case should be self-explanatory.

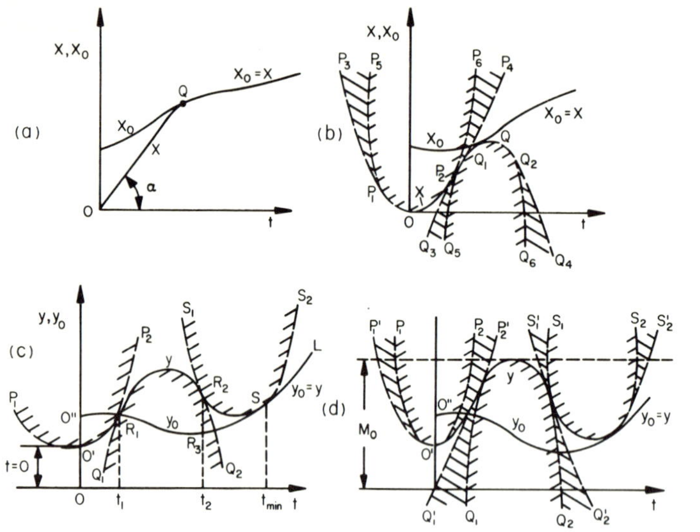

Fig. 3

Appendix I discusses the cases where derivatives of any order are limited. It is shown that when the n-th derivative is limited, the optimal processes consist of n intervals; the modulus of the n-th derivative in each interval must be maximal and the signs of the n-th derivative alternate from the first interval to the last. Depending on the sign of

$$\frac{d^n X}{dt^n}$$

in the first interval, the processes occurring in this case may also be either of the first or the second type.

Finally, there may be a case where the linear combination of derivatives is limited:

$$\left| \frac{d^n X}{dt^n} + a_1 \frac{d^{n-1} X}{dt^{n-1}} + \ldots + a_{n-1}\frac{dX}{dt} + a_n X \right| \leq M. \qquad (8)$$

Such cases are frequent in practice. If, for example, the invariable power part of the system consists of series-connected integrating and inertia links with operators

$$K_1(p) = \frac{k_1}{1 + pT} \quad \text{and} \quad K_2(p) = \frac{\xi_0}{p},$$

and the input magnitude of the power part of the system is limited in modulus, i.e., $|u| \leq M$, than the inequality

$$\frac{1}{\xi} \left| T \frac{d^2 X}{dt^2} + \frac{dX}{dt} \right| = |u| \leq M \qquad (9)$$

is valid, where

$$\xi = k_1 \xi_0$$

The optimal process theorem is proved in Appendix I with the limiting condition of the type (8); this theorem is valid with real roots $p_i \leq 0$ of the equation

$$p^n + a_1 p^{n-1} + \ldots + a_{n-1} p + a_n = 0 \quad (10)$$

It is proved that the optimal process consists of n intervals; the process within every interval is described by the equation

$$\frac{d^n X}{dt^n} + a_1 \frac{d^{n-1} X}{dt^2} + \ldots + a_{n-1} \frac{dX}{dt} + a_n X = \sigma M, \quad (11)$$

and $\sigma = \underline{+}1$, with the signs at σ alternating in successive intervals.*

For the case where complex-conjugate roots are contained in equation (10), the optimal process is complicated. This interesting problem cannot be discussed within the scope of the present paper.

It must be pointed out that it is unnecessary to find the optimal process if a scheme is found for a device that realizes the optimal control law. Within such a scheme the optimal process is realized automatically.

The link whose output value is transmitted to the invariable part of the system need not be a relay or near-relay link. If, for example, in a system consisting of a series-connected inertia and integrating links with operators

$$K_1(p) = \frac{k}{1 + pT} \quad \text{and} \quad K_2(p) = \frac{\xi_0}{p},$$

the condition

$$\left| \frac{d^2 X}{dt^2} \right| \leq M,$$

*If the above form of the optimal process is known, it is possible to obtain equations for the determination of the optimal process parameters by writing in expanded form the conditions (4) and the conjugation conditions at the boundary of adjacent intervals. These equations are **rather** cumbersome; the easiest way to solve them is by means of a computer device, or graphically if $n \leq 4$.

is to be satisfied, then the input value of u of this system changes according to the following law:

$$u = \frac{T}{\xi}\frac{d^2X}{dt^2} + \frac{1}{\xi}\frac{dX}{dt} = \frac{T}{\xi}\sigma M + \frac{1}{\xi}(C + \sigma Mt),$$

where the constant C is different within each interval, i.e. the magnitude u changes not only abruptly but also smoothly within each interval.

The above theorem can be extended to the case when the invariable "power" part of the system is non-linear, but the transformation function is monotone at any value of the stepped input function. In this case the non-linear characteristics may even be other than univalued; they may, for example, show a hysteresis.

4. Structural Scheme

As explained above, to find the optimal process it is necessary to determine the curve $X_0(t)$, i.e. one must know the law of change of the governing influences in the future. If this law is unknown, then the optimal process cannot be constructed in principle. This circumstance causes a principal difficulty in constructing a system in which optimal processes must be realized. Furthermore, the problem includes not only the determination of the optimal process but also the construction of a structural scheme of an automatic control system and the determination of its parameters that insure the realization of the optimal process. Under actual conditions the form of the function $X_0(t)$ is known in advance. It is nevertheless, possible to construct a system realizing optimal processes if it is taken into account that the solution of the contact problem in a phase space is to a certain extent analogous to the solution of the contact problem. Analogously with these devices, a "prognosis unit" must be included in the system Π_0 (Fig. 4) that collects data on the governing influence of $X_0(t)$ and its past performance and predicts the probable future behavior of the function $X_0(t)$ on this basis. On this basis one can define the required optimal form of the process X(t). Since the actual function $X_0(t)$ may differ from the predicted curve, it follows that under actual conditions no exact implementation of the optimal process is impossible.

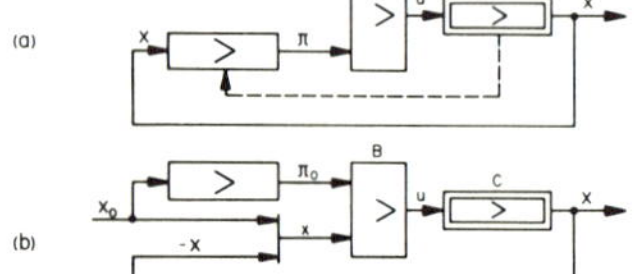

Fig. 4

The scheme of the prognosis unit Π_0 may be based on the hypothesis that $X_0(t)$ belongs to a certain class of functions or on the hypotheses of a statistical character.

If it is assumed that the function $X_0(t)$ is analytical, then its investigation in an infinitely short period of time will supply an exhaustive description of its future behavior. If within the duration of the transient process one can approximate the function $X_0(t)$ by a polynomial with sufficient accuracy, then for a prognosis it is only necessary to know the values of a certain number of derivatives d^iX_0/dt^i at the initial moment, i.e. only the differentiators are required. The prognosis block diagram may be considerably complicated if an inseparable stray interference is added to the signal $X_0(t)$. An investigation of such relatively complex cases is a separate topic that cannot be discussed within the scope of the present paper. Below we shall only discuss an example of the simplest prognosis unit using differentiators without filters.

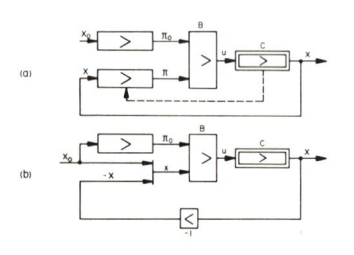

It was explained above that for the determination of the optimal process it is necessary to know also the state of the system, i.e. the coordinate values of its links or the values of X and (n-1) of the derivatives d^iX/dt^i. It is therefore necessary to include in the system the unit П collecting the information on the state of the system received over a channel represented by a dashed line in Fig. 4. This unit may be called a recording unit.

From the units $П_0$ and П the data then flow to the next unit, the computing unit B. This occurs not necessarily over a single channel, but may involve several channels. The computing unit contains a computing-resolving device which finds the required controlling effect u (Fig. 4) on the basis of the data supplied by $П_0$ and П . This controlling effect u must be supplied to the ready part C of the system in order to obtain the optimal process.

The structural scheme may sometimes be simplified by supplying to the unit B the difference $x = X_0 - X$ instead of the output values of the units $П_0$ and П . Such a simplified structural system is shown in Fig. 4b.

An example of the implementation of structural block diagrams of $П_0$ and П as well as B is given below.

5. An Example of the Structural System Implementing the Optimal Process

Let the effects belong to the class

$$X_0(t) = A_0 + A_1 t + A_2 t^2, \tag{12}$$

where A_0, A_1 and A_2 are constants. Since in the course of the transient process for X(t) a large class of effects may be approximated with sufficient accuracy by parabolas, the investigation of the function $X_0(t)$ of the type (12) is of great practical importance. Let an invariable part C of the system represent a series connection of two integrating links with the operator

$$K_0(p) = \frac{\xi_0}{p^2}. \tag{13}$$

It is required that the modulus of the input value supplied to this part of the system must not exceed a certain maximum. Since the controlled magnitude X is the output value of the system C, then the admissible functions are limited by the condition

$$\left|\frac{d^2X}{dt^2}\right| \leq M = \text{const}. \tag{14}$$

This condition must be imposed on the functions (12). Consequently,

$$|2A_2| \leq M. \tag{15}$$

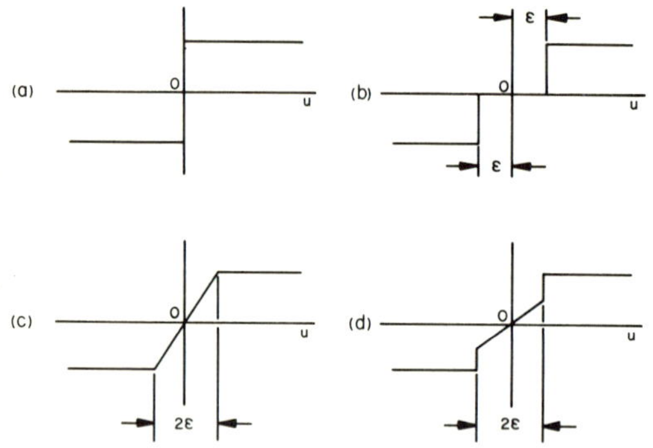

Fig. 5

It is proved in the Appendix II that to obtain the optimal process the magnitude fed to the input lead of the invariable part C of the system must depend on the argument

$$u_0 = x + \frac{y^2 \text{sign } y}{2(M-2A_2 \text{sign } y)} = x + \frac{y^2}{2(M \text{ sign } y-2A_2)} \tag{16}$$

where

$$x = X_0 - X,$$

$$y = \frac{dX_0}{dt} - \frac{dX}{dt} = Y_0 - Y \tag{17}$$

and

$$\text{sign } y = \begin{cases} +1 \text{ at } y > 0 \\ -1 \text{ at } y < 0 \end{cases} \tag{18}$$

The theoretical dependence of the input value of the block C on u_0 must be represented by the function shown in Fig. 5a. In practice, at small values of u_0 this dependence is given the form shown in Fig. 5b, c, and d to insure smooth tracking. Here ε is a small magnitude. The dependence shown in Fig. 5c is assumed below.

Disturbing forces belonging to more restricted classes of $X_0(t) = A_0$ at $t > 0$ and $X_0(t) = A_0 + A_1 t$ at $t > 0$ are obtained if it is assumed that in Equation 12 we have $A_2 = 0$. For these forces the optimal control law according to (16) consists in the dependence on the argument

$$u_0 = x + \frac{y^2 \text{sign } y}{2M} . \qquad (19)$$

This control law was given previously in the paper [1].

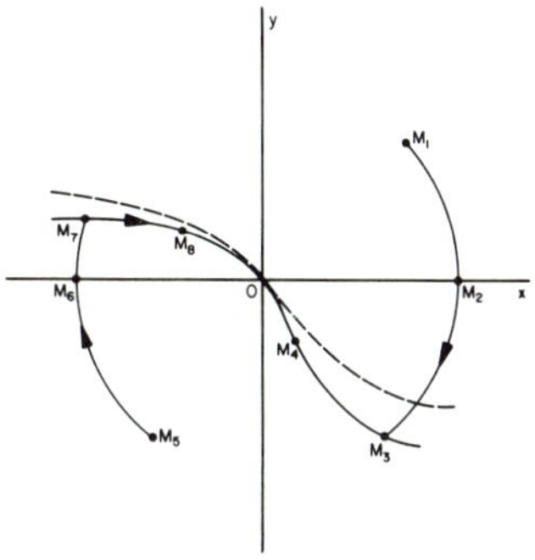

Fig. 6

The pattern of phase trajectories on the phase plane is shown in Fig. 6. The tracing point of the system moves along the (parabolic) trajectory $M_1M_2M_3$, reaching the limiting parabolic trajectory M_3M_4O, which is characterized by equation $u_0 = 0$ or (since sign $y = -1$)

$$x = + \frac{y^2}{2(M+2A_2)} \qquad (20)$$

Further motion proceeds along the parabola M_3M_4O. The trajectory $M_5M_6M_7$ reaches the limiting parabolic trajectory with the equation

$$x = - \frac{y^2}{2(M-2A_2)} . \qquad (21)$$

A dashed line shows the curve

$$x = - \frac{y^2 \text{sign } y}{2M} .$$

At small values of u_0 the curve shown in Fig. 5c has a linear section. For this reason, in practice the trajectories M_3M_4O and M_7M_8O are replaced by narrow curvilinear "corridors" within which at sufficiently small values of u_0 the characteristics of the system change abruptly.

Instead of the controlling signal u_0 one can use a different magnitude of the same sign, for example

$$u_1 = 2u_0(M-2A_2 \text{sign } y) = 2x(M-2A_2 \text{sign } y) + y^2 \text{sign } y. \qquad (22)$$

Fig. 7a shows a structural scheme of a system implementing the control law (22). To simplify the scheme, we shall deal with a real optimal process. The circuit of the invariable part C of the system is outlined by a double line. Its output value X, which is the controlled magnitude, is supplied to the summing device, with a change of sign. The magnitude X_0 is fed to the same device. The difference $x = X_0 - X$ is fed to the input lead of the differentiator D and to one of the inputs of the multiplying link M3. The magnitude $M-2A_2$sign y is received at the second input of the same link, so that at the output of the link the value $2x(M-2A_2$sign y) is obtained. The second input magnitude ($M-2A_2$sign y) is in turn a sum of M = const and an output magnitude of the second multiplying link M3 whose input leads receive the magnitudes sign y obtained from a non-linear converter HП-1 (whose input lead receives y) and the magnitude ($-2A_2$) which is the acceleration $-d^2X_0/dt^2$ that is continuously supplied by means of the double differentiator D^2. The latter plays in the scheme the role of the "predicting" device $П_0$ (cf. Fig. 2b). The determination of the second derivative is difficult in practice and is necessarily connected with additional filtration of interferences that distorts the magnitude d^2X_0/dt^2. In some cases, however, the second derivative can be fed into the system from the outside by means of a special channel without appreciable errors.

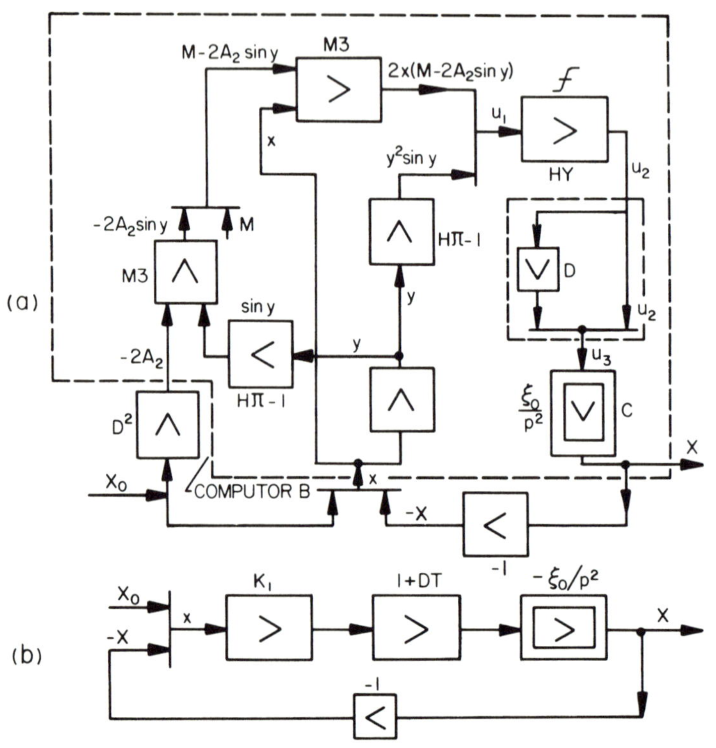

Fig. 7

The sum of the magnitudes $2x(M-2C$ sign y) and y^2 sign y is received at the input lead u_1 of the non-linear amplifier ПY. The magnitude y^2 sign y is obtained at the output lead of the non-linear converter HП-1 to whose input lead the magnitude y is fed. The magnitude u_1 corresponds to the formula (22). The formulas for the control laws (16) and (22) differ from the formula (19) in that the coefficient of a feedback ($M-2A_2$ sign y) depends on the disturbance power $X_0(t)$. The amplifier HY has the characteristics shown in Fig. 5c. For this reason, at large values of u_1, its output magnitude is constant and the differentiation link D, to whose input lead u_2 is coupled, does not operate. It begins to operate only at small values of u_1.

The part of the diagram enclosed by the dashed line is the "computing" device B; it consists of multiplying links, non-linear converters, summing links and differentiators. A diagram for the control laws (16) can be constructed in the same manner; a dividing link will be required in this case.

When the magnitude X approximates X_0, the values of x and y become small; the diagram shown in Fig. 7a can therefore be simplified. In fact, the squares of y can be disregarded. Furthermore, if instead of the function sign x on the non-linear converter a function of the type shown in Fig. 5c is selected, then the term $2x2A_2$ sign v may be disregarded as a magnitude of the second order of smallness. For this reason, u_1 becomes proportional to the magnitude x. Since this case of the differentiator D begins to operate (it is enclosed within the small dahsed-line rectangle in Fig. 7a), then the structural diagram takes the form shown in Fig. 7b. Here T is the time constant of the differentiator.

In the structural diagram for small deviations one must now strive not for a short control time but for a smooth process and a small value of the established error. The operator of the open system shown in Fig. 7b has the form

$$K(p) = \frac{k_1 \xi_0}{p^2} (1+pT) = \frac{\xi(1+pT)}{p^2} . \tag{23}$$

and the characteristic equation of the closed system can therefore be written in the form

$$p^2 + \xi T p + \xi = 0. \tag{24}$$

Thus, the system at small deviations is stable

At $T = 2/\sqrt{\xi}$ the roots of the characteristic equation are equal to each other and the transient process is smooth. The magnitude of ξ is selected on the basis of the condition for small established error with the tracking of the disturbing power of the type (12):

$$x_s = \frac{2A_2}{\xi} \tag{25}$$

Initial calculations show that the system, upon entering the linear region (region of small deviations), remains in that region until some shock or abrupt change in the effect increases the deviation to a large value. In this case the diagram for small deviations will begin to operate and the system, after a brief optimum inclination towards proper motion, will operate smoothly in tracking with a small established error.

CONCLUSIONS

The concepts and methods of system construction considered in the preceding discussion apply to large classes of effects and in general to disturbing powers $X_0(t)$, as well as to various types of invariable parts C of a system with various limitations, etc. In such systems, it is alsoof interest to investigate the deviation of the process from the optimum processes that arise as a result of various causes; for example, the straying of the function $X_0(t)$ beyond the limits of a certain class for which the system is constructed, effect of interferences or change of parameters and characteristics of the system, etc. Furthermore, the concept of the optimal process itself may be formulated in a different way if the problem of error filtration, load effect, etc. is considered.

The theory and principles of system construction discussed in the present paper may be applied, firstly, for the construction of optimal or near-optimal systems, and secondly, for the comparison of the optimal process with processes observed in actual systems for the evaluation of the closeness of an actual system to the optimum system.

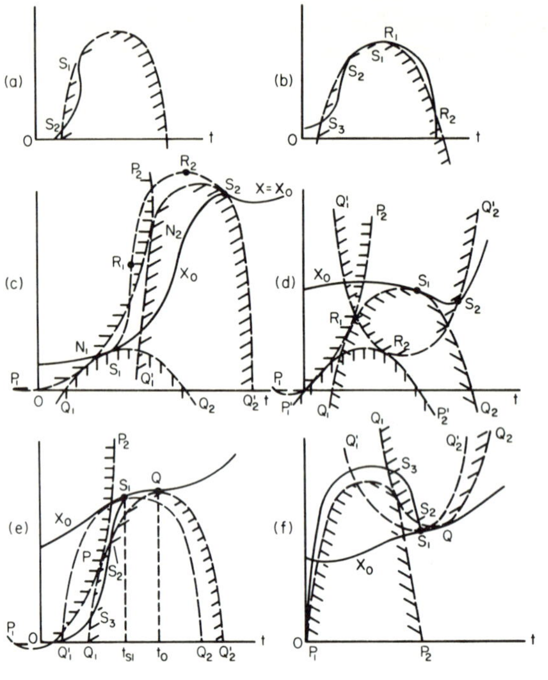

Fig.8

APPENDIX I

Let us prove the validity of the above optimal process method for the case of limitation of the second derivative (5). For the remaining cases the proof is analogous. Let us call the parabolas P_1P_2 and Q_1Q_2 "limiting parabolas". To begin with let us state the virtually self-evident rule: If the curve S_1S_2 (see Fig. 8a and b) touches the limiting parabola at a point S_1 and penetrates inside the shaded area, then it is not admissible in the sense defined above. Likewise such a curve R_1R_2 leaving the shaded area and then re-entering this area is not admissible.

Then, from Fig. 8c, it follows that the existence of two optimal processes ON_1R_1 and ON_2S_2 for a curve X_0 of the type $OR_1R_2S_2$ is impossible; likewise, the existence of two processes ON_1S_1 and ON_2S_2 for a curve X_0 of the type S_1S_2. If both processes exist, then the curve X_0 of the type S_1S_2 entering the shaded area $Q_1'S_2Q_2'$ or the curve X_0 of the type $R_1R_2S_2$ entering the area P_1OP_2 would not be admissible.

It is easy to show by means of the graph of Fig. 8d that simultaneous existence of the processes of the first and second types is impossible. Indeed, if processes OR_1S_1 and OR_2S_2 exist, then the curve X_0, touching both limiting parabolas Q_1Q_2 and $Q_1'Q_2'$, enters one of the two shaded areas and consequently is not admissible.

Let us now examine Fig. 8e. Here the line OPQ is the predicted optimal process. Let another curve exist, $OS_3S_2S_1$, which touches the line $X_0(t)$ at $t_{s1} < t_0$. The curve $OS_3S_2S_1$ must pass to the right of the shaded line OP_2, otherwise it will be inadmissible. Let us prove that this curve cannot be admissible altogether. Let us shift the limiting parabola Q_1Q_2 to the left, forcing it to slide along the curve $X_0(t)$, touching it until the point of contact coincides with S_2. The limiting parabola will then take the position $Q_1'Q_2'$ and the curve $S_1S_2S_3O$ will become a tangent to it at the point S_1 and will enter the shaded area $Q_1'S_1Q_2'$. Consequently the curve $OS_3S_2S_1$ is not admissible, which proves the assertion concerning the minimum control time obtained by means of the process OPQ.

Fig. 8f shows an analogous construction for processes of the second type.

In the same manner it can be proved that the curve having a smaller value of the minimum $|x_d|$ is not admissible. This assertion, unfortunately, is valid only with the limitation of the second derivative, and generally speaking is inapplicable with the limitation of higher derivatives; the process resulting in the least possible control time will not insure the least possible value of the maximum $|x_d|$.

Let us now consider the case of limitation of any n-th derivative ($n > 2$). It is convenient for the proof to think of a certain equivalent scheme (not necessarily coincident with a structural scheme of the invariable part of system) consisting of a sequence of n integrating links with amplification coefficients equal to unity (see Fig. 9a). Let u be the input value of the sequence and X its output value. If the quantity u is limited in modulus, this condition is equivalent to the limitation $|d^nX/dt^n| \leq M$.

Let us prove that in order to obtain the optimal process it is necessary to feed to the input lead of the equivalent scheme the magnitude $u = \sigma M$, where $\sigma = \pm 1$ and the signs of σ alternate in adjacent intervals (which generally speaking are not equal in duration). The number of intervals must equal n. Assuming that such a process is constructed, let us examine Fig. 10a, which shows the graphs of $X_0^{(n-1)}$ and (n-1)-th derivative of the optimal process, i.e. $X^{(n-1)}$. The curve $X^{(n-1)}$ has the form of an inflected line with the slope of each section amounting to either +M or -M. At the point of time $t = t_n$ the curve $X^{(n-1)}$ coincides with the curve $X_0^{(n-1)}$. At the same point of time the equality $X^{(n-2)} = X_0^{(n-2)}, \ldots, X^{(1)} = X_0^{(1)}$ and $X = X_0$ (see Fig. 10b, c and d) is satisfied. At $t > t_n$ the curves X and X_0 coincide.

Let us assume the existence of another curve X_1 with the same initial conditions as those for X but with a shorter control time $t' < t_n$ than that of X. Let us prove that an admissible curve X_1 with such properties cannot exist.

Let us add to the curve X_1 a section of the curve X_0 within the interval $t' \leq t \leq t_n$ and henceforth consider the curve X_1 as such an extended curve given in the interval $0 \leq t \leq t_n$. We then observe that the curve $X_1^{(n-1)}$ cannot intersect each section of the inflected line $X^{(n-1)}$ more than once (otherwise its derivative will exceed M in modulus and the curve will become inadmissible). Then, the curve $X_1^{(n-1)}$ cannot intersect either the first or the last (within the interval $0 \leq t \leq t_n$) of the sections of the inflected line $X^{(n-1)}$; otherwise it will become inadmissible. The number of intersection points of the curves $X^{(n-1)}$ and $X_1^{(n-1)}$ therefore cannot exceed n-2.

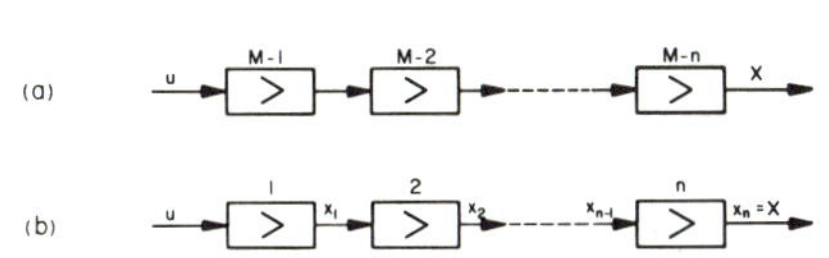

Fig. 9

Let us now consider the curves $X^{(n-2)}$ and $X_1^{(n-2)}$ (Fig. 10b). These curves coincide at points $t = 0$ and $t = t_n$, and their derivatives, as shown above, coincide in no more than n-2 intermediary points. Hence it follows that the curves $X^{(n-2)}$ and $X_1^{(n-2)}$ have no more than (n-3) points of intersection within the interval $0 < t < t_n$ (not including intersection points at the boundaries of this interval). Indeed, we would otherwise have more than n-2 equality points of the derivatives of these curves. It is easy to show in a similar manner that the curves $X^{(n-3)}$ and $X_1^{(n-3)}$ have no more than n-4 points of intersection, etc. Thus, the curves $X^{(2)}$ and $X_1^{(2)}$ have no more than one point of intersection, and the curves $X^{(1)}$ and $X_1^{(1)}$ have no points of intersection (see Fig. 10c). Hence it follows that

$$\int_0^{t_n} X^{(1)} dt \neq \int_0^{t_n} X_1^{(1)} dt, \text{ i.e. the equality } (X_1)_{t=t_n} = (X)_{t=t_n}$$

does not apply; this equality must apply, however, if the curve X_1 has a smaller control time t' than t_n. This contradiction proves the theorem of the impossibility of the existence of an admissible curve X_1 with smaller control time than t_n.

Let us now examine the case of limitation of a linear combination of derivatives when the condition (8) must be satisfied and the roots $p_1, p_2, \ldots, p_n$ of the equation (10) are negative and real (some of them may equal zero). Let us rewrite the equation (10) in the form

$$p^m \prod_{i=1}^{n-m} (1+pT_i) = 0, \tag{26}$$

where $p_i = -1/T_i$ and m is the number of zero roots.

In this case the equivalent scheme may be represented in the form of a sequence of inertia and integrating links (see Fig. 9b), the input value u being limited in modulus $|u| \leq M$, which is equivalent to the condition (8). The sequence of equations of the equivalent scheme may be written in the following form (for simplicity we consider that $m = 0$; if $m > 0$, the proof is analogous):

$$x_1 + T_1 \frac{dx_1}{dt} = u, \quad x_2 + T_2 \frac{dx_2}{dt} = x_1,$$
$$x_{n-1} + T_{n-1} \frac{dx_{n-1}}{dt} = x_{n-2}, \quad X + T_n \frac{dX}{dt} = x_{n-1}. \tag{27}$$

If the curve $X_0(t)$ is given, it is easy to find what the values of $x_i (i=1,2,\ldots n-1$ must be when the equality $X = X_0(t)$ is satisfied. Let us designate these values by x_{i0}. Figure 11a shows, as an example, the curve $x_{10}(t)$. Let $u = \sigma M$, where $\sigma = \pm 1$, the signs of σ alternate in adjacent intervals, and the total number of intervals amounts to n (generally speaking the intervals are not equal to each other). Then the curve x_1 will consist of n exponential sections (see Fig. 11a). Let the control time for the optimal process be $t = t_n$. We assume that another process exists with the same initial condition such that the link output magnitudes are correspondingly $y_1, y_2 \ldots y_n = Y$, the control time being $t' < t_n$. Adding to the functions y_i the sections of the curves x_{i0} in the interval $t' < t < t_n$, we obtain pairs of curves y_i and x_i, which coincide at $t = 0$ and $t = t_n$.

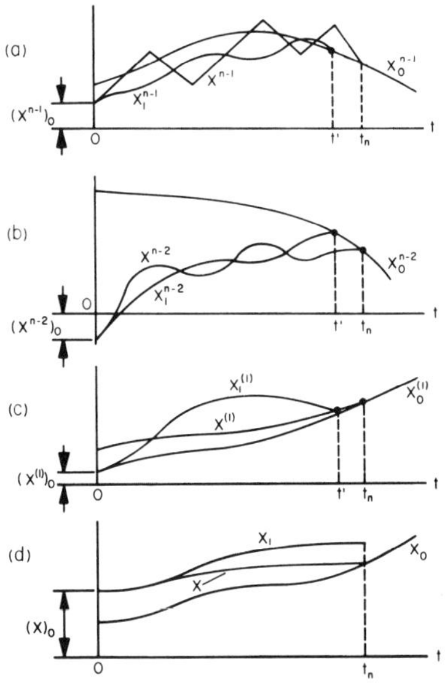

Fig. 10

The curve y_1 cannot intersect either the first or the last sections of the curve x_1, becasue the input magnitude is $|u| \leq M$. For the same reason the curve y_1 can intersect each of the remaining sections no more than once. Consequently, the transition of the curve $x_1 - y_1 = z_1$ through zero is possible no more than in (n-2) points (see Fig. 11b). The difference $z_2 = x_2 - y_2$ is connected with the difference z_1 by the equation

$$z_2 + T_2 \frac{dz_2}{dt} = z_1. \tag{28}$$

The solution of Equation (28) has the form

$$z_2 = (z_2)_{t=0} e^{-\beta_2 t} + \beta_2 e^{-\beta_2 t} \int_0^t z_1(\tau) e^{\beta_2 \tau} d\tau, \tag{29}$$

where $\beta_2 = 1/T_2$.

Since the initial value is $(z_2)_{t=0} = 0$, then, for example, if in the first interval $0 < t < t_1$ the magnitude $z_1 > 0$, then $(z_2)_{t=t_1} > 0$ according to Equation (29). In the next interval $z_1 < 0$; therefore in the second interval the magnitude

$$z_2 = (z_2)_{t=t_1} e^{-\beta_2 (t-t_1)} - \beta_2 e^{-\beta_2 (t-t_1)} \int^t |z_1(\tau)| \; e^{\beta_2 \tau} d\tau$$

decreases monotonely and, consequently, may pass through zero no more than once (see Fig. 11c).

The same assertion can be made with respect to each of the subsequent intervals. The transition through zero is impossible in the last interval, since at its end we have $z_2 = 0$. Therefore, the transition of the magnitude z_2 through zero is possible only in (n-3) points.

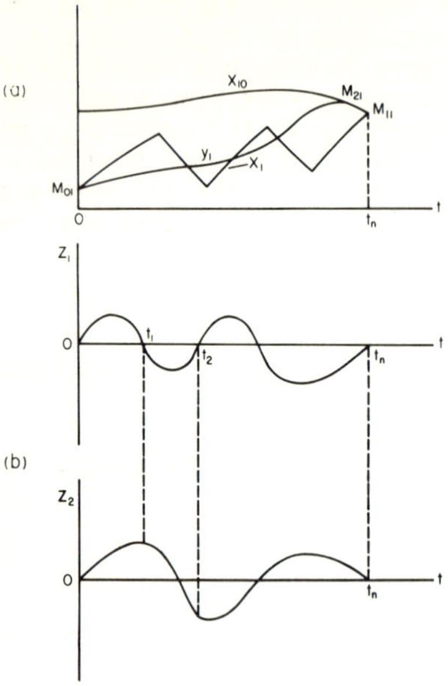

Fig. 11

Passing along the sequence of links successively to the 3-rd,..., (n-1)-th link, we find that the magnitudes $z_i = x_i - y_i$ pass through zero within the interval $0 < t < t_n$ no more than n - i - 1 times. Consequently, the curve z_{n-1} does not pass through zero at all within the interval $0 < t < t_n$.

Because $z_n + T_n\, dz_n/dt = z_{n-1}$ and $(z_n)_{t=0} = 0$, the magnitude

$$(z_n)_{t=t_n} = \beta_n e^{-\beta_n t} \int^{t_n} z_{n-1} e^{\beta_n \tau} d\tau \neq 0$$

(where $\beta_n) = 1/T_n)$, which contradicts the condition $(z_n)_{t=t_n} = 0$.

This contradiction proves that the existence of an admissible curve Y(t) with a smaller control time than that of the optimal process curve X(t) is impossible.

APPENDIX II

For processes shown in Fig. 1 and 3 the conditions can be written (if the second derivative is limited and t_{min} is designated by t_2) as

$$(X_0)_{t=t_2} = \int_0^{t_2} Y dt, \quad (Y)_{t=t_2} = (Y_0)_{t=t_2}. \qquad (30)$$

Let $(Y)_{t=0} = m$. The function Y is represented by the formula (see Fig. 3)

$$Y = m + \sigma M t \qquad (0 < t < t_1),$$

$$Y = m + \sigma[Mt_1 - M(t-t_1)] = m + \sigma(2Mt_1 - Mt) \qquad (31)$$

$$(t_1 < t < t_2),$$

where

$$\sigma = \begin{cases} +1 \text{ for processes of the first type} \\ -1 \text{ for processes of the second type} \end{cases} \qquad (32)$$

From Equation (31) it follows that

$$\int_{t}^{t_0} Ydt = \int_{0}^{t_1} Ydt + \int_{t_1}^{t_2} Ydt = mt_2 - \frac{\sigma M}{2}t_2^2 + 2\sigma Mt_1t_2 - \sigma Mt_1^2. \qquad (33)$$

Let in the general case

$$X_0(t) = \sum_{i=0}^{m} A_i t^i, \; X_0^{(1)} = \sum_{i=1}^{m} iA_i t^{i-1}. \qquad (34)$$

From Equations (30), (31), (33), (34) it follows that

$$- \sigma Mt_1^2 - \frac{\sigma M}{2} t_2^2 + 2\sigma Mt_1t_2 + mt_2 - \sum_{i=0}^{m} A_i t_2^i = 0, \qquad (35)$$

$$- \sigma Mt_2 + 2\sigma Mt_1 + m - \sum_{i=1}^{m} A_i it_2^{i-1} = 0.$$

At the point $t = t_1$ the values of $x = X_0 - X$ and $y = Y_0 - Y$ are equal according to the first equations of (31) and (34).

$$x_1 = (X_0)_{t=t_1} - mt_1 - \frac{\sigma Mt_1^2}{2} = \sum_{i=0}^{m} A_i t_1^i - mt_1 - \frac{\sigma Mt_1^2}{2}, \qquad (36)$$

$$y_1 = (Y_0)_{t=t_1} - m - \sigma Mt_1 = \sum_{i=1}^{m} iA_i t_1^{i-1} - m - \sigma Mt_1.$$

In Equations (35) and (36) the magnitudes x_1 and y_1 can be considered as if they were given, since corresponding apparatus is continuously substituted for them. The magnitudes A_i are replaced in exactly the same manner. Excluding from the four equations of (35) and (36) the three magnitudes m, t_1, t_2, we obtain the identity $(u_0)_{t=t_1} = 0$. The magnitude u_0, which becomes zero at the time point $= t_1$, gives the control law.

Subtracting the second equation of (36) from the second equation of (35) we obtain the equality

$$\sum_{i=2}^{m} iA_i(t_2^{i-1} - t_1^{i-1}) + y_1 = - \sigma M(t_2 - t_1). \tag{37}$$

Since X_0 is an admissible function, then $|d^2X_0/dt^2| \leq M$ or

$$\left| \sum_{i=2}^{m} i(i-1)A_i t^{i-2} \right| \leq M. \tag{38}$$

Since $t_2 > t_1$, the left half of expression (37) must have the same sign as $(-\sigma M)$. Let us show that the sign of the left half is determined by the sign of y_1. For this purpose from Equation (37) we find the quantity $\Delta t = t_2 - t_1$. Since

$$t_2^{i-1} - t_1^{i-1} = (t_2-t_1)(t_2^{i-2} + t_2^{i-3}t_1 + \ldots + t_2t_1^{i-3} + t_1^{i-2}),$$

it follows from (37) that

$$\Delta t = \sum_{i-2}^{m} iA_i(t_2^{i-2} + t_2^{i-3}t_1 + \ldots + t_2t_1^{i-3} + t_1^{i-2}) \; y_1 + \sigma M\Delta t = 0,$$

whence

$$\Delta t = \frac{-y_1}{\sigma M + \sum_{i=2}^{m} iA_i(t_2^{i-2} + t_2^{i-3}t_1 + \ldots + t_2t_1^{i-3} + t_1^{i-2})}. \tag{39}$$

It is possible to select such a time point $t_1 < t_0 < t_2$ that the equality

$$(i-1)t_0^{i-2} = t_2^{i-2} + t_2^{i-3}t_1 + \ldots + t_2t_1^{i-3} + t_1^{i-2}. \tag{40}$$

is satisfied.

The existence of the value t_0 is evident since the inequalities

$$(i-1)t_2^{i-2} > t_2^{i-2} + t_2^{i-3}t_1 + \dots + t_1^{i-2},$$
$$(i-1)t_1^{i-2} < t_2^{i-2} + t_2^{i-3}t_1 + \dots + t_1^{i-2}. \tag{41}$$

are satisfied.

The condition (38), however, must be satisfied for t_0. Consequently, if the value of t_0 is inserted in the expression (38) from (40) we obtain

$$\left| \sum_{i=2}^{m} iA_i (t^{i-3} + t_2^{i-3}t_1 + \dots + t_1^{i-2}) \right| \leq M. \tag{42}$$

From a comparison of formulas (39) and (42) it follows that the sign of the denominator of formula (39) is determined by the sign of σ. Since $\Delta t > 0$, we have

$$\sigma = - \operatorname{sign} y_1. \tag{43}$$

Let us complete the calculation for the simple case

$$x_0 = A_0 + A_1 t + A_2 t^2.$$

In this case the Equations (35) and (36) after the exclussion of m take the form:

$$A_0 + A_1 t_2 + A_2 t_2^2 = 2\sigma M t_1 t_2 + m t_2 - \sigma M t_1^2 - \frac{\sigma M}{2} t_2^2,$$
$$A_1 + 2A_2 t_2 = 2\sigma M t_1 - \sigma M t_2 + m,$$
$$- x_1 + A_0 + A_1 t_1 + A_2 t_1^2 = \frac{\sigma M}{2} t_1^2 + m t_1, \; - y_1 + A_1 + 2A_2 t_1 = \sigma M t_1 + m. \tag{44}$$

Eliminating m from the first and second equations of (44) and then from the third and the fourth equations and subtracting the fourth equation from the second, we obtain three equations

$$
\begin{aligned}
&(A_2 + \frac{\sigma M}{2})t_2^2 - A_0 - \sigma M t_1^2 = 0, \\
&(A_2 - \frac{\sigma M}{2})t_1^2 - y_1 t_1 + x_1 - A_0 = 0, \\
&(2A_2 + \sigma M)(t_2 - t_1) + y_1 = 0.
\end{aligned}
\tag{45}
$$

Eliminating t_2 from the first and last equations* we find

$$
(A_2 - \frac{\sigma M}{2})\, t_1^2 - y_1 t_1 - \frac{2A_0(2A_2 + \sigma M) - y_1^2}{2(2A_2 + \sigma M)} = 0. \tag{46}
$$

Comparing the second equation of (45) and the equality (46), we see that their solutions will coincide only if the equation

$$
x_1 - A_0 = - \frac{2A_0(2A_2 + \sigma M) - y_1^2}{2(2A_2 + \sigma M)}
$$

is satisfied; whence

$$
x_1 = \frac{y_1^2}{2(\sigma M + 2A_2)} \tag{47}
$$

Inserting the value of σ from (43) into the expression (47), we find

$$
x_1 = \frac{y_1^2}{2(-M \operatorname{sign} y + 2A_2)} = - \frac{y_1^2}{2(M \operatorname{sign} y - 2A_2)}. \tag{48}
$$

* In the general case, to exclude these magnitudes it is necessary to equate to zero the corresponding results; in the case at hand the exclusion is made in the simplest way.

This is the equation of the curve on the phase plane at which the transition from acceleration to deceleration or in reverse takes place. For this reason a change in the sign of the signal

$$u_0 = x + \frac{y^2}{2(M \text{ sign } y - 2A_2)} \tag{49}$$

must result in a change in the sign of the magnitude constant in modulus which must be applied to the input terminal of the invariable part C of the system.

The first and the second form of the processes (see Fig. 3) are obtained by means of the control law (49) automatically, since at the boundary between these two forms the magnitude $(u_0)_{t=0}$ becomes zero and changes sign at the transition from the first form to the second.

REFERENCES

1. Fel'dbaum, A. A., Simplest Relay Systems for Automatic Control, Avtomatika i Telemekhanika, 10 (4), 1949.

2. Hopkin, A. M., A Phase-plane Approach to the Compensation of Saturating Servomechanisms. Transactions of the AIEE, 70 (1), 1951.

3. Lerner, A. Ia., Improvement of Dynamic Properties of Automatic Compensators by Means of Nonlinear Couplings, Part I, Avtomatika i Telemekhanika, 13 (2), 1952.

4. Lerner, A. Ia., Improvement of Dynamic Properties of Automatic Compensators by Means of Nonlinear Couplings, Part II, Avtomatika i Telemekhanika, 13 (4), 1952.

5. Fel'dbaum, A. A., Investigation of the Dynamics of Automatic Control Systems by the Method of a Generalized Integral Criterion, Elektrichestvo, (7), 1951.

6. Strelkov, S. P., On the General Theory of Linear Amplifiers, Part I. Avtomatika i Telemekhanika 9 (3), 1948; On the General Theory of Linear Amplifiers, Part II. Avtomatika i Telemekhanika, 10 (4), 1949.

7. Kulebakin. V. S., On the Selection of Optimal Parameters for Automatic Regulators of Control Systems, DAN SSSR, 77 (2), 1951.

8. Ivakhnenko, A. G., On the Methods of Eliminating the Established Error Component of Automatic Control Systems, DAN SSSR 87 (6), 1952.

ON THE "BANG-BANG" CONTROL PROBLEM*

BY

R. BELLMAN, I. GLICKSBERG AND O. GROSS

The RAND Corporation, Santa Monica, Calif.

Summary. Let S be a physical system whose state at any time is described by an n-dimensional vector $x(t)$, where $x(t)$ is determined by a linear differential equation $dz/dt = Az$, with A a constant matrix. Application of external influences will yield an inhomogeneous equation, $dz/dt = Az + f$, where f, the "forcing term", represents the control. A problem of some importance in the theory of control circuits is that of choosing f so as to reduce z to 0 in minimum time. If f is restricted to belong to the class of vectors whose ith components can assume only the values $\pm b_i$, the control is said to be of the "bang-bang" type.

Various aspects of the above problem have been treated by McDonald, Bushaw, LaSalle and Rose. We shall consider here the case where all the solutions of $dz/dt = Az$ approach zero as $t \to \infty$. In this case we prove that the problem of determining f so as to minimize the time required to transform the system into the rest position subject to the requirement that f_1, the ith component, satisfies the constraint $| f_i | \leq b_i$ may be reduced to the case where $f_i = \pm b_i$. Furthermore, we show that if all the characteristic roots of A are real and negative, f_i need change value only a finite number of times at most, dependent upon the dimension of the system.

Finally, an example is given for $n = 2$, illustrating the procedure that can be followed and the results that can be obtained.

1. Introduction. Let z be an n-dimensional vector function of t satisfying the linear differential equation

$$\frac{dz}{dt} = Az + f, \qquad z(0) = c, \tag{1.1}$$

where we assume that:

a. A is a real, constant matrix of order n, whose characteristic roots all have negative real parts;
b. f is restricted to be real, measurable, and to have components satisfying the constraints, $| f_i | \leq 1$.

The first condition is the necessary and sufficient condition that all the solutions of (1.1) approach zero as $t \to \infty$.

The problem we wish to consider is that of determining the vectors f which, subject to the constraint (b), reduce z to zero in minimum time. This is a problem of Bolza of rather unconventional type, and the techniques we shall employ are quite different from the classical ones.

We shall establish two results:

THEOREM 1. *Under the above conditions, an f which reduces z to zero in minimum time exists, and has components f_i for which $| f_i | = 1$.*

*Received December 10, 1954; revised manuscript received March 14, 1955.

THEOREM 2. *If the characteristic roots of A are real, distinct, and negative, a minimizing f exists with components f_i for which $| f_i | = 1$, and each f_i changes sign at most $(n - 1)$ times.*

The statement in Theorem 1 has been assumed in the past on an intuitive basis, see McDonald, [3], and has been established in various cases by Bushaw [1], LaSalle [2], and Rose [4]. The only paper we have had access to is that by Rose, and his methods are distinct from ours. In addition, he is primarily interested in the case where the condition in (*a*) is not satisfied.

Problems of this type arise in connection with many different types of control processes. A discussion of the connection with servomechanisms is sketched in [2].

2. Proof of Theorem 2. We shall consider in detail only the case of Theorem 2, where the characteristic roots of A are real and negative. It will be clear from the treatment of this case how the proof of Theorem 1 goes.

Let X be a square matrix whose columns are the n linearly independent eigenvectors x_j of A, and let λ_j $(j = 1, \cdots, n)$ be the corresponding n distinct, negative eigenvalues of A; clearly, X is non-singular and all its elements are real. Finally, denote by Λ the diagonal matrix whose jth diagonal element is λ_j. We have

$$Ax_j = \lambda_j x_j , \tag{2.1}$$

whence we see that $AX = X\Lambda$; hence

$$X^{-1}AX = \Lambda. \tag{2.2}$$

If now in (2.1) we make the transformation $z = Xy$, we obtain using (2.2),

$$\begin{aligned} y'(0) &= X^{-1}c, \\ y'(t) &= \Lambda y(t) + X^{-1}f(t), \end{aligned} \tag{2.3}$$

or, componentwise,

$$y_i'(t) = \lambda_i y_i(t) + \sum_{j=1}^{n} \alpha_{ij} f_j(t), \tag{2.4}$$

where the α's are the elements of X^{-1}. Solving for $y_i(t)$, we obtain

$$y_i(t) = y_i(0) \exp(\lambda_i t) + \exp(\lambda_i t) \int_0^t \exp(-\lambda_i s) \sum_{j=1}^{n} \alpha_{ij} f_j(s)\, ds. \tag{2.5}$$

Since $z(t) = 0$ is equivalent to $y(t) = 0$, we wish to find the least t for which, for some f, $y_i(t) = 0$, $i = 1, \cdots, n$, i.e., for which

$$-y_i(0) = \int_0^t \exp(-\lambda_i s) \sum_{j=1}^{n} \alpha_{ij} f_j(s)\, ds, \qquad i = 1, \cdots, n \tag{2.6}$$

for some f.

Our first observation is that, given any starting value $y(0) \neq 0$ there exists a $t > 0$ and an f, such that (2.6) is satisfied. In fact, there is a constant vector $f(s) = k$ which does the trick for some t sufficiently large. For substituting $f_j(s) = k_j$ in (2.6), we obtain

$$\sum_{j=1}^{n} \alpha_{ij} k_j = \frac{y_i(0)}{-\int_0^t \exp(-\lambda_i s)\, ds} = \frac{\lambda_i y_i(0)}{\exp(-\lambda_i t) - 1},$$

whence, by virtue of the definition of the α's,

$$k_j = \sum_i x_{ji} \frac{\lambda_i y_i(0)}{\exp(-\lambda_i t) - 1}. \tag{2.7}$$

Since $-\lambda_i > 0$ the right member of (2.7) can be made as small in magnitude as we please for sufficiently large t, and hence we can insure that $|k_j| \leq 1$.

For each $t \geq 0$ we have a linear mapping ρ_t taking f into the n-dimensional vector with ith component

$$\int_0^t \exp(-\lambda_i s) \sum_j \alpha_{ij} f_j(s)\, ds, \tag{2.8}$$

and this mapping clearly takes our basic convex set of f's onto a convex subset $C(t)$ of euclidean n-space. For any f in our basic set there is another, $\underline{f}$, in the set which agrees with f for $s \leq t$ and vanishes for $s > t$, so that, for $t' > t$, $\rho_{t'}\underline{f} = \rho_t \underline{f} = \rho_t f$, by (2.8), and $\rho_t f$ is in $C(t')$. Thus $C(t)$ increases with t.

Now our desired least time is, by (2.6), the least $t \geq 0$ for which $C(t)$ contains the vector $-y(0)$. Since $C(t)$ increases, we have an interval (t_0, ∞) for which $C(t)$ contains this vector, while for $t < t_0$ this is not the case. We can see that $C(t_0)$ also contains this vector as follows.

Denoting for any vector $x = (x_1, x_2, \cdots, x_n)$ the euclidean norm $(\sum_i x_i^2)^{1/2}$ by $\|x\|$, we obtain, using (2.8), a constant $k = k(t_0)$ with the property that for all f and t, t' in a finite interval $[0, t_0]$ we have $\|\rho_t f - \rho_{t'} f\| \leq k |t - t'|$; thus, for $|t - t'|$ small every point of $C(t')$ is close to a point of $C(t)$. Since $-y(0)$ is in $C(t)$ for all $t > t_0$, $-y(0)$ must be at zero distance from $C(t_0)$ so that if we show this set is closed $-y(0)$ must actually be in it. But each $C(t)$ is closed, since by a well known fact about Banach spaces [5], our basic set of f's may be topologized so as to be compact and render each ρ_t continuous. Thus $C(t)$, as the continuous image of a compact set, is compact, hence closed.

Let us return to the fact that $-y(0)$ is not in $C(t)$ for $t < t_0$. From the theory of convex sets [6] this implies that we have a vector θ^t of unit norm, for which, in the usual inner product notation, $(\theta^t, \rho_t f) \leq [\theta^t, -y(0)]$ for every f. Since the vectors of unit norm are compact in the euclidean topology, we may select a sequence t_n increasing to t_0 for which θ^{t_n} converges to some vector θ of unit norm. But since $\rho_{t_n} f$ converges to $\rho_{t_0} f$, $(\theta, \rho_{t_0} f) = \lim (\theta^{t_n}, \rho_{t_n} f) \leq \lim [\theta^{t_n}, -y(0)] = [\theta, -y(0)]$. Thus if f^* denotes an f for which $\rho_{t_0} f^* = -y(0)$ we have $(\theta, \rho_{t_0} f) \leq (\theta, \rho_{t_0} f^*)$ for all f, hence constants $\theta_1, \cdots, \theta_n$, not all zero for which f^* maximizes the expression

$$\sum_i \theta_i \int_0^{t^*} \exp(-\lambda_i s) \sum_j \alpha_{ij} f_j(s)\, ds = \sum_j \int_0^{t^*} (\sum_i \theta_i \alpha_{ij} \exp[-\lambda_i s]) f_j(s)\, ds. \tag{2.9}$$

But this expression clearly has as its maximum

$$\sum_j \int_0^{t^*} \left| \sum_i \theta_i \alpha_{ij} \exp(-\lambda_i s) \right| ds \tag{2.10}$$

achieved by setting $f_j(s) = \operatorname{sgn}(\sum_i \theta_i \alpha_{ij} \exp[-\lambda_i s])$. Thus it is clear that $f_j^*(s) = \operatorname{sgn}(\sum_i \theta_i \alpha_{ij} \exp[-\lambda_i s])$ almost everywhere on the set where $\sum_i \theta_i \alpha_{ij} \exp(-\lambda_i s) \neq 0$.

Our principal result now follows, namely that we can achieve minimal time by restricting f to assume componentwise ± 1 on a finite number of intervals; in fact, in the case considered, each component need change sign *at most* $n - 1$ times. This latter statement is a simple consequence of the fact that unless the continuous function ϕ_i given by $\phi_i(s) = \sum_{i=1}^{n} \theta_i \alpha_{ij} \exp(-\lambda_i s)$ is identically zero (in which case it makes no difference as to our choice of f_i^*), it can have at most $n - 1$ real zeros. This is well known and there is a simple inductive proof.

3. A special case of $n = 2$. Consider the problem as before, with

$$A = \begin{pmatrix} -3 & -2 \\ 1 & 0 \end{pmatrix};$$

thus,

$$z_1' = -3z_1 - 2z_2 + f_1, \qquad z_2' = z_1 + f_2. \tag{3.1}$$

The transformation

$$z_1 = 2y_1 - y_2, \qquad z_2 = -y_1 + y_2 \tag{3.2}$$

reduces the above system to

$$y_1' = -2y_1 + f_1 + f_2, \qquad y_2' = -y_2 + f_1 + 2f_2, \tag{3.3}$$

and we obtain, as before, for the set of admissible starting values, for a given t and f_1, f_2,

$$\begin{aligned} -y_1(0) &= \int_0^t e^{2s}[f_1(s) + f_2(s)]\,ds, \\ -y_2(0) &= \int_0^t e^{s}[f_1(s) + 2f_2(s)]\,ds. \end{aligned} \tag{3.4}$$

From the preceding section, we know that if t^* is minimal, then the optimal f^* is given by

$$\begin{aligned} f_1(s) &= \operatorname{sgn}(\theta_1 e^{2s} + \theta_2 e^{s}), \\ f_2(s) &= \operatorname{sgn}(\theta_1 e^{2s} + 2\theta_2 e^{s}). \end{aligned} \tag{3.5}$$

If we now ask the question "For what set of starting values y is it optimal to choose $f_1 = 1$, $f_2 = 1$ on an *initial interval*?" with a similar question for the other combinations ± 1, it is readily seen that the answers will determine an *optimal policy*. This is clear, since any continuation of an optimal policy must be again optimal with respect to the new starting values. We thus have

$$\begin{aligned} -y_1(0) &= \int_0^{t^*} e^{2s}\{\operatorname{sgn}(\theta_1 e^{2s} + \theta_2 e^{s}) + \operatorname{sgn}(\theta_1 e^{2s} + 2\theta_2 e^{s})\}\,ds, \\ -y_2(0) &= \int_0^{t^*} e^{s}\{\operatorname{sgn}(\theta_1 e^{2s} + \theta_2 e^{s}) + 2\operatorname{sgn}(\theta_1 e^{2s} + 2\theta_2 e^{s})\}\,ds. \end{aligned} \tag{3.6}$$

To answer the first question, for what values of y is it optimal to set $f_1 = f_2 = 1$ on an initial interval, we note that this is equivalent to the conditions

$$\begin{aligned} t^* &> 0, \\ \theta_1 + \theta_2 &> 0, \\ \theta_1 + 2\theta_2 &> 0. \end{aligned} \tag{3.7}$$

Now, since the functions $\theta_1 e^{2s} + \theta_2 e^s$, $\theta_1 e^{2s} + 2\theta_2 e^s$ can each vanish at most once, we see that the above case breaks down into four sub-cases, namely:

$$\text{(a)} \quad \theta_1 \exp(2t^*) + \theta_2 \exp(t^*) > 0, \qquad \text{(b)} \quad >, <, \qquad \text{(c)} \quad <, >, \qquad \text{(d)} \quad <, < \tag{3.8}$$
$$\theta_1 \exp(2t^*) + 2\theta_2 \exp(t^*) > 0.$$

Case (a) is trivial and consists of the arc α' illustrated in Fig. 1. α' is defined parametrically by

$$\begin{aligned} y_1(0) &= 1 - \exp(2t^*) \\ & \qquad\qquad\qquad t^* > 0 \\ y_2(0) &= 3(1 - \exp[t^*]), \end{aligned} \tag{3.9}$$

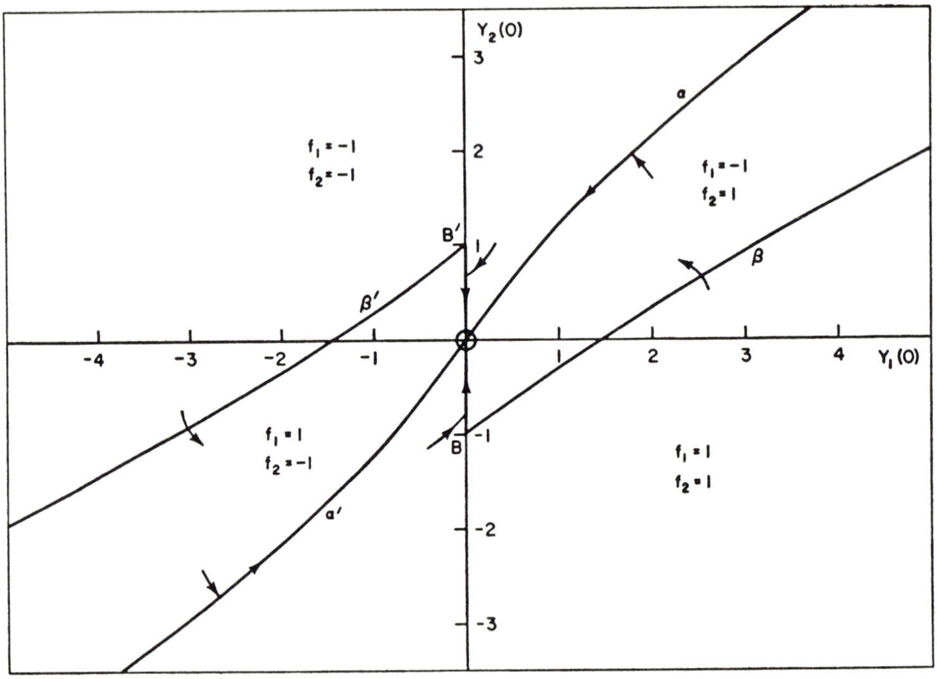

FIG. 1.

as one can readily verify by working out the integrals. Moreover, the curve defines an optimal path, since the solution of the differential equation is, with $f_1 = f_2 = 1$ identically, and $y_1(0)$, $y_2(0)$ defined as above, precisely a sub-arc of α' beginning at $y(0)$ and terminating at the origin.

Case (b) is vacuous, for if we have

$$\begin{aligned} &\theta_1 \exp(2t^*) + \theta_2 \exp(t^*) > 0 \qquad \text{and} \\ &\theta_1 \exp(2t^*) + 2\theta_2 \exp(t^*) < 0, \end{aligned} \tag{3.10}$$

we obtain, by subtraction, and the condition $t^* > 0$, that $\theta_2 < 0$. But, $\theta_1 + \theta_2 > 0$, whence $\theta_1 > 0$. We thus have

$$\begin{aligned} \theta_1 \exp(2t^*) + 2\theta_2 \exp(t^*) &> \theta_1 \exp(t^*) + 2\theta_2 \exp(t^*) \\ &= \exp(t^*)(\theta_1 + 2\theta_2) > 0 \end{aligned} \tag{3.11}$$

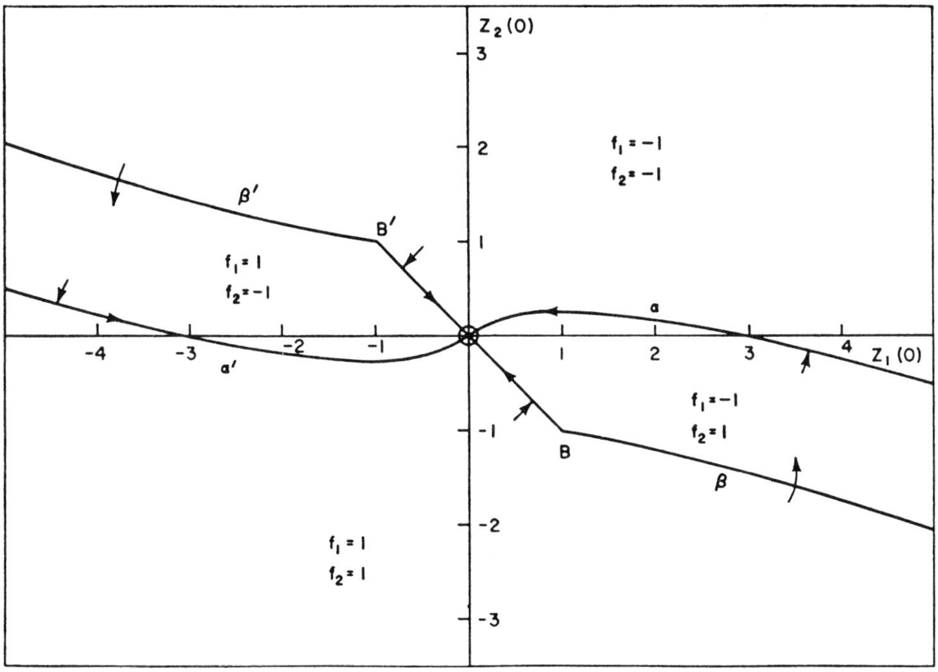

FIG. 2.

which contradicts

$$\theta_1 \exp(2t^*) + 2\theta_2 \exp(t^*) < 0. \tag{3.12}$$

We shall treat case (3.8c) in detail. Case (3.8d) can be treated similarly, but is a trifle more involved, albeit elementary, and will be omitted on those grounds.

We have, upon substituting in (3.6) for case (c):

$$\begin{aligned} -y_1(0) &= \int_0^{\ln(-\theta_2/\theta_1)} \exp(2s)\,ds - \int_{\ln(-\theta_2/\theta_1)}^{t^*} \exp(2s)\,ds + \int_0^{t^*} \exp(2s)\,ds, \\ -y_2(0) &= \int_0^{\ln(-\theta_2/\theta_1)} \exp(s)\,ds - \int_{\ln(-\theta_2/\theta_1)}^{t^*} \exp(s)\,ds + 2\int_0^{t^*} \exp(s)\,ds. \end{aligned} \tag{3.13}$$

Simplifying, we obtain

$$\begin{aligned} -y_1(0) &= (\theta_2/\theta_1)^2 - 1, \\ -y_2(0) &= -2(\theta_2/\theta_1) + \exp(t^*) - 3. \end{aligned} \tag{3.14}$$

If now we set $x^* = \exp(t^*)$, our conditions become

$$\begin{aligned} x^* &> 1, \\ \theta_1 + \theta_2 &> 0, \\ \theta_1 + 2\theta_2 &> 0, \\ \theta_1 x^* + \theta_2 &< 0, \\ \theta_1 x^* + 2\theta_2 &> 0, \\ y_1(0) &= 1 - (\theta_2/\theta_1)^2, \\ y_2(0) &= 3 + 2(\theta_2/\theta_1) - x^*. \end{aligned} \tag{3.15}$$

We easily obtain from the above that $\theta_1 < 0$. By homogeneity, we can set $\theta_1 = -1$, $\theta_2 = \lambda$ and we obtain the equivalent conditions

$$2\lambda > x^* > \lambda > 1 \qquad \text{(A)}$$

$$\left.\begin{aligned} y_1(0) &= 1 - \lambda^2 \\ y_2(0) &= 3 - 2\lambda - x^* \end{aligned}\right\} \qquad \text{(B)}$$

i.e., we wish to find the image of all pairs (x^*, λ) satisfying (A) under the mapping defined by (*B*). Pictorially this is represented by Fig. 3.

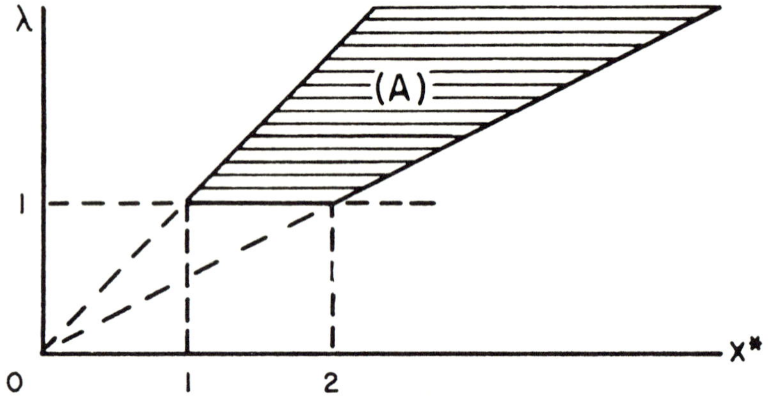

FIG. 3.

On the other hand, the Jacobian of the transformation (B) is given by

$$J_B = \begin{vmatrix} -2\lambda & 0 \\ -2 & -1 \end{vmatrix} = 2\lambda \neq 0 \qquad (3.16)$$

throughout (A); hence the transformation is non-singular and the boundary of the image is the image of the boundary. Making use of this fact we obtain the region for case (3.8c):

$$y_1(0) < 0 \qquad (3.17)$$

and

$$3 - 4[1 - y_1(0)]^{1/2} < y_2(0) < 3 - 3[1 - y_1(0)]^{1/2}. \qquad (3.18)$$

In a similar manner we obtain a region for case (3.8d). The union of cases (3.8a) through (3.8d) is the set of all starting values for which $f_1 = f_2 = 1$ is optimal on an initial interval. In a similar manner we obtain the region $f_1 = 1$, $f_2 = -1$. (Notice that we need not compute the other regions since they can be obtained by skew-symmetry.)

The final result of our calculations is illustrated in Figs. 1 and 2. Figure 2 is the image of Fig. 1 under our initial transformation and gives the optimal policy in terms of our initial starting vector $c = [z_1(0), z_2(0)]$.

In terms of optimal paths (see Fig. 2) we can state the following: A path initiating in the (1,1) region continues with $f_1 = 1$, $f_2 = 1$ until it strikes either the straight segment OB or the parabolic arc β. In the former case f_1 switches from 1 to -1 and the path continues along OB to the origin. In the latter case f_1 switches to -1 at β and the path continues in the $(-1, 1)$ region until it intercepts the parabolic arc α at which f_2 changes from 1 to -1 and α is followed to the origin with $f_1 = f_2 = -1$. Similar remarks hold for the skew-symmetric regions.

Bibliography

1. D. W. Bushaw, Ph.D. Thesis, Department of Mathematics, Princeton University, 1952
2. J. P. LaSalle, Abstract 247t, Bull. Amer. Math. Soc. **60**, 154 (1954)
3. D. McDonald, *Nonlinear techniques for improving servo performance*, Cook Research Laboratories, Bulletin S-2, Chicago, 1950
4. N. J. Rose, *Theoretical aspects of limit control*, Report No. 459, Experimental Towing Tank, Stevens Institute of Technology, November 1953
5. L. Alaoglu, *Weak topologies of normed linear spaces*, Ann. of Math. **41**, 252-267 (1940)
6. T. Bonnesen and W. Fenchel, *Theorie der konvexen Körper*, Ergebnisse der Mathematik **3**, 1, Berlin 1934, New York 1948

L. S. PONTRYAGIN MAXIMUM PRINCIPLE IN THE THEORY OF OPTIMUM SYSTEMS. I

L. I. Rozonoér

(Moscow)

Questions are discussed, which are associated with the proof and use of the L. S. Pontryagin maximum principle in the theory of optimum systems. The work also contains some new results. The problem of optimization for the case of a free right end of a trajectory is examined in the first part of the work. In the second part, the maximum principle is formulated for boundary conditions of a more general type. The connection between the method of dynamic programing and the maximum principle is established in the third part; a method of solving optimization problems in linear discrete systems is given, and a number of considerations concerning the use of the maximum principle in the solution of a definite class of problems associated with the theory of dynamic accuracy of control systems are also discussed.

The problem of creating systems, which are optimum in some prescribed sense, is one of the most important problems of automatic control quality theory. Questions about obtaining optimum laws of control were first seriously posed, apparently, in the theory of the motion of a rocket (see, for example, [17-19]). However, the results obtained here are standard from the viewpoint of general control theory.

The majority of the most important and interesting practical problems lead to nonclassical variation problems, which require new mathematical methods for their solution. The circumstance comes from the fact that the variables in the equation of a real system are (or should be) limited in some way or other. The first most general and important results in this sphere concern theories of systems which insure minimum time of control processes. In 1952-1955, the bases of the theory of processes in linear systems, optimum in relation to rapid action, were developed, mainly in the works of A. A. Feld'baum and A. Ya. Lerner. In particular, the solution of the problem of synthesizing systems, optimum in relation to time, for the case of a linear aperiodic object of arbitrary order with one controlling perturbation, was given in [1-2]. A detailed review of results obtained up to 1956 can be found in [3-5].

In 1956, a principle, leading to the solution of the general problem of finding a control process, optimum for rapid action, was hypothesized by L. S. Pontryagin on the basis of the results of work performed by him, V. G. Boltyanskii, and R. V. Gamkrelidze [6-7]. This principle, which received the name "Maximum Principle," was verified at first for individual types of systems, and in particular, was proved in [8] for the case of linear systems. V. G. Boltyanskii [9] fully proved that the Pontryagin maximum principle was a necessary condition for optimality in relation to rapid action. R. V. Gamkrelidze [8-10] proved theorems of existence and uniqueness and examined the problem of synthesizing controls for linear systems, optimum for rapid action. In [11], the maximum principle was extended to the general case of minimizing an arbitrary functional of the integral function of variable systems. In [12], there is a detailed presentation of basic results obtained by L. S. Pontryagin and his associates.

In examining questions concerned with the theory of optimum systems, it is necessary to note the numerous works of R. Bellman, which are systematically presented in [13] (see also [14]). The method of "Dynamic Programming," developed by R. Bellman, gives a new tool for the solution of nonclassical variational problems, which are closely associated with the Pontryagin maximum principle.

The works of N. N. Krasovskii [15, 16] are also concerned with general questions on the theory of optimum systems; discrete systems, described by finite difference equations, are examined in [16].

The short review presented above is concerned only with papers connected with the maximum principle in some way or other. Hence, many interesting papers were not mentioned.

This paper contains a presentation of the most essential problems in the theory of automatic control which are associated with the proof and use of the Pontryagin maximum principle. The presentation of the majority of the known results (in particular, the proof of the maximum principle) differs somewhat from that in the original works. References to the original works are not given in the text as a rule, so as not to complicate the presentation. Some new results are also contained in this work; a formula for the increment of a functional is based on these results; and also, the sufficient conditions of optimality, formulation of boundary conditions for a number of problems, the connection between the maximum principle and the method of dynamic programming, the formulation and proof of a principle for optimum processes in linear discrete systems, analogous to the maximum principle, result from this formula. The work is published in the form of three separate articles. The optimization problem for the case of a free right end of a trajectory is examined in the first part. In the second part, the maximum principle is formulated for the general case of arbitrary boundary conditions, and the problem of synthesizing optimum systems is discussed. In the third part, the connection between the maximum principle and the method of dynamic programming is established; a method of solving some problems of optimization in discrete systems is given; also, a number of considerations concerning the use of the maximum principle in the solution of a definite class of problems connected with the theory of dynamic precision of control systems are presented (in particular, B. V. Bulgakov's problems about the accumulation of deviations for nonlinear systems).

The most complicated proofs have been placed in appropriate appendices.

1. Statement of the Problem

Let us examine an object of automatic control, which has $\underline{r}$ controlling elements and is described by a system of differential equations of the n-th order:

$$\dot{x}_i = f_i(x_1, \ldots, x_n;\ u_1, \ldots, u_r;\ t) \qquad (i = 1, \ldots, n), \tag{1}$$

where $x_1, \ldots, x_n$ are the parameters of the object, and $u_1, \ldots, u_r$ are the positions of the controlling elements. At each moment, the positions of the controlling elements $u_1(t), \ldots u_r(t)$ must satisfy the inequalities

$$\varphi_j(u_1(t), \ldots, u_r(t)) \leqslant 0 \qquad (j = 1, \ldots, m), \tag{2}$$

which reflect the restrictions which are imposed on the control system. In the future, we will use a geometrical terminology, and we will consider an r-fold space $R(u_1, \ldots, u_r)$. Some point (vector) $\underline{u}$ of the space R corresponds to any given combination of the positions of the controlling elements $(u_1, \ldots, u_r)$. The vector $u(t) = (u_1(t), \ldots, u_r(t))$, given as a time function, will be called the "control" of the object. The control u (t) will be considered piecewise continuous, that is, each of the functions $u_k(t)$ can have a finite number of discontinuities of the first type at the end of an interval of time.

The inequalities (2) isolate some closed* set of points, whose boundaries are given by the equalities $\varphi_j(u_1, \ldots, u_r) = 0$, in the space R. This set will be designed by U, and the inequalitities (2) can be briefly written in the form

$$u(t) \in U, \tag{2'}$$

that is, the vector u (t) must belong to the closed set U of the space R at any given moment. In this case, our

*The set is called closed if it includes its own boundary. The set being examined is closed in so far as conditions (2) permit a sign of the equalities such that the point $\underline{u}$ can be found on the boundary of the set.

choice of the possible controls is limited by condition (2') and by the requirement of piecewise continuity of the functions $u_1(t), \ldots, u_r(t)$. The control u (t), which obeys these two conditions, will be called admissible. When speaking about controls from now on, we will have admissible controls in mind.

We will examine an n-fold phase space $X(x_1, \ldots, x_n)$ of the parameters of the object, along with the space $R(u_1, \ldots, u_r)$, in which the control can be changed. The state of the object is described then by the point (vector) $x(x_1, \ldots, x_n)$ of the space X. If the control u (t) and the initial state of the system $x^0 = (x_1^0, \ldots, x_n^0)$ are given, then the behavior of the system (trajectory x (t) in the phase space X) is uniquely determined from Eqs. (1).

The basic problem of the theory of optimum systems is the choice of a control u (t) such that the behavior of the system will be "best" in some prescribed sense. We will introduce a number of examples of precise statements of problems, in which the sense of the concept "optimum control" is made concrete each time.

It is possible to require that the control u (t) be so selected that the system will go from one fixed state x^0 to another fixed state x^1 in minimum time. The control u (t), which satisfies this requirement, is called optimum for rapid action. The time of transition of the system from state x^0 to state x^1, which determines the criteria of optimality in the given problem, is a functional* given on the controls u (t). The requirement of optimality of the control u (t) means minimization of the value of the functional.

Let us examine another problem. Let it be required that a control u (t) be chosen such that in a given time T the system will go from an initial state x^0 into a state in which one of the variables (for example, x_1) will become as large as possible, and the remaining coordinates will be fixed values. This problem arises, for example, in the calculation of the control law of a rocket, or in putting an artificial satellite of the Earth into a given orbit [20], if it is required that the horizontal velocity of the rocket be maximum at a fixed height and at a given time, for zero vertical velocity and for a given flight range. In the present example, the functional, which determines the criteria of optimality, is the value of the generalized coordinate $x_1(T)$ (horizontal velocity of the rocket) at the time t = T. In a number of cases, there is no necessity to fix the final values of all the remaining coordinates $x_2, \ldots, x_n$. If, for example, only the height and not the flight range plays a role, there is no necessity to impose any restrictions on the latter. Then an analogous problem about the maximum of the functional $x_1(T)$ arises, but it is not necessary for all the remaining coordinates to assume prescribed values. Let us examine, finally, one more problem. It is necessary to choose a control u (t) in such a manner that the integral

$$S = \int_0^T F(x_1, \ldots, x_n; u_1, \ldots, u_r)\, dt$$

becomes minimum (or maximum) during the time of movement T. Here again, different variations are possible. It can be required that the initial and final states of the system be fixed beforehand (for example, in the problem about the flight of an airplane from one fixed point to another, with the least fuel consumption; the function F (x, u) represents fuel consumed per unit time, and the integral represents the full consumption of fuel during the flight). In other cases, the final state of the system does not have any value; it is only important that the integral become the maximum (or minimum) value of all those possible (for example, if it is required that the aggregate being controlled give the maximum quantity of production in the absence of any other conditions; in this case, the function F (x, u) represents instantaneous producitivity, and the integral represents the full production output). The time T, during which optimization of the system is required, can also be either fixed beforehand, or not fixed. If the airplane moves between two points on a schedule, then its flight time is fixed, and minimization of fuel consumption must be required for this time, fixed beforehand. If time does not matter, but only fuel economy is important, then the time must not be fixed beforehand.

The number of examples of such optimization problems can be increased further. However, all these superficially different problems prove to be closely associated mathematically, and require completely analogous methods of investigation. Moreover, one of them can quickly to transformed into others.

*A functional is a correspondence established between functions (or combinations of functions) and numbers. In the given example, a number— the transition time from x^0 to x^1— corresponds to each control u (t) [that is, the combination of functions $u_1(t), \ldots, u_r(t)$] that insures that the system gets to x^1.

We will show, for example, that the problem of optimizing a system with respect to an integral leads to the problem of optimizing with respect to coordinates. Actually, let it be necessary to optimize the magnitude $\int_0^T F(x_1, \ldots, x_n;\ u_1, \ldots, u_r;\ t)\, dt$ (the time T, and also the final values of the coordinates can be either fixed, or free) in an object described by the differential equations (1), with restrictions on the control (2). We will introduce a new variable

$$x_{n+1}(t) = \int_0^t F(x_1, \ldots, x_n;\ u_1, \ldots, u_r;\ t)\, dt,\ x_{n+1}(0) \equiv x_{n+1}^0 = 0.$$

Then one more differential relation can be added to system (1)

$$\dot{x}_{n+1} = F(x_1, \ldots, x_n;\ u_1, \ldots, u_r;\ t),$$

and the problem of optimizing the integral leads to the problem of optimizing the n + 1 st coordinate $x_{n+1}(T)$ at the final moment of time.

The problem about the optimization of some function from the final value of the coordinates $\Phi[x_1(T), \ldots, x_n(T)]$ also leads easily to the problem about optimizing the final value of one coordinate, if the function Φ is differentiable.

To show this, it is sufficient to introduce a new coordinate,

$$x_{n+1}(t) = \Phi[x_1(t), \ldots, x_n(t)],\quad x_{n+1}(0) \equiv x_{n+1}^0 = \Phi(x_1^0, \ldots, x_n^0)$$

and to add the relation to system (1)

$$\dot{x}_{n+1} = \sum_{s=1}^{n} \frac{\partial \Phi(x_1, \ldots, x_n)}{\partial x_s} f_s(x_1, \ldots, x_n;\ u_1, \ldots, u_r;\ t).$$

Let us further note that the problem of optimization with "integral" restrictions of the type

$$\int_0^T F(x_1, \ldots, x_n;\ u_1, \ldots, u_r;\ t)\, dt \leqslant A$$

easily leads to ordinary statements of the problem. Introducing the variable $x_{n+1}(t)$ and adding the relation

$$x_{n+1} = F(x_1, \ldots, x_n;\ u_1, \ldots, u_r;\ t),$$

to (1), we arrive at the ordinary problem, with the additional restriction on the final value of the n + 1st coordinate: $x_{n+1}(T) \leq A$.

The problem about the minimum transition time of the system from one fixed state to another is also a particular case of the problem about the minimization of one coordinate.

Indeed, by combining equation

$$\frac{dx_{n+1}}{dt} = 1,$$

with (1), we may convince ourselves that minimization of time means minimization of the coordinate x_{n+1}. In this case, the final values of the remaining coordinates are given, and the time T, evidently, should not be fixed.

Hence, a broad class of optimization problems leads to the problem concerning optimization of one coordinate of the system. It will be more convenient for us, however, to examine a somewhat more general problem (although one which easily leads to the problem about optimization of one coordinate). To wit, we will pose the problem of optimizing a linear function of the final values of all the coordinates of the system,

that is, the quantities $S = \sum_{k=1}^{n} c_k x_k(T)$, where c_k are certain constants. The quantities S can be treated as the scalar product of the vector x (T) = [x_1 (T),..., x_n (T)], which gives the end point of the trajectory x (t), and the given vector c = (c_1,..., c_k). In other words, we require optimization of the projection of the vector x (T) on the given direction (c_1,..., c_k). By the same token, the requirement of maximum (or minimum) size of S means that we attempt to move the system as much "farther" in the direction of the vector c as possible (or as much "farther" in the direction of the vector − c as possible).

As we have seen, various restrictions can be imposed on the final state of the system (that is, on the position of the final point of the trajectory x (T) in the phase space X). In general, these restrictions can be formulated as a requirement of a transfer of the system to some fixed set G of the phase space X, described by some combination of equalities and inequalities. In particular, if the final values of some coordinates of the system are precisely fixed, and the remainder free, then the set G is a linear manifold in the space X ("linear", "plane," etc).

Hence, we will examine the following problem. It is necessary to select a control u (t) from the group of admissible controls which transfer the system (1) from the point $x(T_0) \equiv x^0$ to the fixed closed set G of the phase space, in such a way that the sum $S = \sum_{i=1}^{n} c_i x_i(T)$ at the given time t = T will assume a minimum (or maximum) value.

In order to be definite, we have formulated a problem in which the control time $T-T_0$ is fixed. However, we will see consequently that in those problems where the time is not given beforehand (in particular, in the problem about minimizing the transition time), completely analogous results obtain.

The control u (t) which makes the functional $S = \sum_{1}^{n} c_i x_i(T)$, minimum (maximum) will be called min-optimum (max-optimum) in S, for brevity.

Mathematically, the problem examined by us is a generalization of Mayer's classical problem in the calculus of variations. However, the presence of restrictions on the positions of the controlling elements, leading to the requirement that the controls u (t) must belong to the closed set U, generally speaking does not permit one to use the methods of the classical calculus of variations. Therefore, the solution of the problem formulated above requires the development of new mathematical methods.

It should further be noted that the theory of optimum systems is not to any degree exhausted by the solution of the problem formulated above. Firstly, various complications in the statement of the problem are possible. In particular, accounting for restrictions, which can be imposed on the phase coordinates x_1,..., x_n, has great practical value. Secondly, in a number of cases problems arise which do not lead to optimization of the final value of the coordinates of the system and which require the solution of variational problems for functionals of another type (for example, the problem about the minimum of the maximum deviation of some coordinate from a given level). These and analogous questions are not discussed in this article.

2. The Problem with the Free Right End of the Trajectory

In this section we will examine a particular case of our basic problem. To wit, we will consider here that the right end of the trajectory x (T) is "free", that is, no restrictions are imposed on the final values of the coordinates (the set G occupies all of the space X). The results, which pertain to the case being examined, prove to be completely analogous to the results obtained in the solution of the general problem, differing from the latter only in details which concern the boundary conditions (transversality conditions) and at the same time permit more simple proofs. Moreover, problems of this type are important in themselves, for example, in a number of questions about the theory of the dynamic precision of control systems or in solving problems of control in mathematical economics. Therefore it is well to examine this simpler problem separately.

Below, we will formulate and discuss results leading to the solution of the problem being examined. Full proofs of the theorems are in the appendix.

We will bring into consideration a combination of n time functions $p_1(t), \ldots p_n(t)$, which form a variable vector $p(t) = (p_1(t), \ldots, p_n(t))$, which has a direction, at time $t = T$, opposite to the direction of the vector $c = (c_1, \ldots, c_n)$, that is

$$p_i(T) = -c_i \quad (i = 1, \ldots, n). \tag{3}$$

We assume here, for simplicity, that the modului of the vectors $p(T)$ and c are equal. The variables $p_i(t)$ are subject to a set of differential equations of the following form

$$\dot{p}_i(t) = -\sum_1^n p_s \frac{\partial f_s(x_1, \ldots, x_n; u_1, \ldots, u_r; t)}{\partial x_i} \quad (i = 1, \ldots, n), \tag{4}$$

by the same token, we give a law which the vector $p(t)$ can be changed in accordance with. Let us note that if any control $u(t)$ is given, the vector $p(t)$ is uniquely determined from Eqs. (4), where conditions (3) play the role of boundary conditions. Indeed, if the control $u(t)$ is known, then, by solving the system of equations

$$\dot{x}_i = f_i(x, u, t) \quad (i = 1, \ldots, n),$$

for which the initial conditions $[x_i(T_0) = x_i^0, i = 1, \ldots, n)]$ are given, we can find the functions $x_i(t)$. Putting these functions in (4), we would have a set of linear differential equations with variable coefficients and with boundary conditions (3), for the magnitudes of $p_i(t)$. The solution of these equations would permit us to determine $p(t)$ as a function of time.

The vector $p(t)$ will be called an "impulse" which maps points at time t.

At each time t, let us examine the scalar product $\sum_1^n p_i(t)\dot{x}_i(t)$ of the vector $p(t)$ and the velocity vector $\dot{x}(t)$ which maps the points. Bringing Eqs. (1) to our attention, we will express this quantity in the form of a function of $2n + r + 1$ variables $x_1, \ldots, x_n$; $p_1, \ldots, p_n$; $u_1, \ldots, u_r$; t:

$$H(x, p, u, t) \equiv \sum_{s=1}^n p_s f_s(x_1, \ldots, x_n; u_1, \ldots, u_r; t). \tag{5}$$

By using the function $H(x, p, u, t)$, which plays a basic role in all further discussion, Eqs. (1) and (4) can be written in the form

$$\dot{x}_i = \frac{\partial H}{\partial p_i}, \quad \dot{p}_i = -\frac{\partial H}{\partial x_i} \quad (i = 1, \ldots, n) \tag{6}$$

with the boundary conditions

$$x_i(T_0) = x_i^0, \quad p_i(T) = -c_i \quad (i = 1, \ldots, n). \tag{7}$$

Let us turn our attention to the fact that Eqs. (6) concur in form with the canonical equations of Hamilton in analytical mechanics. The function H is analogous to the Hamiltonian, and the vector $p(t)$ to the impulse vector, which explains the name given by us to the vector $p(t)$. The connection between the equations of the theory of optimum systems and the equations of mechanics is discussed also in appendix 4.

Now let $u(t)$ be some admissible control, and $x^u(t)$, $p^u(t)$ be the position and impulse which maps the points at time t for the control $u(t)$. Let us put the values of the variables $x_i^u(t)$, $p_i^u(t)$ in the function

H (x, p, u, t). Then we will obtain some function

$$K(t, u_1, \ldots, u_r) \equiv H(x^u(t), p^u(t), u, t),$$

which is a function of r variables $u = (u_1, \ldots, u_r)$ for every fixed time t, that is, points which belong to the closed set U of the space R. We will say that the control u (t) satisfies the maximum (minimum) condition if the function K (t, u) reaches an absolute maximum (minimum) in the set U at any time t ($T_0 \leq t \leq T$), for values of the variables equal to the values of the control at the same time, that is, at $u_k = u_k(t)$ (k = 1,..., r). It appears that fulfilling the maximum (minimum) condition for u (t) is a necessary condition for min-optimality (max-optimality) of the control u (t); this leads to the theorem expressing the Pontryagin maximum principle for our problem. *

Theorem 1. If the control u (t) is min-optimum (max-optimum) in $S = \sum_1^n c_i x_i(T)$, then it satisfies the maximum (minimum) condition.

Hence, the optimum control u (t) must be chosen at each moment so that the function H ($x^u(t)$, $p^u(t)$, u, t), which is a scalar product of the vector $p^u(t)$ and the velocity vector $\dot{x}^u(t)$, is minimized (maximized). Therefore, the geometrical sense of the theorem is that the optimum control tries to "drive away" the image point optimally in some direction determined by the vector $p^u(t)$, at each moment. At the time t = T, when $p^u(T) = -c$, the direction of "maximum dispersal" concurs with the direction of the vector c if we are seeking the maximum of the functional $S = \sum_1^n c_i x_i(T)$, and in the opposite direction to c if the minimum of the functional is sought. This property of the optimum control becomes especially clear in the following example, where the equations of the object have the form:

$$\dot{x}_i = f_i(u_1, \ldots, u_r) \qquad (i = 1, \ldots, n),$$

that is, the right halves of the equations do not depend on the coordinates. Forming the differential equations for the impulse $p^u(t)$, we find that the vector $p^u(t)$ is constant in our case, and is equal to

$$p^u(t) = -c \qquad (T_0 \leqslant t \leqslant T).$$

at any time.

Indeed, $\partial f_s / \partial x_i \equiv 0$, and it follows from Eqs. (4) [or (6)] that $\dot{p}^u(t) = 0$ and, in view of conditions (3) [or (7)], we obtain the equality which is written. Therefore, the direction of "maximum dispersal" is always constant in the given case, and at any time, the control is chosen so that the maximum possible velocity is imparted to the direction of the vector c for max-optimality, and the maximum possible velocity in the direction of the vector $-c$ for min-optimality. Naturally, such a simple control law does not prevail in the general case, since if the right halves of the equations of the object depend on the coordinates, then interval "forces" will act on the image point, and these must be taken into account. The "internal" forces are accounted for by introducing a variable vector $p^u(t)$.

In the future, we will omit the index u in the designations $p^u(t)$, $x^u(t)$.

The maximum principle permits one to form a set of differential equations whose solution determines the

---

*We note that fulfillment of the maximum condition is essential if the functional $S = \sum_1^n c_i x_i(T)$ is to be minimum (and vice-versa). This is connected with the fact that the final value of the vector p (t) was defined as a vector opposite to the vector $c = (c_1, \ldots, c_n)$. One can postulate that p (T) = + c, but in this case the formulation of the theorems would be the reverse of analogous formulations assumed in [6-12], which would lead to confusion.

optimum trajectory and optimum direction. Indeed, the quantities $u_1, \ldots, u_r$ are determined from the maximum (minimum) condition, at any time, as functions of the variables $x_1, \ldots, x_n$; $p_1, \ldots, p_n$; t:

$$u_k = \psi_k(x_1, \ldots, x_n;\ p_1, \ldots, p_n;\ t) \qquad (k = 1, \ldots, r).$$

Putting the expressions obtained in the right halves of Eqs. (6), we will get a set of 2n differential equations with 2n unknown $x_1(t), \ldots, x_n(t)$; $p_1(t), \ldots, p_n(t)$, whose solution, under the boundary conditions (7), will give the optimum trajectory x (t) and impulse p (t). Knowing x (t) and p (t), we obtain the optimum control u (t).

Let us take the simplest example. Let it be required to find the control u (t), which makes the integral

$\frac{1}{2}\int_0^T (x^3 + u^2)\,dt$, maximum, if the equation of the object has the form:

$$\dot{x} = -ax + u, \quad x(0) = x^0,$$

and no restrictions are imposed on the control u (t) (that is, the set U occupies all of the space R– in the given case, the whole real axis $-\infty < u < +\infty$).

Introducing the variables $x_1(t) \equiv x(t)$, $x_2(t) \equiv \frac{1}{2}\int_0^t (x_1^2 + u^2)\,dt$, we get the system

$$\dot{x}_1 = -ax_1 + u, \quad \dot{x}_2 = \frac{1}{2}x_1^2 + \frac{1}{2}u^2.$$

The functional which must be minimized is $S = x_2(T)$, that is, $c_1 = 0$, $c_2 = 1$. According to equality (5), we write the function

$$H(x, p, u) \equiv -ap_1x_1 + \frac{1}{2}p_2x_1^2 + p_1u + \frac{1}{2}p_2u^2$$

and the equations for the impulse (second group of Eqs. (6))

$$\dot{p}_1 = ap_1 - p_2x_1, \quad \dot{p}_2 = 0$$

with the kind of boundary conditions of equalities (7)

$$x_1(0) = x^0, \quad x_2(0) = 0; \quad p_1(T) = 0; \quad p_2(T) = -1.$$

We notice at once that $p_2(t)$ is constant and $p_2 = -1$ always, so that the function H has the form:

$$H = -ap_1x_1 - \frac{1}{2}x_1^2 + p_1u - \frac{1}{2}u^2.$$

According to the maximum principle, the function H must be maximum in u for any values of x and p. In the given case, the maximum of H is reached at the value $u = p_1(t)$. Putting the value of u obtained in the equation of the object, we obtain the following equations for the determination of $x_1(t)$ and $p_1(t)$ (the function $x_2(t)$ does not interest us):

$$\dot{x}_1 = -ax_1 + p_1, \quad \dot{p}_1 = x_1 + ap_1$$

with boundary conditions $x_1(0) = x^0$, $p_1(T) = 0$. The equations are easily integrated:

$$x_1(t) = C_1e^{\lambda t} + C_2e^{-\lambda t}, \quad p_1(t) = D_1e^{\lambda t} + D_2e^{-\lambda t},$$

where $\lambda = \sqrt{a^2 + 1}$ is the root of the characteristic equation, and the constants C_1, C_2, D_1, D_2 depend on x^0. Since $u(t) = p_1(t)$ the optimum control is also determined.

The problem which was examined can evidently be easily solved without the use of the maximum principle, since there are no restrictions on the controls. The given example was introduced only to illustrate the procedure of the solution coming from the maximum principle.

In a very broad class of practically important problems it appears that the maximum of the function $K(t, u) \equiv H[x(t), p(t), u, t]$ is reached at the boundary of the set U, and the optimum control takes its boundary values. In particular, this circumstance always occurs if the functions $u_1(t), \ldots, u_r(t)$ enter the system of equations of the problem linearly. For example, let the equations of the problem have the form:

$$\dot{x}_1 = f_1(x_1, x_2) + u_1, \qquad \dot{x}_2 = f_2(x_1, x_2) + u_2,$$

and the functions $u_1(t)$ and $u_2(t)$ be limited in modulus so that: $|u_1| \leq M_1$, $|u_2| \leq M_2$ (the set U is a rectangle). Then, forming the function

$$H(x, p, u) \equiv p_1 f_1(x_1, x_2) + p_2 f_2(x_1, x_2) + p_1 u_1 + p_2 u_2,$$

we find that the maximum of H is reached at $u_1 = M_1 \operatorname{sign} p_1$, $u_2 = M_2 \operatorname{sign} p_2$. Indeed, H is maximum in u_1 and u_2 when u_1 and p_1, u_2 and p_2 respectively have identical signs (so that the products p_1u_1 and p_2u_2 are positive); in this case, u_1 and u_2 reach a maximum in modulus.* Therefore, the functions $u_1(t)$ and $u_2(t)$ can only "switch" from one boundary position to another, no matter how $p_1(t)$ and $p_2(t)$ change with time; $p_1(t)$ and $p_2(t)$ are determined only at the moment of switching.

Theorem 1, formulated above, which expresses the Pontryagin maximum principle, gives only the necessary conditions of optimality. It is easy to show examples in which the control satisfies the maximum (minimum) condition, but never the less is not optimum. From the viewpoint of the remaining conditions, it appears that the control, which is subject to the maximum (minimum) conditions is optimum, generally speaking, only in a definite local sense, if some additional conditions are not fulfilled, which are connected with the "sharpness" of the maximum (minimum) of the function H [21]. However, for a system whose controls are linear relative to the coordinates

$$\dot{x}_i = \sum_1^n a_{is}(t)\, x_s + \varphi_i(u_1, \ldots, u_r), \quad i = 1, \ldots, n, \tag{8}$$

the following theorem obtains.

Theorem 2. The necessary and sufficient condition of min-optimality (max-optimality) of the control u (t) in system (8) is the fulfillment of the maximum (minimum) condition for u (t).

It must be noted, that if the maximum (minimum) condition is not sufficient, generally speaking, even so, it permits one to determine uniquely the optimum control in the majority of practically important cases. Indeed, if the optimum control exists (which is often evident from physical considerations), and the control satisfying the maximum (minimum) condition is unique, then this unique control is optimum.

APPENDIX

1. Increment of the functional during a change of the control. Let x_i and p_i satisfy the equations

$$\dot{x}_i = \frac{\partial H}{\partial p_i}, \quad \dot{p}_i = -\frac{\partial H}{\partial x_i} \quad (i = 1, \ldots, n), \tag{9}$$

* We designate the function

$$z = \begin{cases} 1 & \text{for } y > 0, \\ -1 & \text{for } y < 0, \end{cases}$$

by the symbol $z = \operatorname{sign} y$, which is not defined when $y = 0$. If at any time $p_1(t) = 0$ and $p_2(t) = 0$, then H does not, in fact, depend on u_1 and u_2, and the maximum principle does not permit one to find the value of the optimum control (see appendix 3.3).

where

$$H(x, p, u, t) \equiv \sum_{1}^{n} p_i f_i(x, u, t). \tag{10}$$

The functions f_i ($i = 1, \ldots, n$) will be considered continuous in all of the arguments (x, u, t), and to have continuous partial derivatives in the arguments (x, u), up to and including the second derivative.

The equality

$$I(x, p, u) \equiv \int_{T_0}^{T} \left[\sum_{1}^{n} p_i \dot{x}_i - H(x, p, u, t) \right] dt = 0, \tag{11}$$

follows from (9) and (10), and is justified if the first group of Eqs. (9) is satisfied under arbitrary controls and boundary conditions. We will choose some control $u(t) \in U$ and examine its increment $\delta u(t)$. Let $x(t)$, and $p(t)$ be a solution of (9) for the control $u(t)$ and some boundary conditions, and $x(t) + \delta x(t)$, $p(t) + \delta p(t)$ be a solution of (9) for the control $u(t) + \delta u(t)$ with the same boundary conditions. Let us examine the difference $\Delta \equiv I(x + \delta x, p + \delta p, u + \delta u) - I(x, p, u)$, in which $\Delta = 0$ always. It follows from (11) that

$$\Delta = \int_{T_0}^{T} \sum_{1}^{n} (p_i \delta\dot{x}_i + \delta p_i \dot{x}_i)\, dt + \int_{T_0}^{T} \sum_{1}^{n} \delta p_i \delta\dot{x}_i dt -$$

$$- \int_{T_0}^{T} [H(x + \delta x, p + \delta p, u + \delta u, t) - H(x, p, u, t)]\, dt. \tag{12}$$

We note that the functions $x(t)$, $p(t)$, $\delta x(t)$, $\delta p(t)$ are continuous, and their derivatives exist and are piecewise continuous.

We will integrate by parts:

$$\int_{T_0}^{T} p_i \delta\dot{x}_i dt = p_i \delta x_i \Big|_{T_0}^{T} - \int_{T_0}^{T} \dot{p}_i \delta x_i dt; \qquad \int_{T_0}^{T} \delta p_i \delta\dot{x}_i dt = \delta p_i \delta x_i \Big|_{T_0}^{T} - \int_{T_0}^{T} \delta x_i \delta\dot{p}_i dt.$$

Hence, keeping (9) in mind, and introducing the vector $y = (y_1, \ldots, y_{2n})$ ($x_i = y_i$, $p_i = y_{n+i}$, $i = 1, \ldots, n$) for brevity, we obtain

$$\int_{T_0}^{T} \sum_{1}^{n} (p_i \delta\dot{x}_i + \delta p_i \dot{x}_i)\, dt = \sum_{1}^{n} p_i \delta x_i \Big|_{T_0}^{T} + \int_{T_0}^{T} \sum_{1}^{2n} \frac{\partial H(y, u, t)}{\partial y_s} \delta y_s dt, \tag{13}$$

$$\int_{T_0}^{T} \sum_{1}^{n} \delta p_i \delta\dot{x}_i dt = \sum_{1}^{n} \frac{1}{2} \delta p_i \delta x_i \Big|_{T_0}^{T} + \frac{1}{2} \int_{T_0}^{T} \sum_{1}^{2n} \delta \frac{\partial H(y, u, t)}{\partial y_s} \delta y_s dt. \tag{14}$$

Using Taylor's formula, we put the last integral in (12) into the form

$$\int_{T_0}^{T} [H(y + \delta y, u + \delta u, t) - H(y, u, t)]\, dt = \int_{T_0}^{T} [H(y, u + \delta u, t) - H(y, u, t)]\, dt +$$

$$+ \int_{T_0}^{T} \sum_{1}^{2n} \frac{\partial H(y, u + \delta u, t)}{\partial y_s} \delta y_s dt + \frac{1}{2} \int_{T_0}^{T} \sum_{s,q=1}^{2n} \frac{\partial^2 H(y + \vartheta_1 \delta y, u + \delta u, t)}{\partial y_s \partial y_q} \delta y_s \delta y_q dt, \tag{15}$$

where $0 < \vartheta_1(t) < 1$. Since

$$\frac{1}{2}\delta\frac{\partial H}{\partial y_s}\delta y_s \equiv \frac{1}{2}\frac{\partial H(y+\delta y, u+\delta u, t)}{\partial y_s}\delta y_s - \frac{1}{2}\frac{\partial H(y, u, t)}{\partial y_s}\delta y_s,$$

by putting (13)-(15) in (12), we get

$$\Delta \equiv \sum_1^n\left(p_i + \frac{1}{2}\delta p_i\right)\delta x_i\Big|_{T_0}^T - \int_{T_0}^T [H(y, u+\delta u, t) - H(y, u, t)]\,dt -$$

$$-\frac{1}{2}\int_{T_0}^T\sum_1^{2n}\left[\frac{\partial H(y, u+\delta u, t)}{\partial y_s} - \frac{\partial H(y, u, t)}{\partial y_s}\right]\delta y_s dt -$$

$$-\frac{1}{2}\int_{T_0}^T\sum_{s,\,q=1}^{2n}\frac{\partial^2 H(y+\vartheta_1\delta y, u+\delta u, t)}{\partial y_s\partial y_q}\delta y\;\delta y_q dt +$$

$$+\frac{1}{2}\int_{T_0}^T\sum_1^{2n}\left[\frac{\partial H(y+\delta y, u+\delta u, t)}{\partial y_s} - \frac{\partial H(y, u+\delta u, t)}{\partial y_s}\right]\delta y_s dt.$$

Using Taylor's formula once more for the integrand of the last integral, and keeping in mind that $\Delta = 0$, we will have

$$\sum_1^n\left(p_i + \frac{1}{2}\delta p_i\right)\delta x_i\Big|_{T_0}^T = \int_{T_0}^T [H(y, u+\delta u, t) - H(y, u, t)]\,dt + \eta, \tag{16}$$

where $\eta = \eta_1 + \eta_2$ and

$$\eta_1 = \frac{1}{2}\int_{T_0}^T\sum_1^{2n}\left[\frac{\partial H(y, u+\delta u, t)}{\partial y_s} - \frac{\partial H(y, u, t)}{\partial y_s}\right]\delta y_s dt,$$

$$\eta_2 = \frac{1}{2}\int_{T_0}^T\sum_{s,q=1}^{2n}\left[\frac{\partial^2 H(y+\vartheta_1\delta y, u+\delta u, t)}{\partial y_s\partial y_q} - \frac{\partial^2 H(y+\vartheta_2\delta y, u+\delta u, t)}{\partial y_s\partial y_q}\right]\delta y_s\delta y_q dt, \tag{17}$$

in which $0 < \vartheta_1 < 1$, $0 < \vartheta_2 < 1$. Fixing the boundary conditions in the form

$$x_i(T_0) = x_i^0, \quad p_i(T) = -c_i \qquad (i = 1, \ldots, n), \tag{18}$$

in view of the fact that $\delta x_i(T_0) = \delta p_i(T) = 0$, we get, finally,

$$\delta S \equiv \sum_1^n c_i\delta x_i(T) = -\int_{T_0}^T [H(x, p, u+\delta u, t) - H(x, p, u, t)]\,dt - \eta. \tag{19}$$

2. Evaluation of the remaining term in the formula for the increment of the functional. First, we will get an evaluation of $\delta x_i(t)$ and $\delta p_i(t)$.

It follows from the first group of Eqs. (9) that

$$\delta\dot{x}_i = f_i(x+\delta x, u+\delta u, t) - f_i(x, u, t) \quad (i = 1, \ldots, n).$$

Since the initial conditions are fixed and $\delta x_i(T_0) = 0$, then

$$\delta x_i(t) = \int_{T_0}^t [f_i(x+\delta x, u+\delta u, t) - f_i(x, u, t)]\,dt.$$

By using the Lipschitz conditions, which always hold for our assumptions, we obtain the inequalities

$$|\delta x_i(t)| \leqslant \int_{T_0}^{t} K \sum_{1}^{n} |\delta x_s(z)|\, dz + \int_{T_0}^{t} K \sum_{1}^{r} |\delta u_k(z)|\, dz \quad (i = 1, \ldots, n),$$

where K is the maximum of the Lipschitz constants for the functions f_i.

Summing and strengthening the inequalities, we have

$$X(t) \leqslant Kn \int_{T_0}^{t} \sum_{1}^{r} |\delta u_k(z)|\, dz + \int_{T_0}^{t} KnX(z)\, dz,$$

where $X(t) = \sum_{1}^{n} |\delta x_i(t)|$. It is easy to show that the inequality

$$X(t) \leqslant a + \int_{T_0}^{T} bX(z)\, dz$$

follows from the inequality

$$X(t) \leqslant ae^{b(t-T_0)}$$

(a and b are positive constants).

Therefore, putting $a = Kn \int_{T_0}^{T} \sum_{1}^{n} |\delta u_k(z)|\, dz$, $b = Kn$ and substituting t for T, we get

$$X(t) \leqslant Kne^{Kn(T-T_0)} \int_{T_0}^{T} \sum_{1}^{r} |\delta u_k(z)|\, dz \quad (T_0 \leqslant t \leqslant T).$$

Thence, we have analogous inequalities for $\delta x_i(t)$:

$$\delta x_i(t) \leqslant M_1 \int_{T_0}^{T} \sum_{1}^{r} |\delta u_k(z)|\, dz \quad (i = 1, \ldots, n; \quad T_0 \leqslant t \leqslant T),$$

where $M_1 = Kne^{Kn(T-T_0)}$ is a constant which does not depend on $\delta u(t)$.

Examining the second group of Eqs. (9), we obtain for $p_i(t)$

$$\delta p_i = -\left[\frac{\partial H(x+\delta x, u+\delta u, p+\delta p, t)}{\partial x_i} - \frac{\partial H(x, p, u, t)}{\partial x_i}\right],$$

in which $\delta p_i(T) = 0$. Therefore, by now using the evaluation for $\delta x_i(t)$, we get, in a completely analogous fashion,

$$\delta p_i(t) \leqslant M_2 \int_{T_0}^{T} \sum_{1}^{r} |\delta u_k(z)|\, dz \quad (i = 1, \ldots, n, \; T_0 \leqslant t \leqslant T).$$

Hence, the evaluation

$$\delta y_s(t)| \leqslant M_1 \int_{T_0}^{T} \sum_{1}^{r} |\delta u_k(z)|\, dz \quad (s = 1, \ldots, 2n, \; T_0 \leqslant t \leqslant T), \tag{20}$$

occurs, where M is a constant which does not depend on $\delta u(t)$. Applying (12) to the remaining members η_1 and η_2 in (9), using the Lipschitz conditions for the functions $\partial H/\partial y_s$ and having the boundedness of the functions $\partial^2 H/\partial y_s \partial y_q$ in mind, we obtain

$$|\eta| \leqslant A\left(\int_{T_0}^{T} \sum_{1}^{r} |\delta u_k(z)|\, \partial z\right)^2 \tag{21}$$

for $\eta = \eta_1 + \eta_2$, without difficulty.

If the function $\delta u(t)$ is different from zero only in the interval $[t_1, t_2]$ of length $t_2 - t_1 = \tau$, then, using the Cauchy-Bunyakovskii (Schwartz) inequality, formula (21) can be re-written in the form

$$|\eta| \leqslant A\tau \int_{t_1}^{t_2} \left(\sum_{1}^{r} |\delta u_k(t)|\right)^2 dt \quad \text{or} \quad |\eta| \leqslant B\tau \int_{t_1}^{t_2} \sum_{1}^{r} \delta u_k^2(t)\, dt \quad (B = rA). \tag{22}$$

3. Proof of theorem 1. To be definite, let us examine the case when the minimum of the functional S is sought. For any change $\delta u(t)$ of the control $u(t)$, the following must hold;

$$\delta S \geqslant 0. \tag{0}$$

Let us assume that the maximum condition does not hold at $t = t^*$, that is, a vector $u^* = (u_1^*, \ldots, u_r) \in U$ exists such that

$$H[x(t^*), p(t^*), u^*, t^*] > H[x(t^*), p(t^*), u(t^*), t^*]. \tag{!}$$

In view of the piecewise continuity of $u(t)$, and the continuity of the functions $x(t)$, $p(t)$, and $H(x, p, u, t)$ some interval $[t', t'']$, which includes t^*, is always found, on which the functions $F_1(t) \equiv H[x(t), p(t), u^*, t]$ and $F_2(t) \equiv H[x(t), p(t), u(t), t]$ are continuous, and consequently, are uniformly continuous (if $t = t^*$ is a discontinuity point of the control $u(t)$, then, by agreeing that $u(t^*) = u(t^* - 0)$, one can take $t' = t^*$). Therefore, the existance of a number $\alpha > 0$ follows from inequality (!), such that the inequality

$$H[x(t), p(t), u^*, t] - H[x(t), p(t), u(t), t] > \alpha \tag{!!}$$

holds for all $t \in [t_1, t_2]$, where $[t_1, t_2]$ are sufficiently small intervals which belong to the interval of continuity $[t', t'']$. Let us now examine the varied control $u(t)$, which is equal to the control $\bar{u}(t)$ everywhere outside the interval $[t_1, t_2]$, and equal to u^* at $[t_1, t_2]$. The control $\bar{u}(t) \in U$ is admissible. Then, using (19), (!!), and (22b), we get

$$\delta S = -\int_{t_1}^{t_2} [H(y(t), u^*, t) - H(y(t), u(t), t)]\, dt - \eta <$$

$$< -\left[\int_{t_1}^{t_2} \alpha\, dt - |\eta|\right] \leqslant -\int_{t_1}^{t_2} \left[\alpha - \tau B \sum_{1}^{r} \delta u_k^2(t)\right] dt.$$

Since $\sum_{1}^{r} \delta u_k^2(t)$ is bounded, it is always possible to choose a sufficiently small $\tau = t_2 - t_1$, for which the integrand is positive and $\delta S < 0$, which satisfies condition (0). The case of the maximum of the functional S is examined analogously. The theorem is proved.

4. Proof of theorem 2. The necessity of the maximum (minimum) condition has been established by theorem 1. We will prove the sufficiency of this condition in the case of linear systems. The Hamiltonian of the system has the form:

$$H = \sum_{i,k=1}^{n} a_{ik}(t)\, p_i x_k + \sum_{1}^{n} p_i \varphi_i(u),$$

and the impulse satisfies the relations

$$\dot{p}_i = -\sum_1^n a_{ki}(t)\, p_k \quad (i = 1, \ldots, n).$$

Let us examine the remaining terms (17) in formula (19) and prove that $\eta \equiv 0$. Indeed, $\partial^2 H/\partial x_i \partial x_j \equiv 0$, $\partial^2 H/\partial p_i \partial p_j \equiv 0$, and the quantities $a_{ij} \equiv \partial^2 H/\partial p_i \partial x_j$ clearly do not depend on x and p. Therefore $\eta_2 = 0$. In the expression for η_1, the differences $\partial H(y, u + \delta u, t)/\partial x_i - \partial H(y, u, t)/\partial x_i$ disappear identically, since $\frac{\partial H}{\partial x_i} \equiv -\sum_1^n a_{ki}(t)\, p_k$ clearly does not depend on u. On the other hand, the change of the impulse $\delta p(t)$ satisfies the relations

$$\delta \dot{p}_i = -\sum_1^n a_{ki}(t)\, \delta p_k \quad (i = 1, \ldots, n),$$

which do not depend on δx and δu. But since the boundary conditions for the impulse are fixed and $\delta p(T) = 0$, then $\delta p(t)$ is identically equal to zero for any t. Therefore, $\eta_1 = 0$. Hence, the formula for the increment of the functional takes the form:

$$\delta S = -\int_{T_0}^{T} [H(y, u + \delta u, t) - H(y, u, t)]\, dt.$$

If the maximum (minimum) condition holds, then the integrand is not positive (not negative), and $\delta S \geq 0$ ($\delta S \leq 0$), Q.E.D.

LITERATURE CITED

[1] A. A. Fel'dbaum, "Optimum processes in automatic control systems," [In Russian], Avtomat. i Telemekh. Vol. 14, No. 5 (1953).

[2] A. A. Fel'dbaum, "On the synthesis of optimum systems with the help of a phase space," [In Russian], Avtomat. i Telemekh. Vol. 16, No. 2 (1955).

[3] A. A. Fel'dbaum, "On the question of synthesizing optimum automatic control systems," [In Russian], Transactions of the Second All-Union Conference on Automatic Control Theory, Vol. 2, Izd-vo. Akad. Nauk SSSR (1955).

[4] A. Ya. Lerner, "Construction of rapid-acting systems with restrictions on the coordinates of the object," [In Russian], see [3].

[5] Itogi nauki. Tekhn. nauki I., "Problems on the theory of nonlinear automatic regulation and control systems" [In Russian], edited by Ya. Z. Tsypkin, Izd-vo. Akad. Nauk SSSR, (chap. 4, paragraph 3, 4) (1957).

[6] V. G. Boltyanskii, R. V. Gamkrelidze and L. S. Pontryagin, "On the theory of optimum processes," [In Russian], Doklady Akad. Nauk SSSR, Vol. 110, No. 1 (1956).

[7] L. S. Pontryagin, "Some mathematical problems arising in connection with the theory of optimum automatic control systems," [In Russian], Session of the Academy of Sciences of the USSR on Scientific Problems of Automating Industry, 15-20 October (1956); "Basic problems of automatic regulation and control," Izd-vo. Akad. Nauk SSSR (1957).

[8] R. V. Gamkrelidze, "On the theory of optimum processes in linear systems" [In Russian], Doklady Akad. Nauk SSSR, Vol. 116, No. 1 (1957).

[9] V. G. Boltyanskii, "The maximum principle in the theory of optimum processes" [In Russian], Doklady Akad. Nauk SSSR, Vol. 119, No. 6 (1958).

[10] R. V. Gamkrelidze, "The theory of processes which are optimum for rapid-action in linear systems" [In Russian], Izv. Akad. Nauk SSSR, ser. matem., Vol. 22, No. 4 (1958).

[11] R. V. Gamkrelidze, "On the general theory of optimum processes," [In Russian], Doklady Akad. Nauk SSSR, Vol. 123, No. 2 (1958).

[12] L. S. Pontryagin, "Optimum control processes" [In Russian], Uspekhi Matem. Nauk, Vol. 13, issue 1 [85] (1959).

[13] R. Bellman, Dynamic Programming. [Princeton University Press, Princeton, N.J., 1957].

[14] Modern Mathematics for Engineers, [Russian translation] edited by E. F. Bakkenbach (chap. 10), [Izd-vo. inostr. lit-ry, M., (1958)].

[15] N. N. Krasovskii, "On the theory of optimum control" [In Russian], Avtomat. i Telemekh. Vol. 18, No. 11 (1957) [See English translation].

[16] N. N. Krasovskii, "On one problem of optimum control" [In Russian], Priklad. Matem. i Mekhan. Vol. 21, issue 5 (1957).

[17] A. B. Kosmodem'yanskii, "Extremum problems for points of variable mass" [In Russian], Doklady Akad. Nauk SSSR, Vol. 53, No. 1 (1946).

[18] H. S. Tsien and R. C. Evans, "Optimum Thrust Programming for a Sounding Rocket," J. Amer. Rocket Soc. Vol. 21, No. 5 (1951).

[19] A. Hibbs, "Optimum Burning Program for Horizontal Flight," J. Amer. Rocket Soc. Vol. 22, No. 4 (1952).

[20] D. E. Okhotsimskii and T. M. Eneev, "Some variation problems connected with launching artificial Earth satellites" [In Russian], Uspekhi Fiz. Nauk Vol. 62, issue 1 (1957).

[21] L. I. Rozonoér, "On the sufficient conditions of optimality" [In Russian], Doklady Akad. Nauk SSSR, Vol. 127, No. 3 (1959).

Received June 5, 1959

L. S. PONTRYAGIN'S MAXIMUM PRINCIPLE IN OPTIMAL SYSTEM THEORY - II*

L. I. Rozonoér

(Moscow)

Questions are treated which are related to the proofs and applications of L. S. Pontryagin's maximum principle in optimal system theory. The work also contains certain new results. The first portion of the work deals with the optimization problem for the case of a trajectory with a free right end. In the second portion, the maximum principle is formulated for a more general type of boundary conditions. The third part establishes the connection between the method of dynamic programming and the maximum principle, provides a method of solving the optimization problem for linear discrete systems, and also presents a number of considerations in the use of the maximum principle for solving a definite class of problems, related to the theory of dynamic accuracy of control systems.

3. The General Problem

We consider the problem, formulated in Section 1 (Part I) of optimization,given arbitrary boundary conditions for the trajectory's right end. The principle special feature of this problem, as compared with the problem considered in Section 2, is this: that in the present case the requirement that the trajectory's right end lie in set G, imposes, by its very nature, an additional limitation on those controls from among which the optimal one is to be chosen. Indeed, the optimal control must here be chosen only from the class of those controls which guarantee that the system will fall in the set G. Naturally, this circumstance gives rise to additional difficulties. It turns out, however, that the action of the maximum (minimum) principle in this case is completely analogous to the principle formulated in Section 2, and the special feature of the problem under consideration here, as cited above, is expressed in the greater complexity of the boundary conditions for the corresponding differential equations. We first give the fundamental result (theorem 3) which asserts the applicability of the maximum principle, and we then give a method of determining the initial conditions.

In the sequel, we shall always assume that the set G in which the end of the trajectory x(t) must lie is closed and convex**.

In the proof of the fundamental theorem (Cf., the Appendix), it is also assumed that the set G has at least one interior point in phase space X, i.e., a point in a sufficiently small neighborhood of which there are contained no points which do not lie in G. It is easily proven that, with this, there are interior points in any arbitrarily small neighborhood of any point of G.

a. The Maximum Principle

We now turn to the exposition of the basic result. Let the initial system of equations have the form:

$$\dot{x}_i = f_i(x_1, \ldots, x_n;\quad u_1, \ldots, u_r; t),\ x_i(T_0) = x_i^0 \quad (i = 1, \ldots, n).$$

---

* Part I of this work was published in Automation and Remote Control (USSR) 20, 10 (1959).

** A set G is said to be convex if the straight line-segment joining any two points of G, lies completely in the set G.

We consider the set of vector functions p(t) which satisfy the relationships

$$\dot{p}_i = -\sum_1^n p_s \frac{\partial f_s(x, u, t)}{\partial x_i} \qquad (i = 1, \ldots, n). \tag{2}$$

Equation (2) (in contradistinction to the problem of Section 2) does not define the functions $p_i(t)$, since the boundary conditions for p(t) are still not fixed. Therefore, even if the control u(t) and the trajectory $x^u(t)$ corresponding to u(t) are given, the vector p(t) is still not uniquely defined by (2).

As before, we introduce the function $H(x, p, u, t) \equiv \sum_1^n p_i f_i(x_1, \ldots, x_n; u_1, \ldots, u_r, t)$, by means of which Eq. (1) and Eq. (2) are written in the form

$$\dot{x}_i = \frac{\partial H}{\partial p_i}, \quad \dot{p}_i = -\frac{\partial H}{\partial x_i}, \quad x_i(T_0) = x_i^0 \quad (i = 1, \ldots, n). \tag{3}$$

Let u(t) be some admissible control, $x^u(t)$ the trajectory corresponding to it, and p(t) some one of the vector functions which satisfy relationships (2). By substituting the values of the variables $x_i^u(t)$, $p_i(t)$ in the function H (x, p, u, t), we obtain the quantity

$$K(t, u_1, \ldots, u_r) \equiv H[x(t), p(t), u, t],$$

which, for each fixed moment of time t, is a function of the point $u = (u_1, \ldots, u_r)$ which lies in the set U of the space R. We say that control u(t) satisfies the maximum (minimum) condition with respect to the vector p(t) if, at any fixed moment of time t ($T_0 \leq t \leq T$), the function K(t, u) attains an absolute maximum (minimum) on the set U for given variables, equal to the values of the control at the same moment of time, i.e., for $u_k = u_k(t)$ ($k = 1, \ldots, r$).

As was shown in Section 2, Part I, the geometric meaning of the maximum (minimum) condition amounts to this: that the control which satisfies this condition tends, at each moment of time, to "accelerate" maximally the representative point in the direction defined by the vector p(t).

We again emphasize that vector p(t) is, on the one hand, not arbitrary and, on the other hand, is still not fixed (in contradistinction to the problem of Section 2, Part I). Therefore, if some permissible control u(t) is given, it is not immediately clear whether one may choose such a vector p(t) that, relative to this p(t), the control u(t) would satisfy the maximum (minimum) conditions. It turns out that an optimal control possesses precisely this property. This fact also constitutes the basic content of L. S. Pontryagin's maximum principle.

In order to formulate exactly the theorem which expresses the maximum principle, we make one more remark. We consider the function $\psi(x) \equiv \sum_1^n c_i x_i$ of points $x = (x_1, \ldots, x_n)$ on the set G. The set of points x^* ($x^*_1, \ldots, x^*_n$), at which the function $\psi(x)$ assumes a value which is a minimum with respect to all other points of G, we denote by G^*. If the set G^* exists, then the following inequality always holds: $\psi^* \equiv \sum_1^n c_i x_i^* < \sum_1^n c_i x_i$ where x^* is an arbitrary point for G^* and $\underline{x}$ is an arbitrary point of G). The functional $S = \sum_1^n c_i x_i(T)$ can not, obviously, assume values less than ψ^*. Then, an arbitrary control which takes the system over into set G^* is min-optimal, since for such a control the functional assumes the least of all its possible values, equal to ψ^*. Therefore, if the time, $T - T_0$, during which the system passes in the necessary optimal way to set G, is given in such a way that the set G^* turns out to be admissible, the problem of minimizing the functional S then reduces to the problem of determining some control which takes the system from the fixed point x^0 to the fixed set G^*. We call this a degenerate problem. It is not considered in the present paper.'

Analogously, we define the case when one deals with a maximum of the function $S = \sum_1^n c_i x_i (T)$. as a degenerate.

The nondegeneracy of the problem may be perceived in practice by comparing the given time $T - T_0$ with the minimal time T^* necessary for translation of the system from point x^0 to the set G^*.

We note further that the problem considered in Section 2, Part I can not be degenerate for any given time T. Indeed, in the given case, the function $\sum_1^n c_i x_i$ is not limited to the set G (occupying the entire space) and, consequently, assumes an extremal value at no point. The matter is analogous in those cases when the set G is open* or is not bounded.

We now formulate the fundamental theorem.

Theorem 3. If, in a nondegenerate problem, the control u(t) is min-optimal (max-optimal) with respect to $S = \sum_1^n c_i x_i (T)$, then there exists a vector function $p^u(t)$ such that u(t) satisfies the maximum (minimum) condition with respect to $p^u(t)$.

Theorem 3 is valid, certainly, in that special case which was considered in Section 2, Part I. Theorem 1 asserts that, in the case of the problem with a free trajectory right end, the vector $p^u(t)$, the existence of which is guaranteed by Theorem 3, is subject to the boundary condition $p^u(T) = -c$. It is now necessary to formulate an analogous condition for the vector $p^u(t)$** in the general problem being considered.

Theorem 3 and the boundary conditions formulated below can be obtained on the basis of the results of work [1], in which the maximum principle with the corresponding transversality conditions was proven under more general assumptions.

b. The Boundary Conditions

Let the point $x^1 = (x_1^1, \ldots, x_n^1)$ be the end of an optimal trajectory x(t). That portion of set G for which $\sum_1^n c_i x_i \leqslant \sum_1^n c_i x_i^1$, we denote by G^-; the portion for which $\sum_1^n c_i x_i \geqslant \sum_1^n c_i x_i^1$, we denote by G^+. The sets G^- and G^+ obviously, are closed and convex and have the hyperplane C, given by the equation $\sum_1^n c_i (x_i - x_i^1) = 0$, for their common boundary. Point x^1, lying in both G^- and G^+, is a boundary point of both sets. For definiteness, we shall now consider the case when one seeks a minimum of the functional $S = \sum_1^n c_i x_i (T)$.

If the control u(t) is min-optimal, then there do not exist controls from the admissible class which would, during the time $T - T_0$, translate the system into set G^- since, for interior points of set G^-, the value of the quantity $\sum_1^n c_i x_i$ is less than for the point x^1. With this, it turns out (Cf., the Appendix) that the vector p(T), at the moment of time t = T, must be orthogonal to some hyperplane A, which is a bracket*** for set G^- at the point x^1 and, moreover, must be directed to that side of hyperplane A where set G^- lies. Therefore, if the equation of

---

* A set G is said to be open if none of the boundary points of set G lies in the set.

** In the sequel, the superscript u will be omitted from $p^u(t)$.

*** A hyperplane A, containing the point x^1, is called a bracket to the convex set G^- at the point x^1 if set G^- lies completely to "one side" of A. It has been proven that a bracket hyperplane may be passed through each boundary point of a convex set.

hyperplane A has the form $\sum_1^n a_i(x_i - x_i^1) = 0$, and the signs of the coefficients a_i are so chosen that set G^- lies on the side of the hyperplane where $\sum_1^n a_i(x_i - x_i^1) \leqslant 0$, then

$$p_i(T) = -a_i \quad (i = 1, \ldots, n) \tag{4}$$

or $p(T) = -a$, if we introduce the vector $a = (a_1, \ldots, a_n)$. Equation (4) generalizes the corresponding conditions for the problem of Section 2, Part I. In fact, two cases of the placement of point $x^1 = x(T)$ are possible: either inside G or on the boundary of G. In the first case (Fig. 1) there may be passed the unique hyperplane A, bracketing G^- and coinciding with hyperplane C, through point x^1. Any other hyperplane A through point x^1 will necessarily "intersect" the set G^- and, consequently, will not be a bracket. Therefore, if the end of the trajectory lies in the interior of set G, the $a_i = c_i$ and $p_i(T) = -c_i$. In the problem considered in Section 2, Part I, this case was always realized, since the set G occupied the entire space and in general, did not have boundary points*.

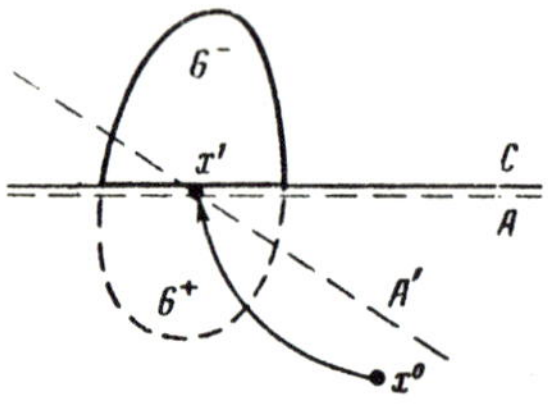

Fig. 1

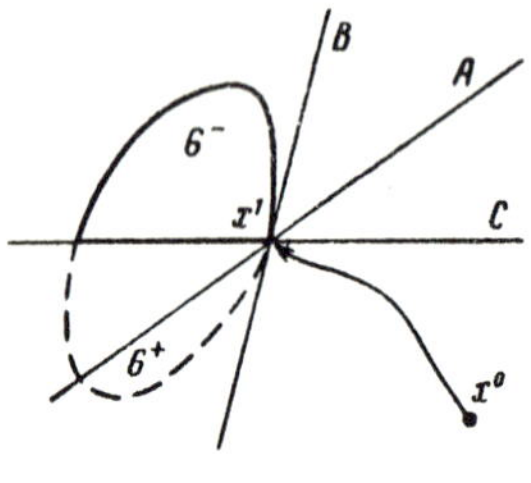

Fig. 2

If the second case holds, and point x^1 is a boundary point of set G, then the bracket hyperplane to G^- is not uniquely defined (Fig. 2). We shall assume that, at point x^1, there exists a unique hyperplane B which is a bracket to set G. The sign of the coefficients b_i of the hyperplane B are so chosen that set G lies on that side of B where $\sum_1^n b_i(x_i - x_i^1) \leqslant 0$. It is then easily seen that no hyperplane A which is a bracket to set G^- can lie in that region of space where the inequalities $\sum_1^n c_i(x_i - x_i^1) < 0$ and $\sum_1^n b_i(x_i - x_i^1) \leqslant 0$.hold simultaneously. By now taking into account that G^- lies on that side of A where $\sum_1^n a_i(x_i - x_i^1) \leqslant 0$, we obtain the following expression for the coefficients a_i:

$$a_i = \lambda c_i + \mu b_i \quad (i = 1, \ldots, n), \tag{5}$$

where $\lambda \geq 0$ and $\mu \geq 0$ are certain nonnegative numbers which do not reduce to zero simultaneously. For $\lambda = 0$, hyperplane A coincides with B and, for $\mu = 0$, with C. If $\lambda >$) (or $\mu > 0$) we can, without loss of generality, set $\lambda = 1$ (or $\mu = 1$). Of both constants are positive, then either of them can be set equal to unity.

This follows from the fact that, to define hyperplane A, the coefficients a_i need only be given to within an arbitrary positive constant (this constant is required to be positive in order that there be no change in the sense of the inequality $\sum_1^n a_i(x_i - x_i^1) \leqslant 0$). Therefore, essentially, only one constant enters into conditions (5).

---

* This case is also always realized in the problem in which the set G is open. For these problems, all the results of Section 2, Part I are completely valid.

Let the set G be given by the inequality $F(x_1, \ldots, x_n) \leq 0$. Then the coordinates of the boundary points of set G (including the coordinates of point x^1) must satisfy the condition

$$F(x_1, \ldots, x_n) = 0. \tag{6}$$

For each boundary point we can find coefficients $b_i(x_1, \ldots, x_n)$ which define the hyperplane B, which is a bracket to G at the point $\underline{x}$. In particular, if the function $F(x_1, \ldots, x_n)$ is differentiable, then the bracket is the hyperplane which is tangent to surface (6) and therefore

$$b_i(x_1, \ldots, x_n) = \frac{\partial F(x_1, \ldots, x_n)}{\partial x_i} \quad (i = 1, \ldots, n).$$

By uniting conditions (4)-(6), we convince ourselves that the coordinates of vectors p(t) and x(t) at time t = T must satisfy the set of relationships

$$\begin{gathered} p_i(t) = -\lambda c_i - \mu b_i[x_1(T), \ldots, x_n(T)] \quad (i = 1, \ldots, n), \\ F[x_1(T), \ldots, x_n(T)] = 0. \end{gathered} \tag{7}$$

We thus obtain n + 1 equations, (7), in which, as was stated above, one additional constant (λ or μ) must enter. Therefore, (7) gives essentially $\underline{n}$ independent relationships. Together with the $\underline{n}$ relationships

$$x_i(T_0) = x_i^0 \quad (i = 1, \ldots, n) \tag{8}$$

we obtain 2n boundary conditions for the solution of system (3) of differential equations, also of order 2n. The control u(t) is eliminated from system (3) by the same method as in the case of the problem of Section 2, since the maximum condition allows one, generally speaking, to express u(t) at each moment of time in terms of x(t) and p(t).

In the case when functional $S = \sum_{1}^{n} c_i x_i(T)$, attains a maximum, boundary conditions (7) and (8) are retained if the inequality giving the set G is written in the form $F(x_1, \ldots, x_n) \geq 0$. To eliminate u(t) from system (3), it is necessary to use the minimum condition.

c. Determination of the Boundary Conditions in Certain Particular Cases

If some coordinate x_s does not enter into the inequality which defines the set G, then the corresponding coefficient b_s in (7) is equal to zero (G is a "cylindrical" body with its generator parallel to the x_s axis and, consequently, the bracketing hyperplane is also parallel to the x_s axis).

In many cases of practical importance the set G lies on some linear manifold of phase space X and, consequently has no interior points in X (since in any arbitrarily small neighborhood of any point of a linear manifold one can find a point which does not lie in the manifold). In particular, this circumstance occurs if some of the coordinates are exactly fixed at time t = T but the set G is given by the system of equations

$$x_s(T) = x_s^1 \quad (s = 1, \ldots, q;\ q < n). \tag{9}$$

We consider this case. Since, in practice, a sufficiently small violation of conditions (9) is always admitted, one could require that instead of (9), the following inequality hold

$$\sum_{1}^{q} (x_s - x_s^1)^2 \leqslant \varepsilon^2, \tag{9'}$$

which, for small ϵ, guarantees that the violation of conditions (9) is sufficiently small and that $|x_s - x_s^1| \leq \epsilon$. Inequality (9') gives a convex and closed domain with interior points in X. However, it turns out to be possible to write simpler boundary conditions than those which follow from (9'). Conditions (9) can be directly considered as the boundary conditions for system (3) by replacing by them the conditions from (7) for the corresponding q. Since, with this, the equations defining G do not depend on the remaining n−q coordinates, then $b_{q+1} = \ldots = b_n = 0$ so that there remains in the result the following set of 2n boundary conditions:

$$\begin{aligned} x_i(T_0) &= x_i^0, \quad i = 1, \ldots, n, \\ x_s(T) &= x_s^1, \quad s = 1, \ldots, q, \\ p_m(T) &= -c_m, \quad m = q+1, \ldots, n. \end{aligned} \tag{10}$$

We now consider the frequently arising problem when it is required to determine the control which gives an extremum to the integral $\int_{T_0}^{T} \Phi(x, u)\, dt$, where, for $t = T_0$ and $t = T$, the values of the coordinates must be fixed:

$$x_i(T_0) = x_i^0, \quad x_i(T) = x_i^1 \quad (i = 1, \ldots, n).$$

The new variable $x_{n+1}(t) = \int_{T_0}^{t} \Phi(x, u)\, dt$ does not enter either into definition of set G or in the right members of the original system of differential equations. By virtue of this latter fact, $\dot{p}_{n+1}(t) = 0$. Since $c_1 = c_2 = \ldots = c_n = 0$, c_{n+1} and $b_{n+1} = 0$, then $p_{n+1}(t) \equiv p_{n+1}(T) = -1$. The system of differential equations and the boundary conditions for them take the following form:

$$\dot{x}_i = \frac{\partial H}{\partial p_i}, \quad \dot{p}_i = -\frac{\partial H}{\partial x_i}, \quad H \equiv \sum_1^n p_s f_s(x, u, t) - \Phi(x, u),$$
$$x_i(T_0) = x_i^0, \quad x_i(T) = x_i^1 \quad (i = 1, \ldots, n). \tag{11}$$

The equation $\dot{x}_{n+1} = \Phi(x, u)$ is excluded, since it gives no additional condition.

d. Optimization Problems in Which the Time of Motion is not Fixed Beforehand

Until now we have considered problems where the time required to implement the optimal process in the system was fixed. On the basis of the results obtained, we can now easily formulate the solution for the problems in which the amount of time taken by the system to transfer from point x^0 to the set G is given beforehand, but must be so chosen that the functional takes a least (greatest) value in comparison with the values which would be obtained for all other possible amounts of this time.

We note first of all that if the problem is degenerate for at least some values of T, then these values of T also provide a minimal (maximal) value of the functional in comparison with all other values, such that the optimization problem with nonfixed time reduces to the degenerate problem. We shall therefore assume that the problem, with arbitrary fixed values of T, is nondegenerate.

It is obvious that all the results given in this section must remain in force for problems with "free" times. Indeed, if the time sought exists and is equal to $\overline{T}$, one can consider the problem with fixed time $T = \overline{T}$, the solution of which would be the solution of the initial problem. However, since the magnitude of $\overline{T}$ is unknown, one additional condition which would define $\overline{T}$ is still required. It turns out that such a condition is the requirement in accordance with which the function H(x,p,u,t) must equal zero at the end of the motion:

$$\sum_1^n p_i(T) f_i[x(T), u(T), T] = 0.$$

If u(T), in correspondence with the maximum (minimum) condition, is expressed in terms of x(T) and p(T) and substituted in (12), the equation obtained gives the additional boundary condition which, in conjunction with boundary conditions (7), allows one to find the solution of system (3) and the optimal time $\overline{T}$.

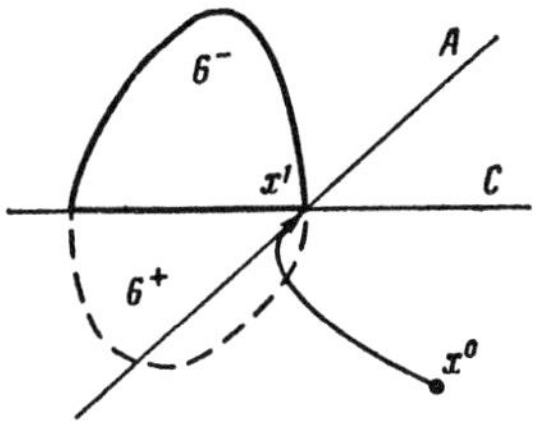

Fig. 3

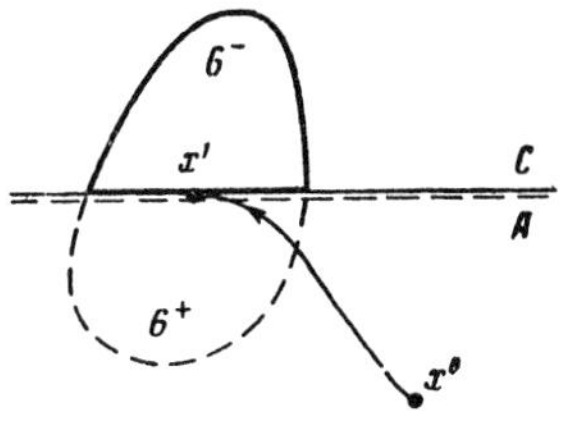

Fig. 4

Condition (12) has a simple geometric meaning. Indeed, the function H is the scalar product of the vector p(t) by the vector $\dot{x}(t)$ for the velocity of the representative point. The scalar product equalling zero means that at the end of the motion the velocity vector must be orthogonal to p(T) and, consequently, must (for example, in the min-optimal case) lie in hyperplane A, which is a bracket for set G^-(Fig. 3). This requirement becomes particularly clear in the case when the end of the optimal trajectory lies in the interior of G (Fig. 4). If the velocity vector were directed to the interior of G^- then, by increasing the time T, one could so arrange matters that the end of the trajectory would lie inside of G^- which is impossible if the control u(t) is min-optimal. If the vector $\dot{x}(T)$ were directed from G^- "outward", this would mean that for a smaller value of T the representative point would be still found interior to G^- which, again is impossible.

e. Problems of Maximal Speed of Operation

We can now turn to the problem of the minimum time of transition from the given point x^0 to the set G. For its solution, it suffices to add the equation $\dot{x}_{n+1} = x$ (where x is an arbitrary positive constant) and to solve the problem of minimizing $x_{n+1}(T)$ for a time not fixed beforehand. It is easily seen that with this we have in boundary condition (7), $c_1 = \ldots = c_n = 0$, $p_{n+1}(T) = -1$ and, in (12) $H \equiv \sum_1^n p_i(T) f_i[x(T), u(T), T] - \alpha = 0$. Moreover, $\dot{p}_{n+1}(t) = 0$ and $p_{n+1}(t) \equiv -1$. Since α is an arbitrary positive constant, we can introduce the function $\overline{H} \equiv \sum_1^n p_i f_i(x, u, t)$, equal to $H + \alpha$ and, finally, we can write the system of differential equations in the form:

$$\dot{x}_i = \frac{\partial \overline{H}}{\partial p_i}, \quad \dot{p}_i = -\frac{\partial \overline{H}}{\partial x_i} \quad (i = 1, \ldots, n) \tag{13}$$

and its boundary conditions in the form

$$x_i(T_0) = x_i^0, \quad p_i(T) = -\mu b_i[x_1(T), \ldots, x_n(T)] \quad (i = 1, \ldots, n),$$

$$F[x_1(T), \ldots, x_n(T)] = 0, \quad \sum_1^n p_s(T) f_s[x(T), u(T), T] > 0. \tag{14}$$

If the set G is a fixed point x^1 then, by substituting $\Phi(x, u) \equiv \alpha > 0$ in formula (11), we easily obtain the following boundary conditions for system (13):

$$x_i(T_0) = x_i^0, \quad x_i(T) = x_i^1 \ (i = 1, \ldots, n), \quad \sum_1^n p_s(T) f_s[x(T), u(T), T] > 0. \tag{15}$$

f. Linear Systems

The maximum principle, as was already mentioned for the case of the particular problem of Section 2, gives, in general, only necessary conditions for optimality. However, for linear systems, described by equations of the form

$$\dot{x}_i = \sum_1^n a_{ik}(t)\, x_k + \varphi_i(u_1, \ldots, u_r) \quad (i = 1, \ldots, n)\ , \tag{16}$$

sufficient optimality conditions can be established which show that the maximum principle, as applied to such systems, is "almost" sufficient. We formulate the corresponding theorem.

As before, we will denote by $b_i(x_1^1, \ldots, x_n^1)$ the coefficients of the hyperplane bracketing set G at the point $x^1 = (x_1^1, \ldots, x_n^1)$ if point x^1 is a boundary point of G. To solve the problem of a minimum of functional S, the signs of the coefficients b_i are so chosen that, for each point $x(x_1, \ldots, x_n) \in G$, the inequality $\sum_1^n b_i(x_1^1, \ldots, x_n^1) \cdot (x_i - x_i^1) \leq 0$, holds, and for solving the problem of a maximum of the functional, the inequality holds with reversed sense. We do not assume now that there is a unique bracketing hyperplane to G at the point x^1, so that we denote by $b_i(x_1^1, \ldots, x_n^1)$ the coefficients of any bracketing hyperplane.

If point x^1 is interior to G, we should set $b_i(x_1^1, \ldots, x_n^1) = 0$. Then, in the case of a minimum of the functional, the following inequality always holds for $x^1 \in G$ and $x \in G$, $\sum_1^n b_i(x_1^1, \ldots, x_n^1)(x_i - x_i^1) \leqslant 0$ (and the inequality with reversed sense for the problem of the maximum of the functional).

Now let x(t) be the trajectory corresponding to control u(T), and let $x(T) = x^1$. Then the following theorem holds*.

Theorem 4. If in system (16), control u(t) satisfies the maximum (minimum) condition with respect to vector p(t), whose coordinates at time t = T take the value.

$$p_i(T) = -\lambda c_i - \mu b_i(x_1^1, \ldots, x_n^1) \quad (i = 1, \ldots, n),$$

where μ is nonnegative and λ is positive, then the control is min-optimal (max-optimal) for $S = \sum_1^n c_i x_i(T)$.

The conditions of Theorem 4 are very "close" to the necessary conditions for optimality expressed by Theorem 3 and formulas (4) and (5) of this section. The sole difference amounts to this that, unlike formulas (4), it is required in the conditions for the theorem just formulated that the constant λ be strictly positive.

The proof of Theorem 4 is given in Appendix II, Section 2°. We remark that the proof rests solely on Theorem 2, on the sufficiency of the maximum principle in linear problems with free-trajectory right ends and, in particular, does not assume that the set G must have interior points.

g. Continuity and Piecewise Differentiability of the Function H

We now formulate a theorem which expresses a very characteristic property of optimal processes. Let the control u(t) be given on the segment $[T_0, T]$ and let x(t) satisfy system (1). Then the following theorem is valid.

Theorem 5. If control u(t) satisfies the maximum (minimum) condition with respect to p(t) then the function $M(t) \equiv H[x(t), p(t), u(t), t]$ is continuous and piecewise-differentiable on the interval (T_0, T) where, at the continuity points of control u(t) the derivative exists and equals

$$\frac{dM}{dt} = \frac{\partial H[x(t), p(t), u(t), t]}{\partial t}.$$

It follows from Theorem 5 that, if the right members of differential Equations (1) do not explicitly depend on time, and if $\frac{\partial H}{\partial t} = \sum_1^n p_i \frac{\partial f_i(x, u)}{\partial t} = 0$, then $\dot{M} = 0$ and (with continuity taken into account) the function

* In the problems where time T is not fixed, the theorem analogous to Theorem 4 apparently does not hold.

H[x(t), p(t), u(t)] is constant. If, in particular, H[x(t), p(t), u(t)] reduces to zero at time t = T as, for example, in formula (12), then the magnitude of H is identically zero for any t.

The constancy of function H, analogous to the Hamiltonian function of analytical mechanics, corresponds to the law of the conservation of energy in conservative mechanical systems (the Hamiltonian function, as is well known, expresses the system's total energy).

h. Singular Controls

The recommended procedure for eliminating the control u(t) from Eqs. (3) by means of the maximum (minimum) condition may turn out to be impossible if the function H, for definite values of x and p, does not in fact depend on u. This may easily be followed in the simplest example of determining the control which, during fixed time T, takes the system described by the equations

$$\dot{x} = u, \quad |u| \leqslant M,$$

from point $x(0) = x^0$ to point $x(T) = x^1$ and minimizes the integral $\frac{1}{2}\int_0^T x^2 dt$. In correspondence with formulas (11), we can write

$$H \equiv pu - \frac{1}{2}x^2, \quad \dot{p} = x.$$

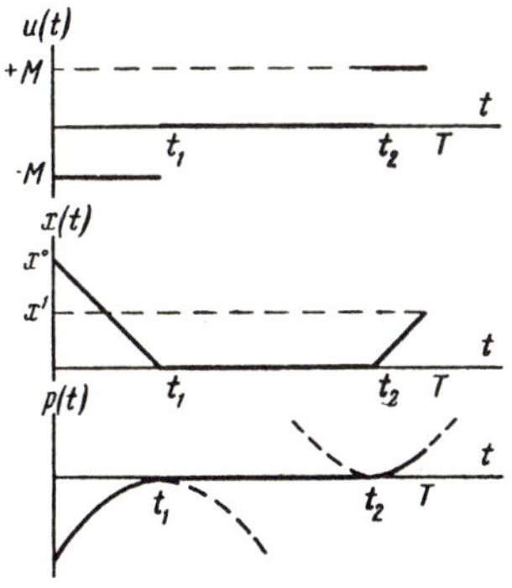

Fig. 5

It follows from the maximum condition that, for $p \neq 0$, the control equals u = M sign p. However, p = 0, the function H does not depend on u. In addition, as may easily be seen, the optimal control, coordinates and pulses, for the condition $T > (x^0 + x^1)/M$, must be changed as shown by Fig. 5. Therefore, on the time interval $[t_1, t_2]$, the function $p(t) \equiv 0$, and the control u(t) is not defined by the maximum condition. Such a control can be called singular. A singular control, if such exists, can be easily detected. Indeed, by first determining for which values of x and p (in the given example, for p = 0) H does not depend on u, we can seek such a control for which this independence would subsist in time. In the given example (since p = 0 = const), $\dot{p} = 0$ and, consequently, x = 0, from which we obtain the singular control u = 0. The function p(t) and, consequently, the control u(t), on the entire segment [0, T], can be defined by the condition of continuity of the singular solution with the nonsingular solutions (in ghe given example, the solution for u = 0 with the solutions for u = ± M). Theorem 5 can also be used. In the given case, for the singular control H = 0 and, for the nonsingular control, $H = M|p| - x^2/2$. Since H = const = 0, we have

$$|p(0)| = \frac{1}{2M}(x^0)^2, \quad |p(T)| = \frac{1}{2M}(x^1)^2,$$

and the signs of the quantities p(0) and p(T) are quickly determined.

i. The Synthesis Problem

We now consider the methods of using the practice the maximum principle of L. S. Pontryagin for solving the problem of designing optimal systems.

The problem of constructing optimal systems may be posed in two aspects. In the first case it may be sufficient to calculate beforehand an optimal control in the form of a function of time for definite, fixed and previously given initial conditions, and thereafter to design a program-controlled system. In the second case, the system's initial conditions may be unknown beforehand, but, nevertheless, it is required that the system realize an optimal process with arbitrary initial conditions. In other words, in this case, the optimal control must be expressed in the form of a function of the current value of the system coordinate and, possibly, of time, $u = \varphi(x, t)$:

$$u_k = \varphi_k(x_1, \ldots, x_n, t) \quad (k = 1, \ldots, r), \tag{17}$$

which allows one, by the use of a regulator with nonlinear connections, to design a system which is optimal for any initial conditions. This problem bears the name of the optimal-system-synthesis problem.

The maximum principle essentially solves the first problem immediately, since the finding of the optimal control in the form of a function of time amounts to the integration of a definite system of differential equations with the corresponding boundary conditions. It should be mentioned, however, that the technical difficulties of integrating the differential equations which flow from the maximum principle require, as a reule that computer technology be called into play. Integration of the equations in closed form turns out to be possible, naturally, in rare cases only.

The synthesis problem ordinarily arises in those problems in which the time of motion is not fixed beforehand. The following procedure for determing the functions (17) derives from the maximum principle. From the maximum (minimum) condition one determines the control in the form of the function $u = \psi(x, p, t)$. With fixed initial conditions, $x(T_0) = x^0$, there are given various initial values of $p(T_0) = p^0$, so chosen that the solution of system (3) of equations, with initial conditions $x(T_0) = x^0$ and $p(T_0) = p^0$, is satisfied together with the required boundary conditions. If the value of p^0 is not thereby defined uniquely, one then chooses the set of values, $p_i^0 (i = 1, \ldots, n)$, for which the functional's value turns out to be extremal. For each fixed set of values of $x_i^0 (i = 1, \ldots, n)$ at the fixed moment of time T_0, there is thus obtained a single set of values of $p_i^0 (i = 1, \ldots, n)$ which provide the optimal process. The function $p^0 = \chi(x^0, T_0)$ is thus defined. Therefore, at time T_0, the following equation holds

$$u(T_0, x^0) = \psi[x^0, \chi(x^0, T_0), T_0].$$

But it is easily seen that this relationship must also hold at any arbitrary moment of time, which can always be taken as the initial moment, by virtue of which the control $\underline{u}$ is defined in a form of the type of (17):

$$u = \psi[x, \chi(x, t), t].$$

In those cases when time does not enter explicitly in the right members of the differential equations, the function φ_k in (17) also turn out to be independent of time.

We now turn our attention to the circumstance that among the variables x_i there may be, not only the coordinates of the controlled object, but also artificially introduced quantities (for example, in the case of an integral extremum, the quantity $x_{n+1}(t) = \int_{T_0}^{t} \Phi(x, u)\, dt$). However, in those cases when the coordinates x_s does not enter explicitly into the right members of the differential equations or into the relationships defining the domain G, the quantity $p_s(t)$ is constant in time and does not depend on the boundary values of the coordinates $x_1, \ldots, x_n$. In addition, x_s does not enter into the function H and, consequently, does not enter into the expression for the control $\underline{u}$ in terms of $\underline{x}$, $\underline{p}$, and $\underline{t}$. Therefore, relationship (17) will also not contain x_s. In particular, in the case of the optimization of the integral $x_{n+1}(T) = \int_{T_0}^{T} \Phi(x, u)\, dt$, only the object's coordinates, and not the quantity x_{n+1}, will enter into (17).

The synthesis problem becomes much more complicated if the artificially introduced coordinate, although not entering explicitly in the equations' right members, does figure in the relationships which define region G. Examples of this are the cases of "integral limitations" of the type $\int_{T_0}^{T} \Phi(x, u)\, dt \leqslant A$, imposed on the control. Here, the introduced parameter $x_{n+1}(t) = \int_{T_0}^{t} \Phi(x, u)\, dt$ enters into the definition of region G: $x_{n+1}(t) \leq A$. Therefore, functions (17) generally turn out to depend on x_{n+1}. In this case, in order to realize an optimal system, one must either have a computing device which determines $x_{n+1}(t)$ at each moment of time, or one must previously compute x_{n+1} in the form of a function of the current, $x_i(i = 1, \ldots, n)$, and initial, x_i^0, coordinate values.

The synthesis problem, to an even greater degree than the problem of determining the control in the form of a function of time, requires the use of computing technology. Even in those cases when it is possible to determine functions (17) in closed form, the form of these functions is ordinarily very complicated. Therefore, a foremost role is played by the problem of synthesizing systems which are sufficiently simple and, in addition, are close to optimal.

Another synthesis procedure, based on the solution of partial differential equations, derives from the dynamic programming method of Richard Bellman.

We will speak of this in the following part of this work [Cf., Automation and Remote Control (USSR) 20, 12 (1959)].

APPENDIX

1°. The Proof of Theorem 3

We define a class Γ of modified controls of a special form. On the interval (T_0, T), we arbitrarily choose $j \geq 1$ moments of time $t = t_k$ and we construct the system of j nonintersecting segments $I_k = [t_k - \tau, t_k]$ of length τ, where the number $\tau > 0$ is sufficiently small ($k = 1, \ldots, j$). We introduce j r-dimensional piecewise-continuous vector functions $\varphi^k(z) \equiv [\varphi_1^k(z), \ldots, \varphi_r^k(z)]$, defined on the segment $[0, 1]$, on $\varphi^k(z) \in U$ $(k = 1, \ldots, j)$.

In addition, to control $u(t)$ we consider the modified control $v(t; \tau, t_1, \ldots, t_j; \varphi^1, \ldots, \varphi^j)$ such that $v = u(t)$ everywhere outside of the segments I_k and $v = \varphi^k[(t_k - t)/\tau]$ on I_k. Control $v(t)$ is obviously admissible. The points t_k and the functions $\varphi^k(z)$ are called, respectively, defining points and defining functions of the control $v(t)$. The class Γ of controls includes all the controls $v(t; \tau, t_1, \ldots, t_j; \varphi^1, \ldots, \varphi^j)$ with arbitrary j, t_k, $\varphi^k(z) \in U$ $(k = 1, \ldots, j)$ and τ sufficiently small.

Let $x(t, [v])$ be the trajectory corresponding to control $\in \Gamma$ and let $\delta x(t, [v]) = x(t, [v]) - x(t, [u])$, where $x(t, [u])$ is the optimal trajectory. For $x(t, [v])$ we have the system of equations

$$\delta \dot{x}_i = f_i(x + \delta x, v) - f_i(x, u) \quad (i = 1, \ldots, n), \tag{18}$$

which, by using Taylor's formula, we can rewrite in the form

$$\delta \dot{x}_i = \sum_1^n \frac{\partial f_i(x, u)}{\partial x_s} \delta x_s + f_i(x, v) - f_i(x, u) + \alpha_i(t, [v]) \quad (i = 1, \ldots, n), \tag{19}$$

where

$$\alpha_i(t, [v]) = \sum_1^n \left[\frac{\partial f_i(x, v)}{\partial x_s} - \frac{\partial f_i(x, u)}{\partial x_s} \right] \delta x_s + \frac{1}{2} \sum_{s\, q=1}^n \frac{\partial^2 f_i(x + \vartheta \delta x, v)}{\partial x_s \partial x_q} \delta x_s \delta x_q \tag{20}$$

and $0 < \vartheta < 1$. By integrating (19) between the limits of T_0 and $t(t_m < t < t_{m+1} - \tau)$, we get

$$\delta x_i(t, [v]) = \int_{T_0}^t \sum_1^n \frac{\partial f_i(x, u)}{\partial x_s} \delta x_s \, dt + \sum_{k=1}^m J_i^k([v]) + \beta_i(t, [v]); \; t \in (t_m, t_{m+1} - \tau) \tag{21}$$

where

$$J_i^k([v]) = \int_{t_k - \tau}^{t_k} \left[f_i\left(x(t), \varphi^k\left(\frac{t_k - t}{\tau}\right)\right) - f_i(x(t), u(t)) \right] dt,$$

$$\beta_i(t, [v]) \equiv \int_{T_0}^{t} \alpha(t, [v])\, dt = \frac{1}{2}\int_{T_0}^{t} \sum_{s,q=1}^{n} \frac{\partial^2 f_i(x + \vartheta\delta x, v)}{\partial x_s \partial x_q} \delta x_s \delta x_q dt +$$

$$+ \sum_{k=1}^{m} \int_{t_k-\tau}^{t_k} \sum_{1}^{n} \left[\frac{\partial f_i\left(x, \varphi\left(\frac{t_k - t}{\tau}\right)\right)}{\partial x_s} - \frac{\partial f_i(x, u)}{\partial x_s} \right] \delta x_s dt.$$

By taking into account the boundedness of $\partial f_i / \partial x_s$ and $\partial^2 f_i / \partial x_s \partial x_q$ on $[T_0, T]$ and also the estimate for δx_s

$$|\delta x_s(t, [v])| \leqslant M\tau, \quad t \in [T_0, T]$$

(where the constant M does not depend on τ), we easily obtain the estimate for β_i:

$$|\beta_i(t, [v])| \leqslant N\tau^2, \quad t \in [T_0, T],$$

where N also does not depend on t and τ, by virtue of which, uniformly in t,

$$\lim_{\tau \to 0} \frac{\beta_i(t, [v])}{\tau} = 0. \tag{22}$$

We now consider the integrals $J_i^k([v])$ (21). If we make the change of variables $z = (t_k - t)/\tau$, we shall have

$$J_i^k([v]) = \tau \int_0^1 [f_i(x(t_k - \tau z), \varphi^k(z)) - f_i(x(t_k - \tau z), u(t_k - \tau z))]\, dz.$$

As $\tau \to 0$, by virtue of the continuity of x(t) and the continuity of u(t) to the left, i.e., $u(t-0) = u(t)$, we get

$$R_i(t_k, [\varphi^k]) \equiv \lim_{\tau \to 0} \frac{J_i^k([v])}{\tau} = \int_0^1 [f_i(x(t_k), \varphi^k(z)) - f_i(x(t_k), u(t_k))]\, dz. \tag{23}$$

It is easily shown that the limit $y_i(t[v]) \equiv \lim_{\tau \to 0} \delta x_i(t,[v])/\tau$ $(i = 1, \ldots, n)$, which we call the variation of trajectory x(t) at the point t, exists for all $t \in [T_0, T]$ different from t_k. Then, by dividing (21) by τ and by taking (22) and (23) into account, we get

$$y_i(t, [v]) = \int_{T_0}^{t} \sum_{1}^{n} \frac{\partial f_i(x, u)}{\partial x_s} y_s dt + \sum_{k=1}^{m} R_i(t_k, [\varphi^k]), \quad t \in (t_m, t_{m+1}). \tag{24}$$

It follows from (24) that, on the intervals (t_m, t_{m+1}), the functions $y_i(t[v])$ satisfy the system of differential equations in the variations

$$\dot{y}_i = \sum_{1}^{n} \frac{\partial f_i(x, u, t)}{\partial x_s} y_s \quad (i = 1, \ldots, n), \tag{25}$$

and, at the points $t = t_k$, experience the jumps

$$y_i(t_k + 0) - y_i(t_k - 0) = R_i(t_k, [\varphi^k]) \quad (i = 1, \ldots, n;\ k = 1, \ldots, j), \tag{26}$$

where, obviously, $y_i(t_1-0) = 0$ (since $\delta x_i(t[v]) = 0$ for $t \in [T_0, t_1-\tau]$). We denote by $y_i^k(t)$ $(t > t_k)$ the solutions of system (25) with the initial conditions $y_i(t_k) = R_i(t_k, [\varphi^k])$. Due to the linearity of the equations, the solution of (25) with conditions (26) is obtained in the form

$$y_i(t, [v]) = \sum_{k=1}^{m} y_i^k(t), \quad t \in (t_m, t_{m+1}). \tag{27}$$

We now determine the $y_i^k(t)$. If $\zeta^q(t) = [\zeta_1^q(t), \ldots, \zeta_n^q(t)]$ $(q = 1, \ldots, n)$ is a fundamental system of solutions of (25), and the matrix $\| \vartheta_i^q(t) \|$ is the inverse of $\| \zeta_i^q(t) \|$, then

$$y_i^k(t) = \sum_{s, q=1}^{n} \zeta_i^q(t)\, \vartheta_q^s(t_k)\, y_s^k(t_k).$$

By taking the initial conditions into account, we get

$$y_i^k(t) = \sum_{s=1}^{n} A_{is}(t, t_k)\, R_s(t_k, [\varphi^k]),$$

with the notation

$$A_{is}(t, t_k) \equiv \sum_{q=1}^{n} \zeta_i^q(t)\, \vartheta_q^s(t_k).$$

By substituting the expression for $y_i^k(t)$ in (27) and introducing the additional notation $B_{is}(t_k) \equiv A_{is}(T, t_k)$, we obtain, for $t = T$

$$y_i([v]) \equiv y_i(T, [v]) = \sum_{k=1}^{j} \sum_{s=1}^{n} B_{is}(t_k)\, R_s(t_k, [\varphi^k]) \quad (i = 1, \ldots, n). \tag{28}$$

The matrix $B_{is}(t_k)$ is defined only by Eqs. (27) in the variations, and does not depend on the choice of the functions $\varphi^k(z)$. The vector $y([v]) \equiv (y_1, \ldots, y_n)$ is linearly expressed in terms of the vectors $R^k \equiv (R_1^k, \ldots, R_n^k)$ $(k = 1, \ldots, j)$.

The points of phase space of the form $x^1 + y([v])$, where $v \in \Gamma$, form a certain set Π. We now prove that Π is convex. Let $y([v'])$ and $y([v''])$ be arbitrary variations of the trajectories obtained with the modified controls v' and v'' with defining points and functions t'_α, $\varphi'^\alpha(z)$ $(\alpha = 1, \ldots, j')$; t''_β, $\varphi''^\beta(z)$ $(\beta = 1, \ldots, j'')$ respectively. By definition

$$\pi' \equiv x^1 + y([v']) \in \Pi, \quad \pi'' \equiv x^1 + y([v'']) \in \Pi.$$

We show that any point of the form

$$\pi \equiv \mu\pi' + (1-\mu)\pi'' = x^1 + \mu y([v']) + (1-\mu)\, y([v'']), \quad 0 \leqslant \mu \leqslant 1, \tag{29}$$

which lies on the line segment joining π' and π'' also lies in Π. For this, obviously, it is necessary to show that there exists a modified control $v \in \Gamma$ such that

$$y([v]) = \mu y([v']) + (1-\mu)\, y'([v'']). \tag{30}$$

We define control $\underline{v}$ in the following manner. As the control's defining points we take the union of the points t'_α and t''_β. The number of defining points of control $\underline{v}$ thus equals $j' + j'' - h$, where $\underline{h}$ is the number of pairs of coincident points t'_α and t''_β. The defining points of control $\underline{v}$ are divided into three classes: 1) the points which coincide with the defining points of control v' and do not coincide with the defining points of control v"; 2) the points which coincide with defining points of control v" and do not coincide with defining points of control v'; 3) the points which coincide simultaneously with defining points of controls v' and v". For the points of the first class, $t_k = t'_{\alpha 1}$ (k and α_1 run through j'−h values), we give the defining functions of control v in the form

$$\varphi^k(z) = \begin{cases} \varphi'^{\alpha_1}\left(\frac{z}{\mu}\right) & 0 \leqslant z \leqslant \mu \\ u(t'_{\alpha_1}) & \mu < z \leqslant 1. \end{cases}$$

For the points of the second class $t_l = t''_{\beta 1}$ (l and β_1 run through j" −h values)

$$\varphi^l(z) = \begin{cases} \varphi''^{\beta_1}\left(\frac{z}{1-\mu}\right) & 0 \leqslant z \leqslant 1-\mu \\ u(t''_{\beta_1}) & 1-\mu < z \leqslant 1. \end{cases}$$

For points of the third class, $t_m = t'_{\alpha 2} = t''_{\beta 2}$ (m, α_2, β_2 run through j values)

$$\varphi^m(z) = \begin{cases} \varphi'^{\alpha_2}\left(\frac{z}{\mu}\right) & 0 \leqslant z \leqslant \mu \\ \varphi''^{\beta_2}\left(\frac{z-\mu}{1-\mu}\right) & \mu < z \leqslant 1. \end{cases}$$

By computing $R_i(t_k, [\varphi^k]$, $R_i(t_l, [\varphi^l])$and $R_i(t_m, [\varphi^m])$ by formula (23), we find that

$$R_i(t_k, [\varphi^k]) = \mu R_i(t'_{\alpha_1}, [\varphi'^{\alpha_1}]),$$

$$R_i(t_l, [\varphi^l]) = (1-\mu) R_i(t''_{\beta_1}, [\varphi''^{\beta_1}]),$$

$$R_i(t_m, [\varphi^m]) = \mu R_i(t'_{\alpha_2}, [\varphi'^{\alpha_2}]) + (1-\mu) R_i(t''_{\beta_2}, [\varphi''^{\beta_2}]).$$

If we now determine $y_i([v])$ by (28), we convince ourselves of the validity of relationship (30). We also note that $x^1 \in \Pi$ since, by giving the modified control $v(t; \tau, t_1, \ldots, t_k; \varphi^1, \ldots, \varphi^k)$ such that; at each defining point t_k, the defining function $\varphi^k(z) \equiv u(t_k)$, we obtain $y_i([v]) = 0$.

Thus, Π is a convex set which includes point x^1. For definiteness, we consider further the case of a minimum of the functional S. The sets G^- and Π have the common point x^1. We now show that, in the nondegenerate problem, none of the points $g^- \in G^-$ (in particular, the point x^1) can be an interior point of Π. Indeed, let, on the contrary, point g^- be interior to Π. If the problem is nondegenerate, the set G^- will have interior points. Otherwise, hyperplane C would be a bracket for set G, and for any point $x = (x_1, \ldots, x_n) \in G$, the inequality

$\sum_1^n c_i(x_i - x_i^1) \geqslant 0$, would hold, this being the condition for a degenerate problem. Therefore, without any limitation on generality, we can assume that g^- is an interior point of G^- since, if g^- were a boundary point of G^-, one could always find another point interior for both G^- and Π (by virtue of the fact that, in any arbitrarily small neighborhood of any point in G^- there are contained points which are interior for G^-). We then find some neighborhood E of point g^-, all the points of which are interior in both Π and G^-. We choose the modified control $v \in \Gamma$ such that $x^1 + y([v]) = g^-$ (this is always possible, since $g^- \in \Pi$). The end of the trajectory $x(t,[v])$ is the point $x^1 + \delta x(T,[v])$, where $\delta x(T,[v]) = \tau y([v]) + \tau \epsilon(\tau)$. Since $\lim_{\tau \to 0} \epsilon(\tau) = 0$, we can always choose a τ sufficiently small so that the point $g \equiv x^1 + y([v]) + \epsilon(\tau) = g^- + \epsilon(\tau)$ lies in E. But points of the form $(1-\mu)x^1 + \mu g$, $0 < \mu \leq 1$, $g \in E$, are interior points of G^-. By choosing $\mu = \tau$, we are led to the conclusion that point $x^1 + \delta x(T,[v])$ is also an interior point of G^-, i.e., in other words, control $v(t; \tau, t_1, \ldots, t_k; \varphi^1, \ldots, \varphi^k)$ takes the system to the interior of set G^-. This contradicts the optimality of control u(t) and point $g^- \in G^-$ cannot be an interior point of Π. We show analogously that point $\pi \in \Pi$ cannot be interior of G^-.

It thus follows that the convex sets Π and G^- can have in common only boundary points, one of which (or the only one of which) is the point x^1, where one of the sets G^- has interior points in phase space X. Therefore, hyperplane A, defined by the expression $\sum_1^n a_s(x_s - x_s^1) = 0$, may be passed through point x^1, thus separating sets G^- and Π. The signs of coefficients a_s can be so chosen that the set Π is located on that side of hyperplane A where $\sum_1^n a_s(x_s - x_s^1) \geqslant 0$. (set G^- is then completely located on the side of the hyperplane where $\sum_1^n a_s(x_s - x_s^1) \leqslant$ ≤ 0). Therefore, for any control $v(t;\ \tau,\ t_1, \ldots, t_k;\ \varphi^1, \ldots \varphi^k) \in \Gamma$, the inequality $\sum_1^n a_s y_s([v]) \geqslant 0$, will hold, i.e.

$$\lim_{\tau\to 0} \frac{\sum_1^n a_s \delta x_s(T,\ [v])}{\tau} \geqslant 0.$$

We now consider the functional $\bar{S} = \sum_1^n a_s x_s(T)$. Then, the requirement that $\lim_{\tau\to 0} \frac{\sum_1^n a_s \delta x_s}{\tau} \geqslant 0$ means that

$$\lim_{\tau\to 0} \frac{\delta\bar{S}}{\tau} \geqslant 0. \tag{31}$$

As a modified control, we select the control $v \in \Gamma$ with only one defining point t_1, such that $\delta u(t) \equiv v(t) - u(t)$ may differ from zero only on the segment $[t_1 - \tau,\ t_1]$. For the control $v(t) = u(t) + \delta u(t)$, inequality (31) holds (as for all controls in Γ). By now introducing the vector p(t) and the function $H(x,\ p,\ u,\ t) \equiv \sum_1^n p_i f_i$ $(x_1, \ldots, x_n;\ u_1, \ldots, u_r;\ t)$, which satisfy the relationships

$$\dot{x}_i = \frac{\partial H}{\partial p_i},\quad \dot{p}_i = -\frac{\partial H}{\partial x_i} \qquad (i = 1, \ldots, n),$$

and by setting $p_i(T) = -a_i$ $(i = 1, \ldots, n)$, we can use, for the functional $\bar{S} = \sum_1^n a_s x_s(T)$, the formula for the increment of functional values (Appendix to Part I). By repeating virtually word for word the argument in the proof of Theorem 1, we can convince ourselves that condition (31) can hold only in the case, when at any moment of time t, the function $K(t,u) \equiv H[x(t), p(t), u, t]$ assumes its maximum value with respect to u.

The case of the maximum of functional $S = \sum_1^n c_i x_i(T)$ is treated analogously. Thus, Theorem 3 is proved.

2°. The Proof of Theorem 4

We carry out the proof for the case when one seeks a minimum of the functional S. The case, where the maximum of the functional is sought, is treated analogously.

Let W_T be the set of points in phase space X which are attainable from point x^0 at time $t = T$ for all the possible controls $u(t) \in U$. We consider the intersection Q of sets G and W_T: $Q = G \cap W_T$. The control u(t) and the trajectory x(t), corresponding to it, are min-optimal if, for each point $x(x_1, \ldots, x_n) \in Q$, the inequality $\sum_1^n c_i x_i(T) \leqslant \sum_1^n c_i x_i$ holds. By denoting $x_i(T) = x_i^1$, we get

$$\sum_1^n c_i(x_i - x_i^1) \geqslant 0. \tag{32}$$

To prove Theorem t, it suffices to show that, if the conditions of the Theorem hold, then inequality (32) is satisfied for each point $x \in Q$.

We use the notation

$$a_i = \lambda c_i + \mu b_i \quad (i = 1, \ldots, n). \tag{33}$$

If the control u(t) satisfies the maximum condition with respect to the vector p(t) which, at time t = T, assumes the value

$$p(T) = -a, \quad a = (a_1, \ldots, a_n),$$

then, in accordance with Theorem 2 of the present work, control u(t) is min-optimal with respect to $S = \sum_1^n a_i x_i(T)$ in the problem with free trajectory right ends, i.e., for each point $x \in W_T$, the following inequality is valid

$$\sum_1^n a_i (x_i - x_i^1) \geqslant 0. \tag{34}$$

On the other hand, for each point $x \in G$ the following inequality holds, by definition,

$$\sum_1^n b_i (x_1^1, \ldots, x_n^1)(x_i - x_i^1) \geqslant 0. \tag{35}$$

Therefore, for each point $x \in Q = G \cap W_T$, inequalities (34) and (35) hold.

But it follows from (33) that, for $\lambda > 0$,

$$c_i = \frac{1}{\lambda} a_i - \frac{\mu}{\lambda} b_i \qquad (i = 1, \ldots, n).$$

We now choose an arbitrary point $x \in Q$ and set up the expression

$$\sum_1^n c_i (x_i - x_i^1) = \frac{1}{\lambda} \sum_1^n a_i (x_i - x_i^1) - \frac{\mu}{\lambda} \sum_1^n b_i (x_i - x_i^1).$$

By virtue of inequalities (34) and (35), inequality (32) follows from this. q.e.d.

3°. The Proof of Theorem 5

For definiteness, we consider the case when the control satisfies the maximum condition. The case of the minimum condition is handled analogously.

We introduce the difference

$$\Delta M \equiv H[y(t+\Delta t), u(t+\Delta t), t+\Delta t] - H[y(t), u(t), t].$$

Now, to shorten the formulas, we introduce the vector $y = (y_1, \ldots, y_{2n})$ $(y_i = x_i;\ y_{n+i} = p_i;\ i = 1; \ldots, n)$. By virtue of the maximum condition

$$H[y(t+\Delta t), u(t+\Delta t), t+\Delta t] \geqslant H[y(t+\Delta t), u(t), t+\Delta t],$$
$$H[y(t), u(t), t] \geqslant H[y(t), u(t+\Delta t), t].$$

From whence follows, for ΔM,

$$\begin{gathered} H[y(t+\Delta t), u(t), t+\Delta t] - H[y(t), u(t), t] \leqslant \Delta M \leqslant \\ \leqslant H[y(t+\Delta t), u(t+\Delta t), t+\Delta t] - H[y(t), u(t+\Delta t), t]. \end{gathered} \tag{36}$$

Because of the continuity of $y_s(t)$ ($s = 1, \ldots, 2n$) in time, and of the continuity of $H(y, u, t)$ over the set of arguments, for $\Delta t \to 0$, the extreme terms in inequality (36) have the limit zero. Consequently, $\lim \Delta M = 0$, which proves the continuity of the function $M(t)$.

Now, let _t_ be a continuity point of control $u(t)$. Then, $\lim_{\Delta t \to 0} u(t + \Delta t) = u(t)$ and, moreover, the derivatives $\dot{y}_s(t)$ ($s = 1, \ldots, 2n$) exist and are continuous. By dividing (36) by Δt and letting Δt approach zero, we convince ourselves that the limits for the extreme terms of the inequality exist and equal

$$\sum_{1}^{2n} \frac{\partial H\,[y(t),\ u(t),\ t]}{\partial y_s}\, \dot{y}_s(t) + \frac{\partial H\,[y(t),\ u(t),\ t]}{\partial t}\,.$$

By virtue of the relationships, $\dot{y}_i = \partial H / \partial y_{n+i}$, $\dot{y}_{n+i} = -\partial H / \partial y_i$ ($i = 1, \ldots, n$), the sum in the previous expression reduces to zero and the limit of both extreme terms equals $\partial H / \partial t$, thanks to which, $dM/dt = \partial H / \partial t$. Consequently, the theorem is proven.

LITERATURE CITED

[1] V. G. Boltyanskii, R. V. Gamkrelidze and L. S. Pontryagin, "Theory of optimal processes," [in Russian] Izv. AN SSSR, seriya matematicheskaya 23, 6 (1959).

Received June 5, 1959

THE MAXIMUM PRINCIPLE OF L.S. PONTRYAGIN IN OPTIMAL-SYSTEM THEORY. PART III

L.I. Rozonoér

(Moscow)

The paper deals with questions related to the proof and employment of L.S. Pontryagin's maximum principle in optimal-system theory. Certain new results are also contained in this work. The first part of the work deals with the optimization problem for the case of free trajectory right ends. In the second part, the maximum principle is formulated for a more general type of boundaryconditions. In the third part, the connection between the method of dynamic programing and the maximum principle is established, a method of solving the optimization problem in discrete linear systems is given, and a number of considerations are presented concerning the use of the maximum principle for solving a definite class of problems which are related to the theory of dynamic accuracy of control systems.

4. Relationship of L.S. Pontryagin's Maximum Principle to R. Bellman's Dynamic Programing Method

We show, in this section, that with certain requirements of a general character there exists a close relationship between the equations deriving from the maximum principle and the corresponding equations from the theory of dynamic programing [1-3].

a) The Optimality Principle

Initially, we give a brief presentation of the idea of the dynamic programing method, using as an example a problem analogous to that considered by us in section 2 of part I. Let it be required to control the system described by the equations

$$\dot{x}_i = f_i(x, u, t), \qquad i = 1, \ldots, n, \qquad u(t) \in U, \tag{4.1}$$

such that a given function, $F[x(T)]$ of the state of the system at a fixed time T will be minimized, given that the system initially starts at point x^0 at time t_0. We denote the optimal control by $u^*(t) \equiv u^*(x^0, t_0, t)$ and the corresponding optimal trajectory by $x^*(t) \equiv x^*(x^0, t_0, t)$. We now consider the position on the optimal trajectory of the representative point $x' = x^*(x^0, t_0, t')$ at some moment of time $t = t'$, $t_0 < t' < T$, and we pose for ourselves the same problem as was formulated above, but with the initial time and initial state now taken to be, respectively, t' and x'. It is now necessary to find the optimal control $u^{**}(t) \equiv u^{**}(x', t', t)$ which minimizes the functional $F[x(T)]$ if the system is in state x' at initial time t'.

It is easily seen that the control $u^*(t)$, which is optimal on the time interval (t_0, T) in the problem with initial state x^0, t_0, must also be optimal on the interval (t', T) in the problem with initial state x', t', i.e., the values of the functional $F[x(T)]$ for the controls $u^*(t)$ and $u^{**}(t)$ must be equal.

*Parts I and II of this work were published, respectively, in Automation and Remote Control 10 and 11 (1959). [See English translation].

Indeed, if this assertion were not correct, and the functional's value for control $u^{**}(t)$ were less than its value for control $u^*(t)$ with the system initially at x', t', then control $u^*(t)$ could always be "improved" in the problem with initial state x^0, t_0, by replacing it by the control

$$v(t) = \begin{cases} u^*(t) & t_0 \leq t < t', \\ u^{**}(t) & t' \leq t \leq T, \end{cases}$$

which would first take the system to point x' and thereafter to the corresponding final state. But since control $u^*(t)$ is, by definition, optimal in the problem with initial state x^0, t_0 and cannot be improved, we arrive at a contradiction, and thus prove our assertion. This very simple fact is the essence of the so-called "optimality principle" which, following R. Bellman ([1], p. 83), we formulate in the following way.

An optimal control has the property that, whatever the initial state and initial control are, the remaining control must constitute an optimal control with regard to the state resulting from the first stage of the control.

Despite its simplicity, the optimality principle in many cases allows one to obtain an equation which ultimately defines the optimal control.

b) Basic Equation of the Dynamic Programing Method

We now derive the proper equation for the problem we are considering. We denote by $S_T(x^0, t_0)$ the value of the functional provided by optimal control $u^*(t)$ ($t_0 \leq t \leq T$) with the system initially at x^0, t_0. In our case, $S_T(x^0, t_0) \equiv F[x^*(x^0, t_0, T)]$. By varying the initial data, x^0, t_0, of the problem, we obtain a function $S_T(x^0, t_0)$ on the points of the $(n + 1)$-dimensional space $L(x_1^0, \ldots, x_n^0, t)$. When it leads to no ambiguities, we shall omit the superscript 0 and write the function S in the form $S_T(x, t)$.

As before, we consider the state x', t' on the optimal trajectory $x^*(t)$ where $x^*(t_0) = x^0$. When motion is along an optimal trajectory from state x^0, t_0, the functional assumes the value $S_T(x^0, t_0)$. By virtue of the optimality principle, controls $u^*(t)$ and $u^{**}(t)$ on the segment (t', T) correspond to one and the same optimal value of the functional, equal to $S_T(x', t')$. But since the functional is defined only by the terminal position of the representative point (at time $t = T$), we have that

$$S_T(x^0, t_0) = S_T(x', t'). \tag{4.2}$$

We consider the optimal control $u^*(t)$ on the segment $[t_0, t']$. It is obvious that, for optimality of the control $u^*(t)$, it is necessary that, to the point x' at time t', there correspond the least value of the function $S_T(x', t')$ in comparison to all other values which could be obtained for all other states reachable from x^0, t_0, at time t' by means of admissible controls $u(t) \in U$. Taking (4.2) into account, we can write this requirement in the following way:

$$S_T(x^0, t_0) = \min_{\substack{u(t) \in U \\ t_0 \leq t \leq t'}} S_T(x', t'), \tag{4.3}$$

bearing in mind for this that x' is a functional on $u(t)$ and, moreover, depends on x^0, t_0.

We now set $t' = t_0 + \tau$, where τ will be considered to be quite small. Then, bearing in mind that $x^*(t_0) = x^0$ and $\dot{x}_i^*(t_0) = f_i[x^0, t_0, u^*(t_0)]$, we write

$$x_i' \equiv x_i^*(t_0 + \tau) = x_i^0 + \tau f_i[x^0, t_0, u^*(t_0)] + \varepsilon,$$

where ϵ is of a higher order of smallness than τ. By assuming the existence and continuity of the partial derivatives of the function $S_T(x, t)$, we can write

$$S_T(x', t') = S_T(x^0, t_0) + \sum_1^n \frac{\partial S_T(x^0, t_0)}{\partial x_i^0}(x_i' - x_i^0) + \frac{\partial S_T(x^0, t_0)}{\partial t_0}(t' - t_0) + \beta,$$

where β is again small in comparison with τ. By using the previous formula for x_i', and by substituting the expression for $S_T(x',t')$ in (4.3), we get

$$S_T(x^0, t_0) = \min_{\substack{u(t)\in U \\ t_0\leqslant t\leqslant t_0+\tau}} \left[S_T(x^0, t_0) + \tau \sum_1^n \frac{\partial S_T(x^0, t_0)}{\partial x_i^0} f_i[x^0, t_0, u^*(t_0)] + \right. \\ \left. + \tau \frac{\partial S_T(x^0, t_0)}{\partial t_0} + \gamma \right].$$

The only terms depending on control u(t) are those containing the f_i and, in addition, the quantity γ which is of a higher order of smallness than τ. Therefore, the terms $S_T(x^0,t_0)$ and $\tau \frac{\partial S_T(x^0, t_0)}{\partial t_0}$ can be "taken out from in front of" the "min" sign. By simplifying and dividing by τ, we get

$$\frac{\partial S_T(x^0, t_0)}{\partial t_0} = - \min_{\substack{u(t)\in U \\ t_0\leqslant t\leqslant t_0+\tau}} \left[\sum_1^n \frac{\partial S_T(x^0, t_0)}{\partial x_i^0} f_i[x^0, t_0, u^*(t)] + \frac{\gamma}{\tau} \right].$$

This equation, just as (4.3), defines the choice of $u^*(t)$ on the segment $[t_0,t']$. By now letting τ approach zero, which also reduces the $[t_0, t_0 + \tau]$ segment to zero, we obtain an equation which determines the choice of $u^*(t)$ at the single point $t = t_0$. Therefore, by letting $u^*(t_0) = u^0$, and bearing in mind that $\lim_{\tau\to 0} \frac{\gamma}{\tau} = 0$, we obtain, finally,

$$\frac{\partial S_T(x^0, t_0)}{\partial t_0} = \min_{u^0\in U} \sum_1^n \frac{\partial S_T(x^0, t_0)}{\partial x_i^0} f_i(x^0, t_0, u^0). \tag{4.4}$$

This relationship is valid for any x^0,t_0. Therefore, the subscript (and superscript) 0 will henceforth be frequently omitted. Furthermore, by using the evident relationship $\max(-\psi) = -\min \psi$ (where ψ is an arbitrary function), we will use Eq. (4.4) in the form

$$\frac{\partial S_T(x, t)}{\partial T} = \max_{u\in U} \sum_1^n \left(- \frac{\partial S_T(x, t)}{\partial x_i} \right) f_i(x, t, u). \tag{4.5}$$

Equation (4.5) is essentially a specific partial differential equation which can be integrated if the corresponding boundary conditions are given. The quantity u can be eliminated from (4.5) if one makes use of the requirement according to which the sum $\sum_1^n \left(- \frac{\partial S_T(x, t)}{\partial x_i} \right) f_i(x, t, u)$ must be maximal for u for any values of x,t and $\partial S_T/\partial x_i$. The elimination of u from (4.5) is carried out in exactly the same way as the elimination of u(t) from the function H in L.S. Pontryagin's maximum principle (cf. section 2, part I and section 3, part II). For this, u is expressed in terms of x,t and $\partial S_T/\partial x_i$:

$$u = \gamma \left(x, t, \frac{\partial S_T}{\partial x_i} \right). \tag{4.6}$$

For example, in the case of the equation

$$\frac{\partial S_T}{\partial t} = \max_u \left[- \frac{\partial S_T}{\partial x_1} (ux_1 + x_2) - \frac{\partial S_T}{\partial x_2} u^2 \right]$$

with the assumption that $\partial S_T/\partial x_2 > 0$, the maximum of the expression $-\frac{\partial S_T}{\partial x_1} x_1 u - \frac{\partial S_T}{\partial x_2} u^2 - \frac{\partial S_T}{\partial x_1} x_2$ as a function of u is attained when $u = -\frac{1}{2} x_1 \frac{\frac{\partial S_T}{\partial x_1}}{\frac{\partial S_T}{\partial x_2}}$, so that after u is eliminated we obtain the equation

$$\frac{\partial S_T}{\partial t} = x_1^2 \frac{\left(\frac{\partial S_T}{\partial x_1}\right)^2}{4 \frac{\partial S_T}{\partial x_2}} - \frac{\partial S_T}{\partial x_1} x_2.$$

The boundary conditions for Eq. (4.5) are very simply found: for t = T, state x,t is simultaneously initial and final, and the functional's value does not depend on the control, and equals

$$S_T(x, T) \equiv F(x_1, \ldots, x_n). \tag{4.7}$$

Now, the solution of Eq. (4.5) can be determined. Indeed, from (4.6) the derivatives $\partial S_T(x,T)/\partial x_i$ are determined for each value of x and, consequently, the right member of (4.5) is also determined. In the same way, we learn the value of the partial derivative $\partial S_T(x,T)/\partial t$ and, for sufficiently small τ, we can find the value of $S_T(x, T-\tau)$ in the form

$$S_T(x, T-\tau) \approx S_T(x, T) - \frac{\partial S_T(x, T)}{\partial t} \tau.$$

Thus, moving step-by-step, we can determine the function $S_T(x,t)$ for any value of t. If the function $S_T(x,t)$ is known then, by means of Eq. (4.6), u is also determined as a function of x,t:

$$u = \varphi(x, t). \tag{4.8}$$

Thus, we have uncovered the partial differential equation and the corresponding boundary conditions*

$$\frac{\partial S_T(x, t)}{\partial t} = \max_{u \in U} \sum_1^n \left(-\frac{\partial S_T(x, t)}{\partial x_i}\right) f_i(x, u, t), \tag{4.9}$$
$$S_T(x, T) \equiv F(x),$$

which allow us to determine the function $S_T(x,t)$ and the min-optimal control as functions of x,t. An analogous equation can be obtained for the case when one is seeking a maximum of the functional F[x(T)]:

$$\frac{\partial S_T(x, t)}{\partial t} = \min_{u \in U} \sum_1^n \left(-\frac{\partial S_T(x, t)}{\partial x_i}\right) f_i(x, u, t), \tag{4.10}$$
$$S_T(x, T) \equiv F(x).$$

The arguments leading to Eqs. (4.9) and (4.10) can in no way be considered as proofs. They should be considered as strictly heuristic, allowing us to surmise how the problem must be solved. However, as will be shown below, with certain assumptions the validity of the final results [i.e., an equation of the type of (4.9) or (4.10)] can be proved.

c) Relationship of the Maximum Principle to the Dynamic Programing Method

The structure of the right members of Eqs. (4.9) and (4.10) recalls the structure of the function

*In the analogous equations [1], the partial derivatives were taken with respect to T, rather than with respect to the initial time t, which leads to a change in sign in the formulas.

$H = \sum_1^n p_i f_i (x, u, t)$ in the maximum principle. We convince ourselves that this similarity is not a casual one by theorem 6, given below, which is formulated for the case of the problem which we considered in section 2, part I [i.e., the problem of optimizing the functional $S = \sum_1^n c_i x_i (T)$].

We introduce the following notation: L is an n-dimensional space with coordinate axes $(x_1, \ldots, x_n, t)$; (x,t) is a point of space L; $u^*(t) \equiv u^*(x^0, t_0, t)$ is a min-optimal (max-optimal) control when the system's representative point is at position x^0 at initial time $t = t_0$; $x^*(t) \equiv x^*(x^0, t_0, t)$ is the corresponding optimal trajectory [so that $x^*(t_0) = x^0$]; $S_T(x,t)$ is the value of the functional $S = \sum_1^n c_i x_i (T)$ on the min-optimal (max-optimal) control if, at time $\underline{t}$, the system is found at point $\underline{x}$.

Theorem 6. In the problem of the min-optimization (max-optimization) of the functional $S = \sum_1^n c_i x_i (T)$ let the function $S_T(x,t)$ be continuous and continuously differentiable in the region Γ of space L.

Then:

1) For all $\underline{t}$ for which $(x^*(t),t) \in \Gamma$, the min-optimal (max-optimal) control $u^*(t)$ satisfies the maximum (minimum) condition with respect to $p(t) = [p_1(t), \ldots, p_n(t)]$, where

$$p_i (t) \equiv -\frac{\partial S_T [x^* (t), t]}{\partial x_i}, \qquad i = 1, \ldots, n,$$

and where

$$\frac{\partial S_T [x^* (t), t]}{\partial t} = H [x^* (t), p (t), u^* (t), t] = \sum_1^n p_i (t) f_i [x^* (t), u^* (t), t];$$

2) The function $S_T(x,t)$ satisfies, in Γ, the partial differential equation

$$\frac{\partial S_T (x, t)}{\partial t} = \max_{u \in U} \sum_1^n \left(-\frac{\partial S_T (x, t)}{\partial x_i}\right) f_i (x, u, t).$$

$$\left\langle \frac{\partial S_T (x, t)}{\partial t} = \min_{u \in U} \sum_1^n \left(-\frac{\partial S_T (x, t)}{\partial x_i}\right) f_i (x, u, t) \right\rangle,$$

where $S_T (x, T) \equiv \sum_1^n c_i x_i$, if $(x,T) \in \Gamma$.

Theorem 6 has a graphic geometric interpretation. In section 2, part I, we recalled that the vector $p(t)$, with respect to which optimal control $u(t)$ satisfies the maximum (minimum) condition, defines the direction of "maximum acceleration" of the system in phase space X. As follows from theorem 6, this direction, at each fixed moment of time $\underline{t}$, is determined in its turn by the gradient of the function $S_T(x,t)$ in phase space X. It thus turns out that, at each fixed moment of time, whatever the position of the representative point, the optimal control tends to "accelerate" the latter in the direction defined by the gradient of the function $S_T(x,t)$.

An analogous partial differential equation can also be obtained in the more general problem considered in section 3, part II. However, the boundary conditions here are significantly more complicated, and we shall not consider them here. In any event, the relationship of the function p(t) to the gradient of the function S is retained even in this more complicated case.*

d) Analogy with the Equations of Analytical Mechanics

The analogy of the equations deriving from L.S. Pontryagin's maximum principle with the canonic equations of analytical mechanics was already cited in section 2, part I and section 3, part II. The establishment of the relationship between the maximum principle and the dynamic programing method shows that this analogy is very profound. The equations deriving from the dynamic programing method are completely analogous with the Hamilton-Jacobi partial differential equations, whereby the function S(x,t) plays the role of the action function. It thus turns out that the connection between the equations of the maximum principle and the equations of the dynamic programing method is analogous to the relationship between the Hamilton canonical equations and the Hamilton-Jacobi equations. The sole difference is that, in optimal system theory, the "control" is explicitly introduced, whereas it is eliminated in analytical mechanics, and is expressed in terms of the coordinates, their derivatives and time. As physical analogies of the control we can use, in particular, the velocities of the system's mass points.

e) The Role of the Requirement of Continuity

In the present work we have always considered problems in which the set U, defining the limitations on the class of admissible controls, does not depend on the running value of the coordinates. Otherwise the maximum principle, in the form in which we have formulated it, turns out to be inapplicable, whereas the equations of the dynamic programing method remain valid in general. This circumstance is explained as follows. The vector p(t) which enters into the formulation of the maximum principle has always been considered by us as a continuous function of time. But if the derivatives $\partial S_T(x,t)/\partial x_i$ are not continuous in the entire space L and, moreover, if the optimal trajectory $(x(t),t)$, $t_0 \leq t \leq T$ intersects a surface of discontinuity of the functions $\partial S_T(x,t)/\partial x_i$ in L, then the functions $p_i(t) \equiv -\partial S_T(x(t),t)/\partial x_i$ also experience a discontinuity. Therefore, it is necessary to generalize the maximum principle so as to allow us to consider discontinuous (in particular, piece-wise-continuous) pulse functions. Such a generalization was made by R.V. Gamkrelidze [4] for the case of optimization with account taken of limitations placed on the system coordinates. The conditions for jumps in the functions $p_i(t)$ were formulated in [4].

Thus, the requirement connected with the continuity of the function $S_T(x,t)$ and its derivatives has a non-formal character. If we follow the mechanical analogy, the requirement that p(t) be continuous corresponds to the requirement of no impulse skips, i.e., the absence of "impact" interaction.

Whether or not the function $S_T(x,t)$ itself is continuous is particularly important. The fact of the matter is that the corresponding partial differential equation is valid, generally speaking, only in the regions of continuity of the functions $\partial S_T/\partial x_i$ in the space L. The condition that $S_T(x,t)$ be continuous allows one to "join" the solutions at the surfaces of discontinuity of the derivatives $\partial S_T/\partial x_i$. The author knows of only one work [5] investigating such questions in which continuity is proven for the optimal values of the functional (time control) in the linear problem of temporal optimization with limitations on the control of the type $|u_k| \leq 1$.

We note further that the existence of singular controls (cf. section 3, part II) is also related to the presence of discontinuities of the derivatives $\partial S_T/\partial x_i$. A singular trajectory occurs precisely along a surface of discontinuity.

f) The Synthesis Problem

As has been mentioned, the knowledge of the function $S_T(x,t)$ allows one to find the control $\underline{u}$ in the form of function (4.8), which rapidly gives a complete solution to the synthesis problem. However, solution of partial differential Eqs. (4.9) and (4.10) in closed form is possible only in the most elementary cases. In practice, therefore, one should attempt to solve the synthesis problem by means of the dynamic programing method only if one has access to a computer. The development of convenient machine algorithms for solving these equations is, therefore, of importance.

*In the general case, the surface S(x,t) = const is the geometric locus of the points which give the same value to the functional when the optimal trajectory begins with them. In particular, in the case of maximizing speed of response, the corresponding surfaces T(x) = const are the "isochrone" surfaces first considered by A.Ya. Lerner.

5. Concerning Optimal Processes in Discrete Systems

In this section we shall consider several optimization problems in discrete automatic control systems, described by finite difference equations. For this, we assume time to be "discrete," i.e., time takes the values $0, \tau, \ldots, m\tau, \ldots$ where τ is some constant having the dimensionality of time. The control processes in such systems can be described by the following system of finite difference equations:

$$x_i^{m+1} = x_i^m + \tau f_i(x_1^m, \ldots, x_n^m, u_1^m, \ldots, u_r^m, m\tau) \quad (i = 1, \ldots, n). \tag{5.1}$$

The symbols x_i^m, u_k^m are the abbreviated notations for the variables x_i and u_k considered at time $m\tau$, i.e., $x_i^m = x_i(m\tau)$, $u_k^m = u_k(m\tau)$. In the sequel we shall consider m as the time variable, assuming the integral values 0, 1, 2, . . .

In system (5.1) we have, as before, denoted by x_i $(i = 1, \ldots, n)$ and u_k $(k = 1, \ldots, r)$ the generalized system coordinates and, respectively, the controlling actions. By introducing the vectors $x^m = (x_1^m, \ldots, x_n^m)$ and $u^m = (u_1^m, \ldots, u_r^m)$, we can write system (5.1) briefly as

$$x^{m+1} - x^m = \tau f(x^m, u^m, m).$$

We shall consider as given the value of vector x^m at time $m = 0$, and shall denote it by x^0. The space $X(x_1, \ldots, x_n)$ in which the generalized system coordinates can vary is called the phase space. A "trajectory" of a discrete system in the phase space is a sequence of isolated points.

As before, we shall call the vector u^m, considered as a vector function of time m, the control. The limitations on the controlling actions are expressed by requirements in accordance with which, at each moment of time m, the control u^m must lie in a closed set U of space $R(u_1, \ldots, u_r)$:

$$u^m \in U \quad (m = 0, 1, 2, \ldots). \tag{5.2}$$

With respect to system (5.1), we can pose various optimization problems, completely analogous to those formulated for continuous systems in section 1, part I. The sole difference is that, in the proper places, the integrals over the continuous time t are replaced by sums over the discrete time m, and derivatives with respect to t are replaced by the differences of variable values at neighboring instants of time m. A wide class of optimization problems (in complete analogy with the problems for continuous systems) can be reduced to the following basic problem. From the set of admissible controls $u^m \in U$ which take the system from point x^0 to a fixed closed set G of phase space X, it is required to so choose the control u^m $(m = 0, 1, \ldots, M-1)$ that the sum $S = \sum_1^n c_i x_i^M$ at a given moment of time $m = M$, assumes a minimum (maximum) value.

The control time here is assumed fixed. Problems in which the time is not given beforehand will not be considered further here.

We remark that the problem formulated above is essentially the problem of minimizing (maximizing) the function S with respect to rM independent variables $u_1^0, \ldots, u_r^0; u_1^1, \ldots, u_r^1; u_1^{M-1}, \ldots, u_r^{M-1}$. Indeed, system (5.1) is a system of recurrence relationships which allow one to determine successively the values of the vectors $x^1, x^2, \ldots, x^M$ in the form of functions of the coordinates of the vectors $u^0, u^1, \ldots, u^{M-1}$ if just the initial value x^0 is given. By thus obtaining the quantities x_i^M $(i = 1, \ldots, n)$ and the function S itself as functions of the variables $u_1^0, \ldots, u_r^{M-1}$, one can determine the extrema of S with the conditions that $u^m \in U$ $(m = 0, \ldots, M-1)$ and $x^m \in G$. However, such a direct method of solving the problem in any complicated case turns out to be inadmissible in practice, due to the mass of computations required, even if a computer is available. Moreover, the necessity arises of providing a uniform method of solution valid for all problems of a given class and allowing the use of a uniform programing scheme. It is, therefore, necessary to seek methods which provide simpler (from the computational point of view) solutions of the problem posed. One of these methods is R. Bellman's dynamic programing method. Below, we present another method, related to an extension to discrete systems of L.S. Pontryagin's maximum principle.

In what follows, we shall consider systems which are linear in the variables $x_1, \ldots, x_n$, i.e., systems of the form

$$x_i^{m+1} - x^m = \tau\left[\sum_{k=1}^{n} a_{ik}^m x_k^m + \varphi_i(u_1^m, \ldots, u_r^m)\right] \quad (i = 1, \ldots, n), \tag{5.3}$$

where the functions φ_i are assumed to be continuous, and the coefficients a_{ik} can depend on the time m.

The limitation of our consideration to linear systems is explained by the fact that the extension of the maximum principle to discrete systems is possible, generally speaking, only in the linear case.*

We turn now to the formulation of the basic results. We consider n functions $p_1^m, \ldots, p_n^m$ of time m which satisfy the relationships

$$p_i^m - p_i^{m-1} = -\tau \sum_1^m p_s \frac{\partial f_s(x^m, u^m, m)}{\partial x_i} \quad (i = 1, \ldots, n), \tag{5.4}$$

where, by virtue of the linearity of the functions f_s,

$$\frac{\partial f_s(x^m, u^m, m)}{\partial x_i} = a_{si}^m. \tag{5.5}$$

We call the vector $p^m = (p_1^m, \ldots, p_n^m)$ the impulse.

By introducing the function

$$H(x, p, u, m) \equiv \tau \sum_1^n p_s f_s(x_1, \ldots, x_n;\ u_1, \ldots, u_r;\ m)$$

and denoting the corresponding first differences by the symbol Δ ($\Delta x_i^l \equiv x_i^{l+1} - x_i^l$, $\Delta p_i^l = p_i^{l+1} - p_i^l$, $l = 0, 1, 2, \ldots$), we can write relationships (5.3) and (5.4) in the form of the system

$$\Delta x_i^m = \frac{\partial H(x^m, p^m, u^m, m)}{\partial p_i^m}, \quad \Delta p_i^{m-1} = -\frac{\partial H(x^m, p^m, u^m, m)}{\partial x_i^m} \quad (i = 1, \ldots, n). \tag{5.6}$$

We now turn our attention to the circumstance that the values of the variables x^m, p^m and u^m at time m define the first differences of the coordinates at the same moment of time, but the first difference of the impulses at the previous moment of time. In other words, by knowing the values of the variables x^m, p^m and u^m at time m we can determine from (5.6) the coordinates at the following moment, m + 1, and the impulse at the previous moment, m − 1.

Let $u^m \in U$ be some admissible control, $x^m \equiv \alpha(m)$ the trajectory corresponding to it and $p^m \equiv \beta(m)$ some one of the vector functions of time which satisfy (5.6). By substituting in the function H the values of x^m and p^m, which are now definite functions of time, we obtain the quantity

$$K(m, u_1, \ldots, u_r) \equiv H[\alpha(m), \beta(m), u, m],$$

which, for each moment of time m, is a function of the point $u = (u_1, \ldots, u_r)$ which lies in set U of space $R(u_1, \ldots, u_r)$. We shall say that control u^m satisfies the maximum (minimum) condition with respect to vector function $p^m \equiv \beta(m)$ if, at each fixed moment of time m ($0 \le m \le M-1$), the function K(m,u) attains an absolute maximum (minimum) on the set U for values of the variables equal to the values of the controls at the same moment of time, i.e., for $u_k = u_k^m$.

*As $\tau \to 0$, the solution of the discrete problem tends, in a definite sense, to the solution of the corresponding continuous problem (cf. [6], where this assertion has been proven for linear systems and limitations of the form $|u_k| \le 1$). Therefore, for sufficiently small τ, the maximum principle turns out to be applicable in a sense.

Just as in the case of continuous systems, we first formulate the results for the problem with free trajectory right ends and then turn to the more general problems.

In the problem with free trajectory right ends, the set G occupies the entire space, which we symbolize by $G \sim X$. The following theorem establishes the discrete analogy to theorem 2 of section 2, part I.

Theorem 7. A necessary and sufficient condition for min-optimality (max-optimality) of control u^m ($m = 0, 1, \ldots, M-1$) in system (5.3) for $G \sim X$ is the holding, for u^m, of the maximum (minimum) condition with respect to the vector functions p^m which satisfy the relationships

$$p_i^{M-1} = -c_i \quad (i = 1, \ldots, n).$$

The proof of theorem 7 is completely analogous to the proof of theorem 2 for continuous systems, and is based on the following formula for the increment of value of function S with a variation of control u^m:

$$\delta S = \sum_1^n c_i \delta x_i^M = -\sum_{m=0}^{M-1} [H(x^m, p^m, u^m + \delta u^m, m) - H(x^m, p^m, u^m, m)] - \eta, \; (5.7) \tag{5.7}$$

where $\delta u^m \equiv (\delta u_1^m, \ldots, \delta u_r^M)$ are the increments of control and $\eta = \eta_1 + \eta_2$ are certain residual terms, where

$$\eta_1 = \frac{1}{2} \sum_{m=0}^{M-1} \sum_{s=1}^{n} \left[\frac{\partial H(y^m, u^m + \delta u^m, m)}{\partial y_s^m} - \frac{\partial H(y^m, u^m, m)}{\partial y_s^m} \right] \delta y_s^m,$$

$$\eta_2 = \frac{1}{2} \sum_{m=0}^{M-1} \sum_{s, q=1}^{n} \left[\frac{\partial^2 H(y^m + \vartheta_1^m \delta y^m, u^m + \delta u^m, m)}{\partial y_s^m \partial y_q^m} - \frac{\partial^2 H(y^m + \vartheta_2^m \delta y^m, u^m + \delta u^m, m)}{\partial y_s^m \partial y_q^m} \right] \delta y_s^m \delta y_q^m.$$

Here, $0 < \vartheta_1 < 1$, $0 < \vartheta_2 < 1$ and, for brevity, we introduced the vector $y = (y_1, \ldots, y_{2n})$ ($y_i = x_i$, $y_{n+i} = p_i$, $i = 1, \ldots, n$). For linear systems of the form of (5.3), the residual term η reduces to zero. The proof of formula (5.7) is carried out in complete analogy with the derivation of the corresponding formula for the increment of the functional's value.

We now turn to the more general problem wherein the "trajectory's" right end lies in some set $G \in X$. It is further assumed that set G is convex and closed.

We first formulate a sufficient condition for optimality. Just as in the analogous continuous problem (section 3f, part II), we shall denote by $b_i(y_1, \ldots, y_n)$ ($i = 1, \ldots, n$) the coefficients of the hyperplane bracketing set G at point $y = (y_1, \ldots, y_n)$. If $\underline{y}$ is an interior point, we then set $b_i(y_1, \ldots, y_n) = 0$. For each point $x(x_1, \ldots, x_n) \in G$ in the problem of minimizing function S we require that the inequality $\sum_1^n b_i(y_1, \ldots, y_n)(x_i - y_i) \leq 0$ hold, whereas we require that the inequality hold with reversed sense in the problem where the function is to be maximized.

Just as in the continuous case, we shall consider nondegenerate problems (section 3a, part II). In a nondegenerate problem, the set $G^* \in G$, on which the function $\psi(x) \equiv \sum_1^n c_i x_i$ assumes its least (greatest) value in comparison with the values for all other points $x \in G$, is not attainable from point x^0 within time M for the controls $u^m \in U$.

Now, if $x^0, x^1, \ldots, x^M$ is an optimal "trajectory," corresponding to control $u^0, u^1, \ldots, u^{M-1}$, the following theorem, establishing a sufficient condition for optimality, is valid.

Theorem 8. If, in system (5.3), control u^m ($m = 0, 1, \ldots, M-1$) satisfies the maximum (minimum) condition with respect to vector p^m, whose coordinates at time $m = M-1$ assume the values

$$p_i^{M-1} = -\lambda c_i - \mu b_i (x_1^M, \ldots, x_n^M) \quad (i = 1, \ldots, n),$$

where μ is nonnegative and λ is positive, then control u^m is min-optimal (max-optimal) with respect to $S = \sum_1^n c_i x_i^M$.

The proof of theorem 8 is based on theorem 7 and is carried out in complete analogy with the proof of theorem 4.

In the formulation of necessary conditions for optimality, it is necessary that one further requirement hold, this requirement amounting to the following. We consider the mapping of r-dimensional space $R(u_1, \ldots, u_r)$ on n-dimensional space $X(v_1, \ldots, v_n)$, given by the functions

$$v_i = \varphi_i (u_1, \ldots, u_r) \quad (i = 1, \ldots, n),$$

which define the right members of Eq. (5.3). We denote by V the set of all points of space X which are images of points which lie in set U of space R. We shall require that set V be convex (which occurs, in particular, if $v_i = b_i u$ and the variable $\underline{u}$ is of bounded modulus).

The following theorem establishes a necessary condition for optimality.

Theorem 9. Let set V be convex. Then, if control $u^m \in U$ $(m = 0, 1, \ldots, M-1)$ in the nondegenerate problem is min-optimal (max-optimal) with respect to $S = \sum_1^n c_i x_i^M$, there then exist vector functions p^m with respect to which control u^m satisfies the maximum (minimum) condition, where the coordinates of vectors p^m at time $m = M-1$ assume the values

$$p_i^{M-1} = -\lambda c_i - \mu b_i (x_1^M, \ldots, x_n^M) \quad (i = 1, \ldots, n),$$

where the constants λ and μ are nonnegative and do not vanish simultaneously.

The proof of theorem 9 is obtained in the following way (for example, for the case of min-optimality). By the conditions of the theorem, the set W_T of the points of space X which are attainable in time M with the control $u^m \in U$ is a convex set. The set G^-, which is the set of those points $x \in G$ for which $\sum_1^n c_i (x_i - x_i^M) \leqslant 0$, is also convex, where the points common to G^- and W_T (in particular, point x^M) can only be boundary points of the two sets. The foregoing defines the hyperplane A which separates sets G^- and W_T and which is a bracket for set W_T. By so choosing the signs of the coefficients a_i $(i = 1, \ldots, n)$ of hyperplane A that the inequality $\sum_1^n a_i (x_i - x_i^M) \geqslant 0$, holds for any point $x \in W_T$, we can convince ourselves that control u^m is min-optimal for $S = \sum_1^n a_i x_i^M$ in the problem with free right ends and, thanks to theorem 7, satisfies the maximum condition with respect to the vector function p^m which, for $m = M-1$, assumes the values $p_i^{M-1} = -a_i$ $(i = 1, \ldots, n)$. The relationships $a_i = \lambda c_i + \mu b_i (x_1^M, \ldots, x_n^M)$ are obtained exactly the same as in the continuous case (section 3, part II).

Theorems 7-9 are used for solving concrete problems by methods completely analogous to the method of using the maximum principle in continuous problems. Specifically, the maximum (minimum) principle allows one to express the control at each moment of time in terms of the coordinates and impulses of the system, thus providing the capability of eliminating the control from Eq. (5.6). The system of 2n finite difference equations thus obtained, with 2n variables and with boundary conditions stated in the formulation of the theorems, defines the optimal trajectory and impulses and, consequently, also defines the optimal control.

6. Use of the Maximum Principle for Solving Certain Problems Connected with the Dynamic Accuracy of Automatic Control Systems

The variational methods developed in optimal system theory have immediate application to the problems connected with the estimation of control processes. This is particularly the case when the problem of dynamic accuracy is so posed that the external stimuli on the system are assumed to be given only by a number of limitations: limitations on modulus, known values of the integral of the squared disturbances, etc. Indeed, the basic problem in the investigation of such cases amounts to choosing, from the class of admissible external stimuli, that one which is the most "dangerous" from the point of view of the accepted criterion of dynamic accuracy. Thus, for example, in B.V. Bulgakov's problem of the accumulation of deviations in linear systems [8-10], one chooses, from the class of modulus-limited external stimuli, those which lead to the maximum deviation of the controlled quantity. In [11, 12], the class of external stimuli is assumed to be given by definite values of the integral of the moduli, or the integral of the squared disturbance, and one then computes the maximum value which the integral of the squared controlled quantity might assume. It is obvious that, in all these cases, a variational problem is essentially solved. An explicit use of variational methods and, in particular, the methods developed in optimal system theory, holds out broad possibilities, both in the sense of the investigation of nonlinear systems and in the sense that the class of admissible external stimuli might be given in significantly more diverse ways.

B.V. Bulgakov's problem on the accumulation of deviations can be formulated in the following way, which is also meaningful for nonlinear systems. Let $u_1, \ldots, u_r$ be the external stimuli acting on the control system described by the differential equations

$$\dot{x}_i = f_i(x_1, \ldots, x_n, u_1, \ldots, u_r; t) \quad (i = 1, \ldots, n). \tag{6.1}$$

All that is known about an external stimulus $u = (u_1, \ldots, u_r)$ is that it satisfies some system of inequalities (in the particular case here, $|u_k| \leq a_k$, $k = 1, \ldots, r$). It is required to find the maximum possible deviation $x_1(T)$ which the controlled quantity x_1 can undergo at time $t = T$.

The problem just formulated is identical with the problem considered by us in section 2, part I, whose theorem 1 gives the capability of solving the problem of accumulation of deviations for nonlinear systems with diverse limitations on the external stimuli. The results already obtained for linear systems are easily obtained as particular cases here.* It turns out that the "impulse" vector considered in the maximum principle is intimately related to the impulsive response of linear systems.

For example, we now show that, by means of the maximum principle, the simplest problem of deviation accumulation is solved for a system with constant coefficients, described by an equation of the form

$$x^{(n)} + a_{n-1}x^{(n-1)} + \cdots + a_0 x = u, \quad |u| \leqslant 1. \tag{6.2}$$

The relationship between the system's impulsive response and the "impulse" vector is particularly clear here. For simplicity of exposition, we shall write the formula for the case when $n = 2$,

$$\ddot{x} + a_1\dot{x} + a_0 x = u, \tag{6.3}$$

bearing in mind that the analogous relationships subsist in systems of higher order. We now write Eq. (6.3) in the form of the system

$$\dot{x}_0 = x_1, \quad \dot{x}_1 = -a_0 x_0 - a_1 x_1 + u,$$

where $x = x_0$ is the coordinate to be controlled. The problem consists of finding the maximum of the function $S = x_0(T)$ for the fixed time T. We must, therefore, solve the problem with free trajectory right ends, whereby $c_0 = 1$ and $c_1 = 0$. In correspondence with the general methodology, we set up the function

*In those cases when the derivatives of the external stimuli enter into the system equations, we should use the results obtained in [4].

$$H = p_0 x_1 - p_1 (a_0 x_0 + a_1 x_1) + p_1 u$$

and the system of equations

$$\dot{p}_0 = -\frac{\partial H}{\partial x_0} \equiv a_0 p_1, \; \dot{p}_1 = -\frac{\partial H}{\partial x_1} \equiv -p_0 + a_1 p_1. \qquad (6.4)$$

The boundary conditions are written in the form

$$p_0 (T) = -c_0 \equiv -1, \; p_1 (T) = -c_1 \equiv 0. \qquad (6.5)$$

Since we seek to maximize the functional, we use the minimum condition. The minimum of function H with respect to u is obviously attained at the boundary points: for $p_1 > 0$, $u = -1$ and, for $p_1 < 0$, $u = +1$, i.e.,

$$u (t) = -\operatorname{sign} p_1 (t). \qquad (6.6)$$

The alternation of the intervals on which the external stimulus assumes the values +1 and −1 is thus determined by the variations in time of the function $p_1(t)$. We now replace system (6.4) by one equation in $p \equiv \equiv p_1(t)$

$$\ddot{p} - a_1 \dot{p} + a_0 p = 0. \qquad (6.7)$$

In (6.7) we carry out the change of variables, $W(t) = -p(T-t)$. Since $\dot{W}(t) = \dot{p}(T-t)$ and $\ddot{W} = \ddot{p}(T-t)$, (6.7) is written in the form of the following equation in the function W (t):

$$\ddot{W} (t) + a_1 \dot{W} (t) + a_0 W (t) = 0 \qquad (6.8)$$

with boundary conditions [by virtue of (6.5)]

$$W (0) = 0, \; \dot{W} (0) = 1. \qquad (6.9)$$

However, as is well known, the solution of Eq. (6.8) with initial data given by (6.9) gives the system's impulsive response. The left members of Eq. (6.8) and the sought-for Eq. (6.3) coincide. Thus, W (t) is the impulsive response of control system (6.3), and component p_1 of the "impulse" vector (p_0, p_1) equals

$$p_1 (t) = -W (T - t). \qquad (6.10)$$

Since $\dot{p}_0 = a_0 p_1$ and $p_0 (T) = -1$, it easily follows that

$$p_0 (t) = -1 + h (T - t), \qquad (6.11)$$

where $h (t) = \int\limits_0^t W (z) \, dz$, i.e., the system's reaction to a unit step function input. The most "dangerous" stimulus, by virtue of (6.6) and (6.10), is determined from the well-known formula

$$u (t) = \operatorname{sign} W (T - t). \qquad (6.12)$$

Also easily solved are problems in which, in addition to the limitation $|u| \leq 1$, there are limitations of the type $\int\limits_0^T |u| \, dt \leqslant A$ or $\int\limits_0^T u^2 \, dt \leqslant A$.* With such limitations, one may seek, not only the maximum deviation of the controlled quantity but also, for example, the maximum value of the integral of the square of this

*We note that, when there are "integral" limitations, we have to deal, generally speaking, with a problem in which the trajectory right ends are no longer free (cf. section 1, part I).

quantity (analogously to [12] where, however, $T = \infty$ and the limitation $|u| \leq 1$ is lacking). In linear cases, the solutions of such problems can be expressed in terms of the system's impulsive response.

The results of section 5 indicate how to expand the above-considered methods for investigating the dynamic accuracy for systems' control of discrete linear systems.

APPENDIX III

Proof of Theorem 6. For definiteness, we consider the case where a minimum of the functions $\sum_1^n c_i x_i(T)$. is sought. The theorem is proved in an analogous way when the case of maximizing the functional is concerned.

As before, we shall assume that the right members of the system

$$\dot{x}_i = f_i(x, u, t) \qquad (i = 1, \ldots, n, u(t) \in U) \tag{III.1}$$

are continuous in the set of arguments (x,u,t) and have continuous first and second partial derivatives with respect to the arguments $(x_1, \ldots, x_n)$.

Let (x^0, t_0) be some point in L, and let $u^* \equiv u^*(x^0, t_0, t)$ and $x^*(t) \equiv x^*(x^0, t_0, t)$ be, respectively, the optimal control and the optimal trajectory corresponding to a minimum of the functional $\sum_1^n c_i x_i(T)$ for a fixed value of T.

Further, at time $t = t'$ $(t_0 \leq t' \leq T)$, let the system be in state $x = x'$. On the segment $[t', T]$ we shall use the control $u^*(t)$. With this, the function $\sum_1^n c_i x_i(T)$ assumes the value $\Phi_T(x', t')$ which depends exclusively on (x', t') since the control $u^*(t)$ is given. By varying the state of the system (x', t'), we obtain the function

$$\Phi_T(x', t') \equiv \Phi_T[x', t', \{u^*(x^0, t_0, t)\}],$$

which has for its value at each fixed point $(x', t') \in L$ the value which the functional assumes on the control $u^*(t)$ $(t' \leq t \leq T)$ for the system's initial state being (x', t'). The symbol $\{u^*(x^0, t_0, t)\}$ (which will be omitted in the sequel) indicates that the function $\Phi_T(x', t')$ is meaningful only if the control $u^*(t)$ is previously given. Let $x(t) \equiv x(x', t', t)$ be the system's trajectory corresponding to control $u^*(t)$ with initial state (x', t'). By definition,

$$\Phi_T(x', t') \equiv \sum_1^n c_i x_i(x', t', T). \tag{III.2}$$

Since the functional to be minimized is defined by the final value only (at time $t = T$) of the system's coordinate, it is then obvious that

$$\Phi_T[x(t), t] = \Phi_T(x', t') \qquad (t' \leqslant t \leqslant T), \tag{III.3}$$

i.e., the values of the functional on the control $u^*(t)$ for initial states lying on the trajectory $x(t) \equiv x(x', t', t)$ are all equal to one another.

It follows, from our assumptions as to the right member of Eqs. (III.1) and from the piecewise continuity of control $u^*(t)$ that the solution $x = x(x', t', t)$ of system (1) is continuous in the set of initial data (x', t') and has all continuous first-order partial derivatives and continuous second-order partial derivatives $\partial^2 x_i / \partial x'_s \partial x'_q$, $\partial^2 x_i / \partial x'_s \partial t'$ $(i, s, q = 1, \ldots, n)$ (cf. [7]).*

*In [7], the proof of the theorem on the continuity and differentiability of the solution with respect to the initial data is carried out on the assumption that the right members of the differential equations are continuous in t. By assuming that, at the points of discontinuity, $u^*(t) = u^*(t+0)$ and by using the so-called theorem on half-interval continuity, one can easily show that the solution of system (1) of equations is differentiable the proper number of times with respect to the initial data even in the case considered, when control $u^*(t)$ is piecewise continuous and has a finite number of first-order discontinuities.

From this follow the continuity and the existence of the corresponding partial derivatives of the function $\Phi_T(x', t') \equiv \sum_1^n c_i x_i(x', t', T)$. By taking this into account, and by then taking the total derivative of Eq. (III.3) with respect to t, we get, by virtue of (III.1),

$$\frac{\partial \Phi_T[x(x', t', t), t]}{\partial t} = -\sum_1^n \frac{\partial \Phi_T[x(x', t', t), t]}{\partial x_s} f_s[x(x', t', t), u^*(t), t].$$

This last relationship holds identically for any x', t' and $t(t' \leq t \leq T)$. Therefore, by setting $t = t'$, and keeping in mind that $x(x', t', t) = x'$ and then discarding the primes, we obtain the identity

$$\frac{\partial \Phi_T(x, t)}{\partial t} = -\sum_1^n \frac{\partial \Phi_T(x, t)}{\partial x_s} f_s[x, u^*(t), t]. \tag{III.4}$$

We now consider the functions

$$p_i(t) \equiv -\frac{\partial \Phi_T[x^*(t), t]}{\partial x_i} \qquad (i = 1, \ldots, n). \tag{III.5}$$

We first note that, by virtue of the well-known relationships

$$\frac{\partial x_i(x^0, T, T)}{\partial x_j^0} = \begin{cases} 1 & i = j, \\ 0 & i \neq j \end{cases}$$

(cf. for example, [7]), we have the equality

$$\frac{\partial \Phi_T(x^0, T)}{\partial x_i^0} \equiv \sum_1^n c_s \frac{\partial x_s(x^0, T, T)}{\partial x_i^0} = c_i \qquad (i = 1, \ldots, n)$$

and, consequently,

$$p_i(T) = -c_i. \tag{III.6}$$

We now derive the system of differential equations which are satisfied by the functions $p_i(t)$. We differentiate (III.5) with respect to t (the corresponding derivatives exist and are continuous):

$$\dot{p}_i(t) = -\frac{\partial^2 \Phi_T[x^*(t), t]}{\partial x_i \partial t} - \sum_{s=1}^n \frac{\partial^2 \Phi_T[x^*(t), t]}{\partial x_i \partial x_s} \dot{x}_s^*(t). \tag{III.7}$$

From (III.1)

$$\dot{x}_s^* = f_s[x^*(t), u^*(t), t] \qquad (s = 1, \ldots, n). \tag{III.8}$$

By differentiating (III.4) with respect to x_i $(i = 1, \ldots, n)$, we get

$$\frac{\partial^2 \Phi_T(x, t)}{\partial x_i \partial t} = -\sum_1^n \frac{\partial^2 \Phi_T(x, t)}{\partial x_i \partial x_s} f_s[x, u^*(t), t] - \\ -\sum_1^n \frac{\partial \Phi_T(x, t)}{\partial x_s} \frac{\partial f_s[x, u^*(t), t]}{\partial x_i}. \tag{III.9}$$

Now, by substituting $x = x^*(t)$ in (III.9), by taking (III.5) into account and by substituting (III.8) and (III.9) into (III.7), we obtain the system of differential equations sought:

$$\dot{p}_i(t) = -\sum_1^n p_s(t) \frac{\partial f_s[x^*(t), u^*(t), t]}{\partial x_i} \qquad (i = 1, \ldots, n). \tag{III.10}$$

But, according to theorem 1 of part I, optimal control $u^*(t)$ satisfies the maximum condition with respect to vector $p(t)$, defined by relationships (III.5) which are subject to system (III.10) of equations and conditions (III.6). Therefore, by substituting $x = x^*(t)$ in (III.4) and by noting that the right member of (III.4) is the expression

$$H[x^*(t), p(t), u^*(t), t] \equiv \sum_1^n p_s(t) f_s[x^*(t), u^*(t), t],$$

we obtain

$$\frac{\partial \Phi_T[x^*(t), t]}{\partial t} = \max_{u \in U} \sum_1^n \left(-\frac{\partial \Phi_T[x^*(t), t]}{\partial x_s}\right) f_s[x^*(t), u, t]. \tag{III.11}$$

In particular, for $t = t_0$, $x^*(t_0) = x^0$,

$$\frac{\partial \Phi_T(x^0, t_0)}{\partial t_0} = \max_{u^0 \in U} \sum_1^n \left(-\frac{\partial \Phi_T(x^0, t_0)}{\partial x_s^0}\right) f_s(x^0, u^0, t_0). \tag{III.12}$$

We now establish the relationship between the functions $\Phi_T(x,t)$ and $S_T(x,t)$. By definition, for any point (x,t) in space L the following equation holds

$$\Phi_T(x, t) \geqslant S_T(x, t), \tag{III.13}$$

for which at points $\underline{x}$, $\underline{t}$ lying along the trajectory we always have:

$$\Phi_T(x, t) = S_T(x, t) \qquad (x = x^*(t)). \tag{III.14}$$

It follows from this that, in the $(n+2)$-dimensional space (z,x,t), the surfaces $z = \Phi_T(x,t)$ and $z = S_T(x,t)$ do not intersect, and have the common curve γ, whose projection on the subspace L gives the optimal trajectory $x = x^*(t)$. In other words, the surfaces $z = \Phi_T(x,t)$ and $z = S_T(x,t)$ are tangent in the curve γ. Now, if the function $S_T(x,t)$ is continuous and differentiable with respect to (x,t) in a neighborhood of the optimal trajectory $x = x^*(t)$ (the continuity and differentiability of the function $\Phi_T(x,t)$ were noted by us above), then the following relationships are valid everywhere on the optimal trajectory

$$\frac{\partial \Phi_T(x, t)}{\partial t} = \frac{\partial S_T(x, t)}{\partial t}, \qquad \frac{\partial \Phi_T(x, t)}{\partial x_i} = \frac{\partial S_T(x, t)}{\partial x_i}$$

$$[i = 1, \ldots, n;\ x = x^*(t)]. \tag{III.15}$$

By assuming, in accordance with the conditions of the theorem that $(x^*(t),t)$ Γ, and by thus guaranteeing that (III.15) holds, we obtain, in correspondence with definition (III.5),

$$p_i(t) = -\frac{\partial S_T[x^*(t), t]}{\partial x_i} \qquad (i = 1, \ldots, n). \tag{III.16}$$

By replacing $\partial\Phi_T/\partial x_i$ and $\partial\Phi_T/\partial t$ in (III.11) by $\partial S_T/\partial x_i$ and $\partial S_T/\partial t$, and by using (III.16), we obtain

$$\frac{\partial S_T [x^*(t), t]}{\partial t} = H(x^*(t), p(t), u^*(t), t]. \qquad \text{(III.17)}$$

Since we have proven that the optimal control satisfies the maximum condition with respect to vector p(t), defined by relationships (III.16), point 1 of theorem 6 is completely proven.

To prove point 2 of the theorem, it suffices to replace the partial derivatives of function Φ_T in (III.12) by the analogous derivatives of the function S_T, in accordance with (III.15). If we note, with this, that the equation obtained remains valid for arbitrary x^0, t_0, and if we discard the superscript (and subscript) 0, we will obtain the identity*

$$\frac{\partial S_T(x, t)}{\partial t} = \max_{u \in U} \sum_{1}^{n} \left(- \frac{\partial S_T(x, t)}{\partial x_s} \right) f_s(x, u, t). \qquad \text{(III.18)}$$

The condition

$$S_T(x, T) = \sum_{1}^{n} c_s x_s \qquad \text{(III.19)}$$

is obvious in view of the definition of function $S_T(x,t)$, if one realizes that, by virtue of continuity, $\lim_{t \to T} S_T(x, t) = S_T(x, T)$. Formulas (III.18) and (III.19) prove point 2. Thus, theorem 6 is completely proved.

LITERATURE CITED

[1] R. Bellman, Dynamic Programing (Princeton University Press, Princeton, New Jersey, 1957).

[2] R. Bellman, J. Glicksberg and O. Gross, "Some aspects of the mathematical theory of control processes," The Rand Corp. Project Rand R-313 (January 16, 1958).

[3] Modern Mathematics for Engineers [Russian translation] edited by B.F. Bekkenback (IL , 1959).

[4] R.V. Gamkrelidze, "Processes optimal with respect to speed of response, with limited phase coordinates," Doklady Akad. Nauk SSSR 125, 3 (1959).

[5] F.M. Kirillova, "On the correctness of the posing of one optimal control problem," Izv. Vysshikh Uchebnykh Zavedenii. Matematika 4 (5) (1958).

[6] N.N. Krasovskii, "On one optimal control problem," Prikl. Matem. i Mekh. 21, 5 (1957).

[7] V.V. Stepanov, Course in Differential Equations [in Russian] (Gostekhizdat, 1954).

[8] B.V. Bulgakov, "On the accumulation of disturbances in linear oscillatory systems with constant parameters," Doklady Akad. Nauk SSSR 51, 5 (1946).

[9] B.V. Bulgakov, Oscillations [in Russian] (Gostekhizdat, 1954).

[10] G.M. Ulanov, "Analysis of automatic control processes given modulus-limited stimuli," in the book: Automatic Control Fundamentals [in Russian], edited by V.V. Solodovnikov, chapter 24 (Mashgiz, 1954).

[11] F.A. Mikhailov, "Integral indicators of automatic control system quality," in the book: Automatic Control Fundamentals [in Russian], edited by V.V. Solodovnikov, chapter 25 (Mashgiz, 1954).

[12] F.A. Mikhailov, "On the limiting values of quadratic estimates of quality, and their application to the choice of parameters of automatic control systems," [in Russian] Trudy of the All-Union Conference on Automatic Control Theory, volume 2 (Izdatelstvo AN SSSR, 1955).

Received June 5, 1959

* In contradistinction to (III.18), one cannot discard the subscript 0 in (III.12) and consider the relationship thus obtained as a partial differential equation defining the function $\Phi_T(x,t)$. Equation (III.12) is not identically valid and, as is clear from (III.11), is valid only for points (x^0, t_0) lying on the optimal trajectory $x = x^*(t)$ which corresponds to some previously fixed optimal control $u^*(t)$.

The 'Bang-Bang' Principle

J. P. LaSalle

Introduction

The control system to be studied is one in which the elements being controlled are linear and in which the steering considered as a function of time enters linearly. The differential equations of such a system are

$$\left(\dot{x} = \frac{\mathrm{d}x}{\mathrm{d}t}\right)$$

$$\dot{x}_i(t) = \sum_{j=1}^{n} a_{ij}(t)x_j(t) + \sum_{k=1}^{r} b_{ik}(t)u_k(t) + f_i(t)$$

$(i = 1, \ldots, n)$. Expressed in terms of matrices and vectors, we have

$$\dot{x}(t) = A(t)x(t) + B(t)u(t) + f(t) \tag{1}$$

where $x(t)$ and $f(t)$ are n-vectors, $u(t)$ is an r-vector, $A(t)$ is an $n \times n$ matrix, and $B(t)$ is an $n \times r$ matrix. The state of the system at time t is described by the n-vector $x(t)$. The function $f(t)$ is some perturbing force. We assume that we can select the steering $u(t)$ as we please subject to the constraint that each component of $u(t)$ satisfy

$$-a_i \leqslant \dot{u}_i(t) \leqslant b_i \quad (i = 1, \ldots, r) \tag{2}$$

where a_i, b_i are positive constants. The problem we wish to consider is as follows: we are given in the n-dimensional phase space of the system a moving particle which at time t is at the point $z(t)$. At time $t = t_0$ the state of the system is $x(t_0) = x_0$. We wish, starting in this initial state, to hit $z(t)$, i.e. to have $x(t_1) = z(t_1)$ at some time $t_1 > t_0$, and we wish to select the steering $u(t)$ so as to do this in minimum time. *Optimal steering* minimizes $t_1 - t_0$. This is a problem in the calculus of variations in which there are constraints on the allowable functions and in which the functional to be minimized is given implicitly. For example, the problem of landing on a satellite in minimum time is a problem of this type. A special case of particular interest is when $f(t) = 0$ and $z(t) = 0$. The initial error is x_0, and we wish to reduce this error to zero as quickly as possible.

Intuitively we feel that optimal steering can only be achieved by at all times using the greatest amount of steering available; i.e. $u_i(t) = b_i(t)$ or $u_i(t) = -a_i(t)$. This we call the 'bang-bang' principle and a control system in which the steering is always an extreme value we call a 'bang-bang' system.

The first person to consider a time-optimal problem of this kind was Bushaw in 1952 in his doctoral dissertation[1] at Princeton University. Bushaw studied the special problem for systems with one degree of freedom. He assumed the bang-bang principle and restricted himself therefore to bang-bang systems. He showed for the special systems he studied, the existence of a best bang-bang system. In 1953 I pointed out[2] that if there is a best bang-bang system then it is the best of all systems subject to the same constraints[2]. For these special systems it is true that optimal steering is unique, and therefore for these systems studied by Bushaw the bang-bang principle does apply: optimal steering is always bang-bang. In this talk we wish to examine this question for more general systems and to discuss some properties of what we call proper systems.

In 1956 Bellman, Glicksberg and Gross[3] gave the first general approach to the time-optimal problem. Unfortunately they restricted themselves more than was necessary, and most practical systems are not of the type they studied. More recently Gamkrelidze[4], Krasovski[5], Pontryagin[6] and LaSalle[7] have studied this problem. Gamkrelidze and Pontryagin study the special problem for autonomous systems of reaching the origin in minimum time. Pontryagin applies his maximum principle to the special problem under more general constraints than those stated above. Krasovski and I study the general problem as stated above.

The 'Bang-Bang' Principle

It is convenient to set $a_i = b_i = 1$, and it is easy to see that there is no loss in generality by doing this. Thus we replace the constraints[2] by

$$|u_i(t)| \leqslant 1 \quad (i = 1 \ldots, r) \tag{3}$$

Also we might as well let $t_0 = 0$. Let us now use $x(t, u)$ to denote the solution of equation 1 satisfying $x(0) = x_0$. Then

$$x(t,u) = X(t)x_0 + X(t)\int_0^t Y(\tau)u(\tau)\,\mathrm{d}\tau + X(t)\int_0^t X^{-1}(\tau)f(\tau)\,\mathrm{d}\tau \tag{4}$$

where $X(t)$ is the principal matrix solution of $\dot{X}(t) = A(t)X(t)$ and $Y(\tau) = X^{-1}(\tau)B(\tau)$. We assume throughout that $A(t)$, $B(t)$ and $f(t)$ are continuous for all $t \geqslant 0$. What we want is to have $x(t_1, u) = z(t_1)$ for some $t_1 \geqslant 0$; i.e. we want

$$w(t_1) = \int_0^{t_1} Y(\tau)u(\tau)\,\mathrm{d}\tau \tag{5}$$

where

$$w(t) = X^{-1}(t)z(t) - x_0 - \int_0^t X^{-1}(\tau)f(\tau)\,\mathrm{d}\tau$$

It is now well known that if there is an allowable steering function satisfying equation 5, then there is an optimal steering function $u^{\star}(t)$ and it is of the form

$$u^{\star}(t) = sgn[\eta Y(t)] \tag{6}$$

for some non-zero n-vector η. The signum is taken by components; i.e. if b is an r-vector, then $a = sgn\, b$ means that $a_j = 1$ when $b_j > 0$ and $a_j = -1$ when $b_j < 0$. We cannot conclude from the form (6) of optimal steering that optimal steering is necessarily bang-bang. In fact, simple examples show that this is not the case. It can be that a component of $\eta Y(t)$ is zero over an interval of positive length, and $u^{\star}(t)$ is then not completely determined by equation 6. We can, however, show that anything that can be accomplished by allowable steering in a given time can be accomplished in the same time by bang-bang steering. This statement will be made precise in a moment. We first need to establish two lemmas.

Lemma 1

Let M be the set of all real-valued measurable functions $\alpha(t)$ on [0, 1] with $|\alpha(t)| \leqslant 1$. Let M^0 be the subset of functions in M with $|\alpha(t)| \equiv 1$. Let $y(t)$ be any n-dimensional function in $L^{-1}([0, 1])$.

Define

$$K = \left\{ \int_0^1 \alpha(t) y(t)\, dt; \quad \alpha \varepsilon M \right\}$$

and

$$K^0 = \left\{ \int_0^1 \alpha^0(t) y(t)\, dt; \quad \alpha^0 \varepsilon M^0 \right\}$$

Then K^0 is closed and $K = K^0$.

Proof—Corresponding to a measurable set E in [0, 1] define

$$\mu(E) = \int_E y(t)\, dt$$

Let R be the range of this vector measure μ, and let $c_E(t)$ be the characteristic function of E. Then $\alpha^0(t) = 2c_E(t) - 1$ is in K^0 and each $\alpha^0(t)$ in K^0 can be represented in this way. Hence we see that $K^0 = 2R - \bar{y}$, where

$$\bar{y} = \int_0^1 y(t)\, dt$$

By a theorem due to Liapunov[8,9] the set R is closed and convex, and therefore K^0 is closed and convex. In order to show that $K = K^0$ we see that we need only show that each z in K is a limit of vectors in K^0. Since K^0 is closed, this will imply that $K \subset K^0$. It is evident that $K^0 \subset K$. Let

$$z = \int_0^1 \alpha(t) y(t)\, dt$$

be any vector in K. Define $\beta(t) = \frac{1}{2}(\alpha(t) + 1)$ and $\bar{z} = \frac{1}{2}(z + \bar{y})$. Note that $0 \leqslant \beta(t) \leqslant 1$ and

$$\bar{z} = \int_0^1 \beta(t) y(t)\, dt \; \varepsilon M$$

Define

$$\bar{z}_m = \sum_{j=1}^{m} \frac{j}{m} \int_{E_j} y(t)\, dt$$

where

$$E_j = \left\{ t; \; \frac{j-1}{m} < \beta(t) \leqslant \frac{j}{m} \right\}$$

Now

$$|\bar{z} - \bar{z}_m| = \sum_{j=1}^{m} \int_{E_j} \left(\frac{j}{m} - \beta(t) \right) y(t)\, dt$$

$$\leqslant \frac{1}{m} \sum_{j=1}^{m} \int_{E_j} |y(t)|\, dt = \frac{1}{m} \int_0^1 |y(t)| dt$$

which shows that $\bar{z}_m \to \bar{z}$ as $m \to \infty$. Letting

$$F_j = \bigcup_{i=j}^{m} E_i$$

we obtain

$$\bar{z}_m = \frac{1}{m} \sum_{j=1}^{m} \int_{F_j} y(t)\, dt$$

Since R is convex, it follows that $\bar{z}_m$ is in R. Therefore $z_m = 2\bar{z}_m - \bar{y}$ is in K^0 and $z_m \to z$ as $m \to \infty$. This completes the proof.

For our purposes we wish to generalize this lemma in the following manner.

Let U be the set of all r-dimensional vector functions $u(\tau)$ measurable on each finite interval $[0, t]$ with $|u_i(\tau)| \leqslant 1$. Let U^0 be the subset of functions $u^0(\tau)$ in U with $|u_i(\tau)| \equiv 1$. With reference to the control problem U is the set of allowable steering functions and U^0 is the set of bang-bang steering functions. Define

$$\Gamma(t) = \left\{ \int_0^t Y(\tau) u(\tau)\, d\tau; \quad u \varepsilon U \right\}$$

and

$$\Gamma^0(t) = \left\{ \int_0^t Y(z) u^0(\tau)\, d\tau; \quad u^0 \varepsilon U^0 \right\}$$

By equations 3 and 4 we see that the state z can be reached in time t using allowable steering if, and only if,

$$w = X^{-1}(t) z - x_0 - \int_0^t X^{-1}(\tau) f(\tau)\, d\tau$$

is in $\Gamma(t)$. The state can be reached in time t using bang-bang steering if and only if w is in $\Gamma^0(t)$. Thus the following lemma is the precise statement of the fact that anything that can be accomplished in time t by allowable steering can also be accomplished in the same time by bang-bang steering.

Lemma 2

$\Gamma^0(t) = \Gamma(t)$ and $\Gamma(t)$ is closed and convex.

Proof—Define

$$\Gamma_j(t) = \left\{ \int_0^t y^j(\tau) u_j(\tau)\, d\tau; \quad u \varepsilon U \right\}$$

and

$$\Gamma_j^0(t) = \left\{ \int_0^t y^j(\tau) u_j^0(\tau)\, d\tau; \quad u^0 \varepsilon U^0 \right\}$$

Since

$$\int_0 Y(\tau) u(\tau)\, d\tau = \sum_{j=1}^{r} \int_0^t y^j(\tau) u_j(\tau)\, d\tau$$

and since the components of $u(\tau)$ in U can be selected independently

$$\Gamma(t) = \Gamma_1(t) + \Gamma_2(t) + \ldots + \Gamma_r(t)$$

and

$$\Gamma^0(t) = \Gamma_1^0(t) + \Gamma_2^0(t) + \ldots + \Gamma_r^0(t)$$

As a consequence of Lemma 1, $\Gamma_j(t) = \Gamma_j^0(t)$ for each j, and therefore, $\Gamma(t) = \Gamma^0(t)$. Also since each $\Gamma_j(t)$ is bounded and by Lemma 1 closed and convex, it follows easily that $\Gamma(t)$ is closed and convex. This completes the proof.

This lemma states with reference to the control problem that if a state can be reached in time t by allowable steering then the state can be reached in time t by bang-bang steering.

Combined with the existence theorem for optimal control that was stated above, we then have the following theorem.

Theorem 1

If there is an allowable steering function u for which

$$x(t_1, u) = z(t)$$

for some $t > 0$, then there is a bang-bang steering function that is optimal.

If it is possible to reach the objective in finite time, then there is a bang-bang steering function that achieves the objective in minimum time. The intuitive hypothesis is usually somewhat stronger than this. The feeling is not only that there is always bang-bang steering that is optimal but that no other type of steering can be optimal. If, at some time, all of the steering is not used, then by using properly the additional steering available it should be possible to reduce the time of reaching the objective. This is not, in general, true since in some cases there is no advantage to having additional steering.

Suppose, however, that the control system has the property that any component of $\eta Y(t)$ zero on an interval of positive length implies $\eta = 0$. This is equivalent to the condition that for each $j = 1 \ldots, r$ the functions $y_1^j(t) \ldots, y_n^j(t)$ are linearly independent on each interval of positive length; $y_i^j(t)$ is the element on the ith row and jth column of $Y(t)$. If this condition is satisfied, then we say that the system is *normal.* In the case of constant coefficients, A and B constant matrices, a system is normal if and only if for each j the vectors b^j, $Ab^j, \ldots, A^{n-1}b^j$ are linearly independent; b^j is the jth column vector in the matrix B (see reference 10). This condition for constant coefficients is a special case of Pontryagin's Condition A[6]. Thus, if a system is normal, optimal steering is uniquely determined by equation 6 and must be bang-bang. For normal systems there is a strict bang-bang principle: optimal steering is always bang-bang.

As an example consider a system of one degree of freedom

$$\ddot{x} + a\dot{x} + bx = u$$

Letting $x_1 = x$ and $x_2 = \dot{x}$, we have the equivalent system

$$\dot{x}_1 = x_2$$
$$\dot{x}_2 = -bx_1 - ax_2 + u$$

Here

$$A = \begin{pmatrix} 0 & 1 \\ -b & -a \end{pmatrix}, \quad B = \begin{pmatrix} 0 \\ 1 \end{pmatrix}, \quad b^1 = \begin{pmatrix} 0 \\ 1 \end{pmatrix} \quad \text{and} \quad Ab^1 = \begin{pmatrix} 1 \\ -a \end{pmatrix}$$

The vectors b^1 and Ab^1 are linearly independent and the system is normal. An example of a system that is not normal is

$$\dot{x}_1 = -x_1 + u_2$$
$$\dot{x}_2 = -2x_2 + u_1 + u_2$$

$$A = \begin{pmatrix} -1 & 0 \\ 0 & -2 \end{pmatrix} \quad \text{and} \quad B = \begin{pmatrix} 0 & 1 \\ 1 & 1 \end{pmatrix}$$

$$b^1 = \begin{pmatrix} 0 \\ 1 \end{pmatrix}, \quad Ab^1 = \begin{pmatrix} 0 \\ -2 \end{pmatrix}, \quad b^2 = \begin{pmatrix} 1 \\ 1 \end{pmatrix}, \quad Ab^2 = \begin{pmatrix} -1 \\ -2 \end{pmatrix}$$

The system is not normal since b^1, Ab^1 are linearly dependent. In fact,

$$\eta Y(t) = \begin{pmatrix} \eta_1 e^t + \eta_2 e^{2t} \\ \eta_2 e^{2t} \end{pmatrix}$$

and the second component vanishes for $\eta_2 = 0$.

Another condition of some importance is obtained by the assumption that $\eta Y(t) \equiv 0$ on an interval of positive length implies $\eta = 0$. A system with this property we call a *proper* system. Although this is not required for this existence theorem (see reference 7), Krasovski[5] restricted himself to the study of proper systems. His method of proof using Krein's results on the L-problem in abstract spaces required this condition.

A system is proper if, and only if, the row vectors $y_1(t) \ldots, y_n(t)$ of $Y(t)$ are linearly independent functions on each interval of positive length. When A and B are constant matrices, this is equivalent to the condition that the set of vectors $b^1 \ldots, b^r$, $Ab^1 \ldots, Ab^r \ldots, A^{n-1}b^1 \ldots, A^{n-1}b^r$ contain a set of n linearly independent vectors (see reference 10). It is obvious that every normal system is proper. From the example above we see that a system can be proper and not normal.

For proper control systems we have a bang-bang principle which is more like what one would suspect: in proper control systems there is always at least one component of optimal steering that assumes an extreme value.

Proper Systems

Previously[10] we investigated some properties of proper control systems of the form (1). Suppose for the moment that there are no constraints on the allowable control functions. We had shown that *proper control systems are completely controllable,* which means that if x_1 and x_2 are any two states and t_1 and t_2 are any two times $t_1 \neq t_2$ then, if the system is in the state x_1 at time t_1, there is a steering function which brings it to the state x_2 at time t_2. Thus with no constraint on the steering functions a proper control system can be steered from any one state to any other, and this can be accomplished as rapidly as desired.

Consider the same general problem discussed in the second section of hitting a moving particle $z(t)$ in the phase space, we wish to obtain a result on optimal steering under a more general constraint. Let the allowable steering functions be those whose values $u(t)$ are in a set U. We shall now show that

Theorem 2

If (1) *is a proper control system and if U is a bounded convex set, then optimal steering has values which are always on the boundary of U; more precisely, if $u^\star$ is optimal, then $u^\star(t)$ cannot be in the interior of U for a positive interval of time.*

Proof—Suppose that $u^\star$ is an optimal steering function and that $t^\star$ is the minimal time. Then

$$w(t^\star) = \int_0^{t^\star} Y(t)u^\star(t)\,dt$$

Suppose further that within some interval $[a, b]$ of positive length within $[0, t^\star]$ that the values of $u^\star(t)$ are interior points of U. Define for any nonzero vector η

$$\delta u^\star(t) = \begin{cases} \varepsilon\, sgn\, [\eta Y(t)], & t \text{ in } [a, b] \\ 0, & \text{otherwise.} \end{cases}$$

Then for $\varepsilon > 0$ and sufficiently small $u^\star(t) + \delta u^\star(t)$ is an allowable steering function. Hence $w(t^\star) + \delta w(t^\star)$, where

$$\delta w(t^\star) = \varepsilon \int_a^b Y(t)\, sgn\, [\eta Y(t)]\,dt$$

is in $\Gamma(t^\star)$. The fact that the system is proper implies that $\eta \delta w(t^\star) > 0$. Since $\Gamma(t^\star)$ is convex due to the convexity of U, it follows that $w(t^\star)$ is an interior point of $\Gamma(t^\star)$. But, just as in reference 10 (see Lemma 3), this implies the existence of a $t < t^\star$ with $w(t)$ in $\Gamma(t)$. This contradicts the optimality of $u^\star$, and completes the proof.

If one assumes that U is a closed and bounded (compact) set of r-dimensional Euclidean space, then it is not difficult to show that, if there is an allowable steering function $u(u(t)\varepsilon U)$ with $z(t) = x(t, u)$, then there is an optimal steering function. If, in addition, U were convex and the system were proper, we should know by Theorem 2 that the values of optimal steering were on the boundary of U.

Consider the special case

$$\dot{x} = Ax + Bu \tag{7}$$

where A and B are constant matrices and the objective is starting initially at x_0 to reach the origin in minimum time. As before, let U be the set of allowable values of the steering function. Then we can prove Theorem 2 for this special problem without any assumptions on U.

Theorem 3

If the system[7] is proper, then optimal steering for the special problem has its values on the boundary of U.

Proof—Let $u^\star$ be optimal steering, and let $t^\star$ be the minimal time to reach the origin. Suppose that for t in $[t_0, t_1]$, $0 \leqslant t_0 < t_1 < t^\star$ $u^\star(t)$ is in the interior of U. Let $x(t, u^\star)$ be the optimal trajectory. Now we can show that we can start at x_0 and reach a point on the optimal trajectory beyond $x(t_1, u^\star)$ in time less than t_1. But this will contradict the optimality of $u^\star(t)$. In the time interval $[t_0, t_1]$ we restrict $u(t)$ to $\|u(t) - u^\star(t)\| < \varepsilon$ and otherwise let $u(t) = u^\star(t)$. Then these $u(t)$ are allowable for ε sufficiently small, and the set of states starting at x_0 that can be reached in time t_1 is a convex set U_1 containing $x(t_1, u^\star)$. Just as in the proof of Theorem 2 it follows that U_1 contains a neighbourhood of $x(t_1, u^\star)$ and hence some $x(t, u^\star)$ with $t > t_1$. This contradiction completes the proof.

For this special problem it is also not difficult to establish that

Theorem 4

If (*a*) *the system is proper,* (*b*) *the uncontrolled system* $\dot{x} = Ax$ *is asymptotically stable, and* (*c*) U *contains a neighbourhood of the origin, then for any initial state* x_0 *there is an allowable steering function that brings the system to the origin in finite time.*

Proof—Let N be a convex neighbourhood of the origin contained in U. Then again it is easy to see from (*a*) that the set of all states from which the origin can be reached in time $t_1 > 0$ using steering with values in N contains a neighbourhood N_1 of the origin. Since the uncontrolled system is asymptotically stable, with no steering the system will reach N_1 in finite time from any initial state, and hence with allowable steering reach the origin in finite time. This completes the proof.

This research was partially supported by the United States Air Force through the Air Force Office of Scientific Research of the Air Research and Development Command, under Contract Number AF49-(638)-382. Reproduction in whole or in part is permitted for any purpose of the United States Government.

References

1 BUSHAW, D. W. *Ph.D. Thesis,* Department of Mathematics, Princeton University, 1952. *Contributions to the Theory of Nonlinear Oscillations,* Vol. IV, *Optimal Discontinuous Forcing Terms.* Princeton, 1958

2 LASALLE, J. P. *Study of the Basic Principle Underlying the 'Bang-Bang' Servo,* Goodyear Aircraft Corporation Report GER-5518 (July 1953). Abstract 247t, *Bull. Amer. math. Soc.* 60 (1954) 154

3 BELLMAN, R., GLICKSBERG, I. and GROSS, O. On the 'bang-bang' control problem. *Quart. Appl. Math.* 14 (1956) 11

4 GAMKRELIDZE, R. V. Theory of time-optimal processes for linear systems. *Bull. Acad. Sci. U.R.S.S.* Ser. Math. 22 (1958) 449 (in Russian)

5 KRASOVSKI, N. N. Concerning the theory of optimal control *Automat. Telemech., Moscow* 18 (1957) 960 (in Russian)

6 PONTRYAGIN, L. S. Optimal processes of regulation. *Progr. math. Sci., Moscow* 14 (1959) 3 (in Russian)

7 LASALLE, J. P. Time optimal control systems. *Proc. nat. Acad. Sci., Wash.* 45 (1959) 573

8 LIAPUNOV, A. Sur les fonctions-vecteurs completement additives. *Bull Acad. Sci. U.R.S.S.* Ser. Math. 4 (1940) 465

9 HALMOS, R. P. The range of a vector measure. *Bull. Amer. math. Soc.* 54 (1948) 416

10 LASALLE, J. P. *Contributions to the Theory of Nonlinear Oscillations,* Vol. V, *The Time-Optimal Control Problem.* Princeton, 1959

The Maximum Principle in the Theory of Optimal Processes of Control

V. G. BOLTYANSKII, R. V. GAMKRELIDZE, E. F. MISHCHENKO and L. S. PONTRYAGIN

Introduction

The use of automatic control contributes very significantly to optimal actuation of a controlled process. At the same time, for every practical technical problem coming within the notion of an optimal process, various qualifications must be attached to this significance, depending upon the aim in view. For example, if the controlled process is most advantageously carried out in a short time interval, then, naturally, under the optimal process, it is made to take place in the minimum possible time—the so-called optimal high-speed process. If the controlled process is to be carried out with the least possible expenditure of energy, fuel, etc., then, it follows, the optimal process is the one which minimizes expenditure of energy, fuel consumption, etc.

Modern automatic control set-ups frequently make use of composite controls, and it is often not possible to work out optimal control experimentally or by numerical methods without a detailed theoretical investigation. This has, for some time now, led to the necessity to develop a general mathematical theory for optimal control processes.

The authors' investigations go in this direction, within the ordinary differential control section of the Mathematics Institute of the Academy of Sciences of the USSR, under the leadership of Academician L. S. Pontryagin.

The paper gives an account of the general optimal problem and presents the principal results obtained by the authors[1–8].

Important results, partially overlapping those given[1–8], have been obtained by Bellman, Glicksberg and Grosse and are summarized in their joint monograph[9]. The recent work of LaSalle[10] merits attention and earlier work by Feldbaum[11], Bushaw[12] and Lerner[13] should also be noted.

Statement of the problem. The maximum principle

Initial considerations

We assume that the controlled object is described by the phase point $x = (x' \ldots, x'')$ of the n-dimensional phase space X^n, the equations of motion of which have the form

$$\dot{x}^i = f^i(x^1 \ldots, x^n;\ u^1 \ldots, u^n) = f^i(x, u) \quad i = 1 \ldots, n \tag{1}$$

Here $u = (u' \ldots, u^n)$ is the control vector. If the control law is given, i.e. n functions $u^1(t) \ldots, u^n(t)$ are given from a certain class of functions, then system 1, under given initial conditions, unambiguously defines the motion of point x in the phase space. The class of functions from which the control functions $u^i(t)$ are chosen depends on the particular technical problem involved. An inherent condition is the requirement that the control vector $u(t) = [u^1(t) \ldots, u^n(t)]$ should relate to a certain fixed, closed region of n-dimensional space, for example to an n-dimensional cube $|u^i(t)| \leqslant 1$.

In the general mathematical statement of the problem (see below), the region of possible significance of the vector $u(t)$ may be an arbitrary (but fixed) sub-set of the n-dimensional space.

Further, the controlling functions $u^i(t)$ can be chosen from a class of piece-wise continuous functions with a finite number of points of discontinuity. This relates to 'inertia-free' control where the controlling parameters can jump instantaneously from one value to another. However, in a number of cases it is necessary to consider the inertia of certain controlling parameters; in this case, some of the functions $u^i(t)$ must be taken as continuous and piece-wise smooth with a finite derivative.

Thus, when formulating the optimal problem, the class of vector functions $u(t)$ from which controls for a given problem are chosen must be clearly defined. This class is called the class of permissible controls.

Having fixed the class of permissible controls, the optimal problem comprises the choosing of a permissible control such that a suitable phase path connects two given points in the phase space and that the chosen control and appropriate phase path minimizes the demand (time, energy, etc.).

Formulation of the optimal problem

Let Ω be an arbitrary sub-set of the n-dimensional linear space. In additional interesting cases Ω may be a closed region (not necessarily finite) with a piece-wise smooth boundary.

The class of permissible controls is designated as a set of all the piece-wise continuous functions $u(t) = [u'(t) \ldots, u^n(t)]$ having discontinuities of the first order, lying on an arbitrary segment $t_1 \leqslant t \leqslant t_2$ of the time axis and, at every instant, taking their values from Ω.

Equation 1 can be rewritten in vector form

$$\dot{x} = f(x, u) \qquad f = (f^1 \ldots f^n) \tag{2}$$

and it will be assumed that the functions $f^i(x, u)$ are definite and continuous for all points $(x, u) \epsilon X^n . \Omega$ and are also continuously differentiated along all coordinates of the vector $x = (x^1 \ldots, x^n)$.

In addition, let it be assumed that the given scalar function $f^0(x, u)$ satisfies the same conditions as the functions $f^i(x, u)$, $i = 1 \ldots, n$.

The optimal problem can be formulated in the following way. ξ_1, ξ_2 are two given points in X^n; from the class of permissible controls, it is necessary to select a control $u(t)$, $t_1 \leqslant t \leqslant t_2$, for which there is a suitable path $x(t)$ from equation 2, defined over the whole segment $t_1 \leqslant t \leqslant t_2$ and joining the points ξ_1, ξ_2: $x(t_1) = \xi_1$, $x(t_2) = \xi_2$, and the integral

$$\int_{t_1}^{t_2} f^0[x(t), u(t)]\, dt \tag{3}$$

reduces to a minimum. (It should be noted that, in this formulation, the segment $t_1 \leqslant t \leqslant t_2$, depending on the choice of the permissible control, is not fixed; only the boundary conditions for the path $x(t)$ are fixed.)

All permissible controls satisfying the formulation of the problem are called optimal controls; the corresponding path is called the optimal path.

Depending on the choice of the function $f^0(x, u)$, the integral 3 can indicate the expenditure of time, energy, fuel, etc., during the course of the process under consideration. For example, if $f^0(x, u) \equiv 1$, then the integral is equal to $t_2 - t_1$, i.e. the process occurs in minimum time.

The necessary conditions which satisfy every optimal control and its corresponding optimal path are given by the fundamental theorem 1, which we call the maximum principle, since its basic content leads to equation 8.

The maximum principle—To formulate the theorem we first consider the vector $\bar{x} = (x^0, x^1 \ldots, x^n)$ of the $(n+1)$ dimensional space X^{n+1}. Obviously, if the coordinates of the vector $\bar{x}$ satisfy the system

$$\dot{x}^i = f^i(x^1 \ldots, x^n, u) = f^i(x, u) \qquad i = 0 \ldots, n \tag{4}$$

with the initial condition

$$x^0(t_1) = 0, \qquad [x^1(t_1) \ldots, x^n(t_1)] = \xi_1$$

then the vector $x = (x^1 \ldots, x^n)$ satisfies control equation 2 and, by the initial condition $x(t_1) = \xi_1$, also the coordinate

$$x^0(t) = \int_{t_1}^{t} f^0[x(\Theta), u(\Theta)]\, d\Theta \tag{5}$$

We define the covariant vector of the space X^{n+1} from $\bar{\psi} = (\psi_0 \ldots, \psi_n)$ and determine the scalar function

$$H(\bar{\psi}, x, u) = \sum_{\alpha=0}^{n} \psi_\alpha f^\alpha(x, u)$$

Equation 4 can now be written in the form

$$\dot{x}^i = \frac{\partial H(\bar{\psi}, x, u)}{\partial \psi_i} \qquad i = 0 \ldots, n \tag{6}$$

We can also write equation 6 for $(n+1)$ cases as

$$\dot{\psi}_i = -\frac{\partial H(\bar{\psi}, x, u)}{\partial x^i} \qquad i = 0 \ldots, n \tag{7}$$

Equations 6 and 7 together form a Hamiltonian system of equations with the Hamiltonian function H. Since $H(\bar{\psi}, x, u)$ does not depend on the coordinate x^0 of the vector $\bar{x}$, $\dot{\psi}_0 = 0$, i.e. $\psi_0(t) = \text{const.}$

If, in the function H, $\bar{\psi}$ and x are taken to be constant but are allowed to vary, H becomes a function of only the one variable u; we will define the exact upper limit of the values of H, when u is changed to the region Ω, by $U(\bar{\psi}, x)$:

$$U(\bar{\psi}, x) = \sup_{u, \varepsilon, \Omega} H(\bar{\psi}, x, u)$$

Theorem 1 (maximum principle)—Let $u(t)$ for $t_1 \leqslant t \leqslant t_2$ be the optimal control $x(t) = [x^1(t) \ldots, x^n(t)]$ the appropriate optimal path of equation 2. A finite, continuous covariant function $\bar{\psi}(t) = [\psi_0(t) \ldots, \psi_n(t)]$ will then be found such that the coordinates $x^1(t) \ldots, x^n(t)$ of the vector $x(t)$ and the coordinate $x^0(t)$, determined by equation 5, satisfy the segment $t_1 \leqslant t \leqslant t_2$ in the Hamiltonian system

$$\left.\begin{aligned} \dot{x}^i &= \frac{\partial H(\bar{\psi}, x, u)}{\partial \psi_i} \\ \dot{\psi}_i &= -\frac{\partial H(\bar{\psi}, x, u)}{\partial x^i} \end{aligned}\right\} i = 0, 1 \ldots, n$$

and the condition of a maximum

$$H[\bar{\psi}(t), x(t), u(t)] = U[\bar{\psi}(t), x(t)] \tag{8}$$

At the same time, it is found that $U[\bar{\psi}(t), x(t)] \equiv 0$ and $\psi_0(t) = \text{const.} \leqslant 0$.

Observation 1—The maximum principle is justified on the basis of assumptions even more general than those given here, namely, the range of possible values of Ω, the control vector, can include an arbitrary Hausdorff topological space, and the class of permissible controls can be expanded to that of finite and measurable controls. This last class is very useful when the maximum principle is applied to the theory of real optimal processes[3,5].

However, on restricting the class of permissible controls to e.g. continuous controls with a piece-wise smooth finite derivative ('inertia' control), the maximum principle ceases to be true. The class of 'inertia' controls can be dealt with with the help of theorems 2 and 3 below.

Observation 2—From theorem 1 it is possible to obtain far-reaching conclusions for linear systems. These results were obtained[2,3,6,9–12] prior to the proof of theorem 1.

Observation 3—If Ω is an open region of the n-dimensional space, the formulated problem is equivalent to Lagrange's problem of variational calculus, and the maximum principle conforms in this case with the well known criterion of Weierstrass. The fundamental difference between our formulation of the optimal problem and Lagrange's lies in the arbitrariness of magnitude Ω. The overwhelming majority of applied problems do not have a solution when Ω is an open number. There is then a solution to the problem only if the region Ω is closed and, as a rule, the optimal control lies on the boundary of Ω. Obviously, in the case of a closed Ω, the criterion of Weierstrass is inappropriate and optimal controls and paths should be sought by means of the maximum principle.

Optimal Problem in the case of Finite Phase Coordinates

Preliminary remarks

It is often necessary to limit not only the range of possible values Ω of the control vector $u(t)$ but also the range of possible values of the phase point x. In other words, it is possible to choose only such permissible controls for which the appropriate phase path of equation 2 lies completely within a fixed, *closed* region G of the n-dimensional phase space X^n.

In this case, the optimal problem comprises the choice of permissible controls such as that the appropriate path lies in the closed region G and links two given points, whereby equation 3 is minimized. In the majority of cases, region G has a piece-wise smooth boundary. For the sake of simplicity we confine ourselves to this condition.

The case of an optimal problem with inertia control, in the sense of observation 1 to theorem 1, is readily brought into the formulated problem. Actually, if $G = X^n$ and the permissible controls $u(t)$ are continuous, piece-wise smooth functions with a finite derivative, whose parameter u we will take as the phase variable and the derivative of u as the controlling parameter; then, instead of equation 2, we have the system

$$\dot{x} = f(x, u) \qquad \dot{u} = v$$

where v is a piece-wise continuous function, and part of the phase coordinates of the generating vector u are included in the region Ω.

Formulation of the problem

We will designate as permissible controls the set of all piece-wise continuous, piece-wise smooth controls with significance in the given (arbitrary) region Ω of n-dimensional space. We define the range of possible values of the phase point by G and assume that G is a closed region with a smooth boundary fixed within the boundary limits of the inequality

$$g(x' \ldots, x^n) = g(x) \leqslant 0$$

where the function $g(x)$ has continuous second partial derivatives within of limits of the boundary $g(x) = 0$ and the vector

$$\operatorname{grad} g(x) = \left(\frac{\partial g}{\partial x^1} \ldots, \frac{\partial g}{\partial x^n}\right)$$

does not become zero anywhere at the boundary. In addition, we will now assume that the functions $f^i(x, u)$, $i = 0 \ldots, n$ are continuously differentiable by all the arguments x^i, u^j within a certain limit of the direct product $G \,.\, \Omega$.

Let there be two points ξ_1, ξ_2 given in the region G. A permissible control $u(t)$, $t_1 \leqslant t \leqslant t_2$ is to be chosen for which the appropriate path $x(t)$ of equation 2 lies completely within the closed region G and links the points ξ_1, ξ_2 while the integral 3 becomes a minimum.

As in section 1, such a control and the appropriate path will be referred to as 'optimal'.

Optimal paths lying on the boundary of region G

We will start with the criterion

$$p(x, u) = \sum_{\alpha=1}^{n} \frac{\partial g(x)}{\partial x^\alpha} f^\alpha(x, u)$$

If the path $x(t)$, $t_1 \leqslant t \leqslant t_2$ of equation 2, appropriate to control $u(t)$, is to lie completely within the boundary $g(x) = 0$ of region G, it is necessary and sufficient that

$$p[x(t), u(t)] = 0, \qquad t_1 \leqslant t \leqslant t_2, \qquad g[x(t_1)] = 0$$

We will call point x of boundary $g(x) = 0$ 'regular', relative to point $u \epsilon \Omega$, if the following conditions 1–3 are fulfilled:

(1) $p(x, u_0) = 0$

(2) the vector $\left(\frac{\partial p(x, u_0)}{\partial u^1} \ldots, \frac{\partial p(x, u_0)}{\partial u^n}\right) \neq 0$

(3) if u_0 is a boundary point of the region Ω, such continuously differentiable functions $q_i(u)$, $i = 1 \ldots, s$ exist that $q_1(u_0) = \ldots = q_s(u_0) = 0$, the vectors

$$\left(\frac{\partial p(x, u_0)}{\partial u^1} \ldots, \frac{\partial p(x, u_0)}{\partial u^n}\right), \quad \operatorname{grad} q_1(u_0) \ldots, \operatorname{grad} q_s(u_0)$$

are independent, and the region Ω will be fixed not far from u_0 by the system of inequalities

$$q_1(u) \leqslant 0 \ldots, q_s(u) \leqslant 0$$

Let $\omega(x)$ denote the set of those values $u \epsilon \Omega$, with respect to which the point x is regular. The path $x(t)$, $t_1 \leqslant t \leqslant t_2$ of equation 2, appropriate to the control $u(t)$ and lying completely within the boundary of region G, will be called regular if, at any instant t of the segment $t_1 \leqslant t \leqslant t_2$,

$$u(t \pm 0) \epsilon \omega[x(t)]$$

Finally, we have the criterion

$$m(\bar{\psi}, x) = \sup_{u \epsilon \omega(x)} H(\bar{\psi}, x, u)$$

If x is a regular point of the boundary $g(x) = 0$ with respect to the point $u \epsilon \Omega$, and $H(\bar{\psi}, x, u) = m(\bar{\psi}, x)$, then, according to Lagrange's law of multipliers, there exist real numbers λ, $\nu_1 \ldots, \nu_s$ such that

$$\frac{\partial H(\bar{\psi}, x, u)}{\partial u^i} = \lambda \frac{\partial p(x, u)}{\partial u^i} + \sum_{\alpha=1}^{s} \nu_\alpha \frac{\partial q_\alpha(u)}{\partial u^i} \qquad i = 1 \ldots, n \tag{9}$$

From these definitions it is possible to formulate the second theorem.

Theorem 2—For every regular optimal path $x(t) = [x^1(t) \ldots, x^n(t)]$, $t_1 \leqslant t \leqslant t_2$ of equation 2, lying completely on the boundary $g(x) = 0$ and appropriate to the optimal control $u(t)$, there will be a continuous non-zero covariant function $\psi(t) = [\psi_0(t) \ldots, \psi_n(t)]$, $t_1 \leqslant t \leqslant t_2$, such that the coordinates $x'(t) \ldots, x^n(t)$ and the variable $x^0(t)$ defined by equation 5 satisfy the segment $t_1 \leqslant t \leqslant t_2$ in equations 10–12 and the further conditions a, b, c:

$$\dot{x}^i = \frac{\partial H(\bar{\psi}, x, u)}{\partial \psi_i} \qquad i = 0 \ldots, n \tag{10}$$

$$\dot{\psi}_i = \frac{\partial H(\bar{\psi}, x, u)}{\partial x^i} + \lambda(t) \frac{\partial p(x, u)}{\partial x^i} \qquad i = 0 \ldots, n \tag{11}$$

$$H[\bar{\psi}(t), x(t), u(t)] \equiv m[\bar{\psi}(t), x(t)] \equiv 0 \tag{12}$$

where the piece-wise continuous, piece-wise smooth function $\lambda(t)$ is uniquely defined from the maximum condition 12 as Lagrange's multiplier in formula 9; and

(*a*) the coordinate $\psi_0(t) = \text{const} \leqslant 0$

(*b*) the vector $\bar{\psi}(t_1)$ is not co-linear to the vector of the normal $\operatorname{grad} g[x(t_1)]$ to the boundary $g(x) = 0$ at the point $x(t_1)$,

(*c*) for any value of t on the segment $t_1 \leqslant t \leqslant t_2$, the vector

$$\frac{d\lambda(t)}{dt} \operatorname{grad} g[x(t)]$$

is directed inwards in the region G or is equal to zero.

Observation 1—The maximum condition 12 reduces to unity (in u) if $\bar{\psi}(t) \equiv 0$, $t_1 \leqslant t \leqslant t_2$, and therefore it becomes void. It is easy to show that, if $\bar{\psi}(t_1) \neq 0$, then $\bar{\psi}(t) \neq 0$ for any value of t; similarly, from $\psi(t_1) = 0$, it follows that $\bar{\psi}(t) \equiv 0$.

Observation 2—For clarification of the significance of condition G, it may be remarked that the system 10–12 has the following trivial solution $u(t), x^0(t) \ldots, x^n(t)$, $\bar{\psi}(t) = \nu\{0, \operatorname{grad} g[x(t)]\}$,

$$\lambda(t) = \nu \qquad t_1 \leqslant t \leqslant t_2$$

where ν is an arbitrary number. If $u(t), x^0(t) \ldots, x^n(t)$, $\bar{\psi}(t)$, $\lambda(t)$ is a solution of the system 10–12, we also have the solution

$$u(t), x^0(t) \ldots, x^n(t), \bar{\psi}(t) + \nu\{0, \operatorname{grad} g[x(t)]\}, \quad \lambda(t) + \nu$$

where ν is an arbitrary number. Regarding observation 1, it is possible to prove that, if $\bar{\psi}(t_1) = \nu\{0, \operatorname{grad} g[x(t_1)]\}$, then

$$\bar{\psi}(t) \equiv \nu\{0, \operatorname{grad} g[x(t)]\}$$

i.e. $\bar{\psi}(t)$ is a trivial solution.

Observation 3—Condition c arises in consequence of the fact that, during derivation of the necessary conditions, the path lying on the boundary $g(x) = 0$ is compared not only with neighbouring paths at the boundary of the region G but with all the nearby paths lying in the closed region G.

Condition of discontinuity

We are still short of one condition enabling us to trace the optimal trajectory uniquely: the condition which such a trajectory has to satisfy at the instant of approach, from inside towards the boundary of the region G (or, on the contrary, by crossing from the boundary to inside the region). We call this the condition of discontinuity for the covariant function $\bar{\psi}(t)$ which can, at this instant, be subject to a discontinuity.

Let $x(t) = [x^1(t) \ldots, x^n(t)]$, $t_1 \leqslant t \leqslant t_2$ be the trajectory of equation 2 lying completely within the closed region G. We will call the point $x(\tau)$ of the trajectory, lying on the boundary $g(x) = 0$, the *junction point* if $t_1 < \tau < t_2$ and if the condition $\varepsilon > 0$ is satisfied, if at least one section of the trajectory $x(t)$—with $\tau - \varepsilon < t < \tau$ or $\tau < t < \tau + \varepsilon$—lies in the open centre of region G. To be precise, we assume that, when $\tau - \varepsilon < t < \tau$, the section does lie in the open centre. We will call the time τ the instant of junction, and consider a path with a finite number of junction points.

The maximum interval of the segment $t_1 \leqslant t \leqslant t_2$, containing a single instant of junction τ, we denote by $\tau_1 < t < \tau_2$. Hence, the section of the path when $\tau_1 \leqslant t \leqslant \tau$ lies in the open centre of the region G (except the end $x(\tau)$ and possibly the beginning $x(\tau_1)$) and therefore satisfies the principle of a maximum. The non-zero function relating to this section

$$\bar{\psi}^-(t) = [\psi_0^-(t) \ldots, \psi_n^-(t)] \qquad \tau_1 \leqslant t \leqslant \tau \tag{13}$$

is continuous and satisfies equations 6–7.

The section $x(t)$, $\tau \leqslant t \leqslant \tau_2$ satisfies either the requirements of theorem 2 (if it lies on the boundary $g(x) = 0$) or the principle of a maximum (if it lies in the open centre of the region G). The relevant, continuous, non-zero function

$$\bar{\psi}^+(t) = [\psi_0^+(t) \ldots, \psi_n^+(t)] \qquad \tau \leqslant t \leqslant \tau_2 \tag{14}$$

satisfies either equations 10–12 or the conditions *a–c* of theorem 2 or the principle of a maximum.

We assume that, at the junction point $x(\tau)$ of the optimal regular path $x(t)$, $t_1 \leqslant t \leqslant t_2$ lying completely within the closed region G, a condition of discontinuity is fulfilled if a section $x(t)$, $\tau_1 \leqslant t \leqslant \tau_2$ of the path exists such that $\tau_1 < t < \tau_2$ is the maximum interval of the segment $t_1 \leqslant t \leqslant t_2$, containing a single instant of junction, and if, for the sections $x(t)$, $\tau_1 \leqslant t \leqslant \tau$ and $x(t)$, $\tau \leqslant t \leqslant \tau_2$, definite higher functions 13, 14 can be selected, such that one of the following two conditions is satisfied

$$\bar{\psi}^+(\tau) = \bar{\psi}^-(\tau) + \mu\{0, \operatorname{grad} g[x(\tau)]\}$$

$$\bar{\psi}^-(\tau) + \mu\{0, \operatorname{grad} g[x(\tau)]\} = 0 \qquad \mu \neq 0$$

If the section $x(t)$, $\tau \leqslant t \leqslant \tau_2$ lies on the boundary $g(x) = 0$, the first condition, according to observation 2 to theorem 2, is equivalent to the identity

$$\bar{\psi}^+(\tau) = \bar{\psi}^-(\tau)$$

The path of equation 2, lying completely within the closed region G, is called regular if its every section lying on the boundary $g(x) = 0$ is regular.

Theorem 3—Let the regular optimal path of equation 2, lying within the closed region G, contain a finite number of points of junction. A condition of discontinuity is then fulfilled at every junction point.

Observation—Well known conditions of refraction of extremals in variational calculus readily follow from this theorem.

A Statistical Problem

Work was started some time ago on the statistical treatment of problems of optimum control. A short summary will be given here of the solution of one such problem; its significance for the theory of optimal control is not yet established. All that can be said is that the result led to setting up and solving a new problem for parabolic equations with a small parameter.

The phase coordinates of the controlled point will be denoted by $z = (z^1 \ldots, z^n)$. Hence point z satisfies the system of equations $\dot{z} = f(z, u)$. Together with the controlled point z in the space $R(z^1 \ldots, z^n)$, let there be a random point Q, i.e. a point whose probability distribution of possible positions in space R obeys Kolmogorov's first differential equation[14]. Let $p(x, \sigma, y, \tau)$ be the probability density of point Q occurring at instant σ in position x and at instant τ in position y. We call point Q random if $p(x, \sigma, y, \tau)$, as a function of x and σ, satisfies the parabolic equation

$$\frac{\partial p}{\partial \sigma} + a^{ij}(x, \sigma)\frac{\partial^2 p}{\partial x^i \partial x^j} + b^i(x, \sigma)\frac{\partial p}{\partial x^i} = 0 \tag{15}$$

Let Σ_z define a certain environment of the controlled point z, moving jointly with z. First let us consider the non-negative function $h(t)$, defined by $0 \leqslant t < \infty$ and not exceeding unity. We shall further define by $\psi_u(x, \sigma, \tau)$ the probability that random point Q occurring at instant σ in position x within the time range $\sigma \leqslant t \leqslant \tau$ will be met by the environment Σ_z of the controlled point z. If the law of control at point z, i.e. the control parameter u, is given as a function of time, $u = u(t)$, then the function

$$\int_0^\infty h(\tau)\frac{\partial}{\partial \tau}[\psi_u(x, \sigma, \tau)]\, d\tau \tag{16}$$

is uniquely defined.

The following problem is set: a control $u(t)$ is to be selected with point z such that function 16 attains an extreme value. The solution of the problem therefore implies the maximum principle as soon as function 16 is known. If Σ_z is a sphere of radius ε with the moving point z as centre (or even an arbitrary environment of point z of small 'radius' ε, bounded by a piece-wise smooth surface, changing with z in a piece-wise smooth manner), then the function $\psi_u(x, \sigma, \tau)$ and, hence, function 16 can be computed. It is found that in this case

$$\psi_u(x, \sigma, \tau) = \varepsilon^{n-2}\psi_u(x, \sigma, \tau) + 0(\varepsilon^{n-2}) \tag{17}$$

whereby we have an effective formula for $\psi_u(x, \sigma, \tau)$. Without writing out the formula here, we will only indicate the method of calculating the probability $\psi(x, \sigma, \tau)$.

Let $q(x, \sigma, y, \tau)$ denote the probability density of random point Q occurring at instant σ in position x and at instant τ in position y while at the same time not meeting the moving sphere Σ_z during the time $\sigma \leqslant t \leqslant \tau$ on its path. The function $q(x, \sigma, y, \tau)$, as a function of the variables x and σ in the region $R - \Sigma_{z(\sigma)}$, satisfies equation 15 and the boundary condition

$$q(x, \sigma, y, \tau)|_{x \varepsilon \mathrm{rp}}\, \Sigma_{z(\sigma)} = 0$$

when $\sigma = \tau$ has the same initial condition as the function $p(x, \sigma, y, \tau)$[15]. It is not difficult to see that

$$\psi(x, \sigma, \tau) = 1 - \int \ldots \int q(x, \sigma, y, \tau)\, dy \tag{18}$$

(where the integral is taken through the region $R - \Sigma_{z(\sigma)}$) is a solution of equation 15, satisfying the conditions

$$\psi(x, \sigma, \tau) \underset{\sigma \to \tau}{\to} 0 \qquad \psi(x, \sigma, \tau)\Big|_{x \varepsilon \mathrm{rp}} \Sigma_{z(\sigma)} = 1$$

References

[1] BOLTYANSKII, V. G., GAMKRELIDZE, R. V. and PONTRYAGIN, L. S. On the theory of optimal processes. *C.R. Acad. Nauk SSSR* 110 (1956) 7

[2] GAMKRELIDZE, R. V. On the theory of optimal processes in linear systems. *C.R. Acad. Nauk SSSR* 116 (1957) 9

[3] GAMKRELIDZE, R. V. The theory of optimal high-speed processes in linear systems. *Bull. Acad. Sci. U.R.S.S.*, (*math*) 22 (1958) 449

[4] BOLTYANSKII, V. G. The maximum principle in the theory of optimal processes. *C.R. Acad. Nauk SSSR* 119 (1958) 1070

[5] GAMKRELIDZE, R. V. On the general theory of optimal processes. *C.R. Acad. Nauk SSSR* 123 (1958) 223

[6] PONTRYAGIN, L. S. Optimal processes of regulation. *Progr. math. Sci., Moscow* XIV (85), (1959) 3

[7] GAMKRELIDZE, R. V. Optimal high-speed processes with finite phase coordinates. *C.R. Acad. Nauk SSSR* 125 (1959) 475

[8] MISHCHENKO, E. F. and PONTRYAGIN, L. S. A statistical problem of optimal control. *C.R. Acad. Nauk SSSR* 128 (1959) 390

[9] BELLMAN, R. E., GLICKSBERG, I. and GROSSE, O. A. Some aspects of the mathematical theory of control processes. *U.S. Air Force Project RAND, Rand Corporation, California, 1958*

[10] LASALLE, I. P. Optimal time control systems. *Proc. Nat. Acad. Sci. Wash.* 45 (1958) 573

[11] FELDBAUM, A. A. On the synthesis of optimal systems with the help of a phase space. *Autom. Telemech., Moscow* 16 (1955) 129

[12] BUSHAW, D. W. Experimental Towing Tank. *Stevens Institute of Technology Report No. 469, Hoboken, N.Y.*, 1953

[13] LERNER, A. Y. On the limit of high-speed systems of automatic regulation. *Autom. Telemech., Moscow* 15 (1954) 461

[14] KOLMOGOROV, A. N. Über die analytischen Methoden in der Wahrscheinlichkeitsrechnung. *Math. Ann.* B104 (1931) 415

[15] FORTET, R. Les fonctions aléatoires du type de Markoff. *J. Math. pures appl.* No. 22 (1943) 177

ANALYTIC CONTROLLER DESIGN. II

A. M. Letov

(Moscow)

Translated from Avtomatika i Telemekhanika Vol. 21, pp. 561-568, May, 1960

Original article submitted December 23, 1959

The solution is presented for the problem of analytic controller design in correspondence with a given optimizing functional. The solution is given for a closed region which contains the boundary of excursion of the controlling organ.

1. Optimal Systems, Defined in a Closed Region

Essential in all automatic control systems is the limitation on the excursion of the controlling organs ξ:

$$|\xi| \leqslant \bar{\xi} \tag{1.1}$$

on the limitation on the magnitude of the velocity of this excursion

$$|\dot{\xi}| \leqslant \bar{f}, \tag{1.2}$$

where $\bar{\xi}$, f are positive numbers.

With such limitations, the system becomes essentially nonlinear, since the presence of the equality sign in (1.1) and (1.2) permits the system to remain on the boundary of the region $\bar{N}$ of its definition. This region is closed. Moreover, it is impossible here to seek an optimal solution to the problem among functions of the class C_1, since there can be discontinuities on the boundary of the function which solves the problem. By taking into account what has just been said, we formulate the following variational problem.

We consider a closed system to be controlled, in which the disturbed motion of the controlled object is given by the equations

$$g_k = \dot{\eta}_k - \Big(\sum_\alpha b_{k\alpha}\eta_\alpha + m_k\xi\Big) = 0 \quad (k = 1, \ldots, n). \tag{1.3}$$

The notation in (1.3) has the same meaning as in [1]. It is assumed that (1.3), in conjunction with the controller equations being sought, are defined in the closed region $\bar{N}$, characterized by (1.1). In this region there are given the sole boundary conditions

$$\begin{aligned}\eta_{10} = \eta_1(0), \ldots, \eta_n(0) = \eta_{n0}, \ \xi(0) = \xi_0;\\ \eta_1(\infty) = \ldots = \eta_n(\infty) = \xi(\infty) = 0\end{aligned} \tag{1.4}$$

They mean simply this: that no matter what transient response arises in $\bar{N}$, it must terminate, for $t^* = \infty$, with the system at the origin of coordinates.

As the criterion of optimality, we take the integral

$$I = \int_0^\infty V dt, \tag{1.5}$$

where V is the positively defined quadratic form

$$V = \sum_k a_k\eta_k^2 + c\xi^2. \tag{1.6}$$

We shall search for such continuous functions $\xi, \eta_1, \ldots, \eta_n$ in Class C (permitting, generally speaking, discontinuities of the first derivatives) which minimize the integral in (1.5).

The problem just formulated belongs to the class of the so-called discontinuous problems of the calculus of variations. To solve such problems there exist various methods of the classical variational calculus, as well as newer methods, presented in the works cited in [1]. Here we shall use the methods of the classical variational calculus, supplemented by a nonlinear transformation which, in optimal problems of the first class [1], was used in [2].*

2. Solution of the Problem

We consider the case when the limitation is as in (1.1), and we set

$$\xi = \varphi(\zeta). \tag{2.1}$$

We define the function $\varphi(\zeta)$ as

$$\varphi(\zeta) = \begin{cases} +\bar{\xi} & \text{for } \zeta \geqslant \zeta^*, \\ \varphi(\zeta) & \text{for } |\zeta| < \zeta^*, \\ -\bar{\xi} & \text{for } \zeta \leqslant -\zeta^*, \end{cases} \tag{2.2}$$

where ζ^* is a given positive number and $\varphi(\zeta)$ is any continuous function whose derivative is continuous for $|\zeta| < \zeta^*$, and which is equal to zero for $\zeta = 0$. In particular, such a condition is satisfied by the function $\varphi(\zeta) = \xi \sin \zeta$ for $\zeta^* = \pi/2$ (Fig. 1).

Transformations (2.1) and (2.2) translate the closed region $N(\xi, \eta_1, \ldots, \eta_n)$ into the open region $\bar{N}(\zeta, \eta_1, \ldots, \eta_n)$ and permit one to use the well-known methods of variational calculus for the solution of ordinary Lagrange problems. The only special feature of this solution is that one must verify that the Weierstrass-Erdmann conditions

* The author's attention was called to the transformation by I. A. Litovchenko, to whom the author expresses his gratitude.

hold at all points of discontinuity of the derivatives. To begin the solution of the problem, we set

$$H = V + \sum_k \lambda_k \left[\dot{\eta}_k - \sum_\alpha b_{k\alpha}\eta_\alpha - m_k\varphi(\zeta)\right]. \qquad (2.3)$$

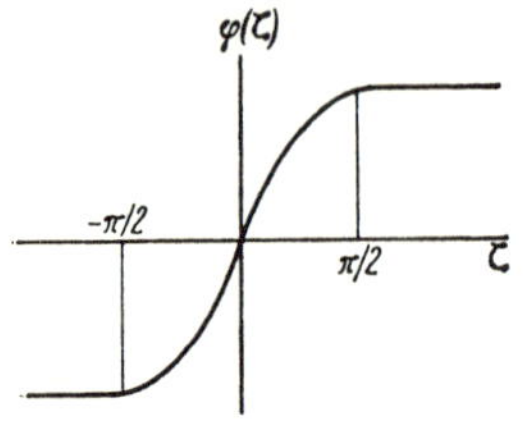

Fig. 1.

On the basis of (2.3), we find that

$$\frac{\partial H}{\partial \dot{\eta}_k} = \lambda_k, \qquad \frac{\partial H}{\partial \eta_k} = 2a_k\eta_k - \sum_\alpha \lambda_\alpha b_{\alpha k},$$

$$\frac{\partial H}{\partial \dot{\zeta}} = 0, \qquad \frac{\partial H}{\partial \zeta} = \left[2c\varphi(\zeta) - \sum_\alpha m_\alpha\lambda_\alpha\right]\frac{\partial \varphi}{\partial \zeta}.$$

The equations of the problem have the form

$$\begin{aligned} \dot{\eta}_k &= \sum_\alpha b_{k\alpha}\eta_\alpha + m_k\varphi(\zeta), \\ \dot{\lambda}_k &= -\sum_\alpha b_{\alpha k}\lambda_\alpha + 2a_k\eta_k, \\ 0 &= \left[2c\varphi(\zeta) - \sum_\alpha m_\alpha\lambda_\alpha\right]\frac{\partial\varphi}{\partial\zeta}. \end{aligned} \qquad (2.4)$$

They coincide to within the factor $\partial\varphi/\partial\zeta$ with the equations [(2.1) and (3.3)] of the analogous problem for the open region $N(\xi, \eta_1, \ldots, \eta_n)$ which was formulated in [1].

Therefore, in addition to the solution obtained in [1] for the open region, we should consider the new solution which corresponds to the equation

$$\frac{\partial\varphi}{\partial\zeta} = 0. \qquad (2.5)$$

By virtue of the definition given by (2.2), we set

$$\varphi(\zeta) = \pm\bar{\xi} \quad \text{for} \quad |\zeta| \geqslant \zeta^*. \qquad (2.6)$$

This latter means that the optimal solution passes over the boundary of the region $\bar{N}(\xi, \eta_1, \ldots, \eta_n)$.

For interior points of the region, the solution found has the form [1]

$$\xi = \sum_{\alpha=1}^{n} p_\alpha\eta_\alpha. \qquad (2.7)$$

Thus, the equation of the controller which corresponds to the functional of (1.5) is written as

$$\xi = \begin{cases} \sum_\alpha p_\alpha\eta_\alpha & \text{for} \quad \left|\sum_\alpha p_\alpha\eta_\alpha\right| < \bar{\xi}, \\ +\bar{\xi} & \text{for} \quad \sum_\alpha p_\alpha\eta_\alpha \geqslant \bar{\xi}, \\ -\bar{\xi} & \text{for} \quad \sum_\alpha p_\alpha\eta_\alpha \leqslant -\bar{\xi}. \end{cases} \qquad 2.8$$

Obviously, this equation corresponds to an ideal nonlinear controller with an infinitely large servomotor speed.

The question of the stability of system (1.3), supplied with the controller defined by (2.8), should be considered separately. It is the subject-matter of an independent problem. As was shown in [1], for a deviation $|\Sigma p_\alpha\eta_\alpha| < \bar{\xi}$, stability is guaranteed; for a deviation $|\Sigma p_\alpha\eta_\alpha| \geqslant \bar{\xi}$ a special investigation is required, leading to the construction of the region of attraction, the boundary of which necessarily lies beyond the limits of $|\Sigma p_\alpha\eta_\alpha| = \bar{\xi}$. Various cases can occur here. Thus, in example 1 of paper [1], where n = 1, $b_{11} = b$, $m_1 = m$ and, $\eta_1 = \eta$, we had the system of equations

$$\dot{\eta} = b\eta + m\xi,$$

$$\xi = \begin{cases} +\bar{\xi} & \text{for} \quad -\frac{k+b}{m}\eta \geqslant \bar{\xi}, \\ -\frac{k+b}{m}\eta & \text{for} \quad \left|1 - \frac{k+b}{m}\eta\right| < \bar{\xi}, \\ -\bar{\xi} & \text{for} \quad -\frac{k+b}{m}\eta \leqslant -\bar{\xi}, \end{cases} \qquad (2.9)$$

where the number k is defined by the formula

$$k = +\sqrt{b^2 + \frac{m^2 a}{c}}. \qquad (2.10)$$

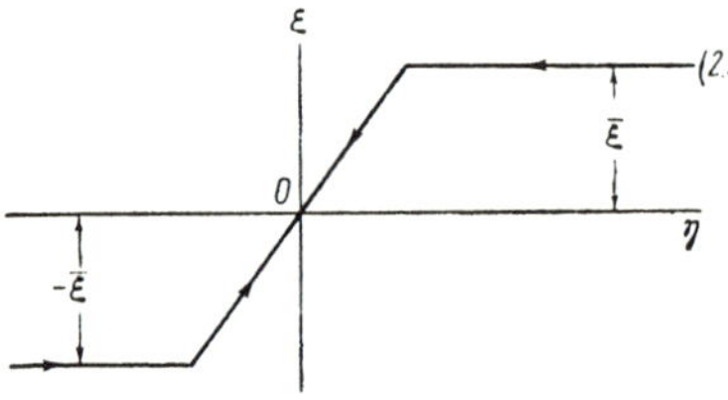

Fig. 2.

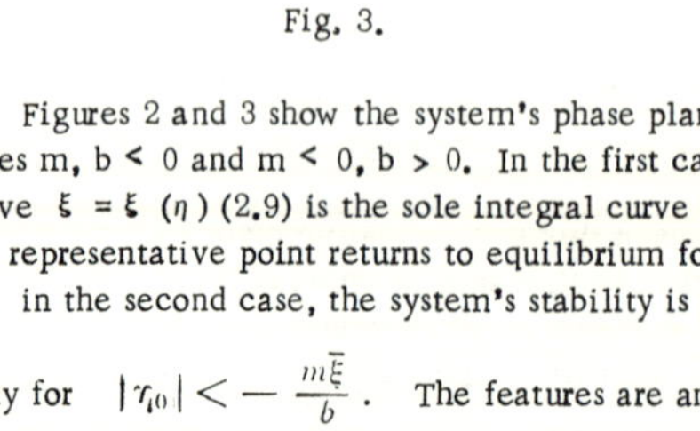

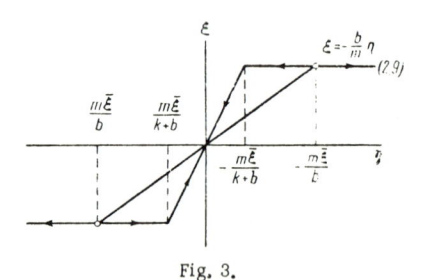

Fig. 3.

Figures 2 and 3 show the system's phase plane for the cases m, b < 0 and m < 0, b > 0. In the first case, the curve $\xi = \xi(\eta)$ (2.9) is the sole integral curve by which the representative point returns to equilibrium for any η_0; in the second case, the system's stability is guaranteed only for $|\eta_0| < -\frac{m\bar{\xi}}{b}$. The features are analogous in the two other cases, in which $m > 0,\ b \gtrless 0$.

It is of interest to note that the choice of sufficiently small weight constants in the function of (1.5) permits an arbitrarily close approach to a relay characteristic of the optimal controller :

$$\xi = \bar{\xi} \operatorname{sign}\left(-\frac{k+b}{m}\eta\right). \quad (2.11)$$

However, the execution of the limiting transfer itself requires additional discussion.

3. Possible Generalizations of the Functional of (1.5)

We now consider the case of optimizing a functional of the form

$$I(\xi) = \int_0^\infty (V + \dot{\xi}^2)\, dt. \quad (3.1)$$

In accordance with transformation (2.1), we have

$$I = [\varphi(\zeta)] = \int_0^\infty \left[\sum_k a_k\eta_k^2 + c\varphi^2(\zeta) + \left(\frac{\partial\varphi}{\partial\zeta}\dot{\zeta}\right)^2\right] dt.$$

The boundary conditions remain as before, i.e., (1.4). We set

$$H = \Sigma a_k\eta_k^2 + c\varphi^2(\zeta) + \left(\frac{\partial\varphi}{\partial\zeta}\dot{\zeta}\right)^2 + \sum_k \lambda_k\left[\dot{\eta}_k - \sum_\alpha b_{k\alpha}\eta_\alpha - m_k\varphi(\zeta)\right]. \quad (3.2)$$

Since

$$\frac{\partial H}{\partial\dot{\zeta}} = 2\left(\frac{\partial\varphi}{\partial\zeta}\right)^2\dot{\zeta}, \quad \frac{\partial H}{\partial\zeta} = \left[2c\varphi(\zeta) + 2\frac{\partial^2\varphi}{\partial\zeta^2}\dot{\zeta}^2\right]\frac{\partial\varphi}{\partial\zeta} - \sum_k \lambda_k m_k\frac{\partial\varphi}{\partial\zeta}.$$

then the equations of the variational problem will have the form

$$\dot{\eta}_k = \sum_\alpha b_{k\alpha}\eta_\alpha + m_k\varphi(\zeta),$$

$$\dot{\lambda}_k = -\sum_\alpha b_{\alpha k}\lambda_\alpha + 2a_k\eta_k, \quad (3.3)$$

$$\frac{d}{dt}\left[2\left(\frac{\partial\varphi}{\partial\zeta}\right)^2\dot{\zeta}\right] = \left[2c\varphi(\zeta) + 2\frac{\partial^2\varphi}{\partial\zeta^2}\dot{\zeta}^2 - \sum_k\lambda_k m_k\right]\frac{\partial\varphi}{\partial\xi}.$$

Consider the last of these equations. After some obvious simplifications, we find that

$$2\left[\frac{\partial\varphi}{\partial\zeta}\ddot{\zeta} + \frac{\partial^2\varphi}{\partial\zeta^2}\dot{\zeta}^2\right]\frac{\partial\varphi}{\partial\zeta} = \left[2c\varphi(\zeta) - \sum_k m_k\lambda_k\right]\frac{\partial\varphi}{\partial\zeta} \quad (3.4)$$

Therefore, (3.3) should be considered for the two cases

$$\frac{\partial\varphi}{\partial\zeta} = 0, \quad (3.5)$$

when the system's motion occurs on the boundary of region $\bar{N}$, and

$$2\left[\frac{\partial\varphi}{\partial\zeta}\ddot{\zeta} + \frac{\partial^2\varphi}{\partial\zeta^2}\dot{\zeta}^2\right] = 2c\varphi(\zeta) - \sum_k m_k\lambda_k, \quad (3.6)$$

when the system's motion takes place on the interior points of region $\bar{N}$. In the first case we have the solution

$$\varphi(\zeta) = \pm\bar{\xi} \quad \text{for} \quad |\zeta| \geqslant \zeta^*. \quad (3.7)$$

In the second case, since $\frac{\partial\varphi}{\partial\zeta}\dot{\zeta} = \frac{d}{dt}\varphi(\zeta)$, Eq. (3.6) reduces to the form

$$2\ddot{\varphi} = 2c\varphi - \sum_k m_k\lambda_k. \quad (3.8)$$

In conjunction with the first 2n equations of (3.3), this determines the controller equation

$$\dot{\xi} = \sum_\alpha p_\alpha\eta_\alpha - r\xi. \quad (3.9)$$

It is essential to note that, inasmuch as Eqs. (3.3) of the variational problem coincide exactly with (2.1) and (3.3) of [1], the equation just found, (3.9), coincides exactly with (4.5) of [1].

On the $\xi, \eta_1, \ldots, \eta_n$ phase space we sketch the two hyperplanes

$$\sum p_\alpha\eta_\alpha = \pm r\bar{\xi}. \quad (3.10)$$

Then, the controller equation being sought will be written as

$$\dot{\xi} = \begin{cases} +\bar{\xi} & \text{for} \quad \dfrac{\Sigma p_\alpha\eta_\alpha}{r} \geqslant \bar{\xi}, \\ \Sigma p_\alpha\eta_\alpha - r\xi & \text{for} \quad \left|\dfrac{\Sigma p_\alpha\eta_\alpha}{r}\right| < \bar{\xi}, \\ -\bar{\xi} & \text{for} \quad \dfrac{\Sigma p_\alpha\eta_\alpha}{r} \leqslant -\bar{\xi}. \end{cases} \quad (3.11)$$

4. The Weierstrass-Erdmann Conditions

To complete the investigation of the necessary conditions for the existence of an optimal solution of the analytic design problem, one should convince oneself that the Weierstrass-Erdmann conditions hold at the nodal points of function ξ.

In the case when one is considering a functional of the form of (3.1), these conditions reduce to the holding of the following equalities:

$$\frac{\partial H^+}{\partial \dot{\eta}_k} = \frac{\partial H^-}{\partial \dot{\eta}_k}, \qquad \frac{\partial H^+}{\partial \dot{\xi}} = \frac{\partial H^-}{\partial \dot{\xi}} \qquad (k = 1, \ldots, n), \tag{4.1}$$

$$H^+ - \sum_k \left(\frac{\partial H}{\partial \dot{\eta}_k}\dot{\eta}_k\right)^+ - \left(\frac{\partial H}{\partial \dot{\xi}}\dot{\xi}\right)^+ = H^- - \sum_k \left(\frac{\partial H}{\partial \dot{\eta}_k}\dot{\eta}\right)^- - \left(\frac{\partial H}{\partial \dot{\xi}}\dot{\xi}\right)^-. \tag{4.2}$$

Here, H is the function in (2.3) or in (3.2), and the "+" and "−" signs denote that the computation of the corresponding functions is carried out to the left or to the right of the nodal points of function ξ.

One easily convinces himself that, if the first n conditions of (4.1) hold, which reduce to the equations

$$\lambda_k^+ = \lambda_k^- \qquad (k = 1, \ldots, n), \tag{4.3}$$

then the two remaining conditions are also satisfied for any functions $\xi, \eta_1, \ldots, \eta_n$ of class C. As for (4.3), it can always be satisfied, as is easily verified, if the optimal system is stable.

Thus, in the example considered in Section 2, the solutions for the optimal controller in the case when have the form $|\xi| \geqslant \bar{\xi}$

$$\begin{aligned} \eta &= c_1 e^{bt} \mp \frac{m\bar{\xi}}{b}, \\ \lambda &= c_2 e^{-bt} \mp \frac{2am}{b^2}\bar{\xi} + \frac{ac_1}{b} e^{bt}, \end{aligned} \tag{4.4}$$

and, in the case when $|\xi| < \bar{\xi}$

$$\begin{aligned} \eta &= \bar{c}_1 e^{-kt} + \bar{c}_2 e^{kt}, \\ \lambda &= \frac{2c}{m^2}[-(k+b)\bar{c}_1 e^{-kt} + (k-b)\bar{c}_2 e^{kt}], \\ \xi &= \frac{1}{m}[-(k+b)\bar{c}_1 e^{-kt} + (k-b)\bar{c}_2 e^{kt}]. \end{aligned} \tag{4.5}$$

From the conditions on the left end (for t = 0)

$$\eta_0 = c_1 \mp \frac{m\bar{\xi}}{b}; \qquad \xi_0 = \pm\bar{\xi}. \tag{4.6}$$

From the conditions on the right end (for t = ∞),

$$\bar{c}_2 = 0. \tag{4.7}$$

The continuity conditions at the nodal points are

$$\bar{c}_1 = c_1 e^{bt_*} \mp \frac{m\bar{\xi}}{b}; \qquad -\frac{k+b}{m}\bar{c}_1 = \pm\bar{\xi}. \tag{4.8}$$

The single condition of (4.3) has the form

$$c_2 e^{-bt_*} \mp \frac{2am\bar{\xi}}{b^2} + \frac{ac_1}{b} e^{bt_*} = -\frac{2c}{m^2}(k+b)\bar{c}_1. \tag{4.9}$$

The last equation of (4.1) and (4.2) reduce to identities.

Equations (4.6), (4.7), and (4.9) define the constants c_1, $\bar{c}_7$, and c_2; (4.8) define c_1 and the time t_*, corresponding to the nodal point of function ξ. We, hence, find that

$$\pm\frac{k}{b}\frac{m\bar{\xi}}{k+b} = \left(\eta_0 \pm \frac{m\bar{\xi}}{b}\right) e^{bt_*}. \tag{4.10}$$

It is easily established that, for m < 0 and b < 0, (4.10) is solvable for $t_* > 0$ for any $|\eta_0| \geqslant \left|-\frac{m\bar{\xi}}{k+b}\right|$; if this latter inequality does not hold, the system does not go beyond the boundary $|\xi| = \bar{\xi}$ and no nodal point exists. In the case when m < 0 and b > 0, the equation has a solution with respect to $t_* > 0$ for any η_0 which satisfy the inequality

$$\left|-\frac{m\bar{\xi}}{k+b}\right| \leqslant |\eta_0| \leqslant \left|-\frac{m\bar{\xi}}{b}\right|$$

This is again the case shown on Figs. 2 and 3. The analogous features also occur for the other combinations of signs of m and b.

If the functional of (3.1) is used as the criterion of system optimality, then the Weierstrass-Erdmann conditions also are met. Indeed, the solution of the system for $|\xi| = \bar{\xi}$ is as follows:

$$\begin{aligned} \eta &= c_1 e^{bt} \mp \frac{m\bar{\xi}}{b}, \quad \xi = \bar{\xi}, \\ \lambda &= c_2 e^{-bt} \mp \frac{2am\bar{\xi}}{b^2} + \frac{ac_1}{b} e^{bt}. \end{aligned} \tag{4.11}$$

With the boundary conditions at infinity taken into account, the solution of the system for $|\xi| < \bar{\xi}$ is

$$\begin{aligned} \eta &= \bar{c}_1 e^{\mu_1 t} + \bar{c}_2 e^{\mu_2 t}, \\ \xi &= \frac{\mu_1 - b}{m}\bar{c}_1 e^{\mu_1 t} + \frac{\mu_2 - b}{m}\bar{c}_2 e^{\mu_2 t}, \\ \lambda &= -\frac{2a}{\mu_1 + b}\bar{c}_1 e^{\mu_1 t} - \frac{2a}{\mu_2 + b}\bar{c}_2 e^{\mu_2 t}. \end{aligned} \tag{4.12}$$

We find from the initial conditions that

$$\eta_0 = c_1 \mp \frac{m\bar{\xi}}{b}, \quad \xi_0 = \bar{\xi}. \tag{4.13}$$

The continuity conditions for the functions ξ and η at the nodal points are

$$\bar{\xi} = \frac{\mu_1 - b}{m}\bar{c}_1 + \frac{\mu_2 - b}{m}\bar{c}_2, \qquad c_1 e^{bt_*} \mp \frac{m\bar{\xi}}{b} = \bar{c}_1 + \bar{c}_2. \tag{4.14}$$

The Weierstrass-Erdmann conditions reduce to the holding of the two equalities:

$$\lambda^+ = \lambda^-, \quad \left[\left(\frac{\partial\varphi}{\partial\dot{\xi}}\right)^2 \dot{\xi}\right]^+ = \left[\left(\frac{\partial\varphi}{\partial\dot{\xi}}\right)^2 \dot{\xi}\right]^- \tag{4.15}$$

or, what amounts to the same thing, to the equalities:

$$c_2 e^{-bt_*} \mp \frac{2am\bar{\xi}}{b^2} + \frac{ac_1}{b} e^{bt_*} = -\frac{2a}{\mu_1 + b}\bar{c}_1 - \frac{2a}{\mu_2 + b}\bar{c}_2,$$

$$\mu_1(\mu_1 - b)\bar{c}_1 + \mu_2(\mu_2 - b)\bar{c}_2 = 0.$$

Equation (4.13) defines the constant c_1; from (4.14) we find that

$$\bar{c}_1 = \frac{1}{\mu_2 - \mu_1}[(\mu_2 - b)\eta^* - m\bar{\xi}],$$
$$\bar{c}_2 = \frac{1}{\mu_2 - \mu_1}[\mu\bar{\xi} - (\mu_1 - b)\eta^*], \quad (4.17)$$

where $\eta^* = \eta(t_*)$. The first equation of (4.16) defines the constant c_2, the second defines the moment of time t_* when the system passes through the nodal point. This last equation, in correspondence with (4.17), takes the form

$$m\bar{\xi}(\mu_1 + \mu_2 - b) = (\mu_1 - b)(\mu_2 - b)\eta^*. \quad (4.18)$$

This last equation means that, at the nodal point, the servomotor speed must vanish, as was also the case with (5.4) of [1].

LITERATURE CITED

[1] A. M. Letov, "Analytic controller design. I," Avtomatika i Telemekhanika 21, No. 4 (1960). †

[2] A. Miele, Aeronat. Sci. 24, No. 2 (1957).

† See English translation.

ANALYTICAL CONTROLLER DESIGN. III

A. M. Letov

Moscow

Translated from Avtomatika i Telemekhanika, Vol. 21, No. 6, pp. 661-665, June, 1960

A solution is given of the variational problem of an optimally controlled system when account is taken of servomotor speed limitations.

1. Servomotor Speed Limitations

In the present paper we shall study the case of analytical controller design when limitations on servomotor speed are taken into account, a problem which was touched on slightly in [1, 2]. Let us pose the problem. We consider a closed autocontrolled system in which the disturbed motion is given by the equations

$$g_k = \dot{\eta}_k - \left(\sum_\alpha b_{k\alpha}\eta_\alpha + m_k\xi\right) = 0 \quad (k = 1, \ldots, n), \quad \dot{\xi} = f(\sigma) \tag{1.1}$$

Here, the η_k are the coordinates, and the $b_{k\alpha}$ are constant parameters of the object of control, while ξ is the coordinate, and the m_k are parameters of the controlling organ. The function $f(\sigma)$ is the subject of our search.

By basing ourselves on well-known attempts [3]*, we shall assume that $f(\sigma)$ lies in functions of class A', for which the following relationships hold:

$$\sigma f(\sigma) > 0, \quad \sigma \neq 0, \quad \left(\frac{df}{d\sigma}\right)_{\sigma=0} > 0. \tag{1.2}$$

The argument of the function, $\sigma = \sigma(\eta_1, \ldots, \eta_n, \xi)$ is also to be determined.

As the criterion of optimality, we consider the functional

$$I[f(\sigma)] = \int_0^\sigma (V + \dot{\xi}^2)\, dt, \tag{1.3}$$

where V is a positive-definite function of the form

$$V = \sum_k a_k\eta_k^2 + c\xi^2. \tag{1.4}$$

We consider the natural boundary conditions:

$$\begin{gathered}\eta_1(0) = \eta_{10}, \ldots, \eta_n(0) = \eta_{n0}, \ \xi(0) = \xi_0, \\ \eta_1(\infty) = \ldots = \eta_n(\infty) = \xi(\infty) = 0.\end{gathered} \tag{1.5}$$

We shall search for those continuous functions ξ, $\eta_1, \ldots, \eta_n$ of class C_1 which, while satisfying (1.1) and boundary conditions (1.5), minimize the functional in (1.3). Equations (1.1) are defined in the open region $N(\xi, \eta_1, \ldots, \eta_n)$, so that the problem just formulated is an ordinary Lagrange variational problem, the procedures for whose solution are well known.

To obtain the equations of the variational problem, we set

$$H = V + f^2(\sigma) + \lambda[\dot{\xi} - f(\sigma)] + \sum \lambda_k g_k. \tag{1.6}$$

We then write the partial derivatives of the function H:

$$\begin{aligned} &\frac{\partial H}{\partial \dot{\eta}_k} = \lambda_k, && \frac{\partial H}{\partial \eta_k} = 2a_k\eta_k - \sum_\alpha \lambda_\alpha b_{\alpha k}, \\ &\frac{\partial H}{\partial \dot{\xi}} = \lambda, && \frac{\partial H}{\partial \xi} = 2c\xi - \sum_\alpha m_\alpha\lambda_\alpha, \\ &\frac{\partial H}{\partial \dot{\sigma}} = 0, && \frac{\partial H}{\partial \sigma} = [2f(\sigma) - \lambda]\frac{\partial f}{\partial \sigma}. \end{aligned}$$

The equations sought have the form

$$\begin{aligned} &\dot{\eta}_k = \sum_\alpha b_{k\alpha}\eta_\alpha + m_k\xi, \quad \dot{\xi} = f(\sigma), \\ &\dot{\lambda}_k = -\sum_\alpha b_{\alpha k}\lambda_\alpha + 2a_k\eta_k \\ &\dot{\lambda} = 2c\xi - \sum_k \lambda_k m_k, \\ &0 = [2f(\sigma) - \lambda]\frac{\partial f}{\partial \sigma} \qquad (k = 1, \ldots, n). \end{aligned} \tag{1.7}$$

2. Solution Abutting the Optimal Curve's Left End

We shall study the solution of the problem for the two cases presented by the last equation of (1.7).

We consider the first case:

$$\frac{\partial f}{\partial \sigma} = 0. \tag{2.1}$$

* In autocontrol systems such as (1.1), the function σ describes the control law, and depends on $\eta_1, \ldots, \eta_n, \xi$.

If we are considering class A' functions, then there exists a positive number σ_* such that, from (2.1), we find

$$f(\sigma) = \pm \bar{f}, \quad |\sigma| \geq \sigma_*. \tag{2.2}$$

Thus, the controller equation is defined everywhere for $|\sigma| \geq \sigma_*$, although the number σ_* itself is still unknown.

Let

$$\Delta(\rho) = |b_{k\alpha} - \rho\delta_{k\alpha}| \tag{2.3}$$

be the determinant system (1.1) for $m_k = 0$. Then Solution (2.2) of system (1.1) is written in the following form:

$$\begin{aligned}\eta_k &= \sum_{s=1}^{n} \Delta_k(\rho_s) C_s e^{\rho_s t} + M_k + N_k t,\\ \xi &= \bar{C} \pm \bar{f}t,\\ \lambda_k &= \sum_{s=1}^{n} \bar{\Delta}(-\rho_s) \bar{D}_s e^{-\rho_s t} + \varphi_k(t),\\ \lambda &= \bar{D} + \psi(t)\end{aligned} \tag{2.4}$$

Here, ρ_k are simple roots of the equation $\Delta(\rho) = 0$, while $-\rho_k$ are simple roots of the equation

$$\bar{\Delta}(\rho) = |-b_{\alpha k} - \rho\delta_{\alpha k}| = 0; \tag{2.5}$$

$M_k + N_k t$, $\varphi_k(t)$, $\psi(t)$ are the corresponding particular solutions arising from the appearance of the line integral for the function ξ; Δ_k are the minors of the determinant in (2.3) and $\bar{\Delta}_k$ are the minors of the determinant in (2.5) corresponding to the elements with ordinal number k in the first row; $\bar{C}_1, \ldots, \bar{C}_n, \bar{C}, \bar{D}, \bar{D}_1, \ldots, \bar{D}_n$ are the $2n + 2$ arbitrary constants. We call the function defined by (2.4) a solution abutting the left (initial) end of the optimal curve ($t = 0$).

This solution will be necessary only for the verification that the boundary conditions hold.

3. Solution Abutting the Optimal Curve's Right End

We now consider the second case presented by the last of Eqs. (1.7)

$$2f(\sigma) = \lambda \tag{3.1}$$

System (1.7) becomes linear with constant coefficients:

$$\begin{aligned}\dot{\eta}_k &= \sum_{\alpha} b_{k\alpha}\eta_\alpha + m_k\xi,\\ 2\dot{\xi} &= 2c\xi - \sum_{k} m_k\lambda_k,\\ \dot{\lambda}_k &= -\sum_{\alpha} b_{\alpha k}\lambda_\alpha + 2a_k\eta_k \qquad (k = 1,\ldots,n)\end{aligned} \tag{3.2}$$

Let

$$\nabla(\mu) = \begin{vmatrix} b_{11}-\mu, \ldots, & b_{1n}, & m_1 \ldots\ldots, & 0 \ldots\ldots, 0\\ \ldots & \ldots & \ldots & \ldots\\ b_{n1}, \ldots\ldots, & b_{nn}-\mu, & m_n, & \ldots 0 \ldots\ldots, 0\\ 0, \ldots\ldots, & 0, \ldots, & 2c, -2\mu^2, & -m_1, \ldots, -m_n\\ 2a_1, \ldots\ldots, & 0, \ldots & 0, \ldots & -b_{11}-\mu, \ldots, -b_{n1}\\ \ldots & \ldots & \ldots & \ldots\\ 0, \ldots\ldots, & 2a_n, & 0, \ldots & -b_{1n}, \ldots, -b_{nn}-\mu \end{vmatrix} \tag{3.3}$$

be the determinant of the system. It is easily proven that, if $\mu_1, \ldots, \mu_n$ are simple roots of the equation $\nabla(\mu) = 0$, then $-\mu_1, \ldots, -\mu_n$ will also be simple roots of this equation. For the proof of this assertion, it suffices to execute the following operations:

1) write the determinant $\nabla(-\mu)$,

2) transpose the middle row downwards,

3) transpose the first n rows downwards,

4) in the determinant thus formed, transpose the middle column to the right, making it the last column,

5) transpose the first n columns to the right.

As the result of these operations, we obtain the determinant

$$\nabla(-\mu) = \begin{vmatrix} -b_{11}+\mu, \ldots, & -b_{n1}, & 0, & 2a_1, \ldots, 0\\ \ldots & \ldots & \ldots & \ldots\\ -b_{1n}, \ldots & -b_{nn}+\mu, & 0, & 0, \ldots, 2a_n\\ -m_1, \ldots, & -m_n, & 2c-2\mu^2, & 0, \ldots, 0\\ 0, \ldots, & 0, & m_1, & b_{11}+\mu, \ldots, b_{1n}\\ \ldots & \ldots & \ldots & \ldots\\ 0, \ldots, & 0, & m_n, & b_{n1}, \ldots, b_{nn}+\mu \end{vmatrix}$$

Now, in order to convince ourselves of the validity of our assertion, it suffices to:

a) take out the minus signs in the first n columns and make them rows;

b) multiply the last n rows by -1 and make them columns.

If, with such transpositions, the column numbers become row numbers and conversely, we obtain, after their termination, the following identity:

$$\nabla(\mu) = \nabla(-\mu). \tag{3.4}$$

To complete the argument, we recall the possibility of so numbering the roots that the following condition holds:

$$\operatorname{Re} \mu_k \leqslant 0 \quad (k = 1, \dots n+1). \tag{3.5}$$

Then, taking the conditions at infinity into account, we write the solution of Eqs. (3.2) in the following form:

$$\begin{aligned} \eta_k &= \sum_{s=1}^{n+1} \Delta_k(\mu_s) c_s e^{\mu_s t}, \\ \xi &= \sum_{s=1}^{n+1} \Delta_{n+1}(\mu_s) c_s e^{\mu_s t}, \\ \lambda &= 2\sum_{s=1}^{n+1} \mu_s \Delta_{n+1}(\mu_s) c_s e^{\mu_s t}, \\ \lambda_k &= \sum_{s=1}^{n+1} \Delta_{n+1+k}(\mu_s) c_s e^{\mu_s t}. \end{aligned} \tag{3.6}$$

Here, the Δ_r are the minors of determinant (3.3) with respect to the elements of r of the first row, and the c_r are constants of integration.

To obtain the controller's equation for the open region, it suffices to take the first n + 2 rows of formulas (3.6) and to eliminate time. This equation has the form

$$\begin{vmatrix} \Delta_1(\mu_1), & \dots, & \Delta_1(\mu_{n+1}), & \eta_1 \\ \cdot & \cdots & \cdot & \cdot \\ \Delta_n(\mu_1), & \dots, & \Delta_n(\mu_{n+1}), & \eta_n \\ \Delta_{n+1}(\mu_1), & \dots, & \Delta_n(\mu_{n+1}), & \xi \\ \mu_1\Delta_{n+1}(\mu_1), & \dots, & \mu_{n+1}\Delta(\mu_{n+1}), & \dot{\xi} \end{vmatrix} = 0. \tag{3.7}$$

After expanding the determinant, we find

$$\dot{\xi} = \sum_{\alpha=1}^{n} p_\alpha \eta_\alpha - r\xi \tag{3.8}$$

which is a linear equation with constant coefficients.

We must now convince ourselves of the possibility of determining the arbitrary constants of integration. Formulas (2.4) and (3.6) contain 3n + 3 constants of integration. For their determination we have the n + 1 initial conditions and the 2n + 2 continuity conditions for the functions $\xi, \eta_1, \dots, \eta_n, \lambda_1, \dots, \lambda_n, \lambda$ at the point σ_*, and also the continuity condition for the function $f(\sigma)$ which we are seeking. We now show how to find this function and the constant σ_* simultaneously.

Let

$$\frac{1}{h}\left(\sum_{\alpha=1}^{n} p_\alpha \eta_\alpha - r\xi\right) = \sigma, \tag{3.9}$$

where h is some positive constant.

Equation (3.8) gives

$$\dot{\xi} = h\sigma. \tag{3.10}$$

To determine the magnitude of σ_* we find

$$h\sigma_* = \bar{f}. \tag{3.11}$$

Thus, the final form of the controller equation is

$$\dot{\xi} = \begin{cases} +\bar{f} & \text{for } \sigma \geqslant \sigma_*, \\ h\sigma & \text{for } |\sigma| < \sigma_*, \\ -\bar{f} & \text{for } \sigma \leqslant \sigma_*. \end{cases} \tag{3.12}$$

4. Two Problems

What has been presented allows us to formulate two problems. The first of them consists of the following. Given that linear system (1.1), (3.9), (3.10) is stable for any deviations. Consequently, nonlinear optimal system (1.1), (3.9), (3.12) is stable at least for any disturbances with respect to σ which satisfy the inequality $|\sigma| \leq \sigma_*$. By virtue of the continuity property of the region of attraction, this system is extended to the limits $|\sigma| = \sigma_*$. It is required to determine the boundaries of the region of attraction.

Second problem: We consider the functional in (1.3), and remove the term $\dot{\xi}^2$ from it. Equations (1.7) of the variational problem then give the solution $f(\sigma) = \bar{f} \operatorname{sign} \sigma$. This solution is compatible with the Weierstrass-Erdmann conditions. It is required to determine the construction of the switching function $\sigma = \sigma(\eta_1, \dots, \eta_n, \xi)$.

5. Example

In the case $n = 1$, $b_1 = b$, $m_1 = m$, $a_1 = a$, we have the characteristic equation

$$\mu^4 - (b^2 + c)\mu^2 + am^2 + cb^2 = 0, \tag{5.1}$$

and the controller equation in the open region is written in the form

$$\dot{\xi} = -\frac{(\mu_1 - b)(\mu_2 - b)}{m}\eta + (\mu_1 + \mu_2 - b)\xi. \quad (5.2)$$

This equation coincides with Eq. (5.4) which was found in [1, 2].

We easily convince ourselves that, in the general case, Eq. (3.8) coincides exactly with Eq. (4.5) of work [1], which was found for an open region, and with Eq. (3.9) of work [2] for regions bounded with respect to the angle of deviation of the controlling organ.

From this there derives the interesting conclusion that, everywhere in the open region, the formula for the optimal controller is the same, and is determined only by the functional adopted as the criterion.

As in work [2], the question as to the stability of system (1.1), (3.12) must be considered separately.

The author is deeply grateful to N. N. Krasovskii for his very useful remarks and advice in regard to the problem considered here.

LITERATURE CITED

1. A. M. Letov, "Analytical controller design. I", Avtomatika i Telemekhanika 21, 4 (1960).†
2. A. M. Letov, "Analytical controller design. II", Avtomatika i Telemekhanika 21, 5 (1960).†
3. A. M. Letov, Stability of Nonlinear Controlled Systems [in Russian] (Gostekhizdat, 1955).

† See English translation.

THE ANALYTICAL DESIGN OF CONTROL SYSTEMS

A. M. Letov

(Moscow)
Translated from Avtomatika i Telemekhanika, Vol. 22, No. 4,
pp. 425-435, April, 1961
Original article submitted November 4, 1960

A method of dynamic programming is obtained for the problem of the analytical design of control systems that are optimum relative to the integral square error.

1. The Method of Dynamic Programming

In [1-13], various methods are described for solving the problem of constructing an optimal system. Solutions obtained in these articles give the law of control as a known function of the time and of the initial and final states of the system. These solutions can be realized by using digital computers operating according to certain algorithms obtained. Discrete time intervals, during which the switching of the controlling unit occurs, are used for the output. In [1-7], the so-called "synthesis problem" is also formulated, i. e., the problem of presenting the control law as a known function of the coordinates of the system. In [14, 15], the authors discuss the simplest case of the solution of this problem, which is given the special name "analytical design."

The problem of the analytical design of control systems was formulated as a problem of classical calculus of variations, in which the law of automatic control is obtained relative to some previously stipulated optimizing functional. The law of control was obtained analytically and written in the form commonly used in actual applications with the corresponding sensing elements and servomotor.

The disadvantage of the methods applying the calculus of variations lies in the fact that they involve writing the equations of the variational problem, and these equations must be actually solved.

In the present article, we use the fact that the dynamic-programming method developed by R. Bellman in [8] permits us to obtain results already known by a new method that is sometimes more conveniently applicable in numerical work, and also to investigate some other possible methods. For clarity, we will describe the basis of the method of dynamic programming by using a simple example. (The original exposition of the method is given in [8]). We will assume that the differential equation

$$\dot{x} = G(x, y) \tag{1.1}$$

is given, with the initial condition $x(t_0) = u$, $t_0 = 0$.

We assume that $G(x, y)$ is a bounded, continuous function of x and y, differentiable with respect to y, defined in the open region $N(x, y)$. Here y is a control function that minimizes the functional

$$I(y) = \int_0^\infty F(x, y)\,dt \tag{1.2}$$

in the class C_1 of functions of x and y. Let y be a function minimizing (1.2). This minimum is some function $\psi(u)$ of the initial state u which we denote by

$$\psi(u) = \min_y I(y). \tag{1.3}$$

Let S be a positive number. We have

$$\psi(u) = \int_0^S F(x, y)\, dt + \int_S^\infty F(x, y)\, dt. \tag{1.4}$$

The essence of R. Bellman's optimization principle lies in the fact that if y = y(t) minimizes the functional $\int_0^\infty F(x, y)\, dt$, then it also minimizes the functional $\int_S^\infty F(x, y)\, dt$ independently of the first integral. The principle expresses the natural condition of calculus of variations according to which any part of an extremal y(t) is also extremal. Using this fact as a basis, R. Bellman developed the following original method. The equality 1.4 can be written in the form

$$\psi(u) = \min_v \left[\int_0^S F(x, y)\, dt + \psi[x(S)]\right]. \tag{1.5}$$

The notation $\min_y$ denotes that the expression (1.5) is minimized by the function y of the class C_1. We will assume that the number S is sufficiently small and that $y(t_0) = v$. If ψ has a derivative for $x \in [x(0), x(S)]$, then according to the mean value theorem we have

$$\psi[u + GS] = \psi(u) + GS\left(\frac{\partial \psi}{\partial x}\right)_{x=\xi},$$

where $0 < \xi < S$. Then

$$\psi(u) = \min_v \left[F(u, v)\, S + \psi(u) + GS\left(\frac{\partial \psi}{\partial x}\right)_{x=\xi} + O(S)\right].$$

Here 0(S) is the remainder, and it is assumed that $\lim 0(S)/S \to 0$ for $S \to 0$. Therefore when $S \to 0$ we obtain

$$\min_v \left[F(u, v) + G(u, v)\frac{\partial \psi}{\partial u}\right] = 0. \tag{1.6}$$

In order that the expression in brackets actually yield a minimum relative to y, its derivative with respect to v must be zero. Therefore

$$F(u, v) + G(u, v)\frac{\partial \psi}{\partial u} = 0, \qquad \frac{\partial F(u, v)}{\partial v} + \frac{\partial G(u, v)}{\partial v}\frac{\partial \psi}{\partial u} = 0. \tag{1.7}$$

After eliminating $\frac{\partial \psi}{\partial u}$, we arrive at the equation

$$F\frac{\partial G}{\partial v} = G\frac{\partial F}{\partial v}, \tag{1.8}$$

relating the values of u and v for any instant of time $t_0 = 0$. The principal aim of the dynamic-programming method is to obtain the functional equations (1.7). We will apply this method in solving the problem of analytical design. However,we first make two observations.

Observation 1. Since the equation (1.8) establishes the relation v = v(u) for any instant t_0 of time, and since as a result of the optimal principle it does not depend on this time, the relation v = v(u) is equivalent to y = y(x) with the equation (1.1), we obtain the complete system. For simplicity, in what follows we will therefore write the functional equation immediately in terms of the original coordinates, since this will not cause any confusion.

Observation 2. In the case when the function G is defined in a closed region $\overline{N}(x, y)$ and the optimal solution can be obtained from the boundary condition, the requirement that the function y(t) be continuous and differentiable can in general be relaxed. The difficulty in solving a problem by the dynamic-programming method lies in the fact that the second of the expressions (1.7) can, in general, not be obtained, since it is uncertain what the expressions $\frac{\partial F}{\partial v}$ and $\frac{\partial G}{\partial v}$ signify along the boundary of $\overline{N}$. The originator of the dynamic-programming method proposes at this stage a very complex method for constructing the optimal solution. We have not applied this method. In the course of the solution of the analytical-design problem in the present work it will be shown that a simple optimal solution can be obtained, in the case of a closed region $\overline{N}$, of the problem for continuous functions y(t), and in a subsequent article for continuous x(t) and discontinuous functions y(t). The value of the method we will describe lies in the fact that it makes it possible to obtain a closed solution for the problem of analytical design in all these cases.

2. A First Order Object of Control

We will start by considering the simplest problem of optimizing the functional (1.2) in the class of functions C_1.

We have the equation of the object of control

$$\dot{\eta} = b\eta + m\xi, \qquad \eta(0) = \eta_0 \tag{2.1}$$

and the optimizing functional

$$I(\xi) = \int_0^\infty (a\eta^2 + c\xi^2)\, dt. \tag{2.2}$$

We write the dynamic programming equations (1.7) in the form

$$\begin{gathered} a\eta^2 + c\xi^2 + (b\eta + m\xi)\frac{\partial\psi}{\partial\eta} = 0, \\ 2c\xi + m\frac{\partial\psi}{\partial\eta} = 0. \end{gathered} \tag{2.3}$$

We thus obtain

$$mc\xi^2 + 2bc\eta\xi - am\eta^2 = 0 \tag{2.4}$$

with the solution

$$\xi = -\frac{k+b}{m}\eta, \quad k = \sqrt{b^2 + \frac{m^2 a}{c}}. \tag{2.5}$$

In the solution of (2.4) for ξ, we reject the solution

$$\xi = -\frac{b-k}{m}\eta,$$

which does not satisfy the requirements of control stability. The solution (2.5) was obtained in [14]. For what follows, it is important to obtain the form of the functional ψ (u). After eliminating ξ from the equations (2.3), we obtain

$$a\eta^2 + b\eta\frac{\partial\psi}{\partial\eta} = \frac{m^2}{4c}\left(\frac{\partial\psi}{\partial\eta}\right)^2. \tag{2.6}$$

This nonlinear differential equation is satisfied by

$$\psi(\eta) = \frac{(b \pm k)c}{m^2}\eta^2 + B(\xi), \tag{2.7}$$

where $B(\xi)$ is an arbitrary function of ξ; we should probably set $B(\xi) = \text{const}$.

3. The Optimal Solution in a Closed Region

We turn again to the equations (2.1), (2.2), and we will investigate their solutions in the closed region $\overline{N}(\xi,\eta)$ characterized by the relation

$$|\xi| \leqslant \bar{\xi}, \tag{3.1}$$

where $\bar{\xi}$ is a given positive number. We will assume that the comparison functions are of the class C, since the optimal solution of the problem can be obtained from the boundary of the region (3.1). The case when $x(t)$ remains continuous while $y(t)$ is discontinuous at a finite number of points will be considered in a subsequent article.

We therefore consider the single-valued nonlinear transformation [15]

$$\xi = \varphi(\zeta). \tag{3.2}$$

The function $\varphi(\zeta)$ is continuous, piecewise differentiable, and defined as *

$$\varphi(\zeta) = \begin{cases} +\bar{\xi} & \text{for } \zeta \geqslant \zeta^*, \\ \varphi(\zeta) & \text{for } |\zeta| < \zeta^*, \\ -\bar{\xi} & \text{for } \zeta \leqslant -\zeta^*. \end{cases} \tag{3.3}$$

The number ζ^* is determined by the form of the function $\varphi(\zeta)$. The transformation (3.2) maps the closed region $\overline{N}(\xi,\eta)$ into an open region $N(\zeta,\eta)$ in which the role of the controlling function passes to ζ.

The functional equations (2.3) in the present case will be

$$a\eta^2 + c\varphi^2 + (b\eta + m\varphi)\frac{\partial\psi}{\partial\eta} = 0,$$

$$\left(2c\varphi + m\frac{\partial\psi}{\partial\eta}\right)\frac{\partial\varphi}{\partial\zeta} = 0. \tag{3.4}$$

The last of the equations (3.4) breaks up into two equations:

$$2c\varphi + m\frac{\partial\psi}{\partial\eta} = 0, \tag{3.5}$$

$$\frac{\partial\varphi}{\partial\zeta} = 0. \tag{3.6}$$

It is evident that when $c \neq 0$, the equation (3.5) taken together with the first equation of (3.4) yields the known solution (2.5). In view of (3.2) and (3.3), this solution exists for

$$\left|-\frac{k+b}{m}\eta\right| < \zeta^*. \tag{3.7}$$

From Eq. (3.6) we also obtain

$$\varphi(\zeta) = \pm\bar{\xi}. \tag{3.8}$$

Then the first of the equations (3.4) becomes an ordinary differential equation for the functional ψ with the solution

$$\psi(\eta) = -\frac{a}{2b}\eta^2 + \frac{2am\bar{\xi}}{b^2}\eta - \frac{am^2 + cb^2}{b^3}\bar{\xi}^3 \ln|-(b\eta + m\bar{\xi})| + D. \tag{3.9}$$

* No specific form of the function $\varphi(\zeta)$ for $|\zeta| < \zeta^*$ is given, since it is not necessary in the present considerations.

For the purpose of analytical design, the expression for the functional (3.9) will be needed only to check on its continuity everywhere in $\bar{N}$. Before doing this, however, we write the control equation

$$\xi = \begin{cases} +\bar{\xi} & \text{for} \quad -\frac{k+b}{m}\eta \geqslant \bar{\xi}, \\ -\frac{k+b}{m}\eta & \text{for} \quad \left|-\frac{k+b}{m}\eta\right| < \bar{\xi}, \\ -\bar{\xi} & \text{for} \quad -\frac{k+b}{m}\eta \leqslant -\bar{\xi}. \end{cases} \tag{3.10}$$

We now assume that the initial deviation η_0 is sufficiently great in absolute value and that the system starts at the boundary of the region $\bar{N}$. We further assume that the system is stable [15]. The expression for the function in this case is obtained from the formula (3.9), where D is an arbitrary constant. Then the functional ψ is a bounded, continuous function of η, since the expression $b\eta = m\bar{\xi}$ is nowhere zero on the boundary. For $|\eta| = |m/(k+b)|\bar{\xi}$, the function $\psi(\eta)$ of (2.7) must take the same value as the function $\psi(\eta)$ of (3.9). This can always be arranged by the proper choice of the constants D and B.

The solution (3.10), although it is the same as the solution obtained in [15] by using the calculus of variations, is interesting because it was obtained by applying a nonlinear transformation of the form (3.3) which avoided the essential difficulties involved in investigating the functional equations, connected with the impossibility of differentiating the expression (1.6) with respect to $v = \xi$ for $\xi = \bar{\xi}$.

4. An nth Order Object of Control

Case of an open region. We consider the general case in which the disturbed motion of the object of control is given by the equations

$$\dot{\eta}_k = \sum_\alpha b_{k\alpha}\eta_\alpha + m_k\xi \qquad (k = 1, \ldots, n),$$
$$\eta_k(0) = \eta_{k0} \tag{4.1}$$

and it is desired to find the function ξ minimizing the functional

$$I(\xi) = \int_0^\infty V\,dt, \tag{4.2}$$

where

$$V = \sum_k a_k\eta_k^2 + c\xi^2 \tag{4.3}$$

is a positive definite quadratic form.

The functional is to be minimized in the class of functions C_1.

The basic functional equation of Bellman has the form

$$\psi(\eta_{k0}) = \min_\xi \left\{ \int_0^S V\,dt + \psi[\eta_k(S)] \right\}. \tag{4.4}$$

When we take the limit when $S \to 0$, we obtain

$$0 = V + \sum_k \left(\sum_\alpha b_{k\alpha}\eta_\alpha + m_k\xi \right) \frac{\partial\psi}{\partial\eta_k}. \tag{4.5}$$

Since the function ξ must make the expression on the right-hand side of (4.5) a minimum,

$$2c\xi + \sum_k m_k \frac{\partial\psi}{\partial\eta_k} = 0. \tag{4.6}$$

The function ψ must therefore satisfy the partial differential equation (4.5), where the integral ψ must be chosen so that it satisfies the relation (4.6).

In order to find such an integral, we simplify Eq. (4.5) by using the equality (4.6). As a result we obtain

$$\sum_k a_k \eta_k^2 + \sum_k \sum_\alpha b_{k\alpha} \eta_\alpha \frac{\partial \psi}{\partial \eta_k} = \frac{1}{4c} \Big(\sum_k m_k \frac{\partial \psi}{\partial \eta_k} \Big)^2. \tag{4.7}$$

The solution of this nonlinear partial differential equation must be sought in the form of a quadratic form in the variables η_k:

$$\psi = \sum_k \sum_\alpha A_{k\alpha} \eta_k \eta_\alpha. \tag{4.8}$$

Here $A_{k\alpha}$ are completely definite numbers which can be found by comparing coefficients after the substitution of the expression (4.8) in the equation (4.7). The substitution of the expression (4.8) in (4.6) gives the equation of a perfect control with a fixed negative feedback [14].

$$\xi = \sum_\alpha p_\alpha \eta_\alpha. \tag{4.9}$$

We will show that (4.9) is the same equation for a perfect control (3.7) obtained in [14]. With this aim in view, we consider the equations (4.5) and (4.6). We will denote the right hand side of Eq. (4.5) by U. Taking (4.9) into account, we must assume that

$$U = U(\eta_1, \ldots, \eta_n) = 0. \tag{4.10}$$

Hence

$$dU = \sum_k \frac{\partial U}{\partial \eta_k} d\eta_k. \tag{4.11}$$

Since the equations (4.1) and (4.9) determine a system of independent solutions η_k, then (4.11) will be satisfied only when the equations

$$\frac{\partial U}{\partial \eta_k} = 0 \qquad (k = 1, \ldots, n). \tag{4.12}$$

are satisfied.

We now use the notation

$$\lambda_k = -\frac{\partial \psi}{\partial \eta_k} \qquad (k = 1, \ldots, n) \tag{4.13}$$

and write the equations (4.12) as

$$2a_k \eta_k - \sum_\alpha b_{\alpha k} \lambda_\alpha - \Big(\sum_\alpha b_{k\alpha} \eta + m_k \xi \Big) \frac{\partial \lambda_k}{\partial \eta_k} = 0.$$

But from (4.1),

$$\Big(\sum_\alpha b_{k\alpha} \eta_\alpha + m_k \xi \Big) \frac{\partial \lambda_k}{\partial \eta_k} = \dot{\lambda}_k,$$

and so along with (4.6) we obtain

$$\dot{\lambda}_k = -\sum_{\alpha} b_{\alpha k}\lambda_\alpha + 2a_k\eta_k,$$
$$0 = 2c\xi - \sum_k m_k\lambda_k \qquad (k = 1, \ldots, n). \tag{4.14}$$

It follows from what has been said that the system of equations (4.14) is equivalent to the system (4.5), (4.6). But the equations (4.14) together with (4.1) are the equations of the variational problem of Lagrange, solved in sections 2 and 3 of the work [14]. The conclusions drawn concerning Eq. (4.9) follow from this. A second, no less important conclusion can now be drawn. Namely, as was shown in [14], the equations (4.1), (4.9) describe a stable control system having a control function that optimizes the functional (4.2) in all nonspecial cases as noted in [14].*

Case of a Closed Region. We again turn to the equations (4.1) and (4.2), and assume that the coordinate ξ is restricted by the inequality (3.1) and that the functional (4.2) is minimized in the class of functions C. If we repeat the reasoning in part 3, we obtain the basic functional equation in the form

$$V + \sum_k \Big(\sum_\alpha b_{k\alpha}\eta_\alpha + m_k\varphi\Big)\frac{\partial\psi}{\partial\eta_k} = 0,$$
$$\Big(2c\varphi + \sum_k m_k \frac{\partial\psi}{\partial\eta_k}\Big)\frac{\partial\varphi}{\partial\xi} = 0. \tag{4.15}$$

As before, we obtain two solutions; the first coincides with the solution (4.9) for the points $|\Sigma p_\alpha\eta_\alpha| < \bar{\xi}$, the second solution $\varphi = \pm\bar{\xi}$ exists for points $|\Sigma p_\alpha\eta_\alpha| \geqslant \bar{\xi}$. In order to check that in both cases the first equation of (4.15) defines a continuous functional, it is necessary, in addition to the solution (4.8), to find the solution of the partial differential equation

$$\sum_k a_k\eta_k^2 + c\bar{\xi}^2 + \sum_k \Big(\sum_\alpha b_{k\alpha}\eta + m_k\bar{\xi}\Big)\frac{\partial\psi}{\partial\eta_k} = 0. \tag{4.16}$$

We will, however, not consider this further.

It is obvious, from comparison, that the dynamic-programming method yields the same result as was obtained in [14, 15] by the methods of calculus of variations with the application of the functional (4.2). This makes it possible to obtain directly the law of control in the form in which it is usually realized with a known selection of sensing elements, transformations, amplifiers, and servomotors.

5. The Case of a Limited Servomotor Velocity

In this case (see [15]), addition to the equations (4.1), we must use the equation

$$\dot{\xi} = f(\sigma), \quad |f(\sigma)| < \bar{f}, \quad \xi(0) = \xi_0, \tag{5.1}$$

where $f(\sigma)$ is a function of the class A [16]. The function $f(\sigma)$ and its argument $\sigma(\eta_1, \ldots, \eta_n, \xi)$ must be chosen to minimize the functional

$$I = \int_0^\infty (V + \alpha\dot{\xi}^2)\,dt \tag{5.2}$$

in the class C of functions of η_1, η_n, and ξ.

* In this connection, see [5, 18].

Reasoning similar to that used above leads to the Bellman equations

$$V + \alpha f^2 + f\frac{\partial\psi}{\partial\xi} + \sum_k\Big(\sum_\alpha b_{k\alpha}\eta_\alpha + m_k\xi\Big)\frac{\partial\psi}{\partial\eta_k} = 0,$$
$$\Big(2\alpha f + \frac{\partial\psi}{\partial\xi}\Big)\frac{\partial f}{\partial\sigma} = 0. \tag{5.3}$$

The desired solution consists of two parts. The first part is determined by the limitations imposed on the velocity, and is obtained from the condition $\partial f/d\sigma = 0$. This means that

$$f(\sigma) = \pm\bar{f}, \quad |\sigma| \geqslant \sigma^*, \tag{5.4}$$

where σ^* is a positive number.

For obtaining the second part of the solution, we have

$$f(\sigma) = -\frac{1}{2\alpha}\frac{\partial\psi}{\partial\xi}, \quad |\sigma| < \sigma^*. \tag{5.5}$$

In combination with the first equation of (5.3), this yields the partial differential equation

$$V + \sum_k\Big(\sum_\alpha b_{k\alpha}\eta_\alpha + m_k\xi\Big)\frac{\partial\psi}{\partial\eta_k} = \frac{1}{4\alpha}\Big(\frac{\partial\psi}{\partial\xi}\Big)^2. \tag{5.6}$$

which can be satisfied by the function

$$\psi = \sum_k\sum_\alpha A_{k\alpha}\eta_k\eta_\alpha + \xi\sum_\alpha B_\alpha\eta_\alpha + R\xi^2. \tag{5.7}$$

The coefficients of the form (5.7) are obtained by the method already described. The equality (5.5) yields a linear function $f(\sigma)$ for $|\sigma| < \sigma^*$, i.e.,

$$f(\sigma) = h\sigma, \quad \sigma = -\frac{1}{2h\alpha}\Big(\sum_k B_k\eta_k + 2R\xi\Big). \tag{5.8}$$

The quantity σ^* is obtained from the condition $h\sigma^* = \bar{f}$.

As in the previous case, we can show that this solution of the problem coincides with the solution obtained in [15].

6. An Example

As an example, we will consider the problem of an aircraft flying at a specified height. With certain assumptions concerning the rate of damping of natural oscillations of the plane relative to its transverse axis, the equations for the disturbed motion can be written as

$$\dot\eta_1 = b_{11}\eta_1 + b_{12}\eta_2 + m_1\xi,$$
$$\dot\eta_2 = b_{21}\eta_1 + b_{22}\eta_2 + m_2\xi, \tag{6.1}$$
$$\dot\eta_3 = \eta_1.$$

The coefficients of the equations are given in terms of the initial parameters of the aircraft by the relations [17]

$$b_{11} = -c_{xc}, \quad b_{12} = 2k_2 c_{yc}, \quad m_1 = -\rho c_{yc}^{\alpha}, \quad \tau = \frac{2m}{\rho SV},$$
$$b_{21} = -c_{yc}, \quad b_{22} = -2k_1 c_{xc}, \quad m_2 = \rho c_{xc}^{\alpha}, \quad \rho = \frac{m_z^{\delta_b}}{m_z^{\alpha}}. \tag{6.2}$$

Here τ is a parameter of the aircraft. In the equations (6.1), η_1 is the inclination of the trajectory, η_2 a dimensionless velocity disturbance, and η_3 a dimensionless disturbance of the height.

The optimizing functional is given by the integral

$$I(\xi) = \int_0^\infty (\eta_3^2 + c\xi^2)\, dt. \tag{6.3}$$

The basic equation for the determination of the functional is

$$\eta_3^2 (b_{11}\eta_1 + b_{12}\eta_2) \frac{\partial \psi}{\partial \eta_1} + (b_{21}\eta_1 + b_{22}\eta_2) \frac{\partial \psi}{\partial \eta_2} + \eta_1 \frac{\partial \psi}{\partial \eta_3} = \frac{1}{4c} \left[m_1 \frac{\partial \psi}{\partial \eta_1} + m_2 \frac{\partial \psi}{\partial \eta_2} \right]^2. \tag{6.4}$$

and the solution of this equation will be sought in the form

$$\psi = \sum_k \sum_\alpha A_{k\alpha} \eta_k \eta_\alpha \qquad (k,\ \alpha = 1,\ 2,\ 3). \tag{6.5}$$

The equations for determining the coefficients are

$$\begin{aligned}
b_{11}A_{11} + b_{21}A_{12} + A_{13} &= \frac{1}{2c}(m_1A_{11} + m_2A_{12})^2, \\
b_{12}A_{12} + b_{22}A_{22} &= \frac{1}{2c}(m_1A_{12} + m_2A_{22})^2, \\
c &= (m_1A_{13} + m_2A_{23})^2, \\
b_{12}A_{11} + (b_{22} + b_{11})A_{12} + b_{21}A_{22} + A_{23} &= \frac{1}{c}[m_1^2A_{11}A_{12} + m_2^2A_{12}A_{22} + m_1m_2(A_{11}A_{22} + A_{12}^2)], \\
b_{11}A_{13} + b_{21}A_{23} + A_{33} &= \frac{1}{c}[m_1^2A_{11}A_{13} + m_2^2A_{12}A_{23} + m_1m_2(A_{11}A_{23} + A_{13}A_{12})], \\
b_{12}A_{13} + b_{22}A_{23} &= \frac{1}{c}[m_1^2A_{12}A_{13} + m_2^2A_{22}A_{23} + m_1m_2(A_{12}A_{23} + A_{13}A_{22})].
\end{aligned} \tag{6.6}$$

The equations (6.6) can be solved by the method of successive approximations, and as a result we obtain

$$\xi = -\frac{1}{c}[(m_1A_{11} + m_2A_{21})\eta_1 + (m_1A_{12} + m_2A_{22})\eta_2 + (m_1A_{13} + m_2A_{23})\eta_3]. \tag{6.7}$$

7. A Relation between Dynamic Programming and Lyapunov's Functions

In a discussion of the contents of the articles [14, 15], N. N. Krasovskii drew my attention to the fact that the functional (4.2), interpreted in these articles as an integral square error, can be considered as a Lyapunov function. N. N. Krasovskii pointed out this relation between Lyapunov functions and optimal systems in [7] and also in [18, 19]. R. E. Kalman noted it later in [13, 20].

We will show here that the relation of Lyapunov functions to the problem of optimizing the integral square error arises naturally from the formulas in section 4. Actually, using (4.9), we will calculate the total derivative of the function ψ defined in (4.8). This function must be positive everywhere that $\Sigma\eta_k^2 \neq 0$. It will have a meaning when the system (4.1) and (4.9) is stable.

Then the basic functional equation (4.5) becomes the partial differential equation we have used for constructing a Lyapunov function with a total derivative given by the formula

$$\frac{d\psi}{dt} = -V, \tag{7.1}$$

so that the functional ψ is the Lyapunov function for our problem. Conversely, we assume that by applying dynamic-programming methods we have found tha functional ψ (4.8). If there is some way of verifying that the function ψ is positive everywhere for $\Sigma\eta_k^2 \neq 0$, then it is a Lyapunov function for the problem. The condition that ψ be positive is the stability criterion for the optimal system. This is of special interest, since the dynamic-programming method can be used to solve simultaneously both the problem of optimizing a system according to the criterion (4.2) and the problem of the stability of the optimal system. An optimal and stable system corresponds to a functional ψ that is positive for $\Sigma\eta_k^2 \neq 0$.

This latter fact is especially important in the case when the system to be optimized is nonlinear

$$\dot{\eta}_k = \Xi_k(\eta_1, \ldots, \eta_n, \xi). \tag{7.2}$$

In this case the basic functional equation will be

$$0 = V + \sum_k \Xi_k(\eta_1, \ldots, \eta_n, \xi)\frac{\partial\psi}{\partial\eta_k} \tag{7.3}$$

and the relation (7.1) remains valid.

The author wishes to thank E. A. Barbashin and N. N. Krasovskii sincerely for their very useful advice and comments.

LITERATURE CITED

1. V. G. Boltyanskii, R. V. Gamkrelidze, and L. S. Pontryagin, "The optimal processes," Dokl. Akad. Nauk SSSR, 110, 1 (1956).
2. R. V. Gamkrelidze, "The theory of optimal processes in linear systems. The theory of optimal processes," Izv. Akad. Nauk SSSR, ser. matem., 24, 1 (1960); Dokl. Akad. Nauk SSSR, 116, 1 (1957). "The theory of processes in linear systems, optimal with respect to rate of action," Izv. Akad. Nauk SSSR, ser. matem., 22 (1958).
3. V. G. Boltyanskii, "The maximum principle in the theory of optimal processes," Doklady Akad. Nauk SSSR, 119, 6 (1958).
4. R. V. Gamkrelidze, "Processes for bounded phase coordinates, optimal with respect to rate of action," Doklady Akad. Nauk SSSR, 125, 3 (1959).
5. N. N. Krasovskii, "The theory of optimal control," Avtomatika i telemekhanika, 18, 11 (1957).*
6. N. N. Krasovskii, "A problem in optimal control," Prikl. matem. i mekh., 21, 5 (1957).
7. N. N. Krasovskii, "A problem in optimal control," Prikl. matem. i mekh., 23, 1 (1959).
8. R. E. Bellman, J. Glicksberg, and O. A. Gross, Some Aspects of the Mathematical Theory of Control Processes. Report No. 313, 1959, RAND Corporation.
9. I. P. LaSall, Time Optimal Control Systems. Proc. National Ac. Sci., vol. 45, No. 4, 1958.
10. Ya. P. Roitenberg, "Some problems in dynamic programming," Prikl. matem. i mekh., 23, 4 (1959).
11. R. Kulikowski, Bulletin de L'Academie Polonaise des Sciences, vol. VII, No. 4, 1959; vol. VII, No. 6, 1959; vol. VII, No. 11, 1959; vol. VII, No. 12, 1959; vol. VIII, No. 4, 1960.
12. C. A. Desoer, The Bong–Bong Servo Problem, Treated by Variational Technique Information and Control, vol. 2, 1959.
13. R. E. Kalman and T. E. Bertram, Control System Analysis and Design Via the Second Method of Lyapunof. Journal of Basic Engineering, June, 1960.
14. A. M. Letov, "Analytical design of control systems," I, Avtomatika i telemekhanika, 21, 4 (1960).*
15. A. M. Letov, "Analytical design of control systems," II and III, Avtomatika i telemekhanika, 21, 5 and 6 (1960).*
16. A. M. Letov, The Stability of Nonlinear Control Systems [in Russian] State Technical Press (1955).
17. I. V. Ostoslavskii and G. O. Kalachev, The Longitudinal Stability of Aircraft [in Russian], Oborongiz (1951).
18. N. N. Krasovskii, "The calculation of optimal control by direct methods," Prikl. matem. i mekh., 2 (1960).
19. N. N. Krasovskii, "The choice of parameters for optimal stable systems," Doklady na Pervom kongresse IFAK (1960).
20. R. E. Kalman, "The general theory of control systems," Doklady na Pervom Kongresse IFAK (1960).

* Original Russian Pagination. See C. B. translation.

OPTIMUM PROCESSES IN SYSTEMS WITH DISTRIBUTED PARAMETERS

A. G. Butkovskii

Translated from Avtomatika i Telemekhanika, Vol. 22, No. 1,
pp. 17-26, January, 1961
Original article submitted May 23, 1960

This article is devoted to the problem of the optimum control of systems whose motion is generally described by nonlinear integral relationships that correlate the command inputs with the output variables of the system to be controlled. It is shown how the obtained results can be applied to the solution of problems in the optimum control of systems described by partial differential equations in the case where the equation solution is expressed by an integral relationship.

Important results in the theory of optimum processes have been obtained by using nonclassical variation methods in investigating lumped-parameter systems that are described by ordinary differential equations [1,2]. However, there is a large number of problems where the systems to be controlled have distributed parameters. Such systems pertain, for instance, to a large number of production-line industrial processes, in particular the heating of metals in through-passage furnaces, the drying of strip and friable materials, continuous etching and deposition of coatings, agglomeration, distillation, etc. The problems in the optimum control of systems with distributed parameters are formulated in [3].

Statement of the Problem

Many problems in the optimum control of systems with distributed parameters can be solved on the basis of the results obtained in considering the following optimum control problem.

Let n coordinates of the vector $Q = Q(t) = [Q_1(t), \ldots, Q_n(t)]$ satisfy the equation

$$Q_i = Q_i(t) = \int_{t_0}^{t_1} K_i(t, \tau, u_1(\tau), \ldots, u_r(\tau))\, d\tau, \tag{1}$$

where

$$K_i(t, \tau, u_1, \ldots, u_r) \quad (i = 1, 2, \ldots, n)$$

are certain given functions of the arguments. The control functions $u_k = u_k(t)$ $(k = 1, 2, \ldots, r)$, are sectionally continuous with respect to t. The control vector $u = u(t) = [u_1(t), \ldots, u_r(t)]$ belongs to a closed region Ω at any instant of time t contained in the $t_0 \leq t \leq t_1$ interval.

It is necessary to find such control $u = u(t) \in \Omega$, $t_0 \leq t \leq t_1$ for which $Q(t_1) = Q_*$ (Q_* is the assigned vector), and the assigned functional

$$Q_0 = \int_{t_0}^{t_1} F(\tau, Q(\tau), u(\tau))\, d\tau \tag{2}$$

assumes the minimum possible value.

Optimum Regime Conditions

The necessary optimum regime condition which the control vector $u = u(t)$ $(t_0 \leq t \leq t_1)$ must satisfy can be formulated by the following maximum theorem.

Theorem 1. Let $u = u(t) \in \Omega$ $(t_0 \leq t \leq t_1)$ represent such control for which $Q(t_1) = Q_*$, where Q_* is the assigned vector. For the optimum control $u = u(t)$, and the corresponding trajectory $Q = Q(t)$, there should exist such a constant nonzero vector $c = (c_0, c_1, \ldots, c_n)$ that $c_0 \leq 0$ and that, for almost all t, $t_0 \leq t \leq t_1$, the function

$$H = c_0 \int_{t_0}^{t_1} \sum_{i=1}^{n} \frac{\partial F(\tau, Q(\tau), u(\tau))}{\partial Q_i} K_i(\tau, t, u)\, d\tau + $$
$$+ c_0 F(t, Q(t), u) + \sum_{i=1}^{n} c_i K_i(t_1, t, u) \tag{3}$$

of the variable $\underline{u}$, $u \in \Omega$, attains its maximum at the point $u = u(t)$.

In certain problems, the point $Q(t_1)$ must belong to a certain multiplicity set M with an arbitrary dimension that does not exceed $n-1$. This is the so-called problem with a mobile right-hand end.

If the point $Q(t_1) \in M$ is known, then, on the basis of the above theorem, optimum control, as applied to the problem with a mobile end, must satisfy the maximum condition. An additional condition determining the point $Q(t_1)$ in the multiplicity set M is the transversality condition [1]. Let $Q(t_1) \in M$ be the optimum trajectory end. We shall say that the transversality condition is satisfied if the $(c_1, \ldots, c_n)$ vector is normal to the plane S, which is tangent to the multiplicity set M at the $Q(t_1)$ point. The necessary condition for the optimum regime in the mobile right-hand end problem can now be formulated in the following manner.

Theorem 2. Let $u = u(t) \in \Omega$ $(t_0 \leq t \leq t_1)$, for which $Q(t_1) \in M$. For the optimum control $u = u(t)$, and the corresponding trajectory $Q = Q(t)$ in the mobile right-hand end problem, it is necessary that there exist a vector $c = (c_0, c_1, \ldots, c_n)$ different from zero, which will satisfy the conditions of theorem 1, and that, moreover, the transversality condition at the point $Q(t_1)$ be satisfied.

The proofs of theorems 1 and 2, which are based on the application of "acicular" variations, and on the properties of convex multiplicity sets [1], are given in Appendix I.

In certain problems, instead of the system (1), systems of the following form must be considered:

$$Q_i = Q_i(t) = \int_{t_0}^{t} K_i(t, \tau, u(\tau))\, d\tau \quad (i = 1, 2, \ldots, n). \tag{4}$$

In this, the condition $Q(t_1) = Q_*$ also must be satisfied for $t = t_1$, and the functional (2) must assume the minimum possible value. This problem represents a particular case of the previous problem if the $K_i(t, \tau, u)$ function in system (1) satisfies the condition

$$K_i(t, \tau, u(\tau)) \equiv 0 \quad (i = 1, 2, \ldots, n), \tag{5}$$

where

$$t \leq \tau \leq t_1.$$

In this case, theorems 1 and 2 are also valid and, because of (5), the function H will assume the following form:

$$H = c_0 \int_{t}^{t_1} \sum_{i=1}^{n} \frac{\partial F(\tau, Q(\tau), u(\tau))}{\partial Q_i} K_i(\tau, t, u)\, d\tau + $$
$$+ c_0 F(t, Q(t), u) + \sum_{i=1}^{n} c_i K_i(t_1, t, u). \tag{6}$$

Application of the Obtained Results

As an example of the utilization of the obtained results in solving problems in the optimum control of systems with distributed parameters, we shall consider two problems.

The first problem pertains to heat-exchange processes where it is necessary to secure, in the minimum time, a temperature distribution in a solid which would be close to the assigned distribution by means of an external temperature field, or to minimize in a certain time deviations (in any sense) of the temperature distribution from a certain assigned distribution.

Assume that the $q = q(x,t)$ function describes the temperature distribution in a solid in dependence on the space coordinate x $(0 \leq x \leq x_1)$ and the time t $(0 \leq t \leq t_1)$, where x_1 and t_1 are certain given values. Further, we shall assume that the heating equations are given by

$$\frac{\partial q}{\partial t} = a \frac{\partial^2 q}{\partial x^2} \quad (0 \leqslant t \leqslant t_1,\ 0 \leqslant x \leqslant x_1). \tag{7}$$

The boundary conditions are

$$\left.\frac{\partial q}{\partial x}\right|_{x=x_1} = \alpha\,[u(t) - q(x_1, t)], \tag{8}$$

$$\left.\frac{\partial q}{\partial x}\right|_{x=0} = 0. \tag{9}$$

The initial condition is

$$q(x, 0) = 0. \tag{10}$$

The optimum control problem consists in determining a control function $u = u(t)$, restricted by the conditions $N_1 \leq u(t) \leq N_2$ $(0 \leq t \leq t_1)$, for which the integral of the square of the solid temperature distribution deviation $q_1 = q(x,t_1)$ from a certain assigned constant temperature q_a assumes the least possible value at the instant of time t_1, i.e.,

$$I = \int_0^{x_1} [q_a - q(x, t_1)]^2\, dx = \min. \tag{11}$$

As is known from the theory of partial differential equations [4,5,6], the function $q = q(x,t)$ that satisfies the conditions (7)-(10) can be represented in the following form:

$$q = q(x, t) = \int_0^{t} \varphi(x, t, \tau)\, u(\tau)\, d\tau, \tag{12}$$

where φ is a known function of its arguments (the Green function method).

The minimization of functional (11) can be reduced (see Appendix II) to the minimization of the functional

$$Q_0 = \int_0^{t_1} [Q_1(\tau) - \gamma R(t_1, \tau)]\, u(\tau)\, d\tau \tag{13}$$

under the following conditions:

$$Q_1(t) = \int_0^{t_1} T(t, \tau)\, u(\tau)\, d\tau, \qquad Q_2 = \int_0^{t_1} d\tau, \tag{14}$$

where R and T are certain known functions, and γ is a number.

In order to find the extremal control function $u = u(t)$, we shall apply theorem 1.

The H function has the following form:

$$H = c_0 \int_0^{t_1} u(\tau)\, T(t, \tau)\, u(t)\, d\tau + c_0\, [Q_1(t) - \gamma R(t_1, t)]\, u(t) + c_1 T(t, t_1)\, u(t) + c_2. \tag{15}$$

From the transversality condition (theorem 2), we have $c_1 = 0$; if we take into account that $c_0 \leq 0$, the function H has a maximum if the following condition is satisfied:

$$u(t) = \frac{1}{2}(N_1 + N_2) + \frac{1}{2}(N_2 - N_1) \times$$

$$\times \operatorname{sign} \left\{ \gamma R(t_1, t) - \int_0^{t_1} [T(t, \tau) + T(\tau, t)]\, u(\tau)\, d\tau \right\}. \tag{16}$$

Condition (16) has the form of an integral equation for the $u = u(t)$ function.

For the $v = v(t)$ function, which is determined by the relation

$$u = \frac{1}{2}(N_2 + N_1) + \frac{1}{2}(N_2 - N_1)\, v, \tag{17}$$

this equation is equivalent to the equation

$$v(t) = \operatorname{sign}\, [a(t) + \int_0^{t_1} b(t, \tau)\, v(\tau)\, d\tau], \tag{18}$$

where $a(t)$ and $b(t,\tau)$ are certain known functions which are expressed in terms of the known functions in Eq. (16), while $|v(t)| \leq 1$ $(0 \leq t \leq t_1)$.

We shall assume that the expression under the symbol "sign" in Eqs. (16) and (18) does not become identically equal to zero, and that there exists a solution $v = v(t)$ which has a finite number of discontinuities in the $(0, t_1)$ interval. In this case, the following method can be used for solving Eq. (18). We shall first check whether the $v(t) \equiv 1$ function or the $v(t) \equiv -1$ function is the solution of this equation for $0 \leq t \leq t_1$. If not, we shall assume that the solution $v = v(t)$ changes its sign only once at the point θ_1 $(0 < \theta_1 < t_1)$, and we shall calculate the expressions Φ_1 and Φ_2 under the symbol "sign" in Eq. (18) as functions of time _t_ and the parameter θ_1. In this, $\Phi_1 = \Phi_1(t, \theta_1)$ is calculated under the assumption that $v = 1$ in the first interval, and $\Phi_2 = \Phi_2(t, \theta_1)$ is calculated under the assumption that $v = -1$ in the first interval. Then, if there exists a solution $v = v(t)$ with a single sign reversal, at least one of the equations $\Phi_1(\theta_1, \theta_1) = 0$, $\Phi_2(\theta_1, \theta_1) = 0$ must have a real solution. If no such solution exists, the solution should be successively sought, first in the class of sectionally constant functions (equal to 1 or -1) with two sign changes, then with three, etc., by successively calculating the Φ_1 and Φ_2 functions in dependence on the parameters $\theta_1, \theta_2, \theta_3$, etc. Finally, at a certain _m_th stage, as a result of the assumptions made, there must exist a solution $v = v(t)$ with sign changes at _m_ points $\theta_1, \theta_2, \ldots, \theta_m$, i.e., there must be a real solution of at least one of the two systems of equations

$$\Phi_1(\theta_i, \theta_1, \ldots, \theta_m) = 0 \quad (i = 1, 2, \ldots, m),$$

or

$$\Phi_2(\theta_i, \theta_1, \ldots, \theta_m) = 0 \quad (i = 1, 2, \ldots, m) \tag{19}$$

$$(0 < \theta_1 < \theta_2 < \ldots < \theta_m < t_1).$$

Here, the $\Phi_1 = \Phi_1(t_1, \theta_1, \ldots, \theta_m)$ function denotes the expression under the symbol "sign" in Eq. (18) in dependence on time _t_ $(0 \leq t \leq t_1)$ under the assumption that $v(t) = 1$ in the first interval for $0 \leq t \leq \theta_1$. The $\Phi_2 = \Phi_2(t, \theta_1, \ldots, \theta_m)$ function denotes the same under the assumption that $v = -1$ in the first interval for $0 \leq t \leq \theta_1$.

Let us now consider the optimum control problem as applied to the process of heat exchange between a stationary and a mobile medium. Such processes take place, for instance, in heating billets in through-passage furnaces.

Let $q = q(x,y,t)$ describe the temperature distribution in an infinitely wide strip with the thickness x_1, which moves with the velocity $\nu = \nu(t) \geq 0$ in the _y_ axis positive direction. The _x_ axis is perpendicular to the plate plane, and the _x_ coordinate varies within the $0 \leq x \leq x_1$ interval. The heating of the material through the plate upper surface takes place in the $0 \leq y \leq y_1$ interval.

The heating equations have the following form:

$$\frac{\partial q}{\partial t} = a\frac{\partial^2 q}{\partial x^2} - \nu\frac{\partial q}{\partial y} \quad (0 \leqslant x \leqslant x_1,\ 0 \leqslant y \leqslant y_1,\ 0 \leqslant t \leqslant t_1). \tag{20}$$

The boundary conditions are

$$\left.\frac{\partial q}{\partial x}\right|_{x=x_1} = \alpha\,[u(t) - q(x_1, y, t)], \tag{21}$$

$$\left.\frac{\partial q}{\partial x}\right|_{x=0} = 0, \tag{22}$$

$$q(x, 0, t) = 0. \tag{23}$$

The initial condition is

$$q(x, y, 0) = q_0(x, y). \tag{24}$$

Here, a and α are positive constant coefficients, and the thickness x_1 of the solid can be a function of

$$\eta = y - \int_0^t \nu(p)\,dp.$$

In this case, the optimum control problem consists in determining a control function $u = u(t)$, restricted by the $N_1 \leq u(t) \leq N_2$ condition, for which the integral of the square of the deviation of the solid average temperature, with respect to its cross section

$$\bar{q} = \bar{q}(y, t) = \int_0^{x_1} q(x, y, t)\,dx,$$

from the assigned temperature q_a, assumes the minimum possible value at the point $y = y_1$ in the time interval from 0 to t_1, i.e.,

$$I = \int_0^{t_1} [q_a - \bar{q}(y_1, t)]^2\,dt = \min. \tag{25}$$

By the nondegenerate substitution of variables

$$\xi = x, \quad \eta = y - \int_0^t \nu(p)\,dp, \quad \tau = t, \tag{26}$$

Equation (20) can be reduced to the one-dimensional heat-conduction equation, and the $q = q(x,y,t)$ function that satisfies conditions (20)-(24) can be represented in the following form [4,5,6]:

$$q = q(x, y, t) = \int_0^{x_1} g(x, t, \xi)\,q_0\Big(\xi, y - \int_0^t \nu(p)\,dp\Big)\,d\xi + \int_0^t \varphi(x, t, \tau)\,u\Big(y - \int_\tau^t \nu(p)\,dp, \tau\Big)\,d\tau. \tag{27}$$

Here, q and φ are certain known functions.

If we assume that t_1 satisfies the condition $\int_0^{t_1} \nu(p)\,dp \leqslant y_1$, then, by taking (27) into account, the average with respect to the temperature cross section $\bar{q} = \bar{q}(y,t)$ will be given by

$$\bar{q} = \bar{q}(y, t) = G(y, t) + \int_0^t k(t, \tau)\,u(\tau)\,d\tau. \tag{28}$$

Here, $G(y,t)$ is a known function representing the first term in (27), averaged with respect to x, and $k(t,\tau)$ is the $\varphi(x,t,\tau)$ function, which is averaged with respect to x.

By denoting $Q_1(t) = \int_0^t k(t, \tau)u(\tau)\,d\tau$ and substituting (28) in expression (25) for $y = y_1$, the problem will be reduced to the minimization of the functional

$$Q_0 = \int_0^{t_1} [\Psi(\tau) - Q_1(\tau)]^2\,d\tau \tag{29}$$

[where $\Psi(\tau)$ is a known function], under the condition that

$$Q_1(t) = \int_0^t k(t, \tau)\,u(\tau)\,d\tau, \qquad Q_2 = \int_0^{t_1} d\tau. \tag{30}$$

We shall now compose the H function. Considering (6), we have

$$\begin{aligned} H &= 2c_0\int_t^{t_1} [\Psi(\tau) - Q_1(\tau)]\,k(\tau, t)\,u(t)\,d\tau + \\ &+ c_0[\Psi(t) - Q_1(t)] + c_1 k(t_1, t)\,u(t) + c_2. \end{aligned} \tag{31}$$

According to the transversality condition, $c_1 = 0$, $c_0 \leq 0$.

It is obvious from (31) that H has a maximum if

$$u(t) = \frac{1}{2}(N_1 + N_2) + \frac{1}{2}(N_2 - N_1)\,\mathrm{sign}\int_t^{t_1} [\Psi(\tau) - Q_1(\tau)]\,k(\tau, t)\,d\tau. \tag{32}$$

By substituting in this expression the $Q_1(\tau)$ value given by (30), we obtain an integral equation with respect to the function u(t) to be determined, the solution of which will define the extremum.

It is obvious from (32) that, in the case where $\Psi(\tau) \equiv Q_1(\tau)$, the first term of the H function becomes identically equal to zero, and that the determination of the optimum control function from the maximum principle becomes impossible. However, it is readily seen from (29) that the functional Q_0 to be minimized is identically equal to zero, i.e., it assumes the minimum possible value. According to the terminology given in [2], this case corresponds to the so-called "particular" trajectory section. The optimum control $u = u(t)$ is, in this case, determined from the solution of the Volterra linear integral equation of the first kind:

$$\Psi(t) = \int_0^t k(t, \tau)\,u(\tau)\,d\tau. \tag{33}$$

The methods used for solving equations of the type given by (33) have been sufficiently treated in the literature [7].

Thus, on the basis of the above reasoning, we can find the optimum control inputs for a number of systems with distributed parameters.

APPENDIX I

<u>Proof of Theorem 1.</u> Let $u = u(t) \in \Omega$ $(t_0 \leq t \leq t_1)$ represent optimum control for which

$$Q_i = \int_{t_0}^{t_1} K_i(t, \tau\;u(\tau))\,d\tau \qquad (i = 1, 2, \ldots, n), \qquad Q(t_1) = Q_* \tag{34}$$

and the functional

$$Q_0 = \int_{t_0}^{t_1} F(\tau, Q(\tau), u(\tau))\,d\tau$$

assumes its minimum value.

Let us determine the control function $u^* = u^*(t)$, which is obtained by varying the control given by $u = u(t)$. For this, we shall select the instants of time $\tau_1, \tau_2, \ldots, \tau_l$ which satisfy the inequalities $t_0 < \tau_1 < \tau_2 < \ldots < \tau_l < t_1$, and which represent continuity points of the control function u(t). We shall select arbitrary non-negative numbers $\delta t_1, \ldots, \delta t_l$, and arbitrary points $v_1, v_2, \ldots, v_l$, belonging to the control region Ω. Consider the half-intervals I_i given by

$$\tau_i - \varepsilon\delta t_i < t \leqslant \tau_i \quad (i = 1, 2, \ldots, l). \tag{35}$$

Assume that ϵ is so small that the half-intervals (35) never intersect each other, and that they are contained within the $t_0 \leq t \leq t_1$ section; then the $u^* = u^*(t)$ control will be determined in the following manner:

If t does not belong to any of the half-intervals $I_1, \ldots, I_l$, then

$$u^*(t) = u(t); \tag{36}$$

if $t \in I_i$ $(i = 1, 2, \ldots, l)$, then

$$u^*(t) = v_i. \tag{36'}$$

Then, the variated trajectory has the following form:

$$Q^*(\tau) = Q(\tau) + \varepsilon\Delta Q(\tau) + \ldots, \qquad Q^* = Q_0 + \varepsilon\Delta Q_0 + \ldots \tag{37}$$

Here, $\Delta Q(\tau)$ and ΔQ_0 are independent of ϵ, and they are given by

$$\begin{aligned} \Delta Q_i(\tau) &= \sum_{j=1}^{l} [K_i(\tau, \tau_j, v_j) - K_i(\tau, \tau_j, u(\tau_j))]\,\delta t_j \\ \Delta Q_0 &= \int_{t_0}^{t_1} \sum_{i=1}^{n'} \frac{\partial F}{\partial Q_i} \sum_{j=1} [K_i(\tau, \tau_j, v_j) - K_i(\tau, \tau_j, u(\tau_i))]\,\delta t_j d\tau + \\ &+ \sum_{j=1}^{l} [F(\tau_j, Q(\tau_j), v_j) - F(\tau_j, Q(\tau_j), u(\tau_j))]\,\delta t_j. \end{aligned} \tag{38}$$

Essentially, the $[\Delta Q_0, \Delta Q(t_1)]$ vector depends on the choice of the τ_i and v_i points, and the δt_i $(i = 1, 2, \ldots, l)$ numbers. (In the case where the same points τ_i correspond to different variations, control variations similar to those used in paragraph 9 of [1] can be introduced.) Moreover, it can be considered that the same number of τ_i and v_i points have been taken for different variations, so that the addition of new τ_i and v_i points for which $\delta t_i = 0$ would not change the control $u^*(t)$ that is being varied.

Let us now consider the multiplicity K of vectors $[\Delta Q_0, \Delta Q_0(t_1)]$ with the origin at the point $[Q_0, Q(t_1)]$ in space (Q_0, Q) which are obtained from the multiplicity of variations of the indicated type. We shall refer to the multiplicity set K by the term "cone of attainability." It can be readily seen that K is a convex cone. Actually, if the points s' and s" belong to cone K, the point $s = \lambda_1 s' + \lambda_2 s''$, where $\lambda_1 \geq 0$, $\lambda_2 \geq 0$, also belongs to cone K, since the point s is obtained by variation which is determined by the joining of τ_i' and v_i' for s', and of τ_i'' and v_i'' for s", while δt_i for the point s is equal to $\delta t_i = \lambda_1 \delta t_i'$ for τ_i', and to $\delta t_i = \lambda_2 \delta t_i''$ for τ_i''. Since Eqs. (38) are linear with respect to δt_i, we find that the point $s \in K$. Further, following a line of reasoning similar to that used in proving lemma 3 in [1], we find that the inside of cone K must not contain a straight line L with the origin at the apex of cone K, and which follows the negative direction of the Q_0 axis in the vector space (Q_0, Q). Hence, it follows that there are such numbers $c_0, c_1, \ldots, c_n$ for which the entire cone K lies in the half-space $\sum_{\alpha=0}^{n} c_\alpha Q_\alpha \leqslant 0$, and the straight line L lies in the half-space $\sum_{\alpha=0}^{n} c_\alpha Q_\alpha \geqslant 0$, i.e., the vector with the coordinates $c_0 = -1, c_1 = 0, \ldots, c_n = 0$ lies in the half-space $\sum_{\alpha=0}^{n} c_\alpha Q_\alpha \geqslant 0$. Consequently, $c_0 \leq 0$, whence we find that

$$\sum_{\alpha=0}^{n} c_\alpha \Delta Q_\alpha \leqslant 0, \quad c_0 \leqslant 0. \tag{39}$$

Let us consider the $[\Delta Q_0, \Delta Q(t_1)]$ vector, which is obtained as a result of varying the control function u(t) at the single point τ_1 $(l = 1)$ and $\delta t_1 = 1$. By taking (38) into account, we have

$$c_0\int_{t_0}^{t_1}\sum_{i=1}^{n}\frac{\partial F}{\partial Q_i}[K_i(\tau,\tau_1,v_1)-K_i(\tau,\tau_1,u(\tau_1))]\,d\tau+$$

$$+c_0[F(\tau_1,Q(\tau_1),v_1)-F(\tau_1,Q(\tau_1),u(\tau_1))]+\sum_{i=1}^{n}c_i[K_i(t_1,\tau_1,v_1)-K_i(t_1,\tau_1,u(\tau_1))]\leqslant 0. \tag{40}$$

Since this inequality is valid for any point $v_1\in\Omega$, the function

$$H=c_0\int_{t_0}^{t_1}\sum_{i=1}^{n}\frac{\partial F}{\partial Q_i}K_i(\tau,t,u)\,d\tau+c_0F(t,Q(t),u)+\sum_{i=1}^{n}c_iK_i(t_1,t,u) \tag{41}$$

must have a maximum for $u\in\Omega$.

Proof of Theorem 2. Let us draw through the point $[Q_0, Q(t_1)]$ in space (Q_0, Q) a plane P that is parallel to space Q. We shall also draw a plane R with the dimension n (parallel to the Q_0 axis) through the plane S (with the $n-1$ dimension in space Q)—which is tangent to the multiplicity set M at the point $Q(t_1)\in M$—and the point $[Q_0, Q(t_1)]$ in space (Q_0, Q). Consider the half-plane T of the plane R that lies in that half of the space divided by the plane P where the negative "end" of the Q_0 axis is located. Due to the fact that the $Q = Q(t)$ $(t_0\le t\le t_1)$ trajectory is the optimum trajectory, the attainability cone K must not contain any straight line L belonging to the half-plane T and having the origin at the point $[Q_0, Q(t_1)]$. In the opposite case, as at the beginning of the proof of lemma 10 from [1], we would arrive at a contradiction to the fact that $Q = Q(t)$ is not optimum, i.e., we could reach the multiplicity set M for a smaller value of Q_0. Cone K and the half-plane T represent convex cones with a common apex at the point $[Q_0, Q(t_1)]$, while the inside of cone K does not intersect with cone T. Therefore, there must exist a plane given by the equation $\sum_{\alpha=0}^{n}c_\alpha Q_\alpha=0$ $(c_0\leqslant 0)$, for which cone T lies in the half-space $\sum_{\alpha=0}^{n}c_\alpha Q_\alpha\geqslant 0$, and cone K lies in the half-space $\sum_{\alpha=0}^{n}c_\alpha Q_\alpha\leqslant 0$. For instance, the plane R, containing the half-plane T which, in turn, by definition, contains the plane S tangent to the multiplicity set M, is such a plane. This proves that the transversality conditions are satisfied.

APPENDIX II

By substituting (12) in (11), squaring, and by expanding into a sum of integrals, we have

$$I=\int_0^{x_1}q_a^2\,dx-2q_a\int_0^{x_1}\left(\int_0^{t_1}\varphi(x,t_1,\tau)\,u(\tau)\,d\tau\right)dx+\int_0^{x_1}\left(\int_0^{t_1}\varphi(x,t_1,\tau)\,u(\tau)\,d\tau\right)^2dx. \tag{42}$$

Let us reverse the order of integration in the second term of the sum, and let us denote $R(t,\tau)=\int_0^{x_1}\varphi(x,t,\tau)\,dx$ and $\gamma = 2q_a$. Let us represent the square of the integral with respect to time in the third term as a double integral, and also reverse the order of integration while denoting $T(t,\tau)=\int_0^{x_1}\varphi(x,t_1,t)\,\varphi(x,t_1,\tau)\,dx.$ Then expression (42) will assume the following form:

$$I=x_1q_a^2-\gamma\int_0^{t_1}R(t_1,\tau)\,u(\tau)\,d\tau+\int_0^{t_1}\int_0^{t_1}T(t,\tau)\,u(t)\,u(\tau)\,dt\,d\tau. \tag{43}$$

It is obvious that (43) can be written thus:

$$I=x_1q_a^2+\int_0^{t_1}\left[\int_0^{t_1}T(t_1,\tau)\,u(t)\,dt-\gamma R(t_1,\tau)\right]u(\tau)\,d\tau. \tag{44}$$

By denoting $Q_1(t) = \int_0^{t_1} T(\tau, t)\, u(\tau)\, d\tau$ and neglecting the constant term $x_1 q_a^2$, we find that the minimization of functional I is equivalent to the minimization of the functional

$$Q_0 = \int_0^{t_1} [Q_1(\tau) - \gamma R(t_1, \tau)]\, u(\tau)\, d\tau \tag{45}$$

under the condition that

$$Q_1(t) = \int_0^{t_1} T(\tau, t)\, u(\tau), \qquad Q_2 = \int_0^{t_1} d\tau. \tag{46}$$

LITERATURE CITED

1. V. G. Boltyanskii, R. V. Gamkrelidze, and L. S. Pontryagin, "Theory of optimum processes. I," Izvest. Akad. Nauk SSSR, Math. Sec. 24, No. 1 (1960).
2. L. I. Rozonoér, "L. S. Pontryagin's maximum principle in the theory of optimal systems. I, II, and III," Avtomatika i Telemekhanika 20, Nos. 10, 11, 12 (1959).
3. A. G. Butkovskii and A. Ya. Lerner, "On the optimum control of systems with distributed parameters," Avtomatika i Telemekhanika 21, No. 6 (1960).
4. S. L. Sobolev, Mathematical Physics Equations [in Russian] (Gostekhizdat, 1954).
5. V. I. Smirnov, Calculus Course [in Russian] (Gostekhizdat, 1951) Vol. 4.
6. Z. S. Agranovich and A. Ya. Povzner, Application of Operational Methods to the Solution of Some Problems in Mathematical Physics [in Russian] (Khar'kov State University Press, 1954).
7. F. Trikomi, Integral Equations [Russian translation] (IL, Moscow, 1960).

Variational Methods in Problems of Control and Programming

LEONARD D. BERKOVITZ

Mathematics Department, The RAND Corporation, Santa Monica, California

Submitted by Richard Bellman

It is shown how a fairly general control problem, or programming problem, with constraints can be reduced to a special type of classical Bolza problem in the calculus of variations. Necessary conditions from the Bolza problem are translated into necessary conditions for optimal control. It is seen from these conditions that Pontryagin's Maximum Principle is a translation of the usual Weierstrass condition, and is applicable to a wider class of problems than that considered by Pontryagin. The differentiability and continuity properties of the value of the control are established under reasonable hypotheses on the synthesis, and it is shown that the value satisfies the Hamilton-Jacobi equation. As a corollary we obtain a rigorous proof of a functional equation of Bellman that is valid for a much wider class of problems than heretofore. A sufficiency theorem for the synthesis of control is also given.

I. INTRODUCTION

A controlled, or programmed, system is one whose state at time t is represented by a real n-dimensional vector $x(t) = (x^1(t), \ldots, x^n(t))$ that is determined by a system of differential equations and initial conditions

$$\frac{dx^i}{dt} = G^i(t, x, u), \qquad x^i(t_0) = x_0^{\,i}, \qquad i = 1, \ldots, n, \tag{1.1}$$

where $u = (u^1(t), \ldots, u^m(t))$. The m-dimensional vector $u(t)$ is called the control function, or control, or the program for the system; it is usually required to satisfy constraints

$$R^j(t, x, u) \geqslant 0, \qquad j = 1, \ldots, r. \tag{1.2}$$

The problem of optimal control, or the programming problem, is to choose the control $u(t)$ so as to bring the system from the given initial state to a terminal state (t_1, x_1), or one of a collection of terminal states $\{(t_1, x_1)\}$, in such a way as to minimize (or maximize) a functional

$$J(u) = g(t_1, x_1) + \int_{t_0}^{t_1} f(t, x, u)\, dt, \tag{1.3}$$

where g is a function defined on the set of terminal states and the integral is evaluated along the solution of (1.1) corresponding to the choice of $u(t)$. A more complete and precise statement of the problem will be given in Section II.

It is generally recognized that in the absence of the constraints (1.2), control problems, as usually formulated, are special cases of the problem of Bolza in the calculus of variations. In attacking problems in which constraints of the form (1.2) are present, as well as constraints of the form

$$\int_{t_0}^{t_1} \varphi^k(t, x, u)\, dt \leqslant C^k, \qquad k = 1, \ldots, K, \tag{1.4}$$

several avenues have been explored. One is the "Maximum Principle" developed by Pontryagin and his collaborators Boltyanski and Gamkrelidze [13] for problems of the following type. The constraints are independent of x and require u to lie in a closed set, the function g is absent, the terminal state x_1 is a prescribed vector, and the terminal time is arbitrary. An extension of the maximum principle to problems in which the time of termination t_1 is fixed, x_1 is free, and g is a linear function of the coordinates was given by Rozonoer [14].

Another approach, which is formal and heuristic in character, is the dynamic programming argument of Bellman [1], who presents a functional equation that the value of the minimum as a function of initial position must satisfy. The terminal condition in this class of problems is t_1 fixed, and x_1 free. Rozonoer [14] has rigorously established the validity of the functional equation presented by Bellman for those problems in this class in which $g = \Sigma_{i=1}^{n} C^i x_1^{\,i}(t_1)$.

A different set of techniques has been used in dealing with linear systems (1.1). The problem of determining a control $u(t)$, subject to the constraints $|u^i(t)| \leqslant 1$, $i = 1, \ldots, m$, that brings $x(t)$ to 0 in minimum time was studied for systems with $G^i = \Sigma_{j=1}^{n} a_{ij} x^j + \Sigma_{j=1}^{m} b_{ij} u^j$ by Bushaw [5], Bellman, Glicksberg, and Gross [2], and Gamkrelidze [6]. The problem of determining u so as to minimize the time required for $x(t)$ to hit a moving particle $z(t)$ for linear systems in which a_{ij} and b_{ij} are functions of time was studied by Krasovskii [8] and LaSalle [10]. The paper by LaSalle gives a brief survey of the other papers cited in this paragraph. Krasovskii [9] has considered the last problem for systems (1.1) of the form $G^i = f^i(t, x) + b^i(t)u$.

In the first part of this paper we shall show how a fairly general control problem with constraints can be reduced to a special type of classical Bolza problem. Necessary conditions from the Bolza problem will be translated into necessary conditions for optimal control. These conditions give more information than the necessary conditions presented by the authors cited, and are applicable to wider classes of problems. For example, it will be seen that the Maximum Principle is a restatement of the Weierstrass condition in the calculus of variations and is applicable to more general problems than those considered in [13] and [14]. Results on "bang-bang" control can be derived from Corollaries 1 and 2 of Theorem 2. We shall not develop this topic here, however.

Theorem 2 of the present paper, which is the main theorem about the necessary conditions, was stated in slightly different form by Hestenes [7] in connection with aircraft climb problems, but was never published by him. Because of the relative unavailability of [7], we shall present the proof of Theorem 2. The constraint conditions of the present paper are slightly different from Hestenes'. We also consider the case of discontinuous f, G^i, and R^i, and give simple criteria for normality in a special class of problems.

In the second part of the paper we study the function $W(t, x)$, which is defined as the value of the minimum (or maximum) of (1.3) as a function of initial position. We determine the differentiability properties of W under reasonable assumptions on the synthesis of control, and show that in its regions of differentiability the function W satisfies the Hamilton-Jacobi equation. By combining this equation with the Weierstrass condition (or Maximum Principle), we can rigorously establish the functional equation of Bellman [1] and obtain a statement about its regions of validity for a very general class of problems.

Our last theorem is a sufficiency theorem that is useful in synthesizing the control. This theorem is a variant of the standard sufficiency theorem in the calculus of variations. A similar theorem was stated by Breakwell [4]; his statement, however, needs an additional hypothesis to be valid and his proof is formal.

We conclude our introductory remarks with the observation that problems in which constraints of the form (1.4) are present can be reduced to problems without these constraints by the introduction of new state variables and associated initial and terminal conditions as follows:

$$\frac{dx^{n+k}}{dt} = \varphi^k(t, x, u), \qquad x^{n+k}(t_0) = 0, \qquad x^{n+k}(t_1) \leqslant C^k, \qquad k = 1, \ldots, K.$$

Vector matrix notation will generally be used. Vectors and matrices will be denoted by single letters. Superscripts will be used to denote the components of a vector; subscripts will be used to distinguish vectors. Vectors will be written as matrices consisting of either one row or one column. We shall not use a transpose symbol to distinguish between the two usages, as it will be clear from the context how the vector is to be considered. If A is a matrix of m rows and n columns, x is an m-dimensional vector and y is an n-dimensional vector, then in the product xA, x must be a row matrix, and in the product Ay, y must be a column matrix. Thus we shall write the inner product of two vectors x and y simply as xy; a quadratic form with matrix A we write as xAx.

The operator (d/dt) will generally be denoted by a prime. Thus, the system (1.1) will be written as

$$x' = G(t, x, u), \qquad x(t_0) = x_1, \tag{1.1}$$

and the constraints (1.2) as $R(t, x, u) \geqslant 0$. (A vector is nonnegative if and only if every component is nonnegative.) If $Z(t, x, u)$ is a vector-valued function that is differentiable on a region $\mathscr{S}$ of (t, x, u)-space, we denote the matrix of partial derivatives $(\partial Z^i/\partial x^j)$ by Z_x; the symbol Z_u has similar meaning. For real valued functions $Z(t, x, u)$, the symbols Z_x and Z_u represent vectors of partial derivatives. We denote the determinant of a square matrix A by $\|A\|$.

Let $\mathscr{D}$ be a bounded region of $(n + 1)$-dimensional (t, x) space and let $\mathscr{U}$ be a region of m-dimensional u-space. Let $\mathscr{S} = \mathscr{D} \times \mathscr{U}$. Let $\mathscr{T}$ be a manifold of class C'', of dimension $p \leqslant n$, lying in $\mathscr{D}$, and given parametrically by equations

$$t = t_1(\sigma), \qquad x = x_1(\sigma), \tag{2.1}$$

where $\sigma = (\sigma^1, \ldots, \sigma^p)$ ranges over an open cube $\mathscr{K}$ in p-dimensional space. Points of $\mathscr{T}$ will henceforth be denoted as (t_1, x_1); we shall call $\mathscr{T}$ the terminal manifold. Let $f(t, x, u)$ be a real-valued function of class C'' on $\mathscr{D}$, let $g(\sigma)$ be a real-valued function of class C'' on $\mathscr{K}$, and let the vector-valued functions $G(t, x, u) = (G^1, \ldots, G^n)$ of (1.1) and $R(t, x, u) = (R^1, \ldots, R^r)$ of (1.2) be class C'' on $\mathscr{S}$. Furthermore, let the constraint vector R satisfy the following *constraint conditions.*

(i) If $r > m$, then at each point of $\mathscr{S}$ at most m components of R can vanish. (2.2)

(ii) At each point of $\mathscr{S}$ the matrix $(\partial R^i/\partial u^j)$, where i ranges over those indices such that $R^i(t, x, u) = 0$, and $j = 1, \ldots, m$, has maximum rank.

Consider the class of all functions $u = u(t)$ that are piecewise C'' (i.e., each component u^i of u is piecewise continuous and has piecewise continuous first and second derivatives) on the closure of the projection of $\mathscr{D}$ on the t-axis, and whose range is contained in $\mathscr{U}$. For each such u we can obtain a continuous solution of (1.1) that defines a curve $\mathscr{K}$, with possible corners, in $\mathscr{D}$. Let $\mathscr{A}$ be the subclass of this class of functions u with the following properties. (i) The curve K is defined and is interior to $\mathscr{D}$ for $t_0 \leqslant t \leqslant t_1$, where $(t_1, x_1) = (t_1, x(t_1))$ is a point of $\mathscr{T}$, and K does not intersect $\mathscr{T}$ for any $t_0 \leqslant t < t_1$. (ii) Along K, the constraints (1.2) are satisfied; i.e., $R(t, x(t), u(t)) \geqslant 0$. The class $\mathscr{A}$, which depends on (t_0, x_0), is called the class of admissible controls. For a given (t_0, x_0) it may be void.

The problem of optimal control is to find an element $u^* \in \mathscr{A}$ that minimizes (or maximizes) the functional

$$J(u) = g(\sigma) + \int_{t_0}^{t_1} f(t, x, u)\, dt \tag{2.3}$$

over all $u \in \mathscr{A}$, where the integral is taken along the curve K corresponding to u, and σ is the parameter value associated with $(t_1, x_1) = (t_1, x(t_1))$. For definiteness we shall henceforth assume that (2.3) is to be minimized.

We note that the problem of optimal control as presented here is equivalent to the problem in which $g \equiv 0$ or the problem in which $f \equiv 0$. The equivalence of these problems can be shown by making transformations similar to those used to show the equivalence of the problems of Bolza, Lagrange, and Mayer in the calculus of variations ([3], pp. 189–190).

III. The Equivalent Bolza Problems

Let $y = (y^1, \ldots, y^m)$ be an m-dimensional vector. To the system (1.1) adjoin the following system of differential equations

$$y' = u, \qquad y(t_0) = 0. \tag{3.1}$$

The following problem of Bolza in $(n + m + 1)$-dimensional (t, x, y) space with differential inequalities as added side conditions is clearly equivalent to the problem of optimal control posed in Section II.

Problem I. Find an arc $(x(t), y(t))$ that minimizes

$$g(\sigma) + \int_{t_0}^{t_1} f(t, x, y')\, dt \tag{3.2}$$

in the class of arcs that are piecewise C'', that satisfy the differential equations

$$G(t, x, y') - x' = 0, \tag{3.3}$$

the differential inequalities

$$R(t, x, y') \geqslant 0, \tag{3.4}$$

and the end conditions

$$\begin{aligned} x(t_0) = x_0, \qquad & y(t_0) \equiv y_0 = 0, \\ t_1 = t_1(\sigma), \qquad & x_1 = x_1(\sigma), \\ y_1 \equiv y(t_1) & = \eta, \end{aligned} \tag{3.5}$$

where $\eta = (\eta^1, \ldots, \eta^m)$.

By means of a device used by Valentine in [15], we obtain the following problem of Bolza, which has no inequality side conditions, and is equivalent to Problem I.

Problem II. Find an arc $(x(t), y(t), \xi(t))$, where $\xi = (\xi^1, \ldots, \xi^r)$, that minimizes (3.2) in the class of arcs that are piecewise C'', that satisfy the differential equations

$$\begin{aligned} G(t, x, y') - x' &= 0, \\ R(t, x, y') - (\xi')^2 &= 0, \end{aligned} \tag{3.6}$$

and the end conditions (3.5) and

$$\xi(t_0) \equiv \xi_0 = 0, \qquad \xi(t_1) \equiv \xi_1 = \tau, \tag{3.7}$$

where $\tau = (\tau^1, \ldots, \tau^r)$, and $(\xi')^2 = ((\xi^{1\prime})^2, \ldots, (\xi^{r\prime})^2)$.

Let $u^* \in \mathscr{A}$ be an optimal control, let K^* be the corresponding curve, and let $x^*(t)$ be the function defining K^*, for $t_0 \leqslant t \leqslant t_1$. Let $y^*(t)$ denote the solution of (3.1) when $u = u^*$. It follows from the preceding discussion that $(x^*(t), y^*(t))$ satisfies (3.3) – (3.5) and minimizes (3.2). Hence the arc defined by $(x^*(t), y^*(t), \xi^*(t))$, where

$$(\xi^*(t)')^2 = R(t, x^*, y^{*\prime}), \qquad \xi^*(t_0) = 0,$$

furnishes a minimum for Problem II. We denote this arc by K_2^*. We assert that at every element $(x^*, y^*, \xi^*, x^{*\prime}, y^{*\prime}, \xi^{*\prime})$ of K_2^*, the equations (3.6) are independent; that is the matrix

$$\begin{pmatrix} G_{y'} & -I & 0 \\ R_{y'} & 0 & -2\Xi' \end{pmatrix} \tag{3.8}$$

has rank $(n + r)$ along K_2^*, where I is the n-dimensional identity matrix and $2\Xi'$ is an $r \times r$ diagonal matrix with entries $2(\xi^i)'$ on the diagonal, $i = 1, \ldots, r$. In order to prove the assertion we first suppose that the first r_1 rows, $0 \leqslant r_1 \leqslant r$ of the submatrix $(R_{y'}\ 0 - 2\Xi')$ have elements $2\xi^i \neq 0$, and the remaining rows have elements $2\xi^i = 0$. This can always be achieved by permuting rows and relabeling. The matrix (3.8) now has the form

$$\begin{pmatrix} A_1 & D \\ A_2 & 0 \end{pmatrix}$$

where D is an $(n + r_1)$ by $(n + r_1)$ diagonal matrix with nonzero entries on the diagonal and 0 is a zero matrix. The matrix A_2 consists of the last $r - r_1$ rows of the matrix $R_{y'}$. For each of these rows, we have $(\xi^i)' = 0$. Consequently, $R^i(t, x^*, y^{*\prime}) = 0$, $i = r_1 + 1, \ldots, r$. From (3.1) we see that this is equivalent to $R^i(t, x^*, u^*) = 0$, for $i = r_1 + 1, \ldots, r$. From the constraint conditions (2.2) we obtain that $r - r_1 \leqslant m$ and that the matrix with elements $\partial R^i/\partial u^j$, $i = r_1 + 1, \ldots, r$, $j = 1, \ldots, m$ has rank $r - r_1$ for (t, x^*, u^*) along K_2^*. Hence, it follows that A_2 has rank $r - r_1$ and (3.8) has rank $(n + r_1) + (r - r_1) = n + r$ as required.

The above argument is actually not restricted to K_2^*; it shows that (3.8) has rank $(n + r)$ at all elements $(t, x, y, \xi, x', y', \xi')$ for which (3.6) holds.

IV. Necessary Conditions for Problem II

Since K_2^* furnishes a minimum for Problem II, and the matrix (3.8) has rank $(n+r)$ wherever Eqs. (3.6) hold, it follows (Bliss [3], McShane [11]) that the following necessary conditions hold along K_2^*.

Theorem 1. *There exist a constant $\lambda_0 \geqslant 0$, an n-dimensional vector $\lambda(t)$, and an r-dimensional vector $\mu(t)$, defined on the interval $t_0 \leqslant t \leqslant t_1$ such that $(\lambda_0, \lambda(t), \mu(t))$ is never zero and such that $\lambda(t)$ and $\mu(t)$ are continuous, except perhaps at values of t corresponding to corners of K_2^*, where they possess unique right and left limits. Moreover, the function*

$$F(t, x, y, \xi, x', y', \xi', \lambda_0, \lambda, \mu) = \lambda_0 f + \lambda(G - x') + \mu(R - \xi'^2) \quad (4.1)$$

satisfies the following along K_2^*.

(i) (Euler-Lagrange equations) *Between corners of K_2^**

$$\frac{dF_{x'}}{dt} = F_x, \qquad \frac{dF_{y'}}{dt} = F_y, \qquad \frac{dF_{\xi'}}{dt} = F_\xi. \quad (4.2)$$

At a corner these equations hold for the unique one-sided limits.

(ia) (Weierstrass-Erdmann) *At a corner of* $K_2^*, F_{x'}, F_{y'}, F_{\xi'}$, *and* $(F - x' F_{x'} - y' F_{y'} - \xi' F_{\xi'})$ *have well defined one sided limits that are equal.*

(ii) (Transversality) *At the end point* $(t_1, x_1^*, y_1^*, \xi_1^*)$ *of* K_2^*,

$$\begin{aligned} (F - x' F_{x'} - y' F_{y'} - \xi' F_{\xi'})t_{1\sigma} + F_{x'} x_{1\sigma} + \lambda_0 g_\sigma = 0, \\ F_{y'} y_{1\eta} = 0, \qquad F_{\xi'} \xi_{1\tau} = 0. \end{aligned} \tag{4.3}$$

(iii) (Weierstrass) *For all* $(t, x, \xi, y, X', Y', \zeta') \neq (t, x, \xi, y, x', y', \xi')$ *and satisfying* (3.6),

$$\varepsilon(t, x, y, \xi, x', y', \xi', X', Y', \zeta', \lambda_0, \lambda, \mu) \geqslant 0, \tag{4.4}$$

where

$$\begin{aligned} \varepsilon = F(t, x, y, \xi, X', Y', \zeta') - F(t, x, y, \xi, x', y', \xi') \\ - (X' - x')F_{x'} - (Y' - y')F_{y'} - (\zeta' - \xi')F_{\xi'}, \end{aligned}$$

the functions $F_{x'}$ *and* $F_{\xi'}$ *being evaluated at* $(t, x, y, \xi, x', y', \xi', \lambda_0, \lambda, \mu)$, *and the arguments* $(\lambda_0, \lambda, \mu)$ *being omitted throughout.*

(iv) (Clebsch) *For every vector* $(\pi, \rho, \kappa) \neq 0$, *where* $\pi = (\pi^1, \ldots, \pi^n)$, $\rho = (\rho^1, \ldots, \rho^m)$ *and* $\kappa = (\kappa^1, \ldots, \kappa^r)$, *that is a solution of the linear system*

$$\begin{aligned} G_{y'} \rho - I\pi = 0, \\ R_{y'} \rho - 2\Xi'\kappa = 0, \end{aligned} \tag{4.5}$$

the following inequality holds

$$\pi F_{x'x'} \pi + \rho F_{y'y'} \rho - 2 \sum_{i=1}^{r} \mu^i (\kappa^i)^2 \geqslant 0. \tag{4.6}$$

V. Necessary Conditions for Problem I

We now follow Valentine [15] and translate the necessary conditions for Problem II into necessary conditions for Problem I. We first consider the Euler equations. From (4.1) we get that

$$F_\xi = 0, \qquad F_{\xi^{i'}} = -2\mu^i \xi^{i'}, \qquad i = 1, \ldots, r. \tag{5.1}$$

Hence it follows from the third equation in (4.2) that $d(\mu^i \xi^{i'})/dt = 0$ along K_2^*. This and the continuity of $F_{\xi'}$ at corners of K_2^* imply that $\mu^i \xi^{i'}$ is constant along K_2^*. From the transversality condition (4.3) we get that $F_{\xi'} \xi_{1\tau} = 0$; from (3.7) we get that $\xi_{1\tau} = I$, where I is the $r \times r$

identity matrix. Therefore, $F_{\xi'} = 0$ at the right end point of K_2^*, and consequently $\mu^i \xi^{i'} = 0$ along K_2^*. It now follows from the second equation in (3.6) that along K_2^*,

$$\mu^i R^i = 0, \qquad i = 1, \ldots, r. \tag{5.2}$$

A similar argument shows that along K_2^*, $F_{y'} = 0$.

We now introduce the function

$$H(t, x, y', \lambda_0, \lambda) = \lambda_0 f(t, x, y') + \lambda G(t, x, y'). \tag{5.3}$$

Clearly,

$$F = H - \lambda x' + \mu(R - \xi'^2). \tag{5.4}$$

The following are immediate consequences of (5.4)

$$F_x = H_x + \mu R_x, \qquad F_{y'} = H_{y'} + \mu R_{y'},$$
$$F_{x'} = -\lambda. \tag{5.5}$$

Since $F_{y'} = 0$ along K_2^*, we get that along K_2^*

$$H_{y'} + \mu R_{y'} = 0. \tag{5.6}$$

From (4.2) and (5.5) we also get that along K_2^*

$$\lambda' = -(H_x + \mu R_x). \tag{5.7}$$

It follows from the vanishing of $F_{y'}$ and $F_{\xi'}$, along K_2^* and from (5.4), (5.5), and the second equation of (3.6), that along K_2^*,

$$F - x' F_{x'} - y' F_{y'} - \xi' F_{\xi'} = H. \tag{5.8}$$

Hence, it follows that the transversality condition becomes

$$\lambda_0 g_\sigma + H t_{1\sigma} - \lambda x_{1\sigma} = 0. \tag{5.9}$$

The relationships used to establish (5.8) and the fact that (t, x, Y', ζ') satisfies the second equation of (3.6) enable us to translate the Weierstrass condition (4.4) into the condition that

$$H(t, x, Y', \lambda_0, \lambda) \geqslant H(t, x, y', \lambda_0, \lambda). \tag{5.10}$$

It is an immediate consequence of (5.4) that (4.6) becomes

$$\rho((H + \mu R)_{y'y'})\rho - 2 \sum_{i=1}^{r} \mu^i(\kappa^i)^2 \geqslant 0. \tag{5.11}$$

If $R^i > 0$ at a point of $K_2{}^*$, then by (5.2), $\mu^i = 0$. If $R^i = 0$ at this point, let $\pi = 0$, let $\rho = 0$, and let κ be a vector whose ith component is equal to one and whose other components are zero. Then $(\pi, \rho, \kappa) \neq 0$, and since $\xi^i = 0$, (π, ρ, κ) is a solution of (4.5). Hence from (5.11), we get $\mu^i \leqslant 0$ at this point. Consequently, we always have

$$\mu^i \leqslant 0 \quad \text{along } K_2{}^*, \qquad i = 1, \ldots, r.$$

Let (t, x, y) be a point of $K_2{}^*$ such that at most r_1, where $r_1 < m$, components of $R(t, x, y')$ vanish; we suppose for definiteness that these are the first r_1 components. It follows from (2.2) – (ii) that the system of linear equations

$$\sum_{j=1}^{m} \frac{\partial R^i}{\partial y^{j'}} \rho^j - 2\xi^i \kappa^i = 0, \qquad i = 1, \ldots, r_1$$

has a solution in ρ and $\hat{\kappa} = (\kappa^1, \ldots, \kappa^{r_1})$ such that $\rho \neq 0$ and $\hat{\kappa} = 0$. It now follows from the second system of equations in (3.6) and the assumption that $R^j > 0$ for $j > r_1$, that the system (4.5) has a solution (ρ, π, κ) such that $\rho \neq 0$ and $\hat{\kappa} = 0$. Let $j > r_1$. Since indices $j > r_1$ correspond to components $R^j > 0$, it follows from (5.2) that $\mu^j = 0$ for $j > r_1$. Hence, each term in the second summation in (5.11) vanishes, and we have from (4.5) that

$$\rho((H + \mu R)_{y'y'})\rho \geqslant 0 \tag{5.12}$$

for any solution vector ρ of the system

$$\sum_{j=1}^{m} \frac{\partial R^i}{\partial y^{j'}} \rho^j = 0, \qquad i = 1, \ldots, r_1. \tag{5.13}$$

The conclusion just stated holds, of course, even if m components of R vanish. In that case, however, the system (5.13) only has the trivial solution.

VI. Necessary Conditions for the Control Problem

The following theorem, in which necessary conditions for optimal control are given, is an immediate consequence of the conclusion obtained in Section V and the use of (3.1) to justify the replacing of the argument y' by u, wherever y' occurs. The function H is now

$$H(t, x, u, \lambda_0, \lambda) = \lambda_0 f(t, x, u) + \lambda G(t, x, u).$$

THEOREM 2. *Let $u^* \in \mathscr{A}$ be an optimal control, let K^* be the corresponding curve, and let $x^*(t)$ be the function defining K^* on $[t_0, t_1]$. Then there exists a constant $\lambda_0 \geqslant 0$, an n-dimensional vector $\lambda(t)$ defined and continuous on $[t_0, t_1]$, and an r-dimensional vector $\mu(t) \leqslant 0$ defined and continuous on the interval $[t_0, t_1]$, except perhaps at values of t corresponding to corners of K^*, where it possesses unique right and left hand limits, such that the vector $(\lambda_0, \lambda(t))$ never vanishes, and such that the following conditions are fulfilled.*

Condition I. Along K^* the following equations hold:

$$x'(t) = H_\lambda, \tag{6.1}$$

$$\lambda'(t) = -(H_x + \mu R_x), \tag{6.2}$$

$$H_u + \mu R_u = 0, \tag{6.3}$$

$$\mu^i R^i = 0, \qquad i = 1, \ldots, r. \tag{6.4}$$

At the end point (t_1, x_1^*) of K^* the transversality condition hold:

$$\lambda_0 g_\sigma + H t_{1\sigma} - \lambda x_{1\sigma} = 0. \tag{6.5}$$

Along K^*, the function H is continuous.

Condition II. For every element $(t, x^*, u^*, \lambda_0, \lambda)$ of K^* and every u such that $u = u(t)$ for some u in $\mathscr{A}$,

$$H(t, x^*, u, \lambda_0, \lambda) \geqslant H(t, x^*, u^*, \lambda_0, \lambda). \tag{6.6}$$

Condition III. At each point of K^* let $\hat{R}$ denote the vector formed from R by taking those components of R that vanish at that point. Let $e = (e^1, \ldots, e^m)$ be a nonzero solution vector of the linear system $\hat{R}_u e = 0$ at a point of K^*. Then $e((H + \mu R)_{uu})e \geqslant 0$ at this point.

Equations (6.1) – (6.4) are the Euler equations, Condition II follows from the Weierstrass condition (5.10), and Condition III follows from the Clebsch condition (5.12). The continuity of H along K^* follows from the continuity of the left member of (5.8) along K_2^*, and the continuity of λ follows from (5.5) and the continuity of $F_{x'}$ (Weierstrass-Erdmann corner conditions). The nonvanishing of (λ_0, λ) along K^* is established as follows. If (λ_0, λ) were zero at a point of K^*, then from (6.3) we would have that $\mu R_u = 0$ at this point. For the sake of definiteness, suppose that the indexing is such that $R^i = 0$ for $i = 1, \ldots, r_1$, where by (2.2) $r_1 \leqslant m$. Hence, by (6.4), $\mu^i = 0$ for $i > r_1$. Thus the condition $\mu R_u = 0$ reduces to a system of linear equations in $\mu^1, \ldots, \mu^{r_1}$ whose coefficient matrix is $(\partial R^i / \partial u^k)$, $i = 1, \ldots, r_1$; $k = 1, \ldots, m$. From (2.2) – (ii), we get that this matrix has rank r_1. Hence $\mu^1 = \ldots = \mu^{r_i} = 0$ is the only solution of the linear system. Thus, we have shown that if (λ^0, λ) is zero at a point, then the vector $(\lambda^0, \lambda, \mu)$ must also be zero, contradicting the assertion of Theorem 1.

If the constraints are specialized, then important simplifications can be effected in the Euler equations.

COROLLARY 1. *Let the constraints be of the form*

$$B^i(t, x) \leqslant u^i \leqslant A^i(t, x), \qquad i = 1, \ldots, m$$

where $A^i > B^i$ *and each* A^i *and* B^i *is of class* C'' *on* $\mathscr{D}$. *Then at each point of* K^*

$$H_{u^i} \begin{cases} \geqslant 0 & \text{if} \quad u^{*i} = B^i \\ = 0 & \text{if} \quad B^i < u^{*i} < A^i \\ \leqslant 0 & \text{if} \quad u^{*i} = A^i, \qquad i = 1, \ldots, m. \end{cases}$$

If we write the constraints as $A^i - u^i \geqslant 0$ and $u^i - B^i \geqslant 0$, $i = 1, \ldots, m$, we obtain a $2m$-dimensional constraint vector with components $A^i - u^i$ and $u^i - B^i$. It follows from the condition $A^i > B^i$ and the form of the constraints that (2.2) is satisfied. The conclusion of the corollary follows from (6.3) and (6.4) by straightforward calculation and use of the condition $\mu \leqslant 0$.

REMARK. If the ith component of u is constrained only from one side, say $u^i \leqslant A^i(t, x)$, then $H_{u^i} = 0$ if $u^i < A^i$ and $H_{u^i} \leqslant 0$ if $u^i = A^i$. Similar statements hold for $u^i \geqslant B^i$.

Another important special case is one in which the constraints are independent of the state, that is $R(t, x, u) \equiv R(t, u)$. Since $R_x = 0$ in this case, we have the following corollary.

COROLLARY 2. *If* R *is independent of* x, *then equation* (6.2) *becomes*

$$\lambda' = -H_x. \tag{6.2$'$}$$

In the problem considered by Pontryagin [13], the constraints required u to lie in a fixed closed set, independent of time t and position x. Equations (6.1), (6.2)′, and (6.6) constitute the "Maximum Principle" as stated by Pontryagin. Our function H is the negative of Pontryagin's, so that his maximum appears as a mimimum in our paper. Note, however, that the Euler equations and Condition II of Theorem 2, which is the Weierstrass condition, give a minimum principle for a wider class of problems.

REMARK. Note that if the A^i and B^i of Corollary 1 are constants, then the results of both corollaries are valid.

VII. Integrable Controls

Instead of considering functions $u = u(t)$ that are piecewise C'', we can consider functions that are merely assumed to be Lebesgue integrable. In this way we can define a class of admissible controls $\mathscr{A}^+$, and we can look for an optimal control u^* in $\mathscr{A}^+$. The curves K corresponding to functions u in $\mathscr{A}^+$ will be defined by absolutely continuous functions $x(t)$, and so will be rectifiable. We can reduce the control problem with constraints to a Bolza problem without constraints as we did before, except that the functions $(x(t), y(t), \xi(t))$ are now absolutely continuous. To this problem we can apply a theorem of McShane (Theorem 16.1, [12]). We can then translate back to the original control problem and obtain the result that the conclusions of Theorem 2, appropriately modified, hold almost everywhere along a curve K^* corresponding to a control u^* that minimizes (2.3) over all u in $\mathscr{A}^+$.

VIII. Normality

A piecewise C'' minimizing curve K^*, or equivalently, the corresponding curve K_2^* of Problem II is said to be *normal* if there are no sets of multipliers with $\lambda_0 = 0$. (See [3], pp. 213–219.) If the minimizing curve is normal, then the multipliers can be chosen so that $\lambda_0 = 1$, and with this choice of λ_0 they are unique. If the curve is not normal, there may be no neighboring curves that satisfy the differential equations, constraints, and end conditions. Necessary and sufficient conditions for normality are given in [3]. These criteria applied to the present problem would involve variations along K_2^* and would generally be difficult to apply in practice. We shall give a condition for normality in the control problem that is sufficient, but not necessary. It is, however, easier to apply in practice, and reduces to a very simple condition in the special case that the terminal manifold $\mathscr{T}$ is n-dimensional.

At (t_1, x_1^*), the end point of K^*, let r_1 components of $R(t_1, x_1^*, u^*(t_1))$ vanish. From (2.2) – (i) we get that $r_1 \leqslant m$. Let $\hat{R}$ denote the r_1-dimensional vector formed from R by taking those components of R that vanish at (t_1, x_1^*), and let $\hat{\mu}$ be the vector formed from μ by taking the corresponding components. Then, from (6.4) we have that $\mu^j(t_1) = 0$ for those components of μ that are not in $\hat{\mu}$. Let M denote the n by p matrix whose typical element is

$$\left(G^i \frac{\partial t_1}{\partial \sigma^j} - \frac{\partial x_1^{\,i}}{\partial \sigma^j}\right), \qquad i = 1,\ldots, n, \qquad j = 1,\ldots, p, \tag{8.1}$$

where the elements are evaluated at the end point of K^*. Let C denote the $(n + r_1)$ by $(m + p)$ matrix

$$\begin{pmatrix} G_u & M \\ \hat{R}_u & 0 \end{pmatrix}$$

where G_u and $\hat{R}_u$ are evaluated at (t_1, x_1^*).

If K^* is not normal, then there exists a set of multipliers $(\lambda_0, \lambda, \mu)$ with $\lambda_0 = 0$. From (6.3) and (6.5) we get that at the end point (t_1, x_1^*) of K^*, the vector $(\lambda, \hat{\mu})$ is a solution of the linear system $(\lambda, \hat{\mu})C = 0$. The following theorem is now a consequence of a standard theorem concerning the solutions of homogeneous linear systems and the fact that (λ, μ) cannot be zero if $\lambda_0 = 0$.

THEOREM 3. *If the rank of C equals $(n + r_1)$, then K^* is normal.*

Note that C can have rank $(n + r_1)$ only when $(n + r_1) \leqslant (m + p)$, and that Theorem 3 is not a necessary condition.

COROLLARY. *If $\mathscr{T}$ is n-dimensional and K^* is not tangent to $\mathscr{T}$, then K^* is normal.*

If $\mathscr{T}$ is n-dimensional, the matrix M is an n by n matrix. By (2.2) – (ii), the r_1 by m matrix $\hat{R}_u$ has rank r_1. Hence, C has rank $(n + r_1)$ whenever M has rank n. Since K^* is not tangent to $\mathscr{T}$, the matrix

$$\begin{pmatrix} 1 & t_{1\sigma} \\ G & x_{1\sigma} \end{pmatrix}$$

has rank $n + 1$. If for each $j = 1, \ldots, n$ we multiply the first column of this matrix by $-\partial t_1/\partial\sigma^j$ and add the result to the jth column we get the matrix

$$\begin{pmatrix} 1 & 0 \\ G & -M \end{pmatrix}.$$

Hence M has rank n and the corollary follows.

IX. DISCONTINUOUS f, G, AND R

Let $\mathscr{M}$ be a manifold of dimension n, lying in $\mathscr{D}$, and dividing $\mathscr{D}$ into two regions, such that some or all of the functions f, G, and R are discontinuous across $\mathscr{M}$. Let the discontinuity of a function be such that the function and its derivatives have unique one-sided limits. Further let us assume that K^* intersects $\mathscr{M}$ at $(t_2, x_2) = (t_2, x_2(t))$ and is not tangent to $\mathscr{M}$ at this point. It can be shown by appropriate modifications of the arguments in [3] (pp. 196–202) that the multipliers λ and μ of

Problem II need not be continuous at $t = t_1$, but will have unique right and left hand limits at (t_2, x_2) as will F and its various partial derivatives when evaluated along K_2^*. Although $F_{x'}$, $F_{y'}$ and $F_{\xi'}$ need not be continuous across $\mathscr{M}$, the expression

$$(F - x' F_{x'} - y' F_{y'} - \xi' F_{\xi'})\, dt + F_{x'}\, dx_2 + F_{y'}\, dy_2 + F_{\xi'}\, d\xi_2$$

has equal right and left hand limits along K_2^* at (t_2, x_2) for all differentials dt_2, dx_2 on $\mathscr{M}$ and all dy_2, and $d\xi_2$. For the original control problem this translates into the condition that

$$(H^+ - H^-)\, dt_2 - (\lambda^+ - \lambda^-)\, dx_2 = 0 \tag{9.1}$$

at (t_2, x_2), where the one-sided limits are evaluated along K^*.

X. Definition of Synthesis

Consider a point (t_1, x_1) of the p-dimensional terminal manifold $\mathscr{T}$, where $0 \leqslant p \leqslant n$. Let $\mathscr{K}'$ denote a region in $(n - p)$-dimensional space over which a vector φ ranges. If $p = n$, then φ is the zero vector. Let $u^*(t; t_1, x_1, \varphi)$ be a function defined in some interval $[t_0, t_1]$, where $t_0 = t_0(t_1, x_1, \varphi)$, such that the following holds.

Assumption 1. (i) The function u^* is piecewise C'' on $[t_0, t_1]$ and its range lies in $\mathscr{U}$. (ii) If u^* is substituted into (6.1) (or equivalently into (1.1)), the resulting differential equation

$$x' = G(t, x, u^*(t; t_1, x_1, \varphi)), \qquad x(t_1) = x_1 \tag{10.1}$$

has a continuous solution $x^*(t; t_1, x_1, \varphi)$ on $[t_0, t_1]$ such that (t, x^*) lies in $\mathscr{D}$ and $R(t, x^*, u^*) \geqslant 0$.

We denote the curve corresponding to $x^*(t; t_1, x_1, \varphi)$ by $K(t_1, x_1, \varphi)$.

We now suppose that the assumptions just made for a particular point (t_1, x_1) hold for all points (t_1, x_1) of $\mathscr{T}$. We have from (2.1) that $(t_1, x_1) = (t_1(\sigma), x_1(\sigma))$, where σ ranges over an open cube $\mathscr{K}$ in a p-dimensional space. Let θ be an n-dimensional vector defined as follows:

$$\theta = (\sigma, \varphi), \qquad \sigma \in \mathscr{K}, \qquad \varphi \in \mathscr{K}'. \tag{10.2}$$

We define functions

$$\begin{aligned} t_0(\theta) &\equiv t_0(t_1(\sigma), x_1(\sigma), \varphi) \\ t_1(\theta) &\equiv t_1(\sigma), \end{aligned} \tag{10.3}$$

and functions

$$\begin{aligned} u^*(t, \theta) &\equiv u^*(t; t_1(\sigma), x_1(\sigma), \varphi) \\ x^*(t, \theta) &\equiv x^*(t; t_1(\sigma), x_1(\sigma), \varphi) \end{aligned} \tag{10.4}$$

for σ in $\mathscr{K}$, φ in $\mathscr{K}'$ and $t_0(\theta) \leqslant t \leqslant t_1(\theta)$. The differential equation (10.1) can now be written as

$$x' = G(t, x, u^*(t, \theta)), \qquad x(t_1(\theta)) = x_1(\sigma). \tag{10.5}$$

Clearly, $x^*(t, \theta)$ is a solution of (10.5). We shall denote the curve $K(t_1, x_1, \varphi)$ by $K(\theta)$.

Let Ω denote the domain of definition of $u^*(t, \theta)$ and $x^*(t, \theta)$; that is the set of points (t, θ) in $(n + 1)$-dimensional space with θ as in (10.2) and $t_0(\theta) \leqslant t \leqslant t_1(\theta)$. Clearly, Ω has nonvoid interior, which we denote by Ω^0. It follows from (2.1) and (10.3) that $t_1(\theta)$ defines a C'' manifold $\mathscr{N}_1$ of dimension n in (t, θ) space and that $\mathscr{N}_1$ is part of the boundary of Ω. We also suppose that $t_0(\theta)$ defines a C'' manifold of dimension n.

A set of functions

$$t = t_i(\theta), \qquad i = 1, 2, \ldots, \alpha,$$

defined and C'' on the region defined in (10.2), with $t_1(\theta)$ as in (10.3) and such that

$$t_0(\theta) < t_{i+1}(\theta) < t_i(\theta), \qquad i = 1, \ldots, \alpha - 1$$

will be said to induce a regular decomposition of Ω. Clearly, each $t_i(\theta)$, $i \geqslant 2$, defines a C'' manifold $\mathscr{N}_i$ of dimension n lying in Ω_0. We let $\mathscr{N}_{\alpha+1}$ denote the manifold defined by $t_0(\theta)$. We define subregions Ω_i of Ω^0 as follows:

$$\Omega_i = E\{(t, \theta) \in \Omega^0 | t_{i+1}(\theta) < t < t_i(\theta)\}, \qquad i = 1, \ldots, \alpha.$$

We shall say that a function $h(t, \theta)$ is piecewise $C^{(k)}$ on Ω if on each subregion Ω_i it agrees with a function $h_{(i)}(t, \theta)$ that is $C^{(k)}$ on $\overline{\Omega}_i$, the closure of Ω_i.

Two more assumptions can now be stated.

Assumption 2. The function $x^*(t, \theta)$ maps Ω^0 in a one-to-one fashion onto a subregion $\mathscr{R}$ of the region $\mathscr{D}$ in (t, x)-space, and maps $\mathscr{N}_{\alpha+1}$ in a one to one fashion onto an n-dimensional manifold that forms part of the boundary of $\mathscr{R}$.

Assumption 3. There exist functions $t_i(\theta)$ that induce a regular decomposition of Ω such that (i) $u^*(t, \theta)$ is piecewise C'' on Ω. (ii) If f, G, or R possess manifolds of discontinuity that lie in $\mathscr{R}$ (as discussed in Section 9), then each of these manifolds is coincident with the image of some set $\mathscr{N}_i$, $i = 2, \ldots, \alpha$. (iii) For each component R^j of the constraint vector R, we either have $R^j(t, x^*(t, \theta), u^*(t, \theta)) \equiv 0$ on Ω_i, or, with the possible exception of a finite number of points, $R^j(t, x^*(t, \theta), u^*(t, \theta)) > 0$ on Ω_i.

We shall denote the image of Ω_i by $\mathscr{R}_i$, $i = 1, \ldots, \alpha$, and the image of $\mathscr{N}_i$ by $\mathscr{M}_i$, $i = 2, \ldots, \alpha + 1$. The function x^* also maps $\mathscr{N}_1$ onto $\mathscr{T}$, whence we may set $\mathscr{M}_1 \equiv \mathscr{T}$. Note, however, that the mapping of $\mathscr{N}_1$ onto $\mathscr{T}$ is not, in general, one to one.

LEMMA 1. *The function $x^*(t, \theta)$ is continuous and is piecewise C'' on Ω. The sets $\mathscr{M}_i$, $i = 1, \ldots, \alpha + 1$ are manifolds of class C''.*

Let $\overset{*}{u}_{(1)}$ denote the function that is C'' on $\bar{\Omega}_1$ and that agrees with u^* on Ω_1. Let $G_{(1)}$ denote the function that is C'' on $\bar{\mathscr{R}}_1 \times \mathscr{U}$ and that agrees with G on $\mathscr{R}_1 \times \mathscr{U}$. We may extend the function $\overset{*}{u}_{(1)}$ to a function $\overset{*}{\tilde{u}}_{(1)}$ that has range in $\mathscr{U}$ and that is C'' on a region containing $\bar{\Omega}_1$ (and hence $\mathscr{N}_1$ and $\mathscr{N}_2$) in its interior. We may also extend $G_{(1)}$ to a function $\tilde{G}_{(1)}$ that is C'' on a region containing $\bar{\mathscr{R}}_1 \times \mathscr{U}$ in its interior. It now follows from (10.5), the properties of $t_1(\sigma)$ and $x_1(\sigma)$, Assumption 3—(i), and standard theorems about the behavior of solutions of differential equations with respect to parameters and initial conditions, that $x^*(t, \theta)$ is C'' on $\bar{\Omega}_1$. Since $\mathscr{M}_2$ is given by $t = t_2(\theta)$ and $x = x_2(\theta) \equiv x^*(t_2(\theta), \theta)$, it follows that $t_2(\theta)$ and $x_2(\theta)$ are C''. The argument just given can be repeated with the appropriate modifications on Ω_2 and $\mathscr{R}_2$, with $t = t_2(\theta)$ and $x = x_2(\theta)$ as the boundary conditions for (10.5). We then get that x^* has the desired properties on $\bar{\Omega}_2$, is continuous on $\bar{\Omega}_1 \vee \bar{\Omega}_2$, and that $\mathscr{M}_3$ is given by $t = t_3(\theta)$, $x = x_3(\theta) \equiv x^*(t_3(\theta), \theta)$. Proceeding inductively in this fashion, we can establish the desired properties for x^*. We note that the sets $\mathscr{M}_i$, $i = 2, \ldots, \alpha + 1$ are given by functions

$$t = t_i(\theta), \qquad x = x_i(\theta) \equiv x^*(t_i(\theta), \theta), \tag{10.6}$$

and hence are manifolds of class C''.

ASSUMPTION 4. For every subregion $\Omega^1 \subset \Omega^0$ whose distance from $\mathscr{N}_1$ is positive, there exists a positive constant $d(\Omega^1)$ such that $\|x_\theta^*(t, \theta)\| \geqslant d(\Omega^1)$ on $\bar{\Omega}^1$. (At boundary points of Ω^1 and at points of $\mathscr{N}_i$, $i \geqslant 2$, the bounding away from zero of the determinant is to be interpreted for the various limits.)

It can be shown that if $\mathscr{T}$ is n-dimensional, then the assumption that each curve $K(\theta)$ is not tangent to $\mathscr{T}$ implies the existence of a constant $d > 0$ such that $\|x_\theta^*(t, \theta)\| \geqslant d$ on all of $\bar{\Omega}$.

It is an immediate consequence of Assumption 4 and (10.6) that the manifolds $\mathscr{M}_i$, $i = 2, \ldots, \alpha + 1$ have dimension n. It also follows from Assumption 4 that the curves $K(\theta)$ are not tangent (from either side) to a manifold $\mathscr{M}_i$, $i \geqslant 2$.

From Assumption 2, it follows that on Ω^0 the relation $x = x^*(t, \theta)$ can be inverted to give a relation

$$\theta = \Theta(t, x), \tag{10.7}$$

where Θ is a single-valued function on $\mathscr{R}$. It further follows from Lemma 1, Assumption 4, and the implicit function theorem that Θ is C'' on each $\bar{\mathscr{R}}_i$, $i \geqslant 2$, and on the set $\bar{\mathscr{R}}_1 - \mathscr{T}$. Since $x^*(t, \theta)$ is one-to-one on $\Omega^0 v \mathscr{N}_{\alpha+1}$, it follows that Θ is continuous on $\mathscr{R}$. From the identity $\theta = \Theta(t, x^*(t, \theta))$ it follows that as (t, x) tends to $\mathscr{T}$ along $K(\theta)$, the function Θ will tend to the value θ. In general, Θ will not tend to a unique limit at points of $\mathscr{T}$. It can be shown, however, that if $\mathscr{T}$ is n-dimensional and the curves $K(\theta)$ are not tangent to $\mathscr{T}$, then Θ is C'' on $\bar{\mathscr{R}}_1$ as well as on $\bar{\mathscr{R}}_i$, $i \geqslant 2$.

ASSUMPTION 5. (i) For every point $(\bar{t}, \bar{x}) = (\bar{t}, x^*(\bar{t}, \theta))$ in $\mathscr{R}$, the control problem (2.3) with initial point $(\bar{t}, \bar{x})$ has a unique solution in which the optimal control is $u^*(t, \theta)$, $\bar{t} \leqslant t \leqslant t_1(\theta)$, and the corresponding curve is $K(\theta)$. (ii) There exists a multiplier vector $(\lambda_0(\theta), \lambda(t, \theta), \mu(t, \theta))$ along each $K(\theta)$ such that $\lambda_0 = 1$ and the functions $\lambda_1(\theta) \equiv \lambda(t_1(\theta), \theta)$ and $\mu_1(\theta) \equiv \mu(t_1(\theta), \theta)$ are C' on $\mathscr{K} \times \mathscr{K}'$.

The existence of multipliers along each $K(\theta)$ follows from Theorem 2; the assumption concerns the properties of λ_0, λ_1, and μ_1.

A function $u^*(t, \theta)$ such that Assumptions 1–5 hold will be called a *normal parametric synthesis* of the control.

REMARK. If $\mathscr{T}$ is n-dimensional and each $K(\theta)$ is not tangent to $\mathscr{T}$, then (ii) follows from the Corollary of Theorem 3 and the transversality condition (6.5).

Define

$$U^*(t, x) = u^*(t, \Theta(t, x)). \tag{10.8}$$

It follows from the preceding discussion that U^* is C'' on each $\bar{\mathscr{R}}_i$, for $i \geqslant 2$, and is C'' on $\bar{\mathscr{R}}_1 - \mathscr{T}$. Along each $K(\theta)$, however, $U^*(t, x)$ does tend to a limit as $\mathscr{T}$ is approached. If $\mathscr{T}$ is n-dimensional and the curves $K(\theta)$ are not tangent to $\mathscr{T}$, then U^* is C'' on $\bar{\mathscr{R}}_1$ as well. We call U^* a *normal synthesis* of the control.

XI. THE FUNCTIONS λ, μ, AND L

LEMMA 2. *The functions $\lambda(t, \theta)$ and $\mu(t, \theta)$ are piecewise C' on Ω. Across every manifold $\mathscr{M}_i$, $i = 2, \ldots, \alpha$, equation* (9.1) *holds. If f, G, and R are continuous across $\mathscr{M}_i$, then so is $\lambda(t, \theta)$.*

Let $\hat{R}$ denote the vector formed by taking those components R^i of R such that $R^i(t, x^*(t, \theta), u^*(t, \theta)) \equiv 0$ on Ω_1. Let $\hat{\mu}$ be the vector obtained from μ by taking the corresponding components. From (2.2) – (ii) we have that $\hat{R}_u$ has maximum rank, say r_1, on Ω_1. Let $\hat{R}_{\hat{u}}$ be an r_1 by r_1 nonsingular submatrix of $\hat{R}_u$. Let $H_{\hat{u}}$ denote the vector obtained from H_u

by selecting the components corresponding to the columns of $\hat{R}_u$ used to obtain $\hat{R}_{\hat{u}}$. In order to simplify the exposition we shall assume that the same submatrix is nonsingular at all points of $\bar{\Omega}_1$. It will be seen from the ensuing discussion that this restriction can be easily overcome.

From (6.3), we get that

$$\hat{\mu} = -(H_{\hat{u}})(\hat{R}_{\hat{u}})^{-1}. \tag{11.1}$$

Since by (6.4), those components of μ that are not included in $\hat{\mu}$ vanish on $\bar{\Omega}_1$, we may write (6.2) along each $K(\theta)$ as follows:

$$\lambda_t(t, \theta) = -H_x + (H_{\hat{u}})(\hat{R}_{\hat{u}})^{-1}\hat{R}_x, \qquad \lambda(t_1, \theta) = \lambda_1(\theta), \tag{11.2}$$

where the arguments of the functions on the right are $(t, x^*(t, \theta), u^*(t, \theta))$. Arguments similar to those used in Lemma 1 can now be used to show that $\lambda(t, \theta)$ is of class C' on $\bar{\Omega}_1$. It then follows from (11.1) that $\hat{\mu}$ is also C' on $\bar{\Omega}_1$. Since the other components of μ vanish on $\bar{\Omega}_1$, the vector μ is C' on $\bar{\Omega}_1$.

The same arguments applied to Ω_2, with $\hat{R}_u$, $\hat{R}_{\hat{u}}$, $H_{\hat{u}}$ and $\hat{\mu}$ appropriately redefined and with the proper initial data $\lambda(t_2(\theta), \theta)$, show that $\lambda(t, \theta)$ and $\mu(t, \theta)$ are C' on $\bar{\Omega}_2$. The initial data $\lambda(t_2(\theta), \theta)$ are defined by continuity or by (9.1) if $\mathscr{N}_2$ corresponds to a manifold of discontinuity of f, G, or R. Proceeding backwards in this fashion we obtain that λ and μ are piecewise C' on Ω and have the requisite continuity properties.

Define

$$L(t, x) = \lambda(t, \Theta(t, x)), \qquad (t, x) \in \mathscr{R}_i, \qquad i = 1, \ldots, \alpha. \tag{11.3}$$

We list the properties of $L(t, x)$ in the following Lemma.

LEMMA 3. *The function L is C' on each $\bar{\mathscr{R}}_i$, $i = 2, \ldots, \alpha$, and on the set $\bar{\mathscr{R}}_1 - \mathscr{T}$. Moreover, if f, G, and R are continuous across a manifold $\mathscr{M}_i$, $i = 2, \ldots, \alpha$, then so is L. Across a manifold $\mathscr{M}_i$,* (9.1) *holds with λ replaced by L, where $+$ now indicates a limit from the interior of $\mathscr{R}_{i-1}$ and $-$ indicates a limit from the interior of $\mathscr{R}_i$. If $\mathscr{T}$ is n-dimensional and the curves $K(\theta)$ are not tangent to $\mathscr{T}$, then L is C' on $\bar{\mathscr{R}}_1$ also.*

The proof of this Lemma, except for the next to the last sentence, is an immediate consequence of Lemma 2 and the properties of $\Theta(t, x)$. It is clear from the properties of f, G, $\lambda(t, \theta)$, $x^*(t, \theta)$ and $u^*(t, \theta)$ that $H(t, x^*(t, \theta), \lambda(t, \theta), u^*(t, \theta))$ is continuous on each of the sets $\Omega_i \cup \mathscr{N}_i$ and $\Omega_{i-1} \cup \mathscr{N}_i$, $i = 2, \ldots, \alpha$. Hence, $H(t, x, L, U^*)$ is continuous on each $\mathscr{R}_i \cup \mathscr{M}_i$ and $\mathscr{R}_{i-1} \cup \mathscr{M}_i$, $i = 2, \ldots, \alpha$. If $\mathscr{M}_i$ is not a manifold of discontinuity of f, G, or R, then by Theorem 2, H is continuous across $\mathscr{M}_i$ along each $K(\theta)$. Hence from the continuity of H on $\mathscr{R}_i \cup \mathscr{M}$ and

$\mathscr{R}_{i-1} \cup \mathscr{M}_i$ it follows that H is continuous across $\mathscr{M}_i$, unrestrictedly in this case. Since L is continuous across $\mathscr{M}_i$ (9.1) holds across $\mathscr{M}_i$ unrestrictedly. A similar argument shows that if $\mathscr{M}_i$ is a manifold of discontinuity of f, G, or R, then (9.1) holds across $\mathscr{M}_i$, also without the restriction that the limits be taken along $K(\theta)$.

XII. The Value and the Hamilton-Jacobi Equation

Let Assumptions 1–5 of Section X hold. Then we can define a function $W(t, x)$ on $\mathscr{R}$ by assigning to each point (t, x) in $\mathscr{R}$ the value that the functional (2.3) with $(t_0, x_0) = (t, x)$ takes along the optimal curve $K(\theta)$ through (t, x). Thus:

$$W(t, x) = W(t, x^*(t, \theta)) = g(\sigma) + \int_t^{t_1(\sigma)} f(t, x^*(t, \theta), u^*(t, \theta))\, dt, \qquad (12.1)$$

where θ and σ are related by (10.2). We shall call W the *value function*, or simply the *value* of the control problem. We summarize the properties of W in the following theorem.

THEOREM 4. *The value W is continuous on $\mathscr{R}$, is C'' on each $\bar{\mathscr{R}}_i$, $i \geqslant 2$, and is C'' on $\mathscr{R}_1 - \mathscr{T}$. On each $\mathscr{R}_i$, $i = 1, \ldots, \alpha$,*

$$\begin{aligned} W_t(t, x) &= -f(t, x, U^*(t, x)) - L(t, x)G(t, x, U^*(t, x)), \\ W_x(t, x) &= L(t, x). \end{aligned} \qquad (12.2)$$

At points of a manifold $\mathscr{M}_i$, $i \geqslant 2$, (12.2) holds for the one-sided limits. If $\mathscr{M}_i$ is not a manifold of discontinuity of f, G, or R, then W_t and W_x are continuous across $\mathscr{M}_i$. Across every manifold $\mathscr{M}_j$, $j = 2, \ldots, \alpha$, the relation

$$W_t^+ \, dt_j - W_x^+ \, dx_j = W_t^- \, dt_j - W_x^- \, dx_j$$

holds for all differentials dt_j, dx_j along $\mathscr{M}_j$.

REMARK 1. If we substitute the second equation of (12.2) into the first, we see that the value satisfies the Hamilton-Jacobi equation on each $\mathscr{R}_i$.

REMARK 2. It follows from the properties of L, U^*, and Θ that both W_t and W_x possess limits as (t, x) tends to $\mathscr{T}$ along a curve $K(\theta)$, even though W_t and W_x do not, in general, possess limits as (t, x) tends to $\mathscr{T}$. If, however, $\mathscr{T}$ is n-dimensional and the curves $K(\theta)$ are not tangent to $\mathscr{T}$, then W is C'' on $\bar{\mathscr{R}}_1$.

REMARK 3. In Assumption 5–(ii) we supposed that along each $K(\theta)$ there was one set of multipliers with $\lambda_0 = 1$. The second equation in (12.2) now shows that if there is one such set satisfying the other requirements of Assumption 5, then it must be unique.

The proof that we now give for Theorem 4 is an extension of an argument used in the calculus of variations to prove the invariance of Hilbert's integral in certain fields.

It is clear from (12.1) that W is continuous. Let

$$t = T_0(s), \qquad x = X_0(s), \qquad 0 \leqslant s \leqslant 1 \tag{12.3}$$

define a curve Γ that does not intersect itself and that, with the possible exception of end points, lies entirely within some $\mathscr{R}_i$. For definiteness we take $i = \alpha$. It follows from Assumptions 2 and 4 that the system of equations

$$T_0(s) = t, \qquad X_0(s) = x^*(t, \theta), \qquad 0 \leqslant s \leqslant 1 \tag{12.4}$$

defines a function $\theta = \theta(s)$ that is C'' on $[0, 1]$. Hence as we traverse Γ as s goes from 0 to 1, we obtain a family of curves $K(s) = K(\theta(s))$, by means of the function $x^*(t, \theta(s))$, where $T_0(s) \leqslant t \leqslant t_1(s)$. Since the manifolds $\mathscr{M}_j$, $j = 1, \ldots, \alpha$, are given by (10.6), it follows that the intersections of the curves $K(s)$ with the manifolds $\mathscr{M}_j$ are given by

$$\begin{aligned} t &= T_j(s) \equiv t_j(\theta(s)), \\ x &= X_j(s) \equiv x^*(t_j(\theta(s)), \theta(s)), \qquad j = 1, \ldots, \alpha. \end{aligned} \tag{12.5}$$

The functions T_j and X_j, $j = 2, \ldots, \alpha$ are clearly C'' on $[0, 1]$. For $j = 2, \ldots, \alpha$, we can compute dX_j/ds from (12.5) in two ways

$$\frac{dX_j}{ds} = x_t^{*+} \frac{dT_j}{ds} + x_\theta^{*+} \frac{d\theta}{ds} = x_t^{*-} \frac{dT_j}{ds} + x_\theta^{*-} \frac{d\theta}{ds}, \tag{12.6}$$

where the superscript $+$ indicates that we are taking limits from the interior of $\mathscr{R}_{j-1}$, and the superscript $-$ indicates limits from the interior of $\mathscr{R}_j$. Equation (12.6) also holds for $j = 0$, without the superscripts $+$ and $-$. From (12.5), (10.2) – (10.5), and standard theorems on the differentiation of solutions of differential equations with respect to initial data, we get that

$$\frac{dT_1}{ds} = t_{1\sigma} \frac{d\sigma}{ds}, \qquad x_\theta^*(t_1(\theta(s), \theta(s)), \qquad \theta(s)) = (-M, 0), \tag{12.7}$$

where M is the matrix (8.1) and 0 is the n by $(n - p)$ zero matrix.

We now consider W along Γ. From (12.1) we get that

$$W(T_0(s), X_0(s)) = g(\sigma(s)) + \int_{T_0(s)}^{T_1(s)} f(t, x^*(t, \theta(s)), u^*(t, \theta(s)))\, dt.$$

Hence dW/ds exists, and

$$\frac{dW}{ds} = \left[g_\sigma \frac{d\sigma}{ds} + f \frac{dT_1}{ds} \right]_{T_1(s)} - \left[f \frac{dT_0}{ds} \right]_{T_0(s)} + \tag{12.8}$$

$$\sum_{j=2}^{\alpha} \left[(f^- - f^+) \frac{dT_j}{ds} \right]_{T_j(s)} + \int_{T_0(s)}^{T_1(s)} \frac{\partial f}{\partial s}\, dt,$$

where $\partial f/\partial s = (f_x x_\theta^* + f_u u_\theta^*)(d\theta/ds)$, the superscripts $+$ and $-$ have the same meaning as in (12.6), and the arguments of the functions are $(t, \theta(s))$. From (6.2) we get that $f_x = -(\lambda_t + \lambda G_x + \mu R_x)$. From (6.3) we get that $f_u = -(\lambda G_u + \mu R_u)$. Hence

$$\frac{\partial f}{\partial s} = -[\lambda_t x_\theta^* + \lambda(G_x x_\theta^* + G_u u_\theta^*) + \mu(R_x x_\theta^* + R_u u_\theta^*)] \frac{d\theta}{ds}. \tag{12.9}$$

The components of the vector $\mu(R_x x_\theta^* + R_u u_\theta^*)$ can be written as follows:

$$\sum_{k=1}^{r} \mu^k (R_x^k x_{\theta i}^* + R_u^k u_{\theta i}^*) \equiv \sum_{k=1}^{r} \mu_k \frac{\partial R^k}{\partial \theta^i}, \qquad i = 1, \ldots, n. \tag{12.10}$$

If at a point (t, θ) in Ω, $R^k(t, x^*(t, \theta), u^*(t, \theta)) > 0$, then by (6.4), $\mu^k(t, \theta) = 0$. On the other hand, since $R^k(t, x^*(t, \theta), u^*(t, \theta)) \geqslant 0$ on Ω, if $R^k = 0$ at (t, θ) then R^k, as a function of (t, θ), has a minimum at this point. Since (t, θ) is interior to Ω, $\partial R^k/\partial \theta^i = 0$ at this point for all $i = 1, \ldots, n$. Hence (12.10) is zero for all (t, θ).

If we set $\partial G/\partial \theta = (G_x x_\theta^* + G_u u_\theta^*)$ then from (10.5) we have $x_{t\theta}^* = \partial G/\partial \theta$. Furthermore, $x_{t\theta}^* = x_{\theta t}^*$. Hence, we may write (12.9) as

$$\frac{\partial f}{\partial s} = -(\lambda x_\theta^*)_t \frac{d\theta}{ds}.$$

Substituting this expression into the integral in (12.8) and performing the integration gives

$$-\left[\lambda x_\theta^* \frac{d\theta}{ds}\right]_{T_0(s)}^{T_1(s)} - \sum_{j=2}^{\alpha} [(\lambda x_\theta^*)^- - (\lambda x_\theta^*)^+]_{T_j(s)} \frac{d\theta}{ds} .$$

If we now use (12.6), (12.7); the relation $x_t = G$, and substitute the resulting expression into (12.8) we get, using the definition of H, that

$$\frac{dW}{ds} = \left[(g_\sigma + Ht_{1\sigma} - \lambda x_{1\sigma}) \frac{d\sigma}{ds}\right]_{T_1(s)} - \left[H \frac{dT_0}{ds} - \lambda \frac{dX_0}{ds}\right]_{T_0(s)} +$$

$$\sum_{j=2}^{\alpha} \left[(H^- - H^+) \frac{dT_j}{ds} - (\lambda^- - \lambda^+) \frac{dX_j}{ds}\right]_{T_j(s)} .$$

From (6.5) we get that the first square bracket vanishes. From Theorem 2 and (9.1) we get that every square bracket in $\Sigma_{j=2}^{\alpha}$ vanishes. Hence, since Γ is arbitrary,

$$dW = - H\, dT + L\, dX \tag{12.11}$$

for arbitrary differentials (dT, dX). The theorem is an immediate consequence of (12.11), the properties of f, G, L, and U^*, Theorem 2, and (9.1).

XIII. An Equation of Dynamic Programming

For each (t, x) in $\mathscr{R}$, let $\mathscr{A}(t, x)$ denote the set of admissible controls u at (t, x). Since U^* is a normal synthesis, it follows from (6.6) that for any (t, x) in $\mathscr{R}_i$, $i = 1, \ldots, \alpha$,

$$H(t, x, L(t, x), U^*(t, x)) = \min_{u \in \mathscr{A}(t,x)} H(t, x, L(t, x), u). \tag{13.1}$$

If we apply (12.2) to (13.1), we get that on $\mathscr{R}_i$,

$$W_t = - \min_{u \in \mathscr{A}(t\ x)} [f(t, x, u) + W_x G(t, x, u)]. \tag{13.2}$$

If (t, x) lies on a manifold $\mathscr{R}_i$, $i = 1, \ldots, \alpha$, then the relations (13.1) and (13.2) hold for the one-sided limits.

Equation (13.2) is the functional equation obtained formally by Bellman [1] for control problems in which $\mathscr{T}$ is the n-dimensional manifold $t_1 =$ constant and f, G, and R are C''. We note that (13.2) holds for more general problems than these. Since (13.1) is a restatement of the Weierstrass condition, since (12.2) says that on each $\mathscr{R}_i$, W satisfies the Hamilton-Jacobi equation, and since Pontryagin's Principle derives from the Weierstrass condition, the relationship between these items and (13.2) is clear.

We remark that computational schemes based directly on (13.1) in the case that $\mathscr{T}$ is of dimension p, with $p < n$, will encounter difficulties because, in general, W_t and W_x do not exist at $\mathscr{T}$. (See Remark 2, Theorem 4.)

XIV. The Problem of Synthesis

Let $u^*(t, \theta)$ and $x^*(t, \theta)$ be as in Assumptions 1 to 4, and let us replace Assumption 5 by the following:

Assumption 6. Along each $K(\theta)$, let Eqs. (6.1) – (6.5) hold with $\lambda_0 = 1$, and let $\lambda(t, \theta)$ and $\mu(t, \theta)$ have the properties described in Theorem 2. Let the functions $\lambda_1(\theta)$ and $\mu_1(\theta)$ be as in Assumption 5. Let the function H be such that (9.1) holds for all manifolds $\mathscr{M}_j$, $j = 2, \ldots, \alpha$.

Assumption 6 consists of those consequences of Assumption 5 that enter into the discussion of Section X. Hence, if we now look upon W as being defined by (12.1), then Theorem 4 still holds. In particular, (12.11) holds. Moreover, if we take Γ to lie entirely on a manifold $\mathscr{M}_i$, $i = 2, \ldots, \alpha + 1$, then the arguments used to establish (12.11) for Γ in some $\mathscr{R}_i$ will show that (12.11) holds for Γ on a manifold $\mathscr{M}_i$, $i \geqslant 2$. For curves Γ on $\mathscr{T} \equiv \mathscr{M}_1$, the validity of (12.11) follows from (6.5). Hence the integral

$$\int_{\Gamma} H(t, x, L, U^*)\, dT - L(t, x)\, dX \tag{14.1}$$

is independent of path in $\mathscr{R}$ for all curves Γ consisting of a finite number of arcs, each arc lying entirely in some $\mathscr{R}_i$ or on a manifold $\mathscr{M}_i$, $i = 1, \ldots, \alpha$.

From the preceding discussion we see that Assumptions 1–4 and Assumption 6 determine for the control problem, the analogue of a field in the calculus of variations with (14.1) as the Hilbert invariant integral. The following theorem can now be established by using the same argument as is used for the analogous fundamental sufficiency theorem in the calculus of variations.

Theorem 5. *Let Assumptions* 1–4 *and Assumption* 6 *hold. Furthermore, let* (6.6) *hold on* $\mathscr{R}$ *for* $u^* = U^*(t, x)$. *Then* $u^*(t, \theta)$ *is a normal parametric synthesis of the control and* $U^*(t, x)$ *is a normal synthesis of the control.*

References

1. Bellman, R. "Dynamic Programming." Princeton Univ. Press, Princeton, New Jersey, 1957.
2. Bellman, R., Glicksberg, I., and Gross, O. On the "bang-bang" control problem. *Quart. Appl. Math.* **14**, 11–18 (1956).
3. Bliss, G. A. "Lectures on the Calculus of Variations." Univ. of Chicago Press, Chicago, Illinois, 1946.
4. Breakwell, J. V. The optimization of trajectories. *J. Soc. Ind. Appl. Math.* **7**, 215–247 (1959).
5. Bushaw, D. W. Optimal discontinuous forcing terms. *In* "Contributions to the Theory of Nonlinear Oscillations," Vol. IV, pp. 29–52. Princeton Univ. Press, Princeton, New Jersey, 1958.
6. Gamkrelidze, R. V. Theory of time-optimal processes for linear systems. *Izvest. Akad. Nauk SSSR* **22**, 449–474 (1958).
7. Hestenes, M. R. A general problem in the calculus of variations with applications to paths of least time. The RAND Corporation, Research Memorandum RM–100, February, 1949.
8. Krasovskii, N. N. On the theory of optimum regulation. *Avtomat. i Telemekh.* **18**, 960–970 (1957) (translated in) *Automation and Remote Control* **18**, 1005–1016 (1958).
9. Krasovskii, N. N. On a problem of optimum control of nonlinear systems. *Priklad. Mat. Mekh.* **23**, 209–229 (1959), (translated in) *J. Appl. Math. Mech.* **23**, 303–332.
10. LaSalle, J. P. The time optimal control problem. *In* "Contributions to the Theory of Nonlinear Oscillations," Vol. V, pp. 1–24. Princeton Univ. Press, Princeton, New Jersey, 1960.
11. McShane, E. J. On multipliers for Lagrange problems. *Am. J. Math.* **61**, 809–819 (1939).
12. McShane, E. J. Necessary conditions in generalized-curve problems of the calculus of variations. *Duke Math. J.* **7**, 1–27 (1940).
13. Pontryagin, L. S. Optimal control processes. *Uspekhi Mat. Nauk* **14**, 3–20 (1959).
14. Rozonoèr, L. I. L. S. Pontryagin's maximum principle in the theory of optimum systems, I, II, III. *Avtomat. i Telemekh.* **20**, 1320–1334, 1441–1458, 1561–1578 (1959), (translated in) *Automation Remote Control* **20**, 1288–1302, 1405–1421, 1517–1532 (1960).
15. Valentine, F. A. The problem of Lagrange with differential inequalities as added side conditions. *In* "Contributions to the Calculus of Variations, 1933–1937," pp. 407–448. Univ. of Chicago Press, Chicago, Illinois, 1937.

On Control Problems with Bounded State Variables

LEONARD D. BERKOVITZ

The RAND Corporation, Santa Monica, California

Submitted by Richard Bellman

I. INTRODUCTION

In a recent paper [1] we showed, among other things, how a fairly general control problem, or programming problem, with constraints can be reduced to a special type of Bolza problem in the calculus of variations. Necessary conditions for the Bolza problem were then translated into necessary conditions for optimal control. These conditions include the maximum principle of Pontryagin [2, 3] for this class of problems and some of the later results of Gamkrelidze [4]. Our results in [1] do not, however, apply to control problems with constraints on the state variables that do not explicitly involve the control variable. Such problems were treated by Gamkrelidze in [4], who modified the arguments in [2] to account for the additional constraints. In this memorandum we shall use the methods of [1] to study such problems, and we shall obtain the results of Gamkrelidze, with one exception, from relevant results in the calculus of variations.

II. FORMULATION OF PROBLEM

We assume that the reader is familiar with [1], and we shall use the notation of [1]. Let θ be a function of class C'' on the region $\mathscr{D}$ of (t, x)-space such that the relation $\theta(t, x) = 0$ defines a manifold $\mathscr{B}^*$ which divides $\mathscr{D}$ into two regions. Let $\mathscr{B}$ be that subset of $\mathscr{D}$ defined by the relation

$$\theta(t, x) \geq 0. \tag{2.1}$$

We shall consider the control problem as formulated in [1] with $g \equiv 0$, and with the added restriction that the curves K resulting from controls u in $\mathscr{A}$ must lie in $\mathscr{B}$. That is, we consider the following problem.

PROBLEM I. Find an element u^* in the class of admissible controls $\mathscr{A}$ that minimizes the functional

$$J(u) = \int_{t_0}^{t_1} f(t, x, u)\, dt.$$

Here, the state of the system is determined by the system of differential equations

$$x' = G(t, x, u), \qquad x(t_0) = x_0;$$

the controls and the state of the system satisfy the constraints

$$R(t, x, u) \geq 0, \qquad \theta(t, x) \geq 0;$$

and the right-hand end point (t_1, x_1) of the trajectory is a point of a p-dimensional manifold, $0 \leq p \leq n$.

It will be clear from what follows and from [1] how one handles the case in which $\mathscr{B}$ is a closed region in $\mathscr{D}$ with piecewise smooth boundary, each piece of which is defined by a relation $\theta_i(t, x) = 0$.

The assumption that $g \equiv 0$ is made in order to simplify a certain portion of the argument below. No loss of generality will result, for the control problem of [1] is equivalent to a control problem in which $g \equiv 0$ and the initial point lies on a line, as the following transformation shows. Let a new coordinate x^{n+1} be introduced by means of the following differential equation and end conditions:

$$\frac{dx^{n+1}}{dt} = 0, \qquad x_1^{n+1} = \frac{g(\sigma)}{t_1(\sigma) - t_0}, \qquad x_0^{n+1} \text{ free.}$$

Let the functional to be minimized be

$$J(u) = \int_{t_0}^{t_1} (f + x^{n+1})\, dt.$$

In Problem I we assumed, as we did in [1], that the left-hand end point (t_0, x_0) is fixed. If (t_0, x_0) is constrained to lie on a p-dimensional manifold $(1 \leq p \leq n)$ in (t, x)-space, the analysis that follows requires the introduction of a transversality condition for the left-hand end point. We leave this to the reader.

We cannot treat Problem I by simply adjoining the constraint (2.1) as an $(r + 1)$-st component to the constraint vector $R(t, x, u)$ and then proceeding to use the analysis of [1]. The reason is that since θ is independent of u, the constraint vector (R, θ) will not satisfy the constraint condition (2.2)-(ii) of [1] at any point of $\mathscr{B}^*$, the manifold defined by $\theta(t, x) = 0$. The constraint conditions for Problem I are the following, which are modifications of those in [1]:

(i) If $r > m$, then at each point of $\mathscr{S} = \mathscr{B}^0 \times \mathscr{U}$, where $\mathscr{B}^0$ denotes the interior of $\mathscr{B}$, at most m components of R can vanish. If $r \geq m$, then at each point of $\mathscr{S}^* = \mathscr{B}^* \times \mathscr{U}$, at most $(m - 1)$ components of R can vanish.

(ii) At each point of $\mathscr{S}$ the matrix $(\partial R^i/\partial u^j)$, where i ranges over those indices such that $R^i(t, x, u) = 0$, and $j = 1, \cdots, m$, has maximum rank. At each point of $\mathscr{S}^*$, if the m-dimensional row vector $\theta_x G_u$ is adjoined to this matrix (where i now ranges from 1 to $m - 1$), the resulting matrix has maximum rank. (2.2)

III. Equivalent Lagrange Problem

Let η be a scalar, and let

$$\gamma(t, x, \eta) = \begin{cases} \eta^4 - \theta(t, x) & \text{if} \quad \eta \geq 0, \\ \theta(t, x) & \text{if} \quad \eta \leq 0. \end{cases} \tag{3.1}$$

The function $\gamma(t, x, \eta)$ is clearly C'' on the region of (t, x, η)-space which is the Cartesian product of the η-axis and $\mathscr{D}$. If we let

$$y' = u, \qquad y(t_0) = 0,$$

then Problem I is readily seen to be equivalent to the following problem of Lagrange in $(n + m + r + 2)$-dimensional (t, x, y, ξ, η)-space.

Problem II. Find an arc $(x(t), y(t), \xi(t), \eta(t))$ that minimizes

$$\int_{t_0}^{t_1} f(t, x, y')\, dt \tag{3.2}$$

in the class of arcs that are piecewise C'' and that satisfy the differential equations

$$\begin{aligned} G(t, x, y') - x' &= 0, \\ R(t, x, y') - (\xi')^2 &= 0, \\ \theta_t + \theta_x x' - \gamma_\eta \eta' &= 0, \end{aligned} \tag{3.3}$$

and also the end conditions

$$x(t_0) = x_0, \qquad y(t_0) = 0, \qquad \xi(t_0) = 0, \qquad \gamma(t_0, x_0, \eta_0) = 0, \tag{3.4}$$

$$t_1 = t_1(\sigma), \qquad x_1 = x_1(\sigma), \qquad \gamma(t_1, x_1, \eta_1) = 0, \tag{3.5}$$

$$\xi_1 = \xi(t_1), \text{ free}, \qquad y_1 = y(t_1), \text{ free}.$$

Note that the last equation in (3.3) and the end conditions imply that $\gamma(t, x, \eta) = 0$ along each arc. Hence, by (3.1), $\theta \geq 0$ along each arc.

Let us suppose that u^* is an optimal control in $\mathscr{A}$, and let K^* be the corresponding curve in (t, x)-space. Let K_1^* be the corresponding arc in (t, x, y, ξ, η)-space. Consider the following $(n + r + 1)$ by $(m + n + r + 1)$ matrix along K_1^*:

$$\begin{Vmatrix} G_{y'} & -I & 0 & 0 \\ R_{y'} & 0 & -2\Xi' & 0 \\ 0 & \theta_x & 0 & -\gamma_\eta \end{Vmatrix}, \tag{3.6}$$

where $2\Xi'$ is an $r \times r$ diagonal matrix with entries $2(\xi^i)'$ on the diagonal. The rank of (3.6) is clearly the same as the rank of the matrix

$$\begin{Vmatrix} G_{y'} & -I & 0 & 0 \\ R_{y'} & 0 & -2\Xi' & 0 \\ \theta_x G_{y'} & 0 & 0 & -\gamma_\eta \end{Vmatrix}. \tag{3.7}$$

Since $\gamma = 0$ along K_1^*, it follows from (3.1) that $\gamma_\eta > 0$ if $\theta > 0$, and that $\gamma_\eta = 0$ if $\eta \leq 0$. Hence, using the constraint conditions (2.2) and arguments similar to those used to determine the rank of (3.8) in [1], we see that the matrix (3.7) has rank $(n + r + 1)$ at all points of K_1^*. Hence (3.6) has rank $(n + r + 1)$.

The above argument is not restricted to K_1^*; it shows that (3.6) has rank $(n + r + 1)$ at all elements $(t, x, y, \xi, \eta, x', \xi', \eta')$ of a curve for which (3.3) and the end condition (3.4) and (3.5) hold.

If $t_1(\sigma)$ and $x_1(\sigma)$ define a p-dimensional terminal manifold for Problem I, then the right-hand end conditions for Problem II and the restriction that (t_1, x_1) is in $\mathscr{B}$ determine a p-dimensional terminal manifold in (t, x, η)-space for Problem II. We suppose that in a neighborhood of the right-hand end points of K_1^*, this manifold is given parametrically as follows:

$$t_1 = t_1(s), \qquad x_1 = x_1(s), \qquad \eta_1 = \eta_1(s).$$

We note that

$$\gamma(t_1(s), x_1(s), \eta_1(s)) \equiv 0. \tag{3.8}$$

Since u^* is an optimal control, it is clear that K_1^* furnishes a minimum for Problem II. From this and from the preceding discussion it follows that the multiplier rule, the Weierstrass condition, and the Clebsch condition as given in Bliss [5] and extended by McShane [6] hold along K_1^*. The function F in this instance is defined as follows:

$$F = \psi_0 f + \psi(G - x') + \mu(R - (\xi')^2) + \nu(\theta_t + \theta_x x' - \gamma_\eta \eta'). \tag{3.9}$$

From the Euler equations

$$\frac{dF_{y'}}{dt} = F_y, \qquad \frac{dF_{\xi'}}{dt} = F_\xi,$$

the continuity of $F_{y'}$ and $F_{\xi'}$, and the relations

$$F_{y'} = 0, \qquad F_{\xi'} = 0 \qquad \text{at} \qquad (t_1, x_1, \eta_1), \tag{3.10}$$

which we obtain from the transversality condition, we deduce as we did in [1] that along K_1^*,

$$F_{\xi_i'} = \mu^i R^i = 0, \qquad i = 1, \cdots, r,$$

$$F_{y'} = \psi_0 f_{y'} + \psi G_{y'} + \mu R_{y'} = 0. \tag{3.11}$$

From the Euler equation $dF_{\eta'}/dt = F_\eta$ we find that between corners of K_1^*,

$$\nu' \gamma_\eta = 0. \tag{3.12}$$

The Euler equation $dF_{x'}/dt = F_x$ takes the form

$$\frac{d}{dt}(-\psi + \nu\theta_x) = \psi_0 f_x + \psi G_x + \mu R_x + \nu(\theta_{tx} + \theta_{xx}x'). \tag{3.13}$$

If we make use of (3.10) in the remaining equations of the transversality condition, we get

$$(F - x'F_{x'} - \eta' F_{\eta'})\, t_{1s} + F_{x'}x_{1s} + F_{\eta'}\eta_{1s} = 0.$$

From (3.3) we obtain that $x' = G$ and that $F = \psi_0 f$ at (t_1, x_1, η_1). Using these relations, Eq. (3.4), and the last equation in (3.3), we can rewrite the preceding equation as follows:

$$(\psi_0 f + \psi G)\, t_{1s} - \psi x_{1s} + \nu(\theta_t t_{1s} + \theta_x x_{1s} - \gamma_\eta \eta_{1s}) = 0.$$

Hence, using (3.8) we find that the transversality condition, in addition to yielding (3.10), gives

$$(\psi_0 f + \psi G)\, t_{1s} - \psi x_{1s} = 0. \tag{3.14}$$

Another necessary condition is the continuity along K_1^* of the expression

$$F - x'F_{x'} - y'F_{y'} - \xi' F_{\xi'} - \eta' F_{\eta'}.$$

If we take (3.3) and (3.10) into account, this expression may be rewritten as follows along K_1^*:

$$\psi_0 f + \psi G + \nu \theta_t. \tag{3.15}$$

Using arguments similar to those used above and in [1], we may rewrite the Weierstrass condition in the following form:

$$\psi_0(f(t, x, Y') - f(t, x, y')) + \psi(X' - x') \geq 0. \tag{3.16}$$

From the Clebsch condition we deduce, as we did in [1], that along K_1^*,

$$\mu \leq 0, \tag{3.17}$$

and that

$$e((\psi_0 f + \psi G + \mu R)_{y'y'})\, e \geq 0 \tag{3.18}$$

for all m-dimensional solution vectors e of the following linear systems: $\hat{R}_{y'}e = 0$ at points that are interior to $\mathscr{B}$; $\hat{R}_{y'}e = 0$ and $\theta_x G_{y'}e = 0$ at points of K_1^* that correspond to points of $\mathscr{B}^*$. The vector $\hat{R}$ is obtained from R by taking those components of R that vanish at the point.

IV. An Interior Segment

We now consider the curve K^* corresponding to the optimal control u^*. We adopt Gamkrelidze's definition [4] and say that the point $(\tau, x(\tau))$ of K^* is a *junction point* if it belongs to K^*, if $t_0 < \tau < t_1$ and if there exists a $\delta > 0$ such that either the segment of K^* for which $\tau - \delta < t < \tau$, or the segment for which $\tau < t < \tau + \delta$ (or both), lies in the interior of $\mathscr{B}$. We call τ a *junction time*. We suppose that K^* has a finite number of junction points. For definiteness, we suppose that if τ is the largest junction time, then the portion of K^* defined for $\tau < t < t_1$ is interior to $\mathscr{B}$. We denote this segment by K_A^* and also use this notation for the corresponding segment of K_1^*.

Since K_A^* is interior to $\mathscr{B}$, it follows that $\eta > 0$. Hence from (3.1) we have $\gamma_\eta > 0$, and so from (3.12) we get that between corners of K_A^*, ν is constant. Moreover, the end condition (3.14) places no restriction on $\nu(t_1)$. Since ν is constant between corners of K_1^*, equation (3.13) can be written as

$$\psi' = -(\psi_0 f_x + \psi G_x + \mu R_x). \tag{4.1}$$

Note that the differential equation (4.1) and the end conditions (3.14) are independent of the values assigned to ν. Using this observation and the fact that the left-hand end point of K_1^* is fixed, we can see by examining the proof in [6] that we can always choose $(\psi_0, \psi, \mu) \neq 0$ at the right-hand end-point (t_1, x_1) of K_1^*. From the constraint condition (2.2)-(ii) and from (3.11) it follows that μ is determined uniquely as a linear function of (ψ_0, ψ) on the interval $\tau \leq t \leq t_1$. Hence, on this interval, (4.1) can be written as a linear differential equation in ψ, and so if $(\psi_0, \psi) = 0$ at any point of K_A^*, then $(\psi_0, \psi) \equiv 0$. Moreover, in this event $\mu \equiv 0$. Since $(\psi_0, \psi, \mu) \neq 0$ at (t_1, x_1), we can therefore conclude that $(\psi_0, \psi) \neq 0$ at every point of K_A^*.

Define

$$H(t, x, u, \lambda_0, \lambda) = \lambda_0 f + \lambda G. \tag{4.2}$$

For $\tau < t < t_1$, let

$$\lambda_0 = \psi_0, \qquad \lambda = \psi, \tag{4.3}$$

and take ν to be a constant on the entire interval $\tau < t < t_1$. (K_1^* may have corners in this interval.) It follows from (4.1)-(4.3), (3.11), (3.14)-(3.18), and from the relation $y' = u$, that Theorem 2 of [1] holds along K_A^*.

V. A Boundary Segment

Let τ' be the largest of the junction times that are less than τ. If there are none, take $\tau' = t_0$. We next suppose that the segment of K^* defined for $\tau' \leq t \leq \tau$ lies entirely in $\mathscr{B}^*$. We denote this segment (and the corresponding segment of K_1^*) by K_B^*. To simplify the exposition we shall suppose that K_B^* has no corners and the same components of R vanish all along K_B^*. If the contrary holds, the argument requires trivial modifications, which we leave to the reader.

Let

$$\phi(t, x, u) = \theta_t + \theta_x G. \tag{5.1}$$

Then along K_B^*, we clearly have

$$\phi = 0. \tag{5.2}$$

On the interval $\tau' \leq t \leq \tau$, let

$$\lambda_0 = \psi_0, \qquad \lambda = \psi - \nu\theta_x. \tag{5.3}$$

If we substitute (5.3) into (3.13) and use the definition of ϕ given in (5.1) and the definition of H given in (4.2), we can rewrite (3.13) as

$$\frac{d\lambda}{dt} = -(H_x + \mu R_x + \nu\phi_x). \tag{5.4}$$

If we substitute (5.3) into the second equation of (3.11) and replace y' by u, we can rewrite this equation as follows:

$$H_u + \mu R_u + \nu\theta_x G_u = 0. \tag{5.5}$$

Similarly, the substitution of (5.3) into the Weierstrass condition (3.16) leads to the relation

$$H(t, x, Y') - H(t, x, y') + \nu\theta_x(X' - x') \geq 0$$

for all admissible (t, x, X', Y'). Since the element (t, x, X', Y') is admissible, it satisfies the last equation of (3.3), and so $\theta_x(X' - x') = \theta_t - \theta_t = 0$. Hence, setting $u = y'$, we can rewrite (3.16) as

$$H(t, x, u) \geq H(t, x, u^*) \tag{5.6}$$

along K_B^* for all admissible u such that $\phi(t, x, u) = 0$.

Finally, equation (3.18) of the Clebsch condition becomes

$$e((H + \mu R + \nu\theta_x G)_{uu})\, e \geq 0. \tag{5.7}$$

From the necessary conditions for Problem II, it follows that there exists a constant $\lambda_0 \geq 0$ and functions (λ, μ, ν) such that (5.4)-(5.7) hold along K_B^*. From the constraint condition (2.2)-(ii), it follows that we may solve (5.5) uniquely for (μ, ν) as linear functions of (λ_0, λ). Substitution of this solution into (5.4) yields a system of linear differential equations for λ. Hence if (λ_0, λ) is determined at a point of K_B^*, then the solution λ of (5.4) and the functions (μ, ν) are uniquely determined along K_B^*.

From the Weierstrass-Erdmann corner condition for Problem II, we see that

$$F_{x'} = -\psi + \nu\theta_x \tag{5.8}$$

is continuous at the junction point $(\tau, x(\tau))$. Thus, if we denote functions along K_A^* by a subscript A and functions along K_B^* by a subscript B, then at $(\tau, x(\tau))$ we have

$$-\psi_A^+ + \nu_A^+\theta_x = -\psi_B^- + \nu_B^-\theta_x. \tag{5.9}$$

Using (4.3) and (5.3), this can be rewritten as

$$\lambda_B^- = \lambda_A^+ - \nu_A^+\theta_x, \qquad \nu_A^+ \text{ arbitrary.} \tag{5.10}$$

This relation and the relation

$$\lambda_{0B} = \lambda_{0A} = \psi_0, \tag{5.11}$$

which follows from (4.3), (5.3), and the constancy of ψ_0, therefore serve to determine $(\lambda_0, \lambda, \mu, \nu)$ uniquely along K_B^*.

From the continuity of (3.15), and from (4.3), (5.3), and (5.2), we readily find that at the junction point $(\tau, x(\tau))$,

$$H^- = H^+ + \nu_A\theta_t. \tag{5.12}$$

With the help of (5.10) and (5.2), this can be rewritten as follows:

$$\lambda_0(f^- - f^+) + \lambda^+(G^- - G^+) = 0,$$
$$\lambda_0(f^- - f^+) + \lambda^-(G^- - G^+) = \nu_A^+(\theta_x G^+ + \theta_t). \tag{5.13}$$

It is readily verified that the vector

$$(\lambda_0, \lambda_B, \mu_B, \nu_B) = (0, \rho\theta_x, 0, -\rho), \tag{5.14}$$

where ρ is any real constant, satisfies (5.4) and (5.5) along any curve K obtained from an admissible control and lying in $\mathscr{B}^*$. Substitution of (5.14) into the relation (5.6) reduces (5.6) to the identity $\rho\theta_t = \rho\theta_t$ along any such curve. From (5.5) and the constraint condition (2.2)-(ii) it follows that (5.14) is the unique solution of (5.4)-(5.6) with $\lambda_0 = 0$, $\lambda = \rho\theta_x$, ρ arbitrary. It is immediate from (5.3) that for Problem II,

$$(\psi_0, \psi_B, \mu_B, \nu_B) = (0, 0, 0, -\rho), \qquad \rho \text{ arbitrary}, \tag{5.15}$$

is the unique vector corresponding to (5.14). The vector (5.15) reduces the Euler equations (3.13) and (3.11), and the Weierstrass condition (3.16) to identities for all admissible curves lying in $\mathscr{B}^*$. We shall refer to (5.14) or (5.15) as a trivial multiplier vector. Note that since ρ is arbitrary, the zero vector is included.

If we have

$$\lambda_0^+ = 0, \qquad \lambda_A^+ = k\theta_x, \qquad k \neq 0, \tag{5.16}$$

at $(\tau, x(\tau))$, for every set of multipliers $(\lambda_0, \lambda_A, \mu_A, \nu_A)$ such that Eqs. (5.4)-(5.7) hold along K_A^*, then it follows from (5.10) and the discussion of the preceding paragraph that along the segment K_B^* we obtain the trivial multipliers (5.14). To avoid this, we proceed as follows. We consider a Problem I′, which we define as Problem I with fixed initial point $(\tau', x(\tau'))$ and fixed terminal point $(\tau, x(\tau))$. It is clear that the segment K_B^* must furnish a relative minimum for Problem I′. For, if some other curve K' furnished a minimum, then we could replace the segment K_B^* of K^* by K' and thereby contradict the minimality of K^*. Since the Lagrange problem corresponding to Problem I′ has fixed end points, it can be seen from the proof in [6] of the necessary conditions that we may take $(\psi_0, \psi(\tau_2)) \neq 0$. Hence there exist nontrivial multipliers (ψ_0, ψ, μ, ν) such that (5.4)-(5.7) hold along K_B^*, even if (5.16) holds. In this event, however, (5.10)-(5.13) are no longer valid.

The following theorem is a consequence of the preceding discussion.

THEOREM 1. *On the interval* $[\tau', \tau]$ *there exists a constant* $\lambda_0 \geq 0$ *and a continuous n-dimensional vector* $\lambda(t)$ *such that* $(\lambda_0, \lambda) \neq (0, \rho\theta_x)$, ρ *arbitrary;*

an r-dimensional vector $\mu(t) \leq 0$, *continuous except perhaps at values of t corresponding to corners of* K_B^*; *and a function* $\nu(t)$ *with the same continuity properties as* μ, *such that along* K_B^*, *(5.4)-(5.7) hold.*

At the junction point $(\tau, x(\tau))$, *either (5.16) holds for every* $(\lambda_{0A}, \lambda_A^+)$, *or the jump conditions (5.10) and (5.12) (and hence (5.11)) hold.*

REMARK 1. This result was obtained by Gamkrelidze [4], who used different arguments. He also presents a result that in our notation reads $d\nu/dt \geq 0$ along K_B^*.

REMARK 2. In Section IV we assumed that the segment K_A^* was interior to $\mathscr{B}$. If we had assumed that the segment K_A^* was in $\mathscr{B}^*$, then we would still conclude that, except for the jump conditions, Theorem 1 holds along K_A^*. This follows from the arguments used to establish the theorem and the observation that the transversality condition (3.14) places no restriction on $\nu(t_1)$.

VI. CONCLUSION

If $\tau' > t_0$, let us suppose that τ'' is the largest junction time that is less than τ'; if there is no such junction time, take $\tau'' = t_0$. The segment of K^* defined for $\tau'' < t < \tau'$ then lies entirely within $\mathscr{B}$. We denote this segment by K_C^*. On this segment we define (λ_0, λ) by means of (4.3), and apply the analysis of Section IV, except for the determination of initial data for (4.1). We now use the continuity of (5.8) at the junction point to determine λ_{0C} and $\lambda_C(\tau'')$, where the subscript C refers to functions along K_C^*. Since we have $(\lambda_0, \lambda_B^+) \neq (0, \rho\theta_x)$, it follows that at $(\tau'', x(\tau''))$, the following jump condition holds:

$$\lambda_C^- = \lambda_B^+ + \nu_C^- \theta_x \neq 0, \qquad \nu_C^- \text{ arbitrary.}$$

Hence the conclusions of Theorem 2 of [1] hold along K_C^*.

Let us now suppose that K_B^*, instead of lying on the boundary as assumed in Section V, is an interior segment. The point $(\tau, x(\tau))$, however, is still assumed to be a junction point. Along K_B^* we now define $(\lambda_{0B}, \lambda_B)$ by (4.3), and we apply the analysis of Section IV, except for the determination of the initial data for $(\lambda_{0B}, \lambda_B)$. To determine λ_{0B} and $\lambda_B(\tau)$ we use the continuity of (5.8) and get

$$\lambda_B^- = \lambda_A^+ + (\nu_B^- - \nu_A^+)\, \theta_x.$$

Since we are free in our choice of ν_B^-, we get

$$\lambda_B^- = \lambda_A^+ + k\theta_x \neq 0. \tag{6.1}$$

Hence Theorem 2 of [1] holds along K_B^*.

Note that in obtaining (6.1), we did not make use of the special fact that ν_A^+ is arbitrary because the segment K_A^* terminates at (t_1, x_1). Moreover, we can choose ν_B^- so that $k \geq 0$.

We summarize the principal results of this paper in the following theorem.

THEOREM 2. *Let $u^* \in \mathscr{A}$ be an optimal control, and let K^* be the corresponding curve. Then there exists a constant $\lambda_0 \geq 0$, an n-dimensional vector $\lambda(t)$, an r-dimensional vector $\mu(t) \leq 0$, and a function $\nu(t)$ such that the following hold: Along a segment of K^* whose end points are junction points and that is in the interior of $\mathscr{B}$, except for the end-points, Theorem 2 of [1] holds. Along a segment whose end-points are junction points and that lies in $\mathscr{B}^*$, Theorem 1 of this paper holds. If $\lambda_0 = 0$, then at a junction point either*

$$\lambda^- + k\theta_x = 0, \qquad k \neq 0, \tag{6.2}$$

or

$$\lambda^+ = \lambda^- + k\theta_x \neq 0. \tag{6.3}$$

If $\lambda_0 \neq 0$, then at a junction point (6.3) holds. At a junction point between two interior segments, we may take k so that (6.2) does not occur, and $k \geq 0$ in (6.3). If (6.3) holds, then the following also holds:

$$H^+ = H^- - k\theta_t. \tag{6.4}$$

From this theorem, several observations can be made. Since these are given by Gamkrelidze [4], there is no need to repeat them here.

REFERENCES

1. BERKOVITZ, L. D. Variational methods in problems of control and programming. *J. Math. Anal. Appl.* **3**, 145-169 (1961).
2. BOLTYANSKII, V. G., GAMKRELIDZE, R. V., AND PONTRYAGIN, L.S. The theory of optimal processes I: The maximum principle. *Izvest. Akad. Nauk. SSSR, Ser. Mat.* **24**, 3-42 (1960).
3. PONTRYAGIN, L. S. Optimal control processes. *Uspekhi Mat. Nauk.* **14**, 3-20 (1959).
4. GAMKRELIDZE, R. V. Optimal processes with bounded phase coordinates. *Izvest. Akad. Nauk. SSSR, Ser. Mat.* **24**, 315-356 (1960).
5. BLISS, G. A. "Lectures in the Calculus of Variations." Univ. of Chicago Press, Chicago, Illinois, 1946.
6. MCSHANE, E. J. On multipliers for Lagrange problems. *Am. J. Math.* **61**, 809-819 (1939).

THE METHOD OF MOMENTS IN THE THEORY OF OPTIMAL CONTROL OF SYSTEMS WITH DISTRIBUTED PARAMETERS

A. G. Butkovskii

(Moscow)

Translated from Avtomatika i Telemekhanika, Vol. 24, No. 9,
pp. 1217-1225, September, 1963
Original article submitted February 20, 1963

In this article, methods are described for the solution of the problem of optimal control by linear systems with distributed parameters by using results concerning the L-problem in the theory of moments. The relation between the results obtained by this method and the results of using the maximum principle are considered. On the basis of the results described, a numerical algorithm is proposed for the determination of optimal control actions. As an example, we consider the process, optimal relative to the time, of heating a massive body, and we calculate its relation with the control process that minimizes the difference between the real and the given distribution. In conclusion, we consider the problem with limitations on the intermediate coordinates of the system, and this problem is also reduced to a moment problem.

We consider a linear system with distributed parameters with a single controlling action

$$Q(x,t) = \int_0^t K(x, t-\tau)\, u(\tau)\, d\tau \qquad (0 \leqslant x \leqslant S,\ 0 \leqslant t \leqslant T) \tag{1}$$

and pose for this system the following problem in optimal control: to find a control action $u(t)$, $|u(t)| \leq L$, $0 \leq t \leq T$, for which the relation

$$Q^*(x) = \int_0^T K(x, T-t)\, u(t)\, dt, \tag{2}$$

is satisfied with $Q^*(x)$ as a given function and the time T as a minimum.

We will show how to reduce this problem to the L-problem of moment theory [1, 2].

We take an arbitrary, complete system of functions $\varphi_i(x)$ ($i = 1, 2, \ldots, 0 \leq x \leq S$) and expand $Q^*(x)$ and $K(x,t)$ in a series of these functions for any fixed time t. Then from (2) we obtain

$$\sum_{i=1}^{\infty} \alpha_i \varphi_i(x) = \sum_{i=1}^{\infty} \varphi_i(x) \int_0^T g_i(T-t)\, u(t)\, dt. \tag{3}$$

In the following we will assume that the functions $g_k(t)$ ($k = 1, 2, \ldots, 0 \leq t \leq T$) are such that the linear combinations $\sum_{k=1}^{n} \lambda_k g_k(t)$ (the numbers λ_k, $k = 1, 2, \ldots$, are not all equal to zero) can be zero only for discrete values of t, and that the number of these values in the interval [0, T] is finite. It is also sufficient to assume that the $g_k(t)$ ($k = 1, 2, \ldots, n$) are linearly independent for any n.

For a solution of (3), it is necessary and sufficient that the infinite set of equations

$$\alpha_i = \int_6^T g_i(T-t)\, u(t)\, dt \qquad (i = 1, 2, \ldots) \tag{4}$$

be satisfied.

The optimal-control problem can here be formulated as follows: to find a function $u(t)$, $|u(t)| \leq L$, $0 \leq t \leq T$, for which the system (4) has a solution, where the time T must be a minimum.

As is known [1, 2], for the solution of this problem for finite n it is necessary and sufficient that

$$\min_{\xi_k^n} \int_0^{T_n} \left| \sum_{k=1}^{n} \xi_k^n g_k (T_n - t) \right| dt = \lambda_n (T_n) = \frac{1}{L} \tag{5}$$

where

$$\sum_{k=1}^{n} \xi_k^n \alpha_k = 1. \tag{6}$$

Here the optimal control for such a "truncated" problem will have the form

$$u_n (t) = L \operatorname{sign} \sum_{k=1}^{n} \bar{\xi}_k^n g_k (T_n^0 - t), \tag{7}$$

where $\bar{\xi}_k^n (k = 1, 2, \ldots, n)$ is the solution of the problem (5), (6), and the optimal time T_n^0 is given by the condition

$$\lambda_n (T_n^0) = \frac{1}{L}. \tag{8}$$

We consider the case when, for $n \to \infty$ the limiting function $\lambda(T) = \lim_{n\to\infty} \lambda_n (T)$ exists and is continuous in T in the range $0 \leq T < \infty$ and $\lambda(T) \to \infty$ for $T \to \infty$ (see Fig. 1). It is then obvious that there is a solution T° of the equation

$$\lambda (T^\circ) = \frac{1}{L}, \tag{9}$$

which has the sense of the time T° of the optimal process for the distributed system (1).

Since the sequence of functions $u_n(t)$ given by the formula (7) is here such that $|u_n(t)| \leq L$ $(0 \leq t \leq T^\circ, n = 1, 2, \ldots)$, it follows that an application of the result in Section 7, Chapter 1 of [3] shows that there is a control $u^0(t)$, $|u^0(t)| \leq L$, that gives the solution of the optimal-control problem stated at the beginning of the article.

The solution of the "truncated" problem for finite n is considered in most cases as an approximate solution of the optimal-control problem. In this case, the distribution function falls optimally (for the minimum time T_n^0) in some neighborhood of the given function $Q^*(x)$.

We will describe a successive-approximation method which can be used to solve the moment problem for a finite n. We will start from the problem defined by (5) and (6); to find numbers $\xi_k^0 (k = 1, 2, \ldots, n)$ and T°, such that

$$\min_{\xi_k} \int_0^{T} \left| \sum_{k=1}^{n} \xi_k g_k (T - t) \right| dt = \int_0^{T} \left| \sum_{k=1}^{n} \xi_k^0 g_k (T^\circ - t) \right| dt = \frac{1}{L} \tag{10}$$

for

$$\sum_{k=1}^{n} \xi_k^0 \alpha_k = 1. \tag{11}$$

We write

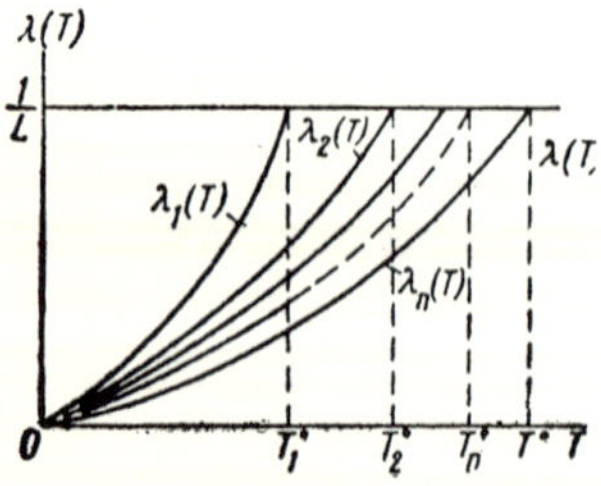

Fig. 1.

$$\rho_\xi (T) = \int_0^{T} \left| \sum_{k=1}^{n} \xi_k g_k (T - t) \right| dt, \tag{12}$$

$$\xi = (\xi_1, \ldots, \xi_n). \tag{13}$$

We take an arbitrary value of the vector $\xi = \xi_0$ satisfying (11), and draw the graph of the function $\rho_{\xi_0}(T)$ as a function of T (Fig. 2). Since $\rho_{\xi_0}(T) \to \infty$ increases monotonically from zero with increasing T, and since $\rho_{\xi_0}(T) \to \infty$ for $T \to \infty$, there exists a value T_0 for which $\rho_{\xi_0}(T_0) = 1/L$, i.e., the graph of $\rho_{\xi_0}(T)$ intersects the horizontal line at the level $1/L$ at a point with abscissa $T = T_0$.

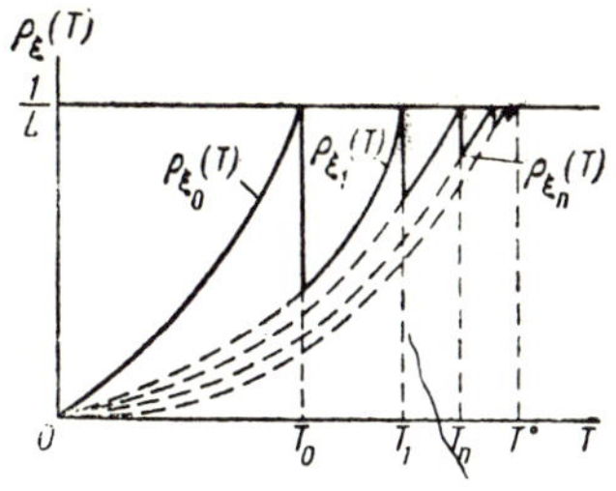

Fig. 2.

For $T = T_0$ $\rho_\xi(T_0)$ is a function of ξ. We find the minimum of $\rho_\xi(T_0)$ relative to ξ for the condition (11). If this minimum is reached on the zeroth-approximation vector ξ_0, then the problem (10), (11) is solved. Such a vector is, however, rarely guessed correctly. There is thus a ξ_1 for which

$$\rho_{\xi_1}(T_0) = \min_{\xi} \rho_\xi(T_0) < \frac{1}{L}.$$

For $\xi = \xi_1$ the graph of $\rho_{\xi_1}(T)$ intersects the $1/L$ level for $T = T_1$.

For $T = T_1$ we again minimize the function $\rho_\xi(T_1)$ relative to ξ with the condition (11), i.e., we find a value ξ_2 satisfying (11) such that

$$\rho_{\xi_2}(T_1) = \min_{\xi} \rho_\xi(T_1). \qquad (14)$$

If $\rho_{\xi_2}(T_1) = 1/L$, then the problem is solved; if not, then the process must be continued. We will now obtain a sequence $T_0, T_1, \ldots$, which converges to T° – the time of the optimal transition process, and a sequence $\xi_0, \xi_1, \ldots$, which converges to the vector ξ° giving the optimal control by means of the formula

$$u_n(t) = L \operatorname{sign} \sum_{k=1}^{n} \xi_k^\circ g_k(T^\circ - t). \qquad (15)$$

Thus the determination of the optimal control action and the time of the optimal process reduces to a successive minimization and determination of the point of intersection of a monotonic curve with the horizontal line at the level $1/L$.

We note that, since the function $\rho_\xi(T)$ for fixed T is a convex function of ξ and since (11) is a linear condition, it follows that the minimization of $\rho_\xi(T)$ relative to ξ can be carried out by any known method (for example by the gradient method or the method of steepest descent, etc.), which leads to the determination of the point of absolute minimum of the function $\rho_\xi(T)$.

Hence the successive-approximation method we have described for finding the optimal control and the time of the optimal process can easily be made automatic by using an optimizer on certain variables and blocks of numerical devices. We show in Fig. 3 the schematic diagram for such a numerical process.

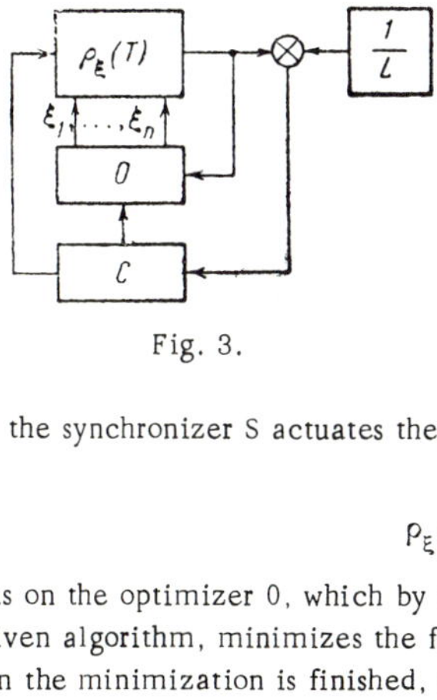

Fig. 3.

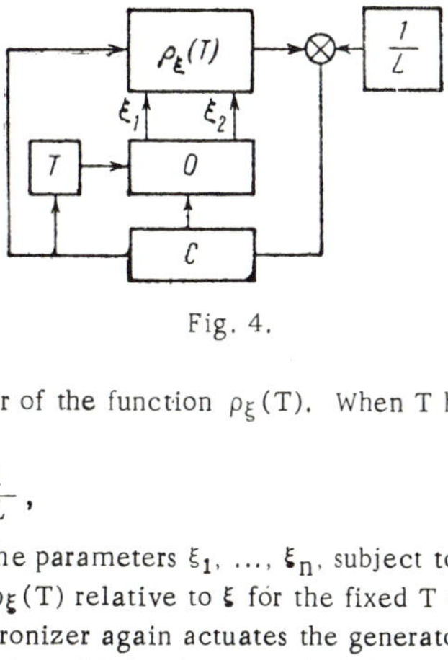

Fig. 4.

For a fixed ξ, the synchronizer S actuates the generator of the function $\rho_\xi(T)$. When T has reached the value for which

$$\rho_\xi(T) = \frac{1}{L}, \qquad (16)$$

the synchronizer turns on the optimizer 0, which by varying the parameters $\xi_1, \ldots, \xi_n$, subject to the condition (11) according to some given algorithm, minimizes the function $\rho_\xi(T)$ relative to ξ for the fixed T obtained from the condition (16). When the minimization is finished, the synchronizer again actuates the generator of the function $\rho_\xi(T)$ of T for fixed ξ, and this generator functions until a value of T has been reached that satisfies (16), etc. As a criterion for the termination of this process, we can use the size of the difference between two successive values T_k and T_{k+1}. For $|T_k - T_{k+1}| < \varepsilon$, where $\varepsilon > 0$ is a given number, the process is stopped.

A consideration of Fig. 2 shows that the logic of the above-described successive-approximation process can be somewhat simplified. In fact the problem (10), (11) can be stated in the following way: to find a vector $\xi = (\xi_1, \ldots, \xi_n)$ such that the intersection of the graph of $\rho_\xi(T)$ with the $1/L$ level occurs for the largest value of T, i.e., we must find

$$\max_{\xi} T = T^\circ \qquad (17)$$

using the condition (16).

In Fig. 4 we show the schematic diagram for a calculating device that realizes the algorithm for the solution of this problem. The synchronizer actuates the generator of the function $\rho_\xi(T)$ of T for fixed ξ and simultaneously actuates the recorder for the time T. When the condition (16) is reached, the value of T for which this condition is satisfied is led to the optimizer. The optimizer varies the parameters $\xi_1, \ldots, \xi_n$, $\xi = (\xi_1, \ldots, \xi_n)$ subject to the condition (11) to maximize the time T. The end of this process can be indicated by the same criterion used in the previous case.

We note a further possibility in designing a calculating device based on the fact that, in the problem (10), (11), it is easy to calculate the gradient of $\rho_\xi(T)$ from the formula

$$\frac{\partial \rho_\xi(T)}{\partial \xi_k} = \int_0^T g_k(T-t)\, \mathrm{sign} \sum_{k=1}^{n} \xi_k g_k(T-t)\, dt. \tag{18}$$

This formula can be realized in a calculating device, and the minimization with the condition (11) can start at any initial point ξ_0. In this case we can thus deal with any inputs without recourse to the direct application of an automatic optimizer.

We now turn to a problem previously considered in [4], and closely related to the above soluble problem. This problem is to find a control u(t) with $|u(t)| \leq L$ such that, for a fixed time T, the integral

$$\int_0^S |Q^*(x) - Q(x, T)|^\gamma dx, \tag{19}$$

with $\gamma \geq 1$, $Q^*(x)$ a given function, and Q(x, t) defined as in (1), takes a minimum value. As was shown in [4], when $\gamma = 2$ and when it is impossible to satisfy the relation (2) for any $t \in [0, T]$ it follows from the maximum principle for systems with distributed parameters [4-6] that an optimal control u(t) satisfies the integral equation

$$u(t) = L \mathrm{sign}\left[B(T, t) - \int_0^T R(T, t, \tau)\, u(\tau)\, d\tau\right], \tag{20}$$

where

$$B(T, t) = \int_0^S Q^*(x) K(x, T-t)\, dx, \tag{21}$$

$$R(T, t, \tau) = \int_0^S K(x, T-t) K(x, T-\tau)\, dx. \tag{22}$$

An approximate method for the solution of such equations is discussed in [4].

When $\gamma \neq 2$, this integral equation has the more complex form

$$u(t) = L \,\mathrm{sign}\left[\int_0^S \left| Q^*(x) - \int_0^T K(x, T-t)\, u(t)\, dt\right|^{\gamma-1} \times K(x, T-t)\, \mathrm{sign}\left(O^*(x) - \int_0^T K(x, T-t)\, u(t)\, dt\right) dx\right].$$

There are two possible reasons why the equality (2) cannot be exactly satisifed: 1) A "hit" on the function $Q^*(x)$ is generally impossible for any $T \geq 0$,2) the time T is so short that a "hit" will not occur.

In case 1, the optimal control always satisfies the integral equation (20).

In case 2, for sufficiently large T, i.e., for $T \geq T^\circ$, where T° is the time of the optimal process in problem (2) the control (20) no longer has any meaning (the expression to the right of "sign" is identically zero), and we must again return to the solution of the problem (2).

As an example, we again consider the heating of a massive body. We must find a control u(t), with the sense of the temperature of the heating medium, $|u(t)| \leq 1$, $0 \leq t \leq T$, such that after a time T the difference between the temperature Q(x, t) $(0 \leq x \leq S)$ and zero be a minimum, i.e., such that the integral

$$\Phi^\circ = \int_0^S Q^2(x, T)\, dx \tag{23}$$

have a minimum value with the conditions

$$\frac{\partial Q}{\partial t} = b \frac{\partial^2 Q}{\partial x^2}, \tag{24}$$

$$-\lambda \frac{\partial Q}{\partial x}\bigg|_{x=0} = \alpha [u(t) - Q(0, t)], \quad \frac{\partial Q}{\partial x}\bigg|_{x=S} = 0, \tag{25}$$

$$Q(x, 0) = Q_0(x) = Q_0 = \text{const}. \tag{26}$$

The solution of Eqs. (24), (25) with the initial condition (26) is [7]

$$Q(x, t) = Q_0 \sum_{k=1}^{\infty} A_k e^{-\mu_k^2 t} \cos \mu_k x + \int_0^t \sum_{k=1}^{\infty} A_k \mu_k^2 e^{-\mu_k^2 (t-\tau)} \cos \mu_k x\, u(\tau)\, d\tau, \tag{27}$$

where $\mu_k (k = 1, 2, \ldots)$ is the sequence of positive roots of the equation $\mu \operatorname{Tg} \mu = \alpha S/\lambda = \mathrm{Bi}$, where α is the heat-exchange coefficient, b is the temperature-transfer coefficient, λ the thermal conductivity, A_k are constants, and the role of the kernel in (1) is played by the sum

$$\sum_{k=1}^{\infty} A_k \mu_k^2 e^{-\mu_k^2 t} \cos \mu_k x = K(x, t). \tag{28}$$

Taking the first infinite series in (27) for t = T as $Q^*(x)$ in the relation (19), and taking into account that $\{\cos \mu_k x\}$ is an orthogonal system, we find that, for sufficiently small values of T, the optimal control u(t) satisfies the integral equation

$$u(t) = \operatorname{sign}\Big[Q_0 \sum_{k=1}^{\infty} B_k e^{-\mu_k^2 (2T-t)} - \int_0^T \mu_k^2 B_k e^{-\mu_k^2 (2T-t-\tau)} u(\tau)\, d\tau\Big], \tag{29}$$

where

$$B_k = \frac{\mu_k \sin^2 \mu_k}{\mu_k + \sin \mu_k \cos \mu_k} \qquad (k = 1, 2, \ldots).$$

However as was shown in [8], we can obtain from any uniform initial distribution $Q_0(x) = Q_0 = \text{const}\,(0 \le x \le S)$ a zero distribution after a time not less than some $T^\circ > 0$, which is the time for the optimal transitional process from Q_0 to zero. In this case, the optimal control $|u(t)| \equiv 1\ (0 \le t \le T^\circ)$, and there is an infinite (countable) number of switchings that accumulate at the point T°. Hence Eq. (29) has a meaning only for $T < T^\circ$. For $T < T^\circ$ the optimal control obtained from the integral equation (29) has a finite number of switchings in the interval [0, T]. For $T \to T^\circ$ the number of intervals of optimal control in the problem (23) tends to infinity. As the numerical solution of (29) shows, each successive interval occupies more than half the time remaining after the previous intervals. Figure 5 shows the dependence of the number of intervals $\underline{n}$ of the optimal process on the parameter T.

The problem of the exact time when zero is reached, as can be seen from (27) for $Q(x, T) \equiv 0\ (0 \le x \le S)$ and the fact that the functions of the system $\{\cos \mu_k x\}$ are linearly independent, reduces to that of the solution of the following moment problem:

$$\frac{1}{\mu_k^2} = \int_0^T e^{\mu_k^2 t} u(t)\, dt \qquad (k = 1, 2, \ldots) \tag{30}$$

for a minimum $T = T^\circ$ and $|u(t)| \le 1\ (0 \le t \le T^\circ)$.

It thus follows from (5) and (6) with $n \to \infty$ that we must find

$$\min_{\xi_k} \int_0^T \Big| \sum_{k=1}^{n} \xi_k e^{\mu_k^2 t} \Big|\, dt = \frac{1}{L} \tag{31}$$

with the condition

$$\sum_{k=1}^{n} \frac{\xi_k}{\mu_k^2} = 1. \tag{32}$$

Hence in this case the nth approximation becomes

$$u_n(t) = L \operatorname{sign} \sum_{k=1}^{n} \xi_k e^{\mu_k^2 t} . \qquad (33)$$

The calculation of the optimal control for the present case by a digital computer showed that, for average values of the parameter Bi, because of the strong convergence of the infinite series in the solution, it is satisfactory in practice to use only the solutions of the moment problems of the third or fourth order. Here the maximum deviation from zero at the end of the transient process is not more than 5% or 1% of the initial value Q_0 respectively. This is shown in Fig. 5 by the fact that almost all the transient time $[0, T°]$ is occupied by only the first three or four intervals.

The above method of determining the optimal process is easily generalized to the case when there are several controlling actions in a system. For example, if (1) has the form

$$Q(x,t) = \int_0^t \sum_{i=1}^{r} K_i(x, t, \tau) u_i(\tau)\, d\tau, \qquad (34)$$

where $|u_i(t)| \leq L$, $i = 1, 2, \ldots, r$, $0 \leq t \leq T$, then the problem reduces to that of finding the vector $\xi = (\xi_1, \ldots, \xi_n)$ and the number T giving the solution of the problem of finding

$$\min_{\xi} \int_0^T \sum_{i=1}^{r} \left| \sum_{j=1}^{n} \xi_j g_{ji}(T, t) \right| dt = \frac{1}{L} \qquad (35)$$

with the condition (6), where $g_{ji}(T, t)$ are the coefficients in the expansion of the ith kernel $K_i(x, T, \tau)$ in a complete system of functions $\varphi_j(x)$.

Here the n-th approximation of the optimal control is

$$u_{jn}(t) = L \operatorname{sign} \sum_{i=1}^{n} \xi_i g_{ij}(T - t) \qquad j = (1, 2, \ldots, r). \qquad (36)$$

Hence, outside the dependence on the number $\underline{r}$ of controlling actions, the minimization need only be carried out relative to one vector ξ.

We now consider the optimal-control problem with limitations on the controlling actions and the coordinates of the system.

Let a control system with distributed parameters be described by the relation (1). Let a further system

$$P(x, t) = \int_0^t F(x, t - \tau) u(\tau)\, d\tau, \qquad (37)$$

be given, where $F(x, t)$ is also a given function ($0 \leq x \leq S$, $0 \leq t \leq T$).

The problem of optimal control relative to the rapidity of action, with restrictions on the controlling action $|u(t)| \leq L$ and on the coordinates of the system $|q(x_1, t)| \leq L$ ($0 \leq x \leq S$, $0 \leq t \leq T$) is stated as follows: let one more function $Q^*(x)$ be given ($0 \leq x \leq S$); it is required to find a permissible controlling action $u(t)$ such that condition (2) is satisifed and

$$|q(x_1, t)| = \left| \int_0^t F(x_1, t - \tau) u(\tau)\, d\tau \right| \leqslant L \qquad (0 \leqslant t \leqslant T), \qquad (38)$$

where x_1 is some fixed point in the interval $[0, S]$ and the time T is to be minimal.

This problem is of great practical importance, since the great majority of real control systems have limitations not only on the controlling action, but also on the system coordinates. For example, in the problem of the heating of a massive body there can be limitations on the gradient of and on the drop in temperature.

The above problem reduces to an L-problem in moment theory in an abstract, linear, normed space [1].

We actually consider the following problem. Let $n (n \leq \infty)$ linearly independent elements $g_1, \ldots, g_n$ of some linear, normed space E be given. We wish to find the necessary and sufficient conditions to impose on the numbers $\alpha_1, \ldots, \alpha_n$, $L (\sum_{k=1}^{n} \alpha_k^2 > 0, L > 0)$ so that there exists a linear functional $l(g)$ satisfying the relations

$$l(g_k) = \alpha_k, \quad \|l\| \leqslant L \quad (k = 1, 2, \ldots, n). \tag{39}$$

As was shown in [1], this problem is closely related to another problem whose solution ensures the existence of a solution to the first problem. This second problem is to find

$$\min_{\xi_k} \left\| \sum_{k=1}^{n} \xi_k g_k \right\| = \lambda \leqslant \frac{1}{L} \tag{40}$$

with the extra condition

$$\sum_{k=1}^{n} \xi_k \alpha_k = 1. \tag{41}$$

The problem (4)-(6) is also essentially a problem of the type (39)-(41).

The linear functional has the form

$$l(g) = \int_0^T g(T - t)\, u(t)\, dt, \qquad \|l\| = \max_{[0, T]} |u(t)|. \tag{42}$$

The problem with the condition (38) can be reduced to the above-considered L-problem, if we take

$$\|l\| = \max_{[0, T]} \left(u(t), \int_0^t F(x_1, t - \tau)\, u(\tau)\, d\tau\right). \tag{43}$$

for the norm of the linear functional.

The whole problem now reduces to the minimization of the expression (40) with the condition (41). Its explicit form will, however, not be as simple as for the problem without any limitations on the coordinates of the system.

For a discrete system with lumped parameters, the above problem is set out in [9].

It can be shown that the norm in E will have the form

$$\|g\| = \min_{\psi(t)} \left[\int_0^T \left| g(\tau) - \int_\tau^T F(x_1, t - \tau)\, d\psi(t) \right| d\tau + \int_0^T |d\psi(t)|\right], \tag{44}$$

where the lower bound is taken for all functions with measure $\psi(t)$. In this case, it is clear that the numerical work involved in the minimization of (40) will be greatly increased, since the function must be minimized, not only over a finite number of parameters, but also over the functions $\psi(t)$.

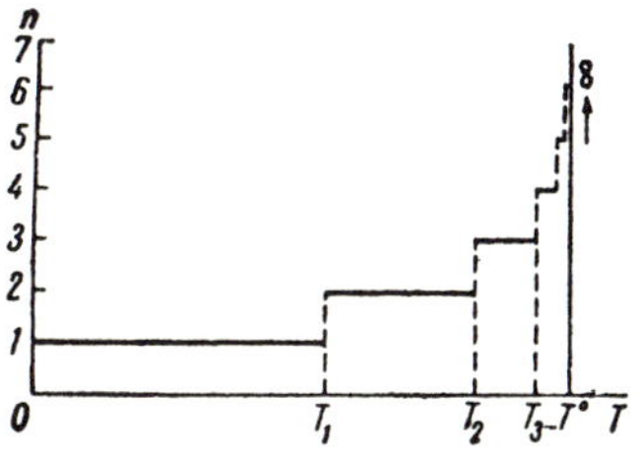

Fig. 5.

Formula (44) is easily generalized to the case when limitations are imposed, not only on one, but on several of the coordinates of the system.

The methods we have considered thus yield a single mathematical procedure that can be used to calculate optimal controlling actions, and it is a procedure that is not dependent on the number of these controls or on the presence or absence of limitations on the intermediate coordinates. It is true that the calculations become formidable when there are limitations on the intermediate coordinates. The method yields a uniform approach to the solution of problems with both lumped and distributed parameters. The necessary information concerning the system to be controlled is also similar for all cases: a knowledge of the eigenfunctions of the system.

We note in conclusion that the method of moments can be generalized to apply to the case when the limitations on the control and on the coordinates are of a more general character than limitations on the absolute value; for example, the control or coordinate vector may be restricted to an arbitrary, closed, convex region possessing interior points.

LITERATURE CITED

1. N. I. Akhiezer, and M. G. Krein, Some Problems in the Theory of Moments [in Russian], GONTI' Khar'kov(1938).
2. N. N. Krasovskii, A contribution to the theory of optimal control, Prikl. matem. i mekhan., Vol. 23, No.4,(1957).
3. S. Kacmarz and G. Steinhaus, The Theory of Orthogonal Series [Russian translation], Fizmatgiz (1958).
4. A. G. Butkovskii, Optimal processes in systems with distributed parameters, Avtomatika i telemekhanika, Vol. 22, No. 1 (1961).
5. A. G. Butkovskii, The maximum principle for optimal systems with distributed parameters, Avtomatika i telemekhanika, Vol. 22, No. 10 (1961).
6. A. G. Butkovskii, A generalized maximum principle for problems in optimal control, Avtomatika i telemekhanika, Vol. 24, No. 3 (1963).
7. A. N. Tihonov, and A. A. Samarskii, Equations of Mathematical Physics [in Russian], Gostekhizdat (1951).
8. Yu. V. Egorov, Some problems in the theory of optimal control, Dokl. AN SSSR, Vol. 145, No. 4 (1962).
9. R. Gabasov, Optimal processes in discrete systems, Avtomatika i telemekhanika, Vol. 23, No. 7 (1962).

I. FLUGGE-LOTZ
H. MARBACH
Division of Engineering Mechanics, Stanford University, Stanford, Calif.

The Optimal Control of Some Attitude Control Systems for Different Performance Criteria[1]

Optimal control functions in the sense of minimum settling time and minimum fuel or energy consumption are derived for several different single-axis attitude control systems. The systems treated differ only in the mechanism used to produce control torque. The torque producing elements considered include, (i) reaction gas jets, with either one or two discrete levels of thrust, (ii) an armature controlled d-c motor, (iii) a two-phase a-c motor. Optimal switching curves for these systems are illustrated in the phase plane, and the optimal choice of system parameter values is discussed.

Introduction

In recent years studies in the theory of optimal control have given considerable emphasis to problems concerned with optimization of the dynamic performance of systems, and in particular to the minimum settling time problem. Problems of this type can be completely formulated if the equations which govern the dynamical behavior of the system are known. On the other hand, for problems in which optimization is to be carried out on the basis of minimum fuel or energy consumption, a complete formulation requires more intimate knowledge of system characteristics.

This paper presents several examples of problems falling in the latter class. Each of these examples will be concerned with the minimization of fuel or energy consumption for space vehicle attitude control systems. Most present-day attitude control systems employ either reaction jets or motor-driven reaction wheels (or both) to develop control torque. Examples of each of these types will be included. It is assumed that, for the purposes of these discussions, the vehicle is adequately represented by a single-axis, pure inertia model.

In order to solve the optimization problems posed in this study the relatively new and quite powerful method afforded by L. S. Pontryagin's maximum principle is used. By means of this method a wide variety of optimization problems, which cannot be handled by the classical calculus of variations, are easily solved. Although a complete solution will in many cases require machine computation, the problems treated here will in each case be solved analytically.

I Pontryagin's Maximum Principle

We shall begin by giving a formulation of the type of optimal control problem to be considered later, and by briefly outlining essential details of the method to be used in obtaining solutions for this type of problem. Pontryagin's maximum principle will be stated here without proof. Detailed proofs may be found in [1],[2] which also gives references to many of the original papers on this principle. Another derivation which appeals to geometrical arguments is given in [2].

The System. We will consider systems which are described by a system of differential equations,

$$\dot{x}_i = f_i(\mathbf{x}, \mathbf{u}, t), \quad i = 1, 2, \dots n, \tag{1}$$

where $\mathbf{x} = (x_1, x_2, \dots x_n)$ is a state vector of the system and $\mathbf{u} = (u_1, u_2, \dots u_r)$ is the control vector. The functions f_i will be considered to be twice continuously differentiable in the arguments $(\mathbf{x}, \mathbf{u})$.

At each instant of time the controls $u_k(t)$, $k = 1, 2, \dots r$, are required to satisfy certain inequalities dictated by the physical constraints of the system. These inequalities can be briefly expressed in the form

$$\mathbf{u}(t) \in U, \tag{2}$$

where U is a closed set in r-dimensional space. For example, with $r = 1$ we might consider a control which is subject to saturation. Such a constraint can be expressed by requiring that, at any instant $|u(t)| \leq 1$. In this case, the set U is simply the closed interval $[-1, 1]$, on the real line.

In addition to the requirement (2), we will require that each $u_k(t)$ is a piecewise continuous function of time. Any control $\mathbf{u}(t)$ which satisfies these two conditions will be designated as an admissible control.

The Control Problem. The control problem to be considered is briefly the following: We wish to find an admissible control $\mathbf{u}(t)$ such that the system is taken, in accordance with (1), from some given initial state $\mathbf{x}(t_0)$ to some fixed final state $\mathbf{x}(t_1)$, and such that system performance is optimum in some specific sense.

The index or cost functional used to evaluate system performance will be taken to have the form,

$$S = \int_{t_0}^{t_1} \phi(\mathbf{x}, \mathbf{u})dt, \tag{3}$$

which encompasses, for example, the minimum time problem with $\phi(\mathbf{x}, \mathbf{u}) = 1$. System performance will be said to be optimum when the integral (3) becomes a minimum with respect to all admissible controls $\mathbf{u}(t)$, and the particular control $\mathbf{u}^*(t)$ which realizes this minimum value (if it exists) will be called the optimal control of the problem. The total time of transition, $T = t_1 - t_0$, from the initial state to the final state, can be either an unknown quantity or a specified constant of the problem.

As noted above, the system of differential equations (1) will be required to satisfy boundary conditions of the type,

$$x_i(t_0) = x_i^0, \qquad x_i(t_1) = x_i^1, \qquad i = 1, 2, \dots n. \tag{4}$$

Problems having boundary conditions of this type are said to have fixed end points, or are commonly referred to as two-point boundary value problems.

The Maximum Principle. Corresponding to the control problem described in the above paragraphs, we introduce a Hamiltonian function[3]

[1] This investigation was conducted at Stanford University under the sponsorship and with the financial assistance of the National Aeronautics and Space Administration.

A grant of the National Science Foundation permitted a desired improvement of the computing facility used in the analog simulation.

[2] Numbers in brackets designate References at end of paper.

Contributed by the Automatic Control Division of The American Society of Mechanical Engineers and presented at the Joint Automatic Control Conference, New York, N. Y., June 27–29, 1962. Manuscript received at ASME Headquarters, April 5, 1962. Paper No. 62—JACC-6.

[3] An alternate definition of the Hamiltonian function, differing from (5) by a minus sign, leads to a "minimum principle," with the advantage that the hamiltonian so defined is minimized for a minimization problem (see [3]).

$$H(\mathbf{x}, \mathbf{p}, \mathbf{u}, t) = \sum_{i=1}^{n} p_i f_i - \phi(\mathbf{x}, \mathbf{u}) \tag{5}$$

where the functions $p_i(t)$ satisfy the system of differential equations,

$$\dot{p}_i = -\frac{\partial H}{\partial x_i}, \qquad i = 1, 2, \ldots n. \tag{6a}$$

Using the Hamiltonian of (5), the original system of differential equations can be expressed as

$$\dot{x}_i = \frac{\partial H}{\partial p_i}, \qquad i = 1, 2, \ldots, n, \tag{6b}$$

with the boundary conditions $\mathbf{x}(t_0) = \mathbf{x}^0$, $\mathbf{x}(t_1) = \mathbf{x}^1$.

Note that, even if the control $\mathbf{u}(t)$ is given as a function of time, equations (6*a*) will not *uniquely* define a vector $\mathbf{p}(t)$ since the boundary conditions have not been specified.

Now let $\mathbf{u}^*(t)$ be some admissible control, and let $\mathbf{x}^*(t)$ be the corresponding solution of (1) emanating from $\mathbf{x}^0$. Then the maximum principle can be stated as follows:

If $\mathbf{u}^*(t)$ is the optimal control, then there exists a vector $\mathbf{p}^*(t)$, satisfying (6*a*), such that, at every instant of time t, $t_0 \leq t \leq t_1$,

$$H(\mathbf{x}^*, \mathbf{p}^*, \mathbf{u}^*, t) \geq H(\mathbf{x}, \mathbf{p}, \mathbf{u}, t)$$

with respect to all admissible controls $\mathbf{u}(t)$, i.e.,

$$H(\mathbf{x}^*, \mathbf{p}^*, \mathbf{u}^*, t) = \operatorname*{Max}_{\mathbf{u} \in U} H(\mathbf{x}, \mathbf{p}, \mathbf{u}, t). \tag{7}$$

In general, the maximum principle gives only a necessary condition for optimality of the control $\mathbf{u}^*(t)$. However, in most cases of practical interest, it gives sufficient information to uniquely define the optimal control. In the case of the two-point boundary value problem formulated above, if a control can be found which satisfies (7) and which uniquely causes the boundary conditions (4) to be satisfied, then this control is usually the unique optimal control for the problem.

The above discussion has dealt strictly with a minimization problem. Problems in which a functional of the type (3) is to be maximized are treated in precisely the same manner with the exception that the hamiltonian (5) is *minimized* with respect to all admissible controls.

II The Optimal Control of a Reaction Jet System

For the first example, we consider a single-axis attitude control system in which control torque is furnished by a suitable arrangement of gas jets (see Fig. 1). The vehicle is represented by a pure inertia and the attitude deviation from some fixed reference is denoted by the variable x_1.

In the absence of disturbing torques, the vehicle motion is described by a simple second order differential equation.

$$\ddot{x}_1(t) = \frac{L(t)}{J}, \tag{8}$$

where control torque is denoted by $L(t)$, and J is the moment of inertia of the vehicle. The saturation level of $L(t)$ is taken to be L_0, i.e., $|L(t)| \leq L_0$, and we define the normalized control $u(t)$ as,

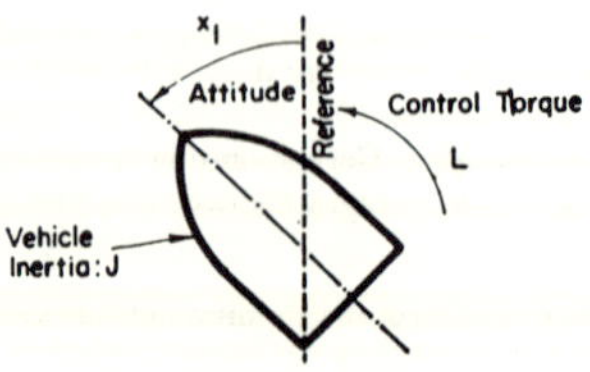

Fig. 1 Single-axis vehicle model

$$u(t) = \frac{L(t)}{L_0}, \quad \text{where } |u(t)| \leq 1.$$

Equation (8) can then be written as,

$$\ddot{x}_1(t) = \frac{L_0}{J} u(t). \tag{9}$$

It will be convenient to define a dimensionless measure of time τ as

$$\tau = \sqrt{\frac{L_0}{J}}\, t,$$

by means of which equation (9) can be written as,

$$x_1''(\tau) = u(\tau),$$

(where the notation $' = d/d\tau$ is used) or, equivalently, as a system of two first order differential equations,

$$\left.\begin{aligned} x_1'(\tau) &= x_2(\tau) \\ x_2'(\tau) &= u(\tau) \end{aligned}\right\} \tag{10}$$

For this case the state vector of the system is $\mathbf{x} = (x_1, x_2)$, and the one dimensional control $u(\tau)$ is constrained to the closed interval $[-1, 1]$.

The function of the control system will be to maintain the vehicle at a fixed attitude. For this simple problem, the desired equilibrium state of the system can always be taken as the origin of the x_1x_2 phase plane.[4]

We are primarily interested here in the minimum fuel consumption problem, but for a later discussion it will be convenient to have at hand the minimum time solution, which is well known in this case. Additionally, the minimum time problem can serve as a simple introduction to the application of the basic concepts.

The Minimum Transition Time Problem. Now suppose that, either through the action of a disturbance or through the command of a new attitude, the system at time $\tau = 0$ is not in the desired state, but in some other state $\mathbf{x}^0$. Then the control problem will be to apply torque to the vehicle such that, at some time $\bar{\tau} > 0$, $\mathbf{x}(\bar{\tau}) = (0, 0)$. We further suppose that this transition from one state to another must be accomplished in the shortest possible time.

The functional (see eq. (3)) which is to be minimized in this problem is simply

$$S(\bar{\tau}) = \int_0^{\bar{\tau}} d\tau = \bar{\tau}, \tag{11}$$

where $\bar{\tau}$ is an unknown quantity.

From (5) and (10), the hamiltonian function for this problem is

$$H = p_1 x_2 + p_2 u - 1, \tag{12}$$

and the system of differential equations (6) becomes

$$\left.\begin{aligned} p_1'(\tau) &= 0, & p_2'(\tau) &= -p_1(\tau) \\ x_1'(\tau) &= x_2(\tau), & x_2'(\tau) &= u(\tau) \end{aligned}\right\} \tag{13}$$

with the boundary conditions $\mathbf{x}(0) = \mathbf{x}^0$, $\mathbf{x}(\bar{\tau}) = \mathbf{0}$.

Applying condition (7) of the maximum principle, we see that the function H is maximized with respect to all admissible controls (i.e., all piecewise continuous functions $u(\tau)$ with $|u(\tau)| \leq 1$) by choosing $u^*(\tau)$ as

$$u^*(\tau) = \operatorname{sgn}[p_2(\tau)].$$

After integrating $p_2'(\tau)$ in (13), we have the result that the optimal control must be of the form,[5]

[4] Equally suitable equilibrium points would be $(2k\pi, 0)$, $k = 1, 2, \ldots$ We will assume that initial conditions are such that there is no ambiguity in designating the origin as the desired equilibrium point.

[5] sgn y (signum of y) is defined as, $\operatorname{sgn} y = y/|y|$.

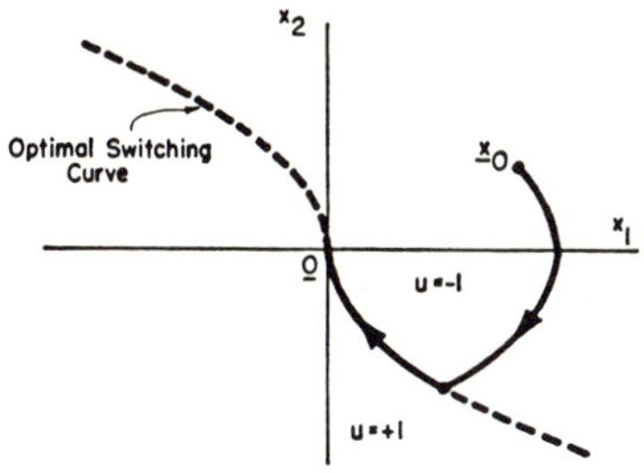

Fig. 2 Phase-plane representation of minimum time solution

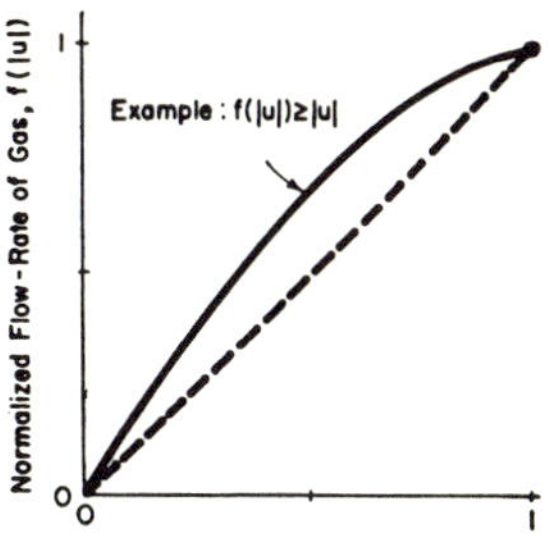

Fig. 3 Flow-rate characteristic of jet system

$$u^*(\tau) = \mathrm{sgn}[-p_1\tau + p_2^0], \tag{14}$$

where p_1 and p_2^0 are undetermined constants.

Now note that, whatever the values of p_1 and p_2^0 happen to be, the following conclusions can be drawn by inspection of (14).

$$\left.\begin{array}{l}\text{(i) } u^*(\tau) \text{ can assume only the values } \pm 1.\\ \text{(ii) The sign of } u^*(\tau) \text{ can reverse at most once.}\end{array}\right\} \tag{15}$$

This describes what is commonly known as a bang-bang, or contactor type control.

Thus, application of the maximum principle to this problem has established the form that the optimal control must take. Given an initial state $\mathbf{x}^0$, conditions (15) provide sufficient information with which to construct a unique optimal solution to equations (10). In the x_1x_2 phase plane this construction can easily be accomplished by an entirely graphical procedure as illustrated in Fig. 2. The solutions (trajectories) of (10) corresponding to $u = \pm 1$ are composed of segments of a parabolic curve. Starting at the initial point $\mathbf{x}^0$ there is one and only one trajectory which proceeds to the origin in accordance with the conditions (15). This unique trajectory is the optimal trajectory for the problem.

For any initial state, the final portion of the corresponding optimal trajectory must lie along either of the two parabolic arcs which pass to the origin. The union of these two arcs forms a curve which divides the x_1x_2 phase plane into two parts and gives the locus of points at which an optimal control must reverse sign. The curve formed in this manner is called the optimum reversal curve.

The Minimum Gas Consumption Problem. In many important vehicle applications, the amount of fuel or energy allotted for control system requirements is limited to such a degree that it becomes necessary to treat fuel economy as the predominant factor influencing system design. In such cases, it is natural to design the control system so that it consumes a minimum amount of fuel or energy, and such that other measures of system performance (e.g., settling time), which are of secondary importance, are merely adequate for the purpose. It is in the framework of these circumstances that the next example will be considered.

Suppose that, at time $\tau = 0$, the single-axis vehicle illustrated in Fig. 1, and described dynamically by the differential equations (10) is in some given initial state $\mathbf{x}^0$. The problem will be to apply control torque to the vehicle, via the gas jets, so that, at some time $\bar{\tau} > 0$, $\mathbf{x}(\bar{\tau}) = (0, 0)$, and such that the total gas expenditure required for this control effort is as small as possible.

In order to be able to formulate a meaningful minimization problem, the total time of transition $\bar{\tau}$ must be either fixed or bounded. For, suppose $\bar{\tau}$ were not bounded. Then it would be theoretically possible to bring the state of the system to the origin with an arbitrarily small expenditure of gas, and consequently a solution to the minimization problem would not exist. If the total time of transition is given in seconds by T, then $\bar{\tau} = \sqrt{L_0/J}\cdot T$.

In contrast to problems concerned with the minimization of either transition time, or some functional depending only on the state of the system, which can be completely formulated knowing only the system dynamics, problems concerned with the minimization of fuel or energy consumption require a somewhat more detailed description of the system. For example, the problem at hand cannot be completely formulated until a precise description is given of how the mass flow rate of the jet system varies as a function of control torque (u).

Although most present-day gas jet systems are of the on-off type, in this study we admit to consideration any variable thrust system which has a mass flow rate characteristic of the following type (see Fig. 3):

Denote mass flowrate by q (slugs/sec), and assume that q is given by

$$q = q_0 f(|u|), \quad 0 \le |u| \le 1, \tag{16}$$

where q_0 is a positive constant, and $f(|u|)$ is non-negative with $f(0) = 0$, and $f(1) = 1$. It is further assumed that, for values of $|u|$ for which $f(|u|)$ is defined, the following inequality holds:

$$f(|u|) \ge |u|. \tag{17}$$

Note that an on-off type jet system satisfies this condition.

The functional to be minimized in this problem can be taken as

$$S = \int_0^{\bar{\tau}} f(|u|)d\tau, \tag{18}$$

where $\bar{\tau}$ is treated as a fixed constant.

Using (18) and (10), the hamiltonian of the problem is written as

$$H = p_1x_2 + p_2u - f(|u|), \tag{19}$$

where the quantities p_1 and p_2 satisfy the relations (see eq. (13))

$$p_1'(\tau) = 0, \quad p_2(\tau) = -p_1\tau + p_2^0,$$

and where p_1 and p_2^0 are unknown constants.

Applying the maximum principle to the Hamiltonian of (19) we must require that, for any instant τ, $0 \le \tau \le \bar{\tau}$,

$$p_2u - f(|u|) = \underset{|u|\le 1}{\mathrm{Max}}\,[p_2u - f(|u|)] \tag{20}$$

Now, from (20) and keeping in mind condition (17), the optimal control u^* can be obtained as a function of the variable p_2, as

$$u^* = \begin{cases} 0, & \text{for } |p_2| < 1\\ +1, & \text{for } p_2 \ge 1\\ -1, & \text{for } p_2 \le -1\end{cases} \tag{21}$$

Therefore, application of the maximum principle has established that the optimal control must be of the on-off type, assuming only the three values, ± 1 or 0. Furthermore, even though $p_2(\tau)$ is not known as a function of time, the mere fact that $p_2(\tau)$ is linear in τ requires that u^* from (21) must proceed in time as a nonrepeating sequence of values of the form (± 1, 0, ∓ 1), or any subsequence thereof. But these simple facts concerning the

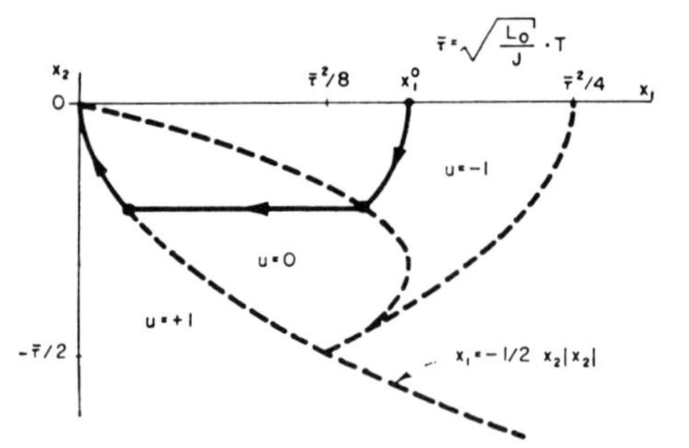

Fig. 4 Optimal switching loci for minimum gas consumption

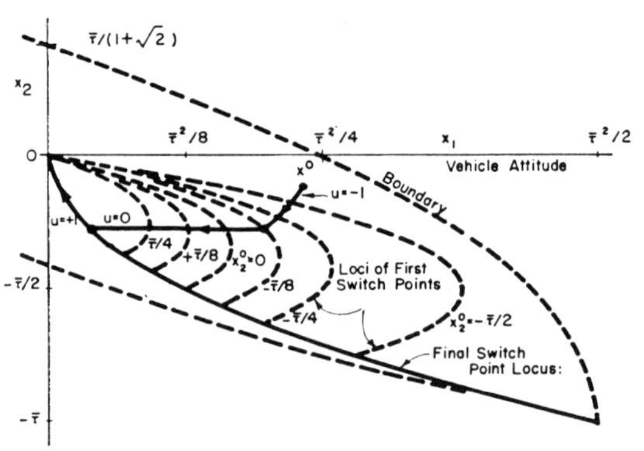

Fig. 5 Optimal switching loci for nonzero initial rate

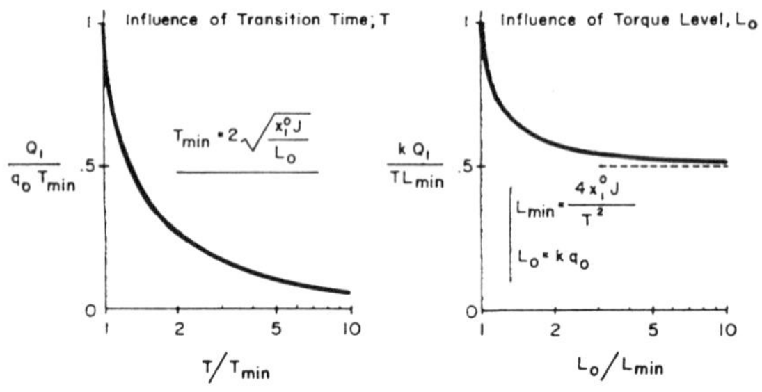

Fig. 6 The influence of transition time and control torque level on gas consumption

nature of the optimal control provide sufficient information with which to construct a unique optimal solution to the problem. Corresponding to any initial state which can be restored to the origin in an interval of time equal to or less than $\bar{\tau}$, there is one and only one control having the required form which will transfer this initial state to the origin. This unique control is the optimal control.

Fig. 4 illustrates the construction of an optimal trajectory in the x_1x_2 phase plane for a case in which the initial attitude rate, x_2^0, is zero. With an initial attitude displacement x_1^0, $0 < x_1^0 < \bar{\tau}^2/4$, the optimal control for this case takes on the successive values $(-1, 0, +1)$. The loci of points at which the control changes values are composed of parabolas in the x_1x_2 plane and lie entirely in the second and fourth quadrants. For an initial displacement $x_1^0 = \bar{\tau}^2/4$ the optimal control is identical to the minimum-time control. For initial displacements greater in magnitude than $\bar{\tau}^2/4$ the problem as originally stated has no solution since the origin cannot be reached in a time interval of length $\bar{\tau}$ with any admissible control.

The locus of first switch points shown in Fig. 4 is derived by imposing the boundary conditions on the system equations (10). The derivation involves only elementary algebra, and is outlined in the Appendix.

The trajectory construction and switching loci given in Fig. 4 apply to any case for which $x_2^0 = 0$. When $x_2^0 \neq 0$ the construction becomes a bit more difficult since for every value of x_2^0 there corresponds a different set of switching loci, although the locus of final switch points is always along the parabolas traced by trajectories bound for the origin. Fig. 5 illustrates a few such optimal switching loci for nonzero initial rate. Note that the problem has a solution only when the initial state lies within a region (again defined by parabolas) in the x_1x_2 plane.

Essentially then, what has been shown here is that for any gas jet system (including continuously variable or discrete thrust systems) having a mass-flow-rate characteristic satisfying condition (17), the on-off control of this system achieves the minimum gas consumption.[6] For such systems the control depends in no way upon the exact nature of the mass flow-torque characteristic. If, on the other hand, we have a gas jet system for which (17) does not hold, and $f(|u|) < |u|$ for some $|u|$, then the on-off control described above is still admissible but no longer optimal. This implies that the gas consumption of a system violating (17) must be less than that of any system satisfying (17) (assuming optimal control and fixed parameters q_0 and L_0). More will be said about this in connection with the two-level gas jet system in a later section.

Up to this point of our investigation the control system parameters ($\bar{\tau}$, q_0, L_0) have been treated as fixed quantities, and the optimal control corresponding to this fixed system has been derived. In most cases, however, there is some liberty beforehand in the choice of these parameter values, and we are now in a position to evaluate the influence of parameters on the gas consumption of an optimal solution.

The case in which initial rate x_2^0 is zero will be considered. For this case, the total gas consumption of an optimal solution is given by,

$$Q_1 = q_0 T \left[1 - \sqrt{1 - \frac{4J}{kq_0} \cdot \frac{|x_1^0|}{T^2}} \right] \tag{22}$$

where Q_1 is the total mass of consumed gas, q_0 is the saturation mass flow rate of the jet system, T is the total transition time in seconds, J is the moment of inertia of the vehicle, and k is a constant.[7]

The dependence of Q_1 on the parameters T and L_0 is illustrated in Fig. 6, from which several conclusions concerning the choice of these parameter values follow immediately. First it is clear that, in order to make Q_1 as small as possible, transition time T should be made as large as possible, consistent with other design objectives. Secondly, for fixed T and initial attitude error, L_0 should be made at least several times greater than that value of L_0 which causes the radical in (22) to become zero (and which corresponds to the minimum-time case). When L_0 and T are made large, the system approaches a pulsed-torque system.

The Two-Level Gas Jet System. In this section we will extend the previous results to encompass the optimal control for minimum gas consumption of a gas jet system which is capable of providing two discrete levels of thrust. The normalized mass flow rate versus control torque characteristic of this two-level system is shown in Fig. 7.

As noted previously, in order to obtain a gas consumption which is less than that obtainable with a simple single-level on-off sys-

[6] That the optimal system should operate in this manner can be easily understood. The system seeks to operate only at maximum specific impulse (thrust per mass rate), but only long enough to accomplish the required task.

[7] It is assumed here that in any system adjustment, saturation torque L_0 is related to q_0 by $L_0 = kq_0$.

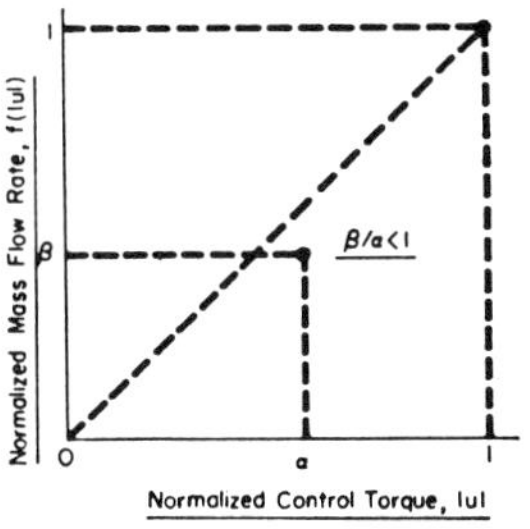

Fig. 7 Flow-rate characteristic of two-level jet system

tem, we must have $f(|u|) < |u|$ for some $|u|$. Thus the two-level system will be more conservative than the one-level system provided only that the ratio β/α is less than unity. This means that the lower level jets must operate at higher specific impulse than the high level jets. If β/α were not less than unity, there would be no justification (in the sense of minimum gas consumption) for adopting a two-level rather than a single-level system.

With precisely the same argument that was used in the previous section, the optimal control u^* for the two-level system is found to be of the following form:

$$u^* = \begin{cases} 0, & \text{for } |p_2| \leq \beta/\alpha < 1 \\ \alpha, & \text{for } \beta/\alpha < p_2 \leq \dfrac{1-\beta}{1-\alpha} \\ 1, & \text{for } p_2 > \dfrac{1-\beta}{1-\alpha} \\ -\alpha, & \text{for } -\dfrac{1-\beta}{1-\alpha} \leq p_2 < -\beta/\alpha \\ -1, & \text{for } p_2 < -\dfrac{1-\beta}{1-\alpha} \end{cases} \tag{23}$$

Again, as in the previous case, the variable $p_2(\tau)$ is found to be a linear function of time. This fact, together with (23), implies that for the two-level system the optimal control u^* must occur in time as a sequence of values of the type

$$\{+1, +\alpha, 0, -\alpha, -1\}$$

or

$$\{-1, -\alpha, 0, +\alpha, +1\} \tag{24}$$

Other sequences obtained by deleting outside members of (24) are also possible. The exact form of the optimal control will, of course, depend on initial conditions.

For the sake of simplicity we will restrict further consideration to cases in which the initial attitude rate x_2^0 of the vehicle is zero. As with the single-level control the problem has a solution only if $x_1^0 \leqq \bar{\tau}^2/4$. The loci of the switching points are determined with equation (24) in the manner indicated in the Appendix, and can be drawn in the x_1x_2 phase plane. These optimal switching loci will depend on the particular values of the parameters α and β. Fig. 8 shows the fourth quadrant of the x_1x_2 phase plane with the optimal switching loci drawn for $\alpha = {}^1/_2$, $\beta = {}^1/_3$ as an example. More generally, for other values[8] of α and β, the loci corresponding to the numbered loci in Fig. 8 are given (in the fourth quadrant) by the following relations:

$$\text{I.} \quad \frac{3}{2}\,x_2^2 - \frac{(\alpha-\beta)(\alpha-2\alpha\beta+\beta)}{\alpha(1-\beta)^2}\,(x_2+\bar{\tau}/2)^2 + \bar{\tau}x_2 + x_1 = 0$$

$$\text{II.} \quad \frac{3}{2\alpha}\,x_2^2 + \bar{\tau}x_2 + x_1 = 0$$

[8] The values of α and β are assumed to correspond to a physically realizable system. This means that β will not be allowed to be zero unless α is also zero.

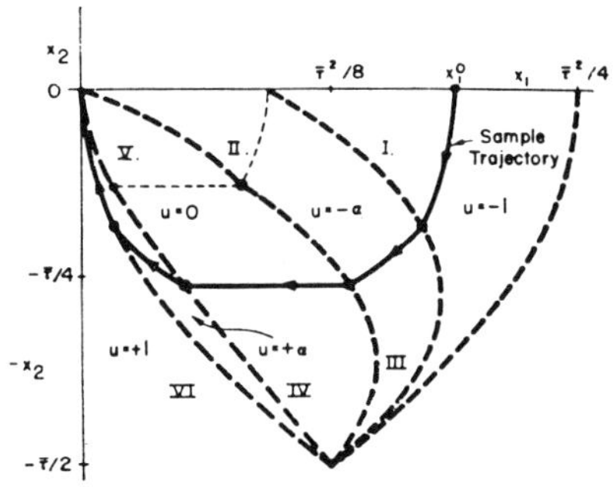

Fig. 8 Optimal switching loci for minimum gas consumption with two-level jet system . . . . . zero initial rate, $\alpha = 1/2$, $\beta = 1/3$

$$\text{III.} \quad \left\{\frac{1}{4\beta}\left[\frac{(1-\beta)^2}{1-\alpha} - 1\right] + 1\right\} x_2^2 + \frac{\bar{\tau}}{2}\left[1 + \frac{(1-\beta)(\alpha-\beta)}{2\beta(1-\alpha)}\right]\cdot x_2 + \frac{\alpha}{2\beta}\,x_1 + \frac{(\alpha-\beta)^2}{4\beta(1-\alpha)}\cdot\frac{\bar{\tau}^2}{4} = 0$$

$$\text{IV.} \quad \frac{1}{2\alpha}\left[\frac{(1-\beta)^2}{1-\alpha} - 1\right] x_2^2 + \frac{(\alpha-\beta)(1-\beta)}{\alpha(1-\alpha)}\cdot\frac{\bar{\tau}}{2}\cdot x_2 + \frac{(\alpha-\beta)^2}{2\alpha(1-\alpha)}\cdot\bar{\tau}^2/4 = -x_1$$

$$\text{V.} \quad x_1 = \frac{1}{2\alpha}\cdot x_2^2$$

$$\text{VI.} \quad x_1 = \frac{1}{2}\,x_2^2$$

The total gas consumption of an optimal solution is obtained by integrating the mass-flow-rate, $q = q_0f(|u|)$, over $[0, \bar{\tau}]$. The result is given by

$$Q_2 = \begin{cases} q_0T\left[1 - C\sqrt{1 - \dfrac{|x_1^0|}{\bar{\tau}^2/4}}\right], & \text{for } r \leqq \dfrac{|x_1^0|}{\bar{\tau}^2/4} \leqq 1 \\ \beta q_0T\left[1 - \sqrt{1 - \dfrac{|x_1^0|}{\alpha\bar{\tau}^2/4}}\right], & \text{for } 0 \leqq \dfrac{|x_1^0|}{\bar{\tau}^2/4} < r \end{cases} \tag{25}$$

where Q_2 denotes the total mass of expended gas for the two-level system, T is the transition time in seconds, and r and C are constants defined as,

$$r = \frac{(\alpha - 2\alpha\beta + \beta)(\alpha-\beta)}{\alpha(1-\beta)^2}$$

$$C = \frac{\alpha(1-\alpha) + (\alpha-\beta)^2}{\alpha(1-\alpha)}.$$

For large initial displacements Q_2 is strongly dependent on the value of the constant C, which is itself determined by the values of α and β. To facilitate the computation of Q_2 for different systems, curves of constant C are drawn in an α, β plane; they are segments of ellipses (see Fig. 9). The reader should be reminded that for realizable systems $\beta \rightarrow 0$ can only occur for $\alpha \rightarrow 0$.

The statement was made previously that the gas consumption of the two-level system (with $\beta/\alpha < 1$) would be less than that of the single-level system. At this point it is possible to evaluate the reduction in gas expenditure obtained by employing a two-level rather than a single-level system. Although the degree of reduction depends on the values of α and β in any particular case, Fig.

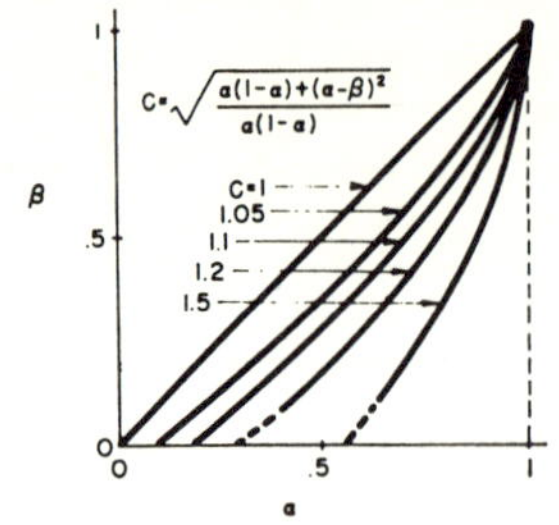

Fig. 9 Curves of constant C . . . . . for realizable systems $\beta \rightarrow 0$ only if $\alpha \rightarrow 0$

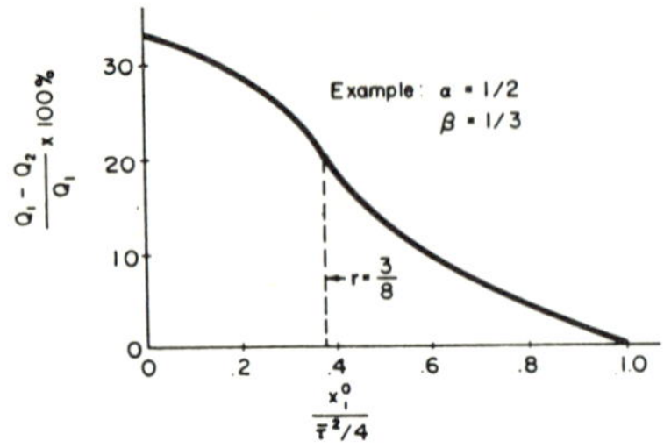

Fig. 10 Gas consumption decrease of two-level system referred to single-level system

10, which is drawn for $\alpha = {}^1/_2$, $\beta = {}^1/_3$, gives a qualitative indication of how gas saving varies with initial attitude displacement. The greatest saving in gas consumption is realized for small attitude deviations, where only the more efficient low-level jets are employed. For large deviations the gas expenditures of both systems are virtually equal. In a particular design study a comparison of this type would indicate whether or not the gas economy of the two-level system could justify the more complex switching logic required.

III A D-C Motor Driven Reaction Wheel System

Another popular technique for controlling attitude entails the use of reaction wheels to develop control torques on the vehicle. The reaction wheels are accelerated with respect to the vehicle by electric motors, and usually either the rotor or the stator of the drive motor serves as the reaction wheel.

In this example we will consider a single-axis model of vehicle and reaction wheel as shown in Fig. 11. We suppose that control torque is provided by a d-c, armature-controlled, permanent magnet servomotor, as illustrated in Fig. 11(a). The motor will be driven by an ideal voltage source which saturates at an output voltage magnitude V_0.

The control problem will be to transfer the vehicle from some fixed initial attitude to some other fixed attitude, and the control will be chosen such that system performance is optimized in a specific sense. It will again be assumed that disturbance torques are negligible, and that the reaction wheel is initially at rest with respect to the vehicle.

We denote vehicle attitude and wheel velocity (with respect to the vehicle) by θ and ω, respectively. Assuming that the wheel is accurately aligned with the vehicle axis, the equations of motion can be written as,

$$\begin{aligned} J\ddot{\theta} &= L \\ I_w(\dot{\omega} + \ddot{\theta}) &= -L \end{aligned} \tag{26}$$

where J and I_w are moments of inertia of the vehicle and wheel, respectively. Combining the above, and with the assumption that the vehicle and wheel are initially nonrotating, we obtain,

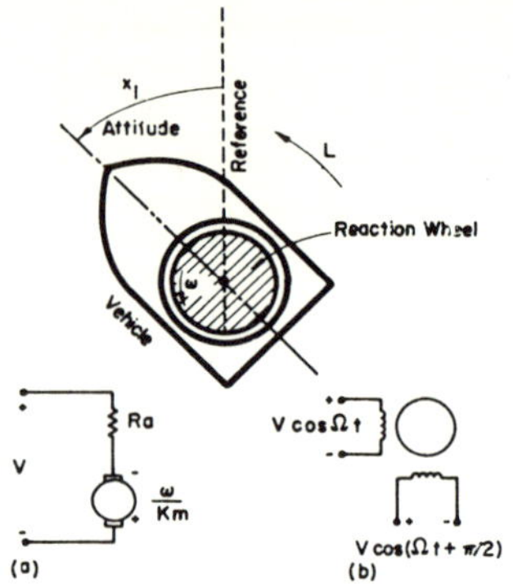

Fig. 11 Vehicle and reaction wheel; (a) d-c servomotor, (b) a-c induction motor

$$\omega = -\frac{J}{I}\dot{\theta}, \tag{27}$$

where

$$I = \frac{I_w}{1 + I_w/J}$$

For the d-c motor being considered, torque is proportional to armature current. The basic equation which relates control torque L to applied armature voltage V is given by

$$L = \frac{K_L}{R_a}\left(V + \frac{\omega}{K_m}\right) \quad \text{(ft-lb)}$$

where R_a is the armature resistance, and K_L (ft-lb/amp) and K_m (rad/volt-sec) are, respectively, the torque and speed constants of the motor.

Substituting for ω from (27) and for L from (26) the motor equation yields the second order differential equation,

$$\tau_m^2\ddot{\theta} + \tau_m\dot{\theta} = \tau_m K_m\left(\frac{I}{J}\right)\cdot V \tag{28}$$

where τ_m is the motor time constant,

$$\tau_m = \frac{K_m I R_a}{K_L} \quad \text{(seconds)}.$$

Equation (28) describes the dynamic behavior of the vehicle in response to the armature control voltage V. It will be convenient to put (28) into a dimensionless form.

Since $0 \leq |V| \leq V_0$ we define the normalized control variable u as,

$$u = \frac{V}{V_0}, \quad \text{with } 0 \leq |u| \leq 1.$$

We introduce the dimensionless measure of time τ, which is defined as

$$\tau = t/\tau_m,$$

and define a normalized attitude variable x_1 as

$$x_1 = \frac{\theta}{\tau_m K_m V_0 (I/J)}$$

By means of these definitions equation (28) can be rewritten in the simple dimensionless form,

$$x_1''(\tau) + x_1'(\tau) = u(\tau)$$

($' = d/d\tau$), or equivalently as a system of two first order differential equations,

$$\left.\begin{aligned} x_1'(\tau) &= x_2(\tau) \\ x_2'(\tau) &= -x_2(\tau) + u(\tau) \end{aligned}\right\} \qquad (29)$$

with the initial conditions, $x_1(0) = x_1^0$, $x_2(0) = 0$.

Equations (29) can now be put into a more convenient uncoupled or normal form. To do this we introduce new coordinates y_1 and y_2, and choose the new coordinate vectors to coincide with the eigenvectors of the coefficient matrix of (29). Following the standard procedure, which is outlined in any good text on matrices, a suitable transformation is found to be the following:

$$\left.\begin{aligned} y_1 &= x_1 + x_2 \\ y_2 &= -x_2 \end{aligned}\right\}. \qquad (30)$$

Then, in terms of the new variables y_1 and y_2, equations (29) can be expressed as

$$\left.\begin{aligned} y_1'(\tau) &= u(\tau) \\ y_2'(\tau) &= -y_2(\tau) - u(\tau) \end{aligned}\right\} \qquad (31)$$

with the initial conditions, $y_1(0) = y_1^0$, $y_2(0) = 0$.

The Minimum Transition Time Problem. Suppose that it is required to transfer the vehicle from an initial attitude y_1^0 to some other fixed attitude in the shortest possible time. The attitude reference will be chosen such that the desired final state coincides with the origin of the y_1y_2 plane. Then the control problem will be to choose an admissible $u(\tau)$ such that the vehicle is taken, in accordance with (31), from the initial state $(y_1^0, 0)$ to the final state $(0, 0)$, and such that the unknown total time $\bar{\tau}$ required to accomplish this transition is a minimum.

The Hamiltonian for this problem is

$$H = p_1u - p_2(y_2 + u) - 1.$$

The functions p_1 and p_2 must satisfy the differential equations,

$$p_1'(\tau) = 0, \text{ and } p_2'(\tau) - p_2(\tau) = 0,$$

and are, $p_1 =$ constant, and $p_2 = p_2^0e^\tau$.

Application of the maximum principle shows that the optimal control must be of the bang-bang type,

$$u^*(\tau) = \operatorname{sgn}[p_1 - p_2^0e^\tau], \qquad (32)$$

assuming only the two values ± 1. Furthermore, (32) implies that $u^*(\tau)$ can reverse sign at most once. This gives all the information needed to uniquely determine the optimal control for any given initial attitude displacement. The complete solution can be constructed in the y_1y_2 phase plane where all optimal trajectories and loci of switch points are composed of segments of a logarithmic curve. The optimal control function for this case can be expressed as

$$u^*(\tau) = -\operatorname{sgn}[y_1 + (\operatorname{sgn} y_2)\ln(1 + |y_2|)].$$

If the argument of the sgn function is set equal to zero we obtain the equation of the optimum switching curve in the y_1y_2 plane (or in the x_1x_2 plane after inverse transformation). In practice this switching curve can be closely approximated with a nonlinear function generator.

Corresponding to an initial attitude displacement x_1^0, the optimal time of transition to the origin is given by

$$\bar{\tau} = |x_1^0| + 2\ln\{1 + [1 - e^{-|x_1^0|}]^{1/2}\}.$$

The Minimum Electrical Energy Consumption Problem. In this example we suppose that it is required to transfer the vehicle from a fixed initial attitude to some prescribed final attitude in a prescribed time $\bar{\tau}$ and with minimum electrical energy consumption of the servomotor.

Again, as in the minimum gas consumption problem for the reaction jet system, a complete formulation of the problem requires specification of further system details besides merely system dynamics. Specifically we require the power $P(\tau)$ delivered to the servomotor to be expressed in terms of system state variables y_1, y_2 and the control u. Since,

$$P(\tau) = \frac{V}{R_a}[V + \omega/K_m],$$

we obtain,

$$P(\tau) = \frac{V_0^2}{R_a}u(\tau)[y_2(\tau) + u(\tau)] \text{ (watts).} \qquad (33)$$

Then the control problem will be to choose an admissible control $u(t)$ such that the vehicle is taken in accordance with (31) from the initial state $(y_1^0, 0)$ to the final state $(0, 0)$, and such that the functional

$$U = \int_0^{\bar{\tau}} u(y_2 + u)d\tau \qquad (34)$$

assumes its minimum value for a given transition time $\bar{\tau} = T/\tau_m$.

The hamiltonian for this problem is

$$H = p_1u - p_2(y_2 + u) - u(y_2 + u) \qquad (35)$$

where the variables p_1 and p_2 must satisfy the differential equations,

$$p_1'(\tau) = 0, \quad p_2'(\tau) - p_2(\tau) = u(\tau). \qquad (36)$$

Applying the maximum principle at this point, we seek a control $u(\tau)$ which at each instant maximizes H with respect to all admissible controls. Since the Hamiltonian H is a nonlinear function of u, one may expect that the optimal solution is not given by a simple bang-bang control.

Setting $\partial H/\partial u = 0$, we find that H is maximized by taking

$$u^* = \begin{cases} \frac{1}{2}(p_1 - p_2 - y_2), & \text{for } |p_1 - p_2 - y_2| \leq 2 \\ \operatorname{sgn}(p_1 - p_2 - y_2), & \text{for } |p_1 - p_2 - y_2| > 2 \end{cases} \qquad (37)$$

From this point the formal solution of the general problem would proceed as follows. By using (37) the control u is eliminated from (31) and (36) yielding a system of four differential equations with four boundary conditions. The solution of this system, when substituted back into (37) will yield the optimal control u^* as a function of τ.

This formal procedure required for the general problem is quite tedious to carry out, at least by hand, and it will be pursued no further here. Rather we shall restrict our consideration to cases in which the optimal control does not saturate at any time during the transition interval. It is easy to show that the optimal control does not saturate whenever a certain inequality involving the values of y_1^0 and $\bar{\tau}$ is satisfied. The required inequality is given by,

$$y_1^0 \leq \begin{cases} \dfrac{2}{3}\cdot\dfrac{\bar{\tau}}{1 + 4/\bar{\tau}^2}, & \text{for } \bar{\tau} \geqq 2 \\ \bar{\tau}^2/6, & \text{for } \bar{\tau} < 2. \end{cases} \qquad (38)$$

If the values of y_1^0 and $\bar{\tau}$ are such that (38) is satisfied, then the formal procedure outlined above permits an immediate solution of the problem, and the optimal control is found to be,

$$u(\tau) = \frac{6y_1^0}{\bar{\tau}^2}\left[\frac{1}{\bar{\tau}}\tau^2 + \left(\frac{2}{\bar{\tau}} - 1\right)\tau - 1\right]. \qquad (39)$$

Corresponding to this control function the system state variables x_1 and x_2 (normalized vehicle attitude deviation and rate) are given as functions of time by (where $y_1^0 = x_1^0$),

$$\begin{aligned} x_1(\tau) &= x_1^0\left[1 - 3\left(\frac{\tau}{\bar{\tau}}\right)^2 + 2\left(\frac{\tau}{\bar{\tau}}\right)^3\right] \\ x_2(\tau) &= \frac{6x_1^0}{\bar{\tau}}\left[\left(\frac{\tau}{\bar{\tau}}\right)^2 - \frac{\tau}{\bar{\tau}}\right] \end{aligned} \qquad (40)$$

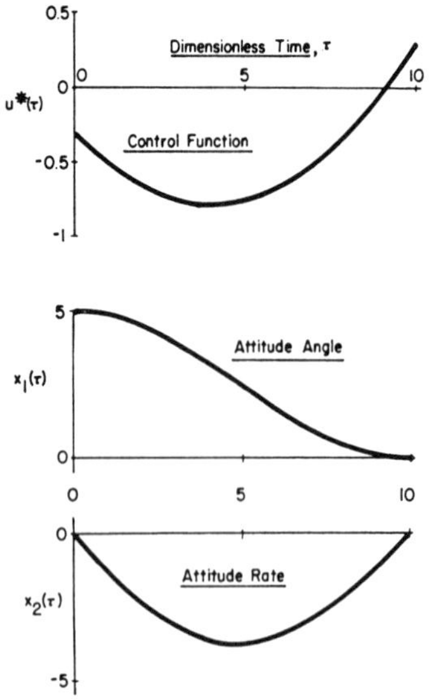

Fig. 12 Minimum energy control for d-c motor reaction-wheel system[9]

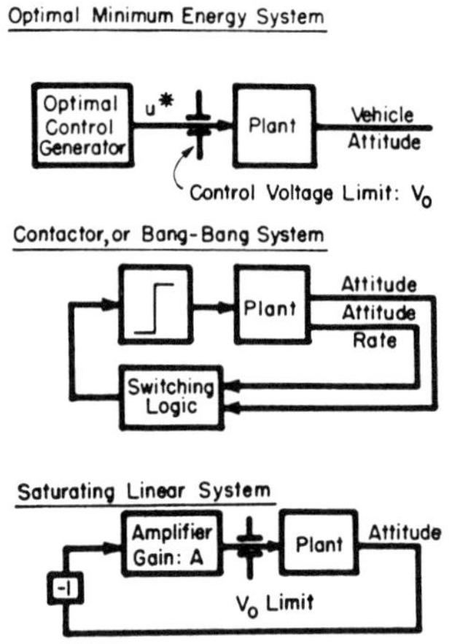

Fig. 13 Systems considered in control energy comparison

The variation of u, x_1, and x_2 with τ for the case $x_1^0 = 5$, $\bar{\tau} = 10$ is illustrated by Fig. 12.

To obtain a solution for the restricted class of problems in which the control never saturates we could just as well have proceeded from the outset with classical techniques of the calculus of variations.

If we had proceeded in the usual manner to minimize the functional (34) with the differential-equation side conditions (31), the procedure would have evolved equations (36) and the upper half of (37). In this approach the variables p_1 and p_2 are interpreted as Lagrange multipliers,[10] and the results are of course identical to those already obtained here. The Lagrange technique, however, fails to indicate how the solution to the general problem can be obtained when the constraint $|u| \leq 1$ is imposed.

In (39) the optimal control is given as a function of time. In most practical cases, however, it is desirable to have the control function expressed in terms of system state variables. For this case the nonsaturating control function can be expressed in terms of x_1 and x_2 (by eliminating τ in (39) and (40)), as

$$u^*(x_1, x_2) = x_2 + \frac{36x_1^0}{\bar{\tau}^3}\left[\frac{2x_1 - x_1^0}{2x_2 - \frac{6}{\bar{\tau}}x_1^0}\right]. \tag{41}$$

Equation (41) gives a control law by means of which the system can be controlled in an optimal fashion. However, it should be kept in mind that this control law is valid only under the conditions for which it was derived. That is, although the control u^* as given in (41) is a function of the system state variables, it is nevertheless essentially an open-loop control and as such is unable to correctly counteract any disturbance torques which might occur during the transition interval. Since disturbances were in no way accounted for in the above derivation we cannot expect that they will be properly handled by the derived control function. An analog simulation of this problem was made where both (41) and (39) were used to generate the control function. Results of this simulation agreed with theoretical results, but verified that system performance is seriously degraded by disturbances when either control function is used.

Corresponding to the nonsaturating optimal control given by either (39) or (41), the total electrical energy consumed by the servomotor during the course of an optimal solution is,

$$U(x_1^0, \bar{\tau}) = \left(\frac{V_0^2\tau_m}{R_a}\right)\frac{12x_1^{0^2}}{\bar{\tau}^3} \text{ (joules)}. \tag{42}$$

Comparison of the Minimum Energy Control to Other Controls. Having obtained the solution of the minimum energy problem formulated in the preceding section, one may wonder how much is really gained by using the optimal control rather than some other popular control technique. In order to answer this question we shall illustrate by means of an example how the optimal control yields a more conservative solution than either a simple, linear (saturating) control or a bang-bang control, for minimum settling time.

For each of the three systems considered in this comparison (see Fig. 13) a common plant (servomotor, inertia wheel, and vehicle) is assumed, a common attitude change is effected by each system, and the total transition time will be identical in each case. We will take $x_1^0 = 5$, $x_2^0 = 0$, $\bar{\tau} = 10$—for these values inequality (38) is satisfied, and the optimal control does not saturate at any time during the transition interval.

In the linear system of this comparison the plant is assumed to be driven by an ideal linear power amplifier which is supplied with a positional error signal, and which saturates at the output voltage magnitude, V_0 (the same saturation level applies to the optimal system). By appropriately adjusting amplifier gain the attitude error (and/or error rate) persisting at the end of the fixed transition period can be varied within limits, however, it is not possible to completely eliminate error in any finite time interval with the linear system. For this system the final attitude error is defined as the error present at the end of the allowed transition period referred to initial error; i.e., $[\theta(T)/\theta(0)] \times 100$ percent, where T is the total transition time.

The contactor, or bang-bang system is adjusted so that transition time is made equal to the fixed value, $\bar{\tau} = 10$. This adjustment is accomplished by reducing the control voltage saturation level to a value $0.58V_0$, approximately.

Representative results of this comparison are given in the following table.

	System	Energy consumption	Final attitude error
I	Optimal: (min energy)	U_0	0
II	Contactor: (min time)	$2.2U_0$	0
III	Linear:	U_0	20%
		$2U_0$	4%

[9] Misprint in the attitude-rate plot; replace "-5" by "-1".
[10] See for example reference [4] for details.

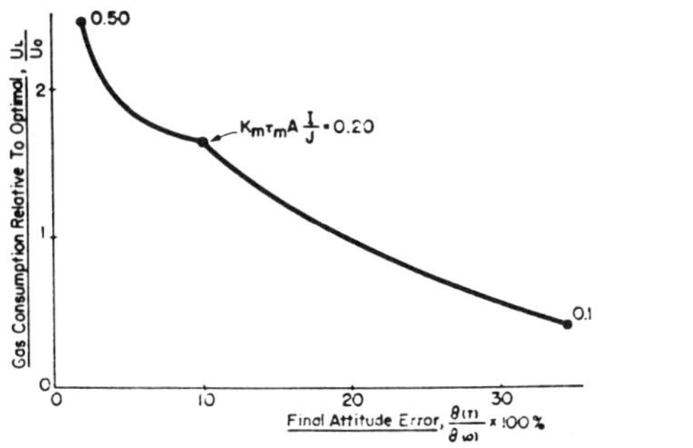

Fig. 14 Energy consumption versus final attitude error for linear system

Systems I and II have finite settling time, but attitude error will persist with the linear system (in theory) after any finite interval of time. As indicated in the previous table, a high degree of performance of the linear system is obtained only with a relatively large expenditure of control energy. This dependence of control energy on system performance is further illustrated by Fig. 14 which is plotted with linear-system normalized loop gain as a parameter along the curve.

Instead of reducing the contactor saturation level such that transition time $\bar{\tau}$ is identical for each of the three systems one might insist that the contactor system be subject to the same saturation level which prevails for the optimal system. For this condition, with $x_1^0 = 5$, the contactor transition time is reduced to $\bar{\tau} = 6.4$, and the energy consumption becomes 6.7 U_0.

The point to be made here is that the energy-optimal system provides a substantially better solution than either of the other two systems considered. Either the minimum-time contactor system or the linear system can be adjusted to consume less than the optimal amount of energy, but only with attendant degradation to system dynamic performance (transition time, accuracy).

IV An A-C Servomotor System

For the final example we consider the problem of the minimum energy control of a reaction-wheel attitude control system in which torque is provided by a two-phase a-c induction motor (Fig. 11(*b*)). The notation and vehicle configuration of Fig. 11 will again be used.

At the outset of this discussion we shall postulate the characteristics of a hypothetical motor. With these characteristics the optimal minimum energy control will be derived for the hypothetical system and conclusions drawn concerning the best choice of system parameters. Finally, actual motor characteristics will be compared with the hypothetical characteristics and it will be pointed out that the derived optimal control can be expected to be nearly optimal for an actual system when operated within a limited range of motor speeds.

The motor is assumed to have symmetrical stator windings to which are applied balanced two-phase control voltages. Incidental effects due to friction, windage, and core loss, and the influence of internal electrical transients are hereafter neglected.

The following motor characteristics are postulated.

1 Torque: Motor output torque is proportional to the squared magnitude of applied control voltage, and independent of motor speed, i.e.,

$$|L| = K_1 V^2 \qquad \text{(ft-lb)}$$

where V is the peak value of stator control voltage, and K_1 is a constant dependent on motor parameters. Denoting the value of $|V|$ at which voltage saturation occurs by V_0, we introduce the normalized control variable u, as

$$u = \frac{V}{V_0}, \quad \text{where } |u| \leq 1. \tag{43}$$

By means of this definition motor torque can be expressed as

$$L = L_0 u^2 \operatorname{sgn} u = L_0 u|u| \tag{44}$$

where $L_0 = K_1 V_0^2$ is the maximum value of control torque magnitude.

2 Power: Total input power to the motor is proportional to the squared magnitude of applied control voltage and independent of motor speed; i.e., $P = K_2 V^2$, where K_2 is a constant determined by motor parameters. By means of (43), total power P is written as

$$P = P_0 u^2, \tag{45}$$

where $P_0 = K_2 V_0^2$ is the power input for maximum control voltage.

Using (44) to describe control torque, the equations of motion for the vehicle are written as

$$\left.\begin{aligned} x_1'(\tau) &= x_2(\tau) \\ x_2'(\tau) &= [u(\tau)]^2 \operatorname{sgn} u(\tau) \end{aligned}\right\} \tag{46}$$

with initial conditions $x_1(0) = x_1^0$, $x_2(0) = x_2^0$.

Again, as in previous examples we have introduced a dimensionless measure of time τ which is defined here as

$$\tau = \sqrt{\frac{L_0}{J}} \cdot t.$$

Now suppose that the vehicle is in an initial state (x_1^0, x_2^0), and that it is desired to transfer this initial state to the origin (0, 0) of the x_1x_2 phase plane. Further suppose that this transition is to be accomplished with the smallest possible expenditure of electrical control energy.

The functional to be minimized can be taken to be

$$S = \int_0^{\bar{\tau}} u^2 d\tau \tag{47}$$

where $\bar{\tau}$ is the total dimensionless transition time $\left(\bar{\tau} = \sqrt{\frac{L_0}{J}} \cdot T,\right.$ where T is the total time in seconds$\left.\right)$, and is treated as a fixed constant.

The Hamiltonian (eq. (5)) for this problem is, from (46) and (47),

$$H = p_1 x_2 + p_2 u^2 \operatorname{sgn} u - u^2 \tag{48}$$

where the variables $p_1(\tau)$ and $p_2(\tau)$ satisfy the differential equations,

$$\left.\begin{aligned} p_1'(\tau) &= 0, \\ p_2'(\tau) &= -p_1. \end{aligned}\right\} \tag{49}$$

Applying the maximum principle to the Hamiltonian of (48), we seek a control u which at each instant τ, $0 \leqq \tau \leqq \bar{\tau}$, maximizes the quantity

$$u^2[(p_2 \operatorname{sgn} u) - 1] \tag{50}$$

with respect to all piecewise continuous controls which satisfy the inequality, $|u| \leq 1$. The desired control u^* which maximizes (50) can be expressed as a function of the variable p_2 as

$$u^* = \begin{cases} +1, & \text{for } p_2 \geqq 1 \\ 0, & \text{for } |p_2| < 1 \\ -1, & \text{for } p_2 \leqq -1. \end{cases} \tag{51}$$

From (49) the variable p_2 must be a linear function of time (τ). This fact, together with relation (51) establishes that the optimal control for this problem must proceed in time as a sequence of values of the type,

$$\{\pm 1, 0, \mp 1\}, \tag{52}$$

or some subsequence thereof.

Having established that u^* must be of the form indicated by (52), we now have sufficient information with which to construct a unique optimal solution for arbitrary initial conditions x_1^0, x_2^0. As a matter of fact, this construction has already been carried out in section II for the minimum gas consumption problem of the reaction-jet system. Figs. 4 and 5 can be used directly for the present problem (by virtue of the normalized form). Fig. 4 shows the loci of optimal switch points in the case where initial rate $x_2^0 = 0$. Fig. 5 indicates how the optimal switching is accomplished when $x_2^0 \neq 0$.

Now consider the case in which the initial angular velocity of the vehicle (x_2^0) is zero. For this case the total electrical energy expended during an optimal transition of the vehicle is given by

$$U = \left(\frac{K_2}{K_1}\right) L_0 T \left[1 - \sqrt{1 - \frac{4x_1^0 J}{L_0 T^2}}\right]. \tag{53}$$

This expression is identical, except for a multiplicative constant, to the analogous relation (eq. (22)) giving total gas consumption for the reaction jet system. Fig. 6 can be consulted for this problem, however, the ordinate normalizing factors will differ for the two problems.

From Fig. 6 (after relabeling the vertical axes $\frac{U}{(K_2/K_1)L_0T_{\min}}$ for 6(a) and $\frac{U}{(K_2/K_1)TL_{\min}}$ for 6(b)) we can draw several conclusions concerning the best choice of values for the parameters T and L_0. In order that energy consumption be made as small as possible, transition time T should be made as large as possible, consistent with other design objectives. And, for fixed values of x_1^0 and T, the ratio $L_0/L_{\min}$ should be at least 2 or 3 if possible. When T and L_0 are made large the system approaches a pulsed-torque system—i.e., control torque is applied to the vehicle in discrete impulses.

Up to this point of the discussion we have been dealing with a hypothetical motor. The above paragraphs describe the optimal control for such a motor. Now, however, it is of interest to compare motor characteristics to those already postulated.

Fig. 15 illustrates the variation of normalized motor torque and input power with slip[11] for a conventionally designed a-c induction motor.[12] With balanced two-phase stator voltages the ordinates of these characteristics are proportional to the square of the applied voltage V, as had been previously assumed. The abscissa in Fig. (15) is $s/\hat{s}$, where $\hat{s}$ is that value of slip for which motor torque is a maximum. We shall be specifically interested here in motors for which the value of $\hat{s}$ is near unity. For motors designed such that $\hat{s} \approx 1$ ($s = 1$ corresponds to zero speed) Fig. 15 indicates that torque and power are roughly constant (i.e., independent of speed) in a limited range of motor speeds centered about zero. Thus, when operated over restricted speed ranges, such motors have torque and power characteristics which approximate the postulated characteristics of the hypothetical motor treated above. It is reasonable to expect, therefore, that the conclusions drawn concerning the optimal minimum energy control of the hypothetical motor will also hold, at least to a first order approximation, for an actual motor. The degree of approximation will of course depend on the range of motor speeds encountered in any particular problem.

It should be noted in this regard that the actual motor speed attained in any particular case will depend inversely on the inertia of the reaction wheel. The use of a wheel having a large moment of inertia will tend to keep motor speeds within the desired range.

More specifically, for an actual motor of the type described

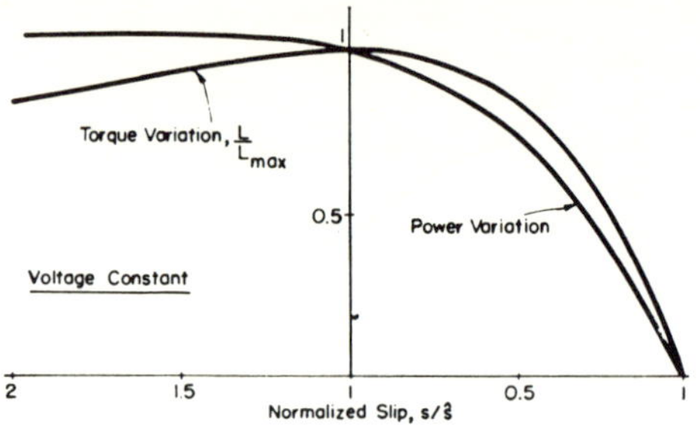

Fig. 15 Normalized induction motor characteristics

previously which is operated within a limited range of speeds, the following conclusions can be made.

(a) An on-off control, occurring as a sequence $\{\pm 1, 0, \mp 1\}$, will result in near-minimum electrical energy consumption.

(b) Assuming an on-off type control, energy is minimized by choosing transition time T and maximum control torque L_0 to be as large as possible.

V Conclusions

For problems of control system optimization with different performance criteria the maximum principle of Pontryagin provides a useful and quite general method of attack. Application of this principle to several examples which are applicable to attitude control problems has established the following results.

(a) Minimum gas consumption of common reaction jet systems is achieved by an on-off type control function. For either a simple, single thrust level system, or for a variable thrust system where specific impulse is greatest at maximum thrust, gas consumption is minimized by using a control which can be either fully on or off. This type of system is most conservative when control torque and settling time are made as large as possible. For systems having two discrete thrust levels, and where specific impulse is greatest at lower thrust, gas consumption is minimized by a control which is either full on, intermediately on, or off. The loci of points at which the optimal control changes values for these cases are parabolas in the phase plane.

(b) The electrical energy consumption of a reaction-wheel system employing a d-c motor is minimized by a control function which may or may not saturate during the control time interval. During periods of nonsaturation the optimal control is described by a quadratic function of time.

(c) For a reaction-wheel system using an a-c induction motor of the type which develops maximum torque near zero speed, electrical energy consumption is approximately minimized by choosing an on-off control function. The degree of this approximation is good for cases in which the motor operates within a limited range of speeds. This type of system is most conservative when control torque and transition time are made as large as possible.

APPENDIX

A brief derivation will be given of the loci of optimal switching points which result in minimum gas consumption for the single thrust level reaction-jet system. These loci are shown in Figs. 4 and 5.

Assume that the initial state (x_1^0, x_2^0) lies in the region for which a solution exists, and for definiteness consider a case for which the optimal control proceeds as the sequence $\{-1, 0, +1\}$, where the switching instants have yet to be determined. Upon starting at $\tau = 0$ the optimal control u^* can be described as

[11] Induction motor slip s is defined as $s = (\omega_s - \omega)/\omega_s$, where ω and ω_s are, respectively, actual motor speed and synchronous speed.

[12] See [5] for derivation—also as general reference for this section.

$$u^*(\tau) = \begin{cases} -1, & \text{for } 0 \leq \tau < \tau_1 \\ 0, & \text{for } \tau_1 \leq \tau < (\tau_1 + \tau_2) \\ +1, & \text{for } (\tau_1 + \tau_2) \leq \tau < (\tau_1 + \tau_2 + \tau_3) \end{cases}$$

where τ_1, τ_2, τ_3 denote the lengths of the time intervals during which u^* remains constant. We use the notation $\mathbf{x}(\tau_1) = \mathbf{x}^1$, $\mathbf{x}(\tau_1 + \tau_2) = \mathbf{x}^2$, $\mathbf{x}(\tau_1 + \tau_2 + \tau_3) = \mathbf{0}$, where we will require that $\tau_1 + \tau_2 + \tau_3 = \bar{\tau}$. Then the following relations follow from a piecewise solution of the system equations (10).

$$\text{(i) } \tau_1 = x_2^0 - x_2^1; \qquad \text{(ii) } \tau_2 = \frac{x_1^2 - x_1^1}{x_2^1};$$

$$\text{(iii) } \tau_3 = -x_2^1; \qquad \text{(iv) } x_1^2 = {}^1/_2(x_2^1)^2 = {}^1/_2(x_2^2)^2.$$

By now requiring that $\tau_1 + \tau_2 + \tau_3 = \bar{\tau}$ we obtain immediately,

$${}^3/_2(x_2^1)^2 + (\bar{\tau} - x_2^0)x_2^1 + x_1^1 = 0,$$

which describes the locus of first switching points in the fourth quadrant. The corresponding locus in the second quadrant is obtained by reflecting about the origin.

The optimal switching loci for the two-level reaction jet system can be derived with an entirely analogous, albeit more tedious, procedure.

References

1 L. I. Rozonoer, "L. S. Pontryagin's Maximum Principle in the Theory of Optimal Systems," *Automation and Remote Control*, vol. 20, October, November, December, 1959, pp. 1288–1302, 1405–1421, 1517–1532.

2 I. Flügge-Lotz and H. Halkin, "Pontryagin's Maximum Principle and Optimal Control," Technical Report No. 130, Division of Engineering Mechanics, Stanford University, Stanford, Calif., September 15, 1961. L (AFOSR TN 1489).

3 R. E. Kalman, "The Theory of Optimal Control and the Calculus of Variations," Technical Report No. 61-3, Research Institute for Advanced Studies, Baltimore, Md., 1961.

4 R. Courant, "Calculus of Variations" (book), New York University Institute of Mathematical Sciences, New York, N. Y., 1957, p. 40.

5 A. Fitzgerald and C. Kingsley, "Electric Machinery" (book), McGraw-Hill Book Company, Inc., New York, N. Y., 1952, pp. 401–407.

DISCUSSION

B. Friedland[13] and H. Ladd[13]

All the workers in the field of optimum control owe a debt of gratitude to the authors for demonstrating that the theory of optimum control has important practical applications—a fact often not recognized by engineers faced with the day-to-day problems of control system design. Professor Flügge-Lotz and Mr. Marbach are to be complimented for their excellent paper.

The problem of minimum fuel consumption in the control of an inertial vehicle has been receiving considerable attention during the past year and perhaps it will be of interest to supplement some of the results of the authors in this regard. If the function $f(|u|)$ has the form of Fig. 3 then the explicit expression for p_2 in terms of the normalized state (x_1, x_2) and the (normalized) time-to-go $T = \bar{\tau} - \tau$ is

$$p_2 = \frac{\nu(T - \nu x_2)}{[T^2 - x_2^2 + \nu(2Tx_2 + 4x_1)]^{1/2}}$$

where

$$\nu = \begin{cases} -\text{sgn}\,(x_1 + {}^1/_2 x_2|x_2|), & x_1 + {}^1/_2 x_2|x_2| \neq 0 \\ -\text{sgn}\, x_2, & x_1 + {}^1/_2 x_2|x_2| = 0 \end{cases}$$

[13] Applied Science Division, Melpar, Inc., Watertown, Mass. At present, Mr. Ladd is with the Missile and Space Division, Raytheon Company, Bedford, Mass.; and Dr. Friedland is with the Aerospace Research Center, General Precision, Inc., Little Falls, N. J.

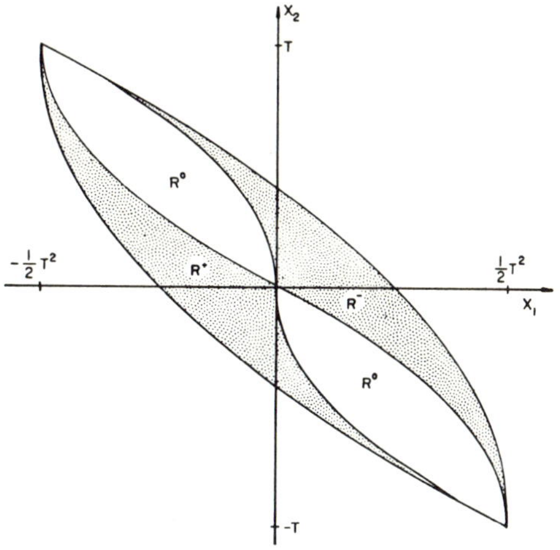

Fig. 16

As a consequence of this expression for p_2 and (21) the phase plane is divided into four regions as shown in Fig. 16. If the state lies in R^+, positive thrust is applied; if the state lies in R^- negative thrust is applied; if the state lies in R^0, no thrust is applied and the vehicle is permitted to coast. If the state lies outside these three regions, the denominator of p_2 is imaginary, and this indicates that it is impossible to reach the origin in the available time-to-go. Note that the region from which the origin can be reached contracts with the time-to-go.

When the amplitude of the thrust is unlimited then the optimum inputs are impulsive, and the control law reduces to

$$u = \begin{cases} [-x_2 - (x_1/T)]\delta(t), & x_1(x_2 + x_1/T) \geqslant 0 \\ 0, & x_1(x_2 + x_1/T) < 0 \end{cases}$$

Graphically, this means that there is a line with slope $-1/T$ in the phase plane such that the first impulse takes the state to the line; then the vehicle coasts until the position error is zero, and finally, a second impulse reduces the velocity error to zero. This conclusion is readily substantiated intuitively. If one is willing to tolerate an oscillatory decay and the use of a little extra fuel this straight line appears to be a reasonably good suboptimum switching line.

The converse problem of minimizing the time to reduce the error to zero subject to a constraint on the available fuel has the following solution for p_2 in terms of the instantaneous state (x_1, x_2)

$$p_2 = \nu\,\frac{\nu(2Mx_2 + 4x_1) - (M^2 - x_2^2)}{\nu(2Mx_2 + 4x_1) + (M^2 - x_2^2)}$$

where ν is defined as above and M is the (normalized) fuel available. This is valid for $M > |x_2|$, or for $M = |x_2|$ and $\nu\,\text{sgn}\, x_2 = -1$. However, for $\nu\,\text{sgn}\, x_2 = +1$ and $M = |x_2|$, the control is $u = 0$. Since the region where $\nu\,\text{sgn}\, x_2 = +1$ and $M = |x_2|$ is just the region R° for $T \geqslant |x_2| + |x_1/x_2| - |x_2/2|$ in Fig. 16, coasting occurs for a time $|x_1/x_2| - |x_2|/2$, at the end of which ν jumps discontinuously to the opposite signum, so that $\nu\,\text{sgn}\, x_2 = -1$ and $p_2 = \nu = -\text{sgn}\, x_2$ is again valid. Note that the case $M = |x_2|$ and $\nu\,\text{sgn}\, x_2 = -1$ corresponds to the case $T = \infty$, while $M = |x_2|$ and $\nu\,\text{sgn}\, x_2 = +1$ corresponds to $T \geqslant |x_2| + |x_1/x_2| - |x_2|/2$.

The expression for impulsive thrust becomes in this case

$$u = \begin{cases} \dfrac{\nu}{2}\,(M - \nu x_2)\delta(t), & x_1 \neq 0 \\ -x_2\delta(t), & x_1 = 0 \end{cases}$$

where

$$\nu = \begin{cases} -\text{sgn } x_1, & x_1 \neq 0 \\ -\text{sgn } x_2, & x_1 = 0 \quad \text{and, of course, } x_2 \neq 0 \end{cases}$$

This control law is valid for $M \geqslant |x_2|$. For $M < |x_2|$ the origin can never be reached. For $M = |x_2|$ and $x_1x_2 > 0$ the origin can never be reached either although this law still applies (corresponding to $T = \infty$). The time taken in the case of impulsive control is

$$T = \frac{2|x_1|}{M + \nu x_2} = \frac{2|x_1|}{M - \text{sgn}(x_1x_2)|x_2|}$$

whereas the time taken in the case of limited control amplitude is

$$T = \frac{M^2 + x_2^2 - 4\nu x_1}{2(M + \nu x_2)}$$

With respect to the minimum electrical energy case, the control law given by (41) involves the initial state x_1^0 and the initial transition time $\bar{\tau}$. It would appear that a more suitable variable would be the time-to-go $T = \bar{\tau} - \tau$. Moreover, (26) and the equation above (28) define a third order system, which reduces to a second order system only when (27) is valid, i.e., when $\omega(0) + J\dot{\theta}(0)/I = 0$. It is preferable to deal with the third order system directly. Introducing a normalized state variable $x_3 = \tau_m\omega I/V_0J$, we obtain the following system

$$x_1' = x_2; \; x_2' = u + x_3; \; x_3' = -u - x_3.$$

The Hamiltonian is

$$H = p_1x_2 + (p_2 - p_3)(x_3 + u) - u(u + x_3)$$

and, it can be shown that the optimum control law is given by

$$u = (p_2 - p_3 - x_3)/2 = -(6/T^2)x_1 - (4/T)x_2 - x_3$$

and is thus realized by feedback, through time-varying gains, of the angle and angular velocity of the vehicle and the velocity of the reaction wheel. The latter can be obtained by monitoring the motor current. If (27) holds, then $x_3 = -x_2$ and the control law simplifies to

$$u = -(6/T^2)x_1 - (4/T - 1)x_2.$$

Authors' Closure

The authors wish to express their sincere appreciation to Dr. B. Friedland and Mr. H. Ladd for their very interesting and informative discussion. An especially interesting aspect of the discussion is that, in each of the cases treated, introduction of the quantity "time-to-go," and implicit use of Dr. R. Bellman's principle of optimality lend additional insight to the problem and lead to clear interpretations of the results. Moreover, "time-to-go" will often be a more naturally significant quantity in applications than a measure of elapsed time.

With regard to the reaction-wheel, minimum energy problem, Dr. Friedland and Mr. Ladd have succeeded in deriving a feedback control function of practical value. It should be mentioned, however, that difficulties are liable to be encountered in attempting to accurately implement a time-variable gain proportional to $1/T$, particularly as T approaches zero. The sophistication required of such an implementation would evidently depend on specific system performance requirements. In this regard, we were able to obtain acceptable results with an analog computer simulation of this control function.

One may perhaps wonder what would happen in a case where, due to either a large initial displacement or an unexpected disturbance, the control function is driven to saturation at some time during the transition interval. It is not difficult to show that in such a case the resulting process is not in general the optimal process. However, a notable feature of the feedback control function is that it gives good results even under saturating conditions.

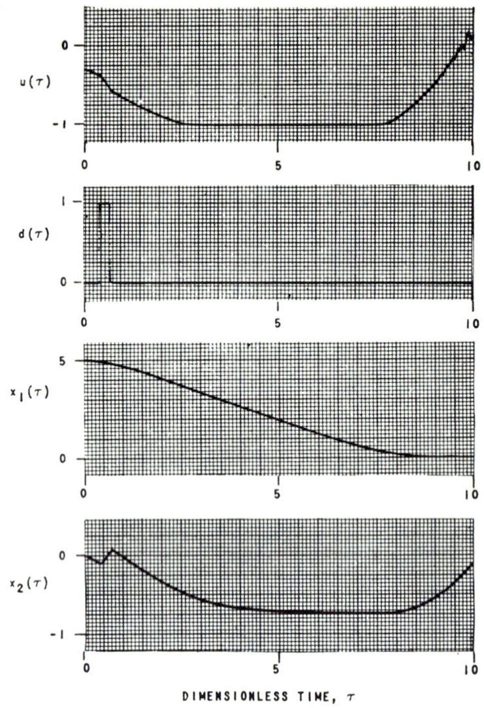

Fig. 17

Let $u = u(\mathbf{x}, T)$, where $T = \bar{\tau} - \tau$, denote the control function as given in the above discussion, and define a "saturating" control function, u_s, as,

$$u_s = \text{sat}(u),$$

where,

$$\text{sat}(u) = \begin{cases} u, & \text{for } |u| \leqq 1 \\ \text{sgn}(u), & \text{for } |u| > 1. \end{cases}$$

Then it is important to note that, for a limited range of initial states (depending on $\bar{\tau}$) and for moderate disturbance torques, the control function u_s will transfer the system to the desired state at the prescribed time even in cases where the control is saturated for a large portion of the transition interval.

Fig. 17, which was taken from an analog computer recording, illustrates such a case. The initial conditions and total transition time are the same as those of Fig. 12 ($x_{10} = 5$, $x_{20} = 0$, $x_{30} = 0$, $\bar{\tau} = 10$). In addition, a disturbance torque $d(\tau)$ of magnitude equal to the motor stall torque (K_LV_0/R_a) acts on the vehicle for a short period of time, and causes the control u_s to saturate. Although the process is not optimal, the positional error is brought to zero at the prescribed time; there is a small final velocity error, which may be attributed to the imperfect realization of the control law. For less extreme cases, in which u_s is saturated for only a small portion of the transition interval, an excellent quasi-optimum process will result.

Optimal Control for Linear Time-Invariant Plants with Time, Fuel, and Energy Constraints

MICHAEL ATHANASSIADES
ASSOCIATE MEMBER AIEE

Summary: The structure of optimum control systems and the form of the optimal control signals are discussed for minimum time, minimum fuel, and minimum energy control of linear time-invariant plants. If the control variables are bounded by 1 in magnitude, then the control signals must have the values +1 or −1 for minimum time response; +1, 0, or −1 for minimum fuel operation; +1, −1 or be linearly related to the state of the plant, between these limits, for minimum energy operation.

DURING THE PAST 5 years the theory of control systems has been influenced by many elegant mathematical techniques, most based on the calculus of variations. One of the best known advances is the "Maximum Principle" of Pontriagin,[1–5] which is related to the "Dynamic Programming" of Bellman.[6] Excellent contributions to the theory and design of optimum control systems can be found in references 7–16 to mention just a few. Most of the papers are of a very mathematical nature, since they were written by mathematicians, and the importance of the principles and techniques involved have not filtered down to the practicing control engineers.

The purpose of this paper is to state the significant theoretical results, and to apply them to some specific problems of engineering importance. These problems are the well-known minimum time problem, the minimum fuel problem, and the minimum energy problem. The controlled plants are linear and time-invariant. The control signals are assumed to be bound by unity in magnitude, due to saturation. In each of the foregoing problems, the structure of the optimum control system is discussed and the shape of the optimal control signals is obtained.

It will be shown that the existing theory leads to a configuration in which the output of the adjoint system passes through a nonlinear element whose output drives the controlled plant. In the case of the minimum energy system, the nonlinear element is of the limiter type. In the case of the minimum fuel system, the nonlinear element is a relay with a dead zone. In the minimum time system the nonlinear element is an ideal relay, as has been apparent since 1950.

Formulation of the Problem

In this section the basic definitions, terminology, and assumptions are stated.

Given the linear time-invariant *plant* described by the matrix differential equation

$$\dot{\mathbf{y}}(t) = \mathbf{A}\mathbf{y}(t) + \mathbf{B}\mathbf{u}(t) \tag{1}$$

where $\mathbf{y}(t) = (y_1, y_2, \ldots, y_n)$ is an n-vector, called the *state* of the plant, equation 1. $\mathbf{u}(t) = (u_1, u_2, \ldots, u_r)$ is an r-vector, called the *control function.* $\mathbf{A}$ is a constant $n \times n$ matrix. $\mathbf{B}$ is a constant $n \times r$ matrix.

In most practical systems the magnitude of each of the control functions $u_1(t)$, $u_2(t), \ldots, u_r(t)$ is limited due to the saturation of the power-amplifying elements. For this reason it is assumed that

$$|u_j(t)| \le c_j \qquad j = 1, 2, \ldots, r \tag{2}$$

where c_j is a constant. For the sake of simplicity, assume that $c_j = 1$, i.e.,

$$|u_j(t)| \le 1 \qquad j = 1, 2, \ldots, r \tag{3}$$

The purpose of the control system is to force the plant from an initial state $\mathbf{y}_o$ to a final desired state $\mathbf{y}_f$ by the appropriate manipulation of the control signals $u_j(t)$. One seeks to find an *optimal control function*, denoted by $\mathbf{u}^o(t)$, so that the functional

$$\int_{t_o}^{t_f} L(\mathbf{y}, \mathbf{u}^o, t)\,dt \tag{4}$$

is minimum, i.e.,

$$\int_{t_o}^{t_f} L(\mathbf{y}, \mathbf{u}^o, t)\,dt \le \int_{t_o}^{t_f} L(\mathbf{y}, \mathbf{u}, t)\,dt \tag{5}$$

for all $\mathbf{u}(t) \ne \mathbf{u}^o(t)$, subject to the magnitude constraint of equation 3.

Examples of systems which may be transformed into equation 1 are plants described by a transfer function containing only poles. For the necessary mathematical manipulations see reference 12.

Theory of Optimal Control

In this section a brief summary of the theoretical results is presented.[1,2,3,5,7,8] The terminology of reference 7 is used.

Using equations 1 and 4, define a scalar function H, called the Hamiltonian, by

$$H(\mathbf{y}, \mathbf{p}, \mathbf{u}, t) = L(\mathbf{y}, \mathbf{u}, t) + \langle \dot{\mathbf{y}}, \mathbf{p} \rangle \tag{6}$$

The term $\langle \mathbf{x}, \mathbf{y} \rangle$ indicates the scalar product of the vectors $\mathbf{x}$ and $\mathbf{y}$, i.e.,

$$\langle \mathbf{x}, \mathbf{y} \rangle = \sum_{i=1}^{n} x_i y_i$$

The n-vector $\mathbf{p}(t)$ is called the *costate.* Its physical significance is discussed later. Substituting equation 1 into equation 6, one obtains

$$H(\mathbf{y}, \mathbf{p}, \mathbf{u}, t) = L(\mathbf{y}, \mathbf{u}, t) + \langle \mathbf{A}\mathbf{y}, \mathbf{p} \rangle + \langle \mathbf{B}\mathbf{u}, \mathbf{p} \rangle \tag{7}$$

Now, determine the *absolute minimum* of the Hamiltonian H, with respect to the control $\mathbf{u}(t)$, subject to the constraints of equation 3. Let

$$H^o(\mathbf{y}, \mathbf{p}, t) = \min_{\substack{\mathbf{u}(t) \\ |u_j| \le 1}} H(\mathbf{y}, \mathbf{p}, \mathbf{u}, t) \tag{8}$$

be the absolute minimum of H. Let $\mathbf{u}^*(t)$ be the control function which minimizes the Hamiltonian, i.e., $H^o(\mathbf{y}, \mathbf{p}, t) = H(\mathbf{y}, \mathbf{p}, \mathbf{u}^*, t)$.

Form the *canonical* equations

$$\frac{\partial H}{\partial y_i} = -\dot{p}_i \qquad i = 1, 2, \ldots, n \tag{9}$$

or

$$\frac{\partial H}{\partial \mathbf{y}} = -\dot{\mathbf{p}}$$

and

$$\frac{\partial H}{\partial p_i} = \dot{y}_i \qquad i = 1, 2, \ldots, n \tag{10}$$

or

$$\frac{\partial H}{\partial \mathbf{p}} = \dot{\mathbf{y}}$$

Equations 9 and 10 represent a total of $2n$ equations where n is the order of the plant equation 1.

Note that since $L(\mathbf{y}, \mathbf{u}, t)$ is not a function of the costate $\mathbf{p}$, it follows that

Paper 62-1185, recommended by the AIEE Feedback Control Systems Committee and approved by the AIEE Technical Operations Department for presentation at the AIEE Summer General Meeting, Denver, Colo., June 17–22, 1962. Manuscript submitted March 16, 1962; made available for printing April 27, 1962.

MICHAEL ATHANASSIADES is with the Lincoln Laboratory, Massachusetts Institute of Technology Lexington, Mass.

This work was performed at Lincoln Laboratory, Massachusetts Institute of Technology, Lexington, Mass., and was carried out with support from the U.S. Army, Navy, and Air Force. The author wishes to thank Dr. Peter L. Falb for the many stimulating discussions and Dr. Fred Schweppe for his critical reading of the paper.

$$\dot{\mathbf{y}} = \frac{\partial}{\partial \mathbf{p}} \{\langle \mathbf{Ay}, \mathbf{p}\rangle + \langle \mathbf{Bu}, \mathbf{p}\rangle\} = \mathbf{Ay} + \mathbf{Bu} \tag{11}$$

which is identical to equation 1, the plant equation.

Write the Hamiltonian H in the form

$$H = L(\mathbf{y}, \mathbf{u}, t) + \langle \mathbf{y}, \mathbf{A'p}\rangle + \langle \mathbf{u}, \mathbf{B'p}\rangle \tag{12}$$

where $\mathbf{A}'$ and $\mathbf{B}'$ are the transposed matrices $\mathbf{A}$ and $\mathbf{B}$, respectively. Equations 9 lead to

$$-\dot{\mathbf{p}}(t) = \mathbf{A}'\mathbf{p}(t) + \frac{\partial L(\mathbf{y},\mathbf{u},t)}{\partial \mathbf{y}} \tag{13}$$

The above system of n differential equations defines mathematically the costate vector $\mathbf{p}(t)$. The vector $\mathbf{p}(t)$, which is the solution of equation 9, depends:

1. On the equation of the plant due to the presence of $\mathbf{A}'$.
2. On the performance function L.

The control $\mathbf{u}^*$ which absolutely minimizes H is a function of $\mathbf{y}, \mathbf{p}$, and t, i.e., $\mathbf{u}^*(\mathbf{y},\mathbf{p},t)$. This functional dependence of $\mathbf{u}^*$ is a *necessary* condition on the control function $\mathbf{u}^o$, which is the one that minimizes

$$\int_{t_o}^{t_f} L(\mathbf{y},\mathbf{u},t)dt$$

The above is the major result of the theory and can be restated as follows: *The optimum control* $\mathbf{u}^o(t)$ *which minimizes the performance index*

$$\int_{t_o}^{t_f} L(\mathbf{y},\mathbf{u},t)dt$$

must necessarily minimize absolutely the Hamiltonian H, given by equation 7. The mathematical steps and extension of the above result may be found in reference 7.

In the following sections the theory is applied to specific problems. These are the problems of minimum time control, minimum fuel control, and minimum energy control.

The Minimum Time Problem

The minimum time problem, or the "bang-bang" problem, has been examined in detail during the past 10 years. The reason that is included in this paper is mostly for the sake of comparison with other optimal systems, and for continuity.

The plant described by equation 1, and the control $\mathbf{u}(t)$, restricted in magnitude by equation 3, are given. It is assumed that the system is controllable, i.e., there exists at least one $\mathbf{u}(t)$, consistent with equation 3, which will force the plant from an initial state $\mathbf{y}_o$ to a final state $\mathbf{y}_f$. With no loss of generality, assume $t_o = 0$. It is desired to determine the optimum control function $\mathbf{u}^o(t)$ which will force the plant from $\mathbf{y}_o$ to $\mathbf{y}_f$ in *minimum time*.

For the minimum time problem,

$$L(\mathbf{y}, \mathbf{u}, t) = 1 \tag{14}$$

since

$$\int_o^{t_f} L dt = \int_o^{t_f} 1 dt = t_f \tag{15}$$

and it is desired to minimize the response time t_f. Substituting equation 14 into equation 7, the Hamiltonian may be determined:

$$H = 1 + \langle \mathbf{Ay}, \mathbf{p}\rangle + \langle \mathbf{Bu}, \mathbf{p}\rangle \tag{16}$$

Before the minimization of the Hamiltonian is carried out, it is instructive to evaluate the costate $\mathbf{p}(t)$. Letting $L=1$ in equation 13, one obtains

$$\dot{\mathbf{p}}(t) = -\mathbf{A}'\mathbf{p}(t) \tag{17}$$

which has the solution

$$\mathbf{p}(t) = e^{-\mathbf{A}'t}\mathbf{p}_o \tag{18}$$

where

$$\mathbf{p}_o \triangleq \mathbf{p}(0) \tag{19}$$

The system of the n equations in equation 17 is called the adjoint system to the controlled plant; see equation 1.

In equation 16 the term $1 + \langle \mathbf{Ay}, \mathbf{p}\rangle$ is independent of $\mathbf{u}(t)$. Hence, one need only determine the absolute minimum of $\langle \mathbf{Bu}, \mathbf{p}\rangle$, under equation 3. Observe that the formal minimization technique,

$$0 = \frac{\partial H}{\partial \mathbf{u}} = \mathbf{B}'\mathbf{p} \tag{20}$$

leads to an unrealistic answer. However,

$$H^o = \min_{\substack{\mathbf{u}(t) \\ |u_j| \leq 1}} H = 1 + \langle \mathbf{Ay},\mathbf{p}\rangle + \min_{\substack{\mathbf{u}(t) \\ |u_j| \leq 1}} \langle \mathbf{u}, \mathbf{B'p}\rangle \tag{21}$$

Define the r-vector $\mathbf{q}(t) = (q_1, q_2, \ldots, q_r)$ by

$$\mathbf{q}(t) \triangleq \mathbf{B}'\mathbf{p}(t) = \mathbf{B}'e^{-\mathbf{A}'t}\mathbf{p}_o \tag{22}$$

Then,

$$H^o = 1 + \langle \mathbf{Ay},\mathbf{p}\rangle + \min_{\substack{\mathbf{u}(t) \\ |u_j| \leq 1}} \sum_{j=1}^{r} u_j(t)q_j(t)$$

$$= 1 + \langle \mathbf{Ay},\mathbf{p}\rangle + \sum_{j=1}^{r} \min_{\substack{\mathbf{u}(t) \\ |u_j| \leq 1}} \{u_j(t)q_j(t)\} \tag{23}$$

The term $u_j(t)q_j(t)$ achieves its minimum value if

$$u_j(t) = -\text{sgn}\{q_j(t)\} \tag{24}$$

Equation 24 is the *optimal control law* for minimum time response. It may be written in vector form:

$$\mathbf{u}(t) = -\text{sgn}\{\mathbf{q}(t)\} = -\text{sgn}\{\mathbf{B}'e^{-\mathbf{A}'t}\mathbf{p}_o\} \tag{25}$$

The conclusions derived from equation 24 are:

1. The optimum control signal for minimum time operation is piecewise constant.
2. The optimum control signal must have only the values $+1$ or -1.
3. The polarity of the control signal depends on the output of the adjoint system.

The exact time equation of the optimal control function would be known if the exact time equation of $\mathbf{p}(t)$ were available. However, knowledge of $\mathbf{p}(t)$ implies knowledge of the initial condition vector $\mathbf{p}_o$. However, the values of $\mathbf{p}_o$ are not completely free since they must be a function of the initial state $\mathbf{y}_o$ and the final state $\mathbf{y}_f$ of the plant. This relationship between $\mathbf{p}_o$, $\mathbf{y}_o$, and $\mathbf{y}_f$ is nonlinear and not known at present. This fundamental difficulty has forced the design engineers to utilize geometrical techniques, such as the concept of the "switching hypersurfaces" described in reference 6.

Fig. 1 represents a conceptual block diagram of the time optimal system. Equipment-wise, the control law equation 24 requires the use of an ideal relay with outputs $+1$ or -1.

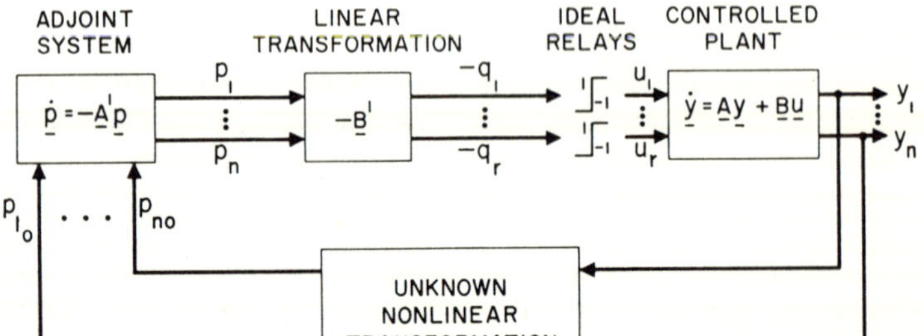

Fig. 1 Conceptual block diagram of a minimum time system

The Minimum Fuel Problem

There are many problems where the control variables $\mathbf{u}(t)$ are directly proportional to rate of flow of mass. For example, the control signal may be the flow from a gas jet for the attitude control of a space vehicle or the exhaust from a missile. Almost invariably in these problems the total fuel available is limited; therefore, it is desirable to accomplish each control correction with a minimum amount of fuel. In this section the form of the minimum fuel control function is discussed. To the author's knowledge, this problem has not been treated in the literature concerning control.

The plant equation 1 and the control $\mathbf{u}(t)$, limited in magnitude by equation 3, are given. Assume that the system is controllable. It is desired to determine the control function which forces the plant from a state $\mathbf{y}_o$ to a state $\mathbf{y}_f$ and which minimizes the functional

$$\int_o^{t_f} \sum_{j=1}^{r} |u_j(t)|\,dt \tag{26}$$

In this problem, the scalar

$$L(\mathbf{y}, \mathbf{u}, t) = \sum_{j=1}^{r} |u_j(t)| \tag{27}$$

is a measure of the total rate of flow of the fuel. Its time integral, equation 26, is a measure of the total consumed fuel. Substituting equation 27 into equation 7, one obtains the Hamiltonian for the minimum fuel problem,

$$H = \sum_{j=1}^{r} |u_j(t)| + \langle\mathbf{Ay},\mathbf{p}\rangle + \langle\mathbf{Bu},\mathbf{p}\rangle \tag{28}$$

Substituting equation 27 into equation 13, one obtains the same adjoint system as for the minimum time problem. Thus,

$$\mathbf{p}(t) = e^{-A't}\mathbf{p}_o \tag{29}$$

Using $\mathbf{q}(t)$, defined by equation 22,

$$H^o = \min_{\substack{\mathbf{u}(t)\\ |u_j|\leq 1}} H = \langle\mathbf{Ay},\mathbf{p}\rangle + \min_{\substack{\mathbf{u}(t)\\ |u_j|\leq 1}} \sum_{j=1}^{r} \{|u_j| + u_j q_j\}$$

$$= \langle\mathbf{Ay},\mathbf{p}\rangle + \sum_{j=1}^{r} \min_{\substack{\mathbf{u}(t)\\ |u_j|\leq 1}} \{|u_j| + u_j q_j\} \tag{30}$$

Consider the minimization of $\{|u_j| + u_j q_j\}$.

Case 1:

If

$$|q_j(t)| \geq 1 \tag{31}$$

then

$$u_j(t) = -\operatorname{sgn}\{q_j(t)\} \tag{32}$$

leads to the minimum value in equation 30, as in equation 3, for $j = 1, 2, \ldots, r$.

Case 2:

If

$$|q_j(t)| < 1 \tag{33}$$

then

$$u_j(t) = 0 \tag{34}$$

leads to the minimum value of equation 30, for $j = 1, 2, \ldots, r$. Thus, for minimum fuel operation, the control law is

$$\left.\begin{array}{ll} u_j(t) = 0 & \text{if } |q_j(t)| < 1 \\ u_j(t) = -\operatorname{sgn}\{q_j(t)\} & \text{if } |q_j(t)| \geq 1 \end{array}\right\} \tag{35}$$

for $j = 1, 2, \ldots, r$; $q_j(t)$ is the jth component of the r-vector $\mathbf{B}'e^{-\mathbf{A}'t}\mathbf{p}_o$.

From the control law equation 35, one may draw the following conclusions:

1. For the minimum fuel problem the optimal control function is piecewise constant.

2. The values of the optimal control function are $+1$, 0, or -1.

Although the exact time equation for $\mathbf{u}_j(t)$ is not provided by the above results, again due to the unknown dependence of $\mathbf{p}_o$ on the state of the plant, the information obtained as to the shape of the control is sufficient to answer certain questions in the preliminary design stage of a minimum fuel system. For example, if gas jets are to be used for attitude control, then one needs a nozzle which will only close or open without any intermediate settings.

Additional information may be extracted regarding the optimal control function from a careful examination of the properties of the signals $q_j(t)$. It is known that if the eigenvalues λ_i of the matrix $\mathbf{A}$ in equation 1 are *real, negative, and distinct*, then the outputs $p_i(t)$ of the adjoint system will be zero *at most* $n-1$ *times*, depending on the value of the initial conditions p_{io}. Since the signals $q_j(t)$ are linear combinations of the $p_i(t)$, as indicated by equation 22, it follows that the $q_j(t)$ will be zero at most $n-1$ times. However, if any of the eigenvalues of $\mathbf{A}$ are complex, one cannot place an upper bound on the times that $p_i(t)$ and $q_j(t)$ will be zero. The functions $q_j(t)$ are continuous. Their magnitude and polarity determine the optimal control functions $u_j(t)$. It follows from the continuity of $q_j(t)$ and equation 35 that control functions of the type

$$u_j(t) = \begin{cases} +1 & 0 \leq t < t_1 \\ -1 & t_1 \leq t < t_2 \\ \cdot & \cdot \\ \cdot & \cdot \\ \cdot & \cdot \end{cases}$$

are not optimal. Hence, if at present, say, $u_j(t) = +1$ is the correct control, and if at some time in the future $u_j(t) = -1$ is required, then the transition from $+1$ to -1 must involve a time element for which $u_j(t) = 0$. However, in certain problems, control sequences of the form

$$u_j(t) = \begin{cases} +1 & 0 \leq t < t_1 \\ 0 & t_1 \leq t < t_2 \\ +1 & t_2 \leq t < t_3 \\ \cdot & \cdot \\ \cdot & \cdot \\ \cdot & \cdot \end{cases}$$

can be optimal.

The conceptual block diagram for a minimum fuel system is shown in Fig. 2. The input to the plant is provided by a relay-type element with a dead zone.

The nonlinear relationship between the initial condition vector $\mathbf{p}_o$ of the adjoint system and the states $\mathbf{y}_o$ and $\mathbf{y}_f$ of the plant is not known. Further research is required along these lines. In reference 18 one can find examples of minimum fuel control for second-order systems. It seems that the concept of "switching sets" will be of value to the design of such systems, although the logic will be more complicated than in the minimum time problem.

The Minimum Energy Problem

There exists a class of problems for

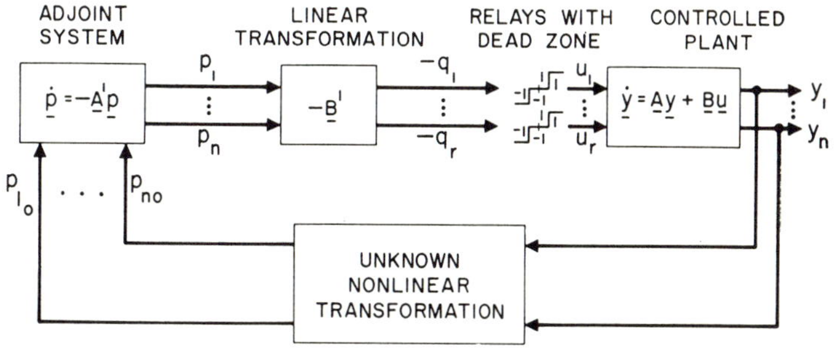

Fig. 2 Conceptual block diagram of a minimum fuel system

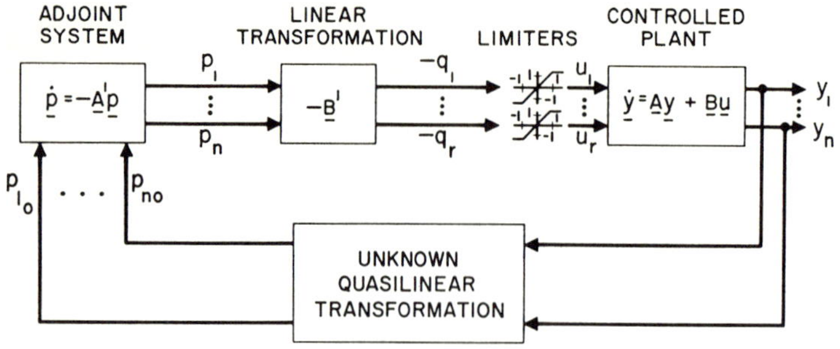

Fig. 3 Conceptual block diagram of a minimum energy system

which the square of the control signal is proportional to power, and the time integral of the square of the control signal is a measure of the energy dissipated. As an example, suppose that the control $u(t)$ is an electric signal deriving its energy from a battery, and it is desired to accomplish a given control action using a minimum amount of energy provided by the battery.

The controlled plant equation 1 and the control $u(t)$, limited by equation 3, are given. References 7, 8, and 9 provide theoretical investigations on this minimum energy problem, whithout the magnitude restriction of equation 3 on the control $\mathbf{u}(t)$. The optimal control $\mathbf{u}(t)$ is sought which will force the plant from the state $\mathbf{y}_o$ to $\mathbf{y}_f$ and which will minimize the functional index of performance

$$\frac{1}{2}\int_o^{t_f}\sum_{j=1}^{r} u_j^2(t)dt \tag{36}$$

Thus,

$$L(\mathbf{y}, \mathbf{u}, t)=\frac{1}{2}\sum_{j=1}^{r} u_j^2(t)=\frac{1}{2}<\mathbf{u},\mathbf{u}> \tag{37}$$

The Hamiltonian for the minimum energy problem is

$$H=\frac{1}{2}<\mathbf{u},\mathbf{u}>+<\mathbf{Ay}, \mathbf{p}>+<\mathbf{Bu}, \mathbf{p}> \tag{38}$$

Using $\mathbf{q}(t)$, defined by equation 22, one obtains

$$H^o=\min_{\substack{\mathbf{u}(t)\\ |u_j|\leq 1}} H=<\mathbf{Ay}, \mathbf{p}>+\sum_{j=1}^{r}\min_{\substack{\mathbf{u}(t)\\ |u_j|\leq 1}}\left\{\frac{1}{2}u_j^2+u_jq_j\right\} \tag{39}$$

To determine the absolute minimum of $\{1/2u_j^2+u_jq_j\}$:

Case 1:

If

$$|q_j(t)|<1 \tag{40}$$

then formal differentiation yields

$$\frac{\partial}{\partial u_j}\left\{\frac{1}{2}u_j^2+u_jq_j\right\}=u_j(t)+q_j(t)=0$$

Hence, the minimum is obtained at

$$u_j(t)=-q_j(t) \qquad j=1, 2, \ldots, r \tag{41}$$

and since in this case $|q_j(t)|<1$, the restriction of equation 3 is satisfied.

Case 2:

If

$$|q_j(t)|\geq 1 \tag{42}$$

then

$$u_j(t)=-\operatorname{sgn}\{q_j(t)\} \tag{43}$$

yields the minimum value for $j=1, 2, \ldots, r$.

Thus the optimal control law for minimum energy response is

$$\left.\begin{aligned} u_j(t)&=-q_j(t) &&\text{if } |q_j(t)|<1\\ u_j(t)&=-\operatorname{sgn} q_j(t) &&\text{if } |q_j(t)|\geq 1\end{aligned}\right\} \tag{44}$$

for $j=1, 2, \ldots, r$.

Now it will be shown that whenever $u_j(t)=-q_j(t)$, the control is a linear function of the state y of the plant. From equation 1 the plant differential equation is

$$\dot{\mathbf{y}}(t)=\mathbf{Ay}(t)+\mathbf{Bu}(t)$$

which is solved to yield

$$\mathbf{y}(t)=e^{\mathbf{A}t}\mathbf{y}_o+\int_o^t e^{\mathbf{A}(t-\tau)}\mathbf{Bu}(\tau)d\tau \tag{45}$$

If equations 40 and 41 hold, then

$$\mathbf{u}(t)=-\mathbf{q}(t)=-\mathbf{B}'e^{-\mathbf{A}'t}\mathbf{p}_o \tag{46}$$

Substituting equation 46 into equation 45 yields

$$\mathbf{y}(t)=e^{\mathbf{A}t}\mathbf{y}_o-e^{\mathbf{A}t}\int_o^t e^{-\mathbf{A}\tau}\mathbf{BB}'e^{-\mathbf{A}'\tau}\mathbf{p}_o d\tau \tag{47}$$

Since $\mathbf{p}_o$ is a constant, equation 47 may be written in the form

$$e^{\mathbf{A}t}\mathbf{M}(t)\mathbf{p}_o=e^{\mathbf{A}t}\mathbf{y}_o-\mathbf{y}(t) \tag{48}$$

where $\mathbf{M}(t)$ is an $n\times n$ matrix. Hence,

$$\mathbf{p}_o=\mathbf{M}^{-1}(t)\{\mathbf{y}_o-e^{-\mathbf{A}t}\mathbf{y}(t)\} \tag{49}$$

Substituting equation 49 into equation 46

$$\mathbf{u}(t)=-\mathbf{B}'e^{-\mathbf{A}'t}\mathbf{M}^{-1}(t)\{\mathbf{y}_o-e^{-\mathbf{A}t}\mathbf{y}(t)\} \tag{50}$$

which implies that the control is linear with respect to the state $\mathbf{y}(t)$ of the plant.

Fig. 3 represents the conceptual diagram of a minimum energy system. The control law of equation 44 implies that the plant is driven by a signal, which is the output of a limiter-type nonlinearity.

Mixed Performance Criteria

The three problems considered in the previous sections had the common characteristic that the performance functional to be minimized was exclusively a function of the control function. This exclusive dependence of L on $\mathbf{u}$ is typical of problems for which a final value is desired, and there is no concern about the shape of the response for points in between.

In this section problems are considered for which the shape of the response is important. In many cases the state $\mathbf{y}$ in equation 1 represents an error state between a desired state and the actual plant state. Consider functionals which are separable; i.e., assume

$$L(\mathbf{y},\mathbf{u},t)=L_1(\mathbf{y},t)+L_2(\mathbf{u}) \tag{51}$$

and the performance index to be minimized is

$$\int_o^{t_f} L_1(\mathbf{y},t)dt+\int_o^{f} L_2(\mathbf{u})dt \tag{52}$$

The Hamiltonian is

$$H=L_1(\mathbf{y}, t)+L_2(\mathbf{u})+<\mathbf{Ay}, \mathbf{p}>+<\mathbf{Bu}, \mathbf{p}> \tag{53}$$

Minimization of H with respect to $\mathbf{u}$ leads to the control laws of equations 24, 34, and 44, if

$$L_2(\mathbf{u})=1,\ L_2(\mathbf{u})=\sum_{j=1}^{r}|u_j|,\ L_2(\mathbf{u})=\frac{1}{2}\sum_{j=1}^{r}u_j^2$$

respectively. Hence, the form of the control functions for optimal response is unchanged. However, the equation of the costate vector $\mathbf{p}(t)$ does change since now $\mathbf{p}(t)$ is the solution of the matrix differential equation

$$\dot{\mathbf{p}} = -\mathbf{A}'\mathbf{p} - \frac{\partial L_1(\mathbf{y}, t)}{\partial \mathbf{y}} \quad (54)$$

It is evident that if the integrand of the performance functional is separable, in the sense of equation 51, then the form of the optimal control signals for the minimum time, minimum fuel, and minimum energy problems remains unchanged.

Conclusions

The theory of optimal control has been used in order to evaluate the form of the optimal control signal and the structure of the control system for the minimum time, minimum fuel, and minimum energy problems. For the minimum time problem it was found that the control signal is the output of an ideal relay-type element. For the minimum fuel problem the control signal is the output of a relay-type element with a dead zone. For the minimum energy problem the control signal is the output of a limiter-type nonlinearity. The role of the adjoint system in the theory and design of optimal systems has been examined and it was found that the unknown nonlinear relationship between the initial conditions of the adjoint system and the state of the plant represents a major obs acle in the actual design of control systems. Further research will be required to remove this obstacle.

References

1. Pontriagin's Maximum Principle and the Principle of Optimality, **C. A. Desoer.** *Journal*, The Franklin Institute, Philadelphia, Pa., vol. 271, no. 5, May 1961, pp. 361–67.

2. The Maximum Principle in the Theory of Optimal Processes of Control, **Boltyanskii, et al.** *Proceedings*, First International Congress on Automatic Control, Moscow, U.S.S.R. 1960, pp. 454–59.

3. Optimum Control Processes, **L. S. Pontriagin.** *Automation Express*, vol. 1, no. 10, 1959, pp. 15–18, and vol. 2, no. 1, 1959, pp. 26–30.

4. The Theory of Optimal Processes in Linear Systems, **R. B. Gamkrelidge.** *Report 61-7*, University of California, Los Angeles, Calif., Jan. 1961.

5. L. S. Pontriagin's Maximum Principle in the Theory of Optimum Systems, **L. I. Rozonoer.** *Automation and Remote Control*, Moscow, U.S.S.R. vol. 20, Oct., Nov., Dec., 1959, pp. 1288–1302, 1405–21, 1517–32.

6. Dynamic Programming (book), **R. Bellman.** Princeton University Press, Princeton, N, J., 1957.

7. The Theory of Optimal Control and the Calculus of Variations, **R. E. Kalman.** *Technical Report 61-3*, Research Institute for Advanced Studies, Baltimore, Md., 1961.

8. Contributions to the Theory of Optimal Control, **R. E. Kalman.** *Boletin de la Sociedad Matematica Mexicana*, 1960, pp. 102–19.

9. On the General Theory of Control Systems, **R. E. Kalman.** *Proceedings*, First International Congress on Automatic Control, 1960, pp. 481–93.

10. The Structure of Optimum Control Systems, **B. Friedland.** *Transactions*, American Society of Mechanical Engineers, New York, N. Y. Series E, *Journal of Basic Engineering*, Mar. 1962.

11. On the Bang Bang Control Problem **R. Bellman.** *Quarterly of Applied Mathematics* vol. 14, 1956, pp. 11–18.

12. Time Optimal Control Systems, **J. P. La-Salle.** *Proceedings*, National Academy of Sciences, Washington, D. C., vol. 45, Apr. 1959, pp. 573–77.

13. Mathematical Aspects of the Synthesis of Linear Minimum Response Time Controllers, **E. B. Lee.** *Transactions on Automatic Control*, Institute of Radio Engineers, vol. AC-5, Sept. 1960, pp. 283–89.

14. A Successive Approximation Technique for Optimal Control Systems Subject to Input Saturation, **Y. C. Ho.** *Transactions*, American Society of Mechanical Engineers, no. 61-JAC-10, 1961.

15. Theory and Design of High Order Bang Bang Control Systems, **M. Athanassiades, O. J. M. Smith.** *Transactions on Automatic Control*, Institute of Radio Engineers, vol. AC-6, no. 2, May 1961, pp. 125–34.

16. The Bang Bang Servo Problem Treated by Variational Techniques, **C. A. Desoer.** *Information and Control*, New York, N. Y., vol. 2, 1959, pp. 333–48.

17. On the Theory of Optimum Regulation' **N. N. Krasovskii.** *Automation and Remote Control* vol. 18, 1958, pp. 1005–16.

18. On Optimal Linear Control Systems which Minimize the Time Integral of the Absolute Value of the Control Function, **M. Athanassiades.** *Lincoln Laboratory Report 22G-4*, Massachusetts Institute of Technology, Lexington, Mass., Mar. 1962.

W. M. WONHAM[1]
Center for Control Theory,
Research Institute for Advanced Studies,
Baltimore, Md.

C. D. JOHNSON[2]
Electrical Engineering Department,
University of Alabama,
Huntsville Center, Huntsville, Ala.

Optimal Bang-Bang Control With Quadratic Performance Index

The following optimal regulator problem is considered: Find the scalar control function $u = u(t)$ which minimizes the performance index

$$J[u] = \frac{1}{2} \int_0^T \langle \mathbf{x}(t), \mathbf{Q}\mathbf{x}(t) \rangle dt,$$

subject to the conditions

$$\dot{\mathbf{x}} = \mathbf{A}\mathbf{x} + u(t)\mathbf{f}, \qquad |u(t)| \leq 1$$
$$\mathbf{x}(0) = \mathbf{x}_0$$
$$(\mathbf{x}_0 \textit{ is unrestricted})$$
$$\mathbf{x}(T) = \mathbf{0} \quad (T \textit{ is free})$$

$\mathbf{Q}$, $\mathbf{A}$ *are constant* $n \times n$*-matrices;* $\mathbf{f}$ *is a constant n-vector. It is shown that optimal control includes both a bang-bang mode and a linear mode, the latter arising from the "singular" solutions of the Pontriagin canonical equations. Conditions are given under which nth-order systems are equivalent, for control purposes, to systems of first or second order. One example of a second-order system is worked in detail and some results of an analog computer study are presented.*

Introduction

Consider the control system defined by

$$\dot{\mathbf{x}} = \mathbf{A}\mathbf{x} + u(t)\mathbf{f} \qquad (\dot{} = d/dt) \tag{1}$$

where $\mathbf{x} = (x_1, \ldots, x_n)$ is the state vector of the plant, $\mathbf{A}$ is an $(n \times n)$-constant matrix, $\mathbf{f} = (f_1, \ldots, f_n)$ is a constant n-vector, and $u(t)$ is the scalar control function.

Optimization of (1) for a quadratic performance index has been studied by several authors. If the index is

$$\int_0^\infty (\langle \mathbf{x}, \mathbf{Q}\mathbf{x} \rangle + u^2)dt$$

and if u is unrestricted in magnitude, it is known [1],[3] [2] that the optimal control law is $u^* = \langle \boldsymbol{\gamma}, \mathbf{x} \rangle$, where $\boldsymbol{\gamma}$ is a constant n-vector. The same problem with the added restriction $|u| \leq 1$ has been discussed by Letov [3] and Chang [4]; it appears, however, that their results are in error [5].

In this paper we consider (1) with performance index

$$\frac{1}{2} \int_0^T \langle \mathbf{x}, \mathbf{Q}\mathbf{x} \rangle dt$$

and the constraint $|u| \leq 1$ (a precise statement of the problem is given later). This problem has also been considered by Chang [6] in the case where $\mathbf{A}$ is stable; his result is apparently incorrect, except in the special case considered in Section 8 of the present paper.

An unusual feature of the solution is that, in general, the control is singular, but of form $u^* = \langle \boldsymbol{\gamma}, \mathbf{x} \rangle$, for states $\mathbf{x}$ in a set R containing the origin; and is bang-bang otherwise. The model is applicable in situations where control cost as measured by $\int u^2 dt$ is unimportant, but where it is desirable to retain the practical advantages of dual-mode control.

2 Statement of the Problem

Let $\mathbf{Q}$ be a positive semidefinite constant matrix, for the moment unrestricted. The problem is to choose u so that the functional

$$J[u] = \frac{1}{2} \int_0^T \langle \mathbf{x}(t), \mathbf{Q}\mathbf{x}(t) \rangle dt \tag{2}$$ [4]

is a minimum, subject to (1) and to the additional conditions

$$\mathbf{x}(0) = \mathbf{x}_0 \qquad (\mathbf{x}_0 \text{ is unrestricted}) \tag{3}$$

$$\mathbf{x}(T) = \mathbf{0} \qquad (T \text{ is free}) \tag{4}$$

and

$$|u(t)| \leq 1 \qquad (0 \leq t \leq T) \tag{5}$$

The function u is supposed to be integrable on the interval $[0, T]$.[5]

It is assumed that the system (1) is controllable; namely, the vectors $\mathbf{f}, \mathbf{A}\mathbf{f}, \ldots, \mathbf{A}^{n-1}\mathbf{f}$ are linearly independent. There is then no loss of generality[6] in assuming that $\mathbf{A}$, $\mathbf{f}$ have the form

$$\mathbf{A} = \begin{bmatrix} 0 & 1 & 0 & \ldots & 0 \\ 0 & 0 & 1 & 0\ldots & 0 \\ & & \ddots & & \\ 0 & \ldots & \ldots & 0 & 1 \\ a_1 & \ldots & \ldots & \ldots & a_n \end{bmatrix}, \qquad \mathbf{f} = \begin{bmatrix} 0 \\ \cdot \\ \cdot \\ \cdot \\ 0 \\ 1 \end{bmatrix} \tag{6}$$

---

[1] This research was supported in part by the National Aeronautics and Space Administration under Contract No. NASr-103, and in part by the United States Air Force under Contract AF 49(638)-1206. Reproduction in whole or in part is permitted for any purpose of the United States Government.

[2] This research was supported in part by the National Science Foundation under Contract No. G-16460 while the second author was associated with the Control and Information Systems Laboratory, School of Electrical Engineering, Purdue University, Lafayette, Ind.

[3] Numbers in brackets designate References at end of paper.

Contributed by the Automatic Control Division of The American Society of Mechanical Engineers and presented at the Joint Automatic Control Conference, Minneapolis, Minn., June 17–21, 1963. Manuscript received at ASME Headquarters, July 19, 1963.

[4] $\langle \mathbf{x}, \mathbf{y} \rangle$ is the scalar product of $\mathbf{x}$ and $\mathbf{y}$.

[5] Piecewise continuity can be too strong a requirement for existence of a solution. A problem of this class in which the optimal control (in the class of integrable functions) is not piecewise continuous is solved in [7].

[6] See Appendix 1.

and that $\mathbf{Q}$ is a diagonal matrix

$$\mathbf{Q} = \mathrm{diag}[q_1, \ldots, q_n], \qquad q_i \geqq 0 \tag{7}$$

3 Canonical Equations

In accordance with the maximum principle [8] define

$$\begin{aligned} H(\mathbf{x}, \mathbf{p}, u) &= \langle \mathbf{p}, \dot{\mathbf{x}} \rangle - \tfrac{1}{2}\langle \mathbf{x}, \mathbf{Qx} \rangle \\ &= \langle \mathbf{p}, \mathbf{Ax} \rangle + \langle \mathbf{p}, \mathbf{f} \rangle u - \tfrac{1}{2}\langle \mathbf{x}, \mathbf{Qx} \rangle \\ &= \sum_1^{n-1} p_j x_{j+1} + p_n \left(\sum_1^n a_j x_j + u \right) - \frac{1}{2} \sum_1^n q_j x_j^2 \end{aligned} \tag{8}$$

If an optimal control u^* exists, it is given by

$$H(\mathbf{x}, \mathbf{p}, u^*) = \max_{|u| \leq 1} H(\mathbf{x}, \mathbf{p}, u) \tag{9}$$

or

$$u^*(t) = \mathrm{sgn}[p_n(t)] \tag{10}$$

provided $p_n(t) \not\equiv 0$. If $p_n(t)$ vanishes on a time interval of positive length $H(\mathbf{x}, \mathbf{p}, u)$ is independent of u on this interval, and u^* is no longer defined by (9). The control is then said to be *singular* [8, 13], and a corresponding arc $\mathbf{x} = \mathbf{x}(t)$ is a *singular subarc*. The determination of u^* on a singular subarc is discussed subsequently. Whether control is singular or not, $\mathbf{x}(t)$ and $\mathbf{p}(t)$ satisfy the canonical equations

$$\dot{x}_i = [\partial H(\mathbf{x}, \mathbf{p}, u)/\partial p_i]_{u=u^*}, \qquad \dot{p}_i = -[\partial H(\mathbf{x}, \mathbf{p}, u)/\partial x_i]_{u=u^*}$$

or in full

$$\begin{aligned} \dot{x}_1 &= x_2 \\ \dot{x}_2 &= x_3 \\ &\cdot \\ &\cdot \\ \dot{x}_{n-1} &= x_n \\ \dot{x}_n &= \sum_1^n a_j x_j + u^* \end{aligned} \tag{11}$$

$$\begin{aligned} \dot{p}_1 &= -a_1 p_n + q_1 x_1 \\ \dot{p}_2 &= -p_1 - a_2 p_n + q_2 x_2 \\ &\cdots \\ \dot{p}_{n-1} &= -p_{n-2} - a_{n-1} p_n + q_{n-1} x_{n-1} \\ \dot{p}_n &= -p_{n-1} - a_n p_n + q_n x_n \end{aligned} \tag{12}$$

When u^* is known as a function of $\mathbf{x}$ and $\mathbf{p}$, (11) and (12) can be solved for the optimal trajectory $\mathbf{x} = \mathbf{x}(t)$. Initial and terminal conditions are given by (3) and (4). Since the terminal time T is free we impose the transversality condition [8] $H(\mathbf{x}(T), \mathbf{p}(T), u^*(T)) = 0$; since H does not depend on t explicitly it follows from (8)–(12) that $H =$ const, and therefore

$$H(\mathbf{x}(t), \mathbf{p}(t), u^*(t)) = 0, \qquad 0 \leqq t \leqq T \tag{13}$$

4 Singular Subarcs

To obtain all possible singular subarcs, let $p_n(t) \equiv 0$ in (12). Then the first $(n - 1)$ equations (11), together with (12), define a free linear system (i.e., independent of u), of formal order $2(n - 1)$. The characteristic equation of this system is

$$\sum_1^n q_k(-\lambda)^{k-1}\lambda^{k-1} = 0 \tag{14}$$

From (14) it is seen that the eigenvalues of the free system occur in pairs $(\lambda_m, -\lambda_m)$. Let Re $\lambda_m \leqq 0$. Setting $\lambda = i\nu$ (ν real) in the left side of (14), there results

$$\sum_1^n q_k(-\lambda)^{k-1}\lambda^{k-1} = \sum_1^n q_k \nu^{2(k-1)} \geqq q_1$$

and therefore Re $\lambda_m < 0$ if $q_1 > 0$. It will be assumed from now on that $q_1 > 0$, $q_n > 0$, and that the $(n - 1)$ eigenvalues λ_m are distinct.

The somewhat artificial restriction $q_n > 0$ is made for simplicity. If $q_j \neq 0$, $q_{j+1} = \ldots = q_n = 0$, the dimension of the singular terminal hyperplane (Section 6) is $j - 1$. Only the case $j = n$ will be considered in this paper.

Consider an $(n - 1)$-parameter family of singular arcs defined by $x_1 = \Sigma\theta_\mu \exp(\lambda_\mu t)$ where the θ_μ are constants of integration and the λ_μ are any $(n - 1)$-distinct eigenvalues in the set $(\pm\lambda_1, \ldots, \pm\lambda_{n-1})$. To each such family there corresponds an integral of (11), (12) of the form

$$\langle \mathbf{c}, \mathbf{x} \rangle = 0 \tag{15}$$

where $\mathbf{c} = (c_1, \ldots, c_n)$ and the c_i are determined by $(n - 1)$-equations

$$\sum_1^n c_i \lambda_\mu^{i-1} = 0 \tag{16}$$

A corresponding singular control u is given by the last equation of (11). Setting

$$u = \langle \boldsymbol{\gamma}, \mathbf{x} \rangle \tag{17}$$

where $\boldsymbol{\gamma} = (\gamma_1, \ldots, \gamma_{n-1}, 0)$, there follows

$$\sum_1^{n-1} \gamma_i x_i = \dot{x}_n - \sum_1^n a_j x_j$$

Thus the γ_i are given by $(n - 1)$-equations

$$\sum_1^{n-1} \gamma_i \lambda_\mu^{i-1} = \lambda_\mu^n - \sum_1^n a_j \lambda_\mu^{j-1} \tag{18}$$

Since the λ_μ are distinct the solution of (18) is unique.[7]

On the arcs of a singular family the p_i can be found from (11), (12) as unique linear combinations of the state variables $x_1, \ldots, x_{n-1}$. The result is $\mathbf{p} = -\mathbf{Bx}$, where the $(n \times n)$-matrix $\mathbf{B}$ depends only on the q_j and on the particular family selected.

5 Optimality of Singular Subarcs

Let $\mathbf{x} = \boldsymbol{\sigma}(t)$, $0 \leqq t \leqq \tau$, denote an arbitrary singular subarc in a hyperplane defined by (15), (16); and put $\boldsymbol{\sigma}(0) = \mathbf{x}_0$, $\boldsymbol{\sigma}(\tau) = \mathbf{x}_1$. Under certain restrictions to be stated later, such an arc is optimal in the following sense. If

$$\mathbf{x} = \boldsymbol{\xi}(t) = (\xi_1(t), \dot{\xi}_1(t), \ldots, \xi_1^{(n-1)}(t))$$

is any trajectory such that $\boldsymbol{\xi}(0) = \mathbf{x}_0$, $\boldsymbol{\xi}(\tau) = \mathbf{x}_1$, then

$$\int_0^\tau \langle \boldsymbol{\xi}(t), \mathbf{Q}\boldsymbol{\xi}(t) \rangle dt \geqq \int_0^\tau \langle \boldsymbol{\sigma}(t), \mathbf{Q}\boldsymbol{\sigma}(t) \rangle dt \tag{19}$$

with equality only when $\boldsymbol{\xi}(t) = \boldsymbol{\sigma}(t)$. That is, the singular control (17) is strictly optimal compared to all controls which transfer the system from $\mathbf{x}_0$ to $\mathbf{x}_1$.

To prove this statement we shall first show that $\langle \mathbf{x}, \mathbf{Qx} \rangle$ is an exact differential on a hyperplane (15). Consider the identity

$$\begin{aligned} \langle \mathbf{c}, \mathbf{x} \rangle^2 &= \sum_1^n c_i^2 x_i^2 + 2 \sum_{i=1}^{n-1} \sum_{j=i+1}^{n} c_i c_j x_i x_j \\ &= \sum_1^n c_i^2 x_i^2 + 2 \sum_{i=1}^{n-1} \sum_{k=1}^{n-i} c_i c_{i+k} x_i x_{i+k} \end{aligned} \tag{20}$$

[7] A control defined by (17), (18) may not be real-valued, or less than 1 in magnitude; $\boldsymbol{\gamma}$, $\mathbf{c}$ are real if any complex λ_μ occur in conjugate pairs.

Since

$$x_{i+k} = x_i^{(k)} \quad (k = 0, 1, \ldots, n - i;\ i = 1, \ldots, n)$$

$$\int x_i x_{i+k} dt = x_i x_{i+k-1} - x_{i+1}x_{i+k-2} + \ldots$$
$$- \begin{cases} (-1)^{k/2}[x_{i+\frac{1}{2}k-1}x_{i+\frac{1}{2}k} - \int x^2_{i+\frac{1}{2}k}dt] & (k \text{ even}) \\ \frac{1}{2}(-1)^{(k+1)/2}x^2_{i+\frac{1}{2}(k-1)} & (k \text{ odd}) \end{cases} \tag{21}$$

Collecting terms in (20) and (21) we obtain

$$\langle \mathbf{c}, \mathbf{x}\rangle^2 = \sum_{i=1}^{n} \left[c_i^2 + 2\sum_{j=1}^{i-1} (-1)^{i+j}c_j c_{2i-j} \right] x_i^2 + 2\frac{d}{dt} V_0(x_1, x_2, \ldots, x_{n-1}) \tag{22}$$

where V_0 is a homogeneous quadratic form in $x_1, \ldots, x_{n-1}$. Empty sums in (22) are defined to be zero. From (20) and (21)

$$V_0(\mathbf{x}) = \frac{1}{2}\sum_{1}^{n-1}\sum_{1}^{n-1} b_{ij}x_i x_j \tag{23}$$

where

$$b_{ij} = (-1)^{\nu}\sum_{k=1}^{\nu} (-1)^k c_k c_{i+j+1-k}, \quad (i, j = 1, \ldots, n-1) \tag{24}$$

Here $\nu = \min(i, j)$ and $c_k \equiv 0$ if $k < 1$ or $k > n$. These equations are valid provided the c_i are normalized by setting $c_1 = q_1^{1/2}$.

Now let the c_i satisfy (16) for $(n-1)$-eigenvalues λ_μ. From (14) and (16)

$$\sum_{k=1}^{n} q_k\lambda_\mu^{k-1}(-\lambda_\mu)^{k-1} = 0 = \left(\sum_{k=1}^{n} c_k\lambda_\mu^{k-1}\right)\left(\sum_{j=1}^{n} c_j(-\lambda_\mu)^{j-1}\right) \tag{25}$$

We restrict attention to those sets $\{\lambda_\mu\}$ such that $\lambda_{\mu'} \neq \pm\lambda_\mu$ if $\mu' \neq \mu$. That is, the set $\{\lambda_\mu\}$ contains one and only one member of each pair $(\lambda_m, -\lambda_m)$, $m = 1, \ldots, n-1$. Then the $(n-1)$th degree polynomials (in λ^2) on each side of (25) have all their zeros in common and so are identical within a constant factor $\rho \neq 0$. Since equations (16) are homogeneous in the c_i we may assume $\rho = 1$. Then

$$\sum_{1}^{n} q_k\lambda^{k-1}(-\lambda)^{k-1} \equiv \left(\sum_{1}^{n} c_k\lambda^{k-1}\right)\left(\sum_{1}^{n} c_j(-\lambda)^{j-1}\right).$$

Equating coefficients of λ^2, there results

$$q_k = c_k^2 + 2\sum_{j=1}^{k-1} (-1)^{k+j}c_j c_{2k-j}, \quad k = 1, \ldots, n \tag{26}$$

Combining (22) and (26), there follows

$$\langle \mathbf{x}, \mathbf{Q}\mathbf{x}\rangle = \sum_{1}^{n} q_k x_k^2 = \langle \mathbf{c}, \mathbf{x}\rangle^2 - 2dV_0/dt \tag{27}$$

Assume finally that any complex λ_μ in the set $\{\lambda_\mu\}$ occurs in conjugate pairs; then the c_i are real. By (27) and the fact that $\langle \mathbf{c}, \boldsymbol{\delta}(t)\rangle = 0$

$$\int_0^{\tau} [\langle \boldsymbol{\xi}(t), \mathbf{Q}\boldsymbol{\xi}(t)\rangle - \langle \boldsymbol{\delta}(t), \mathbf{Q}\boldsymbol{\delta}(t)\rangle]dt$$
$$= \int_0^{\tau} [\langle \mathbf{c}, \boldsymbol{\xi}(t)\rangle^2 - 2dV_0(\boldsymbol{\xi}(t))/dt + 2dV_0(\boldsymbol{\delta}(t))/dt]dt$$
$$= \int_0^{\tau} \langle \mathbf{c}, \boldsymbol{\xi}(t)\rangle^2 dt$$
$$\geq 0$$

Equality holds only if $\langle \mathbf{c}, \boldsymbol{\xi}(t)\rangle = 0$, $0 \leq t \leq \tau$; it is easily seen from the definition of $\boldsymbol{\xi}$ and $\boldsymbol{\delta}$ that the last equation implies $\boldsymbol{\xi} = \boldsymbol{\delta}$.

6 Field of Terminal Subarcs

Consider the family of singular subarcs defined by the $(n-1)$-eigenvalues λ_m with Re $\lambda_m < 0$. Suppose for a moment that the restriction $|u(t)| \leq 1$ is absent. If $\mathbf{x}_0$ is any state on the hyperplane (15) defined by the λ_m and if u^* is defined by (17), then (27) yields

$$J[u^*] = V_0(\mathbf{x}_0) - V_0(\mathbf{x}(T)) \tag{28}$$

Since $\mathbf{x}(t) \to 0$ as $t \to \infty$, the terminal condition (4) is satisfied in the limit $T \to \infty$. As shown in Section 5, the control u^* is optimal; from (28) the functional $J[u] - V_0(\mathbf{x}_0)$ attains for $u = u^*$ its minimum value zero.

To introduce the restriction $|u(t)| \leq 1$, let R be the set of states $\mathbf{x}_0$ such that (i) $\langle \mathbf{c}, \mathbf{x}_0\rangle = 0$ and (ii) if $\mathbf{x}(0) = \mathbf{x}_0$ then

$$|u^*(t)| = |\langle \boldsymbol{\gamma}, \mathbf{x}(t)\rangle| \leq 1, \quad t \geq 0 \tag{29}$$

It is clear that if $\mathbf{x}(0)$ is in R then $\mathbf{x}(t)$ is in R for all $t \geq 0$; evidently (Appendix 2) R is an $(n-1)$-dimensional convex subset of the strip $\langle \mathbf{c}, \mathbf{x}\rangle = 0$, $|\langle \boldsymbol{\gamma}, \mathbf{x}\rangle| \leq 1$. By the foregoing argument, all singular subarcs $\mathbf{x} = \mathbf{x}(t)$ with $\mathbf{x}(0)$ in R are optimal; on these arcs the control u^* given by (17) satisfies (5); and for $\mathbf{x}$ in R

$$J[u^*] = V_0(\mathbf{x}) \tag{30}$$

where V_0 is defined by (23).

From (12), (24), and (26) it can be verified that, for $\mathbf{x}$ in R,

$$p_i = -\partial V_0(x_1, \ldots, x_{n-1})/\partial x_i = -\sum_{j=1}^{n-1} b_{ij}x_j, \quad i = 1, \ldots, n-1 \tag{31a}$$ [8]

and by the definition of R

$$p_n = 0 \tag{31b}$$ [8]

7 Construction of Local Field Containing *R*

To imbed the optimal subarcs covering R in a field,[9] we integrate the canonical equations (11), (12) in reversed time. Let $\mathbf{x}_0$ be a state in R and put $\tau = -t$, $\mathbf{x} = \mathbf{x}(\tau)$, $\mathbf{x}(0) = \mathbf{x}_0$. Let $\mathbf{B}$ be the $(n \times n)$-matrix with elements b_{ij} given by (24), where we define $b_{in} = b_{nj} = 0$. From (31) $\mathbf{p}(0) = -\mathbf{B}\mathbf{x}_0$; from (11), (12)

$$\mathbf{x}(\tau) = e^{-\tau\mathbf{A}}\mathbf{x}_0 + \int_0^{\tau} e^{-(\tau-s)\mathbf{A}}\mathbf{f}u(s)ds, \quad \tau \geq 0 \tag{32}$$

$$\phi(\tau) \equiv -p_n(\tau) = \langle \mathbf{B}e^{\tau\mathbf{A}}\mathbf{f}, \mathbf{x}_0\rangle + \int_0^{\tau} \langle \mathbf{Q}e^{(\tau-s)\mathbf{A}}\mathbf{f}, \mathbf{x}(s)\rangle ds, \quad \tau \geq 0 \tag{33}$$

On a *proper* (i.e., nonsingular) arc, (10) yields

$$u^*(\tau) = -\mathrm{sgn}[\phi(\tau)] \tag{34}$$

except at isolated points where $\phi = 0$.

It will first be shown that, if $|\langle \boldsymbol{\gamma}, \mathbf{x}_0\rangle| < 1$, then (32)–(34) are consistent if $\tau > 0$ is sufficiently small; i.e., proper subarcs can be traced backward from R. We use the identities

[8] If R is regarded as the new terminal manifold, equations (31) are simply the corresponding transversality conditions.

[9] For the terminology see [9].

$$(\mathbf{Q} + \mathbf{BA})\mathbf{f} = c_n \mathbf{c} \quad (35)$$

$$(\mathbf{BA}^2 + \mathbf{QA} - \mathbf{A}^T\mathbf{Q})\mathbf{f} = q_n \boldsymbol{\gamma} \quad (T \text{ denotes transpose}) \quad (36)$$

which can be derived from (16), (18), and (24). From (33), (35), and the fact that $\langle \mathbf{c}, \mathbf{x}_0 \rangle = 0$, there follows

$$\phi(0) = \phi'(0) = 0 \quad (37)$$

At $\tau = 0$, $\phi''(\tau)$ is discontinuous owing to the discontinuity of u^*; from (35) and (36) the one-sided derivatives $\phi''(\pm 0)$ are found to be

$$\begin{aligned} \phi''(-0) &= 0 \\ \phi''(+0) &= q_n(\langle \boldsymbol{\gamma}, \mathbf{x}_0 \rangle - u^*(+0)) \end{aligned} \quad (38)$$

For $\tau > 0$ sufficiently small (34), (37), and (38) yield

$$\begin{aligned} u^*(\tau) &= -\text{sgn}\, \phi''(+0) \\ &= \text{sgn}\,(u^*(+0) - \langle \boldsymbol{\gamma}, \mathbf{x}_0 \rangle) \end{aligned} \quad (39)$$

It is clear that if $|\langle \boldsymbol{\gamma}, \mathbf{x}_0 \rangle| < 1$ then (39) holds for $u^*(\tau) = u^*(+0) = \pm 1$. Let $\mathbf{x} = \mathbf{x}^{\pm}(\tau)$ denote a proper subarc on which $u = \pm 1$. Then (34), (39) show that, on every proper subarc with $|\langle \boldsymbol{\gamma}, \mathbf{x}^{\pm}(0) \rangle| < 1$, the maximum principle (10) is satisfied for all $\tau > 0$ sufficiently small.

On a singular arc, $\langle \mathbf{c}, \dot{\mathbf{x}} \rangle = 0$, or $\langle \mathbf{c}, \mathbf{Ax} + \langle \boldsymbol{\gamma}, \mathbf{x} \rangle \mathbf{f} \rangle = 0$. Hence if $|\langle \boldsymbol{\gamma}, \mathbf{x}_0 \rangle| < 1$ and $\tau > 0$ is small

$$\begin{aligned} \langle \mathbf{c}, \mathbf{x}^{+}(\tau) \rangle &= -\langle \mathbf{c}, \mathbf{Ax}_0 + \mathbf{f} \rangle \tau + o(\tau) \\ &= -(1 - \langle \boldsymbol{\gamma}, \mathbf{x}_0 \rangle)\langle \mathbf{c}, \mathbf{f} \rangle \tau + o(\tau) \\ &= -(1 - \langle \boldsymbol{\gamma}, \mathbf{x}_0 \rangle) q_n^{1/2} \tau + o(\tau) \\ &< 0; \end{aligned} \quad (40a)$$

similarly

$$\langle \mathbf{c}, \mathbf{x}^{-}(\tau) \rangle > 0. \quad (40b)$$

For fixed $\epsilon > 0$, arbitrarily small, let R_ϵ be the set of states $\mathbf{x}_0$ such that (i) $\langle \mathbf{c}, \mathbf{x}_0 \rangle = 0$, and (ii) if $\mathbf{x}(0) = \mathbf{x}_0$ then $|\langle \boldsymbol{\gamma}, \mathbf{x}(t) \rangle| \leqq 1 - \epsilon$ for all $t \geqq 0$.[10] From (40) it follows (Appendix 3) that R_ϵ can be imbedded in a field; namely, if $\langle \mathbf{c}, \mathbf{z}_0 \rangle \lessgtr 0$ and $\mathbf{z}_0$ is sufficiently close to R_ϵ there is a proper subarc $\mathbf{x} = \mathbf{x}^{\pm}(t)$, $\mathbf{x}^{\pm}(0) = \mathbf{z}_0$, with endpoint $\mathbf{z}_1$ in R, along which (34) is true. The trajectory consisting of (i) the proper subarc from $\mathbf{z}_0$ to $\mathbf{z}_1$, and (ii) the singular arc from $\mathbf{z}_1$ to $\mathbf{0}$, is strictly optimal with respect to all admissible arcs from $\mathbf{z}_0$ to $\mathbf{0}$ which lie in the field; this statement follows by standard sufficiency arguments [9], [10], together with the result of Section 5; details are given in Appendix 3.

Existence of an optimal control law $u^* = u^*(\mathbf{x})$ has now been proved for states $\mathbf{x}$ in the local field which contains R_ϵ, in particular for $\mathbf{x}$ sufficiently near $\mathbf{0}$.

Extension of the field by means of (32)–(34) is analogous to the "backward-tracing" procedure which has been used in the time-optimal problem [5]. It is plausible that (32)–(34) define an (n-1)-dimensional *switching surface* in $\mathbf{x}$-space at which $\phi(\tau)$ has (isolated) positive zeros and u^* changes sign; however, a proof of this statement is not available.

Some examples are given in the following sections.

8 Linear Switching

Let the eigenvalues of $\mathbf{A}$ be $\alpha_1, \ldots, \alpha_n$. The result of this section is summarized in the following:

Theorem 1

If (i) *the plant matrix* $\mathbf{A}$ *has* $(n - 1)$*-distinct eigenvalues* α_m *with* Re $\alpha_m < 0$, $m = 1, \ldots, n - 1$; *and* (ii) *the numbers* $q_1, \ldots, q_n$ *are so chosen that*

$$\lambda_m = \alpha_m, \qquad m = 1, \ldots, n - 1 \quad (41)$$

then the optimal control law is

$$\begin{aligned} u^* &= -\text{sgn}[\langle \mathbf{c}, \mathbf{x} \rangle], & \langle \mathbf{c}, \mathbf{x} \rangle \neq 0 \\ &= 0, & \langle \mathbf{c}, \mathbf{x} \rangle = 0 \end{aligned} \quad (42)^{11}$$

If $\alpha_n \leqq 0$, *every state* $\mathbf{x}_0$ *is transferred to the origin by the control* (42); *if* $\alpha_n > 0$, $\mathbf{x}_0$ *is transferred to the origin by* (42) *if and only if*

$$|\langle \mathbf{c}, \mathbf{x}_0 \rangle| < \alpha_n^{-1} c_n \quad (43)$$

A proof is given in Appendix 4.

Linear switching functions of type (42) have been discussed before, notably by Flügge-Lotz [12]. The theorem gives (highly restrictive) conditions under which linear switching is optimal in the sense of (2); under these conditions (1) is equivalent, for control purposes, to a system of first order. It should be noted that $q_i \geqq 0$ cannot always be chosen so that (41) is true; for example, if $n = 3$, (41) can be satisfied only if $|\text{Im}\, \alpha_i| \leqq -\text{Re}\, \alpha_i$, $i = 1,2$.

If $\alpha_n \geqq 0$ the system $\dot{\mathbf{x}} = \mathbf{Ax}$ is unstable if small deviations occur from the plane $\langle \mathbf{c}, \mathbf{x} \rangle = 0$; stabilization is necessary when the control law (42) is instrumented (cf. section 10).

Chang's general result [6] can be written

$$u^* = -\text{sgn}\langle \boldsymbol{\zeta}, \mathbf{x} \rangle$$

where $\boldsymbol{\zeta}$ is a constant n-vector. This result is apparently not correct except in the special case of this section. The principal error in Chang's argument (in the Appendix of [6]) is his assumption that the vector function denoted by $\partial f(\mathbf{x})/\partial \mathbf{x}$, equation (19) of [6], is indeed a gradient; simple examples show that this assumption is false.

9 Singular Control in a Strip

Under the conditions of Theorem 1, $\boldsymbol{\gamma} = \mathbf{0}$ and the set R coincided with the entire plane $\langle \mathbf{c}, \mathbf{x} \rangle = 0$. We now obtain conditions for which $\boldsymbol{\gamma} \neq \mathbf{0}$ and R is the strip defined by $\langle \mathbf{c}, \mathbf{x} \rangle = 0$, $|\langle \boldsymbol{\gamma}, \mathbf{x} \rangle| \leqq 1$; then (1) is equivalent, for control purposes, to a system of second order.

Observe first that the singular arcs are formally tangent to the boundaries $\langle \boldsymbol{\gamma}, \mathbf{x} \rangle = \pm 1$ on the $(n - 3)$-dimensional hyperplanes defined by

$$\begin{aligned} \langle \boldsymbol{\gamma}, \dot{\mathbf{x}} \rangle &= 0 \\ \langle \boldsymbol{\gamma}, \mathbf{x} \rangle &= \pm 1 \\ \langle \mathbf{c}, \mathbf{x} \rangle &= 0 \end{aligned} \quad (44)$$

Let $\mathbf{M}$ be the matrix of coefficients in (44); namely

$$\mathbf{M} = \begin{bmatrix} 0 & \gamma_1 & \gamma_2 & \cdots & \gamma_{n-2} & \gamma_{n-1} \\ \gamma_1 & \gamma_2 & \cdots & \cdots & \gamma_{n-1} & 0 \\ c_1 & c_2 & \cdots & \cdots & c_{n-1} & c_n \end{bmatrix} \quad (45)$$

It is clear that R coincides with the strip only if the rank of $\mathbf{M}$ is less than 3. The case where $\mathbf{M}$ has rank 1 was considered in Theorem 1; we now have

Theorem 2

If (i) *the plant matrix* $\mathbf{A}$ *has* $(n - 2)$*-distinct eigenvalues* α_m *with Re* $\alpha_m < 0$, $m = 1, \ldots, n - 2$; *and* (ii) *the numbers* $q_1, \ldots, q_n$ *are so chosen that*

$$\lambda_m = \alpha_m, \qquad m = 1, \ldots, n - 2 \quad (46)$$

λ_{n-1} *is real and*

$$\lambda_{n-1} \neq \alpha_k, \qquad k = 1, \ldots, n \quad (47)$$

then the matrix $\mathbf{M}$ *has rank 2. All singular subarcs* $\mathbf{x} = \mathbf{x}(t)$, $t \geqq 0$, *such that* $\langle \mathbf{c}, \mathbf{x}(0) \rangle = 0$ *and* $|\langle \boldsymbol{\gamma}, \mathbf{x}(0) \rangle| \leqq 1$, *satisfy the inequality*

$$|\langle \boldsymbol{\gamma}, \mathbf{x}(t) \rangle| \leqq 1, \qquad t \geqq 0 \quad (48)$$

[10] That is, $|\langle \boldsymbol{\gamma}, \mathbf{x} \rangle| \leqq 1 - \epsilon$ on the singular arc starting at $\mathbf{x}_0$. R_ϵ is the set of states $(1 - \epsilon)\mathbf{x}$ with $\mathbf{x}$ in R.

[11] The c_i are normalized by setting $c_1 = +q_1^{1/2}$.

A proof is given in Appendix 5.

If the conditions of Theorem 2 hold, it will be shown that the control law can be expressed as a function only of the variables $\langle \mathbf{c}, \mathbf{x}\rangle$ and $\langle \boldsymbol{\gamma}, \mathbf{x}\rangle$. Let

$$\xi(\tau) = c_n^{-1}\langle \mathbf{c}, \mathbf{x}(\tau)\rangle, \qquad \eta(\tau) = \langle \boldsymbol{\gamma}, \mathbf{x}(\tau)\rangle \tag{49}$$

where $0 \leqq \tau = -t$ and $\mathbf{x}(0)$ is a state in R.

Denote the positive zeros (if any) of $\phi(\tau)$ by τ_k, $k = 1, 2, \ldots$, where $\tau_k < \tau_{k+1}$, and define $\tau_0 = 0$. In the interval $\tau_k < \tau < \tau_{k+1}$, $u^*(\tau) = -\text{sgn}\, \phi(\tau) = (-1)^k u^*(+0)$, $k = 0, 1, \ldots$.

Theorem 3

If the conditions of Theorem 2 hold, then (i) $\phi(\tau)$ *is given by*

$$(D^2 - \alpha^2_{n-1})(D^2 - \alpha_n^2)\phi(\tau) = -q_n\lambda_{n-1}^2 \text{ sgn } [\phi(\tau)] \tag{50}$$

$$\tau_k < \tau < \tau_{k+1}, \qquad k = 0, 1, 2, \ldots$$

$$(D = d/d\tau)$$

At $\tau = 0$

$$\phi(0) = \phi'(0) = 0$$

$$\phi''(+0) = q_n(\eta_0 - u^*(+0)) \tag{51}$$

$$\phi'''(+0) = -q_n\lambda_{n-1}\eta_0$$

At $\tau = \tau_k$, $k = 1, 2, \ldots$

$$\phi^{(r)}(\tau_k + 0) - \phi^{(r)}(\tau_k - 0) = 0, \qquad r = 0, 1, 3$$

$$\phi''(\tau_k + 0) - \phi''(\tau_k - 0) = 2(-1)^{k+1}q_n u^*(+0) \tag{52}$$

(ii) $\xi(\tau)$ *and* $\eta(\tau)$ *are given by*

$$(\lambda_{n-1} - \alpha_{n-1})(\lambda_{n-1} - \alpha_n)\xi(\tau) + \lambda_{n-1}\eta(\tau) + \eta'(\tau) = 0 \tag{53}$$

$$\tau \geqq 0$$

$$(D + \alpha_{n-1})(D + \alpha_n)\eta(\tau) = (\lambda_{n-1} - \alpha_{n-1})(\lambda_{n-1} - \alpha_n)u^*(\tau) \tag{54}$$

$$\tau \geqq 0$$

with initial values $\xi(0) = 0$, $\eta(0) = \eta_0$.

A proof is given in Appendix 6.

It is seen from (50)–(52) that $\phi(\tau)$ is determined for $\tau > 0$ by $u^*(+0)$ and η_0. Equations (53), (54) show that $\eta(\tau)$ and $\xi(\tau)$ are determined by ξ_0, η_0, and $u^*(s)$, $0 < s \leqq \tau$. The control law is therefore a function only of ξ and η and can be studied in the (ξ, η)-plane. In this plane the set R projects onto the segment $\xi = 0$, $|\eta| \leqq 1$.

Equations (50)–(54) hold in particular when $n = 2$. In other words, if for $n = 2$ the control law is $u^* = w(\xi, \eta;\ \alpha_1, \alpha_2, \lambda_1, q_2)$ then for arbitrary n, $u^* = w(\xi, \eta;\ \alpha_{n-1}, \alpha_n, \lambda_{n-1}, q_n)$, whenever the conditions of Theorem 2 are satisfied.

10 Example: Plant With Two Integrations

We shall assume that the conditions of Theorem 2 hold and that $\alpha_{n-1} = \alpha_n = 0$. The problem is then equivalent to the following problem for a system of second order: Minimize

$$\frac{1}{2}\int_0^T (q_1x_1^2 + q_2x_2^2)dt \tag{55}$$

where

$$\dot{x}_1 = x_2, \qquad \dot{x}_2 = u \tag{56}$$

By proper scaling we may take $q_1 = q_2 = 1$; then $\lambda_1 = -1$; $c_1 = c_2 = 1$; $\gamma_1 = 1$.

From (49) $\xi = x_1 + x_2$, $\eta = x_1$; but it is more convenient to express the control law in terms of x_1 and x_2. The set R is the segment, Fig. 1,

$$x_1 + x_2 = 0, \qquad |x_1| \leqq 1 \tag{57}$$

The singular control (17) is

$$u^* = x_1 \tag{58}$$

Under this control the system (56) is unstable; for instrumentation purposes (58) can be replaced by any control such that (56) is stable and (58) holds on R; for example, $u^* = -2x_1 - 3x_2$.

Equation (50) yields

$$\phi^{(4)}(\tau) = -\text{sgn}\, \phi(\tau) \tag{59}$$

Solving (59) with initial values (51)

$$\phi(\tau) = (\tfrac{1}{2}\tau^2 + \tfrac{1}{6}\tau^3)\eta_0 + (\tfrac{1}{24}\tau^4 - \tfrac{1}{2}\tau^2)u^*(+0),$$

$$0 \leqq \tau \leqq \tau_1 \tag{60}$$

and τ_1, the first positive zero of $\phi(\tau)$, is

$$\tau_1 = 2[\eta_0^2 - 3\eta_0 u^*(+0) + 3]^{1/2} - 2\eta_0 u^*(+0) \tag{61}$$

The switching curve is constructed by evaluating x_1, x_2 at the positive zeros of ϕ, for $u^*(+0) = \pm 1$ and $-1 \leqq \eta_0 \leqq 1$. The two segments of the curve which correspond to τ_1 are given by

$$x_1 = \eta_0 + \eta_0\tau_1 + \tfrac{1}{2}u^*(+0)\tau_1^2$$

$$x_2 = -\eta_0 - u^*(+0)\tau_1$$

The curve can be continued beyond these segments on computing further zeros of ϕ by means of (52) and (59).

Some results obtained from an analog computer are shown in Figs. 1–4.

The field of optimal arcs near the origin is shown in Fig. 1. It may be noted that the terminal time T is infinite except for initial states on the two bang-bang arcs which pass through the origin. The "dual-mode" character of optimal control is seen from the typical plot of $u^*(t)$ shown in Fig. 2.

In Fig. 3 the time-optimal switching curve ($x_1 + \frac{1}{2}x_2|x_2| = 0$) is shown for comparison. The performance index (55) was evaluated using both optimal control u^* and time-optimal control u_T^*. The percent increase in J,

$$\Delta = 100(J[u_T^*] - J[u^*])/J[u^*]$$

is shown in Fig. 4 as a function of initial step displacement ($x_2(0) = 0$). Time-optimal control is very nearly optimal for (55) if $x_1(0)$ is large.

If (55) is replaced by

$$\frac{1}{2}\int_0^T x_1^2 dt$$

the singular terminal arc disappears. The solution for that case was derived by Fuller [7], using very special methods. The result is that T is always finite and the switching curve is $x_1 + kx_2|x_2| = 0$ where $k \simeq 0.4446$. Detailed study of the present example (omitted here) shows that the switching curve in Fig. 3 is asymptotic to Fuller's as $|x_1| \to \infty$.

References

1 R. E. Kalman, "Contributions to the Theory of Optimal Control," Boletín de la Sociedad Matemática Mexicana, 1960, pp. 102–119.

2 Ya. Kurtsveil, "Analytical Design of Control Systems," *Automation and Remote Control*, vol. 22, 1961, pp. 593–599.

3 A. M. Letov, "Analytic Controller Design II," *Automation and Remote Control*, vol. 21, 1960, pp. 389–393.

4 Jen-Wei Chang, "A Problem in the Synthesis of Optimum Systems Using Maximum Principle," *Automation and Remote Control*, vol. 22, 1961, pp. 1170–1176.

5 N. N. Krasovskii and A. M. Letov, "On the Theory of Analytical Design of Regulators," *Automation and Remote Control*, vol. 23, 1962, pp. 649–656.

6 Jen-Wei Chang, "Synthesis of Relay Systems From the Minimum Integral Quadratic Deviation," *Automation and Remote Control*, vol. 22, 1961, pp. 1463–1469.

7 A. T. Fuller, "Relay Control Systems Optimized for Various

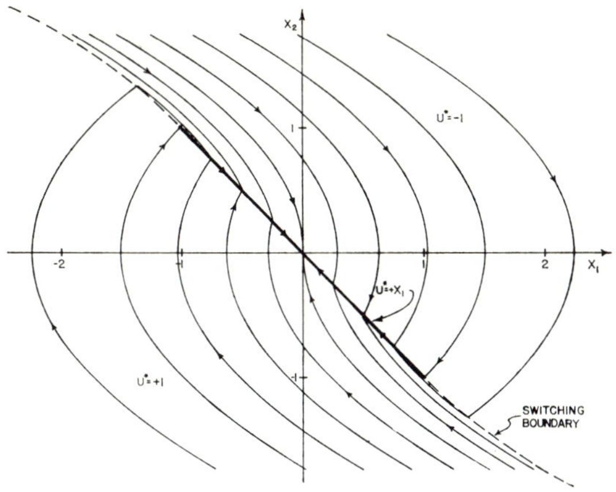

Fig. 1 Field of optimal arcs near x = 0

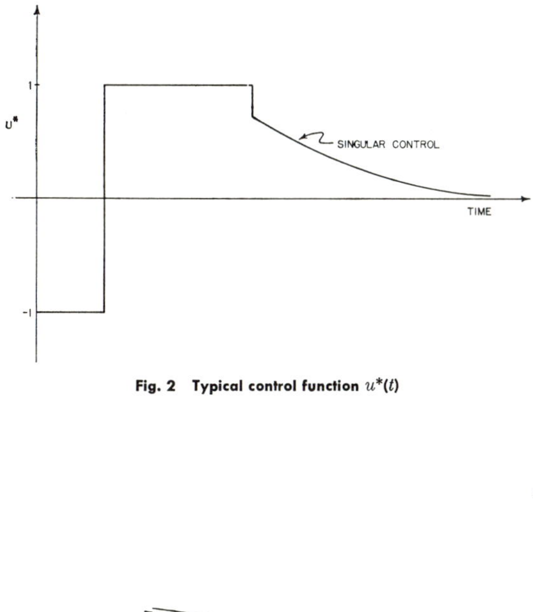

Fig. 2 Typical control function $u^*(t)$

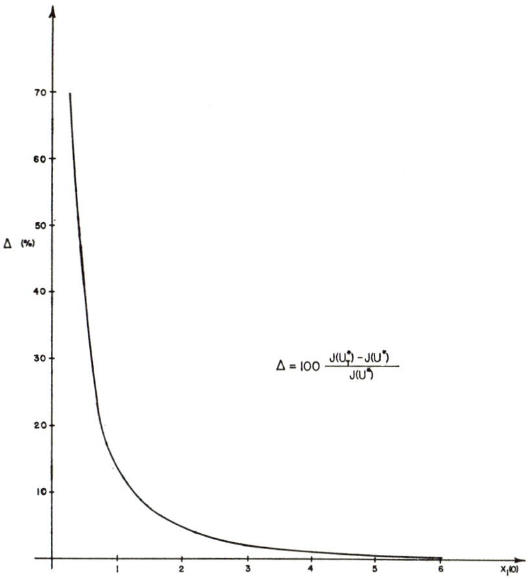

Fig. 4 Comparison of optimal control u^* with time-optimal control u_T^*

Performance Criteria," *Proceedings*, First International Congress IFAC, Butterworths, London, England, 1961, pp. 510–519.

8 L. I. Rozonoer, "Pontriagin's Maximum Principle in the Theory of Optimal Systems," *Automation and Remote Control*, vol. 20, 1959, pp. 1288–1302, 1405–1421, 1517–1532.

9 G. A. Bliss, *Lectures on the Calculus of Variations*, Chicago, Ill., 1961.

10 L. D. Berkovitz, "Variational Methods in Problems of Control and Programming," *Journal of Mathematical Analysis and Applications*, vol. 3, 1961, pp. 145–169.

11 J. P. LaSalle, "The Time Optimal Control Problem Contributions to the Theory of Nonlinear Oscillations," vol. 5, Princeton University Press, Princeton, N. J., 1960, pp. 1–24.

12 I. Flügge-Lotz, *Discontinuous Automatic Control*, Princeton University Press, Princeton, N. J., 1953.

13 C. D. Johnson and J. E. Gibson, "Singular Solutions in Problems of Optimal Control," *Trans. IEEE on Automatic Control*, vol. AC-8, January, 1963, pp. 4–15.

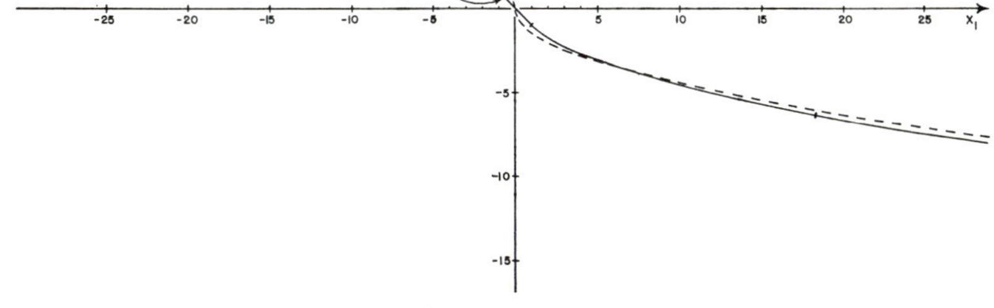

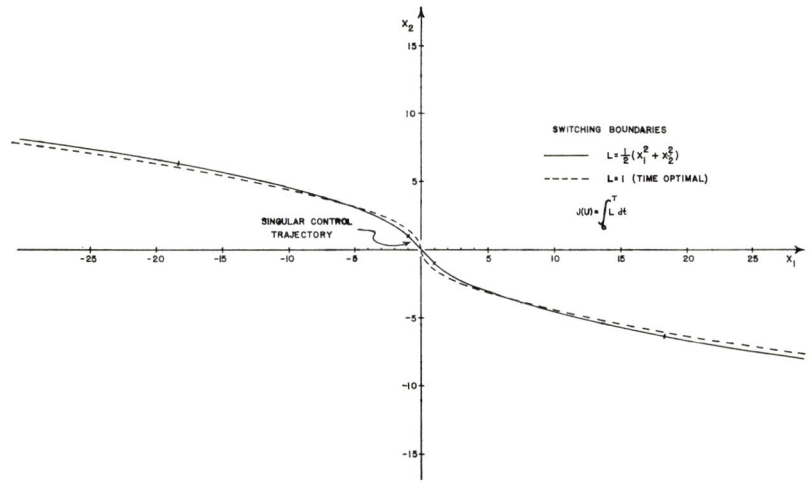

Fig. 3 Optimal switching curves

APPENDIX 1

Note on Controllability

Consider the system (1). It is easily verified that if $\mathbf{A}$, $\mathbf{f}$ have the form (6) then

$$\mathbf{f}, \mathbf{Af}, \ldots, \mathbf{A}^{n-1}\mathbf{f} \tag{62}$$

are linearly independent.

In general, it is known [11] that (62) is a necessary and sufficient condition that, given arbitrary states $\mathbf{x}_0$, $\mathbf{x}_1$, and arbitrary $T > 0$, there exists a control $u(t)$ defined on $[0, T]$ such that if $\mathbf{x}(0) = \mathbf{x}_0$ then $\mathbf{x}(T) = \mathbf{x}_1$. If (62) is true, the system (1) is said to be (completely) *controllable* [11]. Thus all systems of the canonical form (6) are controllable.

It is easy to see that if (1) is controllable and if $\mathbf{K}$ is an arbitrary nonsingular constant matrix, then the system

$$\dot{\mathbf{y}} = \mathbf{K}^{-1}\mathbf{AKy} + \mathbf{K}^{-1}\mathbf{f}u \tag{63}$$

is also controllable.

It will be shown that if (62) is true then there exists a nonsingular matrix $\mathbf{K}$ such that $\mathbf{K}^{-1}\mathbf{AK}$, $\mathbf{K}^{-1}\mathbf{f}$ have the canonical form (6). Let $\mathbf{H}$ be the matrix with column vectors $\mathbf{A}^r\mathbf{f}$:

$$\mathbf{H} = [\mathbf{f}, \mathbf{Af}, \ldots, \mathbf{A}^{n-1}\mathbf{f}] \tag{64}$$

Setting $\mathbf{x} = \mathbf{Hz}$, (1) becomes

$$\dot{\mathbf{z}} = \bar{\mathbf{A}}\mathbf{z} + \bar{\mathbf{f}}u \tag{65}$$

where $\bar{\mathbf{A}} = \mathbf{H}^{-1}\mathbf{AH}$, $\bar{\mathbf{f}} = \mathbf{H}^{-1}\mathbf{f}$. Straightforward calculation shows that

$$\bar{\mathbf{A}} = \begin{bmatrix} 0 & 0 & & & \bar{a}_1 \\ 1 & 0 & & & \cdot \\ 0 & 1 & & & \cdot \\ & & \cdot & & \cdot \\ \cdot & & & & \\ \cdot & & & \cdot & \\ 0 & & & 1 & \bar{a}_n \end{bmatrix}, \quad \bar{\mathbf{f}} = \begin{bmatrix} 1 \\ 0 \\ \cdot \\ \cdot \\ \cdot \\ \\ 0 \end{bmatrix} \tag{66}$$

The elements $\bar{a}_r$ in $\bar{\mathbf{A}}$ are defined by $\bar{a}_r = \langle \mathbf{h}_r, \mathbf{A}^n\mathbf{f}\rangle$, $r = 1, \ldots, n$, where $\mathbf{h}_r$ is the rth row of $\mathbf{H}^{-1}$. Eliminating $z_1, \ldots, z_{n-1}$ from (65) we obtain the following nth order differential equation for z_n:

$$z_n^{(n)} - \sum_{r=1}^{n} \bar{a}_r z_n^{(r-1)} = u \tag{67}$$

Now define $\mathbf{y} = (z_n, \dot{z}_n, \ldots, z_n^{(n-1)})$. Then $\dot{\mathbf{y}} = \mathbf{By} + \mathbf{b}u$, where $\mathbf{B}$, $\mathbf{b}$ have the form (6). The last operation defines a nonsingular matrix $\mathbf{L}$ such that $\mathbf{z} = \mathbf{Ly}$. Set $\mathbf{K} = \mathbf{HL}$; then the transformation $\mathbf{x} = \mathbf{Ky}$ has the required properties.

The foregoing remarks are summarized in the following theorem.

Theorem. *A necessary and sufficient condition that the system* $\dot{\mathbf{x}} = \mathbf{Ax} + \mathbf{f}u$ *be controllable is that there exist a nonsingular matrix* $\mathbf{K}$ *such that* $\mathbf{K}^{-1}\mathbf{AK}$, $\mathbf{K}^{-1}\mathbf{f}$ *have the canonical form* (6). *If* $\mathbf{x} = \mathbf{Ky}$ *then* y_1 *satisfies a differential equation of form* (67).

On setting $\mathbf{x} = \mathbf{Ky}$, $\langle \mathbf{x}, \mathbf{Qx}\rangle$ is transformed to $\langle \mathbf{y}, \mathbf{K}^T\mathbf{QKy}\rangle$. The off-diagonal terms in the latter form can be removed by integrations by parts [cf., (21)].

APPENDIX 2

Properties of R

(i) *R is convex.* On the arcs of the singular family, $\dot{\mathbf{x}} = \mathbf{Sx}$, where $\mathbf{S} = \mathbf{A} + \mathbf{f}\boldsymbol{\gamma}$ and $\mathbf{f}\boldsymbol{\gamma}$ is the matrix with elements $[\mathbf{f}\boldsymbol{\gamma}]_{ij} = f_i\gamma_j$. If $\mathbf{x} \in R$, $\mathbf{y} \in R$, and $0 < \mu < 1$ then

$$|\langle e^{t\mathbf{S}}(\mu\mathbf{x} + (1 - \mu)\mathbf{y}), \boldsymbol{\gamma}\rangle| \leqq \mu|\langle e^{t\mathbf{S}}\mathbf{x}, \boldsymbol{\gamma}\rangle| + (1 - \mu)|\langle e^{t\mathbf{S}}\mathbf{y}, \boldsymbol{\gamma}\rangle| \leqq 1$$

hence $\mu\mathbf{x} + (1 - \mu)\mathbf{y} \in R$.

(ii) *The dimension of R is $(n - 1)$.* Let $\mathbf{x} \in R$ be such that, for some $\epsilon > 0$, $|\langle e^{t\mathbf{S}}\mathbf{x}, \boldsymbol{\gamma}\rangle| \leqq 1 - \epsilon$, $t \geqq 0$ ($\mathbf{x} = 0$ is such a state). If $\mathbf{v}$ is any vector such that $\langle \mathbf{c}, \mathbf{v}\rangle = 0$ then $e^{t\mathbf{S}}\mathbf{v} \to \mathbf{0}$ as $t \to \infty$, and $\langle e^{t\mathbf{S}}\mathbf{v}, \boldsymbol{\gamma}\rangle$ is bounded for $t \geqq 0$. Hence

$$|\langle e^{t\mathbf{S}}(\mathbf{x} + \mu\mathbf{v}), \boldsymbol{\gamma}\rangle| \leqq 1 - \epsilon + |\mu|\,|\langle e^{t\mathbf{S}}\mathbf{v}, \boldsymbol{\gamma}\rangle| \leqq 1$$

if $|\mu|$ is sufficiently small; then $\mathbf{x} + \mu\mathbf{v} \in R$.

APPENDIX 3

(i) *If $\mathbf{z}_0$ is sufficiently near R_ϵ and $\langle \mathbf{c}, \mathbf{z}_0\rangle < 0$ then there is a proper subarc $\mathbf{x} = \mathbf{x}^+(t)$, $0 \leqq t \leqq t_1$, such that $\mathbf{x}^+(0) = \mathbf{z}_0$ and $\mathbf{z}_1 \equiv \mathbf{x}^+(t_1) \in R$.*

Proof. If $\mathbf{y}$ is a state in R_ϵ, then $\langle \mathbf{c}, \mathbf{Ay} + \langle\boldsymbol{\gamma}, \mathbf{y}\rangle\mathbf{f}\rangle = 0$, and $\langle \mathbf{Ay} + \mathbf{f}, \mathbf{c}\rangle = (1 - \langle\boldsymbol{\gamma}, \mathbf{y}\rangle)\, q_n^{1/2} \geqq \epsilon q_n^{1/2} > 0$. Hence for some $\delta > 0$, $||\mathbf{z}_0 - \mathbf{y}|| \leqq \delta$ implies $\langle \mathbf{Az}_0 + \mathbf{f}, \mathbf{c}\rangle = \langle \mathbf{A}(\mathbf{z}_0 - \mathbf{y}), \mathbf{c}\rangle + \langle \mathbf{Ay} + \mathbf{f}, \mathbf{c}\rangle \geqq (\epsilon/2)q_n^{1/2}$. (Here $||\mathbf{z}|| = (\Sigma z_i^2)^{1/2}$.) Define

$$\mathbf{x}^+(t) = e^{t\mathbf{A}}\mathbf{z}_0 + e^{t\mathbf{A}}\int_0^t e^{-s\mathbf{A}}\mathbf{f}\,ds = \mathbf{z}_0 + (\mathbf{Az}_0 + \mathbf{f} + \boldsymbol{\omega}(t))t$$

where $\boldsymbol{\omega}(t) \to \mathbf{0}$ as $t \to 0$. Then for some $\theta > 0$

$$\langle \mathbf{x}^+(t), \mathbf{c}\rangle \geqq -\delta||\mathbf{c}|| + \frac{\epsilon}{2}q_n^{1/2}t + \langle\boldsymbol{\omega}(t), \mathbf{c}\rangle t \geqq -\delta||\mathbf{c}|| + \frac{\epsilon}{4}q_n^{1/2}t \quad \text{if} \quad 0 \leqq t \leqq \theta$$

Since $\boldsymbol{\omega}(t)$ is independent of $\mathbf{z}_0$, θ is independent of δ; thus, if $\delta > 0$ is sufficiently small, we have $\langle \mathbf{x}^+(t_1), \mathbf{c}\rangle = 0$ for some t_1, $0 < t_1 \leqq \theta$. Since $||\mathbf{x}^+(t_1) - \mathbf{y}||$ can be made arbitrarily small by choosing δ sufficiently small, it follows from Appendix 2(ii) that for some $\delta > 0$, $||\mathbf{z}_0 - \mathbf{y}|| < \delta$ implies $\mathbf{x}^+(t_1) \in R$.

A similar proof applies when $\langle \mathbf{c}, \mathbf{z}_0\rangle > 0$ and $\mathbf{x} = \mathbf{x}^-(t)$.

(ii) *Optimality of the field arcs.* Let $\mathbf{x}$ be a state in the local field which contains R_ϵ. Then

$$u^* = u^*(\mathbf{x}) = \begin{cases} +1, & \langle \mathbf{c}, \mathbf{x}\rangle < 0 \\ -1, & \langle \mathbf{c}, \mathbf{x}\rangle > 0 \\ \langle\boldsymbol{\gamma}, \mathbf{x}\rangle, & \langle \mathbf{c}, \mathbf{x}\rangle = 0 \end{cases} \tag{68}$$

Let

$$V(\mathbf{x}) = J[u^*], \qquad \mathbf{x}(0) = \mathbf{x} \tag{69}$$

To each state $\mathbf{x}$ in the field there is associated, by (31)–(34), a unique vector $\mathbf{p} = \mathbf{p}(\mathbf{x})$, continuous in $\mathbf{x}$. Moreover ([3, 4]), $\mathbf{p}(\mathbf{x}) = -\nabla V(\mathbf{x})$ and V satisfies the Hamilton-Jacobi equation

$$H(\mathbf{x}, -\nabla V(\mathbf{x}), u^*(\mathbf{x})) = 0 \tag{70}$$

Let

$$\boldsymbol{\xi} = \boldsymbol{\xi}(t) = (\xi_1(t), \ldots, \xi_1^{(n-1)}(t))$$

be a solution of

$$\dot{\mathbf{x}} = \mathbf{Ax} + \mathbf{f}u \quad (0 \leqq t \leqq T, \quad |u(t)| \leqq 1)$$

such that $\boldsymbol{\xi}(T) = \mathbf{0}$ and $\boldsymbol{\xi}(t)$ is a state in the field for each t. It can be shown ([3, 4]) that (70) implies

$$J[u] \equiv \int_0^T \langle\boldsymbol{\xi}(t), \mathbf{Q}\boldsymbol{\xi}(t)\rangle dt = V(\mathbf{x}_0) + \int_0^T [H(\boldsymbol{\xi}, \mathbf{p}(\boldsymbol{\xi}), u^*(\boldsymbol{\xi})) - H(\boldsymbol{\xi}, \mathbf{p}(\boldsymbol{\xi}), u(t))]dt \tag{71}$$

where $\mathbf{x}_0 = \boldsymbol{\xi}(0)$.

Suppose first that $\langle \mathbf{c}, \boldsymbol{\xi}(t)\rangle \neq 0$, $0 \leqq t < T$. Then $J[u] > V(\mathbf{x}_0)$ unless $u(t) = u^*(\boldsymbol{\xi}(t))$.

Now suppose $\langle \mathbf{c}, \boldsymbol{\xi}(t)\rangle \neq 0$, $0 \leqq t < T_1$, and $\mathbf{x}_1 = \boldsymbol{\xi}(T_1) \in R$ for some T_1, $0 < T_1 < T$. Then

$$J[u] = V(\mathbf{x}_0) - V(\mathbf{x}_1) + \int_0^{T_1} [H(\boldsymbol{\xi}, \mathbf{p}, u^*) - H(\boldsymbol{\xi}, \mathbf{p}, u)]dt + \int_{T_1}^{T} \langle \boldsymbol{\xi}, \mathbf{Q}\boldsymbol{\xi}\rangle dt$$

By (19)

$$\int_{T_1}^{T} \langle \boldsymbol{\xi}, \mathbf{Q}\boldsymbol{\xi}\rangle dt \geqq V(\mathbf{x}_1)$$

with equality only when $u = u^*$. Hence $J[u] > V(\mathbf{x}_0)$ unless $u(t) = u^*(\boldsymbol{\xi}(t))$.

APPENDIX 4

Proof of Theorem 1

Equation (41) implies that the (unique) solution of (18) is $\gamma_1 = \ldots = \gamma_{n-1} = 0$, and therefore $u^* = 0$ for all states $\mathbf{x}$ on the plane $\langle \mathbf{c}, \mathbf{x}\rangle = 0$. It will be verified that the function $\phi(\tau)$ given by (32)–(34) is not zero for any positive value of τ. From (12) and the definition $\phi(\tau) = -p_n(\tau)$ there follows

$$\left(D^n - \sum_1^n a_k D^{k-1}\right)\phi(\tau) = \left(\sum_1^n q_k(-D)^{k-1}D^{k-1}\right)x_1(\tau) \quad (72)$$

where $D = d/d\tau$. By (14) and (41), (72) can be written

$$(D - \alpha_n)\prod_1^{n-1}(D - \lambda_k)\phi(\tau) = (-1)^{n-1}q_n \prod_1^{n-1}(D^2 - \lambda_k^2)x_1(\tau) \quad (73)$$

where α_n is the nth eigenvalue of $\mathbf{A}$. Multiplying (73) by

$$\prod_1^{n-1}(D - \lambda_k)^{-1}$$

we obtain

$$(D - \alpha_n)\phi(\tau) = (-1)^{n-1}q_n \prod_1^{n-1}(D + \lambda_k)x_1(\tau) + \sum_1^{n-1}\theta_k e^{\lambda_k \tau} \quad (74)$$

where the θ_k are constants. Equation (74) holds for all values of τ; but if $\tau < 0$ (i.e., on a singular arc)

$$\phi(\tau) \equiv 0, \qquad \prod_1^{n-1}(D + \lambda_k)x_1(\tau) \equiv 0$$

and so $\theta_1 = \ldots = \theta_{n-1} = 0$. Multiplying (74) by $D + \alpha_n$ we obtain, for $\tau > 0$ sufficiently small

$$(D^2 - \alpha_n^2)\phi(\tau) = -q_n \prod_1^{n}(-D - \alpha_n)x_1(\tau) = -q_n u^*(+0) \quad (75)$$

Solving (75) with initial values (37)

$$\phi(\tau) = -q_n\alpha_n^{-2}u^*(+0)(\cosh \alpha_n\tau - 1) \quad (76)$$

hence $\phi(\tau) \neq 0$ for all $\tau > 0$.

To prove the last statement of the theorem let

$$\xi(t) = c_n^{-1}\langle \mathbf{c}, \mathbf{x}(t)\rangle$$

then (41) implies that, on a proper subarc

$$d\xi/dt - \alpha_n\xi = u(t)$$

Suppose $\xi_0 < 0$: (42) yields $u^* = +1$; then

$$\xi(t) = (\xi_0 + \alpha_n^{-1})e^{\alpha_n t} - \alpha_n^{-1}$$

If $\alpha_n > 0$, $\xi(t) = 0$ for some $t > 0$ if and only if $\xi_0 > -\alpha_n^{-1}$. If $\alpha_n \leqq 0$ we always have $\xi(t) = 0$ for some $t > 0$.

APPENDIX 5

Proof of Theorem 2

We shall find numbers (π, ρ, σ) nonzero and unique (within proportionality), such that

$$\pi\mathbf{c} + \rho\begin{bmatrix}\boldsymbol{\gamma}\\ 0\end{bmatrix} + \sigma\begin{bmatrix}0\\ \hat{\boldsymbol{\gamma}}\end{bmatrix} = \mathbf{0} \quad (77)$$

where $\hat{\boldsymbol{\gamma}} = (\gamma_1, \ldots, \gamma_{n-1})$. We start by proving that $\gamma_1 \neq 0$, $\gamma_{n-1} \neq 0$. The characteristic polynomial of $\mathbf{A}$ is

$$|\lambda\mathbf{I} - \mathbf{A}| = (\lambda - \lambda_1)\ldots(\lambda - \lambda_{n-2})(\lambda - \alpha_{n-1})(\lambda - \alpha_n) \quad (78)$$

and (18), (46), and (78) imply

$$\sum_1^{n-1}\gamma_k\lambda^{k-1} = \gamma_{n-1}(\lambda - \lambda_1)\ldots(\lambda - \lambda_{n-2}) \quad (79)$$

From (18), (47), and (79)

$$\sum_1^{n-1}\gamma_k\lambda_{n-1}^{k-1} = \gamma_{n-1}(\lambda_{n-1} - \lambda_1)\ldots(\lambda_{n-1} - \lambda_{n-2}) = (\lambda_{n-1} - \lambda_1)\ldots(\lambda_{n-1} - \lambda_{n-2})(\lambda_{n-1} - \alpha_{n-1})(\lambda_{n-1} - \alpha_n) \neq 0$$

Hence

$$\gamma_{n-1} = (\lambda_{n-1} - \alpha_{n-1})(\lambda_{n-1} - \alpha_n) \neq 0$$

and (80)

$$\gamma_1 = (-1)^{n-2}\gamma_{n-1}\lambda_1\lambda_2\ldots\lambda_{n-2} \neq 0$$

We set

$$c_1 = q_1^{1/2} \neq 0, \qquad c_n = q_n^{1/2} \neq 0.$$

Now define

$$\pi = \gamma_1\gamma_{n-1}, \qquad \rho = -\gamma_{n-1}c_1, \qquad \sigma = -\gamma_1 c_n \quad (81)$$

Equation (77) becomes

$$\gamma_1\gamma_{n-1}c_k - \gamma_{n-1}c_1\gamma_k - \gamma_1 c_n\gamma_{k-1} = 0, \qquad k = 1, \ldots, n \quad (82)$$

To verify (82) note first that (16) yields

$$\sum_1^n c_k\lambda^{k-1} = c_n(\lambda - \lambda_1)\ldots(\lambda - \lambda_{n-2})(\lambda - \lambda_{n-1})$$

and so

$$c_1 = (-1)^{n-1}\lambda_1\ldots\lambda_{n-2}\lambda_{n-1}c_n \quad (83)$$

Combining (80) and (83) we have that

$$\gamma_{n-1}c_1 + \gamma_1 c_n\lambda_{n-1} = 0 \quad (84)$$

Thus from (18), (46), and (84)

$$(\gamma_{n-1}c_1 + \gamma_1 c_n\lambda_m)\sum_1^n \gamma_k\lambda_m^{k-1} = 0, \qquad m = 1, \ldots, n - 1 \quad (85)$$

Combining (16) and (85)

$$\gamma_1\gamma_{n-1}\sum_1^n c_k\lambda_m^{k-1} = 0 = \gamma_{n-1}c_1\sum_1^n \gamma_k\lambda_m^{k-1} + \gamma_1 c_n\sum_1^n \gamma_{k-1}\lambda_m^{k-1} \quad (86)$$

$$m = 1, \ldots, n - 1.$$

Here $\gamma_0 = \gamma_n \equiv 0$. Since the λ_m are distinct, the polynomials on either side of (86) are identical (within a constant factor which is seen to be unity). Equation (82) now follows by comparing coefficients of λ_m in (86)

The numbers π, ρ, σ defined by (81) are essentially unique; for (77) implies $\pi = -\rho\gamma_1/c_1 = -\sigma\gamma_{n-1}/c_n$, so that $\pi\rho\sigma \neq 0$; i.e. no two row vectors of M are linearly dependent.

Conditions (i) and (ii) are necessary for the result if $\lambda_1, \ldots, \lambda_{n-1}$ are distinct. If M is of rank 2 then $\gamma \neq 0$. It follows that $\rho\gamma_1 \neq 0$ and therefore (π, ρ, σ) are given by (81). Equation (82) implies (85); and from the assumption that the λ_m are distinct we obtain condition (i) and (46). The latter together with (79), (80) imply that (47) holds, and also that λ_{n-1} is given by (84) and is therefore real.

To prove the second statement of the theorem we observe from (77) and (81) that

$$\gamma_1\gamma_{n-1}\langle \mathbf{c}, \mathbf{x}\rangle - \gamma_{n-1}c_1\langle \boldsymbol{\gamma}, \mathbf{x}\rangle - \gamma_1 c_n\langle \boldsymbol{\gamma}, \dot{\mathbf{x}}\rangle = 0 \tag{87}$$

for all $\mathbf{x}$. If $\langle \mathbf{c}, \mathbf{x}\rangle = 0$ then

$$\langle \boldsymbol{\gamma}, \dot{\mathbf{x}}\rangle = -(\gamma_{n-1}c_1/\gamma_1 c_n)\langle \boldsymbol{\gamma}, \mathbf{x}\rangle \tag{88}$$

Since $\boldsymbol{\gamma}$, $\mathbf{c}$ are linearly independent, the equations $\langle \mathbf{c}, \mathbf{x}\rangle = 0$, $\langle \boldsymbol{\gamma}, \mathbf{x}\rangle = \pm 1$, define two $(n - 2)$-dimensional hyperplanes. Equation (88) shows that the singular arcs are never tangent to these hyperplanes. From (84), (88) and the fact that $\lambda_{n-1} < 0$ we have that $\langle \boldsymbol{\gamma}, \dot{\mathbf{x}}\rangle \lessgtr 0$ according as $\langle \boldsymbol{\gamma}, \mathbf{x}\rangle = \pm 1$. Since the vector $\boldsymbol{\gamma}$ points into (out of) the region $|\langle \boldsymbol{\gamma}, \mathbf{x}\rangle| \leqq 1$ at $\langle \boldsymbol{\gamma}, \mathbf{x}\rangle = -1$ $(+1)$ it follows that the singular arcs are directed into the region $|\langle \boldsymbol{\gamma}, \mathbf{x}\rangle| \leqq 1$ at both boundary planes $\langle \boldsymbol{\gamma}, \mathbf{x}\rangle = \pm 1$.

APPENDIX 6

Proof of Theorem 3

Equation (50) follows from (72) by a computation similar to that used in the proof of Theorem 1. If (46) holds, (72) can be written

$$(D - \alpha_{n-1})(D - \alpha_n)\prod_{1}^{n-2}(D - \lambda_k)\phi(\tau) = (-1)^{n-1}q_n\prod_{1}^{n-1}(D^2 - \lambda_k^2)x_1(\tau) \tag{89}$$

or

$$(D - \alpha_{n-1})(D - \alpha_n)\phi(\tau) = (-1)^{n-1}q_n(D - \lambda_{n-1})\prod_{1}^{n-2}(D + \lambda_k)x_1(\tau) + \sum_{1}^{n-2}\theta_k e^{\lambda_k\tau} \tag{90}$$

If

$$\tau < 0, \qquad \phi(\tau) \equiv 0$$

and

$$\prod_{1}^{n-1}(D + \lambda_k)x_1(\tau) \equiv 0$$

Since $\lambda_k + \lambda_{n-1} \neq 0$, $k = 1, \ldots, n - 2$, there follows $\theta_1 = \ldots = \theta_{n-2} = 0$. Multiplication of (90) by $(D + \alpha_{n-1})(D + \alpha_n)$ yields (50).

The first three initial values (51) were derived in Section 6. A computation from (33), (34), and the definition (24) of $\mathbf{B}$ shows that in general

$$\phi'''(+0) = -q_n\langle \boldsymbol{\gamma}, \dot{\mathbf{x}}(+0)\rangle \tag{91}$$

By (84), (88), and the fact that $\langle \boldsymbol{\gamma}, \dot{\mathbf{x}}\rangle$ is continuous, (91) reduces to (51).

Equation (52) follows from (12) by direct computation.

Equation (54) is obtained immediately from (20), (46), and the general solution for $\mathbf{x}(t)$ on a proper subarc; equation (53) follows at once from (80), (83), and (87).

H. O. LADD, JR.
Space and Information Systems Division,
Raytheon Company,
Bedford, Mass.

BERNARD FRIEDLAND
Aerospace Research Center,
General Precision, Inc.,
Little Falls, N. J.

Minimum Fuel Control of a Second-Order Linear Process With a Constraint on Time-to-Run[1]

The optimal control as a function of the instantaneous state, i.e., the optimal "feedback" or "closed-loop" control, is derived for the controlled second-order linear process with constant coefficients

$$\ddot{x} + 2b\dot{x} + c^2x = u$$

for so-called minimum-fuel or minimum-effort operation (i.e., such that the time integral of the magnitude of the control u is minimized), subject to an amplitude limitation on the control $|u| \leqslant L$. The objective is to force the phase state from an arbitrary instantaneous value $(x, \dot{x})$ to the origin within an arbitrarily prescribed time-to-run T. The solution is obtained for the nonoscillatory cases ($b^2 \geqslant c^2 \geqslant 0$) when L is finite, and for arbitrary real b and c when L is infinite; i.e., when the control is not amplitude-limited. The form of the optimal control is shown to be "bang-off-bang" with the most general initial conditions; i.e., during successive time intervals, u is constant at one limit, identically zero, and constant at the limit of opposite polarity. Explicit expressions for the switching surfaces in state space $(T, x, \dot{x})$ at which u changes value and, hence, of the optimal feedback control $u(T, x, \dot{x})$, are given, both with and without amplitude limitation. Without such ($L = \infty$) the optimal control is impulsive and the areas of the impulses in terms of the current state are obtained by a limiting procedure.

Introduction

It is well established [9][2] that when a linear time-invariant process is to be controlled by a scalar amplitude-limited forcing function so as to minimize the time consumed in forcing the phase state between specified values, the optimum control law which results makes this forcing function "bang-bang." That is, there is a surface in the state-space such that for all states on one side of the surface the maximum effort is applied, and for all states on the other side, the (algebraically) minimum effort is applied. Explicit expressions for these switching surfaces are not available, however, except for the second-order case, for which they have been derived, originally by Bushaw [1].

During the past year, there has been considerable interest in control processes in which the forcing function enters into the performance criterion. In particular, as a result of the practical applicability of the results to aerospace-vehicle attitude control, much effort has been devoted to the problem of minimizing fuel consumption, or to achieving optimum performance in the presence of a constraint on available fuel, here defined as being proportional to the integral of the magnitude of the forcing function over the control interval. An integral of this form closely approximates the actual fuel consumed by a reaction-jet actuating system.

Several studies [2, 3, 4, 5, 8] of control problems in which the total fuel is either constrained or to be minimized, and in which the forcing function is limited in amplitude as well, have been made. In the second-order case with real characteristic roots, these studies show that the optimum control law can be characterized as being bang-off-bang, i.e., the state-space is divided by two surfaces into three regions, R^+, R°, and R^-, such that, for all states lying within R^+ the forcing function is at its maximum level, for all states lying in R° the forcing function is zero and the process is permitted to coast, and for all states in R^- the forcing function is at its (algebraically) minimum value. However, none of these efforts has succeeded in deriving the feedback-control law for an arbitrary instantaneous state and for arbitrary values of the coefficients b and c (including the cases of negative damping) nor has a time-to-run constraint been introduced directly. Nevertheless, it is important to introduce a response-time constraint if it is required to force the phase state to the origin, as here. Otherwise, without said constraint, the minimum fuel solution requires in general infinite response time for the overdamped case ($b^2 \geq c^2 \neq 0$), and does not, strictly speaking, always exist for the inertial cases ($b^2 \geq 0$, $c = 0$). The behavior without a time constraint can then be obtained, if desired, by examining the limiting form of our expressions for $T = \infty$.

The specific contribution of the present paper is, then, to give the optimal control $u(T, x, \dot{x})$ as a function of the instantaneous state $(T, x, \dot{x})$; i.e., the optimal feedback, for the class of processes governed by the second-order differential equation

$$\ddot{x} + 2b\dot{x} + c^2x = u \tag{1}$$

where b and c are real constants, and where u is amplitude-limited, thus

$$|u| \leq L$$

This class comprises, in physical parlance, the oscillatory, damped oscillatory, critically damped, overdamped, damped inertial, and inertial one-dimensional systems. The oscillatory cases ($0 \leq b^2 \leq c^2$) receive a solution in the present paper only when there is no amplitude limit on u ($L = \infty$). The solutions for finite L will appear in a subsequent paper. By optimal is to be understood "with minimum fuel consumption, so as to satisfy the ob-

---

[1] A portion of this investigation was conducted while the authors were with the Applied Science Division, Melpar, Inc., Watertown, Mass.

[2] Numbers in brackets designate References at end of paper.

Contributed by the Automatic Control Division of The American Society of Mechanical Engineers and presented at the Joint Automatic Control Conference, Minneapolis, Minn., June 17–21, 1963. Manuscript received at ASME Headquarters, July 30, 1963.

jective of forcing the phase state from an arbitrary initial value $(x_0, \dot{x}_0)$ to the origin within a prescribed time T." As a by-product of the determination of $u(T, x, \dot{x})$, we obtain certain switching surfaces in state-space across which u changes value discontinuously.

The fuel consumed through time t, $M(t)$, is *defined* by

$$M(t) \equiv \int_0^t |u(s)| ds \tag{2}$$

where the starting time t_0 is set to zero as throughout this paper. Since the maximum principle of Pontriagin, specifically as formulated by Rozonoer [6], will be used, an augmented vector state $\mathbf{q} = (q_0, q_1, q_2, q_3)$ must be introduced by the definitions

$$\begin{aligned} q_0(t) &\equiv T - t \\ q_1(t) &\equiv x(t) \\ q_2(t) &\equiv \dot{x}(t) \\ q_3(t) &\equiv M(t) \end{aligned} \tag{3}$$

It follows from equations (1), (2), and (3) that

$$\begin{aligned} \dot{q}_0 &= -1 \\ \dot{q}_1 &= q_2 \\ \dot{q}_2 &= -c^2 q_1 - 2bq_2 + u \\ \dot{q}_3 &= |u| \end{aligned} \tag{4}$$

where the dot refers, of course, to the time derivative.

In terms of equations (3) and (4) the stated problem can now be cast into the following brief form: Determine the forcing function $u(t)$ such that

$$\begin{aligned} &\text{(i)} && |u(t)| \le L, && t \text{ in } [0, T] \\ &\text{(ii)} && \dot{\mathbf{q}} - \mathbf{f}(\mathbf{q}, u) = \mathbf{0} \\ &\text{(iii)} && q_0(0) = T && q_0(T) = 0 \\ & && q_1(0) = x_0 && q_1(T) = 0 \\ & && q_2(0) = \dot{x}_0 && q_2(T) = 0 \\ & && q_3(0) = 0, && [q_3(T) \text{ not specified}] \\ &\text{(iv)} && q_3(T) = M(T) \text{ is minimum.} \end{aligned} \tag{5}$$

Equations (5.ii) are merely equations (4) in vector form. Equations (5.iii) are the boundary conditions which are given by definition in the case of q_0 and q_3.

General Properties of Solution

The general properties of the optimum control will be determined with the aid of the maximum principle of Pontriagin [6]. We first define the Hamiltonian function for the system; namely

$$H \equiv \mathbf{p}^T \mathbf{f}(\mathbf{q}, u) = \sum_0^3 p_i f_i \tag{6}$$

where $\mathbf{p} = \mathbf{p}(t)$ is a certain real vector time function, called the adjoint, *defined* as the simultaneous solution with $\mathbf{q}(t)$ of the eight canonical equations

$$\begin{aligned} \dot{\mathbf{q}} &= \frac{\partial H}{\partial \mathbf{p}} = \mathbf{f}(\mathbf{q}, u) \\ \dot{\mathbf{p}} &= \frac{\partial H}{\partial \mathbf{q}} = -\frac{\partial \mathbf{f}^T}{\partial \mathbf{q}}(\mathbf{q}, u)\mathbf{p} \end{aligned} \tag{7}$$

This set of eight first-order nonlinear ordinary differential equations requires eight boundary conditions for its unique solution in terms of the eight unknowns $\mathbf{p}(t)$ and $\mathbf{q}(t)$ for any given single-valued function $u(t)$. Equations (5.iii) provide seven of these conditions. It will be shown that we can set $p_3(T) = -1$, and this provides the eighth condition. It remains to specify the optimal $u(t)$ so that not only are equations (5) satisfied but they also provide the optimal (fuel-minimizing) trajectory $\mathbf{x}(t) \equiv [T - t, x(t), \dot{x}(t)]$.

The maximum principle asserts that the necessary conditions[3] for optimality are that $H(\mathbf{p}, \mathbf{q}, u)$ be maximum with respect to u in the allowable set $\Omega = \{u: |u| \le L\}$ and that $\mathbf{p}$ and $\mathbf{q}$ be the solutions of equations (7) [in which the control $u^*(\mathbf{p}, \mathbf{q})$ which maximizes H is substituted for u] for the specified boundary conditions; moreover, this maximum value of H is identically zero. Symbolically, define

$$H^*(\mathbf{p}, \mathbf{q}) \equiv H[\mathbf{p}, \mathbf{q}, u^*(\mathbf{p}, \mathbf{q})] = \max_{u \in \Omega} H(\mathbf{p}, \mathbf{q}, u)$$

where $\mathbf{p}$ and $\mathbf{q}$ are the optimal solutions of equations (7). Then

$$H^*(\mathbf{p}, \mathbf{q}) = 0 > H(\mathbf{p}, \mathbf{q}, u), \qquad u \ne u^*$$

Substituting $f_i = \dot{q}_i$ from equations (4) into equation (6) we get explicitly

$$H(\mathbf{p}, \mathbf{q}, u) = -p_0 + p_1 q_2 - p_2(c^2 q_1 + 2bq_2) + p_2 u + p_3|u| \tag{8}$$

It can be shown (from a simple plot of H versus u) that H is maximum with respect to $u \epsilon \Omega$ for a given $\mathbf{p}$ and $\mathbf{q}$ if

$$\begin{aligned} u &= L\ , && \text{when } p_2 \ge -p_3 \\ &= 0\ , && \text{when } p_3 < p_2 < -p_3 \\ &= -L, && \text{when } p_2 \le p_3 \end{aligned} \tag{9}$$

Note that these conditions upon p_2 and p_3 are contradictory unless p_3 is negative, and it will be seen, equation (10), that $\dot{p}_3 = 0$. It follows that p_3 is a negative constant. Since the maximum value of H is identically zero we can multiply equation (8) by an arbitrary *positive* constant. We choose $-(1/p_3)$ which is equivalent to setting $p_3(T) = -1$, as was claimed could be done in the foregoing.

The fact that the optimum control is discontinuous and either maximum, zero, or minimum, is verified by equations (9) which also give the switching surfaces as $p_2 \pm 1 = 0$ or $|p_2| = 1$ (since $p_3 = -1$) where the adjoint state p_2 is to be expressed in terms of the process state $\mathbf{x} \equiv (T, x, \dot{x})$.

In this problem the adjoint differential equations [the last four of equations (7)] are not coupled to the dynamical equations and are linear in $\mathbf{p}$, permitting an immediate solution of $\mathbf{p}(t)$. Explicitly the adjoint equations are

$$\begin{aligned} \dot{p}_0 &= -\frac{\partial H}{\partial q_0} = 0 \\ \dot{p}_1 &= -\frac{\partial H}{\partial q_1} = c^2 p_2 \\ \dot{p}_2 &= -\frac{\partial H}{\partial q_2} = -p_1 + 2bp_2 \\ \dot{p}_3 &= -\frac{\partial H}{\partial q_3} = 0 \end{aligned} \tag{10}$$

from which we see that p_0 and p_3 are constants and $\mathbf{z} \equiv (p_1, p_2)$ has the well-known solution

$$\mathbf{z}(t) = e^{Zt}\mathbf{z}(0)$$

where the matrix Z is defined by

$$Z \equiv \begin{pmatrix} 0 & c^2 \\ -1 & 2b \end{pmatrix}$$

[3] Rozonoer [6] shows that, for *linear systems*, the control u^* which maximizes H is *both* necessary and sufficient to minimize our variable $q_3(T)$, and moreover, that u^* is unique if it exists.

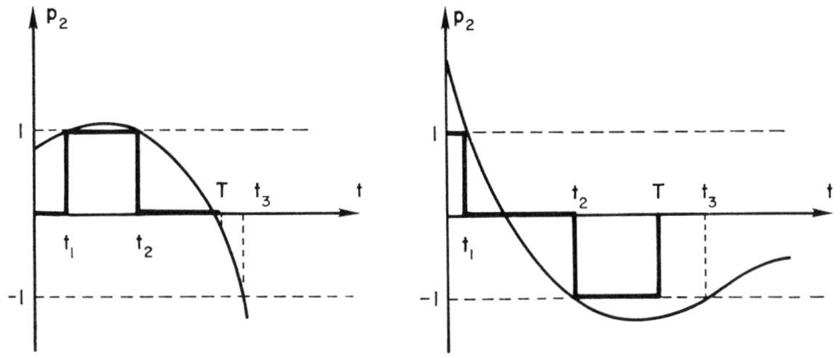

a) POSITIVE OVERDAMPING b) NEGATIVE OVERDAMPING

Fig. 1 Behavior of $p_2(t)$ for most general initial conditions

With no loss of generality we set $c = 1$ (merely renormalizing the unit of time). Since it does not appear in the optimal control law, equations (9), $p_1(t)$ is of no further interest. For p_2 we have explicitly

$$p_2(t) = \frac{1}{2\omega}\left[(\alpha p_{20} - p_{10})e^{\alpha t} + \left(p_{10} - \frac{1}{\alpha}p_{20}\right)e^{(1/\alpha)t}\right] \quad (11)$$

where $\omega \equiv (b^2 - 1)^{1/2}$ and $\alpha \equiv b + \omega$, or, alternatively

$$p_2(t) = e^{bt}\left[\left(\frac{b}{\omega}\sinh \omega t + \cosh \omega t\right)p_{20} - \left(\frac{1}{\omega}\sinh \omega t\right)p_{10}\right] \quad (11a)$$

These expressions are correct for all real values of the damping coefficient b except $|b| = 1$. When $|b| = 1$ (critical damping), a limiting procedure is used to obtain

$$p_2(t) = e^{\nu t}[(1 + \nu t)p_{20} - tp_{10}] \quad (12)$$

where $\nu \equiv \text{sgn } b$. For the damped inertial case ($|b| > c = 0$) we take the limit of equation (11a) for large b to get

$$p_2(t) = e^{2bt}p_{20} - \frac{1}{2b}(e^{2bt} - 1)p_{10} \quad (13)$$

Finally, for the inertial case ($b = c = 0$) a further limiting procedure yields

$$p_2(t) = p_{20} - tp_{10} \quad (14)$$

Examination of equation (11a) with ω real and of equations (12), (13), and (14), shows that there can be at most three times t_1, t_2, and t_3, for which $|p_2(t)| = 1$. However t_3 is never less than T if a solution is to exist at all (see Fig. 1). Consequently, from equations (9), in all of these (nonoscillatory) cases there will be at most two switching times t_1 and t_2 during the interval $[0, T]$ at which the control changes discontinuously. Moreover, with the most general initial values p_{10} and p_{20},[4] the optimal control is bang-off-bang; i.e., during successive time intervals, constant at one limit, at zero, and at the opposite limit. Note that, as must be true physically, the final motion into the origin is always forced, whether with negative, positive, or zero damping. With positive overdamping the origin can be approached arbitrarily close by coasting in a sufficiently large time but never reached in a finite time T.

As mentioned $t_3 \geq T$, if it exists at all. This is because the situation where t_3 arises in negative damping is such that if $t_3 < T$ the final motion is unforced so that the phase state escapes to infinity, while the situation where t_3 arises in positive damping is one where the origin is attained before time $t = T$ and such that if $t_3 < T$, the final motion is forced (necessarily away from the origin).

The appropriate one of equations (11) through (14) provides us with a $p_2(t)$ in terms of p_{20} and p_{10}, which latter must, in turn, be given in terms of the given boundary conditions of the problem equations (5.iii) and $p_3(T) = -1$, before we know the optimal feedback from equations (9). We see that although we have the necessary eight independent boundary conditions needed to solve equations (7) simultaneously they are not all prescribed at the same boundary. We are thus faced with the ubiquitous two-point boundary-value problem of optimum control.

To circumvent this problem, we note that t_1 and t_2 can replace p_{20} and p_{10} as unknown parameters. This is because $p_2(t_1) = \text{sgn } p_{20}$ and $p_2(t_2) = -\text{sgn } p_{20}$ are two independent relations between t_1, t_2, p_{10}, and p_{20}.

Define

$$\mu \equiv \text{sgn } p_{20}$$

Then, from equations (9), for the most general initial conditions defined in the foregoing,

$$\begin{aligned} u(t) &= \mu \quad , \quad 0 \leq t \leq t_1 \\ &= 0 \quad , \quad t_1 < t < t_2 \\ &= -\mu \quad , \quad t_2 \leq t \leq T \end{aligned} \quad (15)$$

where we have set $L = 1$ (which, combined with $c = 1$, results in dimensionless x and t). Substituting u given by equation (15) into equations (4), and integrating from $t = 0$ to $t = T$, making use of the boundary conditions, equations (5.iii), produces the following pair of transcendental equations for t_1 and t_2

$$\begin{aligned} \xi_1 + \xi_2 &= \xi + 1 - \mu y - \mu\nu 2\omega\dot{x} \\ \xi_1^{\epsilon} + \xi_2^{\epsilon} &= \xi^{\epsilon} + 1 - \mu y \end{aligned} \quad (16)$$

where

$$\begin{aligned} \xi_k &\equiv e^{\nu r_+ t_k} \\ \xi &\equiv e^{\nu r_+ T} \\ y &\equiv x + \nu r_- \dot{x} \\ r_+ &\equiv |b| + \omega > 0 \\ r_- &\equiv |b| - \omega > 0 \\ \epsilon &\equiv r_-^2 = r_+^{-2} < 1 (r_+ r_- = 1) \\ \nu &\equiv \text{sgn } b \\ \mu &\equiv \text{sgn } p_{20} \end{aligned}$$

Note that we drop the subscript zero on the starting state $(x_0, \dot{x}_0)$ since it is really any state $(x, \dot{x})$. Also we get the result

[4] These are (i) $|p_{20}| > 1$; (ii) $(p_{10}/p_{20}) > \alpha = b + \omega$; and, when $b < 0$, (iii) $p_2(t^*) = -\text{sgn } p_{20}$ for some $t^* < T$

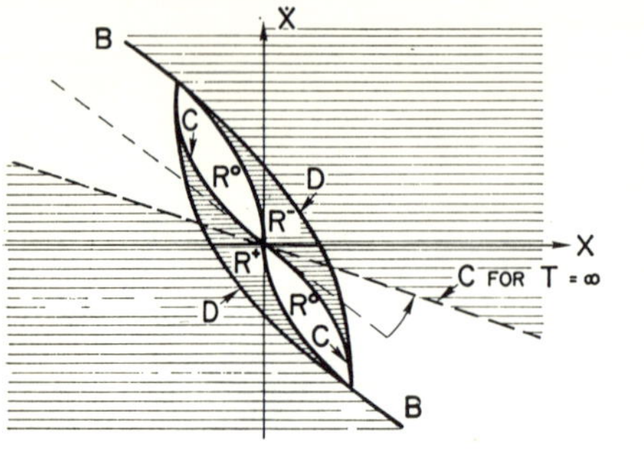

(a) POSITIVE OR ZERO DAMPING

Fig. 2(a) Qualitative behavior of switching surfaces, $L = 1$

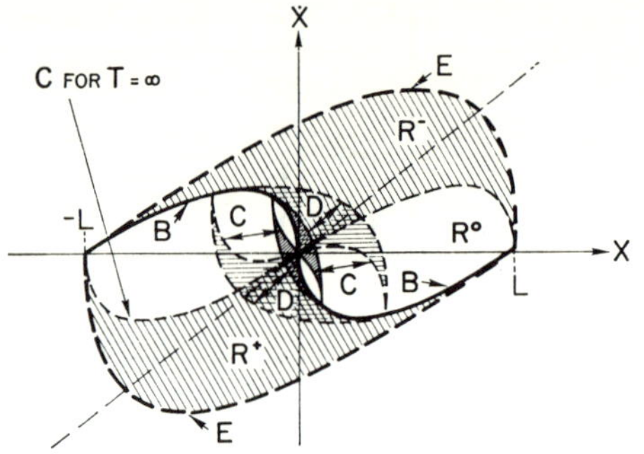

(b) NEGATIVE OVERDAMPING AND CRITICAL DAMPING

Fig. 2(b) Qualitative behavior of switching surfaces, $L = 1$

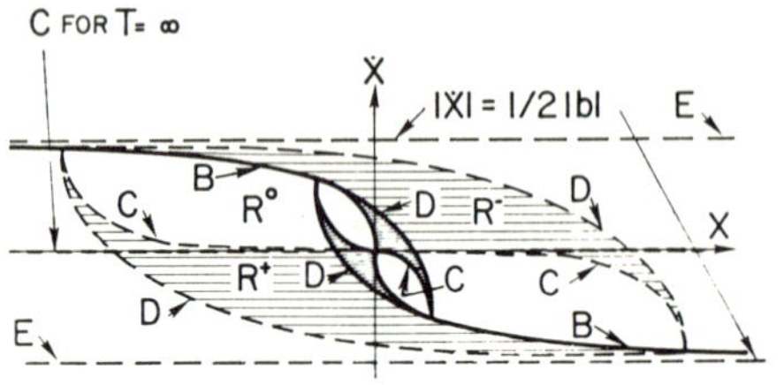

Fig. 2(c) Qualitative behavior of switching surfaces, $L = 1$

$$q_3(T) = M(T) = L[T - (t_2 - t_1)]$$

In the critically damped case ($b^2 = c^2 = 1$, or $b = \nu$) a suitable limiting procedure on equations (16) yields

$$\begin{aligned} \xi_1 + \xi_2 &= \xi + 1 - \mu y \\ t_1\xi_1 + t_2\xi_2 &= T\xi - \mu\dot{x} \end{aligned} \tag{17}$$

where

$$\begin{aligned} \xi_k &\equiv e^{\nu t_k} \\ \xi &\equiv e^{\nu T} \\ y &\equiv x + \nu\dot{x} \end{aligned}$$

In the damped inertial case ($|b| > c = 0$), an independent integration yields

$$\begin{aligned} \xi_1 + \xi_2 &= \xi + 1 - \mu 2b\dot{x} \\ t_1 + t_2 &= T - \mu 2b\left(x + \frac{\dot{x}}{2b}\right) \end{aligned} \tag{18}$$

where

$$\begin{aligned} \xi_k &\triangleq e^{2bt_k} \\ \xi &\triangleq e^{2bT} \end{aligned}$$

Finally, in the inertial case ($b = c = 0$), a limiting procedure on equations (18) yields

$$\begin{aligned} t_1 + t_2 &= T - \mu\dot{x} \\ t_2 - t_1 &= T^2 - \dot{x}^2 + 2\mu\dot{x}T + 4\mu x \end{aligned} \tag{19}$$

Switching and Limiting Surfaces

Equations (16) through (19) are the crucial relations from which analytical expressions for the optimal switching surfaces are derivable in every nonoscillatory case. In fact, if $|b| < 1$ in equations (16), so that r_+ and r_- are complex conjugates, then equations (16) as written yield the surfaces for the oscillatory cases, but only for points $(x, \dot{x})$ within a certain region (within the first "cusp" of the Bushaw minimum-time curve) about the origin. Moreover, the terminal boundary conditions, equations (5.iii), on q_1 and q_2 could have been made quite arbitrary instead of zero so that the solution to the stated problem, equations (5), forces the phase state between arbitrary initial and final values. This has been done, with the result that equations (16) through (19) involve the terminal state $(x_T, \dot{x}_T)$ as well as the initial one $(x_0, \dot{x}_0)$. However, because of the asymmetry of switching surfaces about the origin which results, and for the sake of clarity and simplicity, this generalization will not be presented explicitly in this paper.

It is clear from equations (18) and (19) that t_1 and t_2 can be obtained in these inertial cases as known analytical functions of any initial state $\mathbf{x} = (T, x, \dot{x})$. It follows from the relation that exists between p_{20}, p_{10}, t_1, and t_2 that $p_{20}(\mathbf{x}_0)$ or dropping the subscript zero, $p_2(\mathbf{x})$ can thereby be so obtained, and also $u(\mathbf{x})$ either through equations (9) or (15). Unfortunately, however, equations (16) and (17) are transcendental,[5] so that t_1 and t_2 cannot be given explicitly in terms of $\mathbf{x}$ for these cases, and hence $p_2(\mathbf{x})$ is not available. We circumvent this obstacle by means of the following argument: The requirement that the optimal control assumes the form of equations (9) does not require knowledge of the explicit dependence of p_2 on $\mathbf{x}$, but merely that of the dependence on $\mathbf{x}$ of the equations for the surfaces across which u switches when $|p_2| = 1$.

Having verified the bang-off-bang nature of the optimal control by virtue of the discussion of the nature of $p_2(t)$ in the preceding section, we conclude that there exist two surfaces: $B(\mathbf{x}) = 0$, henceforth called the B-surface, which separates the region R° of unforced motion from the regions R^+ of forced motion, the direction being from unforced to forced motion; and $C(\mathbf{x}) = 0$, henceforth called the C-surface, which separates the same regions when the direction is from forced to unforced motion. In addition, it is physically obvious that there must exist a third surface $D(\mathbf{x}) = 0$, henceforth called the D-surface, enclosing the origin, from outside of which the origin is not attainable within time T. For, it is clear that a phase point $(x, \dot{x})$ sufficiently far from the origin can always be chosen such that, even under continuous power, the origin cannot be attained within a given (i.e., finite) time T, subject to a finite amplitude limit L upon the external force. The intersections of these surfaces with the phase plane $(x, \dot{x})$ at given values of T are shown qualitatively in Fig. 2 for finite L. In this regard, note their behavior for large T. The D-curve (the D-surface's intersection at a given T), with positive or zero damping, Fig. 2(a), expands until in the limit, $T = \infty$, it has receded to infinity, while with negative damping, Figs. 2(b) and 2(c), it expands asymptotically toward a finite limiting curve to be called the E-curve [merely straight lines at $\dot{x} = \pm 1$ for the case of Fig. 2(c)]. This means

[5] Except in equations (16) for certain values of ϵ (namely, $\epsilon = \frac{1}{2}, \frac{1}{3}, \frac{1}{4}$).

Table 1 Expressions for switching and limiting functions, $L = 1$, T finite

	CRITICALLY DAMPED $\lvert b\rvert = c = 1$	OVERDAMPED $\lvert b\rvert > c = 1$	DAMPED INERTIAL $\lvert b\rvert > c = 0$	INERTIAL $b = c = 0$
$B(\underline{x})$	$\mu(1+v\lvert y_v\rvert)\ln(1+v\lvert y_v\rvert)-v\dot{x}$	$\mu v[(1+v\lvert y_v\rvert)^{r_v^2}-(1+v\lvert y_v\rvert)]$ $-v2\omega\dot{x}$	$\mu(e^{4b^2v\lvert y\rvert}-1)$ $-2b\dot{x}$	$x+\frac{1}{2}\dot{x}\lvert\dot{x}\rvert$
$C(\underline{x})$	$\mu[vTe^{vT}-(e^{vT}-v\lvert y_v\rvert)\ln(e^{vT}-v\lvert y_v\rvert)]$ $-v\dot{x}$	$\mu[(\xi_v-v\lvert y_v\rvert)^{r_v^2}-\xi_v^{r_v^2}-v\lvert y_v\rvert)]$ $+2\omega\dot{x}$	$\mu e^{2bT}(1-e^{-4b^2v\lvert y\rvert})$ $-2b\dot{x}$	$x-\frac{\mu}{2}T^2+$ $\frac{\mu}{2}(\dot{x}+\mu T)^2$
$D(\underline{x})$	$vTe^{vT}-$ $(e^{vT}+1-my_v)\ln[\frac{1}{2}(e^{vT}+1-my_v)]$ $-mv\dot{x}$	$v\{\frac{1}{2}(\xi_{-v}^{-1}+1-my_v-m2\omega\dot{x})$ $-[\frac{1}{2}(\xi_v+1-my_v)]^{r_v^2}\}$	$e^{bT}(e^{bT}-2e^{-m2b^2y})$ $+1-m2b\dot{x}$	$m(x+\frac{m}{2}T^2)$ $-\frac{1}{4}(\dot{x}-mT)^2$
DEFENITIONS	$y_v = x+v\dot{x}$ $\mu = v\,\text{sgn}\,y_v,\ y_v \neq 0$ $= 0,\ y_v = 0$ $m = -\text{sgn}\,B,\ B\neq 0$	$y_v = x+vr_{-v}\dot{x}$ $r_v = \lvert b\rvert + v\omega$ $(\omega = \sqrt{b^2-1})$ $\mu = v\,\text{sgn}\,y_v,\ y_v\neq 0$ $=0,\ y_v=0$ $\xi_v = e^{vr_{-v}T}$ $m = -\text{sgn}\,B,\ B\neq 0$	$y = x+\frac{1}{2b}\dot{x}$ $\mu = v\,\text{sgn}\,y,$ $y\neq 0$ $=0,\ y=0$ $m = -\text{sgn}\,B,$ $B\neq 0$	$\mu = -\text{sgn}\,\dot{x},$ $\dot{x}\neq 0$ $=0,\ \dot{x}=0$ $m = -\text{sgn}\,B,$ $B\neq 0$
	$v = \text{sgn}\,b$			

that no matter how much time and fuel are consumed the origin can never be reached from points on or outside this E-curve (the acceleration is precisely zero on the curve).

It is not enough merely to obtain these functions B, C, and D. We must so define them that they are greater than zero always on the same side of their respective surfaces relative to one another, so that a consistent control law, valid for all cases, can be given. This is not a trivial matter and becomes especially difficult when the terminal state is other than the origin. The result for optimum feedback for finite L is

$$
\begin{aligned}
u(\mathbf{x}) &= L = 1 \quad , \quad B \le 0, C \le 0, D \ge 0 \\
&= 0 \quad , \quad BC < 0, D > 0 \\
&= -L = -1 \quad , \quad B \ge 0, C \ge 0, D \ge 0
\end{aligned}
\tag{20}
$$

except for those values of the state $\mathbf{x}$ for which any two of these functions vanish, in which case

$$
\begin{aligned}
u(\mathbf{x}) &= -\text{sgn}\,\dot{x} \quad , \quad \dot{x} \neq 0 \\
&= 0 \quad , \quad \dot{x} = 0
\end{aligned}
\tag{20a}
$$

The *B*-Surface

As mentioned, if the origin is to be attained within a finite time the final portion of every trajectory must be powered. The surface $B(\mathbf{x}) = 0$ has been defined as the locus of states at which unforced motion becomes forced, and this occurs only at the beginning of the final powered portion. Therefore $t_1 = t_2 = 0$ if the instantaneous state is to lie in this surface. Substitution of $t_1 = t_2 = 0$ into equations (16) through (19) thus gives in each case two expressions involving $\mathbf{x} = (T, x, \dot{x})$ one of which can be used to eliminate T, the other then giving $B(x, \dot{x}) = 0$. Thus the surface $B = 0$ is parallel to the T-axis. The curve $B(x, \dot{x}) = 0$ is precisely the switching curve for the bang-bang solution to the time-optimum problem of Bushaw, which is not surprising since the two powered trajectories into the origin are unique, and $B = 0$ by definition coincides with them.

For illustration consider the inertial case of equations (19). With $t_1 = t_2 = 0$, we get

$$
\begin{aligned}
\dot{x} &= \mu T \\
x &= -\mu\tfrac{1}{2}T^2
\end{aligned}
\tag{21}
$$

which is the parametric equation for a parabola. Eliminating T and noting that, since $T > 0$, $\mu = \text{sgn}\,\dot{x}$, we get

$$
B(x, \dot{x}) = x + \tfrac{1}{2}\dot{x}|\dot{x}| = 0 \tag{22}
$$

which is the known expression for Bushaw's switching curve for this case ($b = c = 0$). Recall that the parameter μ in equations (21) was introduced into the integration as the sign of the initial power stroke, and even though the duration of this stroke vanishes when $t_1 = 0$, this definition of μ must be retained. Therefore the sign μ' of the final power stroke must be $\mu' = -\mu = -\text{sgn}\,\dot{x}$ which is, of course, physically correct.

Performing this calculation for the other cases gives the expressions listed in Table 1.

The C-Surface

The surface $C(\mathbf{x}) = 0$ has been defined as the locus of states at which forced motion switches to unforced or coasting motion, and this occurs only at the end of the initial powered period. This surface is thus the locus of all states for which there is no initial power stroke; i.e., $t_1 = 0$. Setting $t_1 = 0$ in equations (16) through (19), thus gives in each case two expressions involving $\mathbf{x} = (T, x, \dot{x})$ and t_2 from which t_2 is eliminated to yield $C(\mathbf{x}) = 0$.

For illustration we again take equations (19). With $t_1 = 0$, we get

Table 2 Expressions for switching and limiting functions, $L = 1$, $T = \infty$

	CRITICALLY DAMPED $\lvert b\rvert = c = 1$	OVERDAMPED $\lvert b\rvert > c = 1$	DAMPED INERTIAL $\lvert b\rvert > c = 0$	INERTIAL $b = c = 0$
$C(\underline{x})$	$y_+ \quad , v = +1$ $\dot{x} + y_- \ln \lvert y_-\rvert \quad , v = -1$	$y_+ \quad , v = +1$ $x - r_-\dot{x} - (\operatorname{sgn} y_-)\lvert y_-\rvert^{r_-^2} , v = -1$	$y_+ \quad , v = +1$ $\dot{x} \quad , v = -1$	$\dot{x}$
$E(\underline{x})$	$-(1 - my_-)\ln\left[\frac{1}{2}(1 - my_-)\right] + m\dot{x}$	$-\frac{1}{2}(1 - my_- - m2\omega\dot{x}) + \left[\frac{1}{2}(1 - my_-)\right]^{r_-^2}$	$1 + m2\lvert b\rvert\dot{x}$	---
REFER TO TABLE 1 FOR DEFINITIONS OF ALL QUANTITIES				

$$t_2 = T - \mu\dot{x} = (T^2 - \dot{x}^2 + 2\mu\dot{x}T + 4\mu x)^{1/2}$$

or

$$C(\mathbf{x}) = x + \mu\tfrac{1}{2}T^2 - \mu\tfrac{1}{2}(T - \mu\dot{x})^2 = 0 \tag{23}$$

where $\mu = -\operatorname{sgn} B(\mathbf{x})$, $B(\mathbf{x})$ being given by equation (22). This follows because μ is the sign of the initial power stroke and B is defined so that when $B \neq 0$ its sign is opposite that of the initial power stroke. The results for the other cases appear in Table 1.

Referring to Fig. 2 we see that the C-surface intersects each branch of the B-surface at the latter's parametric value T, intersects it along the T-axis (the B-surface always intersects the T-axis, also), and remains on that side of the B-surface from which unforced motion proceeds toward the latter.

A curious feature of the C-surface is its behavior for large T. We have already seen, from Figs. 2(b) and 2(c), that the intersection of the D-surface with $T = \infty$ is a certain finite limiting curve, the E-curve, in the case of negative damping. The C-surface also approaches an asymptotic limiting curve at its intersection, in the limit, with $T = \infty$, but it does so for all cases, not just negative damping. In fact, we see from Fig. 2 and Table 2 that $C(\mathbf{x}) = 0$ becomes a definite curve in each case when $T = \infty$. (Comparison with the generating equation for the field of trajectories of the unforced motion,

$$\frac{dq_2}{dq_1} = \frac{d\dot{x}}{dx} = -2b - \frac{x}{\dot{x}}, \quad c \neq 0$$

$$= -2b \quad , c = 0$$

shows that these limiting curves are such trajectories, except for the negatively damped and undamped inertial cases.) This means that given an infinite time to attain the origin one still applies a definite control sequence, even with positive damping, apparently contradicting the assumption in [3] that one does nothing. The answer is that, although it is true with *positive over and critical* damping that no fuel need be expended to asymptotically attain the origin in the actual case of no time constraint ($T = \infty$), nevertheless, as soon as T becomes finite even though very large, our solution applies. In all other cases there is no ambiguity, since the origin will not be attained even asymptotically if nothing is done. With either negative or zero damping in the inertial case, note from Table 2 that the limiting curve is $\dot{x} = 0$, and on this curve motion stops (acceleration is zero), i.e. the phase point rests forever, but a slight overkick will bring it to the origin in a finite time. With negative overdamping, a typical control sequence is as follows when $T = \infty$: In region R^- power with $u = -1$ to the C-limit curve, at which point power is turned off, and along which the phase point then coasts (since it is a coasting trajectory) to $(x, \dot{x}) = (1, 0)$. Here, the acceleration is

$$\ddot{x} = 2|b|\dot{x} - x + u = u - 1$$

Thus, if $u = +1$ is continuously applied, forever, the phase point will rest at $(1, 0)$ forever, while if $u = 0$ or -1 is applied the phase point will escape to infinity. Thus it would seem that this solution is wrong, since it calls for infinite fuel consumption yet never attains the origin, even asymptotically.

The answer again is merely to require T to be finite, even though very large. The optimal sequence will now slightly overcross the C-limit curve before coasting, and the coasting trajectory will reach the B-curve slightly before it reaches the E-curve so that the origin is attained with finite fuel consumption and in a finite time.

The D-Surface

The surface $D(\mathbf{x}) = 0$ has already been introduced as one enclosing the origin from outside of which the origin cannot be reached in the prescribed time, even without an off-power period, and within which the origin can be reached within that time, even with an off-power period. It follows that the D-surface is the locus of states for which the control sequence has no coasting phase, i.e., for $t_2 - t_1 = 0$, so that precisely time T is consumed in reaching the origin while under continuous power. Setting $t_1 = t_2$ in equations (16) through (19) gives in each case two expressions involving $\mathbf{x}$ and t_2 from which t_2 is eliminated to yield $D(\mathbf{x}) = 0$.

For illustration we take equations (19) again with $t_1 = t_2$, to get

$$D(\mathbf{x}) = \mu[(x + \mu\tfrac{1}{2}T^2) - \mu\tfrac{1}{4}(x - \mu T)^2] = 0 \tag{24}$$

where $\mu = -\operatorname{sgn} B(\mathbf{x})$ as before. The expressions for the other cases are in Table 1.

Note that the intersection of the D-surface with the phase plane for a given T, Fig. 2, produces a curve which is identical to the isochrone for that time in the time-optimum problem of Bushaw. This is readily understood, since, by definition, the control law for points *on* the D-surface is just the bang-bang solution of Bushaw, wherein power is applied continuously into the B-surface and thence, with a change of sign, along said curve into the origin.

Furthermore, in the problem converse to ours of minimum time and fixed fuel M, where $M = T$, this same D-surface is an inner boundary within or on which the origin is attained by a control which has no off-power periods.

The E-Curve

In the cases of positive or zero damping the D-curve (the intersection of the D-surface with the phase plane) for a given T expands everywhere to infinity as $T \rightarrow \infty$ while with negative damping this same curve approaches asymptotically a definite limit curve $E(x, \dot{x}) = 0$ for each case as T becomes large, these being identical to the limit curves for the same cases for the unconstrained problem of Bushaw. Physically, the reason for the E-curve is that with negative damping there must always exist a region outside of which the damping force, tending to increase velocity and to drive the phase point to infinity, becomes greater than any finite restoring force due to the amplitude limited control.

Table 3 Expressions for switching functions, $L = \infty$

	OSCILLATORY $b=0, c=1$	DAMPED OSCILLATORY $0<\lvert b\rvert<c=1$	CRITICALLY DAMPED $\lvert b\rvert=c=1$	OVERDAMPED $\lvert b\rvert>c=1$	DAMPED INERTIAL $\lvert b\rvert>c=0$	INERTIAL $b=c=0$
$B(\underline{x})$	$B(\underline{x})=x$ for every case					
$C(\underline{x})$	$\dot{x}+(\cot T)x$	$\dot{x}+(b+\omega\cot\omega T)x$	$\dot{x}+(\frac{1}{T}+v)x$ $=v y_v, T=\infty$	$\dot{x}+(b+\omega\coth\omega T)x$ $=v r_v y_v, T=\infty$	$\dot{x}+\frac{e^{v(T/2)}}{2\sinh(T/2)}x=\dot{x}+\frac{v+1}{2}x,\ T=\infty$	$\dot{x}+\frac{1}{T}x$ $=\dot{x}, T=\infty$
	Here $\omega=\sqrt{1-b^2}$ and $0<T<\frac{\pi}{\omega}$ (no fuel is conserved by waiting longer than $T=\pi/\omega$)					
$D(\underline{x})$	$D(\underline{x})$ does not exist					
REFER TO TABLE I FOR ALL DEFINITIONS						

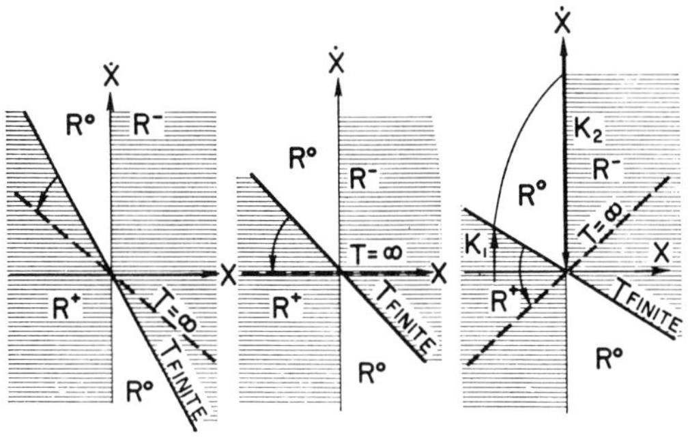

(a) POSITIVE DAMPING (b) ZERO DAMPING OR NEGATIVELY DAMPED INERTIAL (c) NEGATIVELY OVERDAMPED

Fig. 3 Qualitative behavior of switching surfaces, $L = \infty$

Impulsive Control

When the amplitude limitation is absent (i.e., $L = \infty$) inspection of the Hamilton equation (8) shows that the optimal control u is infinite. Therefore, the durations of the powered periods t_1 and $T - t_2$ must go to zero as L increases in such a way that

$$K_1 \equiv \lim_{L\to\infty} Lt_1 \text{ and } K_2 \equiv \lim_{L\to\infty} (T - t_2)$$

remain finite. Otherwise, since K_1 and K_2 are the fuel consumed during, respectively, the initial and final powered strokes, there is no min-fuel solution. It is found that, in fact, this does occur, and consequently the optimal u is impulsive. An impulse is applied initially if in regions $R^{\ddagger}$, transferring the phase state instantaneously to the C-surface which separates $R^{\ddagger}$ from R°. Exactly time T is now consumed in coasting through R° to the B-surface reaching it at the $\dot{x}$-axis so that the position error is zero. A second and final impulse is then applied correcting the residual-velocity error and, of course, consuming zero time. If initially in region R°, there is no initial impulse, and a time $\tau \leq T$ is consumed in coasting to the B-surface, upon reaching which the position error is zero (since it coincides with the $(T, \dot{x})$-plane) and the velocity correction impulse is applied, leaving the process state at $(T - \tau, 0, 0)$. The qualitative aspects of impulsive control are shown in Fig. 3.

Examination of the expressions in Table 1 for the B, C, and D-functions for their limiting forms near the origin of the phase plane, i.e., along the T-axis, yields the corresponding functions for $L = \infty$, since the phase-plane coordinates have been normalized by L^{-1}. We find that, in every case,

$$B(\mathbf{x}) = x$$

$$C(\mathbf{x}) = \dot{x} + (b + \omega \coth \omega T)x \qquad (25)$$

$$D(\mathbf{x}) \text{ does not exist}$$

where the expression for $C(\mathbf{x})$ is valid for all real values of b and c if the appropriate limiting procedures are applied when $b = c$, $c = 0$, and $b = c = 0$. Thus, as mentioned, the solutions for the oscillatory cases are available as well in this impulsive case. The explicit expressions are presented in Table 3. Note that in every case $C(\mathbf{x}) = 0$ is a straight line at a given T of slope $-f(T) = -(b + \omega \coth \omega T)$, and that $B(\mathbf{x}) = 0$ coincides with the $(T, \dot{x})$-plane.

The areas of the initial and final impulses, K_1 and K_2, in terms of the instantaneous state are obtained in each case by a limiting procedure upon equations (16) through (19). In fact, take the limiting forms of these latter equations as $\delta_1 = t_1 \to 0$ and $\delta_2 = T - t_2 \to 0$, and solve simultaneously for $L\,\delta_1$ and $L\delta_2$ to get

$$K_1 = -\mu C(\mathbf{x})$$

$$K_2 = -\mu \frac{\omega e^{-bT}}{\sinh \omega T} x \qquad (26)$$

which yield, since K_1 and K_2 are magnitudes,

$$\mu = -\text{sgn}\, C(\mathbf{x}) = -\text{sgn}\, x \qquad (27)$$

The optimal control law can thus be given as

$$u = \mu K_1 \delta(t) = -C(\mathbf{x})\delta(t), \quad BC \geq 0$$
$$= 0 \quad , \quad BC < 0 \qquad (28)$$

where the B and C-functions are the limiting forms given by equations (25) and, more explicitly, Table 3.

We see that K_2 vanishes if the initial position does, since in this case $u = -\dot{x}\delta(t)$ accomplishes the objective immediately, and K_2 is independent of the initial velocity since the initial impulse always transfers the phase state instantaneously to the C-surface. If in R_0 initially, T in K_2 must be replaced by the actual coasting time τ.

The absence of the D-function in the impulsive control law equation (28) is a reflection of the fact that this law is merely the limiting behavior of the law for $L = 1$, equation (20), very near the T-axis, because the phase-plane coordinates have been normalized by L^{-1} in the latter. Since the D-surface does not intersect the T-axis for $T > 0$, it will not appear in a region arbitrarily close to it.

Since the optimal control without an amplitude is impulsive limitation, it follows that impulsive control is better (consumes less fuel) than any other control. This is readily verified by actually computing the fuel consumed $L(t_1 + T - t_2)$ for those

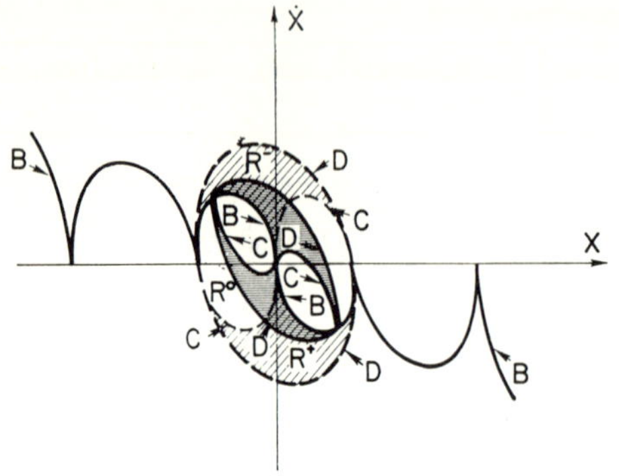

Fig. 4(a) Qualitative behavior of oscillatory solutions, $L = 1$

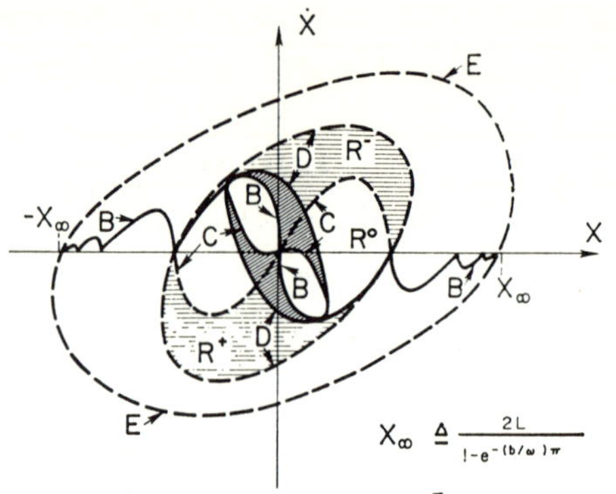

(C) NEGATIVE DAMPING, $-1 < b < 0$, $T \leq \frac{\pi}{\omega}$

Fig. 4(c) Qualitative behavior of oscillatory solutions, $L = 1$

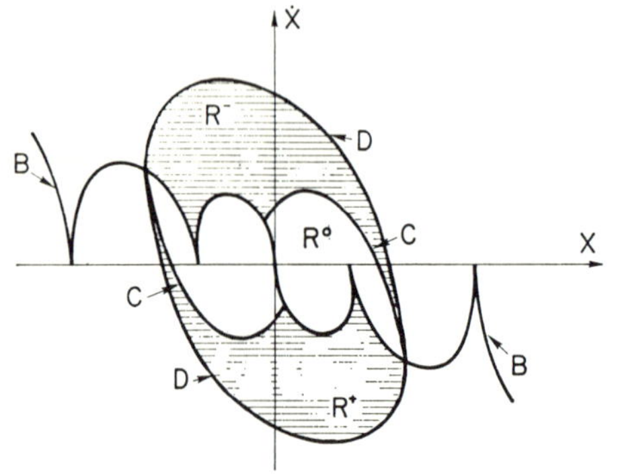

Fig. 4(b) Qualitative behavior of oscillatory solutions, $L = 1$

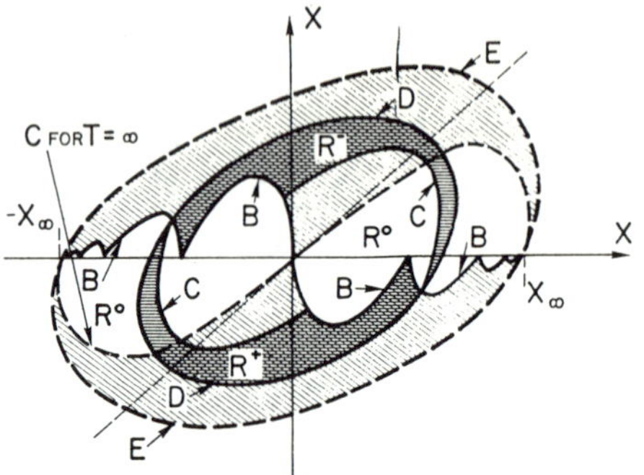

(d) NEGATIVE DAMPING, $-1 < b < 0$, $T > \frac{\pi}{\omega}$

Fig. 4(d) Qualitative behavior of oscillatory solutions, $L = 1$

cases of equations (16) through (19) where t_1 and t_2 are available analytically.

In view of the relative simplicity of the optimal impulsive law, equations (25) and (28), its use in place of the exact expressions in Table 1 might provide a feasible suboptimum control law for finite L, especially when L becomes large; i.e., as the duration of the powered periods become small with respect to the total time T.

Conclusion

The optimal feedback control law for the second-order linear process given by equation (1), has been obtained for the optimality criterion of minimum fuel, the objective being to force the phase state $(x, \dot{x})$ to the origin within a prescribed time, time-to-run T.

The optimal law is given by equations (20) when there is an amplitude limitation on the control, $|u| \leq L = 1$, and by equations (28) when there is none, ($L = \infty$), the optimal control being impulsive in the latter case and bang-off-bang in any case. The explicit dependence upon the state appears through inequality relations between certain functions of the state $B(\mathbf{x})$, $C(\mathbf{x})$, and $D(\mathbf{x})$, which vanish on the several switching and limit surfaces. These functions are given explicitly for the nonoscillatory cases ($b^2 \geq c^2 \geq 0$) when L is finite in Tables 1 and 2, and are given explicitly for all cases when L is infinite in Table 3.

The qualitative nature of the oscillatory solutions appears in Fig. 4. There are in general a number of off-power periods alternating with powered periods of opposite sign in all cases; i.e., with positive negative or zero damping.

The exact number n of switching times which will occur during the remaining course of an optimal trajectory is a complicated function of the instantaneous state $\mathbf{x} = (T, x, \dot{x})$ but is roughly given (within ± 1) by the number of cusps of the B-surface partially or wholly enclosed by the D-surface at that T, Fig. 4. The chief qualitative difference between the nonoscillatory switching surfaces and the oscillatory ones appear only when $T > \pi/\omega$ where $\omega = (1 - b^2)^{1/2}$ is the oscillation frequency. When $T > \pi/\omega$, the C-surface does not intersect the T-axis except at times $T = k\pi/\omega$, so that region $R°$ entirely encloses the T-axis except at these times. This is visible in Fig. 4(b) for positive or zero damping and in Fig. 4(d) for negative damping. There are also limiting expressions for the C and D-surfaces when $T = \infty$ with negative damping just as in the nonoscillatory case, which when graphed are of almost identical appearance. However, the E-curve (D for $T = \infty$) intersects the x-axis at Lx_∞ instead of at L as it does in the nonoscillatory case, where

$$x_\infty = 2(1 - e^{-(b/\omega)\pi})^{-1}$$

The D and B-surfaces are again the isochronic and switching surfaces, respectively, of the time-minimum problem of Bushaw, just as in the other cases.

It should be emphasized that Figs. 2, 3, and 4 show only the intersection of the switching surfaces with the $(x, \dot{x})$-plane at given values of T. Since the C and D-surfaces are not independent of T, if the process starts in R^+, say, when T has one of the values selected in Fig. 2(a), and is powered for a time t_1 until the C-surface is reached, the phase state $(x_1, \dot{x}_1)$ at this time will *not* be the state at which the powered trajectory [projected into the $(x, \dot{x})$-plane] intersects the C-surface in Fig. 2. In fact, as time-to-run T decreases, the C and D-surfaces both shrink and spiral inward, much like the structure of a conch shell, and if the initial state **x** $(T, x, \dot{x})$ lies upon the D-surface there will be no coast phase, by definition, the C-surface being reached only at its common intersection with the D and B-surfaces.

Finally some mention should be made of the problem dual or converse to ours: Minimize the time-to-run with a prescribed amount M of fuel remaining. The Hamiltonian for the dual is identical to equation (8), and so the form of the optimal control is given by equations (9); i.e., is identical to that for our problem. The actual control law involves functions analogous to those of equations (20) including the same B-(Bushaw) function. These functions are obtained, as here, by finding expressions for the switching surfaces between forced and unforced arcs of the trajectory. The D-surface with T replaced by M is no longer a switching surface, but still a boundary, within which M is more than large enough for the Bushaw solution to apply; i.e., continuous power into the origin, and outside of which it will be necessary to coast during some interval (never the initial one) to conserve fuel.

For our problem there is an optimal impulsive control for every point **x**, since the optimal law does not depend on the limiting surface D. In other words, the impulsive control of the origin is always reachable within any real positive time T, from any phase point $(x, \dot{x})$. Physical reasoning argues that this is *not* the case in the dual problem. In fact, as will be shown in a subsequent paper, there is a surface $F(\mathbf{x}) = 0$, where $\mathbf{x} = (M, x, \dot{x})$, enclosing the origin, outside of which the origin is not attainable, even with impulsive control, in the cases of negative and zero damping. This is because the sum of the areas of the two impulses exceeds the available fuel M. Moreover, this surface is obtained by setting $t_1 = 0$ and hence is the analog of the C-surface, not of the D-surface, in our present paper. The off-power region R° reduces to this (outer) curve, and hence the optimal control will always involve an initial power stroke (except for states of measure zero on the curve).

References

1 D. W. Bushaw, *Optimal Discontinuous Forcing Terms*, Contributions to the Theory of Nonlinear Oscillations, S. Lefschetz, editor, vol. 4, Princeton University Press, Princeton, N. J., 1958, pp. 29–52.

2 I. Flügge-Lotz and H. Marbach, "The Optimum Control of Some Attitude Control Systems for Different Performance Criteria," Journal of Basic Engineering, Trans. ASME, Series D, vol. 85, June, 1963, pp. 165–176.

3 M. Athans, "Minimum-Fuel Control of Second-Order Systems With Real Poles," MIT Lincoln Laboratory, Report No. MS-710, Lexington, Mass., October, 1962.

4 G. Boyadjieff, D. Eggleston, M. Jacques, H. Sutabutra, and Y. Takahashi, "Some Applications of the Maximum Principle to Second-Order Systems, Subject to Input Saturation, Minimizing Error, and Effort," to be published in this issue pp. 11–22.

5 L. W. Neustadt, "Minimum Effort Control Systems," *Journal of The Society of Industrial and Applied Mathematics*, series A, vol. 1, 1962, pp. 16–31.

6 L. I. Rozonoer, "L. S. Pontriagin's Maximum Principle in the Theory of Optimum Systems, I, II, III," *Automation and Remote Control*, vol. 20, 1960, pp. 1288–1302; 1405–1421; 1517–1532.

7 B. H. Paiewonsky, *A Study of Time Optimal Control*, Aeronautical Research Associates of Princeton, Inc., ARAP No. 33, Princeton, N. J., July, 1961.

8 M. Athans, "On Optimal Linear Control Systems Which Minimize the Time Integral of the Absolute Value of the Control Function (Minimum-Fuel Control)," MIT Lincoln Laboratory, Report 22G-4, Lexington, Mass., June, 1962.

9 L. W. Neustadt, "Time-Optimal Control Systems With Position and Integral Limits," *Journal of Mathematical Analysis and Applications*, vol. 3, 1961, pp. 406–427.

Solution of an Optimal Control Problem in a Distributed-Parameter System

YOSHIYUKI SAKAWA

***Summary*—This paper treats the problem of optimal control of a typical distributed-parameter system governed by a heat conduction equation. The problem is to minimize the deviation of the temperature distribution from the assigned distribution at a given time.**

Two methods are shown for the solution of the optimal control problem. One is the variational method, and the other consists of reducing the problem to a linear or nonlinear programming problem. Upon use of the variational technique, Fredholm's integral equation of the first kind is derived as a necessary condition for the optimal control. By replacing the minimization of a functional by the minimization of a function of many variables, numerical solutions can be obtained by using the technique of linear or nonlinear programming.

INTRODUCTION

GENERAL AND essential results have been obtained in the theory of optimal processes in lumped-parameter systems, the motion of which is described by a system of ordinary differential equations [1], [2]. Concerning optimal control problems in distributed-parameter systems, Butkovskii and Lerner have initiated fundamental studies [3]–[7]. The processes in such systems are usually described by partial differential equations or integral equations.

Butkovskii has derived a maximum principle for a certain class of distributed-parameter systems describable by a set of nonlinear integral equations [4], [5], [7]. Recently, Wang and Tung gave a general view of the control of distributed-parameter systems [8], [9].

In this paper, a one-dimensional heat conduction system is taken up as a typical distributed-parameter system. It is shown that the solution of the diffusion equation can be obtained by applying the Laplace transform. Two methods are shown for solving the optimal control problem in the distributed-parameter system. One is the variational method, and the other consists of reducing the problem to a linear or nonlinear programming problem. Typical numerical solutions to the problem are also presented.

HEAT CONDUCTION SYSTEM

As a typical distributed-parameter system, a one-dimensional heat conduction system is considered. The process of one-sided heating of metal in a furnace is described by the diffusion equation:

$$\frac{\partial^2 q(x, t)}{\partial x^2} = \frac{\partial q(x, t)}{\partial t}, \tag{1}$$

Manuscript received March 17, 1964; revised July 6, 1964.
The author is with the Dept. of Electrical Engineering, Kyoto University, Kyoto, Japan.

where $q(x, t)$ is the temperature distribution in the metal in dependence on the space coordinate $x(0 \leq x \leq 1)$ and time $t(0 \leq t \leq T)$. The space coordinate x is normalized with respect to the thickness of the metal, and t is normalized so that the coefficient corresponding to the thermal diffusivity in (1) is unity.

The initial and boundary conditions are given by [4]

$$q(x, 0) = 0, \tag{2}$$

$$\left.\frac{\partial q(x, t)}{\partial x}\right|_{x=0} = \alpha\{q(0, t) - v(t)\}, \tag{3}$$

$$\left.\frac{\partial q(x, t)}{\partial x}\right|_{x=1} = 0, \tag{4}$$

where α is the heat transfer coefficient which is assumed to be constant, and $v(t)$ is the temperature of the gas medium. Eq. (3) is the mathematical statement of Newton's law of cooling, *i.e.*, the temperature gradient at the surface $x=0$ is proportional to the temperature difference between the surface $x=0$ and the medium. Eq. (4) shows that the temperature gradient at the other surface $x=1$ is zero.

The temperature $v(t)$ of the medium is controlled by the fuel flow $u(t)$. Namely, the temperature distribution in the metal is controlled through the temperature of the gas medium which is further controlled by the fuel flow. It is assumed that there is the first-order lag from the fuel flow $u(t)$ to the temperature $v(t)$, *i.e.*,

$$\gamma \frac{dv(t)}{dt} + v(t) = u(t), \tag{5}$$

where γ is the time constant of the furnace, and the variable $u(t)$ is normalized properly.

The temperature distribution $q(x, t)$ in the metal is controllable only by means of the fuel flow $u(t)$, which is regarded as the control function of the system. It is necessary to find such a control function $u(t)(0 \leq t \leq T)$ which minimizes the deviation of the temperature distribution from the assigned distribution $q^*(x)$ at a given time T, *i.e.*, the functional

$$I[u(t)] = \int_0^1 \{q^*(x) - q(x, T)\}^2 dx, \tag{6}$$

which is a measure of the deviation, attains a minimum value.

The solution of (1) which satisfies initial and boundary conditions (2), (3), and (4) will be obtained by using the Laplace transform. On applying the transform with respect to t, the partial differential equation is reduced to an ordinary differential equation of variable x. The general solution of the ordinary differential equation is then fitted to the boundary conditions, and the final solution is obtained by the application of the inverse transformation.

Transforming (1), subject to the initial condition (2), yields

$$\frac{\partial^2 Q(x, s)}{\partial x^2} = sQ(x, s), \tag{7}$$

where $Q(x, s) = \mathfrak{L}q(x, t)$. Transforming the boundary conditions (3) and (4) and (5), under the assumption that $v(0) = 0$, yields, respectively,

$$\left.\frac{\partial Q(x, s)}{\partial x}\right|_{x=0} = \alpha\{Q(0, s) - V(s)\}, \tag{8}$$

$$\left.\frac{\partial Q(x, s)}{\partial x}\right|_{x=1} = 0, \tag{9}$$

$$(\gamma s + 1)V(s) = U(s), \tag{10}$$

where $V(s) = \mathfrak{L}v(t)$ and $U(s) = \mathfrak{L}u(t)$.

The general solution of (7) is

$$Q(x, s) = C_1(s) \sinh \sqrt{s}\, x + C_2(s) \cosh \sqrt{s}\, x, \tag{11}$$

where $C_1(s)$ and $C_2(s)$ are arbitrary functions of s. They are determined such that the general solution (11) satisfies the boundary conditions (8) and (9). Thus,

$$\left.\begin{aligned} C_1(s) &= \frac{-\alpha V(s) \sinh \sqrt{s}}{\sqrt{s} \sinh \sqrt{s} + \alpha \cosh \sqrt{s}}, \\ \text{and} \quad C_2(s) &= \frac{\alpha V(s) \cosh \sqrt{s}}{\sqrt{s} \sinh \sqrt{s} + \alpha \cosh \sqrt{s}}, \end{aligned}\right\} \tag{12}$$

are obtained.

Substituting (12) into (11) yields

$$Q(x, s) = V(s) \frac{\alpha \cosh (1 - x)\sqrt{s}}{\sqrt{s} \sinh \sqrt{s} + \alpha \cosh \sqrt{s}}. \tag{13}$$

Since $V(s) = U(s)/(\gamma s + 1)$ from (10),

$$Q(x, s) = U(s) \frac{\cosh (1 - x)\sqrt{s}}{(\gamma s + 1)\left(\dfrac{\sqrt{s}}{\alpha} \sinh \sqrt{s} + \cosh \sqrt{s}\right)}. \tag{14}$$

Defining the following function:

$$G(x, s) = \frac{\cosh (1 - x)\sqrt{s}}{(\gamma s + 1)\left(\dfrac{\sqrt{s}}{\alpha} \sinh \sqrt{s} + \cosh \sqrt{s}\right)}, \tag{15}$$

(14) is written as

$$Q(x, s) = G(x, s)U(s). \tag{16}$$

Eq. (16) shows that the transfer function from the fuel flow $U(s)$ to the temperature distribution $Q(x, s)$ is given by (15).

According to the convolution theorem [10], the inverse transformation of (16) is given by

$$\left.\begin{aligned} q(x, t) &= \int_0^t g(x, \tau)u(t - \tau)d\tau \\ &= \int_0^t g(x, t - \tau)u(\tau)d\tau \end{aligned}\right\}, \tag{17}$$

where $g(x, t) = \mathfrak{L}^{-1}G(x, s)$. Hence, if the function $g(x, t)$ is known, the temperature distribution $q(x, t)$ can be calculated for a given control function $u(t)$.

Defining the following functions:

$$\left.\begin{aligned} M(s) &= (\gamma s + 1)\left(\frac{\sqrt{s}}{\alpha} \sinh \sqrt{s} + \cosh \sqrt{s}\right), \\ N(x, s) &= \cosh (1 - x)\sqrt{s}, \end{aligned}\right\} \tag{18}$$

(15) is written as

$$G(x, s) = \frac{N(x, s)}{M(s)}. \tag{19}$$

It is clear that $N(x, s)$ has no singularities and $M(s)$ has an infinite number of simple zeros at

$$s_0 = -1/\gamma, \qquad s_i = -\beta_i^2 \quad (i = 1, 2, \cdots), \tag{20}$$

where β_i's are the real roots of the transcendental equation:

$$\beta \tan \beta = \alpha. \tag{21}$$

It is easily proved that (21) has no complex roots.

The inverse transform of (19) is given by [10]

$$g(x, t) = \mathfrak{L}^{-1}\frac{N(x, s)}{M(s)} = \sum_{i=0}^{\infty} \frac{N(x, s_i)}{M'(s_i)} e^{s_i t}, \tag{22}$$

where $M'(s_i)$ is the derivative of $M(s)$ at $s = s_i$. By using (18), the function $g(x, t)$ is expressed as

$$g(x, t) = \frac{\kappa^2 \cos \kappa(1 - x)}{\cos \kappa - \dfrac{\kappa}{\alpha} \sin \kappa} e^{-\kappa^2 t} + 2\kappa^2 \sum_{i=1}^{\infty} \frac{\cos (1 - x)\beta_i}{(\kappa^2 - \beta_i^2)\left(\dfrac{1}{\alpha} + \dfrac{1 + \alpha}{\beta_i^2}\right) \cos \beta_i} e^{-\beta_i^2 t}, \tag{23}$$

where $\kappa = 1/\sqrt{\gamma}$.

Necessary Condition for Optimality

In this section, the control function $u(t)$ is assumed to be continuous on the interval $0 \leq t \leq T$. The optimal control problem is stated as follows: Determine the optimal control function $u(t)(0 \leq t \leq T)$, so as to minimize the functional

$$I[u(t)] = \int_0^1 \{q^*(x) - q(x, T)\}^2 dx, \tag{24}$$

where

$$q(x, T) = \int_0^T g(x, T - \tau)u(\tau)d\tau, \tag{25}$$

and $q^*(x)$ is the assigned temperature distribution.

Let $u(t)$ be the optimal control function. Then, the differential of the functional $I[u]$ corresponding to the increment $\delta u(t) = \epsilon\xi(t)$, which is defined by [11]

$$\delta I[u(t), \xi(t)] = \lim_{\epsilon \to 0} \frac{I[u(t) + \epsilon\xi(t)] - I[u(t)]}{\epsilon}, \tag{26}$$

has to vanish, where $\xi(t)$ is an arbitrary continuous function on the interval $0 \leq t \leq T$.

Since

$$I[u(t) + \epsilon\xi(t)] = \int_0^1 \left\{q^*(x) - q(x, T) - \epsilon \int_0^T g(x, T - \tau)\xi(\tau)d\tau\right\}^2 dx, \tag{27}$$

the differential of the functional is evaluated as

$$\delta I[u(t), \xi(t)] = -2\int_0^1 \{q^*(x) - q(x, T)\} \cdot \int_0^T g(x, T - \tau)\xi(\tau)d\tau dx. \tag{28}$$

As the integrand in (28) is continuous on the domain $0 \leq \tau \leq T$, $0 \leq x \leq 1$, the order of integration of (28) can be changed as

$$\delta I[u(t), \xi(t)] = -2\int_0^T \xi(\tau) \int_0^1 \{q^*(x) - q(x, T)\} g(x, T - \tau)dx d\tau. \tag{29}$$

Since $\delta I[u(t), \xi(t)] = 0$ for an arbitrary continuous function $\xi(t)$,

$$\int_0^1 \{q^*(x) - q(x, T)\} g(x, T - \tau)dx = 0, \tag{30}$$

or,

$$\int_0^1 q^*(x)g(x, T - \tau)dx = \int_0^1 g(x, T - \tau) \int_0^T g(x, T - \mu)u(\mu)d\mu dx, \tag{31}$$

must hold in (29).

As the integrand in the right-hand side of (31) is continuous on the domain $0 \leq \mu \leq T$, $0 \leq x \leq 1$, changing the order of the integration once again yields

$$\int_0^1 q^*(x)g(x, T - \tau)dx = \int_0^T u(\mu) \int_0^1 g(x, T - \tau)g(x, T - \mu)dx d\mu. \tag{32}$$

Defining the functions

$$\left.\begin{aligned} \int_0^1 q^*(x)g(x, T - \tau)dx &= f(\tau), \\ \int_0^1 g(x, T - \tau)g(x, T - \mu)dx &= y(\tau, \mu), \end{aligned}\right\} \tag{33}$$

(32) is equivalent to

$$\int_0^T y(\tau, \mu)u(\mu)d\mu = f(\tau) \qquad (0 \leq \tau \leq T). \tag{34}$$

Eq. (34) is Fredholm's integral equation of the first kind, where $y(\tau, \mu)$ is the symmetric kernel due to the definition (33), [12]. Thus, it is concluded that the optimal control function $u(t)$ which is assumed to be continuous, is to satisfy the integral equation (34).

Since the kernel $y(\tau, \mu)$ is symmetric, there exists at least one eigenvalue λ_i which is not zero and satisfies the equation:

$$\phi_i(\tau) = \lambda_i \int_0^T y(\tau, \mu)\phi_i(\mu)d\mu, \tag{35}$$

where $\phi_i(\tau)(0 \leq \tau \leq T)$ is the eigenfunction corresponding to the eigenvalue λ_i. The eigenfunctions ϕ_i's are mutually orthogonal, *i.e.*, if $\phi_i(\tau)$ and $\phi_j(\tau)$ are eigenfunctions corresponding to the eigenvalues λ_i and λ_j, respectively, then

$$\int_0^T \phi_i(\tau)\phi_j(\tau)d\tau = 0, \tag{36}$$

provided that $\lambda_i \neq \lambda_j$ [12].

It has been shown by Picard [11], [12] that the necessary and sufficient condition for the existence of the solution of (34) is that the series

$$\sum_{i=1}^{\infty} \lambda_i^2 c_i^2$$

should be convergent, where

$$c_i = \int_0^T f(\tau)\phi_i(\tau)d\tau. \tag{37}$$

In this case the solution is given by

$$u(\tau) = \sum_{i=1}^{\infty} \lambda_i c_i \phi_i(\tau). \tag{38}$$

In the case where the control function $u(\tau)$ is subject to the constraint of the type $|u(\tau)| \leq 1 (0 \leq \tau \leq T)$, Butkovskii has obtained, by using the maximum principle which he derived, the following integral equation [4], [5], [7]:

$$u(\tau) = \text{sgn}\left\{f(\tau) - \int_0^T y(\tau, \mu)u(\mu)d\mu\right\}. \qquad (39)$$

He has concluded from (39) that the optimal control function $u(\tau)$ must be of bang-bang type [4], [5], [7]. Here note that (34) corresponds to the singular solution [13] of (39). Namely, if (34) holds, the optimal control function can not be determined by (39). Therefore, if a solution of (34) exists and satisfies the constraint $|u(\tau)| \leq 1 (0 \leq \tau \leq T)$, the optimal control function $u(\tau)$ is not of bang-bang type but of continuous type.

Approximate Solution by Using Linear or Nonlinear Programming Technique

Solving the integral equation (34) is not always easy. Moreover, in the case where the control function $u(t)$ is subject to the constraint such as

$$0 \leq u(t) \leq 1 \qquad (0 \leq t \leq T), \qquad (40)$$

it is not guaranteed that the solution of (34) satisfies the constraint (40). In this section, linear or nonlinear programming technique will be used to obtain the approximate solution to the posed problem.

The approximate integration formula using a finite number of values of the integrand is applied to the definite integrals (24) and (25) [14]. It may be Simpson's composite formula or Gaussian integration formula [15]. After applying a numerical integration formula to (24), the approximate performance index $\bar{I}[u]$ is expressed as [15]

$$I[u] \cong \bar{I}[u] = \sum_{i=0}^{n} c_i\{q^*(x_i) - q(x_i, T)\}^2, \qquad (41)$$

where c_i's are the weights assigned to the values of integrand at the points x_i's. The values of x_i's and the weights c_i's are known for each integration formula.

If the Simpson's composite formula is used, the values of x_i's and c_i's are given by [15]

$$\left.\begin{aligned} x_i &= i/n \quad (i = 0, 1, \cdots, n), \\ c_0 &= c_n = 1/3n, \\ c_1 &= c_3 = \cdots = c_{n-1} = 4/3n, \\ c_2 &= c_4 = \cdots = c_{n-2} = 2/3n, \end{aligned}\right\} \qquad (42)$$

where n is an even number. Applying the same integration formula to (25), the approximate value of $q(x_i, T)$ is given by

$$q(x_i, T) \cong \bar{q}(x_i, T) = T \sum_{j=0}^{n} c_j g(x_i, T - \tau_j)u(\tau_j), \qquad (43)$$

where $\tau_j = jT/n$ $(j = 0, 1, \cdots, n)$.

Putting

$$\left.\begin{aligned} Tc_j g(x_i, T - \tau_j) &= a_{ij}, \quad u(\tau_j) = u_j, \\ q^*(x_i) &= q_i^*, \end{aligned}\right\} \qquad (44)$$

and substituting (43) into (41) yields

$$\bar{I}[u] \cong F(u) = \sum_{i=0}^{n} c_i\left(q_i^* - \sum_{j=0}^{n} a_{ij}u_j\right)^2. \qquad (45)$$

The constraint (40) is written as

$$0 \leq u_j \leq 1 \qquad (j = 0, 1, \cdots, n). \qquad (46)$$

Consequently, the minimization problem of the functional (24) is approximately reduced to a minimization of the function (45) of $n+1$ variables u_j's subject to the constraints (46) [14].

Since the performance index (45) is a quadratic function of the variables u_j's and the constraints (46) are linear, the problem becomes a quadratic programming problem [16], [17]. For this problem, an exact solution may be obtained numerically, as in linear programming, in a finite number of iterations of computation. This property is due essentially to the fact that the gradient of the quadratic function $F(u)$ is a linear function of u_j's, and that the constraints are linear.

Although a solution of the quadratic programming problem is obtained in a finite number of iterations of computation, its algorithm is more complicated than that of the simplex method for linear programs. If the performance index is taken as

$$I[u(t)] = \int_0^1 |q^*(x) - q(x, T)|\, dx \qquad (47)$$

instead of (24), the linear programming technique can be used directly. On applying the same procedure as mentioned above, the approximate performance index corresponding to (47) is written as

$$I[u] \cong L(u) = \sum_{i=0}^{n} c_i\left|q_i^* - \sum_{j=0}^{n} a_{ij}u_j\right|. \qquad (48)$$

The problem of minimizing (48) under the constraints (46) can readily be put into a linear programming form by using known techniques [18]. By introducing $2(n+1)$ non-negative auxiliary variables y_i's and z_i's $(i = 0, 1, \cdots, n)$, the minimization of (48) is equivalent to the minimization of

$$L' = \sum_{i=0}^{n} c_i(y_i + z_i), \qquad (49)$$

subject to

$$\left.\begin{aligned} \sum_{j=0}^{n} a_{ij}u_j - q_i^* &= y_i - z_i, \\ y_i \geq 0, \quad z_i &\geq 0. \end{aligned}\right\} \quad (i = 0, 1, \cdots, n) \qquad (50)$$

Here for any u_j's, the minimum value of (49) is attained by setting $z_i = 0$ if

$$\sum_{j=0}^{n} a_{ij}u_j - q_i^*$$

is non-negative and $y_i = 0$ if

$$\sum_{j=0}^{n} a_{ij}u_j - q_i^*$$

is negative. Then, clearly

$$\min L = \min L'. \tag{51}$$

The constraints (46) are written as

$$\left.\begin{array}{l} u_i + w_i = 1, \\ u_i \geq 0, \quad w_i \geq 0. \end{array}\right\} \quad (i = 0, 1, \cdots, n) \tag{52}$$

Thus, the linear programming problem is formulated as follows: Minimize (49) under the constraints (50) and (52). Since $q_i^* \geq 0$ $(i=0, 1, \cdots, n)$, an initial basic feasible solution [17], [19] of the linear program can be taken as

$$\left.\begin{array}{l} u_i = 0, \quad y_i = 0, \quad z_i = q_i^*, \quad w_i = 1 \\ (i = 0, 1, \cdots, n) \end{array}\right\}. \tag{53}$$

Expressing the basic variables z_i's and w_i's in terms of the nonbasic variables u_i's and y_i's yields

$$\left.\begin{array}{l} z_i = q_i^* - \sum_{j=0}^{n} a_{ij}u_j + y_i, \\ w_i = 1 - u_i, \\ (u_i, y_i, z_i, w_i \geq 0). \end{array}\right| \quad (i = 0, 1, \cdots, n) \tag{54}$$

The performance index (49) is expressed, in terms of the nonbasic variables, as

$$L' = \sum_{i=0}^{n} c_i q_i^* - \sum_{j=0}^{n}\left(\sum_{i=0}^{n} c_i a_{ij}\right)u_j + \sum_{i=0}^{n} 2c_i y_i. \tag{55}$$

By using the simplex method [17], [19] and starting with the canonical form (54) and (55), the optimal solution can be reached in a finite number of iterations.

Another way of attaining the reduction to the linear programming problem is to introduce $n+1$ auxiliary variables ξ_i's $(i=0, 1, \cdots, n)$ satisfying the $2(n+1)$ inequalities:

$$\left.\begin{array}{l} \xi_i \geq \sum_{j=0}^{n} a_{ij}u_j - q_i^*, \\ \xi_i \geq -\sum_{j=0}^{n} a_{ij}u_j + q_i^*, \end{array}\right| \quad (i = 0, 1, \cdots, n) \tag{56}$$

which together imply

$$\xi_i \geq \left|\sum_{j=0}^{n} a_{ij}u_j - q_i^*\right|. \tag{57}$$

The performance index in this case is given by

$$L'' = \sum_{i=0}^{n} c_i \xi_i. \tag{58}$$

Clearly the minimum value of (58) is attained when

$$\xi_i = \left|\sum_{j=0}^{n} a_{ij}u_j - q_i^*\right| \quad (i = 0, 1, \cdots, n).$$

Consequently, the minimization of (48) under the constraints (46) is equivalent to the minimization of (58) under the constraints (46) and (56).

For the solution of this linear programming problem it is necessary to introduce further $3(n+1)$ slack variables [19] corresponding to the inequality constraints (46) and (56), hence $4(n+1)$ auxiliary variables must be introduced in all. On the other hand, for the solution of the linear programming problem with the performance index (49), $3(n+1)$ auxiliary variables are necessary. Consequently, the linear programming problem with the performance index (49) is simpler than the problem with the performance index (58).

Numerical Solutions

Figs. 1–4 indicate the results of numerical computation by using a digital computer KDC-I. The performance index (49) was minimized under the constraints (50) and (52), by using the simplex method and starting with the canonical form (54) and (55). Numerical values of the parameters of the system were taken as follows:

$$\left.\begin{array}{l} \alpha = 10, \quad \gamma = 0.04 \ (\kappa = 5), \\ q^*(x) = 0.2 \quad (0 \leq x \leq 1). \end{array}\right\} \tag{59}$$

The number of division of the intervals was taken as $n=20$.

Fig. 1 and Fig. 3 show the optimal control function $u(t)$, in the case where $T=0.2$ and $T=0.4$, respectively. The points denoted by dots in Fig. 1 and Fig. 3 were obtained through the computation. The exact optimal control functions corresponding to those shown in Fig. 1 and Fig. 3 are supposed to be discontinuous in the beginning period and then continuous in the last period.

The curve I in Fig. 2 shows the temperature distribution, at $T=0.2$, with constant control function, *i.e.*, $u(t)=1(0 \leq t \leq 0.2)$. The curve II in Fig. 2 shows the optimal temperature distribution, at $T=0.2$, with the optimal control function as shown in Fig. 1. Fig. 4 shows the temperature distributions in the case where $T=0.4$. Namely, the curve I in Fig. 4 shows the temperature distribution, at $T=0.4$, with constant control function $u(t)=1(0 \leq t \leq 0.4)$. The curve II in Fig. 4 shows the optimal temperature distribution, at $T=0.4$, with the optimal control function as shown in Fig. 3.

As shown in Fig. 2, the optimal temperature distribution (curve II) tolerably deviates from the assigned one in the case where $T=0.2$. But in the case where $T=0.4$, as shown in Fig. 4, the optimal temperature distribution (curve II) coincides with the assigned one very well.

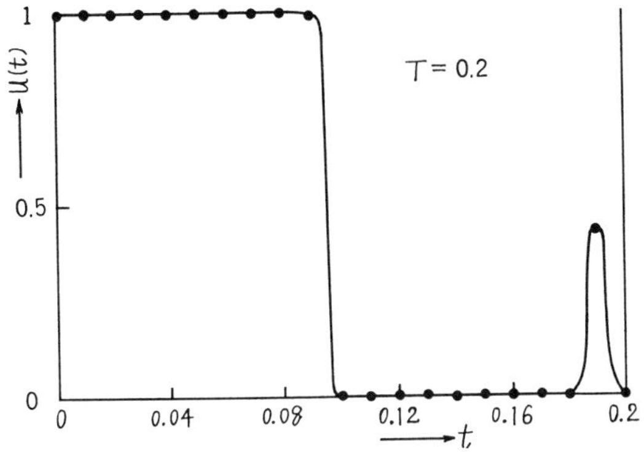

Fig. 1—Optimal control function ($T=0.2$).

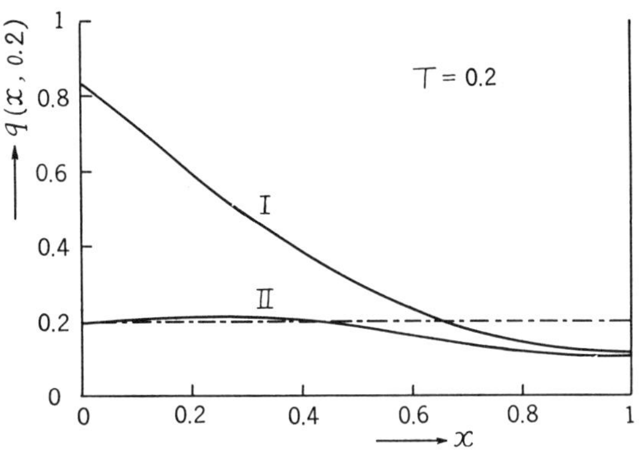

Fig. 2—Temperature distribution with constant control function $u(t)=1$ (curve I), and optimal temperature distribution (curve II), at $T=0.2$.

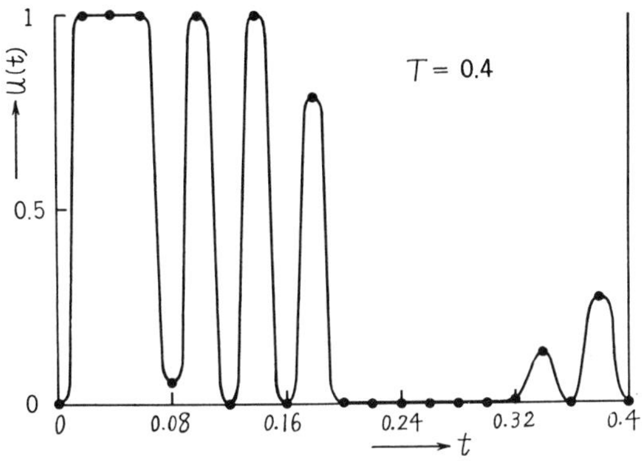

Fig. 3—Optimal control function ($T=0.4$).

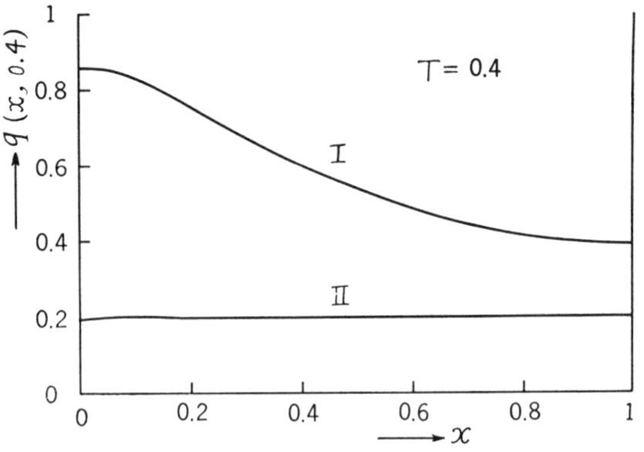

Fig. 4—Temperature distribution with constant control function $u(t)=1$ (curve I), and optimal temperature distribution (curve II), at $T=0.4$.

Eq. (23) was used for computing the values of the parameters a_{ij} which were defined by (44). The infinite series of (23) was approximated by the sum of the first eleven terms of (23), because the infinite series will converge rapidly with the increase of number i. But when $t=0$ in (23), the convergence of the series will be worse. In this case, fortunately, the value $g(x, 0)$ can be obtained by using the initial-value theorem in the Laplace transform, *i.e.*,

$$g(x, 0) = \lim_{s\to\infty} sG(s). \tag{60}$$

By using (15),

$$g(x, 0) = \lim_{s\to\infty} \frac{1}{\gamma\left(\frac{\sqrt{s}}{\alpha}+1\right)e^{x\sqrt{s}}} = 0. \tag{61}$$

Therefore, $a_{in}=0$ $(i=0, 1, \cdots, n)$.

The minimum value of the performance index (48) will decrease with increasing the time T. If such computations are iterated for various values of T, and a curve showing the dependence of min L on the time T is obtained, it is easy to find a value of T at which min L is not greater than a given positive constant ϵ, *i.e.*,

$$\min L \leq \epsilon. \tag{62}$$

Concluding Remarks

In this paper, the computational aspect of solving the optimal control problem in a distributed-parameter system is considered. The analytical results obtained here are available not only for the heat conduction system but also for an arbitrary distributed-parameter system, so long as the state of a system is expressed as (17).

The methods described here appear to be of wider application. For example, the technique of replacing the minimization of a functional by the minimization of a functions of many variables is also applicable for solving the optimal control problem in lumped-parameter system. This problem will be reported later.

Acknowledgment

The author wishes to express his sincere gratitude to Prof. C. Hayashi for his valuable suggestions. The author also wishes to thank K. Goma for his cooperation in preparing the programming of the digital computer.

References

[1] L. S. Pontryagin, V. G. Boltyanskii, R. V. Gamkrelidze, and E. F. Mishchenko, "The Mathematical Theory of Optimal Processes," Interscience Publishers, Inc., New York, N. Y.; 1962.
[2] R. Bellman, "Adaptive Control Processes: A Guided Tour," Princeton University Press, Princeton, N. J.; 1961.
[3] A. G. Butkovskii and A. Ya. Lerner, "Optimal control of systems with distributed parameters," *Avtomatika i Telemekhanika*, vol. 21, pp. 682–691; June, 1960.
[4] A. G. Butkovskii, "Optimum processes in systems with distributed parameters," *Avtomatika i Telemekhanika*, vol. 22, pp. 17–26; January, 1961.
[5] ——, "The maximum principle for optimum systems with distributed parameters," *Avtomatika i Telemekhanika*, vol. 22, pp. 1288–1301; October, 1961.
[6] ——, "Some approximate methods for solving problems of optimal control of distributed parameter systems," *Avtomatika i Telemekhanika*, vol. 22, pp. 1565–1575; December, 1961.
[7] ——, "Optimal control of systems with distributed parameters," *Proc. Second IFAC Congress;* 1963.
[8] P. K. C. Wang and F. Tung, "Optimum Control of Distributed-Parameter Systems," presented at the Joint Automatic Control Conference, Minneapolis, Minn., June 19–21; 1963.
[9] P. K. C. Wang, "Optimum control of distributed parameter systems with time delays," IEEE Trans. on Automatic Control, vol. AC-9, pp. 13–22; January, 1964.
[10] E. F. Beckenbach, "Modern Mathematics for the Engineer, Second Series," McGraw-Hill Book Company, Inc., New York, N. Y.; 1961.
[11] V. Volterra, "Theory of Functionals and of Integral and Integro-Differential Equations," Dover Publications, Inc., New York, N. Y.; 1959.
[12] R. Courant and D. Hilbert, "Methods of Mathematical Physics," Interscience Publishers, Inc., New York, N. Y., vol. I; 1953.
[13] L. I. Rozonoer, "Pontryagin maximum principle in the theory of optimum systems II," *Avtomatika i Telemekhanika*, vol. 20, 1441–1458; November, 1959.
[14] R. Bellman, "Dynamic Programming," Princeton University Press, Princeton, N. J.; 1957.
[15] A. D. Booth, "Numerical Methods," Butterworths Scientific Publications, London, England; 1955.
[16] P. Wolfe, "The present status of nonlinear programming," *in* "Mathematical Optimization Techniques," R. Bellman, Ed., University of California Press, Berkeley and Los Angeles, Calif., pp. 233–249; 1963.
[17] W. S. Dorn, "Non-linear programming—A survey," *Management Science*, vol. 9, pp. 171–208; January, 1963.
[18] L. A. Zadeh and B. H. Whalen, "On optimal control and linear programming," IRE Trans. on Automatic Control, vol. AC-7, pp. 45–46; July, 1962.
[19] S. Moriguchi and T. Miyashita, "Linear Programming," Iwanami-Shoten, Tokyo, Japan; 1959. (In Japanese.)

PART IV

Statistical Methods in Optimal Control

An Optimization Theory for Time-Varying Linear Systems with Nonstationary Statistical Inputs*

RICHARD C. BOOTON, JR.†, ASSOCIATE, IRE

***Summary*—The mean-square optimization problem is stated for time-varying systems with nonstationary statistical input functions. Correlation functions are defined for nonstationary ensembles. The mean-square error is calculated in terms of these correlation functions. The integral equation defining the optimum system is determined by minimization of the mean-square error.**

INTRODUCTION

AS NETWORK THEORY developed, the desirability of extending the now well-known techniques of analyzing systems on the basis of sinusoidal and transient input functions became evident. In answer to this need, a statistical theory leading to the optimum design of constant-coefficient linear systems was created, primarily by Wiener.[1] During recent years, the increasing importance of time-varying systems accentuates the desirability of extending statistical analysis to include time-varying systems. To complete the generalization, the analysis should include nonstationary input functions as well.

Although most of the system-analysis techniques were developed in electrical theory, no mathematical reason exists to distinguish between linear systems with different physical natures. In this paper, a system is defined by a mathematical transformation between two functions. One of the functions is referred to as the "input function," and the result of the transformation is called the "response function," but the system need not exist physically in the form of a "box." The functions can be distances or angles, as in the case of aircraft-control problems, or mechanical (or hydraulic) forces, as in servo problems. In any case, a linear-system problem exists if one variable in a physical situation is derived from another variable by means of a linear transformation.

In Wiener's theory the assumption is made that the input to a system consists of a random signal plus a random noise, each of which is stationary in the sense that its statistical properties do not vary with time. Response of the actual system is compared with the result of a desired, time-invariant, linear operation upon the signal component of the input, and the difference is called the "error." The mean-square value of this error is used as the criterion for optimization. The fundamental mathematical considerations involved in the statistical approach are first, that the input is not one function but one of an ensemble of functions, and second, that the measure of error used to define the optimum system is not the error resulting from one input function but the mean-square error with respect to the ensemble of input functions. Even though the importance of the ensemble concept has been recognized,[2] Wiener's treatment is based upon averages, with respect to time, for a single input function. Unfortunately, the impression seems to have arisen that for stationary ensembles "time averages are equivalent to ensemble averages," meaning that a time average for any function of the ensemble is both independent of the particular function used and also equal to the corresponding ensemble average. This statement is not true, however, for the general stationary ensemble, but only for the special case known as an "ergodic ensemble," for which any function is statistically equivalent to any other function. As Wiener stated his results,[3] they apply only to the ergodic case. Nevertheless, for the general stationary input, the ensemble approach, as presented here, can be used to derive for the optimum system an equation essentially the same as Wiener's, except that all the expressions must be defined by ensemble averages.

This paper generalizes the optimization theory to apply to nonstationary input functions and time-varying desired operations. The input ensemble is described by a set of three correlation functions. The desired response is the result of a time-varying linear operation upon the signal component of the input. For each input function, the error is the difference between this desired response and the actual system response. The optimization criterion is taken as the mean-square value (ensemble average) of the error. Because the input to the system contains noise, a filtering problem exists, even though the desired operation is merely the reproduction of the signal component. If the result of the desired operation depends upon future values of the signal, then the system must be both a filter and a predictor. Other problems, such as the optimum evaluation of derivatives, are specified by suitable choices of the desired operation.

To avoid possible misunderstanding, the range of applicability of the results presented here should be clearly understood. Physical reasoning makes evident, and the equations developed later in this paper prove mathematically, that the characteristics of the optimum sys-

* Decimal classification: 510. Original manuscript received by the Institute, August 15, 1951; revised manuscript received, April 3, 1952.

† Dynamic Analysis and Control Laboratory, Massachusetts Institute of Technology, Cambridge, Mass.

[1] N. Wiener, "Extrapolation, Interpolation and Smoothing of Stationary Time Series, with Engineering Applications," Technology Press, Cambridge, Mass.; 1949.

[2] H. W. Bode and C. E. Shannon, "A simplified derivation of linear least square smoothing and prediction theory," PROC. I.R.E., vol. 38, pp. 417–425; April, 1950.

[3] N. Wiener, *op. cit.*, p. 57.

tem depend upon the statistics of the input during the entire time of interest. This fact is of basic importance in prediction problems. If the future behavior of the statistics of the ensemble is not definitely known, then optimum prediction, in the sense of this paper, is impossible. Under these conditions, mathematical treatment of the prediction problem, if at all possible, is certainly of an order of difficulty greater than in the problem considered in this paper. One of the nonstationary problems to which the results of this paper have already[4] been applied relates to an aircraft-control system in which the ensemble statistics are completely known, although the individual functions are random. Here, there is no ambiguity concerning the determination of the optimum predictor. At the other extreme are problems such as the prediction of the value of a variable associated with the stock market, where separation of the individual variation from an ensemble variation is perhaps indeterminant (or meaningless). Between these extremes problems exist in which the statistical variation can be estimated and approximately optimum predictors determined.

Superposition Integrals

A general expression for the response of any linear system is needed for the construction of an optimization theory. One of the most useful of these expressions is the superposition integral,[5] which, for the constant-coefficient linear system, assumes the well-known form

$$x_R(t) = \int_0^\infty f(\tau) x_I(t - \tau) d\tau, \tag{1}$$

where x_R and x_I denote the response of the system and the input to the system, respectively. The function $f(\tau)$ can be interpreted as the response, after a time τ, to a unit-impulse input function.

Although the superposition integral for time-varying systems is not so well known as the corresponding expression for constant-coefficient systems, the fact that the system response x_R can be expressed in terms of the input x_I as

$$x_R(t) = \int_0^\infty h(\tau, t) x_I(t - \tau) d\tau \tag{2}$$

can be established in essentially the same manner as for the constant-coefficient equation. The principal difference is that the time-varying system is characterized by a function of two variables $h(\tau, t)$, known as the "impulse-response function," whereas for the constant-coefficient system, the impulse response is independent of t and is a function of the one variable τ. The function $h(\tau, t)$ can be shown to be the response, evaluated at a time t, to a unit-impulse input applied at a time $t-\tau$.

[4] Unpublished work at the Dynamic Analysis and Control Laboratory, M.I.T., Cambridge, Mass.

[5] S. Goldman, "Transformation Calculus and Electrical Transients," Prentice-Hall, Inc., New York, N. Y., pp. 112–118; 1949.

Only linear operations are considered in this theory, and thus the desired operation upon the signal component of the input can be expressed in the superposition-integral form

$$x_D(t) = \int_{-\infty}^\infty g(\tau, t) x_S(t - \tau) d\tau, \tag{3}$$

where x_D and x_S denote the desired result and the signal component, respectively. The function $g(\tau, t)$ can be interpreted as an impulse response, in a manner similar to the interpretation of $h(\tau, t)$, except that $g(\tau, t)$ is not necessarily the impulse response of a physical system. Because operations such as prediction, which are operations upon future values of x_S, should be included, the lower limit of the integral in (3) must be minus infinity. In contrast, the response of a physical system, as shown by (2), can depend only upon past values of the input x_I, and thus the lower limit of (2) is always zero.

Correlation Functions

For the purpose of mean-square calculations, the input ensemble is completely specified[6] by three correlation functions. These correlation functions are defined by ensemble averages of products of the input and the signal component of the input. To be precise, if x_I and x_S denote the input function and its signal component, respectively, then correlation functions are defined as

$$\left.\begin{aligned} \gamma_{II}(t_1, t_2) &= \overline{x_I(t_1) x_I(t_2)} \\ \gamma_{IS}(t_1, t_2) &= \overline{x_I(t_1) x_S(t_2)} \\ \gamma_{SS}(t_1, t_2) &= \overline{x_S(t_1) x_S(t_2)} \end{aligned}\right\}, \tag{4}$$

where the bar denotes an averaging operation with respect to the ensemble of input functions.

An alternate set of correlation functions is sometimes used to describe the input ensemble. This set of correlation functions is defined by ensemble averages of products of the signal and noise components of the input. With x_N denoting the noise component of the input, these correlation functions are given by

$$\left.\begin{aligned} \gamma_{SS}(t_1, t_2) &= \overline{x_S(t_1) x_S(t_2)} \\ \gamma_{SN}(t_1, t_2) &= \overline{x_S(t_1) x_N(t_2)} \\ \gamma_{NN}(t_1, t_2) &= \overline{x_N(t_1) x_N(t_2)} \end{aligned}\right\}. \tag{5}$$

The first set of correlation functions can be calculated easily from the second set. Because

$$x_I(t) = x_S(t) + x_N(t), \tag{6}$$

correlation function γ_{II} is obtained by first evaluating

$$\begin{aligned} x_I(t_1) x_I(t_2) &= [x_S(t_1) + x_N(t_1)][x_S(t_2) + x_N(t_2)] \qquad (7) \\ &= x_S(t_1) x_S(t_2) + x_S(t_1) x_N(t_2) \\ &\quad + x_S(t_2) x_N(t_1) + x_N(t_1) x_N(t_2) \end{aligned}$$

[6] This statement should not be taken as an implication that the ensemble of input functions is completely described by the correlation functions defined here. These correlation functions suffice only for mean-square calculations.

An average (with respect to the ensemble) of each side of (7) yields

$$\gamma_{II}(t_1, t_2) = \gamma_{SS}(t_1, t_2) + \gamma_{SN}(t_1, t_2) + \gamma_{SN}(t_2, t_1) + \gamma_{NN}(t_1, t_2). \quad (8)$$

In a similar manner γ_{IS} is evaluated by first multiplying each side of (6) by x_S to yield

$$x_I(t_1)x_S(t_2) = [x_S(t_1) + x_N(t_1)]x_S(t_2) = x_S(t_1)x_S(t_2) + x_S(t_2)x_N(t_1). \quad (9)$$

An average of each side of (9) results in

$$\gamma_{IS}(t_1, t_2) = \gamma_{SS}(t_1, t_2) + \gamma_{SN}(t_2, t_1). \quad (10)$$

Either of the preceding sets of correlation functions, (4) or (5), can be used to describe the input ensemble.

The input ensemble has been described by the correlation functions γ_{II}, γ_{IS}, and γ_{SS}. The statement of the optimization problem is completed by the function $g(\tau, t)$ that defines the desired operation, as shown by (3). In the calculation of the mean-square error that is presented later in this paper, the desirability of defining still another set of correlation functions is indicated. These correlation functions are γ_{ID}, the cross-correlation of the input and the desired response, and γ_{DD}, the autocorrelation of the desired response. They are defined in terms of ensemble averages as

$$\gamma_{ID}(t_1, t_2) = \overline{x_I(t_1)x_D(t_2)} \quad (11)$$

and

$$\gamma_{DD}(t_1, t_2) = \overline{x_D(t_1)x_D(t_2)}. \quad (12)$$

Expressions for these two correlation functions in terms of the given correlation functions and the desired operation are easily derived. Substitution of t_2 for t in (3) and multiplication of each side of the resulting equation by $x_I(t_1)$ yield

$$x_I(t_1)x_D(t_2) = \int_{-\infty}^{\infty} g(\tau, t_2)x_I(t_1)x_S(t_2 - \tau)d\tau. \quad (13)$$

If each side of this equation is averaged,[7] then the correlation function γ_{ID} is given by

$$\gamma_{ID}(t_1, t_2) = \int_{-\infty}^{\infty} g(\tau, t_2)\gamma_{IS}(t_1, t_2 - \tau)d\tau. \quad (14)$$

Similarly, the correlation function γ_{DD} is obtained as

$$\gamma_{DD}(t_1, t_2) = \int_{-\infty}^{\infty}\int_{-\infty}^{\infty} g(\tau_1, t_1)g(\tau_2, t_2)\gamma_{SS}(t_1 - \tau_1, t_2 - \tau_2)d\tau_1\, d\tau_2. \quad (15)$$

Minimization of Error

The error in system performance has been defined as the difference between the desired response and the actual system response, that is,

$$e(t) = x_D(t) - x_R(t). \quad (16)$$

Use of (2) gives the error as

$$e(t) = x_D(t) - \int_0^{\infty} h(\tau, t)x_I(t - \tau)d\tau. \quad (17)$$

The square of the error then is given by

$$[e(t)]^2 = x_D(t)x_D(t) - 2\int_0^{\infty} h(\tau, t)x_I(t - \tau)x_D(t)d\tau + \int_0^{\infty}\int_0^{\infty} h(\tau_1, t)h(\tau_2, t)x_I(t - \tau_1)x_I(t - \tau_2)d\tau_1 d\tau_2. \quad (18)$$

The ensemble-averaged mean-square error is obtained by averaging both sides of (18) with respect to the ensemble of input functions. In terms of the correlation functions previously defined, this mean-square error can be written as

$$M(t) = \gamma_{DD}(t, t) - 2\int_0^{\infty} h(\tau, t)\gamma_{ID}(t - \tau, t)d\tau + \int_0^{\infty}\int_0^{\infty} h(\tau_1, t)h(\tau_2, t)\gamma_{II}(t - \tau_1, t - \tau_2)d\tau_1 d\tau_2, \quad (19)$$

where the assumption is made that the averaging operation commutes with the integration. The mean-square error given by (19) is the error resulting from use of the system with an impulse response of $h(\tau, t)$. In order that this error be the minimum error (and thus $h(\tau, t)$ the impulse response of the optimum system), replacement of $h(\tau, t)$ by $h(\tau, t)+f(\tau, t)$, where $f(\tau, t)$ is any impulse response, must result in a larger value for the mean-square error. Replacement of $h(\tau, t)$ by $h(\tau, t)+f(\tau, t)$ in (19) results, after some simplification, in

$$N(t) = \left\{\begin{aligned} &\gamma_{DD}(t, t) - 2\int_0^{\infty} h(\tau, t)\gamma_{ID}(t - \tau, t)d\tau \\ &+ \int_0^{\infty}\int_0^{\infty} h(\tau_1, t)h(\tau_2, t)\gamma_{II}(t - \tau_1, t - \tau_2)d\tau_1 d\tau_2 \\ &-2\int_0^{\infty} f(\tau, t)\gamma_{ID}(t - \tau, t)d\tau \\ &+2\int_0^{\infty}\int_0^{\infty} f(\tau_1, t)h(\tau_2, t)\gamma_{II}(t - \tau_1, t - \tau_2)d\tau_1 d\tau_2 \\ &+ \int_0^{\infty}\int_0^{\infty} f(\tau_1, t)f(\tau_2, t)\gamma_{II}(t - \tau_1, t - \tau_2)d\tau_1 d\tau_2 \end{aligned}\right\}, \quad (20)$$

where $N(t)$ denotes the mean-square error corresponding to impulse response $h(\tau, t)+f(\tau, t)$. Reference to (19) shows that the sum of the first three terms in (20) is the mean-square error $M(t)$ corresponding to the impulse response $h(\tau, t)$. Substitution of (19) into (20) and use of the fact that last term of (20) is nonnegative[8] yield

[7] The statistical problem is meaningful only if the averaging process commutes with all the operators considered.

[8] The last term of (20) is the ensemble average of $\left[\int_0^{\infty} f(\tau_1, t)x_I(t - \tau_1)d\tau_1\right]^2$, and is thus nonnegative.

$$N(t) \geqq M(t) - 2\int_0^\infty f(\tau, t)\gamma_{ID}(t-\tau, t)d\tau$$

$$+ 2\int_0^\infty \int_0^\infty f(\tau_1, t)h(\tau_2, t)\gamma_{II}(t-\tau_1, t-\tau_2)d\tau_1 d\tau_2. \quad (21)$$

Therefore, the minimizing condition $N(t) \geqq M(t)$ is satisfied if

$$0 = -2\int_0^\infty f(\tau, t)\gamma_{ID}(t-\tau, t)d\tau$$

$$+ 2\int_0^\infty \int_0^\infty f(\tau_1, t)h(\tau_2, t)\gamma_{II}(t-\tau_1, t-\tau_2)d\tau_1 d\tau_2. \quad (22)$$

Because (22) can be written as

$$0 = 2\int_0^\infty f(\tau_1, t)\Big[-\gamma_{ID}(t-\tau_1, t) + \int_0^\infty h(\tau_2, t)\gamma_{II}(t-\tau_1, t-\tau_2)d\tau_2\Big]d\tau_1, \quad (23)$$

the minimizing condition is satisfied for all impulse response functions $f(\tau, t)$ if

$$\gamma_{ID}(t-\tau_1, t) = \int_0^\infty h(\tau_2, t)\gamma_{II}(t-\tau_1, t-\tau_2)d\tau_2 \quad (24)$$

for $0<\tau_1<\infty$.

This equation defines the impulse response of the optimum system. The development here proves the sufficiency of (24) for a minimum. The usual calculus-of-variations methods easily establish its necessity. If (24) has more than one solution, several optimum systems exist, each yielding the same mean-square error. Analysis of this situation is relatively complicated, but the uniqueness of the optimum system can be shown to be equivalent to the completeness of the ensemble of input functions x_I. Fortunately, most physical problems yield unique solutions, and physical reasoning usually makes clear when the optimization procedure merely places a constraint on the system instead of uniquely determining it.

Determination of the Optimum System

At this point, a solution of (24) yielding an explicit expression for $h(\tau, t)$ in terms of γ_{ID} and γ_{II} would complete the determination of the optimum system. Because the general form of (24) is the general form of the integral equation of the first kind, no such explicit solution can be written. Except for the special cases that can be solved analytically, recourse must be made to numerical methods (including machine computation) if actual solutions are desired. Since discussion of these methods is outside the scope of this paper, (24) essentially completes the analysis of the optimization problem presented here.

One special case of the general problem should be mentioned. If the input is stationary, an explicit expression for $h(\tau, t)$ can be obtained in a form similar to the solution of the completely stationary case. The result is a generalization of the completely stationary problem since the desired operation can still be time-varying. If the input x_I is stationary, then a function ϕ exists such that

$$\gamma_{II}(t_1, t_2) = \phi(t_2 - t_1), \quad (25)$$

and (24) can be written as

$$\gamma_{ID}(t-\tau_1, t) = \int_0^\infty h(\tau_2, t)\phi(\tau_1 - \tau_2)d\tau_2. \quad (26)$$

Since (26) can be solved by a method that follows closely the technique used by Levinson[9] in discussing the completely stationary problem, the final solution will be presented without details.

The spectral-factorization theorem proved by Wiener[10] implies that ϕ can be factored in the form

$$\phi(t) = \int_{-\infty}^\infty \phi_+(t-\tau)\phi_-(\tau)d\tau, \quad (27)$$

where

$$\left.\begin{aligned}\phi_+(t) &= 0 \quad \text{if} \quad t<0\\ \phi_-(t) &= 0 \quad \text{if} \quad t>0\end{aligned}\right\}. \quad (28)$$

The correlation function γ_{ID} can be factored as

$$\gamma_{ID}(t_1, t_2) = \int_{-\infty}^\infty \psi(t_2 - t_1 - \tau, t_2)\phi_-(\tau)d\tau. \quad (29)$$

Then the impulse response of the optimum system, that is, the solution of (26), can be shown to be

$$h(\tau, t) = \frac{1}{2\pi i}\int_{-i\infty}^{i\infty} e^{s\tau}\frac{\Psi(s, t)}{\Phi_+(s)}ds, \quad (30)$$

where

$$\left.\begin{aligned}\Psi(s, t) &= \int_0^\infty e^{-s\tau}\psi(\tau, t)d\tau\\ \Phi_+(s) &= \int_0^\infty e^{-s\tau}\phi_+(\tau)d\tau\end{aligned}\right\}. \quad (31)$$

Conclusions

The statistical optimization theory developed by Wiener is extended to include the general case involving a linear time-varying system with a nonstationary input. Statistical characteristics of nonstationary ensembles are defined by ensemble-averaged correlation functions. The mean-square error in the performance of a time-varying linear operation upon the signal component of the input is calculated, and the integral equation defining the optimum system is derived. This integral equation is expressed in terms of functions of time, that is, the impulse response of the system and the cor-

[9] N. Levinson, "A heuristic exposition of Wiener's mathematical theory of prediction and filtering," *Jour. Math. Phys.*, vol. XXVI, pp. 110–119; July, 1947.
[10] N. Wiener, *op. cit.*, p. 53.

relation functions that define both the input functions and the desired operation.

Note should be taken of the fact that, although the optimum system is completely specified by the integral equation derived here, this equation cannot be solved directly in the general case. If actual results are desired, numerical or machine methods of computation must be employed. The development of approximation methods would increase the applicability of the optimization technique. Because little practical application of this optimization theory has been made, no intuitive understanding of the relative importance of the factors involved exists. In some cases a rough solution yields acceptable results, whereas in others, careful determination of the optimum system is essential. Some basis on which to estimate the accuracy required in a particular application would be useful. In work at the Dynamic Analysis and Control Laboratory, the nonstationary optimization theory has been applied to an aircraft-control-system design problem and to the analysis of suppressed-carrier modulation systems.

Acknowledgment

This research, which is a portion of a doctoral thesis,[11] was sponsored by the Bureau of Ordnance of the Navy Department, Bureau of Ordnance Contract NOrd 9661, and was conducted at the Dynamic Analysis and Control Laboratory of the Massachusetts Institute of Technology. The author gratefully acknowledges the support given by Dr. J. A. Hrones, Director of the D.A.C.L., and the benefit of discussions with Dr. W. W. Seifert and M. H. Goldstein, Jr., also of the D.A.C.L.

[11] R. C. Booton, Jr., "Nonstationary Theory Associated with Time-Varying Linear Systems," Thesis (Sc.D.) Dept. of Electrical Engineering, M.I.T., Cambridge, N. Y.; June, 1952.

Optimum Filters for the Detection of Signals in Noise*

L. A. ZADEH†, MEMBER, IRE, AND J. R. RAGAZZINI†, SENIOR MEMBER, IRE

Summary—**A detection system usually contains a predetection filter whose function is to enhance the strength of the signal relative to that of the noise. An optimum predetection filter is defined in this paper as one which maximizes the "distance" between the signal and noise components of the output (subject to a constraint on the noise component) in terms of a suitable distance function $d(x, y)$. In a special case, this definition leads to the criterion used by North, and yields filters which maximize the signal-to-noise ratio at a specified instant of time. North's theory of such filters is extended to the case of nonwhite noise and finite memory (i.e., finite observation time) filters. Explicit expressions for the impulsive responses of such filters are developed, and two examples of practical interest are considered.**

I. Introduction

CONSIDERABLE EFFORT has been devoted in recent years to the development of optimum methods of detection of weak signals in noise. Broadly speaking, the purpose of detection is to establish the presence or absence of a signal in noise, or, more generally, to obtain an estimate of a quantity associated with the signal, *e.g.*, the instant of occurrence of a pulse. In general, a detection system comprises a predetection filter whose function is to enhance the strength of the signal relative to that of the noise, and thereby facilitate the detection process.

A special but rather inclusive type of such filters is the main concern of the present paper. As background, a brief review of the published (or available) work on the detection problem is presented in the following.

In a report published in 1943, North[1] developed a theory of optimum filters—now commonly referred to as "North filters"—based on the maximization of the predetection signal-to-noise ratio. A central result in North's theory is that, in the case of white additive noise, the signal-to-noise ratio is maximized by a filter whose impulsive response has the form of the image of the signal to be detected. A similar result—formulated in terms of so-called "matched" filters—was obtained independently by Van Vleck and Middleton.[2]

More recently, Lee, Cheatham, and Wiesner[3] have described a method of detection of periodic signals based on the use of the correlation analysis. In many respects, the results obtained by this method are essentially equivalent to those obtained by the use of the conventional integration technique, which in turn may be deduced from the theory of North filters. Work along somewhat similar lines has also been reported by Leifer and Marchand.[4]

A more sophisticated approach to detection—closely paralleling the classical Neyman-Pearson theory of testing statistical hypotheses—was initiated by Siegert,[5]

* Decimal classification: R143.2. Original manuscript received by the Institute, December 7, 1951; revised manuscript received June 20, 1952.

† Dep't. of Electrical Engineering, Columbia University, New York 27, N. Y.

1 D. O. North, "Analysis of the Factors which Determine Signa /Noise Discrimination in Radar," Report PTR-6C, RCA Laboratories; June, 1943.

2 J. Van Vleck and D. Middleton, "A theoretical comparison of the visual, aural, and meter reception of pulsed signals in the presence of noise," *Jour. Appl. Phys.*, vol. 17, pp. 940–971; November, 1946.

3 Y. W. Lee, T. P. Cheatham, Jr., and J. B. Wiesner, "Application of correlation analysis to the detection of periodic signals in noise," Proc. I.R.E., vol. 38, pp. 1165–1172; October, 1950.

4 M. Leifer and N. Marchand, "The design of periodic radio systems," *Sylvania Technologist*, vol. 3, pp. 18–21; October, 1950. See also, Proc. I.R.E., vol. 39, pp. 1094–1096; September, 1951.

5 "Threshold Signals," MIT Rad. Lab. Series, McGraw-Hill Book Co., Inc., New York, N. Y., vol. 24, chap. 7; 1950.

and, recently, was further developed by Schwartz.[6] Another statistical theory involving the determination of the *a posteriori* probability distribution of the signal was recently advanced by Woodward and Davies.[7] In many practical situations the usefulness of the latter theory is restricted by the fact that its application requires much more statistical information about the signal and noise than is generally available, while in those cases where the necessary information is available the mathematical computations and the mechanization of the detection process present formidable difficulties. One exception is the case where the noise is additive, white, and Gaussian. In this case the calculations are relatively simple, and the theory leads to the conclusion that the optimum detector consists essentially of a North filter followed by a nonlinear detecting device.

Of the methods mentioned above, the last two are probabilistic in nature, that is, they make use of the probability distributions of the signal and noise. By contrast, detection procedures involving the use of North filters correlation analysis, integration technique, and the like are nonprobabilistic, and hence are inherently much simpler and, in principle, less efficient than the probabilistic procedures.

Despite the theoretical superiority of probabilistic over nonprobabilistic methods, the latter are generally of greater practical utility for two reasons: First, the information about nth-order probability distributions of the signal and noise—which is required by probabilistic methods—is difficult to obtain and to handle for any but the Gaussian type of random function. More important, in many practical cases the pertinent probability distributions are lacking in temporal or spatial stability, or both; in other words, the probability distributions change from day to day or are dependent on the location of the noise source. In such cases, it is clearly unrealistic to base the design of an optimum detector on probability distributions that are assumed to be time and space invariant.

The main advantage of nonprobabilistic methods is that they require relatively little statistical information about the noise—the power spectrum or the correlation function being usually sufficient—and are less critically dependent upon the stability of signal and noise characteristics. Their chief weakness is that they are optimum in only an arbitrary although reasonable sense, and do not make use of such information about the probability distributions as might be available.

The present paper has a twofold purpose: first, to formulate a rather general predetection filtering criterion of a nonprobabilistic type which, through specialization, might be adapted to a wide range of practical cases; and second, using a special form of this criterion, to extend the theory of North filters to the case of nonwhite noise and finite memory (i.e., finite observation time) filters.

In connection with the extension of North's theory, the case of nonwhite noise, it should be noted that such an extension was recently described by Dwork.[8] However, Dwork's results do not resolve the problem of nonwhite noise, since his filters are not, in general, physically realizable. By contrast, the extension described in this paper always leads to physically realizable filters.

II. Criteria of Optimum Filtering

In assessing the performance of filters, predictors, detectors, and many other devices, it is convenient to use a suitable distance function, $d(x, y)$, as a measure of the disparity between two functions $x(t)$ and $y(t)$. For practical purposes, the following three types of distance function are of greatest utility: (The functions $x(t)$ and $y(t)$, appearing below, are assumed to be defined over a long interval of time $(0, T_0)$.)

(a) $d(x, y) = \max\{\,|x(t) - y(t)|\,\}$ = maximum value of the magnitude of the difference between $x(t)$ and $y(t)$.

(b) $$d(x, y) = \frac{1}{T_0}\int_0^{T_0} |x(t) - y(t)|\,dt \tag{1}$$

(c) $$d(x, y) = \left\{\frac{1}{T_0}\int_0^{T_0} [x(t) = y(t)]^2 dt\right\}^{1/2}. \tag{2}$$

Of these, the distance function of type (c) is of widest applicability, and is also the easiest to handle analytically. It will be recognized as simply the rms value of the difference between $x(t)$ and $y(t)$.

In order to place in evidence the similarities as well as the differences between the criteria of optimum performance for the predetection filter on the one hand, and the conventional[9] filter on the other, it will be helpful to consider first a typical conventional filter F whose input, $u(t)$, consists of the sum of a signal $s_i(t)$ and a noise $n_i(t)$, and whose output, $v(t)$, is required to be as close as possible—in terms of a suitable distance function $d(x, y)$—to the input signal $s_i(t)$. Such a filter may be said to be *optimum* if

$$d[v(t), s_i(t)] = \text{a minimum}; \tag{3}$$

for all $s_i(t)$ in some class $S_i = \{s_i(t)\}$ and all $n_i(t)$ in some class $N_i = \{n_i(t)\}$.

For a distance function of type (c), this formulation of optimum filtering reduces to the familiar minimum mean-square-error criterion. For the linear case, the

[6] M. Schwartz, "Statistical Approach to the Automatic Search Problem," Dissertation, Harvard University, 1951. Similar results were reported by D. L. Drukey, "Optimum Techniques for Detecting Pulse Signals in Noise," presented at the IRE National Convention, New York, N. Y.; March 4, 1952.

[7] P. M. Woodward and I. L. Davies, "A theory of radar information," *Phil. Mag.*, vol. 41, pp. 1001–1017; October, 1950. See also, Proc. I.R.E., vol. 39, pp. 1521–1524; December, 1951; and *Jour. IEE* (London), vol. 99, pt. III, pp. 37–51; March, 1952.

[8] B. M. Dwork, "Detection of a pulse superimposed on fluctuation noise," Proc. I.R.E., vol. 38, pp. 771–774; July, 1950.

[9] By conventional filter is meant, here, a network whose function is to separate signal from noise.

output of F, $v(t)$ consists of the sum of the responses of F to $s_i(t)$ and $n_i(t)$, which are denoted by $s_0(t)$ and $n_0(t)$, respectively. Thus, $v(t)=s_0(t)+n_0(t)$, and, on assuming that $s_i(t)$ and $n_i(t)$ are stationary and independent, (3) reduces to[10]

$$\overline{[s_0(t)+n_0(t)-s_i(t)]^2} = \text{a minimum}, \tag{4}$$

where the bar indicates a long-term time average and the classes S_i and N_i consist of stationary random functions having fixed correlation functions $\Psi_s(\tau)$ and $\Psi_n(\tau)$, respectively.

In the case where F is a predetection filter, the situation is different in that the purpose of F is to facilitate the detection of $s_i(t)$, rather than to reproduce $s_i(t)$. Accordingly, in the case of a predetection filter, it is reasonable to assess the performance in terms of the "distance" between the signal component $s_0(t)$ and the noise component $n_0(t)$ in the output of F.[11] More specifically, by analogy with (3), a predetection filter F will be said to be *optimum* if

$$d[s_0(t), n_0(t)] = \text{a maximum}, \tag{5}$$

for all $s_i(t)$ in some class S_i and all $n_i(t)$ in some class N_i, subject to a constraint[12] on $n_0(t)$ (or $s_0(t)$). The constraint may usually be expressed in terms of the "distance" between $n_0(t)$ and the zero signal. Thus, the quantity to be maximized by F becomes

$$R = d[s_0(t), n_0(t)] - \lambda d[n_0(t), 0] = \text{a maximum}, \tag{6}$$

where λ is a constant (Lagrangian multiplier).

The above criterion is, in principle, sufficiently general to cover a wide variety of practical cases. However, only a few types of distance function can be handled analytically. Of these, the most important is the distance function of type (c), with which the expression for R reduces to

$$R = \overline{[s_0(t)-n_0(t)]^2} - \lambda\overline{n_0^2(t)} = \text{a maximum}. \tag{7}$$

In what follows, attention will be confined to the case where $s_i(t)$ is a signal of known form. It is expedient, then, to replace the time averages in (7) by ensemble averages, with t held constant at a fixed value t_0 (relative to a temporal frame of reference attached to the signal $s_i(t)$). Straightforward calculation yields for this case.

$$R = s_0^2(t_0) - \mu\overline{n_0^2(t)} = \text{a maximum}, \tag{8}$$

where μ is a constant equal to $\lambda-1$, and the bar indicates the time average. (It is tacitly assumed that $n_0(t)$ is ergodic, in which case the ensemble and time averages are identical.)

It is readily seen that when F is a linear filter, (8) is equivalent to maximizing the signal-to-noise ratio

$$\rho = \frac{s_0^2(t_0)}{\overline{n_0^2(t)}} = \text{a maximum}, \tag{9}$$

which is the criterion used in North's theory. Thus, when the distance function is of type (c) and F is linear, the general filtering criterion (6) reduces to the North criterion.

It is also clear that the maximization of R, as expressed by (8), is equivalent to the minimization of

$$Q = \overline{n_0^2(t)} - \lambda s_0(t_0) = \text{a minimum}, \tag{10}$$

where λ is a constant (Lagrangian multiplier). From the mathematical point of view, this is the most convenient form of the predetection filtering criterion, and is the one that will be used in the sequel.

In the following sections, explicit expressions for the impulsive responses of linear, physically realizable, and finite as well as infinite memory predetection filters that are optimum in the sense that they minimize Q (or, equivalently, maximize R and the signal-to-noise ratio ρ) will be developed. The assumptions on the signal and noise are: The signal $s_i(t)$ is a specified but otherwise arbitrary function of time, and the noise $n_i(t)$ is ergodic and has a known correlation function $\Psi_n(\tau)$.

By virtue of the similarity between the predetection filtering criterion (10) and the minimum mean-square-error criterion (4), the mathematics of optimum predetection filters is almost identical with that of optimum filters of the Wiener type. However, instead of following the conventional treatment of Wiener filters, a spectrum-shaping technique which circumvents the use of the calculus of variations and, furthermore, avoids the need for the solution of the Wiener-Hopf equation will be used here. It should be noted that variants of this technique have been employed to considerable advantage in the theory of optimum predictors.[13,14]

III. Determination of the Optimum Filter

The principle of the spectrum-shaping technique is illustrated in Fig. 1. Here $u(t)$ and $v(t)$ represent, respectively, the input and output of a filter F, not necessarily linear, which is optimum in the sense that it maximizes (or minimizes) some quantity Q associated with $v(t)$, on condition that the corresponding input $u(t)$ is a member of a specified class of functions of time, $U=\{u(t)\}$. For convenience in terminology, F will be said to be optimum with respect to the criterion Q and the class of inputs U.

It is evident that neither the input nor the output of F is affected by inserting ahead of F a tandem combina-

[10] For reasons of mathematical convenience, $[d(x, y)]^2$ is used, here and elsewhere, in place of $d(x, y)$.

[11] Another reasonable measure is the "distance" between the output $v(t)$ and its noise component $n_0(t)$. For the class of filters considered in the sequel, this measure of performance leads to the same results as the measure used in the text.

[12] Without such a constraint the "distance" could be made as large as desired merely by increasing the gain of F.

[13] H. W. Bode and C. E. Shannon, "A simplified derivation of linear least square smoothing and prediction theory," Proc. I.R.E., vol. 38, pp. 417–425; April, 1950.

[14] L. A. Zadeh and J. R. Ragazzini, "An extension of Wiener's theory of prediction," *Jour. Appl. Phys.*, vol. 21, pp. 645–655; July, 1950.

tion of two linear networks L and L^{-1} which are inverses of one another. (The combination of L and L^{-1} is equivalent to a direct connection.) Now the output of L, which is denoted by $u'(t)$, may be regarded as the input to a composite filter F' which consists of L^{-1} and F. Clearly, if F is optimum with respect to the criterion Q and class of inputs U, then F' is optimum with respect to the criterion Q and class of inputs $U' = \{u'(t)\}$. Consequently, F may be obtained indirectly by first designing a filter F' which is optimum with respect to the criterion Q and class of inputs U' and, then combining F' in tandem with the shaping network L. The advantage of this indirect procedure is that it allows the designer to control the characteristics of the input to F within the limitations imposed by the linearity of the shaping network L. By a proper choice of the shaping network, a complicated optimization problem involving the design of F may, in many cases, be reduced to a simpler problem involving the design of F'.

In applying this approach to optimum filters in the sense of criterion (10), which is equivalent to North's criterion, it is convenient to consider first the relatively simple case in which the filter is not required to have finite memory. This implies that the only condition which the impulsive response must fulfill is that $W(t)$ should vanish for negative t. The case in which the impulsive response is required to vanish outside of a specified interval $0 \leqq t \leqq T$ (finite memory filter) will be considered later in the paper.

Infinite Memory Filters

In this case, it is simplest to use a shaping network L which results in a white noise at the input to F'. The transfer function of such a network may be determined as follows:

If $N(\omega^2)$ is the power spectrum of the input noise $n_i(t)$ and $N'(\omega^2)$ is that of the output of L, then $N'(\omega^2)$ is related to $N(\omega^2)$ by the equation

$$N'(\omega^2) = |H_L(j\omega)|^2 N(\omega^2), \tag{11}$$

where $H_L(j\omega)$ is the transfer function of L. Hence, in order that $N'(\omega^2)$ be a constant, for example unity, it is necessary that

$$|H_L(j\omega)|^2 = \frac{1}{N(\omega^2)} \cdot \tag{12}$$

Expressing $N(\omega^2)$ as the product of two conjugate factors $N_+(j\omega)$ and $N_+^*(j\omega)$ so that $N_+(j\omega)$ and its reciprocal are regular in the right-half of the $j\omega$-plane, it is seen that if $H_L(j\omega)$ is set equal to the reciprocal of $N_+(j\omega)$

$$H_L(j\omega) = \frac{1}{N_+(j\omega)}, \tag{13}$$

then $N'(\omega^2) = 1$. Thus, a shaping network L whose transfer function is given by (13) results in a white noise at the input to F'.

The calculation of $N_+(j\omega)$ is a straightforward algebraic problem, since, in practice, $N(\omega^2)$ is generally of the form

$$N(\omega^2) = \frac{A(\omega^2)}{B(\omega^2)} = \frac{a_0 + a_1\omega^2 + \cdots + a_l\omega^{2l}}{b_0 + b_1\omega^2 + \cdots + b_m\omega^{2m}}, \tag{14}$$

where $A(\omega^2)$ and $B(\omega^2)$ are polynomials in ω^2, and m and l rarely exceed 3. Correspondingly, $N_+(j\omega)$ is of the form

$$N_+(j\omega) = \frac{A_+(j\omega)}{B_+(j\omega)}, \tag{15}$$

where $A_+(j\omega)$ and $B_+(j\omega)$ are real polynomials in $j\omega$ of degrees l and m, respectively. Thus, $A_+(j\omega)A_+^*(j\omega) = A(\omega^2)$ and $B_+(j\omega)B_+^*(j\omega) = B(\omega^2)$, and neither $A_+(j\omega)$ nor $B_+(j\omega)$ has zeros in the right half of the $j\omega$-plane. In terms of these polynomials, $H_L(j\omega)$ reads

$$H_L(j\omega) = \frac{B_+(j\omega)}{A_+(j\omega)} \cdot \tag{16}$$

A simple example will serve to illustrate these relations. Consider a noise whose power spectrum is

$$N(\omega^2) = \frac{\omega^2}{\omega^2 + a^2} \cdot \tag{17}$$

For this case,

$$N_+(j\omega) = \frac{j\omega}{j\omega + a}, \tag{18}$$

and consequently the transfer function of the shaping network is

$$H_L(j\omega) = \frac{j\omega + a}{j\omega} \cdot \tag{19}$$

Now let $W(t)$ and $W'(t)$ be the impulsive responses of F and F', respectively. Referring to Fig. 1, it is seen that $W(t)$ is related to $W'(t)$ by the operational equation

$$W(t) = H_L(p)W'(t). \tag{20}$$

Since $H_L(p)$ is specified by (13), the determination of $W(t)$ is reduced essentially to finding the expression for $W'(t)$. This is a relatively simple problem, as the following analysis indicates:

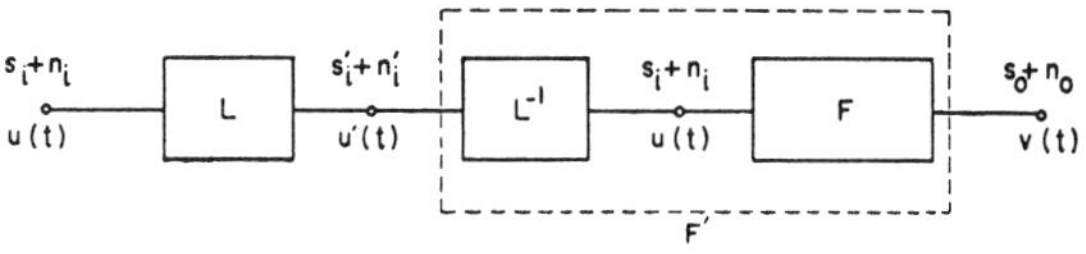

Fig. 1—Principle of spectrum-shaping technique.

Let $s_i'(t)$ and $n_i'(t)$ denote signal and noise components of the input to F'. As a consequence of setting the transfer function of L equal to $1/N_+(j\omega)$, the noise component $n_i'(t)$ is white noise $[N'(\omega^2) = 1]$ while the signal component $s_i'(t)$ is related to $s_i(y)$ (signal component of the input to F) by the operational relation

$$s_i'(t) = H_L(p)s_i(t)$$
$$= \frac{1}{N_+(p)} s_i(t). \qquad (21)$$

So far as F' is concerned, the problem is simply that of determining the impulsive response of an optimum filter in the case where the input noise is white. Thus, the quantity to be minimized by F' is

$$Q = \sigma^2 - \lambda s_0(t_0), \qquad (22)$$

where σ^2 denotes $\overline{n_0^2(t)}$, i.e., the mean-square value of the output noise; $s_0(t)$ is the response of F' to $s_i'(t)$; t_0 is a specified instant of time; and λ is an arbitrary constant. In terms of $W'(t)$, the expressions for σ^2 and $s_0(t_0)$ are

$$\sigma^2 = \int_0^\infty [W'(t)]^2 dt \qquad (23)$$

and

$$s_0(t_0) = \int_0^\infty W'(t)s_i'(t_0 - t)dt. \qquad (24)$$

Substituting these in (22) yields

$$Q = \int_0^\infty \{[W'(t)]^2 - \lambda W'(t)s_i'(t_0 - t)\}dt. \qquad (25)$$

The minimization of Q can easily be achieved without the use of variational techniques by expressing the integrand in (25) as the difference of a perfect square and a constant. Thus, completing the square and setting $\lambda = 2$ (for convenience) yields

$$Q = \int_0^\infty [W'(t) - s_i'(t_0 - t)]^2 dt$$
$$- \int_0^\infty [s_i'(t_0 - t)]^2 dt. \qquad (26)$$

Since the second term on the right is a constant, Q is a minimum when

$$W'(t) = s_i'(t_0 - t), \quad t \geq 0. \qquad (27)$$

In other words, the impulsive response of F is identical, for positive t, with the image of $s_i'(t)$ with respect to $t = t_0/2$. This, as should be expected, is in agreement with the classic result of North's theory in the white noise case.

Once $W'(t)$ is determined, the expression for $W(t)$ can easily be found through the use of (20). Thus, introducing the unit step function $1(t)$ (in order to indicate that $W(t)$ vanishes for $t<0$) and using (20), one obtains the operational relation

$$W(t) = \frac{1}{N_+(p)} 1(t)s_i'(t_0 - t), \qquad (28)$$

where $s_i'(t)$ is given by (21) and $N_+(p)$ is given by (15). This relation constitutes a general expression for the impulsive response of a *physically realizable* optimum filter in the nonwhite noise case.

A more explicit expression for the impulsive response of the optimum filter can readily be found by expressing $s_i'(t)$ in terms of its Fourier transform

$$s_i'(t) = \int_{-\infty}^{\infty} \frac{S(j\omega)}{N_+(j\omega)} e^{j\omega t} df, \qquad (29)$$

where $S(j\omega)$ is the Fourier transform of $s_i(t)$. Substituting this in (28) yields the impulsive response

$$W(t) = \frac{1}{N_+(p)} 1(t) \int_{-\infty}^{\infty} \frac{S^*(j\omega)}{N_+^*(j\omega)} e^{j\omega(t-t_0)} df. \qquad (30)$$

From this, the expression for the transfer function of F is found to be

$$H(j\omega) = \frac{1}{N_+(j\omega)} \int_0^\infty dt\, e^{-j\omega t} \int_{-\infty}^{\infty} df' \frac{S^*(j\omega')e^{j\omega'(t-t_0)}}{N_+^*(i\omega')}, \qquad (31)$$

where

ω' = variable of integration, $f' = \omega'/2\pi$;

$(\ )^*$ = complex conjugate of $(\ )$;

$S(j\omega)$ = Fourier transform of the signal $s_i(t)$ (at the input to F);

$N(\omega^2)$ = power spectrum of the noise $n_i(t)$ (at the input to F);

$N_+(j\omega)$ = factor of $N(\omega^2)$ which, together with its reciprocal, is regular in the right half of the $j\omega$-plane, and is such that $N_+(j\omega)N_+^*(j\omega) = N(\omega^2)$.

Equation (31) is the desired expression for the transfer function of a linear, infinite memory, and physically realizable filter that minimizes Q and also maximizes R and the signal-to-noise ratio ρ at $t = t_0$.

It will be noted that if F is not required to be physically realizable, $W(t)$ need not vanish for $t<0$, and consequently the lower limit in the first integral in (31) should be $-\infty$. Then, (31) reduces to

$$H(j\omega) = \frac{S^*(j\omega)e^{-j\omega t_0}}{N(\omega^2)}, \qquad (32)$$

which is identical with the expression given by Dwork.[8]

Finite Memory Filters

In the finite memory case, the situation is complicated somewhat by the requirement that $W(t)$ should vanish not only for $t<0$ but also for $t>T$, where T is a specified constant. Since $W(t)$ is related to $W'(t)$ by the equation

$$W(t) = H_L(p)W'(t), \qquad (33)$$

the impulsive response of F' is constrained to be such that $H_L(p)W'(t) = 0$ for $t>T$. This constraint is responsible for the complications arising in the process of optimization of F'.

In the infinite memory case just treated, it was found expedient to set the transfer function of the shaping network L equal to the reciprocal of $N_+(j\omega)$, which results in a white noise at the input to F'. The same choice in the finite memory case, however, would make it rather difficult to take into account the constraint imposed on $W'(t)$. Analysis of possible choices for $H_L(j\omega)$ indicates that, in the finite memory case, it is expedient to set $H_L(j\omega)$ equal to the denominator of $N_+(j\omega)$. In other words,

$$H_L(j\omega) = B_+(j\omega), \tag{34}$$

where $B_+(j\omega)$ is defined as in (15). With this expression for the transfer function, the power spectrum of the noise at the input to F' assumes the following form

$$N'(\omega^2) = A(\omega^2) = a_0 + a_1\omega^2 + \cdots + a_l\omega^{2l}, \tag{35}$$

where $A(\omega^2)$ is the numerator of $N(\omega^2)$ (see (14)). Also, the relation between $W(t)$ and $W'(t)$ becomes

$$W(t) = B_+(p)W'(t). \tag{36}$$

In view of this relation, the requirement that $W(t)=0$ for $t>T$ imposes the following constraint on $W'(t)$:

$$B_+(p)W'(t) = 0 \quad \text{for} \quad t > T, \tag{37}$$

which means that, for $t>T$, $W'(t)$ must be a solution of the differential equation $B_+(p)W'(t)=0$.

Turning to the determination of $W'(t)$, one has to express σ^2 and $s_0(t_0)$ in terms of $W'(t)$ and the noise and signal components of the input to F'. If $s_i(t)$ is the signal at the input to F, then the signal at the input to F' is

$$s_i'(t) = B_+(p)s_i(t), \tag{38}$$

and correspondingly at the output of F'

$$s_0(t_0) = \int_0^\infty W'(t)s_i'(t_0 - t)dt. \tag{39}$$

The expression for σ^2 is readily obtained by noting that a term in $N'(\omega^2)$ of the form $a_k\omega^{2k}$ results in a mean-square value component

$$\sigma_k^2 = \int_0^\infty a_k\left[\frac{d^kW'(t)}{dt^k}\right]^2 dt. \tag{40}$$

Hence $N'(\omega^2)$, being the sum of such terms, results in

$$\sigma^2 = \int_0^\infty \left\{a_0[W'(t)]^2 + a_1\left[\frac{dW'(t)}{dt}\right]^2 + \cdots + a_l\left[\frac{d^lW'(t)}{dt^l}\right]^2\right\} dt, \tag{41}$$

which is the desired expression for σ^2.

On substituting (39) and (41) in (22) and restricting the range of integration to $0\leq t\leq T$, the expression for the quantity to be minimized, a, is found to be

$$Q = \int_0^T \left\{a_0[W'(t)]^2 + a_1\left[\frac{dW'(t)}{dt}\right]^2 + \cdots + a_l\left[\frac{d^lW'(t)}{dt^l}\right]^2 - \lambda W'(t)s_i'(t_0 - t)\right\} dt. \tag{42}$$

The determination of a function $W'(t)$ which minimizes this expression is carried out in the Appendix. Once $W'(t)$ has been determined, the impulsive response $W(t)$ of the optimum filter F can be found from the relation

$$W(t) = B_+(p)W'(t), \tag{43}$$

where $B_+(p)$ is defined by (15). The resulting expression for $W(t)$ is given below ($W(t)=0$ outside of the interval $0\leq t\leq T$):

$$W(t) = \frac{1}{N_+(p)}1(t)\int_{-\infty}^{\infty}\frac{S^*(j\omega)e^{j\omega(t-t_0)}}{N_+^*(j\omega)}df + \sum_{\nu=1}^{2l}A_\nu e^{\alpha_\nu t} + \sum_{\mu=0}^{m-l-1}B_\mu\delta^{(\mu)}(t) + \sum_{\mu=0}^{m-l-1}C_\mu\delta^{(\mu)}(t - T), \tag{44}$$

where, to recapitulate,

$W(t)$ = impulsive response of the optimum filter F;

$N(\omega^2)$ = power spectrum of the noise component of the input to F;

$N_+(j\omega)$ = a factor of $N(\omega^2)$ so that $N_+(j\omega)$ and $1/N_+(j\omega)$ are regular in the right half of the $j\omega$-plane, and $|N_+(j\omega)|^2=N(\omega^2)$;

$(\ \ )^*$ = complex conjugate of $(\ \ )$;

$S(j\omega)$ = Fourier transform of the signal component of the input to F;

t_0 = a specified instant of time (relative to the signal);

$2l$ = degree of the numerator of $N(\omega^2)$;

$2m$ = degree of the denominator of $N(\omega^2)$;

A_ν, B_μ, C_μ = undetermined coefficients;

α_ν = roots of the equation $A(-p^2)=0$, where $A(\omega^2)$ is the numerator of $N(\omega^2)$;

T = settling time (length of memory);

$1(t)$ = unit step function;

$\delta(t)$ = unit impulse function;

$\delta^{(\nu)}(t)$ = νth derivative of $\delta(t)$.

In this expression, the terms $\sum_{\nu=1}^{2l}A_\nu \exp(\alpha_\nu t)$ represent the general solution of the differential equation $A(-p^2)W(t)=0$. The terms involving impulse functions of various orders arise from operating with $B_+(p)$ (see (43)) on the discontinuities of $W'(t)$ and its derivatives at $t=0$ and $t=T$. The first term in (44) may be written in a somewhat different but equivalent form which is sometimes advantageous.

$$\text{First term} = \frac{1}{N_+(p)}1(t)s_i'(t_0 - t), \tag{45}$$

where

$$s_i'(t) = \frac{1}{N_+(p)}s_i(t). \tag{46}$$

There remains the question of the undetermined coefficients A_ν, B_μ, and C_μ. The steps leading to the determination of these coefficients can best be formulated by going back to the minimization of the quantity Q,

$$Q = \sigma^2 - \lambda s_0(t_0), \tag{47}$$

which is achieved with the optimum filter. Previously, this quantity was expressed in terms of $W'(t)$, i.e., the impulsive response of F'. Now it will be necessary to express Q directly in terms of $W(t)$.

The expression for σ^2 in terms of $W(t)$ reads[15]

$$\sigma^2 = \int_0^T \int_0^T W(t)W(\tau)\psi_n(t-\tau)dtd\tau, \tag{48}$$

where $\psi_n(\tau)$ is the correlation function of the noise component of the input to F. Similarly, the expression for $s_0(t_0)$ is

$$s_0(t_0) = \int_0^T W(t)s_i(t_0 - t)dt, \tag{49}$$

where $s_i(t)$ is the signal component of the input to F. Substituting these expressions in (47) gives

$$Q = \int_0^T \int_0^T W(t)W(\tau)\psi_n(t-\tau)dtd\tau - \lambda \int_0^T W(t)s_i(t_0 - t)dt. \tag{50}$$

On applying standard variational formulas, it is found that Q is minimized by a $W(t)$, which satisfies the following integral equation:

$$\int_0^T W(\tau)\psi_n(t-\tau)d\tau = s_i(t_0 - t), \quad 0 \leqq t \leqq T. \tag{51}$$

Thus, the impulsive response of F is the solution of integral (51), whose kernel is the correlation function of $n_i(t)$ (the noise component of the input to F), and whose right-hand member is the image of the signal component $s_i(t)$ with respect to $t = t_0/2$. It is of interest to note that when $T = \infty$ this integral equation reduces to the Wiener-Hopf equation which is encountered in Wiener's theory of prediction.[16] (Equation (51) is similar in form to that encountered in an extension of Wiener's theory described in footnote reference 14.)

Now the expression for $W(t)$ obtained previously (see (44)) is, in effect, the solution of the integral (51). Consequently, the undetermined coefficients in (44) may be determined by substituting $W(t)$, as given by (44), into (51) and treating the resulting equation as an identity. This procedure will be illustrated by an example treated in the next section.

By using the fact that $W(t)$ is the solution of (51), it is possible to obtain a simple expression for the signal-to-noise ratio ρ at the output of the optimum filter. Thus, writing σ^2 in the form

$$\sigma^2 = \int_0^T dtW(t) \int_0^T W(\tau)\psi_n(t-\tau)d\tau \tag{52}$$

and noting that $W(t)$ satisfies the integral equation

$$\int_0^T W(\tau)\psi_n(t-\tau)d\tau = s_i(t_0 - t), \quad 0 \leqq t \leqq T,$$

one obtains

$$\sigma^2 = \int_0^T W(t)s_i(t_0 - t)dt, \tag{53}$$

which, in view of (49), is numerically equal to $s_0(t_0)$. (Note that, when $W(t)$ is the solution of (51), $s_0(t_0)$ is a positive quantity.) This implies that *the mean-square value of the noise output of the optimum filter is numerically equal to the signal output at* $t = t_0$. (The numerical equality does not hold unless $W(t)$ is the solution of (51).)

Now the general expression for ρ is $\rho = |s_0(t_0)|^2/\sigma^2$. Making use of the fact that for the optimum filter $\sigma^2 = s_0(t_0)$, the expression for the signal-to-noise ratio at the output of the optimum filter becomes

$$\rho_{max} = s_0(t_0) = \sigma^2. \tag{54}$$

It is easily verified that, if the filter is not required to be physically realizable, (54) reduces to the expression for ρ_{max} given by Dwork.[8]

IV. Illustrative Examples

Two examples of practical interest will serve to illustrate the theory: First, suppose that $s_i(t)$ is a periodic signal of period T_0, consisting of a train of rectangular pulses of unit height and width d. The settling time is assumed to be equal to an integral multiple of T_0, i.e., $T = kT_0$. The instant t_0 is specified as

$$t_0 = (k-1)T_0 + d. \tag{55}$$

In other words, the signal-to-noise ratio is to be maximized at the instant immediately following the occurrence of the training edge of the kth pulse. The power spectrum of noise is assumed to be of the form

$$N(\omega^2) = \frac{1}{\omega^2 + a^2} \cdot \tag{56}$$

The first step in determining the optimum filter is to form the expression for $N_+(j\omega)$. For the specified $N(\omega^2)$, $N_+(j\omega)$ reads

$$N_+(j\omega) = \frac{1}{j\omega + a} \cdot \tag{57}$$

Next, it is noted that $2p = 0$ ($2l$ = degree of the numerator of $N(\omega^2)$) and $2m = 2$ ($2m$ = degree of the denominator of $N(\omega^2)$). Thus $m - l - 1 = 0$, and therefore all terms in (44) involving undetermined coefficients are zero. Consequently, $W(t)$ is given by

$$W(t) = (p + a)1(t) \int_{-\infty}^{\infty} (a - j\omega)S^*(j\omega)e^{j\omega(t-t_0)}df, \quad 0 \leqq t \leqq T; \tag{58}$$

or more simply, (using (45)),

[15] H. M. James, N. B. Nichols, and R. S. Phillips, "Theory of Servomechanisms," Rad. Lab. Series, McGraw-Hill Book Co., New York, N. Y., vol. 24, chap. 6; 1947.

[16] N. Wiener, "The Extrapolation, Interpolation, and Smoothing of Stationary Time Series," John Wiley and Sons, Inc., New York, N. Y.; 1949.

$$W(t) = (p + a)1(t)s_i'(t_0 - t), \qquad 0 \leqq t \leqq T, \quad (59)$$

where

$$s_i'(t) = (p + a)s_i(t). \quad (60)$$

From (59) and (60), the impulsive response of the optimum filter is found to be expressed by

$$W(t) = (a^2 - p^2)s_i(t), \quad 0 \leqq t \leqq T, \quad (61)$$

where $s_i(t)$ is the specified pulse train. The form of $W(t)$ is shown in Fig. 2.

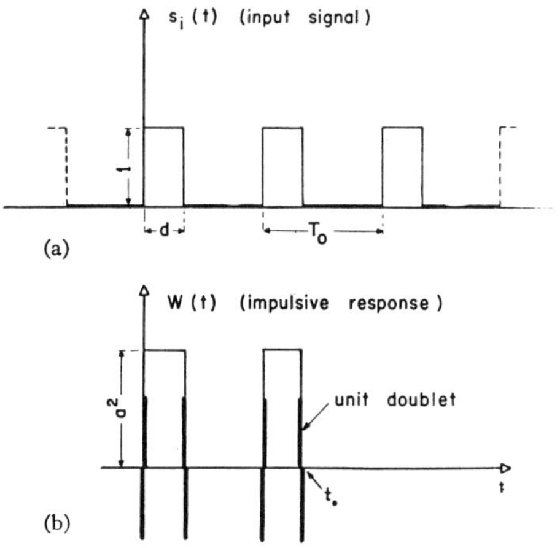

Fig. 2—(a) Form of the signal $s_i(t)$. (b) Form of the impulsive response of the optimum filter.

In the case under consideration, it is worth while to derive the expression for the transfer function $H(j\omega)$ of the optimum filter. From (61), it is readily found that $H(j\omega)$ is given by

$$H(j\omega) = \left(\frac{a^2 + \omega^2}{j\omega}\right)(1 - e^{-j\omega d})(1 + e^{-j\omega T_0} + \cdots + e^{-j\omega(k-1)T_0}); \quad (62)$$

or more simply,

$$H(j\omega) = \left(\frac{a^2}{j\omega} - j\omega\right)(1 - e^{-j\omega d})\left[\frac{1 - e^{-j\omega kT_0}}{1 - e^{-j\omega T_0}}\right]. \quad (63)$$

The bracketed term in this expression represents the transfer function of an ideal "integrator."[17] Thus, the optimum filter consists of a tandem combination of a filter F_1 with transfer function

$$H_1(j\omega) = \left(\frac{a^2}{j\omega} - j\omega\right)(1 - e^{-j\omega d}), \quad (64)$$

and an ideal "integrator" F_2 with transfer function

$$H_2(j\omega) = 1 + e^{-j\omega T_0} + e^{-j2\omega T_0} + \cdots + e^{-j(k-1)\omega T_0}. \quad (65)$$

[17] J. V. Harrington and T. F. Rogers, "Signal-to-Noise improvement through integration in a storage tube," Proc. I.R.E., vol. 38, pp. 1197–1203; October, 1950.

It is of interest to note that the optimum filter has, in general, this structure (that is, a filter followed by an "integrator") whenever the signal $s_i(t)$ is periodic and the power spectrum function $N(\omega^2)$ has a constant for the numerator.

Second Example

In this case the signal $s_i(t)$ is assumed to consist of a single rectangular pulse of unit amplitude and width d. The spectral density function is of the form

$$N(\omega^2) = \frac{\omega^2}{\omega^2 + a^2}. \quad (66)$$

The signal-to-noise ratio is to be maximized at the instant of occurrence of the trailing edge of the pulse. The impulsive response is required to vanish outside of the interval $0 \leqq t \leqq T$.

Following the same procedure as in the preceding example, one finds

$$N_+(j\omega) = \frac{j\omega}{j\omega + a}. \quad (67)$$

Since $2l = 2m = 2$, the unit impulse terms in (44) are zero. The second term, which is the general solution of the differential equation $-p^2W(t) = 0$, is of the form

$$A_0 + A_1t. \quad (68)$$

The first term in (44) may be written as (see (86))

$$\text{first term} = -\frac{(p + a)}{p^2}1(t)s_i'(t_0 - t), \quad (69)$$

where

$$s_i'(t) = (p + a)s_i(t) \quad (70)$$

and

$$s_i(t) = 1(t) - 1(t - d). \quad (71)$$

Calculation of this term yields

$$\text{first term} = 1 - \frac{a^2t^2}{2} \qquad \text{for} \quad t \leqq d$$

$$= -a^2dt + \frac{a^2d^2}{2} \qquad \text{for} \quad t > d. \quad (72)$$

Thus the complete expression for $W(t)$ is

$$W(t) = 1 + A_0 + A_1t - 0.5a^2t^2 \qquad \text{for } 0 \leqq t \leqq d$$

$$= A_0 + 0.5a^2d^2 + (A_1 - a^2d)t \text{ for } d < t \leqq T. \quad (73)$$

It remains to calculate the undetermined coefficients A_0 and A_1. For this purpose, it is necessary to set up the integral (51), of which $W(t)$ is the solution. The kernel of this equation is the correlation function $\Psi_n(\tau)$ of the noise component $n_i(t)$. Using the fact that $\Psi_n(\tau)$ is the inverse Fourier transform of $N(\omega^2)$ (Wiener-Khintchine relation), one readily finds

$$\psi_n = \delta(\tau) = 0.5ae^{-a|\tau|}. \quad (74)$$

Hence, for the case under consideration the integral equation reads

$$\int_0^T W(\tau)[\delta(t-\tau) - 0.5ae^{-a|t-\tau|}]d\tau$$
$$= 1(t) - 1(t-d), \quad 0 \leqq t \leqq T. \quad (75)$$

Substituting $W(t)$ as expressed by (73) into this equation and requiring that $W(t)$ be the solution of (75), yields two linear equations in A_0 and A_1 which, upon solution, give

$$A_0 = \frac{ad(2aT + 2 - ad)}{2(aT+2)} \quad (76)$$

and

$$A_1 = \frac{a^2d(2aT + 2 - ad)}{2(aT+2)}. \quad (77)$$

Substituting these values in (73) yields

$$W(t) = 1 + \frac{ad(2aT+2-ad)}{2(aT+2)} + \frac{a^2d(2aT+2-ad)t}{2(aT+2)} - 0.5a^2t^2 \quad \text{for } 0 \leqq t \leqq d$$
$$= \frac{ad(aT+1)(ad+2)}{2(aT+2)} - \frac{a^2d(ad+2)t}{2(aT+2)} \quad \text{for } d < t \leqq T. \quad (78)$$

This is the desired expression for the impulsive response of the optimum filter. A plot of $W(t)$ for $T=1$ msec, $d=100$ μsec and $a=20{,}000$ sec^{-1}, is shown in Fig. 3. It will be noted that $W(t)$, as given by (78), bears

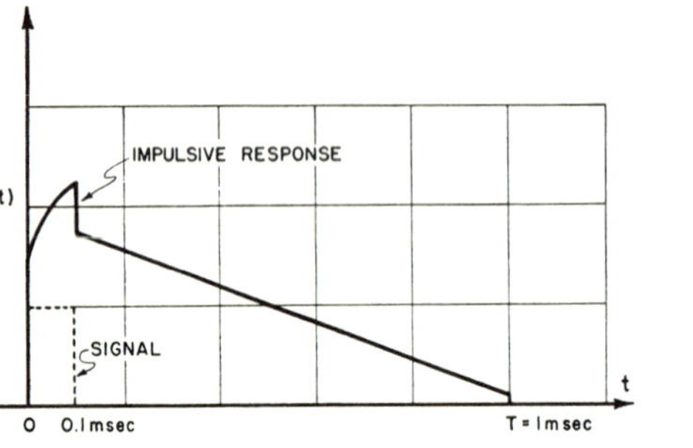

Fig. 3—Impulsive response of the optimun filter for example 2. The signal $s_i(t)$ in this case is a rectangular pulse (indicated by broken lines).

little if any resemblance to the impulsive response suggested by the "matched-filter" formula, namely $W(t) = s_i(t_0 - t)$. This implies that a "matched" filter may be far from optimum in a situation wherein the noise is not white and the filter is required to have a finite memory.

Appendix

The application of a standard variational formula[18] to (42) leads to the differential equation

$$A(-p^2)W'(t) = s_i'(t_0 - t), \quad 0 \leqq t \leqq T, \quad (79)$$

of which $W'(t)$ is a solution. In this equation $A(-p^2)$ represents the numerator of $N(\omega^2)$ with ω^2 replaced by $-p^2$, and

$$s_i'(t) = B_+(p)s_i(t), \quad (80)$$

where $B_+(p)$ is defined in (15).

$W'(t)$ may be written as the sum of two terms, $W_P'(t)$ and $W_G'(t)$, of which $W_P'(t)$ represents a particular solution of (79), while $W_G'(t)$ is the general solution of the homogeneous equation

$$A(-p^2)W'(t) = 0. \quad (81)$$

The general solution $W_G'(t)$ is given by

$$W_G'(t) = \sum_{\nu=1}^{2l} A_\nu' e^{\alpha_\nu t} \quad (82)$$

where the A_ν' are arbitrary constants and the α_ν are the roots of the characteristic equation $A(-p^2)=0$. (If α_ν is a multiple root of order k, then A_ν' is a polynomial of $(k-1)$st degree in t.)

Since a particular solution is not unique, $W_P'(t)$ may be written in various forms which differ between themselves by terms of the form $A_\nu' e^{\alpha_\nu t}$. Two of the more convenient expressions for $W_P'(t)$ are

$$(1) \quad W_P'(t) = \frac{1}{A_+(p)} 1(t) \frac{1}{A_+(-p)} s_i'(t_0 - t)$$
$$= \frac{1}{A_+(p)} 1(t) \int_{-\infty}^{\infty} \frac{S^*(j\omega)}{A_+^*(j\omega)} B_+^*(j\omega) e^{j\omega(t-t_0)} df \quad (83)$$

and

$$(2) \quad W_P'(t) = \frac{}{A(-p^2)} 1(t) s_i'(t_0 - t). \quad (84)$$

Using the first of these expressions, $W'(t)$ reads

$$W'(t) = \frac{1}{A_+(p)} 1(t) \int_{-\infty}^{\infty} \frac{S^*(j\omega)}{A_+^*(j\omega)} B_+^*(j\omega) e^{j\omega(t-t_0)} df + \sum_{\nu=1}^{2l} A_\nu' e^{\alpha_\nu t}. \quad (85)$$

Substituting this in (43) and replacing $A_+(j\omega)/B_+(j\omega)$ by $N_+(j\omega)$, one obtains the expression for $W(t)$ given by (44). The impulsive terms in (44) arise from operating with $B_+(p)$ on the discontinuities of $W'(t)$ and its derivatives at $t=0$ and $t=T$.

When (84) rather than (83) is used to represent $W_P'(t)$, the first term in (44) is replaced by

$$\text{first term} = \frac{B(p)}{A(-p^2)} 1(t) s_i'(t_0 - t). \quad (86)$$

(This change affects only the undetermined coefficients A_ν). In the case of the second example in section 4, this form of the first term is more convenient to work with than that appearing in (44).

[18] Courant-Hilbert, "Methoden Der Mathematischen Physik," Interscience Publishers, Inc., New York, N. Y., vol. I, p. 163; 1931.

OPTIMAL CONTROL UNDER CONDITIONS OF LAGGING FEEDBACK

N. N. Krasovskii

(Sverdlovsk)

Translated from Avtomatika i Telemekhanika, Vol. 24, No. 8,
pp. 1021-1036, August, 1963
Original article submitted December 7, 1962

The problem of determination of the optimal control law ξ° is discussed which will make the integral used to estimate process quality a minimum when the system is subject to random influences and the feedback signal is arriving with a lag. A criterion for a system being in an optimum condition has been formulated which is based on the concepts of the Lyapunov functions method [1], and on the principles of dynamic programming [2]. An efficient way for calculation of the optimal control ξ° is described which minimizes the rms error.

1. Preliminary Remarks

Let us examine the system of automatic control which is represented in the block diagram below. In this system, A is the object to be controlled, B is the "regulator" (the element carrying out the control action), C is the device wherein the comparison takes place, and D is the link in which the lag occurs. The function z(t) represents a vectorial quantity in the output of the object A which is to be regulated; $x(t) = z(t) - z^\circ(t)$ is the error function, ξ is the control action of the regulator (or the regulatory action), and $\eta(t)$ is a random function of the Markov kind [3] which is a determining factor in the state of object A. Factor $\eta(t)$ may be due to an accidental load imposed on A at random or to an accidental variation of a parameter of A. The quantity $\dot{\varphi}$ is a pulse-type disturbance of the kind characterized as "white noise" [3]. The quantity h denotes a constant lag, and we always have $h > 0$.

Let the motion of the system be described by the equation:

$$\dot{x} = f[t, x(t), \eta(t), \xi] + \dot{\varphi}, \tag{1.1}$$

where x and f stand for the vectors $\{x_i\}$ and $\{f_i\}$ in n-dimensional space; and η and ξ are scalars. The functions $f_i[t, x, \eta, \xi]$ are given. Let us assume that provisions are made for the values of $\xi(t)$ to be "remembered" (or stored) by the regulator B. The problem consists in determining the optimal control ξ°, that is, the control which will make the quantity

$$J = M\left\{\int_0^T \omega[\tau, x(\tau), \xi(\tau)]\,d\tau + \psi[x(T)]\right\} \tag{1.2}$$

a minimum. In the above formula ω and ψ are given nonnegative functions, and $M\{\nu\}$ is the symbol for mathematical expectation. It is required to find ξ° in the shape of a function of quantities which will describe the state of the system and which it is possible to determine. Thus, the problem under consideration is really a problem of synthesis of an optimal system [4], or a problem of analytical design of an optimal regulator [5]. We must, however, note that the problem may contain additional conditions which limit ξ°, such as, for instance, that there must be $|\xi^\circ| \leq 1$, or limitations for ξ° may follow from the minimum conditions for this quantity (1.2).

As was shown by [6], the problem of optimal control can be classified according to the properties of the object A and according to the nature of the information on the current state of A coming in to regulator B during the course of the control process. The classification follows:

I. Object A has a completely definite behavior, and

I*. Regulator B receives sufficiently complete information on the current state of A. Or

I••. Insufficient information on the current state of A is supplied to regulator B. Problems of class I are treated in papers [4, 5, 7-9].

II. The behavior of object A is of a probabilistic nature, and the following subclasses are possible:

II• At any instant t in the course of the process, sufficiently complete information on object A is supplied to regulator B, and the future behavior of object A at any time $\tau > t$ is according to a probability of the Markov type. Or

II•• Insufficient information on the current state of A is supplied to regulator B, and this information supply can not be improved by means of a rational selection of control action ξ°. Or

II••• The insufficient information on the current state of A can be supplemented by information obtained by means of a rational selection of ξ°.

To problems of Class II•, papers [2, 8-10], among others, are devoted, and to problems of class II••, papers [8, 11]. Class II••• corresponds to the dual control cases treated in [6] or to the selfadapting cases treated in [12].

The problem studied by us here belongs to class II••; the lag $h > 0$ excludes the possibility of exact information on the state of object A reaching regulator B at every instant of control action, and the lag h is assumed to be completely independent of control ξ.

2. Formulation of the Problem

Let us formulate the problem in a more exact way. We shall examine the process x(t) during the time span $0 \leq t \leq T$ $(T < \infty)$. The statistical properties of the random functions $\eta(t)$ and φ are supposed to be known, and so is is the description of the initial state of the system in terms of probability. In other words, we assume that the distribution of the random quantities x(0) and $\eta(0)$ is known. Let us denote this distribution by the arbitrary symbol H. For all instants $t \in [0, T]$ [meaning all t in the set of values from 0 to T in which the pertinent parameters are measurable -- Publisher] we know for regulator B the values of $x(t-h)$, $\eta(t-h)$ and $\xi(\vartheta + t)$ $(-h \leq \vartheta < 0)$ when $t \geq h$, or the values of $\xi(\vartheta)$ $(0 \leq \vartheta < t)$, when $t < h$. Knowing these quantities makes it possible to compose a probability description of the state of object A at various instants t, that is to give the probability distribution of the random quantities x(t) and $\eta(t)$.

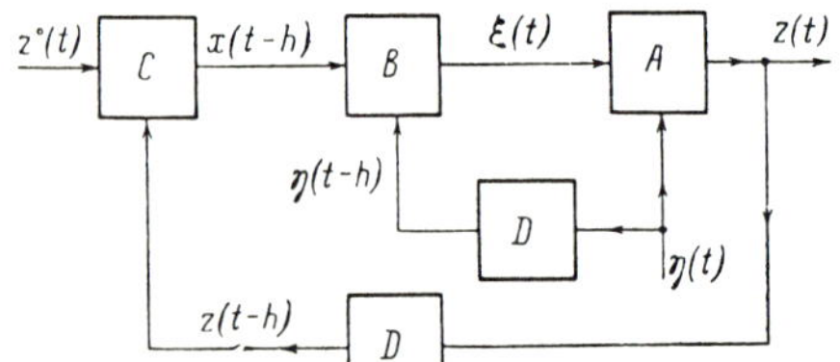

Let us introduce the following quantities:

$$\lambda(t) = \begin{cases} H, \ \xi(\vartheta) & (0 \leqslant \vartheta < t) \text{ when } t < h, \\ x(t-h), \ \eta(t-h), \ \xi(t+\vartheta) & (-h \leqslant \vartheta < 0) \text{ when } t \geqslant h. \end{cases} \tag{2.1}$$

The quantity

$$\min \{J_t \text{ over all } \xi(\tau) \ (t \leqslant \tau \leqslant T)\}, \tag{2.2}$$

where

$$J_t = M \left\{ \int_t^T \omega[\tau, x(\tau), \xi(\tau)] \, d\tau + \psi[x(T)] \right\}$$

can now be considered as a functional of $\lambda(t)$, that is, as a function of function $\lambda(t)$ which in turn is determined according to (2.1) by the values of components H and $\xi(\vartheta)$ when $t < h$, and by the values of $x(t-h)$, $\eta(t-h)$, and $\xi(t+\vartheta)$ when $t \geq h$. According to the rules of the theory of dynamic programming [2], the optimal control ξ° must be sought in the form of a functional

$$\xi^\circ = \zeta^\circ[t, \lambda(t)], \tag{2.3}$$

that is, we must be able to determine for every instant t the value of the optimal control ξ° from quantities which are components of $\lambda(t)$, and which it is possible to determine by measurements on regulator B; these quantities are H and $\xi(\vartheta)$ for $t < h$ and $x(t-h)$, $\eta(t-h)$, and $\xi(t+\vartheta)$ for $t \geq h$.

We shall henceforth call the functionals $\xi = \zeta\ [t, \lambda(t)]$, where $\lambda(t)$ is defined by (2.1), simply "controls."

Let us examine Eq. (1.1). If we substitute in the equation $\zeta\,[t, \lambda(t)]$ for ξ, then (1.1) becomes a stochastic differential equation. The following integral equation can serve as an exact interpretation of this differential equation:

$$x(t) = x(0) + \int_0^t f\,[\tau, x(\tau), \eta(\tau), \zeta[\tau, \lambda(\tau)]]\,d\tau + \int_0^t d\varphi\,[\tau, x(\tau)]. \tag{2.4}$$

Let us examine the meaning of $d\varphi$ a little closer. Let us assume that $d\varphi = R[t, x(t)]dy$, where $R = \| r_{ij}[t, x(t)] \|_1^n$ is an $n \times n$ matrix, and dy is an $\underline{n}$ dimensional vector $\{dy_i\}$ with components dy_i, independent of each other, each of which represents a Brownian movement [3]. Hence the $y_i(t)$ values are Gaussian probability processes for which we have:

$$M\,\{y_i(t_2) - y_i(t_1)\} = 0,$$

$$M\{[y_i(t_2) - y_i(t_1)][y_j(t_2) - y_j(t_1)]\} = \delta_{ij}\,|t_2 - t_1| \quad (\delta_{ii} = 1, \ \delta_{ij} = 0 \text{ when } i \neq j).$$

The matrix $R = \| r_{ij} \|_1^n$ determines the second moments of the random scatter of the quantities $dx_i(t)$, namely:

$$M\,\{dx_i(t)\,dx_j(t)\} = \sum_{k=1}^{n} r_{ik}(t, x)\,r_{jk}(t, x)\,dt = \sigma_{ij}(t, x)\,dt.$$

The white noise disturbance $\dot{\varphi} = d\varphi/dt$ can be treated as a random assembly of small pulses acting with a high average frequency.

Equation (2.4) differs from the usual stochastic equations describing processes similar to the diffusion process (see [3]) in one respect, namely by the quantity $\lambda(\tau)$ on the right side which produces aftereffects in the system. However, this does not prevent us from obtaining the solution of equation (2.4) by the method of successive approximations while still maintaining sufficient generality with respect to the assumptions about f, H, η, R, and ζ. Without going into details, let us assume that the functions f, H, η, and R satisfy the necessary requirements, and let us limit the multiplicity of feasible controls $\{\zeta\}$ in the ensemble $\zeta[t, \lambda(t)]$ only to such controls for which it is possible to construct a solution of equation (2.4) which will make all (or nearly all) x(t) realizations of the process-to-be-controlled continuous. Let us note that the conditions for existence of such a solution are satisfied in any case for the problem which will be examined in section 4, where the function f_i are linear, H has a normal distribution, functions R and ζ are assumed to be sufficiently smooth, and $\eta(t)$ is either a process with entirely discrete parameters (completely dissociated states) or a process of the diffusion type [3].

The multiplicity of $\{\zeta\}$ can in some instances be narrowed down still further by imposing additional restraints on $\xi = \zeta$ according to the requirements of the problem at hand (as for instance, that there must be $|\xi| \leq 1$).

Equation (1.1) and its exact expression (2.4) can be visualized more clearly by the following interpretation: Let us assume, for instance, that $\eta(t)$ is a discrete-parameters Markov process [3] whose realizations $\eta P(t)$ are constant value functions within small limited ranges. Suppose a control $\xi = \zeta[t, \lambda(t)]$ has been selected, and at the instant $t = \tau$ we have: $\lambda(\tau) = \lambda^*$, $x(\tau) = x^*$, and $\eta(\tau) = \eta^*$. Then there is a bunch of random realizations $xP(t)$ $(t \geq \tau)$ which emanates from point $x(\tau) = x^*$. The quantity $\eta(t)$ will maintain its value $\eta(\tau) = \eta^*$ within the span $\tau \leq t \leq \tau + dt$ with a probability $p(\eta^*, dt) = 1 - p(\eta^*)dt + 0(dt)$, and, therefore, it can be stated that, when $dt > 0$ is sufficiently small, there is a probability close to one that quantity $x(\tau)$ will have the following random increment

$$dx(\tau) = f\,[\tau, x^*, \eta^*, \zeta\,[\tau, \lambda^*]]\,dt + R\,[\tau, x^*]\,dy(t). \tag{2.5}$$

In other words, during time dt the vector x(t) has shifted by a quantity $f(\tau, x^*, \eta^*, \zeta[\tau, \lambda^*])dt$ and with a scatter due to the term $R[\tau, x^*]dy(t)$; and this scatter is taking place according to a normal distribution around an average of zero and with a second order moments matrix $\| \sigma_{ij}[\tau, x^*]dt \|$.

We shall designate henceforth by the symbol $x^{\xi}[t \mid \lambda(\tau)]$ $(t \geq \tau - h$ for $\tau \geq h$, or $t \geq 0$ for $\tau < h)$ the random quantity x(t) which represents a solution of equation (1.1) when the initial condition is $\lambda(\tau)$ and the control is ξ. And $\xi(t)$ $[t \geq \max(\tau - h, 0)]$ can be here, either a definite function of time $\xi(t)$, or it can be equal to $\zeta[t, \lambda(t)]$ where ζ is any kind of control operation. However, it is assumed all the time that when $t < \tau$ the control $\xi(t)$ coincides with that control $\xi(t)$ which is a component of $\lambda(\tau)$ in accordance with (2.1). Similarly, the symbols $\eta[t \mid \eta(\tau)]$ with $\tau > 0$ and $[\eta(t) \mid H]$ at $\tau = 0$ will stand for the random quantity $\eta(t)$ with the understanding that the initial conditions H prevail. And the symbol $\lambda^{\xi}[t \mid \lambda(\tau)]$ will stand for the random quantity $\lambda(t)$, when in $\lambda(t)$ of (2.1) the components $x(t-h)$ and $\eta(t-h)$ for $t \geq h$ are $\eta[t-h \mid \eta(\tau-h)]$, $\eta(\tau-h) \in \lambda(\tau)$, and $x[t-h \mid \lambda(\tau)]$. And furthermore it is assumed that when $\xi = \zeta[t, \lambda(\tau)]$, then within the range $\tau \leq \vartheta < t$ we have control $\xi(\vartheta) = \zeta(\vartheta, \lambda[\vartheta \mid \lambda(\tau)])$, and for $\vartheta < \tau$ we have as the control the $\xi(\vartheta)$ which is a component of $\lambda(\tau)$ according to (2.1).

Now we can formulate our problem.

Problem 2.1. It is required to find among the feasible controls $\{\zeta[t, \lambda(t)]\}$ the optimal control $\xi^{\circ} = \zeta^{\circ} \times [t, \lambda(t)]$, which satisfies the condition

$$\min_{\zeta} J[\tau, \lambda(\tau); \zeta] = J[\tau, \lambda(\tau); \zeta^{\circ}] \quad (\zeta \in \{\zeta\}) \tag{2.6}$$

at all $\tau \in [0, T]$ and at all $\lambda(\tau)$ (2.1) containing as components $\xi(\vartheta)$ in the form of functions which are continuous within limited ranges. In formula (2.6)

$$J[\tau, \lambda(\tau); \zeta] = M\left\{\int_{\tau}^{T} \omega[t, x^{\xi}[t \mid \lambda(\tau)], \zeta[t, \lambda^{\xi}[t \mid \lambda(\tau)]]\, dt + \psi[x^{\xi}[T \mid \lambda(\tau)]]\right\} \quad (\xi(t) = \zeta[t, \lambda(t)]). \tag{2.7}$$

3. Criterion of Optimal Condition

Let us first introduce some definitions and denotations. By the symbol $M\{\mu \mid \nu\}$ we shall denote the conditional mathematical expectation of the quantity μ under the condition ν; by the symbol $\xi[\vartheta, t, \lambda(t)]$ we shall denote the component $\xi[t+\vartheta]$ for $t \geq h$, and the component $\xi(\vartheta)$ for $t < h$ in accordance with (2.1). The identity $\xi[\vartheta; t_1; \lambda(t_1)] \equiv \xi[\vartheta; t_2, \lambda(t_2)]$ will mean that the components $\xi[\vartheta; t_1, \lambda(t_1)] \in \lambda_1(t_1)$ and $\xi[\vartheta; t_2, \lambda(t_2)] \in \lambda(t_2)$ coincide with each other in the common part of those spans in which their value has been determined. Specifically, $\xi[\vartheta; h, \lambda(h)] \equiv \xi[\vartheta; t, \lambda^*(t)]$ at $t < h$ means that $\xi[\vartheta] = \xi^*[\vartheta]$ at $0 \leq \vartheta < t$, where ξ is $\in \lambda(h)$ and ξ^* is $\in \lambda^*(t)$. We will call a functional $u[t, \lambda(t)]$ continuous with respect to <u>t</u> and λ for $t > h$ or for $t < h$, if small changes of <u>t</u> and $\lambda(t)$ produce only small changes in $u[t, \lambda(t)]$. And the smallness of the change in $\lambda(t)$ is judged on the basis of the smallness of the changes in the $\lambda(t)$ components as measured by any of the conventional systems of units.

We will consider a functional $u[t, \lambda(t)]$ to be continuous for all values of <u>t</u>, if it is continuous with respect to <u>t</u> and $\lambda(t)$ for $t < h$ and $t > h$, and if at the same time the following condition is satisfied:

$$\lim_{t \to h-0} \{u[t, \lambda^*(t)]\} = M\{u[h, \lambda(h)] \mid \xi[\vartheta; h, \lambda(h)] \equiv \xi[\vartheta; t, \lambda^*(t)]\} \text{ .(3.1)} \tag{3.1}$$

This additional condition is caused by the fact that in transition of <u>t</u> through the point $t = h$ the quantity $\lambda(t)$ changes its character. Condition (3.1) means that the value of functional $u[t, \lambda^*(t)]$ for $t \to h - 0$ coincides with the mathematical expectation (average value) of functionals $u[h, \lambda(h)]$ over all those $\lambda(h)$ whose $\xi(\vartheta)$ component is equal to that of $\lambda^*(t)$, that is, over all those $\lambda(h)$ into which seemingly $\lambda(t^*)$ is split up in transition over the point $t = h$ because of the fact that beginning at the instant $t = h$ additional information on the quantities $x(t-h)$ and $\eta(t-h)$ is arriving in the regulator, and therefore $\lambda(t)$ is changing its character.

Let us denote the average derivative of functional $u[t, \lambda(t)]$ at point τ, $\lambda(\tau)$ for a series of solutions of equation (1.1) for control $\xi = \zeta[t, \lambda(t)]$ by the symbol $[dM\{u\}/dt \mid \tau, \lambda(\tau); \zeta]$ [10, 14]. Let us explain the meaning of this quantity a little further: suppose at the instant $t = \tau$ we have a value $\lambda(\tau)$. This initial condition creates the random quantity $\lambda^{\zeta}[t \mid \lambda(\tau)]$. Then for $t \to \tau + 0$, we have

$$(dM\{u\}/dt \mid \tau, \lambda(\tau); \zeta) = \lim (t-\tau)^{-1} [M\{u[t, \lambda^{\zeta}[t \mid \lambda(\tau)]] - u[\tau, \lambda(\tau)]\}$$

The quantity $dM\{u\}/dt$ is connected with the concept of an infinitely small generating operator of the probability process, even though in our case it is computed not for a Markov process, but for a process having an aftereffect.

Now let us formulate the "sufficient" conditions for optimality of control $\zeta^{\circ}[t, \lambda(\tau)]$.

Criterion 3.1. Suppose we have succeeded in finding functionals $v[t, \lambda(t)]$ and $\zeta^\circ[t, \lambda(t)]$ which satisfy the following conditions:

1) the quantity ζ° is continuous with respect to t and λ for $t < h$ and $t > h$;

2) the quantity v is continuous for all values of t;

3) the following equality is valid:

$$v[T, \lambda(T)] = M\{\psi[x^\xi[T \mid \lambda(T)]\}; \tag{3.2}$$

4) the derivative $dM\{v\}/dt$ averaged over the motion (1.1) satisfies the following conditions:

$$\left(\frac{dM\{v\}}{dt} \mid \tau, \lambda(\tau), \zeta^\circ\right) = -M\{\omega[\tau, x^\xi[\tau \mid \lambda(\tau)], \zeta^\circ[\tau, \lambda(\tau)]]\},$$

$$\left(\frac{dM\{v\}}{dt} \mid \tau, \lambda(\tau), \zeta^\circ\right) + M\{\omega[\tau, x^\xi[\tau \mid \lambda(\tau)], \zeta^\circ[\tau, \lambda(\tau)]]\}$$

$$= \min_\zeta \left(\frac{dM\{v\}}{dt} \mid \tau, \lambda(\tau), \zeta\right) + M\{\omega[\tau, x^\xi[\tau \mid \lambda(\tau)], \zeta[\tau, \lambda(\tau)]]\} \quad (\zeta \in \{\zeta\}). \tag{3.4}$$

When all the above conditions are satisfied then $\xi^\circ = \zeta^\circ[t, \lambda(t)]$ is the optimal control which solves problem 2.1 and the following equality is valid:

$$J[\tau, \lambda(\tau); \zeta^\circ] = v[\tau, \lambda(\tau)]. \tag{3.5}$$

Let us outline a proof of this criterion. Suppose the control $\xi = \zeta^\circ$ has been selected as a suitable one, and the quantity $\lambda(\tau) = \lambda^*(\tau)$ has been determined. We set up the following expression:

$$V[t, \lambda^*(\tau); \zeta^\circ] = M\{v[t, \lambda^{\zeta^\circ}[t \mid \lambda(\tau)]] \mid \lambda(\tau) = \lambda^*(\tau)\} \quad (t \geqslant \tau). \tag{3.6}$$

If process $\eta(t)$ and solution $x(t)$ of equation (2.4) have sufficient regularity as was assumed [see paragraph starting: "Eq. (2.4) differs" on p.933], the quantity $V[t, \lambda^*; \zeta^\circ]$ is a continuous function of t. Computing the derivative dV/dt from (3.6) in a manner used in a similar case described in [10, 14], we obtain:

$$\frac{dV[t, \lambda^*(\tau); \zeta^\circ]}{dt} = M\left\{\left(\frac{dM\{v\}}{dt} \mid t, \lambda^{\zeta^\circ}[t \mid \lambda^*(\tau)]; \zeta^\circ\right) \mid \lambda^*(\tau)\right\}.$$

Because of (3.3) we now have:

$$\frac{dV[t, \lambda^*(\tau); \zeta^\circ]}{dt} = -M\{\omega[t, x^{\zeta^\circ}[t \mid \lambda^*(\tau)], \zeta^\circ[t, \lambda^{\zeta^\circ}[t \mid \lambda^*(\tau)]]] \mid \lambda^*(\tau)\}. \tag{3.7}$$

Integrating (3.7) and taking into account (3.2) we obtain the following:

$$v[\tau, \lambda^*(\tau)] = V[\tau, \lambda^*(\tau); \zeta^\circ] = M\left\{\left[\int_\tau^T \omega[t, x^{\zeta^\circ}[t \mid \lambda^*(\tau)],\right.\right.$$

$$\left.\left.\zeta^\circ[t, \lambda^{\zeta^\circ}[t \mid \lambda^*(\tau)]]]\, dt + \psi[x^{\zeta^\circ}[T \mid \lambda^*(\tau)]]\right] \mid \lambda^*(\tau)\right\}. \tag{3.8}$$

For $\xi = \zeta[t, \lambda] \not\equiv \zeta^\circ[t, \lambda]$ we follow the same procedure, but use instead of equation (3.7) the following inequality:

$$\frac{dV[t, \lambda^*(\tau); \zeta]}{dt} \geqslant -M\{\omega[t, x^\zeta[t \mid \lambda^*(\tau)], \zeta[t, \lambda^\zeta[t \mid \lambda^*(\tau)]]] \mid \lambda^*(\tau)\}, \tag{3.9}$$

which follows from condition (3.4). We then obtain:

$$v\,[\tau,\lambda^*(\tau)] = V\,[\tau,\lambda^*(\tau),\zeta] \leqslant$$

$$\leqslant M\left\{\left[\int_{\tau}^{T} \omega\,[t, x^{\zeta}[t\,|\,\lambda^*(\tau)],\ \zeta\,[t,\lambda^{\zeta}\,[t\,|\,\lambda^*(\tau)]]\right] dt + \psi\,[x^{\zeta}\,[T\,|\,\lambda^*(\tau)]]]\,|\,\lambda^*(\tau)\right\}. \qquad (3.10)$$

Relationships (3.8) and (3.10) prove the validity of criterion 3.1.

Note. A rigorous proof of criterion 3.1 must include a continuity check of the quantity $V[t, \lambda^*(\tau), \zeta]$ with respect to t; a rigorous foundation must be laid for equation (3.7) and inequality (3.9), and it also is necessary to show that the integration of these expressions is justified. We are not going to discuss these questions in detail, but we will however remark that for the cases discussed in section 4 below the necessary proof on all questionable points raised here comes through in the affirmative.

4. Analytical Construction of an Optimal Regulator for a Linear System

Let us examine the system described by the linear equation

$$\frac{dx}{dt} = A\,(t)\,x\,(t) + b\,(t)\,\eta\,(t) + m\,(t)\,\xi + \frac{d\varphi}{dt}, \qquad (4.1)$$

where $A(t)$ is the $n \times n$ matrix $\|a_{ij}(t)\|_1^n$; $b = \{b_i(t)\}$ and $m = \{m_i(t)\}$ are n-dimensional vectors. We are assuming that the matrix R which determines the noise $d\varphi/dt$ is dependent only on time, and therefore the matrix of the random scatter second moments also is a function of time only. Thus, we have:

$$M\,\{(dx_i - dx_i^*)\,(dx_j - dx_j^*)\} = \sigma_{ij}\,(t)\,dt.$$

The quantity dx_i^* here represents the variation of the average value of $x_i(t)$, that is $dx_i^* = [A(t)x^*(t) + b(t)\,\eta^*(t) + m(t)\xi^*]dt$, if at the instant t the respective functions have the values $x^*(t)$, $\eta^*(t)$, and $\xi^*(t)$. We assume also that the initial distributions $x(0)$ and $\eta(0)$ are normal.

Let us seek a minimum for the functional

$$J = M\left\{\int_0^T \left[\sum_{i,j=1}^{n} \omega_{ij}\,(t)\,x_i\,(t)\,x_j\,(t) + \xi^2\,(t)\right] dt + \sum_{i,j=1}^{n} \psi_{ij} x_i\,(T)\,x_j\,(T)\right\}, \qquad (4.2)$$

where $\Sigma\omega_{ij}x_ix_j$ and $\Sigma\psi_{ij}x_ix_j$ are nonnegative forms.

We examine first the case when $\eta(t) \equiv 0$, that is, we examine the problem of finding the minimum of quantity

$$J\,[\tau,\lambda\,(\tau),\zeta] = M\left\{\left[\int_{\tau}^{T}\left[\sum_{i,j=1}^{n}\omega_{ij}\,(t)\,x_i\,(t)\,x_j\,(t) + \xi^2\,(t)\right] dt + \sum_{i,j=1}^{n} \psi_{ij} x_i\,(T)\,x_j\,(T)\right]\Big|\,\lambda\,(\tau)\right\} \qquad (4.3)$$

for the system

$$\frac{dx}{dt} = A\,(t)\,x\,(t) + m\,(t)\,\xi + \frac{d\varphi}{dt}. \qquad (4.4)$$

We will show how in this case the functionals $v[t, \lambda(t)]$ and $\zeta^\circ[t, \lambda(t)]$ must be constructed so as to satisfy the conditions of criterion 3.1. We seek functional $v[t, \lambda(t)]$ in the following form:

$$v\,[\tau,\lambda\,(\tau)] = M\left\{\sum_{i,j=1}^{n} \alpha_{ij}\,(\tau)\,x_i^{\xi}\,(\tau\,|\,\lambda\,(\tau))\,x_j^{\xi}\,(\tau\,|\,\lambda\,(\tau))\,|\,\lambda\,(\tau)\right\} + \gamma\,(\tau), \qquad (4.5)$$

where $\alpha_{ij}(t)$ are time functions that are to be determined.

First of all, let us verify that (4.5) really is a functional of $\lambda(\tau)$. To prove this we will show that $\underline{v}$ (4.5) can be computed from a given value of time instant τ and given values of the components $\lambda(\tau)$. To simplify the writing, let us assume for the time being that A is constant, even though all following discussions remain valid also in the case when A varies with time. The difference between the case when A is independent of time and the case when A(t) is a function that varies with time consists only in that in the former case the solution for the nonhomogeneous equation

$$\frac{dx}{dt} = Ax + m(t)\,\xi \tag{4.6}$$

when $x(0) = x_0$ can be written down using the Cauchy formula in the more compact form:

$$x(t) = F(t)\,x_0 + \int_0^t F(t-\vartheta)\,m(\vartheta)\,\xi(\vartheta)\,d\vartheta, \tag{4.7}$$

Function F(t) in (4.7) is the coefficients matrix of the system of homogeneous equations

$$\frac{dx}{dt} = Ax \tag{4.8}$$

[F(0) = E is the identity, or unit matrix]. If A(t) is a function of time, then

$$x(t) = F(t, t_0)\,x(t_0) + \int_0^t F(t, \vartheta)\,m(\vartheta)\,\xi(\vartheta)\,d\vartheta,$$

where $F(t, t_0)$ is the matrix of the fundamental set of solutions for the homogeneous system $dx/dt = A(t)x$ which becomes a unit matrix at $t = t_0$.

So let us have for the present A = const. Let us suppose at first that $\tau \geq h$, and that throughout the span $\tau - h \leq t < \tau$ in equation (4.4) noise $d\varphi/dt$ is absent. Let us denote by the symbol $x^*[\tau \mid \lambda(\tau)]$ a solution of equation (4.6) computed for the instant of time τ and corresponding to the value of $\lambda(\tau)$ at that instant. When $\tau \geq h$ the quantity $\lambda(\tau)$ is composed as follows:

$$\lambda(\tau) = \{x(\tau - h),\ \xi(\vartheta + \tau)\ (-h \leqslant \vartheta < 0)\}.$$

Taking into account that during the time interval $\tau - h \leq t < \tau$ in equation (4.6) control $\xi(t) = \xi(\vartheta + \tau) \in \lambda(\tau)$, was in force, and, having chosen $t = \tau - h$ as the starting point of our count we can write down solution (4.7) as follows:

$$x^*(\tau \mid \lambda(\tau)) = F(h)\,x(\tau - h) + \int_{-h}^{0} F(-\vartheta)\,m(\tau + \vartheta)\,\xi(\tau + \vartheta)\,d\vartheta. \tag{4.9}$$

When $\tau < h$, then the quantity $\lambda(\tau)$ is composed of $\{H, \xi(\vartheta)\ (0 \leq \vartheta < \tau)\}$. In this case even in the absence of noise $d\varphi/dt$ the solution of equation (4.6) is a random quantity because of the random straying value of the initial condition x(0). In this case we denote by the symbol $x^*[\tau \mid \lambda(\tau)]$ the mathematical expectation of the $x(\tau)$ solution of equation (4.6). Since the random solution x(t) is calculated by formula (4.7) with $\xi(\vartheta)$ replaced by $\in \lambda(\tau)$, we obtain by averaging (4.7) over $x_0 = x(0)$ the following:

$$x^*(\tau \mid \lambda(\tau)) = M\{x(\tau)\} = F(\tau)\,M\{x(0)\} + \int_0^{\tau} F(\tau - \vartheta)\,m(\vartheta)\,\xi(\vartheta)\,d\vartheta \quad (\tau < h), \tag{4.10}$$

in which $M\{x(0)\}$ is determined by the probability distribution H of the initial conditions x(0). Because of the noise $d\varphi/dt$, in reality the random quantity $x^{\xi}[\tau \mid \lambda(\tau)]$ follows a normal distribution law around a center point (mean value) of $x^*[\tau \mid \lambda(\tau)]$, determined by (4.9) or (4.10). The mathematical expectation $M\{x^{\xi}[\tau \mid \lambda(\tau)]\} = x^*[\tau \mid \lambda(\tau)]$ and the matrix $\|\varepsilon_{ij}(\tau)\|_1^n$ of the second moments of the scatter around the center point can be computed in a known manner [3] from the values of $\sigma_{ij}(t)$ and of the second moments matrix of the initial distribution H of x(0). Thus we obtain the following:

$$\varepsilon_{ij}(\tau) = M\{(x_i^{\xi}(\tau\mid\lambda(\tau)) - x_i^*)(x_j^{\xi}(\tau\mid\lambda(\tau)) - x_j^*)\} = \int_{-h}^{0}\Big(\sum_{l,k=1}^{n} f_{ik}(-\vartheta) f_{jl}(-\vartheta)\Big)\sigma_{l,k}(\tau+\vartheta)\,d\vartheta \quad \text{for} \quad \tau \geqslant h \tag{4.11}$$

and

$$\varepsilon_{ij}(\tau) = M\{(x_i(0) - M\{x_i(0)\})(x_j(0) - M\{x_j(0)\})\} + \int_{0}^{\tau}\Big(\sum_{l,k=1}^{n} f_{ik}(\tau-\vartheta) f_{jl}(\tau-\vartheta)\Big)\sigma_{l,k}(\vartheta)\,d\vartheta \quad \text{for} \quad \tau < h. \tag{4.12}$$

Therefore

$$x^{\xi}(\tau\mid\lambda(\tau)) = x^*(\tau\mid\lambda(\tau)) + x(\tau), \tag{4.13}$$

where vector x^* is determined by equations (4.9) and (4.10), and vectors $x(\tau)$ are distributed,normally random quantities with average values of zero and matrices of second moments $\|\varepsilon_{ij}(\tau)\|_1^n$ according to (4.11) and (4.12).

Substituting (4.13) into (4.5),which determines $\underline{v}$, we obtain the following:

$$v[\tau, \lambda(\tau)] = \sum_{i,j=1}^{n} \alpha_{ij}(\tau) x_i^*(\tau\mid\lambda(\tau)) x_j^*(\tau\mid\lambda(\tau)) + \sum_{i,j=1}^{n} \alpha_{ij}(\tau)\varepsilon_{ij}(\tau) + \gamma(\tau), \tag{4.14}$$

in which the vectors x^* are determined by (4.9) and (4.10). Formulas (4.14), (4.9), and (4.10) show clearly how the quantities of (4.5) depend on $x(\tau - h)$, $\xi(\tau + \vartheta)$ or H and $\xi(\vartheta)$,which are components of the quantities $\lambda(t)$.

We will show now that the coefficients $\alpha_{ij}(t)$ and $\gamma(t)$ can be so chosen that they will satisfy conditions (3.1)-(3.4) of criterion (3.1). We shall henceforth use everywhere for $\underline{v}$ not the explicit form given in (4.14), but the symbolical form of (4.5), which is more convenient to handle. We will compute now the averaged value of the derivative $dM\{v\}/dt$. Using the formula of iterated conditional mathematical expectations [3], the validity of the following equation can be verified:

$$\left(\frac{dM\{v\}}{dt}\,\Big|\,\tau, \lambda(\tau); \zeta\right) = M\left\{\left[\frac{dM\Big\{\sum_{i,j=1}^{n} \alpha_{ij}(t) x_i^{\xi}(t\mid\lambda(\tau))\, x_j^{\xi}(t\mid\lambda(\tau)) \mid x(\tau\mid\lambda(\tau))\Big\}}{dt}\right]_{t=\tau}\Bigg|\,\lambda(\tau)\right\} + \frac{d\gamma}{dt}. \tag{4.15}$$

The quantity enclosed in square brackets in the above formula has been computed in paper [14] for a process of similar nature. Using this computation we obtain for our case:

$$\left\{\frac{dM\Big\{\sum_{i,j=1}^{n} \alpha_{ij}(t) x_i(t) x_j(t) \mid x(\tau)\Big\}}{dt}\right\}_{t=\tau}$$

$$= \sum_{i,j=1}^{n}\left\{\left(\frac{d\alpha_{ij}(t)}{dt}\right)_{t=\tau} + \sum_{k=1}^{n}(\alpha_{ik}(\tau)a_{kj} + \alpha_{jk}(\tau)a_{ki})\right\} x_i(\tau)\,x_j(\tau)$$

$$+2\sum_{i,j=1}^{n}\alpha_{ij}(\tau)\,x_j(\tau)\,m_i(\tau)\,\xi(\tau) + \sum_{i,j=1}^{n}\alpha_{ij}(\tau)\,\sigma_{ij}(\tau) \quad (\xi(\tau) = \zeta[\tau, \lambda(\tau)]). \tag{4.16}$$

Averaging (4.16) in accordance with equation (4.15) we obtain

$$\left(\frac{dM\{v\}}{dt}\,\Big|\,\tau, \lambda(\tau); \zeta\right) = \sum_{i,j=1}^{n}\left\{\left[\left(\frac{d\alpha_{ij}(t)}{dt}\right)_{t=\tau} + \sum_{k=1}^{n}(\alpha_{ik}(\tau)a_{kj} + \alpha_{jk}(\tau)a_{ki}\right] x_i^* x_j^*\right.$$

$$\left. + 2\alpha_{ij}(\tau)\,x_j^* m_i(\tau)\,\xi(\tau)\right\} + q(\tau) + \left(\frac{d\gamma}{dt}\right)_{t=\tau}, \tag{4.17}$$

wherein function $q(\tau)$ can be expressed in a well known manner in terms of $\alpha_{ij}(\tau)$, and x_i^* are the components of vectors (4.9) or (4.10).

Substituting (4.17) into criterion condition (3.3), we obtain the first equation for v and $\xi^\circ = \zeta^\circ[t, \lambda]$. The second equation is obtained by differentiation of the first equation over ξ and taking into account that at $\xi^\circ = \zeta^\circ[t, \lambda]$ (3.4) reaches a minimum. Eliminating ξ from the two equations, we obtain an equation for v. Considering that in the latter equation the coefficients at similar expressions of x_i^* and x_j^* must be equal, we obtain a series of differential equations for the coefficients $\alpha_{ij}(\tau)$ of the following shape:

$$\frac{d\alpha_{ij^*}(t)}{dt} = -\sum_{k=1}^{n} (\alpha_{ik}(t)\, a_{kj} + \alpha_{jk}(t)\, a_{ki})$$

$$+ \sum_{k;\, l=1}^{n} [\alpha_{kj}(t)\, m_k(t)\, \alpha_{li}(t)\, m_l(t)] - \omega_{ij}(t) \qquad (i = 1, \ldots, n;\ j = 1, \ldots, n). \tag{4.18}$$

Equations (4.18) must be solved for the span $0 \leq t \leq T$ and the initial condition: $\alpha_{ij}(T) = \psi_{ij}$, as follows from condition (3.2). Let us point out that conditions (3.1) of the continuity of $v[t, \lambda(t)]$ are in our case (4.5) fulfilled for all t automatically, provided the quantities $\alpha_{ij}(t)$ are continuous with respect to t. Equations (4.18) have a solution which is definite and unique for the span $[0, T]$ and satisfies the conditions $\alpha_{ij}(T) = \psi_{ij}$. Therefore, the coefficients $\alpha_{ij}(t)$ can always be determined from equations (4.18) by any numerical method (or by means of a model). After coefficients $\alpha_{ij}(t)$ have been determined, the quantity $\gamma(t)$ can be determined from the equation

$$\frac{d\gamma}{dt} = -q(t), \qquad \gamma(T) = 0. \tag{4.19}$$

The quantity $\xi^\circ = \zeta^\circ[t, \lambda(t)]$ is determined from the equation:

$$\xi^\circ = \zeta^\circ[t, \lambda(t)] = -\sum_{i,\, j=1}^{n} \alpha_{ij}(t)\, m_i\, x_j^*(t \mid \lambda(t)), \tag{4.20}$$

wherein vector x^* is determined by means of formulas (4.9) and (4.10).

Thus, we see that the problem of determining the optimal control $\xi^\circ = \zeta^\circ[t, \lambda(t)]$ is solved in the case under consideration as effectively as the problem of Cauchy is solved for equation (4.18).

Note. Equations (4.18) and conditions $\alpha_{ij}(T) = \psi_{ij}$ coincide with those equations and conditions, which would be obtained for the coefficients of the optimal Lyapunov function [5, 14]

$$v[t, x] = \sum_{i,j=1}^{n} \alpha_{ij}(t)\, x_i(t)\, x_j(t),$$

when solving for the minimum value of the quantity

$$J = \int_0^T \Big[\sum_{i,j=1}^{n} \omega_{ij}(t)\, x_i(t)\, x_j(t) + \xi^2(t) \Big] dt \tag{4.21}$$

in motions of the system (4.6), under the condition that control ξ can be selected in the form of a function $\xi = \zeta[t, x(t)]$ of the ordinary coordinates $x(t)$, that is, if the problem to be solved is one concerning the minimum of quantity (4.21) in motions (4.6) in the absence of lag of the feedback signal.

In that case the optimal control ξ° would be represented by the following expression:

$$\xi^\circ = \zeta^\circ[t, x(t)] = -\sum_{i,j=1}^{n} \alpha_{ij}(t)\, m_i x_j(t). \tag{4.22}$$

Hence, the optimal control (4.20) for a problem solved taking into account that the feedback signal is lagging has the same structure as the optimal control (4.22) for a similar problem without lag of the feedback signal, but with one difference: namely, while the components of (4.22) contain ordinary coordinates $x(t)$ characterizing the system, in (4.20) there stand in their place the quantities $x^*(t \mid \lambda(t)) = M\{x^\xi(t \mid \lambda(t)) \mid \lambda(t)\}$, which represent the average value of the random quantities $x^{\xi}[t\,|\,\lambda(t)]$ computed on the basis of a known value of $\lambda(t)$. We may point out that the quantity $x^{*}[t\,|\,\lambda(t)]$ can also be considered as the best rms prediction [3] of the random quantity $x^{\xi}[t\,|\,\lambda(t)]$ with the known value of $\lambda(t)$ taken into account. Thus, in this case the solution of the problem of finding the minimum of of quantities (2.7) in motions of the system (1.1) in the presence of a lagging feedback signal, of an initial scatter of the quantity $x(0)$, and of a noise action $d\varphi/dt$ can be separated into two parts: 1) solution of a similar problem, but in the absence of feedback signal lag and any probabilistic factors, and 2) solution of the problem of the best rms prediction $x^{*}[t|\,\lambda(t)]$ for the quantity $x^{\xi}[t\,|\,\lambda(t)]$ on the basis of available information on $\lambda(t)$ (the forecast covering the time span $\Delta t = h$ when $t \geq h$, and the span $\Delta t = t$ when $t < h$). The optimal control (4.20) for the original problem (with feedback lag) is obtained from optimal control (4.22) by introducing into the control formula (4.22) in place of the variables $x(t)$ their best rms prediction values $x^{*}[t|\,\lambda(t)]$. We also see that the magnitude of the random scatter $\|\varepsilon_{ij}(t)\|_1^n$ does not affect the form of the optimal control. The quantities $\sigma_j(t)$ and $\varepsilon_{ij}(t)$ enter only in the expressions for $\gamma(t)$, and consequently affect only the quantity

$$\min J[\tau, \lambda(\tau), \zeta].$$

Thus, for the case $\eta(t) \equiv 0$ the problem of constructing the optimal control $\xi^{\circ} = \zeta^{\circ}[t, \lambda(t)]$ is solved. Let us now take up the solution of this problem for the case when $\eta(t) \not\equiv 0$. We shall limit ourselves to two particular cases: 1) the probability process $\eta(t)$ is a Markov process with mutually independent, completely discrete parameters [3], and 2) the probability process $\eta(t)$ is of the diffusion type [3]. In the first case, we will describe the random changes of $\eta(t)$ by the functions $q(t, \mu, \nu)$ and $q(t, \mu)$, which have the following meaning:

$$P[\eta(t) = \mu \,|\, \eta(\tau) = \mu] = 1 - q(\tau, \mu)(t - \tau) + o(t - \tau),$$

$$P[\eta(t) = \nu \neq \mu \,|\, \eta(\tau) = \mu] = q(\tau, \mu, \nu)(t - \tau) + o(t - \tau), \tag{4.23}$$

wherein the symbol $P[A\,|\,B]$ denotes conditional probability. The quantities $o(t-\tau)$ in (4.23) are infinitesimally small quantities of higher order than $(t-\tau)$. In the second case, we assume that the increment $\eta(t) - \eta(\tau)$ of the process is composed of the sum of the small increments $d\eta(\vartheta)$ within the range of $\tau < \vartheta < t$ with $d\eta(\vartheta) = \mu[\vartheta, \eta(\vartheta)]\,d\vartheta + \sigma[\vartheta, \eta(\vartheta)]\,dy(\vartheta)$, the quantities μ and σ here are known functions, and $y(\vartheta)$ describes the Brownian motion process [3]. The distributions of the quantities $x(0)$ and $\eta(0)$ will be considered to be independent.

In the case $\eta(t) \not\equiv 0$ it will be our aim to find a functional of the following form:

$$v[t, \lambda(t)] = M\left\{\sum_{i,j=1}^{n} \alpha_{ij}(t)\, x_i^{\xi}(t|\lambda(t))\, x_j^{\xi}(t\,|\,\lambda(t))\right\} + \sum_{i=1}^{n} \beta_i\, M\{x_i(t\,|\,\lambda(t))\} + \gamma, \tag{4.24}$$

where β_i and γ are functions of time $\underline{t}$ only when $t < h$, and are functions of time $\underline{t}$ and the quantities $\eta(t-h) \in \lambda(t)$ (2.1) when $t \geq h$.

Let us set up the equations which are needed for determination of $\alpha_{ij}(t)$, β_j, and γ. The derivative $dM\{v\}/dt$ has in this case the following form:

$$\begin{aligned}\left\{\frac{dM\{v\}}{dt}\,|\,\tau, \lambda(\tau), \zeta\right\} &= M\left\{\left(\frac{dM\{\Sigma\alpha_{ij}(t)\,x_i(t)\,x_j(t)\,|\,x(\tau)\}}{dt}\right)_{t=\tau} |\,\lambda(\tau)\right\} \\ &+ \sum_{i=1}^{n} \beta_i\, M\left\{\left(\frac{dM\{x_i(t)\,|\,x(\tau)\}}{dt}\right)_{t=\tau} |\,\lambda(\tau)\right\} + \sum_{i=1}^{n} M\{x_i(\tau)\,|\,\lambda(\tau)\} \\ &\times \left[\left(\frac{dM\{\beta_i\}}{dt}\right)_{t=\tau} |\,\lambda(\tau)\right] + \left[\left(\frac{dM\{\gamma\}}{dt}\right)_{t=\tau} |\,\lambda(\tau)\right],\end{aligned} \tag{4.25}$$

where

$$\frac{dM\{\Sigma\alpha_{ij}x_i x_j\}}{dt} = \sum_{i,\,j=1}^{n}\left[\frac{d\alpha_{ij}}{dt} + \sum_{k=1}^{n}(\alpha_{ik}a_{kj} + \alpha_{jk}a_{ki})\right]x_i x_j$$

$$+2\sum_{i,\,j=1}^{n}(\alpha_{ij}m_j x_j \xi + \alpha_{ij}b_j x_i \eta) + \sum_{i,\,j=1}^{n}\alpha_{ij}\sigma_{ij}$$

$$(\xi = \zeta[\tau, \lambda(\tau)]). \tag{4.26}$$

This differs from the corresponding expression (4.16) for the derivative of M in the preceding case only by the following terms in the sum $2\Sigma\alpha_{ij}(\tau)b_j(\tau)x_i(\tau)\eta(\tau)$, which are now:

$$\left(\frac{dM\{x_i(t)\mid x(\tau)\}}{dt}\right)_{t=\tau} = \sum_{j=1}^{n} a_{ij}x_j(\tau) + b_i(\tau)\eta(\tau) + m_i(\tau)\xi(\tau), \tag{4.27}$$

$$\left(\frac{dM\{\beta_i\}}{dt}\right)_\tau = \begin{cases}\left(\dfrac{d\beta_i(t)}{dt}\right)_{t=\tau} & \text{for } \tau < h\\ \left(\dfrac{dM\{\beta_i(t, \eta(t-h))\}}{dt}\right)_{t=\tau+0} & \text{for } \tau \geqslant h,\end{cases} \tag{4.28}$$

$$\left(\frac{dM\{\gamma\}}{dt}\right)_\tau = \begin{cases}\left(\dfrac{d\gamma(t)}{dt}\right)_{t=\tau} & \text{for } \tau < h,\\ \left(\dfrac{dM\{\gamma[t, \eta(t-h)]\}}{dt}\right)_{\tau=\tau+0} & \text{for } \tau \geqslant h.\end{cases} \tag{4.29}$$

Then, in the case of the discrete-parameters process, we have:

$$\left(\frac{dM\{\lambda[t, \eta(t-h)]\}}{dt}\right)_\tau = \left(\frac{\partial\lambda}{\partial t}\right)_\tau$$

$$+\int_{-\infty}^{\infty}\lambda[\tau, \nu]\,d_\nu q[\tau-h, \eta(\tau-h), \nu] - q[\tau-h, \eta(\tau-h)]\,\lambda[\tau, \eta(\tau-h)]. \tag{4.30}$$

And in the case of the diffusion process, we have

$$\left(\frac{dM\{\lambda[t, \eta(t-h)]\}}{dt}\right)_\tau = \left(\frac{d\lambda}{dt}\right)_\tau + \left(\frac{\partial\lambda}{\partial\eta}\right) \times \mu[\tau-h, \eta(\tau-h)] + \frac{1}{2}\left(\frac{\partial^2\lambda}{\partial\eta}\right)\sigma^2[\tau-h, \eta(\tau-h)]. \tag{4.31}$$

These formulas are similar to those obtained in papers [10, 14].

Averaging the quantities (4.26) and (4.27) over the $x[\tau \mid \lambda(\tau)]$ values and substituting the expressions for the averages so obtained as well as (4.28)-(4.31) into the right side of (4.25), we obtain an explicit expression for the derivative $dM\{v\}/dt$, which we shall not write down here. Substituting this expression and $\xi^\circ = \zeta^\circ[\tau, \lambda(\tau)]$ into equation (3.3), we find the first equation for $\underline{v}$ and ζ°

$$\left[\frac{dM\{v\}}{dt}\mid \tau, \lambda(\tau), \zeta^\circ\right] + M\left\{\sum_{i,\,j=1}^{n}\omega_{ij}(\tau)x_i(\tau)x_j(\tau)\mid\lambda(\tau)\right\} + \zeta^\circ[\tau, \lambda(\tau)])^2 = 0. \tag{4.32}$$

Differentiating this equation with respect to ζ° we obtain the second equation for $\underline{v}$ and ζ°, which is

$$2\zeta^\circ + \frac{\partial}{\partial\zeta^\circ}\left[\frac{dM\{v\}}{dt}\mid\tau, \lambda(\tau), \zeta^\circ\right] = 0. \tag{4.33}$$

After elimination of ζ° we set the coefficients of equal dimensions with respect to x_i^* equal, and so find the equations for $\alpha_{ij}(t)$, β_i, and γ.

Let us point out first of all that the equations for $\alpha_{ij}(t)$ obtained here are exactly the same as those obtained above for the case $\eta(t)\equiv 0$. Thus, the values of $\alpha_{ij}(t)$ here can be determined just the same as in the case $\eta(t)\equiv 0$, and the values of $\alpha_{ij}(t)$ can be considered now to be known quantities. This being the case, that part $\xi_1^\circ = \zeta_1^\circ[t, \lambda]$ of control ξ° which is dependent on $x^\bullet[\tau \mid \lambda(\tau)]$ can now be determined, and it is found that this part of ξ° has the same shape as control (4.20) obtained as a solution of the problem in the case of $\eta(t) \equiv 0$, namely:

$$\xi_1^\circ = \zeta_1^\circ[\tau \mid \lambda(\tau)] = -\sum_{i, j=1}^{n} \alpha_{ij}(\tau)\, m_i(\tau)\, x_j^*(\tau \mid \lambda(\tau)). \tag{4.34}$$

Having determined the quantities $\alpha_{ij}(t)$ we can now take up the determination of the quantities β_i. The equations for β_i can be obtained from the general equation for $\underline{v}$ by setting equal the expressions containing β_i serving as multipliers of the first-power terms of $x_i^\bullet[\tau \mid \lambda(\tau)]$. However, it is more convenient to determine the β_i on the basis of the following interpretation (similar to the method used in [10]): Let us consider the system of auxiliary equations:

$$\frac{dr_i}{dt} = \sum_{j=1}^{n} a_{ij} r_j - m_i(t) \left(\sum_{k, l=1}^{n} \alpha_{kl}(t)\, m_l(t)\, r_k \right), \tag{4.35}$$

which is obtained from system (4.6) by setting $\xi = \zeta_1^\circ[t, r]$ (4.34), where $r = x^\bullet$. Then the equations for β_i can be written down (without giving a proof of this here) as follows:

$$\left(\frac{dM\{[\Sigma\beta_i[t, \eta(t-h)]\, r_i(t)\}}{dt} \mid \tau, \eta(\tau - h), r(\tau) \right)_{(4.35)}$$

$$= -2 \sum_{i, j=1}^{n} \alpha_{ij}(\tau)\, b_j^\eta(\tau)\, r_i(\tau)\, M\{\eta(\tau) \mid \eta(\tau - h)\} \qquad (\tau \geqslant h) \tag{4.36}$$

or

$$\left(\frac{d(\Sigma\beta_i(t)\, r_i(t))}{dt} \right)_{(4.35),\, \tau} = -2 \sum_{i, j=1}^{n} \alpha_{ij}(\tau)\, b_j(\tau)\, r_i(\tau)\, M\{\eta(\tau)\} \quad \text{for} \quad \tau < h, \tag{4.37}$$

where the symbol $[dM(\Sigma)/dt]_{(4.35)}$ indicates that the derivative is computed subject to the condition that $r(t)$ is a solution of the system of equations (4.35). Equation (4.36) must be solved for the time span $h \le \tau \le T$, under the condition that

$$\beta_i[T, \eta[T - h]] = 0 \tag{4.38}$$

at all values of $\eta[T-h]$. The initial conditions for $\beta_i(t)$ at $t = h - 0$ are determined from the solution $\beta_i(t, \eta[t-h])$ at $t = h$ by reason of the continuity conditions (3.1) of functional $\underline{v}$. Let us describe the procedure for calculation of the β_i quantities in detail.

Suppose first that $\tau \ge h$. We denote by the symbol $r[t \mid r(\tau)]$ a solution of system (4.35) which at $t = \tau$ becomes equal to the vector $r(\tau)$. Then, integrating (4.36) over $\underline{t}$ from $t = \tau$ to $t = T$ and taking into account (4.38), we obtain the following equation:

$$\sum_{i=1}^{n} \beta_i[\tau, \eta(\tau - h)]\, r_i(\tau) = 2 \int_{\tau}^{T} (\Sigma\alpha_{ij}(t)\, b_i(t)\, r_j(t \mid r(\tau))\, M\{\eta(t) \mid \eta(\tau - h)\})\, dt. \tag{4.39}$$

System (4.35) is a linear system whose solution for $r[t \mid r(\tau)]$ can be written down in the form $r[t \mid r(\tau)] = G[t, \tau]r(\tau)$ wherein $G[t, \tau] = \| g_{ij}(t, \tau) \|_1^n$ is the fundamental solutions matrix of equations (4.35) which becomes a unit matrix for $t = \tau$. Substituting this expression for $r[t \mid r(\tau)]$ into equation (4.39), and considering that the terms on the right and on the left side of (4.39) with the same $r_i(\tau)$ must be equal, we obtain the following series of formulas for $\beta_i[\tau, \eta(\tau-h)]$:

$$\beta_i [\tau, \eta (\tau - h)] = 2 \int_{\tau}^{T} \Big(\sum_{k, l=1}^{n} \alpha_{kl} (t)\, b_k (t)\, g_{li} (\tau, t)\, M\{\eta (t) \mid \eta (\tau - h)\}\Big) dt$$

$$(i = 1, \ldots, n;\ \tau \geqslant h). \tag{4.40}$$

Consequently, to determine the coefficients $\beta_i[\tau, \eta(\tau - h)]$ it is sufficient to know how to calculate the quantities α_{kl}, and g_{li}, and how to make a prediction $M\{\eta(t)| \eta(\tau-h)\}$ of the average value of $\eta(t)$ $(t \geq \tau)$, knowing the value of $\eta(\tau - h)$.

For $\tau < h$, in a similar manner from equation (4.37) the following formula is deduced:

$$\beta_i (\tau) = \int_{\tau}^{h} \Big(\sum_{k, l=1}^{n} \alpha_{kl} (t)\, b_k (t)\, g_{li}\, (\tau, t)\, M\{ \eta (t)\}\Big) dt + M\{\beta_i [h, \ \eta (0)]\}, \tag{4.41}$$

where the quantities $M\{\eta(t)\}$ and $M\{\beta_i[h, \eta(0)]\}$ are determined by the initial distribution H of the quantities $\eta(0)$ and $x(0)$.

Thus, we have verified the possibility of determining the quantities β_i in such a manner that the equation for $\underline{v}$ is satisfied. Setting equal the terms in the equation for $\underline{v}$ that do not contain x_i^*, we obtain equations for $\gamma(\tau)$ when $\tau < h$, and for $\gamma[\tau, \eta(\tau - h)]$ when $\tau \geq h$. After the quantities $\alpha_{ij}(t)$ and β_i have been determined, there are, in principle, no difficulties encountered in the solution of the resulting equations, provided the predictions $M\{\eta(t) | \eta(\tau - h)]\}$ can be made. We shall not describe the solution of the equation for γ, since the value of γ has no effect on the regulation law. The only effect that γ has is on the magnitude of the quantity min J $[\tau, \lambda(\tau), \zeta]$, inasmuch as γ is a term in the expression for $v[\tau, \lambda(\tau)] = \min J[\tau, \lambda(\tau), \zeta]$; generally, the larger the scatter of the random quantities $x(t)$ and $\eta(t)$ is, the greater is the value of γ which is added to the quantity $J[\tau, \lambda(\tau), \zeta^\circ]$. Substituting the known values of $\alpha_{ij}(t)$ and β_j into equation (4.33), we find the following expression for the optimum control ξ°:

$$\xi^\circ = \zeta^\circ [\tau, \lambda (\tau)] = - \Big[\sum_{i, j=1}^{n} \alpha_{ij} (\tau)\, m_i (\tau)\, \overset{*}{x}_j (\tau | \lambda (\tau))\Big] - \frac{1}{2} \sum_{i=1}^{n} \beta_i m_i (\tau), \tag{4.42}$$

wherein the vector x^* is determined by equations (4.9) and (4.10), and the quantities β_i by equations (4.40) and (4.41).

Let us point out that the conditions of continuity of $\underline{v}$ stipulated in criterion 3.1, with our choice of the quantities α_{ij}, β_i, and γ, are satisfied automatically if these quantities are continuous functions of their independent variables, but for this to be true it is only necessary that the quantity $M\{\eta(t) \mid \eta(\tau - h)\}$ be a continuous function of τ and $\eta(\tau - h)$; and this quite generally is the case.

An analysis of solution (4.42) for the problem of mathematical synthesis of optimal regulation leads us to the following conclusion (see note in section 4 above): the optimal control ξ° (4.42) for the problem with a random load $\eta(t)$ and with feedback lag is chosen for every instant $t = \tau$ to be of the same form as the optimal control that would result from solution of a similar problem for a completely determined system without feedback lag and with a predetermined definite load $\eta(t)$, but with the known quantities $x(\tau)$ in the optimal regulation formula of the completely determined system replaced for the stochastic case by the probabilistic quantities $x[\tau | \lambda(\tau)]$, and the predetermined definite load replaced by the prediction $M\{\eta(t) \mid \lambda(\tau)\}$ for $t > \tau$. Unfortunately, this convenient conclusion does not have universal applicability, the applicability depending on certain particular features of every given problem.

5. Example

Let us illustrate the general method of procedure of section 4 by a simple example: let us examine the problem of finding the minimum for functional

$$J = M\left\{\int_0^T (x_2^2(t) + \xi^2(t))dt\right\} \tag{5.1}$$

where x_1 and x_2 are motion coordinates of a system described by the following differential equations:

$$\frac{dx_1}{dt} = x_2, \qquad \frac{dx_2}{dt} = -x_1 + \eta(t) + \xi + \dot{\varphi}, \tag{5.2}$$

Here $\eta(t)$ is a Markov process with states completely dissociated in behavior, and with two feasible states $\eta_1 = 1$, and $\eta_2 = -1$ in existence. The transition probability from one state to the other [see (4.23)] is:

$$P[\eta(t) = \eta_i \mid \eta(\tau) = \eta_j,\ i \neq j] = p(t-\tau) + o(t-\tau) \qquad (p = \text{const}). \tag{5.3}$$

The initial conditions are assumed to be known exactly, namely: $x_1(0) = x_2(0) = 0$, and $\eta(0) = \eta_1 = 1$. The noise $\varphi(t)$ is supposed to be the scalar Brownian movement $\varphi(t) = y(t)$, discussed in connection with formula (2.4). The delay $\underline{h}$ in this case is supposed to be equal to π.

According to (4.24) we wish to determine a functional of $\underline{v}$ in the following shape:

$$v[t, \lambda(t)] = M\{\alpha_{11}(t)x_1^2(t \mid \lambda(t)) + 2\alpha_{12}(t)x_1(t \mid \lambda(t))$$
$$\times x_2(t \mid \lambda(t)) + \alpha_{22}(t)x_2^2(t \mid \lambda(t))\} + \beta_1 M\{x_1(t \mid \lambda(t))\} + \beta_2 M\{x_2(t \mid \lambda(t))\} + \gamma(t). \tag{5.4}$$

In system (5.2) $m_1 = 0$, and $m_2 = 1$ [see (4.1)]. And comparing (5.1) with (1.2) we see that $\omega_{11} = \omega_{12} = \omega_{21} = 0$, $\omega_{22} = 1$, and $\psi_{ij} = 0$ (for i, j = 1, 2). Thus the equations for $\alpha_{ij}(t)$ corresponding to (4.18) are as follows:

$$\frac{d\alpha_{11}}{dt} = 2\alpha_{12} + \alpha_{22}^2, \qquad \frac{d\alpha_{22}}{dt} = -2\alpha_{12} + \alpha_{22}^2 - 1, \qquad \frac{d\alpha_{12}}{dt} = -2\alpha_{11} + 2\alpha_{22} + 2\alpha_{12}\alpha_{22}. \tag{5.5}$$

After the $\alpha_{ij}(t)$ functions are determined by solving equations (5.5) under the boundary conditions $\alpha_{ij}(T) = 0$, we can determine the β_i quantities by means of (4.40) and (4.41). The respective formulas in our case assume the following shape:

$$\beta_i(\tau, \eta(\tau-\pi)) = 2\int_\tau^T [\alpha_{12}(t)g_{1i}(\tau, t) + \alpha_{22}(t)g_{2i}(\tau, t)]\,\eta(\tau-h)\,e^{-2p(t-\tau+h)}\,dt \quad \text{for } t \geqslant h,$$

$$\beta_i(\tau) = 2\int_t^T [\alpha_{12}(t)g_{1i}(\tau, t) + \alpha_{22}(t)g_{2i}(\tau, t)]\,e^{-2pt} \qquad \text{for } t < h, \tag{5.6}$$

In the above $\eta(\tau)e^{-2p(t-\tau)}$ has been inserted for the general expression $M\{\eta(t) \mid \eta(\tau)\}$, and the quantities $g_{ij}(\tau, t)$ represent the elements of the fundamental solutions matrix of the following system of equations corresponding to the system of equations (4.35):

$$\frac{dr_1}{dt} = r_2, \qquad \frac{dr_2}{dt} = -r_1 - (\alpha_{12}r_1 + \alpha_{22}r_2). \tag{5.7}$$

As a result we obtain for the optimal control ζ° the following expression:

$$\zeta^\circ[t, \lambda(t)] = -\alpha_{12}(t)x_1^*(t \mid \lambda(t)) - \alpha_{22}(t)x_2^*(t \mid \lambda(t)) - \frac{1}{2}\beta_2, \tag{5.8}$$

where

$$x_1^*(t \mid \lambda(t)) = \int_0^t \sin(t-\vartheta)\,\xi(\vartheta)\,d\vartheta,$$
$$\qquad\qquad\qquad\qquad \text{for } t < h = \pi,$$
$$x_2^*(t \mid \lambda(t)) = \int_0^t \cos(t-\vartheta)\,\xi(\vartheta)\,d\vartheta$$

and

$$x_1^*(t \mid \lambda(t)) = -x_1(t-\pi) - \int_{-\pi}^{0} \sin\vartheta\,\xi(t+\vartheta)\,d\vartheta,$$

$$x_2^*(t \mid \lambda(t)) = -x_2(t-\pi) + \int_{-\pi}^{0} \cos\vartheta\,\xi(t+\vartheta)\,d\vartheta \qquad \text{for } t \geqslant h = \pi.$$

This has been arrived at on the basis that the matrix F(t) [see (4.8)] of the fundamental set of solutions for the system of equations $dx_1/dt = x_2$ and $dx_2/dt = -x_1$ is

$$F(t) = \begin{pmatrix} \cos t & \sin t \\ -\sin t & \cos t \end{pmatrix}.$$

The quantity β_2 is determined by formulas (5.6).

LITERATURE CITED

1. A. M. Lyapunov, The General Problem of Stability of Motion [in Russian] (Gostekhizdat Press, 1950).
2. R. Bellman, J. Glicksberg, and O. Gross, Some Problems of the Mathematical Theory of Control Processes [Russian translation] (Inostr. Liter. Press, 1962).
3. J. L. Doob, Stochastic Processes [Russian translation of book published by Wiley, New York, 1953] (Inostr. Liter. Press, 1956).
4. A. A. Fel'dbaum, Computer Devices in Automatic Systems [in Russian] (Fizmatgiz Press, 1959).
5. A. M. Letov, "Analytical construction of regulators" I, IV. Avtomatika i Telemekhanika, 21, No. 4 (1961); 22, No. 4 (1961).
6. A. A. Fel'dbaum, "Collection of information in closed systems of automatic control." Izv. AN SSSR, Otd. Tekhn. n., Énergetika i avtomatika, No. 4 (1961).
7. A. Ya. Lerner, Principles of Construction of Fast Acting Tracking Systems and Regulators, Library on Automation, Vol. 25, Gosénergoizdat Press (1961).
8. L. S. Pontryagin, V. G. Boltyanskii, R. V. Gamkrelidze, and E. F. Mishchenko, Mathematical Theory of Optimal Processes [in Russian] (Fizmatgiz Press, 1961).
9. I. V. Girsanov, "Minimax problems in the theory of diffusion processes." Dokl. AN SSSR, 136, No. 4 (1960).
10. N. N. Krasovskii, "Root-mean-square optimal stabilization in case of damped random disturbances." Prikl. Mathem. i Mekhan., 25, No. 5 (1961).
11. Ts'ien Süeh-sên, Technical Cybernetics [Russian translation] (Inost. Liter. Press, 1956).
12. R. Bellman, Adaptive Control Processes. Project. Rand. (1961).
13. E. B. Dynkin, Markov Processes and Operator Halfgroups. Theory of Probabilities and Its Application [in Russian] (1956), Vol. 1, No. 1.
14. N. N. Krasovskii and É. A. Lidskii, "Analytical construction of regulators in systems with random properties." I-III. Avtomatika i Telemekhanika, 22, Nos. 9-11 (1961).

PART V

Self-Optimizing Control

Principles of Optimalizing Control Systems and an Application to the Internal Combustion Engine

C. S. Draper and Y. T. Li

Section I

GENERAL PRINCIPLES OF OPERATING SYSTEMS

1.1 Introduction

Optimum performance from operating systems becomes of increasing importance as competition in the modern world becomes more severe. The benefits of achieving the best possible production from an industrial plant are as apparent as the advantages of drawing the ultimate pound of thrust from the gas turbine power plant of a military aircraft. This goal of forcing optimum performance from equipment is usually approached by use of manual adjustments and regulators which vary the essential inputs in accordance with relationships intended to produce the desired results. Practical difficulties appear when this method is used, because of engineering compromises and tolerance variations that cause the operation of any given controlled system to deviate from the standard assumed for design purposes. Regulators work under the handicap that best operation depends upon the continued existence of standard behavior by the controlled system with no "checking up" on results by feedback from the output to the adjustments of the controlled inputs. It is the object of this paper to discuss optimalizing controllers which are based upon the use of feedback arrangements for driving the input adjustments of controlled systems toward optimum performance by means of signals that represent the system output. Controllers of this kind may be designed for any operating system that actually exhibits an optimum performance condition as its inputs are varied. It is unnecessary to build particular input-output functions into control equipment of this type because it automatically compensates for changes in the controlled system. Many arrangements may be used to achieve optimalizing control characteristics. This paper outlines the general principles of optimalizing controllers, discusses a number of typical systems and describes experimental results from a controller operating with a single-cylinder internal combustion engine.

1.2 Elements of a Typical System

Operating systems, by definition, have the property of establishing functional relationships between a number of independent quantities called inputs and a number of dependent quantities called outputs. Strictly speaking, the term input should be applied only to things or states of things that are measurable and for this reason fall into the class of physical quantities. However, in practice, it is convenient to extend the input definition to include supplies of material or energy whose rates of flow are measurable. The ambiguity caused by this extension in a primary definition is undesirable but should not introduce difficulty if it is understood that in any given situation the context will determine whether the term input refers to a material (such as air or gasoline) or to a rate of flow of the material which is measurable and, therefore, truly a physical quantity.

Inputs to a system are classed as actuating inputs if their presence is essential for operation of any sort, and modifying inputs if their action is to change the relationships between the actuating inputs and the outputs. Figure 1* is a functional diagram illustrating the organization of components in a typical operating

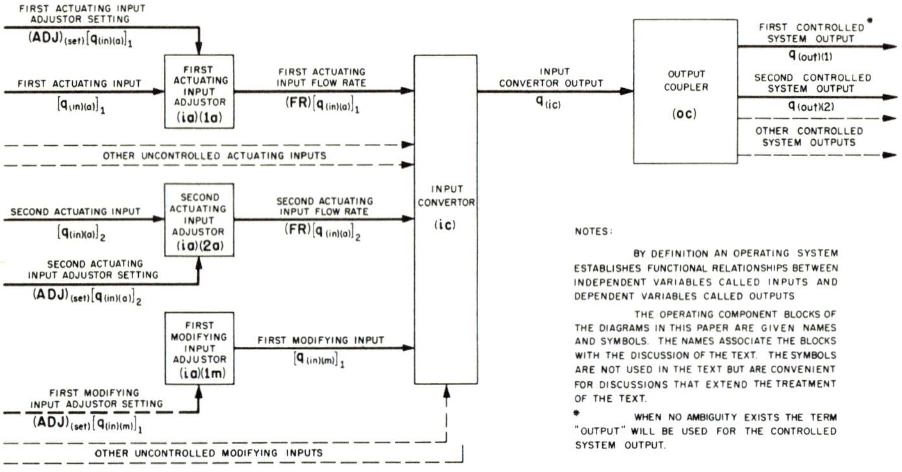

Fig. 1. Functional diagram showing the components of a generalized operating system.

system. Two actuating inputs and one modifying input are shown as determing two outputs. Light, dashed lines are used to indicate that in general other inputs and outputs may be present in addition to those specifically shown in the figure. Adjustors are shown as operating to control the flow rates of the actuating input materials and to make modifying input settings. The actuating inputs enter the input convertor, which produces the interactions necessary to generate the input convertor output. This output is taken by the output coupler, and transformed into the controlled system outputs, which are transferred to operating components beyond the chain shown in Fig. 1.

1.3 The Internal Combustion Engine as an Example of an Operating System

The internal combustion engine is an example of a system with operating components that correspond functionally to those of Fig. 1. The layout diagram of Fig. 2 shows that fuel may be considered as the first actuating input, air as the second actuating input, and ignition timing as the first modifying input. The fuel valve is the first actuating input adjustor, the air throttle is the second actuating input adjustor, and the ignition timing adjustment is the first modifying input adjustor. The flow rates of the first and second actuating inputs correspond to the fuel flow rate and the air flow rate, respectively. The combustion chamber and

* The operating component blocks of the diagrams in this paper are given names and symbols. The names associate the blocks with the discussion of the text. The symbols are not used in the text but are convenient for discussions that extend the treatment of the text.

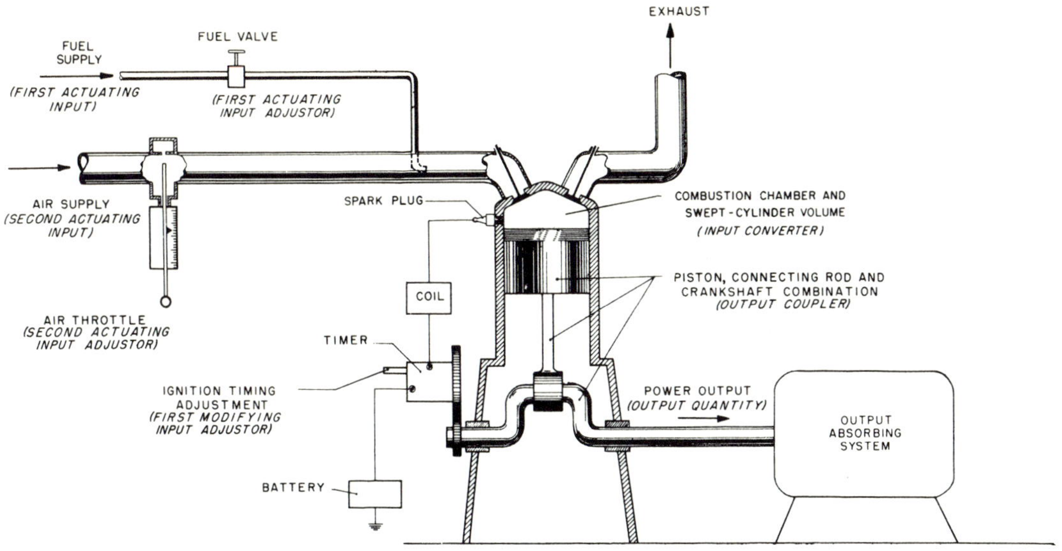

Fig. 2. Layout diagram for a reciprocating piston engine as an operating system.

swept-cylinder volume provide the input convertor function by supplying an enclosure in which chemical energy is changed, first into heat and then into mechanical output. The piston, connecting rod, and crankshaft act as the output coupler that serves to transfer the mechanical energy output of the cylinder gases into the mechanical work of rotation which is supplied to an output absorbing system.

When a given load requirement is imposed on a system like that represented in Fig. 1, one of the actuating inputs must be adjusted to a level determined principally by the load. In order for operation to exist at all, the other actuating inputs must have more or less exact relationships to this primary control input, and the modifying inputs must also be adjusted within certain fairly well-defined tolerance limits. With input settings made within ranges that allow the system to function, the remaining problem is to refine the input adjustments so that the required output is obtained with minimum flow rates of the costly input materials, or the maximum output is obtained for given flow rates of these materials. This desirable situation is possible only if the controlled system has characteristics that allow the operation to approach an optimum condition as the input adjustments are properly modified.

1.4 Graphical Representation of the Optimum Operating Condition

The reciprocating piston internal combustion engine is an example of a system with characteristics that permit the realization of an optimum operating condition. Figure 3 is a photograph of a three-dimensional model showing the performance surface that represents the relationships between brake mean effective pressure as the dependent output and ignition timing and fuel-air ratio as independent variables subject to the conditions that engine speed and fuel flow rate are both held constant. The data summarized in Fig. 3 represent performance

* The C F R engine is a single-cylinder test engine developed by the Cooperative Fuel Research committee (now the Coordinating Research Council, Inc.) for fuel rating. For details see the C. R. C. Handbook (Coordinating Research Council, Inc., 30 Rockefeller Plaza, New York, N.Y., 1950), p. 32.

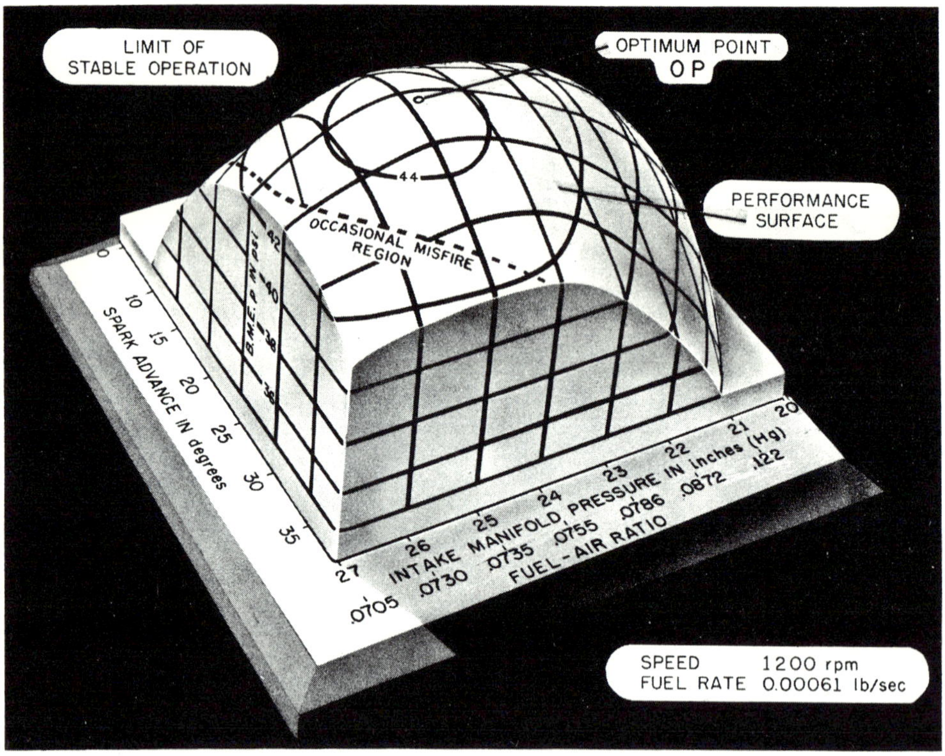

Fig. 3. Static performance characteristics of the C R F engine.

of the C F R engine* to which the optimalizing controller described later in this paper was applied as a typical performance example. The essential feature of the performance surface shown in Fig. 3 is that an optimum point (OP) exists. It is this point that must be approached by changes in spark advance and air flow during the process of adjusting for optimum performance with fuel flow and engine speed held constant. The surface of Fig. 3 is marked with a dashed line that represents the operational limit imposed by the occurrence of occasional misfires. An optimalizing controller applied to the engine whose performance is shown by Fig. 3 would operate by searching out the optimum point through changes in spark advance and air throttle settings made in response to a feedback signal representing the brake mean effective pressure (bmep) as the essential controlled system output. Details of an optimalizing controller that automatically carries out this search are given later in this paper to illustrate operation for this type of equipment.

In practice, the design of optimalizing controllers for operating systems with characteristics of the general type illustrated by the surface of Fig. 3 is complicated by the fact that the output is generally dependent upon more modifying and actuating inputs than those describable by any single three-dimensional diagram. For example, the output of the internal combustion engine, whose operation is partly described by Fig. 3, not only depends upon air flow and spark advance but is also affected by the temperature, pressure and humidity of the input air, fuel temperature, cylinder temperature, exhaust gas pressure and other factors. In addition to these modifying inputs, engine speed and fuel flow are quantities that must be taken into account by the operation of any optimalizing controller for internal combustion engines. To extend the description of engine performance characteristics at constant speed beyond that given in Fig. 3, a curve family like that of Fig. 4 may be plotted to show the effects of spark advance and air flow on brake mean effective pressure for various fuel flow rates. This curve family, in effect, sets up the problem for any system designed to control the engine whose performance is described.

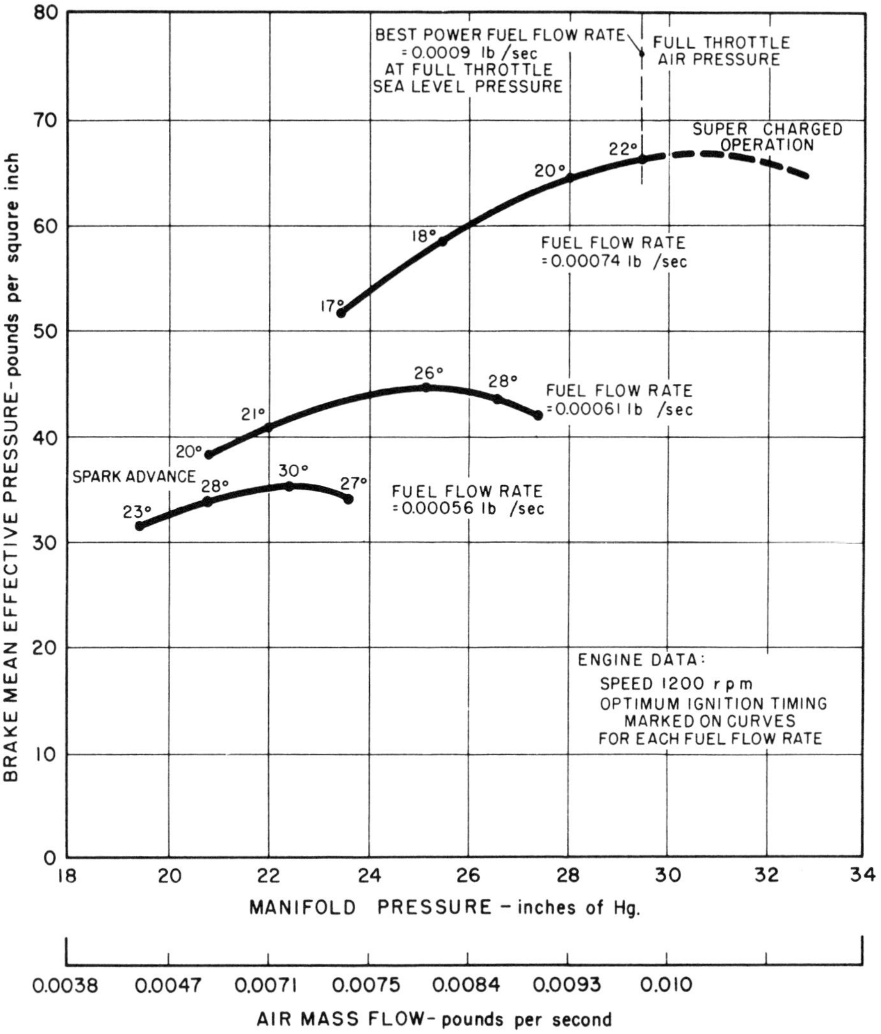

Fig. 4. Variation of the optimum operating conditions with fuel flow rate at a constant speed for the CRF engine.

Section II

METHODS OF REALIZING OPTIMUM PERFORMANCE

2.1 Introduction

In general, there are three approaches to the problem of achieving optimum performance from operating systems which have characteristics that permit optimalizing control:

A. Independent manual adjustment of the inputs to produce the optimum operating conditions. For the internal combustion engine characteristics illustrated in Figs. 3 and 4 this means that, with a fixed speed and fixed fuel flow, the maximum brake mean effective pressure will be obtained from a certain combination of spark advance and air flow that may be achieved by independent manual adjustments.

B. The use of interconnecting regulators between the input adjustors and between some variable connected with the output and the inputs to produce the combinations of input adjustments shown in performance curves similar to those of Figs. 3 and 4. Regulators for systems of this type must be designed to reproduce the input relationship required by the characteristic curves for optimum performance. The conventional internal combustion engine is an example of a regulator-equipped system. In this example, the carburetor acts as an interconnecting regulator that controls the fuel flow rate to match the air flow rate for good performance. The air flow rate is directly adjusted by the throttle position to establish the required power output from the engine.

C. The use of optimalizing controllers as feedback components designed to receive signals functionally related to the system output and to generate corrections for the input settings which automatically cause the system to approach optimum operating conditions. Controllers of this type are discussed in this paper.

2.2 Independent Manual Adjustment

The functional diagram of Fig. 1 illustrates a typical system that would require independent manual adjustments of inputs to achieve optimum operation. The necessary adjustments might be made either on the basis of recorded data like that of Figs. 3 and 4, or by repeating the input adjustment setting on a trial-and-error basis until optimum operating conditions occur. This method tends to be cumbersome; it is often the only possible procedure for laboratory tests, but it is not generally satisfactory or even possible for many practical applications.

2.3 Interconnecting Regulators

The second approach to the problem of achieving optimum operation is to choose one actuating input as the basic variable for establishing the general output level, and to use interconnecting regulators for making other input adjustments that cause the system to approach its optimum performance condition. In certain cases, operation is improved by introducing additional regulators controlling selected input adjustments in accordance with output changes. The successful application of this method depends upon the practicability of designing regulators that incorporate the functional relationships required to match the input adjustments to each other and to the output for optimum performance. Figure 5 is a functional diagram illustrating a system made up of a controlled system, consisting of an input convertor with an output coupler, and a number of interconnecting

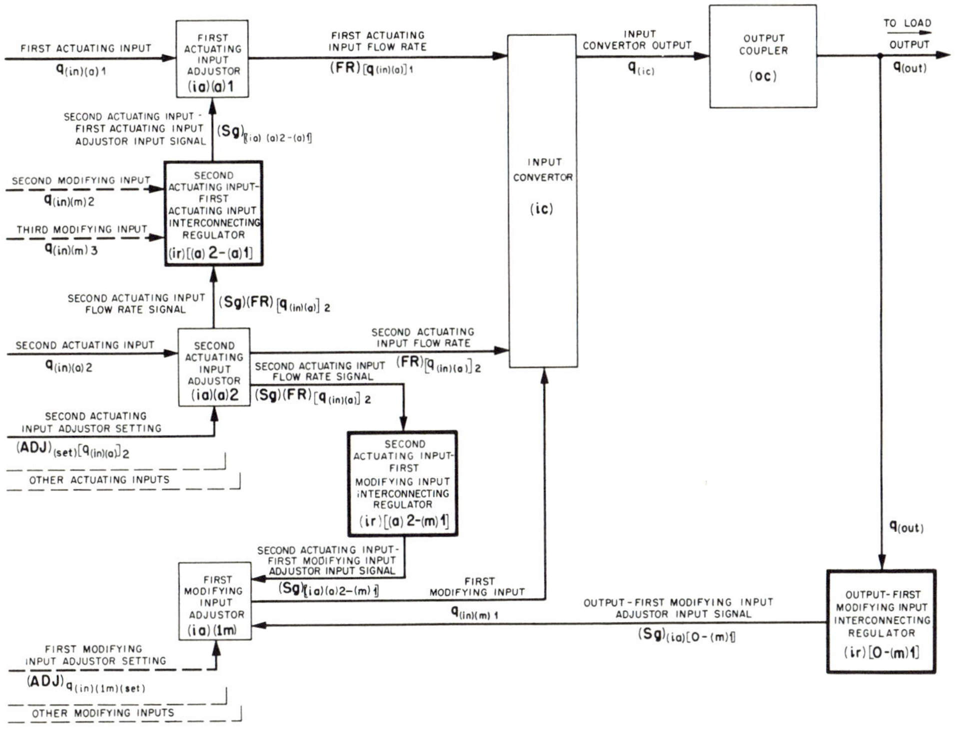

Fig. 5. Functional diagram for an operating system with inputs adjusted by interconnected regulators.

regulators designed to set the input adjustments for optimum performance. The second actuating input is chosen as the basic variable to be changed in setting up a required output level. The first actuating input is adjusted by an interconnecting regulator that also receives several modifying inputs not represented in the system of Fig. 1. In addition to this interconnecting unit, a second regulator is shown between the output and the first modifying input adjustor, while a third regulator is placed between the second actuating input adjustor and the first modifying input adjustor.

Conventional internal combustion engines are often designed from the standpoint of control to have the general functional features illustrated in Fig. 5. The carburetor acts as an interconnecting regulator between air flow, which is the basic actuating input, and fuel flow, which is a second actuating input. In Fig. 5, air would correspond to the second actuating input, and fuel to the first actuating input. The essential regulator action of the carburetor causes the ratio of the fuel flow rate to the air flow rate not only to remain within the range permitting engine operation but also to approach its value for optimum operation* to a degree depending upon the quality of the engine and carburetor designs. Automobile carburetors are usually designed for smooth running rather than for maximum economy or maximum power output. Aircraft engine carburetors, on the other hand, often include refinements intended to give operation approaching either best economy or maximum power as required for particular situations. For example, absolute air pressure may be received by the carburetor as an additional modifying input in order to compensate for the effects of altitude on the fuel-air ratio. As another example, automobile carburetors often use temperature as a modifying input to enrich the mixture and thus smooth out operation when the engine is cold (the "automatic choke"). In addition to the carburetor, which is an air-fuel interconnecting regulator with provisions for receiving certain modifying inputs in some cases, automobile engines often include a regulator component sensitive to crankshaft speed and an additional regulator component sensitive to manifold pressure, which combine their output signals to adjust the ignition timing. In the functional diagram of Fig. 5, these regulators correspond to the output - first modifying input interconnecting regulator and the second actuating input - first modifying input interconnecting regulator, respectively.

The success of any given interconnecting regulator system depends upon the feasibility of designing and constructing operating components to exactly produce the functional relationships required for optimum operation of the system. For example, the complex interactions of the many variables that affect engine performance introduce difficulties in the design of carburetors as interconnecting regulators for input adjustors. These difficulties are due to the many modifying inputs that should be recognized for best carburetor operation and to the complexity of the optimum functional relationships among these quantities. In practice. an additional complicating factor is that the required functions for ideal regulation often vary in unpredictable ways during operation so that they are not accurately known for a given controlled system at an arbitrary instant of time.

For the reasons noted, practical limits exist to the level of performance that is to be expected from systems controlled by interconnecting regulators alone, even though great effort is made to design the best possible equipment. The practical compromises with ideal performance that have to be made because of design complications or difficulties of construction tend to prevent a regulator from reaching optimum controlled system performance. This departure from optimum performance is especially serious if environmental conditions shift outside the ranges provided for in the regulator design.

2.4 Optimalizing Control

The third possibility for producing best performance from a controlled system is to use an optimalizing controller, which is essentially a closed-chain feedback arrangement that forces the relationships among input adjustment

* In the internal combustion engine optimum operation may be either (1) best economy for a given power output level, or (2) maximum power level for a given engine without regard for fuel economy.

settings to depend directly on the system output without the use of detailed assumptions as to performance characteristics. This arrangement will continue to produce the best possible performance even if considerable changes occur in the uncontrolled modifying inputs.

Figure 6 is a functional diagram showing the essential components of a generalized optimalizing controller applied in a typical system. In practice,

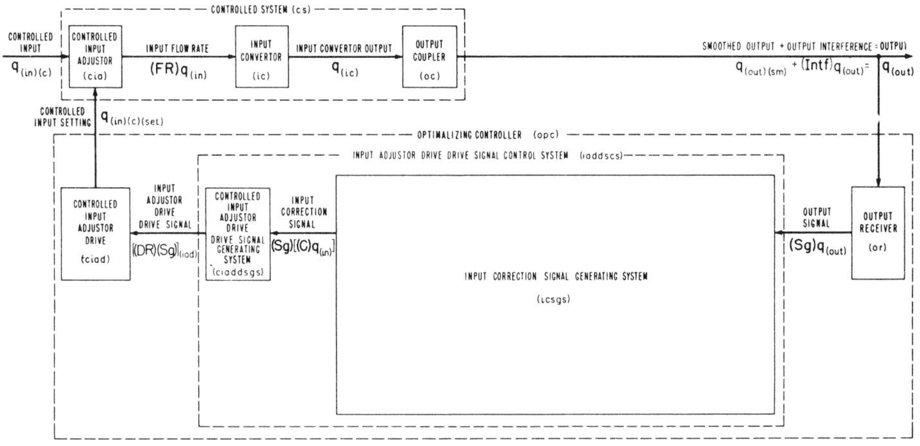

Fig. 6. Essential components of a generalized optimalizing controller acting upon an operating system with a single controlled input.

optimalizing control action may be required for a number of inputs, but to facilitate the present discussion the controlled system of Fig. 6 is shown with a single output depending upon a single controlled input. This means that the diagram applies only to situations in which all other inputs except the controlled input are constant or in which operation is primarily determined by a single input. The optimalizing controller appears as the feedback branch of a closed-chain operating system. This feedback branch may be considered as made up of three links. The first link is the output receiver, which receives the output to be controlled and produces a corresponding output signal, which has a form adapted to act as the input to the input adjustor drive drive signal control system. The output of this component is supplied to the controlled input adjustor drive, which generates a controlled input setting that closes the loop from the controlled system output to the controlled input. The input adjustor drive drive signal control system includes two principal operating components: the input correction signal generating system, which receives the output signal and produces the input correction signal, and the controlled input adjustor drive drive signal generating system, which receives this correction signal. The optimalizing controller causes changes of the controlled input setting that are related to variations of the output level in a way that causes the output to approach its optimum performance level. When the controlled system is an internal combustion engine, the action of the optimalizing controller is to cause the engine to search out and maintain operation near the peak point of a performance surface like that shown in Fig. 3.

Optimalizing controllers offer certain advantages over regulators for the control of systems with complex performance characteristics. The primary characteristic of the optimalizing controller is that it uses the controlled system itself as an instrument for determining the existing relationship between its output and its controlled input. Beyond the assumption that some optimum performance condition exists, no knowledge either of the form of the input-output relationship or of quantitative data to describe this function for the controlled system is required for the controller design. This means that the optimalizing controller is always able to search out optimum performance, no matter how environmental conditions or the controlled system itself may change, so long as an optimum condition actually exists. This fact distinguishes optimalizing controller systems from regulator systems because the latter require that the controlled system maintain the characteristics used in the regulator design.

Section III

GENERAL PRINCIPLES OF OPTIMALIZING CONTROL SYSTEMS

3.1 Output Deviations and Their Graphical Representation

In general controllers of all kinds are actuated by the output deviation of the controlled system. This quantity is, by definition, the algebraic difference between the actual level of the controlled output and some output reference level. The meaning of the output deviation for the case of a simple regulator acting on a system with a single, essential input is illustrated in Fig. 7. The performance of the controlled system for one set of environmental conditions is represented by a characteristic curve. For example, the plot of Fig. 7 might represent the relationship between the speed of an internal combustion engine and the fuel mixture flow rate under one particular load condition while the other inputs are held constant.*

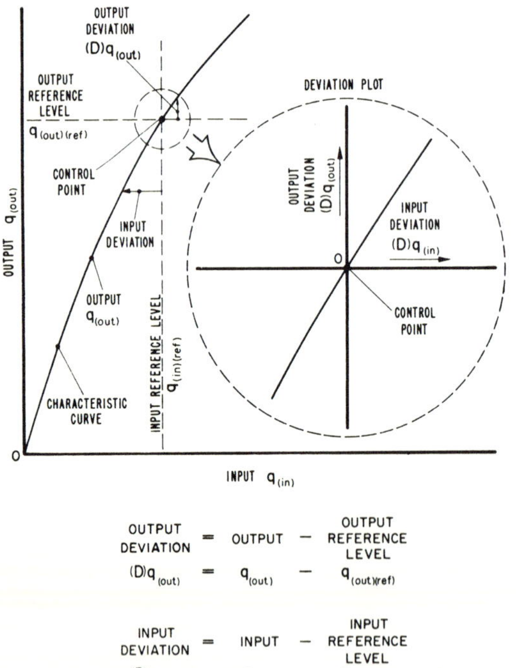

$$\text{OUTPUT DEVIATION} = \text{OUTPUT} - \text{OUTPUT REFERENCE LEVEL}$$

$$(D)q_{(out)} = q_{(out)} - q_{(out)(ref)}$$

$$\text{INPUT DEVIATION} = \text{INPUT} - \text{INPUT REFERENCE LEVEL}$$

$$(D)q_{(in)} = q_{(in)} - q_{(in)(ref)}$$

Fig. 7. Performance diagram for a simple regulator acting upon an operating system with a single controlled input.

The simplest control situation exists in the case of a regulating system which has a constant output reference level, independent of controlled system operating conditions. This situation might be represented by the horizontal, dashed line of Fig. 7. The actuating input for the regulator is a signal corresponding to the output deviation generated by some suitable receiver to represent the output deviation that is shown in Fig. 7 by an arrow pointing upward from the output reference level toward the characteristic curve.

In practice, effective controller operation must limit input

* This curve is a special case of a group of characteristic curves required to represent the performance of any controlled system under all load and environmental conditions.

and output changes to magnitudes that are relatively small compared with the total operating range of the controlled system. This fact makes it possible to describe controller performance by means of deviation plots, with the origin of the plot arbitrarily chosen in the region of primary interest. This choice of the origin means that the coordinate ranges to be plotted become relatively small, so the scales of deviation plots may be greatly expanded. An illustrative deviation plot is given in Fig. 7 with the origin arbitrarily taken at the control point, which represents the desired output from the system. Figure 7 also gives defining relationships for input and output deviations.

The output reference level for a controlled system is not necessarily constant or independent of operating conditions. For example, the output reference level for an optimalizing controller is the optimum output reference level, which is not constant but is automatically varied, depending upon the location of the optimum point of the characteristic curve for the controlled system. This situation is represented by the diagram of Fig. 8. To facilitate discussions of optimalizing controller performance a plot output reference level and a plot input reference level may be arbitrarily chosen so that the deviation plot origin is located in the region of primary interest. The word "plot" used to describe a deviation implies that the deviations are taken with respect to an origin that is chosen for convenience in representing the operation. Deviations with respect to other reference levels are generally useful for performance studies and will be defined as required. Definitions of plot output deviation and output deviation are illustrated in Fig. 8.

For the purpose of optimalizing controller operation a signal of some kind is required to represent the output of the controlled system. This fact is recognized in Fig. 8, where the ordinate of the characteristic curve is labeled both as output and output signal. The use of a single curve for both of these quantities implies that scales have been chosen in Fig. 8 to make this simplification possible in the plot. The actual controller input must be a signal representing the output deviation. In practice it is not feasible to generate an accurate signal of this kind because of the difficulty of continuously producing a signal level accurately representing the output optimum level. However, by proper controller design an indicated optimum output reference may be generated to serve as the reference level for the production of the indicated output deviation signal, which may be used as the essential optimalizing controller input. A graphical representation of the indicated output deviation signal is given in Fig. 8.

For convenience, the discussions of control systems given in this paper are carried out in terms of curves plotted near an origin of coordinates. This means that either the plots describe situations in which the variables concerned do not change greatly from levels near zero, or the deviation coordinates are used to place expanded curves arbitrarily in the region of operation of primary importance. To simplify the terms used in discussions and the labels for curves, no distinction is made between the coordinate markings on performance characteristic plots* and performance deviation plots. When any given figure represents deviations, this fact is noted on the plot.

* By definition, performance characteristics are plotted with the zero level of the characteristic curve included on the plot.

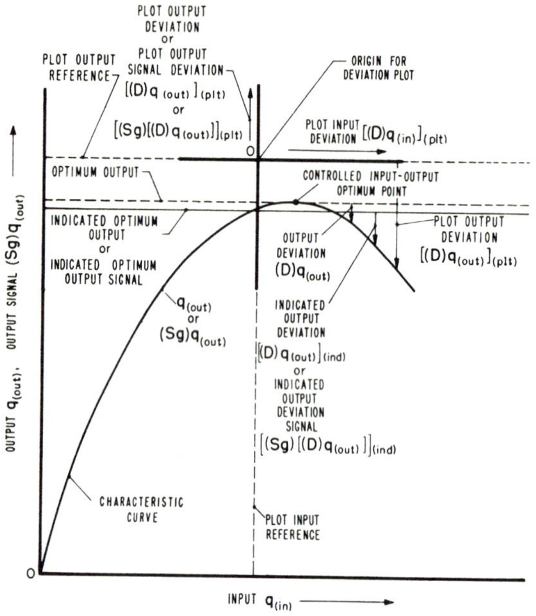

PLOT OUTPUT DEVIATION	=	OUTPUT	−	PLOT OUTPUT REFERENCE
$[(D)q_{(out)}]_{(plt)}$	=	$q_{(out)}$	−	$[q_{(out)(ref)}]_{(plt)}$
OUTPUT DEVIATION	=	OUTPUT	−	OPTIMUM OUTPUT
$(D)q_{(out)}$	=	$q_{(out)}$	−	$[q_{(out)}]_{(opt)}$
INDICATED OUTPUT DEVIATION	=	OUTPUT	−	INDICATED OPTIMUM OUTPUT
$[(D)q_{(out)}]_{(ind)}$	=	$q_{(out)}$	−	$[q_{(out)(opt)}]_{(ind)}$
INDICATED OUTPUT DEVIATION SIGNAL	=	OUTPUT SIGNAL	−	INDICATED OPTIMUM OUTPUT REFERENCE SIGNAL
$[(Sg)[(D)q_{(out)}]]_{(ind)}$	=	$(Sg)q_{(out)}$	−	$[(Sg)[q_{(out)(opt)}]]_{(ind)}$

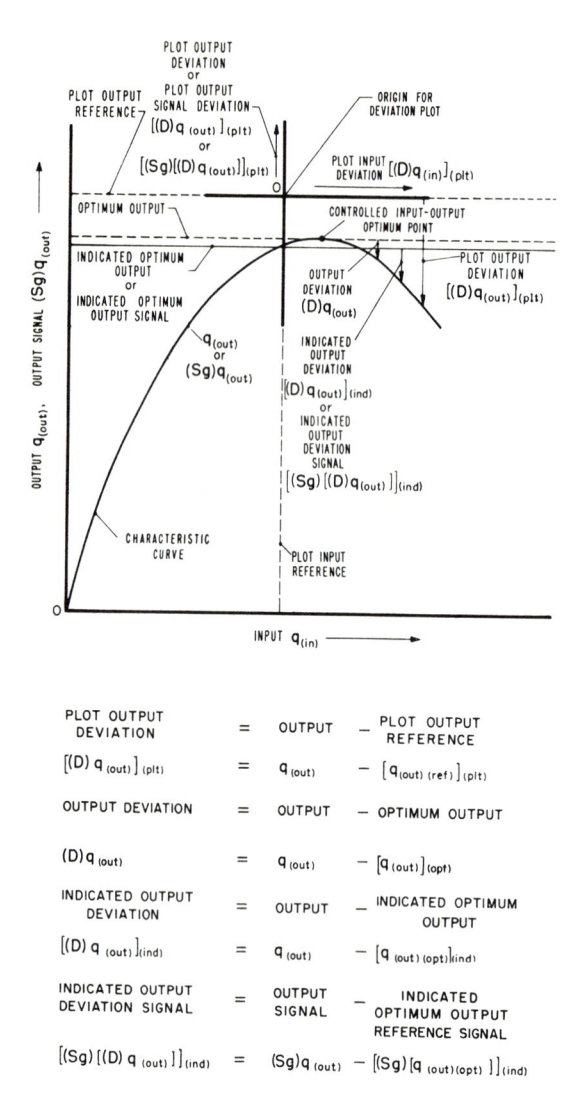

Fig. 8. Reference levels and deviations associated with optimalizing control.

3.2 Typical Performance Characteristics of Optimalizing Control Systems

Plots illustrating typical performance characteristics of a system adapted for optimalizing control are given in Fig. 9. Plot 9a is generally similar to the deviation plot of Fig. 8 with the simplifications of notation described above. The plot of Fig. 9b shows the variation of the controlled input - output sensitivity characteristic of the controlled system as a function of the controlled input. This sensitivity is, by definition, equal to the partial derivative of the output with respect to the controlled input and, as a consequence, represents the slope of the output - controlled input characteristic of the controlled system with all other inputs held constant. Because this slope has the nature of a derivative, it is independent of the shifts in location of the origin. Consequently it is the same for the plots of controlled input - output performance characteristics and for all deviation curves with constant reference levels.

Optimalizing control may be applied to any operating system with a performance characteristic like that illustrated in Fig. 9a. The action of a controller must be to to change the controlled input in such a way that operation is driven toward the optimum point which, in Fig. 9a, is the maximum point of the controlled input - output characteristic curve. At this point the tangent to the characteristic curve is horizontal, and the controlled system sensitivity is zero, as shown in Fig. 9b. This fact, and the circumstance that the controlled system sensitivity reverses its sign at the optimum point, make it possible to use a deviation signal based on sensitivity with zero for the reference level as the essential input for optimalizing controllers.

Optimalizing control may not only be made to depend upon the controlled system sensitivity but may also be based upon the indicated output deviation signal, as this quantity is defined in Figs. 8 and 9a. This deviation may be used as the input to a controller which operates by changing the controlled input level in the proper direction to reduce the indicated output deviation.

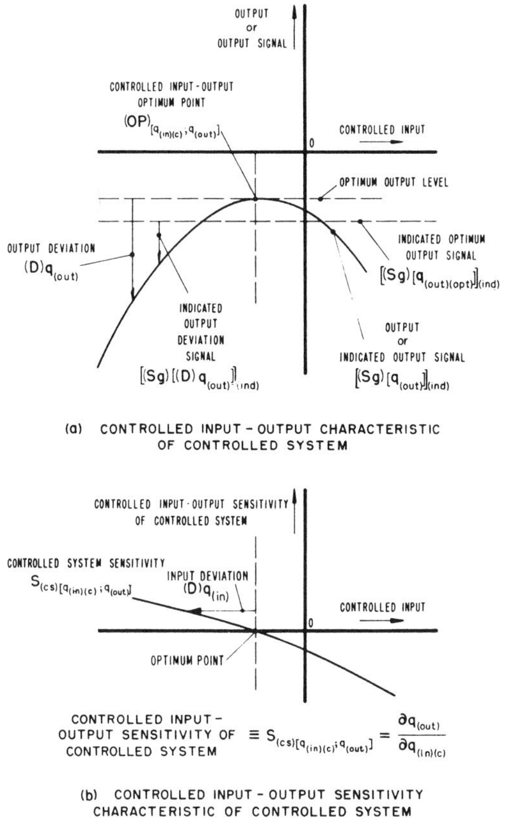

Note: 1) Plot a) is a deviation plot.
2) Plot a) origin is chosen near the optimum point.
3) The characteristics of a) and b) apply only to situations in which the controlled system has a single essential input, or in which all inputs except the controlled input are held constant.

Fig. 9. Typical performance characteristics of an operating system adapted for optimalizing control.

Signals representing the output of a controlled system are ordinarily easy to obtain. Thus the principal problem in the design of a controller using output deviation as its input is to generate an indicated optimum output signal that is a close representation of the actual optimum output level as this quantity varies with controlled system operation. When controlled system sensitivity signals are used for control purposes, the reference level is naturally zero and, for this reason, is easy to realize in practice. On the other hand, the problem of generating signals that satisfactorily represent controlled system sensitivity is not simple. The several possible approaches to this problem lead to various types of optimalizing controllers.

3.3 Classes of Optimalizing Controllers

Optimalizing controllers may be divided into two classes depending upon the type of input signal that is used. These classes, with sub-classes, are listed below:

A. Input-output sensitivity operated controllers.
   1) Sensitivity signal input controllers.
   2) Continuous test signal controllers.
   3) Output sampling controllers.

B. Peak holding controllers.

All optimalizing controllers of the first type work by using the controlled system itself to generate a signal that represents its controlled input - output sensitivity, and then taking the deviation of this signal from zero to produce the controller input signal. In controllers of the sensitivity signal input type, suitable input changes are applied to the controlled system for driving the operating conditions toward the optimum point, and the sensitivity signal input for the controller is derived from the direction and magnitude of the output changes caused by the applied input changes. Continuous test signal controllers apply a relatively small-amplitude test input change, independent of the input correction adjustment to the controlled system, and use the corresponding output variation to give a measure of sensitivity. Output sampling type controllers obtain signals representing controlled system sensitivity by comparing the average output changes that occur during successive time intervals because of a given controlled input change.

Optimalizing controllers of the peak holding type operate by continuously searching for an indicated optimum output level which is used in the generation of the indicated output deviation signal. These various controller types are discussed with more detail in later sections.

3.4 The Limitation of Optimalizing Control Interference Effects

Optimalizing control depends directly or indirectly upon indications of the controlled input - output sensitivity for the controlled system. Because this sensitivity is associated with the slope of the static characteristic curve, data from more than one operating point* are necessary in order to generate a proper signal for control purposes. In practice this means that a test signal of some type that varies with time may be applied to cause changes in the controlled input. The effect of this test signal on the output is to produce a hunting zone that represents the cost of using optimalizing control. It is generally desirable to keep the hunting zone as small as possible by a minimum input variation for the test signal.

In order to measure successfully the effect of the test signal on the output, it is necessary for the test function input variation with time to be made up of frequency components that can be distinguished from interference effects. The relative amplitudes of the output frequency components making up the interference spectrum for a typical operating system are represented by the curve of Fig. 10.

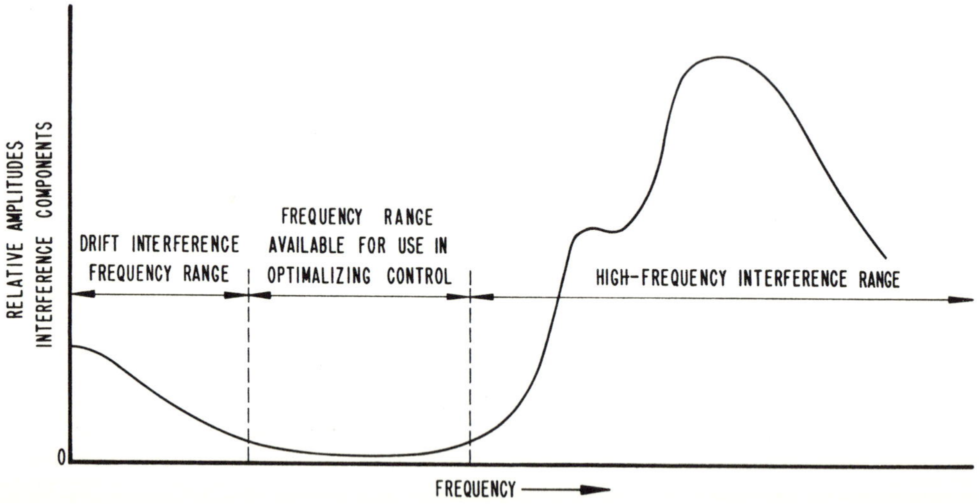

Fig. 10. Relative amplitude as a function of frequency for the random interference components of a typical operating system.

* An operating point is a point on the characteristic curve that corresponds to the instantaneous operating conditions of the controlled system. The operating point is discussed in detail in Appendix I.

Drift interference components are associated with slow changes in the environment or internal conditions of the operating system and, for this reason, are made up of relatively low frequencies. High-frequency interference components occur above some frequency limit determined by systematic and random output variations that accompany operation. Satisfactory optimalizing control depends upon the existence of some frequency range substantially free from strong interference components in between the low- and high-frequency ranges. The corresponding design control problem is to realize equipment based on test functions formed of frequency components that may be satisfactorily distinguished from the existing output interference without causing unacceptably large hunting effects. In general, the test function must be made up of input variations that are fast enough to be separable from drift interference and at the same time are slow enough to prevent confusion with high-frequency interference effects. The practical minimum limit for the output hunting zone is determined by the success achieved in meeting these conditions.

Analysis of Peak-Holding Optimalizing Control

H. S. TSIEN* AND S. SERDENGECTI†

California Institute of Technology

SUMMARY

The peak-holding optimalizing control is analyzed under the assumption of first-order input linear group and output linear group. Design charts are constructed for determining the required input drive speed and the consequent hunting loss with specified time constants of the input and output linear groups, the hunting period, and the critical indicated difference for input drive reversal.

INTRODUCTION

Optimalizing control was invented by C. S. Draper, Y. T. Li, and H. Laning, Jr.[1, 2] Their basic idea can be summarized as follows: In almost all engineering systems, within the restrictions of operation, there is an optimum state of the system for performance. For instance, in an internal combustion engine, within the restriction of producing the load torque at the specified speed, there are optimum settings for the manifold pressure and the ignition timing for minimum fuel consumption. Another example is an airplane under cruising condition; then under the restriction of engine cruising r.p.m. and assigned altitude, there is an optimum combination of trim setting and engine throttle for maximum fuel economy or maximum miles per gallon of fuel. But more important than the existence of an optimum operating state is the fact that the optimum operating state cannot be exactly predicted in advance because of the natural changes in the environment of the engineering system: In the case of the internal combustion engine, it is the changes in the temperature and the humidity of the air; in the case of the airplane, it is unavoidable changes in the aerodynamic properties of the airplane and the engine performance with age. Therefore if the purpose is to operate always near the optimum state in spite of the "drift" of the system, then the control device for the engineering system must be so designed as to search out automatically the optimum state of operation and to confine the operation close to this state. This is the basic idea of optimalizing control.

The application of Draper's optimalizing control to the general cruise control of airplanes was discussed by Shull.[3] Shull emphasized the possible elimination of extensive flight testing of new airplanes for performance determination, because the optimalizing control will automatically measure the performance whenever the airplane is flown. This in itself would constitute a great saving. But moreover, in critical circumstances such as flight through icing atmosphere, the ability of the optimalizing control to extract the best performance of a radically changed system (through ice deposition on the airplane) could be of utmost importance.

There are two fundamental problems in the theory of optimalizing control. One of the problems is the dynamic effects of the controlled system on the performance of the control. The other problem is the elimination of the noise interference. The two problems are somewhat interrelated, because if large deviations from the optimum state or the optimum operating point and hence large loss can be tolerated, then the noise interference will not be critical. The basic design aim of optimalizing control is to have the smallest loss or to operate as close to the optimum state as possible without the danger of having the control misled by the noise interference. Both of these problems were considered by the original inventors of optimalizing control. The noise problem is essentially the problem of detection of a sinusoidal variation under heavy random interference, a subject of much current research. The purpose of the present paper is to solve completely the first problem of dynamic effects under the assumption that the dynamic properties of the controlled system can be approximated by a first-order linear system. We shall begin with the brief review of the operating principles of an optimalizing control of the peak-holding type—a type least affected by the noise interference.[1, 2]

PRINCIPLE OF OPERATION

The heart of an optimalizing control system is the nonlinear component that characterizes the optimum operating condition of the controlled system. For simplicity of discussion, it is assumed that this basic component has a single input and a single output. For the time being the dynamic effects will be neglected and the output is assumed to be determined by the instantaneous value of the input. Since there is an optimum point, output as a function of input has a maximum at the output y_0 at the input x_0, as shown in Fig. 1. It is convenient to refer the output and the input to the optimum point and put the physical input as $x + x_0$ and the physical output as $y^* + y_0$. The optimum point is then the point $x = y^* = 0$. The purpose of an optimalizing control is then to search out this optimum point and to keep the system in the immediate neighborhood of this point. In this neighbor-

Received April 30, 1954.

* Robert H. Goddard Professor of Jet Propulsion, Daniel and Florence Guggenheim Jet Propulsion Center.

† Daniel and Florence Guggenheim Jet Propulsion Fellow.

hood, the relation between x and y^* can be represented as

$$y^* = -kx^2 \tag{1}$$

where k is a characteristic constant of the controlled system.

The operation of a peak-holding optimalizing control, neglecting the dynamic effects, then would be as follows: Say the input x is below the optimum value and is thus negative. The input drive is then set to increase the input at a constant rate. At the time instant 1 (Fig. 2) the input changes from negative to positive and passes through the optimum point. The output y^* is thus maximum at the time instant 1 and is decreasing after the instant 1. Now if an output sensing instrument is so designed as to follow the output exactly when the output is increasing, but hold to the maximum value after the maximum is passed and the output starts to decrease; then there will be a difference between the reading of this output sensing instrument and the output itself after the time instant 1. This difference is shown in the lower graph of Fig. 2. When this difference is built up to a critical value c at the time instant 2, the input drive is tripped and the direction of the input drive is reversed, but still at the same constant rate as before. After the instant 2 then, the input decreases and the output increases till a maximum in output is again reached at the time instant 3. At time instant 3, the input, of course, again passes from positive to negative, and the indicated difference between the output sensing instrument and the output itself again builds up. At the time instant 4, the difference reaches the critical value c again, and the input drive direction is again reversed. At the time instant 5, the input x becomes zero again and another maximum of the output is reached. The period of input variation is thus the time interval from the instant 1 to the instant 5, and the input, when plotted as a function of time, consists of a series of straight line segments forming a saw-tooth variation. The period of output variation is the time interval from the instant 1 to the instant 3, and the output, when plotted as a function of time, consists of a series of parabolic arcs. The periodic variations of input and output are called the hunting of the system, and the period of output variation is called the hunting period T. The period of input variation is thus $2T$.

The extreme variation of output Δ (Fig. 2) is called the hunting zone. If a is the amplitude of the saw-tooth variation of the input (Fig. 2), then due to Eq. (1),

$$\Delta = ka^2 \tag{2}$$

The difference between the maximum output and the average output of the hunting system is called the hunting loss D (Fig. 2). Because of the fact that the output is a series of parabolic arcs,

$$D = (1/3)\Delta = (1/3)ka^2 \tag{3}$$

For this idealized case, the critical indicated difference c between the output sensing instrument and the output itself is equal to Δ, the hunting zone. It is then clear from this discussion that in order to reduce the hunting loss for better efficiency of the system, one must try to reduce the hunting zone or the amplitude of input variation. Unfortunately the critical indicated difference is also reduced by such modification, and a limit is set by the noise interference on the proper tripping operation of the input drive.

The dynamic effects are so far neglected. But in any physical system, this is not possible because of the ever present inertial and damping forces. The output y^* given by Eq. (1) has to be considered then as the fictitious "potential output" but not the actual output y measured by the output indicating and sensing instrument. y^* is equal to y only when the period T of hunting becomes extremely long. The relation between y^* and y is determined by the dynamical effects. For the conventional engineering systems, these dynamical effects are determined by a linear relation. For instance, in the case of an internal combustion engine, the potential output is essentially the corrected effective pressure generated in the engine cylinders, while the actual output is the brake mean effective pressure of the engine. The dynamical effects are here mainly due to the inertia of the piston, the crankshaft, and other moving parts of the engine. For small changes in the operating conditions of the engine, such dynamical effects can be represented as a linear differential equation with constant coefficients.

Since the reference level of input and output is taken to be the optimum input x_0 and the optimum output y_0, the physical potential output is $y^* + y_0$ and the physical actual output is $y + y_0$. Thus the relation between the physical potential output and the physical actual output can be written as an operator equation

$$y + y_0 = F_0(d/dt)\,(y^* + y_0) \tag{4}$$

where F_0 is generally the quotient of two polynomials in the time differential operator d/dt. In the language of the Laplace transform then $F_0(s)$ is the transfer function. Let the linear system which transforms the potential output to actual output be called the output linear group. Then $F_0(s)$ is, specifically, the transfer function of the output linear group. By implication however, when the dynamical effects are negligible or when $s = 0$, the potential output is equal to the actual output. Therefore

$$F_0(0) = 1 \tag{5}$$

Since the optimum output y_0 only varies extremely slowly by the drift of the controlled system, during a time interval of many hunting periods y_0 can be taken as a constant. Then the condition of Eq. (5) simplifies Eq. (4) to

$$y = F_0(d/dt)y^* \tag{6}$$

In a similar manner, let x^* be the "potential input" that is actually the forcing function generated by the optimalizing control system but not the actual input

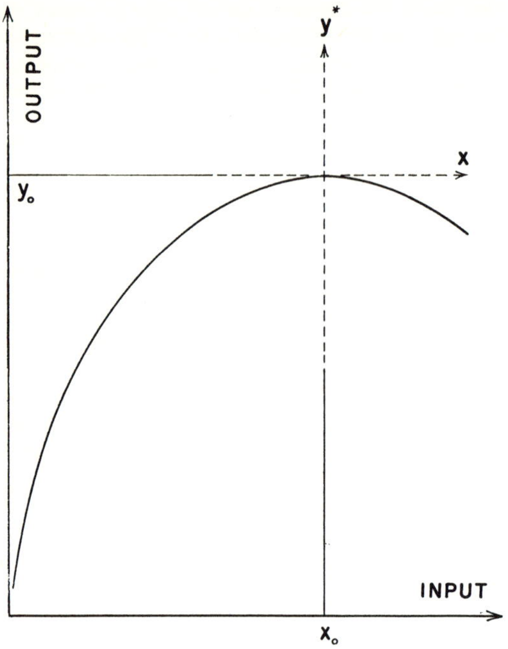

FIG. 1. Input-output characteristic of controlled system.

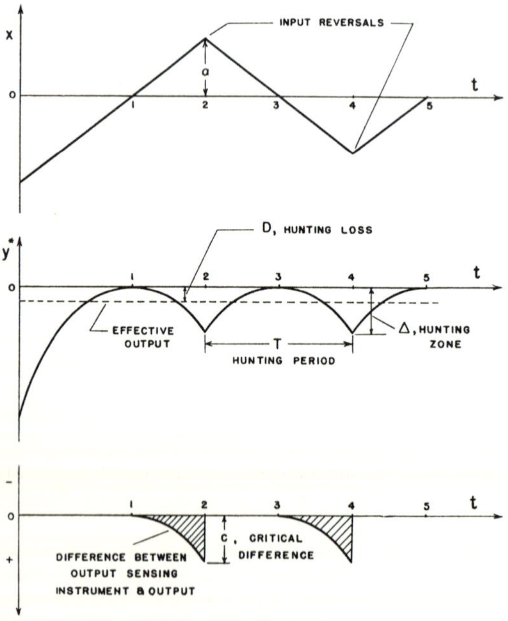

FIG. 2. Typical performance diagram for an ideal peak-holding optimalizing control system.

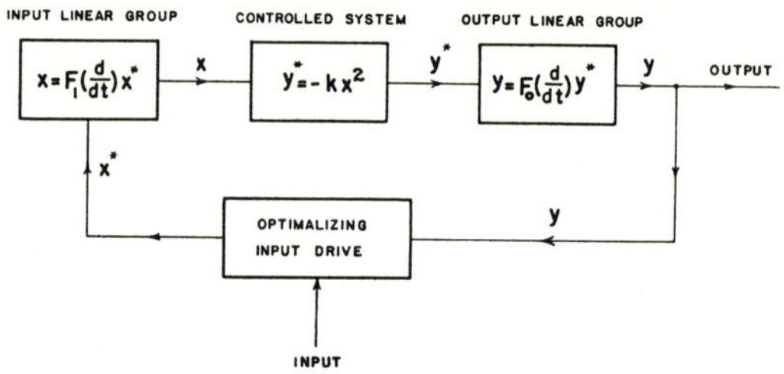

FIG. 3. Block diagram of a complete peak-holding optimalizing control system.

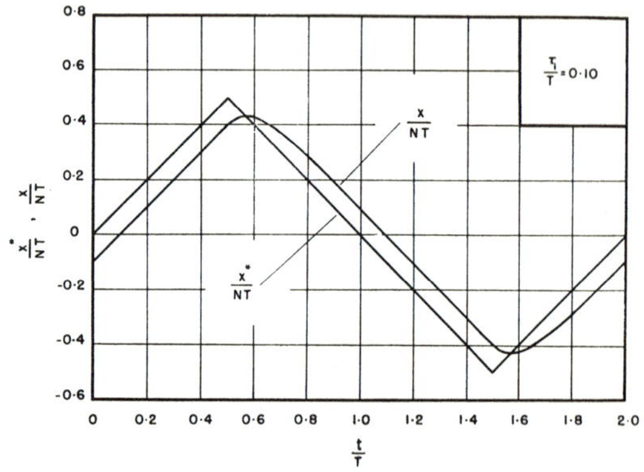

FIG. 4. "Potential" input and actual input for value of $\tau_i/T = 0.1$.

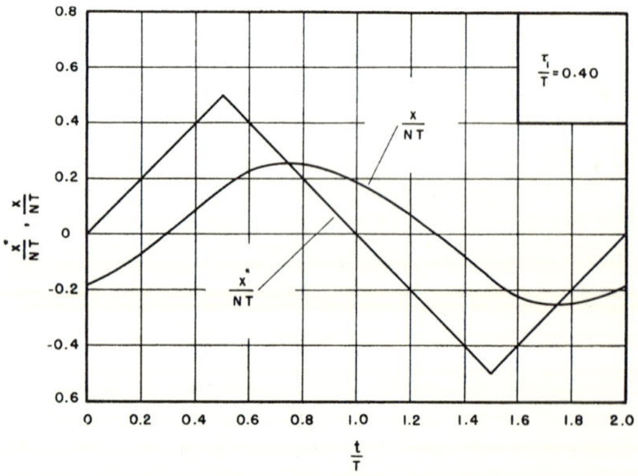

FIG. 5. "Potential" input and actual input for value of $\tau_i/T = 0.4$.

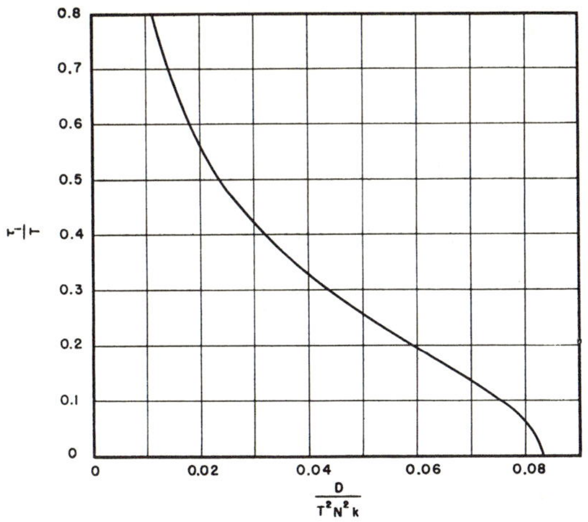

FIG. 6. Variation of dimensionless hunting loss, $D/(T^2N^2k)$ with τ_i/T.

x. It is x^* that has the saw-tooth form shown in Fig. 2, but not x. The relation between x^* and x is determined by the inertial and dynamical effects of the input drive system. This input drive system can be called the "input linear group" of the optimalizing control. The operator equation between the potential input x^* and the actual input x is

$$x = F_i(d/dt)x^* \tag{7}$$

$F_i(s)$ is thus the transfer function of the input linear group. Similar to Eq. (5), the meaning of potential and actual inputs implies

$$F_i(0) = 1 \tag{8}$$

Thus a simple representative block diagram of the complete optimalizing control system can be drawn as shown in Fig. 3. The nonlinear components of the system are thus the optimalizing input drive and the controlled system itself.

FORMULATION OF THE MATHEMATICAL PROBLEM

The general relation between the input x and the output y is determined by the system of Eqs. (1), (6), and (7), with the potential input x^* specified as a saw-tooth curve with period $2T$ and amplitude a. Let ω_0 be the hunting frequency defined by

$$\omega_0 = 2\pi/T \tag{9}$$

then x^* can be expanded into a Fourier series,

$$x^* = \frac{8a}{\pi^2}\sum_{n=0}^{\infty}\frac{(-1)^n}{(2n+1)^2}\sin(2n+1)\frac{\omega_0 t}{2} = \frac{8a}{\pi^2}\sum_{n=0}^{\infty}\frac{(-1)^n}{(2n+1)^2}\frac{1}{2i}\left(e^{[(2n+1)/2]i\omega_0 t} - e^{-[(2n+1)/2]i\omega_0 t}\right) \tag{10}$$

Therefore by using Eq. (7), the actual input x is given by

$$x = \frac{8a}{\pi^2}\sum_{n=0}^{\infty}\frac{(-1)^n}{(2n+1)^2(2i)}\times\left[F_i\left(\frac{2n+1}{2}i\omega_0\right)e^{[(2n+1)/2]i\omega_0 t} - F_i\left(-\frac{2n+1}{2}i\omega_0\right)e^{-[(2n+1)/2]i\omega_0 t}\right] \tag{11}$$

By using Eqs. (11) and (16), the actual output y is given by

$$\begin{aligned} y = \frac{16a^2k}{\pi^4}\sum_{n=0}^{\infty}\sum_{m=0}^{\infty}\frac{(-1)^{n+m}}{(2n+1)^2(2m+1)^2}\times \Big\{ & F_0[(n+m+1)i\omega_0]F_i\left(\frac{2n+1}{2}i\omega_0\right)\times F_i\left(\frac{2m+1}{2}i\omega_0\right)e^{(n+m+1)i\omega_0 t} - F_0[(n-m)i\omega_0]\times \\ & F_i\left(\frac{2n+1}{2}i\omega_0\right)F_i\left(-\frac{2m+1}{2}i\omega_0\right)e^{(n-m)i\omega_0 t} - F_0[-(n-m)i\omega_0]F_i\left(-\frac{2n+1}{2}i\omega_0\right)\times \\ & F_i\left(\frac{2m+1}{2}i\omega_0\right)e^{-(n-m)i\omega_0 t} + F_0[-(n+m+1)i\omega_0]\times F_i\left(-\frac{2n+1}{2}i\omega_0\right)F_i\left(-\frac{2m+1}{2}i\omega_0\right)\times e^{-(n+m+1)i\omega_0 t}\Big\} \end{aligned} \tag{12}$$

By comparing Eqs. (11) and (12), it is seen that the input has half the frequency of the output. This is, of course, to be expected from the basic parabolic relation of input and output as specified by Eq. (1).

The average of the actual output y with respect to time t, being here referred to the optimum output y_0, gives directly the hunting loss D. Equation (12) shows that this average value is the sum of terms with $n = m$ from the second and the third terms of that equation. Therefore, using Eq. (5),

$$D = \frac{32a^2k}{\pi^4}\sum_{n=0}^{\infty}\frac{1}{(2n+1)^4}F_i\left(\frac{2n+1}{2}i\omega_0\right)\times F_i\left(-\frac{2n+1}{2}i\omega_0\right) \tag{13}$$

This equation can be easily checked by observing that when the dynamic effects are absent, $F_i \equiv 1$, then the series can be easily summed and $D = (1/3)a^2k$ as required by Eq. (3). Equation (13) also shows that the average output and hence the hunting loss are independent of the output linear group. This agrees with the one's physical understanding: Only detailed time variation of the output is modified by the dynamics of the output linear group. In the case of an internal combustion engine, the average output specifies the power of the engine. The dynamics of the output linear group is determined by the inertia of the moving parts. The power of the engine is certainly independent of the inertia of the moving parts.

Equations (11) to (13) fully determine the performance of the optimalizing control system once the values of a, k, and ω_0 are specified and the transfer functions $F_i(s)$ and $F_0(s)$ of the input linear group and the output linear group are given. The following sections give the detailed calculations and results for the case of first-order input and output groups.

First-Order Input and Output Groups

The frequency ω_0 of the optimalizing control is usually low, and the important dynamic effects come from the inertia in the input and the output linear groups. Then these linear groups can be closely approximated by first-order systems. In other words, their transfer functions are

$$F_i(i\omega) = 1/(1 + i\omega\tau_i) \qquad (14)$$

$$F_0(i\omega) = 1/(1 + i\omega\tau_0) \qquad (15)$$

where τ_i and τ_0 are the characteristic time constants of the input linear group and the output linear group, respectively. It is evident that these transfer functions satisfy the conditions of Eqs. (5) and (8).

By substituting Eq. (14) into Eq. (11), the actual output x is given by

$$x = \frac{8a}{\pi^2}\sum_{n=0}^{\infty}\frac{(-1)^n}{2i(2n+1)^2}\left[\frac{e^{[(2n+1)/2]i\omega_0 t}}{1+(2n+1)i(\omega_0\tau_i/2)} - \frac{e^{-[(2n+1)/2]i\omega_0 t}}{1-(2n+1)i(\omega_0\tau_i/2)}\right] \qquad (16)$$

When the summation is carried out, Eq. (16) yields the following equations for the input x:

$$x = NT\left[\frac{t}{T} - \frac{\tau_i}{T} + \frac{\tau_i}{T}\frac{e^{-[(t/T)/(\tau_i/T)]}}{\cosh(T/2\tau_i)}\right] \quad \text{for } -\frac{1}{2} \leqslant \frac{t}{T} \leqslant \frac{1}{2} \qquad (17a)$$

and

$$x = -NT\left[\frac{t}{T} - \left(1 + \frac{\tau_i}{T}\right) + \frac{\tau_i}{T}\frac{e^{(1-t/T)/(\tau_i/T)}}{\cosh(T/2\tau_i)}\right] \quad \text{for } \frac{1}{2} \leqslant \frac{t}{T} \leqslant \frac{3}{2} \qquad (17b)$$

where N is the constant input drive speed—i.e.,

$$N = 2a/T \qquad (18)$$

By using these equations, the variation of actual input x with respect to time can be calculated for any specified data. Examples of such calculations are shown in Figs. 4 and 5 for $\tau_i/T = 0.1$ and $\tau_i/T = 0.4$, respectively. Both show the expected effect of rounding-off of the sharp corners of the saw-tooth curve and a time delay. It is of interest to note that while the delay is almost equal to τ_i itself for small τ_i/T, the delay is less than τ_i for larger τ_i/T.

With the first-order transfer function of Eq. (14), the hunting loss given by Eq. (13) becomes

$$D = \frac{32a^2k}{\pi^4}\sum_{n=0}^{\infty}\frac{1}{(2n+1)^4\{1 + [(2n+1)/2]^2\omega_0^2\tau_i^2\}} \qquad (19)$$

By carrying out the summation, Eq. (19) gives the hunting loss as

$$D = (N^2T^2k/12)\,[1 - 12(\tau_i/T)^2 + 24(\tau_i/T)^3\tanh(T/2\tau_i)] \qquad (20)$$

Fig. 6 shows a dimensionless plot of this equation.

To calculate the actual output y, both Eqs. (14) and (15) have to be substituted into Eq. (12)—i.e.,

$$y = \frac{4T^2N^2k}{\pi^4}\sum_{n=0}^{\infty}\sum_{m=0}^{\infty}\frac{(-1)^{n+m}}{(2n+1)^2(2m+1)^2}\times\left\{\frac{e^{i(n+m+1)\omega_0 t}}{[1+(n+m+1)i\omega_0\tau_0]\,[1+(2n+1)i(\omega_0\tau_i/2)]\,[1+(2m+1)i(\omega_0\tau_i/2)]} - \frac{e^{i(n-m)\omega_0 t}}{[1+(n-m)i\omega_0\tau_0]\,[1+(2n+1)i(\omega_0\tau_i/2)]\,[1-(2m+1)i(\omega_0\tau_i/2)]} - \frac{e^{-i(n-m)\omega_0 t}}{[1-(n-m)i\omega_0\tau_0]\,[1-(2n+1)i(\omega_0\tau_i/2)]\,[1+(2m+1)i(\omega_0\tau_i/2)]} + \frac{e^{-i(n+m+1)\omega_0 t}}{[1-(n+m+1)i\omega_0\tau_0]\,[1-(2n+1)i(\omega_0\tau_i/2)]\,[1-(2m+1)i(\omega_0\tau_i/2)]}\right\} \qquad (21)$$

By changing the summation indices, Eq. (21) can also be written as

$$y = \frac{4T^2N^2k}{\pi^4}\left(\sum_{s=-\infty}^{\infty}\frac{(-1)^{s-1}e^{is\omega_0 t}}{(1+is\omega_0\tau_0)}\times\sum_{n=0}^{\infty}\frac{1}{(2n+1)^2[(2n+1)-2s]^2\,[1+(2n+1)i(\omega_0\tau_i/2)]\,\{1-[(2n+1)-2s]i(\omega_0\tau_i/2)\}} + \sum_{s=-\infty}^{\infty}\frac{(-1)^{s-1}e^{-is\omega_0 t}}{(1-is\omega_0\tau_0)}\sum_{n=0}^{\infty}\frac{1}{(2n+1)^2[(2n+1)-2s]^2\,[1-(2n+1)i(\omega_0\tau_i/2)]\,\{1+[(2n+1)-2s]i(\omega_0\tau_i/2)\}}\right)$$

or

$$y = \frac{8T^2N^2k}{\pi^4}\left\{-\sum_{n=0}^{\infty}\frac{1}{(2n+1)^4[1+(2n+1)^2(\omega_0\tau_i/2)^2]} + \sum_{s=1}^{\infty}\frac{(-1)^{s-1}e^{is\omega_0 t}}{(1+is\omega_0\tau_0)} \times \right.$$

$$\sum_{n=0}^{\infty}\frac{[(2n+1)^2+4s^2]\,[(1+i\omega_0\tau_i s)+(\omega_0\tau_i/2)^2(2n+1)^2]+8(\omega_0\tau_i/2)^2s^2(2n+1)^2}{(2n+1)^2[(2n+1)^2-4s^2]^2\,[1+(\omega_0\tau_i/2)^2(2n+1)^2]\,[(1+i\omega_0\tau_i s)^2+(\omega_0\tau_i/2)^2(2n+1)^2]} + \sum_{s=1}^{\infty}\frac{(-1)^{s-1}e^{-is\omega_0 t}}{(1-is\omega_0\tau_0)}\sum_{n=0}^{\infty} \times$$

$$\left.\frac{[(2n+1)^2+4s^2]\,[(1-i\omega_0\tau_i s)+(\omega_0\tau_i/2)^2(2n+1)^2]+8(\omega_0\tau_i/2)^2s^2(2n+1)^2}{(2n+1)^2[(2n+1)^2-4s^2]^2\,[1+(\omega_0\tau_i/2)^2(2n+1)^2]\,[(1-i\omega_0\tau_i s)^2+(\omega_0\tau_i/2)^2(2n+1)^2]}\right\} \tag{22}$$

The last two summations in Eq. (22) are complex conjugate of each other, thus

$$y = \frac{8T^2N^2k}{\pi^4}\left\{-\sum_{n=0}^{\infty}\frac{1}{(2n+1)^4\,[1+(2n+1)^2(\omega_0\tau_i/2)^2]} + 2\mathrm{Rl}\sum_{s=1}^{\infty}\frac{(-1)^{s-1}e^{is\omega_0 t}}{(1+is\omega_0\tau_0)}\sum_{n=0}^{\infty} \times \right.$$

$$\left.\frac{[(2n+1)^2+4s^2]\,[(1+i\omega_0\tau_i s)+(\omega_0\tau_i/2)^2(2n+1)^2]+8(\omega_0\tau_i/2)^2s^2(2n+1)^2}{(2n+1)^2[(2n+1)^2-4s^2]^2[1+(\omega_0\tau_i/2)^2(2n+1)^2]\,[(1+i\omega_0\tau_i s)^2+(\omega_0\tau_i/2)^2(2n+1)^2]}\right\} \tag{23}$$

where Rl means the real part of the expression following it. In order to carry out the summation with respect to the index n, Eq. (23) is resolved into the following partial fraction form:

$$y = \frac{8T^2N^2k}{\pi^4}\left(-\sum_{n=0}^{\infty}\frac{1}{(2n+1)^4[1+(2n+1)^2(\omega_0\tau_i/2)^2]} + 2\mathrm{Rl}\sum_{s=1}^{\infty}\frac{(-1)^{s-1}e^{is\omega_0 t}}{(1+is\omega_0\tau_0)} \times \right.$$

$$\left\{\frac{1}{4s^2(1+is\omega_0\tau_i)}\sum_{n=0}^{\infty}\frac{1}{(2n+1)^2} + \frac{(\omega_0\tau_i/2)^4}{2(1+is\omega_0\tau_i)^2\,[1+is(\omega_0\tau_i/2)]}\sum_{n=0}^{\infty}\frac{1}{[1+(\omega_0\tau_i/2)^2(2n+1)^2]} + \right.$$

$$\frac{(\omega_0\tau_i/2)^4}{2(1+is\omega_0\tau_i)\,[1+is(\omega_0\tau_i/2)]}\sum_{n=0}^{\infty}\frac{1}{[(1+i\omega_0\tau_i s)^2+(\omega_0\tau_i/2)^2(2n+1)^2]} -$$

$$\left.\left.\frac{[1+is\omega_0\tau_i+4(\omega_0\tau_i/2)^2s^2]}{4s^2(1+is\omega_0\tau_i)^2}\sum_{n=0}^{\infty}\frac{1}{[(2n+1)^2+(i2s)^2]} + \frac{2}{(1+is\omega_0\tau_i)}\sum_{n=0}^{\infty}\frac{1}{[(2n+1)^2+(i2s)^2]^2}\right\}\right) \tag{24}$$

By using the summation formulas given in the Appendix, the sums with respect to n can be evaluated and the result is, noting that $\tan \pi s = 0$ for integer values of s,

$$y = \frac{8T^2N^2k}{\pi^4}\left(-\left[\frac{\pi^4}{96} - \frac{\pi^2}{8}\left(\frac{\omega_0\tau_i}{2}\right)^2 + \frac{\pi}{4}\left(\frac{\omega_0\tau_i}{2}\right)^3\tanh\frac{\pi}{\omega_0\tau_i}\right] + \right.$$

$$\left.2\mathrm{Rl}\sum_{s=1}^{\infty}\frac{(-1)^{s-1}e^{is\omega_0 t}}{(1+is\omega_0\tau_0)}\left\{\frac{\pi^2}{4}\,\frac{1}{(4s^2)\,(1+is\omega_0\tau_i)} + \frac{\pi}{4}\,\frac{(\omega_0\tau_i/2)^3\tanh[\pi/(\omega_0\tau_i)]}{(1+is\omega_0\tau_i)^2\,[1+is\,(\omega_0\tau_i/2)]}\right\}\right) \tag{25}$$

Eq. (25) is again resolved into partial fractions in order to carry out the summation with respect to s, viz.,

$$y = \frac{8T^2N^2k}{\pi^4}\left[-\left[\frac{\pi^4}{96} - \frac{\pi^2}{8}\left(\frac{\omega_0\tau_i}{2}\right)^2 + \frac{\pi}{4}\left(\frac{\omega_0\tau_i}{2}\right)^3\tanh\frac{\pi}{\omega_0\tau_i}\right] + \right.$$

$$\frac{\pi}{2}\left(\frac{(\omega_0\tau_0/2)^3}{[(\omega_0\tau_0/2)-(\omega_0\tau_i/2)]}\left\{\frac{2(\omega_0\tau_i/2)^3\tanh[\pi/(\omega_0\tau_i)]}{[(\omega_0\tau_0/2)-(\omega_0\tau_i/2)][\omega_0\tau_0-(\omega_0\tau_i/2)]} - \pi\right\}\mathrm{Rl}\sum_{s=1}^{\infty}\frac{(-1)^{s-1}e^{is\omega_0 t}}{(1+is\omega_0\tau_0)} + \right.$$

$$\frac{(\omega_0\tau_i/2)^3}{[(\omega_0\tau_0/2)-(\omega_0\tau_i/2)]}\left\{\pi - \frac{2(\omega_0\tau_i/2)^2\tanh[\pi/(\omega_0\tau_i)]}{[(\omega_0\tau_0/2)-(\omega_0\tau_i/2)]}\right\}\mathrm{Rl}\sum_{s=1}^{\infty}\frac{(-1)^{s-1}e^{is\omega_0 t}}{(1+is\omega_0\tau_i)} - \frac{\pi}{2}\left(\frac{\omega_0\tau_0}{2}+\frac{\omega_0\tau_i}{2}\right) \times$$

$$\mathrm{Rl}\sum_{s=1}^{\infty}\frac{(-1)^{s-1}ie^{is\omega_0 t}}{s} + \frac{\pi}{4}\mathrm{Rl}\sum_{s=1}^{\infty}\frac{(-1)^{s-1}e^{is\omega_0 t}}{s^2} - \frac{(\omega_0\tau_i/2)^4\tanh[\pi/(\omega_0\tau_i)]}{[2(\omega_0\tau_0/2)-(\omega_0\tau_i/2)]}\mathrm{Rl}\sum_{s=1}^{\infty}\frac{(-1)^{s-1}e^{is\omega_0 t}}{[1+is(\omega_0\tau_i/2)]} -$$

$$\left.\left.\frac{2(\omega_0\tau_i/2)^4\tanh[\pi/(\omega_0\tau_i)]}{[(\omega_0\tau_0/2)-(\omega_0\tau_i/2)]}\mathrm{Rl}\sum_{s=1}^{\infty}\frac{(-1)^{s-1}e^{is\omega_0 t}}{(1+is\omega_0\tau_i)^2}\right)\right] \tag{26}$$

The result of carrying out the summations in Eq. (26) and simplifying the expressions is,

$$y = 2T^2N^2k\left[-\left\{\frac{1}{2}\left(\frac{t}{T}\right)^2 - \left(\frac{\tau_i}{T}+\frac{\tau_0}{T}\right)\left(\frac{t}{T}\right) + \left[\frac{1}{2}\left(\frac{\tau_i}{T}\right)^2 + \frac{\tau_i\tau_0}{T^2} + \left(\frac{\tau_0}{T}\right)^2\right]\right\} + \right.$$

$$\frac{1}{2}\left(-\frac{(\tau_0/T)^2}{(\tau_0/T-\tau_i/T)}\left\{\frac{2(\tau_i/T)^3\tanh(T/2\tau_i)}{[(\tau_0/T)-(\tau_i/T)]\,[2(\tau_0/T)-(\tau_i/T)]} - 1\right\}\frac{e^{-(t/T)/(\tau_0/T)}}{\sinh(T/2\tau_0)} + \right.$$

$$\left.\left.\left\{\frac{t}{T} + \frac{(\tau_i/T)^2}{[(\tau_0/T)-(\tau_i/T)]}\right\}\frac{2(\tau_i/T)^2\,e^{-(t/T)/(\tau_i/T)}}{[(\tau_0/T)-(\tau_i/T)]\cosh(T/2\tau_i)} + \frac{(\tau_i/T)^3}{[2(\tau_0/T)-(\tau_i/T)]}\,\frac{e^{-(2t/T)/(\tau_i/T)}}{\cosh^2(T/2\tau_i)}\right)\right] \tag{27a}$$

for $-(1/2) \leqslant t/T \leqslant 1/2$ and

$$y = 2T^2N^2k\left[-\left\{\frac{1}{2}\left(\frac{t}{T}\right)^2 - \left(\frac{\tau_0}{T} + \frac{\tau_i}{T} + 1\right)\left(\frac{t}{T}\right) + \left[\frac{1}{2}\left(\frac{\tau_i}{T}\right)^2 + \frac{\tau_i\tau_0}{T^2} + \left(\frac{\tau_0}{T}\right)^2 + \frac{\tau_0}{T} + \frac{\tau_i}{T} + \frac{1}{2}\right]\right\} + \right.$$
$$\frac{1}{2}\left(-\frac{(\tau_0/T)^2}{[(\tau_0/T) - (\tau_i/T)]}\left\{\frac{2(\tau_i/T)^3 \tanh(T/2\tau_i)}{[(\tau_0/T) - (\tau_i/T)]\,[2(\tau_0/T) - (\tau_i/T)]} - 1\right\}\frac{e^{(1-t/T)/(\tau_0/T)}}{\sinh(T/2\tau_0)} + \right.$$
$$\left.\left.\left[\frac{t}{T} + \frac{(\tau_i/T)^2}{(\tau_0/T) - (\tau_i/T)} - 1\right]\frac{2(\tau_i/T)^2 e^{(1-t/T)/(\tau_i/T)}}{[(\tau_0/T) - (\tau_i/T)]\cosh(T/2\tau_i)} + \frac{(\tau_i/T)^3\, e^{2(1-t/T)/(\tau_i/T)}}{[2(\tau_0/T) - (\tau_i/T)]\cosh^2(T/2\tau_i)}\right)\right] \tag{27b}$$

for $1/2 \leqslant t/T \leqslant 3/2$.

In Eqs. (27a) and (27b), there are apparent singularities whenever $\tau_0/T = \tau_i/T$ and $2\tau_0/T = \tau_i/T$; that is, the value of output y seemingly cannot be determined for these values of time constants. However this is deceptive. By using a simple limit procedure or by direct evaluation of Eq. (25) for these two cases, it can be shown that this is not the case. For example, for $\tau_i/T = \tau_0/T$

$$y = 2T^2N^2k\left\{-\frac{1}{2}\left(\frac{t}{T}\right)^2 + 2\left(\frac{\tau_i}{T}\right)\left(\frac{t}{T}\right) - \frac{5}{2}\left(\frac{\tau_i}{T}\right)^2 + \left[-\left(\frac{\tau_i}{T}\right)^2 - \frac{1}{2}\left(\frac{t}{T}\right)^2 + \right.\right.$$
$$\left.\left.\left(\frac{\tau_i}{T}\right)\left(\frac{t}{T}\right) + \frac{1}{8}\right] e^{-[(t/T)/(\tau_i/T)]}\,\mathrm{sech}\,\frac{T}{2\tau_i} + \frac{3}{2}\left(\frac{\tau_i}{T}\right)e^{-(t/T)/(\tau_i/T)}\,\mathrm{csch}\,\frac{T}{2\tau_i} + \frac{1}{2}\left(\frac{\tau_i}{T}\right)^2 e^{-(2t/T)/(\tau_i/T)}\,\mathrm{sech}^2\,\frac{T}{2\tau_i}\right\} \tag{28}$$

for $-(1/2) \leqslant t/T \leqslant 1/2$, and, for $2\tau_0/T = \tau_i/T$,

$$y = -2T^2N^2k\left\{\frac{1}{2}\left(\frac{t}{T}\right)^2 - \frac{3}{2}\left(\frac{\tau_i}{T}\right)\left(\frac{t}{T}\right) + \frac{5}{4}\left(\frac{\tau_i}{T}\right)^2 + \left[\left(\frac{\tau_i}{T}\right)\left(\frac{t}{T}\right) + 2\left(\frac{\tau_i}{T}\right)^2 + \frac{1}{2}\left(\frac{\tau_i}{T}\right)\mathrm{ctnh}\,\frac{T}{\tau_i} + \right.\right.$$
$$\left.\left.\frac{1}{8}\left(\frac{\tau_i}{T}\right)\mathrm{ctnh}\,\frac{T}{2\tau_i}\right]\frac{e^{-[(2t/T)/(\tau_i/T)]}}{\cosh^2 T/2\tau_i} + \left(\frac{\tau_i}{T}\right)\left(2\,\frac{t}{T} - 4\,\frac{\tau_i}{T}\right)\frac{e^{-[(t/T)/(\tau_i/T)]}}{\cosh T/2\tau_i}\right\} \tag{29}$$

for $-(1/2) \leqslant t/T \leqslant 1/2$.

An analysis for the continuity of Eqs. (27a) and (27b) at $t/T = 1/2$ shows that the values of y and its derivative with respect to t are the same at $t/T = 1/2$ whether they are computed from Eq. (27a) or from Eq. (27b).

Now the computation of the potential output y^* can be accomplished by letting $\tau_0/T = 0$ in Eqs. (27a) and (27b). Thus,

$$y^* = 2T^2N^2k\left[-\frac{1}{2}\left(\frac{t}{T}\right)^2 + \left(\frac{\tau_i}{T}\right)\left(\frac{t}{T}\right) - \frac{1}{2}\left(\frac{\tau_i}{T}\right)^2 - \left(\frac{t}{T} - \frac{\tau_i}{T}\right)\left(\frac{\tau_i}{T}\right)\frac{e^{-[(t/T)/(\tau_i/T)]}}{\cosh(T/2\tau_i)} - \frac{1}{2}\left(\frac{\tau_i}{T}\right)^2\frac{e^{-[(2t/T)/(\tau_i/T)]}}{\cosh^2(T/2\tau_i)}\right] \tag{30a}$$

for $-(1/2) \leqslant t/T \leqslant 1/2$ and

$$y^* = 2T^2N^2k\left\{-\frac{1}{2}\left(\frac{t}{T}\right)^2 + \left(1 + \frac{\tau_i}{T}\right)\left(\frac{t}{T}\right) - \frac{1}{2}\left(1 + \frac{\tau_i}{T}\right)^2 - \left(\frac{\tau_i}{T}\right)\left[\frac{t}{T} - \right.\right.$$
$$\left.\left.\left(\frac{\tau_i}{T} + 1\right)\right]\frac{e^{(1-t/T)/(\tau_i/T)}}{\cosh(T/2\tau_i)} - \frac{1}{2}\left(\frac{\tau_i}{T}\right)^2\frac{e^{[2(1-t/T)]/(\tau_i/T)}}{\cosh^2(T/2\tau_i)}\right\} \tag{30b}$$

for $1/2 \leqslant t/T \leqslant 3/2$.

These expressions check with the result of direct calculation of y^* by Eqs. (1) and (17).

Figures 7 and 8 show the dimensionless plots of actual output y and potential output y^* for the particular values of τ_0/T and τ_i/T. In these figures it is clearly seen that the dynamic effects not only decrease the output of the system but also introduce a time lag and lower the maximum output of the system. Figure 8 with $\tau_i/T = 0.4$, $\tau_0/T = 0.6$, has the maximum value of y almost at the very instants of input drive reversal points, $t/T = n + (1/2)$. This is indeed an extreme case.

Design Charts

From the principle of operation of the peak-holding optimalizing control, it is seen that the most important quantity to be specified for its design is the critical indicated difference c between the reading of the special output sensing instrument and the output itself. By definition, c is the difference of the maximum of the actual output y and the value of y at the tripping instant of the input drive. The instant of reversing the input drive is typified by $t/T = 1/2$. If the corresponding instant of maximum y is t^*, then the critical indicated difference c is calculated as

$$c = y(t^*/T) - y(1/2) \tag{31}$$

by using any one of Eqs. (27), (28), or (29). Since the instant of input drive reversal must come after the instant of maximum output, $t^*/T < 1/2$.

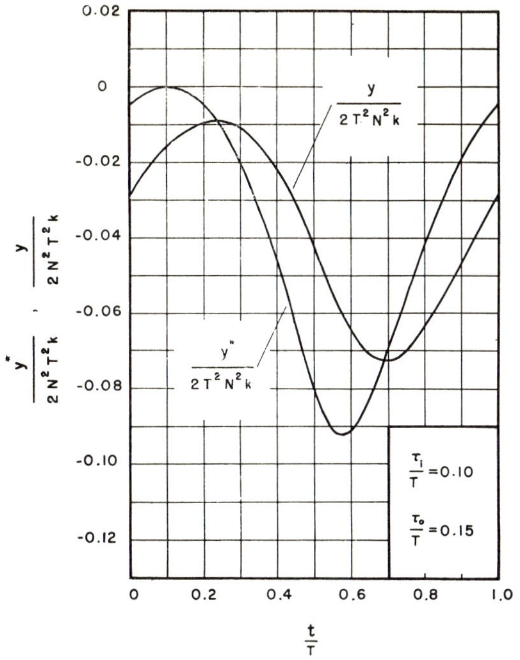

FIG. 7. "Potential" output and indicated output for values of $\tau_i/T = 0.1$ and $\tau_0/T = 0.15$.

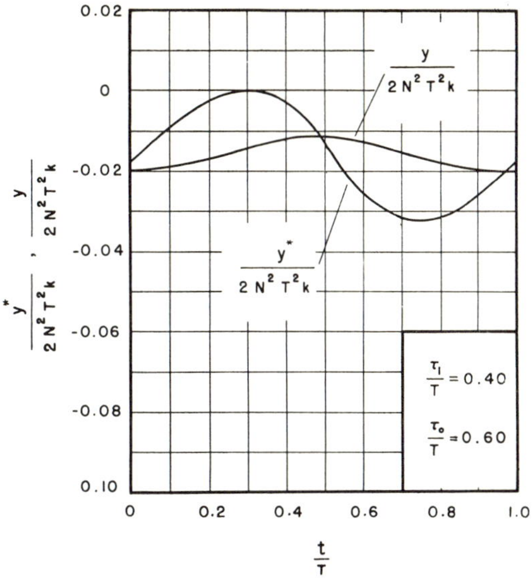

FIG. 8. "Potential" output and indicated output for values of $\tau_i/T = 0.4$ and $\tau_0/T = 0.6$.

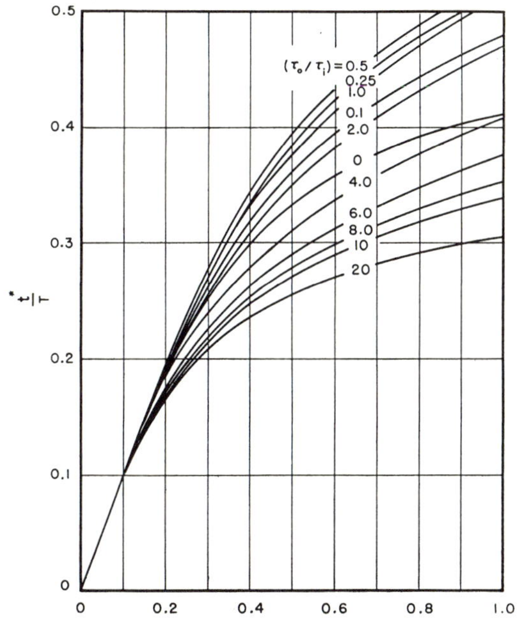

FIG. 9. Maximum output occurrence instant, t^*/T in interval $(0 \leq t/T \leq 1/2)$ versus $(\tau_0 + \tau_i)/T$ with τ_0/τ_i as parameter.

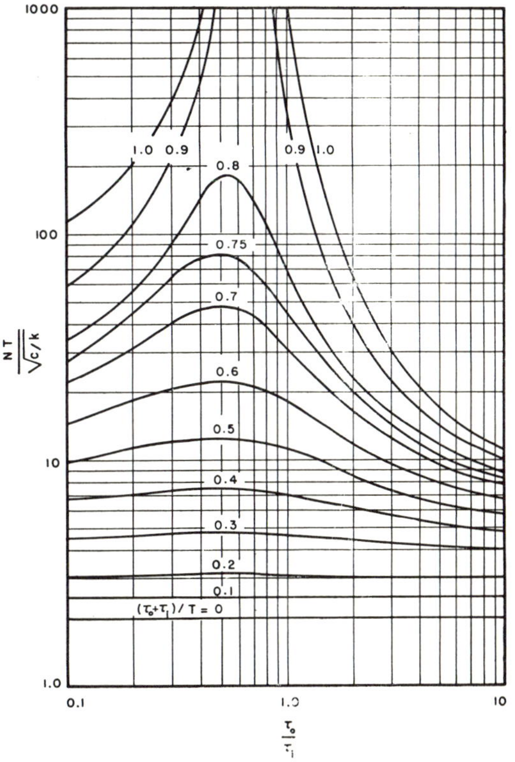

FIG. 10. Critical indicated difference parameter, $TN/\sqrt{c/k}$ versus τ_0/τ_i with $(\tau_0 + \tau_i)/T$ as parameter.

To determine t^*, one may use the condition of zero slope—i.e., $dy/dt = 0$. Then Eq. (27a) gives

$$
\begin{aligned}
-\left[\frac{t^*}{T} - \left(\frac{\tau_0}{T} + \frac{\tau_i}{T}\right)\right] + \frac{(\tau_0/T)}{2[(\tau_0/T) - (\tau_i/T)]}\left\{\frac{2(\tau_i/T)^3 \tanh (T/2\tau_i)}{[(\tau_0/T) - (\tau_i/T)]\,[2(\tau_0/T) - (\tau_i/T)]} - 1\right\}\frac{e^{-[(t^*/T)/(\tau_0/T)]}}{\sinh (T/2\tau_0)} + \\
\left\{1 - \left(\frac{t^*}{T}\right)\left(\frac{T}{\tau_i}\right) - \frac{(\tau_i/T)}{[(\tau_0/T) - (\tau_i/T)]}\right\}\frac{(\tau_i/T)^2\, e^{-(t^*/T)/(\tau_i/T)}}{[(\tau_0/T) - (\tau_i/T)] \cosh (T/2\tau_i)} - \\
\frac{(\tau_i/T)^2\, e^{-[(2t^*/T)/(\tau_i/T)]}}{[2(\tau_0/T) - (\tau_i/T)] \cosh^2(T/2\tau_i)} = 0 \qquad (32)
\end{aligned}
$$

This transcendental equation for t^*/T may be solved by iteration. For instance, for small τ_0/T and τ_i/T, only terms within the first brackets are of importance, then $t^*/T \simeq (\tau_0 + \tau_i)/T$. This is already recognized by Draper and co-workers.[1,2] The complete results of calculation are shown in Fig. 9, which shows that t^*/T is almost only a function of $(\tau_0 + \tau_i)/T$ with minor modifications from the parameter τ_0/τ_i, the ratio of characteristic times of the output linear group and the input linear group. Values of t^*/T beyond 1/2 are not shown, as clearly then the maxima of the output will occur after the corresponding input drive reversal points and proper operation of the control will be difficult if not impossible.

With t^*/T determined, Eq. (31) gives c by substituting Eq. (27a). However the specified quantities of an optimalizing control are k, the characteristics of the controlled system, and τ_i, τ_0, the characteristics of the linear group. From considerations on the noise interference, the designer can make an appropriate choice of the period T and the critical indicated difference c for input drive reversal. Therefore the quantities that the designer wishes to know, after he has the values of k, τ_i, τ_0, T, and c, are N, the input drive speed, and D, the hunting loss. Thus the result of calculation with Eq. (31) should be written as follows:

$$
\begin{aligned}
\frac{TN}{\sqrt{c/k}} = \Bigg(\left[\frac{1}{4} - \left(\frac{t^*}{T}\right)^2\right] + 2\left(\frac{\tau_i}{T}\right)\left(\frac{\tau_0}{\tau_i} + 1\right)\left(\frac{t^*}{T} - \frac{1}{2}\right) - \frac{(\tau_0/\tau_i)^2\,(\tau_i/T)}{[(\tau_0/\tau_i) - 1] \sinh (\tau_i/\tau_0)(T/2\tau_i)} \times \\
\left\{\frac{2(\tau_i/T) \tanh (T/2\tau_i)}{[(\tau_0/\tau_i) - 1]\,[2(\tau_0/\tau_i) - 1]} - 1\right\}\left(e^{-[(t^*/T)/(\tau_0/\tau_i)\,(\tau_i/T)]} - e^{-\{1/[2(\tau_0/\tau_i)\,(\tau_i/T]\}}\right) + \\
\frac{2(\tau_i/T)}{[(\tau_0/\tau_i) - 1] \cosh (T/2\tau_i)}\left\{\left[\frac{t^*}{T} + \frac{(\tau_i/T)}{(\tau_0/\tau_i) - 1}\right] e^{-[(t^*/T)/(\tau_i/T)]} - \left[\frac{1}{2} + \frac{(\tau_i/T)}{(\tau_0/\tau_i) - 1}\right] e^{-(T/2\tau_i)}\right\} + \\
\frac{(\tau_i/T)^2\left(e^{-[(2t^*/T)/(\tau_i/T)]} - e^{-(T/\tau_i)]}\right.}{[2(\tau_0/\tau_i) - 1] \cosh^2 (T/2\tau_i)}\Bigg)^{-(1/2)} \qquad (33)
\end{aligned}
$$

When N is determined, Eq. (20) then gives the hunting loss D.

Figures 10 and 11 are the design charts for peak-holding optimalizing control computed from the equations of the preceding analysis. Figure 10 gives $TN/\sqrt{c/k}$ as a function of τ_0/τ_i with $(\tau_0 + \tau_i)/T$ as parameter. Figure 11 gives relative hunting loss D/c again as a function of τ_0/τ_i with $(\tau_0 + \tau_i)/T$ as parameter. The peaks of curves near $\tau_0/\tau_i = 1$ indicate a sort of resonant effect between the input linear group and output linear group. The hunting loss for fixed $(\tau_i + \tau_0)/T$ and c is smaller for τ_0/τ_i away from unity. For fixed τ_i, τ_0, and c, clearly the way to reduce the hunting loss is by increasing the period T.

Concluding Remarks

The present analysis gives the necessary input drive speed N and the hunting loss D for any specified hunting period T, time constants τ_i and τ_0 for the input linear group and the output linear group, and the chosen critical indicated difference c. T and c are fixed by considerations on the noise interference. The analysis shows that whenever the hunting period is relatively short with respect to the time constants τ_i, τ_0, or whenever $(\tau_i + \tau_0)/T$ is relatively large, the hunting loss will be large, especially when τ_i and τ_0 are nearly equal. To avoid such unfavorable condition, the designer should improve his input drive system so as to reduce the constant τ_i. τ_0 is, however, a constant of the intrinsic characteristic of the controlled system, due to, say, the inertia of the moving parts of the system. τ_0 is thus not at the disposal of the designer of the control system. However, suppose there is a compensating circuit between the output y and optimalizing input drive unit (Fig. 3), such that the effects of the output linear group is completely compensated. Then the effective signal for input drive reversal is not the actual output y, but the potential output y^*. In other words, the value of τ_0 is made to be effectively zero. Even if complete compensation is not achieved, the effective value of τ_0 can still be greatly reduced. For difficult cases then, such a compensating unit should certainly be added to reduce the hunting loss. This will be just a minor complication when compared with the additional equipment required for satisfactory noise filtering.

Appendix

Typical Summation Formulas

Rl and Im mean, respectively, the "real part of" and the "imaginary part of" the expression following it.

$$(1)\quad \sum_{n=0}^{\infty} \frac{1}{(2n+1)^2} = \frac{\pi^2}{8}$$

$$(2)\quad \sum_{n=0}^{\infty} \frac{1}{(2n+1)^4} = \frac{\pi^4}{96}$$

$$(3)\quad \sum_{n=0}^{\infty} \frac{1}{[1+(2n+1)^2 z^2]} = \frac{\pi}{4z} \tanh \frac{\pi^2}{2z}$$

$$(4)\quad \mathrm{Rl} \sum_{s=1}^{\infty} \frac{(-1)^{s-1} e^{is\omega_0 t}}{1+i2sb} = \frac{1}{2} - \frac{\pi}{4b} \frac{e^{-[(\omega_0 t)/(2b)]}}{\sinh \pi/2b} \quad \text{when } -\pi < \omega_0 t < \pi$$

$$= \frac{1}{2} - \frac{\pi}{4b} \frac{e^{\pi/b}}{\sinh \pi/2b} \times e^{-[(\omega_0 t)/(2b)]} \quad \text{when } \pi < \omega_0 t < 3\pi, \text{ etc.}$$

$$(5)\quad \mathrm{Im} \sum_{s=1}^{\infty} \frac{(-1)^{s-1} e^{is\omega_0 t}}{s} = \frac{\omega_0 t}{2} \quad \text{when } -\pi < \omega_0 t < \pi$$

$$= \frac{\omega_0 t}{2} - \pi \quad \text{when } \pi < \omega_0 t < 3\pi, \text{ etc.}$$

$$(6)\quad \mathrm{Rl} \sum_{s=1}^{\infty} \frac{(-1)^{s-1} e^{is\omega_0 t}}{s^2} = \frac{\pi^2}{12} - \left(\frac{\omega_0 t}{2}\right)^2 \quad \text{when } -\pi < \omega_0 t \leq \pi$$

$$= 2\pi\left(\frac{\omega_0 t}{2}\right) - \left(\frac{\omega_0 t}{2}\right)^2 - \frac{11}{12}\pi^2 \quad \text{when } \pi < \omega_0 t < 3\pi, \text{ etc.}$$

$$(7)\quad \mathrm{Rl} \sum_{s=1}^{\infty} \frac{(-1)^{s-1} e^{is\omega_0 t}}{(1+i2sa)^2} = \frac{1}{2} - \frac{\pi}{4a^2} \frac{e^{-[(\omega_0 t)/(2a)]}}{\sinh^2 (\pi/2a)} \times \left(\frac{\omega_0 t}{2} \sinh \frac{\pi}{2a} + \frac{\pi}{2} \cosh \frac{\pi}{2a}\right) \quad \text{when } -\pi < \omega_0 t < \pi$$

$$= \frac{1}{2} - \frac{\pi}{4a^2} \frac{e^{\pi/a} e^{-[(\omega_0 t)/2a)]}}{\sinh^2 (\pi/2a)} \times \left[\left(\frac{\omega_0 t}{2} - \pi\right) \sinh \frac{\pi}{2a} + \frac{\pi}{2} \cosh \frac{\pi}{2a}\right] \quad \text{when } \pi < \omega_0 t < 3\pi, \text{ etc.}$$

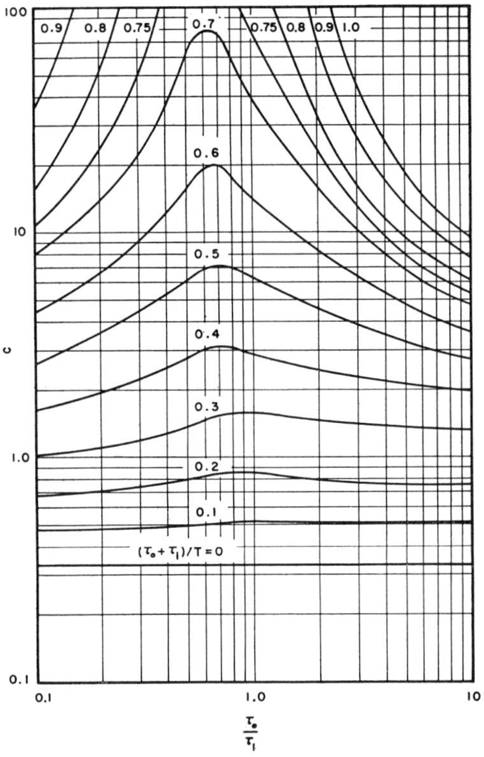

FIG. 11. Relative hunting loss, D/c versus τ_0/τ_i with $(\tau_0 + \tau_i)/T$ as parameter.

REFERENCES

[1] Draper, C. S., and Li, Y. T., *Principles of Optimalizing Control Systems and an Application to the Internal Combustion Engine,* American Society of Mechanical Engineers Publication, September, 1951.

[2] Li, Y. T., *Optimalizing System for Process Control. Instruments,* Vol. 25, pp. 72–77, January, 1952; pp. 190–193, 228, February, 1952; pp. 324–327, 350–352, March, 1952.

[3] Shull, R., Jr., *An Automatic Cruise Control Computer for Long Range Aircraft,* Trans. I.R.E., Professional Group on Electronic Computers, pp. 47–51, December, 1952.

Design of a Self-Optimizing Control System

By R. E. Kalman,[1] New York, N. Y.

This paper examines the problem of building a machine which adjusts itself automatically to control an arbitrary dynamic process. The design of a small computer which acts as such a machine is presented in detail. A complete set of equations describing the machine is derived and listed; engineering features of the computer are discussed briefly. This machine represents a new concept in the development of automatic control systems. It should find widespread application in the automation of complex systems such as aircraft or chemical processes, where present methods would be too expensive or time-consuming to apply.

Introduction

The art of the design of systems for the automatic control of dynamic processes of many different kinds (such as airplanes, chemical plants, military-weapon systems, and so on) has been reduced gradually to standard engineering practice during the years following World War II. In the simplest possible setting, the problem that the engineer faces in designing such automatic control systems is shown in Fig. 1. It is desired that the output of the process $c(t)$, which may be position, speed, temperature, pressure, flow rate, or the like, be as close as possible at all times to an arbitrarily given input $r(t)$ to the system. In other words, at all instants of time it is desired to keep the error $e(t) = r(t) - c(t)$ as small as possible. Control is accomplished by varying some physical quantity $m(t)$, called the control effort, which affects the output of the process.

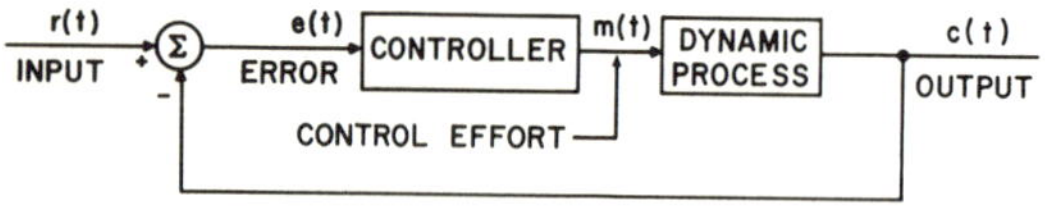

Fig. 1 Block Diagram of Simplest Control Problem

As long as the deviations from an equilibrium value of $r(t)$, $c(t)$, and therefore of $e(t)$ and $m(t)$, are small, the system can be regarded as approximately linear and there is a wealth of theoretical as well as practical information on which engineering design may be based. (When the system is not linear, present-day knowledge supplies only fragmentary suggestions for design; however, nonlinear effects are frequently of secondary importance.) It is generally agreed that the design of high-performance control systems is essentially a problem of matching the dynamic characteristics of a process by those of the controller. Practically speaking, this means that if the dynamic characteristics of the process are known with sufficient accuracy, then the characteristics of a controller necessary to give a certain desired type of performance can be specified. Usually, this amounts to writing down in quantitative terms the differential equations of the controller. Thus the design procedure can be divided roughly into the following distinct stages:

I Measure the dynamic characteristics of the process.
II Specify the desired characteristics of the controller.
III Put together a controller using standard elements (amplifiers, integrators, summers, electric networks, and so on) which has the required dynamic characteristics.

This subdivision of effort in designing a control system is oversimplified, but it will be a convenient starting point for the following discussion.

It has been pointed out by Bergen and Ragazzini (1)[2] that if a high degree of flexibility is desired in design stage (III), it is advantageous to use a sampled-data system. In principle, a sampled-data system is one where the controller is a digital computer. It is probably no exaggeration to say that, because of the great inherent flexibility of a digital computer, *any* desired controller characteristics is practically realizable. The use of a digital computer for the controller reduces stage (III) to a straightforward operation, like that of transcribing a handwritten manuscript by means of a typewriter.

Since the theory of linear control systems is well developed, stages (I–II) also can be made to consist of more-or-less standard procedures. Quick and convenient design even in stage (III) demands or at least suggests a digital computer; so the question arises whether or not stages (I–II) also can be reduced to completely mechanical operations which can be performed by a digital computer. Accordingly, the problem considered in this paper can be stated as follows:

To design a machine which, when inserted in the place of the controller in Fig. 1, will automatically perform steps (I–III), and set itself up as a controller which is optimum in some sense. The design of this machine is to be based on broad principles only. Its operation should require no direct human intervention but merely the measurements of $r(t)$ and $c(t)$.

In other words, such a machine, if it can be built, eliminates the lengthy, tedious, and costly procedure of engineering design—it is only necessary to connect the machine to *any* process. Thus the machine would seemingly eliminate the need for the control-systems engineer, but the latter can be reassured by the fact that the design of the machine itself is a far more ambitious and challenging undertaking than that of conventional control systems.

An even more decisive advantage of the machine over present-day design procedures is the following: In carrying out steps (I–III) it is generally taken for granted that the dynamic characteristics of the process will change only slightly under any operating conditions encountered during the lifetime of the control system. Such *slight* changes are foreseen and are usually counteracted by using feedback. Should the changes become large, the control equipment as originally designed may fail to meet performance specifications. Instances where difficulties of this type are encountered are:

(*a*) Changes of aircraft characteristics with speed.
(*b*) Chemical processes.
(*c*) Any large-scale control operation, where the nature of the system can be affected by uncontrolled and unforeseen factors.

By contrast, the machine can *repeat* steps (I–III) continually and thereby detect and make corrections in accordance with any

[1] Department of Electrical Engineering and Electronics Research Laboratories, Columbia University; formerly, Engineering Research Laboratory, E. I. du Pont de Nemours & Company, Wilmington, Del.

For presentation at the Instruments and Regulators Division Conference, Evanston, Ill., April 8–10, 1957, of The American Society of Mechanical Engineers.

Note: Statements and opinions advanced in papers are to be understood as individual expressions of their authors and not those of the Society. Manuscript received at ASME Headquarters, January 14, 1957. Paper No. 57—IRD-12.

[2] Numbers in parentheses refer to the References at the end of the paper.

changes in the dynamic characteristics of a process which it controls. Such a control system operates always at or near some "optimum," provided only that changes in the dynamic characteristics of the controlled process do not occur very abruptly. It may be said that the machine adapts itself to changes in its surroundings—this may be regarded as an extension of the principle of feedback. The author prefers to call this property of the machine "self-optimization." The word "ultrastability" has been suggested also in a similar context by Ashby (2).

In the stated degree of generality, the problem is certainly not at a stage at present where any clear-cut ("unique") solution can be expected. Therefore this paper does not treat the general problem but presents a specific approach which leads to a practically satisfactory solution. This point is of considerable interest, since some earlier speculations relating to the problem were mostly of theoretical nature, without an attempt to appraise the difficulties (cost, complexity, and so on) of practical implementation (2–5). A machine based on the principles discussed in what follows actually has been built and will be described briefly in a later section.

It should be emphasized that the machine has been designed from a practical engineering point of view, rather than deduced from some law of physics or mathematics. The various single elements in the design of the machine are based on known principles. The choice between alternate possibilities in each stage of the design has been guided by efficiency and cost considerations. It is claimed that the over-all design uniting these principles in one machine is new and represents a major advance in regard to practicality over suggestions contained in the current literature.

General Design Considerations

From the technological point of view, it is clear that the machine discussed in the preceding section must be a computer. There are two possible choices, analog or digital computer. The latter choice is preferable. The reason is this. An analog computer is basically a method of simulating simple dynamic processes as they occur in the physical universe. The machine in question is required to simulate the actions of man, not of nature. This requires much greater flexibility and at the present state of computer technology such flexibility is provided only by digital computers.

The words "digital" and "analog" used here refer to the *external* characteristics of computers. Mathematically speaking, an analog computer performs the operations of analysis, such as differentiation, integration, computing logarithms, and so on, while a digital computer performs only arithmetic operations; namely, addition and multiplication. An analog computer operates on continuous functions (of time), the digital computer deals with discrete numbers. As far as the *internal* construction of these machines is concerned, it may happen that a computer which is called analog by its user contains discrete components (such as very fast counting circuits); and a computer which is called digital by its user may contain continuous components (such as potentiometers). Following these remarks, the computer that is described later may be called externally digital, internally analog.

In a digital computer, mathematical operations must be expressed (using approximations of various types) in numerical form. For instance, a function such as e^x must be computed by means of a series, which involves only repeated addition and multiplication. Another example is measuring the dynamic characteristics (transfer function or impulse response) of a process. Mathematically, this leads to the problem of solving an integral equation for which no satisfactory analog computing technique exists at present. On a digital computer the problem reduces to solving a set of simultaneous algebraic equations which is much simpler than solving an integral equation.

These considerations suggest the first fundamental design requirement:

(*A*) *The machine must be a digital computer.*

Recall now that the machine has a twofold job; namely, design and control. (i) It must measure the dynamic characteristics of the process and then determine the best form of the controller. (ii) It must control the process by providing the required control action $m(t)$. It is naturally desirable to keep these distinct functions independent. Therefore:

(*B*) *The operations necessary for designing a suitable controller must not be allowed to interact with the control action itself.*

It will be seen later that this requirement cannot be satisfied completely; the degree to which it must be relaxed to provide satisfactory operation is one of the unanswered questions at present.

Special Design Considerations

There are several practical requirements, all quite self-evident, which must be satisfied if the machine is to fulfill the expectations presented in the Introduction. All of these are related to design problem (I).

The functioning of the machine must not be critically dependent on obtaining measurements with high accuracy. Determination of the dynamic characteristics of the process is based on knowledge of $m(t)$ and $c(t)$. Since the first of these is actually produced by the machine itself, it may be assumed to be known with arbitrary accuracy; $c(t)$, however, corresponds to some physical quantity such as temperature, flow, and so on, whose determination is always accompanied by errors due to the imperfect operation of measuring equipment. These errors are called *measurement noise.* The standard method of reducing measurement noise is to take a large number of measurements. This leads to the requirement:

(*C*) *The determination of the dynamic characteristics of the process must be based on a large number of measurements so as to minimize the effects of measurement noise.*

As pointed out in the Introduction, one of the potential advantages of such a machine is that it can constantly repeat the entire design procedure and thereby adjust itself in a manner corresponding to any changes in process characteristics. But because of requirement (*C*), the determination of process characteristics requires a large number of measurements, taking a (possibly) long period of time. Since the system characteristics at the end of a series of measurements may be appreciably different from what they were at the beginning of the series of measurements, it is clear that older measurements ("obsolete data") should not be regarded as being as good as more recent measurements. This may be stated as:

(*D*) *Among any two measurements of $c(t)$, the more recent one should be given the higher weight: Measurements of $c(t)$ made infinitely long ago should be given zero weight.*

The cost, size, probability of breakdown, and so on of the machine is roughly proportional to the number of computations it has to perform per unit time. Therefore other things being equal, the number of computations should be as small as possible:

(*E*) *The methods of numerical computation to be used in the machine should be highly efficient.*

This last requirement will make it possible also to choose between alternative methods of computation.

Computation of Transfer Function From Measurements

Sampling. We now examine in detail the problem of measuring the dynamic characteristics of the process to be controlled. To do this, the functions $m(t)$ and $c(t)$ must be known. Since, according to requirement (A), the machine is to be a digital computer, it is necessary to replace $m(t)$ and $c(t)$, which are continuously varying functions of time, by sequences of numbers which are discretely varying functions of time. This process is known as *sampling.* The most common way of doing this is to perform measurements periodically. Let the sampling instants be $t = kT$, $k = 0, 1, 2, \ldots$, where T is called the sampling period. Then sampling replaces $m(t)$ and $c(t)$ by the sequences of numbers

$$\begin{matrix} m(0), & m(T), & m(2T), \ldots, & m(kT), \ldots \\ c(0), & c(T), & c(2T), \ldots, & c(kT), \ldots \end{matrix} \qquad k = 0, 1, \ldots \quad [1]$$

In order to simplify the notation, we frequently will write $m_k = m(kT)$ and $c_k = c(kT)$ from now on. As a result of the sampling process, all experimental information about the functions $m(t)$ and $c(t)$ is contained in the Numbers [1]. The sampling process is illustrated in Fig. 2.

The theory of linear control systems in which some of the controlled quantities are subject to sampling (the so-called sampled-data systems) is well developed. For further information, see Ragazzini and Zadeh (6) and Truxal (7).

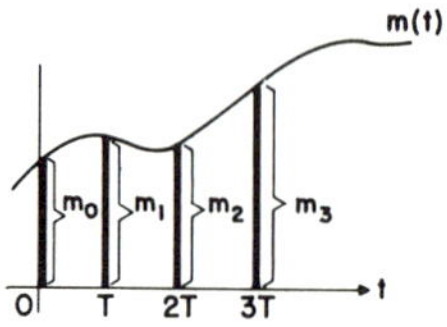

FIG. 2 SAMPLING PROCESS

Step Response of the Process. If the process is *linear, time-invariant and stable,* it is well known that $c(t)$ is related to $m(t)$ by the convolution integral

$$c(t) = \int_{-\infty}^{t} h(t-u)dm(u) \quad [2]$$

where $h(t)$ is the step-function response of the process; $h(t) = 0$ when $t < 0$. Once $h(t)$ (or one of its equivalent forms, for instance, its Laplace transform) is known, the dynamic behavior of the process in question is completely characterized. But to find $h(t)$ given $m(t)$ and $c(t)$ by means of Equation [2] requires solving an integral equation which is a very difficult task.

If we consider now the closed-loop system shown in Fig. 1, it is clear that the input $m(t)$ to the process is the output of the self-optimizing controller. Therefore $m(t)$ must depend on the output of a digital computer; in other words, $m(t)$ must be a function of time which is completely determined by its values m_k at the sampling instants. To construct a function $m(t)$ from the series of numbers m_k which has a definite value at every instant of time calls for some method of interpolation. The simplest and practically most frequently used method (6, 7) is to hold the value of $m(t)$ constant after each sampling instant until the next sampling instant. In mathematical notation

$$m(t) = m_k, \qquad kT \leqslant t < (k+1)T \quad [3]$$

Assuming that $m(t)$ is given by Equation [3], it is easy to show that the convolution integral Equation [2] reduces to the sum

$$c(t) = \sum_{l=-\infty}^{lT<t} h(t-lT)(m_l - m_{l-1}) \quad [4]$$

Noting that $h(kT) = 0$ for all $k < 0$, and considering only sampled values of $c(t)$ and $h(t)$, Equation [4] can be rewritten in the simpler form

$$c_k = \sum_{l=-\infty}^{l=k} (h_{k-l} - h_{k-l-1})m_l = \sum_{l=-\infty}^{l=k} g_{k-l}m_l \quad [5]$$

where the g_k's are recognized as the samples of the response of the system to a unit pulse. According to Equation [5], the dynamic behavior of the process is now represented by the sequence of numbers

$$g_0 = h(0), \quad g_1 = h(T) - h(0), \ldots, \quad g_k = h(kT) - h[(k-1)T], \ldots$$

Moreover, if the input-output sequences [1] are known after some sampling instant, say, $k = 0$, then the numbers g_k can be determined by solving an infinite set of simultaneous linear algebraic equations given by Equation [5]. Since $h_k \rightarrow$ const with $k \rightarrow \infty$ (otherwise the process would not be stable and therefore Equation [5] would not be valid at all) it can be assumed in practice that $h_k = h_N$ for all $k > N$ if N is sufficiently large. This assumption means that $g_k = 0$ for all $k > N$ so that only a *finite* set of linear algebraic equations has to be solved to get the g_k.

But even with this simplification it would be quite inefficient to represent the process by means of the g_k because this would require a large amount of storage in the digital computer. For instance, if the step response of the process is

$$h(t) = 1 - \exp(-t/\tau)$$

$$g_0 = 0, \qquad g_k = [\exp(T/\tau) - 1]\exp(-kT/\tau), \qquad k \geq 1$$

then approximately $N = 5\tau/T$ numbers are necessary if the error due to neglecting the terms g_k, $k > N$ is to be less than 1 per cent. If fast control is required, the time constant of the closed-loop system must be much less than τ; on the other hand, the response of the closed-loop system on the average cannot take place in less T seconds. Thus τ/T must be large, which means that a large number of values of g_k must be stored. This and other practical considerations to be discussed later indicate that the numbers g_k do not represent the dynamic characteristics of a process efficiently.

Pulse Transfer Function. A different way to represent a dynamic process is to assume that there is a linear differential equation relating $m(t)$ to $c(t)$. Consequently, m_k and c_k may be assumed to be related by means of a linear difference equation

$$c_k + b_1c_{k-1} + \ldots + b_nc_{k-n} = a_0m_k + a_1m_{k-1} + \ldots + a_qm_{k-q} \quad [6]$$

where the a_i and b_i are real constants and b_0 has been set arbitrarily equal to unity. If the differential equation relating $m(t)$ and $c(t)$ is known, the Difference Equation [6] can be derived readily using the theory of sampled-data systems. Such a derivation shows that in general $q = n$. By rearranging Equation [6], it follows that c_k can be expressed in terms of previous inputs and outputs

$$c_k = a_0m_k + a_1m_{k-1} + \ldots + a_nm_{k-n} - b_1c_{k-1} - \ldots - b_nc_{k-n} \quad [6a]$$

Usually $a_0 = 0$, since most physical systems do not respond instantaneously. The theoretical difference between Equations [6a] and [4] is that in the latter case in principle all past inputs are needed to determine the present output while in the former case only a finite number of past inputs and outputs is needed. The practical difference is that when the system is known to be governed by a difference equation, much fewer a_i and b_i than g_k are needed to represent the system.

Using the notation $z^ic_k = c_{k+i}$ (where i is any integer), it is possible to write down the following basic relationship between the g_k defined by Equation [5] and the a_i and b_i defined by Equation [6]

$$G(z) = \frac{a_1 z^{-1} + \ldots + a_n z^{-n}}{1 + b_1 z^{-1} + \ldots + b_n z^{-n}}$$
$$= g_1 z^{-1} + g_2 z^{-2} + \ldots + g_k z^{-k} + \ldots \ldots \ldots [7]$$

where the right-hand term is obtained by the formal expansion of the rational fraction $G(z)$ by long division according to ascending powers of z^{-1}. The first term, g_0, is missing because it was assumed that $a_0 = 0$ which implies that $h_0 = g_0 = 0$. The function $G(z)$ is called the *pulse transfer function* of the process (6, 7). It has the same role in the analysis of linear sampled-data systems as the transfer function (Laplace transform of a differential equation) in the analysis of linear continuous systems.

The number of the a_i and b_i used to represent the process is based also on an assumption as to what the value of n should be. This is a matter of approximation; in other words, n should be chosen sufficiently large so that the a_i and b_i represent the process with some desired accuracy. But the characteristics of the process are not known in advance so that some initial guess must be made about n in setting up the machine. It is, of course, possible in principle to let the machine check the adequacy of this initial guess once experimental data about the process are available. For simplicity, however, the machine discussed in this paper was designed to operate with a fixed choice of n ($n = 2$).

Finally, it should be recalled that use of the numbers g_k is feasible only if the process is stable. No such restriction is inherent in the representation by Equation [6].

To summarize, the first step in the design of the machine is:

(i) *The dynamic characteristics of the process are to be represented in the form of Equation [6], the coefficients of which are to be computed from measurements. The number $n = q$ is assumed arbitrarily. In general, the higher n, the more accurate the representation of the process by the Difference Equation [6].*

Method of Determining Coefficients. According to design requirement (C), the coefficients in Equation [6] must be determined from a large number of measurements. This can be done as follows: Suppose we make a particular guess for the a_i and b_i at the Nth sampling instant. Let us denote these assumed values by $a_i(N)$ and $b_i(N)$, and compute all the past values of c_k using this particular set of coefficients and Equation [6a]. Denoting by $c_k^*(N)$ the values of the output computed in this way, we have

$$c_k^*(N) = -b_1(N)c_{k-1} - b_2(N)c_{k-2} - \ldots - b_n(N)c_{k-n}$$
$$+ a_1(N)m_{k-1} + a_2(N)m_{k-2} + \ldots + a_n(N)m_{k-n} \ldots\ldots [8]$$
$$k = 0, 1, \ldots, N$$

A convenient measure of how good this choice of coefficients, in the light of past measured data, is the mean squared error

$$\frac{1}{N}\sum_{k=0}^{k=N} \epsilon_k^2(N) = \frac{1}{N}\sum_{k=0}^{k=N} [c_k - c_k^*(N)]^2 \ldots\ldots [9]$$

where $\epsilon_k^2(N)$ represents the squared error between measured values c_k in the past and the predicted values $c_k^*(N)$ based on a certain choice of coefficients made at the Nth sampling instant; choosing the coefficients $a_i(N)$ and $b_i(N)$ in such a fashion that the mean squared error Equation [9] is a minimum called *least-squares filtering*. In general, any method for determining the $a_i(N)$ and $b_i(N)$ differs from least-squares filtering only in the form of the appropriate expression to be minimized. The advantage of least-squares filtering is that the computations can be carried out fairly simply (see Appendix), which is usually not the case if other types of error expression are used.

In view of design requirement (D), the more recent measurements should receive greater weight than very old ones, since the process dynamics may change with time. To meet this requirement, we proceed as follows: Let $W(t)$ be a continuous, monotonically decreasing function of time such that

$$\left.\begin{array}{c} W(0) = 1 \\ 0 < W(t) < 1, 0 < t < \infty \\ W(\infty) = 0 \\ \int_0^\infty W(t)dt < \infty \end{array}\right\} \ldots\ldots\ldots\ldots [10]$$

A function satisfying such conditions is called a *weighting function.* Writing W_k for $W(kT)$, the final criterion of determining the coefficients may be stated as follows: Choose $a_i(N)$, $b_i(N)$ in such a way that the expression

$$E(N) = \sum_{k=0}^{k=N} \epsilon_k^2(N) W_{N-k} \ldots\ldots\ldots\ldots [11]$$

is a minimum. In other words the errors which would have been committed with the present choice of the coefficients $N - k$ sampling periods ago are to be weighted by a number $0 < W_{N-k} < 1$. Practically speaking, this means that the coefficients are calculated by disregarding errors which would have been committed in predicting the output a very long time ago (when the process may have been different) but trying to keep errors in predicting recent outputs small. None of these considerations, however, determines the precise form of the function $W(t)$; this question will be settled later so that an efficient computation procedure is obtained. We now state the second step in the design of the machine:

(ii) *The coefficients a_i and b_i should be determined anew at each sampling instant so as to minimize the weighted mean-square error $E(N)$.*

Numerical Solution of Weighted Least-Squares Filtering Problem. The explicit process necessary to determine the $a_i(N)$ and $b_i(N)$ requires, even after numerous simplifications, lengthy and somewhat involved calculations. These are discussed and recorded in detail in the Appendix. Only a few remarks are given here:

1 It is necessary to compute a number of so-called pseudo-correlation functions in order to write the error expression $E(N)$ in a simple form. These pseudo-correlation functions embody all measurement data up to the Nth sampling instant which is necessary to compute $E(N)$. To compute $E(N + 1)$, it is necessary to modify the pseudo-correlation functions so as to include the data received at the $(N + 1)$st sampling instant. It turns out that this process can be carried out in a simple way only if W_k is the unit pulse response (cf. Equations [5] and [7]) of a linear system governed by a difference equation. Then computation of the pseudo-correlation functions is carried out by passing products of measured values of m_k and c_k through a linear low-pass filter.

2 In order to apply Equation [6] to characterize a process, it is necessary that m_k and c_k be measured with respect to two reference values m_r and c_r such that, if m_r is a constant input to the system, c_r is the output in the steady state. Since the correct choice of such reference levels is not known in general, they must not enter into the computations of the type of Equation [6a]. In practice, the reference levels are usually determined by extraneous considerations such as calibration and range of measuring instruments. One way of avoiding the effect of incorrect reference levels (so-called *bias errors*) is to pass m_k and c_k through identical high-pass filters. After a sufficiently long period of time the bias errors, which are equivalent to a constant input to the filter, will be attenuated by an arbitrarily large factor at the output of an appropriately designed high-pass filter.

After the pseudo-correlation functions have been obtained, the determination of the coefficients reduces to solving a set of simultaneous linear algebraic equations. To do this efficiently, an iteration procedure is used; it turns out that high-pass filtering m_k and c_k (which is equivalent approximately to subtracting the instantaneous mean value of these series of numbers) is a necessary requirement to insure the convergence of the iteration procedure.

The third step in the design is as follows:

(iii) *The calculations necessary for determining the coefficients consist of modifications of the classical least-squares filtering procedure and are given in the Appendix.*

Optimal Adjustment of Controller

Once the pulse-transfer function of the process to be controlled has been obtained, the synthesis of an "optimal" controller as a set of difference equations becomes a routine task (1, 8, 9).

It is not easy to agree, however, on what constitutes optimal control. The design of an optimal controller depends in general on two considerations:

(*a*) The nature of the input and disturbance signals to the system.

(*b*) The performance criterion used.

For instance, the inputs to the system may consist of step functions of various magnitudes; the performance criterion may be the length of time after the application of the step required by the control system to bring the error within prescribed limits. Or the input may consist of signals which are defined only in the statistical sense, in which case a reasonable performance criterion is the mean squared value of the error signal.

To include in the design of the machine means by which the machine can decide what class of input signals it is subjected to and what type of optimal controller should be used appears to be too ambitious a task at the present time. For this reason, in the practical realization of the machine (see the section Description of Computer), a prearranged method of optimizing the controller was used.

This method was described in a recent note by the author (8). The input signals are to consist of steps. The controller is to be designed in such a fashion that the error resulting from a step input becomes zero in minimum time and remains zero at all values of time thereafter. As a result of these assumptions the optimal controller is described by a difference equation whose coefficients are simple multiples of the coefficients of the pulse transfer function (see Equation [25] in the Appendix.)

We note the last step in the design:

(iv) *The choice of an optimal controller is largely arbitrary, depending on what aspect of system response is to be optimized. The determination of the coefficients in the describing equations of the controller is a routine matter if the coefficients of the pulse-transfer function are known.*

Summary of Machine Organization

Since the describing equations of the self-optimizing controller are somewhat involved, it is helpful to visualize the various computation processes as shown in Fig. 3.

Numbers in brackets indicate equations which characterize the particular operations performed. It should be remembered, of course, that there are many pseudo-correlation functions, coefficients, and so on, to be computed, some of which are indicated only in a schematic fashion.

It is perhaps worth while to emphasize that the closed-loop system consisting of the self-optimizing machine and the process is highly nonlinear. The principal nonlinear operations are:

(*a*) The multiplications before the input to low-pass filters whose outputs are the pseudo-correlation functions.

(*b*) The determination of controller coefficients.

These nonlinear operations have made it necessary to design the self-optimizing machine step by step. There exists at present no general theory for the design of nonlinear control systems of this type.

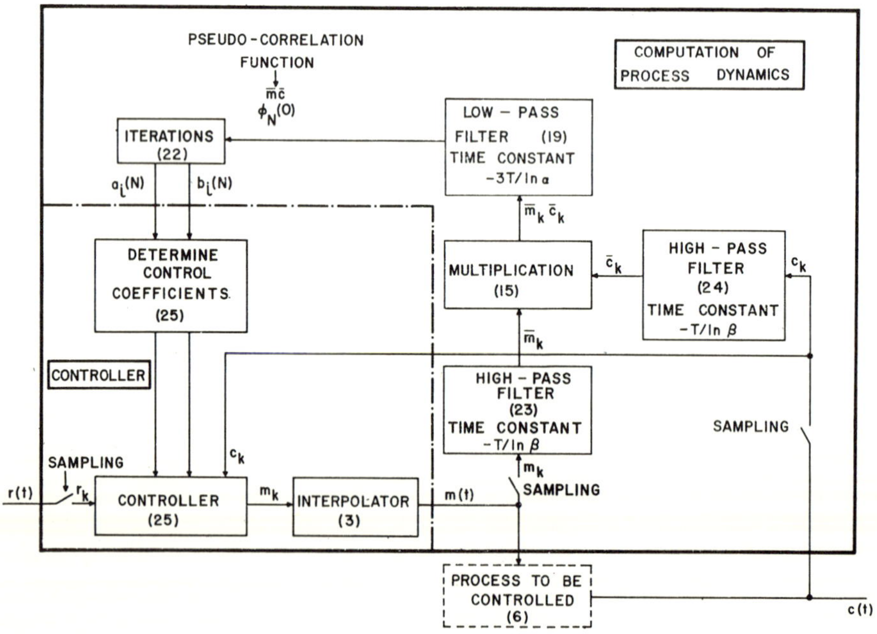

Fig. 3 Block Diagram of Computation Steps for Self-Optimizing Controller

Unsolved Questions

According to the preceding discussion, the operation of the self-optimizing system depends mainly on the accuracy of the computation of the pulse-transfer function from measurement data. Now suppose that the system is under very good control and that the input and disturbances to the system are nearly constant. In that case m_k and c_k will vary only very slightly about their equilibrium values. As a result, the numbers $\bar{m}_k$ and $\bar{c}_k$ (approximately the deviations of m_k and c_k from equilibrium) which are the inputs to the computation process determining the transfer function will be small and of roughly the same order of magnitude as the measurement noise. Under such circumstances, the transfer function cannot be computed very accurately. If the transfer function is not known accurately, then the controller cannot be set up accurately either and the system will not be operating optimally. But then the control will be less good and the deviations from the equilibrium values will increase. This, in turn, will improve the signal-to-noise ratio of the quantities $\bar{m}_k$ and $\bar{c}_k$; the computation of the transfer function will be more accurate, control action more nearly optimal, and so on. This shows that the operation of the system is limited basically by measurement noise. The fluctuations around the equilibrium condition must always be large enough to measure the transfer function with reasonable accuracy even in face of measurement noise. Thus the operation of the system depends on not being entirely at rest; if it were, it is impossible to say anything about the dynamic characteristics of the controlled process. A more precise answer to the problem involved here calls for further study.

Let us now examine qualitatively the effect of the choice α and β (cf. Fig. 3 and Appendix, Equations [19, 23, 24]) on this aspect of system performance. If α is very close to unity, the computation of the pulse-transfer function involves a large number of samples of $\bar{m}_k$ and $\bar{c}_k$ so that even if the system is at rest, i.e., $\bar{m}_k$ and $\bar{c}_k$ are practically zero, the computation of the pulse-transfer function is not affected for a long time, because the system "remembers" results of old measurements. On the other hand, if the process dynamics change rapidly in time, then α should be chosen fairly small because otherwise the computed transfer function will not be the actual transfer function. Thus α is a design parameter whose choice depends somewhat on the nature of a particular situation encountered. There is no reason, of course, why the system cannot adjust α also, but this is a problem beyond the scope of this paper.

The choice of β is guided by similar considerations. If the inputs to the system change slowly then β should be very close to unity for then the low-frequency components in m_k and c_k (slow "drift" about equilibrium point) will be very heavily attenuated. If the system is a more lively one, i.e., m_k and c_k fluctuate appreciably in time due to the effect of inputs or disturbances acting on the system, the β should be chosen smaller to improve the transient response of the high-pass filter. Thus β is another design parameter for the self-optimizing system.

Additional possibilities for improving these aspects of system operation should be considered in future work. More complicated weighting-functions and high-pass filters, suspending the operation of transfer-function computation when signal-to-noise levels become too low, putting in periodic test signals to check the operation of various parts of the computer, and the like, are some topics for future research.

Description of Computer

As soon as the operations discussed in the foregoing sections have been reduced to a set of numerical calculations (see Appendix) the machine has been synthesized in principle. This means that any general-purpose digital computer can be programmed to act as the self-optimizing machine.

In practical applications, however, a general-purpose digital computer is an expensive, bulky, extremely complex, and somewhat awkward piece of equipment. Moreover, the computational capabilities (speed, storage capacity, accuracy) of even the smaller commercially available general-purpose digital computers are considerably in excess of what is demanded in performing the computations listed in the Appendix.

For these reasons, a small special-purpose computer was constructed which could be called externally digital and internally analog according to the terminology in the section General Design Considerations. Briefly, this computer is organized as follows:

The computer operates on numbers whose absolute values do not exceed unity. Each number is represented by a 60-cycle-per-sec (cps) voltage. Numbers are stored on multiturn potentiometers, by positioning a given potentiometer by means of a servo arrangement in such a fashion that its output voltage (with unit excitation) is a 60-cps signal of the required magnitude and sign. Numbers are added by feeding corresponding voltages into electronic summing circuits. Two numbers a and b are multiplied by the following well-known method: If output of the potentiometer with unit excitation is b, then the output of the potentiometer with excitation a will be ab. The storage locations and summers can be interconnected in such a fashion that, in any one step of computation, the computer is capable of performing any one of the following types of operations

$$\left.\begin{array}{ll} & a_1b_1 + a_2b_2 + \ldots + a_7b_7 = x \\ \text{or} & \\ & a_1b_1c_1d_1 + a_2b_2c_2 + a_3b_3c_3 = x \\ \text{or} & \\ & a_1b_1c_1d_1e_1f_1g_1h_1 = x \end{array}\right\} \quad \ldots\ldots\ldots [12]$$

and so on

where each quantity appearing on the left-hand side of Equations [12] is an arbitrary number; x is the desired result of the computation. The fact that several additions and multiplications can be performed simultaneously is very convenient from the standpoint of programming the computer. Usually, each of Equations [12] must be broken up into several parts in programming them on a general-purpose computer.

The front view of the computer, which is roughly of the size of an average filing cabinet, is shown in Fig. 4. Only connections for input-output signals appear on the front panel. The programming of the computer is achieved by inserting wires into a "patch panel" on top of the computer which is shown in Fig. 5. Almost every signal voltage inside the computer is brought out to some contact on the patch panel. This arrangement makes it possible to interconnect the basic components of the computer in any manner desired and also facilitates troubleshooting and maintenance. The disadvantage of a patch-panel type of programming is that the change of program is a time-consuming operation; however, this is of minor significance since the machine is intended to operate with a fixed program in any typical application. The control panel shown in Fig. 5 also contains means for changing the sampling rate and reading numbers into any one of the storage locations in the computer.

The wiring necessary to connect computer components with the patch panel, together with associated relays, timing and checking circuits takes up approximately one third of the volume of the computer. Another one third of the volume is required for the electronic circuits performing summation and multiplication and

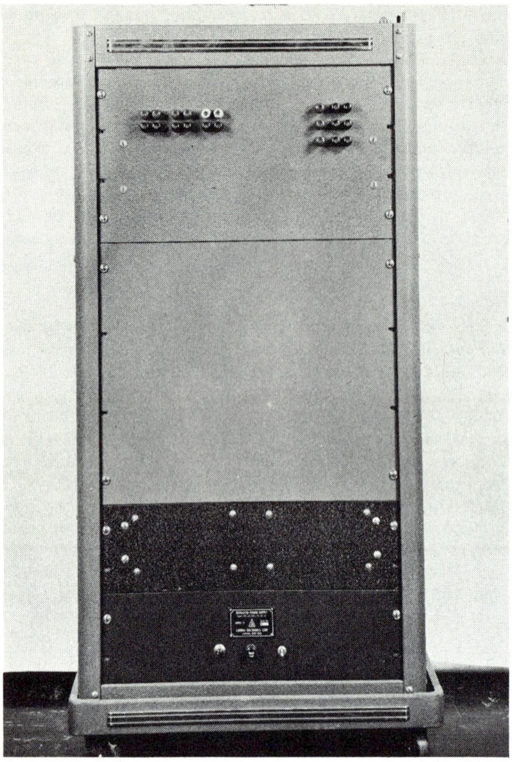

Fig. 4 Front View of Computer

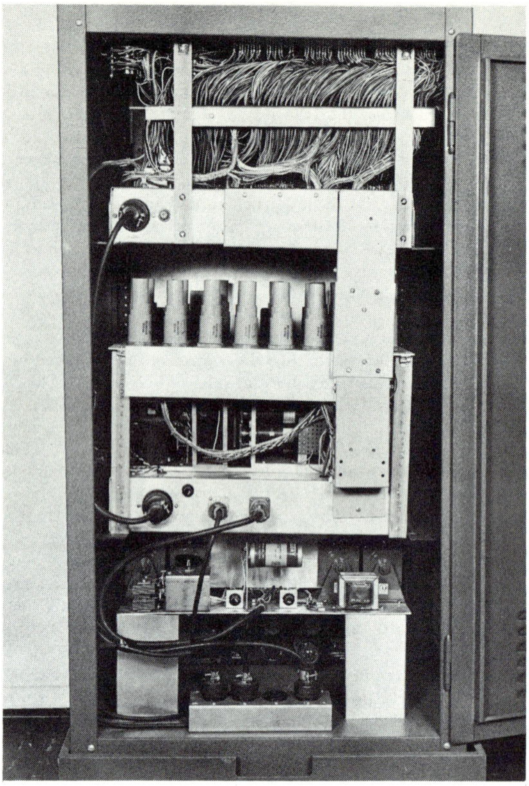

Fig. 6 Rear View of Computer

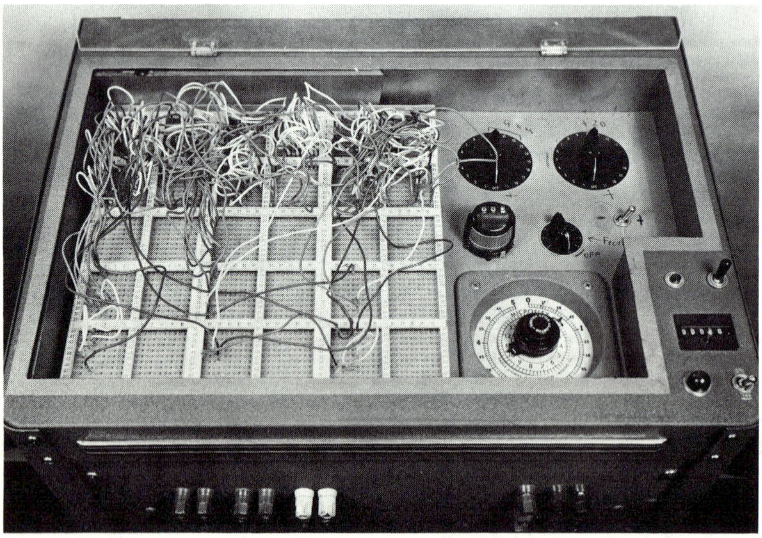

Fig. 5 Control Panel of Computer

the storage potentiometers. The remaining one third of space is taken up by power supplies. The internal arrangement of the computer is shown in the rear view of Fig. 6.

The computer described shows that the practical realization of a self-optimizing machine is well within the technological means available at the present time. Actually, the computer described was constructed in 1954/1955. The computer also represents savings in cost and complexity over currently available general purpose digital computers. On the other hand, when self-optimizing control of a large-scale installation is desired, in other words, when there are several dynamic processes to be controlled simultaneously and possibly in an interdependent fashion, then the general-purpose digital computer is much better matched to the problem both in terms of cost and computational capability.

Conclusions

This paper shows the feasibility of mechanizing much of the process by which automatic control systems for standard applications are being designed today. The amount of numerical computations necessary for accomplishing this is relatively modest (after the numerous simplifications discussed) and can be readily implemented in practice at moderate cost.

More importantly, however, the machine described here is an ideal controller since it needs merely to be interconnected with the process to be controlled to achieve optimum control after a short transitory period and hold it thereafter even if the process characteristics change with time. The task of the control engineer of the future will be not to design a specific system, but to improve the principles on which machines of the type described here will operate. Unlike his predecessor, the stock in trade of the new control-systems engineer will not be the graph paper, the slide rule, or even the analog computer but a firm and deep-seated understanding of the fundamental principles, physical and mathematical, on which automatic control is based. The drudgery of computing will be taken over by machines but the challenge of thinking remains.

Acknowledgments

The research reported here was supported by the Engineering Research Laboratory, E. I. du Pont de Nemours & Co., Wilmington, Del., to whom the author is indebted for permission to publish this paper. The author wishes also to thank various members of the Engineering Research Laboratory for their help and interest during the progress of this work, and to Dr. J. R. Ragazzini, Columbia University, for several stimulating discussions.

References

1 "Sampled-Data Processing Techniques for Feedback Control Systems," by A. R. Bergen and J. R. Ragazzini, Trans. AIEE, vol. 73, part II, 1954, pp. 236–247.

2 "Design for a Brain," by W. R. Ashby, John Wiley & Sons, Inc., New York, N. Y., 1952.

3 "Possibilities of a Two Time Scale Computing System for Control and Simulation of Dynamic Systems," by H. Ziebolz and H. M. Paynter, Proceedings of the National Electronics Conference, vol. 9, 1953, pp. 215–223.

4 "Determination of System Characteristics From Normal Operating Records," by T. P. Goodman and J. B. Reswick, Trans. ASME, vol. 77, 1955, pp. 259–268.

5 "Self-Optimizing Systems," by E. G. C. Burt, preprint for International Control Systems Conference, Heidelberg, Germany, September, 1956.

6 "The Analysis of Sampled-Data Systems," by J. R. Ragazzini and L. A. Zadeh, Trans. AIEE, vol. 71, part II, 1952, pp. 225–234.

7 "Automatic Feedback Control System Synthesis," by J. G. Truxal, McGraw-Hill Book Company, Inc., New York, N. Y., 1955.

8 R. E. Kalman, discussion of reference (1), Trans. AIEE, vol. 73, part II, 1954, pp. 245–246.

9 "Digital Controllers for Sampled-Data System," by J. E. Bertram, Trans. AIEE, vol. 75, part II, 1956, pp. 151–159.

10 "Introduction to Numerical Analysis," by F. B. Hildebrand, McGraw-Hill Book Company, Inc., New York, N. Y., 1956.

11 "Numerical Analysis," by W. E. Milne, Princeton University Press, Princeton, N. J., 1949.

Appendix

The following is the detailed derivation of the complete set of equations characterizing the self-optimizing controller in the special case when $n = 2$ in the Difference Equation [6]. Using these equations, any digital computer may be programmed to act as a self-optimizing controller. When $n > 2$, the required equations can be obtained similarly.

First of all, instead of performing the computations required to minimize Equation [11] at every sampling instant, they may be performed at every qth (where q is a positive integer) sampling instant. This does not affect the reasoning in the section Method of Determining Coefficients, and results in considerable simplification in the required computations. With this change, the error expression Equation [11] becomes

$$E(N) = \sum_{j=0}^{j=N/q} \epsilon_{qj}^2(N) W_{N-qj} \qquad [13]$$

where $k = qj$ and N is a number divisible by q.

Now assume that $n = 2$ in Equation [6]. Using the recurrence relation Equation [8], $\epsilon_{qj}^2(N)$ can be written as

$$\left.\begin{aligned} \epsilon_{qj}^2(N) &= [c_{qj} - c_{qj}^*(N)]^2 \\ &= c_{qj}^2 + b_1^2(N)c_{qj-1}^2 + b_2^2(N)c_{qj-2}^2 \\ &\quad + 2b_1(N)c_{qj}c_{qj-1} + 2b_2(N)c_{qj}c_{qj-2} \\ &\qquad\qquad + 2b_1(N)b_2(N)c_{qj-1}c_{qj-2} \\ &\quad - 2a_1(N)c_{qj}m_{qj-1} - 2a_2(N)c_{qj}m_{qj-2} \\ &\quad - 2b_1(N)a_1(N)c_{qj-1}m_{qj-1} \\ &\qquad\qquad - 2b_1(N)a_2(N)c_{qj-1}m_{qj-2} \\ &\quad - 2b_2(N)a_1(N)c_{qj-2}m_{qj-1} \\ &\qquad\qquad - 2b_2(N)a_2(N)c_{qj-2}m_{qj-2} \\ &\quad + a_1^2(N)m_{qj-1}^2 + a_2^2(N)m_{qj-2}^2 \\ &\qquad\qquad + 2a_1(N)a_2(N)m_{qj-1}m_{qj-2} \end{aligned}\right\} \qquad [14]$$

The measured values of c and m occur in Equation [14] always in terms of the type

$$c_{qj-r}c_{qj-s} \qquad c_{qj-r}m_{qj-s} \qquad m_{qj-r}m_{qj-s} \qquad [15]$$

where $r, s = 0, 1, 2$. If we now let

$$q = n + 1 = 3$$

then it is clear that factors of the same type will be multiplied by the same coefficients in Equation [14], regardless of the value of j. This property does not arise when $q < 3$. Using the symmetry introduced by the particular choice of q, $E(N)$ can be put in a simpler form by defining the *pseudo-correlation functions*

$$\left.\begin{aligned} \phi_{N-r}^{cc}(r - s) &= \sum_{j=1}^{j=N/3} c_{3j-r}c_{3j-s}W_{N-3j} \\ \phi_{N-r}^{cm}(r - s) &= \sum_{j=1}^{j=N/3} c_{3j-r}m_{3j-s}W_{N-3j} \\ \phi_{N-r}^{mm}(r - s) &= \sum_{j=1}^{j=N/3} m_{3j-r}m_{3j-s}W_{N-3j} \end{aligned}\right\} \qquad [16]$$

With these definitions, $E(N)$ can be written as follows, arranging the terms in the same fashion as in Equation [14]

$$\left.\begin{aligned} E(N) = {} & \phi_N^{cc}(0) + b_1^2(N)\phi_{N-1}^{cc}(0) + b_2^2(N)\phi_{N-2}^{cc}(0) \\ & + 2b_1(N)\phi_N^{cc}(-1) + 2b_2(N)\phi_N^{cc}(-2) \\ & \qquad + 2b_1(N)b_2(N)\phi_{N-1}^{cc}(-1) \\ & - 2a_1(N)\phi_N^{cm}(-1) - 2a_2(N)\phi_N^{cm}(-2) \\ & - 2b_1(N)a_1(N)\phi_{N-1}^{cm}(0) \\ & \qquad - 2b_1(N)a_2(N)\phi_{N-1}^{cm}(-1) \\ & - 2b_2(N)a_1(N)\phi_{N-2}^{cm}(1) - 2b_2(N)a_2(N)\phi_{N-2}^{cm}(0) \\ & + a_1^2(N)\phi_{N-1}^{mm}(0) + a_2^2(N)\phi_{N-2}^{mm}(0) \\ & \qquad + 2a_1(N)a_2(N)\phi_{N-1}^{mm}(-1) \end{aligned}\right\} \quad \text{..[17]}$$

Remark. The conventional definition of correlation functions is

$$\phi_N^{cc}(r) = \frac{1}{N}\sum_{k=0}^{k=N} c_k c_{k+r}$$

To evaluate this function iteratively, as is done in Equation [19] for pseudo-correlation functions, it would be necessary to compute

$$\phi_N^{cc}(r) = c_N c_{N+r}/N + (N-1)\phi_{N-1}^{cc}(r)/N$$

Since the factor $(N-1)/N$ cannot be calculated accurately enough as $N \to \infty$, such an iterative calculation would be impractical.

The pseudo-correlation functions can be evaluated iteratively as follows: Suppose that, in addition to meeting Conditions [10], the weighting function W_k is a sequence of numbers such as the g_k given by Equation [7]. Then it follows that the pseudo-correlation functions can be regarded as the output of a linear system governed by a difference equation, whose input consists of products such as Equation [15]. In particular, if we let

$$W^{3j} = \alpha^j \qquad (0 < \alpha < 1) \text{.............} [18]$$

then every pseudo-correlation function satisfies a first-order difference equation of the type

$$\phi_{3j-r}^{cm}(r-s) - \alpha\phi_{3(j-1)-r}^{cm}(r-s) = c_{3j-r}m_{3j-s} \text{...} [19]$$

According to Equation [17] the determination of the coefficients of the pulse-transfer function requires first that all input-output data (the measured values of c and m) be consolidated into the pseudo-correlation functions. Because of the recurrence relation Equation [19], the computation of the latter is quite simple, since to get the pseudo-correlation functions at the Nth sampling instant requires only the knowledge of the same functions at the end of the $(N-3)$th sampling instant, plus the values of c_{N-2}, c_{N-1}, c_N, m_{N-2}, m_{N-1}. Once the new pseudo-correlation functions have been computed, the data measured during the preceding three sampling periods can be discarded and the system is ready to receive new data. Thus the use of the pseudo-correlation functions and the choice of a suitable weighting function greatly simplifies the implementation of mean-square filtering.

In order that $E(N)$ be a minimum with respect to the a_i and b_i, it is *necessary* that the partial derivatives

$$\frac{\partial E(N)}{\partial a_i} = 0 \qquad \frac{\partial E(N)}{\partial b_i} = 0 \quad (i = 1, 2, \ldots, n) \text{....} [20]$$

vanish. The proof that these conditions are also *sufficient* to insure the existence of a minimum of $E(N)$ is quite difficult. Refer to Milne (11) for discussion of a closely related problem.

The Conditions [20] lead to four linear equations in the coefficients $a_1(N)$, $a_2(N)$, $b_1(N)$, $b_2(N)$ as follows

$$\left.\begin{aligned} & a_1(N)\phi_{N-1}^{mm}(0) + a_2(N)\phi_{N-1}^{mm}(-1) - b_1(N)\phi_{N-1}^{cm}(0) \\ & \qquad - b_2(N)\phi_{N-2}^{cm}(1) = \phi_N^{cm}(-1) \\ & a_1(N)\phi_{N-1}^{mm}(-1) + a_2(N)\phi_{N-2}^{mm}(0) \\ & \qquad - b_1(N)\phi_{N-1}^{cm}(-1) - b_2(N)\phi_{N-2}^{cm}(0) = \phi_N^{cm}(-2) \\ & -a_1(N)\phi_{N-1}^{cm}(0) - a_2(N)\phi_{N-1}^{cm}(-1) \\ & \qquad + b_1(N)\phi_{N-1}^{cc}(0) + b_2(N)\phi_{N-1}^{cc}(-1) = -\phi_N^{cc}(-1) \\ & -a_1(N)\phi_{N-2}^{cm}(1) - a_2(N)\phi_{N-2}^{cm}(0) \\ & \qquad + b_1(N)\phi_{N-1}^{cc}(-1) + b_2(N)\phi_{N-2}^{cc}(0) = -\phi^{cc}(-2) \end{aligned}\right\} \text{..[21]}$$

Any method for solving linear simultaneous equations can be used for finding the a_i and b_i from Equation [21]. However, the standard elimination methods (which, incidentally, are much more efficient than solving Equation [21] by Cramer's rule) require a rather large amount of storage and somewhat lengthy computations. These disadvantages become increasingly worse as n increases. However, an exact computation of a solution of Equation [21] is very wasteful in that, if a solution of Equation [21] at the $(N-3)$th sampling instant is available, then that solution is also an excellent guess for the solution of Equation [21] at the Nth sampling instant since the correlation function can have changed only slightly, unless a very small value of α is used. This suggests an *iteration* procedure for solving Equation [21], of which the simplest is the so-called Gauss-Seidel method (10).

Applying the Gauss-Seidel method to Equation [21] leads to the equations

$$a_1(N) = \frac{-a_2(N-3)\phi_{N-1}^{mm}(-1) + b_1(N-3)\phi_{N-1}^{cm}(0) + b_2(N-3)\phi_{N-2}^{cm}(1) + \phi_N^{cm}(-1)}{\phi_{N-1}^{mm}(0)} \text{...} [22a]$$

$$a_2(N) = \frac{-a_1(N)\phi_{N-1}^{mm}(-1) + b_1(N-3)\phi_{N-1}^{cm}(-1) + b_2(N-3)\phi_{N-2}^{cm}(0) + \phi_N^{cm}(-2)}{\phi_{N-2}^{mm}(0)} \text{.....} [22b]$$

$$b_1(N) = \frac{a_1(N)\phi_{N-1}^{cm}(0) + a_2(N)\phi_{N-1}^{cm}(-1) - b_2(N-3)\phi_{N-1}^{cc}(-1) - \phi_N^{cc}(-1)}{\phi_{N-1}^{cc}(0)} \text{............} [22c]$$

$$b_2(N) = \frac{a_1(N)\phi_{N-1}^{cm}(1) + a_2(N)\phi_{N-2}^{cm}(0) - b_1(N)\phi_{N-1}^{cc}(-1) - \phi_N^{cc}(-2)}{\phi_{N-2}^{cc}(0)} \text{....................} [22d]$$

If desired, the cycle of iterations just written down can be repeated to obtain better accuracy.

A necessary and sufficient condition for the convergence of the iteration Equations [22] is that the diagonal coefficients in Equations [21], i.e., $\phi_{N-1}^{mm}(0)$, $\phi_{N-2}^{mm}(0)$, $\phi_{N-1}^{cc}(0)$, $\phi_{N-2}^{cc}(0)$ should be larger in absolute value than any of the other coefficients in the same equation. To insure rapid convergence, it is highly desirable that the diagonal coefficients be as large as possible compared to the off-diagonal coefficients.

A glance at Equation [19] shows that the pseudo-correlation

functions just mentioned are always the sum of positive numbers because the right-hand side of Equation [19] is always positive, being a square. To make the pseudo-correlation functions corresponding to the off-diagonal elements in Equations [21] smaller in absolute value than the diagonal elements, the right-hand side of Equation [19] for these functions must be alternatively positive and negative. This can be achieved by subtracting from each c_k and m_k the average (mean) values of these quantities over a long period of time. Unless this is done, c_k and m_k might vary only slightly about a large average value in which case all the correlation functions will be approximately equal and the iteration Equation [22] will not converge fast enough, if at all.

To estimate the mean of a time series in a very reliable way is not an easy problem. In the present case, however, sophisticated statistical methods are not required because the precise knowledge of the mean is not important. The simplest procedure then is to put both c_k and m_k through identical high-pass filters which remove the slowly varying components (i.e., the mean) of these quantities. When the mean is constant in time, it is equal to the zero frequency component of the signal. The simplest high-pass filter on numerical data is represented by the difference equation

$$c_k - c_{k-1} = \bar{c}_k - \beta \bar{c}_{k-1} \qquad (0 < \beta < 1) \ldots\ldots [23]$$

where $\bar{c}_k$ is approximately equal to $c_k -$ mean (c_k). The closer β is to 1, the better the removal of the mean if the latter is constant. On the other hand, if the mean varies β should be somewhat smaller for best results. A similar equation holds for $\bar{m}_k$

$$m_k - m_{k-1} = \bar{m}_k - \beta \bar{m}_{k-1} \qquad (0 < \beta < 1) \ldots\ldots [24]$$

A simple substitution in Equation [6] shows that $\bar{c}_k$ and $\bar{m}_k$ are related by the same difference equation as c_k and m_k. This is because if two quantities are linearly related, the relationship remains undisturbed if both quantities are put through identical linear filters. Thus the removal of the mean represented by Equations [23] and [24] does not affect the computation of the pulse-transfer function of the process to be controlled, except for greatly improving the convergence of the iteration process Equations [22]. Hence all pseudo-correlation functions should be computed using the $\bar{c}_k$ and $\bar{m}_k$.

It remains to show how the equations of the controller can be obtained from the knowledge of the coefficients of the pulse-transfer function. As mentioned earlier, the controller is to be digital. Using a method of synthesis due to the author (8), which yields the optimum design if the closed-loop system is to respond to a unit step input in minimal time without overshoot (for a given fixed sampling period T), the numbers necessary to specify the controller are very simply related to the coefficients of the pulse-transfer function of the process which is to be controlled. In fact, the difference equation specifying the controller is

$$[a_1(N) + a_2(N)]m_k - a_1(N)m_{k-1} - a_2(N)m_{k-2} = e_k + b_1(N)e_{k-1} + b_2(N)e_{k-2} \ldots\ldots [25]$$

where

$$e_k = r_k - c_k$$

Equation [25] is valid for $N + 1 \leq k \leq N + 3$, after which a new set of coefficients must be used from the next determination of the pulse-transfer function. It should be noted that Equation [25] holds only if the (continuous) transfer function of the process is approximately $H(s) = K/(s + a)(s + b)$ with $a, b, K > 0$. If, for instance, $a = 0$, the form of Equation [25] is different. For methods of synthesizing digital controllers which are optimal in some other sense, see references (1, 9).

For convenience, the time sequence of computations to be performed during a cycle of $q = 3$ sampling periods is listed as follows.

$k = N - 2$

(1) Compute m_{N-2} using [25]
(2) Compute $\bar{c}_{N-2}$ using [23]
(3) Compute $\bar{m}_{N-2}$ using [24]
(4) Compute $\phi_{N-2}^{\bar{m}\bar{m}}(0)$, $\phi_{N-2}^{\bar{c}\bar{c}}(0)$, $\phi_{N-2}^{\bar{c}\bar{m}}(0)$ using Equation [19]

$k = N - 1$

(1) Compute m_{N-1} using [25]
(2) Compute $\bar{c}_{N-1}$ using [23]
(3) Compute $\bar{m}_{N-1}$ using [24]
(4) Compute $\phi_{N-1}^{\bar{m}\bar{m}}(0)$, $\phi_{N-1}^{\bar{m}\bar{m}}(-1)$, $\phi_{N-1}^{\bar{c}\bar{c}}(0)$, $\phi_{N-1}^{\bar{c}\bar{c}}(-1)$ $\phi_{N-1}^{\bar{c}\bar{m}}(0)$, $\phi_{N-1}^{\bar{c}\bar{m}}(-1)$, $\phi_{N-2}^{\bar{c}\bar{m}}(1)$ using Equation [19]

$k = N$

(1) Compute m_N using [25]
(2) Compute $\bar{c}_N$ using [23]
(3) Compute $\bar{m}_N$ using [24]
(4) Compute $\phi_N^{\bar{c}\bar{c}}(-1)$, $\phi_N^{\bar{c}\bar{c}}(-2)$, $\phi_N^{\bar{c}\bar{m}}(-1)$, $\phi_N^{\bar{c}\bar{m}}(-2)$ using Equation [19].
(5) Compute $a_1(N)$, $a_2(N)$, $b_1(N)$, $b_2(N)$ using [22]

STATISTICAL THEORY OF GRADIENT SYSTEMS OF AUTOMATIC OPTIMIZATION FOR OBJECTS WITH QUADRATIC CHARACTERISTICS

A. A. Fel'dbaum

(Moscow)

(Translated from: Avtomatika i Telemekhanika, Vol. 21, No. 2, pp. 167-179, February, 1960)

Original article submitted June 12, 1959

The paper formulates the problem of investigating gradient systems of automatic optimization in the presence of random factors. Methods are given for determining the steady-state error and estimating the duration of the transient response for gradient systems with several input variables. The results are illustrated by examples of systems with one and with two variables.

INTRODUCTION

The near future will be marked by a significant development of self-adjusting (adaptive) systems. Great value,therefore,inheres in the development of a theory of automatic serach, which is the basic process in such systems, and which differs essentially from the process of error liquidation in automatic-control systems. One of the classes of adaptive systems which promises to be of importance practically is that of automatic optimization systems. We present below the theory of one of the forms of such systems.

The problem of an automatic optimization system consists of automatically finding and maintaining a minimum of some quantity y with, generally speaking, additional conditions imposed. The quantity y is a function of the variables u_i:

$$y = y(u_1, u_2, \ldots, u_m). \tag{1}$$

The process of automatic search for a minimum is slowed when there is random noise present, and the minimum itself will be determined, and maintained, with some error under these circumstances. The duration of the transient response of the search process, and the steady-state error, are the fundamental symptomatic indicators of the system's process.

The most general problem consists of synthesizing such a controlling portion which will implement the best (in some sense) process of automatic search. We shall consider below the more restricted problem of determining the indicators of the process for a given controlling portion, and also of choosing the optimal values of this portion's parameters.

In the automatic serach for a minimum, tentative movements are made – "experiments" with the object, as it were – and thereafter the operational movement is made on the basis of an analysis of the results of the tentative trial motions. Various combinations of operationa and trial movements are possible. In the sequel, we consider systems of the discrete type in which, during one cycle, a series of trial steps is taken, and then followed by an operational step; in the following cycle, there is again taken a series of trial steps followed by an operational step, etc.

Figure 1 shows an example of an automatic optimization system. Here, C is the controlling portion; at the output of part F_0 of object 0 there is the quantity y which must be minimized. It is joined, in part F of the object, by an error z. At the object's input, the controlling quantities u_i are joined by random-noise quantities, z_{0i}. The sums thus obtained

$$x_i = u_i + z_{0i} \tag{2}$$

are applied to the input of part F_0 of the object. In carrying out trials on the ith input variable, one adds to the quantity x_i the quantity $+\alpha_{0i}$ in the first trial interval and $-\alpha_{0i}$ in the second trial interval. Thus, a trial consists of two intervals. If the total number of input variables is m, the entire cycle is composed of 2m intervals. We shall assume that the variations of the object's input quantities require the expenditure of no time, but that the carrying out of an "experiment," as a result of which the quantity y appears at the object's output, requires some time interval of constant duration.

The presence of the noise z_{0i} at the input gives rise to a random displacement of the minimum point y in the space $u_1, u_2, \ldots, u_m$, which imitates a slow "drift" of the characteristics,which occurs in actual objects. It is possible to set $z_{0i} = \gamma_i n$, where n is discrete time or the number of cycles ($n = 0, 1, 2, \ldots$) and the γ_i are random variables. The noise z at the object's output (for example, in a measuring block) is a random noise of comparatively high frequency. We shall suppose that the increments of these quantities are independent random variables with known distribution law $\psi(v)$, zero mean value and finite dispersion σ^2. Such a form for the noise was introduced for these systems in [1].

The Markov Process in a Gradient System of Automatic Optimization

Let the dependence of the output y' of portion F_0 of the object on the input quantities x_k' be described by the formula ·

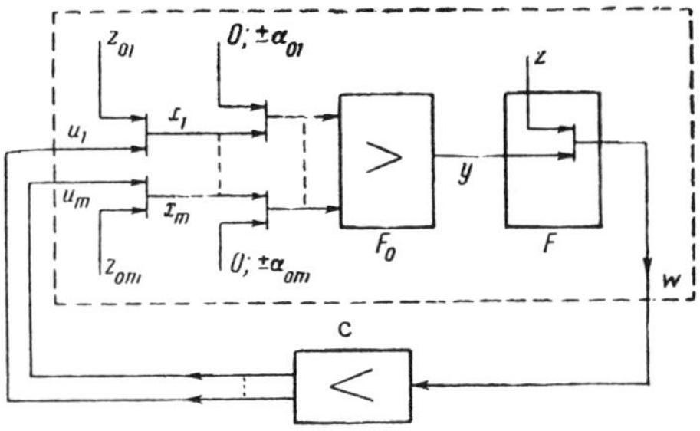

Fig. 1.

$$y' = \sum_{i,k=1}^{m} b'_{ik} x'_i x'_k + \sum_{k=1}^{m} c'_{ik} x'_k + d'. \quad (3)$$

By applying a linear transformation to each variable separately, we can take this formula to the form

$$y = f(x_1, \ldots, x_m) = \sum_{i,k=1}^{m} b_{ik} x_i x_k, \quad (4)$$

where $b_{ik} = b_{ki}$. We shall assume that quadratic form (4) is positive definite. Then y has a unique minimum at the origin of coordinates.

During the ith pair of intervals, whose ordinal numbers within the cycle are j and $j+1$, where $j = 2i - 1$, measurements are made of the quantity y. We denote the values of the quantities x_i in the jth interval by $x_i^{(j)}$, and the value of y by $y^{(j)}$. In the first interval of the ith pair, there is the quantity $x_i^{(j)} + \alpha_{0i}$ at the ith input, while the second interval finds the quantity $x_i^{(j+1)} - \alpha_{0i}$ at this input.

After these two intervals, we determine the difference

$$\Delta_i y_n = f(x_{1,n}^{(j)}, \ldots, x_{i,n}^{(j)} + \alpha_{0i}, \ldots, x_{m,n}^{(j)}) - f(x_{1,n}^{(j+1)}, \ldots, x_{i,n}^{(j+1)} - \alpha_{0i}, \ldots, x_{m,n}^{(j+1)}). \quad (5)$$

The subscripts n denote that the measurements were made in the nth cycle. The corresponding quantity at the output of controlling portion C (Fig. 1) is defined by the expression

$$\Delta_i w_n = \Delta_i y_n + \Delta_i z_n = \Delta_i y_n + v_i. \quad (6)$$

The gradient method consists of this: that after a series of trials, as a result of which one determines the direction of the gradient of the quantity y – the vector with components $\partial y / \partial x_i \cong \Delta_i y_i$, the operational step is taken in this direction. Obviously, the increments of the quantities $u_{i,n+1} - u_{i,n}$, where n is discrete time, must be proportional to the quantities $\Delta_i w$, found in the nth cycle:

$$u_{i,n+1} - u_{i,n} = -\alpha_i (\Delta_i w_n) = -\alpha_i (\Delta_i y_n + v_i). \quad (7)$$

By taking into account (2) and (5), and the formula $z_{0i} = \gamma_i n$, we find that

$$x_{i,n+1} = x_{i,n} + \gamma_i - \alpha_i [f(x_{1,n}^{(2i-1)}, \ldots, x_{i,n}^{(2i-1)} + \alpha_{0i}, \ldots, x_{m,n}^{(2i-1)}) - f(x_1^{(2i)}, \ldots, x_i^{(2i)} - \alpha_{0i}, \ldots, x_m^{(2i)}) + v_i] \quad (8)$$

Here, we have denoted $x_{i,n}^{(1)}$ simply by $x_{i,n}$. Since

$$x_i^{(j)} = x_i^{(1)} + \gamma_i \frac{j-1}{2m} = x_i + \gamma_i \frac{i-1}{m},$$

$$x_i^{(j+1)} = x_i + \gamma_i \frac{2i-1}{2m}, \quad (9)$$

then

$$x_{i,n+1} = x_{i,n} + \gamma_i - \alpha_i \Big[f\Big(x_1 + \gamma_1 \frac{i-1}{m}, x_2 + \gamma_2 \frac{i-1}{m}, \ldots, x_i + \gamma_i \frac{i-1}{m} + \alpha_{0i}, \ldots, x_m + \gamma_m \frac{i-1}{m}\Big) - f\Big(x_1 + \gamma_1 \frac{2i-1}{2m}, \ldots, x_i + \gamma_i \frac{2i-1}{2m} - \alpha_{0i}, \ldots, x_m + \gamma_m \frac{2i-1}{2m}\Big) + v_i \Big]. \quad (10)$$

For brevity, we denote $x_{i,n} = \xi_i$ and $x_{i,n+1} = x_i$; we introduce the vector $\mathbf{x}$ in the m-dimensional space Ω_x, the vector ξ with coordinates ξ_i in the space $\Omega_\xi = \Omega_x$ and the vector γ with coordinates γ_i and the vectors ξ_{0i}, again in space Ω_x. Then (10) can be rewritten in the form

$$x_i = \xi_i + \gamma_i - \alpha_i \Big\{ f\Big(\xi + \alpha_{0i} \xi_{0i} + \gamma \frac{i-1}{m}\Big) - f\Big(\xi - \alpha_{0i} \xi_{0i} + \gamma \frac{2i-1}{2m}\Big) + v_i \Big\}. \quad (11)$$

We now take the form of function f(x) [cf., (4)] into account. By substituting (4) in (10) or (11), we obtain after some transformation,

$$x_i = \gamma_i - \alpha_i v_i + \sum_{j=1}^{m} A_{ij} \xi_j + B_i, \quad (12)$$

where

$$A_{ij} = \delta_{ij} + \frac{\alpha_i}{m} \sum_{\substack{k=1 \\ k \neq i}}^{m} b_{kj} \gamma_k + \alpha_i b_{ji} \Big(\frac{\gamma_i}{m} - 4\alpha_{0i}\Big),$$

$$B_i = \frac{4i-3}{2m} \alpha_i \Big\{ \frac{1}{2m} \sum_{\substack{j,k=1 \\ j,k \neq i}}^{m} b_{jk} \gamma_j \gamma_k + \Big(\frac{\gamma_i}{m} - 2\alpha_{0i}\Big) \sum_{\substack{j=1 \\ j \neq i}}^{m} b_{ji} \gamma_j + b_{ii} \gamma_i \Big(\frac{\gamma_i}{2m} - 2\alpha_{0i}\Big) \Big\}. \quad (13)$$

Here, $\delta_{ij} = 1$ for $i = j$ and $\delta_{ij} = 0$ for $i \neq j$; i.e., δ_{ij} is a Kronecker delta.

The sequence $x_{i,n}$ ($n = 0, 1, 2, \ldots$), or the vector x_n, is a random Markov process (cf. [2,3]) since the probability distribution for x_{n+1} depends on the value of x_n.

Initially, let the γ_i be fixed quantities. In view of the independence of the γ_i and the v_i, we can compute the distribution $W(\gamma)$ for γ at any subsequent stage. Further, let the v_i now be all zero. We first investigate the convergence of the automatic search process when the random noises are lacking. Equation (12) can be rewritten as:

$$\mathbf{x} = A\xi + \mathbf{B}, \quad (14)$$

where A is the matrix with elements A_{ij}, and B is the vector with coordinates $\gamma_i + B_i$. If the system converges to a steady state x_{ste}, then this latter state may be found from the equation

$$x_{ste} = A x_{ste} + B. \quad (15)$$

Let E be the unit matrix, and let the inverse $(E-A)^{-1}$ of the matrix E-A exist. Then

$$x_{ste} = (E - A)^{-1} B. \quad (16)$$

We consider the differences

$$x_{n+1} - x_{ste} = \Delta_{n+1}, \quad x_n - x_{ste} = \Delta_n. \quad (17)$$

If follows, from (14), (16), and (17) that

$$\Delta_{n+1} = A\Delta_n. \quad (18)$$

The necessary and sufficient conditions for the convergence of the search process, i.e., for the holding of the condition $\Delta_n \to 0$ as $n \to \infty$, are the inequalities

$$|\lambda_k| < 1, \quad (19)$$

where the λ_k (k = 1, . . ., m) are the roots of the characteristic equation $|A - E\lambda| = 0$ of the matrix A. As is well known, these inequalities reduce to condtions of the Routh-Hurwitz type. We shall assume that these conditions are satisfied.* With this, the speeds γ_i can not be arbitrary; the vector γ must lie within a certain region Ω_γ of the m-dimensional space.

We turn now to the general equation, in which random noise is present. Let the transition probability from the point $\xi = \{x_{1,n}, x_{2,n}, \ldots, x_{m,n}\}$ in the interval $x_i \leq x_{i,n+1} \leq x_i + dx_i$ (i = 1, . . . , m) equal $\varphi(\xi, x)$. $dx_1 \ldots dx_m = \varphi(\xi, x)\, d\Omega_x$, where $d\Omega_x = dx_1, \ldots, dx_m$.

Then, $p_{n+1}(x)$, the probability density that x_{n+1} appear in the interval $x_i \leq x_{i,n+1} \leq x_i + dx_i$ (i = 1, . . . , m), is defined by the formula

$$p_{n+1}(\mathbf{x}) = \int_{-\infty}^{+\infty} \ldots \int_{-\infty}^{+\infty} \varphi(\xi, x)\, p_n(\xi)\, d\xi_1 \ldots d\xi_m =$$

$$= \int_{\Omega_\xi} \varphi(\xi, \mathbf{x})\, p_n(\xi)\, d\Omega_\xi, \quad (20)$$

where $d\Omega_\xi = d\xi_1, \ldots d\xi_m$. If this linear integral transformation has a fixed point to which the sequence $p_n(x)$ tends, then by denoting

$$P(\mathbf{x}) = \lim_{n \to \infty} p_n(\mathbf{x}), \quad (21)$$

we may find this function from the linear integral equation

$$P(\mathbf{x}) = \int_{\Omega_\xi} (\xi, \mathbf{x}) P(\xi)\, d\Omega_\xi. \quad (22)$$

We find $\varphi(\xi, x)$, assuming now that the γ_i are fixed. From (12) we get

$$v_i = \frac{1}{\alpha_i}\left[\gamma_i - x_i + \sum_{j=1}^{m} A_{ji}\xi_j + B_i\right]. \quad (23)$$

The conditional probability that $x_{i,n+1}$ is found in the interval $x_i \leq x_{i,n+1} \leq x_i + dx_i$ if $x_{j,n} = \xi_j$ (j = 1, . . . , m) equals $\psi(v_i)\, dx_i / \alpha_i$, where the v_i are determined from (23). Since, for different x_i, the v_i are independent, we have that

$$\varphi(\xi, \mathbf{x}) = \prod_{i=1}^{m} \frac{\psi(v_i)}{\alpha_i} = \prod_{i=1}^{m} \frac{1}{\alpha_i} \psi\left\{\frac{1}{\alpha_i}\left[\gamma_i - x_i + \right.\right.$$

$$\left.\left. + \sum_{j=1}^{m} A_{ij}\xi_j + B_i\right]\right\}. \quad (24)$$

Determination of the Indicators of the Automatic Search Process

We now find the mathematical expectation of the random variable y_n, by which we understand the arithmetic mean over the nth cycle:

$$M[y_n] = \int_{\Omega_x} \frac{1}{2m}\sum_{i=1}^{m} \left[f\left(\mathbf{x} + \alpha_{0i}\xi_{0i} + \gamma\frac{i-1}{m}\right) + \right.$$

$$\left. + f\left(\mathbf{x} - \alpha_{0i}\xi_{0i} + \gamma\frac{2i-1}{2m}\right)\right] p_n(\mathbf{x})\, d\Omega_x. \quad (25)$$

We consider separately the expression in the square brackets. By substituting (2) for f(x) we obtain, after some transformations,

$$\frac{1}{2m}\sum_{i=1}^{m}\left[f\left(\mathbf{x} + \alpha_{0i}\xi_{0i} + \gamma\frac{i-1}{m}\right) + f\left(\mathbf{x} - \alpha_{0i}\xi_{0i} + \gamma\frac{2i-1}{2m}\right)\right] =$$

$$= \sum_{j,k=1}^{m} b_{jk} x_j x_k + \left(1 - \frac{1}{2m}\right) \sum_{j,k=1}^{m} b_{jk} \lambda x_j{}_k + C, \quad (26)$$

where

$$C = \frac{\frac{2}{3}(m+1)(4m-7) + 5}{8m^2} \sum_{j,k=1}^{m} b_{jk}\gamma_j\gamma_k +$$

$$+ \frac{1}{m}\sum_{i=1}^{m} b_{ii}\alpha_{0i}^2 - \frac{1}{2m^2}\sum_{i,j=1}^{m} b_{ij}\alpha_{0i}\gamma_j. \quad (27)$$

Therefore,

$$M[y_n] = \int_{-\infty}^{\infty} \ldots \int_{-\infty}^{\infty} \left\{ \sum_{j,k=1}^{m} b_{jk} x_{j,n} x_{k,n} \right.$$

$$\left. + \left(1 - \frac{1}{2m}\right) \sum_{j,k=1}^{m} b_{jk} x_{j,n} \gamma_k + C \right\} +$$

$$p_n(x_{1,n}; x_{2,n}; \ldots; x_{m,n})\, dx_{1,n}\, dx_{2,n} \ldots dx_{m,n} \quad (28)$$

or

$$M[y_n] = \sum_{j,k=1}^{m} b_{j,k} \int_{\Omega_x} x_j x_k\, p_n(\mathbf{x})\, d\Omega_x +$$

$$+ \left(1 - \frac{1}{2m}\right) \sum_{j,k=1}^{m} b_{jk}\gamma_k \int_{\Omega_x} x_j\, p_n(\mathbf{x})\, d\Omega_x + C, \quad (29)$$

* The stability conditions for continuous gradient systems, derived in [6], have well-known similarities to those given above for $\gamma_i = 0$.

since

$$\int_{\Omega_x} p_n(\mathbf{x})\, d\Omega_x = 1.$$

We introduce the notation

$$I_{jk,\,n} = \int_{\Omega_x} x_j x_k p_n(\mathbf{x})\, d\Omega_x,$$

$$J_{j,\,n} = \int_{\Omega_x} x_j p_n(\mathbf{x})\, d\Omega_x. \tag{30}$$

Then,

$$M[y_n] = \sum_{j,\,k=1}^{m} b_{jk} I_{jk,\,n} + \left(1 - \frac{1}{2m}\right) \sum_{j,\,k=1}^{m} b_{jk} \gamma_k J_{j,\,n} + C. \tag{31}$$

Equations (30) for the integrals can be found from (20). We multiply both members by $x_j x_k d\Omega_x$ and integrate over Ω_x. Then, $I_{jk,\,n+1}$ appears in the left member of the equation, and the expression takes the form:

$$I_{jk,\,n+1} = \int_{\Omega_x} x_j x_k \left[\int_{\Omega_\xi} \varphi(\xi, \mathbf{x})\, p_n(\xi)\, d\Omega_\xi\right] d\Omega_x =$$

$$= \int_{\Omega_x} x_j x_k \left[\int_{\Omega_\xi} \prod_{i=1}^{m} \frac{\psi(v_i)}{\alpha_i} p_n(\xi)\, d\Omega_\xi\right] d\Omega_x. \tag{32}$$

We now reverse the order of integration, and change from the variables $x_1, x_2, \ldots, x_m$ to the new integrand variables $v_1, v_2, \ldots, v_m$. Since $dx_i = -\alpha_i dv_i$, and the change in sign of the differential compensates for the changes in the signs of the limits of integration, we then find, by letting $d\Omega_v = dv_1 \ldots dv_m$, that

$$I_{jk,\,n+1} = \int_{\Omega_\xi} p_n(\xi) \Big[\int_{\Omega_v} \sum_{i=1}^{m} \psi(v_i)\, (\gamma_j - \alpha_j v_j + \sum_{\nu=1}^{m} A_{j\nu} \xi_\nu + B_j)\, (\gamma_k - \alpha_k v_k + \sum_{\nu=1}^{m} A_{k\nu} \xi_\nu + B_k)\, d\Omega_v\Big] d\Omega_\xi = \int_{\Omega_\xi} p_n(\xi)\, L_{jk}\, d\Omega_\xi. \tag{33}$$

We now consider the interior integral L_{jk} included within the square brackets. By expanding the parentheses in it, we obtain

$$L_{jk} = \int_{-\infty}^{+\infty} \cdots \int_{-\infty}^{+\infty} \left[\prod_{i=1}^{m} \psi(v_i)\right] \Big[\alpha_k \alpha_j v_k v_j + v_j \Big(-\alpha_j \gamma_k - \alpha_j \sum_{\nu=1}^{m} A_{k\nu} \xi_\nu - \alpha_j B_k\Big) + v_k \Big(-\alpha_k \gamma_j - \alpha_k \sum_{\nu=1}^{m} A_{j\nu} \xi_\nu - \alpha_k B_j\Big) + \tag{34}$$

$$+ (\gamma_j \gamma_k + \gamma_k B_j + \gamma_j B_k + B_k B_j) + (\gamma_j + \gamma_k) \sum_{\nu=1}^{m} (A_{k\nu} + A_{j\nu})\, \xi_\nu + (B_j + B_k) \sum_{\nu=1}^{m} (A_{k\nu} + A_{j\nu})\, \xi_\nu + \sum_{\mu,\,\nu=1}^{m} A_{k\nu} A_{j\mu} \xi_\mu \xi_\nu\Big]\, dv_1, \ldots, dv_m.$$

Now, we take into account that

$$\int_{-\infty}^{+\infty} \psi(v_i)\, dv_i = 1, \qquad \int_{-\infty}^{+\infty} v_i \psi(v_i)\, dv_i = 0, \tag{35}$$

and denote the dispersion of the noise at the output by

$$\sigma^2 = \int_{-\infty}^{+\infty} v_i^2 \psi(v_i)\, dv_i. \tag{36}$$

By taking (35) and (36) into account, we may rewrite (34) in the form

$$L_{jk} = \delta_{jk} \alpha_k^2 \sigma^2 + (\gamma_j \gamma_k + \gamma_j B_k + \gamma_k B_j + B_k B_j) + \sum_{\nu=1}^{m} [(\gamma_j + B_j) A_{k\nu} + (\gamma_k + B_k) A_{j\nu}]\, \xi_\nu + \sum_{\mu,\,\nu=1}^{m} A_{k\nu} A_{j\mu} \xi_\mu \xi_\nu. \tag{37}$$

By substituting (37) in (33), we obtain

$$I_{jk,\,n+1} = \delta_{jk} \alpha_k^2 \sigma^2 + (\gamma_j \gamma_k + \gamma_j B_k + \gamma_k B_j + B_j B_k) + \sum_{\nu=1}^{m} [(\gamma_j + B_j) A_{k\nu} + (\gamma_k + B_k) A_{j\nu}]\, J_{\nu,\,n} + \sum_{\mu,\,\nu=1}^{m} A_{k\nu} A_{j\mu} I_{\mu\nu,\,n}. \tag{38}$$

It is possible to write $m(m+1)/2$ such equations for determining $I_{jk,\,n+1}$ from $I_{\mu\nu,\,n}$. The m quantities $J_{\nu,n}$ ($\nu = 1, \ldots, m$) also appear in these equations. These latter quantities can be found from (20) in an analogous way. Indeed, by multiplying this expression by $x_{j,n+1} d\Omega_x$ and integrating over Ω_x, we arrive at the formula

$$J_{j,\,n+1} = \int_{\Omega_x} x_j \left[\int_{\Omega_\xi} \varphi(\xi, \mathbf{x})\, p_n(\xi)\, d\Omega_\xi\right] d\Omega_x =$$

$$= \int_{\Omega_x} x_j \left[\int_{\Omega_\xi} \prod_{i=1}^{m} \frac{\psi(v_i)}{\alpha_i} p_n(\xi)\, d\Omega_\xi\right] d\Omega_x = \tag{39}$$

$$= \int_{\Omega_\xi} p_n(\xi) \left[\int_{\Omega_x} x_j \prod_{i=1}^{m} \frac{\psi(v_i)}{\alpha_i} d\Omega_x\right] d\Omega_\xi = \int_{\Omega_\xi} p_n(\xi)\, L_j\, d\Omega_\xi.$$

With this,

$$L_j = \int_{\Omega_x} x_j \prod_{i=1}^{m} \frac{\psi(v_i)}{\alpha_i} d\Omega_x = \int_{-\infty}^{\infty} \cdots \int_{-\infty}^{\infty} \prod_{i=1}^{m} \psi(v_i)\, (\gamma_j - \alpha_j v_j + \sum_{\nu=1}^{m} A_{j\nu} \xi_\nu + B_j)\, dv_1 \ldots dv_m = \gamma_j + \sum_{\nu=1}^{m} A_{j\nu} \xi_\nu + B_j. \tag{40}$$

By substituting (40) in (39), we find that

$$J_{j,\,n+1} = \int_{\Omega_\xi} p_n(\xi)\,(\gamma_j + \sum_{\nu=1}^{m} A_{j\nu}\xi_\nu +$$

$$+ B_j)\,d\Omega_\xi = (\gamma_j + B_j) + \sum_{\nu=1}^{m} A_{j\nu} J_{\nu,\,n}. \qquad (41)$$

Using (41), we can determine $J_{j,\,n+1}$ from the $J_{\nu,\,n}$, and then substitute the result in (38). The presence of the noises v_i is completely unreflected in (41). For $v_i = 0$, the distribution densities reduce to unit pulse functions, but (41) remain unchanged by this. Therefore, the necessary and sufficient conditions for convergence for the sequence $J_{\nu,n}$ as $n \to \infty$ remain the same inequalities (19). The sequence of second moments $I_{jk,\,n}$ of the distribution also converges for $v_i \neq 0$.

In fact, the presence of the noise v_i in (38) is reflected by the additive terms $\delta_{jk}\,\alpha_k^2\,\sigma^2$. For $\sigma^2 = 0$ (absence of noises v_i), conditions (19) are necessary and sufficient for convergence of the sequence $I_{jk,n}$. It is obvious that the presence of the additional terms $\delta_{jk}\,\alpha_k^2\sigma^2$ only changes the steady-state value, but has no effect on the fact of convergence, since the transformation matrix of the $I_{jk,\,n}$ [cf. (38)] depends only on the A_{jk}. Therefore, inequalities (19), when random noises v_i are present, also guarantee convergence of the first and second moments and, consequently, convergence of the sequence $M[y_n]$ [cf. (31)].

We set

$$I_{jk} = \lim_{n\to\infty} I_{jk,\,n}; \quad J_j = \lim_{n\to\infty} J_{j,\,n};$$

$$\eta = \lim_{n\to\infty} M\,[y_n]. \qquad (42)$$

It follows, from (31), (38), and (41), that the quantities I_{jk}, J_j, and η are defined by (43), (44), and (45):

$$I_{jk} = \delta_{jk}\,\alpha_k^2\sigma^2 + (\gamma_j\gamma_k + \gamma_j B_k + \gamma_k B_j + B_j B_k) +$$

$$+ \sum_{\nu=1}^{m} [(\gamma_j + B_j)\,A_{k\nu} + (\gamma_k + B_k)\,A_{j\nu}]\,J_\nu +$$

$$+ \sum_{\mu,\,\nu=1}^{m} A_{k\nu}A_{j\mu}I_{\mu,\,\nu} \quad (j,\,k = 1,\,\ldots,\,m). \qquad (43)$$

$$J_j = (\gamma_j + B_j) + \sum_{\nu=1}^{m} A_{j\nu}J_\nu \; (j = 1,\,\ldots,\,m), \qquad (44)$$

$$\eta = \sum_{j,\,k=1}^{m} b_{jk}I_{jk} + \left(1 - \frac{1}{2m}\right)\sum_{j,\,k=1}^{m} b_{jk}\gamma_k J_j + C. \qquad (45)$$

Thus, the problem of determining the mathematical expectation η of the quantity y in the steady-state mode is solved. A consequence of (43), (44), and (45) is that the error is defined only by the dispersion σ^2 of the noise, and does not depend on the form of the function ψ (v). This property is a consequence of the quadratic characteristic of the object. The mathematical expectation of the deviations from the minimum (in the given case, $y_{min} = 0$) in the steady state may be considered as a certain measure of the error in this mode. As for the duration of the transient response, its mathematical expectation may also serve as its measure. This criterion was introduced in [4].

However, another measure turns out to be simpler — not the mathematical expectation of the duration of the transient response, but the duration of the transient response for the mathematical expectation, which is not the same thing. Consider the dependence of $M[y_n]$ on n [cf. (31)]. This is a transient response in some equivalent discrete system which may be studied by the ordinary methods, for example by frequency methods, integral methods, etc. In the simple cases (cf., below), one can obtain an expression for the duration of the transient response in such equivalent systems.

If the vector γ is not fixed, but has some probability distribution $W(\gamma)$, we may then, by denoting $d\Omega_\gamma = d\gamma_1 \ldots d\gamma_m$, average the values of η over Ω_γ in accordance with the formula

$$\eta_{av} = \int_{\Omega_\gamma} \eta W(\gamma)\,d\Omega_\gamma. \qquad (46)$$

It may be more advantageous for computational purposes to use (45), where the maximum expected values of the γ_i are substituted.

Example of a Simplest System (m = 1)

We illustrate the use of the formulas obtained by the example of a simple system with one input variable. We set

$$\alpha_1 = \alpha,\; \alpha_{01} = \alpha_0,\; x_1 = x,\; \xi_1 = \xi,\; \gamma_1 = \gamma,\; b_{11} = b,\; B_1 = B,\; A_{11} = A.$$

In this case, (19) for search stability takes the form $|A| < 1$ or, in accordance with (13),

$$|A| = |1 - 4\alpha\alpha_0 b + \alpha\gamma b| < 1. \qquad (47)$$

It is clear from this that the speed γ must not go beyond certain limiting values, i.e., $\gamma_1 \leq \gamma \leq \gamma_2$, where $(\gamma_1, \gamma_2) > 0$.

Equation (45) takes the form

$$\eta = bI_{11} + \frac{b\gamma}{2}J_1 + b\left(\alpha_0^2 - \gamma\frac{\alpha_0}{2} + \frac{\gamma^2}{8}\right). \qquad (48)$$

The integrals I_{11} and J_1 are determined from (43) and (44), which are rewritten in the form

$$I_{11} = \alpha^2\sigma^2 + (\gamma + B)^2 + 2A\,(\gamma + B) + A^2 I_{11}, \qquad (49)$$

$$J_1 = \gamma + B + AJ_1. \qquad (50)$$

Here, in accordance with the second of Eqs. (13),

$$B = -\alpha b\gamma\frac{1}{2}\left(2\alpha - \frac{\gamma}{2}\right) = \alpha b\gamma\left(\frac{\gamma}{4} - \alpha_0\right). \qquad (51)$$

From these expressions, we find that

$$J_1 = \frac{\gamma + B}{1 - A},\quad I_{11} = \frac{\alpha^2\sigma^2 + (\gamma + B)^2}{1 - A^2} + 2A\frac{(\gamma + B)^2}{(1 - A)(1 - A^2)} \qquad (52)$$

The transient response is determined by (31), (38), and (41), which take the following form:

$$\eta_n = bI_{11,n} + b\left(\alpha_0^2 - \frac{\gamma\alpha_0}{2} + \frac{\gamma^2}{8}\right) + \frac{b\gamma}{2} J_{1,n},$$
$$I_{11,n+1} = \alpha^2\sigma^2 + (\gamma + B)^2 + 2A(\gamma + B) J_{1,n} + A^2 I_{11,n},$$
$$J_{1,n+1} = \gamma + B + AJ_{1,n}. \qquad (53)$$

We set

$$A_0 = \alpha_0\sqrt{\frac{b}{\sigma}}, \quad \delta = \gamma\sqrt{\frac{b}{\sigma}}, \quad k = \alpha\alpha_0 b, \quad \varepsilon = \frac{\eta}{\sigma}. \qquad (54)$$

Then, after substitution of the values of I_{11} and J_1 from (49) and (50), (48) assumes the form

$$\varepsilon = \left(A_0 - \frac{\delta}{4}\right)^2 + \left(\frac{\delta}{k}\right)^2 \frac{1}{\left(4 - \frac{\delta}{A_0}\right)^2} + \left(\frac{k}{A_0}\right)^2 \frac{1}{1 - \left(1 - 4k + \frac{k\delta}{A_0}\right)^2}. \qquad (55)$$

We rewrite stability condition (47) in the form

$$\left|1 - 4k + k\frac{\delta}{A_0}\right| < 1.$$

$$\text{Если } j = 1 - 4k + k\frac{\delta}{A_0}, \text{ то } k\left(4 - \frac{\delta}{A_0}\right) = 1 - j = q. \qquad (56)$$

If $j = 1 - 4k + k\frac{\delta}{A_0}$, then $k(4 - \frac{\delta}{A_0}) = 1 - j = q$.

In a stable system, $-1 < j < 1$ and $0 < q < 2$. The boundary of stability is reached for

$$K_{bo} = \frac{2}{4 - \delta/A_0} \qquad (57)$$

The other boundary is obtained from the condition that $k > 0$, i.e.,

$$4 - \frac{\delta}{A_0} > 0. \qquad (58)$$

Thus, the region of stability has the form shown in Fig. 2.

As an example, let us set $\delta = 0.2$. For this value, and by giving A_0, we find from (55) the minimal value ϵ_{min} as a function of k. Let it be attained for $k = k_{opt}$ (Fig. 3). If we trace the curve $\epsilon_{min} = \epsilon_{min}(A_0)$ (Fig. 4a) and the curve $k_{opt} = k_{opt}(A_0)$ (Fig. 4b), we can find the minimum possible value of the steady-state error $\epsilon_{\min\,min}$ and the values of the parameters A_0 and k which correspond to it. It is clear from Fig. 4 that $\epsilon_{\min\,min} \approx 0.3$, $A_0 = 0.4$, and $k = 0.15$.

The optimal parameter values depend on the fact that for very large steps the error increases due to the significant deviations from the minimum; however, for very small steps the system can not compensate the effect of the "drift" γ of the characteristics, thanks to which the error again increases. One easily convinces oneself that

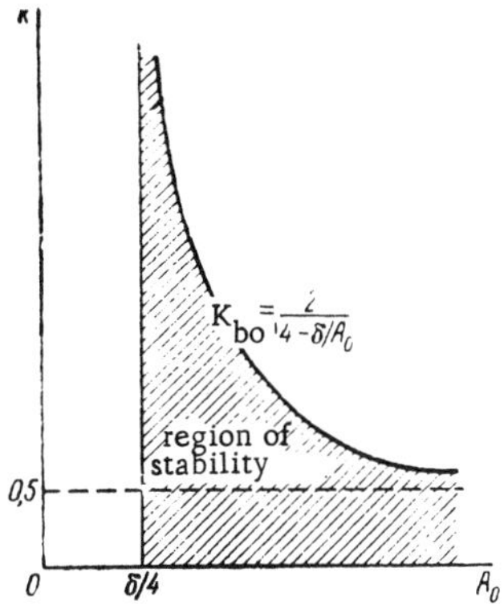

Fig. 2.

for $\gamma = 0$, the optimal values of α and α_0 are infinitesimally small and, in the limit, the error ϵ tends to zero.

We now find the duration of the transient response where, for simplicity, we limit ourselves to the case when $\gamma = 0$. Then from (51) and (53), we find that $B = 0$ and

$$\eta_n = bI_{11,n} + b\alpha_0^2, I_{11,n+1} = \alpha^2\sigma^2 + A^2 I_{11,n}, A = 1 - 4k. \qquad (59)$$

The steady-state values turn out to be

$$I_{11} = \frac{\alpha^2\sigma^2}{8k(1-2k)}, \quad \eta = \frac{b\alpha^2\sigma^2}{8k(1-2k)} + b\alpha_0^2. \qquad (60)$$

Since

$$I_{11,n} = \alpha^2\sigma^2 + A^2 I_{11,n-1} = \alpha^2\sigma^2 + A^2[\alpha^2\sigma^2 + A^2 I_{11,n-2}] = \cdots$$
$$\cdots = \alpha^2\sigma^2[1 + A^2 + \cdots + A^{2(n-1)}] + A^{2n} I_{11,0} =$$
$$= \alpha^2\sigma^2\frac{1 - A^{2n}}{1 - A^2} + A^{2n} I_{11,0} = I_{11}(1 - A^{2n}) + A^{2n} I_{11,0}, \qquad (61)$$

the difference

$$\theta_n = \eta_n - \eta = b(I_{11,n} - I_{11}) = bA^{2n}(I_{11,0} - I_{11}). \qquad (62)$$

It may be that at the initial moment $I_{11,0} < I_{11}$, if the initial value of x is, for example, at the origin of coordinates. However, if we assume that the system is significantly distant from the steady-state position at the initial moment of time, we can assume that $I_{11,0} - I_{11} > 0$. Then, the quantity θ_n tends to zero with increasing n, while remaining positive. We now find the discrete time n_0 after whose expiration the following relationship is valid:

$$\frac{\theta_n}{\lambda} \leqslant 1, \qquad (63)$$

where the constant $\lambda \ll 1$ is some admissable threashold.

It follows from (60), (62), and (63), that

$$n_0 = \frac{1}{2}\,\frac{\ln\lambda(I_{11} + \alpha_0^2) - \ln(I_{11,0} - I_{11})}{\ln A} \qquad (64)$$

The quantity n_0 serves as a measure of the duration of the transient response in the system.

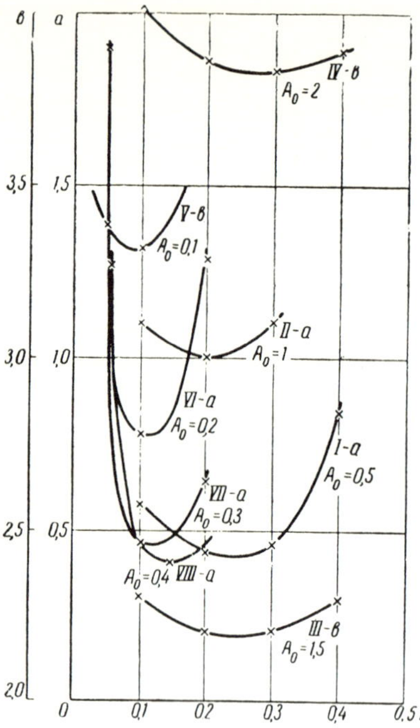

Fig. 3.

Example of a System with Two Variables (m = 2)

Let the object's equation have the form:

$$y = x_1^2 + 2\beta x_1 x_2 + x_2^2. \tag{65}$$

For $|\beta| < 1$, the unique minimum of the function y is found at the origin of coordinates. This case corresponds to m = 2, $b_{11} = b_{22} = 1$, and $b_{12} = \beta$ in the general formulas. We further set $\gamma_i = 0$, $\alpha_1 = \alpha_2 = \alpha$, $\alpha_{01} = \alpha_{02} = \alpha_0$, $\alpha_1\alpha_{01} = \alpha_2\alpha_{02} = k$. Then, from (13), we find that

$$A_{11} = A_{22} = 1 - 4k, \quad A_{12} = A_{21} = -4\beta k. \tag{66}$$

Equation (45) takes the form:

$$\eta = I_{11} + 2\beta I_{12} + I_{22} + \alpha_0^2, \tag{67}$$

and I_{11}, I_{12}, and I_{22} are found from (43), which can be written in the following forms:

$$\begin{aligned} &I_{11} 8k(1-2k) + 8\beta k(1-4k) I_{12} - 16\beta^2 k^2 I_{22} = \alpha^2\sigma^2, \\ &I_{11} 4\beta k(1-4k) + 8k(1-2k-2\beta^2 k) I_{12} + I_{22} 4\beta k(1-4k) = 0 \\ &-16\beta^2 k^2 I_{11} + 8\beta k(1-4k) I_{12} + I_{22} 8k(1-2k) = \alpha^2\sigma^2. \end{aligned} \tag{68}$$

In these equations, the quantities I_{11} and I_{22} enter in identical fashion, as was to be expected. We set

$$8\beta k(1-4k) = D, \quad 8k(1-2k-2\beta^2 k^2) = E. \tag{69}$$

Then, solving (68), we find that

$$I_{11} = I_{22} = \frac{\alpha^2\sigma^2 E}{E^2 - D^2}, \quad I_{12} = \frac{\alpha^2\sigma^2 D}{D^2 - E^2} \tag{70}$$

and, as follows from (67),

$$\eta = \frac{2\alpha^2\sigma^2(E - \beta D)}{E^2 - D^2} + \alpha_0^2. \tag{71}$$

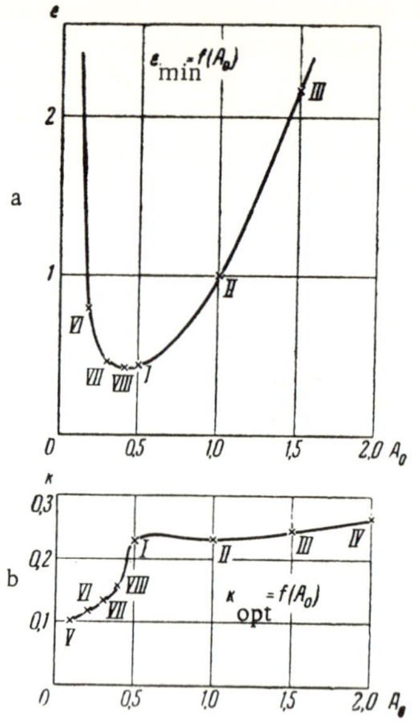

Fig. 4.

We now introduce the relative error from the random noise (for this, we assume that $\alpha_0\alpha = k$)

$$\frac{\eta - \alpha_0^2}{\left(\frac{\sigma}{\alpha_0}\right)^2} = \frac{2k^2(E - \beta D)}{E^2 - D^2} = \theta(k, \beta). \tag{72}$$

By substituting the values of E and D from (69), we find that

$$\theta(k, \beta) = \frac{k(1-2k)}{4} \times$$

$$\times \frac{1 - \beta^2}{(1-2k)^2 - 4\beta^2 k(1-2k) + 4\beta^4 k^2 - \beta^2(1-4k)^2}. \tag{73}$$

We find the stability conditions from the characteristic equation $|A - E\lambda| = 0$, or

$$\begin{vmatrix} A_{11} - \lambda & A_{12} \\ A_{21} & A_{22} - \lambda \end{vmatrix} = 0. \tag{74}$$

By substituting the values of A_{ij} here, we arrive at the equation

$$(1 - 4k - \lambda)^2 - 16\beta^2 k^2 = 0, \tag{75}$$

whose roots are

$$\lambda_{1,2} = (1 - 4k) \pm 4\beta k. \tag{76}$$

The search is stable if $|\lambda_{1,2}| < 1$. It follows from this that k must be found within the limits

$$0 < k < \frac{1}{2(1 + |\beta|)}. \tag{77}$$

For a given k, the quantity β may vary within the limits

$$|\beta| < \frac{1}{2k} - 1. \tag{78}$$

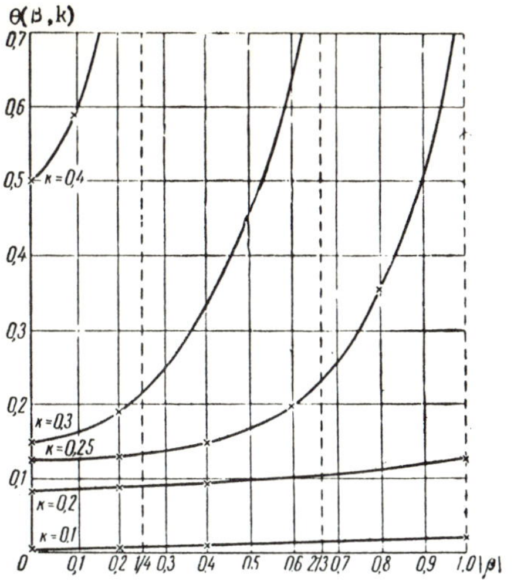

Fig. 5.

Figure 5 shows the function $\theta(\beta, k)$. It is clear from the graphs that the error from the random noise, generally speaking, increases with increasing $|\beta|$. Indeed, for $\beta = 0$ the lines y = const on the (x_1, x_2) plane are concentric circles. With increasing $|\beta|$, they become ellipses whose axes are turned by 45° with respect to the coordinate axes. The greater $|\beta|$ is, the more "elongated" these ellipses become, which worsens the conditions for minimum search and increases the steady-state error from the random noise.

For $\alpha \to 0$ and $\alpha_0 \to 0$, the total steady-state error can be made arbitrarily small. Certainly, if $\gamma_i \neq 0$, there exist optimal values of α and α_0 which are greater than zero. The essential dependence of the error on α_0 and α (or k) (Fig. 5) shows that automatic tuning of α_0 and α, providing a minimum of the error, is advantageous in automatic optimizers [5].

The author wishes to express his gratitude to B. M. Levitan for his counsel in carrying out this work.

LITERATURE CITED

[1] A. A. Fel'dbaum, "Steady-state processes in the simplest discrete extremal systems with random noise present," Avtomatika I Telemekhanika, 20, 8 (1959).†

[2] V. I. Romanovskii, Discrete Markov Chains [in Russian] (Gostekhizdat, 1947).

[3] T. A. Sarymsakov, Basic Theory of Markov Processes [in Russian] (Gostekhizdat, 1954).

[4] A. A. Fel'dbaum, "On the effect of random factors on automatic search processes," Proceedings of the Conference on the Theory and Application of Discrete Automatic Systems [in Russian] (IAT AN SSSR, Moscow, 1958).

[5] A. A. Fel'dbaum, "An automatic optimizer," Avtomatika i Telemekhanika 19, 8 (1958). †

[6] A. A. Krasovskii, "The dynamics of continuous extremal control systems," Izvest. Akad. Nauk, OTN, Energetika i avtomatika No. 3 (1959).

† See English Translation

DUAL-CONTROL THEORY. I

A. A. Fel'dbaum

Moscow

Translated from Avtomatika i Telemekhanika, Vol. 21, No. 9, pp. 1240-1249, September, 1960

Original article submitted March 23, 1960

Some fundamental problems in communication theory and control theory are compared. The problem of designing an optimum (in the statistical sense) closed-loop dual-control system, is formulated. Its solution, as well as examples and some generalizations, will be given in parts II, III, and IV.

Introduction

A general block diagram of signal transmission, as investigated in communication theory is shown in Fig. 1. The transmitted signal x^* proceeds from the transmitting device A to the communication channel H^*. The mixing of signal and interference (noise) h^* now takes place. The resultant signal y^* represents a mixture of the transmitted signal and the interference. The resultant signal proceeds to the input of receiver B. The optimum receiver problem consists in obtaining the signal $\underline{x}$ at its output, such that it is, in a specified sense, closest to the transmitted signal x^* or to some transformation of the signal x^*. The mathematical side of the problems related to such systems has been the subject of important investigations by A. N. Kolmogorov [1], N. Wiener [2], C. E. Shannon [3], and A. Wald [4]. This type of system was investigated in the works on communication theory by V. A. Kotel'nikov [5], D. Middleton, D. Van Meter [6], and others. The cited works differ in their various approaches to the problem, but are all basically concerned with the investigation of the scheme represented by the block diagram in Fig. 1. The results obtained in the above-cited works, and in particular the Kolmogorov-Wiener theory, have proved useful in formulating the statistical theory of automatic-control systems. This theory has been expounded in the books of V. S. Pugachev [7], J. H. Laning, Jr., and R. H. Battin [8], and others. The fullest consideration has been given to the theory of linear systems. If a system is linear, then whatever the closed-loop system, it is easy to obtain an open-loop system equivalent to it. That is why the automatic-control systems, which, as a rule, are

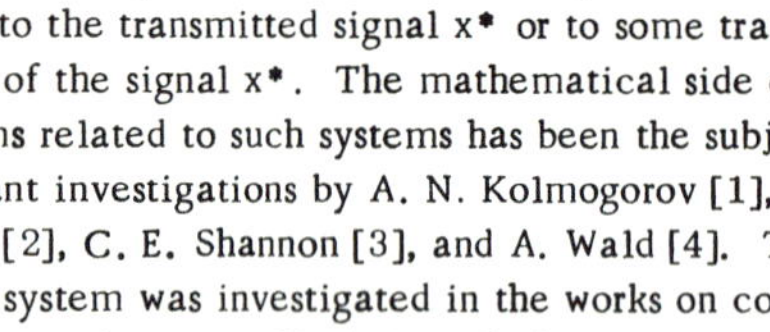

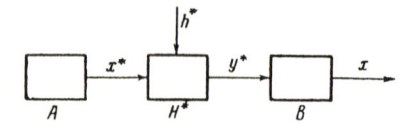

Fig. 1.

closed-loop systems, enable one to use the scheme as in Fig. 1, provided that the system is linear. Some complications and difficulties arise when the interference does not appear at the input of the system, but at the input of the controlled object – the latter being inside the closed-loop network. This also creates difficulties which are not, however, of a fundamental nature. More serious difficulties arise due to the bounds to which the power of the system's signals are subjected. The problem becomes more involved when the controlled object is nonlinear or it is required that an optimum control system, which often proves to be nonlinear, is designed. It is not always possible to proceed from an open nonlinear system to an equivalent closed-loop one; furthermore, this is an extremely involved process. In such a case, the open-loop scheme depicted in Fig. 1 cannot be used in practice. A number of attempts have been made to reduce approximately nonlinear systems to equivalent linear ones (see, for example, the paper of I. E. Kazakov [9]). Such studies are of considerable practical value but do not, in their present state, provide a means of estimating how close the obtained approximation is to the true solution; neither do they enable one to synthesize the optimum system.

In order to be able to solve optimum problems of the control theory, a fundamentally different approach is required. Firstly, a different block diagram replacing that depicted in Fig. 1 is needed. Before selecting a common scheme to be used in automatic-control theory, it seems advisable to have a preliminary survey of certain basic concepts of the theory.

Figure 2, a shows the controlled object B with $\underline{x}$ as its output, $\underline{u}$ as the controller, and $\underline{z}$ as the disturbance (interference). When the system has several inputs and outputs, one can regard $\underline{x}$, $\underline{u}$, and $\underline{z}$ as vector quantities.

The output $\underline{x}$ depends on $\underline{u}$ and $\underline{z}$. This dependence can be described either by a linear or a nonlinear operator, and in a particular case of memoryless systems, only by a function. The interference $\underline{z}$ is generally a function of time. Thus, since a change in the system's characteristics can be considered a particular result of interference (e.g., the parametric effect), then hereafter everything in the system's characteristics that changes with time will be attributed to interference. If, for example, x depends on u as in

$$x = [a_0 + f_0(t)]\,u^2 + [a_1 + f_1(t)]\,u + a_2 + f_2(t), \quad (1)$$

then the vector

$$z = \{z_0, z_1, z_2\},$$
$$z_0 = f_0(t),\ \ z_1 = f_1(t),\ \ z_2 = f_2(t) \quad (2)$$

gives the interference or disturbance, and the formula

$$x = [a_0 + z_0]\,u^2 + [a_1 + z_1]\,u + a_2 + z_2 \quad (3)$$

represents a particular operator.

If the object has memory and if, for example, its motion can be described by a differential equation of the nth order, then its state is considered as one of the characteristics of the object as described by the value of the vector x in the n-dimensional phase space.

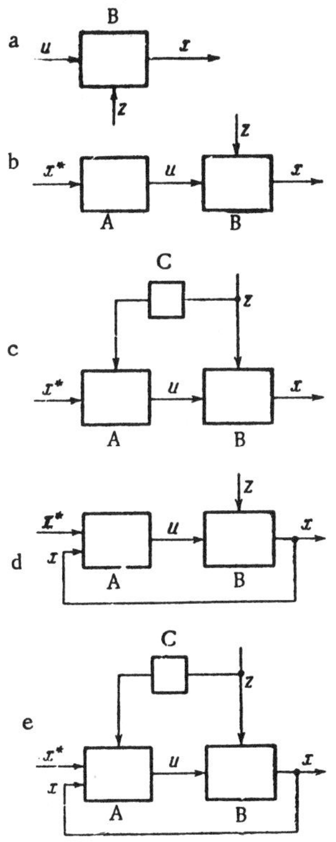

Fig. 2.

Complete information about a system thus consists of information about its operator, interference (noise), and the state of the system. The controlling device may be given and is considered as known. The open-loop systems are automatic-control systems of a simple type. A block diagram of an open-loop system is shown in Fig. 2, b and is of the same character as the one given in Fig. 1. The exciting quantity x* enters the input of the regulating member A, determining how the output quantity x should vary. The output u of the regulating device enters the input of the object B under control. The output x of the controlled object B does not proceed in this case to the regulating member A.

The required rule of change in x can only be implemented when full information about the controlled system is available, i.e., when its operator and state x are known, at least at the initial moment of time, as well as the interference z. The latter should be known a priori at all moments of time, including future moments. The required rule of change in x must be one of the admissible ones, such that it can be implemented for the given class of initial states of the system and for a class of controlling motions u staying within acceptable bounds.

The above conditions, and, in particular, the a priori full knowledge of the controlled system, cannot be satisfied in practice. This is why an accurate implementation of the required control rule cannot be obtained. Sometimes the interference z is not known a priori, but it is possible to measure it with a device C (see Fig. 2, c) and to introduce the outcome of the measurement into the controlling member A. One can then find in the latter the required controlling rule u. Such a scheme is also an open-loop one. But the scheme depicted in Fig. 2,c differs in some ways from the scheme with complete a priori information about the system, as now future magnitudes of the interference z remain unknown. Because of this, the exact implementation of the required rule of variation of the controlling quantity x is not always feasible.

When the state x of the system is not known, then, generally speaking, it is not possible to implement the required rule of the change in x. To be able to attain the required variation in x, or one near to it, a feedback network is needed to feed the output quantity x to the input of the controlling member A (see Fig. 2, d). Having compared x and x*, the controlling member generates the regulating action u, bringing x to its required value. The block diagram of Fig. 2, d is a closed-loop scheme, and is of the utmost importance in the automatic-control theory.

A closed-loop network offers far-reaching possibilities not available in an open-loop system. For example, it may be possible for a class of objects B of control to obtain a process x close to the one required even when the interference z remains unknown and incapable of measurement. Let, for example, the interference z, together with the controlling action u, be applied at the input of the controlled object B, the latter representing an inertia member. If the quantity $x^* = x$ is to be attained, the regulating member can be implemented in the form of an amplifier of high gain $k \gg 1$, the difference $x^* - x$ being sent to its input.

It is not difficult to see that the requirement $x^* = x$ will be satisfied approximately, whatever the continuously varying interference z, provided k is sufficiently high and the bounds of variability of u are such that the interference z can be compensated by u.

This principle of neutralizing the interference can be generalized and applied to cases considerably more involved, combining the system's accuracy with its stability. A detailed analysis of the applicability of this principle was carried out by M. V. Meerov in his monograph [10].

When the interference z can be measured, it is possible to implement a combined system (see Fig. 2, e) of measurement of the state of the controlled system x as well as of its interference. Such systems are of considerable practical value. We shall not, however, concern ourselves with them but shall limit the study to the "pure" type of closed-loop systems, considering them as being of primary importance.

The input quantity x^* may be previously unknown; usually, neither do we have any prior knowledge of the interference z. Consequently, these processes become random, and, in a favorable case, the a priori information is limited to our knowledge of their statistical characteristics. Such processes may be regarded as belonging to a class of curves $x^*(\lambda)$ and $z(\mu)$ where λ and μ are parameter vectors$(\lambda_1, \ldots, \lambda_q)$and $(\mu_1, \ldots, \mu_m)$, respectively, with their probability distributions either known or unknown.

In communication channels connecting the blocks of a system, the errors of measurement or noise can be regarded as subsidiary random processes as well, with either known or unknown characteristics. Thus, the analysis of a control system and the synthesis of the regulating member can be regarded as problems of a statistical nature. The problem should be solved for an over-all block diagram in which all the above features of an automatic-control system are reflected. Such a block diagram is depicted in Fig. 3; it is the subject of the present paper as well as that of further papers in this series.

The input quantity x^* proceeds to the input of the controlling member A through channel H^* where it becomes mixed with noise h^*. Thus, the quantity y^* entering the input of A is generally not equal to the actual value of the input quantity x^*. There also exists a class of systems with the external input x^* altogether absent. Generally speaking, however, it cannot be neglected. A similar mixing takes place of the state x of controlled object B and noise h in channel H; quantity y entering A will not, as a rule, be equal to x. The regulating action u proceeds next from A to controlled object B having previously passed through channel G where it was mixed with noise g. The quantity v proceeding to the controlled object is not, as a rule, equal to u.

Dual Control

One cannot neutralize, in a general case, the interference z by a regulation u if the interference z is not known. Its direct measurement is not, as a matter of fact, often possible. In such a case, an open-loop system is useless. But the closed system in Fig. 3 shows how z can be indirectly determined by measuring the input and the output, in and out of object B, by studying its characteristics. The input of controlling member A enters both the input v and the output x of the object or, in any case, the quantities u and y related to v and x. The examination of the quantities u and y provides information on the characteristics of object B. It should be understood that this information is never complete, as the noises g and h render an exact measurement of B's characteristics impossible; if the actual form of the object's operator is not known either, a full determination of its characteristics would not be possible even in the absence of noise, unless the determination time is infinitely great. The lack of complete information on the disturbance z can assume the form of an a posteriori probability distribution of its parameters. Although the latter does not provide precise values of the parameters, it is more accurate than an a priori distribution, as the former reflects the real character of the interference.

If the random process can be measured directly, one is able eventually to specify its statistical characteristics more accurately. The method which provides such improvement with the aid of dynamic programming was discussed in examples by R. Bellman and R. Kalaba [11, 12] and also by M. Freimer [13]. One is able to find the characteristics of the process x^* more accurately in the open part of the block diagram in Fig. 3, or in a similar scheme in Fig. 1.

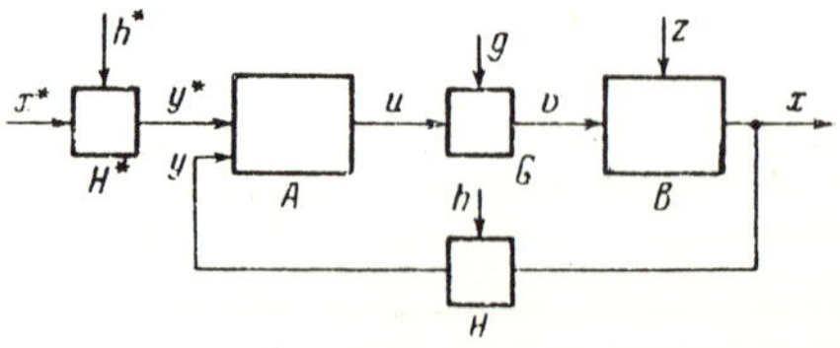

Fig. 3.

This formulation of the problem is characteristic for an open system. In a closed system its formulation becomes totally different. It is shown that some processes in the system of Fig. 3 may occur which have no counterpart in open-loop systems. Whereas open systems can only be studied by passive observations, the study may develop into an active one in closed systems. In order to improve the investigation one may vary the signals u (or v) which act on the controlled object B. The object is, as it were, "reconnoitered" by signals of an enquiring character whose purpose it is to promote a more rapid and more accurate study of the object's characteristics and of the methods of controlling it.

However, the controlling movements are necessary not only to study or to learn the characteristics of the object or the ways of controlling it, but also to implement the regulation, to direct the object to the required state. Thus, the controlling effects in the general block diagram in Fig. 3 must be twofold: they must, to a certain extent, be investigating as well as directing.

The control whose regulating effects are of this twofold character will in the sequel be called dual control; the papers in the present series will be devoted to tne theory of dual control.

Dual control is particularly useful and even indispensible in cases where the operator and the interference z in the object B are complex, and the object is thus distinguished either by its complexity or by the variability of its characteristics. Some typical examples of systems with dual control are to be found in automatic search systems, in particular, in automatic optimization systems (see, for example, [14 and 15]). In these systems, the investigating or "trial" part can usually be separated easily from thecontrolling or "operating" part of the signal, either by the difference in their frequency ranges or because they interweave in time. Such a separation, however, need not always take place; an effect can be twofold in character by virtue of being partly diagnostic and partly regulating.

Thus, in dual-control systems, there is a conflict between the two sides of the controlling process, the investigational and the directional. An efficient control can only be effected by a well-timed action on the object. A delayed action weakens the control process. But the control can only be effective when the properties of the object are sufficiently well known; one needs, however, more time to become familiar with them. A too "hasty" controlling member will carry out the operational movement without making proper use of the results of trial investigations performed on the object. A too "cautious" system will bide its time unnecessarily long and process the received information without directing the object to its required state at the right time. In each case, the control process may not prove the best one and may not even prove to be up to the mark. Our problem is to find out, one way or another, which combination of these two sides of the regulation would prove to be most suitable. The operations must be so selected as to maximize a criterion of the control's quality.

As shown above, the incomplete information about the object will be expressed by the presence of the probability distributions of potentially possible characteristics of the object. The regulating member compares, as it were, the various hypotheses on the object, with probability of its occurrence being attached to each hypothesis. These probabilities vary with time. There may be a control method such that the most probable hypothesis will always be selected and, therefore, assuming that it is valid, the optimum control method will be attained. Such a control system is not generally optimum in the absolute meaning of the word as the complete information on the object has not been utilized. The probability distribution of the different hypotheses extracted from the experiments is distorted as the probability 1 was ascribed to one of them and the probability 0 to others. A better control method will be one whereby the probabilities of all the hypotheses would be taken into account.

The probability distribution of hypotheses will vary with time, the higher probabilities concentrating more and more in the region of those hypotheses which approach the true characteristics of the object. The pace of concentration and, therefore, the success of the subsequent regulating movements, depends on the character of the preceding regulating movements, on how well they have "sounded" the object. Thus, two factors should be taken into account by the controlling member which decides the specific amount of regulating movement at any given moment of time:

(a) The loss occurring in the value of the quality criterion due to the fact that the outcome of the operation at a given moment, and at subsequent moments of time, will cause a deviation of the object either from the required state or from the best attainable one. The average value of this loss shall be called the action risk.

(b) The loss occurring in the value of the quality criterion due to the fact that the magnitude of the controlling action has not proved the best to obtain information on the characteristics of the object; in view of this, the subsequent actions will not be the best posssible ones either. The average value of this loss shall be called the investigation risk.

It will be shown that for a certain class of systems, the total risk will be equal to the sum of the action and investigation risks.

All systems of automatic search (see [14])are characterized by trial actions. Dual control, therefore, is applicable to all systems of automatic search and, in particular, to automatic optimization systems. It can also be applied to other types of closed-loop systems which do not belong to the automatic search class at all. To illustrate the difference between the two types of dual-control systems, a few examples will be given.

Figure 4,a shows a system which operates as follows: the main regulating member A implements the control of object B, either in an open- or in a closed-loop network (the closed one is indicated by a dashed line). The

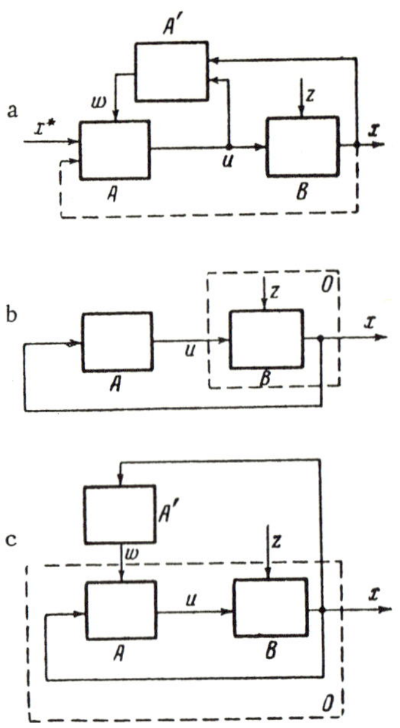

Fig. 4.

regulating movements u are of the investigational and action type simultaneously. The quantities u and x, from the input and the output of object B, respectively, enter an additional controlling member A'. The latter receives the characteristics of object B from the results of the investigations; subsequently, in accordance with an algorithm given in advance and fed into the device from outside, the parameters of controlling member A are so computed that its controlling action is optimal. Having the results of the computation, the additional regulating action w establishes the computed optimum parameters in the main controlling member A. This process may repeat itself periodically.

Such systems contain investigational movements; however, the automatic search is absent. The parameters of member A are established, not via automatic search, but from an algorithm given in advance, from a function of the determined characteristics of object B. There is no investigational component in the operation w. The channel w is not usually found in a closed network, as the change in the coefficients of A has no effect on the coefficients of B.

A block diagram of an automatic optimization system is presented in Fig. 4,b. Here the action u is dual in character, investigating object B as well as directing it to its optimum mode of action. The latter corresponds to an extremum of quantity Q dependent on x. The optimum mode is found by means of automatic search. The latter is conducted in such a way that the information received from the investigating action u and from the output x of the system is analyzed in controlling member A. This permits determination of the regulating part of the same action u on the same object B whose input and output were investigated, so that the same quantity x which was being investigated can be changed in the right direction.

The combination of the investigating and directing operations has, so far, not constituted the whole search, but only one of its distinct features. There is no search in the system depicted in Fig. 4,a; it takes place, however, in the system of automatic optimization shown in Fig. 4,b. But both systems are of the dual-control type.

In Fig. 4,b the controlled object is inside a dashed rectangle denoted by O. In this case, it does not differ from object B. The dual control, however, can also be applied to control the entire automatic system, considered as a complex object. For example, in Fig. 4,c the complex object O inside the dashed rectangle comprises the controlling member A and the object B of control. The auxiliary controlling member A' investigates the process x and, with the aid of the controlling process w, can vary the algorithm of regulation implemented by member A. The w processes are twofold in character. The investigation of changes in the algorithm of member A and their effect on the process x results in regulating processes w, bringing the algorithm of member A to such a form that the process x will either prove admissible, favorable, or optimum, depending for what purpose the system will be used. Here an automatic search takes place in the closed network of processes $w \rightarrow x \rightarrow u$.

Statement of the Synthesis Problem of an Optimum System of Dual Control

The problem of designing an optimum, in the specified meaning of the word, controlling member A, as shown in Fig. 3, is formulated below. It is advisable when formulating the problem to make use of certain concepts of the theory of games and of A. Wald's [4] theory of statistical decisions (see D. Blackwell and M. A. Girshick [16], and also Chow [17]). In solving the variational problem as stated later in the present series of papers, use is made of the concepts of R. Bellman's dynamic programming (see, for example, [18]). In the subsequent parts of this series, the mathematical exposition may appear somewhat cumbersome but is actually quite simple. The main contents of the papers deals with further development of the concepts of automatic control briefly described above.

Consider the scheme presented in Fig. 3. The following limitations of the statement of the problem are introduced.

1) A discrete-continuous system is investigated in which the time but not the level is quantized. All magnitudes occurring in the system are considered at discrete moments of time $t = 0, 1, 2, \ldots, n$ only. Any

magnitude at the sth moment of time will carry the index s. Thus, the considered quantities are x^*_s, x_s, y_s, v_s, g_s, etc.

Such limitation enables one to simplify the computation. Moreover, in many cases this actually occurs. The transition to the continuous time can in some cases be accomplished in an intuitive manner by making the time interval between the discrete values approach zero (see Part III). One meets with considerable difficulties in more fully examining the passage to the limit.

2) The time interval, or the number of cycles n within which the process is being investigated, is assumed to be a fixed constant. In certain cases no major difficulties arise when proceeding to the limit with $n \to \infty$. A wider generalization relating to a variable number n of cycles not known beforehand would be of interest, but will not be tackled in the present paper.

3) A Bayesian problem, in which a priori densities of random variables are given, is considered. Other formulations, for example, minimax, are also of considerable interest, but far more difficult to solve. This problem could also be formulated in relation to the concept of the so-called "inductive probability" (see, for example, the paper of L. S. Schwartz, B. Harris, and A. Hauptschein [19]).

We assume that h^*_s, h_s, g_s, are sequences of independent random variables with identical distribution densities $P(h^*_s)$, $P(h_s)$, $P(g_s)$. Further, let $z_s = z(s, \mu)$, and $x^*_s = x(s, \lambda)$ where μ and λ are random parameter vectors with coordinates μ_i and λ_i, respectively:

$$\mu = (\mu_1, \ldots, \mu_m), \qquad \lambda = (\lambda_1, \ldots, \lambda_q). \tag{4}$$

The a priori probability densities $P(\mu)$ and $P(\lambda^*)$ are given.

4) The object B is assumed to be memoryless; in other words, the values x_s of its output depend only on the values of the input quantities z_s and v_s at the same moment of time:

$$x_s = F_0(z_s, v_s). \tag{5}$$

The functions F_0 and z_s are assumed to be finite and single-valued, continuous and differentiable.

A generalization relating to objects with memory and with x_s depending on x_r, z_r, v_r $(r < s)$ will be given in Part IV. It should be pointed out that memoryless objects are of great practical value. Namely, if the input data (initial conditions or values of parameters) are given for a certain model, and one is able to carry out experiments using this model and also to register the results, then such an object becomes equivalent to a memoryless one.

5) A simple criterion W of quality is introduced.

Let the partial loss function corresponding to the sth time moment be of the form

$$W_s = W(s, x_s, x^*_s). \tag{6}$$

Moreover, let the total loss function W for the total time be equal to the sum of partial loss functions (such a criterion shall be called a simple one):

$$W = \sum_{s=0}^{s=n} W(s, x^*_s, x_s). \tag{7}$$

The smaller the mathematical expectation of W, the better is the system. It shall be called optimum when its average risk R (i.e., the mathematical expectation M of the quantity W) is minimal. The amount of risk is given by the formula

$$R = M\{W\} = \tag{8}$$

$$= M\left\{\sum_{s=0}^{s=n} W(s, x^*_s, x_s)\right\} = \sum_{s=0}^{s=n} M\{W_s\} = \sum_{s=0}^{s=n} R_s.$$

Each $R_s = M\{W_s\}$ will be called a partial risk due to the sth cycle.

There may be many types of simple criteria, for example,

$$W_s = \alpha(s)[x_s - x^*_s]^2. \tag{9}$$

Criteria of practical importance need not always be simple, and generalizations relating to other criteria would therefore be of interest.

The formulation of the optimum strategy problem in terms of risks is not the only one in existence. There exist a number of studies in which closed systems are investigated from the point of view of the information theory (see, for example, R. L. Dobrushin's paper [20]). As the primary aim of a control system does not lie in transmitting information but in designing required processes, the formulation of the problem in the language of statistical decisions fits in better with the intrinsic nature of the problem.

6) All the quantities occurring in the sth cycle will be regarded as scalar. Our object, therefore, has only a single input v and a single output x. The exposition becomes more involved with generalizations relating to objects with several inputs and outputs (see Part IV).

7) We assume that the manner by which the signal and the noise are combined in H*, H, or G blocks is

known and invariable, and that the blocks are memoryless. Thus,

$$\begin{aligned} v &= v(u, g), \\ y^* &= y^*(h^*, x^*), \\ y &= y(h, x). \end{aligned} \tag{10}$$

Therefore, the conditional probabilities $P(y^*|x^*)$ and $P(y|x)$ and $P(v|u)$ make sense.

8) We assume that the controlling member A generally possesses a memory and that, moreover, for the sake of generality, the algorithm of its action is a random one, i.e., the part A exhibits random strategy.

We introduce the vectors ($0 \leq s \leq n$):

$$\begin{aligned} \mathbf{u}_s &= (u_0, u_1, \ldots, u_s), \\ \mathbf{y}_s^* &= (y_0^*, y_1^*, \ldots, y_s^*), \\ \mathbf{y}_s &= (y_0, y_1, \ldots, y_s). \end{aligned} \tag{11}$$

The controlling member can now be characterized by the probability densities

$$P_s(u_s) = \Gamma_s(u_s, \mathbf{u}_{s-1}, \mathbf{y}_s^*, \mathbf{y}_{s-1}) \quad (0 \leqslant s \leqslant n). \tag{12}$$

The problem consists in finding a sequence of functions F_s such that the average risk R (see [8]) becomes minimal.

LITERATURE CITED

1. A. N. Kolmogorov "Interpolation and extrapolation of stationary random sequences," Izvest. AN SSSR Ser. Matem. 5, 1 (1941).
2. N. Wiener, Extrapolation, Interpolation, and Smoothing of Stationary Time Series (J. Wiley and Sons, New York, 1949).
3. C. E. Shannon, "A mathematical theory of communication," Bell System Techn. J. 27, 3 (1948).
4. A. Wald, Statistical Decision Functions (J. Wiley and Sons, New York; Chapman and Hall, London, 1950).
5. V. A. Kotel'nikov, Theory of Potential Noise Stability [in Russian] (Gosénergoizdat, 1956).
6. D. Van Meter and D. Middleton, Modern Statistical Approaches to Reception in Communication Theory. Trans. IRE, IT-4 (Sept., 1954).
7. V. S. Pugachev, Theory of Random Functions and Its Applications to Automatic Control [in Russian] (Gostekhizdat, 1957).
8. J. H. Laning, Jr. and R. H. Battin, Random Processes in Automatic Control (McGraw-Hill, New York, 1956).
9. I. E. Kazakov, "An approximate statistical analysis of accuracy of essentially nonlinear systems," Avtomat. i Telemekh. 17, 5 (1956).*
10. M. V. Meerov, The Synthesis of Networks of Automatic Control Systems of High Accuracy [in Russian] (Fizmatgiz, 1959).
11. R. Bellman and R. Kalaba, On Communication Processes Involving Learning and Random Duration. IRE National Convention Record, Part 4 (1959).
12. R. Bellman and R. Kalaba, On Adaptive Control Processes. IRE National Convention Record, Part 4 (1959).
13. M. Freimar, A Dynamic Programming Approach to Adaptive Control Processes. IRE National Convention Record, Part 4 (1959).
14. A. A. Fel'dbaum, Computers in Automatic Systems [in Russian] (Fizmatgiz, 1959).
15. A. A. Fel'dbaum, Problems of statistical theory of automatic optimization, Proc. of the 1st. International Congress of Automatic Control (IFAC) [in Russian] (Moscow, 1960).
16. D. Blackwell and M. A. Girshick, Theory of Games and Statistical Decisions [Russian translation] (IL, 1959).
17. C. K. Chow, An Optimum Character Recognition System Using Decision Functions. IRE Trans. EC-6, No. 4 (1957).
18. R. Bellman, "Dynamic programming and stochastic control processes," Information and Control 1, 3 (Sept., 1958).
19. L. S. Schwartz, B. Harris, and A. Hauptschein, Information Rate from the Viewpoint of Inductive Probability. IRE National Convention Record, Part 4 (1959).
20. R. L. Dobrushin, "Transmission of information in channels with feedback," Teor. Ver. i ee Prim. 3, 4 (1958).

*See English translation.

DUAL CONTROL THEORY. II

A. A. Fel'dbaum

Moscow

Translated from Avtomatika i Telemekhanika, Vol. 21, No. 11,
pp. 1453-1464 , November, 1960
Original article submitted March 23, 1960

Basic formulas are derived and the optimum control algorithm is determined in the general case, first for an open-loop and then for a closed-loop nonlinear system of dual control [1].

Similarities and differences between the solutions for open and closed systems are indicated.

1. Derivation of the Risk Formula in Open-Loop Systems

We start first by deriving the formulas for an open system shown in Fig. 1. This is done to demonstrate certain methods which have led to the obtained results; also to compare certain characteristics of the open and closed systems. The open system is basically more simple than the closed one, and this makes the derivation of the formulas easier in the former case.

The problem is stated as follows [1]: all quantities are functions of discrete time at the time moments 0, 1, ..., s, ..., n, where n is fixed. The input is

$$x_s^* = x_s^*(s, \boldsymbol{\lambda}), \tag{1}$$

where $\boldsymbol{\lambda}$ is the parameter vector

$$\boldsymbol{\lambda} = (\lambda_1, \ldots, \lambda_q) \tag{2}$$

with an a priori probability density $P_0(\boldsymbol{\lambda}) = P(\boldsymbol{\lambda})$. The input x* becomes mixed with noise h* in the channel or system H*, at whose output y* is obtained. Statistical properties of the noise, and the method of combining the signal and the noise in H* are known. Consequently the conditional probability $P(y^*_s/x^*_s)$ is also known, being identical for all s, as the probability density $P(h^*_s)$ of the noise is assumed as not varying with s*.

The characteristic of the controlled object B is given by the formula

$$x_s = F_0(z_s, v_s), \tag{3}$$

where F_0 is a known function, and

$$z_s = z_s(s, \boldsymbol{\mu}), \tag{4}$$

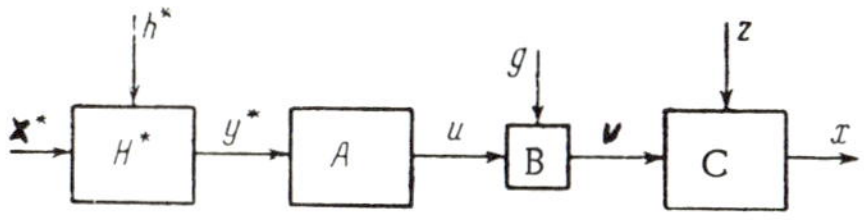

Fig. 1

in which $\boldsymbol{\mu}$ is the parameter vector

$$\boldsymbol{\mu} = (\mu_1, \mu_2, \ldots, \mu_m) \tag{5}$$

with given a priori probability density $P_0(\boldsymbol{\mu}) = P(\boldsymbol{\mu})$. The quantity v_s is obtained at the output of the channel G, in which quantity u_s is mixed in a known manner with the noise g_s, whose probability density $P(g_s)$ does not vary with s. Thus, the conditional probability density $P(v_s | u_s)$ is also known. It is now required to find such a sequence of probability densities $\Gamma_s(u_s | \mathbf{y}^*_{s-1})$, that the average risk, that is, the mathematical expectation of the quantity

$$W = \sum_{s=0}^{s=n} W_s(s, x_s^*, x_s), \tag{6}$$

will be minimum.

Therefore, the minimum of the quantity

$$R = M\{W\} = \sum_{s=0}^{s=n} M\{W_s\} = \sum_{s=0}^{s=n} R_s \tag{7}$$

is required. The function Γ_s is the required algorithm of the controlling member A.

Further notation is introduced. Let $P(x_s | u_s)$ be the conditional probability density of x_s with given u_s. This function can be computed from the formulas (3) and (4), when the probability density $P(\boldsymbol{\mu})$ is known. In addition, let $P(\mathbf{y}^*_{s-1} | \mathbf{x}^*_{s-1})$ be the conditional probability density of the vector

$$\mathbf{y}_{s-1} = (y_0^*, y_1^*, \ldots, y_{s-1}^*) \tag{8}$$

when the vector

$$\mathbf{x}_{s-1}^* = (x_0^*, x_1^*, \ldots, x_{s-1}^*) \tag{9}$$

is known.

It follows from the properties of the channel H* that

$$P(\mathbf{y}_{s-1}^* | \mathbf{x}_{s-1}^*) = \prod_{i=0}^{i=s-1} P(y_i^* \mid x_i^*). \tag{10}$$

* All external noises are regarded as independent.

The vector $\mathbf{x}^*_{s-1}$ depends on s and $\boldsymbol{\lambda}$, and therefore $P(\mathbf{y}^*_{s-1} | \mathbf{x}^*_{s-1})$ depends also on s and $\boldsymbol{\lambda}$.

We denote by $\Omega(x_s, v_s, u_s, \mathbf{y}^*_{s-1})$ the region of variation of the parameters x_s, v_s, u_s, $\mathbf{y}^*_{s-1}$. An infinitely small element of this region is denoted by

$$d\Omega(x_s, v_s, u_s, \mathbf{y}^*_{s-1}) = dx_s\, dv_s\, du_s\, dy^*_0 \ldots dy^*_{s-1}. \quad (11)$$

At first we shall write down the expression for the conditional partial risk r_s at the sth moment, understanding by the latter the magnitude of the risk R_s when the vector $\mathbf{x}^*_s$ is kept fixed or, what amounts to the same, when the vector $\boldsymbol{\lambda}$ remains fixed. Then

$$r_s = M\{W_s | \mathbf{x}^*_s\} = \int_{\Omega(x_s, v_s, u_s, \mathbf{y}^*_{s-1})} W_s(s, x^*_s, x_s) P(x_s | v_s) \times P(v_s | u_s) \Gamma_s(u_s | \mathbf{y}^*_{s-1}) P(\mathbf{y}^*_{s-1} | \mathbf{x}^*_{s-1})\, d\Omega(x_s, v_s, u_s, \mathbf{y}^*_{s-1}). \quad (12)$$

Let $\Omega(\boldsymbol{\lambda})$ be the region of variation of the vector $\boldsymbol{\lambda}$ and $d\Omega(\boldsymbol{\lambda})$ an infinitely small element of it. The partial risk R_s is given by the formula

$$R_s = \int_{\Omega(\boldsymbol{\lambda})} r_s P(\boldsymbol{\lambda})\, d\Omega(\boldsymbol{\lambda}) = \int_{\Omega(x_s, u_s, v_s, \mathbf{y}^*_{s-1}, \lambda)} W_s(s, x^*_s, x_s) P(x_s | v_s) \times P(v_s | u_s) \Gamma_s(u_s | \mathbf{y}^*_{s-1}) P(\mathbf{y}_{s-1} | \mathbf{x}^*_{s-1}) P(\boldsymbol{\lambda})\, d\Omega(x_s, u_s, v_s, \mathbf{y}_{s-1}, \boldsymbol{\lambda}) =$$

$$= \int_{\Omega(x_s, u_s, v_s, \mathbf{y}_{s-1})} P(x_s | v_s) P(v_s | u_s) \Gamma_s(u_s | \mathbf{y}^*_{s-1}) \left\{ \int_{\Omega(\lambda)} W_s[s, x^*_s(s, \boldsymbol{\lambda}), x_s] \times P(\mathbf{y}^*_{s-1} | \mathbf{x}^*_{s-1}) P(\boldsymbol{\lambda})\, d\Omega(\boldsymbol{\lambda}) \right\} d\Omega(x_s, u_s, v_s, \mathbf{y}^*_{s-1}). \quad (13)$$

The expression in the braces represents an integral over the region $\Omega(\boldsymbol{\lambda})$, as W_s and $P(\mathbf{y}^*_{s-1} | \mathbf{x}^*_{s-1})$ generally depend on $\boldsymbol{\lambda}$. Having performed the integration, we obtain a function ρ_s in the braces depending on x_s, s, $\mathbf{y}^*_{s-1}$. The dependence on s is shown in the index s, and therefore one can write

$$\rho_s = \rho_s(x_s, \mathbf{y}^*_{s-1}) = \int_{\Omega(\lambda)} W_s[s, x^*_s(s, \boldsymbol{\lambda}), x_s] \cdot P(\mathbf{y}^*_{s-1} | \mathbf{x}^*_{s-1}) P(\boldsymbol{\lambda})\, d\Omega(\boldsymbol{\lambda}). \quad (14)$$

Then

$$R_s = \int_{\Omega(x_s, v_s, u_s, \mathbf{y}^*_{s-1})} P(x_s | v_s) P(v_s | u_s) \Gamma_s(u_s | \mathbf{y}^*_{s-1}) \times \rho_s(x_s, \mathbf{y}^*_{s-1})\, d\Omega(x_s, v_s, u_s, \mathbf{y}^*_{s-1}). \quad (15)$$

From (7) the total risk R is determined from the expression

$$R = \sum_{s=0}^{s=n} R_s = \sum_{s=0}^{s=n} \int_{\Omega(x_s, v_s, u_s, \mathbf{y}^*_{s-1})} P(x_s | v_s) P(v_s | u_s) \times \Gamma_s(u_s | \mathbf{y}^*_{s-1}) \rho_s(x_s, \mathbf{y}^*_{s-1})\, d\Omega(x_s, v_s, u_s, \mathbf{y}^*_{s-1}). \quad (16)$$

The functions Γ_s are to be selected in such a way that the value of R is a minimum.

2. Determination of Optimum Strategy for Open-Loop Systems

It can be seen from the formula (16) that the selection of functions Γ_s for fixed s only affects the component R_s corresponding to the sth time moment. In this way the total risk is identical with action risk and one is allowed to select Γ_s such that it minimizes a single R_s in (15). As the function Γ_s represents probability density, we have

$$\int_{\Omega(u_s)} \Gamma_s(u_s)\, d\Omega(u_s) = 1. \quad (17)$$

The expression for R(s) is rewritten as follows:

$$R_s = \int_{\Omega(u_s, \mathbf{y}^*_{s-1})} \Gamma_s(u_s | \mathbf{y}^*_{s-1}) \left\{ \int_{\Omega(x_s, v_s)} P(x_s | v_s) P(v_s | u_s) \times \rho_s(x_s, \mathbf{y}^*_{s-1})\, d\Omega(x_s, v_s) \right\} d\Omega(u_s, \mathbf{y}^*_{s-1}). \quad (18)$$

The integral in the braces represents a function of u_s and $\mathbf{y}^*_{s-1}$ which we shall denote by $\xi_s(u_s, \mathbf{y}^*_{s-1})$, that is,

$$\xi_s(u_s, \mathbf{y}^*_{s-1}) = \int_{\Omega(x_s, v_s)} P(x_s | v_s) P(v_s | u_s) \rho_s(x_s, \mathbf{y}^*_{s-1})\, d\Omega(x_s, v_s). \quad (19)$$

Then

$$R_s = \int_{\Omega(\mathbf{y}^*_{s-1})} I(\mathbf{y}^*_{s-1})\, d\Omega(\mathbf{y}^*_{s-1}),$$

where

$$I(\mathbf{y}^*_{s-1}) = \int_{\Omega(u_s)} \Gamma_s(u_s | \mathbf{y}^*_{s-1}) \xi_s(u_s, \mathbf{y}^*_{s-1})\, d\Omega(u_s) = (\xi_s)_{av} \int_{\Omega(u_s)} \Gamma_s(u_s | \mathbf{y}^*_{s-1})\, d\Omega(u_s) = (\xi_s)_{av} \geqslant (\xi_s)_{min}. \quad (20)$$

One can take the average value $(\xi_s)_{av}$ outside the integration in accordance with the integral mean value theorem. The function Γ_s represents probability density and hence its integral over the region $\Omega(u_s)$ equals unity.

It follows from the expression (20) that a minimum value of $I(\mathbf{y}^*_{s-1})$ is $(\xi_s)_{min}$. It is not difficult to show that I attains this value if the function Γ_s is chosen accordingly. In fact, let u^*_s be the value of u_s corresponding to the minimum (for instance, the least of all local minima) of the function $\xi_s(u_s)$ in the region $\Omega(u_s)$. We assume that such a value exists either within or on the boundary of the region.

Consider the function

$$\Gamma_s(u_s) = \delta(u_s - u^*_s), \tag{21}$$

where δ is the unit impulse function (otherwise Dirac's δ-function). Formula (21) provides the optimum algorithm of the member A, as substituting (21) into the left-hand side of (20) and using a well-known property of δ-function, we find

$$I = \int_{\Omega(u_s)} \Gamma_s(u_s \mid \mathbf{y}^*_{s-1})\, \xi_s(u_s, \mathbf{y}^*_{s-1})\, d\Omega(u_s) =$$

$$= \int_{\Omega(u_s)} \delta(u_s - u^*_s)\, \xi_s(u_s, \mathbf{y}^*_{s-1})\, d\Omega(u_s) =$$

$$= \xi_s(u^*_s) = \min_{u_s \in \Omega(u_s)} \xi_s(u_s) = (I)\min \tag{22}$$

The minimum values of I for each $\mathbf{y}^*_{s-1}$ provide also the minimum of R_s.

Thus, the optimum strategy, as seen from the formula (21), does not prove random but regular. The value of u_s should be taken as equal to a u^*_s. As seen from the formula (20), the value u^*_s which minimizes the function $\xi_s(u_s, \mathbf{y}^*_{s-1})$ depends on $\mathbf{y}^*_{s-1}$. In other words, as

$$\xi_s(u^*_s, \mathbf{y}^*_{s-1}) = \min, \tag{23}$$

the quantity u^*_s is a function of $\mathbf{y}^*_{s-1}$:

$$u^*_s = u^*_s(\mathbf{y}^*_{s-1}). \tag{24}$$

This makes also the function Γ_s in the formula (21) depend on $\mathbf{y}^*_{s-1}$:

$$\Gamma_s = \delta(u_s - u^*_s) = \delta[u_s - u^*_s(\mathbf{y}^*_{s-1})]. \tag{25}$$

Thus, the optimum strategy proves regular; it is determined in the general case from all the preceding

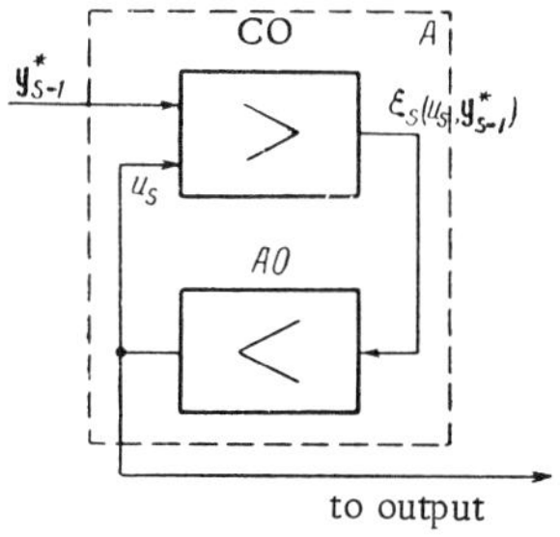

Fig. 2

values of y^*_i ($i = 0, \ldots, s-1$). It should be shown that the regularity of the optimum decisions occurs in a wide group of problems in Wald's general theory of statistical decisions.

The integral $\xi_s(u_s, \mathbf{y}^*_{s-1})$ can be evaluated with the aid of a computer CO (Fig. 2). The block diagram of the optimum controlling member can then be represented as shown in Fig. 2. The automatic optimizer AO selects a value u_s such that ξ_s becomes least. This value is now sent to the output of the block A. Were it possible to determine the value of u^*_s analytically as a function of $\mathbf{y}^*_{s-1}$, the block A could be constructed differently. However, the formula for $\xi_s(u_s, \mathbf{y}^*_{s-1})$ is as a rule most difficult to obtain explicitly and that is why the computer CO must perform automatically the integrations with respect to x_s and v_s, as shown in the formula (18). In this way the minimization of the integral ξ_s can be achieved directly.

3. Derivation of Risk Formula for Closed-Loop Systems

Consider now a block diagram of a closed system shown in Fig. 3. In order to simplify the exposition we neglect the interference h^* in the channel H^* (see, for example, Fig. 1 or Fig. 3 of [1]); x^* is thus assumed known. It was shown previously how the interference h^* should be taken into consideration, and should such a need arise, this can be done without any real difficulties. Our notation remains the same. In addition, there is also the feedback channel H with interference h_s which has a constant in time density distribution $P(h_s)$.

The way in which the signal and noise combine in the channel H is given and the conditional probability density $P(y_s \mid x_s)$ can therefore be found, and consequently the conditional probability density

$$P(\mathbf{y}_s \mid \mathbf{x}_s) = \prod_{i=0}^{i=s} P(y_s \mid x_s). \tag{26}$$

In a closed system it is necessary to take into account also the vectors

$$\begin{aligned} \mathbf{x}^*_s &= (x^*_0, x^*_1, \ldots, x^*_s), \\ \mathbf{y}_s &= (y_0, y_1, \ldots, y_s), \\ \mathbf{u}_s &= (u_0, u_1, \ldots, u_s), \\ \mathbf{v}_s &= (v_0, v_1, \ldots, v_s), \\ \mathbf{x}_s &= (x_0, x_1, \ldots, x_s). \end{aligned} \tag{27}$$

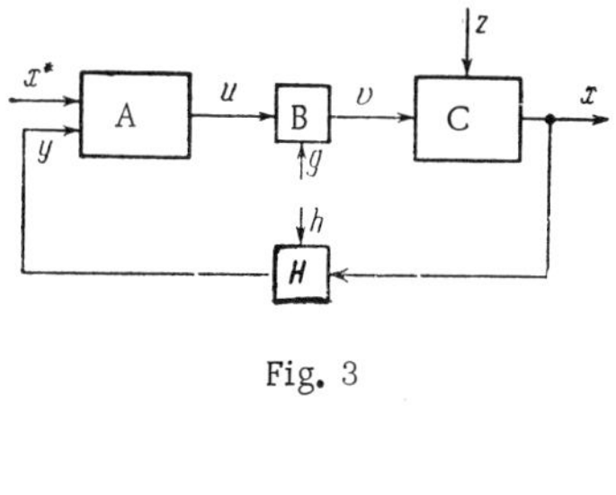

Fig. 3

The determination of the optimum controlling member A is reducible to the determination of its strategy, random in the general case, ensuring the minimizing of the risk R. The function $\Gamma_s(u_s \mid \mathbf{x}_s^*, \mathbf{y}_{s-1}, \mathbf{u}_{s-1})$, is assumed to represent random strategy, that is, the conditional probability density of u_s when the vectors $\mathbf{x}_s^*$, $\mathbf{y}_{s-1}$, and $\mathbf{u}_{s-1}$ remain fixed. Now Γ_s is a function of $\mathbf{x}_s^*$, $\mathbf{y}_{s-1}$, and $\mathbf{u}_s$.

First we shall write down the expression for the conditional partial risk r_s and we shall now understand by it the risk R_s when all the preceding motions of the system A are known, that is, when the vectors $\mathbf{x}_s^*$, $\mathbf{y}_{s-1}$, and $\mathbf{u}_{s-1}$ are fixed. Thus,

$$r_s = M\{W_s \mid \mathbf{x}_s^*, \mathbf{y}_{s-1}; \mathbf{u}_{s-1}\} =$$

$$= \int_{\Omega(x_s, v_s, u_s)} W_s(s, x_s^*, x_s) P_s(x_s \mid v_s) \times$$

$$\times P(v_s \mid u_s) \Gamma_s(u_s \mid \mathbf{x}_s^*, \mathbf{y}_{s-1}, \mathbf{u}_{s-1}) \, d\Omega(x_s, v_s, u_s). \tag{28}$$

In this formula $P_s(x_s \mid v_s)$ is understood to represent the conditional probability density of the output $\underline{x}$ from the object B when its input $\underline{v}$ is known; as shown below, this probability need not be the same for different $\underline{s}$.

If one considers the values of r_s corresponding to different trials of the system, then generally speaking the vectors $\mathbf{u}_{s-1}$ and $\mathbf{y}_{s-1}$, not known beforehand, can for different trials assume different values. Therefore, in computing the average partial risk R_s it is necessary, when averaging r_s, to take into account the joint probability distributions $P(\mathbf{u}_{s-1}, \mathbf{y}_{s-1})$ of the vectors $\mathbf{u}_{s-1}$ and $\mathbf{y}_{s-1}$, which in the general case are not statistically independent of one another. Thus,

$$R_s = M\{r_s\} =$$

$$= \int_{\Omega(x_s, v_s, u_s, \mathbf{y}_{s-1})} W_s(s, x_s^*, x_s) P_s(x_s \mid v_s) P(v_s \mid u_s) \times$$

$$\times \Gamma_s(u_s \mid \mathbf{x}_{s-1}^*, \mathbf{u}_{s-1}, \mathbf{y}_{s-1}) P(\mathbf{u}_{s-1}, \mathbf{y}_{s-1})$$

$$d\Omega(x_s, v_s, \mathbf{u}_s, \mathbf{y}_{s-1}). \tag{29}$$

The values of the quantities u_i and y_i ($i = 0, \ldots, s-1$) are memorized in the controlling member A. Thus the input and the output of B are known — admittedly not exactly, but with some error due to the presence of $\underline{g}$ and $\underline{h}$, the input and the output interference respectively. This knowledge enables one to obtain a more accurate probability density of the parameter vector $\boldsymbol{\mu}$ on which in turn depends the interference z_s acting on the object B. The better $\boldsymbol{\mu}$ is known, the more fully determined is the method of regulating the object. One can derive a Bayesian formula in order to determine the a posteriori probability density of vector $\boldsymbol{\mu}$ in the $\underline{s}$th beat. Consider the probability density† $P(\boldsymbol{\mu}, \mathbf{u}_{s-1}, \mathbf{y}_{s-1})$ of a joint event consisting in a simultaneous occurrence of the vectors $\boldsymbol{\mu}$, $\mathbf{u}_{s-1}$ and $\mathbf{y}_{s-1}$. Let $P(\mathbf{u}_{s-1}, \mathbf{y}_{s-1} \mid \boldsymbol{\mu})$ be the conditional joint probability density of the vectors $\mathbf{u}_{s-1}$ and $\mathbf{y}_{s-1}$ when $\boldsymbol{\mu}$ is kept fixed and $P(\boldsymbol{\mu} \mid \mathbf{u}_{s-1}, \mathbf{y}_{s-1})$ is the conditional probability density of $\boldsymbol{\mu}$ when the vectors $\mathbf{u}_{s-1}$ and $\mathbf{y}_{s-1}$ are fixed. The latter is the required a posteriori probability density of the vector $\boldsymbol{\mu}$. Then, of course,

$$P(\boldsymbol{\mu}, \mathbf{u}_{s-1}, \mathbf{y}_{s-1}) = P(\mathbf{u}_{s-1}, \mathbf{y}_{s-1} \mid \boldsymbol{\mu}) P(\boldsymbol{\mu}) =$$

$$P(\boldsymbol{\mu} \mid \mathbf{u}_{s-1}, \mathbf{y}_{s-1}) P(\mathbf{u}_{s-1}, \mathbf{y}_{s-1}). \tag{30}$$

$P(\boldsymbol{\mu})$ denotes the a priori probability density of vector $\boldsymbol{\mu}$. Hence the formula is obtained giving the a posteriori probability density of vector $\boldsymbol{\mu}$:

$$P(\boldsymbol{\mu} \mid \mathbf{u}_{s-1}, \mathbf{y}_{s-1}) = \frac{P(\boldsymbol{\mu}) P(\mathbf{u}_{s-1}, \mathbf{y}_{s-1} \mid \boldsymbol{\mu})}{P(\mathbf{u}_{s-1}, \mathbf{y}_{s-1})} =$$

$$= \frac{P(\boldsymbol{\mu}) P(\mathbf{u}_{s-1}, \mathbf{y}_{s-1} \mid \boldsymbol{\mu})}{\int_{\Omega(\boldsymbol{\mu})} P(\mathbf{u}_{s-1}, \mathbf{y}_{s-1} \mid \boldsymbol{\mu}) P(\boldsymbol{\mu}) \, d\Omega(\boldsymbol{\mu})}. \tag{31}$$

In the latter formula $\Omega(\boldsymbol{\mu})$ denotes the range of variability of vector $\boldsymbol{\mu}$ and $d\Omega(\boldsymbol{\mu})$ its infinitely small element.

In formula (31) a special role is played by the likelihood function $P(\mathbf{u}_{s-1}, \mathbf{y}_{s-1} \mid \boldsymbol{\mu})$. The probability densities of quantities are called likelihood functions when the vector $\boldsymbol{\mu}$, whose values are subject to hypothesis testing, is kept fixed. We obtain the likelihood function for the closed-loop system shown in Fig. 3. Obviously, we have

$$P(\mathbf{u}_{s-1}, \mathbf{y}_{s-1} \mid \boldsymbol{\mu}) = P(u_0, y_0 \mid \boldsymbol{\mu}) P(u_1, y_1 \mid \boldsymbol{\mu}, u_0, y_0) \times$$

$$\times P(u_2, y_2 \mid \boldsymbol{\mu}, \mathbf{u}_1, \mathbf{y}_1) \ldots P(u_{s-1}, y_{s-1} \mid \boldsymbol{\mu}, \mathbf{u}_{s-2}, \mathbf{y}_{s-2}). \tag{32}$$

A typical factor on the right-hand side is a probability density

$$P(u_i, y_i \mid \boldsymbol{\mu}, \mathbf{u}_{i-1}, \mathbf{y}_{i-1}) =$$

$$= P(y_i \mid \boldsymbol{\mu}, u_i, \mathbf{u}_{i-1}, \mathbf{y}_{i-1}) P(u_i \mid \boldsymbol{\mu}, \mathbf{u}_{i-1}, \mathbf{y}_{i-1}) =$$

$$= P(y_i \mid \boldsymbol{\mu}, i, u_i) P(u_i \mid \boldsymbol{\mu}, \mathbf{u}_{i-1}, \mathbf{y}_{i-1}) =$$

$$= P(y_i \mid \boldsymbol{\mu}, i, u_i) \Gamma_i(u_i \mid \mathbf{u}_{i-1}, \mathbf{y}_{i-1}). \tag{33}$$

Thus $P(y_i \mid \boldsymbol{\mu}, u_i, \mathbf{u}_{i-1}, \mathbf{y}_{i-1})$ depends neither on $\mathbf{u}_{i-1}$ nor on $\mathbf{y}_{i-1}$, but only on $\boldsymbol{\mu}$, on the beat index $\underline{i}$ and on the value of u_i. In addition, $P(u_i \mid \boldsymbol{\mu}, \mathbf{u}_{i-1}, \mathbf{y}_{i-1})$ does not depend on $\boldsymbol{\mu}$ but only on $\mathbf{u}_{i-1}$ and $\mathbf{y}_{i-1}$ and this is precisely the stochastic algorithm Γ_i of the controlling member A.

†In a number of subsequent formulas the dependence of the probability density on $\mathbf{x}_s^*$ is not stated explicitly but it is always implied.

By substituting the expression (33) into (32) we find that

$$P(\mathbf{u}_{s-1}, \mathbf{y}_{s-1} \mid \boldsymbol{\mu}) = \left[\prod_{i=0}^{s-1} P(y_i \mid \boldsymbol{\mu}, i, u_i)\right]$$

$$\left[\prod_{i=1}^{s-1} \Gamma_i(u_i \mid \mathbf{u}_{i-1}, \mathbf{y}_{i-1})\right] P_0(u_0). \qquad (34)$$

Here $P_0(u_0)$ is the initial probability density of $\underline{u}$ which also should be given.

Now one is able to substitute the likelihood function obtained in (34) into the a posteriori probability density formula (31). We obtain

$$P_s(\boldsymbol{\mu}) = P(\boldsymbol{\mu} \mid \mathbf{u}_{s-1}, \mathbf{y}_{s-1}) =$$

$$P(\boldsymbol{\mu}) \frac{\left[\prod_{i=0}^{s-1} P(y_i \mid \boldsymbol{\mu}, i, u_i)\right] \prod_{i=0}^{s-1} \Gamma_i}{P(\mathbf{u}_{s-1}, \mathbf{y}_{s-1})}. \qquad (35)$$

In the above formula the following notation has been introduced:

$$\Gamma_0 = P_0(u_0). \qquad (36)$$

Knowing the a posteriori probability density $P_s(\boldsymbol{\mu})$ one is able to determine more precisely the expression of the probability density $P_s(x_s \mid v_s)$ which appears in the formula (29). From the formulas (3) and (4) we find that

$$x_s = F_0(z_s, v_s) = F(s, \boldsymbol{\mu}, v_s). \qquad (37)$$

The quantities $\underline{s}$ and v_s which appear in the function F are parameters. This formula enables one to find the conditional probability density $P_s(x_s \mid v_s)$ when $P_s(\boldsymbol{\mu})$ is known.

Since

$$\int_{(\Omega v_s)} P_s(x_s \mid v_s) P(v_s \mid u_s) d\Omega(v_s) = P_s(x_s \mid u_s) =$$

$$= \int_{\Omega(\boldsymbol{\mu})} P(x_s \mid \boldsymbol{\mu}, u_s) P_s(\boldsymbol{\mu}) d\Omega(\boldsymbol{\mu}), \qquad (38)$$

the expression (29) giving R_s can be re-written in the following way:

$$R_s = \int_{\Omega(x_s, \mathbf{u}_s, \mathbf{y}_{s-1})} W_s(s, x_s^*, x_s)$$

$$\left[\int_{\Omega(v_s)} P_s(x_s \mid v_s) P(v_s \mid u_s) d\Omega(v_s)\right] \times$$

$$\times \Gamma_s(u_s \mid \mathbf{x}^*_{s-1}, \mathbf{u}_{s-1}, \mathbf{y}_{s-1})$$

$$P(\mathbf{u}_{s-1}, \mathbf{y}_{s-1}) d\Omega(x_s, \mathbf{u}_s, \mathbf{y}_{s-1}) =$$

$$= \int_{\Omega(x_s, \boldsymbol{\mu}, \mathbf{u}_s, \mathbf{y}_{s-1})} W_s(s, x^*_s, x_s) P(x_s \mid \boldsymbol{\mu}, u_s)$$

$$P_s(\boldsymbol{\mu}) \Gamma_s(u_s \mid \mathbf{x}^*_{s-1}, \mathbf{u}_{s-1}, \mathbf{y}_{s-1}) \times$$

$$\times P(\mathbf{u}_{s-1}, \mathbf{y}_{s-1}) d\Omega(x_s, \boldsymbol{\mu}, \mathbf{u}_s, \mathbf{y}_{s-1}). \qquad (39)$$

Substituting the formula (35) for $P_s(\boldsymbol{\mu})$ and cancelling $P(\mathbf{u}_{s-1}, \mathbf{y}_{s-1})$ we obtain

$$R_s = \int_{\Omega(x_s, \boldsymbol{\mu}, \mathbf{u}_s, \mathbf{y}_{s-1})} W_s(s, x_s^*, x_s) P(x_s \mid \boldsymbol{\mu}, u_s) P(\boldsymbol{\mu}) \times$$

$$\times \prod_{i=0}^{s-1} P(y_i \mid \boldsymbol{\mu}, i, u_i) \prod_{i=0}^{s} \Gamma_i d\Omega(x_s, \boldsymbol{\mu}, \mathbf{u}_s, \mathbf{y}_{s-1}). \qquad (40)$$

The total risk is given by

$$R = \sum_{s=0}^{s=n} R_s = \sum_{s=0}^{s=n} \int_{\Omega(x_s, \boldsymbol{\mu}, \mathbf{u}_s, \mathbf{y}_{s-1})}$$

$$W_s(s, x_s^*, x_s) P(x_s \mid \boldsymbol{\mu}, u_s) P(\boldsymbol{\mu}) \times$$

$$\times \prod_{i=0}^{s-1} P(y_i \mid \boldsymbol{\mu}, i, u_i) \prod_{i=0}^{s} \Gamma_i d\Omega(x_s, \boldsymbol{\mu}, \mathbf{u}_s, \mathbf{y}_{s-1}). \qquad (41)$$

Let us compare the expressions (16) and (41) of risks in open and closed systems. In the formula (16) only the $\underline{s}$th component R_s was influenced by the function Γ_s; the total risk associated with Γ_s was exclusively an action risk. In the formula (41), however, the function Γ_s influenced not only the term R_s (action risk) but also all the other components R_i where $i > s$. As regards Γ_s, the sum $\sum_{i=s+1}^{n} R_i$ represents the investigation risk. In fact, the selection of Γ_s influences the character of the process in the subsequent beats, as it causes either a better or a worse investigation of the characteristics of the object B; the latter amounts to the determination of the probability density $P_s(\boldsymbol{\mu})$. Thus the total risk regarded as a function of Γ_s ($0 \leq s \leq n$) represents the sum of the action risk and the investigation risk. As regards Γ_n only a single action risk occurs.

When the object B has memory the selection of Γ_s influences not only R_s but also the terms R_i when $i > s$ even when the additional investigation of the object B has not taken place (see Paper IV in this series). Consequently, in this case the action risk is expressed by a more involved formula, and the interconnection between the action and the investigation risks proves also to be more involved.

4. Determination of Optimum Strategy in Closed Systems

It is required to select the functions Γ_i in the formula (41) such that the risk R be minimum. As Γ_i represents probability densities they must satisfy the condition (17).

To be able to select Γ_n we consider the last component R_n of R:

$$R_n = \int_{\Omega(x_n, \boldsymbol{\mu}, \mathbf{u}_n, \mathbf{y}_{n-1})}$$

$$W_n(n, x_n^*, x_n) P(x_n \mid \boldsymbol{\mu}, u_n) P(\boldsymbol{\mu}) \times$$

$$\times \prod_{i=0}^{n-1} P(y_i \mid \boldsymbol{\mu}, i, u_i) \prod_{i=0}^{n-1} \Gamma_i \Gamma_n \, d\Omega(x_n, \boldsymbol{\mu}, \mathbf{u}_n, \mathbf{y}_{n-1}). \qquad (42)$$

We assume that $\Gamma_0, \ldots, \Gamma_{n-1}$ are given, and only Γ_n is to be selected such that R_n becomes minimum provided a constraint as in (17) is satisfied:

$$\int\limits_{\Omega(u_n)} \Gamma_n(u_n, \mathbf{u}_{n-1}, \mathbf{y}_{n-1})\, d\Omega(u_n) = 1. \quad (43)$$

In order to simplify the expression (42), put

$$\alpha_n = \alpha_n(\mathbf{u}_n, \mathbf{y}_{n-1}) =$$

$$= \int\limits_{\Omega(x_n, \mu)} W_n(n, x_n, x_n^*)\, P(x_n \mid \mu, u_n)$$

$$P(\mu) \prod_{i=0}^{n-1} P(y_i \mid \mu, i, u_i)\, d\Omega(x_n, \mu). \quad (44)$$

Further, put

$$\beta_k = \prod_{i=0}^{k} \Gamma_k; \quad (45)$$

then

$$R_n = \int\limits_{\Omega(u_n, \mathbf{u}_{n-1}, \mathbf{y}_{n-1})}$$

$$\alpha_n(u_n, \mathbf{u}_{n-1}, \mathbf{y}_{n-1})\, \beta_{n-1} \Gamma_n\, d\Omega(\mathbf{u}_n, \mathbf{y}_{n-1}) =$$

$$= \int\limits_{\Omega(\mathbf{u}_{n-1}, \mathbf{y}_{n-1})} \beta_{n-1} \varkappa_n(\mathbf{u}_{n-1}, \mathbf{y}_{n-1})\, d\Omega(\mathbf{u}_{n-1}, \mathbf{y}_{n-1}), \quad (46)$$

where

$$\varkappa_n(\mathbf{u}_{n-1}, \mathbf{y}_{n-1}) =$$

$$\int\limits_{\Omega(u_n)} \alpha_n(u_n, \mathbf{u}_{n-1}, \mathbf{y}_{n-1})\, \Gamma_n(u_n, \mathbf{u}_{n-1}, \mathbf{y}_{n-1})\, d\Omega(u_n). \quad (47)$$

If the Γ_n is selected such that for <u>any</u> set of vectors $\mathbf{u}_{n-1}$ and $\mathbf{y}_{n-1}$ the quantity κ_n remains least, then the integral (46) will also be minimum (bearing in mind that the quantity β_{n-1} is assumed known. By regarding the vectors $\mathbf{u}_{n-1}$ and $\mathbf{y}_{n-1}$ in the formulas (44) and (47) as parameters, one is able to find a value u_n^* such that the function α_n is minimum. We put

$$\gamma_n^* = \alpha_n(u_n^*, \mathbf{u}_{n-1}, \mathbf{y}_{n-1}) = \min_{u_n \in \Omega(u_n)} \alpha_n(u_n, \mathbf{u}_{n-1}, \mathbf{y}_{n-1}). \quad (48)$$

The quantity u_n^*, of course, depends on $\mathbf{u}_{n-1}$ and $\mathbf{y}_{n-1}$:

$$u_n^* = u_n^*(\mathbf{u}_{n-1}, \mathbf{y}_{n-1}). \quad (49)$$

Then the optimum function Γ_n satisfying the condition (43) is

$$\Gamma_n(u_n, \mathbf{u}_{n-1}, \mathbf{y}_{n-1}) = \delta(u_n - u_n^*), \quad (50)$$

because in this case

$$\varkappa_n = \alpha_n(u_n^*, \mathbf{u}_{n-1}, \mathbf{y}_{n-1}) = (\alpha_n)_{\min} = (\varkappa_n)_{\min} \quad (51)$$

This follows from the considerations similar to those given above when the conditions (19), (20), and (21) were derived.

Now the optimum function Γ_{n-1} will be determined. Consider the sum of the last two terms R_{n-1} and R_n. First of all, we introduce the function

$$\alpha_k = \alpha_k(u_k, \mathbf{u}_{k-1}, \mathbf{y}_{k-1}) =$$

$$\int\limits_{\Omega(x_k, \mu)} W_k(k, x_k^*, x_k)\, P(x_k \mid \mu, u_k) \times$$

$$\times P(\mu) \prod_{i=0}^{k-1} P(y_i \mid \mu, i, u_i)\, d\Omega(x_k, \mu) \qquad (0 \leqslant k \leqslant n). \quad (52)$$

There the expression $\prod_{i=0}^{k-1} P(y_i \mid \mu, i, u_i)$ equals unity when $k = 0$.

Now the sum of the last two terms becomes

$$S_{n-1} = R_{n-1} + R_n =$$

$$= \int\limits_{\Omega(\mathbf{u}_{n-1}, \mathbf{y}_{n-2})} \alpha_{n-1} \beta_{n-1}\, d\Omega(\mathbf{u}_{n-1}, \mathbf{y}_{n-2}) +$$

$$+ \int\limits_{\Omega(\mathbf{u}_n, \mathbf{y}_{n-1})} \alpha_n \beta_n\, d\Omega(\mathbf{u}_n, \mathbf{y}_{n-1}). \quad (53)$$

When $i \leq n-2$, the Γ_i are assumed to be known and Γ_n is always selected in accordance with the formula (50). Then

$$S_{n-1} = \int\limits_{\Omega(\mathbf{u}_{n-2}, \mathbf{y}_{n-2})} \beta_{n-2} \Bigg\{ \int\limits_{\Omega(u_{u-1})} \Gamma_{n-1} \alpha_{n-1}\, d\Omega(u_{n-1}) +$$

$$+ \int\limits_{\Omega(u_{n-1}, y_{n-1})} \Gamma_{n-1} \alpha_n(u_n^*, \mathbf{u}_{n-1}, \mathbf{y}_{n-1})\, d\Omega(u_{n-1}, y_{n-1}) \Bigg\}. \quad (54)$$

This quantity is least when the expression within the braces is least; we write the latter in full as

$$\varkappa_{n-1}(\mathbf{u}_{n-2}, \mathbf{y}_{n-2}) =$$

$$= \int\limits_{\Omega(u_{n-1})} \Bigg\{ \Gamma_{n-1} \alpha_{n-1} + \int\limits_{\Omega(y_{n-1})}$$

$$\Gamma_{n-1} \alpha_n(u_n^*, \mathbf{u}_{n-1}, \mathbf{y}_{n-1})\, d\Omega(y_{n-1}) \Bigg\} d\Omega(u_{n-1}) =$$

$$= \int\limits_{\Omega(u_{n-1})} \Gamma_{n-1}(u_{n-1}, \mathbf{u}_{n-2}, \mathbf{y}_{n-2}) \times$$

$$\times \Bigg\{ \alpha_{n-1} + \int\limits_{\Omega(y_{n-1})}$$

$$\alpha_n(u_n^*, \mathbf{u}_{n-1}, \mathbf{y}_{n-1})\, d\Omega(y_{n-1}) \Bigg\} d\Omega(u_{n-1}). \quad (55)$$

Now consider the function

$$\gamma_{n-1} = \gamma_{n-1}(\mathbf{u}_{n-1}, \mathbf{y}_{n-2}) = \alpha_{n-1} +$$

$$+ \int\limits_{\Omega(y_{n-1})} \alpha_n(u_n^*, \mathbf{u}_{n-1}, \mathbf{y}_{n-1})\, d\Omega(y_{n-1}). \quad (56)$$

We find the value u_{n-1}^* which is the minimum value of this function. This value obviously depends on $\mathbf{u}_{n-2}$ and $\mathbf{y}_{n-2}$:

$$u_{n-1}^* = u_{n-1}^*(\mathbf{u}_{n-2}, \mathbf{y}_{n-2}). \quad (57)$$

Then the most suitable function Γ_{n-1} such that it ensures the minimum of κ_{n-1} and satisfies the condition (17) will be

$$\Gamma_{n-1}(u_{n-1}, \mathbf{u}_{n-2}, \mathbf{y}_{n-2}) = \delta(u_{n-1} - u^*_{n-1}). \quad (58)$$

By applying analogous arguments one can determine the whole sequence of the functions Γ_i using the following procedure.

We introduce the function

$$\gamma_{n-k} = \alpha_{n-k} + \int\limits_{\Omega(y_{n-k})} \gamma_{n-k+1}(u^*_{n-k+1}, \mathbf{u}_{n-k}, \mathbf{y}_{n-k})\, d\Omega(y_{n-k}), \quad (59)$$

where $\gamma_n = \alpha_n$. Let the minimum of γ_{n-k} over u_{n-k} be denoted by γ^*_{n-k}:

$$\gamma^*_{n-k} = (\gamma_{n-k})_{u_{n-k}=u^*_{n-k}} =$$

$$= \min_{u_{n-k}\in\Omega(u_{n-k})} \gamma_{n-k}(u_{n-k}; \mathbf{u}_{n-k-1}, \mathbf{y}_{n-k-1});$$

$$u^*_{n-k} = u^*_{n-k}(\mathbf{u}_{n-k-1}; \mathbf{y}_{n-k-1}). \quad (60)$$

Then the optimum function Γ^*_{n-k} is given by the formula

$$\Gamma^*_{n-k} = \delta(u_{n-k} - u^*_{n-k}), \quad (61)$$

where δ is the unit impulse function. Then

$$(S_{n-k})_{\min} = \left(\sum_{i=0}^{i=k} R_{n-i}\right)_{\min} =$$

$$= \int\limits_{\Omega(\mathbf{u}_{n-k-1}, \mathbf{y}_{n-k-1})} \beta_{n-k-1}\gamma^*_{n-k}\, d\Omega(\mathbf{u}_{n-k-1}, \mathbf{y}_{n-k-1}). \quad (62)$$

In this way Γ_i are determined when $i = n, n-1, \ldots, 1$. As far as the determination of $\Gamma_0 = P_0(u_0)$ is concerned, this function may be given beforehand and then no selection is required. If the best Γ_0 can be chosen, the selection takes place in accordance with the procedure shown above. When $k = n-1$ we arrive at the formula

$$(S_1)_{\min} = \int\limits_{\Omega(u_0, y_0)} P_0(u_0)\gamma^*_1(u_0, y_0)\, d\Omega(u_0, y_0). \quad (63)$$

The total risk therefore when all Γ_i $(i = 1, \ldots, n)$ are optimal, is expressed by the formula

$$R = R_0 + (S_1)_{\min} =$$

$$= \int\limits_{\Omega(x_0, \mu, u_0)} W_0(0, x^*_0, x_0) P(x_0 \mid \mu, u_0) \times$$

$$\times P(\mu) P_0(u_0)\, d\Omega(x_0, \mu, u_0) +$$

$$+ \int\limits_{\Omega(u_0, y_0)} P_0(u_0)\gamma^*_1(u_0, y_0)\, d\Omega(u_0, y_0) =$$

$$= \int\limits_{\Omega(u_0)} P_0(u_0)\Big[\alpha_0(u_0) +$$

$$+ \int\limits_{\Omega(y_0)} \gamma^*_1(u_0, y_0)\, d\Omega(y_0)\Big]\, d\Omega(u_0), \quad (64)$$

where

$$\alpha_0 = \alpha_0(u_0) =$$

$$= \int\limits_{\Omega(x_0, \mu)} W_0(0, x^*_0, x_0) P(x_0 \mid \mu, u_0) P(\mu)\, d\Omega(x_0, \mu). \quad (65)$$

We put

$$\gamma_0 = \gamma_0(u_0) = \alpha_0(u_0) + \int\limits_{\Omega(y_0)} \gamma^*_1(u_0, y_0)\, d\Omega(y_0). \quad (66)$$

It can be seen from the formula (64) that the quantity R becomes minimum when

$$\Gamma_0 = P_0(u_0) = \Gamma^*_0 = \delta(u_0 - u^*_0), \quad (67)$$

where the value u^*_0 makes the function $\gamma(u_0)$ minimum.

The value u^*_0 is dependent on the a priori probabilities, also generally on the given data, but not on observations which are not available at the initial moment of time.

Thus in the case of a closed system as well, the optimum strategy proves to be not random but a regular one. This conclusion is naturally valid within the bounds of the limitations accepted when formulating this theory.

The determination of sequence of functions γ_{n-k} may prove rather tedious in actual examples if electronic computers are not used. Even so, it has only been possible so far to solve only relatively simple problems in which the memory capacity necessary to memorize the functions is not too great.

The obtained system with the optimum control algorithm Γ^*_i is, generally speaking, a dual control system in which the u_i serve not only as directing but also as investigating operations. In the absence of investigation, the probability density $P_s(\mu)$ would remain equal to $P_0(\mu)$ and the investigation risk would be null.

It may happen that in a partidular case of a dual control system the process of investigating the object proceeds in the same way, no matter what the values of the regulating operations within the admissible bandwidth; what is only required is that the regulating operations take place. Such a system (an example is given in the next paper) is called neutral. In a neutral system the investigation risk is independent of the quantity u_i, but $P_s(\mu)$ is not identical with $P_0(\mu)$ but varies with s.

LITERATURE CITED

1. A. A. Fel'dbaum, "Theory of dual control. I," Avtomat. i Telemekh. 21, No. 9 (1960). ‡

‡See English translation.

THE THEORY OF DUAL CONTROL. III

A. A. Fel'dbaum

Translated from Avtomatika i Telemekhanika, Vol. 22, No. 1,
pp. 3-16, January, 1961
Original article submitted April 18, 1960

We shall study two examples of the synthesis of an optimal system for dual control. In the first example, we study a system of automatic stabilization with a linear object in which the performance criterion is the mean-square error. In the second example, we study an automatic system which searches for the minimal output value for an object that has a parabolic characteristic. The analysis is performed on the basis of the theory presented in the preceding papers [1,2] in this series.

Remarks on the Synthesis of Optimal Dual-Control Systems

In [1,2] we formulated the statement of the problem for the case of synthesizing optimal dual-control systems, and presented a general method for solving this problem. In the analysis below we study examples of the application of the general theory to individual problems.

The method of solution consists of formulating a series of functions γ_{n-k} ($k = 0, 1, \ldots, n$), and finding those values u^*_{n-k} of the control input which minimize the functions γ_{n-k}. Assume the minimal value of the function γ_{n-k} with respect to u_{n-k} is denoted by γ^*_{n-k}. The function γ_{n-k-1} is formed from γ^*_{n-k} by integrating the output value y_{n-k} of the object which is measured by the control unit, and by adding the function α_{n-k-1}. Thus, the scheme for the basic computations involves a series of alternate integrations and minimizations which is clearly depicted in Fig. 1.* The results of the computations are the optimal inputs u^*_s.

In order to find the optimal control input u^*_0 at the initial instant $t = 0$, it is necessary to pass through the entire chain of computations shown in Fig. 1. At the instant $t = s$ the volume of the computations required for determining u^*_s is reduced, since it is necessary to perform only a portion of the chain of computations shown in Fig. 1 — from the end of u^*_n to the determination of u^*_s. The latter quantity is determined as a function of the vectors $\mathbf{u}_{s-1}$, $\mathbf{x}^*_s$, and $\mathbf{y}_{s-1}$; i.e., it is determined as a function of all the preceding values of the quantities at the input and output of the control section of the system. These values are memorized in the control section.

Depending on the complexity of the computations performed in the chain depicted in Fig. 1, the following cases may be encountered:

a. The entire chain of minimizations and averagings can be performed (either exactly or approximately) analytically. In that case, it is possible to compute the functions

$$u^*_s = u^*_s(\mathbf{u}_{s-1}, \mathbf{x}^*_s, \mathbf{y}_{s-1}) \qquad (s = 0, 1, \ldots, n) \tag{1}$$

in advance and to introduce the ready control law in the form of (1) into the control section A of the system. This case is treated in the first example in this paper. However, such a possibility is encountered only in the simplest examples.

---

*Figure 1 indicates integration with respect to x_i, since, in the subsequent examples, $h_s = 0$ and $y_i = x_i$.

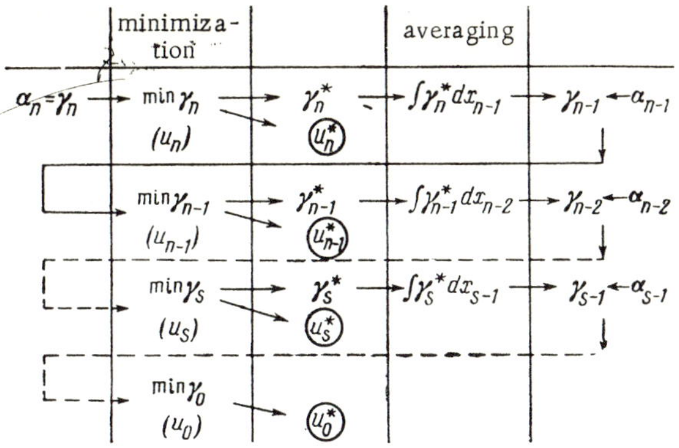

Fig. 1.

b. It is impossible to perform the entire chain of computations in advance, and to obtain ready formulas of the type (1). This is the more general case. Such a problem is treated in the second example. In this case, the theory provides the possibility of achieving the synthesis of an optimal dual-control system. Here we design a control section A for the system, such that it automatically performs (either completely or partially) the computations shown in Fig. 1.

The Synthesis of the Optimal Control Section for the Automatic Stabilization System

The block diagram of the system is shown in Fig. 2. The output quantity x of the controlled object B is applied to the input of the control section A of the system. The standard input x^* (which is assumed constant), is applied to the other input of the section. The output quantity u from the section A of the system consists of the control input, which is applied to the input of the object B, together with a random constant bias μ and a random noise g. The values g_s of the noise at the instants $t = s$ are a series of independent random quantities with the same distribution density $q(g_s)$. The a priori distribution density $P(\mu) = P_0(\mu)$ is specified by the random quantity μ. The object B has a linear characteristic of the following form:

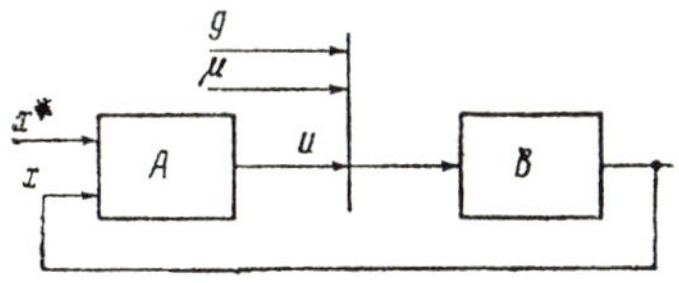

Fig. 2.

$$x_s = u_s + g_s + \mu. \tag{2}$$

The specific loss function is determined by the expression

$$W_s = (x_s - x^*)^2. \tag{3}$$

The over-all loss function is written as

$$W = \sum_{s=0}^{n} W_s = \sum_{s=0}^{n} (x_s - x^*)^2, \tag{4}$$

where the number of cycles n is specified. It is necessary to synthesize a control section A, such that the risk R (the mathematical expectation of the function W) is minimal.

In accordance with the general theory, it is required to find the probability density $P(y_i | \mu, i, u_i)$. Since, in this problem, $y = x$, μ is a scalar quantity, and the specified probability density is independent of i, we shall write it as $P(x_i | \mu, u_i)$. It is obvious that, in this problem,

$$P(x_i | \mu, u_i) = q(x_i - u_i - \mu). \tag{5}$$

In order to determine the optimal strategy, it is necessary to find the function $\alpha_k (0 \leq k \leq n)$, which is given by the expression

$$\alpha_k = \int_{\Omega(x_k, \mu)} W_k P_0(\mu) \prod_{i=0}^{k} P(x_i \mid \mu, u_i) \, d\Omega(x_k, \mu) =$$
$$= \int_{-\infty}^{+\infty} \int_{-\infty}^{+\infty} (x^* - x_k)^2 P_0(\mu) \prod_{i=0}^{k} q(x_i - u_i - \mu) \, dx_k \, d\mu. \tag{6}$$

We shall study the case where $P_0(\mu)$ and $q(g_s)$ are normal distributions with zero average values. Then

$$P_0(\mu) = \frac{1}{\sigma_\mu \sqrt{2\pi}} \exp\left\{-\frac{\mu^2}{2\sigma_\mu^2}\right\}, \qquad q(g_s) = \frac{1}{\sigma_g \sqrt{2\pi}} \exp\left\{-\frac{g_s^2}{2\sigma_g^2}\right\}. \tag{7}$$

From (6) and (7) we find

$$\alpha_k = \frac{1}{(\sigma_g)^{k+1} \sigma_\mu (2\pi)^{\frac{k}{2}+1}} \int_{\mu=-\infty}^{+\infty} \exp\left\{-\left[\frac{\mu^2}{2\sigma_\mu^2} + \sum_{i=0}^{k-1} \frac{(x_i - u_i - \mu)^2}{2\sigma_g^2}\right]\right\} \times$$
$$\times \left[\int_{x_k=-\infty}^{+\infty} (x^* - x_k)^2 \exp\left\{-\frac{(x_k - u_k - \mu)^2}{2\sigma_g^2}\right\} dx_k\right] d\mu. \tag{8}$$

We shall make use of the formula ([3], p. 188)

$$\int_{-\infty}^{+\infty} e^{-px^2+2qx} x^{a+1} \, dx = \frac{1}{2^a p} \sqrt{\frac{\pi}{p}} \frac{d^a \left(q e^{\frac{q^2}{p}}\right)}{dq^a}, \tag{9}$$

where a is a positive integer, and p and q are rational.

For a = 1, we obtain

$$\int_{-\infty}^{+\infty} x^2 e^{-px^2+2qx} \, dx = \frac{1}{2p} \sqrt{\frac{\pi}{p}} \, e^{\frac{q^2}{p}} \left(1 + \frac{2q^2}{p}\right). \tag{10}$$

We shall find the integral I_k in the square brackets of formula (8):

$$I_k = \int_{-\infty}^{+\infty} (x^* - x_k)^2 \exp\left\{-\frac{(x_k - u_k - \mu)^2}{2\sigma_g^2}\right\} dx_k = \exp\left\{-\frac{l_k^2}{2\sigma_g^2}\right\} \int_{-\infty}^{+\infty} z^2 \exp\left\{-\frac{z^2}{2\sigma_g^2} + 2\left(-\frac{l_k}{2\sigma_g^2}\right) z\right\} dz, \tag{11}$$

where

$$x_k - x^* = z, \qquad x^* - u_k - \mu = l_k. \tag{12}$$

Making use of formula (10), we find

$$I_k = \sigma_g^3 \sqrt{2\pi} \, [1 + (x^* - u_k - \mu)^2] \tag{13}$$

from (11) and (12).

Then

$$\alpha_k = \frac{1}{\sigma_g^{k-2} \sigma_\mu (2\pi)^{\frac{k+1}{2}}} \left[\int_{-\infty}^{+\infty} \exp\left\{-\left[\frac{\mu^2}{2\sigma_\mu^2} + \sum_{i=0}^{k-1} \frac{(x_i - u_i)^2 - 2\mu (x_i - u_i) + \mu^2}{2\sigma_g^2}\right]\right\} d\mu + \right.$$
$$\left. + \int_{-\infty}^{+\infty} \exp\left\{-\left[\frac{\mu^2}{2\sigma_\mu^2} + \sum_{i=0}^{k-1} \frac{(x_i - u_i)^2 - 2\mu (x_i - u_i) + \mu^2}{2\sigma_g^2}\right]\right\} (x^* - u_k - \mu)^2 \, d\mu\right]. \tag{14}$$

The first of the integrals in the square brackets of (14) can be found if we use the formula ([3], p.185)

$$\int_{-\infty}^{+\infty} e^{-px^2 \pm qx}\, dx = e^{\frac{q^2}{4p}} \sqrt{\frac{\pi}{p}}. \tag{15}$$

The second integral in the square brackets can be determined by assuming $\mu + u_k - x^* = z$. Finally, the formula for α_k is obtained in finite form.

We shall assume

$$u_k - x^* = w_k, \quad \sum_{i=0}^{k-1} (x_i - u_i) = \Sigma_{k-1},$$

$$\varepsilon_k = \frac{1}{2\sigma_\mu^2} + \frac{k}{2\sigma_g^2}, \quad \sum_{i=0}^{k-1} (x_i - u_i)^2 = \theta_{k-1}, \tag{16}$$

$$a_k = \frac{1}{\sqrt{2}\sigma_g^{k-2}\sigma_\mu (2\pi)^{\frac{k-1}{2}} \sqrt{\varepsilon_k}}, \quad b_k = \frac{\sqrt{\pi}}{2\sigma_g^{k-2}\sigma_\mu (2\pi)^{\frac{k+1}{2}} (\varepsilon_k)^{\frac{3}{2}}}.$$

Then

$$\alpha_k = \left\{a_k + b_k + \frac{2b_k}{\varepsilon_k}\left(w_k\varepsilon_k + \frac{\Sigma_{k-1}}{2\sigma_g^2}\right)^2\right\} \exp\left\{-\frac{\theta_{k-1}}{2\sigma_g^2} + \frac{\Sigma_{k-1}^2}{4\sigma_g^4 \varepsilon_k}\right\}. \tag{17}$$

The quantity u_k, which is contained in w_k, is present in only one of the multipliers, and is not included in the exponential term. This fact greatly simplifies the minimization of α_k with respect to u_k.

We shall now perform the series of computations indicated in Fig. 1. In formula (17) we shall write $k = n$ and find the minimum of the function $\gamma_n = \alpha_n$ with respect to u_n. It is obvious that the condition governing the minimum is written as

$$w_n\varepsilon_n + \frac{\Sigma_{n-1}}{2\sigma_g^2} = 0, \tag{18}$$

whence we find the optimal value u_n^* for the control input:

$$u_n^* = x^* - \frac{\sum_{i=0}^{n-1} (x_i - u_i)}{2\sigma_g^2 \varepsilon_n}. \tag{19}$$

Then we find

$$\gamma_n^* = \alpha_n^* = (a_n + b_n) \exp\left\{-\frac{\theta_{n-1}}{2\sigma_g^2} + \frac{\Sigma_{n-1}^2}{4\sigma_g^4 \varepsilon_n}\right\}. \tag{20}$$

After that we find the function γ_{n-1} (cf. [2]):

$$\gamma_{n-1} = \alpha_{n-1} + \int_{x_{n-1}=-\infty}^{+\infty} \alpha_n^*\, dx_{n-1} =$$

$$= \left\{a_{n-1} + b_{n-1} + \frac{2b_{n-1}}{\varepsilon_{n-1}}\left[w_{n-1}\varepsilon_{n-1} + \frac{\Sigma_{n-2}}{2\sigma_g^2}\right]^2\right\} \exp\left\{-\frac{\theta_{n-2}}{2\sigma_g^2} + \frac{\Sigma_{n-2}^2}{4\sigma_g^4 \varepsilon_{n-1}}\right\} + \tag{21}$$

$$+ \int_{-\infty}^{+\infty} (a_n + b_n) \exp\left\{-\frac{(x_{n-1} - u_{n-1})^2 + \theta_{n-2}}{2\sigma_g^2} + \frac{[\Sigma_{n-2} + (x_{n-1} - u_{n-1})]^2}{4\sigma_g^4 \varepsilon_n}\right\} dx_{n-1}.$$

We denote the integral in this formula by J_{n-1}. Using formula (15), we determine this integral:

$$J_{n-1} = (a_n + b_n)\sqrt{\frac{\pi}{\left(\frac{1}{2\sigma_g^2} - \frac{1}{4\sigma_g^4 \varepsilon_n}\right)}} \times$$
$$\times \exp\left\{-\frac{\theta_{n-2}}{2\sigma_g^2} + \frac{\Sigma_{n-2}^2}{4\sigma_g^4 \varepsilon_n} + \frac{\Sigma_{n-2}^2}{16\sigma_g^8 \varepsilon_n^2\left(\frac{1}{2\sigma_g^2} - \frac{1}{4\sigma_g^4 \varepsilon_n}\right)}\right\} \tag{22}$$

In this formula, we encounter the quantity

$$\frac{1}{2\sigma_g^2} - \frac{1}{4\sigma_g^4 \varepsilon_n} = \frac{1}{2\sigma_g^2} - \frac{1}{\frac{2\sigma_g^4}{\sigma_\mu^2} + 2n\sigma_g^2}.$$

This quantity is positive, since $n \geq 1$ and $\frac{2\sigma_g^4}{\sigma_\mu^2} > 0$. It should be noted that J_{n-1} is independent of u_{n-1}. Therefore, in formula (21), only the first term α_{n-1} depends on u_{n-1}; this facilitates minimization of γ_{n-1} with respect to u_{n-1}.

In this case, only α_{n-1} depends on u_{n-1}, and $\int \gamma_{n-1}^* \, dx_{n-1}$ is independent of u_{n-1}; this means that only the operational risk for $t = n - 1$ depends on u_{n-1}, whereas the adaptive risk is independent of the quantity u_{n-1}, even though it is nonzero. Thus, the system under study is neutral [2], and in it the process of adapting to the object proceeds identically for any value of u_{n-1}, and, in general, for u_s $(0 \leq s < n)$.

Minimizing α_{n-1} with respect to u_{n-1}, we find the condition governing the minimum in the same form as Eq. (18):

$$w_{n-1}\,\varepsilon_{n-1} + \frac{\Sigma_{n-2}}{2\sigma_g^2} = 0, \tag{23}$$

whence it follows that

$$u_{n-1}^* = x^* - \frac{\sum_{i=0}^{n-2}(x_i - u_i)}{2\sigma_g^2 \varepsilon_{n-1}}. \tag{24}$$

Reasoning analogously, we find that, in general, γ_s^* is independent of w_s, and depends only on the difference $x_{s-1} - u_{s-1}$. Therefore, the substitution $z = x_{s-1} - u_{s-1}$ liquidates dependence on u_{s-1} in the integral J_{s-1}. Therefore, for any $s - 1$, only α_{s-1} depends on u_{s-1}, and the formula for determining u_s^* is written as

$$u_s^* = x^* - \frac{\sum_{i=0}^{s-1}(x_i - u_i)}{2\sigma_g^2 \varepsilon_s}. \tag{25}$$

Substituting the value of ϵ_s from (16), we find the optimal control law in the following form:

$$u_s^* = x^* - \frac{\sum_{i=0}^{s-1}(x_i - u_i)}{s + \left(\frac{\sigma_g}{\sigma_\mu}\right)^2} \quad (s = 0, 1, \ldots, n). \tag{26}$$

This formula has a simple meaning. If the noise g_s were to be equal to zero, then (Fig. 2) we would need only two values (namely x_i and u_i) for determining the bias μ; here $\mu = x_i - u_i$. It is obvious that, after this measurement, the value of u_{i+1}, which must be introduced, is equal to $x^* - \mu = x^* - (x_i - u_i)$. If the noise g_s exists, then, for large s, it is natural to determine μ in the form of the arithmetic mean of all the measurements of $(x_i - u_i)$, i.e., $\mu_{av} \approx \frac{\sum_{i=0}^{s=1}(x_i - u_i)}{s}$. Then we introduce the value

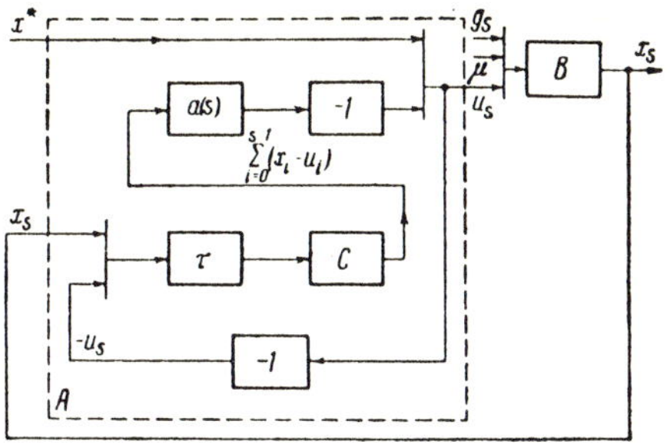

Fig. 3.

$$u_s = x^* - \mu_{av} = x^* - \frac{\sum_{i=0}^{s-1}(x_i - u_i)}{s}. \tag{27}$$

The exact formula (26) differs from formula (27), which is derived from simple considerations, only for small s. For sufficiently large s, the two formulas coincide.

This example is the simplest one, and is illustrative in nature, since the measurement of the difference $(x_i - u_i)$ makes it possible to determine the value of $\mu + g_s$, and then to determine the bias μ as if it had been measured directly with the error g_s. The same result would be obtained in the problem under study in the case of a nonlinear, mutually single-valued characteristic for the object. However, even in linear systems, the synthesis of an optimal control section A is appreciably complicated when two coordinates μ_1 and μ_2 of the vector $\boldsymbol{\mu}$ are present, if the characteristic of the object has, for example, the form

$$x_s = \mu_2(u_s + \mu_1 + g_s). \tag{28}$$

The general theory cited in [2] makes it possible to solve this problem in principle.

From the optimal control law (26) it is not difficult to formulate the block diagram of the control system (cf. Fig. 3). The sign (−1) denotes an inverter (i.e., a sign-changing block). The letter τ denotes a block that produces a delay of one cycle, and the letter C denotes an adder with storage. The result of the summing (it is assumed that n is not so great that the adder overflows) is the quantity $\sum_{i=0}^{s-1}(x_i - u_i)$, which is subjected to multiplication by $\left[s + \left(\frac{\sigma_g}{\sigma_\mu}\right)^2\right]^{-1}$ in the block a(s), and then is subjected to sign inversion.

It is of definite interest to extrapolate this scheme to the case of a continuous system. We shall assume that the duration of a cycle is $\Delta t = t/s$, and shall make s go to infinity while maintaining $t = \text{const}$. Then $\Delta t \to 0$. Assume that we have the problem of synthesizing a control system for the case where the noise g(t) is stationary white noise with the spectral density S_0. However, white noise is not the limit of a series of independent random quantities with finite dispersion, since its dispersion is infinitely great:

$$\sigma^2 = \frac{1}{2\pi}\int_{-\infty}^{+\infty} S_0\, d\omega = \infty.$$

Therefore, it is possible to obtain white noise in the limit for $\Delta t \to 0$ from a series of quantities g_s only in the case where the dispersion of these quantities is correspondingly increased. Assume the correlation function for the noise is written as

$$\begin{aligned} K_g(\tau) &= \frac{S_0}{\Delta t}\left(1 - \frac{|\tau|}{\Delta t}\right) = \sigma_g^2\left(1 - \frac{|\tau|}{\Delta t}\right) \quad \text{for} \quad -\Delta t \leqslant \tau \leqslant \Delta t; \\ K_g(\tau) &= 0 \quad \text{for} \quad |\tau| > \Delta t. \end{aligned} \tag{29}$$

Then the spectral density is

$$S_g(\omega) = 2\int_0^{\Delta t} K_g(\tau)\cos\omega\tau\, d\tau =$$

$$= \frac{2\sigma_g^2}{\omega}\sin\omega\Delta t - \frac{2\sigma_g^2}{\omega^2\Delta t}[\omega\Delta t\sin\omega\Delta t + \cos\omega\Delta t - 1]. \tag{30}$$

For $\Delta t \to 0$, the function $S_g(\omega)$ tends toward $\sigma_g^2\Delta t$:

$$\lim_{\Delta t\to 0} S_g(\omega) = \lim_{\Delta t\to 0}\sigma_g^2\Delta t = \lim_{\Delta t\to 0}\frac{S_0}{\Delta t}\Delta t = S_0. \tag{31}$$

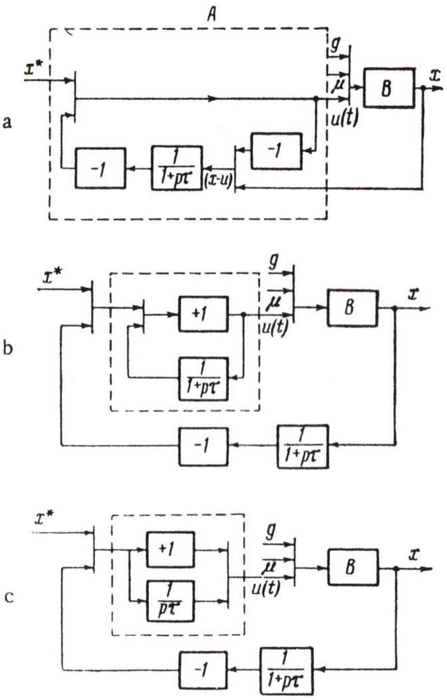

Fig. 4.

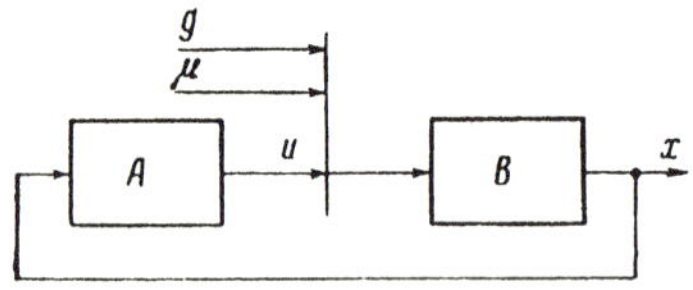

Fig. 5.

We shall rewrite formula (26) as follows:

$$u_s^* = x^* - \frac{\sum_{i=0}^{s-1} (x_i - u_i)\,\Delta t}{s\Delta t + \frac{\sigma_g^2 \Delta t}{\sigma_\mu^2}}. \tag{32}$$

For $\Delta t \to 0$ the quantities in this formula tend toward the following limits:

$$\sigma_g^2 \Delta t \to S_0, \qquad \sum_{i=0}^{s-1} (x_i - u_i)\,\Delta t \to \int_0^t (x - u)\,dt. \tag{33}$$

Since $s\Delta t = t$, it follows that, in the limit, we obtain the following optimal control law from (32):

$$u^*(t) = x^* - \frac{\int_0^t (x-u)\,dt}{t + \frac{S_0}{\sigma_\mu^2}} = x^* - \frac{\int_0^t (x-u)\,dt}{t + a}, \tag{34}$$

where $a = S_0/\sigma_\mu^2$. The second term in this expression can be obtained at the output of a filter with the transient response

$$u_{\text{out}} = \frac{1}{t+a}\int_0^t u_{\text{in}}\,dt = \frac{t}{t+a}, \tag{35}$$

if we apply the quantity $u_{\text{in}} = x - u$ to its input.* This transient response is not an exponential. The transfer function K(p) for such a filter is expressed in terms of an integral exponential function, and cannot be represented in the form of a finite sum of fractionally rational functions. However, it is possible approximately to replace the filter having the transient function (35) with an inertial section having the time constant $T \approx 1.1\,a$. Then a system which is close to optimal will be of the form illustrated in Fig. 4a. Converting this system to an equivalent one, we successively obtain the systems shown in Figs. 4b and 4c. The latter variant is a section which introduces the integral into the channel of the system, and has an inertial section in the feedback loop. It is of interest to compare these systems with similar ones which were obtained on the basis of completely different concepts by I. B. Reswick [4] and O. T. M. Smith [5].

The Synthesis of the Optimal Control Section for an Automatic Search System

We shall study an example of applying the theory of dual control for synthesizing an optimal automatic search system. The block diagram for the system is shown in Fig. 5. Assume that the characteristic for the object B is written as

$$x_s = (u_s + g_s + \mu)^2. \tag{36}$$

It is required that the value of x prove to be as close as possible to the minimum as a result of automatic search. The constant bias μ at the object's input is not known a priori, and is a random quantity with a specified a priori probability density $P(\mu) = P_0(\mu)$. The noise g_s, just as in the preceding example, consists of a series of independent random quantities with a zero average value and the same probability density $P(g_s) = q(g_s)$.

* In determining the transient function, it was assumed that $u_{\text{in}} = 1 = \text{const}$.

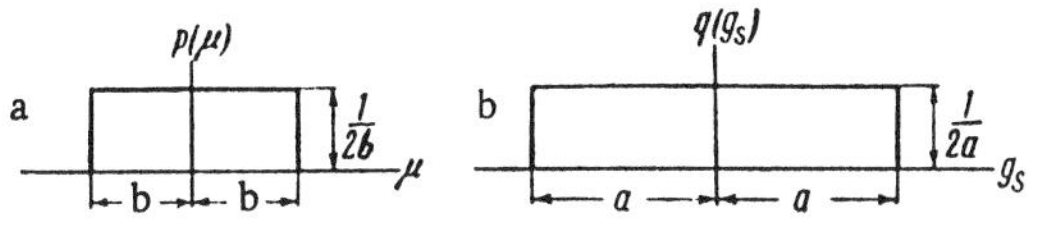

Fig. 6.

In order to determine the required value of the control input, we establish n trial values of u_s at the instants $s = 0, 1, \ldots, n-1$. Then, for $s = n$, we establish the final working value $u = u_n$, after which search ends. It is required to establish the series of trial values u_s $(s = 0, 1, \ldots, n-1)$, and the working value u_n in such a way that the mathematical expectation for the deviation of x_n from the minimum is minimal. Such a search will be an optimal search performed according to the extrapolation method.

The loss function for the problem under study will be written as

$$W_s = \vartheta_s x_s = \vartheta_s (u_s + g_s + \mu)^2, \tag{37}$$

where

$$\vartheta_s = \begin{cases} 0, & s < n, \\ 1, & s = n. \end{cases} \tag{38}$$

The problem consists of determining an algorithm for the control section A which is such that the risk $R = R_n = M\{W_n\}$ will be minimal. Therefore, for any sth cycle $(s < n)$ the entire risk is the adaptive risk, and the operational risk is equal to zero. Moreover, for $s = n$, the over-all risk is the operational risk. Further, the function α_s is equal to zero for $s < n$. The quantity

$$R = R_n = \int\limits_{\Omega(x_n, \mu, \mathbf{u}_n, \mathbf{x}_{n-1})} x_n P(x_n \mid \mu, u_n) P(\mu) \prod_{i=0}^{n-1} P(x_i \mid \mu, u_i) \times \prod_{i=0}^{n} \Gamma_i d\Omega(x_n, \mu, \mathbf{u}_n, \mathbf{x}_{n-1}) \tag{39}$$

is to be minimized.

In accordance with general theory, it is necessary to study the auxiliary function

$$\gamma_n = \alpha_n = \int\limits_{\Omega(x_n, \mu)} x_n P(x_n \mid \mu, u_n) P(\mu) \prod_{i=0}^{n-1} P(x_i \mid \mu, u_i)\, d\Omega(x_n, \mu). \tag{40}$$

If the quantities μ and g_s are normally distributed, then it follows that, from Eq. (40), it is possible to obtain the function α_n in finite form by integration. However, even in this case, only the first minimization (with respect to u_n) is not beset with difficulty. The subsequent integrations and minimizations already cannot be performed analytically. For other distribution laws, $P(\mu)$ and $q(g_s)$, the situation is complicated even at the first stage of the computations. In the analysis below we shall study the case where the densities $P(\mu)$ and $q(g_s)$ correspond to uniform distribution (Fig. 6). Assume also that the condition $b < a$ is satisfied. The meaning of the parameters a and b is clear from Fig. 6. Assume that

$$\eta_s = u_s + \mu + g_s. \tag{41}$$

Then $\eta_s^2 = x_s$, and $2\eta_s d\eta_s = dx_s$. From this it follows that*

$$\Pr(x' < x_s < x' + dx_s) = \Pr\left(\sqrt{x'} < \eta_s < \sqrt{x'} + \frac{dx_s}{2\sqrt{x'}}\right) + \Pr\left(-\sqrt{x'} < \eta_s < -\sqrt{x'} + \frac{dx_s}{2\sqrt{x'}}\right), \tag{42}$$

or

$$\Pr(x' < x_s < x' + dx_s) = \Pr\left(\sqrt{x'} - u_s - \mu < g_s < \sqrt{x'} - u_s - \mu + \frac{dx_s}{2\sqrt{x'}}\right) + \Pr\left(-\sqrt{x'} - u_s - \mu < g_s < -\sqrt{x'} - u_s - \mu + \frac{dx_s}{2\sqrt{x'}}\right). \tag{43}$$

* The letters Pr are the abbreviation for "probability."

Thus,

$$P(x_i \mid \mu, u_i) = [q(\sqrt{x_i} - u_i - \mu) + q(-\sqrt{x_i} - u_i - \mu)] \frac{1}{2\sqrt{x_i}}. \tag{44}$$

Assume

$$\begin{gathered} \sqrt{x_i} = \zeta_i, \\ Q_i = q(\zeta_i - u_i - \mu) + q(-\zeta_i - u_i - \mu) = \\ = q(-\zeta_i + u_i + \mu) + q(\zeta_i + u_i + \mu). \end{gathered} \tag{45}$$

Then

$$P(x_i \mid \mu, u_i) = \frac{1}{2\zeta_i} Q_i(\zeta_i, u_i + \mu). \tag{46}$$

Substituting this expression and the value of $P(\mu)$ into (40), we find

$$\alpha_n = \frac{1}{2b} \int\limits_{\mu=-b}^{b} \int\limits_{\zeta_n=0}^{\infty} \zeta_n^2 Q_n(\zeta_n, u_n + \mu) \prod_{i=0}^{n-1} \frac{1}{2\zeta_i} Q_i(\zeta_i, u_i + \mu)\, d\mu\, d\zeta_n. \tag{47}$$

Here we should take into account the fact that $dx_n = 2\zeta_n d\zeta_n$. Formula (47) can be written in the following form:

$$\alpha_n = \frac{1}{2b} \int\limits_{\mu=-b}^{b} I_n(\mu) \prod_{i=0}^{n-1} \frac{1}{2\zeta_i} Q_i(\zeta_i, u_i + \mu)\, d\mu, \tag{48}$$

where

$$I_n(\mu) = \int\limits_{\zeta_n=0}^{\infty} \zeta_n^2 Q_n(\zeta_n, u_n + \mu)\, d\zeta_n. \tag{49}$$

In the latter integral, the upper limit may be finite, since $Q_n = 0$ for $\zeta_n > a + 2b$.

The computation of the integral $I_n(\mu)$ yields the formula

$$I_n(\mu) = \frac{a^2}{3} + (u_n + \mu)^2. \tag{50}$$

Therefore,

$$\alpha_n = \frac{1}{2b} \left(\prod_{i=0}^{n-1} \frac{1}{2\zeta_i} \right) \left[\frac{a^2}{3} \int\limits_{-b}^{b} \prod_{i=0}^{n-1} Q_i(\zeta_i, u_i + \mu)\, d\mu + \right.$$

$$\left. + \int\limits_{-b}^{b} (u_n + \mu)^2 \prod_{i=1}^{n-1} Q_i(\zeta_i, u_i + \mu)\, d\mu \right]. \tag{51}$$

We shall assume that

$$I_{0,n} = \int\limits_{-b}^{b} \prod_{i=0}^{n-1} Q_i(\zeta_i, u_i + \mu)\, d\mu, \qquad I_{1,n} = 2\int\limits_{-b}^{b} \mu \prod_{i=0}^{n-1} Q_i(\zeta_i, u_i + \mu)\, d\mu,$$

$$I_{2,n} = \int\limits_{-b}^{b} \mu^2 \prod_{i=0}^{n-1} Q_i(\zeta_i, u_i + \mu)\, d\mu. \tag{52}$$

Then formula (51) will become

$$\alpha_n = \frac{1}{2b} \left(\prod_{i=0}^{n-1} \frac{1}{2\zeta_i} \right) \left[\frac{a^2}{3} I_{0,n} + u_n^2 I_{0,n} + u_n I_{1,n} + I_{2,n} \right]. \tag{53}$$

Differentiating α_n with respect to u_n, we find the optimal value of u_n^*:

$$u_n^* = -\frac{I_{1,n}}{2I_{0,n}} \tag{54}$$

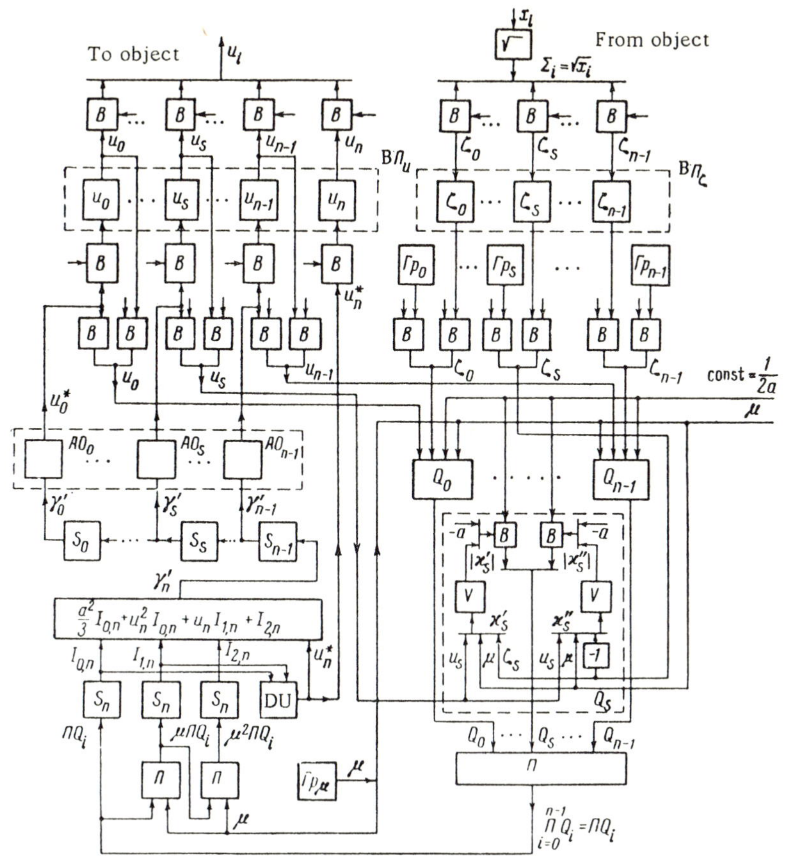

Fig. 7.

and the corresponding value of α_n^*:

$$\alpha_n^* = (\alpha_n)_{u_n = u_n^*} = \frac{1}{2b}\left(\prod_{i=0}^{n-1}\frac{1}{2\zeta_i}\right)\left[\frac{a^2}{3} I_{0,n} + I_{2,n} - \frac{I_{1,n}^2}{4I_{0,n}}\right]. \tag{55}$$

The expressions $I_{0,n}$, $I_{1,n}$, $I_{2,n}$ in the form of formulas are so complex that it is simpler to determine the integrals in the actual control section A. The further integrations and minimizations in formula (55) can also be performed only within A, since the formulas cannot be obtained in finite form. However, the over-all sequence of computations can be realized by a computer device whose block diagram is shown in Fig. 7. This is the block diagram for an optimal control system. The blocks in this system can, in principle, be either analog or digital, and the diagram proper can be replaced by its equivalent program on a universal digital computer.

In the block diagram shown in Fig. 7 we have used the following notation: B are rectifiers which are controlled by a control and synchronization block not shown in the figure; Γp are generators which produce "triangular" waves at various frequencies; V are the modulus blocks for which the output quantity is equal to the absolute value of the input quantity; S_i are integrating blocks (a more detailed diagram of the integrating block is shown in Fig. 8); AO_i are automatic optimizers with respect to one variable; Π are the product blocks; DU is a dividing unit; $B\Pi_u$ is the memory block for the u_i values; $B\Pi_\zeta$ is the memory block for ζ_i values; √ is a block whose output quantity is $\zeta_i = \sqrt{x_i}$, where x_i is the input quantity.

The generator Γp_μ applies a voltage to the bus μ, which varies over the limits $-b \leq \mu \leq b$ according to a "triangular" curve; here $\left|\frac{d\mu}{dt}\right|$ = const. The blocks $Q_0, Q_1, \ldots, Q_s, \ldots, Q_{n-1}$ form the corresponding functions in accordance with Eq. (45). As an example, Fig. 7 shows the block diagram for the section Q_s in more detail; here Q_s is the sum of the output signals from two rectifiers B. Each of these output signals is equal to $\frac{1}{2}a$ or zero, depending on the conditions

$$|\varkappa_s'| = |u_s + \mu + \zeta_s| \lesseqgtr a, \qquad |\varkappa_s''| = |u_s + \mu - \zeta_s| \gtreqless a. \tag{56}$$

The terms q in expression (45) are obtained at the outputs of the rectifiers.

All of the functions Q_s ($s = 0, 1, \ldots, n-1$) are applied to the block Π, where the product $\prod_{i=0}^{n-1} Q_i = \Pi Q_i$ is produced. The resulting product, and also the products $\mu \Pi Q_i$ and $\mu^2 \Pi Q_i$, are applied to integrating blocks where integration with respect to μ is performed during a half-cycle of the voltage from the generator Γp_μ. The resulting values $I_{0,n}$, $I_{1,n}$, and $I_{2,n}$ are applied to the input of the block, which computes the function

$$\gamma_n' = \frac{a^2}{3} I_{0,n} + u_n^2 I_{0,n} + u_n I_{1,n} + I_{2,n} \tag{57}$$

[i.e., that factor in the function $\alpha_n = \gamma_n$ which depends on u_n in accordance with formula (53)]. At the output of the dividing unit DU, the normal value of u_n^* as computed according to Eq. (54) is determined; the quantity u_n^* is applied to the input of the block γ_n'. Therefore, at its output, we obtain the value $\gamma_n'^*$ corresponding to $u_n = u_n^*$. The function γ_n' is integrated in the block S_{n-1} during one half-cycle of the generator Γp_{n-1}, i.e., it is integrated with respect to the coordinate ζ_{n-1}, which, for the time being, arrives from the generator Γp_{n-1}. As a result, we obtain the function γ_{n-1}'. In order to integrate we must first multiply α_n^* [cf. (55)] by $2\zeta_{n-1} d\zeta_{n-1}$, and then integrate. Therefore, only the square bracket in formula (55) must participate in the integration. The multipliers $1/\zeta_i$ must not be taken into account.

The output signal γ_{n-1}' of the block S_{n-1} is transmitted to the input of the automatic optimizer AO_{n-1}, which chooses the value of u_{n-1}^* in such a way as to ensure the minimum for γ_{n-1}'. The next integration over a half cycle of the generator Γp_{n-2} in the integrator S_{n-2} makes it possible to obtain the function γ_{n-2}', etc. The chain of optimizers automatically selects the values of $u_0^*, u_1^*, \ldots, u_{n-1}^*$, which minimize the functions $\gamma_0', \gamma_1', \ldots, \gamma_{n-1}'$, respectively.

The value of u_0^* chosen in this manner is applied to the memory block $B\Pi_u$ and stored in the cell u_0. From this it is transmitted to the object at the instant $t = 0$. As soon as the value u_0 is memorized in the $B\Pi_u$ and is applied to the object, the computation of u_0 can be ceased, and from then on u_0 is applied to the block Q_0 only from the memory block. Analogously, at the instant following the memorization of the value u_1, the latter begins to be applied to the block Q_1 only from the memory block $B\Pi_u$, etc. Gradually, during the process of operation of the network, all of the cells u_i in the memory block are filled. Before the last cycle, the cell u_n is filled. In exactly the same way, all of the cells ζ_i in the memory block $B\Pi_\zeta$ are gradually filled. As soon as the value ζ_s has appeared at the output of the object at the instant $t = s$, it is stored in the sth cell of the ζ_s memory block, and from that instant the block Q_s is subjected not to the output signal of the generator Γp_s, but to the constant value ζ_s which is measured by the block.

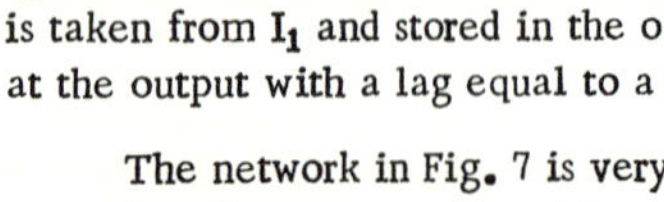

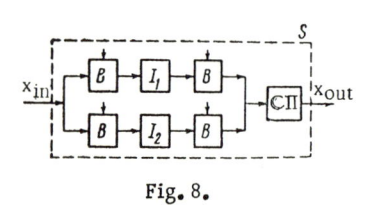

Fig. 8.

Figure 8 shows the block diagram of the integrator S. During the first half-cycle, the upper branch of the integrator I_1 operates (starting from zero) and accumulates the value of the integral. During the second half-cycle, the lower branch operates with an analogous integrator I_2, and during that time the accumulated reading is taken from I_1 and stored in the output memory cell CΠ. Thus, we obtain the required value of the integral at the output with a lag equal to a half-cycle of the corresponding generator.

The network in Fig. 7 is very complex. Its basic shortcoming, however, is not its complexity, but the necessity of an extremely rapid operation of a number of sections. The number of memory cells in the network is small; the number of blocks which perform the basic operations is also small, but the fundamental frequency must be very great. Assume, for example, that $n = 3$. If the generator Γp_{μ} operates at a frequency of $f = 5$ Mc, then, during a half-cycle (i.e., during a period $T = 10^{-7}$ sec), the integrators S_n produce the values $I_{0,n}, I_{1,n}, I_{2,n}$. The quantity γ_n^* is applied to the integrator S_{n-1} with exactly the same lag. For integration with respect to ζ_{n-1}, it is required that no less than 10-20 values of γ_n^* correspond to a half-cycle of generator $\Gamma p_{n-1}(\Gamma p_2)$. Assuming that 20 half-cycles of Γp_{μ} must be used for one half-cycle of the generator Γp_2, we obtain a frequency of 250 kc for the latter. Thus, during one of its half-cycles (i.e., during a period $T_2 = 2 \cdot 10^{-6}$ sec), the value γ_2^* is produced. In order to compute $u_{n-1}^* = u_2^*$, it is necessary to pass over the entire scale $-b \leq u_2 \leq b$ while testing not less than 10 to 20 positions on the scale. Therefore, the computation of u_2^* requires a time equal to $T_2^* = 20T_2 = 40 \cdot 10^{-6}$ sec. Reasoning analogously, we find that integration for obtaining γ_1^* requires a time equal to $T_1 \approx 20T_2^* = 8 \cdot 10^{-4}$ sec, and for obtaining u_1^* it requires a time equal to $T_1^* \approx 20T_1 = 1.6 \cdot 10^{-2}$ sec. Integration for the purpose of forming γ_0^* requires a time $T_0 = 20T_1^* = 32 \cdot 10^{-2}$ sec, and a time $T_0^* = 20T_0 = 20 \cdot 0.32 = 6.4$ sec is required to obtain u_0^*. Thus, even the very high carrier frequency of 5 Mc (and at that for a relatively small value $n = 3$) cannot assure a short time for determining the first value u_0. Of course, the subsequent values u_i will be determined more rapidly. If we were to determine the value of u_n^* not according to formula (54) but by minimization of γ_n^*, then the time for determining u_0 would prove to be still greater.

This example demonstrates that, as far as possible, we should attempt an approximate solution of the problem involving the analytical determination of the values u_i^* since the computation of these values in a computer requires an extremely high speed of response. Modern digital machines cannot insure the required speed of response when complex problems are solved. This example also indicates the importance of papers in the field of designing ultrahigh-speed computers as far as the synthesis of optimal control systems is concerned.

However, we should keep in mind the fact that, for the principle of computer operation cited above, the operating time is of the order of a^n, where $a = \text{const}$. Therefore, as n increases, the time increases extremely rapidly. If we perform the greater portion of the computations in advance, and feed already formulated functions into the computer, then the operation is accelerated. However, under these conditions, it is necessary to remember functions of n variables, and thus the volume of the memory will be equal to a number of the order of b^n, where $b = \text{const}$. Only the approximation of functional relationships in the form of functions of a definite type with a comparatively small number of unknown parameters, combined with an acceleration of the operation of computers and the development of approximate methods for solving problems, will create the practical possibility of designing optimal dual-control devices in cases which involve any appreciable complexity.

LITERATURE CITED

1. A. A. Fel'dbaum, "Theory of dual control. I," Avtomatika i Telemekhanika 21, No. 9 (1960).
2. A. A. Fel'dbaum, "Theory of dual control. II," Avtomatika i Telemekhanika 21, No. 11 (1960).
3. I. M. Ryzhik, Tables of Integrals, Sums, Series, and Products [in Russian] (State Technical Press, 1948) 2nd edition.
4. I. B. Reswick, "Disturbance-response feedback. A new control concept," Trans. ASME 78, No. 1 (January, 1956).
5. O. T. M. Smith, Feedback Control Systems (McGraw-Hill, New York, 1958).

THE THEORY OF DUAL CONTROL. IV

A. A. Fel'dbaum (Moscow)

Translated from Avtomatika i Telemekhanika, Vol. 22, No. 2, pp. 129-142, February, 1961
Original article submitted June 6, 1960

A generalized algorithm is derived for the optimal strategy of a dual-control system for an object with several inputs and outputs, and a memory. An example is given of the application of the algorithm. In conclusion, we consider the directions that further development of the theory of dual control should take.

Derivation of a Generalized Algorithm for the Optimum Strategy of Dual Control

In the second paper of this series (see [1]), an algorithm was derived for the optimal strategy of a dual control, where it was assumed that the object of control did not have a memory, and had one output and one input. We consider below a generalization of this theory to an object with a memory and with several inputs and outputs.

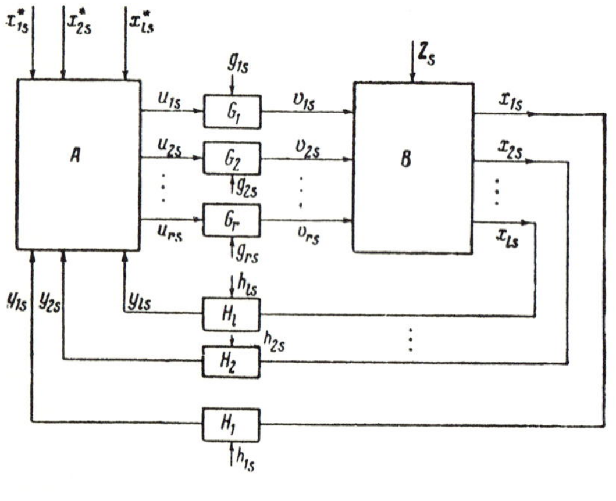

Fig. 1.

The block diagram of the system we are considering is shown in Fig. 1. All quantities will be assumed to be functions of a discrete time t = s (s = 0, 1, . . . , n). The controlling parameters $u_{1s}, u_{2s}, \ldots, u_{rs}$ from the output of the control section A, arrive at the controlled object B through transmission channels $G_1, G_2, \ldots, G_r$, in which the useful signal is mixed with the interference components $g_{1s}, g_{2s}, \ldots, g_{rs}$, respectively. At the object B, the controlling quantities $v_{1s}, v_{2s}, \ldots, v_{rs}$ arrive from the transmission channels. Moreover, the object is subjected to the interference $\mathbf{Z}_s$, which is generally a vector, i.e., it is the combination of interferences applied, perhaps, at various parts of the object B:

$$\mathbf{Z}_s = \mathbf{Z}_s(s, \boldsymbol{\mu}), \tag{1}$$

where $\boldsymbol{\mu}$ is the parameter vector

$$\boldsymbol{\mu} = (\mu_1, \mu_2, \ldots, \mu_m). \tag{2}$$

The outputs $x_{1s}, x_{2s}, \ldots, x_{ls}$ from the object B pass through channels $H_1, H_2, \ldots, H_l$ to the input of the control section A. In the channels $H_1, H_2, \ldots, H_l$ the interference $h_{1s}, h_{2s}, \ldots, h_{ls}$ acts, and so the outputs $y_{1s}, y_{2s}, \ldots, y_{ls}$ from the channels generally differ from the inputs $x_{1s}, x_{2s}, \ldots, x_{ls}$ to these channels. In the control section A, the quantities $y_{1s}, y_{2s}, \ldots, y_{ls}$ can generally be compared with certain given quantities $x_{1s}^*, x_{2s}^*, \ldots, x_{ls}^*$. In certain cases (for example, in obtaining the minimum of some quantity $\underline{x}$), such a comparison can be omitted.

In particular cases, for certain inputs, there will be only one scalar quantity x_s at the object output; such a

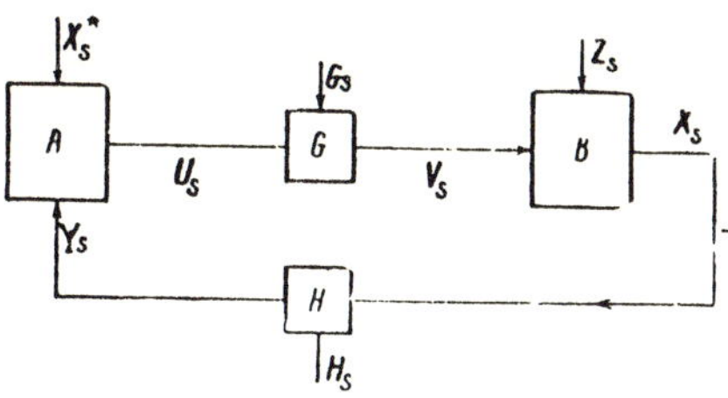

Fig. 2.

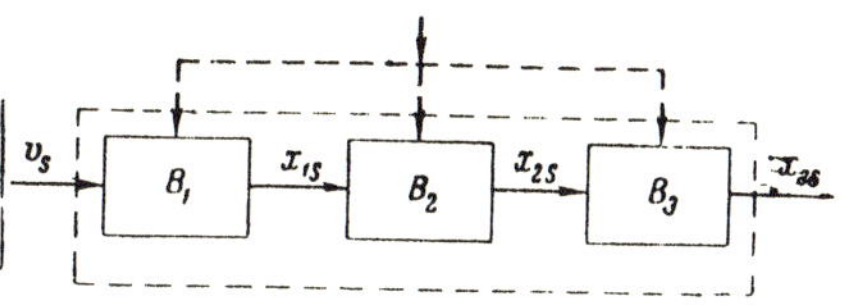

Fig. 3.

case is found in systems of automatic optimization. In other types of systems, the controlling action u_s is transmitted to the object through only one channel, while several quantities x_{is} $(i = 1, \ldots, l)$ are measured at the output.

We introduce vectors made up of the values of our parameters all taken for the same time t = s:

$$\begin{aligned} &\mathbf{X}_s^* = (x_{1s}^*, x_{2s}^*, \ldots, x_{ls}^*), && \mathbf{X}_s = (x_{1s}, x_{2s}, \ldots, x_{ls}), \\ &\mathbf{Y}_s = (y_{1s}, y_{2s}, \ldots, y_{ls}), && \mathbf{U}_s = (u_{1s}, u_{2s}, \ldots, u_{rs}), \\ &\mathbf{V}_s = (v_{1s}, v_{2s}, \ldots, v_{rs}), && \mathbf{G}_s = (g_{1s}, \ldots, g_{rs}), \\ &\mathbf{H}_s = (h_{1s}, \ldots, h_{ls}). \end{aligned} \tag{3}$$

These space vectors must differ from the time vectors, which are denoted by lower-case letters:

$$\begin{aligned} &\mathbf{x}_{is}^* = (x_{i0}^*, x_{i1}^*, \ldots, x_{is}^*), \qquad \mathbf{x}_{is} = (x_{i0}, x_{i1}, \ldots, x_{is}); \\ &\mathbf{y}_{is} = (y_{i0}, y_{i1}, \ldots, y_{is}) \qquad (i = 1, 2, \ldots, l); \\ &\mathbf{u}_{js} = (u_{j0}, u_{j1}, \ldots, u_{js}); \quad \mathbf{v}_{js} = (v_{j0}, v_{j1}, \ldots, v_{js}) \qquad (j = 1, 2, \ldots, r). \end{aligned} \tag{4}$$

If this vector notation is used, then the system in Fig. 1 can be represented as in Fig. 2.

The equations for the object B can have arbitrary form; there is the condition, however, that they must, in principle, be solvable, and so the vector $\mathbf{X}_s$ can be determined as a function of the vector $\boldsymbol{\mu}$ and the vectors $\mathbf{V}_k$ $(k = 0, 1, \ldots, s)$

$$\mathbf{X}_s = \mathbf{X}_s(\boldsymbol{\mu}, \mathbf{V}_0, \mathbf{V}_1, \ldots, \mathbf{V}_s). \tag{5}$$

We will consider various particular cases. Let, for example, the motion of the object be described generally by the nonlinear, finite difference equations

$$x_{i, s+1} = F_i(s, \mathbf{Z}_s, x_{1s}, \ldots, x_{ls}, v_{1s}, \ldots, v_{rs}) = F_i(s, \boldsymbol{\mu}, \mathbf{X}_s, \mathbf{V}_s) \tag{6}$$

or

$$\mathbf{X}_{s+1} = \mathbf{F}(s, \boldsymbol{\mu}, \mathbf{X}_s, \mathbf{V}_s), \tag{7}$$

where $\mathbf{F}$ is the vector with components $F_1, \ldots, F_l$. When the initial values $\mathbf{X}_0$ and $\mathbf{V}_0$ of the vectors $\mathbf{X}$ and $\mathbf{V}$ are specified, then from this formula we obtain the vector

$$\mathbf{X}_1 = \mathbf{F}(0, \boldsymbol{\mu}, \mathbf{X}_0, \mathbf{V}_0) = \mathbf{F}_1(\boldsymbol{\mu}, \mathbf{V}_0). \tag{8}$$

If we know $\mathbf{X}_1$, we can find the vector

$$\mathbf{X}_2 = \mathbf{F}(1, \boldsymbol{\mu}, \mathbf{X}_1, \mathbf{V}_1) = \mathbf{F}_2(\boldsymbol{\mu}, \mathbf{V}_0, \mathbf{V}_1)$$

etc. To sum up, we obtain a formula of the type (5) for the vector $\mathbf{X}_s$.

As another example, we can use the block diagram shown in Fig. 3 for the object B. The parts B_1 and B_3 of the object are linear, with transfer functions

$$x_{1s} = \sum_{k=0}^{s} a_{1k}(s, \mu) v_{s-k}; \qquad x_{3s} = \sum_{k=0}^{s} a_{3k}(s, \mu) x_{2, s-k}. \tag{9}$$

The section B_2 is noninertial nonlinear, with the equation

$$x_{2s} = F(s, \mu, x_{1s}). \tag{10}$$

The dependence of x_{2s} on x_{1s} is continuous and single-valued (but its inverse is not necessarily single-valued).

From Eqs. (9) and (10), it is obvious that we can express x_{1s}, x_{2s}, and x_{3s} as functions of μ and $\mathbf{v}_s = (v_0, v_1, \ldots, v_s)$, i.e., we can obtain a relation of the type (5).

We will first of all assume that such a relation has been obtained by some method or other.

We introduce the space-time matrices

$$\bar{\bar{U}}_s = \begin{vmatrix} u_{10}, & u_{11}, & \ldots, & u_{1s} \\ u_{20}, & u_{21}, & \ldots, & u_{2s} \\ \vdots & & & \vdots \\ u_{r0}, & u_{r1}, & \ldots, & u_{rs} \end{vmatrix} = \begin{vmatrix} \mathbf{u}_{1s} \\ \mathbf{u}_{2s} \\ \vdots \\ \mathbf{u}_{rs} \end{vmatrix} = |\mathbf{U}_0, \mathbf{U}_1, \ldots \mathbf{U}_s|, \tag{11}$$

$$\bar{\bar{V}}_s = \begin{vmatrix} v_{10}, & \ldots, & v_{1s} \\ \vdots & & \vdots \\ v_{r0}, & \ldots, & v_{rs} \end{vmatrix} = \begin{vmatrix} \mathbf{v}_{1s} \\ \mathbf{v}_{2s} \\ \vdots \\ \mathbf{v}_{rs} \end{vmatrix} = |\mathbf{V}_0, \mathbf{V}_1, \ldots, \mathbf{V}_s|, \tag{12}$$

$$\bar{\bar{X}}_s = \begin{vmatrix} x_{10}, & \ldots, & x_{1s} \\ \vdots & & \vdots \\ x_{l0}, & \ldots, & x_{ls} \end{vmatrix} = \begin{vmatrix} \mathbf{x}_{1s} \\ \vdots \\ \mathbf{x}_{ls} \end{vmatrix} = |\mathbf{X}_0, \ldots, \mathbf{X}_s|, \tag{13}$$

$$\bar{\bar{X}}^*_s = \begin{vmatrix} x^*_{10}, & \ldots, & x^*_{1s} \\ \vdots & & \vdots \\ x^*_{l0}, & \ldots, & x^*_{ls} \end{vmatrix} = \begin{vmatrix} \mathbf{x}^*_{1s} \\ \vdots \\ \mathbf{x}^*_{ls} \end{vmatrix} = |\mathbf{X}^*_0, \ldots, \mathbf{X}^*_s|, \tag{14}$$

$$\bar{\bar{Y}}_s = \begin{vmatrix} y_{10}, & \ldots, & y_{1s} \\ \vdots & & \vdots \\ y_{l0}, & \ldots, & y_{ls} \end{vmatrix} = \begin{vmatrix} \mathbf{y}_{1s} \\ \vdots \\ \mathbf{y}_{ls} \end{vmatrix} = |\mathbf{Y}_0, \ldots, \mathbf{Y}_s|. \tag{15}$$

We choose a loss-function for the system, of the form

$$W = \sum_{s=0}^{n} W_s, \tag{16}$$

where

$$W_s = W(s, \mu, \mathbf{X}^*_s, \mathbf{X}_s). \tag{17}$$

An explicit dependence of W_s on μ can exist. For example, if in the system of Fig. 1 there is a unique output x_s given by

$$x_s = \mu_{r+1} + \sum_{i, j=1}^{r} a_{ij}(v_{is} - \mu_i)(v_{js} - \mu_j), \tag{18}$$

where a_{ij} = const, v_{js} is the input to the object, and the second term on the right-hand side of Eq. (18) cannot be negative, then the minimum possible value of x_s is μ_{r+1} (for $v_{is} = \mu_i$). The deviation of x_1 from the minimum is given by the difference $x_s - \mu_{r+1}$. In the given case, we can therefore take $W_s = x_s - \mu_{r+1}$, and demand the minimization of the mathematical expectation of the corresponding quantity W.

Let the a priori probability density for the vector μ be given, let it be denoted by $P(\mu) = P_0(\mu)$, and let the probability density $P(g_{js})$ $(j = 1, \ldots, r)$ also be given. We will assume that the $P(g_{js})$ are independent of s and, generally speaking, that they are different for different values of j. In the same way, let the probability densities $P(h_{is})$ $(i = 1, \ldots, l)$ be independent of s and different for different values of i.

We will assume that the channels G and H have no memory. Therefore,

$$v_{js} = v_j(g_{js}, u_{js}), \qquad y_{is} = y_i(h_{is}, x_{is}). \tag{19}$$

If we have the above information, we can find the conditional probability densities $P(y_s | x_s)$ and $P(v_s | u_s)$, and also $P(\mathbf{Y}_s | \mathbf{X}_s)$ and $P(\mathbf{V}_s | \mathbf{U}_s)$. We can then find the conditional probability densities

$$P(\mathbf{y}_s | \mathbf{x}_s) = \prod_{i=0}^{s} P(y_s | x_s), \qquad P(\mathbf{v}_s | \mathbf{u}_s) = \prod_{i=0}^{s} P(v_s | u_s), \tag{20}$$

and also the conditional probability densities $P(\overline{\overline{\mathbf{Y}}}_s | \overline{\overline{\mathbf{X}}}_s)$ and $P(\overline{\overline{\mathbf{V}}}_s | \overline{\overline{\mathbf{U}}}_s)$.

The algorithm for the controlling section A of the system is characterized by the probability density Γ_s of its output vector $\mathbf{U}_s$, which, generally speaking, depends on all the previous inputs of the controlling section:

$$P_s(\mathbf{U}_s) = \Gamma_s = \Gamma_s(\mathbf{U}_s | \overline{\overline{X}}{}^*_s, \overline{\overline{Y}}_{s-1}, \overline{\overline{U}}_{s-1}). \tag{21}$$

We pose the problem of finding a sequence of functions Γ_i $(i = 1, \ldots, n)$, and an initial probability density $\Gamma_0 = P(\mathbf{U}_0)$, such that the risk R is a minimum, where R is the mathematical expectation of the loss-function W.

We can write the expression for R in various forms. We give below an expression for R which has a form which is the most convenient for finding the optimal strategy. This expression is a generalization of a similar formula, given in Section II of the present series of papers. The method of derivation that we use here is somewhat different — it is shorter, but somewhat more formal.

From the equalities (17) and (7), we obtain

$$W_s = W[s, \mu, \mathbf{X}^*_s, \mathbf{X}_s(s, \mu, \overline{\overline{V}})] = W(s, \mu, \mathbf{X}^*_s, \overline{\overline{V}}). \tag{22}$$

We will limit our derivation of the expression for R to the case of a fixed matrix $\overline{\overline{X}}{}^*_s$. Let the general conditional probability density $P(\mu, \overline{\overline{U}}_s, \overline{\overline{V}}_s, \overline{\overline{Y}}_{s-1} | \overline{\overline{X}}{}^*_s)$ for the coupled random vectors and matrices be known.

Here $\overline{\overline{Y}}_{s-1}$ occurs, since, on the basis of (20), $\overline{\overline{U}}_s$ is related to $\overline{\overline{Y}}_{s-1}$. Then the specific risk R_s, corresponding to the instant $t = s$, is

$$R_s = M\{W | \overline{\overline{X}}{}^*_s\} = \\ = \int_{\Omega(\mu, \overline{\overline{U}}_s, \overline{\overline{V}}_s, \overline{\overline{Y}}_{s-1})} W(s, \mu, \mathbf{X}^*_s, \overline{\overline{V}}_s) P(\mu, \overline{\overline{U}}_s, \overline{\overline{V}}_s, \overline{\overline{Y}}_{s-1} | \overline{\overline{X}}{}^*_s) \, d\Omega(\mu, \overline{\overline{U}}_s, \overline{\overline{V}}_s, \overline{\overline{Y}}_{s-1}) \tag{23}$$

Further, if we use a known theorem concerning the multiplication of probabilities, we obtain

$$P(\mu, \overline{\overline{U}}_s, \overline{\overline{V}}_s, \overline{\overline{Y}}_{s-1} | \overline{\overline{X}}{}^*_s) = P(\mu) P(\overline{\overline{V}}_s, \overline{\overline{U}}_s, \overline{\overline{Y}}_{s-1} | \mu, \overline{\overline{X}}{}^*_s). \tag{24}$$

Here we assume that μ and $\overline{\overline{X}}{}^*_s$ are independent.

We consider the second factor on the right-hand side of (24):

$$P(\overline{\overline{V}}_s, \overline{\overline{U}}_s, \overline{\overline{Y}}_{s-1} | \mu, \overline{\overline{X}}{}^*_s) = P(\overline{\overline{U}}_s, \overline{\overline{Y}}_{s-1} | \mu, \overline{\overline{X}}{}^*_s) P(\overline{\overline{V}}_s | \overline{\overline{U}}_s, \overline{\overline{Y}}_{s-1}, \mu, \overline{\overline{X}}{}^*_s) = \\ = P(\overline{\overline{U}}_s, \overline{\overline{Y}}_{s-1} | \mu, \overline{\overline{X}}{}^*_s) P(\overline{\overline{V}}_s | \overline{\overline{U}}_s), \tag{25}$$

since the probability density of the matrix $\overline{\overline{V}}_s$ is completely determined for one fixed $\overline{\overline{U}}_s$ only, and supplementary information concerning μ and $\overline{\overline{X}}{}^*_s$ does not change it.

Further,

$$P(\overline{\overline{U}}_s, \overline{\overline{Y}}_{s-1} | \mu, \overline{\overline{X}}_s^*) = P(U_0, Y_0 | \mu, X_0^*) P(U_1, Y_1 | \mu, U_0, Y_0, \overline{\overline{X}}_1^*) \times$$
$$P(U_2, Y_2 | \mu, \overline{\overline{U}}_1, \overline{\overline{Y}}_1, \overline{\overline{X}}_2^*) \ldots P(U_i, Y_i | \mu, \overline{\overline{U}}_{i-1}, \overline{\overline{Y}}_{i-1}, \overline{\overline{X}}_i^*) \ldots \tag{26}$$
$$P(U_{s-1}, Y_{s-1} | \mu, \overline{\overline{U}}_{s-2}, \overline{\overline{Y}}_{s-2}, \overline{\overline{X}}_{s-1}^*) P(U_s | \mu, \overline{\overline{U}}_{s-1}, \overline{\overline{Y}}_{s-1}, \overline{\overline{X}}_s^*).$$

We consider a typical factor of this product ($0 < i < s$):

$$P(U_i, Y_i | \mu, \overline{\overline{U}}_{i-1}, \overline{\overline{Y}}_{i-1}, \overline{\overline{X}}_i^*) =$$
$$P(Y_i | \mu, \overline{\overline{U}}_i, \overline{\overline{Y}}_{i-1}, \overline{\overline{X}}_i^*) P(U_i | \mu, \overline{\overline{U}}_{i-1}, \overline{\overline{Y}}_{i-1}, \overline{\overline{X}}_i^*) = \tag{27}$$
$$P(Y_i | i, \mu, \overline{\overline{U}}_i) \Gamma_i(U_i | \overline{\overline{U}}_{i-1}, \overline{\overline{Y}}_{i-1}, \overline{\overline{X}}_i^*).$$

The probability density $\mathbf{Y}_i$ is actually determined for fixed μ and $\overline{\overline{U}}_i$, and the supplementary fixing of $\overline{\overline{Y}}_{i-1}$ and $\overline{\overline{X}}_i^*$ does not change it.

The second factor is Γ_i – the probability density of U_i (see [21]), which depends only on $\overline{\overline{U}}_{i-1}$, $\overline{\overline{Y}}_{i-1}$, and $\overline{\overline{X}}_i^*$. We note the fact that, in the formula for $P(\mathbf{Y}_i)$, it depends on i.

If we substitute (27) in (26), we obtain

$$P(\overline{\overline{U}}_s, \overline{\overline{Y}}_{s-1} | \mu, \overline{\overline{X}}_s^*) = \prod_{i=0}^{s} \Gamma_i \prod_{i=0}^{s-1} P(Y_i | i, \mu, \overline{\overline{U}}_i). \tag{28}$$

Here we set

$$\Gamma_0 = P_0(U_0, X_0^*). \tag{29}$$

We now substitute (28) in (25), (25) in (24), and (24) in (23), and the expression for R_s becomes

$$R_s = \int_{\Omega(\mu, \overline{\overline{V}}_s, \overline{\overline{U}}_s, \overline{\overline{Y}}_{s-1})} W(s, \mu, X_s^*, \overline{\overline{V}}_s) P(\mu) P(\overline{\overline{V}}_s | \overline{\overline{U}}_s) \prod_{i=0}^{s-1} P(Y_i | i, \mu, U_i) \times$$
$$\prod_{i=0}^{s} \Gamma_i(U_i | \overline{\overline{U}}_{i-1}, \overline{\overline{Y}}_{i-1}, \overline{\overline{X}}_i^*) d\Omega(\mu, \overline{\overline{V}}_s, \overline{\overline{U}}_s, \overline{\overline{Y}}_{s-1}). \tag{30}$$

The general risk R is given by

$$R = \sum_{s=0}^{n} R_s. \tag{31}$$

In the particular case when the object B has one input and one output, the space-time matrices in formula (30) become time-vectors, and the space vectors become scalars. The expression (30) now takes the form

$$R_s = \int_{\Omega(\mu, \mathbf{v}_s, \mathbf{u}_s, \mathbf{y}_{s-1})} W(s, \mu, x_s^*, \mathbf{v}_s) P(\mu) P(\mathbf{v}_s | \mathbf{u}_s) \prod_{i=0}^{s-1} P(y_i | i, \mu, \mathbf{u}_i) \times$$
$$\prod_{i=0}^{s} \Gamma_i(u_i | \mathbf{u}_{i-1}, \mathbf{y}_{i-1}, \mathbf{x}_i^*) d\Omega(\mu, \mathbf{v}_s, \mathbf{u}_s, \mathbf{y}_{s-1}). \tag{32}$$

Even this expression is more general than formula (40) of the second paper of this series. Actually, W depends here not on the scalar v_s, but on the vector $\mathbf{v}_s$, and, because of this, it is necessary to take into account the probability density $P(\mathbf{v}_s | \mathbf{u}_s)$. Moreover, $P(y_i)$ depends here not on the value of u_i, but on the vector $\mathbf{u}_i$, i.e., on all the "previous history" of the input to the object B.

In order to determine the optimum strategy, we consider, as in paper II, the specific risk R_n, and assume in the meanwhile that the probability densities Γ_i ($i = 0, 1, \ldots, n-1$) are fixed. We set

$$\alpha_k = \alpha_k(\overline{\overline{U}}_k, \overline{Y}_{k-1}, X_k^*) =$$

$$\int_{\Omega(\mu, \overline{V}_k)} W(k, \mu, X_k^*, \overline{V}_k)\, P(\mu)\, P(\overline{V}_k \mid \overline{U}_k) \prod_{i=0}^{k-1} P(Y_i \mid i, \mu, \overline{U}_i)\, d\Omega(\mu, \overline{V}_k). \tag{33}$$

For k = 0 we set the quantity $\prod_{i=0}^{k} P(Y_i)$ equal to one. We also set

$$\beta_k = \beta_k(\overline{\overline{U}}_k, \overline{\overline{X}}_k^*, \overline{Y}_{k-1}) = \prod_{i=0}^{k} \Gamma_k. \tag{34}$$

Then

$$R_n = \int_{\Omega(\overline{\overline{U}}_n, \overline{Y}_{n-1})} \alpha_n(U_n, \overline{\overline{U}}_{n-1}, X_n^*)\, \beta_{n-1}\Gamma_n\, d\Omega(\overline{\overline{U}}_n, \overline{Y}_{n-1}) =$$

$$\int_{\Omega(\overline{\overline{U}}_{n-1}, \overline{Y}_{n-1})} \beta_{n-1}\varkappa_n(\overline{\overline{U}}_{n-1}, \overline{Y}_{n-1}, \overline{\overline{X}}_n^*)\, d\Omega(\overline{\overline{U}}_{n-1}, \overline{Y}_{n-1}), \tag{35}$$

where

$$\varkappa_n(\overline{\overline{U}}_{n-1}, \overline{Y}_{n-1}, \overline{\overline{X}}_n^*) =$$

$$\int_{\Omega(U_n)} \alpha_n(U_n, \overline{\overline{U}}_{n-1}, \overline{Y}_{n-1}, X_n^*)\, \Gamma_n(U_n, \overline{\overline{U}}_{n-1}, \overline{Y}_{n-1}, \overline{\overline{X}}_n^*)\, d\Omega(U_n). \tag{36}$$

We now take into consideration the fact that the choice of Γ_n, as for all the probability densities, must satisfy the condition

$$\int_{\Omega(U_n)} \Gamma_n(U_n, \overline{\overline{U}}_{n-1}, \overline{Y}_{n-1}, \overline{\overline{X}}_n^*)\, d\Omega(U_n) = 1. \tag{37}$$

It is necessary to select the quantity Γ_n, satisfying condition (37), so that the quantity R_n is a minimum. But this latter quantity will be minimized, if, for any $\overline{\overline{U}}_{n-1}$ and $\overline{Y}_{n-1}$, the quantity κ_n is minimized, and this will be ensured if we choose

$$\Gamma_n = \delta(U_n - U_n^*). \tag{38}$$

Here δ is the unit impulse function. The quantity U_n^* is determined by the condition

$$\gamma_n^* = \alpha_n(U_n^*, \overline{\overline{U}}_{n-1}, \overline{Y}_{n-1}, X_n^*) = \min_{U_n \in \Omega(U_n)} \alpha_n(U_n, \overline{\overline{U}}_{n-1}, \overline{Y}_{n-1}, X_n^*). \tag{39}$$

It is evident that

$$U_n^* = U_n^*(\overline{\overline{U}}_{n-1}, \overline{Y}_{n-1}, X_n^*). \tag{40}$$

Therefore, the optimal strategy Γ_n is not random, but regular. The choice of the optimal controlling action U_n^* is given by the formulas (39) and (40).

In a similar way, when we consider the sum of the terms $R_{n-1} + R_n$, and then the sum $R_{n-2} + R_{n-1} + R_n$, etc., we can find the optimal strategies Γ_i (i = n − 1, n − 2, . . .). A similar proof was given in section II of [1]. The result is the following: we introduce the function

$$\gamma_{n-k} = \alpha_{n-k} + \int_{\Omega(Y_{n-k})} \gamma_{n-k+1}^*\, d\Omega(Y_{n-k}), \tag{41}$$

with $\gamma_n = \alpha_n$, and

$$\gamma_{n-k}^* = (\gamma_{n-k})_{U_{n-k} = U_{n-k}^*}, \tag{42}$$

and the value of U^*_{n-k} is obtained from the condition

$$\gamma_{n-k}(U^*_{n-k}, \overline{\overline{U}}_{n-k-1}, \overline{\overline{Y}}_{n-k-1}, X^*_{n-k}) = \min_{U_{n-k}\in\Omega(U_{n-k})} \gamma_{n-k}(U_{n-k}, \overline{\overline{U}}_{n-k-1}, \overline{\overline{Y}}_{n-k-1}, X^*_{n-k}). \tag{43}$$

Then the optimal strategy Γ^*_{n-k} is given by

$$\Gamma^*_{n-k} = \delta(U_{n-k} - U^*_{n-k}), \tag{44}$$

i.e., it is regular, where U^*_{n-k} is obtained from condition (43), and is a function of $\overline{\overline{U}}_{n-k-1}$, $\overline{\overline{Y}}_{n-k-1}$, and X^*_{n-k}.

If, as in the first part of paper II of this series, the action X^*_{n-k} passes through a noisy channel before entering the control section A, then the optimal strategy becomes more complicated, since it is necessary to include a method for calculating the a posteriori probability density $P_{n-k}(X^*_{n-k})$. The quantity must be calculated by taking into account the preceding values of X^*_{n-k-i} $(i > 0)$, i.e., all the matrices $\overline{\overline{X}}^*_{n-k}$. Therefore, in this case, Γ^*_{n-k} will depend, generally speaking, on all the matrices $\overline{\overline{X}}^*_{n-k}$. In posing such a problem and result, we refer to the case when the aim of the control is not completely explicit, and this aim becomes clearer and clearer during the control process.

An Application of the Generalized Formulas

As an example of the application of the formulas we have derived, we will consider the problem of synthesizing an algorithm for optimizing the control section A for a system of automatic stabilization. The block diagram of the system is shown in Fig. 4. The controlled object B consists of a part B_1 that possesses a memory, and a part B_2 that has no memory. The equations for these parts are:

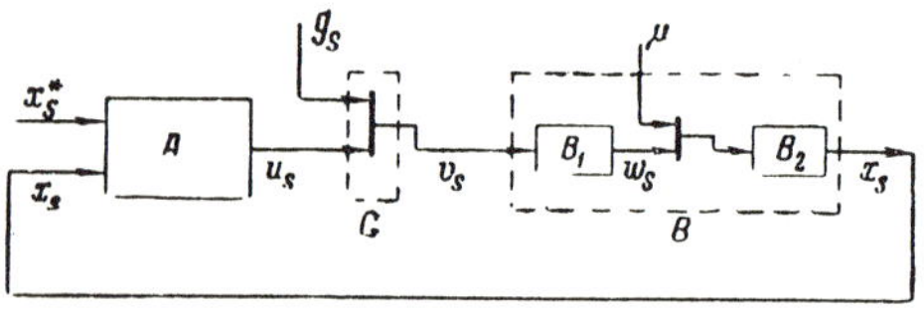

Fig. 4.

$$w_s = \sum_{k=0}^{s} a_k v_{s-k}; \qquad x_s = \mu + w_s. \tag{45}$$

Here a_k are given constants, and μ is a random quantity with a given a priori probability density $P(\mu) = P_0(\mu)$. The general equation for the object B can be written in the form

$$x_s = \mu + \sum_{k=0}^{s} a_k v_{s-k}. \tag{46}$$

The sequence of independent random variables g_s all have the same probability density $q(g_s)$. The functions $P(\mu)$ and $q(g_s)$ are given by the normal-distribution formulas

$$P(\mu) = \frac{1}{\sigma_\mu \sqrt{2\pi}} \exp\left(-\frac{\mu^2}{2\sigma_\mu^2}\right), \quad q(g_s) = \frac{1}{\sigma_g \sqrt{2\pi}} \exp\left(-\frac{g_s^2}{2\sigma_g^2}\right). \tag{47}$$

The quantity u_s is added to the noise g_s in the block G. The output of this block is

$$v_s = g_s + u_s. \tag{48}$$

We will write the specific-loss function in the form

$$W_s = (x_s - x_s^*)^2, \tag{49}$$

and the general loss function will be

$$W = \sum_{s=0}^{n} W_s = \sum_{s=0}^{n} (x_s - x_s^*)^2. \tag{50}$$

In the particular case of systems with one input and one output, from formula (33) we obtain for the function α_k the expression

$$\alpha_k = \alpha_k(\mathbf{u}_k, \mathbf{y}_{k-1}, x_k^*) =$$

$$\int_{\Omega(\mu, \mathbf{v}_k)} W(k, \mu, x_k^*, \mathbf{v}_k) P(\mu) P(\mathbf{v}_k | \mathbf{u}_k) \prod_{i=0}^{k-1} P(y_i | i, \mu, \mathbf{u}_i) \, d\Omega(\mu, \mathbf{v}_k) \tag{51}$$

In the example considered,

$$\alpha_k = \int_{\Omega(\mu, \mathbf{v}_k)} \left(\mu - x_k^* + \sum_{\rho=0}^{k} a_\rho v_{k-\rho}\right)^2 \frac{1}{\sigma_\mu \sqrt{2\pi}} \exp\left(-\frac{\mu^2}{2\sigma_\mu^2}\right) P(\mathbf{v}_k | \mathbf{u}_k) \times \prod_{i=0}^{k-1} P(y_i | i, \mu, \mathbf{u}_i) \, d\Omega(\mu, \mathbf{v}_k). \tag{52}$$

We will now find expressions for $P(\mathbf{v}_k | \mathbf{u}_k)$ and $P(y_i | i, \mu, \mathbf{u}_i)$.

It follows from (48) that

$$P(v_i | u_i) = q(v_i - u_i) = \frac{1}{\sigma_g \sqrt{2\pi}} \exp\left[-\frac{(v_i - u_i)^2}{2\sigma_g^2}\right]. \tag{53}$$

From the independence of the random variables g_i ($i = 0, 1, \ldots, k$), it follows that

$$P(\mathbf{v}_k | \mathbf{u}_k| = \prod_{i=0}^{k} P(v_i | u_i) = \frac{1}{\sigma_g^{k+1} (2\pi)^{\frac{k+1}{2}}} \exp\left[-\frac{\sum_{i=0}^{k} (v_i - u_i)^2}{2\sigma_g^2}\right]. \tag{54}$$

We now find that $P(y_i | i, \mu, \mathbf{u}_i) = P(x_i | \mu, \mathbf{u}_i)$. This change in notation follows from the fact that in the example we are considering $y_i = x_i$, instead of the vector $\boldsymbol{\mu}$ we have the scalar μ, and, finally, the object of control is independent of <u>i</u>.

It follows from (46) that

$$x_i - \mu = \sum_{\rho=0}^{i} a_\rho v_{i-\rho} = \sum_{\rho=0}^{i} \nu_\rho, \tag{55}$$

where

$$\nu_\rho = a_\rho v_{i-\rho} = a_\rho (u_{i-\rho} + g_{i-\rho}) = a_\rho u_{i-\rho} + a_\rho g_{i-\rho}. \tag{56}$$

From this it is evident that the quantity ν_ρ is normally distributed, with a mean value $a_\rho u_{i-\rho}$ and a variance $(a_\rho \sigma_g)^2$. Since $u_{i-\rho}$ and μ are taken to be fixed, and the values ν_ρ are independent for fixed $u_{i-\rho}$, it is not difficult to show that x_i is also normally distributed with a mean value

$$(x_i)_{\text{mean}} = \mu + \sum_{\rho=0}^{i} a_\rho u_{i-\rho} \tag{57}$$

and a variance

$$\sigma_i^2 = \sum_{\rho=0}^{i} a_\rho^2 \sigma_g^2 = \sigma_g^2 \sum_{\rho=0}^{i} a_\rho^2. \tag{58}$$

Therefore,

$$P(x_i | \mu, \mathbf{u}_i) = \frac{1}{\sigma_i \sqrt{2\pi}} \exp\left[-\frac{\left(x_i - \mu - \sum_{\rho=0}^{i} a_\rho u_{i-\rho}\right)^2}{2\sigma_i^2}\right]. \tag{59}$$

The substitution of the expressions (54) and (59) in (52) yields

$$\alpha_k = \alpha_k(\mathbf{u}_k, \mathbf{x}_{k-1}, x_k^*) = \int_{\Omega(\mu, \mathbf{v}_k)} (\mu - x_k^* + \sum_{\rho=0}^{k} a_\rho v_{k-\rho})^2 \frac{1}{\sigma_\mu \sqrt{2\pi}} \times$$

$$\exp\left(-\frac{\mu^2}{2\sigma_\mu^2}\right) \frac{1}{\sigma_g^{k+1}(2\pi)^{\frac{k+1}{2}}} \exp\left[-\frac{\sum_{i=0}^{k}(v_i - u_i)^2}{2\sigma_g^2}\right] \frac{1}{(2\pi)^{\frac{k}{2}}} \left(\prod_{i=0}^{k-1} \frac{1}{\sigma_i}\right) \times$$

$$\exp\left[-\sum_{i=0}^{k-1} \frac{\left(x_i - \mu - \sum_{\rho=0}^{i} a_\rho u_{i-\rho}\right)^2}{2\sigma_i^2}\right] d\Omega(\mu, \mathbf{v}_k). \tag{60}$$

If the object has no memory, and $a_0 = 1$, $a_\rho = 0$ $(\rho > 0)$, then it is not difficult to show that the expression becomes formula (8) of paper III of the present series.

On the basis of (58) we can write

$$\prod_{i=0}^{k-1} \sigma_i = \sigma_g^k \prod_{i=0}^{k-1} \left(\sum_{\rho=0}^{i} a_\rho^2\right)^{\frac{1}{2}} = \sigma_g^k A_{k-1} \tag{61}$$

where A_{k-1} denotes the product.

Formula (61) can now be written

$$\alpha_k = \alpha_k(\mathbf{u}_k, \mathbf{x}_{k-1}, x_k^*) = \frac{1}{\sigma_\mu \sigma_g^{2k+1} A_{k-1} (2\pi)^{k+1}} \times$$

$$\int_{\mu=-\infty}^{\mu=\infty} \int_{v_0=-\infty}^{v_0=\infty} \cdots \int_{v_k=-\infty}^{v_k=\infty} (\mu - x_k^* + \sum_{j=0}^{k} a_j v_{k-j})^2 \times$$

$$\exp\left[-\frac{\mu^2}{2\sigma_\mu^2} - \frac{\sum_{j=0}^{k}(v_j - u_j)^2}{2\sigma_g^2} - \sum_{i=0}^{k-1} \frac{\left(x_i - \mu - \sum_{\rho=0}^{i} a_\rho u_{i-\rho}\right)^2}{2\sigma_i^2}\right] d\mu\, dv_0 \ldots dv_k. \tag{62}$$

In this integral, the quantities x_k^*, x_i, and u_i are parameters. We make a change of variables, and introduce the new variables λ_j and the parameters $x_k^{(0)*}$, $x_i^{(0)}$, B_{k-1}, C_{k-1}, and D_{k-1}:

$$\lambda_j = a_{k-j}(v_j - u_j) \quad (j = 0, \ldots, k), \qquad \lambda_{k+1} = \mu - \frac{B_{k-1}}{2C_{k-1}}, \tag{63}$$

$$x_k^{(0)*} = x_k^* - \sum_{j=0}^{k} a_{k-j} u_j, \qquad x_i^{(0)} = x_i - \sum_{j=0}^{i} a_{i-j} u_j \quad (i = 0, \ldots, k-1),$$

$$B_{k-1} = \sum_{i=0}^{k-1} \frac{x_i^{(0)}}{\sigma_i^2}, \qquad C_{k-1} = \frac{1}{2}\left(\sum_{i=0}^{k-1} \frac{1}{\sigma_i^2} + \frac{1}{\sigma_\mu^2}\right) > 0,$$

$$D_{k-1} = \sum_{i=0}^{k-1} \frac{(x_i^{(0)})^2}{2\sigma_i^2} > 0, \quad E_k = \frac{B_{k-1}}{2C_{k-1}} - x_k^{(0)*}.$$

Then, after transformation, the formula (62) becomes

$$\alpha_k = \frac{\exp\left(-D_{k-1} + \frac{B_{k-1}^2}{4C_{k-1}}\right)}{\left(\prod_{j=0}^{k} a_{k-j}\right)\sigma_\mu \sigma_g^{2k+1} A_{k-1} (2\pi)^{k+1}} \int_{\lambda_0,\ldots,\lambda_{k+1}=-\infty}^{\lambda_0,\ldots,\lambda_{k+1}=\infty} \cdots \int \left(\sum_{i=0}^{k+1} \lambda_i + E_k\right)^2 \times$$

$$\exp\left(-\frac{1}{2\sigma_g^2}\sum_{i=0}^{k}\lambda_i^2 - C_{k-1}\lambda_{k+1}^2\right) d\lambda_0\, d\lambda_1 \ldots d\lambda_k\, d\lambda_{k+1} =$$

$$\frac{\exp\left(-D_{k-1} + \frac{B_{k-1}^2}{4C_{k-1}}\right)}{\left(\prod_{j=0}^{k} a_{k-j}\right)\sigma_\mu \sigma_g^{2k+1} A_{k-1} (2\pi)^{k+1}} I_k. \tag{64}$$

The integral I_k can be reduced to the following form (see [2], p. 238):

$$I_k = \frac{(2\pi)^{\frac{k+1}{2}} (\sqrt{2}\sigma_g)^{k+1}}{\sqrt{C_{k-1}}} \frac{1}{\theta} \int_{-\infty}^{\infty} (t + E_k)^2 \exp\left[-\left(\frac{t}{\theta}\right)^2\right] dt, \tag{65}$$

where

$$\theta^2 = 2\sigma_g^2 (k+1) + \frac{1}{C_{k-1}}. \tag{66}$$

Since we have

$$\int_{-\infty}^{\infty} (t + E_k)^2 \exp\left[-\left(\frac{t}{\theta}\right)^2\right] dt = \theta\sqrt{\pi}\left(\frac{\theta^2}{2} + E_k^2\right), \tag{67}$$

then it follows that

$$I_k = \frac{2^{k+1}\sigma_g^{k+1} (\pi)^{\frac{k}{2}+1}}{\sqrt{C_{k-1}}} \left[\sigma_g^2 (k+1) + \frac{1}{2C_{k-1}} + E_k^2\right]. \tag{68}$$

If this expression is substituted in (64), we obtain

$$\alpha_k = \frac{\exp\left(-D_{k-1} + \frac{B_{k-1}^2}{4C_{k-1}}\right)\left[\sigma_g^2 (k+1) + \frac{1}{2C_{k-1}} + E_k^2\right]}{\left(\prod_{j=0}^{k} a_{k-j}\right)\sigma_\mu \sigma_g^{k} A_{k-1} (\pi)^{\frac{k}{2}} \sqrt{C_{k-1}}}. \tag{69}$$

In this formula, only E_k depends on u_k, since

$$E_k = \frac{B_{k-1}}{2C_{k-1}} - x_k^{(0)*} = \frac{1}{2C_{k-1}} \sum_{i=0}^{k-1} \frac{\left(x_i - \sum_{j=0}^{i} a_{i-j} u_j\right)}{\sigma_i^2} - x_k^* + \sum_{j=0}^{k} a_{k-j} u_j. \tag{70}$$

From this and (69) it follows that the minimum of α_n relative to u_n is obtained if u_n^* is such that $E_n = 0$. Therefore,

$$u_n^* = \frac{1}{a_0}\left[x_n^* - \frac{1}{2C_{n-1}} \sum_{i=0}^{n-1} \frac{\left(x_i - \sum_{j=0}^{i} a_{i-j} u_j\right)}{\sigma_i^2} - \sum_{j=0}^{n-1} a_{n-j} u_j\right] = \frac{K_n}{a_0}, \tag{71}$$

where K_n denotes the quantity in the square brackets.

The optimal strategy in the nth cycle has thus been obtained.

In the transition from n to (n − 1), we must integrate $\gamma_n^* = \alpha_n^*$ with respect to x_{n-1}, add the function α_{n-1} to the integral, and then find the value of u_{n-1}^* that minimizes the resulting expression. It is clear from (69) that for $E_n = 0$ the function α_n depends on u_{n-1}, since this quantity enters into the expressions D_{n-1} and B_{n-1}. However, when we use the substitution

$$x_{n-1} - \sum_{j=0}^{n-1} a_{n-1-j} u_j = x_{n-1}^{(0)} \tag{72}$$

and integrate with respect to the new variable $x_{n-1}^{(0)}$ in the range $(-\infty, \infty)$, we see that $\int_{-\infty}^{\infty} \alpha_n^* \, dx_{n-1}$ does not depend on u_{n-1}. Therefore, the minimizing of γ_{n-1} with respect to u_{n-1} reduces to the minimizing of α_{n-1} with respect to u_{n-1}. Similar reasoning shows that, in general, u_k^* can be obtained by minimizing α_k, and this reduces to the condition $E_k = 0$. From this we obtain the optimal strategy in any sth cycle

$$u_s^* = \frac{1}{a_s}\left[x_s^* - \frac{1}{2C_{s-1}} \sum_{i=0}^{s-1} \frac{\left(x_i - \sum_{j=0}^{i} a_{i-j} u_j\right)}{\sigma_i^2} - \sum_{j=0}^{s-1} a_{s-j} u_j\right] = \frac{K_s}{a_s}, \tag{73}$$

where K_s denotes the quantity in the square brackets.

The physical sense of the solution we have obtained becomes clearer when we note that

$$\mu = x_i - w_i = x_i - \sum_{j=0}^{i} a_{i-j} v_j =$$

$$x_i - \sum_{j=0}^{i} a_{i-j}(u_j + g_j) = \left(x_i - \sum_{j=0}^{i} a_{i-j} u_j\right) - \sum_{j=0}^{i} a_{i-j} g_j. \tag{74}$$

The last term in this expression is random, and its variance depends on i. The expression in brackets is the mean value. Thus, the second term in the formula for K_s gives the value of the random quantity μ. The various results of measuring μ enter this value with different weights, since the variance is different for different measurements.

The last term in the formula for K_s represents the mean value of the results of the previous action u_j ($j < s$), which still has an effect because of the presence of the memory in the object at the instant s. It is natural that, in the determination of u_s^*, this residue must be taken into account. Thus, all the terms of the formula (73) have a clear physical meaning.

It can be shown that when $a_p < a_0 \epsilon^p$, where $|\epsilon| < 1$, and for a sufficiently large value of s, the middle term in the formula for K_s reduces to

$$\frac{1}{s} \sum_{i=0}^{s-1} \left(x_i - \sum_{j=0}^{i} a_{i-j} u_j\right),$$

i.e., to the arithmetic mean of the measurements of μ.

In principle, we can extend the results we have obtained to the case of a continuous system. If, in the continuous case, the coupling between w(t) and v(t) is, for example, described by an equation for an inertial link with transfer function $(1 + p\tau_0)^{-1}$, then

$$w(t) = \int_0^t b(\tau)\, v(t - \tau)\, d\tau, \tag{75}$$

where

$$b(t) = \frac{1}{T_0} \exp\left(-\frac{t}{T_0}\right). \tag{76}$$

In order to make this problem discrete, we set

$$w(t) \approx \sum_{\rho=0}^{s} b(t_\rho) v(t - t_\rho) \Delta t = \sum_{\rho=0}^{s} a_\rho v(t - t_\rho) = \sum_{\rho=0}^{s} a_\rho v_{1-\rho}, \tag{77}$$

where

$$a_\rho = b(t_\rho) \Delta t = \frac{\Delta t}{T_0} \exp\left\{-\frac{\rho \Delta t}{T_0}\right\} \tag{78}$$

$$a_0 = \frac{\Delta t}{T_0}.$$

If we substitute the values of a_ρ in the formula (73) for the optimal strategy, let Δt tend to zero, and set $s\Delta t = t$, we could obtain in the limit the optimal strategy for the continuous case, as in the example in paper III of the series. However, as is also clear from physical considerations, such a limiting operation causes $a_0 \to 0$ and the quantity u_n^* in formula (71) to tend to infinity. The same result is obtained for the other u_s as well. But, for real physical systems, only those solutions for which the value of u_s is bounded have a meaning. We must therefore introduce into the discrete case a further condition, for example, of the type

$$|u_s| \leqslant M. \tag{79}$$

With this condition, however, the optimal strategy changes. For example, instead of (71),we must write

$$u_n^* = \frac{K_n}{a_0} \quad \text{for} \quad \left|\frac{K_n}{a_0}\right| \leqslant M, \qquad u_n^* = \operatorname{sign} \frac{K_n}{a_0} \quad \text{for} \quad \left|\frac{K_n}{a_0}\right| > M. \tag{80}$$

The investigation of this problem shows that now $\int \gamma_n^* dx_{n-1}$ depends on u_{n-1}, and this results in a very much more involved calculation.

SUMMARY

The basic content of this series of papers on the theory of dual control is as follows.

A. A new, very general, and practically important problem has been posed. This problem reduces, in its essentials, to that of finding an optimal method of control in an indefinite situation, with incomplete a priori information concerning the object of control (or even concerning the aim of the control), in a closed system with active accumulation of information.

B. A general method of solving this problem and certain of its generalizations was found. This method consists of a succession of alternate minimizations and integrations.

C. Examples were given, from which it followed that only in very simple cases could the solution be completed without the use of computers. In the general case, the control section must contain a very complicated computing device.

The further development in this region was considered, and the following conclusions were reached.

1. Generalizations to cases not yet investigated. Thus, for example, the general solution obtained for a fixed number n of cycles can be extended to include the case when the number of cycles is not fixed beforehand. Examples were given of this in papers III and IV. The extension to the problem of minimizing the time of search is also possible. For example, let $W_s = 0$ for $s < n$, i.e., the weight of the risk is R_n. Then, without fixing n, we can find an optimal strategy $U_s^* = U_s^*(\overline{U}_{s-1}, \overline{Y}_{s-1}, \overline{X}_s^*)$, such that the number of steps n is minimized, as a result of which the risk R_n is less than, or equal to, a certain given quantity. The method of solution of this problem is based on formulas obtained for fixed n, but the general method of solution is more complicated than for fixed n.

It is also of interest to extend the results to the establishment of a regime that has properties equivalent to the consideration of a specific risk of the type

$$R = \lim_{n \to \infty} \frac{1}{n+1} \sum_{s=0}^{n} R_s. \tag{81}$$

Related to this extension is the interesting problem of finding in what cases, with an infinite number of trials, can complete information concerning the object be obtained, i.e., to obtain the limiting a posteriori probability density $P_s(\mu)$ in the form of a δ-function.

Finally, it is interesting to generalize to a continuous system. This does not present any insurmountable difficulties if we do not demand a rigorous approach. Then the method of calculating the set of functions γ_s^* ($s = 0, 1, \ldots, n$) reduces to the solution of a partial differential equation. The idea of taking such a limit exists in the literature (see, for example, [3,4]). One must, however, take into account that, in the case of digital calculating devices, the problem must again be made discrete.

2. The search for practical methods of constructing systems that approximate closely to optimal. This can be related to approximate methods of solving the equations obtained for the strictly optimal strategy by investigating particular types of systems, and establishing their degree of approximation to the optimal solution. This region of development is very important, since, in complex cases, the exact solution is inapplicable in practice because of the complicated computing devices that are necessary.

Finally, other basic problems can be posed, and these will lead to new methods of investigation, and new results.

The present series of papers has therefore described only the first necessary stage of investigations into new, very interesting, and promising regions in the theory and technique of automatic control.

LITERATURE CITED

1. A. A. Fel'dbaum, "The theory of dual control. I, II, and III," Avtomatika i Telemekhanika 21, 9, 11 (1960); 22, 1 (1961).
2. I. M. Ryzhik, Tables of Integrals, Sums, Series, and Products [in Russian] (Gostekhizdat, 1948) 2nd edition.
3. C. W. A. Merriam, III, "Class of optimum control systems," J. Franklin Inst. 267, No. 4 (April, 1959).
4. L. I. Rozonoér, "L. S. Pontryagin's maximum principal in the theory of optimal systems. I, II, and III," Avtomatika i Telemekhanika 20, Nos. 10, 11, and 12 (1959).

Index